CADOGAN

"Cadogan Guides really need no introduction and ~~...~~ covered ... they give the explorer, the intellectual c ~~...indeed any visitor~~ – all they need to know to get the very best from their visit ... it makes a good read too by the many inveterate armchair travellers."

—*The Book Journal*

"The quality of writing in this British series is exceptional ... From practical facts to history, customs, sightseeing, food and lodging, the Cadogan Series can be counted on for interesting detail and informed recommendations."

—*Going Places* (US)

"Standouts these days are the Cadogan Guides ... sophisticated, beautifully written books."

—*American Bookseller Magazine*

"Entertaining comparisons, with sharp insights, local gossip and far more of a feeling of a living author ... The series has received plaudits worldwide for intelligence, originality and a slightly irreverent sense of fun."

—*Saturday Telegraph*

Other titles in the Cadogan Guides series:

AMSTERDAM
AUSTRALIA
BALI
BERLIN
CENTRAL AMERICA
ECUADOR,
   THE GALAPAGOS
   & COLOMBIA
GREEK ISLANDS
INDIA
IRELAND
ITALIAN ISLANDS
MEXICO
MOROCCO
NEW YORK
NORTHEAST ITALY
NORTHWEST ITALY
PORTUGAL
PRAGUE
ROME
SCOTLAND

SOUTH OF FRANCE: PROVENCE,
   CÔTE D'AZUR &
   LANGUEDOC-ROUSSILLON
SOUTH ITALY
SOUTHERN SPAIN: GIBRALTAR &
   ANDALUCÍA
SPAIN
THAILAND
TUNISIA
TURKEY
TUSCANY, UMBRIA & THE MARCHES
VENICE

Forthcoming:

CENTRAL ASIA
CYPRUS
GERMANY
MALTA
MOSCOW & ST PETERSBURG
PARIS
SICILY

ABOUT THE AUTHOR

For the past four years, James Henderson has watched the Caribbean from a top floor flat in London and from the window of tiny island-hopping planes; he travels there as much as possible, braving flash tropical downpours and droughts, coups d'etat, jerk, pot-holes, rum punches and island-fever, and the attentions of over-zealous aloe masseuses, jumbies and coconut salesmen. Half English and half Scots he has also lived in the UK, USA, Cyprus and the Arabian Gulf, and has wandered Europe, Pakistan and Afghanistan.

He has lingered longest in the Caribbean, still watching for the Green Flash and writing features for the *Financial Times*.

PLEASE HELP TO UPDATE THIS BOOK

The Caribbean and its multi-million dollar tourist industry are constantly changing. Each year new hotels open up, a new chef arrives at a restaurant or moves on, PR companies embellish island-histories yet further, crowds drift from one bar to the next ... even beaches migrate in the Caribbean. It is hard to keep track of the changes, impossible to test them all out (and even then it might be a particularly good/bad night).

And so we need your thoughts to create as complete a picture as possible for each update. If you had a particularly pleasing (or upleasant) experience, we would like to hear about it. Similarly, if you feel that you have some ideas for the guide, send them in. Be as opinionated as you like. Writers of the best letters each year are awarded a complimentary guide of their choice from the series.

CADOGAN GUIDES

THE
CARIBBEAN

JAMES HENDERSON

CADOGAN BOOKS
London

THE GLOBE PEQUOT PRESS
Old Saybrook, Connecticut

Cadogan Books Ltd
Mercury House, 195 Knightsbridge, London SW7 1RE

The Globe Pequot Press
6 Business Park Drive, PO Box 833, Old Saybrook, Connecticut 06475–0833

Cover design by Keith Pointing, adapted by Ralph King
Cover illustration by Povl Webb
Maps © Cadogan Books Ltd,
drawn by Thames Cartographic Services Ltd

Series Editor: Rachel Fielding

First published in 1990
Second revised edition October 1992

A Catalog record for this book is available from the Library of Congress
ISBN 1–56440–003–4

British Library Cataloguing in Publication Data
Henderson, James
    Caribbean—2nd rev. ed.—(Cadogan Guides)
    I. Title II. Milne, Lucy III. Series
    917.2904
    ISBN 0–947754–39–3

Photoset in Ehrhardt on a Linotron 202
Printed and bound in Great Britain by
Redwood Press Limited, Melksham, Wiltshire

CONTENTS

v

Part V: The Bahamas *Pages 621–59*

Further Reading *Page 601*

Index *Pages 661–669*

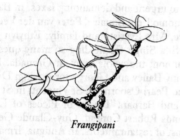

Frangipani

LIST OF MAPS

ACKNOWLEDGEMENTS

Once again, thanks goes to all West Indians, native and adoptive, who make travelling in the islands such fun; for all the lifts (cars, bikes, boats and planes), beers, beds for the night; to all the voluble taxi-drivers, limers and tourism officials who responded so kindly to hours of questions, and then replied to urgent and demanding faxes. In Barbados, Hugh Foster and Robert Goddard; Aruba, Antonio Leo; Bonaire, Peter van der Veen and Jo; Curaçao, Erwin Eustacia, Cynthia Scudmore, Mrs Evaristo and family; Ethylyn John in Tobago; Richard Tomwing in Trinidad and Sita Singh for fielding so many questions, the Lees and their children for the bamboo cannon; the whole team in Grenada, Edwin Frank and Natalie Evans, Llewelyn Simon, Jenny Bailey and George for driving; Dennis in Mayreau, Julie in Bequia and Janet Woods and Pearl Osborne in St Vincent; in St Lucia, Maria Monplaisir, Nova Alexander and Jane and Barbara Tipson of Pieces of Eight; in Dominica, Steve Johnson. In the French Islands Robert Conrad, Guy-Claude Germain, Bernadette Davis, Elise Magras and a whole host of restauranteurs. In Antigua, Irma Tomlinson, Mrs Tongue and family, John Shears of Seahorse Studios; in Montserrat, Leona Midgette; in Nevis, Elmeader Prentice and the Milnes Gaskells; Goldwyn Caines in St Kitts and particularly Clare and Paul Rawson at Rawlins. In the Dutch Windwards, Cornelius de Weever, Maxine Suares and Glen Holm. In Anguilla, Amelia Donna Banks. For a tour of the Virgin Islands, Luce Smith, and rude-boy Dave for beer and bunk; Bob Kirkpatrick, Arlene Stevens and B. J. Harris. In Puerto Rico thanks to Salvador Soto and to visitors Kate, James, Fiona and Sophy for bringing my Christmas stocking and for a break in the routine; in the Dominican Republic, Rodolfo Espinal, the ladies at Asonahores and the lady at the Hostal Nicolas Nader whose name I forget; in Haiti, Margaret Guercy and Richard Moss at the Oloffson Hotel; in Jamaica, Jacquie Goldson and Pat, Peter Bailey of Sense, Jan and Alex at Hedonism and travelling companions Sophie and Ben for a memorable birthday. Finally, in the Bahamas, the ladies in the word-processor room, Monique Knowles and Eileen Fielder; in the Turks and Caicos, Elis Malcolm.

Back in London thanks is due to tourist board members and others who sat through a further bombardment of questions and kindly read through the text, also those who took the trouble to write with Caribbean tales of joy (and sometimes woe); Grace Shorey and Michael Wagner, Ms Coral Bayley from Preston Candover, Christian Noel, Karen Mills, Miss H. J. Shires for impression of her island-hopping tour, Veronica Gibbons and Feolla Chastanet, the Vastags, Susan Steele and Roger Cravens, Clarita Richards and Susan Groom, Mark Bowers and Ruth Buckmaster, Christine Oliver, Jacqui Wilkinson and the girls at the Puerto Rico Tourist Office, Melanie Friedersdorf for her comments on a few islands; Georges Metaxas for assistance with the French Caribbean, Jocelyn Green, Jan Murray of Traveller's Tree and Michaela Bergman and Hugh Miller; Paulette Buchanan Calder and Fenella Kennedy, Deirdre Kirwan-Taylor, Nikky Toppin and Franz Hepburn.

And finally, a big thanks to all those who have helped or watched, supportive as the second edition slowly took form: in particular to all the members of my family who squeezed me in again; to my editor Rachel Fielding; and finally to Louisa McDonnell for casting a constant eye over it all, and Stephen and Meg Davies for respectively proof-reading and indexing.

INTRODUCTION

The legend goes that if you eat the *cascadura* fish of Trinidad, you will return to the island. There is indeed something enchanting about all the islands of the Caribbean, and they have captivated travellers from the temperate zones for centuries. Here you will be bombarded by vibrant unfamiliar sensations; the sweet flavours of ripened fruits—mango, soursop or sweet banana—and the fragrance of jasmine and frangipani on the night air. Only the strongest colours stand out in the glare of the Caribbean sun—the impossibly bright plumage of a scarlet ibis and the shimmering fluorescence of a hummingbird. But above all it is always pleasantly warm—the blanket of the sun's heat is whipped by sea breezes and the sea never has a cold edge.

The Caribbean is known as a hedonist's destination, where you have an 'all-over body holiday'. You can simply lie back and absorb the sun's warmth, dive in euphoric, suspended animation and feast your eyes on a glittering seascape of corals and tropical fish, feel the surge of a windsurfer beneath you as you race off on the trade winds, savour the taste of *piña colada*—a thoroughly 20th-century rest-cure.

But beyond the beach and body culture, the coconut oil and cocaine, you will discover a West Indies that pulses to a different beat. It is a land of creole, callaloo and calypso—rhythmic, vibrant, compelling.

The pace of life is unaccustomedly laid-back. It is shambolic and often infuriating and at times service is so absurdly slow that you feel like an unwitting player in a farce. The islanders will just look on in bemusement at the worries of a slave to the second hand. And yet, Caribbean life is demonstrative and always lively. There is a theatre of the street, which turns a bus trip or a visit to the market into an adventure. It is an easy place to travel, because if you want company, you simply stop and talk to somebody. They'll spin a yarn or two, but they are unusually open and friendly.

The West Indians are masters of street talk and you can expect to be on the receiving end of a 'limer's' quip or two. Heckling is an art form. It is difficult for a visitor even to understand at first, let alone respond in kind, but you can guarantee that you will hear peals of distinctive West Indian laughter all around you. Music is played everywhere, loudly, and people set up vast speakers in the road and dance just for the hell of it. Practically every island has its own rhythm—*soca, salsa, ska*!

There can be few more uplifting sights than the appearance of the islands, great grey stains on the horizon, at the end of a month-long Atlantic crossing. Few have the opportunity of seeing it nowadays, but for Columbus it was the fulfilment of a dream, and the mythical continent of Atlantis became a reality.

Since its discovery and colonization by the Europeans, the Caribbean has become an extraordinary melting pot of cultures, with echoes from all over the world: Parisian chic, a parish church from rural England, cable TV and large cruising cars, minarets and Hindu prayer flags, and of course the strongest reminders of Africa in the faces, the spirit religions and the relentless drum-based rhythms. And yet the flashes are only momentary, because they have metamorphosed, *creolized* into something uniquely West

Indian—Christmas carols to a reggae beat, a face with Dutch features and ebony black skin, Martinican *créole*, which sounds so like French, but which evaporates as soon as you think you have understood it. Each island has its distinctive characteristics and the variety is striking, even across just a few miles of sea.

Two hundred years ago the Caribbean was immensely rich. The fertile islands were turned into sugar factories—the wealth of the West Indies was enough to kick-start the industrial revolution—and the imperial armies would come thousands of miles to fight over them, erecting the vast fortresses that still litter the islands. But that heyday is long past. Today the islands struggle to keep financially afloat and their economic mainstay is the notoriously fickle industry of tourism.

The Caribbean is highly developed and it can be quite difficult now to find an isolated beach. It has some of the smartest and most exclusive resorts in the world, and receives visitors by the jumbo-load. In the last 20 years, tourism has changed the face of the islands beyond all recognition. Yet there is still nothing to beat sitting at a rickety beachside hut in the evening warmth, surrounded by palm fronds that reach down to scratch the ground, and waves that clap and hiss on the sand, watching the last of the golden light fading in the sky.

Guide to the Guide and a Little Geography

For a picture of the Caribbean islands, imagine a dinosaur skeleton, standing between the North and South American continents. It is perched in the middle of the Caribbean Sea, its body at Hispaniola, supported by feet in Jamaica and it stretches out its head and neck (Cuba) towards the Gulf of Mexico. In the east, the arc of the Lesser Antilles makes up the links of its prehensile tail, of which the final vertebra, Trinidad, is firmly embedded in South America.

The area has a variety of names: *Caribbean* comes from the indigenous tribe of American Indians, the Caribs, who inhabited the Lesser Antilles (see p. 3) until the arrival of the Europeans; the origin of the term *West Indies* lies with Columbus himself, who discovered the islands while attempting to find a route via the west to India; and *Antilles* is from Antillia, supposedly a corruption of Atlantis, the lost continent that was presumed to lie beyond the Azores.

The string of islands encloses the Caribbean Sea, separating it from the Atlantic Ocean, and over the millennia they have sprouted on the rift of the Atlantic and Caribbean tectonic plates. The Tropic of Cancer cuts through the middle of the Bahamas, passing just a few miles north of Havana in Cuba.

There are 28 different political units in the Caribbean and the Bahamas, among them independent countries, crown colonies, overseas departments, a territory and a commonwealth. This guide book approaches them in a rough geographical order, tracking along the island-chain from the southeast to the northwest, but collecting them according to language and nationality and the old groupings of the colonial administration. For convenience and in order to emphasize their cultural unity, the French West Indies are treated as one group (even though they are spread over 300 miles), as are the two groups of the Netherlands Antilles, which are separated by some 600 miles of the Caribbean Sea. Strictly speaking the archipelago of the Bahamas is geographically not a part of the Caribbean, but they are included in this book as the islands and their people have a similar heritage, and of course visitors have much the same reason for going there as they do to the Caribbean.

   Introductions to the different island groups are given in the text. Each island is then divided up according to the same format, leading with an introduction and history, followed by any 'topics' that are particularly striking about the island and a section on flora and fauna. Then there are the practical 'getting to and around the island' and tourist information sections, followed by information on the beaches, beach bars and sports. Next comes a description of island sights and finally there is a selection of festivals, the best hotels, restaurants and bars.

The Caribbean at a Glance

Here is a thumbnail sketch of the islands, including recent changes.

Anguilla: Laid back, superb sand. Still uncrowded (though there are projects afoot for large, mid-range hotels). Known for its enclaves of high luxury, but there are cheaper places to stay. Eating out quite pricey, but good beach restaurants and bars.

Antigua: The chosen retreat of a number of wealthy expatriates with the hotels and restaurants to serve them. Fairly expensive; easy to reach; superb sand—active beaches with watersports as well as countless miles of undisturbed strand. Known for its sailing, out of English Harbour and Falmouth Harbour in the south.

Aruba: Fantastic beaches, developed with a string of high rise hotels; continuing to build—big names such as Holiday Inn and Hyatt Regency. Not really the place for a quiet, off-beat holiday; but international standards of comfort and well organized with cabarets and casinos. Easily accessible from the States (though more difficult from the UK). The Arubians are also a mellow bunch.

The Bahamas
Nassau, Cable Beach and Paradise Island: the principal tourist resort and cruise ship terminal. Crowded and hardly relaxed (unless you are in one of the expensive private enclaves such as Lyford Cay). Good bars and restaurants and everything you might want in the way of watersports. Most package holidays end up here.

Freeport/Lucaya: a purpose-built resort area with big hotels and some good beaches.

The **Family Islands**: hundreds of cays and sandbars; some of the least explored islands in the whole area—scattered with hotels, each isolated on their own magnificent strip of sand. Superb sailing, deep-sea fishing, bone fishing and scuba diving.

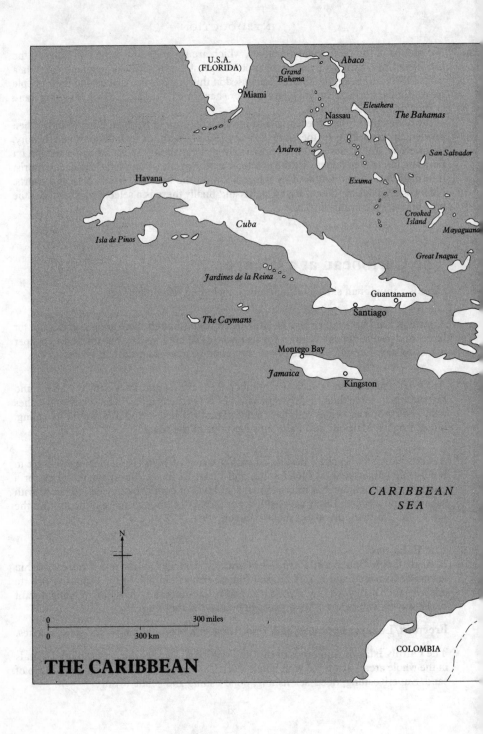

U.S.A.
(FLORIDA)

Miami

*Grand
Bahama*

Abaco

Eleuthera

Nassau

The Bahamas

Andros

San Salvador

Havana

Exuma

Cuba

*Crooked
Island*

Isla de Pinos

Mayaguana

Jardines de la Reina

Great Inagua

Guantanamo

The Caymans

Santiago

Montego Bay

Jamaica

Kingston

*CARIBBEAN
SEA*

N

0   300 miles
0   300 km

COLOMBIA

THE CARIBBEAN

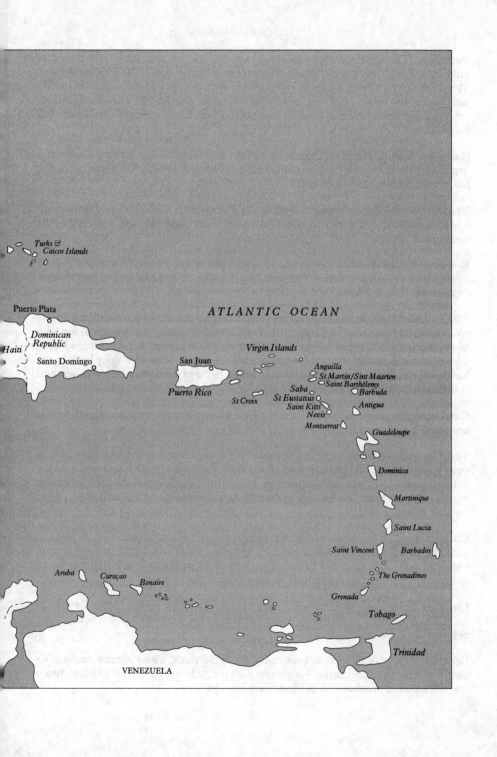

Turks &
Caicos Islands

Puerto Plata

ATLANTIC OCEAN

Dominican
Republic

Haiti

Santo Domingo

Virgin Islands

San Juan

Anguilla
St Martin/Sint Maarten
Saint Barthélemy

Puerto Rico

Saba
St Eustatius
Saint Kitts
Nevis

Barbuda

Antigua

St Croix

Montserrat

Guadeloupe

Dominica

Martinique

Saint Lucia

Saint Vincent

Barbados

The Grenadines

Aruba

Curaçao

Bonaire

Grenada

Tobago

Trinidad

VENEZUELA

Barbados: The gentleman of Caribbean tourism and second home to a crowd of English sophisticates; some of the Caribbean's best known hotels along the west coast. The south coast offers a lower-key atmosphere with riotous nightlife. The Bajans are still among the most charming people in the area despite the island's economic problems. Excellent beaches, good restaurants and bars. Easily accessible and caters well for all tastes.

Barbuda: Tiny, attached to Antigua, one of the least known islands in the Caribbean. Just superb sand, a couple of outrageously expensive hotels and a lazy Caribbean life that has not changed in about fifty years.

Bequia: A charming and pretty island in the Grenadines, well developed, with small hotels and restaurants along the waterfront around the main bay, and scattered in the small coves. Airstrip.

Bonaire: A slumberstruck coral outcrop with little except some of the world's finest diving; an ideal retreat. Great diving lodges to stay in; a surprising string of good restaurants. Building fast.

The British Virgin Islands: Easy-going islands with the feel of a sophisticated play-ground. Good restaurants and bars on **Tortola** (the main island) and a nautical feel with all the passing yachts—the Virgin Islands have excellent sailing. Across Francis Drake Channel are the nearly deserted **Norman Island, Cooper Island** (nothing but a beach bar) and the second island, **Virgin Gorda,** with a string of excellent hotels and beaches. **Anegada** is very low key.

Carriacou: Classic small island life in the Grenadines. Superb beaches, superb sailing and some hip bars.

The Cayman Islands: Grand Cayman: highly developed and fairly American in style—hotels are big and modern—a well-organized rest-cure, easily accessible from the States. Some of the best scuba diving in the world. The Caymanians are a charming bunch. **Cayman Brac** and **Little Cayman**: castaway island life; good small hotels, more brilliant diving.

Cuba: Selling its tourism hard at the moment and building extensively. If you are prepared to be a dutiful package tourist, spending your time in the resorts and on packaged bus tours, then the island offers a typical Caribbean beach holiday. As an independent traveller's destination it is hard work at the moment.

Curaçao: Easily accessible and extremely cosmopolitan (the senior Dutch Caribbean island), with a string a good bars and restaurants and a lively crowd. Beaches not brilliant, but good diving. Some nice small hotels.

Dominica: Least developed and poorest of the Windwards, with a natural charm of its own. Supreme flora and fauna—rainforest with over a hundred species of birds. Just a few golden-sand beaches and life extremely low key.

The Dominican Republic: Spanish-speaking; one of the largest Caribbean countries, with a huge tourist industry (over a million visitors each year), but beyond the tourist ghettos are cool coastal towns on superb beaches and lively island life. Also relatively cheap.

Grenada: Volcanic peaks and rainforests; fruit and spice plantations; easy-going islanders; less developed than St Lucia. Good beaches in the south of the island. Easy to reach; some good small hotels, with a full range from luxury to budget. Also see **Carriacou**.

The Grenadines: Strung between St Vincent and Grenada; fantastic sea, beaches and sailing; a good mix of attractive tourist islands—including island-enclaves of super-luxury—and accessible West Indian life; island-hopping possible. **Canouan** has fine anchorages and hidden coves; **Mayreau** is secluded with beaches on all sides; the **Tobago Cays** are uninhabited islets in paradise. **Union Island** is the local transit point. See also **Bequia, Carriacou, Mustique, Palm Island, Petit St Vincent** and **Young Island**.

Guadeloupe: Highly developed French island, with a large tourist industry, particularly Grande-Terre in the east (for the beaches). Less crowded, Basse-Terre has golden sand beaches in the north west, but also rainforest for walking. Charming offshore islands: **Marie Galante** and **La Désirade** are very low key; **Terre de Haut** in The Saints is pretty and well developed.

Haiti: Hardly a typical tourist island; politics prevent it. For the traveller, though, quite simply one of the most compelling countries in the world. French and the African influence; naive art, markets and voodoo.

Jamaica: Largest of the former British Islands; easily accessible and with a full range of tourist hotels (super-luxury to friendly guest houses); good bars and restaurants. Beyond the coastal resorts fascinating island life in music and a vibrant culture.

Martinique: The most developed (and visibly the most prosperous) French Caribbean island; Martinicans are chic and their restaurants excellent—in town and in the resorts. Beaches best in the south, where most of the tourist industry is concentrated.

Montserrat: Slow and sedate; just a few comfortable hotels and villas. Not much nightlife or even beaches in the typical Caribbean mould— reliable peace.

Mustique: Best known as an exclusive holiday domain for the rich and famous; just a series of luxurious, privately owned villas, one hotel and a beach bar. Airstrip.

Nevis: Undeveloped Leeward Island with slow and gentle small-island life; just a few bars and restaurants. Some good beaches and some classic Caribbean plantation hotels.

Palm Island: An island-resort in the southern Grenadines; reached by boat, just a few villas, a beach and an easy life.

Petit St Vincent: An island-resort in the southern Grenadines, reached by boat, or by helicopter; just a few villas where you communicate by flag and call room service to your beach-hammock.

Puerto Rico: Smallest of the Greater Antilles, a Spanish-speaking American territory (English also widely spoken). Large tourist industry on the northern shore—good bars and restaurants in San Juan; National Parks, mountains, rainforest. Delightful offshore islands: **Vieques** and **Culebra.**

Saba: A tiny outcrop with very gentle, easy-going islanders. Not much to do, but a pretty and reliable retreat. Building steadily; no beaches but good diving.

Saint Barthélemy (St Barts): A champagne playground, as only the French would conceive. Some charming hotels and fine restaurants; very expensive and going strong despite the recession. Barely any West Indian culture to distract you from the essentials of gourmet dining, sunning and posing.

St Kitts: The larger and marginally more developed partner of Nevis in the Leeward Islands; an easy-going West Indian atmosphere. Beaches and the traditional Caribbean resort hotels in the south; in the north some of the Caribbean's finest plantation hotels.

St Lucia: Most developed of the volcanic Windwards, with some pretty smart hotels along its good beaches. Still building, large hotels in some cases, and for the moment it holds the development quite well. Lovely hideaway hotels among the coves of the leeward coastline. Easy to join in with local life.

Saint Martin: The larger and (marginally) less developed French half of the island shared with Dutch Sint Maarten. Good beaches, some good hotels, a number of nice (if expensive) guest houses and excellent restaurants; Gallic atmosphere; quite expensive.

Saint Vincent: An unspoilt, quite poor, English-speaking Windward Island; grand natural fertility and just a few comfortable, family-run hotels. A good starting point for a tour of the Grenadines.

Sint Eustatius: A tiny outcrop, whose heyday was really two centuries ago. Very peaceful, a writer's retreat.

Sint Maarten: The more developed (Dutch) half of an island shared with French Saint Martin. Excellent beaches, good sports, casinos and good shops; also good restaurants (with an endless choice of others in the French half) and bars. Too developed for some, but the locals swear by it.

Tobago: Partnered with Trinidad, Tobago is a lovely, low-key tropical island. Tourism is concentrated in the southwest but elsewhere idyllic spots are still to be found in isolated coves beneath the tumbling rainforests.

Trinidad: Trinidad is industrialized, crowded, and strong on culture—lively home to carnival, steel pan and calypso. Spectacular natural life—over 400 species to be found in the rainforest and the coastal swamps.

The Turks and Caicos Islands: At the south-eastern limit of the Bahamas, the Turks and Caicos lie in two groups. Providenciales is the most developed and most accessible; the rest are in varying states of undevelopment, ideal for a lazy retreat. Spectacular beaches throughout and diving superb.

The US Virgin Islands
St Thomas: highly developed and easily reached from the mainland US. Big hotels and endless shopping in Charlotte Amalie. Gets crowded, but good restaurants and bars. Good transit point.

St Croix: larger and less developed, still some nice hotels and restaurants. The island has recovered from Hurricane Hugo.

St John: least developed of the US Virgins—much of it is National Park. Good bars and restaurants on the coasts. Also frequented by passing yachties.

Young Island: A tiny, forested blip just a couple of hundred yards off St Vincent's southern coast; just a charming West Indian hotel.

The Best of the Caribbean

Backchat: rude boy stands, Trinidad; Coronation market, Kingston, Jamaica.
Beaches:
Walking beaches: 7-Mile Beach, Grand Cayman; Negril Beach, Jamaica; north coast of Providenciales, Turks and Caicos.
Isolated beach: Anse de la Roche, Carriacou.
Beach to sail to: Tobago Cays in the Grenadines; Stocking Island, off Great Exuma in the Bahamas; the cays off Jost van Dyke.
Windsurfing beaches: Silver Sands, Barbados; Cabarete, north coast of the Dominican Republic.

Botanical gardens: St Vincent; Andromeda in Barbados; Jardins de Balata in Martinique.

Day's sail: Sir Francis Drake Passage, BVI.

Dive sites: Cayman walls; Bahamian walls and caves; and Bonaire slopes.

Drinks: *bastidas* (fresh fruit milk-shakes) in the Dominican Republic; Barbadian fruit punches.

Duty-free ports for shopping: Philipsburg, Sint Maarten; Charlotte Amalie, St Thomas, USVI.

Factories: Hacienda Buena Vista coffee factory, Puerto Rico and Mavis Bank, Jamaica; Dougaldston Estate, and Nutmeg Co-op, Gouyave, Grenada; cigar factories, Cuba; the salt flats of Bonaire; Curaçao Liqueur Factory, Curaçao.

Forts: the Citadel in Haiti; Brimstone Hill in St Kitts; El Morro, Santiago de Cuba; El Morro, San Juan.

Islands:
Island-resorts: Petit St Vincent in the Grenadines and Peter Island, BVI (both for high luxury); Young Island off St Vincent (for its West Indian charm).
Island to be marooned on: Jost van Dyke, BVI; Mayreau in the Grenadines (when the cruise ship's not in the bay).
Small but developed islands: Bequia, Grenadines; Terre de Haut, in the Saints off Guadeloupe; Harbour Island, Eleuthera, Bahamas.

Markets: Port au Prince, Haiti; St George's, Grenada; floating market, Willemstad, Curaçao.

Natural wonders: the evening flight of the scarlet ibis, Caroni Swamp, Trininidad; bio-luminescent bay, Vieques, Puerto Rico.

Picturesque ports: Admiralty Bay, Bequia, Grenadines; English Harbour, Antigua; Gustavia, St Barts.

Plantation house hotels: Rawlins Plantation, St Kitts (and others on St Kitts and Nevis); Hacienda Gripinas, Puerto Rico; Caribbee Inn, Carriacou; Ivor Lodge, Jamaica.

Rainforest retreats: Asa Wright Nature Centre, Trinidad; the whole island of Dominica; El Yunque rainforest, Puerto Rico.

Restaurants:
Gourmet: Papiamento, Aruba; Graycliff, Nassau.
Local: Casita Blanca, Puerto Rico; Bistro Nu, Saint Martin; Blue Crab, Scarborough, Tobago; Mamma's, Grenada, for opossum or armadillo with green fig and breadfruit.
Waterfront charm: the French Restaurant, St Vincent; Mangos, Anguilla; Pisces, St Lawrence Gap, Barbados.

Rum punch at sunset: Admiralty Bay, Bequia; Pigeon Point, Tobago; Les Anses d'Arlets, Martinique.

Secluded bay: Marigot bay, St Lucia.

Towns: Colonial Havana, Cuba; Old San Juan, Puerto Rico; St George's harbour, Grenada.

Views: from Firefly, Noel Coward's House in Jamaica; from the middle of Sir Francis Drake Channel, BVI; from Fort Charlotte, St Vincent, across the Grenadines; the Pitons, St Lucia.

West Indian fast food: Jamaican jerk centres; Store Bay, Tobago for crab and dumpling; Baxter's Road, Barbados (night only) for battered kingfish; Trinidad Breakfast Sheds for rice and peas; Plaza Biejo, Willemstad, Curaçao for a *toetoe* or iguana soup.

Part I
GENERAL INFORMATION

Hummingbird

Getting to the Caribbean
By Air
From the UK

British Airways has the widest range of services between the UK and the Caribbean. Antigua, Barbados, Grenada, Jamaica, Puerto Rico, St Lucia and Trinidad are served direct from London Heathrow or Gatwick.

The cheapest official fares require 21 days advance booking, and there are penalties for changing reservations. Peak fares are charged in December, and between July and September. The highest fares are to the most southerly destinations, Grenada and Port of Spain in Trinidad; peak season costs around £800 return, low season £700. Fares to other destinations in the Caribbean are about £700 peak, £600 off season. Lower fares are often available through travel agents, see flights only section below.

Other scheduled carriers are BWIA, based in Trinidad, which serves Port of Spain, Barbados and Antigua, and Air Jamaica.

From the USA

American Airlines, has the most extensive service from the States, flying to most of the islands, usually out of New York (JFK) or Miami, often two flights a day. Connections to the smaller islands can be made in San Juan (Puerto Rico), their Caribbean hub, or in Sint Maarten, Antigua, Barbados and Nassau. They fly direct to smaller islands such as St Kitts, St Lucia and Tortola/Beef Island in the British Virgin Islands.

Continental fly from New York (Newark) to Kingston (Jamaica), Port of Spain (Trinidad), Antigua and the Virgin Islands. **Delta** flies to Nassau and San Juan from Miami and **TWA** and **US Air** fly to San Juan in Puerto Rico. Air Jamaica, ALM and BWIA also have a number of flights to cities all over the Caribbean and Viasa, the Venezuelan national carrier, makes some stops as it flies south.

Fares from the USA vary little from one carrier to another. The seasons are strictly observed: mid-December to mid-April is high season, late June to mid-September is the summer peak, while the rest of the year is low season. Sample midweek round-trip fares to Grenada from Miami and most other East Coast cities are $450 high season, $400 summer peak and $380 low season. From the Midwest add around $150, from the West Coast $250. These require advance booking, and cancellation charges apply. Supplements are payable for weekend travel, departure taxes, US customs fees and so on. With luck and a bit of scouting around you can get a seat on a charter flight, which will mean perhaps a third off the scheduled price.

From Canada
Air Canada flies direct, usually out of Toronto, but occasionally Montreal, to a number of destinations in the Caribbean, including Jamaica (Montego Bay and Kingston), Antigua, Guadeloupe and Martinique, St Lucia, Barbados and Port of Spain in Trinidad. In the Bahamas, the destinations are Freeport, Nassau and Governor's Harbour (Eleuthera). You might also consider making a connection in the States.

BWIA fly from Toronto in Canada to Port of Spain, stopping over in Antigua, Barbados or Grenada. There are plenty of charter flights servicing the vacation packages.

Further details on flights to and between the islands are listed under the 'Getting To' sections in each island.

Tour Operators and Travel Agents
Most holidays to the Caribbean are sold as scheduled or charter packages, and with these you can get anything from a two-week, two-destination package at two different luxury resorts at opposite ends of the Caribbean Sea, through sporting holidays and the proliferation of honeymoon packages (complete with nuptial underwear if you want), to the charter packages that take advantage of the low season rates, giving you a return flight and two weeks' accommodation for less than the price of a normal return airfare.

It is worth using tour operators because they can get discounts both with the airlines and the hotels: in most cases they are able to arrange a package more cheaply than an independent traveller. A well-informed travel agent can sift through the multiplicity of packages and find the best one for you and many will also tailor a trip to your special interests. Many of the tour companies include obligatory **insurance** in their packages, but travel agents will always sell you a policy. Check your existing policies—it is worth insuring against medical problems, cancelled flights and lost luggage.

In the UK
The biggest Caribbean tour operator in the UK is **Caribbean Connection**, which offers a wide-ranging selection of hotels and villas in the different destinations;

2

Concorde House, Forest St, Chester CH1 1QR (tel 0244 341131). **Elegant Resorts of the Caribbean**, Lion House, 23 Watergate Row, Chester CH1 2LE (tel 0244 329671, fax 0244 41085) also offer top of the range packages and have knowledgeable staff; as do **Thomas Cook** Faraway Holidays, PO Box 36, Thorpe Wood, Peterborough, Cambridgeshire PE3 6SB (tel 0733 330336, fax 0733 505784), who have a series of comfortable World Travel Service lounges throughout the country. Smaller operators include the friendly **Caribtours** at 161 Fulham Rd, London SW3 6SN (tel 071 581 3517, fax 225 2491) who give a personalized service; **Harlequin Worldwide**, who tailor-make to off-beat destinations as well as the big Caribbean hotels (tel 0708 852780, fax 0708 854952) at 2 North Road, South Ockendon, Essex RM15 6QJ; and **Silk Cut Faraway Holidays**, Meon House, Petersfield, Hants GU32 3JN (tel 0730 65211, fax 60263), who offer a villa programme as well as an extensive range of hotels.

The specialist Caribbean travel agent and tour operator **Transatlantic Wings** are at 70 Pembroke Rd, London W8 6NX (tel 071 602 4021, fax 603 6101). **Caribbean Independence** (tel 0371 874848) specializes in trips to Puerto Rico and the British and American Virgin Islands. There are a couple of Cuba specialists mentioned in that island's section.

If your main desire is to get to the West Indies for as little money as possible, you can travel with one of the charter package companies and the best prices are in summer. Some of the cheapest are offered by **Airtours** at Wavell House, Holcombe Rd, Helmshore, Rossendale, Lancs BB4 4NB (tel 0706 260000, fax 0706 212144). Charters are also offered by **Intasun**, Intasun House, Cromwell Ave, Bromley, Kent BR2 9AQ (tel 081 290 1900) and **Thomson Holidays**, Greater London House, Hampstead Rd, London NW1 7SD (tel 021 632 6282, fax 071 387 8451).

There are a number of **flights only** specialists, who offer discounted prices on scheduled and some charter flights to the Caribbean, often used by West Indians on a trip back home. Contact **Caribbean Gold** (tel 081 741 8889), **Newmont Travel** (tel 071 254 6546, 081 743 5885), **Hoffman Travel** (tel 071 733 7071) and **Stoke Newington Travel** (tel 071 254 0136). **Caribbean Connection** also have a flights only office called the Reunion Club (tel 071 631 3650).

Special Interest Holidays
Honeymoon packages (with wedding if you want it) get ever more popular and many tour operators will arrange one for you. Honeymoon specialists include **New Beginnings** at Rawdon House, High St, Hoddesdon, Herts EN11 8TE (tel 0992 447244), **Thomas Cook, Caribbean Connection** and **Caribtours**. Some tour operators are offering twin destination holidays, perhaps with a week in another Caribbean island or in Florida.

Holidays with a specialist interest, particularly for watersports, are easily arranged through the regular tour operators. Other specialists include **Twickers World** at 22 Church St, Twickenham, Middx TW1 3NW (tel 081 892 7606), who offer **diving** holidays to the Caribbean islands of Aruba, Bonaire and the Caymans as well as the Peter Hughes Dive operations all over the area. The **Barefoot Traveller** (tel 0932 845580) arranges birdwatching holidays in Trinindad and Tobago, as well as diving in the Eastern Caribbean. The **Traveller's Tree** at 116 Crawford St, London W1H 1AG (tel 071 935 2291, fax 071 486 2587) runs tours specialising in **natural history**, including

3

the islands of Dominica and Carriacou and Grenada. **DB Jazz Tours** (0789 267532) arranges some music tours to the Caribbean. And **Jungle Art** arranges a two-week painting holiday on the island of Tobago, with ten lessons in a range of locations. Contact Langley Travel (tel 081 950 1680).

For **sailing** holidays you can contact the charter companies direct, or go through the tour operators. Crewed yachts, both sailing and motor yachts (gin palaces) are available through **Crestar**, Colette Court, 125–6 Sloane St, London SW1X 9AU (tel 071 730 9962, fax 071 824 8691) and **Camper and Nicholsons**, 31 Berkeley St, London W1X 5FA (tel 071 491 2950, fax 071 629 2068). They will help to arrange your flights to the Caribbean, and transfers (by helicopter onto the yacht's landing pad if you want). Price from US$7000 to about $200,000.

When the England **cricket** team tours the West Indies there are a number of companies offering tours, often with former players as guides. Contact the tourist boards.

In the USA

Tour operators working out of the **USA** include Fly AAway Vacations with American Airlines (toll free 800 433 7300) and American Express Vacations (toll free 800 241 7700), Horizon Tours (tel 800 525 7760), Travel Impressions (toll free 800 632 6721), Thomson Vacations (toll free 800 222 6400) and GoGo Tours, with offices all over the country (head office 201 934 3500 or toll free in New York City 800 526 0405).

Special Interest Holidays

Divers can contact Aqua Adventures, at 114 East 32nd St, Suite 501, New York, NY 10017 (tel 212 686 6210 or toll free 800 654 7537), which runs tours to over fifty of the Caribbean's dive-sites. Oceanic Society Expeditions at 275 Park Ave South, New York, NY 10010 (tel 212 673 3120) runs **natural history** tours to islands including Trinidad and Tobago. Most tour companies will arrange a **honeymoon** for you in the Caribbean.

By Sea

Cruise liner is a popular way of travelling around the Caribbean, and it enables you to visit as many as four or five different islands in a week, without the hassle of delayed flights or even packing your suitcase. Most depart from Miami or Fort Lauderdale and a few are based in San Juan, Puerto Rico and they sail all year round. Cruise-ship companies include Chandris Fantasy Cruises, with four liners (UK tel 071 588 2598, US toll free 800 621 3446), Cunard (UK tel 071 491 3930, US toll free 800 854 0500), Norwegian Cruise Lines (UK tel 071 493 6041, US toll free 800 327 3090), Princess Cruises (UK tel 071 831 1881, US toll free 800 421 0880).

The possibilities of independent travel to the Caribbean by sea are more limited and may not be convenient anyway because of the time involved. If you are prepared to pay the fairly steep rates you can travel on the Geest Line that sails out of Barry docks, PO Box 20, Barry, South Glamorgan CF6 8XE (tel 0446 700333). Price about £2700 for the full 23 day round-trip, £1900 if you fly one way. It no longer seems possible to work a passage out to the islands, even swabbing the decks, unless you have a merchant marine card.

However, a large number of **yachts** make the Atlantic crossing to the Caribbean towards the end of the year (after spending the summer in the Mediterranean), arriving in time for the winter sailing season. You might be able to pick up a yacht on the south coast of Britain, in the south of France, in Gibraltar, or even in the Canaries any time from September (just after the hurricane season). Try the yacht club noticeboards and yachting magazines. The Cruising Association, Ivory House, World Trade Centre, London E1 (tel 071 481 0881) has a crewing service, connecting skippers and crew once a month (£14 for the year's membership) You negotiate from there with the captain.

Experience is not necessarily required. Most yachts will charge you just enough to cover food or nothing at all, but there are one or two sharks around who have been making outrageous charges for what can be quite a hard three-week sail. If you are worried about the crossing, catamarans are more comfortable. The return journey across the Atlantic generally takes place at the end of April, fairly soon after Antigua Race week, and the ports of Antigua are the best places to look if you wish to make the eastward crossing.

In the same way the American yachting community migrates down to the Caribbean over the winter. Once again, try yacht club noticeboards, the yachting magazines and the ports on the eastern seaboard.

Entry Requirements and Customs
British citizens do not need a visa to any of the Commonwealth Caribbean countries or the French or Netherlands Antilles or to the Dominican Republic or Haiti. To enter Cuba you must have a tourist card (£10). Americans and Canadians travelling as tourists do not need a visa to enter any Caribbean country, but they must buy a tourist card when entering the Dominican Republic US$15, and Cuba US$10. In many countries proof of identity is enough, though a passport is the best document. Business visitors should consult the Embassy before departure. Citizens of other countries do not usually need a visa, except sometimes to Puerto Rico and the US Virgin Islands (same regulations as US).

The Caribbean may be known for being laid-back. Their immigration authorities are most definitely not, however. Invariably they will require an onward ticket and they will hold your passport until you produce one. You will also be asked for your address on the island on the immigration form. This is almost a formality as they rarely check up, but it eases entry to put something down. Addresses of hotels and guest houses are at the back of each separate island chapter.

Most countries levy a departure tax, payable when you leave, sometimes in hard currency (listed in the separate island sections).

Drugs not issued on prescription are illegal in the Caribbean, and people do occasionally end up inside for possession of user quantities. Customs officials operate a strict policy against them and they search bags going in and out of the countries. Alcohol and tobacco allowances vary from island to island. While on an island you will probably be approached by 'oregano salesman' with an offer of marijuana (weed, ganja etc.) and occasionally cocaine. You will not be popular if you are caught.

Specialist Bookshops
In London the following shops have a wide selection of travel books including Caribbean material:

5

Daunt's bookshop at 83 Marylebone High St, London W1M 4DE (071 224 2295)—they will send you a reading list of their material.
The **Travel Bookshop** at 13 Blenheim Crescent, London W11 2EE (tel 071 229 5260).
Stanfords at 12–14 Longacre, London WC2E 9LP (tel 071 836 1321) who are also map specialists.

In the USA, try:

British Travel Books, 40 West 57th Street, New York, NY 10019 (tel 212 765 0898).
Rand McNally Map Travel, 444 North Michigan Ave., Chicago, IL 60611.
The Complete Traveller, 4038 Westheimer, Houston, TX 77027.
Traveller's Bookstore, 22 West 52nd Street, New York, NY 10019 (tel 212 664 0995).
Travel Logs, 222 West 83rd Street, New York, NY 10024 (tel 212 799 8761).
Travel Merchandise, 1425 K Street NW, Washington, DC 20005 (tel 202 371 6656).

Getting Around the Caribbean

Island Hopping

One of the great things about a holiday in the Lesser Antilles is the great variety of islands so close to one another. The views are fantastic and in the Eastern Caribbean you can see from one island to the next right the way down the chain, from Anguilla to Grenada. Twenty minutes' flying can get you from a French overseas *département* to independent islands that have a strong British heritage, from industrially developed countries to tiny blips with just a few shacks and palm trees. For suggested island-hopping trips and itineraries around the bigger islands, see the separate sections: the Grenadines, the Virgin Islands, Puerto Rico, the Dominican Republic, Jamaica, Cuba and the Bahamas.

Days' sails and convenient flight timings for a day's visit are available to the islands around Sint Maarten—Saba, Statia and St Barts. To Anguilla, your best bet is to go by ferry from Marigot. Cuba has been opening up short hops from the surrounding islands: Jamaica, the Bahamas and the Cayman Islands.

By Air

Most Island Hopping nowadays is by **plane**, and although the aircraft look a bit like coffins with wings on and do feel slightly alarming, they get you there. And of course the views as you fly over the islands are fantastic. These small planes are affectionately known as the islands' bus service and they will simply miss out a destination if nobody wants to get on or off. The main centres for travel around the Caribbean are Miami, San Juan in Puerto Rico, and in the Eastern Caribbean, Sint Maarten, Antigua and Barbados.

However, island hoppers will experience more grief in airline offices than any other places in the Caribbean. Planes are often overbooked, and those booked in advance may well leave half empty. Standby often works. You must reconfirm obsessively if you want to guarantee your seat and if you miss a flight you will find that the whole of the rest of the itinerary might be cancelled. A dose of judicious anger may help you get what you want. Most airlines are usually quite amenable, though, about excess luggage, except when the plane is full.

National airlines will often have an island-hopping service with smaller planes. The biggest carrier in the Eastern Caribbean is **LIAT** (Leeward Islands Air Transport, 'Leave Island Any Time', 'Likeable Interested Attentive Tolerant', 'Lost in Air Transit' or 'Luggage in Another Town', depending on whose story you believe), which operates to islands between Puerto Rico and Port of Spain, Trinidad. LIAT offers an 'Super Caribbean Explorer' ticket allowing you a month with unlimited stops in one direction for US$357, and a 'Caribbean Explorer', twenty-one days with three stops at US$199 peak times (1 July–31 Aug and 15 Dec–31 Jan) and US$169 in low season. **BWIA** (pronounced Beewee) is based in Trinidad and flies to many of the Eastern Caribbean islands including Antigua and Puerto Rico. Their 'Hopper' ticket allows you unlimited travel in one direction for 30 days, cost US$330.

Air Martinique operates from Martinique and flies to Dominica in the north, to Barbados and to St Lucia, St Vincent and the Grenadine islands of Mustique, Canouan and Union Island. **Air Guadeloupe** flies south to Dominica and north to Antigua and Sint Maarten. The last option is to **charter** a small plane, which can work out at a good price if there are enough people. All Caribbean airports have a charter company on call.

The small propeller planes (usually Twin Otters or Islanders) carry about 20 passengers. Flight can be a bit of a novelty; planes this size tend to bounce off clouds—there are vertical streams of air within them which will leave your stomach a hundred feet above you in a matter of a second or so. If you do find a penetrable cloud, you might find it coming through the overhead blowers.

The Caribbean also has some pretty hairy airstrips. Some are very short—you will know about this just after landing when the reverse thrust makes the whole plane shudder and the instrument panel becomes a blur. Others are hairy because there is an obstacle course for the pilot to negotiate on approach to landing. The top two airstrips in the area are:

St Barthélemy in the Leeward Islands, where there are two approaches: from the seaward (marginally preferable) where you get a close inspection of some second-degree jungle and the local cemetery just before you land; and over land, for which they stop the traffic on the road in case the plane's wheel takes off a driver's hat. But the most spectacular of them all is the strip on Saba, just 400 yards long (shorter than any self-respecting aircraft carrier) and with a hundred-foot drop at either end. Taking off is exciting, landing here has a stress quotient. People say: 'they only use half the runway'. Just pray that it is the first half.

By Boat

Until thirty years ago all the islands of the Caribbean were linked by elegant old sloops and schooners once or twice a week. These have mostly gone now, but it is still sometimes possible to hitch a ride on the **freighters** which bring provisions and manufactured goods into the islands. Go to the dock and ask around. If you are making the ride between Grenada and Trinidad, you can usually get a lift on the magnificent sloops that tie up in St George's harbour Grenada.

7

Ferries connect all the Virgin Islands; the French islands of Martinique and Guadeloupe (via Dominica); the islands off Guadeloupe; and all the Grenadines (see separate island sections). Another possibility is to travel by hitching on a **yacht**, which you can catch at the main centres (USVI, Antigua, Martinique, St Lucia and some of the Grenadines). If you go down to the marina and ask around, you may come up with something as the crews are often happy to take along the occasional passenger who is prepared to help out.

For details of car-hire, public transport, taxis etc. see the 'Getting Around' sections on each island.

Health

In the 18th century if you were caught in a cholera epidemic, you could have looked foward to a tonic of diluted sulphuric acid and tincture of cardamom or ammoniated tincture of opium. There are references to 'this fatal climate' on gravestones and memorials throughout the Caribbean. Today however, the Caribbean is basically a very healthy place.

Malaria is still a problem in Haiti and a little bit in the Dominican Republic, so you are advised to take preventative medicines when visiting those countries—the course usually begins a week before you arrive and continues for four weeks after you leave the area. **Hepatitis** occurs rarely and so you can have an injection giving some cover against Hepatitis A, which is caught mainly from water and food.

There is quite a high incidence of venereal diseases around the Caribbean, including HIV, which some reckon started in Haiti (there is little evidence that this is true, though it is prevalent there). The risks from casual sex are clear. If you are travelling to the less developed islands and wish to take sterile needles (and possibly plasma), make sure they are packed up to look official otherwise customs might begin to wonder.

Warnings
Sun-burn can ruin your holiday and so it is worth taking it easy for the first few days. You are recommended to keep to short stints of about 15–20 minutes at first in the hottest part of the day (11 am–3 pm). Take high protection-factor suncream. Sun-hats are easily bought. Be particularly careful if you go snorkelling, because the combination of the sun and the cooling water is lethal. Take sunglasses.

Traditional West Indian methods of soothing sun-burn include the application of juice of **aloe**, a fleshy cactus-like plant, which is used a lot in cosmetics. Break a leaf and squeeze out the soothing juice. Manufactured alternatives include calamine lotion. And if you will be spending most of your time in and out of the water you might take some talcum powder for your feet.

There are very few poisonous things in the Caribbean, but you may well come across the **manchineel tree**, which often grows on the beach. These are tall, bushy trees with a fruit like a small apple, known by Columbus's men as the apple of death. Do not eat them! Steer clear of the tree itself because the sap is poisonous. You should not even shelter under them in the rain because the sap will blister your skin.

Mosquitoes are of course a plague, though many tourist areas are treated to get rid of them. They can cause dengue fever (in the Greater Antilles) and of course malaria (in

8

Hispaniola only). Burn mosquito coils, and off the beaten track you might consider taking a mosquito net (there will probably already be nails in the walls where others have had the same idea). Of the many insect repellents, the strongest (the basis for most of them) is DET (pronounced Deet).

Less potentially harmful, but equally as irritating, are the tiny invisible **sand-flies** which plague certain beaches after rain and towards the end of the afternoon. In 1631, Sir Henry Colt wrote: 'First you have such abundance of small knatts by ye sea shore towards ye sun goinge down yt bite so as no rest cann be had without fyers under your Hamaccas'. For a barely visible insect, they pack a big bite.

Climate

Colonists knew the Bahamas as the 'isles of perpetual June'—generally speaking the climate over the whole area is impeccable. The temperature varies just a few degrees across the year from Nassau, the capital of the Bahamas in the north to Port of Spain in Trinidad, more than 1000 miles farther south. In the larger islands it will occasionally reach 100°F. Temperatures drop considerably at night and so you might need a thin jersey on a winter evening.

Average winter and summer temperatures, °C(°F)

	Nassau (Bahamas)	Kingston (Jamaica)	San Juan (Puerto Rico)	St John (USVI)	Port of Spain (Trinidad)	Willemstad (Curaçao)
Winter	21(69)	25(77)	26(78)	25(76)	26(79)	27(80)
Summer	27(80)	28(82)	28(82)	28(82)	27(80)	28(82)

There are just two main seasons, which vary very slightly between Nassau in the north and Port of Spain; wet (May or June and October or November) and the dry season. The difference is very slight. Tropical showers are frequent all year round in the Caribbean. They will drench you in a matter of seconds. You may consider taking a waterproof, but remember that the sun will dry you out almost as quickly as you got wet.

Hurricanes

Hurricanes are the severest natural disaster in an area of otherwise benign weather and recent years have seen some bad ones (Hurricane Gilbert in 1988 wasted Jamaica and the Cayman Islands, but both have been quickly rebuilt and the worst hurricane this century, Hurricane Hugo in 1989, flattened Guadeloupe and St Croix.) Turning anti-clockwise in the northern hemispheres, hurricanes rise near the coast of Africa, and, fed by warm winds over the water, they get a couple of thousand miles run-up before they carve their way through the islands, at the same time delivering a massive deluge of rain, which cause yet more destruction. If you hear that one is on the way, find the strongest concrete bunker possible and shelter in it with everybody else. If all suddenly goes quiet for a while you are in the eye (the very centre of the hurricane), batten down the hatches because it will start again in a few minutes. If you are in a sailing boat, the best place to head for is a mangrove swamp. The most likely month for hurricanes is September. The traditional rhyme runs:

June too soon, July stand by, September remember, October all over.

The Green Flash

Every fan of the Caribbean pursues the Green Flash relentlessly: it is one of the islands' most elusive and ephemeral moments, best sought on a palm beach, rum punch in hand. It occurs over the sea, only rarely, during a totally cloudless sunset, at the very moment that the last tip of the sun disappears over the horizon. It usually lasts for about half a second, and never for more than a second and a half: a tiny green strip the width of the sun on the surface of the sea.

Time Zones

Apart from Club Med enclaves (which have their own time schedule for some reason), the whole of the Eastern Caribbean (Barbados up to the Virgin Islands) and Puerto Rico and the Dominican Republic are four hours behind GMT. Haiti, Jamaica, Cuba, the Caymans and the Bahamas work to Eastern Standard Time (five hours behind GMT).

'Caribbean Time' is an expression you will hear all over the islands and it refers to the West Indians' elastic and entirely unpredictable schedules. Businesses can be punctual, but in restaurants and shops they will have little sympathy with a slave to the second hand. The Jamaicans say 'soon come', which means any time from now to tomorrow.

Electricity

In most Caribbean islands the electrical supply is 110 or 120 volts at 60 cycles, and so American electrical appliances need no adaptor (British and French visitors will need to take one). The French islands work to 220 volts and the Dutch islands at 110. The British islands are mixed; those that have been developed recently tend to be on the American standard (BVI and Anguilla), but some of the British Caribbean islands have a 230 or 240 volt supply at 50 cycles per second. Some hotels work on the American system, though, so it is worth checking before you go. If hotel rooms are not fitted with electrical appliances, ask at the front desk, where they may well keep some stashed away.

Photography

You will find that many West Indians either dive for cover or start remonstrating violently at the very sight of a camera—enough lobster-red tourists have photographed the quaint natives here to last an age. Some will talk about their soul and others about the money you will have to pay. If you see a good shot and go for it, you can usually talk your way out of trouble, but if you stop and chat first then most people will let you photograph them.

In the middle of the day, the brightness of the Caribbean sun bleaches all colour out of the landscape except the strongest tropical colours, but as the afternoon draws in you will find a stunning depth of colour in the golds and greens. The heat in the islands is also a problem with film (put it in the hotel fridge), as are the X-ray machines at the airports. The officials will swear that no damage will be done, but it is best that it goes through in a X-ray proof bag, or is searched by hand.

Money

Generally speaking the Caribbean is not cheap. Flights are quite expensive to begin with and then if you stay on the tourist circuit you will find yourself paying prices not unlike Europe or the USA. However, if you get off the tourist track and stay in local West Indian guest houses in town and eat local food, you will pay considerably less in most islands. All the same, do not expect to stay anywhere for much less than US$15.

A few Caribbean countries have their own currency, but many of the smaller islands share a denomination, often according to the past colonial set-up. The US dollar, however, is the currency in universal demand around the area and so many countries have pegged their currency to it. Where the greenback is not officially allowed to circulate freely, there is usually a black market for exchange.

Prices in the tourist industry throughout the Caribbean are quoted in US dollars and it is even possible in places to spend a couple of weeks working exclusively in that currency (in tourist hotels and their watersports concessions, restaurants and shops). However, if you go off the beaten track, it is a good idea to have local notes and change. It is also a good idea to take small denominations.

Hustling is fairly widespread in the Caribbean. All visitors are presumed to have a few dollars that they would not mind releasing (they could afford the flight after all). You are vulnerable particularly in the first 48 hours or until you have a bit of colour. Also you will probably be accosted if you go to the downtown area and on any public beach. A firm and polite no to whatever is offered (from a reefer to an aloe massage) is the easiest way to guarantee your peace.

These are the official currencies in the different islands:
Barbados—Barbados dollar, fixed to US dollar (US$1=BDS$1.98), US currency also accepted.
Trinidad and Tobago—Trinidad and Tobago dollar, fixed to US dollar (US$1=TT$4.25), US currency not officially valid.
Windward and Leeward Islands (the former British islands of Grenada, St Vincent, St Lucia, Dominica, Antigua and Barbuda, St Kitts and Nevis and the Crown Colonies of Montserrat and Anguilla)—the Eastern Caribbean dollar, fixed to US dollar (US$1=EC$2.65), US currency also accepted.
French Antilles (Martinique, Guadeloupe, St Martin, St Barthélemy)—French Franc, US dollar also accepted in tourist areas.
Netherlands Antilles (Sint Maarten, Saba, Statia, Curaçao and Bonaire)—Netherlands Antillean Florin or Guilder, fixed to US dollar (US$1=NAFl1.77), US dollar freely accepted.
Aruba—Aruban Florin, fixed to US dollar (US$1=AFl1.77), US dollar freely accepted.
British and US Virgin Islands—US dollar official currency.
Puerto Rico—US dollar.
Dominican Republic—Dominican Peso, fixed to the US dollar (US$1=RD$12 approx). US dollars accepted in all tourist areas.
Haiti—Haitian Dollar, made up of five gourdes; officially fixed to US dollar (US$1=5 gourdes), but the US dollar trades at about 8 gourdes. US dollar is accepted under the counter. Tourist hotels accept US dollars.
Cuba—Cuban Peso, fixed artificially to US dollar in tourist areas (US$1=Cuban$1) and this has led to a black market.
Jamaica—Jamaican dollar, fixed to US dollar (US$1=J$20 approx). Now fluctuates on the open market.

11

Cayman Islands—Cayman Islands dollar, fixed to US dollar (US$1=80 Cayman cents or CI$1=US$1.25).
Turks and Caicos—US dollar.
Bahamas—Bahamian dollar, fixed at par to US dollar, which is freely accepted all over the Bahamas.

Exchange

The banks give the best rate of exchange. At the hotels you will usually receive a lesser rate. The exchanges in most islands will accept hard currency **traveller's cheques**—Sterling, French Franc, Deutschmark and Canadian Dollar, but the most popular is of course the US Dollar, particularly if you are going to a country where the dollar is an alternative currency. You will also get a better rate of exchange. Some banks are beginning to charge for the exchange of traveller's cheques, however. Take plenty of small denomination cheques and remember to record the number so that you can be refunded if you lose them. **Credit cards** are widely accepted in anything that is connected with the tourist industry—hotels, restaurants and tourist shops. If you need to, you can draw cash on a credit card at the bank—there are AMEX and VISA representatives on all the islands. **Personal cheques** are rarely accepted. Service charges in the Caribbean are usually 10%, unless otherwise indicated.

Language

English is spoken in the tourist industry in most Caribbean countries, mainly because of the large number of American visitors. Most islands have a *patois*, an everyday language based on the original official colonial language; these are often incomprehensible to the visitor.

English is the official language of all the British Commonwealth Caribbean countries—Barbados, Trinidad and Tobago, the Windward Islands (Grenada, St Vincent, St Lucia, Dominica), the Leeward Islands (Antigua, Montserrat, St Kitts and Nevis and Anguilla), the British Virgin Islands, Jamaica, the Caymans, the Turks and Caicos and the Bahamas.

French is the official language of the French Antilles, Martinique, Guadeloupe, St Martin and St Barts, but English is widely spoken in the hotels. French is also the official language of Haiti, though few people speak it outside the main towns because they talk *kreyol*. English is spoken in the bigger hotels.

Dutch is the official language of the Netherlands Antilles, but *Papiamento* is spoken in the Dutch Leeward Islands (ABC Islands) and English is traditionally the language of the Dutch Windwards.

Spanish is the language of Puerto Rico, the Dominican Republic and Cuba. English is widely spoken in Puerto Rico, but few people speak it outside the hotels in either Cuba or the Dominican Republic.

Flora and Fauna

Columbus himself was the first European to be captivated by the extraordinary beauty of the West Indies. The volcanic islands of the Lesser Antilles and the windward coasts of the Greater Antilles are incredibly fertile, watered by constant showers from the Atlantic winds. There are many rainforests in the Caribbean islands. A gardener's most useful tool is a machete, to keep back what use to be known as the *green hell*. Growth is so rampant that fences turn into hedges and even telegraph wires fur up in no time.

Trees

There are many varieties of **palm** tree in the Caribbean and you will see coconut palms everywhere, including the beaches of course—beware of sitting under them, though, because people have been killed by falling coconuts. In many Caribbean gardens you will often find the golden palm, that looks like a fountain of greenery, and the sago palm, very dark green, with scratchy fronds like a comb. In St Barts they use the sabal palm (**latanier** in French) for weaving rushwork. But the most impressive palms of all are the tall cabbage, and particularly the royal palm, both of which grow to over 100 feet in height and cast off a spike that points directly upwards. The royal palm is cultivated for the heart of palm that is put into salads.

In the forests you will see bamboo that grows up to 60 feet, sometimes grown in alleys, and endless ferns that perch in the treetops like an explosion of greenery. The shape of the silver-backed fern will be stencilled on you if you slap it onto your skin.

Many of the fruit-bearing **trees** that grow so well in the islands' fertile soil were imported in the 18th century, as a commercial proposition, or to provide food for the slaves. The banana and some of its many relatives, the plantain and green fig, came from the Indian Ocean area. In Europe you only see a few of the hundred odd varieties; some ripen too quickly for the two-week shipment, particularly the delicious miniature banana. In the southern Caribbean they still grow nutmeg and cocoa, which was made fashionable in Europe by Marie-Thérèse d'Espagne when she became Queen of France. Breadfruit, with fruits like vast green cannonballs (also its relation the breadnut) was unpopular with the slaves at first, but has since become a staple. The fruit of the ackee tree tastes a bit like scrambled egg and is eaten at breakfast. 'Ground provisions' include yam, tannia, eddoe, cassava and christophene, all of which you will see on display at the Caribbean markets.

Flowers

The Caribbean is perhaps most famous for its flowers and gardens and you will see explosions of tropical colours all year round, with orange, pink and purple bougain-villaea, 200 species of brightly coloured hibiscus (one of which is known as *choublac* in Haiti, and is used to blacken shoes) and scarlet poinsettia. More exotic flowers are passion flowers, heliconia, shaped like a lobster claw, the chenille plant (also called red hot cat tail because of its shape) and the bird of paradise flower, like a bird's face with topknot plumage. You will see the ubiquitous plastic-looking anthurium everywhere. There are also hundreds of orchids in the Caribbean, one of which is grown commercially to produce vanilla. The local names for plants vary of course from island to island and between the languages, but there are some colourful and amusing names: *mother-in-law's tongue* grows in a sprout of fearsome twisted green tongues.

Many of the trees in the West Indies also flower, including the scarlet of the African tulip tree, white or yellow frangipani and the cannonball tree, whose delicate flowers

13

Hibiscus

drop to earth at dusk, unlike the night-blooming *cereus* (a flower), which dies with the daylight. Lignum vitae and jacaranda bloom a lilac colour and the two tall pouis leave the ground smothered in pink or yellow petals. Perhaps most impressive of the flowering trees are the tall immortelle, which comes out in an orange bloom early in the year and the poinciana. The *flamboyant*, otherwise known as the tourist tree, comes out in a flush of scarlet in June and July. And other local trees are the chicle tree, which provides a rubber-like substance that the Amerindians chewed on, and the calabash or gourd tree, whose large wooden fruits are used as bowls and cups. In the ABC islands look out for the lopsided divi-divi tree which grows with the direction of the wind.

There are **Botanical Gardens** throughout the islands, used for propagation of food and of important medicinal and commercial plants (quinine, arrowroot, camphor and spices such as cinnamon, clove, allspice). The oldest and most famous are the gardens in St Vincent, but there were gardens in most islands at one stage and some of them are still in commercial use.

Fauna

The animal life of the Caribbean is quite limited and all the domestic animals that you see were imported by the colonists—including the ubiquitous goat. Only a few indigenous land animals survive and it is rare to see an armadillo or a jutia (a rat like creature). Reptiles of all sorts exist, from the tiny little tree frogs that keep you awake at night chirruping, toads that croak so loud that they sound like a generator, to the prehistoric, tank-like five-foot iguanas and the crocodiles that live in the swamplands. There are a few snakes, but only one or two of them are poisonous—if you see a pair of eyes glowing at night in Martinique or St Lucia watch out, because it will be the venomous *fer-de-lance*. There are plenty of insects, including mosquitoes, marching columns of termites and on the beaches irritating tiny sand flies that appear towards dusk.

Birdlife

The birds of the Caribbean are spectacular and incredibly varied. Not only are there plenty of indigenous species, many with plumage of startling tropical colours, but migratory species also pass through in the winter months as they keep away from the winter cold (both north and south). In the gardens you will find small and daring tanagers and bananaquits (which will have a go at the food on your table if you look away) as well as the yellow orioles and characters called grackles. There are also a large number of hummingbirds. Trinidad alone has about 15, but you will see these beautiful creatures in the rainforests and in the gardens. The 'doctor bird' or red-billed streamertail (it has a long double tail) is the Jamaican national bird.

Many of the Windward Islands have their own parrots that hide high up in the rainforest; sadly many are endangered because they have been hunted near to extinction and then exported as pets. Other forest dwellers are the black and yellow trogons and fluorescent green honeycreepers. There are woodpeckers, cuckoos and warblers in the larger islands. Shore birds include pelicans, which you will see offshore, perched on a rock digesting their meal, boobies, terns, magnificent frigatebirds and the scissor-tailed red-billed tropicbird.

Swamps have the greatest diversity of birdlife and here you will find many sorts of herons, waders and ducks as well as sandpipers and the odd tiny water-tyrant. Oddest of all are the purple gallinule and the wattled jacana, with overlong toes that allow it to walk over lilies. Finally, one of the most spectacular sights that you can witness in the West Indies is the evening flight of the scarlet ibis, which only takes place in the Caroni Swamp in Trinidad. Another fine sight is the pink flamingo, which nests only in Great Inagua in the Bahamas and on Bonaire in the ABC islands.

For the birdlife, Trinidad is undoubtedly the most exciting island to visit (it supposedly has more species than Canada, which is not unlikely because most Canadian birds probably spend the winter here), but all the Greater Antilles also have an excellent variety. Over the last few years there has been an increase in awareness of the natural habitat in the countries of the Caribbean, along with the establishment of natural parks or increased powers for those that already exist. There should be excellent opportunities for enthusiasts, but not all islands have the organization to cope well with visitors. The best islands to visit for a general impression of the flora and birdlife are Trinidad (rainforest and swamplands), Dominica (rainforest) and Puerto Rico.

Sports

Beaches

The Caribbean is famous for its beaches and on most islands you will find the idyll of a palm-fringed strip with warm water that laps in small waves and of course a supreme sunset. The best sand tends to be on the low coral islands like the Bahamas and the Leewards, but you will also find magnificent, often secluded, coves tucked between the vast headlands of the mountainous islands in the Eastern Caribbean and the Greater Antilles. Swimming is safe in most places, but do not swim alone, and beware the undertow on the Atlantic side of the Lesser Antilles.

If all you want from the Caribbean on your holiday is a beach, then the best islands for being alone on uninterrupted miles of blinding white sand, with gin-clear shallows and an aquamarine sea before you are Anguilla, Antigua and Barbuda, the Family Islands in the Bahamas and the Caicos Islands in the Turks and Caicos. A bit better known and often more crowded, are the British Virgin Islands, Barbados and the Grenadines. For more information there are individual 'beaches' paragraphs in the individual island sections.

Beach Watersports

On the smaller islands there is usually at least one beach that is has all the **watersports** and where the big hotels are collected. Here you can get anything from a windsurfer and a few minutes on waterskis to a parasail flight, a trip on a pedalo or a high-speed trip around the bay on an inflated sausage (it'll shut the kids up anyway). Glass-bottom boat tours are usually available too. Wetbikes or jetskis have made their mark in the West Indies and are available for hire at most centres and in most hotels you are able to hire small sailboats such as hobie cats and sunfish. Hotels set on their own beach will invariably have a selection of watersports, though not usually as complete as above. Prices vary considerably across the Caribbean and are listed in the island sections. Most things can be booked through the hotels or their beach concessionaires. There is not really that much beach culture in the islands, but you will often find a small beach bar, where you can get hold of a rum punch or a beer or a small local snack. Rum cruises and sunset tours aboard a resurrected galleon complete with boozatorium and lots of walking the plank are available on the larger and more touristed islands.

Diving

The Caribbean and the Bahamas have some of the best corals and fish in the world. The variety is stunning, from the world's third largest barrier reef just a few miles off the coast of Andros in the Bahamas, to the colourful seascapes of Bonaire and the Caymans to warm and cool water springs under the sea off the volcanic islands.

The reefs are incredibly colourful. You will see yellow and pink tube sponges and purple trumpet sponges, sea feathers and seafans (gorgonians) that stand against the current alongside a forest of staghorn, elkhorn and black coral and the more exotic species like the domes of startlingly white brain coral, star corals and yellow pencil coral. Near the surface the corals are multi-coloured and tightly bunched as they compete for space; then as you descend the yellows and the reds and whites fade, leaving the purples and blues of larger corals that lean out into the deep sea to catch the last of the light.

Many islands have laws to protect their reefs and their fish (there are hardly any places left in the Caribbean where you are allowed to use spearguns). In certain islands you are asked not to buy coral jewellery because it will probably have been taken illegally from the reef. One of the few dangerous things on the reef are fire corals, which will give you a nasty sting if you touch one.

Other underwater life includes a stunning array of crustaceans and of course tropical fish. On the bottom you will find beautifully camouflaged crabs that stare at you goggle eyed, starfish, lobsters, sea anenomes and pretty pink and white feather duster worms. Around them swim angelfish, squirrelfish, surgeonfish, striped sergeant majors, grunts

16

and soldierfish. Above them little shoals of wrasses and blue tang shimmy in the bubbles. If you get too close, puffer fish blow themselves up like a spiky football, smiling uncomfortably. And beware the poisonous stonefish.

At night a whole new seascape opens up as some corals close up for the night and others open up in an array of different colours. While some fish tuck themselves into a crevice in the reef to sleep (eyes kept open), starfish, lobsters and sea urchins scuttle around the seabed on the hunt for food. If you stop breathing for a moment, you will hear the midnight parrotfish crunching on the coral polyps, spitting out the broken down fragments of reef that eventually turn into sand.

The best areas for diving in the Caribbean are Bonaire off the coast of South America (for its slopes with excellent and colourful corals), the Cayman Islands (noted for its sheer walls) and some of the Bahamas and the Turks and Caicos. There are also a number of liveaboard dive boats based around the Bahamas and the Caymans. Other islands with good reputations include the Virgin Islands and smaller places such as Saba and Dominica. Cozumel off the Yucatan peninsula (not dealt with in this book) is also reputed to have excellent diving.

Most dive-shops in the Caribbean are affiliated to PADI (many also to NAUI) and they will expect you to present a certificate of competence if you wish to go out on to the reefs straight away, but all islands except the smallest have lessons available in the resorts if you are a novice. An open-water qualifying course (which allows you to dive in a pair with another qualified open-water diver) takes about a week, but with a resort course you can usually get underwater in a morning. You will have a session in the swimming pool before you are allowed to dive in the open sea.

The **snorkelling** is also good off many of the islands and most hotels have equipment for their guests and on hire to non-residents. Beware, if you go snorkelling on a sunny day soon after you arrive, because the water and the sun make a fearsome combination on unprotected skin (wear a shirt, perhaps). In most places you can arrange glass-bottom boat tours and snorkelling trips.

For those who would like to see the deeper corals, but who do not dive, there are submarines in Barbados, St Thomas in the USVI, Grand Cayman and the Bahamas, St Barts and St Martin.

Fishing

A sport that is traditionally renowned in certain areas, but which is now possible in all Caribbean islands is **deep-sea** or **big game fishing**. Docked at the yachting marina, the boats are huge, sleek and gleaming cruisers with high towers for visibility, usually equipped with tackle and bait and 'fighting chair'. Beer in hand you trawl the line behind the boat waiting for a bite and then watch the beast surface and fight as you cruise along, giving line and steadily hauling it in.

The magnificent creatures that you are out to kill are fish such as the blue marlin, which inhabits the deepest waters and can weigh anything up to 1100 lbs and measure ten feet in length. Giant or bluefin tuna can weigh up to 1000 lbs. Wahoo, around 100 lbs, is a racer and a fighter and the white marlin can weigh up to 150 lbs. Perhaps the most beautiful of them all is the sailfish, with a huge spiny fan on its back, which will jump clean out of the water in its desperate attempts to get free.

The best known areas are the ports off the Gulf Stream, on Bimini, and traditionally around Havana (though things are quieter there now), but you can easily charter a boat from the north coast of Jamaica and from Puerto Rico and the Virgin Islands (there are deep waters offshore). The most famous story about fishing is *The Old Man and The Sea* by Ernest Hemingway, which is set in a small fishing village east of Havana.

Bonefishing takes place in the shallows not far from the shore. Fish that you cast for not far offshore are blackfin and allison tuna, bonito, dorado and barracuda and smaller fish such as snapper and grouper, all of which end up on your dinner table if you wish to taste them.

Windsurfing

Because of the warmth and the constant winds off the Atlantic Ocean, the Caribbean offers superb windsurfing, particularly when the winds are at their highest in the early months of the year. The sport is well developed—a number of championship competitions have been held in the Caribbean—and you can hire a board on any island. 'Clinics' and instruction are usually available. The best places to go are Aruba, the southern coast of Barbados and the north coasts of Puerto Rico and the Dominican Republic (Cabarete). The sport is also very popular in the French islands.

Yachting

There is a marina on most islands where you can find a crewed sailboat if you wish to go for a day's **yachting** (or longer in many places). The volcanic islands are particularly good for this, because as you sail along the coast, you see the vast and fertile landscape move gradually above you, but there are many popular sailing areas in the Caribbean and the Bahamas. Tried and trusted are the Grenadine Islands between St Vincent and Grenada, Antigua, the British Virgin Islands (centred around Sir Francis Drake Passage, one of the most beautiful spots in the whole area) and the Bahamas. See sections under the Virgin Islands and the Grenadines. The British Yacht Cruising Association can be contacted on 0705 219844.

Other Sports

The mountainous islands of the Caribbean literally collect water and many have large rivers where you can find waterfalls and rockpools that make excellent **river bathing**. There is a problem in some islands including St Lucia with bilharzia (in lakes and slow flowing rivers) so you are not advised to swim there, but the other Windwards are clear. In Jamaica, where there is good river bathing you can also take a **rafting** trip on the larger rivers—quite expensive, but good fun.

Sports based on land include **tennis**, which is well served all over the Caribbean, with courts in a high proportion of the hotels and some island clubs. If there is no court at your hotel, arrange with another through the front desk, or simply wander in and ask. Hotels generally charge a small fee and they usually have racquets and balls for hire. **Riding** is also offered on the majority of the islands and this is a good way to see the rainforest and the sugar flats if you think that your calves might not be up to the hike. In Jamaica and the Dominican Republic you can even get a game of polo.

On the larger islands and those with a developed tourist industry there are **golf** courses open to visitors on payment of a green fee (except in some hotels where it is included in the package). If you decide to play, be flexible because the courses will often give priority to hotel guests. Most courses have equipment for hire.

There is good **walking** in the Caribbean islands, which are cut and crossed with traditional trails used by the likes of the *porteuses* (see Martinique) and the farmers of today. The rainforest is fascinating to walk in anyway because the growth is so incredibly lush. Many of the Eastern Caribbean islands have an active volcano in whose crater you can climb—or you could make the walk to the boiling lake in Dominica's Valley of Desolation.

The heat will be most bearable between dawn, usually at around 6 am, and 10 am, before the sun gets too high and then between 4 pm and dusk. However, the higher you go, the cooler it gets, and the temperature in the forest is not bad anyway. It gets dark quickly in the Caribbean, so be careful to be back by 6 pm otherwise you may find yourself stranded, at the mercy of the spirits of the Caribbean night. It often rains of course, so take a waterproof coat and high up in the hills you will need a jersey underneath because the winds make it very cold. Big heavy boots are not necessary. Gym-shoes or sneakers are usually enough, unless you are headed into very steep and slippery country, when you should have some ankle support—perhaps a pair of light tropical boots. There are tour companies on all the larger islands who will transport you to and from your hotel and provide a guide.

There are a number of islands with extensive **cave** systems which have been carved out of the limestone rock by the dripping of water. The best caves are in the Greater Antilles, though some have been overdeveloped (with electric buggies, hard hats and probably even canned music by now) but not all are open to the public. For hard-core speleologists there are excellent opportunities for exploring uncharted pot-holes in the larger islands, such as where whole rivers disappear underground in the *karst* limestone country.

Caribbean Rhythms

People joke that the West Indians change the roll of their gait as they move along the street, switching rhythm to each successive stereo system that they pass. A bit of an exaggeration, but music has been central to Caribbean life since slave days when it was a principal form of recreation, and you will hear it all day, every day. You'll see three-year-olds in the first throes of rhythm and sixty-year-olds who will take a turn on the living room floor with an easy grace. In Santo Domingo the shoeshine boys will strike up on their boxes with brushes and tins of polish. Buses are like mobile discotheques. At Carnival they dance for days.

There are almost as many beats as there are islands in the Caribbean and they go on changing and developing over time. The roots are audible in many cases—you will see marching bands dressed in their red tunics playing 'Oh when the Saints' *reggae* style, Indian flourishes appear in Trinidadian *calypso*, the Latin beat is so clear in Cuban and Puerto Rican *salsa* and the vocals of rap appear in calypso and Jamaican *dancehall*. But in all the Caribbean sounds, the rhythm is relentlessly fast and the beat is as solid as the African drums from which it is derived.

19

The West Indians will use anything to make music. At carnival the crowds shuffle along to the sound of a couple of drums and a cowbell. Even garden forks have been tuned up in Curaçao. But the best example of them all is the steel drum in Trinidad, which was invented in the yards of Port of Spain after the last war. Discarded biscuit tins and oil drums were bashed out and then tuned up and an orchestra was created.

As you travel around, you will see speakers set up in the street just for the hell of it. Cars practically bulge with the beat and they can often be heard before they can be seen coming along the road. If you are invited to a *fête*, go, because they are a wild side of West Indian life. Dance is all lower carriage movement, shuffle-stepping and swaying hips and is incredibly energetic.

The rhythms of one island often spread to another. The main popular rhythms and their countries of origin are as follows:

Soca (soul-calypso)—Trinidad, where calypso itself started, see pp. 60–1, Barbados and other islands nearby have begun to produce their own calypsonians, some of them very good.

Zouk—Martinique and Guadeloupe, with a bustling double beat.

Salsa—two different sorts, one each from Cuba and Puerto Rico, the latter influenced by the 'Neo-Riceñans' (Puerto Ricans in New York).

Merengue—the Dominican Republic, also a strongly Latin sound.

Compas—Haiti, a bit rougher, but not dissimilar to the zouk of the French Antilles, also echoes of West Africa.

Any of the Caribbean **carnivals** is worth attending if you happen to be on the island and you can often join in if you do go by asking around (usually for a small fee to cover the cost of the costume). It is worth crossing half the world to get to the **Trinidad Carnival** (many Trinidadians do), which takes place at the beginning of Lent. Also there are steel band and calypso competitions. Other music festivals include the Cuban **Jazz Festival** in February (Cuba is good for music, because of the many different sorts) and the **Merengue Festival** in Santo Domingo in July. At around the same time, reggae fans cross the world for **Reggae Sunsplash** in Montego Bay, Jamaica.

A Caribbean Calendar of Events

The big festivals in the Caribbean are Independence day celebrations and Carnival, usually pre-Lenten, but sometimes at the end of the sugar harvest (*cropover* in Barbados and the *zafra* in Cuba), with other religious festivals in the Catholic islands (the *fiestas patronales* of Martinique and Guadeloupe, Puerto Rico, the Dominican Republic and Haiti). Other get-togethers are centred around music—calypso, merengue, reggae, jazz (see below) and around the sea, with sailing and fishing competitions. Finally, there are other cultural events, from dance in Jamaica and story-telling in St Lucia and Dominica, Indian festivals in Trinidad to gastronomic blowouts in the French islands.

Whatever the official reason, they become another excuse for an organized party and they usually involve a *jump-up* (more Caribbean dancing) which will wind through the streets or in a stadium, dancing to a shuffle step. It is often a bit like an oversized picnic, with cook-ins going on on the sidelines, where a half oil-barrel is turned on its side to make a brazier. Here chicken and fish are barbecued and then sprinkled with hot pepper sauce and soldier crabs are roasted in their shells.

The summer months are the best if you want to see the West Indians at play (they think the temperature is better) and so there are a number of festivals in June, July and August. Things also get booked up then. However, once you are there, you will invariably be made welcome by the islanders.

January

At **New Year** singers stroll from house to house chanting in Aruba, Grenada holds a sailing regatta and the Bahamas kick off the New Year with their **junkanoo** celebrations. Early in the month there is a **Maroon** Festival in Jamaica, some of which dates from the 18th century. Look out for the **Three Kings' Day** in Puerto Rico on 6 Jan, also celebrated in Martinique with gastronomic flair as **La Fête des Rois**. St Barts holds a Music Festival.

January also sees the culmination of the St Kitts Carnival, but most of the pre-Lenten **Carnivals** are just getting underway with weekend warm-ups and the early stages of calypso and beauty-queen competitions. There are also windsurfing competitions in Barbados and the Dominican Republic.

February

Grenada holds its **Independence Day** celebrations on 7th, with *jump-ups* up and down the hills of St George's, followed by St Lucia on 22nd and the Dominican Republic on 27th. In the first week is the **Miami—Montego Bay yacht race** and on 18th there is a **street fair** in Holetown, Barbados, commemorating the first settlement of the islands in 1627. There is a **jazz festival** in Havana in February or March.

Carnivals culminate in a three-day *jump-up*, calypso competitions and masked parades in the streets on Shrove Tuesday (Mardi Gras) or Ash Wednesday. Aruba, Bonaire, Carriacou, Curaçao, Dominica, Dominican Republic, Guadeloupe, Haiti, Martinique, St Lucia, Saint Barthélemy, Saint Martin, Trinidad and Tobago.

March

Montserrat celebrates **St Patrick's Day** on 17th and in Trinidad **Phagwah** sees street parades in which people spray each other with bright red dye. March 30th is the Anniversary day of the transfer to American ownership in the USVI.

April

The Netherlands Antilles commemorate Queen Beatrix's official Birthday with parties on 30 April and there are also celebrations for **Easter**, including a **Fish Festival** in Oistins Town on Barbados and **goat and crab races** in Tobago. Many of the **sailing** competitions get underway, including the Family Islands Regatta in the Exumas, Bahamas, the Bequia Regatta in the Grenadines, Grenada's regatta and the famed International Sailing Week in Antigua. The Cayman Islands hold a regatta and a couple of small carnivals (**Batanabo** mid-month and **Brachanal** in Cayman Brac a week later). Jamaica holds a Carnival week and you can also see the Easter season of their National Theatre Dance Company. St Thomas also holds a carnival at the end of the month.

May

Anguilla Day is celebrated on 30 May with sailing races and Long Island in the Bahamas holds a **regatta**. In Jamaica a carnival is held at Negril, with junkanoo parades

21

as well as popular dance music in the streets. **Abolition Day** is remembered with picnics and fêtes in the French islands on 27th and St Martin holds a **Food Festival** with *jump-ups* as well as classic cooking.

June
The **Bomba y Plena** Festival of African music and dance is held in Ponce, Puerto Rico at the beginning of the month and the **Goombay** Festival kicks off with street parades and reviews in the Bahamas. In St Lucia Aqua Action is staged at the Whitsun weekend. In the Cayman islands it is Million Dollar Month (a fishing competition) and regattas include a week's sailing in Tobago and **Regatta Time** in the Abacos in the Bahamas. **Carnival** week or Vincie Mas takes place towards the end of the month in St Vincent and the Grenadines and the beginnings of **Cropover** in Barbados get underway.

July
The Bahamas celebrates **Independence** on 10th and of course the French Antilles fête **Bastille Day** on 14th. The big events in Cuba are around 26 July, when the anniversary celebrations of the Moncada Garrison attack and then **Carnival** are held. The USVI celebrate emancipation on 3rd. There are carnivals in Saba and Sint Eustatius and late in the month in Antigua and Barbuda. Music is particularly strong in July, with **Reggae Sunsplash** in Jamaica, the **Merengue Festival** in the Dominican Republic and then in Barbados the Carnival-like **Cropover**, which culminates with Kadooment Day. The annual Trinidad to Tobago **powerboat race** and the **Bimini Blue Marlin Tournament** take place towards the end of the month.

August
Most of the former British islands hold festivities on 1st, the date of emancipation, which in Jamaica also coincides with the **Independence Day** celebrations on the first Monday in August. **St Barts** also celebrates its saint's day on 24th and Trinidad and Tobago *jump-ups* up with Independence celebrations on 31st. The extraordinary and colourful **Fête des Cuisinières** takes place on 11th, St Laurent's day (the patron Saint of cooks) in Guadeloupe, with parades of dishes and blow-outs. Anguilla holds its **carnival week** at the start of the month. There are plenty of regattas with the **yoles rondes** sailing races in Martinique, the **Carriacou** regatta, races at **Canouan** in the Grenadines, the **Anegada** race in the BVI late in the month and in the **Turks and Caicos**.

September
St Kitts and Nevis celebrate **Independence** on 19th and St John, USVI, holds its **carnival** near the beginning of the month.

October
There is an annual **regatta** in Bonaire (mid-month) and in the Caymans **Pirates' Week** with all sorts of festivities is held towards the end of the month. Puerto Plata in the Dominican Republic has a **merengue festival** in the second week. Trinidad holds a **steelband competition** early in the month. Also in Trinidad **Divali**, the Hindi Festival of lights, is very colourful and is held in October or November.

November
Dominica celebrates **Independence** on 3rd and Barbados on 30th. Sint Eustatius

commemorates the first salute to the American flag on 16th and nearby Saint Martin/ Sint Maarten get together in **Concordia Day** on 11th. Trinidad holds the yearly **Pan Jazz Festival.** Late November sees the beginning of the Antigua sailing season with the **Nicholson's boat show.**

December
Saba celebrates its flag day on 7th and St Lucia's **National Day** is on 13th. The **ARC** Rally arrives in the island about the same time after an Atlantic crossing. There are jazz and guitar festivals in alternate years in Martinique. St Kitts starts **Carnival Week** on about 20th and the Bahamas set **junkanoo** into motion, a celebration which lasts into the New Year. All Caribbean islands celebrate Christmas; **Nine Mornings** in St Vincent sees a week of celebrations in the run up to it; and of course the New Year itself is yet another good excuse for another *jump-up*. Well worth a visit to see the Puerto Ricans in a riot of excess is the **Hatillo Festival of Masks** on 28th.

Shopping

Shopping is one of the Caribbean's biggest industries, but hardly any of the things that are sold here originate in the area. Though there are objects of cultural value to be found, particularly in the larger islands, most of it is shipped in to satisfy the collector passions of long-distance shoppers. On the shelves of all the airco boutiques and the newer shopping malls that have begun to infest the area you can find jewels and precious stones, perfumes, photographic equipment, clothes, Cuban cigars etc.

The islands follow roughly speaking the patterns of their nation, with the French the leaders in perfumes and designer clothes and the Dutch, always great traders, with well-priced photographic equipment from the Far East. St Thomas, a traditional and particularly attractive port in the US Virgin Islands, where almost anything is on sale, is in danger of becoming one outsize emporium. The lure is, of course, the reduced prices (in comparison to the mainland) and every shop announces itself as 'duty-free' or 'in-bond'. The best duty-free shopping-centre islands in the Caribbean (some of which have been trading like this for hundreds of years) are Sint Maarten, St Thomas in the USVI and Nassau and Freeport in the Bahamas.

There is quite an active art scene now in many of the island and galleries are mentioned in the text. There are occasionally things of interest in the craft markets, but particularly on the bigger islands—Jamaica, Haiti and the Dominican Republic—you will find some highly original work. The best known of course is the *naive* work from Haiti.

Where to Stay

The West Indies had some of the finest and most luxurious hotels in the world. You can stay at island resorts where you communicate by flag, on endless beaches which are deserted at dawn, in 18th-century plantation splendour with a view across the canefields, and in high-pastel luxury in the Caribbean's newest resorts. Many of the islands offer top-notch hotels, but try the Grenadines and the Virgin Islands for isolated island

23

settings, Barbados for grand and long established hotels set in magnificent gardens, St Kitts and Nevis for plantation splendour, St Barts for chic, Anguilla for sumptuous, small island charm and Jamaica for reliable luxury.

There are some venerable gentlemen and grand dames of Caribbean tourism, who run luxurious enclaves which have seen generations of return guests since the Second World War, when Caribbean tourism began to take off. In Barbados and Jamaica are hotels such as the Sandy Lane, the Half Moon Club and Round Hill. They are invariably expensive, but they still offer a sophistication which was a hallmark of the Caribbean (mostly gone now). There are also some charming island-resorts which offer low-key but still sophisticated seclusion. You will find these in the Grenadines and the Virgin Islands. You will also find some faded old beach club hotels, remnants from the 60s, just a small number of rooms around a central house on the beach. The most modern Caribbean hotels tend to be large, humming palaces with blocks of rooms decorated in a symphony of bright pastel colours set against white tile floors.

All-Inclusives

This tradition has developed considerably in recent years. As the name implies, the rate is all-inclusive, and once you have paid the initial bill you do not have to pull out your wallet again. It is easier to budget of course, but it may discourage you from leaving the hotel and exploring, or going out to try the restaurants for dinner. All-inclusives have sprung up all over the Caribbean and they have begun to improve the service that they offer. Some have gone up-market, offering champagne and *à la carte* dining instead of the traditional buffet style meals. Jamaica and St Lucia are the specialists and the Sandals chain now has many resorts; there are all-inclusives that specialize in looking after children.

There is still a holiday-camp atmosphere about some all-inclusives, though, and their names give a good indication of their theme—Hedonism II and Couples (with the symbol of a pair of lions humping). These seem to encourage riotous behaviour, high-pressure fun factories—with as much alcohol as you can drink, dancing on the tables, mirrors on the bedroom ceiling and crash courses in marriage.

West Indian Inns

Dotted sporadically around the Caribbean are some magnificent old gingerbread-style homes, often former plantation houses, that have been converted into inns with mid-range prices, ideal for the independent traveller with a bit of cash. Some of the best are the *paradores* in Puerto Rico, often family-run hotels in charming old buildings hidden in the rainforest or in the towns, and the inns tucked into the hillsides of Charlotte Amalie on St Thomas.

Villas, Apartments and Condominiums

There are also **villas** all over the islands, most of them relatively modern and well-equipped. You can cater for yourself, or arrange for a cook. Contact them through the individual island villa rentals organizations or the tourist boards. The Caribbean now copes reasonably well with self-catering or efficiency holidays and so there are a large number of **apartments** on all the islands, some built in one building like a hotel, others scattered in landscaped grounds. Finally, **condominiums** are also springing up in many islands, answering to those who wish to invest in their vacation.

Guest Houses

These are the cheapest option and they are more fun, cheaper, and have far more character than bottom of the range tourist hotels. They are used by West Indian travellers and businessmen and are usually presided over by an ample and generous mother figure (something of a West Indian institution, she has not changed much for about two hundred years, see Barbados Hotels) and staying in them can be a good way to be introduced to local West Indian life in just a few days. In some you may notice a remarkable turnover of guests as these guest houses often rent rooms out by the hour as well as by the night.

In the major yachting centres you can sometimes persuade the yachties to give you a berth on the charter boats while they are in dock. Simply go down to the marina and ask around and you may come up with something.

Camping

Rules vary throughout the islands with regard to camping and though it is generally not encouraged, particularly on the beaches, there are camp-sites on the larger islands (the French Antilles and Cuba are quite well organized for camping). As a general rule, permission has to be obtained from the police before camping is permitted.

Categories

MAP means Modified American Plan (with breakfast and dinner included in the price) and **EP** means European Plan (no meals). You may also come across **CP**, Continental Plan, with room and breakfast and **AP**, or American Plan, with a room and all meals. Also see **all-inclusive** above. The high season is mid-December or January until mid-April and prices will be highest then. 'Off-season' travel will bring reductions of as much as 30% in some cases, making some of the idyllic places suddenly affordable.

One serious problem with the Caribbean is that holidays invariably seem to revolve around the couple and so single travellers will often find themselves paying the same as a couple for a room. You can try bargaining, but it is unlikely to do any good.

Note: **All prices quoted in this book are for a double room in the peak winter season unless otherwise stated.**

Eating Out

Caribbean hotel food is notoriously bad. The British may have something to do with this because so many of the islands ended up as her colonies—a quick trip to the French Antilles will tell a different story entirely. The tourist hotels have brought a uniformity that is acceptable to most visitors—a universal and lacklustre 'international' style. Things are improving, though and some good restaurants have opened up recently. Also a number of famous chefs have made their way down to the Caribbean and so you can dine on delicious food in tropical splendour. You can expect to pay as much or more for this as you would at home. There are only about ten restaurants and hotel dining rooms in the whole Caribbean which have a dress-code (a jacket for dinner, but usually not even a tie). Barbados has one or two, but otherwise you have no need to pack a tie unless you know you are going somewhere extremely smart and you do not want to be caught out.

It is worth getting out in search of West Indian food. It has its own distinctive flavours, it is cheaper and the restaurants are usually more fun. It is also worth seeking out the beach bars, where you will have barbecued local fish and vegetables.

Gastronomes should really head for the French islands, where there is a strong tradition of creole cookery with luxurious sauces, but in the Dutch islands you will find echoes of Indonesia and Holland in the *rijstafel* and Edam cheese. The tastes of India have come through strongest in Trinidad, but curry goat and *roti* (an envelope of dough with a meat or vegetable filling) have reached everywhere now. The Spanish islands are best known for their aromatic sauces and stews. Caribbean food is traditionally quite spicy and they can be quite heavy on the meats in their cook-ups. Beware of bottles marked *pick a peppa*. Fish is abundant, and often delicious, as are seafoods such as lobster and crab and an island favourite, conch.

Other foods that have become popular are made of ingredients that were originally hardship foods, often fed to the slaves because they were cheap. The Jamaican national dish is *ackee and saltfish*, and now that things can be refrigerated and food is no longer salted to preserve it, salted cod is expensive and difficult to get hold of. *Rice 'n peas* (or peas 'n rice depending on which island you are in) is another standard meal in the cheaper restaurants in the British islands and it is particularly good when served with coconut milk. *Oil-dung* is a pot of vegetables cooked in coconut oil.

West Indian dishes are usually served with traditional vegetables, many also brought as slave food. Try breadfruit, fried plantain (like a banana) and cassava (originally an Arawak food) and the delicious christophene. Callaloo, made from spinach, is a traditional West Indian soup which you will find everywhere. The Caribbean is of course famous for its **fruits**—which taste especially good in the ice-creams—juicy mangoes with strands that get stuck in your teeth, sweetsop or sugar apple, soursop (which tastes like a cross between a citrus and a banana) and delicate black pineapples, which are sweeter than the ones obtainable in Europe because they are allowed to ripen on the stem. Less well known are mammee apple, golden apple, papaya, bitter tamarind and guava. There are as many citrus fruits as you can imagine, and others which are cross-fertilized. The Dominican Republic makes the best fruit drinks, like fresh fruit milk-shakes, called *bastidas* (better than Puerto Rican *piña coladas*).

Drinking

Rum and Red Stripe
Rum is the Caribbean 'national' drink—50 years ago bars kept their bottles of rum on the counter free of charge and it was the water you had to pay for. Distilled from sugar molasses, it is produced all over the islands and though it often tastes like rocket fuel, it gives the West Indians their energy for dancing, so it cannot be all bad. Look out for Appleton's in Jamaica, Mountgay in Barbados, Barbancourt in Haiti and the varieties of Rhum St James in Martinique.

Far more so than wine, the West Indians prefer a cool beer and almost every island brews its own, usually under licence from the major drinks companies. Some of the best known are Red Stripe and Crucial Brew from Jamaica, Banks from Barbados and Carib from Trinidad. Non-alcoholic drinks that the West Indians often make are ginger beer, sorrel, the red Christmas drink and a disgusting concoction made from tree-bark called mauby juice.

Cocktails

The Caribbean is of course famous for its cocktails such as *Piña Colada* (pineapple and coconut cream and rum) and *Daquiri* (crushed ice, rum and fruit syrup whisked up like a sorbet), making the best use of the exotic fruits. The *Cuba Libre*, first mixed after the Cuban Revolution in 1959, is made of rum with lemon and cola, and Hemingway's *Mojito* is made with white rum, fresh mint and Angostura Bitters. The *planter's punch*, traditionally drunk all over the Caribbean, is made from rum and water with a twist of lime and sugar, topped with ground nutmeg. Fruit punches are also good, particularly in Barbados.

Soft Drinks

Life in the Caribbean sun is still hot work, though, and so the West Indians have an array of drinks on sale in the street. *Snow cones* and *Sky juice* are made with crushed ice (scraped off a huge block), water and a dash of fruit concentrate. You swill it around with a straw and the effect is something like a cold ribena. You have to be careful not to drink the water and the concentrate too quickly otherwise you are just left with a mound of ice crystals. In some islands you get weird and wonderful toppings with condensed milk and crushed peanuts.

Each island has its own system. In Jamaica the vendors walk around pushing brightly-painted handcarts and they present the drink to you in a little plastic gold-fish bag rather than a cup. In Trinidad they use silver carts like mobile soup-kitchens and they crush the ice by machine, and in the Dominican Republic and Haiti they have tricycles mounted with an ice-box and a whole array of concentrate bottles (the water is often dodgy here, so you could go for a *bastida* instead). In Puerto Rico, which is part of the United States, drinks come in vending machines, of course. There are the usual cans all over the Caribbean, but a particularly good soft drink is the Trinidadian *Bentley*, lemon and lime with a dash of bitters.

Another option available in all the islands is coconuts, which are often sold in the street. Do not be alarmed when the vendor pulls out a two-foot machete, because he will deftly top the coconut with a few strokes, leaving just a small hole through which you can drink. Get an older coconut if you can, because the milk will be fuller and sweeter. Once you have drunk the milk, hand it back to the vendor, who will split it for you so that you can eat the delicious coconut slime that lines the inside (it eventually turns into the white coconut flesh). You will also be offered sugar-cane juice, either as a liquid, or in the sticks themselves, which you bite off and chew to a pulp (very sweet).

Water

The water in most islands in the Caribbean is drinkable from the tap, but to make sure, particularly in the larger islands, you are advised to drink the water served by the hotel to begin with. However, in Haiti and the Dominican Republic you should definitely only drink bottled water. Do not drink iced drinks off the street in these two countries either, because the ice will not have been made with purified water. Get a soft drink or a coconut instead.

There is a shortage of water in many of the flatter islands, and so, even in expensive hotels, you may find that nothing comes out when you turn on the tap. You are always asked to conserve water where possible.

Part II
HISTORY

Hair-braiding

Caribbean Indians

Virtually no indigenous Caribbean Indians survive today, but when the Europeans first arrived in the New World there were two principal races of Amerindians living in the islands. In the north were the tribes of the Arawaks, spread over the Greater Antilles and the Bahamas, and to the south the islands of the Eastern Caribbean were inhabited by the Carib Indians, who had worked their way up along the chain of the Lesser Antilles from South America as far as the Leeward Islands.

The Amerindians are thought to have made their way over from Asia to the American continent about 40,000 years ago, fanning out into different areas to become Eskimos, the North American Indians and the settled tribes of South America. A few hundred years BC the Arawaks (from the South American coastal area), started to island hop along the Lesser Antilles, settling the Windwards and the Leewards and eventually coming to the Greater Antilles. The Arawaks were to live in peace on the islands for a thousand years or so, until the Caribs, a belligerent tribe who originated in the Amazon jungle, started to force them out. When Columbus arrived, the Caribs had got as far as the northernmost of the Lesser Antilles and were just making to raids on Puerto Rico. If the Spaniards had not arrived and taken over the killing of the Arawaks, then the Caribs would probably have done so.

Arawaks

The Spaniards found different tribes of Arawaks: on Puerto Rico the *Borinquens*, in Hispaniola, Jamaica and Cuba the *Tainos* (the Indians shouted this word, supposedly

28

meaning peace in their language, when they first saw the Spanish ships) and in the Bahamas the *Lucayans*. A tribe called the *Guanahatabeyes* had already found their way to Cuba, probably from Florida, and lived in the caves inland, but very little is known about them.

The Arawaks were the first to discover the tropical island idyll and they led a very peaceable existence in their hammocks, fishing occasionally and snorting tobacco at three-day dance parties. They lived off the food they could catch—fish, manatee, doves and parrots, animals like iguana and fruits—and kept just a few crops like cassava and maize. They were adept hunters. To catch ducks they would allow gourds (fruits like wooden footballs) to float downstream in a river into the flock so that they would become used to them, and then they would swim with a gourd on their head, grabbing the ducks by the feet and pulling them under as they floated past. They also used to attach a cord to a remora, a little sucker fish with a grip so tight that it could hang on to a turtleshell while they pulled it in.

The height of beauty in an Arawak was a pointed skull with hair worn in a topknot, and so babies' heads were pressed with slats of wood, giving them huge foreheads. This reputedly made their heads so hard that they could stop a Spanish sword. Like the Caribs, Arawaks had thick and glossy black hair which they oiled and wore long. They wore few clothes but they decorated themselves with feathers, tattoos and beads. Only married women would cover themselves at all. Their only domestic animal was a little dog, an alcos, that could not bark, and possessions meant little to them, so they happily gave away what they had to the early Spanish visitors. In their simplicity they were fascinated by the mirrors and bells that they were given in return. Theft was regarded as the worst of crimes and those caught were slowly skewered to death with a pole.

They lived in small communities near the sea, in conical thatched shelters and they were led by a *cacique* or chieftain. The *cacique*, who was also the spiritual leader, would preside over the religious ceremonies, calling them together on a conch shell and then forcing himself to vomit so that he would be pure enough to communicate with the gods. Then began day-long sessions of dance, stupor and games (some played with a shuttle-cock and others like volleyball), all fired by maize alcohol and the Arawak drug, a powder blasted up the nostrils through a metre-long, double-pronged tube called a *tabaco*; the Arawak for tobacco was *cohiba*, and the habit of smoking comes from them—the Spaniards were terrified to see these people with firebrands hanging out of their mouths. Tobacco, syphilis and the hammock are some of the few Arawak bequests to the Europeans.

All the tribes had similar spiritual beliefs, in a male and a female God. They worshipped them in the form of *zemes*, figures of animals or humans carved in wood and stone, which also represented the forces in their lives—rain, wind, fire and hurricanes. They believed that after death they went on to *coyaba*, a plentiful land without sickness or hurricanes, where they feasted and danced all day long.

Columbus noted that the Arawaks were gentle, generous and honest, but today there is nothing left of them, except a few Arawak features in the faces of the Cubans and the Dominicans. In their search for gold, the Spaniards managed to wipe them out within fifty years. They took them off to work in their gold-mines and in the pearl beds off South America. The Arawaks, who believed firmly in an afterlife, preferred to commit suicide.

Caribs

Somebody has done a pretty mean PR job on the Caribs (the European powers had to justify their ruthless genocide), but they were hardly humanitarian. Their love for alcohol was so great that they would have no qualms about killing the crew of a ship which might have brandy aboard. They were also a fearsome enemy—in their *piragua* canoes, which could hold as many as a hundred men, they could paddle as fast as a sailing ship and they would attack on the high seas.

They never harmed women, merely taking them to live with them, but for men they reserved a special ceremony—the barbecue. They would prepare the unfortunate captive by slitting his legs and back and stuffing the cuts with pimentoes and herbs before despatching him with a club and putting him on the spit. A Carib victim would insult his captors by saying that he had eaten so many of the others' relatives that barbecuing him was tantamount to eating their own flesh and blood. There was even a pecking order of European meals. The French were regarded as the most delicate and tasty, followed by the English and the Dutch, but the Spaniards were so stringy and disgusting as to be almost inedible.

On land the men were expert hunters and were excellent shots with bows and arrows. They could split a coin at a hundred yards and astonished early visitors by the speed with which they fired arrow after arrow in succession. They would capture parrots alive by burning red pepper beneath them until they suffocated and they could entrance an iguana out of its hole by whistling monotonously. Fish were shot or poisoned with dogwood bark and simply collected when they floated to the surface.

The Carib features were similar to other South American Indians and they were stocky. They painted their skin bright red and adorned themselves with parrot feathers and necklaces strung with the teeth of their victims. But their pride was their long blue-black hair which was oiled by the women after breakfast.

The women worked around the *carbet*, a round palm-thatch house and living area. They tended crops such as yucca (cassava) and sweet potato and prepared meals of the fish or animals caught by the men. Many of the women were Arawak captives and so they spoke a different language among themselves. The Caribs had a hazy conception of good and evil spirits in the world but were completely uninterested in religious matters. Missionaries gave up in the end—the Caribs got baptized simply for the presents that they would receive.

Columbus

Columbus is well known as the discoverer of America. One Caribbean calypso singer objected in song that this view was simply Eurocentric arrogance because American Indians clearly beat him to it by just thousands of years. However, his voyages were to have an importance that changed the world.

In fact he was sailing for the Indies: Cathay (China) and Cipangu (Japan), as mentioned by Marco Polo, to reopen the spice trade with the East. Discovery of other islands—the existence of islands in the Atlantic, including Antillia (later used in the word Antilles), had been suspected since Biblical times—was a secondary concern for him. Strictly speaking he failed in his quest, but it was clear to all, even by the time that he died, how significant his discoveries in the New World were.

Cristoforo Colombo (or Cristobal Colon in Spanish) was born in the 1450s in Genoa, the son of a weaver, but he chose his career as a sailor while still a young man and travelled throughout the Mediterranean on trading voyages. Eventually he sailed further afield, to Iceland and along the coast of West Africa.

Columbus was largely self-taught. He was obviously an intelligent and forceful man, but without formal schooling he was inflexible and jumped to illogical geographical conclusions: for example, he decided at one stage that the world was pear-shaped. All the same, he was a bold and accomplished explorer and a fine navigator. He was persuasive and even charismatic in court, impressing Queen Isabella so much that she helped him despite the advice of her courtiers. But he was domineering in authority and this was his downfall. He may have carried it off on board ship, persuading his lieutenants to 'see' land and allaying a potentially mutinous crew, but he was a hopeless administrator of the colonies.

If he was a visionary, and he stuck to his plan for years before he was granted the opportunity to carry it out, his dreams also tipped into fantasy and self-delusion. He considered himself chosen by God, with a mission to bring Christianity to the New World and he was paranoid about others encroaching on what he considered his domain. He was vain and he insisted on huge public honour in reward for his service to the Crown of Spain. He was ennobled, granted the titles of *Admiral of the Ocean Sea* and *Viceroy of the Indies*, as well as huge financial rewards from any future trading with the area.

But he fulfilled the dreams of the age. The world was outgrowing its Mediterranean confines as the Portuguese began to explore the coast of Africa. And the ancient spice routes to the east had been closed with the fall of Constantinople in the 1450s. Columbus was a master mariner who had sailed all the seas and was acquainted with all the available maps from his cartographic work. Slowly the plan came into being. He would try to reach the east by sailing west.

He tried all the major European powers for a sponsor and had to attend the Spanish court for six years before Ferdinand and Isabella granted him a commission to sail. Freed of the last of the Moors and in confident mood in 1492, they gave him three caravels, the *Santa Maria*, the *Niña* and the *Pinta*.

On 3 August 1492 Columbus set off from Palos, touching the Canaries and then heading off into the ocean, navigating due west. According to his calculations (which he had massaged to his favour), he expected to come to Japan or China after about 2500 miles (about where America is). They sailed with the wind behind for over a month, through the Sargasso Sea, into the unknown. Steadily the crew became more rebellious (fearing they might not get home). On 12 October 1492, they sighted land, one of the Bahamian islands.

Columbus called the island San Salvador in honour of the Saviour, but clearly he had not found Japan, so after a few days he set off in search of it, asking along the way for gold. He touched Cuba and then his flagship was wrecked off Hispaniola and he was forced to leave about 40 men behind when he sailed for Spain, where he announced that he had reached Asia. On Palm Sunday 1493 Columbus was received with all the pomp and glory that he craved. He was treated almost as an equal to the monarchs in court.

A second expedition was sent the same year, with 1500 settlers to colonize the island of Hispaniola. Administrative problems began almost at once and were compounded when Columbus left his brother Diego in charge during his exploration of Cuba and Jamaica.

Columbus led a third voyage in 1498, arriving in Trinidad in the south, narrowly missing the continent of South America. From here he sailed to Hispaniola by dead reckoning (no mean feat; a journey of 800 miles throught uncharted waters). He found the colony in disarray and was forced to treat with the rebels. Eventually his viceregal authority was revoked and he was shipped back to Spain in chains.

He was treated kindly by Ferdinand and Isabella and eventually he was permitted to return to the New World on a fourth journey in 1502, with the express undertaking that he was not to set foot on Hispaniola. In some ways his last trip was the most successful—he made contact for the first time with the more developed Indian cultures of the Central American seaboard and he discovered gold in larger quantities (the shape of things to come). However he was shipwrecked on the coast of Jamaica and had to wait a year before he was rescued and made it back to Spain.

Columbus died in Spain in 1506, faintly ridiculed because of all his problems in the Indies, his eccentric behaviour and his excessive claims against the Crown. Though his experience as a seaman had probably told him otherwise, he maintained to his death that he had discovered the Far East.

Columbus (his remains at least) made yet more journeys after his death. He was brought to Santo Domingo in 1544 by his daughter-in-law and then removed (or not, as the case may be; see Hispaniola) to Spanish soil (Cuba) at the time of the Haitian invasion in 1796, perhaps returning to Seville a century later. In honour of the 500th anniversary of the discovery, Columbus has made yet another journey to a specially constructed crypt in the enormous Faro a Colon, a megalithic lighthouse in the shape of a cross in Santo Domingo.

Buccaneers, Pirates and Privateers

The Papal edicts or 'Bulls' that quickly followed the discovery of the New World by Columbus ordained that all land, discovered or undiscovered, west of a line 100 leagues beyond the Azores, should be an exclusive Spanish preserve (the line cuts off the eastern tip of Brazil and so the Portuguese were allowed to settle there). *No peace beyond the line* was declared, and any ships found in the waters were regarded as pirates. The crews officially would be killed if captured. But this did not stop the searovers from the other European nations, who had heard of the massive riches that the Spaniards were pillaging from the Indian settlements on the Spanish main. Already by 1540 many of these 'privateers', working under contracts to their governments, started to creep into the Caribbean.

Jack Hawkins (son of a seafaring father who had brought an Indian chief from South America to the English court) made three voyages to the Caribbean in the second half of the century and on his final voyage he took the young Francis Drake. He was working a trade route via Africa that was later to become very familiar—he collected Africans to sell to the Spaniards in the New World as slaves. Others, including French pirates *Pie de Palo* (Timberleg) and Jacques Sores, were less interested in trade as privateers and more interested in what they could seize by besieging and ransoming Spanish settlements. Drake returned at the end of the century, as did Walter Raleigh, on his search for the Golden *El Dorado*.

In the early 1600s large numbers of pirate ships operated in the Caribbean and some of the sailors ended up settling the north coast of Hispaniola, killing cattle and curing it for sale to passing ships. They were called **buccaneers**, because of the *boucan*, the oven in which they smoked the meat. Searovers, misfits and deserters came to join them, jumping ship or deserting from their indentureships on the plantations. They lived in small groups, sharing all their property (even wives if they had them) and wore loose clothes with a leather belt that was slung with knives. They were renowned for their shooting. As the century progressed they moved across to the island of Tortuga off the north coast of Haiti, overlooking the Windward Passage between Cuba, Hispaniola and the Bahamas, which became their stronghold and from where they would set off in search of Spanish ships.

They called themselves the *Brethren of the Coast* and they took to sea as far afield as Madagascar and the Indian Ocean as pirates. The lure of this life on the edge was, of course, easy money, and when the money from the previous expedition ran out, they were ruthless and cunning about getting more, attacking any ships that they could find, taking the loot and selling it in their ports at St Thomas in the Virgin Islands, Port Royal in Jamaica and later Nassau in the Bahamas. They were fearsome fighters, putting the fright into professional soldiers and sailors and they were renowned for their cruelty. Once again they worked in small crews, with laws amongst themselves.

Père Labat tells of a French *filibuster*, a privateer rather than a pirate, for whom he said mass in 1694. During the service, they fired a salvo of cannons at the Elevation of the Holy Sacrament and at the Benediction and then contributed handsomely to his coffers from the profits of their latest venture. These privateers divided the prizes equally amongst themselves, with a slightly larger share for the captain, quartermaster, surgeon and pilot, with a bonus for the man who first sighted the prize. Money was put aside for a wounded member of the crew and compensation was paid—600 ecus for a limb, 300 for a finger or an eye—and they were cared for out of captured loot.

Henry Morgan was one of the most colourful of the privateers/pirates and he worked out of Port Royal at the height of its infamy in the late 1600s. He soon became the 'admiral' of the buccaneers (elected by them). He invented the strategy of attacking towns far inland and he even took the most fortified Spanish city, Puerto Bello (by using a human shield of monks and nuns to storm the walls). His men would then loot, ransack and rape their way through the town and, loaded down with pieces of eight, they would return to Port Royal for more revelry. Morgan was notoriously cruel and became hugely wealthy. Eventually, after double-crossing many of his buccaneers, he became Lieutenant Governor of Jamaica and had a hand in stamping out piracy in the region.

Edward Thatch or Blackbeard was the most notorious pirate of the 1700s and one of the 'sweet trade's' greatest showmen. He dressed outrageously and cultivated a monstrous appearance with a huge black beard and fuses fizzing in his hair when he went into battle. At one stage he led a whole squadron of boats around the islands. He was known occasionally to fire on his companions just to keep them guessing, while quaffing his favourite *rumfustion*, a mix of beer, gin, sherry, rum and gunpowder.

Stede Bonnet was a gentleman and a man of letters of Barbados, a Justice of the Peace who bought his own ship and took to the seas, after providing for his family. Jack Rackham actually had two women in his crew, Anne Bonney and Mary Read, who were reputed to be as violent as their male colleagues. A man could be killed for cowardice and the captain lose his command if the crew thought he had failed in attacking a prize, so the pirates were always bold and brave, and they would regularly take on ships far larger than their own. One Captain Moidore loaded up his cannons with gold coins when he ran out of shot. L'Ollonois, a Frenchman, executed the whole crew of a ship at one point, licking their blood off his sword and then tore out the heart of a man and ate it. He was dismembered and roasted himself in the end.

The Slave Trade and the Middle Passage

As the sugar industry developed in the Caribbean, there was a massive demand for labour to work the canefields. Indentured servants from Europe were tried, but they did not cope well in the heat and so they went for Africans. The Spaniards had imported a few Africans in the 16th century, but it was not until the islands of Barbados and Martinique started to cultivate the crop that the slave trade grew. A triangular trade route grew up between the ports of Europe and the southern facing coastline of West Africa, with manufactured goods making their way to Africa on the first leg, payment in kind for the slaves they took on board. The last stretch, from the West Indies back to Europe, was made with a cargo of sugar hogsheads on board.

The most notorious leg of the journey was the fearsome *Middle Passage*, from the African coast to the West Indies, which lasted anything from six to twelve weeks. The slaves, from the Coromantee, Eboe, Mandingo and Yoruba tribes, taken from their villages in night-raids or sold into slavery as prisoners of war and then held captive in the vast fortresses that lined the Gold and Ivory Coasts, were loaded on board. They were chained to one another in the hold, each with a space so cramped that they could not sit up. As the ship pushed off, the crew stood by with lighted torches, threatening to set light to it and all the people on board if the slaves rebelled. Once out of sight of land, the slaves were allowed to exercise for just a few minutes each day, still chained in pairs, before being returned to the festering hold again. On average, about 12% died on each trip, some from disease but others preferred to commit suicide by jumping overboard to certain drowning in their pairs.

In the last few days before arriving in the Caribbean, they were fattened up and as the ship drew into port, the frightened slaves were brought up on deck, where they were oiled to make them look healthy. They were then paraded through the streets singing on the way to the market where they were auctioned.

Part III
THE LESSER ANTILLES

Flying fish on the Careenage

BARBADOS

Barbados stands alone, out in the Atlantic, about 100 miles beyond the rest of the Eastern Caribbean, a coral island with some of the finest golden sand beaches anywhere and perhaps the most agreeable climate in the West Indies. It is one of the Caribbean's most popular destinations. Just 21 miles by 14, Barbados is often dismissed as small and flat, but away from the crowded coastal areas, the gentle cane-covered country rises to the thousand foot heights of Hackleton's cliff above the Atlantic. Its British heritage, stronger here than in any other island, has given it the name 'Little England' in the past. There is even an isolated area of rugged hills in the northeast familiarly known as Scotland.

'The whole place has an appearance of cleanliness, gentility and wealth which one does not find in any other island.' So thought Père Labat, a Dominican monk and roving gastronome who visited Barbados at the height of its prosperity in 1700, and much of his opinion still stands. Education, literacy and health care, the social services in general, are the best in the English-speaking Caribbean and the poor are better off in Barbados than in most of the neighbouring islands. Barbados commands a position of influence out of proportion to its size, the source of the renowned Bajan (native Barbadian) self-esteem. Altogether, the national motto 'Pride and Industry' is quite appropriate for the Bajans.

Barbados has a population of 258,000, the most dense in the area. Most Bajans live along the sheltered west coast of the island and in the massive extended suburb of the south coast that runs to the capital, Bridgetown. Just a few villages are tucked away inland. The population is over 90 per cent of African descent, but there are small communities of white Bajans, a visible and influential business community and the 'poor whites', descendants of indentured servants who have scraped a living from the land for centuries. There are not many Bajans of mixed race, but if the island has a problem, it is the residue of a rigid system of colour prejudice.

Barbados's colonial legacy is fading now (since Independence in 1966) as it thrusts on and modernizes, but the island has taken more from England than any other island in the area. The 300-year connection has left a delightful and often old-fashioned charm in the manners, the buildings and even the language. Classically beautiful plantation houses stand in the swathes of sugar-cane; cricketers in whites play beneath palm trees. You can even hear traces of a West Country accent in Bajan speech.

At times, though, it seems that Little England has managed to inherit some of the worst British foibles: pomposity and cliquish social attitudes. Functionaries will address you in clipped and hushed tones about a dress code (jacket and tie) in some clubs, which comes as a bit of a surprise in the Caribbean.

Barbados is crowded, so if you are looking for beach-bound Caribbean seclusion this is hardly the place to come, but it has an established and well organized tourist industry and so it is easy to have a good holiday here. Its famous west-coast hotels, long favoured by a crowd of international sophisticates, have given it the nickname the millionaires' playground.

History

The history of Barbados is bound inextricably with that of England and with the fortunes of West Indian sugar. In an area where islands changed hands with almost every war, colonial Barbados had 300 years of uninterrupted British rule. It was the first in the Caribbean to exploit sugar successfully, and even today many of the roads are lined each side with curtains of tall green cane.

The island was named by Portuguese visitors who passed by in the 1580s. They called the island *los Barbudos* or the 'bearded ones' after the long matted and straggly shoots thrown off the upper branches of the banyan trees that grew near the coast. There had been native Amerindian settlements on Barbados, but by the time the Europeans arrived they had left.

Barbados was claimed for England in 1625, and was settled two years later, in an expedition sent by Sir William Courteen. They found the island uninhabited except by some wild boars left by early visitors as food for shipwrecked mariners. After wrangling and intrigue in the court of King Charles I, with the Earls of Pembroke and Carlisle in dispute over rights of colonization, and a parallel armed battle on the island itself between the Windward and the Leeward men, the settlement flourished, assisted by a family of 40 Arawaks from Guiana who demonstrated how to cultivate tropical plants.

The colony exploded, and within 30 years Barbados was overcrowded. Fortune hunters flooded in; indentured servants put themselves in servitude for years with a promise of land at the end of their term. Refugees came from the Civil War in England; others were deported by the notorious Judge Jeffreys for their part in the Monmouth

Rebellion and sold into slavery. *To be Barbadosed* was a recognized punishment in 17th-century England.

In an early piece of industrial espionage, the Dutch brought sugar-cane to Barbados. They taught the Barbadians how yield could be increased by *ratooning*, in which the cane was planted not sticking out of the ground but laid flat and buried; and they introduced boiling techniques. At first the crop was used only for producing rum, but it soon became clear how profitable sugar was for export to Europe. And so by the 1650s the whole of Barbados was planted with cane, even to the exclusion of growing provisions—cultivating sugar was so profitable that the Barbadians preferred to pay the price of imported food. *Good merchantable muscovado sugar* was used as currency for barter at this time, even for the Governor's salary. Willoughby Fort in Bridgetown was constructed as a defence against pirates in 1656 at a price of 80,000 pounds of sugar.

Whistler, a soldier, visited Barbados in the 1650s and described the population like this:

> 'The island is inhabited with all sortes, with English, French, Dutch, Scotes, Irish, Spaniards, they being Jues, with ingones (Indians) and Miserabell Negors borne to perpetual slavery thay and theyer seed; ... This Iland is the dunghill whar our England dost cast forth its rubidg. Rodgs (rogues) and Hors and such like peopel are those that are generally broght heare.'

The whores and rogues were sent out to provide manpower for the cultivation of sugar. Many of them moved on, leaving the 'Miserabell Negors', the African slaves who were already being brought over in their thousands from the west coast of Africa and whose descendants make up the majority of the Bajan population today.

The empire builders were so successful with their sugar that Barbados came to be called 'the brightest jewel in the English Crown' at the end of the 17th century. The monopoly did not last, despite Barbadian efforts to protect their markets, as other islands started to cultivate the crop. Expensive equipment forced out the smallholders and the plantations became fewer, larger and more profitable. Their fortunes waxed and waned with war and peace in the 18th century, as Britain, France and Spain vied for supremacy in the Americas. Fortunes were handsomely augmented by the usual Caribbean trade of smuggling, avoiding port taxes. Père Labat wrote that the captain of his barque worked hard unloading during the day, but far harder at night.

Barbados's unconquered history was due mainly to its position out in the Atlantic. Ships had to beat upwind towards it and could be seen from miles off, and it was formidably protected by a string of forts down the west coast. It was the headquarters of the British forces in the Caribbean for many years. But it was not only from outside that the island was threatened. The plantation slaves plotted rebellion from the beginning and they were ruthlessly treated when found out. The most famous revolt is *Bussa's Rebellion*, in 1816, caused by thoughts of freedom at the time of the abolition of the slave-trade in 1807. It was initiated by torching the canefields and was put down with the loss of nearly 300 lives. Many more rebel slaves were deported to Honduras.

In 1838 the slaves were finally freed (after a four-year 'apprenticeship' period in which they were paid minimally, but had to remain on their plantations) and the industry faltered. Many of the freed slaves emigrated because there was no land for them other than on the plantations.

As sugar beet was developed in Europe, the sugar industry nearly collapsed, but after 50 years in the doldrums, West Indian sugar was given preferential treatment and it was profitable again by 1910. Sugar and the rum produced from it is still very important to Barbados. The national coat of arms shows a fist grasping two canes, and the Bridgetown coat of arms has three rum puncheons, used by the likes of Père Labat's captain as the standard currency for barter.

The 20th century brought further pressure for political change and the growth of trades unions. Eventually universal franchise came in 1951. After the failure of Federation in 1962, Barbados took Independence on 30 November 1966, remaining within the British Commonwealth. Today Barbados is led by Prime Minister Erskine Sandiford of the Democratic Labour Party. He was re-elected with a majority of eight in early 1991.

Life has changed radically since Independence and the influence of the United States has clearly replaced that of Britain. There is still a small sugar industry as well as a small manufacturing sector, some off-shore finance and data processing, but by far the biggest earner in the Barbados economy is tourism.

Recent years have been hard on the Barbados economy and they have felt the recession badly. Public employees were laid off or forced to take a wage cut and the island narrowly avoided a devaluation of its currency.

Cricket and the Constitution

The two most hallowed institutions to be adopted during 300 years' association with Britain are cricket and Parliament. Barbados is the home of players like Sir Frank Worrell (the first black captain of the West Indies team) and Sir Gary Sobers and more recent names such as Malcolm Marshall and Gordon Greenidge. Wes Hall is now Minister of Tourism and Sports. The island provides many international players and, despite its size, it has won the regional championship more times than all the other islands combined. If a Test Match is being played while you are visiting, be sure to go along (you will find that the rest of Barbados life stops for it anyway).

Founded in 1637, the Barbados Assembly is the third oldest Parliamentary body in the British Commonwealth, after Bermuda and Westminster itself. The destruction of their official building, the State House, in a fire in 1668, meant that the Legislative Assembly spent 60 years conducting its business in taverns.

The late 19th century was a time of political crisis in the West Indies because Britain was keen to impose direct rule from London, bypassing the islands' assemblies. Barbados was the only Caribbean colony to keep its legislative powers intact.

Barbados has a bicameral Parliamentary system, with elections held every five years to the 28-seat House of Assembly. 21 Senate members are appointed by the Governor General Dame Nita Barrow on the advice of the senior politicians.

Flora and Fauna

When the Europeans first arrived in 1627, Barbados was entirely forested, but the trees were stripped within 20 years as cultivation went ahead. Turner's Hall Wood in the north of the island is the only place where the original forest remains (see p. 50).

There are few wild animals, though you will come across green monkeys (more brown with green patches), which were brought over from Africa 300 years ago. Other animals can be seen in the Barbados Wildlife Reserve in the north of the island. Birdlife is more varied. In the remote northern areas you can see three hummingbirds—the Antillean crested hummingbird, the purple-throated carib and the green-throated carib, as well as colourful tanagers and kingbirds. In the inland swamps you can see sandpipers, terns and warblers, and along the coast you will see solitary pelicans digesting their meal on an isolated rock.

One pleasure in Barbados is the domestic and hotel gardens, which are all impeccably kept, festooned with tropical plants that flower all year round, palms and flowering trees like the flamboyant that explodes into scarlet in the summer months.

GETTING TO BARBADOS

Barbados is geographically distinct from the rest of the Caribbean, but the island is well served by air. The Barbados government is a partner in the LIAT airline, and there are regular services to other islands and to Guyana and Venezuela on the South American mainland. All air tickets sold in Barbados are supplemented with a 20% government tax. There is a departure tax of Bds$25.

By Air

From the UK: during the winter, British Airways provides the opportunity to travel to Barbados on Concorde, for a' fare of over £2600 each way. The time saving is not quite what you might expect for an aircraft travelling at twice the speed of sound; on the outbound leg, a refuelling stop is made at Shannon in southern Ireland, and the journey time is only eighty minutes less than the non-stop 747 flight. The return leg is non-stop, however, allowing the usual 8-hour journey time to be almost halved.

Subsonic services on British Airways operate on most days from Gatwick. BWIA has two or three flights each week from Heathrow. There are also numerous charter services operated by tour companies. BWIA also fly from Köln, Frankfurt and Munich in **Germany**, Stockholm and Zurich.

From the USA: the best gateways on the American mainland are Miami and New York, and connections are also possible through San Juan on Puerto Rico.

From other Caribbean Islands: services are less frequent, and fares higher, than within the Caribbean proper. For example, the shortest hop—to St Vincent—costs over US$100. Fares can be trimmed by using the services of British Airways, which flies 747s to St Lucia and Port of Spain. To fill up jumbo jets which might otherwise be half-empty, BA sells reduced rate tickets.

By Boat

Sea connections with other islands are infrequent and irregular. There are Geest Line freighters between Barbados and Antigua, Grenada, St Vincent, St Lucia and Dominica. The same line (tel 0446 700333 in the UK) has services to and from the port of Barry in South Wales. A one-way fare is around £1250.

Within the Caribbean: Eric Hassell & Co. (tel 436 6102) have a regular sailing to St Lucia. You might also catch a passage to another island if you go to the shallow draft dock and ask. Departure tax by sea Bds$6.

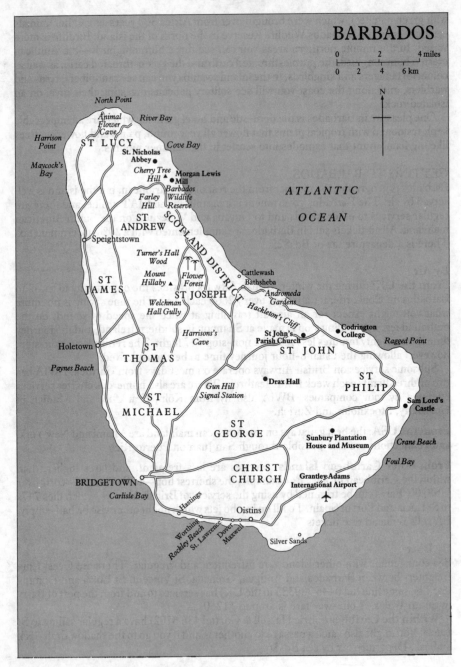

BARBADOS

GETTING AROUND BARBADOS

Barbados has a relatively efficient bus system, emanating mostly from Bridgetown, which is a lively way to get around. It is served both by dull blue and yellow **public** buses and **private** minibuses. Public buses display their destination on their front and operate to a schedule (West Indian time) at the cost of Bds$1.50 for a ride. The main public bus terminal is in Fairchild St, just across Charles Duncan O'Neal bridge from Trafalgar Square. To go north you leave from the Lower Green Station, at the end of Broad St near St Mary's Church.

The **private buses** also have names on the front but these are more likely to be *Street Demon, Black Starliner* or *Thunder Run*, depending on the driver's self-esteem. To travel north to Speightstown along the west coast, private buses leave from the Lower Green Station near the public bus terminus and the south and east of the island is served by a terminal in Probyn St, not far from the Fairchild St Terminal. Stereo systems on board the buses have recently been banned. Schoolchildren liked them so much that they were playing truant and spending their lunch-money on a ride. Z-Vans, small minibuses, have taken over as the mobile discotheques.

It is important to stand at a recognized bus stop if you want to hail one. Bus drivers are warned about picking up passengers elsewhere because they end up in court for doing so, as can be seen from a series of ironic bus names like *Chief Justice, The Advocate* and *Not Guilty*.

As a good tourist, you will be expected to travel by **taxi**. Make sure to fix the price beforehand, though, because taxis are not metered in Barbados. Sample prices are **airport** to Bridgetown—Bds$26, Speightstown—Bds$50 and from **Bridgetown** to St Lawrence Gap—Bds$13, Holetown—Bds$20, Speightstown—Bds$27 and Bathsheba—Bds$38. A taxi driver would be only too pleased to give a tour of the island, for around US$90 for a day for four people. Many of them are knowledgeable and charming and if you're lucky they might bring along some coconut cakes and home-made sorrel, or mauby juice, a traditional drink made from bark.

Island **bus tours**, a day trip to the hills of Scotland for instance and the views of the east coast, can be arranged through the **LE Williams Tour Co.** (tel 427 1043) or **Bartic Tours** (tel 428 5980) for about US$45. They will pick you up at your hotel. For a cheaper option, contact the **United Taxi Owners Association** in Bridgetown (tel 426 1496) or the **Barbados Transport Co-op** (tel 436 2486), who will offer any number of tours to suit you.

A good way to explore the countryside is by **hire car**, or by the trusted favourite, a mini moke. If you do set off, make sure to have a good road map because it is surprising quite how easily you can get lost in Barbados's endless fields of sugar-cane. In the winter season there is often a waiting list for vehicles (up to three days), so consider arranging a car when you book your holiday. Firms also give better deals for a three-day hire. Expect to leave a hefty deposit with the hire company unless you present a credit card. Car hire here is expensive, expect to pay US$45 per day for a mini-moke and marginally more for a large car. Some of the 40-odd local car hire firms are: **Sunny Isle Motors** in Worthing (tel 435 7979), or **Dear's Garage** in Bridgetown (tel 429 9277) and in Hastings (tel 427 7853), who have a large selection of cars. Otherwise shop around the smaller firms. For a moped, contact **Fonseca's** in Rockley (tel 435 8206).

To drive in Barbados (this takes place on the left as a rule) you need a special visitor's driving licence, which can be purchased at the airport on arrival on presentation of a valid driving licence, or at any police station, cost Bds$10.

TOURIST INFORMATION
The Barbados Board of Tourism has offices in:
UK: 263 Tottenham Court Rd, London W1P 9AA, tel (071) 636 9448/9.
USA: 800 Second Ave, New York, NY 10017, tel (212) 986 6516 or 3440 Wilshire Blvd, Suite 1215, Los Angeles, CA 90010, tel (213) 380 2198, toll free (800) 221 9831.
Canada: 615 Dorchester Blvd West, Suite 960, Montreal, Quebec H3B 1P5, tel (514) 861 0085 and 20 Queen St West, Suite 1508, Box 11, Toronto, Ontario, M5H 3R3, tel (416) 979 2137, toll free (800) 268 9122.
Germany: Rathenau Platz 1A, 6000 Frankfurt Am Main 1, tel (069) 280 982/3.
Sweden: Barbados Board of Tourism, c/o Hotel Investors (Sweden) Ltd, Nybrogatan 87, 5—114—41, Stockholm (tel 468 662 8584, fax 662 8775).
France: Caraïbes, 102 des Champs Elysées, 75008 Paris (tel 42 62 62 62, fax 40 74 07 01).

On the island you can get tourist information and assistance with hotels at the main **Tourist Offices** in Harbour Road, west Bridgetown (tel 427 2623), at the airport (tel 428 0937) and at the Deep Water Harbour, where the cruise ships dock (tel 426 1716). All the big hotels have desks that can help out as well and tickets for shows are available through **Box Office Barbados** (tel 426 2626). If you need further assistance on current events and tips about where to find shopping bargains, there is a plethora of magazines and leaflets, including *Ins and Outs of Barbados*, *Time Out in Barbados* and broadsheets like *The Visitor* and the *Sunseeker*.

The two main Barbadian **newspapers** are the *Advocate* and the *Nation*, and as well as good coverage of local and international news they list forthcoming events. **The Investigator** will plug you in to the most scurrilous island gossip. The **bookshops** of Barbados are very well stocked with books on the Caribbean and most magazines anyone would want to read. Try the Cloister Bookstore on the Wharf or Cave Shepherd on Broad St.

In a medical **emergency**, contact the Queen Elizabeth Hospital, on Martindales Road in the north of Bridgetown (tel 436 6450) or dial 119.

Useful addresses: British High Commission, Lower Collymore Rock, St Michael, (tel 436 6694); US Consul General (tel 431 0025); the Canadian High Commission, Bishop Court, Hill Pine Road, (tel 429 3550).

The **IDD code** for Barbados is 809, followed by a seven-digit island number, beginning 42 or 43. On-island dial all seven digits.

MONEY
The Barbados currency is the Barbados dollar, which like many others in the Caribbean is fixed to the US dollar (rate US$ = Bds$1.98) which gives an easy approximate exchange rate of one Bbd$ to US50c. It is worth carrying Barbados dollars because they are used in most transactions on the island. You will also get slightly better value even after the exchange. US and Canadian dollars will be accepted, but make sure to establish which currency you are dealing in. Credit cards are widely accepted by the hotel and restaurants and tourist areas generally.

Banking hours are 9–3, with an additional 3–5.30 on Fridays only, but you can change money any time at the hotels (for a marginally less favourable rate).

SHOPPING
Opening hours are weekdays 8–6 and Saturdays 8–midday. If you wish to shop for Bajan or Bajan designed products, try the **Best of Barbados**, which has branches throughout the island, or **Fairfield Greathouse Pottery**, which is set in an old boiling house in St Michael.

FURTHER READING
Some books written by Barbadian authors are *In the Castle of my Skin*, by George Lamming, about a black Barbadian boy growing up and *Christopher*, by Geoffrey Drayton about the stifling life of a white Barbadian boy. Edward Braithwaite's collections of poetry include *Rights of Passage*.

A ripping good yarn, good beach material, is Thomas Hoover's *Caribbee*, set in the time when Barbados had a tavern for every 20 inhabitants. There are many well written histories of the island and plenty of photographic lifestyle books.

BEACHES
The beaches of Barbados are excellent and they offer something for every taste, from the fine golden sand and calm water of the protected west coast, round the southern point where the water is a little livelier and the sand becomes coral pink, to the east coast where the sea is positively rough, and huge breakers bring in the full force of the Atlantic. The west coast is the home to wetbikes and waterskiers and the sports get more adventurous with rougher water and the wind round the coastline, with the best windsurfing in the south and surfing on the east coast. For an out-of-the-way beach go to the north, beyond hotel country or to the southeast, where coves are cut into the cliffs. There are fewer hucksters on the main beaches now, but you will probably be offered the traditional array of services, including hair-braiding, tropical shirts and African carvings. They can be quite persistent (and very persuasive) when they get going, so if you do not want to buy you may have to do a bit of stonewalling. Barbadian modesty prevents nude and even topless bathing.

On the more or less continual stretch of west coast beach, north of Bridgetown, the most popular areas are at **Paradise Beach, Payne's Bay, Treasure Beach** and **Heywood's Beach**, just north of Speightstown. The whole ten-mile tourist stretch is redolent with the aroma of bodies gently sizzling in coconut oil, but it never gets too crowded. It is a good place to arrange a waterskiing trip (about Bds$40 for 15 minutes), try parasailing, or take out a small sailing boat. Negotiate with one of the concessionaires and hotel watersports shops based on the beaches. Be careful of the tall and bushy *manchineel* trees all along the coast. Their fruit were called the apples of death by Columbus, because they cause a nasty rash and swelling. Beyond the hotel strip you will find relative seclusion at **Six Men's Bay**, where Bajans build fishing boats or at **Maycock's Bay**.

On the south coast, your local stretch of sand is likely to be **Accra, Rockley** or **Worthing Beach**, in the extended suburb, and no more than a few yards from the nearest bar. The beaches at St Lawrence Gap have a similar feel. Farther round the coast is a series of bays, less frequented but attractive pink sand strands beneath the cliffs.

Just short of the airport, **Silver Sands Beach** is one of the liveliest beaches on the island and at competition time it attracts a crowd of the Barbados body beautiful and the winter influx of nut-brown poseurs and straw-haired surf bums. Beyond the airport things get a bit more secluded. Try **Foul Bay**, named so because of its reputation as an anchorage rather than its setting and **Harrismith Beach**, or **Crane Beach**, just beneath the surreal hotel of the same name. **Bottom Bay** is also charming and cut off.

On the east coast the surf comes pounding in and swimming is often dangerous, but it is spectacular to view, from **Ragged Point** in the southeast through Bathsheba and Cattlewash to **Gay's Cove** and **River Bay** in St Lucy parish to the north, where the Bajans come for an outing. Surfing is possible on the south coast but most popular on the east coast, from Bathsheba to Duppies, or Crab Hill, in the far north.

Beach Bars

The **Bamboo Beach bar** is a popular spot just south of Holetown, a shady retreat from the sun on a boarded veranda above the waves. It is lively in the early evening as a crowd of white Bajans catch a beer and a chat on the way home. **Rumours**, just to the north of Holetown, has a list of cocktails as long as your arm. The fruit punch is excellent if you want something soft. Steel band on Fridays. In Worthing on the south coast you will find a mixed crowd of Bajans and visitors at the **Carib Beach Bar**. Snacks by day and also very lively at night.

WATERSPORTS

Windsurfing is most challenging on the south coast—experienced windsurfers should head for the area around Oistins. The best winds are at Barbados's most southerly point, around Silver Sands beach, host of the the 1991 World Championships, where **Mistral** keeps an outfit over the winter months (when the tradewinds are at their highest). Another popular place for windsurfing is the **Barbados Windsurfing Club Hotel** on Maxwell Beach (also Mistral), which offers equipment hire and instruction. Windsurfers will get a gentler ride on the west coast, where you can also get small sailing boats (sunfish) in most of the large hotels (about Bds$40 for an hour).

If you would like to go **sailing**, perhaps to cruise up the west coast, this can be arranged through the yachts docked at the Careenage in Bridgetown. Try the catamaran *Tiami* (tel 425 5800), or the 44 ft monohull *Limbo Lady* (tel 435 8206). Piracy and profligacy of a rum-soaked nature can be found on the **Jolly Roger**. Lots of *shiver me timbers* and walking the plank, for Bds$65 (reservations tel 436 6424). For a more stately ride in an old riverboat, try the **Bajan Queen** (tel 436 2149).

For a deep-sea fishing charter after swordfish or marlin, try **Jolly Roger Watersports** (tel 422 2335), or individual boats on the Careenage, among them *Blue Jay* (tel 422 2098).

The most popular **diving** is on the protected west coast, but if you are staying on the south coast there is no need to go up there, because Barbados is surrounded by reefs (though many of them are not in pristine condition). Average prices are Bds$70 for a one-tank dive. Companies offering equipment and qualified instruction are **Willie's Water Sports** with plenty of operations on the west coast (tel 422 1834) and **Shades of Blue** (tel 425 1060) near Holetown. On the south coast there is **Sandy Beach Water**

Sports at Worthing (tel 435 8000) and there are also one or two places in Hastings, for example **Underwater Barbados** (tel 426 0655).

Snorkelling equipment can be hired from any of the diving shops and most hotels. Good places to **snorkel** on the reefs are the **Folkstone National Marine Park**, near Holetown on the west coast, where the reefs are protected. Also try Carlisle Bay opposite the Government buildings and off the Heywoods resort near Speightstown. Trips in a glass-bottomed boat on the west coast can be organized through most west-coast watersport shops. And for a view of deeper Barbados corals without getting wet, contact **Atlantis Submarine** (tel 436 8929); reserve a couple of days in advance in the season.

OTHER SPORTS
On **land** there are three **golf** courses. The best known is the 18-hole championship course at **Sandy Lane** (tel 432 1145), green fees around US$80.

Many of the hotels have **tennis** courts where you can play, usually for a fee of about US$6 per hour. There are even **squash** courts in Barbados. Contact the Barbados Squash Club (tel 427 7193) or Rockley Resort above.

Walkers can find satisfying hikes in the hilly district of Scotland and along the rugged east coast. If you wish to set off alone, maps are easily available in town. The Barbados National Trust organizes walks to many different sites of natural and historical interest each Sunday (tel 426 2421), starting 6 am and 3 pm and lasting about 3 hours (details in the local newspapers, adm free). If you would prefer to explore on **horseback** or fancy a canter along the beach at dawn, contact the Brighton Stables (tel 425 9381) in St Michael, or Beau Geste Stables (tel 429 0139) for a ride through the canefields to Francia Plantation.

Spectator sports include the **horse-racing** on alternate Saturdays at the Garrison Savannah south of Bridgetown and even **polo** (Barbados Polo Club, tel 432 1802) on the west coast). But of course, **cricket** is the Barbadian national sport, and you will come across weekend matches all over the island, and less formal games being played by children in the backstreets of the towns—stop and watch, you may even be thrown the ball and told to bowl. Details of forthcoming League matches and international Tests, held in the Kensington Oval north of Bridgetown, can be found in the newspapers, or through the Barbados Cricket Association (tel 436 1397).

Bridgetown

Set on the broad sweep of Carlisle Bay on the southwest coast of Barbados, Bridgetown is a thriving Caribbean capital with over 100,000 population. Grand old colonial structures jostle with purposeful glass-fronted and modern pastel offices, while hucksters fill the streets, touting their wares from trays.

The heart of the city is the old harbour at the **Careenage**, an inlet surrounded by warehouses that takes its name from the process of *careening* a boat, in which a weight would be tied to its mast to upturn it, revealing the hull to be cleaned and painted. The lighters that once loaded the ships at anchor in the bay from here are now gone because Barbados has a deep-water harbour, but the jetties of the careenage buzz with café life and local fishing craft and pleasure boats. It is still a working harbour and is all quite

45

picturesque nowadays, when the daily catch of flying fish is landed in the late afternoon, but about 300 years ago it was an offence worthy of prosecution to disturb the waters of the Careenage because the smell was so bad.

Presiding over the scene is a statue of **Lord Nelson** in full uniform, erected in 1813, following his death at the Battle of Trafalgar. Nelson had been based in the West Indies for several years, and the Barbadians were grateful to him as the 'preserver of the West Indies'. The Barbadian tribute to him preceded the Statue in London by 27 years.

Traditionally he faces any danger that threatens Barbados and so he has always faced the sea. In a recent redevelopment, however, he was inexplicably turned around. In the present economic difficulties, Bajan wags claim that he now faces the twin threats of the Government buildings and the Central Bank.

As in London, he stands in **Trafalgar Square**, once known as **the Green** in English fashion, originally the position of the pillory and the ducking stool. On the north side of the square are the **Public Buildings**, which were recently cleaned up to reveal bright coral rock. They house the Barbados Parliament, two long rounded buildings constructed of Barbadian coral rock with green-louvred shutters and red tin shades. Opened in 1874, they are Italian Renaissance in style but have pointed arches. In the **House of Assembly** there is a stained glass window commemorating the monarchs of England, from James I to Victoria, including a portrait of Cromwell, interesting in itself because of Barbados's royalist sympathies during the Civil War. Two minutes' walk east of Trafalgar Square is **St Michael's Cathedral**, rebuilt with money raised in a lottery in 1789 after the early wooden structure was destroyed in the hurricane of 1780. It became a Cathedral when William Hart Coleridge arrived in 1825 as the first Bishop of Barbados. Among the sculpted memorials and tablets is a font that dates from 1680 and is decorated with a greek palindrome: NIφON ANOMH MAMH MONA NOφIN, meaning: *Wash the sin, not just the skin.*

On Magazine Lane, leading up to the functional buildings of the Law Courts and the Public Library, presented to Barbados by Andrew Carnegie in 1906, is the recently restored 19th-century **Synagogue** on the site of the original 17th-century building constructed by Jews who had escaped from Brazil and obtained permission to settle in Barbados on hearing that Cromwell had granted freedom of worship. Just inside the graveyard can be seen the bemusing headstone commemorating a certain **Benjamin Massiah**, no doubt a local celebrity, who 'performed the office of circumciser with great Applause and Dexterity'.

Now behind Nelson is **Broad Street**, Bridgetown's main thoroughfare and business street, where elaborate colonial edifices that might belong in an English south coastal town are interspersed with shopping centres and banks.

Following **Bay Street** to the south you will skirt Carlisle Bay, where yachts lie at anchor off the beach and the esplanade. A hundred years ago this area was a poor quarter renowned for smuggling and so the Government bought it out and built the esplanade. Bay Street itself is still a tatty area of old wooden buildings and pokey bars that works by night as Bridgetown's red light district.

Not far along the route is the Roman Catholic **St Patrick's Cathedral**. Barbados is mostly protestant, but St Patrick's was built in 1897 in response to the demands of the catholic Connaught Rangers, an Irish Regiment stationed on the island. Farther on, the area opens out and the wooden town houses take on gingerbread pointings with the intricacy of lacework.

The Barbadian flag was first raised in place of the Union Jack on the **Garrison Savannah**, a 50-acre park surrounded by trees a couple of miles from central Bridgetown. It takes its name from its original use as a military ground before the troops were withdrawn in 1905. Military barracks, in varying states of repair, surround the Savannah. The original Guard House, with its green-domed clock tower, is occupied by the **Savannah Club**. Nowadays, as well as the parades, the Savannah hosts sports such as racing, rugby and cricket. Today's military, the Barbados Defence Force, still occupies one of the buildings, the 18th-century St Anne's Fort across the road at the south of the Savannah.

Barbados Museum

At the northern end of the Savannah, in the handsome setting of the former garrison jail, is the **Barbados Museum**, which gives an enlightening view of Barbadian history from its start as a coral-encrusted shelf, inhabited by various Amerindian tribes, to the archetypal sugar island and on to *Bimshire* and Independence. There are some particularly good displays in the Aall maps and prints gallery, and some peep-in views of old-time Barbados. Naturally there is an exhibit of a prisoner's cell. The temporary exhibition gallery has revolving exhibits of local artists and there is a hands-on children's gallery. Open Mon–Sat, 10–6, adm.

Markets

Bridgetown's two main covered markets are **Fairchild Market**, just across Charles Duncan O'Neal Bridge from Trafalgar Square and **Cheapside Market**, near to St Mary's Church in the west of town. Vendors tout tropical fruits and vegetables shipped in from the Windwards as well as tourist T-shirts. Both are worth a visit any day bar Sunday and are particularly lively on Saturdays. Swan St in the centre of town is also a busy shopping market on weekdays. Just south of Cheapside market is the **Rasta Mall**, rastaman stalls painted in red, gold and green selling anything from the speeches of Haile Selassie to herbal medicines. Following the Princess Alice Highway out of town you will come to **Pelican Village**, a sort of artisan's mall selling paintings, wickerwork and clothes.

The West Coast—North to Scotland and St Lucy

Highway 1, or the spring Garden Highway, where the Parade of Bands is held at *Cropover*, leads out of Bridgetown to the north, along the west coast of the island, to Speightstown, Barbados's second town. Winter home to transient millionaires, the west coast is all hotels and expensive villas muscling in for frontage on the 15-mile strip of extremely fine beaches. Interspersed you will find rum-shops, restaurants and the best sunset beach bars.

Until the Second World War, people would avoid the area and make the journey by boat. It was considered unhealthy because of the coastal swamps, but since the fifties, people have flocked here from all over the world for a rest-cure. Barbados's most exclusive hotels are situated here. In tourist jargon it is referred to as the Gold Coast, recently updated to the Platinum Coast.

If you still go by boat you will pass the deep-water harbour on the point in Bridgetown, immediately recognizable by its triple silos that store the Barbados sugar before export and then, travelling north, you will pass the **West India Rum Refinery**, where you will catch the smell of rum blowing over the water. Visits can be made on Wed and Fri, tour with lunch and tasting, Bds$55 (tel 425 9066).

On land, the road passes the Kensington Oval, the island's stadium where the cricket internationals are held, and then passes the walls of Cave Hill Campus, one of three that make up the **University of the West Indies**. Buried in the grounds is Sir Frank Worrell, the Barbadian cricketer who you will see pictured on the Barbadian $5 note.

Following the west coast road, which winds over the headlands and occasionally touches the seafront, you come to **Holetown**, seven miles north of the capital, where the first European settlers made their home. It is apparently so-called because the sailors who put in here were reminded of 'the Hole' on the River Thames. It was here that Captain John Powell claimed the island for England. His sign, *'James K. of E. and of this island'*, was placed in 1625 on a fustic tree, and has now disappeared, but the event is recalled by a memorial in the town. Originally the town was called Jamestown, the name of the Parish and the Holetown church, **St James's**, one of the oldest on the island, which has recently been restored. The bell, supposedly brought to Barbados after an attack on Martinique, is inscribed, *'God Bless King William 1696'*.

Inland, just off Highway 2, is **Harrison's Cave**, a series of underground rivers and limestone caverns hung with stalactite shark teeth that drip on to glutinous stalagmites, due to join up in a couple of million years. It is all a bit overplayed, with hard hats, strict guides, fat-wheeled buggies, and yet another handicraft shop, but the 500,000-year-old caverns are genuinely a stimulating sight. Open 9–4 (tel 438 6640), adm expensive.

Welchman Hall Gulley is a couple of miles farther along Highway 2, a cleft in Barbados's limestone *cap* that drips with tropical greenery, a canopy that nearly blocks out the sun and drops lianas down on to the array of shrubs and trees. On the short walk through the gulley you might think that you have descended to the depths of Barbados, but when you come out into the open you are presented with a fantastic view over northern Barbados and the Atlantic. The gulley and the caves were used by runaways and escapers of all sorts. Open 9–5, (tel 438 6671), adm Bds$5.

Back on the coast, **Speightstown** (pronounced rather like *Spikestong*), is about 12 miles north of the capital. Very early on the town was a thriving port, used to land goods for the northern part of Barbados, before good roads were built. The town was even known as *Little Bristol* because it had links with Bristol, then England's second largest port. Its name even derives from a Bristol man, William Speight, a member of the Barbados Parliament in 1639.

Scotland and St Lucy in the North

Barbados's imposed sophistication evaporates with the last hotel just north of Speight-stown, giving way to fishing villages in the bays and the simple attractive parish of **St Lucy** and leading up to the cliffs of the north coast. The land is covered in caves and sugar-cane, plains that descend from the mountainous **Scotland District** in the centre

One of sour, two of sweet, three of strong, four of weak

of the island. It was to Scotland that the catholics, *barbadosed* by Cromwell, were sent to keep them out of the way. Some of their descendants are still there, in the communities of *poor whites* as they are known.

At the most northerly point in the island is **Animal Flower Cave**, a series of caverns thrashed out by the force of the waves, which can be approached from the land by steps. Ghostly lumps of rock are silhouetted against the sea outside and at high tide the waves gush through blow-holes. The name derives from sea anemones that grow there and which look like flowers when they open out their tendrils. If you disturb them, the yellow and green anemones snap back into the rock and the blue and brown into their little tubes, adm. In the nearby Pirate's Tavern, covered in visiting cards, you can get a drink and escape the heat.

A popular place for surfing when the waves are up is the beach at **Duppies** (a West Indian word for ghosts). Not far away is the home of Barbados's most popular rum, the **Mount Gay Rum Distillery**, its name taken from the nearby Gay's Cove.

Inland from Speightstown you come to the rugged and mountainous **Scotland District**, where crags tower above sparsely grassed moorland. Escaped slaves would come to lie up in the hope of casting off for St Vincent, 100 miles directly downwind, and visible on the clearest days from Mount Hillaby. It also found favour with the planters, who built some of the finest plantation houses here.

The roads are rough in the remoter areas of Scotland District, because deforestation has loosened the soil, causing occasional landslides and blocking them off. However, the views are spectacular. Just in from the coast, beyond Mile and a Quarter (the distance from Speightstown) you come to **All Saints**, one of the oldest churches on the island, though the original was destroyed in the hurricane of 1831. In the graveyard is the tomb of William Arnold, one of the first settlers to set foot on the island in 1627.

One of the best views is from **Cherry Tree Hill**, from where one can look north to St Lucy and south over the island as far as **Hackleton's Cliff** in the parish of St Joseph. Just beneath it is a cool avenue of casuarina and mahogany trees where the Bajans come to take their picnics.

There is another fine view of Scotland from **Farley Hill**, with its shell of a 19th-century country mansion, renowned as the smartest in Barbados in the late 1880s, when the owner Sir Graham Briggs held lavish receptions. Unfortunately it was gutted by fire in the sixties but not before it was used as the Fleury home in the film of Alec Waugh's *Island in the Sun*, starring Harry Belafonte and Joan Collins. Since then it has been purchased by the Barbados Government and the gardens, with their magnificent royal palms and other labelled trees and plants, have been restored as a National Park. It is a little sad, but peaceful. Gardens open until dusk, adm.

St Nicholas Abbey

Just a couple of miles away is **St Nicholas Abbey**, one of the two oldest mansions on the island and among the only three Jacobean houses surviving in the whole of the Americas (along with Drax Hall, also in Barbados, and Bacon's Castle in Virginia, USA). Built around 1650 by a Colonel Berringer, it is not an Abbey at all, but it is a fine stone building with curved gables (a reminder of the Dutch influence in Barbados in the early days of settlement). One oddity is that the house has fireplaces, as though the inhabitants feared cold nights in the hills of Scotland. It was a working plantation up to the forties. Open Mon–Fri, 10–3:30. Do not miss the twice-daily (11 am and 2 pm) showing of a film of Barbados in the 1930s, which includes footage of the Bridgetown Careenage, loading rum puncheons, *mauby ladies* pouring drinks from a barrel on their head and shots of Barbados's windmills (tel 422 8775), adm.

St Andrew's Parish

Old prints of Barbados show the island dotted with windmills and at one time about 500 were employed in crushing cane. Among the ruins there is only one that survives intact, the **Morgan Lewis Mill** in the hills of St Andrew's Parish. It is maintained in working order as a museum by the Barbados National Trust, with its crushing gear on view. Open Mon–Sat, 9–5, (tel 422 9222) adm Bds$5.

St Andrew's Parish is the least populous in Barbados and boasts the highest point on the island, **Mount Hillaby**, 1160 ft above sea level. It also has Barbados's only untouched forestland, **Turner's Hall Wood**, on a ridge leading from Mount Hillaby, the last remnant of the forest that once covered the whole of Barbados. The wood has a variety of trees including the sandbox, the buttressed locust tree, which has a pod with foul-smelling but reasonable tasting flesh and the *jack-in-a-box* tree that takes its name from its seed which stands erect in a pod. You might also see a grey kingbird or a carib grackle.

The Sugar Heartland—Bridgetown to the Atlantic Coast

Highways 3 and **4**, pass through Barbados's sugar-cane heartland, the roads curtained either side by the 12-foot grass-like crop. The roads are a maze linking small villages of colourful clapboard houses, *chattel houses* to the Bajans, and some of the island's finest plantation houses. The east coast is popular among Bajans escaping from Bridgetown for their holidays. The land rises steadily from west to east, culminating in a cliff that gives broad and sweeping views of the windward coastline.

The first important landmark on Highway 4 out of Bridgetown is the award-winning **Banks Brewery**. Visits can be made on certain days; contact them on (tel 429 2113). **Francia** Plantation House, set in open tropical gardens with a panoramic view of the west coast, is a Bajan family home with echoes of Brazil in some architectural features and in the imported hardwood. West Indian prints and maps as well as a three-way seat for a pair of lovers (the third seat is for the girl's chaperone). There is a dripstone, which provided clean and filtered water. Open Mon–Fri, 10–4 (tel 429 0474), adm.

Gun Hill Signal Station is one of a string of semaphore stations that could link the whole of Barbados within minutes. Set up in 1818, the military were able to warn of impending trouble from the sea, by using flags by day and coloured lanterns at night, and also pass the message quickly of uprisings among the slaves or even advise that a ship had arrived in port with merchandise. The communication tower at Gun Hill has been restored and provides a fine view of the island all around, as well as a map of the other stations in the network and some military memorabilia.

On approach to the signal station you will see an odd-looking white lion on the side of the hill. Gun Hill was used as for convalescence for troops suffering from malaria and yellow fever. They tended to recover because the climate was fresher away from the sea at this height. During his recuperation in 1868, a Col. Wilkinson sculpted the Gun Hill Lion (hardly a masterpiece). Open Mon–Fri, 9–5, adm.

Drax Hall, set in massive trees just off Highway 4, contends with St Nicholas Abbey in the parish of St Peter to be the oldest building on the island. It is of simpler Jacobean design than its rival and has a fine early Jacobean mastic-wood staircase. It is still privately owned, by the Drax family who built it in the 1650s. It is said that Colonel William Drax was the first man to plant sugar-cane in Barbados on this estate. He had arrived with 300 pounds and vowed that he would not return to England until he could afford an estate with an annual income of £10,000. Not only did he do this, but as a moderate roundhead during the Civil War, he was knighted by Cromwell and then four years later granted a baronetcy by Charles II, for 'devoted services to the King'. The house is not open to the public except once a year under the auspices of the National Trust.

Close by is **Villa Nova**, a classical Bajan Great House swallowed in a profusion of tropical greenery. The coral-stone house is surrounded by a gallery to allow breezes through the open rooms while excluding the rain. On view is Chippendale furniture and the desk of former owner, Sir Anthony Eden. In the garden is a cannonball tree and an African tulip tree with flowers like hanging trumpets, (tel 433 1524), adm.

There is an extremely fine view from **St John's Parish Church**, which stands on the cliff 800 ft above the Atlantic coast. Rebuilt in 1836 after the 1831 hurricane, the original 1667 church was constructed at a cost of 100,000 pounds of sugar.

St John's also has a strange history concerning its early vestryman Ferdinando Paleologus, who came to Barbados as a refugee after fighting on the side of the Royalists in the Civil War. His ancestors had been the Christian Emperors of Constantinople until they were driven out by the Turks in the 15th century. His remains were discovered in the destruction of the 1831 hurricane, head pointing west according to the Greek custom, and they were moved and reinterred in a vault with Greek columns and an inscription that is similar to the one on his father's grave in Llandulph, Cornwall:

THE CARIBBEAN

Here Lyeth ye body of
Ferdinando Paleologus
Descended from Ye Imperial Line
Of Ye Last Christian
Emperors of Greece
Churchwarden of this Parish
1655–1656
Vestryman, Twentye Years
Died Oct. 3, 1678

To the southeast, on a shelf in the descending cliff is **Codrington College**, a magnificent coral-stone seminary with an arched portico and views down to Consett Bay. Approached through an avenue of mighty cabbage palms, living columns up to 100 feet in height, it is set in a garden of tropical plants with a lake. It was built in the early 18th century with money from a bequest from Christopher Codrington, a Governor-General of the Leeward Islands whose grandfather was one of the earliest settlers of Barbados.

A story is attached to two of the cabbage palms in the avenue, planted in 1879 by Prince Albert and Prince George who were on a visit to the island. One palm flourished, but the other did not. When the news came that Prince Albert had died, the local Bajans showed no surprise and said, 'We knew he die soon. His cabbage die!'.

Hackleton's Cliff runs parallel to the coastline and commands another of Barbados's fine panoramas with views both north and south along the windward coastline from about 1000 feet above the sea.

Just inside the parish of St Joseph is a former signal station, the **Cotton Tower**, a link in the semaphore chain from Gun Hill. It stands above a gully, the Devil's Bowling Alley, and has cracking views over Scotland.

The windward coast of Barbados is lined by reefs sometimes up to 3 miles offshore, making it impossible for all but the smallest shipping to put in here. But the reefs have little effect on the Atlantic breakers that barrel in and crash on the poised rocks the size of houses on the coastline, eroding it at the rate of a foot a year. A typical windward coast settlement is **Bathsheba**, a slightly ragged fishing village dotted with houses and windblown palm trees, set on a bay popular with surfers because of its waves. It is still possible to see the fishing boats making their way out to sea through the reefs.

Andromeda Gardens above the village are full to bursting with tropical plants from all over the world, ranging from tiny orchids to the tree that gave Barbados its name, the banyan, or bearded fig tree.

Started in 1954 and recently bought by the Barbados National Trust, you follow paths through a valley alive with the smells and colours of a tropical explosion (the plants are labelled). You will see the native *frangipani*, with bright red and yellow petals, orchids that look like five-winged purple and white butterflies and *ravenala madagascariensis*, the traveller's tree, a fan of broad leaves. Open daily, adm.

The east coast road leads north into the parish of St Andrew, following the track of the old railway to its terminus at Belleplaine, where the Bajans would come on their picnics earlier this century. Inland there is another garden, the **Flower Forest**, paths through more tropical splendour and views of Scotland in the distance. Tropical plants include breadfruit, golden apple and mango, as well as spices and citrus. Open 9–5, adm.

52

Suburbs and the South Coast

Like the west coast, the south coast of Barbados is gilded with beaches, mounds of golden sand on which the waves clap and rush. Just behind them are apartment-blocks and hotels jostling for space in the extended suburbs that contain the homes of the Bajan *bons bourgeois*. It does not have the sophistication of the west coast but has a lively atmosphere and good nightlife.

Highway 7 runs through the endless suburb from central Bridgetown to Oistins Town (about 5 miles), throwing off lanes that seek out the *gaps* and the coves. The areas have names like Hastings, Worthing and Dover, perhaps a reminder of home for nostalgic colonists in centuries past, but certainly less demure than their British counterparts.

Oistins, where the sea flashes with colourful Barbadian fishing boats, is a fishing centre and Barbados's third largest town. It comes alive each day at one o'clock in the afternoon when the catch is brought in and sold. According to Ligon, a visitor in the 1650s, it was called 'Austins Bay, not in commemoration of any Saint, but of a wilde mad drunken fellow, whose lewd and extravagant carriage made him infamous in the Iland'. It was in Oistins Town in 1652, at **Ye Mermaid's Inn**, that the 'Magna Carta of Barbados', the articles of capitulation, were signed by the Royalists, surrendering Barbados after a long siege to the Commonwealth Commissioners sent by Cromwell.

Farther along the coast is a notorious house in Long Bay, the crenellated **Sam Lord's Castle**, solidly built in 1820 (it was undamaged in the 1831 hurricane but scaffolding on the walls ended up three miles away). It is now surrounded by a hotel complex, but it is famous for the legend that surrounds its first owner, Sam Lord, a story that becomes more embellished with each telling.

Lord was a greedy man, who was suspected of murdering to gain inheritance and who was found out mistreating his wife cruelly, but he is also credited with causing shipwrecks on the reefs below his house, luring ships in to land by hanging lanterns in his windows/his palm trees/the horns of his cattle/the antlers of his deer (delete as applicable). Then, so the story goes, he would offload the booty and bring it to his castle by way of an underground passage (conspicuously absent today).

He became an extremely rich man, favoured by a series of sudden deaths, but he was busily chasing yet another inheritance when he was uncovered. He had locked up his wife before a journey to England to talk her family into giving him some of her money, but she escaped and managed to get there before him and he was arrested. However, a case brought against him was inconclusive. He is remembered in a book by Lt. Colonel Drury, *The Regency Rascal*, and whatever the legend that surrounds him he was undoubtedly an extravagant rogue whose only bequests were debts, an impressive £18,000 in 1845 to go with his magnificent castle. It is suitably and lavishly decorated according to the period, with plasterwork ceilings and mahogany trimmings, Regency furnture and an extremely fine staircase. Open in the day, adm. (It is often crowded because it works as the hotel lobby as well.)

Ragged Point is the most easterly place on the island, a limestone cliff thrashed by the Atlantic. A lighthouse, built to deny Sam Lord his loot, is now defunct, but the view is majestic. Culpepper Island nearby is the only remaining offshore cay, now that the others have been swallowed up by land reclamation.

Off Highway 5, the direct route back towards Bridgetown, is the **Sunbury Plantation House and Museum** (tel 423 6270), where the pleasant lawned garden is set with coaches and iron farm machinery. The house, originally constructed in the 1660s, is restored in Georgian style to the state of a plantation house at the height of Barbados's sugar prosperity. You can dine in the house in plantation splendour, arranged through the hosts who live in Sunbury. If you do not feel like being quite so grand, there is a medium-priced restaurant in the grounds for lunch and afternoon tea.

FESTIVALS
The highlight of the Barbadian Festival year is the *Cropover*, which culminates on first Monday in August on Kadooment Day, celebrating the last of the cane harvest. It is a show along Carnival lines, with players dressed in colourful costumes parading the streets, struggling to keep moving to the relentless calypsos. Over the Easter Weekend, the town of Oistins on the south coast celebrates its *Fish Festival*, and in February Holetown comes alive, in celebration of the first settlers who put in there in 1627. In January, October and November, street fairs are held St Lawrence Gap and Speight-stown. In November, *NIFCA*, the National Independence Festival of the Creative Arts, stages performing arts and there is an annual culinary exhibition in October.

WHERE TO STAY
As the nerve centre of the British presence in the Eastern Caribbean, Barbados has a tradition of hotels going back 200 years. The best known was the 19th-century *Ice House*, patronized because it brought cool drinks to Barbados, but most were famous for a series of prodigious creole landladies who kept houses of varying states of disorder: *Sabina Brade, Hannah Lewis* who would complain of her lumbago and *Betsy Austin*, a lady of massive size and earthy language, who would become violent if her bill was questioned.

For many of the tavern girls 'of erect figure and stately carriage ... without shoes or stockings, in a short white jacket and thin short petticoat ... a white turban on the head, neck and shoulders left bare', it was a business profitable enough to buy their freedom from slavery.

But the most popular image is that of the gargantuan *Rachel Pringle*, an expansive matriarch, dressed in voluminous silk, of almost unmovable disposition, whose caricature by the cartoonist Rowlandson can be seen all over the island.

The 20th-century tourism boom came early to Barbados and the island offers a good holiday across the board, from a cheap summer package to a luxurious winter excursion or honeymoon. Package tours have come recently to Barbados, filling a surfeit of rooms in the summer months and bringing in extra foreign exchange.

Barbados offers probably the best range of hotels in the Caribbean and prices are fairly high in season because of its reputation, however it is possible to find a good deal in the summer months. As well as hotels, there are self-catering flats and also villas for hire. If you take one of these, maid-service is always available. Many are air-conditioned, but some give you the choice of a fan. Contact **Bajan Services Ltd** at Seascape Cottage, Gibbs, St Peter, Barabados (tel 809 422 2618, fax 422 5366) or in Britain **Caribbean Journeys**, Ashley Wood House, Burchetts Green, Maidenhead, Berks SL6 6RB (tel 0628 524268, fax 822190) who cover many two to eight bedroom villas.

The smart set go to the *Platinum Coast*, which runs north along the west coast from Bridgetown to just beyond Speightstown. Some of the finest hotels in the Caribbean are here, set in gardens of tropical splendour and giving on to the gentle bays with golden strands, a fine place to see the Green Flash at sunset.

The busy south coast is more active and with one or two exceptions the hotels are older and less luxurious. There is also a large selection of self-catering flats and areas with small guest houses. All except the smallest hotels and the guest houses will have a pool and watersports equipment available to their guests. Many have tennis courts. Bear in mind that all accommodation bills in Barbados will be supplemented with a 5% government tax and in almost all cases with a 10% service charge as well.

Hotels

EXPENSIVE

The **Sandy Lane** in St James (tel 432 1311, fax 432 2954), for so long one of the best-known and most luxurious hotels in the Caribbean, has just spent millions to keep the ambience just so. Guests are whisked from the airport to this classical, coral-stone enclave, north and south wings either side of an amphitheatrical courtyard, set on 300 yards of beachfront on the delightful Payne's Bay. It is large, with 121 ocean-view rooms and very expensive, at US$600–750 for a double room in season, with breakfast and another meal (MAP). The **Royal Pavilion** (tel 422 5555, fax 422 3940), farther north in St James has a similar feel of manicured luxury in the best traditions of Barbados hospitality, again with a certain formality (no children in winter). All 75 rooms look on to the ocean from deep balconies, and cost US$445–485 per night in season. Guests have the use of the larger and less formal Glitter Bay resort next door. A charming small hotel is the **Cobbler's Cove** (422 2291, fax 522 1460) on the coast just south of Speightstown. It is dressed in pink, with 39 suites of varying luxury, beachfront and garden, culminating in the Camelot Suite, almost a legend in sumptuary, above the main house. Double room from US$480–570 in season (MAP). Guests return years after year to the **Coral Reef Club** (tel 422 2372, fax 422 1776) just north of Holetown, a family-run hotel with the stately grace of old-time Barbados. The 71 individual rooms are set in coral-rock cottages scattered around luxuriant gardens of sago palm and casuarina. The hotel retains a certain old-time formality too, with a jacket and tie required at dinner in season, when rooms cost US$310–360 a double, MAP also. Slightly more casual, wrapped in bougainvillaea, are the suites of the **Sandpiper Inn** nearby (tel 422 2251, fax as Coral Reef), double room US$280–$515.

MODERATE

A surreal shade of turquoise runs as a leitmotif through the **Crane Beach Hotel** (423 6220, fax 423 5342) on the southeast coast in St Philip, from the absurdly rich sea to the clifftop pool with its classical columns and balustrades. Established over a hundred years ago, the hotel takes its name from a crane that once winched goods from the classic cove below. The 18 rooms and suites (four set in a miniature castle) are luxurious and start at $190. Another haven of antique Barbadian luxury, yet further afield, can be found at Cattlewash on the east coast, at the **Kingsley Club** (tel 433 9422, fax 433 9226). Earlier this century, well-to-do Bajans would escape the turmoil of Bridgetown to this traditional timber-frame villa. Now it is an ideal writer's retreat and professional's rest-cure, as you can tell by the faded copies of Architectural Digest and Forbes Magazine. Eight double rooms at US$92 in winter. The **Island Inn Hotel**

(tel 436 6393) in Aquatic Gap, just south of Bridgetown, is set in the old stone walls and tin roofs of the former British Military rum store. Not the thundering of barrels any more, but more likely the clinking of glasses beneath the breadfruit tree in the courtyard. 25 rooms at US$120 in winter. And there is a similar old-time grandeur at the **Ocean View Hotel** in Hastings (tel 427 7821, fax 427 7826) which has presided over its fine view since 1901. Antique furniture, four posters and creaking floorboards, with a charming waterfront restaurant, double room US$121 in season.

CHEAP

As the name suggests, the **Benston Windsurfing Club Hotel** (tel 428 9095) in Maxwell, caters specially for windsurfers, with good rates on rooms and equipment alike. It can be spotted by the line of sailboards beating out and back from the coast. Double room US$60. For a classic Caribbean **Guest House**, dingy and welcoming, try the **Rydal Waters Guest House** on 3rd Ave, Worthing (tel 435 2433); 6 rooms US$20 and $30. Nearby **Shells Guest House** (tel 435 7253) and the **Crystal Waters** (tel 435 7514), which also have a local Bajan feel, charge about the same. In Maxwell, the **Villa Marie** (tel 428 2863) has a lively atmosphere and double rooms at about $30.

EATING OUT

Bajan Food

As in many of the Caribbean islands, some Bajan traditional dishes have a slave heritage. And so *cou-cou*, a dish made from cornmeal and okra, is served with salt fish, once a hardship food. In Barbados 'peas and rice' are a staple and often flavoured with coconut. Besides the traditional *pepperpot stew*, a four-day boil-up, there is also plenty of seafood, including crab and *sea-egg*, the roe of the white sea-urchin, which is supposely an aphrodisiac.

The best-loved fish in Barbados is the flying fish, winged fish that flit and glide over the waves, sometimes for distances up to 100 yards, which you may well see if you go out sailing. You can also see them brought in to the Careenage in the late afternoon, in season between December and June. Served with a spicy flavouring, flying fish is something of a national dish and is delicious.

Bajan Drink

'The chiefe fudling they make in the iland is Rumbullion, alias Kill Divill and this is made of suggar canes distilled, a hot hellish and terrible liquor'.

Barbados produces some of the finest **rum** in the world. Brewed from molasses, the thick liquid left over from the sugar-boiling process, many rums are still left to mature in oak, taking on a darker colour with age. Mountgay is the best known, try their special 5-year-old, but others worth trying are Cockspur Old Gold and VSOR. Local white rums include Alleyne's. There are hundreds of 'rum shops' on the island, mostly small clapboard shacks, where you will find the Barbadians 'liming', passing the time of day. If you would like to see the distillation process, you can join a 'Where the Rum comes From' tour (tel 435 6900).

Barbados produces superb fruit punches, fresh fruit and juices crushed with ice, and free from the usual pints of sticky grenadine syrup that obliterates the taste elsewhere. More traditional drinks include **mauby** juice, a bitter drink made by boiling bark and spices—100 years ago *mauby ladies* would ply the streets of Bridgetown with an urn on their heads, offering drinks to quench a midday thirst. The 20th-century equivalent is a snow-cone in a plastic cup. You will also find delicious home-brewed **ginger beer**, boiled up from grated root ginger and **sorrel**, a sweet concoction made from the red flowers of the sorrel plant. It is known as the Christmas drink all over the Caribbean. The Bajan beer is the award-winning **Banks** brew.

Restaurants
Barbados has some extremely fine restaurants, known both for good food and for charming locations: terraces on the waterfront just above the waves and the garden setting of Bajan galleries, verandas threatened by explosive tropical flora. Many of the hotels also have fine kitchens and it you are staying at one of the Elegant Resorts of Barbados you may try the others out. No restaurants outside the hotels require a jacket and tie, though there may be a dress-code of trousers and a sleeved shirt. There is an encrustation of pizza huts and steak houses, but you can of course eat Bajan style, taking away in a polystyrene box. Eating out in Barbados is not cheap and a hefty bill will be supplemented by a 10% service charge and a 5% government tax. Credit cards are widely accepted. You are advised to reserve a table in the winter season.

EXPENSIVE
Only the quiet clink of cutlery will rise above the murmur of the night air at **Bagatelle Great House** (tel 421 6767), where you dine in the coral-stone rooms of one of the oldest plantation houses in Barbados. French cuisine with a twist of the Caribbean in the spices or ingredients; try Dijon steak flambéed in local sugar-cane brandy or Bajan catch in local ginger and yoghurt. Finish off with chocolate Amaretto. About Bds$100 without wine for a five course dinner. For the island's finest waterfront dining try **Carambola** (tel 432 0832), where twenty tables are strung out above the calm waters of St James, under awnings and umbrellas. Jumbo shrimp sizzling in sweet pepper and maltese sauce or kingfish on onions and herbs in red wine. French menu, closed Sun, main dish from Bds$45. At **La Cage aux Folles** (tel 424 2424) there are dishes from all over the world—marinaded, grilled and glazed chinese duck, yogurtlu lamb kebab or local catch amandine with slivered almonds. Main dish Bds$55 and up. Closed Tues. And at the **Chateau Creole** (tel 422 4116) you might try the Guyanese shrimp saki, or Drunken chicken, marinaded in local Bajan rum. Main course Bds$50. Back on the coastline you can get a slightly cheaper dinner above the waves at **The Fathoms** (tel 432 2568) at the top end of Payne's Bay. Start with octopus, or sea-egg (an aphrodisiac) and move on to other creatures of the deep; shrimp brochette in orange champagne or barracuda basking in dill and mustard. Main course Bds$30.

MODERATE
Just south of Bridgetown in Aquatic Gap, **Brown Sugar** (tel 426 7684) is set in an extended veranda festooned with greenery, hanging vines and mini-rockpools. Pepper chicken, Jamaican jerk and crab-back with lime and parsley for Bds$20–26. The best waterfront setting on the south coast is at **Pisces** (tel 435 6564), a white wicker dining room wrapped in greenery just above the calm waters of St Lawrence Gap. Dolphin diable in mustard and yoghurt and specials of exotic fish, as the name suggests. Otherwise, try the delicious chicken in a guava sauce. Main course Bds$30. **David's**

Place (tel 435 6550) is just across the small bay and you will get a fine Bajan serving of mellow pumpkin fritters or the original Bajan pepperpot. Main dish Bds$25, closed Mon. Perhaps the best Bajan meal on the island is served at **Shirley's Restaurant** (tel 422 1316), on the waterfront in downtown Speightstown. Shirley used to work at the Sandy Lane Hotel and now the hotel managers come to her. Superb cou-cou and flying fish, hot pepper sauce tempered to taste, or chicken as only the West Indians know how. Full meal Bds$45 approx, closed Sun. Another good local spot is the **Rose Bud Restaurant** (tel 435 8051) on Main Rd, Worthing, where the locals lime before a creole chicken and plantain. Main course Bds$12–20. You might also try the **Pot and Barrel** (tel 423 4107), near Sam Lord's Castle in St Philip. Sunday lunch is a popular moment to eat out in Barbados and many of the hotels offer a buffet. One of the best known is at the **Atlantis Hotel** in Bathsheba (tel 423 1526) above the dramatic east coast of the island.

CHEAP
You can find a cheap burger at one of the beach bars, including the **Sandy Bank** in' Hastings. And you might try **Muster's** in the centre of town (favoured by the taxi-drivers), for the best in cou-cou and steam fish. Finally, **Baxter's Road**, on the northern road out of Bridgetown, is an excellent place to get a nightime snack. The street is lined with hole-in-the-wall bars and golfing umbrellas, under which expansive Bajan ladies fry up on charcoal braziers. They start at about midnight and carry on until about 4 or 5 in the morning.

BARS AND NIGHTLIFE

A French priest who came to Barbados in the 1650s claimed that there were 100 taverns for a population of 2000. The ratio of one for every twenty people may have gone down a bit since the 17th century, when even the Barbados Assembly used to meet in the pub, but evenings in Barbados can be very lively. Generally speaking the best areas are Bridgetown and the south coast, particularly around St Lawrence Gap. Bajan entertainment for Bajans tends to be in rum shops, usually local wooden houses with their shutters pinned open. It is worth stopping at one (try **Muster's** in town and in Weston on the west coast try **John Moore's**, the Little Man's Club, where you can catch a game of dominoes), but otherwise there is a host of bars that are more like home. Many of the big hotels have a discotheque; clubs often charge an entry fee.

Many of the daytime beach bars (listed under beaches) liven up at night. Also worth a try are the **Sugar Reef** bar at Accra beach and the **Pelican beach bar** in Carlisle Bay. The **Villa Marie** in Maxwell attracts a young crowd of pool players.

If you want something a little more chichi, Barbados even has a small collection of wine bars, where the Bajan bon-bourgeois congregate over a glass of Chablis with garlic bread and grilled goat's cheese; try **Nico's** in Holetown or the **39 Steps** in Hastings.

The trick with Barbados **night-life** is to bar-hop with the Bajans. Each different club has its night. In town there is a clutch of clubs behind the waterfront at the Careenage— the **Warehouse** discotheque, large black and white dancefloor, international music, Thurs and Sat. The **Dry Dock** close by is a little more stately—armchairs, polished deck and a harbour view to go with the jazz on Fridays. On Carlisle Bay **Harbour Lights** is a lively waterfront bar with a dancefloor; popular Wed and Fri. In St James you will find the **Coach House**, which has music on Thurs.

St Lawrence Gap is the most popular area for clubs, and the day's lightly grilled flesh comes in for a nightime roasting here. The **Ship Inn** is most popular, where visitors and young Bajans dance or pulsate, depending on how much room there is; most nights. Next door is **After Dark**, which is frequented mostly by Bajans; sometimes jazz in the courtyard. If you are feeling peckish, head off to Baxter's Road.

For pure and wholesome Bajan entertainment, you might go to a weekend **Bram**—details in the paper (a picture of the host, location and admission price); boozing and bit of wining and grinding to the latest soca and Jamaican dub.

For those who prefer a more formal setting, there are a number of shows depicting Barbadian life and history. The best is probably *1627 and all that . . .* which celebrates Bajan history from the beginning and takes place twice a week, Thurs and Sun, in the Barbados Museum. For Bds$82 you have a tour of the museum, and dinner, and see the show. The Plantation Restaurant in the old boiling house of the Balls Estate in St Lawrence stages a couple of shows, the *Plantation Tropical Spectacular* (Mon, Sat) and *Barbados by Night (Wed, Fri) with fire-eating and flaming limbo, adm Bds$85 for drinks and dinner. Reservations (tel 435 6900). Yet more formal entertainment, classical concerts and plays, are usually held in the* **Frank Collymore Hall** in Bridgetown.

TRINIDAD AND TOBAGO

The twin-island state of Trinidad and Tobago is an unusual mix of two completely different Caribbean strains. Trinidad exudes the excitable bustle of a large island and an extraordinarily cosmopolitan heritage. And just a few miles away, Tobago is in the image of the Caribbean idyll, a beach-bound paradise with all the calm and peace of the West Indies of 50 years ago.

Trinidad and Tobago may be truly Caribbean in spirit, but are geologically closer to South America. The northern range of mountains in Trinidad, just 7 miles off the continent, slipped away from the mainland about 10,000 years ago. Trinidad is the largest of the Lesser Antilles (1864 square miles, about 50 miles by 50). Unlike the other Antilles to the north, it is not volcanic and its heartlands are low agricultural plains. Tobago is a cumulus of forested peaks that broke off from South America millions of years ago. It lies 22 miles off the northeastern tip of Trinidad and has an area of 116 square miles.

There are 1.2 million people on the two islands, which makes it the most populous country in the Lesser Antilles (Tobago has just 45,000 of this population). The two islands were unwilling partners when they were first lumped together by the British Government in 1898, but they have grown closer, even if there is some dissent. Tobagonians sometimes complain that they are politically neglected and they joke that Port of Spain is a den of thieves where you need eyes in the back of your head just to survive. In Trinidad, they laughingly claim the Tobagonians are a bit backward.

Oil brought prosperity to Trinidad this century and with it came trade unions and political change, often accompanied by violence. In 1956 the country voted the People's National Movement (PNM) into power, led by the charismatic leader Eric Williams, who was Prime Minister until his death in 1982.

Trinidad and Tobago has long been a political leader in the Caribbean. Until the failure of the West Indian Federation in 1962, Chaguaramas on Trinidad was to have been the seat of the Caribbean Parliament. Williams led Trinidad and Tobago to independence from Britain on 31 August 1962. In 1976 the country became a Republic, recognizing a President as Head of State rather than the Queen, though it has remained within the British Commonwealth. There are two houses of Parliament, a 33-seat upper House and a 31-seat House of Representatives. The country is led by Mr Patrick Manning of the People's National Movement, who have 16 of the seats. The United National Congress is in opposition.

The oil business took a downturn in the eighties and there have been austerity programmes and cutbacks in Government spending in recent years. Despite the difficulties, this is not enough to dampen the Trinis' spirit and some are claiming that there is an upswing in the economy despite the world difficulties. As far as they are concerned, the *fête* goes on and on.

Carnival, Calypso, Steel Pan

The country is also a cultural leader. Steel pan, and the calypso, a relentless song of stinging social comment, were born here. Carnival or *Mas* is one of the three biggest in the world and is the model for most others held in the Caribbean. The *Trinbagonians* must also take the responsibility for inventing the *limbo* dance.

Carnival

On Shrove Tuesday the streets of Port of Spain seethe with the *bacchanal*—fluorescent satin flashes by as a frenzied army of imps advances in lines, each brandishing a trident. At their head is a massive devil with glowing eyes, a vast black mannequin with a demonic smile held aloft, sparkling with sequins. The Savannah and the length of Frederick Street reverberate to a killing beat—vast articulated lorries stacked 30 feet high with

Panyard, Port of Spain

60

speakers, followed by a sea of people shuffle-stepping in waves. It is the Parade of Carnival Bands and at Trinidad Carnival, each band (like a pageant) can contain as many as a thousand 'players'.

In the weeks after Christmas the Trinidadians stage spectacles of calypso, steel bands, beauty pageants and fêtes all over the country—all culminating in a two-day *jump-up* in Port of Spain in which hundreds of thousands of people take part.

Mas (short for masquerade) was introduced by the French settlers who came to Trinidad at the end of the 18th century; they would move in masked processions from one open-house to the next. At first it was the preserve of the plantocracy and the wealthy traders, but with emancipation in 1838, the slaves made the event their own. They danced in the streets with lighted torches celebrating *Canboulay* (from *cannes brûlées*), or the burning of the canefields. Drums led the processions and any instrument was used to make a tune: tin kettles, shack-shacks, even bottles and biscuit tins.

In Victorian times the celebrations were frowned upon by the government and many official attempts were made to curb them, but these often ended in rioting (another meaning of the word bacchanal) as bands of revellers and groups of police armed with sticks took each other on.

Early in the 20th century the tradition of dressing up was revived and the drum-driven masquerade once again became the centrepiece of the Carnival. Steel bands led the processions in the years after the Second World War and now you will hear the relentless sounds of *soca* music as the engine-house of the pageant.

Mention Rio or New Orleans to a Trinidadian and they will laugh and assure you that carnival in those cities is just a fashion show. People leave their jobs to get back to *Mas* here, and without exception they follow the creole maxim 'tré le vie' (from *tuer la vie*, meaning something like dance till you drop). Despite one or two horror stories of people being mugged for their stone-washed jeans and being left without their wallet or their trousers, Carnival is accessible to outsiders. It simply must be seen to be believed.

The best moments to see are the calypso and steel band competition finals and then *jouvert* (pronounced jouvay), a dawn dance in which hundreds of thousands shuffle in the streets, smeared with mud or oil to steel band music (beware if you wander by in a white suit). It is a crush and it is deafening, but there is nothing like it. The 'roadmarch tunes' of any particular year become ingrained on your memory as you hear them played over and over again; they will bring back the feeling of Carnival for years. Finally you can watch the *Parade of Bands*, the centrepiece of Carnival, in which the bands perform and are judged on the Savannah. Better still, join in. If you wish to 'play Mas', you can turn up at a Mas Camp ten days ahead of time and a buy a costume in which to play for between US$50 and $100.

Carnival Calendar of Events

A typical Carnival calendar stages *calypso tents*, *panorama* (steel band) and Carnival King and Queen competition heats on the weekends before the beginning of Lent.

Friday before Lent—King and Queen of Bands Competition. *Calypso Competition* finals.
Saturday—*Panorama* final, Junior Carnival Parade and Competition.
Sunday—*Dimanche Gras*, a day of fêtes.
Monday—*Jouvert* (a *jump-up* 4–10 am), Procession of Carnival Bands.
Tuesday—*Mardi Gras*, Parade of Carnival Bands from 9 am until late.

Calypso

The sounds that accompany Carnival—the relentless beat on the *Roadmarch* as the masqueraders dance through the streets and in the lively sparring in the concert-halls—are *calypsos*. They are Trinidadian-born songs of life and love—witty, lyrical, melodic, full of gossip and often political, but above all entertaining and with as many styles as there are calypsonians (also known as *kaisonians*).

The roots of the calypso are obscure, but they were first sung in French creole in Trinidad during the last century. Early this century they became a source of popular entertainment and as they started to reach a larger audience they were sung in English. Since they became popular in Trinidad, other islands in the area have adopted the form.

They are a verbal newspaper of sorts and they deal with contemporary issues, commenting on politics, satirizing life's institutions (from love to the IMF) and passing on juicy bits of gossip. They are often irreverent or just plain rude, they have a fearsome cutting edge when it comes to ridicule and they have been known to vote governments out.

But the *calypsonian* is also a performer, daring, outspoken and often overtly sexual, as seen in the annual calypso competition in the run-up to Carnival. The big calypsonians will spar with each other in their songs, ridiculing their opponents in their lyrics. They belong to a *calypso tent* (no longer a tent but a group of like-minded singers who club together in a hall) where they perform the songs that they write. Judges select a number of calypsonians from each tent to go on to the National Calypso Monarch Competition.

The finals are something like a variety show as the performers act out their theme. Calypsos must be timely and witty, but the style can range from that of a raconteur to a pantomime artist. The repertoire is endless.

After the war, the calypsos were often backed by steel pan, but since the late seventies, this has been replaced by *soca* music (from soul-calypso), a much faster beat played on more conventional modern instruments. Above the definite African drumbeat can be heard the strains of European rock and often odd blends of Indian or Chinese sounds.

The names of the calypsonians are colourful: early singers included *Atilla the Hun*, *Lord Executor* and the *Roaring Lion*. Other self-appointed Lords include *Lord Melody* and *Lord Kitchener*, who stand alongside the *Calypso Rose*, *The Mighty Chalkdust* (a schoolteacher), *Cro-Cro* and *Black Stalin*. But the mightiest (another popular prefix) of them all is the *Mighty Sparrow*, whose reign as Calypso King lasted for years—he was first crowned monarch in 1956 and was winner of the Roadmarch as recently as 1984.

Steel Pan

As you walk along the street in Port of Spain, you might hear a rising, tremulous thunder of plinks and clangs. Suddenly you will hear a beat and the rhythm emerges: energetic, compulsive, like notes on velvet.

Steel pan, played on the stretched lids of oil-drums, was invented in Trinidad and was first heard at the end of the Second World War. It was back street music that came from the poorest areas of Port of Spain and initially it was frowned upon by the authorities. The *pan-yards* gave themselves names like *Desperadoes* and *Renegades* and they fought regularly amongst themselves and with the police.

But the movement picked up in popularity and then became more respectable. It soon replaced *tamboo-bamboo* as the music for the Carnival roadmarch and has only been superseded by *soca* in the last few years. Many pan-yards are still active in Trinidad and it is definitely worth going along (just walk in) if you hear them playing. Pan competitions are held annually at Carnival and every other year at the World Steelband Festival (alternating with School Pan). Pan Jazz is a yearly festival held in November in which steel bands play alongside world famous jazz musicians.

TOURIST INFORMATION
The **Trinidad and Tobago Tourism Development Authority** offices are in:
UK: 8a Hammersmith Broadway, London W6 7AL (tel 081 741 4466, fax 081 741 1013).
USA: 25 West 43rd St, Suite 1508, New York, NY 10036 (tel 212 719 0540, fax 719 0988, toll free 800 232 0082).

FURTHER READING
The most eloquent form of expression in Trinidad life is probably the calypso, but there is a flourishing literature that first grew in the 1930s.

The earliest book set on Tobago (and one of the earliest English novels) is of course *Robinson Crusoe* by Daniel Defoe (published in 1719), which tells the story of a ship-wrecked sailor who lives on the island for nearly 30 years. Life can be just about as secluded today as it was then.

Eric Williams, for a long time Trinidad and Tobago's Prime Minister and an accomplished historian was the author of *Capitalism and Slavery, From Columbus to Castro*, also *A History of the Peoples of Trinidad and Tobago*, written at the time of Independence. Together with CLR James (who died in 1989 in London) he changed the perspective of West Indians towards their history and culture in the 30s, heralding the birth of West Indian Independence. CLR James was author of *Beyond A Boundary*, a charming autobiographical book about cricket and Trinidad life in the twenties. His *Black Jacobins* is an extremely angry view of the Haitian Revolution.

In *The Wine of Astonishment*, Earl Lovelace tells of the changes in town life during the war, when the Americans were in Trinidad.

The Lonely Londoners by Samuel Selvon tells of life in London in the 50s and 60s as the first West Indians started to come to Britain. His *Ways of Sunlight* is a collection of short stories of rural life in Trinidad and 'hard times' in London.

Novelist VS Naipaul was born in Trinidad of a Brahmin family. His works set in Trinidad include *The Mystic Masseur* and *The Suffrage of Elvira*, two satires of the elections in 40s and 50s and *A House for Mr Biswas*, which portrays the dissolution of traditional Trinidadian life. *Miguel Street* uses the eyes of a young boy to paint a charming picture of the characters in a Port of Spain street.

TRINIDAD

In the faces of Trinidad you will see echoes from around the globe; African, (East) Indian, European, Middle Eastern (called Syrian), Chinese and South American. It is an extraordinary mixture, made yet more complex as the races have intermingled.

You will hear names like Harris Mohammed and Winston Chang and see people wearing saris and shalwar kameez. Even the traditional Caribbean rhythm (*soca* in this area) will sometimes have strains of Indian and Chinese, as heard in *chutney* in 1991. On the skyline Hindu prayer flags and the domes of minarets stand among the classically English parish church towers.

The two largest sectors of the population are the African and the Indian, each of which is about about 40 per cent. Other races include European and quite a few Chinese, though many have left in recent years. Around 15 per cent of the islanders are of mixed descent and sometimes it is difficult to tell their heritage because it is so varied. Generally speaking it is a benevolent mix.

The island is highly industrial for the Caribbean. Oil is still the main earner and after a slump in the early 80s when the OPEC cartel was broken, business has begun to pick up again. Other industries include asphalt and the export of manufactured goods. Despite the fertile soil, the agricultural sector is small. The intention is for tourism to increase. The attempted coup in 1990 set the economy back a little, but it suffered less from the Gulf War than other countries.

Nearly half of the population live in the east-west corridor that runs between the capital, Port of Spain, and the town of Arima beneath the northern range of mountains. The south of the country is industrial, given over to oil fields and vast tracts of sugar cane.

Trinidad has never done anything by halves and the expansive nature of the islanders which produces such lively Carnival celebrations has been known to spill over into violence. Politics occasionally erupts in strife. The islanders have been called *Trickida-dians*, in line with this reputation for being rough and cheeky and you are advised to be careful. Trinidad is not a typical tourist enclave, but with such a variety of cultural and natural assets, it offers far more to the traveller who wants to go off the beaten track.

History

In its early history Trinidad was *Iere* or 'the land of the hummingbird' and was home to Arawak Indians from mainland South America. Unlike their cousins farther north, the Iere Arawaks managed to resist the cannibalizing Caribs who came by in waves about AD 1000, escaping the *boucan* (on which meat was smoked).

The island was christened by Columbus himself in 1498. He sighted three peaks in the southeast of the island as he arrived in the New World for the third time and he called the island Trinidad as a special devotion to the Holy Trinity. The Indians continued to resist any attempts to settle and they kept the Spaniards off the island for 100 years until 1592.

At the beginning of the 17th century, explorers began to use the island as a base for expeditions into the South American jungle in search of *El Dorado*.

Trinidad was officially a defensive Spanish outpost, but it was usually ignored in favour of the islands in the Greater Antilles and so it did not attract many settlers to develop the fertile lands. There was just a small and beleaguered garrison. The island's small trade in tobacco was banned (at one stage the word *Trinidado* was used to refer to tobacco in the same way that the word *Virginia* is used nowadays). The governing *Cabildo*, often called 'illustrious', could not even afford the ceremonial clothes. A priest was sent once a year to say Mass, but usually the only visitors to the island were on raiding parties.

In 1783 efforts were made to develop the vast areas of untouched land in Trinidad and the Spanish king issued a *cedula* (decree) to encourage immigration. Grants of land were given to the 'subjects of powers and nations in alliance with Spain'. Catholics came from French colonies, some of them fleeing the revolutionaries and the slave uprisings in Saint Domingue (now Haiti) and they set up cocoa and sugar plantations. Though it has nearly died out, it is still just possible to hear the French creole spoken in the mountains east of Port of Spain.

On 18 February 1797, the British fleet sailed into Port of Spain harbour and the Governor, Chacon, had no choice but to scuttle his five ships and hand over the island. After 200 years as a Spanish island, Trinidad now became a British colony.

It was already a mix—a mainly French population administered by the British according to Spanish laws. The new British Governor, Picton, tried to develop it into another sugar island, despite the growing lobby against slavery and revolts all over the Caribbean. Next door South America was in turmoil and he had his hands full controlling the lawless population. His solution was to erect on the Government House lawn a set of gallows which he used liberally.

Emancipation came in 1834 and the freed men and women moved away from the cocoa walks and canefields, prefering to live in town or farm a small plot of land. Large stretches of land were still unworked and so the government encouraged immigration again. In 1845 the first East Indians arrived on indentureships—their return passage paid in return for five years' work on a plantation. In all, by 1917, when indentureship was stopped by the Indian government, 145,000 Indians had come to Trinidad. Some went home when their time was up, but many took up the alternative offer of five acres of land and settled in the remote country areas, where their descendants are still today. The Indian workers were treated far better than their African counterparts had been 100 years before, and their families were allowed to remain intact.

Adding further to the racial mix, Chinese workers came, renowned for their work in the canefields of Java and the Philippines and conspicuous in their pigtails, blue smocks and broad conical hats. In the 20th century the mix was completed by the arrival of settlers from the Middle East, many of them Syrians and Lebanese.

Throughout the 20th century Trinidad has suffered sporadic outbursts of political violence. Trade unions rallied the workers to confront the colonial authorities over the minimum wage in the 30s, culminating in riots. In 1970 the capital was brought to a standstill by Black Power protests and bands of guerrillas took to the hills. Most recently in July 1990, Muslim activists led by Abu Bakr took over the Parliament Building and the TV studio in Port of Spain, holding the Prime Minister and his Cabinet at gunpoint. The coup took most Trinidadians by surprise (many were watching the football at the time) and it turned out that the coup leaders did not have the anti-government following they expected, so it quickly collapsed.

Flora and Fauna

The flora and fauna of Trinidad is related to that of South America and is consequently richer and more varied than other islands. The vegetation looks neolithic after the explosive lushness of the Windwards—vines and lianas grow to an immense thickness and the trees grow up to 200 feet high clinging to the steep land. The rainforest flits and squawks all day long with incredibly colourful butterflies and birdlife.

Among the yellow and pink pouis, and 100-foot bamboo sprouts, you will find heliconia and chaconia (the crab-claw-shaped Trinidadian national flower) and even venus fly-traps. There are 2200 species of flowering plants and trees.

By comparison mammals are relatively limited, though the 108 species is an abundance for a Caribbean island. They all originate in South America, so you might see an agouti, an opossum, an ocelot and even an armadillo.

There are also a number of snakes (47) that have been washed over from the continent, of which four are poisonous, including the *fer de lance* and the coral snake. You are advised to be careful when walking in some of the more remote areas.

But the birdlife on Trinidad is the most spectacular—there are about 425 species that make an appearance during the year. The island is on a migratory route and like tourists they fly down here to escape the cold weather. Among the nocturnal oilbirds and white-bearded or golden-headed manakins, macaws and violaceous trogons (yellow breasted with a blue collar and a blue and white stripey tail), there are 27 herons and 18 humming-birds, which flash with fluorescence as they come to suck at a flower on the veranda.

The swamps have an enormous variety of birdlife and water-borne life (from groupers to spectacled caymans and tree crabs). In among the mangroves, with a network of roots like a thousand flying buttresses, you will find oysters that are then sold as an evening snack on the Savannah. And in the evenings the trees in the Caroni Swamp light up with egrets and the colourful scarlet ibis, Trinidad's national bird (see p. 74).

Places to see the Trinidad wildlife include the **Asa Wright Nature Centre** in the northern range, where you can see toucans and honeycreepers and the famed nocturnal oilbirds that feed on fruit, snatched from the tree while flying at night. If a swamp does not sound too outlandish, try the **Caroni Swamp Bird Sanctuary**. Tours can be arranged with extremely knowledgeable guides through **Nanan Tours**, Bamboo Grove Settlement No. 1, Butler Highway, Valsayn (tel 645 1305).

There is little coral on Trinidad's shores because of the freshwater outflow from the Orinoco (go to Tobago for coral), but one of the world's largest species of turtle, the Leatherback (it can weigh up to 1200 lbs and is about seven feet long) comes to nest on both islands between April and June—on Matura Beach on the east coast of Trinidad and at Turtle Beach on Tobago.

Trinidad has large reserves of oil beneath its surface and these find odd ways of coming to the surface. There is no actual volcano on the island, but the gases seep up through bubbling mud flues—at the Devil's Woodyard near Princes Town for example—and the island has one of the Caribbean's oddest underworld phenomena in the Pitch Lake in the south of the island near La Brea.

GETTING TO TRINIDAD

Trinidad has some of the best air links in the Caribbean. It has its own airline—BWIA, often referred to as Bee-wee—and is served by numerous others. Flights to and from places in South America, such as Guyana and Venezuela, are easily arranged.

A departure tax of TT$50 is payable.

By Air
From the UK: British Airways and BWIA have several services each week direct from London Heathrow and Gatwick. Other **European** cities served by direct flights include Stockholm, Cologne, Frankfurt, Munich, Zurich and Amsterdam.

From the USA: BWIA links Miami and other US cities including New York with Port of Spain and American Airlines run services from Los Angeles and Chicago. In **Canada**, Air Canada and BWIA fly from Toronto.

From other Caribbean Islands: BWIA, LIAT and some foreign airlines link Trinidad to all the major destinations within the Caribbean.

By Boat

There is an occasional ferry from La Guiria in Venezuela, across the Dragon's Mouth and you might even try your luck in catching a schooner to Grenada in the Windward Islands.

GETTING AROUND TRINIDAD

Once you are past the Piarco airport taxi-touts, who are among the Caribbean's most persistent, travel in Trinidad is easy. If you do go by taxi the trip to Port of Spain will cost around TT$90, but it is possible to do it for TT$1.50 on the public transport bus which leaves every hour. Piarco is 17 miles from Port of Spain and it takes at least an hour to cover the distance.

There are two **bus** systems on the island: the government-run **PTSC** and the hundreds of private minibuses, or *maxi-taxis* as the contrary Trinidadians prefer to call them. Both systems start running at dawn and continue until late evening.

PTSC is extremely cheap and links all the major towns for less than TT$5. Being the government transport network, the buses have no plush seats or stereo systems like the private buses and maddeningly it is impossible to get tickets outside weekday office hours (they must be bought in the terminal office). They run a regular, if infrequent, schedule, leaving Port of Spain from the former railway station on South Quay.

Maxi-taxis are really mobile discotheques, usually audible before they come into view—crowded and extremely noisy, and one of the best bits of Trinidad that you will come across. They will take you to most towns and they are colour-coded according to their destination. When you reach your destination, shout *Driver, Stop!* (you will have to shout to be heard above the stereo system).

Faster, more comfortable, a little more expensive, but not nearly such fun are **share-taxis**, private cars that follow fixed routes to and from town; the longest run costs TT$3. Most leave from the same point as the maxi-taxis: **Independence Square** for the east and west, and **Woodford Square** for St Ann's and St James. Jeeps for the north coast leave from **George St**. There are no specific stops, so when you want to get out, just tell the driver. Drivers leave when the vehicle is full. If you go farther afield in a share-taxi, make sure of the price before you get in.

Normal **taxis** are in plentiful supply and can be fixed up in the main squares and at all the hotels. Some sample prices are: **airport** to central Port of Spain—TT$90, Asa Wright Centre—TT$90; and from downtown **Port of Spain** to Maracas—TT$100, Caroni Bird Sanctuary—TT$85 and Asa Wright Centre—TT$140. To call a taxi: St Christopher's Taxi Co-op (tel 624 3560).

Tours around Port of Spain and the island can be fixed through tour operators. Try **Twin Island Tours** (tel 622 2813), 177 Tragarete Rd, Port of Spain, **Travel Trinidad and Tobago** on Independence Sq (tel 625 2201) or through the taxi drivers at the hotels. A two-hour tour around the city costs about TT$100, over to Maracas—TT$200, to the Caroni Bird Sanctuary—TT$180 and to the Pitch Lake—TT$250 (6 hours).

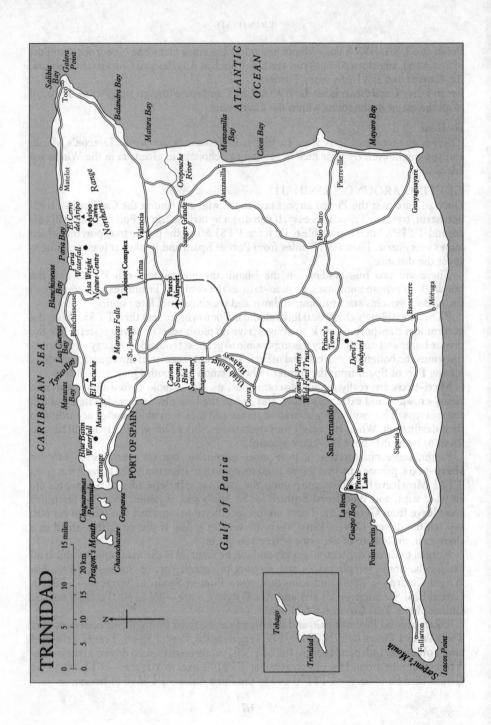

Trinidad is a big place and is worth exploring. There are plenty of vehicles for **hire**. The roads are OK, though if you plan to go off the beaten track, it might be worth taking a four-wheel drive. Licences from UK, France, Germany, USA and Canada are valid in Trinidad and Tobago, and driving is on the left (when driving carry your licence with you at all times along with your passport). Do not drive in downtown Port of Spain except for sport.

Expect to pay from US$45 per day, tax included, for the smallest car. Rental companies include: **Auto Rentals** on Tragarete Rd, Port of Spain (tel 623 3063), **Carr Rentals**, 34 Sydenham Ave, St Ann's (tel 624 1028) and **Singh's** at 7 Wrightson Rd (tel 625 4247). A number of them have outlets at Piarco airport.

TOURIST INFORMATION

The main **Trinidad Tourism Development Authority** is at 134–8 Frederick St (top end) in central Port of Spain (tel 623 1932). They will give advice about accommodation and help with arranging trips to all over the island. On arrival it is definitely worth checking with the very helpful office at Piarco airport.

In a medical **emergency**, the Port of Spain General Hospital is on Charlotte St in the centre of town (tel 625 7869). The international direct dial telephone code for both islands is 809, followed by the 7-digit local telephone number. If you are phoning between the islands dial just the seven figures.

MONEY

The currency is the Trinidad and Tobago dollar (TT$); it is the only legal tender on the island and the authorities are quite strict about it. It is fixed to the US$ like other Caribbean currencies and the current exchange rate is US$1 = TT$4.25. The US dollar, though in demand throughout the country, is not legal. All currency must be changed at the official rate in banks or hotels and a (recent) receipt must be presented if you wish to change money back when you leave the country. The black market for the exchange of US dollars has tailed off recently.

Banking hours are Mon–Thurs, 9–2 and Fri, 9–2 and 3–5. **Shops** open 8–6:30 and until noon on Saturdays. Keep your exchange receipts.

BEACHES

Trinidad's beaches do not have the precious picture-postcard feel of other Caribbean islands—try Tobago for that; here the beaches are rugged and more spectacular, and unlike Tobago, few hotels are built on them. If you are staying in Port of Spain, you will have to travel quite a few miles to get to one. Some beaches have changing facilities and you can buy a drink and a snack on all except the most remote. At Maracas Bay the thing to have is a 'shark and bake'—a fish sandwich—with a Solo soft drink.

The closest beaches to Port of Spain are on the north coast, a short ride over the Saddle. **Maracas Bay** is the first, a huge sweeping strand enclosed by vast headlands, which funnel the waves on to the shelved sand and enormous palm trees. Red flags mean a strong current. Close by is **Tyrico Bay**, where the waves are often big enough to surf. Also popular with Trinidadian weekenders is **Las Cuevas** Bay, named after the underwater caves (there are changing rooms available) and the open **Blanchisseuse Bay**, with a fishing village and forest down to the water. Buses run as far as Las Cuevas (depart

George St, downtown), but only occasionally to Blanchisseuse. **Paria Bay**, a couple of miles beyond Blanchisseuse itself, is a cracker and is usually deserted.

It is a problem to go farther afield by public transport and so you are best off in a hire car. A trip to the northeastern part of the island is long but very rewarding because of the scenery and the secluded strands. On the east coast is **Balandra Bay**, where the waves crash in with the full force of the Atlantic and yet more remote is **Salibia Bay** on the Toco coast, just beyond Galera Point. With a view towards Tobago, the beach has clear green water and makes good swimming. Snacks and drinks are available.

On the east coast there are endless miles of white sand backed by coconut and manchineel trees. The beaches face the Atlantic and so the waves can be big. **Manzanilla Bay** runs south to **Cocos Bay** (island lore explains that a boatload of coconuts from Brazil was washed up here) and **Mayaro Bay** runs down to the southern corner of Trinidad. There are one or two hotels and shops can provide food and drink, but you may prefer to choose a spot cut off from anywhere, of which there are plenty.

RIVER BATHING
The rivers and rockpools in Trinidad's northern range provide some excellent river bathing if you want a change. Perhaps the easiest to reach is the **Blue Basin Waterfall** in Petit Valley off the Diego Martin Valley, west of Port of Spain. At 300 ft high, **Maracas Falls** are worth a visit and can be found a mile off the road that runs north out of St Joseph. The **Paria Waterfall**, off the Arima to Blanchisseuse road can be reached along a track that follows the river into the rainforest for an hour. There is a waterfall and a pool at the Asa Wright Nature Centre and there is good swimming in the Caura River at Eldorado Village and in the Oropouche River at the eastern end of the range.

SPORTS
Trinidad is not as well organized as its sister island to cater for the traditional Caribbean watersports, and most of the popular Trinidadian sports are **land-based**. On Saturdays and Sundays the Savannah in central Port of Spain will be crowded with football and hockey matches; running round the outside is the **racetrack** (the stands at the finish-line are also used for the culmination of the Carnival Parade), where there are regular meets.

Endless games of **cricket** are also played on the Savannah, some more formal than others, and if you hang around to watch, you might be invited to join in. If you go to watch a match at the main Queen's Park Oval stadium, make sure to get into the *rude boy stand*, where the banter is liveliest.

Outside the Hilton Hotel, **tennis** courts can be arranged through the Trinidad Country Club (tel 622 3470). There are a number of **golf** courses on the island, of which the closest to Port of Spain is the 18-hole St Andrew's course at **Moka** just beyond Maraval (tel 629 2314).

Trinidad also has some of the most exciting wildlife in the Caribbean, with 450-odd birds, over 600 species of butterfly and 700 orchids (see Flora and Fauna) and there are plenty of **walking tours** to take it all in. It is even possible to go **hunting** for armadillo or quenk (wild hog).

For **watersports**, go to the **Yacht Club** in the Bayshore area west of Port of Spain or the **Yachting Association**, beyond Carenage. You might be able to persuade an owner to lend you a windsurfer or take you out on his yacht. **In-Joy** Tours (tel 622 8974) will take you out to the islands off Chaguaramas. They also arrange **deep-sea fishing**; you sail to the islands at Columbus's 'Dragon's Mouth' and into the Caribbean Sea, where you can cast for kingfish, wahoo and tarpon.

Scuba diving in Trinidad is limited as some of the waters are clouded by the outflow from the Orinoco River from South America and the fresh water discourages the coral growth. Contact the **Scuba Shop** in Marabella (tel 658 2183).

Port of Spain

Like so many Caribbean capitals, Port of Spain (population 300,000) is set on the sea and is framed by hills. It lies in the northwest of the island on the Gulf of Paria, in the crook of the Charaguaramas peninsula. It is not a particularly attractive city, but it is the heart of the island and it buzzes. Some of the most Caribbean's elaborate and beautiful gingerbread houses can be found here, though they are steadily becoming overshadowed by the burgeoning concrete buildings of the modern city.

The streets are mayhem, with share-taxis stopping at will and buses nosing for position among them; hucksters line the pavements of Frederick Street, their trestletables stacked with cassettes and mirror-shades or yards of T-shirts and underpants. Everywhere there is the smell of batter snacks frying and the cry of peanut and snow-cone vendors. As in any large city, you are advised to be careful after dark. For every thousand charming Trinidadians, there is a tricky one. However, you'll need your wits about you to enjoy the city anyway, because it is very lively.

The original capital of the island was positioned inland at St Joseph as a defensive measure, but it was moved to the coast in 1757 when the new Governor found his Residence uninhabitable. The new town expanded rapidly as the island population soared at the end of the century and trade picked up. The town was almost completely destroyed by a fire in 1808 and then laid out by Governor Woodford in 1813. Echoes of the British influence remain in the hefty colonial architecture and the spiked metal railings in the squares.

Gingerbread house

The business centre of the town is just above the waterfront, around **Independence Square** (not really a square at all, but a long wide street, known as Marine Square until Independence in 1962) and from here the two other main thoroughfares of Charlotte St and Frederick St run north.

The latter touches **Woodford Square**, the heart of Trinidadian politics. Riots have occurred here, but its most important moments were as the 'University of Woodford Square', when it saw the birth of Independence politics in the 50s. On the western side, the **Red House** is now the seat of the Trinidad and Tobago Parliament. It was first painted red in 1897 for Queen Victoria's Diamond Jubilee and has been repainted and called so ever since. This was the building taken over by the militant Muslims in their 1990 coup attempt. The two chambers can be visited and there is a spectacular bright blue ceiling. Open during office hours, adm free.

At the very top of Frederick St you will find the **National Museum and Art Gallery** (tel 623 6419), which exhibits Trinidadian life throughout the ages, from the Arawaks and early Spaniards to angostura, asphalt and oil. It also has a display of last year's carnival costumes and drawings of the Trinidad countryside by Michel Cazabon. Upstairs are more modern Trinbagonian paintings and a display of characters from island folklore, incluing *Papa Bois*, a friendly spirit who saves animals from hunters with the blow of a horn, the *Soucouyant*, an old hag who turns herself into a ball of fire and will suck your blood, and *La Diablesse*, who leads intoxicated men astray after a party and with a shriek of laughter dumps them in a thorn bush. Open 10–6, adm free.

The Trinidadian claim that the **Savannah** is the biggest roundabout in the world is probably true—it has a two and a half mile circumference. Once it was used to graze cattle that would terrorize the inhabitants, but now it is used as a sports ground. According to CLR James (*Beyond a Boundary*), it is big enough to contain 30 full-size cricket pitches, but at least some of them are given over to hockey, football and horse-racing. The culmination of Carnival takes place here too. At the roadside there is always a crowd of vendors with fresh fruit—sliced pineapple, oranges and coconuts—to quench a thirst, and at night there are fast food caravans serving oysters and burgers.

On the western side of the Savannah are the **Magnificent Seven**, a row of incredibly elaborate and imposing mansions. Built early this century, they are a hodge-podge of styles, and include a mock Rhineland castle, a Moorish creation called Whitehall, and a mansion in the style of the French Second Empire known as the Gingerbread House.

At the northeastern corner of the park are the **Royal Botanical Gardens**, a 70-acre retreat from the bustle of Port of Spain. They were laid out by Governor Woodford in 1820 and he moved his residence up here because they were so pleasant. Among the pink and yellow *pouis* is a *cannon-ball* tree (with fruit like a wooden cannon ball, but the most ephemeral flowers that drop to earth at dusk), and the *raw beef* tree, which seeps red sap like a joint when the bark is cut (it has a fence around it now because it was so badly cut up). You will see the oddly-shaped *chaconia*, the national flower of Trinidad and Tobago, and there is also a large orchid collection. Open during daylight hours, adm free.

Nearby is the **Emperor Valley Zoo**, named after a butterfly that once lived here, which exhibits Trinidad's deer and other indigenous animals like agouti and raccoon, as well as some tropical snakes. Toucans and macaws are on display. Open 9.30–5, adm. The official residences of the President of the Republic and of the Prime Minister are in the gardens.

The heights above the town are dominated by the usual series of forts, which still give magnificent views. **Fort Picton** and **Fort Chacon** stand in the east, above the crowded suburb of Laventille. **Fort George** is an hour's drive into the hills to the west. The main Port of Spain **market**, one of the liveliest places in town, is on Beetham Highway, which heads out of the town towards the airport.

Over the Saddle Road to the North Coast

The Saddle Road runs north out of Port of Spain, from the northwest corner of the Savannah, through the wealthy suburb of **Maraval**, and then winds into the hills of the northern range. The scenery is majestic and makes the drive worthwhile even before you descend to the rural north coast. Maracas Bay, with its palm trees a hundred feet high, is a popular picnic place at the weekends. It is possible to reach the **Maracas Falls** and Trinidad's second peak **El Tucuche** from here, but it is quite a hike. The fishing villages of **Las Cuevas** and **Blanchisseuse** overlook the sea but are usually less crowded than Maracas Bay (See Beaches).

The Chaguaramas Peninsula

The route west out of Port of Spain passes a vast transhipment terminal and scrubby hills before coming to Chaguaramas, one of the areas which was leased to the Americans during the Second World War. The American presence on the island had a considerable effect on the Trinidadians because they paid so highly and because they spawned a large entertainment industry. *Working for the Yankee Dollar* was the catch-phrase of a calypso that spoke about the Trini girls deserting their menfolk for the rich American sailors.

Beyond the peninsula are five off-shore islands in the **Bocas del Dragon** (the Dragon's Mouth), named by Columbus in 1498, where rich Trinidadians have built villas for themselves. On **Gasparee** are some caves with stalactites and stalagmites. **Chacachacare** is the biggest of the islands and has some strange red-brick buildings that once were a leper colony.

The Eastern Main Road

Running out of Port of Spain to the east as far as Arima, the corridor along the Eastern Main Road is the most populous area of the island outside the capital. Just out of the town is the **Angostura** factory, where the famous bitters are produced. An unrevealed number of spices and barks are selected by just four people and then percolated in alchohol to produce the bitters. Tours can be arranged (tel 623 1841, Marketing Department), adm free. The road skirts the southern side of the lush Northern Range of mountains on the left and as you approach St Joseph, originally the capital of the island, the St Augustine campus of the University of the West Indies is on the right. Overlooking the plain from 800 feet up in the foothills is the Mount St Benedict Monastery. There is now also a school there and a Catholic seminary and you can stay there in the small guest house.

The **Lopinot Complex**, a restored 19th-century estate, is close by on the right. In 1800, the Comte de Lopinot fled the troubles in Saint Domingue (now Haiti) and he settled the plantation he cut out of the jungle in the Arouca Valley. Early in the year the *immortelle* trees flame bright orange in the valley. Today, the cocoa walks and cashew and coffee plantations that they shaded have been brought back to life in a working museum. Visits to the caves on the estate are also possible. Open until about 5, adm free.

Arima has a strong Amerindian influence deriving from a community of Arawaks that lived here 200 years ago. There is a small museum devoted to the Indians in Cleaver Woods Park, just west of the town.

One of the island's most appealing spots is the **Asa Wright Nature Centre** (tel 667 4655), 1200 ft up in the hills above Arima, about an hour and a half from Port of Spain. It houses a Research Station, but also has accommodation for amateur naturalists, who can witness the amazing colour and variety of the squawking, screeching rainforest. The estate house was built in 1908 and has a view across a valley where you can realistically expect to see twenty-five species of birds before breakfast. The balcony at the Nature Centre is one of the most charming places in the whole Caribbean.

Five trails (varying between a few minutes and three hours) have been cut into the forest around the main house, and you will possibly see species such as the white-bearded or the golden-headed manakin, toucans and honeycreepers, as well as some of Trinidad's 18 fluorescent hummingbirds and its 600-odd butterflies. The most famous inhabitant is the nocturnal oilbird, who comes out only at night and feeds on fruit that it picks from the trees while in flight. They were once hunted by the Arawaks for their oil, but now are protected and live in remote regions in caves. Open to outsiders 9–5, adm US$6 adults, $4 children.

If you wish to climb **El Cerro del Aripo** (3083 ft), Trinidad's highest peak, get a guide in Aripo as the trail is difficult and quite long. You will be completely swallowed by the rainforest and have a good chance of seeing hummingbirds and maybe even Trindad's rare piping guan. The Aripo caves are extensive, with a forest of monstrous stalactites and stalagmites, and a colony of oilbirds' nests.

Beyond Aripo the main road turns south, but if you take a left you come to the east coast at Salybia, close to **Matura Beach**, where the Leatherback turtle nests by crawling up on to the sand and digging a hole with its flippers before laying between 100 and 150 eggs. From here, the road passes on to the northeastern point of the island to the rugged Toco coast.

The South of the Island

The southern plains of Trinidad contain the agricultural lands, covered in green swathes of sugar-cane, and the industrial and oil heartland that has made Trinidad rich in the last two decades (you will see the drill heads pecking at the ground like huge metal chickens).

Take the eastern main road out of Port of Spain and then turn south on the Uriah Butler Highway towards Chaguanas and San Fernando. The road skirts the **Caroni Swamp**, a National Park and bird sanctuary, which contains an enormous abundance of birdlife, about half the island's total species. One of the island's most spectacular sights takes place here every evening, when the **scarlet ibis**, Trinidad's national bird, flies in to roost. You can take a leisurely tour at dusk as they arrive and for a moment whole trees will seem to be on fire with the scarlet of the ibis in flight. The extremely knowledgeable guides will give you all sorts of snippets about swamp life—among the mangroves you might see a spectacled cayman (an alligator) or *cyclopes didactylus* (a two-toed sloth) or perhaps a greater ani (pronounced Arnie, no doubt a tougher version of Schwarzenegger). The tour starts around 4.30 pm, in good time for dusk, cost around TT$25 per person, depending on the size of your party, restless children not recommended.

The highway continues to the town of **Chaguanas**, which has mushroomed in the last ten years. The population is mostly of East Indian descent and in the main street you will find the **Lion House**, once the home of VS Naipaul. From here the road passes sugar mills and the factories of heavy industry at Point Lisas and the tangle of silver pipes at Point-a-Pierre, the island's main oil refinery. It was bought by the Trinidad and Tobago Government from Texaco in 1984 when the oil company withdrew. On the lakes within the refinery compound, the **Point-a-Pierre Wild Fowl Trust** researches Trinidad wildlife and encourages endangered species to nest on the island—100-odd birds nest there during the year.

San Fernando, an urban sprawl with a population of 60,000, is Trinidad's second, slightly calmer city. The San Fernando Hill gives a good view of the city and the surrounding countryside and the **fish market** down by the bus station is worth a visit in the late afternoon.

The Pitch Lake

In the 'deep south', as it is jokingly known, is one of the Caribbean's most extraordinary phenomena, the **Pitch Lake**. According to a legend of Iere, a chief once killed a sacred hummingbird, which so angered the gods that they punished him by engulfing his village in pitch. Although the 'lake' often turns up old artefacts in its continual stirring—from prehistoric tree trunks to biscuit tins—it has not yet produced a whole village to verify the legend.

As you approach the Pitch Lake through the town of La Brea, the side of the road is covered with splodges of black goo and an infestation of weeds. The lake itself is 100 acres of tar, slightly springy underfoot, with folds like a cake mix that move very, very slowly. When you step on it you leave an imprint and then very gradually you sink. Stay there for an hour or two and you will be stirred into the mix.

More recent history has Sir Walter Raleigh caulking his ships with it—'most excellent good and melteth not with the sun as the pitch of Norway'. However, when he brought it back to England and asphalted Westminster Bridge for the opening of Parliament, it did melt, clagging the carriage wheels and the horses' hoofs. Since then, Trinidad pitch has been used with more success on roads all over the world. Towns as far flung as Cairo, Bombay, Singapore and London were laid with it, as well as Port of Spain.

Once it was tried as fuel for street lighting, but the smoke and the stench were so overpowering that it had to be stopped (though it was used to fumigate the town after a small-pox epidemic in 1920). It was even tried as a covering to prevent weeds growing in the city, but it turned out to be such a potent fertilizer that the streets were infested in no time.

Old prints show the 19th-century mining methods. A pick axe was used, and then a shovel to load up the carts with stringy black goo. Today it is more like a vehicle ballet, with JCBs scooping up the bitumen and dumping it in railway carriages. They run alongside the railway as near as they can, but with the lake constantly in motion it is difficult to get close.

The cake mix itself has seeped from the oil sands that lie beneath Trinidad and is apparently 'uniform in composition—made up of celloidal clay-30%, bitumen-54%, salt water-3% and ash-36%.' As Quentin Crewe points out in *Touch the Happy Isles*, any composition which adds up to 123% has to arouse some doubts.

It is the largest lake of its kind in the world, but stories that this monstrous cauldron is of unfathomable depth and constantly self-replenishing are not true. A hole dug one day may be gone the next as the lake settles, but the level is steadily dropping.

The Pitch Lake's main attraction is really in its history and mystery—visiting it is quite like wandering around on a bouncy car park. Open any time in daylight (remember that the round trip is about 6–8 hours by bus from Port of Spain), for a look at the small museum and a guided tour of the lake itself, on which you will learn more fantastic stories from the guide (adm free, but a guide will ask for TT$70 or so). Take a flat pair of shoes, because high heels might get you swallowed up.

From La Brea, the southern main road continues along the peninsula to Icacos Point, from where you can see Venezuela about ten miles away. Columbus was supposed to have dropped anchor at Los Gallos when he arrived in Trinidad in 1498. At **Siparia** there is a black Virgin which has become a focus of pilgrimage for Trinidadians of all religions, not just Christian. Her festival is on the Sunday after Easter when she is carried around the town in procession.

The Atlantic Coast

At Valencia, the eastern main road turns south to Sangre Grande and reaches the Atlantic coast at Manzanilla (the Spanish word for the poisonous manchineel tree which grows here). But this coast is more noted for its coconuts, because there are literally miles and miles (nearly 50 miles) of them. In the season, the beaches towards **Guayaguayare** are covered in chip-chip shells, which make a favoured local dish, and off the southeastern tip of the island are the oil-rigs which brought Trinidad its wealth in the 70s. From the sea you can see the three peaks which inspired Columbus to call the island Trinidad.

As you drive back inland towards San Fernando through the canefields, you might pass the villages of Third Company and Sixth Company, named after black American Regiments who were brought to Trinidad in the middle of the last century when the island was crying out for settlers. There is no mention of the Second Company because they were lost at sea.

Close to Princes Town is the **Devil's Woodyard**, one of Trinidad's mud volcanoes. The mud exudes through cracks in the earth's surface, cooling as it emerges in a cone and occasionally bubbling with gas. The site is considered holy by some Hindus.

FESTIVALS
The most colourful festival outside Carnival is **Divali** (pronounced Deewali), the festival of lights, which was brought to Trinidad by Hindus as a celebration in honour of Lakshmi, the goddess of light. In November, hundreds of thousands of *deyas*, little clay pots with coconut oil candles (and increasingly electric lights) are kept alight all night to

show her the way. People throw open their houses and entertain guests with sitars and dancing and huge vegetarian meals.

Phagwa is the Hindu New Year celebration, which takes place in March. It has taken on the Carnival style of floats in the street with dancing and is celebrated by Trinis of all racial origin now. If you see a band of dancers covered in red food dye, they are out celebrating Phagwa.

Hosay (Hussein) is a Muslim festival that remembers the martyrdom of Hussein (it brings in the Muslim New Year, but the date varies in the Christian calendar). Processions of tassa drummers follow models of Hussein's tomb through the streets and you will occasionally still see fire-eating and jugglers throwing sticks of fire. The Trinidadian Muslims also celebrate **Eid ul Fitr** to mark the end of Ramadan. Dates vary according to the Islamic calendar.

WHERE TO STAY

Trinidad does not have many resort hotels in the typical Caribbean mould. Most hotels are in Port of Spain itself, but there are some notable exceptions in the mountains around the town. VAT is charged on all rooms at 15% and most places charge 10% extra for service. If you are in Trinidad during Carnival, room prices will rise by anything from 30–70%.

Though there are few beach hotels, the Trinidadians have built villas for themselves on the beaches, particularly in the northeast of the island and it is possible to rent these at the weekend, or during the week when they are more likely to be free. Check in the local paper.

EXPENSIVE

For the views alone, the **Trinidad Hilton**, PO Box 442, Port of Spain (tel 624 3211), is worth a visit. It is set on a hill in up-town Port of Spain and many of the rooms look out over the city, over the Savannah and the 'Magnificent Seven' and to the hills in the west. Strangely, it is the ground floor that has the best view, as the Trinidad Hilton was built upside down, the higher the floor number, the further it is down the hill. 'Executive Floors' are on offer to business travellers and there are plenty of facilities for holiday-makers. US$137–156. Two restaurants (see below).

MODERATE

The **Kapok Hotel**, 16–18 Cotton Hill, St Clair (tel 622 6441, fax 622 9677), is a smaller, modern hotel at the northwest corner of the Savannah. Within easy reach of the city-centre, it takes its name from a silk cotton tree that grows outside. Friendly, rooms decorated with prints of the West Indies, the pool in a palm courtyard at the back. US$75–135. Two restaurants include the Café Savannah (local and Caribbean food) and the Tiki village, with Chinese and Polynesian food and a good view across the capital. The **Hotel Normandie**, PO Box 851, St Anns (tel 624 1181), is close to the Botanical Gardens to the north of the Savannah. Its address at 10 Nook Avenue gives an idea of the cosy and friendly atmosphere. It is a concoction of styles—covered balconies, dormer windows and an octagonal spire and it is situated on a former plantation, La Fantaisie, from which the restaurant (see below) takes its name. The inner courtyard is a riot of banana and golden palm set around a swimming pool. One or two rooms are a little dark, but the newer loft apartments are very comfortable. US$70–90. Buried in the rainforest of the northern range is another favourite Trinidadian spot, the **Asa Wright Nature Centre**, Spring Hill Estate, PO Box 10, Arima (no phone there, but tel 667 4655, fax 667 4655 for reservations). Take afternoon tea on the veranda of the main house, amidst the sound of toucans, tufted coquettes (hummingbirds) and butterfly wings. Stay in the main house or in the simple garden rooms. There is a swimming pool. US$180 a double per day in winter, full board.

CHEAP
'In peace awhile here rest most welcome Guest'. The **Pax Guest House**, Mount St Benedict, Tunapuna (tel 602 4084) is set beside a monastery in the hills above the Eastern Main Road. There are 14 simple rooms, not all with private bathrooms, and the verandas have a magnificent view of the valley and the hills beyond, walking trails and even laboratory facilities if you want them. US$50 for full board.

Guest Houses
A charming spot in the Woodbrook area is **La Maison Rustique** (tel 622 1512). It is hardly 'rustic', the name comes from its address at 16 Rust St; it is more of a town house, set in a garden of colourful tropical flora. Tranquillity with enormously attentive service. Double US$60, single $35, includes breakfast. In the residential district of Maraval is **Monique's**, 114 Saddle Road (tel 628 3334), with the typical feel of a West Indian family house. The seven rooms all have private baths and air-conditioning, and guests are welcome to collect for the evening meal. The house is on the main drag into town, worked by the two-dollar share-taxis that will drop you in the centre of town. Single room US$35 and a double $40. Other guest houses include the **Kestours Sports Villa**, 58 Carlos St (tel 628 4028), a modern house surrounded by the fading gingerbread splendour of Woodbrook, a suburb of Port of Spain. Room rates start at US$15 for a single. Meals can be provided. **Hillcrest Haven**, 7A Hillcrest Avenue (tel 624 1344), is a quiet guest house in Cascade, just northeast of the Savannah, behind the Hi-Lo Supermarket. The accommodation is very simple, with electric fans and share-baths. US$15 for a single. Note that prices tend to rise during Carnival and that a minimum length of stay may be required. Finally there are plenty of really cheap places to lay your head, though as with many Caribbean islands, they tend to double as knocking shops. One of the cleaner ones not used for this purpose is **Schultzi's** on Fitt St, Woodbrook, just off Ariapita Avenue. You can also try **La Calypso**, 46 French St, off Tragarete Rd (tel 622 4077); very simple, fairly clean.

Bed and Breakfast
Another inexpensive way to stay, and it has the distinct advantage of seeing the Trinis in their homes, is in the bed and breakfasts. These are quite carefully vetted by the Tourism Development Authority and prices start at about US$20 per night for a single and US$15 each in a double. Facilities vary, but all provide breakfast and most can fix an evening meal if requested. Details can be obtained in the Tourism Office in Port of Spain and at Piarco airport, or the **Bed and Breakfast Association of Trinidad and Tobago**, PO Box 3231, Diego Martin Post Office (tel 628 3731, fax 627 0856). Bed and breakfasts are available all over the northern part of the island, particularly in Port of Spain.

EATING OUT

A Tour of Snacks and Sweetmeats

You can live in Trinidad without ever sitting down to a formal meal—snacks are available all day everywhere. You can start right outside the airport when you arrive, perhaps with a *Pow!* (the Chinese word for bread), a little white fluffball of dough, colour-coded with a spot for salt or sweet, or with one of Trinidad's most popular snacks, a *roti*, an envelope of unleavened bread with a filling of anything from curry shrimp to lentils. Spices are optional, but be wary, as Trinidadians like their food hot. *Doubles* are similar; they are folded *bara* (more unleavened bread) with *channa* (split peas). *Aripa* is a cornflour pattie with mince stuffing, and *pastel* is a mix of peppers, raisins and beef wrapped in a dasheen leaf or more likely foil, nowadays. *Aloo pie* (from the Indian for potato) is a doughy potato mix. Batter snacks include *phulori*, split peas in batter balls and *sahina*, made with spinach, which you can dip into mango chutney, sweet or hot, or into pepper sauce, firebrand style. The stalls are invariably run by charming and chattering ladies, who do their frying on outdoor ovens.

So much for the first course. You can follow the savoury mouthfuls with a whole volley of sweet snacks. Perhaps go for a *pamie* (pronounced pay-me), sweet coconut in a pattie or wrapped in a banana leaf, or try *pone*, a creation of cassava flour, sugar and coconut. Then there are *bene balls*, crisp lumps of sesame snap, and for the very brave there are *tamarind balls*, sluggish lumps with unverifiable specific gravity, a torture of sweet and bitter.

Restaurants

Things have changed a bit since the late 40s when Patrick Leigh Fermor visited Trinidad and decided that 'Hotel cooking in the island is so appalling that a stretcher may profitably be ordered at the same time as dinner'. In fact, hotels have some good food, though this should not discourage you from getting out to enjoy Trinidad's culinary diversity. As you would expect, the variety is overwhelming.

Trinidad's restaurants tend to be active and noisy, full of friendly crowds as well as diners out for a smart evening. You can expect a charge of 15% for VAT and in some places a service charge of 10%

EXPENSIVE

The **Tiki Village** (tel 622 6441) at the Kapok Hotel is top for its cuisine and also for its setting. You get a fine view of Port of Spain by night to go with a vast array of Polynesian and Chinese dishes. Try Steak Samoa or Jar doi yuk pien (Sezchuan radish). Main course TT$50 and up, best to reserve. The **Café Savannah** downstairs is another popular meeting point for a meal out. Try the Soucouyant lobster (in garlic) or the Saga boy chop in tamarind sauce. TT$40 and up, closed Sun. The **Boucan** at the Hilton (tel 624 3211) is named after the oven used by the Arawak Indians to cure meat and some dishes are cooked over guava wood here. The menu is international with a twist of Trinidadian creole. Main course TT$50. You will find a taste of Trinidad's French heritage in the nouvelle cuisine creole of **La Fantaisie** (tel 624 1181) at the nearby Hotel Normandie. Main course from TT$45.

MODERATE

The **Sea Belle** (tel 622 3594) is a seafood restaurant tucked away in the outskirts of Port of Spain, unmarked at 27 Mucurapo Rd. A trusty crowd of regulars keeps returning for the seafood crêpe and crab-back. There are also some more exotic local fish on offer; ask for tile-fish, flounder or local salmon. Main course from TT$35, closed Sun. Farther out in Chaguaramas you will find the **Anchorage** (tel 634 4334), on Pointe Gourde Rd, particularly popular at the weekend when the Trinis flood out of town. Wooden tables and chairs on a terrace above the sea. TT$35 for a main course. A hip spot in town, frequented by cabinet ministers and cabinet makers, is **Rafters** (tel 628 9258) at 6A Warner St, just off the Maraval Rd. It is set in an old dry goods store, its shutters and windows still intact; simple snacks one side, with callaloo, seafood platters and creole dishes à la carte next door. Dinner main course from TT$40. In the Maraval area just up from Port of Spain is the **Orchid** (628 7007), 100 Saddle Rd. The tables are set either side of a dance floor. Try *fig for so*—green figs aplenty or *drunken parandero*, a Trinidadian rum trifle. Closed Sun, main dish TT$35.

There are two fun spots to get a lunch. Try the **Verandah**, 16 Grey St, St Clair (tel 622 2987), in the setting of an old creole house, with tables above the garden on the veranda. The ice-creams are particularly good. Or try **Veni Mange** at 13 Lucknow St in St James (no phone), where two Trinidadian sisters, Allyson Hennessy and Rosemary Hezekiah, are renowned for their soups. Also try avocado and shrimp salad or a crab-back. It is more expensive, with a main dish costing about TT$50. Both are open for lunch only, during the week. Make a reservation at the Verandah. A **Chinese** meal is a popular evening out in Trinidad. **Hong Kong**, on Tragarete Rd, is brightly dressed up in Chinese decor of red velvet and golden dragons. The food is straight Chinese, plus a few dishes with West Indian ingredients—dasheen pork and sweet and sour lambi. Main dish TT$35. The **New Shay Shay Tien** on Cipriani Blvd also serves Chinese food, only until 8.30.

CHEAP

For a good **Indian** meal (Trinidad style) in a swish setting, try **Monsoon** on Tragarete Rd. Purple and green neon clash and you can take away or sit in and eat creations such as conch paratha and dhalpuri, TT$20. **Mangals** at 13 Queens Park East also has a take away service. You will also find a number of **snack-wagons** on the eastern side of the Savannah where you can pick up a batter chicken or fish for a few dollars.

For a distinctly Trinidadian feel there is the **Breakfast Shed** on the waterfront not far from the Holiday Inn Hotel, offering home-style rice and peas with fried plantain at very good prices. It caters for local workers, who come in from the wharf nearby, so opening hours are 5–3, but best to get there before 2.

In **San Fernando**, try **Belle Bagai**, 36 Gransaul St, tables set on a veranda, for a creole lunch, TT$15. **Soongs Great Wall** on the Circular Rd is a popular Chinese restaurant in the town, TT$30 and up.

PUBS AND CLUBS

Like the restaurants, Trinidad bars (often called pubs here) are lively, particularly at the weekends when Port of Spain drops everything for a drink. You will find cocktail bars, where Trinidad-produced *Angostura Bitters* add the zing to the traditional Caribbean rum punch and a profusion of rum shops, fired by VAT 19, and the two local brews, heavy and dark **Carib** and the lighter, malty **Stag** beers.

How do you make the roof of a shopping mall a place worth visiting? Dress it up as a transatlantic liner; wooden decks with railings and overhead trampolines to keep off the rain. Add live music (Wed–Sat), from jazz to the big names in calypso, and then serve some outrageously strong cocktails to go with the light snacks. Well worth a try: **Moon over Bourbon Street** (closed Mon, Tues) in the West Mall, ten minutes out of town towards Chaguaramas.

Another spot for an afternoon drink with a view is **Wazo Deyzeel** (Trinidad's French heritage is audible in there somewhere). You will find it in St Ann's, on Carib Way, off Sydenham Avenue. **Rafters** on Warner St has a video bar and a lively crowd, mainly black Trinidadians, collects at the **Cricket Wicket** on Tragerete Rd, opposite the cricket stadium.

Clubs have their night, for boozing, and if there's room, a quick turn on the dancefloor. On Thursdays and Sundays, try the **Pelican**, just beneath the Hilton, where you can leave your car number-plate as a memento of your visit. On Fridays it is the **Bedrock** and on Saturdays the place to go to join the press is **Genesis**.

The **Mas Camp Pub** on the corner of French St and Araipita Ave in Woodbrook is something of an institution. Here you will find anything from ballroom dancing to calypso singing; each night different and well worth checking out for the best in local entertainment. For a more regular dancing club, try the **Attic** on Saddle Rd in Maraval. All styles of dance music—Latin music or a Caribbean compendium. Alternatively, try **Upper Level** and **Wall Street**.

TOBAGO

Tobago is a classic West Indian haven, completely without the glaring flamboyance of her sister island Trinidad. So many islands in the Caribbean have pushed on and encouraged development, changing fast, but in Tobago the change is measured. The traditional rural West Indian life is still just visible there.

Farmers, Tobago

81

Geographically Tobago is more similar to the Windward Islands than to Trinidad. A single spine of thickly forested mountains (up to 1890 ft) runs down the middle of the island, casting off spurs that reach out as headlands into the sea, enclosing huge crescent bays.

And historically Tobago has been more closely associated with the Windwards too. Like them it was a plantation island and in its 18th-century heyday it was so wealthy that people would use the phrase 'as rich as a Tobago planter'. It was also battled over incessantly. In the 19th century, when sugar failed and the island went bankrupt, it was simply appended to Trinidad.

The population of Tobago (about 45,000) is radically different from Trinidad's, as it is almost entirely African in origin. About 9000 people live in the capital, Scarborough, on the south side of the island. The main sources of employment are farming, fishing, the government and tourism. There is virtually no industry on Tobago.

You will see the shacks of subsistence farmers and the villas of international holidaymakers (many of them from Trinidad also) side by side here. Tourism is slightly more established here than in Trinidad, mainly in the southwest corner of the island, but it has by no means swamped traditional life. Tobago's heyday may have gone—the cannons at Fort King George point only at windsurfers and yachts—but her charm lies in her calm unaffected manner, just as so much of the Caribbean used to be.

History

Some claim that Columbus sighted Tobago as he emerged through the Dragon's Mouth from the Gulf of Paria on his third voyage in 1498, and called it Bellaforma. However, he did not stop there, but continued west along the South American coastline. Tobago never became a Spanish island and until the late 18th century it was not really a 'possession' at all. The island saw so many invasions, settlements and sieges that it changed hands more often than any other in the area.

The Dutch were the first to claim it in 1628, but all their expeditions were harried by canoes full of Caribs and Spaniards from Trinidad. King James I of England then granted the island to his godson Jacobus, Duke of Courland (a principality in modern-day Latvia), but each one of the six Courlander settlements failed too. Working on the same claim that the English flag had been planted on the island in 1580 by some passing sailors, James's successor, Charles I, decided to grant the island to the Earl of Montgomery. To complete the picture, the French made similar claims, grants and settlements—Louis XIV made the leader of a French-backed expedition, Dutchman Adraien Lampsius, the Baron of Tobago.

The settlements were intended to cultivate plantations of tropical produce for Europe and to begin with their main crop was tobacco. Tobago's name derives from the same Carib word as tobacco, though this was not what the Caribs called the plant. (To them 'tobacco' was the yard-long, double-pronged tube that they used to blast their powdered drugs up each other's noses.) Still, smoking was popular in Europe by the late 1500s and *freighting smoke* was a profitable occupation even though the shippers had to run the gauntlet of the Spanish navy, who had instructions to root out the trade.

Towards the end of the century, in an attempt to stop the fighting, Tobago was declared a neutral island. The Treaty of Aix la Chapelle in 1684 allowed the island no defences and it was supposedly free for all nations to come and go. Within years the treaty was nicknamed the 'Pirates' Charter' because along with settlers came pirates who were being chased out of their traditional hunting grounds around Jamaica and the Bahamas. Man o' War Bay in the northeast was renowned for its 'safe retreat and commanding situation for cruize and plunder'.

Tobago was an attractive prize and while some fought for her, others tried to gain the island by legal means. At one stage it was the cause of one of the Caribbean's most touching love stories, set in the court of Marie Antoinette in France.

A Swedish diplomat named Staël was wooing a Mademoiselle Necker, a courtesan, and she told him that she would only consent to marry him if he were an ambassador. The Queen gave him her support and wrote to King Gustavus requesting that he be made one. The King wrote back saying that he would consent, but that in return Staël must get him an island in the Caribbean, preferably Tobago. Staël bargained at the court, but the best he could do was St Barthélemy in the Leeward Islands, in return for a warehouse in Gothenburg, because the French government would not relinquish Tobago. However, the Queen intervened once again with King Gustavus and secured the ambassadorship. Staël won the hand of Mlle Necker.

The 19th century saw a spiralling decline of the sugar industry, and as a result of the emancipation of the slaves in 1834 and the cultivation of sugar-beet in Europe. All the estates on the island became dependent on a single British firm, Messrs A M Gillespie and Co, which eventually went bankrupt in 1884, leaving Tobago ruined. The land was sold off at ten shillings an acre and so the former slaves were able to buy themselves plots of land on which to grow their crops. Tobago became a very poor agricultural island.

For many years Tobago looked north in political matters. In the 19th century it had been one of the Windward Islands and, unlike Trinidad, which had remained under direct rule from London, it had always had some elected representation on its Governing Council. Now that it was in debt, it was simply attached to Trinidad, first as an economic arrangement, but then just placed under its control, as a 'ward', uninvited and largely unwanted.

With this heritage, many of the Tobagonians feel that their island has been neglected in the past. There was no regular link until a steamer started to make a trip in 1910—before that the mail was rowed the 22 miles over from Toco in Trinidad. Electricity did not reach the island until the 1950s and Eric Williams himself admitted in 1957 that the problem was 'one of stark poverty'. Many Tobagonians have left the island to look for a better life in Trinidad and elsewhere, but things have taken an upturn since a Tobagonian, ANR Robinson, became Prime Minister of Trinidad and Tobago in 1986.

The Tobagonians are independent in their outlook. They may be poor, but unlike the Trinidadians, most people here own the land which they cultivate and money is now coming to the island, brought by their cousins who have been working abroad.

GETTING TO TOBAGO

By Air: Crown Point airport in Tobago is now served by international flights from: **Britain**, weekly on BWIA and from the USA: there are daily services from Miami and New York. There are about ten daily flights between Trinidad and Tobago for TT$125 return, by BWIA and LIAT. There are regular flights to Aruba, Barbados and to

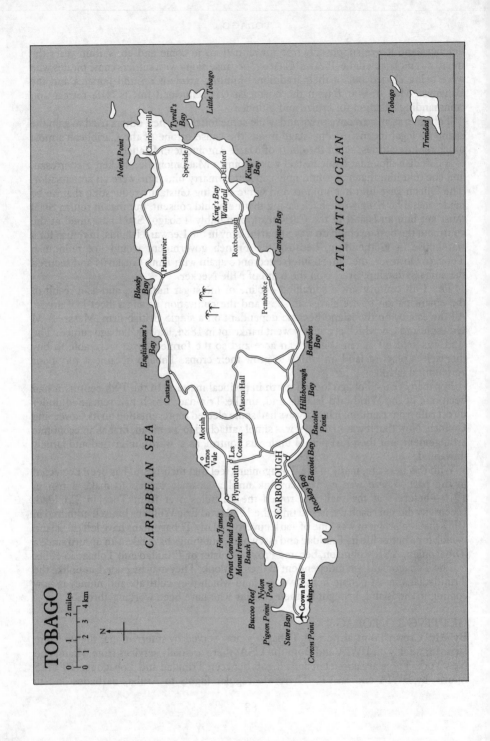

TOBAGO

0   1   2 miles
0   1   2   3   4 km

N

CARIBBEAN SEA

North Point

Charlotteville
Tyrell's Bay

Little Tobago

Speyside
Delaford
King's Bay

Bloody Bay

King's Bay Waterfall

Parlatuvier

Roxborough

Carapuse Bay

Englishman's Bay

Pembroke

Castara

Barbados Bay

Moriah

Mason Hall

Hillsborough Bay

Amos Vale

Les Coteaux

Bacolet Point

Plymouth

SCARBOROUGH

Bacolet Bay

Fort James
Great Courland Bay
Mount Irvine Beach

Rockley Bay

Buccoo Reef
Nylon Pool
Pigeon Point

Store Bay

Crown Point Airport

Croton Point

ATLANTIC OCEAN

Tobago

Trinidad

Grenada and St Lucia. Flights do get very booked up at weekends and there are often long delays for a crossing which is just over ten minutes. BWIA do a one-day excursion. **By Boat**: There is also a daily ferry (except Sat) from Port of Spain to Tobago. Return trips leave from Scarborough and are generally overnight. Crossing time is approximately 5 hours. Prices vary from TT$80 for a cabin on the *Panorama* to TT$50 economy on the *Tobago*. Tickets on sale until 8.30pm, but not at weekends.

GETTING AROUND TOBAGO

The government-run **bus** system (PTSC) runs all the major routes from Scarborough. It is extremely cheap and runs to a schedule, every half hour to Crown Point, but only once an hour or two elsewhere. Tickets must be bought in advance. There are no ticket offices open at weekends, so remember to stock up with them.

A good alternative are the **share-taxis** (private cars) that ply the more popular roads around the western end of the island. These pause for the few seconds it takes to fill with passengers, opposite the ferry terminal on Carrington St. Ask around for your destination: from Scarborough to Crown Point—TT$6, Plymouth—TT$3, Buccoo—TT$4. A few **maxi-taxis** run the road to Speyside and Charlotteville (TT$8), departing from James Park on Burnett St. **Hitching** works adequately, but check whether the driver will expect you to pay before you get in.

Plenty of regular **taxis** are available at the airport, the taxi-stand in Scarborough and through all the hotels. They are quite expensive. Some sample prices are: Crown Point airport to Pigeon Point—TT$25, Scarborough—TT$50, Plymouth—TT$45 and Charlotteville around TT$150. A tour by taxi costs around TT$85 per hour, or TT$250 for a half-day's excursion. The Taxi Cab Co-op can be reached on 639 2707.

If you wish to reach the bays at the eastern end of the island or see Tobago in its variety, you need to get hold of a **hire car**. Four-wheel drive is useful as the remoter roads sometimes turn into muddy tracks. Driving is on the left, and a licence from the UK, France, Germany, USA and Canada is valid in Trinidad and Tobago. When driving, you are supposed to carry it with you at all times along with your passport.

Car hire firms include **Baird's Rentals** on Lower Sangster Hill, Scarborough (tel 639 2528) and **Peter Gremli** on (tel 639 8400). **Banana Rentals** at the Kariwak Village has scooters and bicycles as well as cars and four-wheel drives. Expect to pay around US$35 per day for a car.

TOURIST INFORMATION

The **Tobago Division of Tourism** has an office in the Mall in Scarborough (tel 639 2125, fax 639 3566), with a desk at Crown Point airport and at the cruise ship terminal.

In a medical **emergency**, the Tobago County Hospital is on Fort Street in Scarborough (tel 639 2551). The **international dialling code** for Tobago is 809 followed by the seven-figure island number. If phoning from Trinidad or on the island, dial the seven figures.

MONEY

The currency is the Trinidad and Tobago dollar (TT$) with an exchange rate of US$1 = TT$4.25. Although it is accepted by certain hotels, the US dollar is not legal tender. All currency should be changed at the official rate in banks or hotels and a (recent) receipt must be presented if you wish to change money back when you leave the country. Credit cards are widely accepted in the tourist areas.

Banking hours are Mon–Thurs, 9–2 and Fri, 9–1 and 3–5. **Shops** open 8–6.30 and until noon on Saturdays.

BEACHES

At the western end of Tobago you will find typical Caribbean picture-postcard beaches: white sand, palm trees and fluorescent windsurfers. And yet, go further east and there are secluded coves with curves of golden sand with fishing villages.

The liveliest beach on the island is at **Pigeon Point**, where the Tobago body-beautiful roam. Miles of soft sand to walk, palms for shade and some watersports on offer— windsurfing, waterskiing, wetbikes—as well as a snack bar. To round off the idyll, there is a splendid view of the sunset. The beach is on private land and so you are asked to pay an entry fee of TT$5. Trips can be made to Buccoo Reef from here and most hotels lay on a bus service to drop you and pick you up again.

Smaller but also lively is **Store Bay**, at the western tip of the island close to Crown Point. There are changing rooms and across the road are some breakfast sheds, local Tobagonian snack shops, which will provide food and drink to combat the sweltering heat of a good day's sunbathing. Trips can be arranged out to Buccoo Reef from here as well. Store Bay is the destination of the annual Trinidad to Tobago **Great Race** in which power boats race from Port of Spain to Tobago on 30 July.

Towards Plymouth, just beyond the Mount Irvine Beach, is **Back Bay**, a tiny secluded strip of sand beneath a cliff. At the southern end of Great Courland Bay, a wide strip where the Turtle Beach Hotel has sports and snacks on offer, is **Turtle Beach** itself, named after the turtles that come there to lay their eggs.

As the north coast becomes more rugged, the road comes to the **Arnos Vale Hotel**, where there is a small beach and a good snorkelling reef, and then it passes to a series of stunning bays, each with a small fishing village on the beach, enclosed within the arms of massive headlands.

At Castara there are a few shacks under the palm trees and you can get a snack and a drink. Probably the most beautiful of them all is **Englishman's Bay**, a classic West Indian beach in a crescent curve, where the royal blue water stands out against the green forestland and the palms. It is very secluded and you will find the path down to it on the straight piece of road half a mile beyond Castara. Take a picnic.

At **Parlatuvier** there is a small village where life is sedate and a little farther on you will come to the isolated **Bloody Bay**, which takes its name from a conflict in which the sand ran red with blood.

The south coast has a few similar bays where the waves chase one another in to the beach. As you leave Scarborough, you come to **Bacolet Bay**, with coconut palms and a dark-sand beach which was the setting for the film *Swiss Family Robinson*. Past Hillsborough and Barbados and Roxborough Bays you eventually come to **King's Bay**, with palms and grey sand, where the headlands are so high that when you swim you seem to be enclosed by mountains. The end of the line (when the roads close in the wet season anyway) is at Man O' War bay, a stunning corner of sand beneath the headlands along from Charlotteville.

BEACH BARS
Pigeon Point has a beach bar from paradise on the sand beneath the palms and a thatch shelter on the jetty from where you can watch the sunset. In crowded Store Bay you will find the Taxi Co-op Pub, where the drivers take a bit of time off. Most isolated bays have at least one waterfront rum-shop. In Speyside try **Jemma's** for a fruit juice above the water (she does not sell alcohol) or the **Fisherman's Association Bar**.

SPORTS
Buccoo Reef, off the western tip of the island, is Tobago's main underwater sight and it attracts scuba divers, snorkellers and boat-borne non-swimmers alike. In the vast area of coral heads just a few feet below the surface—forests of seafan and staghorn coral and lobes of white brain coral—you will find black and yellow rock beauties, parrotfish and angelfish loitering, or schools of silver grunts dipping and darting in unison.

Considerable damage has been done to Buccoo Reef over the years by careless visitors and souvenir hunters, and although there has been legislation for some time it has not been properly enforced. However, the reef is still a spectacular sight if you want to check out the grunts and groupers, and it is well worth the TT$20 visit. Take a swimming costume and make sure that the boat has a mask your size for snorkelling when you get there. Trips leave from Store Bay and from Pigeon Point, but times vary, so check beforehand. The **Nylon Pool**, on the way out to the reef, is an off-shore sandbar where the pale turquoise water is thigh deep and the warm sand caresses your toes.

Scuba: the reefs are best at the eastern end of the island and most operators will take you up there. There is a good variety of sites from shallow snorkelable reefs to drift dives on which you can see barracudas and maybe even a manta ray. Contact **Dive Tobago** at Store Bay (tel 639 2266), **Tobago Dive Experience** in Crown Point (tel 639 0343) or **Tobago Scuba** (tel 660 4327) in Speyside, where equipment, instruction and dives are available. A single-tank dive costs around US$35. Also **Man Friday Diving** (tel 660 4676) in Charlotteville. **Snorkelling** reefs are at Buccoo, Arnos Vale, the Blue Waters Inn at the eastern end and at Charlotteville.

Windsurfing is best arranged at Pigeon Point beach or through one of the hotels (e.g. Turtle Beach or Mount Irvine), where there will often be small sailing boats that you can borrow. If you want a day's **sail** aboard a yacht, try *Chlöe* or the catamaran *Loafer* (tel 639 8555). There are also operators offering a 'reef and rum punch' tour. **Deep-sea fishing** tours, casting for marlin, sailfish and dorado in season can be fixed up through Dillon Tours and Charters, aboard *Super Cool* (tel 639 8765).

On land there is an 18-hole **golf** course at the Mt Irvine Hotel (tel 639 8871). This hotel also has **tennis** courts.

If you would like to take a bird-watching or plant-watching **hike** into the rainforest between Roxborough and Parlatuvier or to the mangrove swamps, then Tobago has a number of operators. Contact David Rooks at PO Box 58 in Scarborough (tel 639 9408), Pat Turpin at the Man O War Bay Cottages in Charlotteville (tel 660 4327) or countryman Adolphus James (tel 639 2231).

Scarborough
Scarborough, Tobago's main town, clambers over the side of a hill above Rockley Bay, on the southwest corner of the island. Despite its 19,000 population it is ramshackle and

sleepy—most Tobagonians say that they only ever come to town when they have to collect something off the ferry. Even so, Carrington St can get pretty lively when all the rum shops and roti-sellers are open.

Fort King George stands sentinel 400 feet above the town and has commanding views east along the coastline and west as far as Trinidad. Since being abandoned in 1854, the dark arched buildings are in decay and sitting among the cannons is quite peaceful now. There is a small Fine Art gallery in the fort and museum, where you can see Amerindian, pirate and colonial artefacts—buttons and bottles from Tobago's history. Open 9–6 weekdays, till 1pm weekends, adm free.

Walking down the hill you come to the old stone colonial buildings and homes, including the Tobago **House of Assembly**, completed in 1825. On **Gun Bridge**, the railings are made from rifle barrels, flanked by cannon.

From here, where the market was once located, steep alleyways lined with rusting tin shacks lead down to the newest part of town. The modern concrete official buildings are in the Scarborough Mall, which was thrown up in the 60s. Behind it are the bus station and the new market square, which is quite lively in the mornings with vendors and limers. Along the waterfront where the ferry docks, Carrington Street is crowded with breakfast sheds, which start up at seven in the morning and serve snacks all day. Behind the town are the Scarborough **Botanical Gardens**, good for sitting out and recovering from the hassle of the metropolis Scarborough. Open during daylight hours, adm free.

Around the Island

The west end of the island is most attractive for its reefs, beaches and natural life, though you may hear elaborate stories about Robinson Crusoe's life (his 'cave' is just below Crown Point airport) from a fellow that claims he saw him there not long ago.

Above Great Courland Bay, **Plymouth** is Tobago's second town—a village really, with a few shops and a petrol station. Once it was important enough to have its own fort, **Fort James**, named after Jacobus of Courland, who sent settlements to this bay in the 17th century.

From Plymouth you can return to Scarborough, or continue along the north coast. In the tiny fishing villages of Castara and Parlatuvier you will see the fishermen drying their nets and waiting for the turn of the tide. Returning via Moriah or Les Coteaux, you will see Tobago at its most rural and traditional. This is the rich plantation land of 200 years ago and you will still see the buildings and gear poking out of the undergrowth from time to time.

Windwardside

The south coast of Tobago is known as Windwardside because of the Atlantic trades that blow for most of the year. As you head east, the country becomes steadily more rugged and overgrown and the road switchbacks and chicanes as it clambers on the hillsides and drops down into the bays. The settlements get steadily more scarce and you will see just a few houses in a plot of beaten earth with a breadfruit tree for shade. In plantation days, each estate would carry its produce down to the nearest bay, from where it would be picked up by ship. The distance to Charlotteville in the northeast of the island is about 15 miles, but it can easily take two hours or more.

At Studley Park you can take a left turn on to a winding road that disappears into the rainforest, passing the Hillsborough dam and then descending to Mason Hall. A mile after you leave the coast, you can walk to the **Green Hill Waterfall** just off the road. Farther along the coast, **Carapuse Bay** takes its name from the turtle shell or carapace, a legacy from the 17th century, when turtlers would come to the island. Turtles were a valuable source of meat, particularly as they could be kept alive on their backs for up to three weeks until the meat was needed.

At King's Bay, a magnificent horseshoe harbour almost enclosed by mountains, you will find the **King's Bay Waterfall**, where water cascades from all directions into a rockpool.

Speyside at the eastern end of the island looks out into Tyrell's Bay and Little Tobago. It is also known as Bird of Paradise Island, because in 1909 Mr Ingram, the owner of the island, brought a colony from New Guinea, where they were becoming extinct. The mating dance was a spectacular sight, with cries and wings held aloft to reveal a golden plumage that was kept constantly shimmering by strutting and side-stepping. Despite the assurances of the boatowners trying to persuade you to take a trip out there, no birds are left there now. The last one was sighted in 1983.

Charlotteville is a classic West Indian fishing village, with red-roofed houses stacked above one another on the slopes like an amphitheatre. The sale of the catch is announced each day with the blow of a conch. The road beyond Cambleton to Parlatuvier is passable only in the dry season.

FESTIVALS
Like its counterpart in Trinidad, the Tobago Carnival culminates with Mardi Gras at the beginning of Lent, and you can catch a calypso tent for a month beforehand. The end of Lent is celebrated as well, with goat and crab races and a general jump-up. In August the island hosts the Tobago Heritage Festival.

WHERE TO STAY
With better beaches, Tobago has more typical Caribbean beach resort hotels than Trinidad, but it also has some superb West Indian hideaways tucked away in a cove or in the hills. If you wish to hire a villa, contact **Tobago Villas**, PO Box 301 (tel 639 8737). Hotels in Tobago add 15% VAT to all bills and most charge 10% for service.

EXPENSIVE
The plushest place to stay in Tobago is the **Mount Irvine Bay Hotel**, PO Box 222, (tel 639 8871). Its setting, on the north shore west of Scarborough, is impressive, with rooms looking out over the ocean or the lush golf course. A double room in peak season costs US$150–600. The **Grafton Beach Resort** on Stone Haven Bay (tel 639 0191, fax 639 0030) also proffers high-grade luxury in sumptuous rooms and beach-bound relaxation (endless watersports) right outside. Double room in season US$200–250.

MODERATE
Set in its own valley a little further up the coast (due north of Scarborough), the **Arnos Vale** Hotel (tel 639 2881, fax 639 4629) has a charm dating from the days of Tobago's pre-eminence as a plantation island. 30 rooms scattered on the verdant hillsides around the old estate house and in a block down by the pool and very private beach. Double room

US$130 in season. The **Richmond Great House** (tel 660 4467) also echoes with the plantation splendour of old-time Tobago. The timber-frame estate house has been restored by a Tobagonian professor of African history. Seven rooms lead off the breezy central dining area and look out onto the tropical gardens and pool above Richmond on the south coast. US$75 a double room in season. **Arcadia** (tel 639 1695, fax 639 4433) is approached through an avenue of royal palms, a modern Tobagonian villa in classical tropical surroundings, on the hilltop above Scarborough. Just three bedrooms and a congenial bar and dining-room. Isolation for US$65 a double in season. The five **Man O War Bay** cottages (tel 660 4327, fax 660 4328) overlook the waves along the bay from 'downtown' Charlotteville. Smothered in greenery, they are the ultimate in West Indian seclusion. Double rate $80. At Batteaux Bay, Speyside, is the **Blue Waters Inn** (tel 660 4341, fax 660 5195), where there are 28 rooms set in cabanas and in a block. There is a good restaurant serving local food and excellent snorkelling right offshore. Double room US$90 in season. Of the hotels around Crown Point, at the western extreme of the island close to the airport, perhaps the best value is the **Kariwak Village** (tel 639 8545), where comfortable cabanas stand around a pool in tropical greenery. Although not right on the beach, it is friendly with a restaurant and pool. A double room in peak season costs around US$75.

CHEAP

There are other, cheaper options. Around Scarborough there are some cheap and simple guest houses, such as the **Della Mira** on Windward Road (tel 639 2531), where a simple double room in winter costs US$45, though the noise from the adjacent club can be disturbing. Around Crown Point you find friendly service and simple rooms at **Wood's Castle** (tel 639 0803) for TT$100 in season. Also try **Jeffrey's Place**. Opposite the airport, **Jetway** has rooms for a similar price.

For bed and breakfast in private homes, a good way to see Tobagonian life, contact the Tourist Office in Scarborough about the Bed and Breakfast Association, or Mr Lloyd Anthony, Tony's House, Carnbee (tel 639 8836, fax 639 3566). The cost is generally US$20–25 per person.

EATING OUT

There are some good restaurants outside the hotels in Tobago and it is worth the effort of visiting them. There are the usual VAT (15%) and service (10%) charges.

EXPENSIVE

You will find the best in in island seafood and a very friendly hostess on the veranda at the **Blue Crab** (tel 639 2737) at the corner of Robinson and Main Streets. Pumpkin soup and fish chowder followed by the daily catch or flying fish creole. Mangos, bananas and avocados from the garden and all the local vegetables. You must ring to reserve (and request any dish you want). Closed Thurs, main dish TT$65–85. The **Old Donkey Cart House** (tel 639 3551) has an alluring setting in a floodlit tropical garden. Shrimp and crab cocktail followed by seafood pasta, washed down with German wine (the owner is German). Main dish TT$45–60, closed Wed. Close by is **Rouselle's**, for good West Indian fare, rice and peas and curry goat, and a spot of liming at the bar. Another seafood restaurant, **Dillons** is set in an air-conditioned dining room in a modern villa in the Crown Point area, where you sometimes eat to the accompaniment of a steel band. Try

90

the lobster thermidor, glazed in brandy and mushroom, or crayfish, grilled with café de Paris butter. Main course TT$65 and up, closed Mon. At **Papillon** Restaurant (tel 639 0275) at the Old Grange Inn in Mount Irvine you can eat on the breezy terrace. Local conch cooked in coconut, or a sea food casserole in ginger wine, with generous servings of plantain and ground provisions, followed by Tobago pone for pudding. About TT$50–70.

CHEAP

Jemma's is a classical West Indian kitchen on the waterfront in Speyside (both lunch and dinner). Chicken or fish, cooked to creole perfection. She is a Seventh Day Adventist, so she will sell you no alcohol, but you can take your own if you want. Finally, at **Store Bay** you will find a clutch of snackettes where you can take away the famous Tobago crab and dumpling on a polystyrene plate or a curry goat or 'buss up shut' (paratha bread, or 'bust up shirt')—Miss Esmie, Sylvia, Alma, Joicy's, Miss Trim and Miss Jean, all in a row. About TT$15, open until about 10pm.

BARS AND NIGHTLIFE

The hotels sometimes stage live entertainment which you are welcome to attend. You can always wander in to other hotel bars, but there are local bars worth a look too. In town, Carrington St is lively most nights—try the **Kings Well Inn** at the eastern end. There are any number of rum shops around the island, the **Fountain** at Moriah and **John Grant** at Crown Point for example. And for a drink with a difference, go to **Teeside**, where you can taste 30 different sorts of tea.

There are one or two **clubs** in town. Huge **La Tropicale**, set high above the waves, often has music, also **Club Christie** in uptown Scarborough off St James Park (Fri, Sat). On Sunday night you might try 'Sunday School' at Buccoo, a jump-up that kicks off late.

91

The Windward Islands
Grenada, St Vincent and the Grenadines, St Lucia and Dominica

Banana Grove, St Lucia

The four independent nations of the Windward Isles stand like a line of Titans in the Southern Caribbean. Each one in sight of the next, these massive fertile peaks soar thousands of feet from the water, separating the Atlantic Ocean from the Caribbean Sea.

In fact the islands are a series of volcanic peaks on a mountain range below the surface of the water. They lie along a fault-line on the seabed, where the Atlantic crust is gradually forcing its way under the Caribbean plate and the magma is throwing up lava through volcanoes. Though the eruptions have calmed down somewhat over the last few millions of years, the volcanoes are still relatively active, each of them blowing about once a century and causing earthquakes that reverberate along the whole chain of the Lesser Antilles. On one day in 1867, weird happenings on Grenada in the far south of the chain, where the harbour water swelled and contracted as though the underworld were breathing, were echoed by seismic activity as far north as the Virgin Island of St Thomas.

Each one of the Windwards has its *Soufrière*, a sulphurous volcanic vent, and you will be greeted by its smell. The St Vincent volcano and those on nearby Martinique and Guadeloupe are the most violent as they tend to blast out volumes of lava and super-heated gases that collapse mountains and destroy anything in their path, as well as a plume of gas and a shower of pumice stones. On the other islands things are a little less extreme. There are volcanic steam-baths that constantly let off sulphurous fumes so digusting that they kill off all the plant-life, and fumaroles. In the Grenadines there is an underwater volcano (Kick 'em Jenny), now quite close to the surface, whose activity has been spotted by pilots flying over the area.

An American seer has predicted that the 1990s are to be an active time for the Windward Islands. According to her, one island will appear in the decade—presumably

Kick 'em Jenny—but more worryingly she has predicted that another island will disappear.

The Windward Islands are all similar in their appearance and they are some of the most beautiful and fertile in the Caribbean. They rise sheer from the water to serrated volcanic peaks, usually stacked with rain-clouds formed as the Atlantic winds are forced up their slopes. Their height gives them their own micro-climates. The rainfall here is measured in feet, and it crashes down the hills in torrents and waterfalls. It also feeds the dripping, sweltering rainforest: a monstrous tangle of trees, creepers, bushes and ferns clambering over one another in botanical pandemonium. The islands are so fertile that clumps of bamboo will grow to 60 feet in height, creaking even when there is no wind. The gardener's most useful tool is the machete.

The Windwards are smack in the middle of the hurricane belt and in the season are occasionally visited by these outsize whirlwinds. The Windwards are often the first point of contact with land after a 2000-mile run-up across the Atlantic. Hurricanes are indescribably destructive—Gilbert in 1988 pushed a 5000 tonne ship 500 yards inland; 'Big Master David' in 1979 left 80 per cent of Dominicans homeless. Not only do they destroy the houses and crops, but torrential rains sweep away roads and collapse bridges.

Human history in the Windwards is split-second in terms of the volcanoes and plate tectonics and is reckoned to have started about 2000 years ago, when the Arawaks first touched the islands on their migration north from the South American mainland. For a 1000 years they led a peaceful existence centred around agriculture and fishing. Pieces of their pottery are still to be found in the islands today, as are their rock-carvings.

Around AD 1000, their peace was disturbed by the Caribs, another South American Indian tribe, who followed them along the island chain. The newcomers were cannibals and they made short work of the gentle Arawaks as they bludgeoned and barbecued their way north, fattening up the men and adopting the women as their wives. At the time of Columbus's arrival in the New World, they had island-hopped as far as the Virgin Islands and were beginning to raid *Borinquen*, now Puerto Rico.

On the earliest maps of the Americas, the Windward Islands are marked as the *Cannibal Isles*, such was the terror which they conjured up in the minds of sailors. The Spaniards gave them a wide berth and headed for the less hostile islands of the Greater Antilles.

But as the age of Empire began, so the Europeans encroached on the Lesser Antilles, conducting a war that would lead to the genocide of the Caribs. The mountainous Windwards became the heartland of Carib resistance to the invaders. A treaty of 1660 supposedly ensured that they would be left alone on St Vincent and Dominica on condition that they kept the peace elsewhere, but the governments connived with the colonists' campaign of extermination because the land was proving to be so valuable.

The Caribs from Dominica and from St Vincent, where a mixed race of Caribs and escaped African slaves, the *Black Caribs*, conducted a ruthless campaign right up to the beginning of the 19th century.

But the 18th century was also the height of French and British rivalry. Every war in Europe sent shock-waves to the Caribbean and the islands were batted back and forth like shuttlecocks. In turn, the two nations would tear up and down the island chain, ransacking the colonies and annexing them, only to hand them back at the next treaty.

Despite blockades, the islands were extremely valuable to the colonists as they brought in a vast wealth in sugar. Their importance can be seen in the Treaty of Paris in 1763, when the French traded their rights in the whole of Canada in order to retain a foothold in the islands by keeping Martinique, the most prosperous of their islands, between St Lucia and Dominica. By the early years of the 19th century, the final pattern was fixed—Martinique was French and the Windward Islands were in British hands.

Behind the wars and the empire building, the issues were rather different for the islanders themselves, to whom the colonial armies were an ambivalent presence. There is some French influence in each of the Windwards. Many of the place-names are French, as are the *anses* (bays) and *mornes* (hills) and in some islands you will still hear French creole, which still survives even though the official language has been English for nearly 200 years.

If the 18th century was a turbulent and prosperous one, the 19th saw a steady decline to obscurity and poverty in the Windwards. Their major industry, sugar, became uncompetitive as sugar beet was grown more economically in Europe, and attempts at other crops met with limited success. A highlight was emancipation in 1834. Unlike Barbados, where there was no unowned land, and the former slaves were effectively forced to continue working the plantations to make a living, the freed slaves on the Windwards voted with their feet, preferring to take a plot of land in the hills where they could be their own masters. The islands became backwaters, declining to the point where Dominica had only a fortnightly postal service.

The Windwards (except Dominica, which did not join the Windwards until 1939) were grouped under a Governor in St George's, Grenada and in 1874, Crown Colony status was enforced and rule was transferred to London. As the political scene changed after the Second World War, universal franchise came in 1951 and internal self-government in 1967. The Windward Islands ceased to exist as a political unit in 1960 as the islands were on the path to Independence. All four nations remain within the British Commonwealth and the Queen is represented by a Governor General. The highest court of appeal is the Privy Council in London.

Attempts to link the islands in a Federation had failed as early as 1763 and again in 1885. The Windwards were a part of the short-lived West Indian Federation in 1958 and since 1981 they have been part of the Organisation of Eastern Caribbean States, which promotes economic integration between the smaller Commonwealth countries in the area.

The islands are partly agricultural, depending mainly on bananas and other small-scale agricultural industries such as nutmeg in Grenada and arrowroot in St Vincent. They are also industrially undeveloped, in sharp contrast to the nearby French islands, which are developed to be like mainland France. However, they need dollars to buy in essentials like medicines and some foods, not to mention desirable luxuries, and so there is a persistent need to find sources of foreign income. The largest industry of course is tourism, which contributes most of the badly needed foreign exchange.

The society is changing. Where the old people have lived a tough farmer's existence attached to the land, the youth of today are unwilling to live like this. Many would prefer to take their chances in town. On an island like St Lucia, a large proportion of the population lives in the capital, Castries. There is a burgeoning middle class and civil service in all the islands.

The islands are small and friendly and you will find that people say good morning and chat when they get on a bus. If you ever want a chat, you simply stop anyone you come across in the street.

Bananas

A familiar sight in the Windwards is the messy swathes of banana trees, their leaves tousled, arched in irregular directions. Look closely and you may see them lashed together for support with a network of string, their dark green fruits, or 'hands', protected by blue plastic bags.

The banana is native to China and Malaya and had made its way to the Canary Islands by 1510. It botanical name is *Musa Sapientum*, or the *muse of wise men*. According to Indian legend, sages would sit under the huge leaves for shade and savour the fruit. They had lost their popularity with Caribbean colonists by the start of the 19th century, when they were regarded as a suspect fruit because of their colour and shape. They were thought 'to excite urine and to provoke venery'. However, the banana became popular again and it has been an important export crop in the Windwards since the 1950s. The packing stations are all over the islands and you will see farmers carrying the fruit down the hill in time for the weekly visit of the *Geest* ships that make the three week round trip from Europe. Boxes of *Windward Islands Bananas* are a common sight in the markets in Britain.

There are many varieties of banana, the most widely-known being the *gros michel*, large and yellow when ripe. Less known is the smaller and sweeter canary banana or rock fig (considered *l'amie de la poitrine* by Père Labat), which is about four inches long. But the most exotic and sweetest of them all is the *secret fig*, which grows no longer than about two inches. There are unsweet varieties such as *plantain*, delicious when fried, and other starchy vegetables, the *green fig* and the fatter *bluggo*.

In fact bananas do not grow on trees at all, but a stem of unripe leaves packed closely like a cigar. As each new leaf forces its way up, it stands erect like a bright green scroll and gently unfurls, bending gracefully as it is superseded by another. The leaves, sometimes 10 foot long by 2, start off with a beautiful green sheen that makes water dance like mercury, and as they age they become shredded and look like an untidy head of hair.

When a plant bears fruit, it throws out a long trunk with a purple heart at the tip, which opens to reveal little black teeth in rows. These teeth are the end of the fruit, which swell until the bunches appear like so many fingers sticking up. A trunk may have about ten hands of bananas, or finger rolls as they are known. Each plant flowers only once, after which it is removed and another shoot takes its place in the same spot. The blue plastic bags protect the maturing bananas from the scratches of lizard claws, insects and birds.

GRENADA
Carriacou and Petit Martinique

Grenada and its Grenadines lie in the south of the Caribbean, at the foot of the Windward Islands chain, about 90 miles from Trinidad and the South American coast. The island of Grenada itself is typical of the Windwards in its tropical beauty, towering

Sloops in St George's Harbour

mountains covered in explosive rainforest, inlets and bays on the coast furred with palms and white sand beaches.

In the north Grenada (pronounced Gre-nay-der) is linked to the island of St Vincent by the Grenadines, a 60-mile string of volcanic islets and cays, towering peaks that soar out of the water and sandbars that barely make it to the surface. Two of the inhabited Grenadines, Carriacou and Petit Martinique, belong to Grenada, and altogether the three islands make up a population of about 91,000.

Grenada's capital, St George's, is the prettiest harbour town in the whole Caribbean. It is set in a massive volcanic bowl, and its slopes are lined with red-tiled roofs that descend to the edge of the bay, where yachts and old-fashioned schooners sit in dock.

Grenada calls itself the *Spice island of the West* because its fertile soil produces spices for markets all over the world. In the valleys of the mountainous interior you will see the fruit and spice plantations and the *cocoa walks*, where orange *immortelle* trees stand aflame above them. The *nutmeg*, from which come the spices nutmeg and mace, is the island's most famous spice and its fruit appears on Grenada's flag.

The island is quiet in the Caribbean style, but not so long ago Grenada (just 12 miles by 21) was thrust into the international news because of its revolution and the subsequent invasion that put the might of the United States on to a tiny Caribbean island in October 1983. The revolution still remains in the minds of some of the islanders, but the return to customary Caribbean quiet did not take long.

History

From the earliest sightings travellers have spoken of Grenada's physical beauty and fertility. To 16th-century Spanish sailors coasting the Windwards it was a reminder of home, the hills above the city of Granada.

Early attempts to settle *Camerhogne* failed at the hands of the Carib Indians. Englishmen came in 1609 in the ships *Diana*, *Penelope* and *Endeavour*, but they were chased off, as were the settlers sponsored by the Frenchman de Poincy.

96

By 1650 though, the Caribs actually invited the Frenchman from Martinique, Du Parquet, to settle the island. He came with 'two hundred men of good stamina', arriving to a salute of guns and promptly erecting a cross and building a fort. Eventually he bought the island from the Caribs for 'cloth, axes, bill-hooks, knives, glass beads, mirrors and two large bottles of *eau-de-vie* (brandy) for the chief himself'. It was not long before the Caribs decided the deal was not a good one after all. By 1654 they were locked in a duel with the French for possession of the island. Reinforcements came for the French from Martinique by ship and for the Caribs from St Vincent and Dominica by canoe.

It was an extremely brutal time. The Caribs roamed the island killing French hunters and then made an attack on the French settlement. But, armed only with bows and arrows against the guns of the French, the Caribs were forced back to the north of the island where rather than be captured and killed, they threw themselves off a cliff to their deaths.

A new owner, the Comte du Cerillac, sent a brutal governor who so abused his power that the islanders tried him and sentenced him to be hanged. At this he pleaded noble birth, which stipulated that he should be beheaded. There was no executioner on Grenada, so the islanders eventually had him shot.

In the early 1700s the island became an important French colony, as a refitting station on the route from Martinique, the French headquarters in the Caribbean, to South America, and as a plantation island. But endless rounds of 18th-century wars affected the islands and Grenada was blockaded and captured as the navies whittled through the islands. As the island changed hands, the names were changed from French to English and back again; Fort Royal became St George's and Gouyave on the west coast became Charlotte Town. Some of the names stuck, but many of the original French names also remain in Grenada even today. Despite the difficulties brought by the wars, it remained prosperous and was thought of as 'the second of the English Islands' (after Barbados).

It was not long before the French were back. Grenada was taken almost by mistake because an attack on Barbados was made impossible by bad weather. Admiral d'Estaing entered St George's harbour and the Irish troops of his ally Count Arthur Dillon attacked by land. The island surrendered.

Hard on his heels came the British Admiral, *Foulweather Jack* Byron, but even though some of his ships made it into the harbour, he could not draw the 'mere gasconade of a vapouring Frenchman' into battle and so the French won Grenada again. The British Governor and the island's colours were shipped off to France. The latter were strung up above the High Altar in Notre Dame and the former was eventually returned to Britain.

By the time the British were back again, the British Grenadians were vengeful over their treatment at French hands. They confiscated church lands and made the French Grenadians submit to the *Test*, an oath demanding a rejection of Transubstantiation, impossible for a Catholic. Many chose to emigrate to Trinidad, where the Spaniards were crying out for settlers. Much of Trinidad's French heritage dates from these Grenadian refugees. But on the island itself the grievances increased, fired by the harsher treatment of the slaves under the British and by the French Revolution, which was being spread from Guadeloupe by Victor Hugues (see p. 205). Eventually it erupted into open rebellion in 1795.

97

Fédon's Rebellion

The revolt was led by Julien Fédon, a mulatto planter. From Guadeloupe the revolutionaries brought back 'arms and ammunition, caps of liberty, national cockades and a flag on which was inscribed in large characters, *Liberté, Egalité ou la Mort*'. The rebels overran the whole island, killing prisoners along with suspected collaborators. Their first strike was on the east coast, at La Baye, near modern Melville, where British settlers were taken from their beds and shot, and at Charlotte Town, where the Governor himself, Sir Ninian Home, was captured trying to return to St George's. He was one of 51 hostages taken to the rebel mountain stronghold, eventually to be slaughtered on Fédon's personal instructions as the rebels came under threat from the advancing British troops.

St George's never fell to the rebels but it took a year before reinforcements under Sir Ralph Abercromby defeated the guerrillas. Their leaders were captured and executed immediately or exiled to Honduras, but Fédon himself was never taken. Some think he drowned in an attempt to escape to Trinidad, but others think that he made it to Cuba. His estate at Belvidere, from where he ran the insurrection, is just below one of Grenada's mountain peaks, which is now known as Fédon's Camp. By the end of the conflict, Grenada was left in ruins.

When the slaves were freed in 1838 they took over small plots of Grenada's fertile land. Unlike the other Windwards, Grenada remained reasonably prosperous during the decline of the 19th century. Agriculture was the economic mainstay; bananas and cocoa were grown, as they can still be seen, among lesser known spices such as cinnamon, bay leaf, allspice and ginger.

Like most of the British islands, Grenada became a Crown Colony in 1877, ruled directly from Britain with a resident Governor. Grenada was the senior Windward island and the Governor of the Windward Islands resided here, in the house where the Governor General of the island resides today.

With the failure of Federation, when attempts to unite all the British Caribbean islands into one country foundered in 1962 and after a later failure to unite with Trinidad and Tobago, Grenada became an Associated State of Britain in 1967. They were not long in deciding on Independence and Grenada became an independent nation within the British Commonwealth on 7 February 1974.

Grenada's first leader was Eric Gairy, a volatile and charismatic man whose political heritage was in the oil-fields of the Caribbean island of Aruba. Elected as early as 1951, he was fondly thought of by many Grenadians as the champion of workers' rights against the colonial government. He was to stay in Grenadian politics for the next 30 years; but after Independence his leadership became steadily more corrupt, wasteful and bullying, a secret army called the *Mongoose Gang* unofficially imposing his will.

In the early 70s the New Jewel Movement was formed. Initially clandestine, to avoid harassment from the overbearing government, this socialist movement steadily gained ground, allying itself with the disillusioned opposition to Gairy, including the influential and traditionally conservative business class.

Revolution and Invasion

On 13 March 1979, with Gairy out of the country, 38 armed members of the NJM stormed the army barracks at True Blue on the south coast of the island and in a bloodless coup the NJM was in power. With popular support, they began a social experiment unprecedented in the Commonwealth Caribbean. Considerable strides forward were made in health care and in education, with general economic growth over the next four years. However, the gradually repressive nature of the People's Revolutionary Government's programmes became clearer: the press was stifled, political detainees were held untried and the Grenadian Revolution began to excite international disapproval.

Grenadian foreign policy and their closer ties with Cuba and the eastern bloc led to their isolation by the USA and other islands in the Caribbean. Under this pressure from outside and facing straitened economic circumstances on the island, the PRG foundered in a split from within.

The leader, Maurice Bishop, was placed under house arrest by the other members of the Central Committee, but eventually his supporters brought him to St George's, where they congregated at Fort George. Bernard Coard and others of the opposing faction of the PRG sent down troops who fired on the crowd to disperse it, killing about 60 people, then shooting Bishop and five of his close associates inside the fort. The whole island was placed under a 24-hour curfew for four days until US 82nd Airborne Division arrived on 25 October 1983.

Massive aid and assistance came in the first couple of years and President Reagan himself made a visit in February 1986, but it has tailed off now that Grenada has acquiesced. Many Grenadians do think of the invasion as the 'rescue mission' and are grateful to Reagan for sending troops. Others will never forgive the United States for what seemed to them an unwarranted show of force against a small country by a big power in whose backyard Grenada happened to be. There is still considerable support for Maurice Bishop, if not for his deputies.

Grenada remains within the British Commonwealth and has two Houses of Parliament, a 13-member Senate and a 15-member House of Representatives elected for five-year terms. The Prime Minister is Nicholas Braithwaite of the National Democratic Congress.

The Spice Island of the West

Grenada was known as the Isle of Spice—the source of the island's prosperity at the turn of the century. It is still a profitable business even though Grenada's third share of the world market in nutmeg is now gone and prices on the world markets fluctuate.

Nutmeg is the island's principal spice, and it is even commemorated on the colourful Grenadian flag. In the past nutmeg has been used as a charm to ward off illness and today it is locally used in remedies against colds as well as in *Vicks*. In the Second World War, oil of nutmeg was in demand for aircraft engine oil because it does not freeze at high altitudes.

Nutmeg was introduced into Grenada in 1843, supposedly at a party where it was added as a mystery ingredient to the top of the regular planter's punch—the party was no doubt a success, but more importantly, Grenadians have never drunk a punch without nutmeg since.

The tree is evergreen and grows up to 60 feet in height. Its fruit looks like a yellow apricot and the Grenadians will tell you that no part of it goes to waste. When it ripens,

99

the flesh splits open, revealing a brown nut covered with a wax netting, and it drops to the ground. The fruit must be collected immediately to prevent it from rotting and then the parts are separated.

The outer flesh goes into making jams or preserves and the nut, which contains the nutmeg itself, is processed to make the spice nutmeg. Finally, the red netting is used to make a second spice, *mace*. It is not commonly known that the two spices come from the same plant. A London bureaucrat caused great hilarity among the estate workers when he sent notice that the international market price of nutmeg was on the decrease and that of mace increasing and so cultivators would be advised to hold on the first and to step up production of the latter. The two biggest nutmeg factories are in Gouyave and Grenville.

Another tree seen all over the island is the **cocoa** tree, *theobroma* or *Food of the Gods*, with hand-sized, purple pods sprouting indiscriminately from trunk and branches. They grow in *cocoa walks*, as the valley plantations were called, alternate male and female trees up to 30 feet high, which go on producing for up to 100 years, usually in the shade of the the much larger *immortelle* tree, famed for its orange blooms.

The pods are collected and broken open to reveal a (delicious) white sticky-sweet gel and up to 20 cocoa beans. The beans are then fermented, piled into a wooden sweating box with a little water and turned regularly, while the white pulp degrades. Next the brown beans are laid out on to huge trays, or *boucans*, where they are dried in the sun, again constantly being turned, or *danced*, by the workers, who shuffle through them in lines. At this stage they begin to smell of bitter unsweetened cocoa. From here they are exported, as Grenada has no large processing plant. For local consumption, some beans are processed and the oily product is rolled into sticks, which can be boiled up to make cocoa for breakfast.

Other spices cultivated in Grenada are **cinnamon** bark, bundles of which can be bought in the markets rolled up in pink ribbon, **cloves** and **pimento**, or **allspice**, so-called so because it tastes like cinnamon, clove and nutmeg all at once. **Ginger, bay leaves** and **vanilla** are also grown. Many are used in confectionery and the flavouring of food or as a preservative. Apart from local use for their alternative medicinal properties (bay rum is used to quell fevers and oil of ginger is said to reduce pain), many are exported for use in the pharmaceutical industry.

Flora and Fauna

Like the other Windward Islands, much of the interior is too wild and remote to be inhabited and so there are large tracts of rainforest that are untouched, but which you can explore by a series of trails (many start out from the Grand Etang in the National Park, where no building is allowed anyway). You will see huge gommier and mahogany trees, grappled by creeping vines and lianas that threaten to throttle the path and if you go higher, beyond the montane forest into the elfin woodland, there are wild grasses and ferns. Living in the forest are a few animals, including mona monkeys, opossum and a species of nine-banded armadillo and many birds, including tanagers and the odd hawk.

There are a number of mangrove areas in Grenada, including Levera in the northeast and La Sagesse estuary in the southeast (a national park area), which have an entirely different bird life. Here you may see coots and flycatchers and the more traditional seabirds such as pelicans and boobies. The national flower of Grenada is the bougainvillaea.

GETTING TO GRENADA
Grenada has reasonable international air links to Point Salines airport in the southwest of the island, both from Europe and the States. If there is no direct flight, it is nearly always possible to make a connection the same day, either via Barbados, Trinidad or St Lucia. A departure tax of EC$25 is payable by all adults who stay more than 24 hours; children aged 10–16 pay half as much, those under 10 years are exempt.

By Air
From the UK: one direct flight a week on British Airways from Gatwick. BWIA fly via Barbados and in the winter months these are supplemented by charter flights. The best place to connect is Barbados (or Trinidad or St Lucia).
From Europe: Stockholm, Frankfurt, Cologne and Zurich are linked to Grenada via Barbados, Paris via Martinique.
From the USA: American Airlines flies daily via Puerto Rico and BWIA has daily direct flights from Miami and New York.
From other Caribbean Islands: LIAT connects Grenada with Barbados, Tobago, St Vincent and several of the Grenadines, including Carriacou and Union Island. BWIA flies between Grenada and Trinidad.

By Boat
There are many ferry services a week (not quite one a day) between Grenada and Carriacou; the journey time is four hours. The schedule is fairly flexible and depends on which boats are running. Check the Carenage in St George's or at the Tourist Board. The one-way fare is EC$25, EC$50 return. From Windward in Carriacou you can take a boat to Petit Martinique (Mon, Wed, Fri). There is also a twice-weekly link from Carriacou to Union Island: Mon, Thurs, departure about midday, EC$10 single.

GETTING AROUND GRENADA
Buses run all the main roads in Grenada and can be flagged down from the side of the road with a frantic downward pointing finger. They leave when the driver feels like it, from the main Market Square on the Esplanade side of town, starting at dawn and running until about seven in the evening and infrequently into the night. On Sundays, after the morning run to church, Grenadian bus-drivers wash their vehicles and will come out for no man. Some prices are **St George's** to Gouyave—EC$4, Grenville—EC$4 and to Sauteurs—EC$5. To the Grand Anse area, or L'Anse aux Epines, it is a dollar and twenty-five cents ride.

The alternative is to go by **taxi**, which is easily arranged at a hotel, in town or at the major beaches. As usual, the drivers are a mine of information and are happy to give an impromptu tour. Sample rates, set by the Grenada Board of Tourism, are: from **St George's** to Grand Anse—US$7, L'Anse aux Epines—US$12, to Point Salines Airport—US$12, to the Grand Etang—US$30 return, and to Gouyave and Dougaldston—US$40 return. To hire a taxi by the hour costs US$20, and about US$150 for four people for a day's outing.

Car hire is another possibility and a good way to see the island if you are prepared to brave the vagaries of the Grenadian road and can remember to keep to the left. You will

101

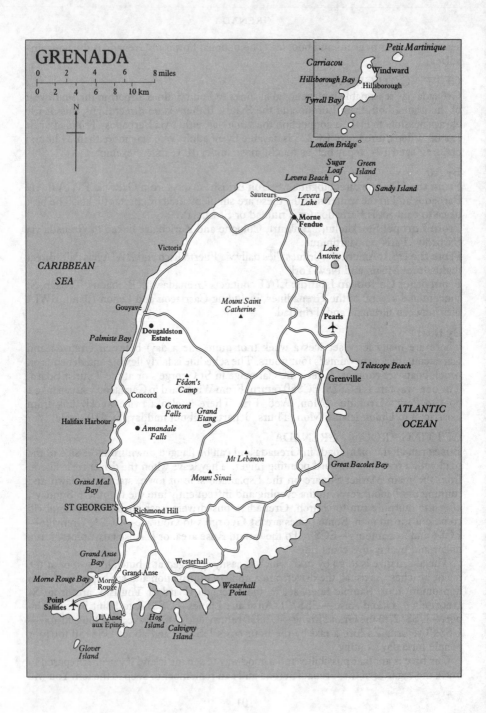

need a visitor's licence, which can be bought from the police, or rental companies, on the Carenage on presentation of a valid licence from home for EC$30. Rental cars, at about US$40 per day, are available from **Royston's**, at Blue Horizons on Grand Anse (tel 444 4316), **Spice Isle**, the Avis rental in St George's (tel 440 3936), **David's Car Rentals** (tel 440 2399) and **Maitland's** (tel 440 1807), which also rents out motorbikes.

TOURIST INFORMATION
In **Britain**, the Grenada Board of Tourism is at 1 Collingham Gardens, London SW5 0HW (tel (071) 370 5164/5). In the **United States** you can contact them at 141 East 44th St, Suite 701, New York, NY 10017 (tel (212) 687 9554 or toll-free (800) 638 0852) and in **Canada** at 439 University Avenue, Suite 820, Toronto, Ontario M5G 1Y8 (tel (416) 595 1339).

The main **Grenada Board of Tourism**, Box 293 (tel 440 2001) is in St George's, on the waterfront in the Carenage, and there is a smaller office at Point Salines airport. Both are helpful with accommodation and advice about the island. Open 8–4 in St George's and 7–11 at the airport.

The *Grenadian Voice*, *The Informer* and *The Grenadian Today* are the island's weekly newspapers and they list local events as well as coverage of Caribbean news. There is also a wide selection of foreign newspapers and magazines on sale in St George's.

The **IDD code** for Grenada is 809, followed by a seven-digit island number. In a **medical emergency**, contact St George's Hospital (tel 440 2051/2/3).

MONEY
The Grenadian currency is the Eastern Caribbean dollar (shared with a number of other British Commonwealth Caribbean countries), which is fixed to the US dollar at a rate of about EC$2.69 = US$1. It is important to be sure which currency you are dealing in, as a bargain may suddenly turn out to be nearly 3 times better or a taxi fare considerably more expensive. **Banking hours** are Mon–Fri, 8–noon, some until 2; and 3–5 Fri. **Shops** are open 8–noon and 1–4 weekdays, Sat morning until noon. For local and Caribbean crafts, try **Imagine** in the Grand Anse Shopping Centre.

BEACHES
Grenada has plenty of beaches, Caribbean-style strands mounded with silken white sand, and the tiny secluded coves bristling with coconut palms that are so typical of the mountainous Windward Islands. Easily the best known is **Grand Anse**, two miles of pristine sand where many of the island's hotels are located, a dollar and twenty-five cents ride by local bus. There are more secluded strands beyond Grand Anse, towards the western tip of the island; for instance **Morne Rouge Bay**, sometimes known as BBC Beach after a defunct discotheque, an attractive stretch of sand in a deep cove and **Dr Groom** and **Magazine beach**. Another popular beach area is **L'Anse aux Epines** (when spoken, it sounds something more like *Lansapeen*), to the south of the Grand Anse area, also easy to reach on the bus.

Along the southern and eastern coasts, beaches can be found at **Westerhall Point**, in an attractive bay at **La Sagesse**, at **Bacolet Bay** and at **Telescope Beach** near Grenville. At the northeastern tip of the island are the two good strands which look out into the Atlantic. **Bathway Beach** is safe for swimming because it has an offshore reef,

103

but the water at **Levera Beach** is rougher. Take a picnic to this area. On the west coast, the Grenadians like **Palmiste Bay** and **Grand Mal Bay**.

BEACH BARS

There are some good seaside haunts with a secluded bar where you can get a rum punch and a lobster salad. At BBC Beach you will find the **Sur la Mer** restaurant, an ideal liming spot with a cracking view of the sunset through the fishnets and shutters. **Aquarium**, off the airport road is set back from a quiet cove and attracts a friendly crowd of visitors and locals. **La Sagesse** bay is a lovely cove tucked away on its own in the southeast of the island, very isolated. There is a small bar and restaurant in the trees and the smell of nutmeg hangs in the air from the shells strewn on the ground. On Grand Anse beach, the **Green Parrot Café** is well worth a visit in the day, for a beer with a lively crowd. Farther down is the noisy **Cotbam**, but preferable is the smaller **Umbrella Beach House**, under the police station next door, a quieter spot for a burger and a beer.

WATERSPORTS

Sailing up the sheltered coast of Grenada in the lee of the rainforested mountains and putting in to one of the many coves or cruising the stretch of Grenadine Islands to the north make Grenada a very popular area. It is also possible to visit some of the tiny islands that lie off the Grenada coast, perhaps Calvigny and Hog Island in the south, or Sugar Loaf and Green Island off the northeastern tip.

Yachts are available, skippered or uncrewed, from a day to a week or more. Island yacht charter firms are: **Grenada Yacht Services** (tel 440 2883), working from the Lagoon in St George's, and on the south coast, **The Moorings** at Secret Harbour (tel 444 4439) in Mount Hartmann Bay and in the beautiful setting of L'Anse aux Epines Bay, is **Spice Island Marine Services** (tel 444 4257). It is also a port of entry to Grenada. It is also possible to arrange **deep-sea fishing** trips through them, best between November and March. Aslo try **Evans Chartering Services** (tel 444 4422).

Windsurfing and other beach sports (waterskiing or perhaps a spot of parasailing) are best arranged through the hotel concessionaires at Grand Anse.

Scuba diving and resort course instruction can be arranged through the **Dive Grenada** (tel 444 4371) at the Ramada Renaissance Hotel, or at **Grenada Aquatics** (tel 444 4129) both on Grand Anse Beach. A one-tank dive costs in the region of US$40. Grenada is surrounded by reefs on all sides, some of the better known are Bass Reef and Wibble Reef in the southeast. You can also dive the liner *Bianca C*, at 600-ft the longest upright wreck in the world. It was scuttled after a fire in the Carenage. You can dive the upper decks and even take a turn around the swimming pool. **Snorkellers** will find good shallow seascapes in L'Anse aux Epines and at Molinière north of St George's.

Like most islands, Grenada also offers a rum-soaked picnic excursion, lunch and punch and maybe even a look at a reef. Try the **Rhum Runner** (tel 440 2198) for an afternoon of pirate profligacy. If you would like to put a jet-ski to work, try **Dorset Watersports** on Grand Anse Beach.

OTHER SPORTS

One of the pleasures of visiting Grenada lies in its natural beauty and it is well worthwhile taking a walk through the tropical rainforests, perhaps to one of the waterfalls. **Henry's Tours** (tel 444 5313) offer well-organized walks, reaching some off-beat parts of the island, including *Fédon's Camp*, the summit from which Julien Fédon led his rebellion in the 18th century. **New Trends Tours** (tel 444 1236) and **Arnold's Tours** (444 1167) also offer a variety of bus-borne island-tours.

There are **tennis courts** at many of the hotels and at the Richmond Hill Tennis Club in Richmond Hill (tel 440 2537) and at the Tanteen Tennis Club (tel 440 3010). **Golfers** can play a nine-nole course near Grand Anse, the Grenada Golf and Country Club (tel 444 4128).

St George's

The capital of Grenada is the prettiest town in the Caribbean. Stacked on the hillside are warehouses, homes and churches, their ochre-tiled roofs glowing in the evening light against the rich tropical green of Grenada's slopes. Named after King George III, the town is sprinkled with fine old creole houses, built of brick in soft shades of rose, yellow and beige and embellished with elaborate ironwork balconies and porches that were used to keep sedan chair passengers from getting wet in the rain. Brightly coloured schooners tie up at the wharves of the Carenage.

In fact, the main town is built over the backbone of a hill, spilling over either side of the ridge, all linked up by a network of cobbled streets and stepped alleys. At Carnival in St George's the floats have to be winched up the cobbled streets and then held back from running away down the other side. Dating from the late 18th century, when the original buildings were mostly destroyed in fires, St George's has two main halves, the Carenage that overlooks the inner harbour, and the Esplanade, fronting on to the Caribbean Sea.

Once, St George's Harbour was an inland lake, but now it can take ocean-going vessels. It was the crater of a volcano, from which the sides have crumbled. It is extinct, but not entirely dormant, as was shown by a curious and alarming incident in 1867, when volcanic activity was felt throughout the Caribbean. At five in the afternoon the level of the water in the Carenage suddenly dropped by five feet and the Green Hole started to bubble and steam, letting off sulphurous gases. Moments later, the level of the sea rose to about four feet above the normal, only to be sucked down and to rise again a number of times. One of the best views of the town can be had from a water-taxi trip across the harbour (price EC$1).

The **Carenage** is the centrepiece of the town, the curved harbour lined with old mercantile buildings on the waterfront, still used by businesses today. One of the finest old creole houses is the former **Antilles Hotel**, originally a French military barracks and one of the oldest buildings on the island. Next door, on the corner of Young Street, is the **Grenada National Museum** in another French barrack building, where Arawak petroglyphs are on view, alongside Empress Josephine's marble bathtub (she spent her childhood on the nearby island of Martinique), copper kettles and a rum still from the days of sugar and newspaper clippings of the recent political turmoil. Opens weekdays, 9–3, adm.

Forts and churches dominate the heights of St George's and many of them stand on Church Street, running along the ridge that looks down on both sides of the town. Close to Fort George, which overlooks the harbour mouth is the **Scot's Kirk**, the Presbyterian Church, erected in 1831. A little farther up is the **St George's Parish Anglican Church**, rebuilt in 1825 on the site of an original 1763 French Roman Catholic Church.

105

It contains plaques commemorating the victims of the Brigand's War, or Fédon's Rebellion, and the 51 hostages, including the Governor, Ninian Home, who were murdered by the 'execrable banditti'.

Still on Church Street is **York House**, the Grenadian House of Parliament. Open to visitors on weekdays, 9–3.30, adm free. But the best position is commanded by the **Roman Catholic Cathedral** (many Grenadians are still Catholic from French days), built in 1818 and remembered for its Angelus that tolled in the morning, midday and evening.

The other half of St George's is the **Esplanade** or Bay Town, which looks on to the Caribbean Sea. It was hard work getting over the ridge to the market from the Carenage and so at the end of the 19th century a tunnel was constructed, linking the two. The Sendall tunnel, named after the Governor, is over 100 yards long and still used now for heavy traffic.

The Esplanade itself is in decay, lines of old warehouses on the seafront, but you find the **fish market** here, alive when the catch is brought in at the end of the day. The main St George's **market** is a couple of blocks inland from the Esplanade, on open ground between Granby and Hillsborough Streets. It is a typical Caribbean ironwork-covered market bulding, but most of the activity takes place out on the square, golf umbrellas sheltering the vendors and their produce—root vegetables and tropical fruits (and of course Grenadian spices)—from the sun and from passing rainstorms. The best day to visit is Saturday, in the morning, but it is lively on any weekday morning (closed Sunday). If you have not been waylaid already by the spice women who ply the streets of St George's, then at the back of the square on Grenville St you can visit the **Minor Spices Society**, which smells of the cinnamon, cloves and saffron on sale here.

Well worth a visit in this area of town is the **Yellow Poui Art Gallery** on Cross St. Named after a Caribbean tree, it features West Indian art, particularly impressive for its primitivist paintings, and West Indian scenes by foreign painters and sculptors. Look out for Grenadians Michael Paryag and Elinus Cato and Carriacouans Canute Caliste and Frankie Francis.

Only two of the forts remain of what was once a protective ring of defences on the heights above St George's. **Fort George** dominates the harbour mouth, with a fine view of the Carenage and of the open sea, and it is now the main St George's police station. Constructed in 1706, it spent a spell more recently as Fort Rupert (called after the father of Maurice Bishop who was killed in a riot in 1974). It was here that Maurice Bishop himself and his colleagues were shot on 19 October 1983. Cannon still poke over the battlements and underground there is a warren of tunnels and caverns, supposedly leading to a series of underground passageways from one fort to the next (now blocked off). It is possible to visit the fort at the weekend.

On the rising ground that forms the backdrop of St George's harbour, among the homes of prosperous Grenadians, is **Marryshow House**, a creole building that was once the home of the Grenadian political leader and architect of the West Indies Federation. Higher still is **Government House**, with a fine view over the harbour and town. Built in 1802, it is now the residence of the Governor General. But the most spectacular view can be seen after a stiff climb up **Richmond Hill**, which commands the harbour and looks along the coast as far as Point Salines in the southwest. Once there were four forts, started by the French after they captured the island in 1779 and completed by the British. Fort Frederick is in reasonable repair and there is a campaign to restore Fort Matthew and Fort Lucas. The island prison is in the former military hospital.

There are two botanical gardens in St George's. At the foot of Richmond Hill, on the outskirts, are the old **Botanical Gardens**, established in 1886. There was a zoo, but it has now closed and the gardens are sadly not in good repair, though they are still a pleasant place to sit and rest. Behind Richmond Hill are the **Bay Gardens**, set in the grounds of a former sugar mill, where you will see a huge range of Caribbean flora—vivid blooms of purple, pink and scarlet among the endless shades of green. Open daylight hours, adm. It is well worth finding a guide to tell you about the many species on display.

The West Coast

The Grenadian coastline is a series of headlands and bays, folds of land thrown off from the volcanic peaks and valleys carved out by rivers, where Grenada's spice plantations have grown. The road follows the coastline, all hairpins and switchbacks and overhung by cliffs, initially laid out by the French in the 18th century. The names recount the island's mixed history—Halifax Harbour, Beauséjour Bay, Happy Hill and Molinière.

From St George's the Esplanade road leads up the west coast, passing the old communal loo on the bayfront and on to **Queen's Park**, an open ground used for cricket and football matches on the outskirts of the town.

Halifax Harbour is a sheltered inlet and good natural harbour which is popular with sailors today, just as it was once with the corsairs and the naval fleets apparently used by the French fleet in their eternal battles with the British.

Inland from Concord, following the Black Bay River upstream among the nutmeg and cocoa plantations, are the **Concord Falls**, a series of three waterfalls lost in the undergrowth. It is possible to drive to the lowest one, but the other two must be reached on foot, the first 25 minutes, and the next an hour and a half's walk. However, each fall has a pool in which you can swim after the climb. In high season you will probably not be

Cocoa drying in the boucans on Dougaldston Estate

107

alone, but it is a pleasant walk. It is even possible to walk up to Grand Etang (about five hours' climb). Back on the coast, **Black Bay** is named after its appearance, which is black volcanic rather than white coral sand.

The Dougaldston Estate
Just outside Gouyave is the Dougaldston Estate, a charming old plantation of clapboard and shingle buildings and dilapidated farm machinery, where cocoa and nutmeg are grown among allspice, tonka beans and coffee. In years past the estate would ring to the sound of violins as the workers *danced* the cocoa beans to dry them evenly in the *boucans*, shuffling in lines and turning the cocoa beans with their feet. The boucans, vast trays that are pulled out from beneath one another to catch the sun, are on wheels so that they can be rushed back beneath the building in case of rain. In the main building, heavy with the smells of cinnamon, cloves and nutmeg, the old processes can be seen, worked by the Grenadian ladies. It is possible to buy the spices on display.

Gouyave (French for guava) is a little farther along the coast. Set on a promontory, the town is run down, the old creole houses past their best now, but it is alluring in its faded prosperity. Travelling in the 40s, Patrick Leigh Fermor came across a sweepstake here, in which the first prize was a free funeral for the ticket holder or for any friend or relation.

The biggest building in Gouyave is the **Grenada Nutmeg Cooperative Association**—floors full of sacks, tea chests and machinery, the air redolent with the sweet-spice smell of nutmeg. The nutmeg arrives as a 'nut', which is covered with a netting of red wax. The wax is mace, which is stored for six months and is graded as the spice itself, or used as a preservative in food or cosmetics, to be exported in tea chests. The 'nut' is put through a crusher which removes the shell and then the kernels are graded by throwing them into water. Those that float are used in pharmaceuticals, but the good ones sink and they make the spice nutmeg that ends up floating on a rum punch. These are then stored in hessian sacks, stencilled with huge brushes and black ink.

Set on a sweeping bay on the north coast is the village of **Sauteurs**, the island's third largest town and the scene of one of the saddest moments in Grenada's history, when the retreating Caribs were surrounded by the French troops and threw themselves to their death in the sea rather than be killed. And so in French, the place became known as *Le morne des Sauteurs*, Leaper's Hill.

Towards the northeastern point of the island is **Levera Bay**, a strip of white sand with fine views of the offshore islands. Nearby is Levera Lake, like Lake Antoine to the south, an extinct volcanic crater and at Bedford Point itself are the ruins of an old fort.

The South Coast
With its pristine beaches so close to St George's, the southwestern tip of Grenada is the hotel heartland. The countryside is flatter than the island interior and most of Grenada's sugar was grown here. The southern coastline is a long succession of deep bays and promontories, where many wealthy Grenadians have chosen to build their homes and cruising yachts put in for shelter. Farther east the coast becomes remoter, but judging by the names it has a romantic history *Morne Delice, Mamma Cannes, Perdmontemps*, and *Après tout*.

A couple of miles south of the town, **Grand Anse** is the most popular beach on the island. It is about two miles of blinding white satin sand. A number of hotels front on to the beach, but it does not usually get too crowded. Farther round the point are a number of small bays, pleasant and secluded, though the peace will occasionally be interrupted by planes passing overhead as they come in to Point Salines airport at the southwestern tip of the island.

Just along the southern coast is another popular bay, once called Prickly Bay by the English, but now usually known by its French equivalent, *L'Anse aux Epines*. It has some fine hotels and apartments, spread out on the thin strip of sand and on the clifftops. Visible out to sea south of Grenada is Glover Island, operated as a whaling station in 1925 by the Norwegians.

Calvigny Point was the site of the main camp of the People's Revolutionary Army in the time of Maurice Bishop, and the area saw considerable military activity during the American invasion. Beyond the charming fishing village of Woburn, **Fort Jeudy**, now an expensive housing estate, speaks of earlier conflicts, when a fort used to guard the entrance to Egmont Harbour. Not much farther on, at Westerhall, is the **Westerhall Rum Distillery**. Also close by is the isolated **La Sagesse Nature Centre**, set on its own huge bay. There are trails and guides to help you explore the countryside around here.

The coast road winds through the former plantations and past secluded beaches such as **Bacolet Bay** until it reaches **Marquis**, just south of Grenville. This settlement was the first target in Fédon's rebellion, where the English inhabitants were dragged from their beds and killed.

Over the Grand Etang to the East Coast

To a Grenadian 'over the Grand Etang' means going over the mountains and through the centre of the island, more roads that wind and switchback as they climb steadily into Grenada's staggeringly lush interior, mountains dressed in elfin woodland, valleys planted with cocoa trees, which come aflame in the early months of the year when the *immortelle* trees are in full orange bloom, and with the yellow of the *Yellow Poui* tree. The best road to take from St George's goes along the St John's River, past the race course in Queen's Park, but it is possible to go via Government House and left at the roundabout, from where the road climbs to the oddly named Snug Corner and eventually to the Grand Etang itself. Remember to look behind as you climb for some of the island's most spectacular views, as far as Point Salines in the southwest.

Just off the road are **Annandale Falls**, a 30-foot cascade (only really impressive in the rainy season) that races into a bathing pool, surrounded in tropical greenery. The valley was the scene of considerable fighting in the recent invasion.

At the summit of the range is the **Grand Etang** (Big Pond), another extinct volcano crater. Set in a Government Reserve, its water is cold and metallic blue (estimates of its depth vary from 14 feet to fathomless). There is a small **museum** nearby, once a government-run rest house and occupied by the PRG as an army barracks until 1983, where the Caribbean's geological past is clearly described: two chains of volcanic islands created by the shifting of the Atlantic and Caribbean tectonic plates. There are also short walking tours around the Grand Etang and into the rainforest in the mountains, where you will see explosions of bamboo, tree-top ferns and creeping vines. You might also see birds like Grenada's hummingbirds, tanagers and the occasional cuckoo, as well as armadillos and opossums. Open Mon–Sat, 8–4, adm free.

Some way off is **Morne Fédon**, also called Mt Qua Qua. Much of the fighting in the 1795 rebellion led by Fédon, who owned the estate at Belvidere just below the mountain, took place in this area. The mountain stronghold was situated on the three spurs of the peak, each named after one of their slogans, *Champ la Liberté, Champ l'Egalité* and *Champ la Mort*. It is a couple of hours' hike to get there.

Descending into the windward side of Grenada the road passes among tiny villages clinging to the hillsides down to the cocoa receiving station at Carlton, where the beans are processed and prepared for shipment. A short walk off the road in St Margaret's you will find the Seven Sisters Falls, worth a detour for a swim, though you should ask permission to walk over the private land. Eventually coming to the coast at **Grenville**, in a large bay sheltered by reefs. It is still referred to as la Baye, as it is known in French. There are a few solid stone structures that speak of its former position of importance, the 'second city' to St George's. The countryside is known as Grenada's *lifeblood*, the island's breadbasket and is dotted with plantation houses. In the town itself, the covered market and fish market are the centres of town activity and graceful Grenadian sloops can often be seen at the waterfront, calling in on their trips between the Grenadines and Trinidad. There is also a nutmeg factory in Grenville that is worth a visit (see Gouyave, p 108).

Just north of the town is the old airport at Pearls, closed when the controversial airport at Point Salines was opened in 1984. This area was once inhabited by Arawak Indians and their pottery is still being dug up, mostly pots decorated with animal faces that were handles. Children might offer these ghostly little faces to you, but it is illegal to take them out of the country.

A little farther north is the **River Antoine Rum Distillery**, on a plantation dating from the 18th century, complete with crushing gear still driven by a water wheel. You can also sample the fearsome rum they produce. Lake Antoine is the crater of a volcano reckoned to be extinct, though underground forces are still at work just beyond here, at the mineral springs, which emit wisps of sulphurous gas from hot springs.

Morne Fendue

On the road to the north-coast town of Sauteurs is one of Grenada's most charming spots, Betty Mascoll's **Morne Fendue**, an old plantation house full of family memorabilia. It is an enchanting place to visit. Nutmeg shells laid out on the drive give off a heady smell of spice as you drive up. There are three rooms for rent, but it is best known for its lunch, traditional Caribbean callaloo and island specialities, taken on the veranda with fine views of the Grenadian landscape.

FESTIVALS

Carnival in Grenada is celebrated in August rather than at the beginning of Lent, but it is still three days of dancing in the street with carnival parades and calypsonians. If you would like to 'play mas' (ie buy a costume and shuffle-step with the parades), contact the Tourist Boards for the name of a band. They also have a *jump-up* on the anniversary of Independence Day, 7 February.

If you are in the area in August, make sure you go over to Carriacou for the **Sailing Regatta**, a week of drinking and dancing, with sailing events for local boats but which also have some outside entrants, as well as onlookers from the world over.

WHERE TO STAY
Grenada is a good place to visit at the moment, for prices and for the island itself. The island has certainly been opened up by Point Salines airport, whatever its other uses might have been. For a while over the revolution period the tourist trade dropped off, but now it is bounding along, the international pastel revolution has come instead, all airco, jacuzzis and satellite televisions. All hotels have to charge an 8% government tax on the bill and most will also add 10% service as well.

There are few hotels outside St George's and the southwestern corner of the island, though it is possible to find cheap guest house accommodation around the island. The tourist board publications have a listing of the most off-beat spots. There are a number of villas for rental on the island, some of which are administered by **Grenada Realtors Limited**, PO Box 124, St George's (tel 444 4255).

The **Spice Island Inn**, PO Box 6, St George's (tel 444 4258, fax 444 4807) has 56 suites, each with their own whirlpool and a view over Grand Anse Beach towards St George's and the mountains beyond. Smooth Caribbean luxury in high pastel, jacuzzi and champagne. Expensive at US$300–400 a double in season. **Secret Harbour**, PO Box 11 (tel 444 4548, fax 444 4819, US 800 334 2435), lives up to its name; it is a reclusive string of villas overlooking Mt Hartman Bay at L'Anse aux Epines. There is a view through the arches from your four-poster and low-key luxury in the main house, where the vaulted brick is inlaid with mosaics and topped with terracotta tiles, like a Spanish colonial palace above the harbour. The beach is uninspiring, but all watersports are available through the Moorings next door. No children. Double room US$200. You can tailor-make sailing trips to the Grenadines with a stay in the hotel. **Twelve Degrees North**, PO Box 241, on L'Anse aux Epines Bay (tel 444 4580, fax 444 4580), is an extremely fine getaway, a collection of one- and two-bedroom apartments on the clifftops above the beach. So named because it lies exactly 12 degrees north of the equator, it takes a maximum of 20 people, children not allowed. There is a pool and palm-thatch honour bar, with stunning sunset views. All with maid service, one-bedroom apartments go for US$150 per night in winter and a two-bedroom apartment for US$200 in winter. The **Calabash** Hotel, PO Box 382 (tel 444 4334, fax 444 4804) is a charming and friendly hotel at the head of L'Anse aux Epines bay. The 28 breezy suites are set in an arc around the lawn of coconut palms and calabash trees running down to the beach. The dining area is open to the air, screened by creeping plants and primitive paintings. winter rooms, full meal plan only, cost US$250 and in summer they are $120, with good deals for children.

If you like a big plush resort which is brisk and active with plenty of sports, try the **Ramada Renaissance**, PO Box 441 (tel 444 4371, fax 444 4800), which is set in a manicured garden at the St George's end of Grand Anse beach. A double room costs US$185 in season.

The **Flamboyant Hotel** (tel 444 4247, fax 444 1234) at the far end of Grand Anse beach is a mixture of old-time West Indian villas (fans and wooden floors) with the more recent Caribbean (rooms in blocks). All view St George's in the distance and although all are comfortable the older rooms are preferable. US$105 for the suites, $85 the rooms.

111

INEXPENSIVE
In the north of the island is **Morne Fendue**, also known as Betty Mascoll's Plantation House. The setting is one of former plantation splendour, a family home presided over by Betty Mascoll herself, the extremely knowledgeable and charming hostess. There are only three rooms, though there are always plenty of people passing by for the renowned Morne Fendue lunch. A double room starts at US$65, year round. At **La Sagesse Nature Centre**, PO Box 44 (tel 444 6458, fax 444 4847), in the remote southeastern corner of the island, you can escape to the quiet of a banana estate and a charming bay enclosed by massive headlands. Just three rooms, at US$70 a night in winter. Grenada's best view for breakfast, with the morning light setting the red roofs of St George's aglow, is from the balcony of the **Hotel Balisier**, PO Box 335 (tel 440 2346), on Richmond Hill high above St George's, a local West Indian inn. Built on the battlements of a fort, it is quiet and decorated with West Indian scenes painted by the owner. If the hill is too steep to make it up there every night (double rooms with a view are US$105 in season, and US$65 in summer), do not miss an evening cocktail there as the sun goes down over St George's harbour mouth.

Guest Houses
Above the Lagoon, with a view across the water to the Carenage, there is **Mamma's Lodge**, Box 248, Lagoon Rd, Belmont (tel 440 1459), the modern West Indies at its most plush and airco. Patronised mostly by West Indians themselves, the ten rooms are luxurious (deep pile wallpaper and carpets) and go for US$35 per night for a double all year round. The **Windward Sands Inn** (tel 444 4238) has nine rooms and is just a short walk from Grand Anse Beach, as is **Roydon's**. Both simple but comfortable rooms, US$60. There are one or two guest houses in St George's, including **Mitchell's Guest House** (tel 440 2803) on Tyrell St and **Simeon Inn** (tel 440 2537) on Green St higher up, simple rooms, both about US$20.

EATING OUT
It might be that the Grenadians have retained their flair for cooking from the days when the French owned the island. At any rate, the abundance of island produce makes Grenada a good place for classic West Indian fare; callaloo, breadfruit, christophene and green fig, as well as the more exotic *tatou* (armadillo) and *manicou* (opossum). There is 'international fare' on offer, often in hotels, for those who feel too far from home in the West Indies, but Grenada has some charming and inexpensive restaurants, some of which are in the more 'local' hotels. Expect a service charge of 10% plus 8% VAT to be added to your bill.

EXPENSIVE
At **Canboulay** (tel 444 4401) on Morne Rouge, the hill behind Grand Anse beach, the theme of Caribbean carnival runs through the whole restaurant—in masks and the strong colours (peach, turquoise and Caribbean green) and in the names of the dishes (*jab jab* and *moko jumbie*, a shrimp on stilts). Adventurous combinations of European dishes and local ingredients; for example breadfruit vichyssoise and callaloo in a crêpe. Five courses for EC$80, closed Mon. **La Belle Créole** (tel 444 4316) is set on a breezy veranda at Grand Anse, at the Blue Horizons Cottage Hotel. Twenty quiet tables between the arches with fans whirring overhead and fine West Indian fare in a menu that

varies nightly; okra soup (with an inimitable texture of velvet stringiness), cream of breadnut soup. Full meal for EC$80 plus taxes. Down on the waterfront at the head of Grand Anse beach is **Coconuts** beach restaurant (tel 444 4644). Eye the sunset with a rum punch or listen to the shrill night air that accompanies a creole menu with a French Caribbean lilt. Main dish EC$35 plus. Also on the water, but in L'Anse aux Epines, is the **The Boatyard** (tel 444 4662) set in an open veranda overlooking the water. International menu, local catch, creole and burgers, EC$30.

MODERATE
A classic West Indian setting, and traditional local fare, can be found at **Mamma's** (tel 440 1459), on Lagoon Road, going south out of town. Sadly the inspirational Mamma has died, but her daughter has taken over. The Special (the only order) brings a compendium of local dishes, from oildown (four or five vegetables boiled in coconut milk), to yam, breadfruit, turtle, booby (a local seabird) and fish broth (one of a number of local aphrodisiacs). Specials EC$45. **Tropicana**, on the way into town, is set on a veranda lit up with fairy lights. The menu is local and Chinese, main dish EC$10–40. You can also get a local meal or a seafood platter for lunch at a good price at the **Cactus Seafood Grill** at Point Salines. There are plenty of local restaurants around the town for lunch or a simple dinner. **Rudolf's** collects a local crowd; pub-style benches and an egg-box ceiling, steaks, seafood and omelettes, EC$15–50. **Nutmeg** (tel 440 2539) is an upstairs lounge with a fine view of the Carenage. Nutmeg callaloo and club sandwiches, EC$15–40.

BARS AND NIGHTLIFE
Most of the hotels and restaurants have bars, but straw-haired beach bums and medical students collect at the **Green Parrot Café** in Grand Anse–walkways over the lily-ponds to islands where you sit under bamboo shelters. Simple meals but a young and lively bar. Still one of the best spots on the island is the bar at the hotel **Balisier** where you get a stunning view of the sunset over the town at Happy Hour. There are also plenty of bars in town. **007**, the floating bar on the Carenage, can get quite busy, or you can try the **Hole in the Wall** opposite for a shot of local white rum (Clarke's Court of varying percentage proof). Other rum shops, good also for a Carib beer and a game of dominoes include **Aboo's** on the Carenage, **Ye Olde Farm House**, opposite the Yellow Poui Gallery and **Pitch Pine** on the Esplanade waterfront.

Grenada's main discotheques are the **Sugar Mill** south of Grand Anse and **Fantasia** at BBC beach. The hotels also have live shows and steel bands. If you would like to see the Grenadians jumping up—banks of speakers set out in the street and chicken legs being barbecued on upturned braziers—try Gouyave on a Sunday night.

Carriacou and Petit Martinique

These two inhabited islands lie at the northern limits of Grenadian territory. Strictly speaking, the border with St Vincent slices the top off the two islands, but they have not come to blows recently over it.

Among the smaller uninhabited islands are Les Tantes and the Sisters and one that even calls itself London Bridge. The underwater volcano by the name of Kick 'em Jenny, perhaps a corruption of the French *Cay qui me gêne*, is so called because the water around it is renowned for being very rough (sea-sickness pills advised if you go anywhere near it). LIAT pilots who fly over here have reported seeing movement under the water and the seismic instruments in Trinidad regularly detect it. Many reckon that it is growing slowly as it belches and that another Grenadine might appear eventually.

CARRIACOU

Carriacou is gentle and quiet (just 8 miles by 5), with a population of about 6000. It is mountainous, though not high enough to have the tropical lushness of Grenada itself, but it is bordered with the supreme white-sand beaches of the Grenadines. Tiny islets lie off its shores, nothing more than sand and a few palm trees.

The first settlers of Carriacou (from the Indian Kayryouacou) were French turtlers fishing in the abundant waters or taking the turtles on the island's fine sand beaches as they came to lay their eggs. Soon it was settled as a plantation island, growing mainly cotton, but also supporting two sugar estates that provided the island with rum.

The island is well known for its tradition of boat-building; though few are built any more, the brightly painted sloops with gracefully curved bows were built here. And it is also known for smuggling, something of a Caribbean tradition. Shippers, legal or otherwise, are called *traffickers* hereabouts and they take produce down to Trinidad or Barbados, returning with tinned food, snacks and manufactured goods. Cargoes from Sint Maarten and the other duty-free islands and the odd consignment of whisky and foreign brand cigarettes do occasionally go astray in a cove en route. The islanders usually get a few hours' notice when the coastguard leaves St George's and so the contraband gets hidden away in the hills. The mainstay of the declared economy is agriculture, vegetables sent to market in Grenada and sheep and goats, looking confused, tied up in bags so that only their heads protrude, on their way to market in the other islands.

You will find almost every conceivable alcohol in Carriacou, but the island's special drink is *jackiron*, or the jack, which has the peculiar and disarming quality of making ice sink in it, quite apart from being extremely strong.

The liveliest and most spectacular moment in the Carriacouan calendar is the annual **Regatta**, to which yachts come from all over the world, usually to be beaten by sailors from the next door island of Petit Martinique. There are also celebrations on Independence Day on 7 February and at Carriacou's **Carnival** at the beginning of Lent.

Carriacou schooners
It is fascinating to see the boats being made in **Windward**, on the east coast of the island. Skeletal hulls of cedar steadily take shape, not so many big ships any more, but many smaller boats. The work is done by hand, a tradition supposedly bequeathed by a Scots ancestry of Glaswegian shipwrights. The launching ceremony is a major festivity and well worth a visit if you hear of one. The blood of a goat is sprinkled on the boat as it is blessed and then it is launched, loaded to the gunwales with locals in their Sunday best.

Getting to Carriacou is part of the fun—coasting Grenada's leeward (western) side from St George's gives spectacular views of the fertile slopes that tumble from Mount St

Catherine, and then there is a horizon dotted with the Grenadines. It is possible to go by yacht or by the boats that leave from the Carenage, best of all on one of Carriacou's own graceful schooners (about EC$25). If you are travelling on through the Grenadines, boats head for Union Island on Mon and Thurs, about midday (EC$10 plus departure tax).

Alternatively, go by air and experience Lauriston, one of the Grenadines' gentler airstrips (no mountains to negotiate on approach), though you might be surprised to find that the island's main road runs diagonally across the middle of it.

Carriacou is rimmed with fine white **beaches**, many of which will be deserted. Look to the west coast, or on a still day try the windward (east) coast. The best find of all is **Anse la Roche**, off the track north from Bogles. Getting there is half the fun and is something like a treasure hunt. On the track north from Bogles look for a gnarled tree leaning over the road; turn left down to a dried pond and a ruin; then down the hill at a black rock which you recognize because it usually has a conch shell perched on the top. It is an idyllic cove. Round the northern point is another superb beach in Windward Bay. Beyond the airport is a fine deserted strip called **L'Esterre** and on the south side of the island there is a good harbour at **Tyrrel Bay** and strips of sand which make for good sunbathing.

It is fun to take a trip to one of the sandbars in Hillsborough Bay, tiny islets with just a few palms: **Mabouya** (from the Indian for evil spirits), **Jack A Dan**, whose name is a mystery, and **Sandy Island**, often indistinguishable in the haze, which is sadly silting away at the moment. A boat can be hired from the jetty.

There is a **scuba** dive shop on the island, at the Silver Beach Resort. The operator Tanky will take you to Pagoda City, to the caves at Kick 'em Jenny or to loiter among a school of barracuda. Novice instruction available (tel/fax 443 7882). For a **sailing** trip ask at the hotels or contact Dave at the Blue House behind the Fish Centre in Windward.

Stretched along the seafront, **Hillsborough** is the only settlement that constitutes a town. The centre of activity is the jetty, which comes alive on a Monday when the boats bring mail and provisions. The two streets contain all the island's official buildings (including immigration if you come by boat) and banks. There is a museum, with a display of Carib history and even a small botanical garden, now in disrepair, where huge palms tower over the walkways.

Above the town is the great house of **Belair**, with its windmill tower, from where the view stretches both ways along the chain of the Grenadines, south to Grenada and as far as St Vincent in the north. The area was also used by the PRG as their principal army base during their tenure in the early 1980s. An island tour can be fixed up through Carriacou Tours (tel 443 7134) US$6.

PETIT MARTINIQUE

The 600 inhabitants of this tiny island, lying about three miles east of Carriacou, are also fishermen and boat-builders, reputedly even more closely involved in smuggling than their neighbours. When a customs officer tried to land there once they threw him off. Their island is called so because, like the island of Martinique, there are snakes. It is said that rival colonies would introduce snakes on to other islands to make life more difficult for the settlers.

Not surprisingly, the islanders are fiercely independent. There are boats on Mon, Wed (the doctor's trip) and Fri. Otherwise you can hire a boat in Windward.

WHERE TO STAY AND EAT
The **Caribbee Inn** (tel 443 7380, fax 443 7999) at Prospect towards the northern end of Carriacou is one of the Caribbean's gems. The setting is the old West Indies—four poster beds, muslin nets, ceiling fans that whip the sea breezes through louvred windows and a magnificent view of Hillsborough Bay. Just ten rooms. Personable, with an honour bar and a fine kitchen preparing local ingredients in French and creole style—local catch court bouillon and plantain. Suite US$120, room US$90 in winter. The **Silver Beach Resort** (tel 443 7337), on the sand in Hillsborough bay, has a faded beach club feel about it. The 18 rooms are in garden cottages and a block, just out of the town to the north. Some watersports, double room US$75–100. **Cassada Bay Resort** (tel 443 7494, fax 443 7672) is remote and the breezy wooden cabanas are perched on the hillside, with superb views through the southern Grenadines to Grenada fifteen miles away. 16 rooms, US$90–120. There are some cheaper places to stay in Hillsborough, in modern concrete villas: **Ade's Dream House** (tel 443 7733) has seven rooms and a slightly chaotic feel, set above a rum shop, US$20. Simpler yet is the **Traveller's Inn**, straight inland from the pier, also above a rum shop, US$15. In **Petit Martinique** you can stay at the **Sea Side View Holiday Cottages** (tel 443 9210), just four rooms overlooking the island of Petit St Vincent and the Grenadines. Simple and low key, EC$55 per person.

There are a number of **restaurants** outside the hotels in Carriacou. In Hillsborough itself, try **Callaloo** (tel 443 8004) for a garlic butter grilled fish and sailing scenes painted on calabashes, EC$30 a main course. The **Roof Gardens** or **Paradise Store** will serve you local rice 'n peas or a roti to go for EC$15.

There are a couple of restaurants in Tyrrel Bay, where most yachts put in. The **Pizzeria Aquilana** (tel 443 7197, VHF channel 16, 68) offers pizzas—lambi, rasta, *capriciosa* and other Italian dishes, EC$12–20. Also with a veranda view of the yachts in harbour is the **Oystershell** (channel 16). Chicken or fish, lobster and lambi, EC$20–25. **Turtle Dove** (tel 443 7194), up the hill in Hermitage will fix you a good West Indian chicken or fish, or coo-coo, EC$30.

On the beachfront in Tyrrell Bay are a couple of palm thatch lean-tos where you can sit with a rum punch and watch for the Green Flash. Finally there is one of the coolest and most unlikely bars in the islands on the waterfront in Hillsborough. The **Hillsborough Bar** looks like an English pub and disco (it was built by two lads from Birmingham). Plenty of drinking, occasional dancing and a weekly film viewing night.

ST VINCENT and THE GRENADINES

Today, a sailor's paradise, once St Vincent and the Grenadines was the heartland of Indian resistance to the domineering European powers and red-painted Caribs would ply between the islands in their war canoes. Now more peaceful craft cruise the waters of the Grenadines, 30 island havens strung out over 60 miles, a short hop by yacht from one to the next.

In the north, St Vincent stands in the sea like a massive cut emerald with facets of lush forested slopes stacked irregularly, rising to the central mountain range of Morne Garu. At 18 miles by 11, this fertile island is the smallest link in the Windward Islands. It is dominated by the mighty Soufrière, a distinctly active volcano, which last blew in 1979, showering the island with ash adding yet more fertilizer to the rich land. A pencil could take root in the deep brown earth of the Mesopotamia Valley and in Kingstown are the oldest botanical gardens in the Americas, 20 acres of spectacular tropical abundance of scarlet, yellow and purple blooms.

Many of the 108,000 islanders live a simple life depending on the land or the sea. With little industry, there is high unemployment and agriculture is still the economic mainstay. The principal exports are bananas, coconut products and arrowroot, a starch once used by the Indians as an antidote to poisoned arrows and now used in biscuits and computer paper. Fruit and vegetables are sent to nearby Barbados, where there is a greater market as much of its agricultural land is planted with sugar.

St Vincent itself is still relatively undeveloped: there are not too many tourists and it is as yet unscarred by the high-rise concrete monstrosities of mass development. Some of the Grenadines depend on tourism, though, and an hour's sail will take you from simple island life to the most expensive island luxury. In centuries past, the Grenadines would be leased out for 100 years on West Indian charters and turned into plantations. Nowadays, developers lease them to create some of the most exclusive resorts in the world.

The tropical island idyll is perfected here, seclusion with a view over dazzling white sand to islands that fade to grey on the horizon. You can be so isolated that you have to communicate by flag. Two hundred years ago the message might have been 'Bear to leeward, danger, reefs'. Now, with room service just at hand to pamper you, you are more likely to string up: 'Orange juice, coffee and croissants' or 'We do not want to be disturbed'.

History

With little strategic value, inhospitable St Vincent was given a wide berth by the early European visitors. *Hairoun* was wild even among the *Cannibal Isles*. It was a Carib stronghold, and Europeans would all too often be confronted by a shower of arrows and the barbecue spit. As the Europeans picked off the other islands in their quest for empire, St Vincent became a sanctuary for the Caribs, left as a European no-man's-land as late as 1750, where the Carib race could live out the last of their days.

St Vincent also became a refuge for slaves, who first arrived in 1675, when a slave-ship was wrecked off Bequia, and as word got out, escaping Africans made their way over from St Lucia, Grenada and Barbados to join them. The slaves would cast off on rafts and drift 100 miles with the wind in a desperate bid for freedom.

The Africans mixed with the local Indians, the *Yellow Caribs*, to create a 'tall and stout' race known as the *Black Caribs*. This fierce new tribe took over the resistance to the European colonizers and eventually dominated the original Yellow Caribs, taking their land. Faced with extinction at the hands of their cousins, the Yellow Caribs promptly invited the French to settle St Vincent in 1719.

The French settlers brought African slaves to work plantations. Fearing for their freedom, the Black Caribs retreated to the hills, where they distinguished themselves from the newcomers with bands around their calves and upper arms and by deforming their babies' skulls in old Carib style with tightly bound slats of wood, giving them sloping foreheads.

The Black Caribs kept the colonizers at bay for another 50 years. In the Treaty of Aix-la-Chapelle in 1748, St Vincent was too hot to handle and so officially it was left neutral, with an unwritten clause that the European powers would fight over it later. By 1763 it was British. The new owners wanted the Black Carib land for their plantations and so they went in and took it in the First Carib War.

But soon afterwards the French were in control. They came in three sloops of war in 1779, unchallenged by the merchants of St Vincent, who were wide-eyed at the opportunity of trade. The soldiers were all at work on the Governor's plantation up north and the key to the battery was lost in any case, so the invaders just landed and took the place over. In moments the island had surrendered.

Four years later the British were back, and they were faced with another Black Carib uprising in the 1790s in the Second Carib War, or *Brigands' War*, whipped up by the revolutionary Victor Hugues in Guadeloupe. Duvallé, a violent leader, swept down the east coast, burning the plantations and killing the British planters by passing them through the crushing gear in the sugar-mills. On the west coast the overall chief, Chatoyer (also Chattawar), spared them the destruction, save a single sideboard which he sliced with his cutlass to show his intentions. Their armies came together like pincers in the south and they fortified themselves on the hills above Kingstown.

Chatoyer was killed in combat with the Militia Colonel Alexander Leith as Dorsetshire Hill was stormed. On his body was found a silver gorget, a present from Prince William, later King William IV, who had met him on a visit to the West Indies in the ship *Pegasus*. Chatoyer had dreamed of forging an island home for the Black Caribs, but his dreams died with him.

For a year the Black Caribs held on, attacking the British from the heights and slinking back into the jungle, but eventually, in 1797, General Abercromby gained the upper hand and threatened them with surrender or extinction. He razed their settlements and destroyed their crops, and 5000 gave themselves up. They were deported to Roatan Island in the Bay of Honduras (their descendants can still be found there, a thriving community). The Caribs living in the north of the island today are descended mainly from the few Yellow Caribs to survive the wars, forced to the north coast as the settlers took their fertile land.

With the cannon silenced and the colonial map fixed in the early 1800s, St Vincent ended up in British hands and became another quiet agricultural island, growing sugar, Sea Island cotton and arrowroot, of which they held a large share of the world market.

Governed as part of the colony of the Windward Islands, St Vincent and the Grenadines became an Associated State of Britain in 1969 and then took its Independence on 27 October 1979, remaining within the Commonwealth. Today the country is led by the Bequian Prime Minister James Mitchell and the New Democrats Party, elected in 1984 and returned to power in 1989. His party holds all 15 seats.

Flora and Fauna

St Vincent is extraordinarily fertile and if you visit the upper valleys you will find a whole new world of explosive tropical vegetation. Close to Kingstown is the Mesopotamia (Marriaqua) Valley, where you will see all the produce growing that later makes its way to market. You will see hummingbirds and tropical mockingbirds among the heliconias and anthuriums in the Montreal Gardens at the top of the valley.

Another fertile area is Buccament Valley, inland from Layou on the west coast, where vast forests of bamboo rise to 60 feet and the rainforest begins, an infestation of creeping vines and lianas that clamber over gommier and mahogany trees. There are trails in the Vermont area and it is here that you have the best chance of spotting the endangered St Vincent parrot (*Amazona Guildingii*) around dawn. Unique to the island, it has a white and yellow head, a tawny brown body with blue wing-tips and a tail of green, blue and yellow. The female is more colourful than the male and usually lays two eggs. There are thought to be only about 450–500 of these protected birds left.

In the north of the island is the Soufrière, where the vegetation is different again, as rainforest gives way on the heights to elfin woodland, home to the rufous-throated solitaire.

GETTING TO ST VINCENT AND THE GRENADINES
There are no direct flights from outside the Caribbean to St Vincent and the Grenadines and so most visitors arrive via Barbados, where there is a special transit desk for passengers bound for the islands, or via St Lucia or Grenada. LIAT fly between St Vincent and Grenada, calling in at Bequia, Mustique, Canouan, Union Island and Carriacou. Air Martinique serves Mustique and Union Island twice a day and Mustique Airways flies to Mustique from Barbados and St Vincent. Light planes can also be chartered in the other islands, through **St Vincent and the Grenadine Air** (tel 456 9334). There are **ports of entry** at Kingstown, Arnos Vale airport and Wallilabou bay in the northeast and in the Grenadines you can register in Bequia and Union Island. There is a departure tax of EC$15.

GETTING AROUND ST VINCENT
The south coast of St Vincent and the major valleys are well served with **dollar-buses**, always a lively and crowded part of Vincentian life. You get to know your fellow passengers pretty well. The buses are cheap to travel and they each have a name on their bonnet: *Borderclash, Conquering Lion, Ragamuffin, Road Runner* and *Jah Guide Everytime* and *Stay Cool Behind*. Buses can usually be waved down along the route with a downward pointing finger and an expectant face. To be dropped off you must shout *DRIVER! STOP!*, usually to the hilarity of the other passengers. Buses leave from the new terminal on the Kingstown waterfront.

Buses on the coastal roads are sporadic so it is best to leave plenty of time to get there and back, but they run to **Villa** until as late as 11 pm. Some fares are: **Kingstown** to Villa (Aquatic Club)—EC$1.50, Mesopotamia—$2.50, Georgetown—$4 and to Layou—$2 and Wallilabou—$3.

Taxis are of course readily available, at a rate fixed by the St Vincent Government of EC$35 per hour. They can be arranged from hotels or found in the Market Square.

119

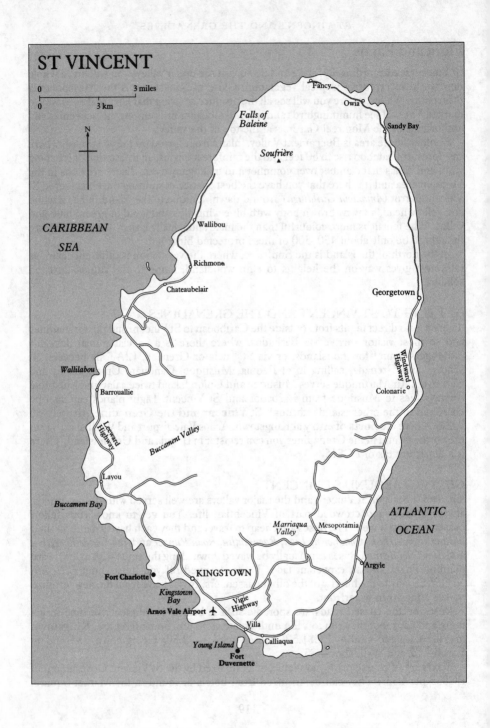

ST VINCENT

0 ——————————— 3 miles
0 ——————————— 3 km

N

*Falls of
Baleine*

Fancy
Owia
Sandy Bay

Soufrière ▲

*CARIBBEAN
SEA*

Wallibou

Richmond

Chateaubelair

Georgetown

Wallilabou

Barrouallie

*Leeward
Highway*

Buccament Valley

Colonarie

*Windward
Highway*

Layou

Buccament Bay

*Marriaqua
Valley*

Mesopotamia

*ATLANTIC
OCEAN*

Fort Charlotte
KINGSTOWN

Argyle

*Kingstown
Bay*
Arnos Vale Airport ✈

Vigie
Highway

Villa

Young Island
Fort
Duvernette

Calliaqua

Kingstown to the airport—EC$15, to Villa—$20, Mesopotamia—$35 and George-
town—$70, to Fort Charlotte—$10, Layou—$35. From Arnos Vale airport to the
Villa/Young Island area costs EC$20.

To drive a **hire car** in St Vincent you need to purchase a local driver's licence, price
EC$10 (on production of a valid licence from home) from the Licensing Authority on
Halifax Street. Cars can be hired at a daily rate of about US$40 from: **Lucky Car
Rentals Ltd** in Kingstown (tel 62422), **Kim's Rentals Ltd** (tel 61884) and **Sunshine
Rentals** (tel 65380) in Arnos Vale. Driving is on the left and if you get lost do not hesitate
to stop a Vincentian and ask for directions.

TOURIST INFORMATION
In **Britain** the St Vincent and the Grenadines Tourist Office is at 10 Kensington Court,
London W8 5DL (tel 071 937 6570, fax 937 3611) and in the **USA** 801 Second Ave,
New York, NY 10017, (tel 212 687 4981, fax 949 5946, US 800 729 1726). In **Canada**
they can be contacted at: Suite 504, 100 University Ave, Toronto, Ontario, Canada M5J
1V6 (tel 416 971 9666, fax 971 9667).

The main Tourist Office on the islands is on Egmont Street in Kingstown (tel 457
1502), and there is a Tourist Information desk at **ET Joshua airport** in Arnos Vale (tel
458 4685). For those making connecting flights via Barbados, there is the **St Vincent
and the Grenadines Desk** at the Barbados International Airport, (tel 428 0961) open
from 1 pm until the last flight of the day bound for St Vincent has left.

The Tourist Board put out a magazine, the **Visitor's Guide**, with useful information
(including ferry timings to the Grenadines) and current standard prices for taxis, etc.

If you have a medical **emergency**, contact the General Hospital in Kingstown (tel 456
1185). The **IDD code** for St Vincent and the Grenadines is 809, and this is followed by a
seven-digit local number, usually beginning with 456/7/8. At the time of publication you
need only dial five digits when on-island, but it is expected to change to the full seven.

MONEY
The currency of St Vincent and the Grenadines is the Eastern Caribbean dollar
(EC$2.69 = US$1), but the US dollar and traveller's cheques are widely used in tourist
restaurants and hotels. Major credit cards are also accepted in the tourist centres. Be
sure which currency you are dealing in, for example in taxis. For the best exchange rate
banks are open 8–1, Mon–Thur, with extended hours on Friday afternoon until 5pm.
For those passing through the island on their way to the Grenadines, there is an Bureau
de Change at ET Joshua Airport, open daily except Sun until 5pm. **Shops** open 8–noon,
1pm–4pm, Sat 8–noon.

BEACHES
Steep-sided and volcanic, St Vincent has mainly black sand beaches, except in the south
where the coast slopes more gently out towards the Grenadine Islands and where the
wave action on the coral reefs pushes up whiter sand. The liveliest beaches on St Vincent
are in the south, close to Kingstown at **Indian Bay, Villa** and at **Blue Lagoon**. These
thin strips of sand are both popular among the Vincentians at weekends and have bars to
retreat to nearby after a hard day's lying about in the sun.

The east coast, with the big breakers coming in from the Atlantic, is quite rough and so for seclusion and the afternoon sun it is best to go to the leeward coast with its sheltered bays with black sand and fishing villages. The nicest bays among them are **Peter's Hope** and **Kearton's Bay** near Barroualie; also **Buccament Bay** and **Richmond** at the limit of the Leeward Highway. Consider taking a picnic, though it is possible to buy a drink and a snack in the villages along the coast.

BEACH BARS

Beachcombers is just along from Villa, a timber-frame veranda set back from the beach, where you can get a drink and a grill pizza or a lime pie. Most of the restaurants at **Villa** are open during the day for light meals and drinks. Way up the leeward coast you will find the **Anchorage** bar in Wallilabou Bay, a waterfront terrace overlooking the bay and overshadowed by massive headlands.

SPORTS

St Vincent is not that developed, but you can find most **watersports** on Villa Beach or at Blue Lagoon. You can hire a **windsurfer** (about US$15 per hour) and water-skiing can be arranged from **Villa Beach**, opposite Young Island, where there is very attractive coral within reach of snorkellers. Try **Mariners Watersports**.

Diving can be arranged at **Dive St Vincent** (tel 74174, fax 74948), with trips up the sheltered western side of St Vincent with wrecks, caves and vertical drop-offs from 60 ft. St Vincent is not that well known as a diving destination, but there are some excellent coral reefs on its leeward shores and the fish life of the Grenadines is superb—you will see whole schools of silverfish and graceful pouting angelfish striped with yellow and blue. There is also a dive-shop in Wallilabou, **Carib Divers** (tel 67023, fax 74948), from which you can reach pristine walls and barrel sponges so big you could sit in them. You can arrange a ten-dive roll-over package with these two operators and their counterpart in Union Island, **Grenadines Dive**, particularly useful for sailors.

Sailing

The Grenadines are one of the world's top sailing destinations. The islands look fantastic, yellow or green-grey in the distance against an aquamarine sea and steel blue sky. Dolphins play at the prow of your yacht and schools of gar fish jump up ahead, 20 silver flashes sewing their way through the water. But the big attraction is to moor in a deserted bay where the water is crystal clear and the beach is pristine white and the Grenadines can provide this too.

Charters are available in the Grenadines, bareboats or crewed, for a day, a week or a month. Some companies working out of St Vincent and the Grenadines are: **Barefoot Yacht Charters**, (tel 69334) on Blue Lagoon, beyond Calliaqua on the south coast and **Mariners Watersports and Yacht Charters Ltd**, PO Box 639 (tel 458 4228). Both these companies will arrange day trips through the Grenadine Islands. It is advisable to book well in advance for the winter season, but in the summer you will just be asked to prove that you can sail.

Walking and Hiking

Walking in St Vincent's fertile country is a pleasure, enjoyed by visitors for more than 200 years. It is an adventurous three-hour hike up through seasonal forest, rainforest, and elfin and montane woodland to the lip of the **Soufrière**, from where there is a cracking view of the steaming crater and across the island.

If a 4000ft climb seems daunting, there are other trails beyond the water station at the head of **Buccament Valley**, past the casino at Peniston, off the Leeward Highway, where there is a chance of seeing the St Vincent parrot.

The lush mountainsides of St Vincent are cut with tumbling and racing streams, perfect for a walk through the forest and a dip. The most spectacular are the **Falls of Baleine** in the north of the island (these must be approached by sea and there are plenty of operators who will take you there), but others can be found at Trinity, up from Wallilabou and inland from here at Hermitage. On the Windward coast there is good walking around Colonaire and there are rockpools which make for good swimming in the South Rivers Valley, unless of course somebody has got there before you to do their washing or to take a bath. **Paradise Tours** (tel 85417) run inland trips to climb the Soufrière, parrot-spotting in Vermont and a view of petroglyphs.

Kingstown

The capital of St Vincent is set on the mile-wide sweep of Kingstown Bay at the southwest corner of the island. A town of about 25,000, it is surrounded by a ring of steep ridges spiked with palm trees, running from Cane Garden Point in the south to Berkshire Hill, where Fort Charlotte commands a magnificent view of the 60-mile string of the Grenadines. Downtown in quaint cobbled streets, modern glass-fronted shops stand out among the faded grandeur of old stone warehouses in the business centre. Vaulted walkways keep off the rain, the arches supporting the wooden upper storeys of the houses and sharply sloping tin roofs, all strung together by a profusion of telephone wires.

On the higher ground of Kingstown Vale stand the old colonial houses, once majestic in their open tropical gardens. Now they are jostled for space as the Kingstown suburbs encroach. Overlooking the town from their perches on the heights are the modern houses of today's wealthy Vincentians, some of whom have returned to their island and built homes after working abroad for years.

Down on the waterfront Kingstown is busy; cargoes of tinned food and timber are hauled aboard and stacked under tarpaulin at the **Deep Water Pier** and the **Grenadines Wharf**, where the boats depart for the journey south to the Grenadines. Along the waterfront the modern colossus is the new Government Offices and the National Bank, towering above the town. Beyond them are the bus terminal and the new Fish Market, where men in stained working coats pour out boxes of sprats and slap coloured snappers on the marble slabs.

But the heart of the town is still the **Market Square**, off Halifax Street, where the bustle spills out of the covered market building on to the pavements and the square itself. In the bustle, trays of sweets are thrust under your nose and the market ladies, their skirts rolled up over their knees, remonstrate with buyers, selling their fruits and vegetables from the piles on blankets before them.

Officialdom keeps its distance from all this activity on the other side of Halifax Street, behind the iron railings and the imposing stone façade of the **Law Courts**, where the 15-member St Vincent Parliament meets.

The Kingstown skyline of steep sloping roofs is broken by church towers. **St George's Anglican Cathedral**, a brightly painted Georgian church with a castellated clock-

123

tower, was built in 1820 as the Cathedral of the Anglican diocese of the Windward Islands, partly from government money that came from the sale of Carib lands. The stained-glass window with the red angel was supposedly commissioned by Queen Victoria for St Paul's Cathedral, in honour of her first great grandson (later King Edward VIII), but she rejected it on the grounds that in the Bible the angels were dressed in white. It was given to Bishop Jackson by Dean Inge of St Paul's and he brought it to St Vincent. Inside, a tablet commemorates Major Alexander Leith, a hero of the Brigands' War of 1795, who killed the Carib leader Chattawar.

The most surprising architectural feature of Kingstown is the **Roman Catholic Church**, presbytery and school. Built in 1823 and enlarged in 1877 and 1891, it is a riot of styles in dark brick, a hodge-podge of Romanesque arches and Gothic pointings that would be more at home in deepest medieval Europe.

The St Vincent Botanical Gardens

On the steep slopes facing into Kingstown Valley, just off the road north to Layou, are the **Botanical Gardens**, the oldest in the Americas and one of the delights of the Caribbean. The walkways and lawns are bordered by an overwhelming abundance of tropical splendour: bushes with fluorescent flowers, trees with heavy aromas and palms that soar and sway overhead.

Founded in 1765, the gardens were run commercially in order to propagate useful species from all over the world in the Caribbean, and were connected to the Botanical Gardens at Kew in London. It was to the West Indies that Captain Bligh was headed on his fateful voyage in the *Bounty* in 1787. He was on a commission for the Society of West Indian Merchants to bring the breadfruit tree from the South Seas to St Vincent, where it could be used as food for the slaves on the plantations. Cast adrift with 18 loyal officers by his mutinous crew, he sailed 4000 miles to Timor without the loss of a life.

Six years later, this time in the ship *Providence*, he succeeded in bringing over 400

St Vincent Botanical Gardens

specimens of the breadfruit tree to St Vincent intact, and offshoots of them still grow in the gardens today. Ironically, the slaves would not touch the new food when it first arrived, but nowadays the huge perennial tree, with its lustrous dark green leaves shaped like medieval flames, can be seen all over the Caribbean. The starchy fruit starts life as a small green lollipop and then turns over with the weight, swelling to the size of a cannonball and dropping to the ground with a thud. Boiled and fried, it is a popular supplement to the 20th-century Caribbean diet.

The guides are helpful (basically you will not escape without one). In their jargon they offer an 'educational tour', one worth taking because even if their botanical knowledge is often a little shaky, they do know all the amusing plants to show off, telling stories and crushing leaves for the aroma—cinnamon, citronella, camphor and clove. The gardens are open from the early morning until dusk and there is no admission charge, but depending on the number of people, you might give a guide EC$15 for an hour's tour.

The Gardens are well worth a visit, a fascinating hour even for botanical novices. They are full of gems like the *sandpaper tree*, with leaves as rough as emery paper and the velcro tree, *flambago*, related to flax, to which material sticks. And there is the waterproof *lotus lily*, on which water rolls in beads like mercury (put them underwater and the waterproof pink leaves take on a silver sheen and then come out dry). There is the tree of life, or *lignum vitae*, whose wood is so hard that it was used to replace iron as bearings for propellor shafts, the *sealing-wax* or *lipstick* palm that seeps bright red, *love lies bleeding* and the *mahogany* tree, whose pods explode, releasing a shower of whirling seeds like a sycamore. At sundown, when the white-painted trunks of the palms loom in the obscurity, the flowers of the cannonball tree that open in the day fall to the ground, and the air is heavy with the aroma of jasmine.

Above the Botanical Gardens today is the house of the Governor General and in a pretty West Indian house in the grounds is the **St Vincent Museum**, with fierce and sublime faces in stone and pottery left by the Arawaks and Carib Indians and later artefacts from the Black Carib wars of the 18th century. The chattering and squawking that rings in the gardens comes from the blue-brown St Vincent parrot, of which a few are kept in an aviary, after recovery from illegal hunters. Gardens open dawn–dusk, museum Wed 8–11 and Sat 4–6, adm. The museum also opens on other days if there is a cruise ship in town.

Fort Charlotte

The lumbering giant on the Berkshire Hill promontory is worth a visit if only for the fantastic view north along the leeward coast, on to Kingstown and over the Grenadine Islands scattered to the south. It is a pleasant half-hour walk from town, mostly uphill, and on the way you must pass over **Old Woman's Point**.

'It received its name in the seventeenth century from a virago of Indian birth from Guadeloupe who, having 'tormented her husband to death,' married again within eight days, and repairing to St Vincent spent her honeymoon in a cottage under the point. Tiring of her second husband, she beat out his brains with a conch-shell and then, to escape justice, fled to the territory of the Caribs. There she lived until she aroused the jealousy of the wives of a powerful Carib chief. She then returned to her cottage and remained there until the English erected a battery on the spot, when she retired to the house of a Spanish priest near by.

Here many jovial parties were held, and the gay spirits of Kingstown were wont to visit the house for refreshment and recreation. 'A bottle of wine or rum secured admission.' It was a tradition that the wicked old woman, who lived to a great age, was eventually carried off this earth into the unknown during a terrific hurricane which swept over the island.'

Sir Algernon Aspinall, *Pocket Guide to the West Indies*, 1907

Constructed at the turn of the 19th century and taking its name from George III's queen, Fort Charlotte was once the island's main defence, with barracks for 600 men and 34 cannon. For all this hardware and manpower, the Fort saw action only once, an argument between two men just outside the gates, in which a Private Ballasty killed Major Champion in 1824. The perpetrator was tried and hanged on the same spot.

The Fort stands 630 feet above the sea, and is approached by way of a steep causeway and through an arch. Only three of the cannon remain and the barracks now house a museum of the Carib Wars. It is illustrated with a series of paintings by Lindsay Prescott, picturing the important moments such as the death of the Carib Chief Chatoyer and the deportation of the Black Caribs in 1797. The Fort is open during office hours (roughly speaking); adm.

The South Coast

Leaving Kingstown valley to the east you come to the airport at Arnos Vale. From here the road (the Vigie Highway) leads inland to the **Marriaqua Valley**, usually known as **Mesopotamia** after a town that is spread along the sides of this extraordinarily lush valley. Its steep ground is terraced and the rivers come together at the spectacular Yambou Gorge. Kids play cricket in the road by the pastel-coloured houses perched on the hillsides among a profusion of greens: banana, breadfruit and coconut.

The ridge at the **Vigie** (French for 'look out') gives spectacular views of Kingstown from above. The Carib camp was situated here in the war of 1795–96 and it was fortified with earth-filled sugar hogsheads (cone-shaped stones through which molasses was dripped after boiling). Higher up, lost in the mountains, are the **Montreal Gardens**, with walkways through the tropical foliage, nutmegs and citrus. The gardens specialize in anthuriums, grown here commercially and seen all over the West Indies, with a heart-shaped leaf like a vividly coloured plate and a long thin protrusion.

Following the coastline from ET Joshua airport, the Windward Highway leads past the expensive houses of St Vincent's prime residential area to **Villa Point**, the enclave of tourist hotels and restaurants on St Vincent.

Opposite Villa, a little way out to sea is **Young Island**, one of the Caribbean's best hotels (see Where to Stay). Young Island takes its name from a Governor Young who brought a black charger with him to St Vincent in the 18th century. The horse was admired by a chief of the Black Caribs, whereupon the gallant Sir William Young said, 'It is yours!' The chief took him at his word and rode off on it. Some time later, the Governor was with the Carib chief again on the balcony of Government House in Calliaqua and he admired the island off the coast. Not to be outdone, the Carib, who owned the island, said at once, 'Do you like it? It is yours!'. It has remained Young Island ever since.

The island is private, but a few guests are allowed over when the hotel is not full. Perhaps it is best to go over in the evening for a cocktail. There is a telephone on the dock at Villa Point to call reception.

Fort Duvernette, behind Young Island, is an outcrop of rock that rises a sheer 200 feet out of the water and is covered in dark green vegetation, marked on old maps as *Young's Sugar Loaf.* There are two batteries, still with their ten mortars and cannon from the reigns of George II and George III, covering the southern approaches to St Vincent, though it is now favoured for its beauty than for any strategic significance. A staircase to the heights is cut out of the rock, and is worth the climb for the view across to the Grenadines. Visits can be arranged though the Young Island Hotel.

A little farther along the coast is the quiet town of **Calliaqua**, once St Vincent's capital and the residence of the Governor in Sir William Young's day.

The Windward Highway to Georgetown

The Windward road cuts in from the south coast beyond Calliaqua and emerges on the Atlantic at Argyle. Immediately the sea is rougher, with huge ocean breakers. This fertile sloping land originally belonged to the Carib Indians but the European plantations steadily ate into it. As the road twists along the coastline the skeletons of the old plantation prosperity are just visible; the buildings and aqueducts are disappearing, overwhelmed by the tropical undergrowth. New plantations, acres of bananas and coconuts, can also be seen at every turn of the road.

Inland from Argyle, a short walk off the road to Mesopotamia that passes through the Yambou Gorge, are some **rock carvings**, squiggles and ghostly faces carved by the Arawak Indians, who lived on the island until about AD 1000.

Georgetown, 22 miles and a good hour's drive from Kingstown, was once a prosperous centre, servicing the plantations of the Windward Coast. Now it is an empty town, its buildings run down. Beyond Georgetown, in the shadow of the Soufrière Volcano, the road becomes rougher and four-wheel drive is advised. It crosses the **Rabacca Dry River**, a river course in a rainstorm and the path for lava after a volcanic explosion, and passes into the Orange Hill Estate, at 3200 acres one of the largest coconut plantations in the world. In the villages of **Sandy Bay** and **Fancy** live the descendants of the Yellow Caribs. Even though they have now mixed and have considerable African blood, their Indian heritage of lighter skin and pinched eyes is still clearly visible. There is little employment and the people live mainly on what they produce on the land. Generally, the northern part of the island area is extremely poor, with little hope of improvement.

At **Owia** on the isolated northeastern tip of the island, about an hour beyond Georgetown on the rough roads, is a large pond fed by the sea, but protected from it by a barrier of rocks, a good place to stop for a swim. There is an arrowroot factory in the town which may be visited, adm free.

The Soufrière Volcano
Dominating the whole of the northern end of the island is the St Vincent **Soufrière** Volcano, 3000 ft high and definitely still active, blowing occasionally in a pall of smoke, thunder and flame.

The Soufrière spat fire in 1718 and then blew properly in 1812, spewing into the air ashes and sand that floated down on the island leaving a white covering inches thick like snow. The pall of smoke was illuminated by darting electric flashes and accompanied by violent thunder, an earthquake and a stream of lava overflowing from the boiling crater. The cloud even plunged Barbados, 100 miles away, into darkness.

Then it was quiet for another 90 years until 1902 when it blew again (in tandem with the cataclysmic explosion at St Pierre on Martinique), killing 2000, mostly the descendants of the Caribs living on St Vincent's northern shore. On this occasion it rained stones for miles downwind, bombarding the fleeing Vincentians. The streams ran thick with ash and the noise was so terrible that people thought that the island was sinking.

It was quiet until 1971, when a minor eruption created an island of lava in the crater lake, but on Good Friday, 13 April 1979, the Soufrière blew once more; a vast cloud of ash rose 20,000 feet into the sky, explosive gases boiled over the crater lip and raced down the mountainside, destroying any crops and houses in its way.

Farmers in St Vincent spoke of extraordinary abundance following the eruption— outsize fruits that came out of season because the ash acted as a fertilizer. Now the Soufrière is dormant again and the forest has taken over once more.

The best places to approach it from are the Rabacca Dry River on the east coast, just north of Georgetown, and Richmond, north of Chateaubelair on the leeward coast, which is a gentler climb. It is about three hours' walk to the summit and you are advised to arrange a guide and to take a picnic.

The Leeward Highway to Chateaubelair

The Leeward Highway winds along the west coast of the island, climbing over massive ridges and promontories and dropping into deep coves, good shelters for passing yachtsmen, where small fishing villages of pretty clapboard houses sit on black, volcanic sand beaches. Inland the valleys are steep sided and draped in greenery.

About three miles from Kingstown the road passes the majestic Peniston or Buccament Valley. At the head of the valley there are nature trails that lead up into the depths of the rainforest in the hills. The road rejoins the coast at **Layou**, where there is a petroglyph, Arawak impressions scratched on a 20 ft rock. It can be reached on foot by a ten-minute walk over private land and so visitors should ask permission. The road then passes on to the fishing port of **Barrouallie**, and just off the road not far up river from **Wallilabou**, you will find a fall that pours into a small rockpool, ideal for a midday dip. Ask around for directions.

The road continues through the town of Chateaubelair and eventually comes to an end at **Richmond** where there is an attractive bay and beach with just a few houses.

The Falls of Baleine

In the far north of the island are the **Falls of Baleine**. The river races down through the tropical forest on the slopes of the Soufrière volcano and drops into a rockpool in a 60 ft spray of warm water. Visits are best made by boat which can be an idyllic day out from Kingstown, coasting the leeward side of St Vincent, past all the fishing villages and landing on the northern tip of the island. From there it is a short walk in the river bed to the rockpool and the falls themselves where you can swim. Expect to pay about US$40 for the day's outing, which can be arranged through one of the watersports companies on the south coast (see Sports).

FESTIVALS

Carnival, or **Vincy Mas** as it is called, at the end of June or in early July is the main event in the Vincentian calendar. A month of calypso competitions culminates in *jump-up* in the streets of Kingstown, steel bands and wild pageants of dancers all fired by rum and *Hairoun*, the Vincentian beer.

WHERE TO STAY

For the moment, St Vincent remains relatively undeveloped, untouched by international hotel corporations and their concrete plant. Most of the hotels are owned by the Vincentians themselves and some are set in attractive old-fashioned houses, family homes and the old warehouses of Kingstown, and have the friendly atmosphere of West Indian inns. The island's largest hotel has just 31 rooms. Apart from the few in Kingstown, the hotels are mainly on the white sand beaches of the south coast, where the Vincentians prefer to live. The main centre is at **Villa**, about 15-minutes' ride from Kingstown.

It is possible to live quite cheaply in St Vincent in the guest houses, where the rooms cost under US$40 per night, double or single. There is never a problem finding a room in St Vincent, but you are advised to book ahead for the more exclusive retreats like Young Island and trusted faithfuls on the Grenadines. A 5% government tax will be added to all hotel bills and most hotels charge a 10% service charge on top too.

EXPENSIVE

Two hundred yards off the south coast of St Vincent is **Young Island**, PO Box 211 (tel 458 4826, fax 457 4567), luxury in true Vincentian style and one of the Caribbean's loveliest hotels. 29 cottages of local stone topped with palm thatch roofs are set on the slopes of the tiny island, looking over the white-sand beach to the lush Vincentian coast or to the Grenadines. Each with its own terrace, the rooms are screened with wooden louvres and decorated with dark stained wood and bamboo furniture, ventilated by ceiling fans. The pool meanders among the garden of golden palm and ginger lily (with its distinctive red flower), and small huts with palm thatch look on to the beach. Behind Young Island is Fort Duvernette, where cocktail parties and barbecues are held each week. There is a tennis court on the island and sailing and windsurfing are laid on. For the true tropical island idyll, Vincentian-style, expect to pay US$410–550 for a double room at the peak of the season, decreasing to $240–380 per day in the summer. There are also good 'Lovers Packages' on offer in the low season, but whenever you go do not miss the hammocks on the beach, slung under a palm thatch roof, big enough for two.

MODERATE

The **Sunset Shores Beach Hotel**, PO Box 849 (tel 458 4411, fax 457 4800) looks over to Young Island from the mainland. It is a bit pre-fab, with blocks around a pool, but it is just off the beach and has the facilities of a resort. Low-key and friendly, and quite comfortable, double room in season US$95–130.

Villa itself is a charming stretch of family holiday homes built on the seafront opposite Young Island earlier this century, each similar in style with tall, gently sloping corrugated tin roofs. Most are now restaurants or hotels and the area has a friendly seaside feel. At the far end of the Villa walkway is the **Mariner's Inn**, PO Box 868 (tel 458 4287) which retains some of the old-time feel of the Villa strip in colonial days. There are 20 rooms in the main house and a block, overlooking the hotel's boat bar and the sea. A double room in season costs US$75. Just along from here is the **Umbrella Beach Hotel**, PO Box 530 (tel 458 4651, fax 457 4948) which has a friendly holiday feel. The rooms are self-contained with kitchen and patio, and impeccably priced at US$48 year round. More off the beaten track in style and location is **Petit Byahaut** (tel/fax 457 7008), hidden in a cove on the leeward coast where the emerald water is enclosed by huge headlands. It is accessible only by boat. Rooms are permanent tents with beds, hammocks and showers, ranged on the hillside above the bay. Watersports, including scuba, can be arranged, but if all you want is peace and seclusion, that is there too. US$85 year round.

For those who wish to stay in Kingstown itself, perhaps in order to catch the mail-boat early in the morning to get to an island in the Grenadines, there is a clutch of West Indian inns among the columns and arches and the cobbled streets of the capital. The **Heron Hotel**, PO Box 226 (tel 457 1631), stands in the centre of Kingstown. Once the town house and warehouse of a planter who lived in the north of the island, the Heron Inn has old-fashioned island charm and the 12 rooms are air-conditioned, a double room costing US$60 in winter. Similar in colonial style and West Indian charm is the **Cobblestone Inn**, where rooms cost US$50–70 for a double all year round.

Guest Houses

There are also plenty of guest houses, some set on the heights above the town, in old colonial houses built there for the fine view of the town and harbour. The most attractive is the **Kingstown Park Guest House**, PO Box 41 (tel 456 1532), supposedly built for the French Governor General in the 18th century, a wooden creole mansion with creaking floors and good West Indian cooking in the dining room downstairs. The rate per person per night is about US$15 all year round. There is a homely charm about the **Bella Vista Inn** (tel 487 2757), a friendly West Indian Guest House also in Kingstown Park. Prices for the simple rooms start at US$15 per person in winter, breakfast and dinner available.

EATING OUT

Outside a few top restaurants and hotel dining rooms, Vincentian food is solidly West Indian. Some restaurants will take credit cards, but ask beforehand. As always, restaurants also double as bars and you will find the Villa strip particularly lively. There is a 5% government tax to add to all bills and most restaurants will charge 10% for service.

EXPENSIVE

The food is excellent at the **French Restaurant** (tel 84972), which is set on the waterfront in one of the pretty houses in Villa. You are served on the veranda, a French and Caribbean menu, lobsters picked from the pool in the garden and prepared in cognac or in a crêpe (delicious), or curry de lambi. Finish off with a banana flambéed at the table. It is important to reserve in season, main dish from EC$35.

MODERATE

The **Lime and Pub** (tel 84227) is also on the waterfront at Villa, on a raised platform festooned with greenery and with a tree growing through it. International menu with some seafood. Sea spiny lobster flambéed in Pernod with creole rice, or the original Caribbean crab-back. EC$35–60. Jana's **Dolphin** next door opens daily for dinner. You can sit inside in alcove seats or on the open veranda. Mostly European dishes, but also sesame chicken wings in honey and ginger and buljol, salted codfish marinated in lime and herbs. EC$10–30. **Basil's Too** (tel 84205), after Basil's in town also has an attractive setting on the Villa waterfront. Seafood and continental menu. Try the day's catch cooked in dill or good old Caribbean barbecue chicken. EC$25 plus.

In Kingstown there are two good local restaurants with lively bars attached, both upstairs on Grenville St. **Aggie's** serves a variety of seafood, including whelks and conch, often in a creole sauce of garlic, onion, chives and thyme, as well as local souse. EC$20–30. **Sid's** is decorated with the cricketing memorabilia of the owner, who also serves West Indian food. EC$15–25. On Halifax St you can grab a roti or a sandwich at lunchtime from the **Bounty**. If you are in Georgetown, **Ferdie's** Restaurant offers good West Indian fare (chicken or fish with local vegetables) at EC$18–25. On the opposite side of the island in Wallilabou bay is the Wallilabou **Anchorage** with a terrace of the waterfront where you can grab a local dish or a salad.

BARS AND NIGHTLIFE

Night-life is pretty quiet in St Vincent and is centred on the hotels, which stage steel bands occasionally and Villa, a natural gathering place where you will find visitors and passing sailors ashore for a beer and a game of darts. Try the **Lime and Pub**, which has a video bar and **Basil's Too**, which often has a discotheque and hosts a live band on Saturdays in season.

In Kingstown there are any number of rumshops in which to sit and have a *Hairoun* or an award-winning EKU beer, both of which are brewed in St Vincent. You might also try a *sea-moss* (made with seaweed and milk), or one of St Vincent's extremely powerful rums. **Aggie's** and **Sid's** collect a amusing crowd of locals.

Vincentians move on to the **Attic**, sumptuous and quite sophisticated, for jazz, above Kentucky Fried Chicken on the corner of Melville St.

The Grenadines

Scattered over the 80 miles between the volcanic peaks of St Vincent and Grenada are the Grenadines, 30 tiny islands and cays, reefs and sandbars that just cut the surface of the Caribbean Sea. Here you will find some of the finest beaches in the world—glaring white strips of sand on an aquamarine sea, protected by a rim of offshore reefs, where lines of silver breakers glint in the haze. Each one is an hour's sail from the next: the island-hopper's paradise.

Life for the locals is a much tougher prospect. Many of the islanders are poor, earning as little as US$5 for a day's work when they can get it, with expensive imported food to buy. Unemployment is high and the inhabitants of the Grenadine islands do feel neglected occasionally, as in 1979, just after Independence, when there was an uprising on Union Island and forty of the islanders staged an armed revolt.

There is a traditional connection with the sea; the islanders have long gone away to work on the big ships and many more who stay in the islands make their living from fishing. And on the smaller islands there is something of a 'when the boat comes in'

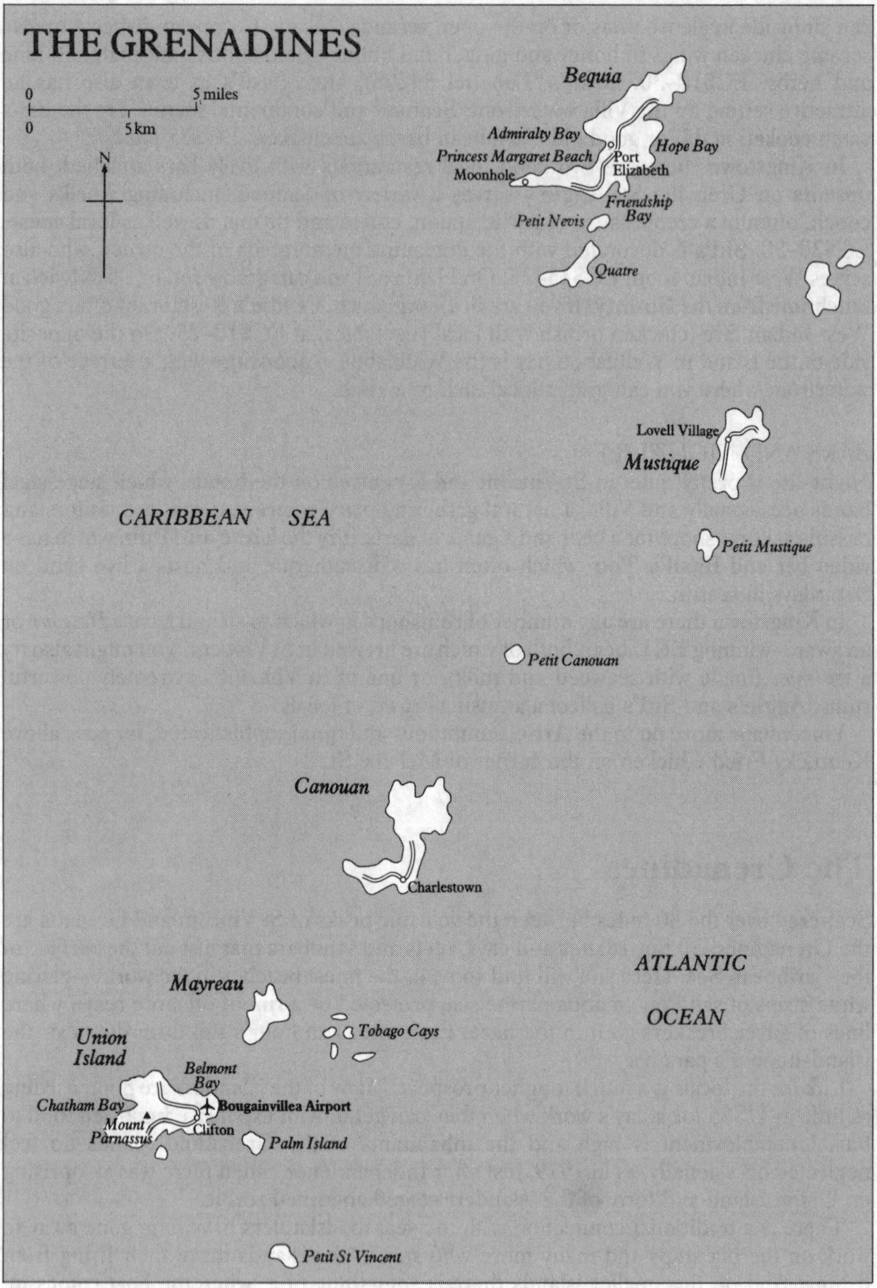

THE GRENADINES

0 _____ 5 miles
0 _____ 5 km

N

Bequia

Admiralty Bay
Princess Margaret Beach
Moonhole
Port Elizabeth
Hope Bay

Petit Nevis
Friendship Bay

Quatre

Lovell Village
Mustique

Petit Mustique

CARIBBEAN   SEA

Petit Canouan

Canouan

Charlestown

ATLANTIC

OCEAN

Mayreau

Tobago Cays

Union
Island
Belmont
Bay
Chatham Bay
Bougainvillea Airport
Mount
Parnassus
Clifton

Palm Island

Petit St Vincent

mentality. Life revolves around the dock when the mail boat makes its twice weekly visit, bringing the mail, as well as the weekly supply of soft drinks, beer, gas bottles and sheets of galvanized tin and sacks of cement for building.

There are also some charming places to stay, many of them very expensive island resorts, just a few rooms on an isolated cove. And then there are developed islands like Mustique, with luxury villas, and Bequia, with a string of small family hotels strung along the waterfront.

GETTING AROUND IN THE ISLANDS

Island-hopping by plane gives some cracking views of the Grenadines. It is a good way to get around, but there are some pretty hairy airstrips: Union Island now has a new strip but Canouan can still be exciting (crosswinds), as can Mustique (a steep descent that leads to a bouncy landing). But the islands are typically low-key and you may come across nonchalant signs like:

CAUTION—AIRCRAFT

LOOK LEFT

Mayreau, the Tobago Cays, Palm Island and Petit St Vincent have no airstrip and so you have to go by boat.

It is fun to travel by the local mail boat and the many smaller craft that do the island run. The mail boat, the *MV Snapper*, makes two sailings a week each way between Kingstown and Union Island, touching Bequia (1 hour), Canouan (2 hours), Mayreau (1 hour) and on to Union Island (½ hour). It travels south on Mondays and Thursdays and north on Tuesdays and Fridays. Fares are impeccable: from St Vincent to Bequia— EC$10–12, to Canouan—EC$13, to Mayreau—EC$15 and to Union Island—EC$20.

BEQUIA

Bequia (pronounced Beck-way) is a neat and pretty Caribbean hideaway. Largest of the St Vincent Grenadines (an amoeboid 5 miles by 2), it lies nine miles from Kingstown, or about an hour's sail away to the south. The approach to the main town of Port Elizabeth is glorious as the rocky headlands glide by on both sides towering above you. Sunset from the head of Admiralty Bay, through the masts of the yachts riding at anchor is quite simply one of the finest sights of the Caribbean.

The island is quite developed—pretty pastel boutiques and t-shirts strung up at the waterfront like washing—but it holds it well. The Vincentians themselves come on holiday here and think that the place is special. It is a pleasure in itself to stroll along the waterfront in the Belmont area, a narrow walkway that passes between the sea and the pastel-coloured wooden villas and inns, many of them built in the 1920s and 30s. An airstrip has recently been built on the island and it remains to be seen whether it will change the picture-postcard feel of the place. On the more secluded Atlantic coast you may come across tropicbirds and the scissor-tailed frigatebird.

The 5000 Bequians themselves are quiet and independent, still claiming to be a bit wary of 'Vincentians', who might almost come from a world away. There is a small community of white Bequians stuck up on the hill above Mt Pleasant. They have isolated themselves up there for years, but the younger generation have moved down now and are more visible in the community.

THE CARIBBEAN

The island is well served from St Vincent. At least two **motor vessels** make a daily trip to Kingstown during the week, departing early in the morning and returning soon after midday. The mail boat *MV Snapper* stops there four times a week too.

As you enter the harbour, Admiralty Bay, chosen by the British Navy as a port, but never occupied because of a lack of water, you will see some dwellings cut into the cliffs, with arches descending to the waterfront. They are known as Moonhole, after the natural arch in the rock, but they are private houses and the residents do not take kindly to people poking around uninvited.

There is a small **Tourist Office** by the pier in Port Elizabeth (tel 458 3286). Irregular dollar-buses (costing EC$1.50) ride out in both directions from Port Elizabeth, taking you up to the Spring Bay area or down to Paget Farm in the southwest.

The best **beaches** on the island lie on the south side of Admiralty Bay, the sumptuous golden sand of **Lower Bay**, with a couple of bars, easily reached by sea-taxi (EC$10) or land-taxi, and the more secluded inlet of **Princess Margaret Beach**, a little walk over the headland. On the south coast is the huge half-moon of **Friendship Bay**, with the hotel bar to retreat to and its views to Petit Nevis (an island still ocasionally used by whalers from Bequia to section their catch). East coast coves worth a visit are at **Industry Bay** (also called Crescent Bay) and **Spring Bay**. There are **beach bars** on nearly all the beaches on Bequia, pleasant spots to take time out from the sizzling and snorkelling. On Lower Bay try **De Reef** and **Teresa's** and on Friendship Bay you will find a waterfront bar with chairs swinging from the ceiling to help you with your balance after a few rum punches. In Industry Bay, check out the **Cresent Bay Inn** bar. People have been known to skinny-dip at Hope Bay.

Dive Bequia, PO Box 16, Bequia (tel 458 3504), operates out of the Plantation House Hotel in the Belmont area and **Sunsports** (tel 458 3527) out of the Gingerbread Complex, offering instruction as well as underwater camera rental. There are fine reefs around the island, starting at 30 ft and a one-tank dive costs about US$40. **Sailing** trips can be arranged among the islands to the south through **Grenadines Adventure Sailing** (tel 458 3695) or at the Frangipani and **deep sea fishing** trips can be arranged through *Illusion* (tel 83425).

WHERE TO STAY
Many of Bequia's small hotels (only one has as many as thirty rooms) are set in the island's fine old buildings, restored forts or old family holiday homes. They have charm and character, lost in tropical gardens on the heights or down on the seafront in Belmont overlooking Admiralty Bay and the yachts at anchor. As the island becomes more accessible, it is worth reserving a room on Bequia, particularly in the winter season.

The **Old Fort**, Mount Pleasant, PO Box 16 (tel 459 3440, fax 458 3824) is set in a restored plantation house, with a fort's eye view of the Grenadines as far south as Grenada. It is a private, isolated mock-fortress in tropical gardens high in the hills where peacocks, dogs and donkeys roam. Excellent dinners served on the terrace. Rooms at US$120 a double in season. The Sunny Caribbee **Plantation House Hotel**, PO Box 16 (tel 458 3425, fax 458 3612), is pastel-pink prettiness taken to perfection; gingerbread cabins set in a garden of palm and hibiscus on a strip of sand on Admiralty Bay. Sports include diving, watersports and tennis. Bungalows on the beachfront cost US$295–395 in season for a double room. There is a 12% service charge. With its magnificent setting

134

overlooking the east coast, **Spring on Bequia** (tel 458 3414) offers seclusion on an old plantation estate, surrounded by orchards. The 12 rooms, each with their own terrace, are in three buildings of Bequian stone, with distinctive shingle roofs copied from Martiniquan great houses. There is a freshwater pool and tennis court and the beach at Spring Bay which is just a short walk away. In winter a basic double room costs US$110–165 and in summer it is $115. A little untypical in Bequia for its modern resort feel is the **Friendship Bay Hotel**, on the south coast (tel 458 3222), pleasantly decorated cabins with their own terrace overlooking the circular bay, where watersports, diving, windsurfing and sailing are arranged. The main building and fine dining room stand above on the hill giving fine views of Petit Nevis. Daily rates vary from US$140 a double in winter, including breakfast and dinner. On the waterfront in Belmont the **Frangipani** (tel 458 3255) has kept the atmosphere of an old family home. It is the house of the Prime Minister, James Mitchell. Built in the 30s, it has a garden of mango trees, copper sugar kettles and plenty of red and white *frangipani*. The cottages and rooms, in the house itself, vary in price between US$50 and $100 in winter for a double.

At the bottom end of the scale Bequia has some bargains. In town, straight opposite the jetty, is **Julie's and Isola's** guest house, where rooms come at around US$45 for a couple and $30 for a single year-round. The **Old Fig Tree Guest House** (tel 458 3201) offers rooms for around US$25. If you want to be on the beach, away from the relative bustle of Port Elizabeth, try the **Keegan's Guest House** (tel 458 3675), nine rooms at US$50 (includes breakfast and dinner) or **Lower Bay Guest House** (458 3675), lost in a tropical garden, where a double room costs US$20 and a single $15 any time of the year.

EATING OUT
The hotel restaurants are a safe bet and many offer good local menus as well as the international fare, but recently a number of restaurants have sprung up, in which you will be served excellent local creole dishes and Bequian curries, accompanied by a volley of tropical vegetables. Most restaurants double as bars.

Daphne Cooks It (tel 83271) gives the finest creole food—local soups, frittered vegetables and exotic fruit sorbets—in a side-street just beyond the pier in Port Elizabeth. Ring to reserve a table (and a dish) EC$45. Another lovely spot for local food is **Dawn's Creole Tea Garden** (tel 83154), up the hill at the far end of Lower Bay (follow all the signs). Varieties of fresh fish in Dawn's creole sauce (clove, ginger and nutmeg), accompanied by breadfruit, sweet potato and plantain. Four course fixed dinner for EC$45 or a shortened version for $35. On the Belmont waterfront, the **Gingerbread House** has an upstairs view of the yachts in harbour through a filigree of mock-gingerbread fretwork. Salads by day, scallops in Vermouth cream by night and curries gingerbread style, spicy or mellow in coconut, EC$35–50. Live music three times a week, when a crowd packs the bar. At **Mac's Pizzeria** you can eat on a timber veranda above a luxurious tropical garden. Leisurely, good pizzas and salads for EC$20–30. The **Green Boley**, both bar and restaurant just down the walkway, has Caribbean rhythms and a local crowd and serves an excellent tropical juice or a local meal (fish or chicken) or a roti for EC$15.

Two **bars** are the **Harpoon Saloon**, which has a cracking view of the sunset from the northern side of Admiralty Bay and on the Belmont waterfront the **Whaleboner**, where you can get a cocktail while sitting on a massive whale vertebra (surprisingly comfortable). The hotels have an occasional *jump-up*.

MUSTIQUE

The island of Mustique, which takes its name from the French word for mosquito but thankfully has little more to do with them than that, has a lore all of its own. Its image is one of almost absurd exclusivity, an enclave reserved for the very rich; famous, notorious or anonymous. Names as incongruous as Princess Margaret and Mick Jagger have made this place their retreat.

Flights to Mustique come from Barbados and from St Vincent, mostly chartered. Air Martinique flies a scheduled service twice a day from St Vincent for US$30.

The island is run as a company, **The Mustique Company**, into which shareholders buy, by making the considerable investment of building a house on the island (quite a commitment as the going rate is about a million dollars). The company takes care of the infrastructure of Mustique, including health care and the education of the children on the island.

Incredibly neat, Mustique has a sedate exterior, pricked by the occasional character to be found at Basil's Bar. It is possible to come across the transient millionaires around the island, if you can spot them among the roving sailing-bums.

Lovell Village is the recognizably West Indian part of the island and it is here that many of the people employed by the Mustique Company live, as well as the fishermen, some of whom were here for generations before the company arrived.

Some of the most pleasant **beaches** scattered around the island are: **Endeavour Bay** in the north of the island and **L'Ansecoy Bay**, where the rusted carcass of the *Antilles* cruise liner can be seen. Secluded **Macaroni Bay** is on the east coast, mounds of bright white sand and one or two umbrella shades. **Gelliceaux Bay** is a pleasant cove with shallow water, secluded in the south of the island. Diving is arranged through **Dive Mustique** which works from the beach near the Cotton House Hotel.

The island is small enough to walk around in a couple of hours (look out for the iguanas, which are pretty big and for the mysterious miniature cattle which leave their prints when they come to drink at the pools by night), but if that seems too energetic then it is possible to hire a horse and ride round. Mini-mokes and mopeds are also available for hire from the company; enquire at the main office near the airport. If price is an object do not bother. It is not far to walk anyway.

WHERE TO STAY

Visitors to Mustique generally take a villa, one of the 30-odd luxurious piles dotted around the island. They vary in style from an Etruscan palace to chi-chi gingerbread cottages, with two rooms and more. All come with maid service, gardeners and cooks, in fact all that is needed to ensure the ultimate rest-cure. With names like *Nirvana*, *Serendipity* and *El Sueño* you get the idea that this might be as near to heaven as the developed world of the late 20th century can offer. The villas are not cheap. Prices for a two-bedroom villa start at US$2750 per week in winter and $2000 in summer; three bedrooms range from US$3500 to 5000 in winter and from $2500 to 4000 in the summer. Four bedroom villas start at $5000 in summer and $3000 in winter, and five bedrooms are $7000 or more in the winter and $5000 in summer. Contact **Mustique**

Villa Rentals, PO Box 349, St Vincent. In Britain they can be contacted at Chartham House, 16a College Ave, Maidenhead, Berks SL6 6AX (tel 0628 75544, fax 0628 21033).

There is one hotel on the island, the **Cotton House Hotel**, a former 18th-century plantation house and seat of present day luxury. 25 sumptuous rooms are scattered over a rolling hill, among the grassland and hibiscus. All have balconies overlooking the Grenadines and St Vincent, or with a view west for incomparable sunsets. The pool stands, crenellated and pillared, on the heights, overlooking the Jagger and Bowie investments. The main building is exquisite—pink, white and perfect. All this for US$550–730 per couple per night in winter and a snip at US$300–400 in summer.

For those who might feel a little extravagant staying at the Cotton House there is a cheaper alternative in **Firefly** (tel 458 4621), the Mustique Guest House, with fine views over the Grenadines to the south. The cry goes that you do not have to be a millionaire to stay on Mustique because you can come here, but if you do, be sure to come with plenty of loot even so. Board and breakfast costs US$80 for a double in season ($85 for a single) and US$70 in the summer (single $55).

BARS
Basil's Bar is a popular haunt, on Wednesdays particularly, when the yachts bring their passengers ashore and the millionaires venture out from their villas. It is a seaside bar from paradise, bamboo cane and a rush-work roof, jutting out into the water on stilts, from where you can admire the sunset and the views of the Grenadines over the gin palaces that bob in the bay. Entry to the *jump-up* on Wednesday night costs about US$20 and drinks will set you back about US$5. There is a local bar with a pool table in Lovell Village, the **Piccadilly** pub where cheap(er) meals and beer can be found.

CANOUAN

Crescent-shaped Canouan lies 25 miles from St Vincent and measures three miles by one and a half. It is home to less than 840 people, mostly farmers and fishermen. There are a few shops to stock up at if you are passing by on a boat, and fine anchorages all around the island, the principal one being off the main settlement, Charlestown, in **Grand Bay** but the island has many hidden coves and beaches to explore. Other bays include **Rameau** and **Corbay**. An attractive stone church stands on its own, up in the north of the island, away from the main town, which abandoned it and went south after a hurricane in 1921.

WHERE TO STAY
The **Canouan Beach Hotel**, PO Box 530, Kingstown (tel 458 8888, 458 8875) is not far from the airstrip, cottages with 43 rooms among the mangrove and hibiscus, set on a spit of land with glaring white sand either side and a fine view of the other Grenadines. Prices per week, with full board and free watersports (windsurfing, sailing and diving) US$1200–1600.

The **Crystal Sands Beach Hotel** (tel 458 8015, fax 458 8309) is also a stone's throw from the airport, with a bar that gives on to the beach. Ten double rooms are arranged in five cottages, self-contained but with a joining door. Watersports on offer, double room in season US$55 all year.

There are two small guest houses on the island; **Villa la Bijou** (tel 456 4099), six rooms in a converted house, share baths and spectacular views of the Grenadines from the outsize terrace, cost US$80 per person in season (includes board with breakfast and one other meal) and the **Anchor Inn Guest House** (tel 458 8568), just three rooms near the beach in Grand Bay, double rate US$45 year round. It is also permitted to camp out in Canouan.

MAYREAU

With just 180 inhabitants and no airstrip, this island of a square mile and a half, 30 minutes in a boat from Union Island, is nearly the most secluded of them all (the Tobago Cays nearby win that claim). There are no roads or cars and there is not even a jetty big enough to take the mail boat, so the week's supplies are offloaded into smaller boats. Cows making a journey from Mayreau are winched up on to deck, and if alighting here they are simply herded off into the bay and left to swim for it. Electricity has not really reached Mayreau yet (except in the two hotels).

Mayreau has beaches, though, on all sides. The best known are at **Saline Bay** and **Salt Whistle Bay**, a particularly good anchorage on the leeward coast. But there are many others; snorkelling is recommended at the northern point and on the windward beaches, where the sand is framed with sea grape bushes. Head windward on the day that the cruise ship puts in and dumps its passengers on the leeward coast, or alternatively take advantage of the island's views from the high ground, north to Canouan, east to the Tobago Cays and south to the majestic peaks of Union Island.

The **Salt Whistle Bay Resort** (boatphone 493 9609, or call on VHF channel 16), contact 1020 Bayridge Drive, Kingston Ontario, Canada K7P 2S2 (tel 613 634 1963, fax 613 384 6300, US 800 263 2780), is set on a stunning half-mile half-moon bay. It is about as remote as you will get; 27 luxurious rooms with old-time elegance in stone cottages hidden among a sandy garden of palms. Some watersports but mostly a quiet retreat, for which it is ideal. It is expensive, at US$420 a double in winter and $270 in summer, which includes meals.

Dennis's Hideaway is set on the hillside in the middle of Mayreau's town, three plush rooms in modern West Indian style and a huge balcony. He will also feed you on the small veranda restaurant, which collects a crowd of passing yachtsmen in the evenings. US$35 a double.

TOBAGO CAYS

The Tobago Cays (pronounced keys) are five uninhabited islets set in the circle of Horseshoe Reef, an underwater world as spectacular as the island scenes above the surface. The water is crystal clear all around, out to the limit of the reef, which is marked by a circle of silver breakers. You will cruise in between the reefs and drop anchor in the shallows of a pristine white sand beach.

Any yachting cruise in the Grenadines will stop off here on request and you can take a day trip to the Cays from Union Island. You are unlikely to be the only yacht in the area in high season (December until April) and despite their status as a marine park, there have sadly been recent reports of rubbish in this corner of paradise.

Devotees of the Tobago Cays talk of them as the closest thing to heaven and somehow it is true. It is among these 30 islands and cays that you will find that well-known bit of real estate, beloved of Bacardi drinkers, the dazzling strip of sand with a single palm tree.

UNION ISLAND

Mid-way down the Grenadines is spectacular-looking Union Island, parched yellow slopes draped down from the sharp peaks of the oddly-named Mount Parnassus and Mount Olympus. It is a sailing centre and yachts crowd in the bay off the main town of Clifton. Union Island is something of a gateway in the area because the airport serves as dropping-off point for boat connections to the other islands nearby: Mayreau, the Tobago Cays, Palm Island and Petit St Vincent. It is also possible to sail on from here to Carriacou in the Grenadian Grenadines (twice weekly ferry), for about EC$10. Union Island is a **Port of Entry** to St Vincent and the Grenadines. Passengers arriving at the privately-operated Bougainvillaea airport have to pay a charge of EC$26.

There is a certain listlessness in Union Island and life is quite clearly a struggle for the 2000 islanders, though the government provides some employment and there is money coming in from tourism. **Big Sand** beach in Belmont Bay has shallow water and fine sand screened by bushes, but perhaps the best place to go for a secluded day at the beach is over the hill at **Chatham Bay** with miles of undisturbed (as yet) strand. There are no facilities in these places, so be sure to take water and a picnic if you will want them.

There is a small **Tourist Office** in Clifton. Union Island is a popular place to start yacht tours around the Grenadines and these can be arranged through the Anchorage Yacht Club below. **Grenadines Dive** (tel 458 8138, fax 458 8398) works out of the Sunny Grenadines Hotel, charging US$45 for a single dive with equipment.

WHERE TO STAY AND EAT

There are three hotels on Union Island, along the waterfront at Clifton, overlooking the open bay where the charter yachts dock. The **Anchorage Yacht Club** (tel 458 8244, fax 458 8365), with ten air-conditioned rooms in a garden of palms looking out over a passable beach towards Palm Island. There is a constant bustle and turnover, Grenadine style, of yacht crews and passengers, many of them French-speaking from the islands to the north. Be careful after the usual intake of rum punch, as the sharks kept in the pool at the waterfront seem to loom ever larger as the evening draws on. The restaurant, on an open terrace, serves French food. A double room in season costs US$90, or $200 for a self-catering cabana, and in summer the prices reduce to $80 and $150. At the other end of Clifton is the **Sunny Grenadines Hotel** (tel 458 8327, fax 458 8398), 18 rooms in small units with ceiling fans, set among the palm trees with a lively bar that gives on to a rickety wooden jetty, perfect for lounging in the evening light. Double rooms come at US$85–115 all year round, a single costs $55. Local food, including curry conch and steamed snapper, EC$30 a main dish. The **Clifton Beach Hotel** (tel 458 8235) and the nearby Guest House provide simple and clean fan-ventilated rooms at good prices, run by an island family whose influence seems limitless. In winter the 25 rooms cost US$33 and a single $20, and in summer they are $40 and $16. The Guest House offers rooms at about US$25.

There are one or two restaurants in Clifton outside the hotels. Try **T&N Restaurant, Bar, Variety Store and Bike Rentals**, upstairs in Clifton, for local dishes of chicken and fish creole at EC$25. The **Lambi Supermarket, Bar and Restaurant** is on the waterfront; regular Caribbean dishes, including of course lambi (conch), of which the pink shells are set into the wall.

Finally, a cool spot for an ital juice (perhaps soursop or papaya), wanties and oil-dung (a vegetable boil up in coconut milk) is **Roots Corner** behind T&N, with a red, gold and green sitting area. The **Eagle's Nest** is the local club.

PALM ISLAND

Until recently with a population of just two cows, Palm Island, or Prune Island as it used to be known, is a purpose-built island resort, the work of John Caldwell and his wife Mary who took the island on a lease of 99 years in 1966 after sailing the world in small yachts. The island is a casual paradise, without imposed sophistication and yet with afternoon tea at four each day. 24 fan-ventilated rooms in stone cabins face out to sea, overlooking the magnificent **Casuarina** beach, that runs the length of the sheltered west coast. Just over 100 acres in size, the island is strewn with palm trees and lies about a mile from Union Island, a short hop in the motor launch. There are no telephones or televisions—hospitality Caldwell-style will help you escape all that. In the winter season a double room (with all meals) costs US$320, reduced to $210 in the summer (tel 458 4808, fax 458 8804).

PETIT ST VINCENT (PSV)

Petit St Vincent, a self-contained island resort (tel 458 4801, fax 458 8801, US 800 654 9326), is the most southerly of the St Vincent Grenadines and from here it is possible to see people walking about on Petit Martinique, part of Grenada. But this is about as close to the crowds as you will get on PSV (as habitués know it), because this island resort specializes in seclusion. You get peace at a price at PSV. You can even have room service at your beach hammock. It seems rich and exclusive, but with a good anchorage it is also popular with the yachting fraternity and so they mix in here with customary Caribbean ease.

Exertion is a walk to the beach and, since the island is completely surrounded by them, that will not be too far. The cottages are spread out for maximum seclusion. You communicate to room service by flag, simply by placing an order in the post box, raising the flag and retiring to further inactivity. If you do wish to stretch some muscles, there is a tennis court and watersports are laid on.

If prices concern you, however, then this place might not be for you, as such luxury comes at an undisclosed sum in the winter season (about US$650 per couple per night) with reductions to $350 in the summer months.

ST LUCIA

Hold St Lucia, and the rest may perish!

The call to arms on behalf of St Lucia was raised so often that she become known as the Fair Helen of the West Indies. Desire to possess her moved whole armies and led to her changing hands 14 times. She is a charmed isle, not so much for her strategic value nowadays, but for her people, among the friendliest and most forthcoming in the Caribbean and for her natural beauty: hidden coves, tropical abundance and the *Pitons*, twin volcanic pyramids from the south seas.

Lying between Martinique and St Vincent, St Lucia (pronounced St Loosha) is another island peak in the Windward chain, with slopes that soar from the sea to a central mountain spine crested by Morne Gimie (3117 ft), and fall away in forest-clad hills to lush valleys of bananas, tropical overgrowth and beaches mounded with golden sand. 27 miles by 14, St Lucia has an active volcano, a fumerolle called *la Soufrière*, a bubbling and stinking morass which has the dubious distinction of being the only drive-in volcano in the world.

The 145,000 St Lucians are mostly of African descent, brought to the island as slaves, and more than a third live in the capital, Castries, which shambles over the hills above a sheltered harbour in the northeast of the island. St Lucia is the most developed of the Windward Islands and has some industry, but many of the islanders still live a simple West Indian existence, tied to the land, producing sustenance and a small living from agriculture. Bananas are the biggest crop and they account for about 70% of export earnings. There are about 2000 banana farmers and on market day the children from the country stay away from school to help their parents on the small farms by carrying a couple of boxes of bananas down to the processing plant.

Tourism has had a late start here but it is developing fast. The island is becoming popular and has 318,000 visitors a year, many flooding ashore on day release from the cruise ships that loom in Castries harbour like floating skyscrapers.

The Pitons, St Lucia

But the tangled and romantic history of St Lucia is still visible through the encrustation of hotel plant and the service infrastructure and the island is littered with the ghostly
fortresses of forgotten wars. The French possessed St Lucia for many years and their
influence remains in the *mornes*, mountain-peaks, and *anses*, the sheltered bays, and
every visitor will hear the strains of the local *patois* spoken in the streets, tantalizingly like
French for a moment and yet impossible to pin down. The population is mostly Catholic
and there are even flashes of French mannerisms in the way that they act. Now that the
British colonial connection is ended, the French are providing development assistance.

English is the official language and it is important to speak it in order to 'get on'.
Parents will bring up their children to speak English even though they might talk in patois
between themselves.

The 18th-century war-cry 'To St Lucia! To St Lucia!', is being raised again and the
seaborne invaders are coming in droves, swamping Castries, storming the heights of
Morne Fortune, and throwing up the concrete forts of the 20th century. Go soon, before
the calm and beauty of Fair Helen has gone.

History

Santa Lucia first appears on a royal *Cedula* of 1511 marking out the Spanish domain in
the New World, and then on a Vatican globe of 1520. It is not known who discovered it,
or why it was named after the virgin-martyr of Syracuse, but the St Lucians celebrate St
Lucy's day, 13 December, as their national day.

Hewanorra, as the Caribs called St Lucia, was a favoured hide-out for the pirates and
privateers of the 16th century. They came to scourge the Spaniards in the Indies and
men like Frenchman François de Clerc (better known to the Spaniards as *Pie de Palo*
because of his wooden leg), would hide at Pigeon Island in the north of the island, on the
look-out for shipping to plunder, just as the admirals of the European navies would 200
years later. In 1553 he left for a grand tour in which he sacked the major towns in Santo
Domingo, Puerto Rico and Cuba.

Attempts to settle St Lucia began at the turn of the 17th century. The first, in 1605,
really happened by accident, when the *Olive Blossom* limped to St Lucia after being blown
off course on the Atlantic crossing. She was headed for the Guianas in South America,
but, short of supplies, 67 of her passengers took their chances in St Lucia and bought
huts and food from seemingly friendly Carib Indians. The Caribs soon changed their
tune, though, and after five weeks of hostilities just 19 of the settlers were still alive, so
they made a final purchase of a canoe and paddled off to South America.

Another English attempt in 1639 survived 18 months unmolested before the Caribs
attacked. The Indians winkled them out of their fort by burning red pepper in the wind, a
trick they used to catch sleeping parrots. Almost all were killed.

Just as Charles I of England granted St Lucia and other islands officially in the
Spanish domain to the Earl of Carlisle in 1627, so Cardinal Richelieu felt free to offer
islands 'not possessed by any Christian prince' to the French West India Company in
1642 and soon the French settlements in the West Indies began to appear. The scene
was set for the next 200 years; settlements, battles and treaties, a rivalry that would see St
Lucia change hands a ridiculous 14 times. Once the Caribs were wiped out, the island
steadily turned from a rabble of deserters, loggers and turtlers to a prosperous colony,
cultivating sugar.

142

With Louis XVI guillotined in January 1793 in Europe, Britain and the Republic were at war again in the Caribbean and the revolutionaries raised the *tricolore* in St Lucia. With its revolutionary sympathies and a guillotine erected in the capital, the island became known as *St Lucie la Fidèle*. The British fought their way back into Castries in 1796, but the 'Armée française dans les bois' (a kind of forest-based guerrilla force), held the rest of the island to ransom for another year. The subsequent war and treaty left St Lucia in British hands. The slaves were emancipated in 1834.

In 1885 Castries became one of the two principal coaling stations in the British West Indies, along with Kingston, Jamaica, filling 1000 steam-ships a year and gaining yet more importance when the Panama Canal was opened in 1914. Women would be seen climbing the gangways with 110lb baskets of coal on their heads, smoking pipes or singing shanties.

After the Second World War, as the West Indian islands moved towards political self-determination, St Lucia became self-governing in 1967 and then took Independence on 22 February 1979. The country is still a member of the British Commonwealth, with an elected Parliament after the Westminster model. At present the island is governed by the United Workers Party under Prime Minister Julian Hunte, holding eleven seats to the St Lucia Labour Party's six.

St Lucia's economy depends mainly on tourism, but bananas also contribute to foreign exchange earnings. Most are shipped out by *Geest* and are sold in Britain as Windward Island Bananas. The small St Lucian farmers are concerned that the EC single-market agreement of 1992 threatens this special relationship.

Flora and Fauna

Like all the Windwards St Lucia has exuberant flora; coastal mangrove swamps (near Savannes on the southeast coast) at sea level where you can see the mangrove cuckoo and the tropical mockingbird and warblers, and plains flown over by hawks and herons; the white bird that keeps a silent vigil by the grazing cows is the cattle egret, who found his way over from Africa earlier this century. In the higher reaches of rainforest you will find St Lucia's hummingbirds: the Antillean crested hummingbird and the purple-throated hummingbird. The upper rainforest is also home to the endangered St Lucia parrot. On the off-shore islands you will come across tropicbirds and magnificent frigatebirds.

There are far fewer animals, but one to look out for if you are rootling around the undergrowth is the highly poisonous *fer-de-lance* snake, which snoozes by day (apparently they exist, but are very rarely seen). Turtles also come to lay their eggs on St Lucian beaches between March and August.

GETTING TO ST LUCIA
Flights from outside the Caribbean serve Hewanorra International Airport near the south coast and 40 miles (over an hour's ride) south of Castries. If you are flying within the Caribbean, it is probably better to aim for Vigie Airport just outside the capital. There is a departure tax of EC$20 for points in the Caribbean, plus Guyana and Venezuela. For all other destinations it is EC$27.

Cruise passengers are well looked after, following the opening of a new tender jetty at Pointe Seraphine in Castries.

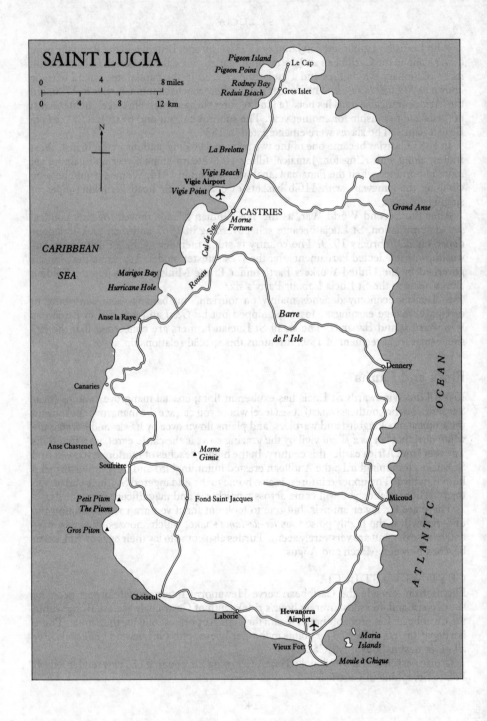

SAINT LUCIA

0   4   8 miles

0   4   8   12 km

N

Pigeon Island
Pigeon Point
Le Cap
Rodney Bay
Reduit Beach
Gros Islet

La Brelotte

Vigie Beach
Vigie Airport
Vigie Point

CASTRIES
Morne
Fortune

Grand Anse

CARIBBEAN

Cul de Sac

SEA

Marigot Bay
Hurricane Hole

Roseau

Anse la Raye

Barre
de l' Isle

Dennery

Canaries

Anse Chastenet

▲ *Morne*
Gimie

Soufrière

Petit Piton ▲
The Pitons

Fond Saint Jacques

Micoud

Gros Piton ▲

ATLANTIC

OCEAN

Choiseul

Laborie

Hewanorra
Airport

◇ *Maria*
Islands

Vieux Fort

Moule à Chique

By Air
From the UK: BWIA has three flights a week to St Lucia and British Airways two. On days when no direct flights are operating, the best connections are via Barbados.
From the USA: BWIA has a daily direct flight from Miami and New York, and American Airlines fly daily from Puerto Rico, where connections can also be made.
From Canada: Air Canada flies weekly from Montreal and Toronto.
From other Caribbean Islands: Most flights come into Vigie in the north of the island and there are links to most major islands nearby. LIAT (tel 452 3051) flies to Barbados, north to Antigua and south to Trinidad and also Caracas. Air Martinique (tel 452 2463) originates in Martinique and flies south to the Grenadines. American Eagle (tel 452 1820) has a daily link to San Juan, Puerto Rico. If you wish to charter a plane try Helenair (tel 809 452 7196) and Eagle Air Services (tel 452 1900).

GETTING AROUND ST LUCIA
Private **minibuses** (the old wooden lorries have now been discarded for Japanese vans) run all the main routes around the island. Gros Islet and the north are served frequently and buses continue until as late as 10pm (longer on a Friday night), leaving from Darling Rd. Buses heading south leave from around Bridge St, departing on and off until the late afternoon. For a day trip to Soufrière you must be quite careful because the last bus back to Castries leaves at midday, after which time you will have to take the longer route via Vieux Fort. Some sample prices are: **Castries** to Gros Islet—EC75c, to Dennery—$2 and to Soufrière or Vieux Fort—$5. 75c will get you to the top of Morne Fortune.

Island tours around St Lucia can be arranged through **Solar Tours** in Choc Bay (tel 452 5898) and **Barnards Travel** (tel 452 1615).

Taxis can be arranged easily enough at hotels and in town or at the airport; if you are lucky the driver will give you an impromptu guided tour. By the hour a taxi costs about EC$50, and a day tour in a taxi can be shared for about EC$250 between four people. A few sample one-way fares are: **Castries** to Vigie airport—EC$10, and to Hewanorra airport, near Vieux Fort—EC$120, to Rodney Bay—$20, the Cap in the north—$30 and to La Toc, just south of Castries—$10.

Car hire gives more independence for exploring the inland byways like the rainforest road out of Soufrière and the route to Grand Anse northeast of Castries. A temporary driving licence is required, costing EC$30 on presentation of a valid licence from home to the police at either airport or in Castries. An international driving licence is valid. Driving is on the left, generally.

Many hire companies have desks at the airports and typically they will require a deposit of US$100. Cars cost from US$40 per day, from **Carib Touring Auto Rentals** on Laborie St (tel 452 2689 or 452 3184) and **Avis** in Castries (tel 452 2202 or 452 2700) or **National**, nearer to Gros Islet (tel 450 8721 or 450 8028). You can hire motorbikes through **Wayne's Motorcycle Centre** in Vide Bouteille (tel 452 2059), and bicycles through **Ryan's Bicycle Rental** in Rodney Bay (tel 450 8489).

If you would like to tour the island by helicopter—in half an hour you can fly between the Pitons, hover in rainforested valleys and dive-bomb yachts—contact **St Lucia Helicopters** (tel 453 6950), departure from Point Seraphine.

TOURIST INFORMATION
The St Lucia Tourist Board can be contacted at:
UK: 10 Kensington Court, London W8 5DL (tel 071 937 1969, fax 937 3611).

USA: 9th Floor, 820 Second Ave, New York, NY 10017 (tel 212 867 2950, fax 212 370 7867).
Canada: 151 Bloor St West, Suite 425, Toronto, Ontario M5S 1S4 (tel 416 961 5606, fax 416 961 4317).
Germany: Postfach 2304, 6380 Bad Homburg 1 (tel 06172 30 44 31, fax 049 6921 5900).
France: ANI, 53 rue François Ier, 7ième Etage, Paris 75008 (tel 47 20 39 66, fax 47 23 09 65).

In St Lucia itself write to the main Tourism Office in the **Point Seraphine Shopping Complex**, across the harbour from downtown Castries, where the cruise ships dock, PO Box 221 (tel 452 4094). There are also helpful tourist information offices at **Vigie** airport, close to Castries (tel 452 2595) and at **Hewanorra** airport in the south (tel 454 6644). The Tourist Board puts out two publications; *Visions of St Lucia* a glossy magazine with practical details and feature articles and the monthly broadsheet, *the Tropical Traveller*, for a more topical view. *The Voice* newspaper is published in Castries twice a week, on Wednesdays and Saturdays, with local news and events.

MONEY
The official currency of St Lucia is the Eastern Caribbean dollar and although US dollars are widely accepted in tourist areas, *dollars* usually refer to the Eastern Caribbean dollar. The conversion rate is EC$2.69 = US$1, so it is worth establishing which currency you are working in. Hotels and the larger restaurants will be happy to quote US$ prices; banks give a better exchange rate than the hotels if you want cash, though. **Banks** are open Mon–Fri, 8–1pm with an extra stint on Friday afternoons, 3–5. **Shops** are open weekdays 8.30–12.30 and 1.30–4, Sat 8–noon. The IDD code for St Lucia is 809, followed by a seven figure number. On-island you must dial all seven digits.

FURTHER READING
One of the English-speaking Caribbean's most celebrated authors is St Lucian, the poet and playwright Derek Walcott. Another St Lucian author is Garth St Omer, whose works include *The Lights on the Hill*. If you can track down a copy of *St Lucia, Tours and Tales*, by Harriet Durham and Florence Lewisohn, do so, because it gives a well-presented and amusing background to the island. And you might even find a copy of the *St Lucia Diary of Lt JH Caddy*, a military man who served time in the West Indies in the 1830s. A revealing description of his life riding out, dining out and occasional military manoeuvres during his stay in St Lucia in 1833–34, published by the St Lucia Archaeological and Historical Society.

BEACHES
St Lucia's best white-sand beaches lie on the protected leeward coast at the northern end of the island. Most beaches in the middle of the island, where the mountainsides drop steeply into the ocean, have black volcanic sand.

The finest and most popular of all is in the wide sweep of the historic **Reduit Beach** in Rodney Bay, miles of mounded sand so soft that you stumble trying to get through it. It is a 20-minute ride from the capital, and most watersports are available through the hotel concessionaires. If you feel sunstroke coming on, there is a whole array of bars and restaurants to retreat to behind the beach. There are one or two more secluded strips of sand on **Pigeon Island**, across the bay.

On the route back to town is **La Brelotte**, where you will find the Windjammer resort in a steep-sided bay, and worth a couple of hours in the afternoon sun. Just outside Castries is **Vigie Beach**, a two-mile stretch with hotels at intervals, with sand that slopes gently away into the crystalline water. A particularly charming half-moon bay, mounded with golden sand, is at **La Toc** bay just south of Castries. There are a number of secluded coves on the west coast south of Castries that can only be reached by boat.

Anse Chastanet, close to Soufrière on the leeward coast, is an idyllic cove with grey sand that is sheltered between massive headlands. In the south, to the windward side of the island, is **Anse des Sables**, a shallow and open bay swept by the Tradewinds that is renowned for windsurfing.

BEACH BARS
Some of the best beach bars are connected to the hotels. **Anse Chastanet** has a wonderful tropical bar and a superb view over the grey sand to the sunset. There are three or four along Reduit Beach, but for a change you could always sail over to **Les Pigeons** on Pigeon Point, which has a nice setting above the water; sandwiches, omelettes and soft drinks. There are a couple of excellent bars beneath the palm trees in **Marigot Bay** and if you happen past **Anse Jambette**, just further south, while it is open, that is well worth hoving to for.

WATERSPORTS
Sailing: all down its west coast, St Lucia is indented with coves that make protected harbours for yachts. Charter expeditions can be arranged around the island, or farther afield, perhaps to the Grenadines in the south, in bare boats or crewed. Two charter companies work out of Rodney Bay: **Sunsail Stevens** (tel 450 8648) and **Trade Wind Yacht Charters** (tel 450 8424). Distinctive for their white hulls and blue markings, yachts from **The Moorings** can be hired from Marigot Bay, about half an hour's drive south of Castries (tel 451 4256).

There are three marinas on the island, and although they are functional now, each has its historical and romantic lore. In the north, Rodney Bay marina lies behind Reduit beach. In Vigie cove behind Point Seraphine is a smaller marina convenient for Castries and a few miles south of here is Marigot Bay. If you are crossing the Atlantic, the Atlantic Rally for Cruisers takes place in November/December each year and culminates in St Lucia. Contact World Cruising Ltd, PO Box 165, London WC1B 5LA (tel 071 405 9905, fax 071 831 0161).

If you do not feel like taking out a 60-footer, **windsurfers** are available at the main beaches through hotel watersports shops, about US$13 an hour. The best winds are in the south of the island, near Hewanorra Airport. Small sailing boats like sunfish and Hobie cats are also available.

At the bigger hotels there are the facilities for **waterskiing**, costing about US$20 for a 20-minute session, and if you would like a parachutist's eye view, then **parasailing** can be arranged for EC$80. Banana rides and glass-bottom boat trips can also be fixed up through Jacob's Watersports (tel 450 8281) at the St Lucian Hotel.

For a day cruise of yo-ho-ho down to the Pitons, try the 140 ft square-rigged brigantine *Unicorn* departing Vigie Cove in Castries harbour at 9.30am, returning at 4.30pm. The *Unicorn* played the slave-ship in the television series *Roots*. The motor yacht *Vigie* offers a more sedate variation on a theme.

Diving is excellent, with visibility up to 100 feet and colourful coastal marine life, wrasses and grunts by the group. Instruction and equipment (including underwater cameras) are available through the large operators. Most of the diving takes place on the west coast; two popular areas are Anse Cochon and Anse Chastanet near Soufrière, the home of **Scuba St Lucia** (tel 459 7354, or 450 8009 at the St Lucian Hotel) where the reefs start at 15 feet below the surface. Also recommended is **Buddies** (tel 452 5288) in Rodney Bay marina. A single-tank dive costs around US$35. Most hotels will provide **snorkelling** gear for a minimal fee if you wish to chase after an angelfish or a stretched trumpetfish.

For a **deep-sea fishing** trip, trailing a line for marlin or sailfish, contact **Mako Watersports** in Rodney Bay (tel 450 0412) or **Captain Mike's Watersports** in Vigie Cove (tel 452 7044).

There are two nine-hole **golf** courses on St Lucia, one in the Cap Estate near the northern tip (tel 450 8523, green fee EC$30) and the other in the La Toc Valley (tel 452 3081, green fee EC$25). Clubs, carts and caddies are available for rent. **Tennis** is available at all the big hotels and most will let you play on their courts.

Hire of horses and riding instruction is available through **Trim's Riding Stables** on the Cap Estate in the north of the island (tel 450 8273, price about US$15 per hour). Rides will take you for a picnic and a canter along the beach in a secluded cove on the Atlantic coast, less visited by cars which find the roads a little testing.

Castries

If history was replayed as you cruised into Castries harbour, the hills around you would swarm with troops, the air hang heavy with the smell of gunpowder and the ground and the harbour would be stained scarlet with blood. Castries was one of the most bitterly contested places in the whole of the Caribbean.

The town lies on the protected leeward coast of the island, at the head of an irregular and almost landlocked bay, framed by forested hills that rise in folds into the distance. The harbour mouth is guarded by **Vigie Point** (French for look-out), covered in yellow-brick barrack buildings and the graveyards of campaigns past—you get a good view of them as you come in for the final wobbly descent into Vigie airport.

Castries takes its name from the Maréchal de Castries, a French colonial minister, who was Governor of the island in 1784. The name stuck, despite being rejected at the time of the French Revolution, when it was known as *Félicité-ville*. Set out on a grid-iron pattern, the centre of the town is mostly modern, concrete and functional. Near the market on Jeremie Street there is even an area of neo-brutalist housing estate imported from 60s England. But despite Castries's rather unfortunate habit of burning down (1796, 1812, 1927 and 1948), it has a few pockets of old creole architecture, mostly in the southeast corner of the town at the top end of Chaussee Road. Their balconies overhang the pavement on sturdy wooden stilts and the gingerbread patterns on the eaves here are more intricate and prettier than on any island in the Eastern Caribbean except for Trinidad.

The centre of the town is **Columbus Square**, flanked on one side by the **Roman Catholic Cathedral**. The Cathedral was built in 1897 and is dedicated to the Immaculate Virgin. It is decorated with biblical paintings in which all the characters are depicted as African. On the south side of the square the elaborate façades are a relic of old-time Castries, and among them is the ever-popular restaurant, Rain.

The liveliest area of town however is the **Market**, five minutes' walk away on Jeremie Street, a magnificent old red iron-market erected at the turn of the century. It is jumbled full of furniture, straw bags and sweetmeats. The streets are alive with the chatter of the market ladies from the country, who sit watching over piles of eddoe, tannia, christophene and yam.

Morne Fortune (pronounced Fortunay and supposedly meaning the *Hill of Good Luck*) looms above the town, and it is here that the fiercest battles took place in the 18th century. Nowadays the soldiers would be fighting their way through the scarlet and purple blooms of the bougainvillaea in the private gardens as the road winds its way back and forth to the summit. The old imposing military hulks, barracks, stables and gun emplacements, have been taken over by the modern-day establishment as official buildings. Close to the summit stands the partially restored Fort Charlotte, which dates from the late 18th century.

Nearby is Government House, the official residence of the Governor General, built of red stones with smart white trimmings in the 1890s. It had something of a habit of killing Governors. As Sir Algernon Aspinall relates in his *Pocket Guide to the West Indies*, one inhospitable Governor Farquharson was obliged to entertain a Bishop and when it was time to retire he said, 'I suppose your lordship has heard of the insalubrity of this place; every room in the house has already witnessed the death of some Governor, but none of them has had the honour of killing a Bishop; so, my Lord, you have only to make your selection.' The Bishop departed immediately and ironically Governor Farquharson died of fever in the house two years later.

The Morne dominates the town and from the top you get one of the finest views in the West Indies. To the north it looks over the ant-size aircraft landing at Vigie airport and then out to Pigeon Point. On clear days it is quite possible to see as far as Martinique. The view is also spectacular to the south, where the *Pitons* are visible in the distance.

North from Castries to the Cap

As you head north out of town you will see a white pyramid, the new Alliance Française on the opposite side of the bay, past the fish market. Follow further around behind it and you will come to Point Seraphine, the cruise ship dock and shopping centre, where you can score a few duty-free bargains.

Time was, not so long ago, when the cars had to be cleared off the road to allow planes to land at Vigie airport, which handles short-haul island-hopper flights. Now the airstrip runs alongside **Vigie Beach**, so if you want some last minutes of sun and sand before leaving, there is two miles of protected bay here. It is the site of many a forgotten invasion and the fortifications that opposed them, 18th-century strongholds that now lie buried under the bastions of the 20th-century Caribbean tourist hotels. The island opposite the Halcyon Beach Club is called **Rat Island**, a former nunnery, now deserted.

From the top end of Choc Bay a side road branches through the hills to the other side of the island, towards the attractive half-moon bay of Grand Anse on the Atlantic coast. The family of the Empress Josephine had a sugar estate at Paix Bouche on the windward side of the island. Despite Martiniquan insistence to the contrary, the St Lucians claim that Josephine was born in St Lucia.

The coastal road re-emerges from the rolling hills on **Rodney Bay**, named after the British admiral who made St Lucia his headquarters in the late 18th century, where you will see gin palaces lie at anchor in formation, just as Rodney's warships did 200 years ago.

On the bay stands the village of **Gros Islet**, famed for its parties on Friday nights when the few streets of simple clapboard houses seethe with dancers until the early hours. It was proudly called *Révolution* when St Lucia was holding out at the time of the French Revolution. The 'islet' (Pigeon Island) from which the town takes its name is in fact no longer an island. It was joined to the mainland in the early 70s by an artificial causeway, part of a vastly expensive tourist development programme that foundered, leaving just a few abandoned foundations and a perfectly protected and stunning bay.

Pigeon Point, Pigeon Island that was, lies a mile across the bay, a barren outcrop with two peaks that the British fortified as soon as they took the island from the French in 1778. The stone ramparts and defences are still visible, 18th-century gun batteries and gun slides, 19th-century barracks and cookhouses. Since the earliest visitors came to St Lucia, Pigeon Island has been used as a vantage point to watch over Martinique, visible 20 miles away. Pirates used it as a spot to look for Spanish sails and the British watched for French convoys. Pigeon Point is a National Park and there is a museum with its war memorabilia from past French–British conflicts. Open Mon–Sat, 9–4, adm.

At the northern tip of the island is the **Cap Estate**, an expensive residential area with smart villas and a golf course. In the prosperous days of the 18th century the town in this area, now defunct, was known as *Dauphin*, again too much for revolutionary sentiment and so it became *La Nation*. Well worth a visit in this area is the gallery of the St Lucian born artist, Llewelyn Xavier. Go straight ahead at the second roundabout, past the house that looks like a banana and it is a white building up on the left. Artists on view include locals Derek Walcott and Roy Lawaetz (as well as Xavier himself), Mr Canute Caliste from Carriacou and several Haitians, but the trip is worthwhile for the view alone, which takes in both the Atlantic coast and the Pitons. Admission free, paintings from a few hundred dollars.

South to Soufrière

The route to Soufrière from Castries follows a tortuous path on the leeward coast of the island, a series of switchbacks struggling up over the headlands and cruising down into the river valleys where fishing villages nestle among the palms. Alternatively, take a yacht and coast down-island for three hours and you will see the road straggle southward against the backdrop of St Lucian mountains, so often shrouded by passing rainstorms. Whichever way you go, the journey culminates in one of the most exciting views in the whole of the Caribbean, the twin peaks of the *Pitons* that soar from the sea's edge like vast tropical pyramids.

On land the journey starts at the summit of Morne Fortune, and drops into **Cul de Sac**, a wide valley once riffling with sugar cane and now carpeted with banana trees. The *Geest* freighters call weekly for bananas for shipment to Britain.

Past the industrial estate and up into the heights, the route south opens into another huge valley, at **Roseau**, again filled with bright green banana leaves that splay gracefully in an arch until their tips reach the ground. As you descend you come to the turning to the hidden **Marigot Bay**, an idyllic hideaway in a steep-sided harbour festooned with palm trees, where yachts sit serenely on the calm of Hurricane Hole, an extremely safe anchorage. It is here that *Dr Dolittle* with Rex Harrison, and Sophia Loren's *Fire Power*, were filmed. A small boat-taxi links one side to the other. In 1778, Admiral Barrington is supposed to have eluded d'Estaing by bringing his fleet into the bay and camouflaging the ships with palm fronds. Back on the main road, the best view of the Roseau valley is from the heights just as you leave it to drive farther south.

The two fishing towns of **Anse la Raye** and **Canaries** lie on river mouths at the sea's edge. From here the road cuts deeper into the undergrowth, a profusion of majestic ferns that sprout from the deep brown earth and ancient lianas that hang from high above.

Finally the road clears another summit and emerging from the dank rainforest you see the twin points of the **Pitons** standing out in the glare of the sun. As you descend the mountain these two pyramids move beside one another above the town of Soufrière. Seen from the sea the Pitons soar majestically right from the water's edge, but the view is better from above the town because of their identical shape.

Piton means 'spike', and these two pyramids look as though they come from the south seas. They have long been a landmark for sailors and are thought to be spines of lava forced out of volcanic craters which have gradually eroded.

The town of **Soufrière** lies in a valley beneath the *Petit Piton* (2461 ft). It is one of the oldest settlements in St Lucia, a thriving port in the mid 18th century, and takes its name from the volcanic vent nearby that emits sulphurous clouds. For a while in the 1790s it held the honoured republican name of *La Convention*, after the revolutionary tribunal in Paris.

The town is quite tatty and obviously poor, but there are some attractive old stone façades and wooden creole homes surviving from French times, their eaves a gingerbread filigree beneath corrugated iron roofs. The inhabitants are friendly, though some country people on a visit to town may regard you a bit suspiciously. On Saturday morning there is a market on the seafront and perhaps you will see cocoa beans drying in the sun on the pavement, before they are processed into cocoa paste.

The walls of the bay are extremely steep, dropping straight away thousands of feet. For those brave enough to swim in a fathomless place like this, the water has warm and cold patches, released by the volcano beneath the surface.

Inland from Soufrière, the road comes to the **Sulphur springs** at Diamond, where a path through tropical gardens of cocoa and cinnamon trees leads into a cleft and to a small waterfall gushing into a small rockpool. The water descends straight from the volcano above, where it leaves the ground at 106° Fahrenheit and has discoloured the river bed orange and gold with the volcanic mud. It is reputed to have considerable curative powers, 'efficacious in cases of rheumatism and kindred ills', and in 1784 the Governor, Baron de Laborie, had the water analysed. Louis XVI was so impressed that he gave a grant for the construction of some baths for his troops in the Windward Islands. It is still possible to bathe in the warm water, as the buildings have been restored. Curative water to drink, brought down from higher up the mountain, is also available and is good for ailments because of the mineral-rich volcanic mud. Gardens and the changing rooms, adm.

The road to Diamond continues inland, climbing steadily into the St Lucia rainforest and losing itself in Fonds St Jacques, now a nature reserve, where among the wild orchids and the montane woodland you might catch a glimpse of the endangered St Lucia parrot among the flitting hummingbirds.

Travelling south from Soufrière, the road climbs for a couple of miles to the **Soufrière volcano**, St Lucia's well-behaved solfatara. In the collapsed crater is a bubbling and steaming morass an acre in size, devoid of plant-life, with grey mudpools that hiss and smell gently of stink-bomb.

There was a vapour explosion at the Soufrière in 1766, but nothing too violent has happened since then. It is not expected to erupt because it constantly lets off steam. Paths are clearly marked and you are not advised to walk around on it because the mudpools have been known to move suddenly (one person was swallowed to the waist and ended up with third degree burns on his bum). You may see a couple of rusty pipes sticking out of the ground, an attempt to tap the heat for power generation.

As the tourist brochures say, the Soufrière is a drive-in volcano. For the tourists who dare venture forth from the protection of their car, there are guides who will ply them with more Soufrière 'lore' for a small fee.

From the mountain heights of the Pitons, the road steadily descends to the southern plains that once blew with sugar-cane, to **Vieux Fort** at the farthest tip of the island. The road passes through fishing villages of **Choiseul**, with its black and white cemetery and **Laborie**. Both are quiet and unaffected West Indian towns, full of clapboard houses on stilts, standing in neat yards in the shadow of breadfruit trees. You will probably see the signs as you arrive: 'Do a kind deed if you can', and perhaps you will arrive on the day when the open-air butcher is at work, boiling up black puddings for passers-by. At Choiseul, the Arts and Crafts Development Centre displays and sells local handiwork including rocking chairs and carvings. There is a small restaurant if you want to stop for lunch. Creole food at EC$10.

Vieux Fort

Named after a fortress mentioned by a 17th-century island-hopping monk, Abbé Raynal, windswept Vieux Fort stands on an open bay, looking south towards St Vincent. Vieux Fort is St Lucia's second town. It was here that the sugar industry was first set up in 1765, but now the town is quiet and the few streets seem empty. Hewanorra International Airport nearby was first built by the Americans in the Second World War as a refuelling point on their routes between the United States and Europe; now it receives long-haul flights in both directions.

Sticking out into the rough water between the Atlantic and the Caribbean by Vieux Fort is the **Moule à Chique** peninsula, offering fine views towards St Vincent, a grey-green stain about 25 miles away to the south.

The **Maria Islands** lie off the Atlantic coast just out of Vieux Fort and are kept as a nature reserve. Those interested in discovering the delights of the *kouwès* snake (this is the only place on the globe that this species of grass snake lives) and the wheeling world of frigatebirds and brown noddies should contact the Interpretive Centre, in a small **museum** of natural life at the end of the Hewanorra runway opposite the islands. The museum is open Wed–Sun, 9.30–5, adm.

Vieux Fort to Castries—North along the Windward Coast

The Windward road winds along the rough Atlantic coast, over the spurs and the valleys thrown off by the central spine of mountains and passes through the plantations that provide St Lucia's food and export fruit. The centres are the towns of **Micoud** and **Dennery**. At Dennery is one of the island's largest banana plantations, where you will see the huge bright green leaves unscroll and become steadily shredded by the wind as they age. From here the road cuts inland, over the **Barre de l'Isle** ridge, among the lianas and bushy ferns high up in the rainforest and then descends into Cul de Sac valley before climbing the back of Morne Fortune and dropping into Castries.

FESTIVALS

The St Lucians celebrate Independence on 22 February and their National day on 13 December with a round of fêtes and *jump-ups*, but the highlight of the St Lucian cultural calendar is **Carnival**, a pre-Lenten blow-out of street-parties led by bandwagons (artics stacked with speakers) and whipped up by calypsonians. Well-known island figures dress up and play to the crowds and the beat in the streets of Castries gets so strong that even the buildings seem to rock in time with the dancers (in fact, parts of Castries are built on reclaimed land and they really do move).

On 22 November the patron saint of music, St Cecilia, is remembered by island calypsonians and panmen. During the day they ride through the streets playing from vans and then in the evening they collect for competitons. The **Rose** and the **Marguerite** (on 30 August and 17 October) are also musical celebrations, set around an imaginary court and its retinue, each with its flower cockade. They stage a ball, and they are led by a chanterelle and a band (banjo, quattro, boom boom and drum). Well worth attending if you are on-island.

WHERE TO STAY

The majority of St Lucia's hotels are on the beaches of the northern leeward coast, facing the calm Caribbean Sea and the sunset. Some are humming hives of high-pressure luxury, classic Caribbean beach resorts, but St Lucia also has some lovely smaller hotels offering seclusion tucked away in the island's coves. All bills will be supplemented by a government tax of 8% and most hotels also levy a 10% service charge.

EXPENSIVE

The white arches and orange tiles of the **Windjammer Landing Villas Beach Resort**, PO Box 1504 (tel 809 450 0913, fax 450 0907) stand out starkly against the greens of La Brelotte Bay north of Castries. There are 114 luxurious one-, two- and three-bedroom villas, some with their own plunge pool, sunning area and maid service. Tennis and watersports by day and in the evening you can dine by the swimming pool at Rosie's on crayfish or lobster thermidor in Calvados. Rates from US$260 per couple per night. The **Royal St Lucian Hotel**, PO Box 997 (tel 809 450 9999, fax 450 9639) stands in the middle of Reduit Beach, a mansion with a marble foyer giving on to the pool and Pigeon Island. The 85 suites are in the wings, a study in twentieth century sumptuousness from the king-sized beds down to the third phone in the bathroom. The hotel dining room serves some of the best food on the island. Rooms are quite expensive at US$265 a night for a couple.

St Lucia has recently gone in for the all-inclusive concept of hotel in which you pay a fee on or before arrival and then do not pull out your wallet again.

The newest and smartest on St Lucia is the **Jalousie Plantation** (contact in Miami 305 856 7083, fax 858 4677). The resort has a magnificent setting between the Pitons, giving onto a palm-backed beach. The rooms are in cottages, each with their own covered veranda, private pool and TV and there is a slightly rarified ambience about the central areas. Sports include tennis and riding and the usual watersports. US$290 per person per night. **Le Sport**, PO Box 437 (tel 450 8551, fax 450 0368, US 800 544 2883, UK 800 590794) devotes itself to a scheduled body-holiday for office-weary execs. The hotel is set on an isolated, steep-sided cove in the north of the island and as the name suggests, there are plenty of sports, both land and waterborne. And for less energetic rejuvenation, you can try the Moorish relaxation palace (algae bubble baths and seaweed wraps, loofa rubs, swiss needle showers and massage). Calorised cuisine or plain old chocolate indulgence. Daily price per person, US$190–380. You will notice **Couples**, PO Box 190 (tel 452 4211) by the pairs of bicycle-borne lovers and the hotel insignia of two lions humping near the end of the airport runway. It is an all-inclusive resort for couples only, set on Choc Beach; endless watersports, dance till you drop and extra-curricular courses in how to get married on your holiday in St Lucia. Highly spoken of for a romping good vacation. Rates are by the week, inclusive of food and all sports, per couple: US$328 per couple per day.

There are some excellent small hotels hidden in the indentations of St Lucia's leeward coastline. The **Marigot Bay Resort**, PO Box 101 (tel 451 4357, fax 451 4353) has 30 cottages and rooms set on the slopes of the magical steep-sided Marigot Bay. There are two restaurants, diving and sailing and superb views of the sunset through the yacht masts and the scratchy combs of the coconut palms. Prices range from US$140 to $155 in winter, with very good rates in summer. A little farther down the coast, the **Anse Chastanet Beach Hotel**, PO Box 7000 (tel 459 7000, fax 459 7700) is set on a pretty bay just north of Soufrière. The rooms stand directly on the grey sand beach, where there is a friendly palm-thatch bar, or on the hillside looking towards the twin peaks of the Pitons. There is tennis and watersports, but Anse Chastanet specializes in diving and arranges good packages for this. Double room from $170 in season. The most spectacular position of all, though, is claimed by the **Ladera Hotel**, PO Box 255 (tel 459 7323, fax 459 7954) at 1000 feet above the sea and with a stunning view through the Pitons themselves. There are seven villas and eight suites built of mahogany and greenheart and face stone, and fitted with tropical furniture, including four-poster beds and dressers. Some have their own pool otherwise the central pool and the Dasheene restaurant and bar share the view. Double rate US$160–320 in winter, with good reductions in summer. The **Hummingbird Beach Resort** (tel 459 7232) is an intimate spot just above the beach and the palm trees. The ten rooms overlook the pool and restaurant hung with coral and flags and cost US$55–130 a double year round. If you would like to be near Reduit beach without spending too much, try the **Islander Hotel**, PO Box 907 (tel 452 0255, fax 450 0958), which has comfortable rooms with kitchenettes, each one festooned in tropical greenery and its own beach bar, close to all the activity of Rodney Bay. Double US$100 in winter.

Guest Houses
There are any number of guest houses in St Lucia. Some will provide meals, but many are simple, without a pool and generally they do not accept credit cards. **E's Serenity Lodge** (tel 452 1987) is clean and comfortable, set in a modern villa in Sunny Acres just north of Castries. It is friendly and serves breakfast and dinner if you want. Double room US$40–50 in season. Most of the way up the Morne you will find **Bon Appetit** (tel 452 2757). Superb view, double room US$40–50. Not far off, **Mrs Dubois** has four rooms above La Toc Bay for US$33 a double (tel 452 2201), restaurant attached. The cheapest deal in town is **Lee's Guest House** (tel 452 2193), rooms US$17. Near Gros Islet you can try the friendly **La Panache** guest house (tel 450 0765), on a hill above the town, double $25.

In Soufrière you can stay at the **Home** Guest House (tel 459 7318) where a double room costs US$30, and in Vieux Fort, perhaps as a stop on arrival at Hewanorra or just before leaving, try **Kimitrai** (tel 454 6328), with rooms at US$35 for a double, or the **Southern Comfort Inn** (tel 454 6088) at US$25.

EATING OUT
St Lucia's French heritage extends into the food and the West Indian ingredients take on new life in such creole dishes such as *Soupe Germou* (pumpkin and garlic soup) and *Pouile Dudon* (treacle and coconut chicken stew). As in any other of the islands, it is worth getting a spread of the vegetables, cooked in all the different ways—plantain boiled and fried, breadfruit, yam and christophene. Most large or hotel restaurants will take credit cards and traveller's cheques; local ones will accept EC (Eastern Caribbean) dollars willingly and US dollars at a pinch.

Close to the top of the Morne you will find one of the most sympathetic spots on the island, the tiny dining room at **Bon Appetit** (tel 452 2757). The six tables have a view as far as Martinique and the walls are decorated with murals painted by the hostess, who cooks. The menu is international—seafood crêpe to start or heart of palm, followed by shrimp in garlic butter, thyme and sherry. Remember to reserve a table in season, main course EC$50 plus. Slightly down the hill, the **Green Parrot** maintains another all-encompassing view of Castries, orchestrated by the patron and island luminary, Chef Harry. He oversees a French and creole menu as well as entertainment on Wednesdays and Saturdays. *Stuffed Pussy* is a popular dish for its name, but you might try soup *A la la* or *doward St Jaques*, all with St Lucian vegetables; yam frites, coquettes, gombo, chou à pomme and germou. Four course dinner, EC$80 plus 18%.

EXPENSIVE
The well-known **San Antoine** (tel 452 4660) is a restaurant with ambience, set in a 19th-century stone great house. You begin with cocktails at the bar looking out through the trees, and then move through to the refined, candle-lit dining room. The menu is French and international —poisson grillé aux trois fruits (mango, banana and orange) or fruits de mer flambés (shrimp, cream, sweet pepper, onion, garlic and brandy). Luncheon too. EC$40–60 a main course. Closed Sun out of season. **Rain** (tel 452 3022),

with its green gables and verandas, is a St Lucian keynote, a green and white clapboard masterpiece inspired by a Somerset Maugham story. Overlooking Columbus Square in the centre of town, it is a popular meeting place for cocktails, before pizzas and burgers 'à la blackboard' downstairs, 'à la carte' dining upstairs, or the 'Champagne Banquet of 1885', a seven-course extravaganza that celebrates the year of the building's birth. An entrée upstairs comes at about EC$40 and lunch on the terrace about half this.

MODERATE
Just outside Castries is a charming veranda setting above the water at **Jimmie's** (tel 452 5142). The fare is seafood and local vegetables cooked in European style, as well as small fish caught in pots (cages) not served by other restaurants. Try angel fish, doctor fish and gozier (big eye). EC$35. Also out of town, try **D's** Restaurant (tel 453 7931), which is popular with businessmen for lunch (EC$25 for a kebab or a mixed grill), and in the evening when you can have chicken in a coconut cream or local catch delicately grilled. About EC$30 a main dish.

There are some excellent restaurants in Rodney Bay, many of them with the added advantage of a waterfront setting on the Rodney Bay marina. There is always a crowd at the **Charthouse** (tel 450 8115), set in a timber-frame house hung with ferns and palms. Breezy and lively, the Charthouse specializes in steaks and ribs (hickory smoked) and local fish. Reservations recommended, closed Sun, main dish EC$30–80. The **Eagles Inn** (tel 450 0650) sits on the waterfront, looking across the channel to the village of Gros Islet. Quiet and relaxed with French creole food. Excellent red snapper and flying fish St Lucia (in lime butter and seasoning). Closed Fri, main course EC$30 plus. Close to the marina itself is the **Bistro** (tel 450 9494) which has a charming outdoor setting on a marine veranda, with red-chequered tablecloths on the wooden tables. Happy mix of yachties and businessmen, menu on the blackboard—mushroom and artichoke lasagne, chicken cheese and crab in puff pastry and even a Lancashire Hotpot, EC$35 and up. If you think you would like an air-conditioned speakeasy with a feeling of mock-gangster-ism, then try **Capone's** (tel 450 0284) nearby, where the menu is Italian. Start with a Prohibition Punch, followed by gambera all Romanov (shrimp in vodka cream) or chicken in cream and pineapple. EC$40–70, bill comes in a violin case. If you cannot remember the code-word (Al sent me), then there is a pizzeria next door. **The Lime,** just off the road to the St Lucian Hotel, offers less expensive dinners and daytime snacks on a veranda of encroaching greenery. Fish grilled or sautéd in lime butter, fixed price EC$45. You can find the best in local fare at **Laurel's**, on a terrace above the road to the Windjammer resort.

In the **Soufrière** area you can try the hotel dining rooms—Anse Chastanet, the Humming Bird and Dasheene at the Ladera. Otherwise **The Still** opens for a West Indian lunch, tropical juices and locally raised seafood and vegetables. It is friendly, but is occasionally invaded by busloads of cruise-ship passengers. You might also try **Captain Hook's** for local fare in West Indian sized portions. **Marigot Bay** is an idyllic stopover, where you can linger over a fish in creole sauce or a salad at **Dolittle's** or **Odin's** down in the bay or at **Jay-Jay's** up above.

VERY CHEAP
You will find endless snacks and pastries on offer in St Lucia, some of them fried on braziers in front of you. A *float* is a deep-fried dough cake and you will find variations

such as codfish or corned beef fritters. Finish off with a coconut pattie or a delicious St Lucian fruit cake. In Castries there are also a number of take-away vans where you can get a juice and a local meal in a polystyrene box in the daytime.

BARS AND NIGHTLIFE
St Lucia is pretty quiet in the week, though the hotels (the Green Parrot and Wind-jammer among them) do arrange tourist shows if you wish to see a few thighs singed under the limbo pole and hear the velvet notes of a steel band. The Royal St Lucian has occasional jazz evenings.

Most bars in St Lucia are attached to restaurants, but a popular spot in town is **Kimlan's**, where you can watch the crowds on Columbus Square from the balcony. And there is a long list of cocktails in **Rain**, on the other side of the square. On the waterfront on Rodney Bay is the **A-Pub**, frequented by white St Lucians and semi-permanent yachtsmen; darts, backgammon and the occasional karaoke, and close by, the **Lime** is a popular gathering point at the weekends and particularly on Wednesday nights before the crowd moves on to **Splash**, the discotheque at the St Lucian Hotel. Other dis-cotheques include the Fisherman's Wharf at the Halcyon Beach Club, and the Blue Moon, next to the Halcyon Beach Club. Club Monroe is a much more St Lucian affair, off the road to Reduit from Castries, where you will hear local music and the heavy tones of Jamaican dub and dancehall.

But the best-known party in the island is the weekly *jump-up* on Friday nights at **Gros Islet**, where four or five clubs spill out on to the street, speakers turned into the road pumping out *soca*, *reggae* and the latest *zouk* from Martinique, visible just a few miles to the north. It has become a bit of a tourist event, but it is still quite fun. You can pick up grilled fish and chicken legs, cooked in braziers on the street and served with hot pepper sauce. A less crowded variation on the theme is outside **Jay-Jays** on the road that leads down into Marigot Bay.

DOMINICA

Dominica is practically all mountains and rainforest; a jumble of peaks and spurs so rugged and dramatic that the island has its own micro-climate. Of all the islands that Columbus is supposed to have described to Ferdinand and Isabella of Spain by crum-pling a piece of parchment and throwing it on to the table with a 'like this, your Majesties', Dominica is the one he would be most likely to recognize today. Wags claim that it has hardly changed since he was here 500 years ago.

In its 29 miles by 16, Dominica has mountains over 4500 ft, higher than anything on the British Isles. The water-laden winds of the Atlantic Ocean clamber up its slopes and then stack in huge clouds on the mountaintops, poised immobile before they ditch their load. The rainfall here is measured in tens of feet and romantics will tell you there is always a rainbow somewhere in the mist-veiled peaks of the island. The vegetation is explosive—a garden untended for ten years will be five foot under with trees as thick as your leg and the natural life is unparalleled. Dominica is overwhelmingly green.

Dominica (pronounced *Domineeker*) is the least developed of the Windward Islands and for all the fertility, it is hard to make a living. Many parts of the island are very poor and you will see more subsistence farmers working small plots cut out of the hillside than on the other islands. For years it was difficult enough to get to the island and relatively recently new roads have opened up parts that before could only be reached on horseback. Vans travel between the villages selling anything from tinned milk to Sunday dresses.

Apart from its wildlife, Dominica's most remarkable heritage is that it is home to the last surviving traces of the Carib race. To the Caribs, the island was *Waitukubuli* or 'tall is her body' and the wild terrain meant that it was the last island to be settled by Europeans. Once proud and warlike, the Caribs were left in peace on Dominica for a while, but ultimately they could not defend their homeland from the newcomers. There are no native Carib-speakers left, but their descendants are easily recognized in Dominica by their Amerindian features.

A quarter of the island's 71,000 population live in the capital Roseau, on the protected Caribbean coast. The island lies between two French islands, Guadeloupe to the north and Martinique to the south, and over the centuries this has had its effect. The official language may be English, but French *patois* can be heard all over the island and most of the population is Catholic.

In a part of the world renowned for its 'palm-fringed and dazzling white-sand beaches', Dominica is an odd-man out. It is unpretentious and its beauty lies rather in its spectacular interior, rightfully calling itself the *Nature Island of the Caribbean*. Even 500 years after Columbus crumpled his parchment, patches of Dominica are still 'unexplored jungle'.

History

Waitukubuli was christened on 3 November 1493, as Columbus made land after five weeks at sea on his second voyage to the New World. It was a Sunday, and to give thanks for the safe passage of his fleet the explorer called his new discovery Dominica.

As the heartland of the 'Cannibal Isles', Dominica was given a wide berth by the Spaniards, and only pirates, fishermen and foresters braved its coasts. For a while the Spaniards considered making a harbour where their ships could re-fit and take on water after the Atlantic crossing, but they did not reckon on the opposition of the man-eating Caribs.

The Europeans were kept at bay for 200 years. Dominica was officially a neutral island as late as 1748, left 'to the undisturbed possession of the native Indians' (Treaty of Aix-la-Chapelle), and a retreat for the Caribs squeezed out of the neighbouring islands. But Dominica's position between the two French colonies of Martinique and Guadeloupe meant that it was too important to be disregarded for long, and in the 1750s the French moved in. The campaign against the Caribs was so ruthless and thorough that there were just 400 survivors, who retreated still further to the windward coast where they would be left alone.

Dominica was caught in the crossfire of the European conflicts like the other Windwards, blockaded each time war was declared and encouraged to plant madly in times of peace. Traditionally, the French settlers planted coffee and the British sugar. The island was also a *free port* and for a while did a brisk trade as a slave market. In 1763, after the Treaty of Paris granted the island to Britain, the French lands were promptly sold to

English planters and the £313,666 that the sale realized were pocketed by George III, 'to make up for the lack of a dowry from Queen Charlotte'!

Dominica's mountainous and fertile interior offered easy sanctuary for runaway plantation slaves, or *maroons*, who hid out in small communities in the hills. Initially they were happy with just their freedom, but rallied by leaders with names such as Congo Ray, Jacko, Zombie and Jupiter, they soon began to steal cattle and torch estate buildings, encouraging other slaves to join them. The island militia was first sent out against them in 1785, flushing them out in the network of tracks in the hinterland.

As the French Revolution took its effect in the Caribbean, French Royalists fled to Dominica from Martinique and Guadeloupe. Republican revolutionaries followed them and offered freedom to the island slaves if they rose up against the British (slaves on the French islands had been freed in 1794). They sent in arms to the maroons and there was an invasion from Guadeloupe in June 1795, but the hills were cleaned out again and it was repulsed.

With the French in the ascendancy again in Europe in the early 19th century, Dominica was threatened once more along with the other British Caribbean islands. In 1805, armed ships appeared in Roseau Bay, flying the Union Jack. At the last moment they tore it down and ran up the *tricolore* instead. Admiral La Grange was besieging the island for France and he blockaded Roseau. After chasing up and down the island, La Grange ransomed the town for £12,000, took all the slaves he could lay his hands on and sailed off to St Kitts.

Maroons were still hiding out in the hills and they rose up again in a guerrilla war between 1812 and 1815. Eventually crushed by the Rangers, the leaders were hanged, but their memory remains in the peak near the town of Belles, *Morne Nègres Marrons*.

With Emancipation in 1834, Dominica became a refuge for French slaves from the neighbouring islands, where slavery had been reintroduced in 1802. Until 1848, when the French banned it once again, the slaves would make the perilous journey on homemade rafts at night in their bid for freedom. Dominica's freed slaves moved away from the plantations, preferring instead to cut a plot of land out of the fertile interior, growing the produce they needed and selling the surplus at market. The new Dominicans were self-reliant and independent, with a spirit that would erupt into violence at times—there were riots when the government demanded taxes for roads or even called a census.

Despite its size and fertility, the island was particularly poor. But some industries were able to flourish, the most notable being *Rose's*, now part of the Cadbury Schweppes group, which provided lime juice for British ships. The drink became popular beyond the requirements for naval rations and in 1875 a factory was set up in Roseau to extract lime juice from the thousands of acres that were planted with the fruit. For a while, Dominica was by far the world's largest producer of limes and the fruit brought in about half of the country's export earnings. Since the Second World War this has declined and bananas have taken their place.

Despite spending most of its colonial life in the Leeward Isles, in federation with Antigua and Montserrat and islands further north, Dominica is much more similar to the Windward Islands and it became one of them in 1939. In 1951 the vote was given to all Dominicans over the age of 21 and the island became self-governing in 1967.

In the ground-swell of the new political freedom, the Dominica Labour Party, led by

Edward Le Blanc, rallied the new voters and was thrust to power. The 70s saw social unrest as demonstrations, racist attacks and strikes held the island to ransom and a state of emergency was declared more than once. The *Dreads*, called so because they wore their hair in dreadlocks, took to the hills, hiding out as the maroons had done 200 years before.

On 3 November 1978, 485 years to the day after the island was discovered by Columbus, Dominica took its independence from Britain. Then a few months later Hurricane David arrived—Roseau was literally flattened, there were 37 deaths and 80 per cent of the population were left homeless. The political unrest continued; an emergency government had to be installed and then there were two coup attempts and an invasion party was arrested in the States.

Today Dominica has steadied politically after a decade of rule by the Dominica Freedom Party, headed by Miss Eugenia Charles, first elected in 1980 as the Caribbean's first woman Prime Minister, and most recently in 1990, when she was returned to the 21-seat Parliament with a majority of one.

The Nature Isle—Dominican Flora and Fauna

Much of Dominica is 100 feet deep in tropical rainforest, undergrowth, overgrowth and canopy so thick that it is dark at midday. Trees vie with each other to grow tallest, stretching up to reach the sunlight, while lianas and creeping vines take an easier route, grappling the tree-trunks and using them to climb. In the branches sit orchids and ferns that explode in graceful curves. The forest gushes with water, it squawks and chirrups and is a botanist's utopia. With so many species in such good condition, it has been called a living museum.

The **Morne Trois Pitons National Park**, a 17,000-acre reserve of rainforest in the centre of the island, is the Caribbean's oldest nature reserve and it contains many of the island's natural attractions. There are several marked **walking trails** in the park and guides are readily available. On paths the best footwear is a strong pair of sneakers, perhaps with ankle support, but if you are walking up rivers, take the local red, gold and green plastic sandals, nicknamed 'Toyotas' (because they hold the road well). Also remember a waterproof, a picnic and if you are out for a long day, take a jersey too. As with anywhere, you are advised to take little money and jewellery with you when you go off the beaten track in Dominica.

Off the transinsular road there is the **Emerald Pool**, a tame cascade falling into a rockpool and the **Middleham Trails**, leading to lost waterfalls. At the head of the Roseau Valley are the **Trafalgar Falls** and from the nearby town of Laudat it is possible to reach the **Titou Gorge** and the **Freshwater** and **Boeri** Lakes. Other visits to falls include a walk up the **Sasari River** from La Plaine and the **Victoria Falls** above Delices. A very long day's walk will take you to the smelly and steaming **Valley of Desolation** and the **boiling lake**, high in the mountains. (See around the island, pp. 166–70 for more detail about the sights.)

More information and help with guides can be found at the **Division of Tourism** (tel 44 82351) or the **Division of Forestry** office (tel 44 82401 ext 417), situated in the Botanical Gardens in Roseau. Tours can be arranged through **Dominica Tours** (tel 44 82638) and **Ken's Hinterland Adventure Tours** (tel 44 84850). Also **Antours**, PO

Box 428, Roseau (tel 44 86460, fax 44 8 6780). Tour operators have a wide range of suggestions to add to those above.

Some 135 species of bird live in Dominica or migrate with the tourists for the better weather during the winter season. Among the common bananaquits and bullfinches, the exotic flycatchers and fluorescent hummingbirds, Dominica has two parrots that are endemic to the island. Both are endangered, and the sisserou is portrayed on the national flag. The sisserou, or imperial parrot, is one of the largest parrots in the world and has a purple breast and green wings. The smaller red-necked amazon or jacko is a little less scarce and might be seen racing by in a flash of scarlet. To have a hope of seeing the parrots (a trip can be arranged through one of the operators above) you may have to get up extremely early and hike into the hills to a special hide. Another bird almost unique to Dominica is the siffleur montagne which whistles its single melancholy note every few minutes in the rainforest.

As all over the Caribbean, fauna is much more limited. Agouti and a rare three-foot iguana scurry around the heights and in the constant susurration of island insects you may see cockroaches wiggle antennae four inches long. Out at night you may come across luminous flickering points that are fireflies and maybe the blacksmith beetle, which clanks.

There are five species of snake, none of them poisonous. One of the rarest but most surprising is the shy boa constrictor, known as *tête chien* because of the shape of its head. Outside the Amazon basin it is found only in Dominica and it has been known to grow to 20 feet long and as thick as a man's leg. There is an early story of a Dominican who was resting under a tree and woke up to find his leg inside one of these snakes up to the thigh. Friends helped him extricate himself, putting wedges on the snake's teeth and chopping it up into pieces to release him.

It might be possible (depending on the season) to arrange to catch crayfish and frogs, later served as mountain chicken. Hunting for frogs takes place at night, with the aid of burning torches that have a fatal attraction for the animals.

GETTING TO DOMINICA

The two airports on Dominica are Melville Hall (code DOM) and Canefield (DCF). Neither accepts jet aircraft. Melville Hall is inconveniently located on the eastern side of the island, 35 miles northeast of Roseau, and so you are probably best to aim for Canefield, on the west coast just north of the capital.

Since only propeller aircraft can fly to Dominica, passengers from outside the Caribbean have to connect from another island, of which the best are Sint Maarten, Antigua, Barbados and St Lucia. Air Caribe Dominica Ltd (tel 809 44 92998) has three or four daily flights from St Maarten, a single flight to Barbados and a link three times a week to St Lucia. LIAT has about 10 flights a day, originating in Antigua or Barbados and Air Martinique and Air Guadeloupe fly from their respective homes. There is a departure tax of EC$20 and a $5 airport security tax.

By **boat**, there is a weekly service to and from Barry in South Wales on Geest Line. Caribbean Express runs a link four times a week between Martinique and Guadeloupe which touches Dominica (Mon, Wed, Fri, Sat). Fare to: Martinique–EC$106, Guadeloupe–$126. Reserve a seat in season and during school holidays. Contact Dominica Booking Agents (tel 44 82881).

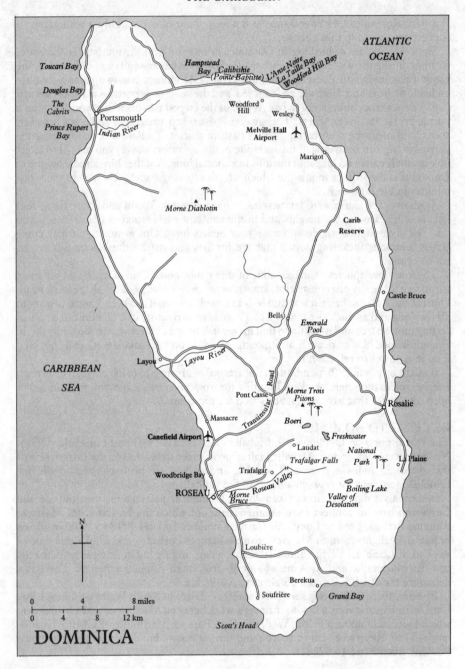

ATLANTIC
OCEAN

Toucari Bay

Hampstead Bay *Calibishie (Pointe-Baptiste)* *L'Anse Noire Bay* *La Taille Bay* *Woodford Hill Bay*

Douglas Bay

The Cabrits

Woodford Hill

Wesley

Prince Rupert Bay

Portsmouth

Indian River

Melville Hall Airport

Marigot

▲ *Morne Diablotin*

Carib Reserve

Castle Bruce

Bells

Emerald Pool

CARIBBEAN

SEA

Layou

Layou River

Transinsular Road

Pont Cassé

Morne Trois Pitons

▲

Rosalie

Massacre

Boeri

Canefield Airport ✈

🐚 *Freshwater*

Laudat

National Park

La Plaine

Trafalgar Falls

Woodbridge Bay

Trafalgar

Roseau Valley

ROSEAU

Morne Bruce

Boiling Lake

Valley of Desolation

N

Loubière

Berekua

0   4   8 miles

Soufrière

Grand Bay

0   4   8   12 km

Scott's Head

DOMINICA

GETTING AROUND DOMINICA
Public transport is mostly by Japanese van, with teenage minders leaning out of them to shout for passengers, and by unwieldy government bus. The major routes are all served, but only infrequently after noon and hardly at all on Sundays (it is possible to get stranded in outlying areas, because the buses tend to go to Roseau in the morning and return in the early afternoon). However, **hitching** works quite well (you may be lucky enough to get a ride in one of the old Bedfords with the colourful wooden cages on the back). Though they would probably not take it, drivers might appreciate being offered a couple of dollars for the ride.

Buses travelling **south** go from near the Old Market Square; for the **Roseau Valley** from the top of King George V St, opposite the Police Headquarters, and those headed **north** leave from near the New Market, next to the West Bridge. Sample bus prices, all set by the government, are: **Roseau** to Soufrière—EC$3, Laudat—$2, Canefield Airport—$1.50, Castle Bruce—$6, Portsmouth—$7.

Taxis also have fixed rates, costing EC$35 from **Roseau** to Trafalgar Falls and to Canefield airport. The trip to Melville Hall airport is charged by the car, at EC$130, for a maximum of four people. For an island tour, taxis can be hired for about EC$45 per hour.

Hire cars are available in Roseau from **Valley Rent a Car** on Goodwill Road (tel 44 83233), **Wide Range Car**, 81 Bath Road (tel 44 82198) and **STL Car Rental** (tel 44 82340). Hire costs around US$40 per day. You will need a local driver's licence, which can be obtained from the Traffic Dept in Roseau, price EC$20.

TOURIST INFORMATION
UK: you can contact the Dominica Tourist Office at 1 Collingham Gdns, London SW5 0HW (tel 071 835 1937).

USA: contact the Caribbean Tourism Association, 20 East 46th St, New York, NY 10017 (tel 212 682 0435).

On the island itself, the **Dominica Tourist Board** is reached at Box 73, Roseau, Dominica (tel 44 82351, fax 44 85840). For tourist **information** there is a kiosk at the Old Market Place on the waterfront and one at each of the airports.

The main hospital in Roseau is the **Princess Margaret Hospital** (tel 44 82231). For emergency services, dial 999. The **IDD code** for Dominica is 809 and this is followed by a seven-digit island number, beginning with 44. When you are on-island, dial only the last five digits of this number. It is best to address letters to the Commonwealth of Dominica, because otherwise they often end up in the Dominican Republic.

MONEY
The currency of Dominica is the EC$ (US$1 = EC$2.69). Prices are often published in both dollar currencies, so it is worth knowing which currency you are dealing in. **Banks** open daily 8–3, staying open until 5 on Fridays. **Shopping hours** are 8–4 in the week, often with a stop for lunch 1pm–2pm and Saturdays 8–1pm.

WRITERS AND ARTISTS
The writer Jean Rhys (1890–1979) came from Dominica. Her family owned an estate in Grand Bay and she was born in Roseau, but left the island when she was 16, moving to Europe. Many of her books include nostalgic memories of the Dominica of her

childhood. Fame came with *Wide Sargasso Sea* (1966), some of which is set in the oppressive atmosphere of colonial Dominican society at the turn of the 19th century. Another Dominican authoress and politician, Phyllis Shand Allfrey, wrote the novel *The Orchid House*, also set on the island. The story of a private soldier's life is recorded in *Redcoats in the Caribbean* by James Aytoun, published by Blackburn Recreation Services Dept for the Cambridgeshire Regiment.

Dominica was very fortunate in the visit of the Italian painter, Agostino Brunias, who stayed on the island for many years in the late 18th century, recording the Dominican way of life and events. His paintings are extremely lively, giving a fascinating view of the dress of free creoles, the plantations, vendors' stalls, dances and women washing clothes in the streams, much of which can still be seen in its different form today.

BEACHES AND RIVER-BATHING

Dominica has no white coral-sand beaches in the typical Caribbean mould and most beaches tend to be dark volcanic grey or jet black. There are some golden-sand beaches in the coves on the northeastern coast of the island, overhung with cliffs, where you will often be alone. Take a good map and all you need in the way of food and drink, and head for **Hampstead Bay**, **Calibishie** (Point Baptiste), where there is a good stop at the **Almond Beach Bar** or farther round at **L'Anse Noir**, **La Taille Bay** and **Woodford Hill Bay**. Black-sand beaches include **Douglas Bay**, **Prince Rupert Bay** in the northwest, and **Castaways**, where you will find a bar. In places near Roseau, the waterfront is made up of fist-sized rocks that clatter as they race and recede with the waves. **Spider's Bar** is across the road from the sea at Loubière.

Perhaps preferable to sea-bathing is swimming in Dominica's **rivers**. There is plenty of flowing water on the island. So much, in fact, that they sell it to drier islands such as Antigua and St Maarten to the north. Waterfalls are also a good bet, because there is usually a pool beneath them. Some good places to swim are at the Trafalgar and Middleham Falls (an hour's walk), the Rosalie river on the east coast and the White River in La Plaine, whose source is the boiling lake. Otherwise, ask around. For a full day's outing you can float and clamber down the **Layou River**, starting at Belles in the rainforest on the transinsular road and working your way down through the Layou flats towards the west coast.

WATERSPORTS

Watersports are not that developed in Dominica and if you wish to go **windsurfing** you will have to contact one of the hotels (try the Anchorage or Castaways). If you would like to take a day's sail, contact **Dominica Tours** (tel 44 82638).

Dominica has a growing reputation for **diving**, though. Dives take place on the reefs along the leeward coast, mainly in the south near Scott's Head in Soufrière bay, where there is a new Marine Park and also in the Marine Park in Douglas Bay just north of the Cabrits. Brain corals, black corals and sponges are all on view, and you will also see schools of soldierfish and triggerfish, as well as individual angelfish in yellow and velvet blue. Dominican oddities include hot and coldwater springs under the surface (at Champagne in Soufrière Bay you will see and and feel the warm bubbling water, discoloured with sulphur and iron) and clear water beneath cloudy river outflows. Wrecks also occasionally turn up too. Dives (about US$40 per tank), equipment hire and instruction can be arranged through **Dive Dominica Ltd**, at the Castle Comfort Guest House (tel 44 82188) just south of Roseau, **Dominica Dive Resorts** (tel 44 82638), who have an operation both in the north and south of the island; and the **Dive Centre** at Castaways Beach Hotel in Mero (tel 44 96244).

Snorkelling is good off the north coast, for instance at Hodge's Bay and Douglas Bay and particularly in Soufrière Bay. Equipment can be hired at the watersports shops or at the hotels.

Roseau

Roseau, Dominica's capital, has 20,000 inhabitants, about a quarter of the population, and is the only sizeable town on the island. Towered over by the mountainous hinterland of Dominica, the town stands at the mouth of the Roseau river, taking its name from the French word for the reeds that grew here, which the Caribs would use to poison the tips of their arrows. Lacking a proper harbour, it was never intended to be the island's capital, but Portsmouth in the north was considered unhealthy and so the administrators moved here in the late 18th century.

Roseau is a traditional West Indian waterfront town. It was extensively rebuilt after Hurricane David in 1979, but it has not been redeveloped in concrete; many of the old creole houses have been rebuilt as they were. Only the occasional satellite dish stands out among the shanties and the streets of traditional warehouses near the waterfront. With strong stone foundations and shuttered doorways that let through the breeze, the old storehouses and shops are topped with wooden upper storeys and steep roofs, many of them embellished with trelliswork. Some have balconies over the pavement, supported by sturdy wooden columns, giving welcome shelter in Roseau's regular tropical rainstorms. Although the town looks a little neglected, its roofs rusted and the buildings a bit run down, these attractive houses give Roseau a charming atmosphere.

Wherever you go in Dominica people seem to greet you, usually in French *patois*, but the liveliest spot in Roseau is the market. Next to the river-mouth, it is ominously entitled **Roseau Market . . .** as though the dots concealed its secrets. There is a large covered area of tables, but the Dominicans mostly prefer to spread out their produce—guava, grapefruit and golden apple—on the ground in the open, using golf umbrellas to protect them from the sun and plastic sheeting at the ready for when it rains.

The market was moved here in the 70s, from its original site a few hundred yards away at the other end of the waterfront, beneath the old Fort Young. **Dawbiney Market Plaza** has now been taken in hand by the Tourist Board and has been restored much as it was. Trading took place here, along with all of Dominica's public executions.

Walking north on Castle Street and Virgin Lane, you come to the Roman Catholic **Cathedral of the Assumption**, built in dark stone with Romanesque arches and completed in 1841. Even though the majority of Dominica's population was Catholic, the official Anglican government would grant no money for the building of the Cathedral. Summoned by a bell, the faithful would come out at night and carry stones from the Roseau river to the site.

Fort Young is now a hotel, but once was Roseau's main defence. It was erected in 1775 and visitors to the hotel will still see a few slim and elegant-looking cannons hanging around the foyer and grounds.

165

THE CARIBBEAN

Behind the town, at the foot of Morne Bruce, are the **Botanical Gardens**, which date from 1891. Landscaped with open lawns, it must be the only place of its kind that appears less fertile than the country surrounding it. There are 150 species, including a giant boabab tree that came down in 1979, when Hurricane David uprooted over half the garden's species, still lying on top of the yellow school bus that it crushed. It has even begun to flower again.

A path climbs **Morne Bruce** from the gardens, 500 feet up through the creaking bamboo, to the crown-like Catholic memorial. The Morne takes its name from the 18th-century engineer who fortified it and it gives an excellent view across the town, covering the bay. Most of the buildings have fallen down now. Earlier this century the Morne was thought to be haunted as troops would be heard marching and a bugle sounded on dark nights.

The Roseau Valley

The extension of King George V St leads out of the town and across a clattering wooden suspension bridge into the Roseau river valley, straight into the Dominican heartland. The bridge may seem high, but the Roseau river has been known to rise 20 feet in as many hours. Some of Roseau's more prosperous citizens have retreated into the cooler heights of the valley, side by side with farmers who manage to terrace and cultivate the absurdly steep valley walls.

At the head of the valley, five miles up river from Roseau, just beyond the village of Trafalgar, are the **Trafalgar Falls**, two spectacular cascades that tumble 90 feet from the lip of a gorge, water whipped into a maelstrom by upward winds, splattering down among titanic black boulders and orange iron-discoloured rocks. The vegetation is prodigious and provides pockets of quiet as you climb, before you emerge into the blanket of fine spray and white noise that fills the gorge, a deafening hiss and roar that drops into the pools of hot and cold water. The falls are smaller now that some of the water has been harnessed for hydro-electricity.

The Trafalgar Falls are easy to reach on a short outing from town and you can drive to within ten minutes of them. Take a swimming costume and gymshoes if you like clambering over rocks and consider getting a guide (for perhaps EC$10), who will know the quick routes through the gargantuan orange and black boulders. You might need a jersey for your return because it can also get a bit cold and wet in the wind.

Twin pipes lead down from the falls, carrying water to a hydro-electric generating station, passing **Papillote Wilderness Retreat**, where a hotel is set in a 12-acre garden of Dominican profusion and rushing water spewed out by ornamental iguanas. Paths lead among forests of white-leafed hibiscus, bromeliads and aroids, and orchids like butterflies, all sheltered by vast sprays of bamboo overhead. There is also a naturally heated mineral bath, for which the water comes from the springs higher up the mountain. This is a good place to stop for lunch on the veranda (tel 44 82287).

Morne Trois Pitons National Park

At the head of a side valley is the village of Laudat, the best dropping off point for the 17,000-acre reserve. You can reach the **Freshwater Lake** by vehicle, a couple of miles

166

beyond Laudat. The lake is at 2500 ft and was haunted variously by a vindictive mermaid who would lure travellers to drown them and according to Oldmixon in 1708 by 'a vast monstrous Serpent, that had its Abode in the before-mentioned Bottom (an inaccessible Bottom in the high mountains). They affirm'd, there was in the Head of it a very sparkling Stone, like a Carbuncle of inestimable Price; that the Monster commonly veil'd that rich jewel with a thin moving skin, like that of a Man's Eyelid, and when it went to drink or sported itself in the deep Bottom, it fully discovered it, and the Rocks all about receiv'd a wonderful Lustre from the Fire issuing out of that precious Gem.'

Three quarters of an hour's walk beyond the Freshwater Lake, towards the Morne Trois Pitons, the island's second highest peak, is the **Boeri Lake**, in the crater of an extinct volcano. The vegetation thins at this height and the rainforest gives way to montane and elfin growth, giving good views, on days when the rainclouds are not obscuring them.

But Dominica's volcanic heartland is the **Valley of Desolation**, appropriately named because nothing can grow there—even Dominican vegetation is killed off by sulphur emissions. This foetid area, among the jumble of (almost) extinct volcanoes, four hours' walk away and over two mountains, is laid with titanic boulders and sulphurous cesspools of diabolic colours. The volcano beneath it all erupted last in 1880, showering Roseau with volcanic ash.

At its centre is the **Boiling Lake**, a seething and bubbling morass like an angry jacuzzi, constantly steaming at between 180 and 200°F, and fed by (occasionally poisonous) gases from underneath that make the whole lake rise by several feet. It has been known to measure about 70 yards across, but it is smaller now. It also disappears down the plug-hole occasionally, re-emerging with a geyser spout and monumental rumbling.

South from Roseau

The road south from Roseau leads along the coast through the suburbs of Charlotteville and Castle Comfort, past a clutch of the island's hotels. In the 18th century a string of forts and batteries ran along the coast to the southern tip at Scotts Head and it was here that the French General de Bouillé made his advance when he attacked the island in 1778.

From Loubière, an impossibly steep road branches inland, climbing to the oddly named Snug Corner and over the summit, descending beneath the cliffs to the citrus orchards and banana plantations at **Bereuka** on Grand Bay, where fort ruins stand beneath the vast cliffs of the windward coast.

Eventually you come to the valley of **Soufrière**, one of the earliest areas of the island to be settled by the French. The town takes its name from the sulphur outlets farther up the valley, which flow into the river and provide heated water for bathing or washing clothes. It is a pleasant walk up the river among the 60-foot bamboo trees that creak constantly and over to Grand Bay on the Atlantic side of the island, but if you feel like refreshing yourself with a drink be careful because you might scald your hand.

The southern point of the island is dominated by Scotts Head, a spit of land jutting into the Caribbean Sea. There is little left of Fort Cacharou that once dominated it, but it was attacked many times in the past. On one occasion Dominicans sympathetic to the French got the British soldiers drunk and spiked their guns with sand, enabling the

French to overrun the fort with ease. The view from Scotts Head to Martinique, 20 miles south, and back along the leeward coast of Dominica, is stunning.

North from Roseau—the Leeward Coast

Despite being proposed in the 18th century, the road link from Roseau to Portsmouth, Dominica's second town in the north of the island, was one of the last to be completed, with some cuttings into the cliff-face up to 50 feet deep. The journey had to be made via the other side of the island or by boat until well into this century. The leeward coast is supposedly in the 'rain-shadow' of Dominica's central mountain range, meaning that it is dry (by Dominican standards). However, it can still pour without a moment's notice.

The road follows the coast, passing Woodbridge Bay, the cruise-ship dock and the deepwater port, where goods for the capital are unloaded. Just before the airport at Canefield is the **The Old Mill Cultural Centre**, in the grounds of an old plantation. The gardens contain an aqueduct and water-wheel as well as less ancient steam-driven cane-crushing gear. In the museum, **Lavi Dominik**, are displays of Dominica's pre-Columbian history, with exhibits of Carib lifestyle and weaving, representations of the colonial age in the work of Agosto Brunias and the Porters as well as an exhibit of the old Parliamentary mace, presented to the House of Assembly in 1770 and used for the 208 years before Independence in 1978, when another mace of local wood was adopted in Parliament.

Just beyond Canefield is the settlement of **Massacre** (pronounced more as in French than as in English), the site of a sad episode that took place between two half-brothers, one half Carib, the other European, in the early 1600s. *Indian Warner* was born in St Kitts, son of Governor Warner by a Carib woman, but had to flee when his father died and so he went to Dominica, becoming a Carib chief. The massacre took place when his brother Phillip was sent by the Governor of the Leeward Islands on a campaign to 'put down' the Caribs in 1674. Phillip and his troops are supposed to have feasted with the Caribs and he initiated the massacre by stabbing his brother.

Soon the leeward road passes beneath Dominica's highest peak, **Morne Diablotin** (4747 ft), which takes its name from a diabolically ugly bird that once lived on its slopes, prized of hunters in the 18th century. With webbed feet and black and white plumage, the Diablotin (black-capped petrel) was about the size of a duck and nested in the ground, flying down to the sea to fish at night. The view from Morne Diablotin is superb, but more often than not it is obscured by the clouds that hang on Dominica's mountains.

The road continues to Dominica's second town of **Portsmouth**, crossing the **Indian River** just before the town. It is possible to arrange canoe trips up the river, where the banks are tangled with mangrove roots and the canopy is festooned with flying tropical overgrowth.

Portsmouth, another tired-looking town of 3000 inhabitants with dilapidated wooden buildings, stands at the head of Prince Rupert's Bay, sheltered in the north by the promontory of the Cabrits. The bay itself takes its name from the royalist prince who arrived in the West Indies in 1652 to find that Barbados and the Leeward Islands were in the hands of the Commonwealth. Two centuries ago the bay would see as many as 400 navy ships at anchor if a campaign was brewing. Because of its harbour, Portsmouth was supposed to become the capital of Dominica, but the swampy land was malarial and so the British colonists took off to the old Carib settlement at Roseau instead.

On the northern side of the bay is the promontory of the **Cabrits National Park**, two hills scattered with the fortifications of Fort Shirley. The Fort, dating from the 1770s, has been restored to its fearsome brimstone glory after more than 100 years of decay since it was abandoned in 1854 by the British. The restoration received an award from American Express. The word *Cabrits* derives from the Spanish word for goat— animals that would be left here as fresh meat for future arrivals low on stocks after the Atlantic crossing. Marked trails cover the promontory and there is a small museum, adm free.

From Portsmouth a side road leads north past the anchorages at Douglas Bay and Toucari Bay. It was from an estate just north of Toucari that John Mair and friends watched the Battle of the Saints in April 1782. They were breakfasting in the portico as the battle began. (See Guadeloupe, p. 226.)

The main road around the island leads inland from Portsmouth, winding into the hills, violent Dominican fertility alternately soaked and shined upon at half-hourly intervals, and rejoining the north coast after five miles. In this area Dominica's best beaches can be found in the coves that look out on to the islands of Marie Galante and the Saints. Beneath bright orange and muddy cliffs are beaches of large-grained golden sand, sometimes flecked with jet black magnetic particles (see Beaches, p. 164).

The road continues to the villages of Wesley and Marigot, settled by Antiguans and other Leeward Islanders who came as construction labourers and settled here when their work was finished. Unlike most Dominican villages they speak English and not French creole as their first tongue.

The Transinsular Road to the East Coast

The grandly-named Transinsular Road, formerly known by the even grander name of the Imperial Road, winds a laborious way into the Dominican highlands from Canefield airport. For years, journeys to the Atlantic coast had to be made by boat or on horseback along paths throttled by vegetation, but the Imperial Road commenced its journey to windward in 1909, setting off into the jungle and only emerging on the Atlantic coast in the late 50s.

It always seems to be raining up in Dominica's hinterland and you will certainly see a few rainbows among the peaks. The road also gives an excellent way to see some of Dominica's extraordinary fertility (you cut through the northern part of the Morne Trois Pitons National Park). There are whole slopes covered with elephant ears and creeping vines, fluorescent green ferns so large that they might fly away and waterfalls that descend from heights invisible from below in the spray.

The **Middleham Trails** lead off the main road and cross over the hills to the Roseau Valley at Laudat, via the Middleham Falls, a stunning waterfall of 150 metres in height. At Pont Casse the road splits three ways, left to the Layou Valley and back down to the Leeward Coast and right to Castle Bruce and the southeast corner of the island. The transinsular road continues straight to the Atlantic coast just short of Marigot and Melville Hall airport. At **Belles** it is possible to join the higher reaches of the Layou

River for a day-long hike and swim through flats and gulleys that emerge on the Layou road a couple of miles short of the west coast. Take a pair of gym-shoes and a swimming costume and arrange for someone to meet you at the bottom.

Back on the Castle Bruce road a tamer walk through the jungle can be made at the **Emerald Pool**. Walkways are carefully marked out and lead down to the small pool, where a tiny cascade races into the warm and dank recess and roots like knotted fingers grapple rocks furred with moss. However, do not expect it to be isolated enough to go skinny-dipping.

The road passes beneath Dominica's second peak, **Morne Trois Pitons**, and then throws off another branch that leads to **Rosalie** and to **La Plaine**. The latter was the scene of riots at the end of the 19th century, when the villagers protested at the imposition of land taxes.

Atlantic breakers pound the windward shore, where there are cliffs hundreds of feet high. Before the road was built, stores had to be winched up from the bays below. In Dominican creole, the Atlantic coast is known as *au vent*, literally 'in the wind', a reference to the Tradewinds.

Carib Territory

The Caribs retreated to the Atlantic coast of Dominica in the 18th century when the Europeans took over the island. In the 100 years to 1750 their numbers had reduced from about 5000 to 400 and they knew their struggle was lost, so they took up a peaceful life as far as possible from the invaders.

The Carib Territory itself (then called the Carib Reserve), was not created until 1903, when the Governor Hesketh Bell allotted some 3700 acres to the few hundred remaining Caribs. A hereditary chief was presented with a mace and an official sash and was referred to as 'King'. However, he was implicated in a smuggling racket in the 30s and the position went into abeyance until 1952, when the 'Chief' was reintroduced as an elected post within the local government system.

The Caribs have adopted a West Indian lifestyle, living in clapboard houses on stilts rather than their original *carbets* (pointed thatch huts) and they make a living in a similar way to other Dominicans. They do maintain some Carib traditions, such as building canoes, dug out from trees that they fell high up in the forest, and their skilful weaving of rushes and reeds. They sell woven baskets, mats and ornaments. One curious object is known as the *wife-leader*. It is a mesh of interwoven reeds that tightens when you put it over your finger and pull it, trapping you.

There are not reckoned to be any pure-bred Caribs left in the Territory, but the Carib features, not dissimilar to faces from the Far East, are immediately recognizable. Carib hair, dark and sleek and once the pride of their ancestors, is still much admired by Dominicans today (many of whom have tight African curls).

FESTIVALS
Dominica maintains a traditional **Carnival** in the days before Lent (still called Masquer-ade from the French celebrations) with feasting and revelling in the streets and bands of players dressed in fantastic costumes. Other celebrations include **Independence Day** (3 November), which is strong on folk arts, including music and dance as well as the

usual *jump-up*. In **conte**, or story-telling, raconteurs compete with one another in telling humorous anecdotes of everyday life. **Domfesta** is an annual festival of local arts, crafts and performing arts held in July and August. The village of Soufrière holds an occasional *jump-up* in the streets, called **Korné Korn La**, with chicken and battered fish cooked in braziers; ask around to see if one is on while you are in Dominica.

WHERE TO STAY

Dominica's hotels are mainly small, family-run affairs, many of them in the old-time buildings around the coast or hidden among the island's overbearing foliage (as you sit on the veranda you can practically see it grow). Except in the most popular hotels in season, there is usually no difficulty in finding a room. If you wish to hire a villa, contact the Tourist Board. The government levies a tax of 5% and most hotels charge service of another 10%.

MODERATE

The **Fort Young Hotel**, PO Box 519 (tel 44 85000, fax 44 85006) in the southern part of Roseau, is the island's finest. It is set in the old stonework of the fort that guarded the Roseau approaches for a couple of centuries. The attractive courtyard is still laid with flagstones and the pool and bar are lost in foliage. There are 27 comfortable rooms on the battlements, most with a sea view. Double rate in winter US$95–105. The **Reigate Hall Hotel** (tel 44 84031, fax 44 84034) is reached via a tortuous road up King's Hill and has a superb view over the Roseau valley to the town and the sea beyond. Old-time Dominica prevails in the original stone of the old house and the heavy furniture of the central area and 17 rooms. Double rate US$95

Back on the coast, there is a small cluster of hotels a mile south of Roseau in Castle Comfort, all with a fine view out west to the horizon. There is no beach here really, but smooth fist-size rocks that clatter and jangle as the waves move over them. The **Anchorage**, PO Box 34 (tel 44 82638, fax 44 85680) has 36 rooms above the open harbour where yachts often put in. It is a friendly, family-run hotel. Rooms cost US$85–100. Nearby, the **Evergreen Hotel**, PO Box 309 (tel 44 83288, fax 44 86800) is built on the site of one of Roseau's many forts, with ten rooms lined in stone, the best and airiest overlooking the sea. With breakfast and dinner, rooms cost US$90 for a double.

Castaways, PO Box 5 (tel 489 6244, fax 489 6246, US 800 626 0581), is Dominica's best beach hotel, set on black sand at Mero, a few miles north of Roseau. There is a large and attractive terrace with the bar and the Almond Tree restaurant, from which the wings run on either side, containing 27 rooms in all. There is a fantastic view of the sunset from the palm-thatch beach bar down below. Also, a dive shop, double rooms in winter US$90–150. Just north of here is the striking **Lauro Club**, PO Box 483 (tel 44 96602, fax 44 96603) at Salisbury, a riot of oddly coloured cottages on the clifftops; *Tango, Quadrille, Calypso* and *Lambada* are comfortable and brightly decorated, with views along the coast to Scott's Head. Just ten rooms with pool, bar and restaurant up above. Double room US$100–130. The **Coconut Beach Hotel** (tel 445 5393) is just south of Portsmouth on Prince Rupert Bay, on a long strip of grey sand where wooden ships are sometimes built. It is small, with six rooms and five cottages and a bar frequented by sailors washed in on the tide. Cottages cost US$100 and double rooms $65–85.

171

Dominica has some extremely fine **rainforest retreats**. The rooms are often quite basic, but the settings are supreme. In the heights of the Roseau Valley, near the village of Trafalgar, is the **Papillote Wilderness Retreat**, PO Box 67 (tel 44 82287), which is practically throttled by its 12 acres of garden. Eight rooms and suites, overlooking the falls. The restaurant is on the garden terrace and serves local food. Room rates US$60 for a double. The **Springfield Plantation**, PO Box 41 (tel 44 91401), has a supreme setting, buried in rainforest off the Imperial Road. Plantation machinery hangs around the wooden verandas and the rooms are dotted about the main house and cottages that have steadily increased in size and number since the 30s. It is cool at 1700 feet above the sea and it often rains. With so much water around, freshwater bathing is arranged in nearby river pools. Rooms are available from US$55–125 for a double year-round. The **Layou Valley Inn**, PO Box 196 (tel 44 96203, fax 44 85212), is hidden in the hills of the Dominican heartland and has superb views over the multiple greens of the rainforest of the upper Layou valley. With just five rooms and good home cooking, this is a nature-lover's retreat. Rooms cost from US$40. The **Roxy Mountain Lodge**, PO Box 265 (tel 44 84845), in the mountains at Laudat, a good starting-point for the National Park, has six rooms at US$25 basic, but with meals available.

Finally, **Pointe Baptiste**, c/o Mrs G Edwards, Calibishie (tel 445 7322) has one of the loveliest settings in the Caribbean. On the clifftops of the north coast, the main house is a classic wooden West Indian house with a huge balcony, from where you look towards Marie Galante and Guadeloupe. There is a golden sand beach just below and an old-fashioned aura so rarely found anywhere nowadays. Maid service, villa rates US$960 per week (for six people) in season.

In Roseau there are a number of small hotels and guest houses, including **Vena's** on Cork Street (tel 44 83286), the birth-place of the Dominican novelist Jean Rhys, which offers simple rooms from US$30. **La Tropical** Guest House, at 51 Old St (tel 44 88015, fax 44 87665), upstairs from **Wykie's** Bar has seven simple rooms at US$25 a double. A friendly haunt where chat and cheap rooms are available is the **Kent Anthony Guest House** in the middle of town on Marlborough St (tel 44 8 2730). Rooms cost about US$20 per night. Another alternative, in a similar price-range, is the **Continental Inn** on Queen Mary Street (tel 44 8 2214). For cheap accommodation in **Portsmouth**, go to the **Indian River Inn**, where rooms cost around US$20.

EATING OUT
Dominican Food
Eating out is something of a problem in Dominica, particularly after dark, when there are very few restaurants open outside the hotels. However, you will get good traditional Caribbean fare: callaloo or pumpkin soup followed by fish or a curry goat sitting among prodigious quantities of local vegetables such as plantain, green fig and breadfruit. Dominica also has one or two specialities, such as *mountain chicken* or *cwapaud* (in fact breaded bullfrog legs), crab-backs stuffed with land-crab meat and tiny fish in cakes called *tee-tee-ree*, which are caught at the river-mouth in a sheet. There is a government tax of 5% and most restaurants add a service charge of 10%.

Restaurants
The evening out for subdued old-Roseau ambience is **La Robe Creole** on Fort St (tel 44 82896), set in a stone town-house with arched windows and doors. The waitresses

172

wear the traditional *madras* costume from which the restaurant takes its name. Steamed shrimp with a cream sauce and mountain chicken bathed in coconut, followed by banana flambéed at your table. Mainly a creole menu, main course EC$45 and up. A livelier spot is the **Orchard** Restaurant on King George V St, set in another town house, but with a breezier West Indian atmosphere inside—a lino floor and simple table settings. Regular Dominican fare, lambi or goat, chicken or fish, with ground provisions and guava pie. EC$25. In the hotels you might try the **Almond Tree** at Castaways and the **Lauro Club**, where you can get fish in lime butter and guava cheese (not cheese at all, but a sugar fruit ball) in a bright painted dining room on the cliffs, EC$35 a main course. Also the **Ocean Terrace** at the Anchorage Hotel for international and some local food.

The guest houses around Roseau will fix you a dinner of callaloo soup and roti or chicken and chips for a few EC$. Try **The World of Food** at Vena's, where the open dining room gives on to a paved garden and a mango tree, or **Kent Anthony's**.

There is a little more variety at lunch. **Guiyave** (tel 44 82930) has a pretty setting with a green and white balcony upstairs overlooking Cork St. Baked chicken with glazed spinach followed by local ice-cream, main dish EC$25. The **Cartwheel Café** is down on the waterfront (Bay St) and serves local meals.

Roseau has plenty of *snackettes*, usually teeming with the schoolkids on their lunchtime break, where you can get a lunchtime pattie and a fruit juice—sorrel, soursop, lime and tamarind according to the season—followed by a coconut cake. Finally, do not forget **Al's**; twelve different flavours of ice cream, open until 10pm.

BARS AND NIGHTLIFE

Some of the hotels have happy hours, barbecues and a band in season, but otherwise you will rely on Dominican entertainment; rum shops, discos and local fêtes. There are limitless rum shops on the island, where you will be welcome to try out a few of the Dominican rums: *Red Cap, Soca rum, D Special* and if you can find it some *Mountain dew*.

Wykie's bar on Old St is a favourite with island-execs and passers-through, a cosy creole town house with a small veranda, all lined with bamboo. Just north of the town, the **Good Times** bar is right next door to the Warehouse discotheque. Part bar—daquiri and rum punch—and part restaurant—chicken or fish with salad (Wed–Sun). Another discotheque is **Aquacade** near the airport in Canefield.

If you are going on an island-tour, there are some waterfront bars worth pausing at for a juice or a beer. Some of the best are **Spider's** in Loubière, **United Brothers** in Taru and the **Almond Bar** in Calibishie on the north coast.

173

The French Antilles

Martinique, Guadeloupe, St Martin and St Barthélemy

Mid-way down the chain of the Lesser Antilles are the islands of Martinique and Guadeloupe, the two large French outposts in the Caribbean. The French half of St Martin and the island of St Barts lie 150 miles to the north in the Leeward Islands.

The familiar verve of the French is ever-present in these islands. Chic customers glide by shops filled with Christian Lacroix and Yves St Laurent, and lovers linger over a meal under coloured awnings while citizens play *boules* on the dusty town squares. There is a certain *coquetrie* in the dress and manner—on the *autoroutes* you will find yourself competing with Peugeots and Citröens driven with a nonchalance both French and Caribbean (a fearsome combination). In Fort de France, the capital of Martinique, there is even a Parisian haste, a *je m'en foutisme* untypical of the Caribbean. The illusion of being in France is only spiked by the unfamiliar bristle of palm trees and the variety of skin tones among the faces.

But familiar Caribbean strains run through French islands too. The air pulses to the sound of the relentless French Caribbean rhythm, *zouk*. Away from the towns, the slopes are blanketed in typical Caribbean rainforest and the flatlands with sugar-cane or bananas sewn up in blue plastic bags. There the islanders walk at a relaxed and graceful pace, carrying the twin tools of the West Indies, the machete and the umbrella. You will see the *blanchisseuses* with their white washing spread all over the rocks at the riverside, keeping up a constant chatter of *créole*, the mix of French and African that has developed in the islands. The markets, under red corrugated-iron roofs, are typical Caribbean mayhem.

Politically, France has taken a radically different approach to its colonies from Britain. Instead of encouraging a gradual move to independence, France has embraced her Caribbean islands, taking them into her *République* and giving them the status of overseas *Départements*, equal to that of *Savoie* or *Lot-et-Garonne*. Martinique and Guadeloupe are *Régions* in their own right, with the extra powers and responsibilities brought by decentralization in 1985. They are administered by a *Préfet* appointed by the French government. Their people vote in French elections and they each send three Deputies and two Senators to the National Assembly in Paris.

In standard of living alone, the contrast with neighbouring islands is striking, and it could never be maintained without direct support from Paris. Most French Antilleans appreciate the benefits and would not change their situation, except to gain the maximum self-government while under the French umbrella, but there are some who envy the other islands their autonomy. Independence movements have expressed themselves in graffiti campaigns and have occasionally erupted into violence, with bomb attacks.

But the official line is that life should be French, with all the benefits that brings. Milk costs the same as it does in the *métropole*, as continental France is called, and so does a car. There is National Service. Rumour has it that they even fly in croissants.

To some Frenchmen the islands seem like an expensive burden, but then they are also a bridge-head in the Americas. Besides, most of the money sent here is used to buy French goods. And of course it is nice to go on holiday there; the language is familiar and they know they can trust the food.

History

The earliest French involvement in the Caribbean was as pirates and privateers in the 16th century. In fact it was a French pirate who had revealed to the whole of Europe what wealth the Spaniards were gaining in the New World. Jean Fleury captured, off the Azores in 1523, two Spanish ships which contained the riches of Montezuma's palace in Mexico, a prize worth millions.

Life *beyond the line* was dangerous, because capture by the Spaniards meant certain death, but men like François le Clerc (known to the Spaniards as *pie de palo* because of his wooden leg) ran a fleet of ten ships and scoured the Caribbean Sea and the Bahamas for plunder. In 1553, he sacked nearly every major town, ransoming hundreds of thousands of pounds. Many of the buccaneers, who centred on the island of Tortuga off Hispaniola in the seventeenth century, were Frenchmen and this led to the establishment of France's most successful colony in St Domingue, now Haiti.

It was on a privateering expedition in 1624 that the first French colony accidentally came into being. Pierre d'Esnambuc, after a fight with a Spanish galleon off the Cayman Islands, was forced to put in for repair at St Christopher, where the British had just established a colony. He made friends with the Governor Sir Thomas Warner and helped to protect him from the Caribs. Two years later he was back, and they settled the island together.

From this *Mother colony of the West Indies* both nations looked farther afield, despite the continued onslaught of the Caribs. De Poincy, a Grand Cross and Bailiff of the Order of the Knights of Malta, whose name is remembered in the *poinciana* tree all over the Caribbean, directed the expeditions. In the name of the *Compagnie des Iles d'Amerique*, the French boldly set out for the hostile Windward Islands of Martinique and Guadeloupe, planting settlements there in 1635.

In 1647, the age of *l'or blanc* began and sugar-cane, introduced by Dutch Protestants fleeing the Inquisition in Pernambuco, soon blanketed the islands. With a sharp eye for new technology, the French soon developed into the leading exporters of refined sugar to the voracious European markets. The industry required labour so slaves were brought over in their hundreds from Africa.

Development went forward apace and in 1669, the seat of government was moved from St Kitts to Martinique, a shift that was to guarantee the island's predominance over the other French colonies into the 20th century. Most of the trade was conducted through St Pierre on Martinique.

Steadily, the French expanded their domain southwards, settling a swathe of islands from Guadeloupe to Grenada. French buccaneers settled on St Barts and the Virgin Islands and from Tortuga they moved into the western area of Hispaniola, which eventually became St Domingue (now Haiti), and which later overtook Martinique and became the most prosperous colony in the world. For the expanding empires, land was valuable and they would snatch whatever they could get.

The French and British were at loggerheads in the Eastern Caribbean and they harried one another's colonies mercilessly. During the Seven Years' War, the British ripped through the islands and captured Martinique and Guadeloupe. It was considered so vital to retain a foothold in the Caribbean that at the Treaty of Paris in 1763, the French were prepared instead to relinquish all their claims to land in India, Louisiana and Canada (which simply had to be written off as 'quelques arpents de neige'—a few tracts of snow). But with the British overstretched in the American War of Independence a few years later, the French in their turn whittled through the islands, reclaiming all their old colonies.

The French Revolution had profound effects in the islands. The traditions of *Egalité* and the Rights of Man had particular significance in the Caribbean because they could hardly tolerate slavery. The islands shuddered at the ideas emanating from their capital and each colony turned out differently.

In Martinique the planters and royalists remained in the ascendancy and preferred to maintain the old prosperous regime by calling in their old enemies, the English, but in Guadeloupe, the revolutionaries gained the upper hand. There was a reign of terror; the slaves were liberated, the planters put to death or exiled and the plantations, symbols of the *ancien régime*, were destroyed (there are no pre-revolutionary buildings left in Guadeloupe).

And the humanitarian ideas emanating from Paris proved to be the death of France's most prosperous colony, St Domingue. In 1794 it erupted in an armed rebellion by the slaves, a war of liberation that led to the founding of the world's first black republic, Haiti.

Following the Napoleonic Wars, the other islands were returned to France and they have remained in her hands ever since.

Schoelcher and the Abolition of Slavery
The re-introduction of slavery in 1802 caused terrible disruption in Guadeloupe, where many of the former slaves preferred to die rather than lose their freedom. But in 1834 slavery was abolished in the British colonies. St Lucia and Dominica were free, and so slaves on the French islands put out on rafts in a break for freedom.

Victor Schoelcher was born in Paris in 1804 and eventually entered the family firm of porcelain-makers. In 1829 he undertook a journey on behalf of the firm to Mexico, Cuba and the southern States. His business was not particularly successful, but having witnessed the depredations of slavery his life was changed for good.

On his return to France he embarked on a career as a polemicist and pamphleteer, steadily mobilizing the public imagination through his works. He continued for 15 years, but there were powerful lobbies against him, and it became clear that only a political reversal in France could affect the situation in the Caribbean colonies.

As it had been 60 years before, it was a revolution that overturned the law and in 1848 Schoelcher, the committed Republican, had his chance. On 27 April the law was passed abolishing slavery in the French colonies once and for all. Schoelcher was put in charge of dismantling it and he went to the Antilles. He was elected deputy of Guadeloupe.

After Emancipation, the French Antilles, like the British islands, were short of labour for the canefields as the freed slaves took to the land. By 1870, some 80,000 East Indians, or *Z'indiens*, as they are known in creole, came as indentured labourers. Their faces are less visible nowadays, but there are some Hindu temples dotted around the islands.

The French colonies in the Caribbean followed the vagaries of the various *Empires* and *Républiques* of French politics until 1946, when Martinique and Guadeloupe were elevated to the status of *Départements*. They are governed by an elected island assembly, the Conseil Régional and a Governor appointed in France.

Language and Culture

French colonization was a more thorough-going affair than that of the British and despite the occasional revolts at being thought of as 'black Frenchmen' with no culture of their own, the French Antilles have a deep pride in French culture and their own creole version of it.

It is often said how beautiful the people of Martinique and Guadeloupe are. The faces show a greater variety of colour than the British islands. Though the French islands always had a slightly higher proportion of whites, the settlers were clearly also less prudish about taking an African mistress. The mix of racial strains is much more thorough (though still not as thorough as the mix in the Spanish islands) and it has created some strikingly beautiful faces; the creole beauties of Martinique were renowned all over the Caribbean.

And 100 years ago these *doudous* (from *douce chérie*) were as chic as their metropolitan counterparts. They presented themselves with characteristic Gallic flair, bedecked in reams of brightly coloured cotton and yards of lace petticoat, with a *foulard* thrown over their shoulder. You can still see the chequered *madras* material in the two large islands.

But the focal point of the impression was the construction of the hat. This too was fashioned of bright silk material, often yellow and checked and there was supposedly a code in its design:

Tête à un bout (one point): my heart is for the taking.

Tête à deux bouts: my heart is taken.

Tête à trois bouts: my heart is taken, but there might be room for another.

The French Antilles were one of the leading centres of *Négritude*, a French black consciousness literary movement that was born in the 1930s. Martiniquans Etienne Lero and Aimé Césaire, together with Léopold Senghor of Senegal, re-examined the position of the black man, formerly the slave and his relation to the white man, the colonial master. Aimé Césaire became famous with his *Cahier d'un retour au pays natal* in 1939 and a later play *La Tragédie du Roi Christophe*. He has been active in the politics of Martinique as the mayor of Fort de France since the Second World War.

Créole is the mixed language that has developed in many parts of the French colonial world. The Caribbean islands which have seen a French presence each have a version of their own: Martinique and Guadeloupe creole are incomprehensible to the Haitians, once also French subjects.

The language is also heard in many of the Windwards (Dominica, St Lucia and occasionally Grenada), which the French have owned at one time or other, and even as far away as Trinidad, taken there by French Royalists fleeing the *patriotes* in revolutionary times.

There are creoles in French Guyana in South America and in Réunion, the two other French overseas Départements, and also in Mauritius. In the French Leeward Islands, St Martin and St Barthélemy, however, where the language has traditionally been English, they speak either English or pure French.

The creole language is a classical Caribbean melting pot, a pidgin formed by early settlers from different countries in order to communicate with each other and then steadily changed by the influx of African slaves, none of whom spoke a common language because they were purposely split up to destroy their traditions.

French is clearly audible in creole. For tantalising moments the stream will let you hold on to words and even phrases, but suddenly it will whiplash and escape your grasp, chasing off in a flurry of unaccustomed vowels and peculiar utterances. In the same way, in the rhythm and intonation, and in the sharp un-Gallic sounds, are distinct echoes and resonances of African languages.

But French is the official language of the islands, used in the schools and by the authorities. As in the Windward Islands, you must speak the official language to 'get on', and so it is mainly the country people who speak creole. There is little written in the language because it has always had an oral tradition, particularly in song.

TOURIST INFORMATION
For detailed information, write to the **Office Inter-Régional du Tourisme des Antilles et de la Guyane Françaises**, 12 rue Auber, 75009 Paris (tel 42 68 11 07).

There are no Tourist Offices outside France devoted specifically to the French Antilles; they come under the **French Government Tourist Offices**:

UK: 178 Piccadilly, London W1V 0AL (tel (071) 499 6911). There is an answering machine at this number, so you are probably best to write, envelope marked French Antilles.

USA: French Government Offices, 628 5th Ave, New York, NY 10020 (tel (212) 757 1125) and French Government Offices in the following cities: Beverly Hills (tel (213) 272 2661), Chicago (tel (312) 337 6301), Dallas (tel (214) 720 4010) and San Francisco (tel (415) 986 4161).

Canada: 191 Ave McGill College, Suite 480, Montreal, Quebec, H3A 2W9 (tel (514) 514 89 06) and 1 Dundas St W, Suite 2405, Toronto, Ontario, M5G 1Z3 (tel (416) 593 4717).

Germany: Westendstrasse 47, Postfach 2927, D 600 Frankfurt/Main (tel 697 52029).

Because of the many American visitors, English is quite widely spoken in the French Antilles. However, it is important to understand French if you are to deal with officialdom or if you want to go off the beaten tourist track. In the villages on Martinique and Guadeloupe, and the islands off Guadeloupe, like Marie Galante and the Saints you will hear creole or French and little else. Also, museums (and menus) are in French.

The islands of St Martin and St Barts have a stronger English-speaking heritage.

MARTINIQUE

Martinique has traditionally been the flagship of French culture in the Caribbean. It was the richest of the colonies and in the last century its social hub, St Pierre, the *Paris of the Lesser Antilles*, was renowned all over the Americas. The fashion followed Paris to the letter, and the great plays of the age were staged in the St Pierre Theatre.

Though the spirit of St Pierre died in 1902, when the city was destroyed in a cataclysmic volcanic explosion, Martinique is still that little bit more chic. The island is more developed than its confrères, and with 385,500 citizens, a third of whom live in the capital Fort de France on the southeast coast, it is the most populous island in the Lesser Antilles after Trinidad.

Martinique is a central link in the island chain, lying between the Windward Islands of Dominica and St Lucia. It measures 48 miles by 19 at its widest point (75 by 30 km) and has an area of 1080 square km. It seems larger because it is so highly developed. The north is dominated by the steep volcanic mountain of Mont Pelé (4656 ft) and from there the land steadily falls away south to the central sugar plains of Lamentin and Fort de France, before rising again into the *mornes* (hills) of the southern peninsula. The island is of volcanic origin, except the south where age-old coral limestone formations have been pushed up out of the sea.

The French heritage constantly bombards the eyes, from the billboards to *boules* on the town-square. The Martiniquans have a surprisingly faithful attachment to France, stronger than their compatriots in Guadeloupe, whom they consider a little wild and unpredictable.

Despite subsidies from France that amount to a total of about 70% of the island's GNP, Martinique receives a lot from tourism, which brings in approximately as much as the rest of Martinique's exports combined, valued in 1989 at about a billion francs. The next principal earner is agriculture: one-third of the land is under cultivation and you will see banana plantations everywhere and sugar-cane, which is used for sugar and rum.

History

Martinique was discovered at the turn of the 15th century, on Columbus's first, second or fourth voyage, depending whose history you believe (it was actually his first landfall on his fourth voyage). Columbus apparently thought the island was inhabited by a tribe of Amazons because he was greeted only by women shouting *Madanina*. The Carib men must have been away raiding another island.

Similarly, the origins of the name Martinique have been obscured by zealous historians. It may have been named for St Martin, but most think that the name derives from the Carib word Madinina, thought to mean *the island of flowers*.

With or without menfolk, the island was left to the Caribs until 1635, when the Breton d'Esnambuc arrived from St Kitts with 100 colonists and settled on the leeward coast near Le Carbet. They planted a cross and erected a fort, and after years of running battles with the Caribs they came to an arrangement in which the French lived on the Caribbean coastline and the Caribs on the Atlantic side.

Just as Barbados became the leading British island, so Martinique became the leading French colony in the 1650s. The islanders became fantastically rich growing sugar and smuggling it out to Europe, and they had an uneasy relationship with the French Crown. In 1717 the Governor tried to enforce the *exclusif* (a law stipulating that trade from Martinique must be made exclusively with France) and he found himself taken prisoner with his Intendant and simply sent back to France as an unwanted nuisance. A more conciliatory governor was sent out to replace him, one who was prepared to turn a blind eye to the smuggling.

In the 18th century Martinique changed hands a number of times, like all the islands in the area, snatched by roving navies and swapped with other prizes at the end of each successive war. A new storm rose on the horizon as the ideas of the Revolution reverberated in the Caribbean. Martinique was divided along traditional lines; the townspeople, or *patriotes*, adopted the cockade and allied themselves with the revolutionaries, and the planters struck for the Royalists. Initially the *patriotes* took the island, rallied by the Revolutionary Lacrosse from St Lucia. General de Rochambeau and the Revolution came to the island in triumph; Fort Royal became République-ville. But within a year the planters had turned the tables and had contrived to get the British in, restoring the *ancien régime* and their prosperity. Martinique was relatively stable for the next 20 years under British rule and did not see the troubles that occurred in the other colonies of Guadeloupe and Saint Domingue.

In the first half of the 19th century, forces were mobilized against slavery in France initially by Cyrille Bissette, a Martiniquan, and then by Schoelcher (see p. 176). Slave riots took place in Le Carbet, St Pierre and in Grande Anse. With the coming of the Second Republic, the abolition of slavery in the French islands was proclaimed on 27 April 1848.

1902 was a momentous date for the colony because of the eruption of Mont Pelé, which completely destroyed St Pierre, then the commercial and cultural centre of the island. Fort de France took its place. In 1946, Martinique became a *département* with the same status and responsibilities as any other in *le métropole* and in 1985 it became a *Région*.

Three Crowned Heads

In the 17th century, a Françoise d'Aubigné, the daughter of a colonial functionary, spent her childhood at the northern parish of Le Prêcheur, just as the colony was becoming prosperous. When she returned to Europe, she embarked on a course that would take her to the royal court of France. She became Madame de Maintenon and in 1684 she secretly married Louis XIV.

Martiniquan legend relates a story of two young cousins, Yéyette and Aimée, who were walking one evening when they came across an old woman known in the area as a fortune-teller. They gave their palms to be examined and eventually she made her pronouncement: 'You', she said to the first, 'will be an Empress, and you', talking to Aimée, 'will be more than an Empress.' She walked off, refusing to respond to their pleas for more detail.

Aimée Dubuc de Rivery was soon sent to a convent in France to complete her education and the incident was forgotten. But on her return journey to Martinique she was caught in a storm off the European coast and was taken captive by Barbary pirates. The Bey of Algiers sold the passengers of the ship as slaves, but kept Aimée because he was captivated by her beauty. Eventually he made a present of her to the Grand Turk in Constantinople.

There, she penetrated the deepest secrets of the seraglio, to become the favourite of the Sultan, lover of his successor and finally the Sultana Validé, adoptive mother of Emperor Mahmoud II.

Her cousin Yéyette was born Marie-Rose Joséphine Tascher de la Pagerie, in Trois-Ilets in 1763. Her family had fallen on hard times, but when offered an advantageous match, her parents married her off to the son of a former governor, Alexandre Vicomte de Beauharnais, and she too went to France.

At one stage Joséphine was condemned to death as a noble, but she was set free when Robespierre fell and within a few years she married Napoleon Bonaparte, General of the French army in Italy. On 2 December 1804 she became his Empress.

Many consider Joséphine a shallow woman, and it is somewhat surprising that the Martiniquans should be so proud of her, particularly as she was behind the re-introduction of slavery in the French islands in 1802. Such is their attachment to France.

Flora and Fauna

Martinique has the best of both worlds, the verdant profusion in the mountainous rainforests and the open plains that now blow with sugar-cane and bananas, and where cattle once were allowed to run wild in buccaneer-style farming.

The rainforest is fantastic and well worth seeing, either simply by driving through it, or on a visit to the **Balata Gardens** just north of Fort de France.

The island is unfortunate, however, in suffering from a scourge that most of the Windwards do not—the *fer de lance* snake. Called *trigonocephalus* because of its triangular head, it grows up to six feet long and has a pair of eyes that are supposed to glow orange in the night.

It is curious that it came to be here in the first place, as its nearest relatives are somewhere in South America. In the times of fierce competition during the sugar years, snakes were sometimes surreptitiously introduced into the islands to make other plant-ers' jobs more difficult, but the *fer de lance* has been here since before the Europeans arrived.

Though the snake is extremely poisonous to humans, it poses little danger to visitors because it steers well clear of any tourist habitations. However, if you are rootling around in the undergrowth or stealing a stem of bananas, then watch it.

GETTING TO MARTINIQUE

By Air
From Europe: Air France has daily flights from Paris and weekly connections from other French cities including Lyon, Toulouse, Bordeaux and Nantes. These are supple-mented by charters operated by Nouvelles Frontières and other companies from the French capital plus several other cities in France. There are no direct flights from other European countries; travellers can connect in Paris, North America or other Caribbean airports.
From the USA: American Airlines has frequent services to its hub at San Juan, Puerto Rico, from where there are connections to many Caribbean islands. Eastern Airlines flies from Miami, as does Air France. From Canada there are daily flights from both Montreal and Toronto on Air Canada.
From other Caribbean Islands: the island's carrier, Air Martinique, flies propeller aircraft linking Martinique with Union Island, Mustique, St Vincent, Barbados, St Lucia, Dominica, Antigua and St Martin, but not with the nearby French island of Guadeloupe; Air France has the monopoly on this route. LIAT also serves islands to the north and south of Martinique, originating in Antigua and Grenada. An airport security tax of FR10 is payable by all passengers leaving Martinique.

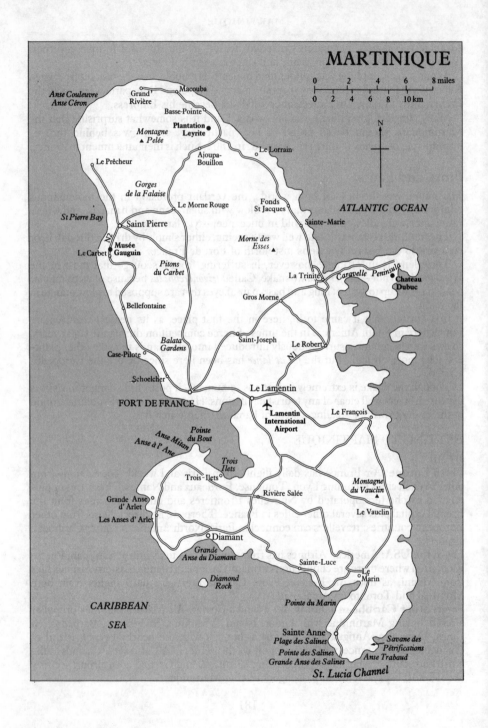

MARTINIQUE

0	2	4	6	8 miles
0	2	4	6	8	10 km

N

ATLANTIC OCEAN

Anse Couleuvre
Anse Céron

Grand
Rivière

Macouba

Basse-Pointe

**Plantation
Leyrite**

Montagne
▲ Pelée

Le Prêcheur

Ajoupa-
Bouillon

Le Lorrain

Gorges
de la Falaise

Le Morne Rouge

Fonds
St Jacques

St Pierre Bay

Saint Pierre

Sainte-Marie

N2

**Musée
Gauguin**

Le Carbet

Morne des
Esses ▲

Pitons
du Carbet

La Trinité

Caravelle Peninsula

Château
Dubuc

Bellefontaine

Gros Morne

Balata
Gardens

Saint-Joseph

Le Robert

Case-Pilote

N1

Schoelcher

Le Lamentin

FORT DE FRANCE

**Lamentin
International
Airport**

Le François

Pointe
du Bout

Anse Mitan
Anse à l' Ane

Trois
Ilets

Trois-Ilets

Rivière Salée

Montagne
du Vauclin ▲

Grande Anse
d' Arlet

Les Anses d' Arlet

Le Vauclin

Diamant

Grande
Anse du Diamant

Sainte-Luce

Diamond
Rock

Marin

CARIBBEAN

SEA

Pointe du Marin

Sainte Anne
Plage des Salines

Savane des
Pétrifications

Pointe des Salines
Grande Anse des Salines

Anse Trabaud

St. Lucia Channel

By Sea
The Compagnie Général Maritime runs a weekly service between Dunkerque or Le Havre and Fort de France, taking a little over three weeks. Within the French Caribbean, **Caribbean Express** (tel 60 12 38) in the CGM building on Ave Maurice Bishop, runs a hydrofoil link from Martinique to Guadeloupe, touching Dominica. The *Diamant Express* departs from Fort de France five times a week.

GETTING AROUND MARTINIQUE

If you wish to get a bus from the airport into Fort de France (no buses run the route directly), you must cross the main road, beyond the car park in front of the terminal building, and flag down a *taxi collectif* on the other side.

Public **buses** are a cheap way of travelling around the island and they depart from **le Parking**, on the waterfront at Fort de France, or from the main square in other towns. You will find both public buses, which follow a vague time schedule, and *taxis collectifs* (TCs), share-taxis that run a fixed route and do not depart until they are full. At the terminus, ask around and you will be directed to the first one headed in your direction.

Public buses are only allowed to stop at official stops, but you might be able to flag down a TC on the roadside if you are lucky. *Arrêt!*, loud enough to be heard above the noise of the stereo system, is the word used to indicate that you want to get off. The buses run from 5 am until about 7 pm and the TCs a little longer. On Sundays and on public holidays the public transport system packs up in mid-afternoon and you can quite easily be left isolated. Some prices are: **Fort de France** to airport—Fr8.50; to St Pierre—Fr15; to St Anne—Fr28.

Island tours are easy to organize in full-day and half-day tours (usually taking in a meal as well). Three tour operators are: **Caribtours**, Pointe du Bout, Trois-Ilets (tel 66 02 56), **STT Voyages** at 23 rue Blénac, Fort de France (tel 71 68 12) and **Madinina Tours**, 89 rue Blénac (tel 70 65 25).

The tourist areas on the other side of Fort de France bay (Pointe du Bout, Anse Mitan, Anse à l'Ane) are best served by **ferry** (vedette). The vedettes leave from the waterfront next to the Savane, close to Fort St Louis, and keep up a regular schedule to Pointe du Bout from 6 am until about midnight; 20-minute crossing, return fare Fr19.

Taxis are also readily available at the **Parking** downtown or the airport and can be ordered at any hotel. Taxi companies include: **Taxis Savane** (tel 60 62 73) and **Radio Téléphone** (tel 41 19 29). Their rates are fixed at around Fr3 per kilometre after an initial charge, with higher rates after dark. Some examples are: from **Lamentin airport** to: city-centre—Fr70, Pointe du Bout—Fr150, St Anne—Fr260. Taxi-drivers are willing to take day tours (many of them speak English). If divided between four people, the Fr500 for a day's drive is reasonable value, but be sure to fix the price beforehand.

For maximum mobility, plenty of **hire cars** are available. In comparison with other islands nearby, Martinique's roads are good, though the islanders tend to drive with an abandon both French and Caribbean. Driving is on the right and your own licence is valid for the first 20 days, after which time an international driving licence is required. Maps are usually handed out by the hire companies. Found at the airport, in Fort de France and in the tourist centres, the hire companies offer cars from about US$45 per day, a little above average for the Caribbean. Major credit cards are accepted as deposit, otherwise expect to put down about US$350. Some companies include:

THE CARIBBEAN

Europcar-International in Fort de France (tel 73 33 13) and at the Zone Industrielle du Lamentin (tel 51 20 33), near the airport, and **Hertz**, 24 rue Ernest Deproge, Fort de France (tel 60 64 64). A slightly cheaper option is **Parking**, 55 rue Lazare-Carnot, Fort de France (tel 71 89 27).

You can rent motorbikes and scooters through **Funny Rent Motorcycles** (general tel no 63 33 05), with outlets all over the island. If you would like to explore the island by **mountain bike**, contact **VT Tilt** at Pointe du Bout 97229, Trois Ilets (tel 66 01 01). As well as the northern rainforest, they run tours through Les Anses d'Arlets and the beaches of the southern coast.

TOURIST INFORMATION
The Martinique Tourist Office is on the waterfront in Fort de France, on the Boulevard Alfassa (tel 63 79 60), and is open weekdays 7.30–12.30 and 2.30–5.30, and Sat 8–noon. There is also a tourist office in the airport at Lamentin (tel 51 28 55). (see French Antilles p. 178 for tourist offices abroad)

With its suitably sexy slogan *Une Histoire d'Amour entre Ciel at Mer* (a love story between the sky and the sea), the Martinique Tourist Board puts out several publications, including *Choubouloute*, providing useful information such as taxi prices and ferry times and the restaurant guide *Ti Gourmet*, to help you get to grips with the all-important island dining experience.

The American Consulate in Martinique is at 14 rue Blénac, Fort de France (tel 63 13 03).

In the case of a medical **emergency**, contact the Hôpital Zobda Quitman (tel 55 20 00) and if you need to contact the police, call 55 30 00. The **IDD** code for Martinique is 596, followed by a six-digit local number.

MONEY
The currency of Martinique is the French franc. US dollars are accepted in the larger hotels, but it is more convenient to carry francs for shops and restaurants. Major credit cards are also accepted in tourist areas and in Fort de France. Traveller's cheques in dollars or francs are accepted in many shops in town. Sometimes payment by credit card or by traveller's cheque will mean a discount on prices. Service is included in restaurant bills on the island, and tipping is the standard 10–15%. **Banks** are open for exchange on weekdays, 7.30–12 noon and 2.30–4. There is a bank in all the main towns. **Shops** are open 8.30–6, with a long break for lunch in the heat of the day (usually 12–2.30).

FURTHER READING
Two Dominican Monks
Two Dominican monks, **Père Dutertre** and **Père Labat**, visited Martinique in the 17th century and wrote memoirs of their trips. Their stories and observations about life make fascinating reading.

Père Dutertre was a soldier and romantic who turned to the Church late in life and came to the Caribbean in the 1650s. He was fascinated by the novelties of the New World and on his return he wrote his *Histoire Générale des Antilles Habitées par les Français*. The work is full of observations about the natural life of the islands and of the Carib Indians, whom he makes into naturally egalitarian and melancholic dreamers, probably one of Rousseau's sources for his idea of the *noble savage* a hundred years later.

184

Père Labat spent 10 years in the Caribbean until 1705, living mainly in Martinique, but undertaking missions all over the area, which he relates in his *Nouveau Voyage au Iles de l'Amérique*. In his book you will find him tending souls by spiritual means or defending them with a cannon instead, celebrating mass for buccaneers and chatting with enemy admirals. He details the system of compensation among the buccaneers for the loss of a limb, he invents a new system for distilling sugar into rum, and being a confirmed gastronome, his writing is sprinkled with descriptions of meals of sumptuous proportions. His interest is inexhaustible, he is unfailingly humorous, earthy, adventurous and an incorrigible busy-body.

Strangely, he is wrongly accused by folk tradition in Martinique of introducing slavery into the island. A hundred years ago, his name was used as a threat against naughty children: *Moin ké fai Pè Labatt vini pouend ou!* (I'll make Père Labat come and take you away) and his ghost would apparently be seen walking the *mornes* above St Pierre at night because his soul could find no rest. Certainly he was sanguine about the treatment of slaves—he ordered one man to be given 300 lashes—but it was a cruel age.

He had a number of close shaves too. At one point his ship was captured by Spanish pirates after he had refused to fire the only cannonball because it was needed to crush the garlic. He was about to be put to death, but a moment later he found all his captors on their knees around him. While rootling through his luggage they had found a cross of the Holy Inquisition. Of course it was there completely by chance, he claims, but it was enough to set him free.

There is an abridged English translation of his work, *The Memoirs of Père Labat*, by John Eaden, published in 1931.

Lafcadio Hearn

The traveller **Lafcadio Hearn** lived near St Pierre for two years in the late 1880s and he painted a series of tender pictures of Martiniquans and their lives: the *blanchisseuses* (launderesses) who rise at 4.30 am when the local alarm clock, the cabritt bois (a cricket), stops chirruping, covering the rocks on the River Roxelane with the washing that they beat and scrub; the *porteuses* who carry supplies weighing up to 120 pounds on their heads, singing as they cross the mountain range in the heat of the day; a man infatuated by the *guiablesse* (a zombi), who leads him to his death when he tries to kiss her. It is all a bit romanticized, but his *Two Years in the West Indies* is a charming book and gives an unforgettable picture of Martinique before St Pierre was destroyed by Mont Pelé.

BEACHES

Martinique has beaches to suit every taste—busy strips with hotels and watersports or the more isolated palm-fringed coves with fishing villages. Most lie on the protected Caribbean coast, but there are one or two hidden in the nooks and crannies of the Atlantic shore. The sand is better in the south, where the terrain is gentler and coral has been able to grow on the coast. Beaches are public in Martinique (which means you can go anywhere as long as you officially do not overstep the high-water mark) and most hotels do not mind outsiders, though one or two discourage them for the benefit of their guests. Most charge for the use of their beach-chairs.

The best beach on the island is right at the southern tip, the **Grand Anse des Salines**, which gets crowded at the weekends, but can be fairly free during the week. There is a bar and a restaurant, le Point de Vue at the far end of the sand, where you can retreat and soak up the scene over a creole platter. Just beyond here is the more secluded **Grande Terre** beach and further round the coast is **Anse Trabaud** and **Point Macré**, both worth a detour for greater seclusion. They are protected from the full force of the Atlantic by offshore reefs.

On the Caribbean side, around St Anne, the **Pointe du Marin** is a very popular beach and it attracts the body-beautiful. All watersports are available here and there is a line of little cafés and restaurants above the beach where you can linger over an *Orangina* and a lobster salad. There is a Fr5 admission charge for cars. Just south of the town is the more secluded **Plage des Salines**, adm free.

Near St Luce there are a number of good spots, including the **Plage corps du Garde**, where there are facilities and as you head farther west to Diamant you come to two miles of strand that is constantly washed with breakers. And around the western tip you will find a string of cracking coves in the **Anses d'Arlet**. A bar worth pulling over for is the palm-thatched **Anse Noir** between Anse Noir and Anse Dufour. Also look out for **Edouard's Bar** in Petite Anse d'Arlet, a hip spot with a hip owner.

Three areas can be reached from Fort de France by ferry: **Anse Mitan**, a fine strip of white sand with a host of hotels and bars to retire to if the sun becomes too hot; **Pointe du Bout**, man-made beaches crowded with high-pressure vacationers, and **Anse à l'Ane**, a 500-yard strip of brown sand between two headlands. All three hire out watersports equipment and become quite crowded at weekends.

If you are in the north of the island, your nearest beaches are in the lee of the Caravelle Peninsula, but only go on a calm and sunny day because otherwise the sea will be rough. However, you might go north beyond Le Prêcheur, where **Anse Céron** and **Anse Couleuvre** are secluded coves with black sand and coconut palms. Take a picnic.

WATERSPORTS

Windsurfing (*planche à voile*) is a popular sport on Martinique and you can hire equipment on all the major beaches (about US$20 per hour). The winds are best in the winter season and boardsailors will go out all along the Caribbean coast and occasionally in the Atlantic bays where the winds are strongest. **Surfissimo** (tel 71 54 42) is a general watersports shop for rental in Fort de France. At Anse Mitan you can hire a windsurfer from **Sun Martinique** (Tel 66 02 22) and in St Anne, contact **Alizé Fun Dillon** (tel 76 70 73). On the Atlantic coast there is the Club Nautique du Vauclin (74 50 83) and AGEPAL in Trinité (tel 58 24 32). **Waterskiing** and **jetskiing** can be arranged at the large resort areas.

Coasting the Caribbean shore of Martinique in a yacht is a fun day out from Fort de France bay, and there are coves where you can pause for a swim both north and south, for example down to Les Anses d'Arlet. Yachts can be hired through **Caraïbe Evasion** (tel 66 02 85) in the Pointe du Bout marina and **Bambou Yachting** in Le Marin (tel 62 46 57). If you would prefer a picnic cruise or dinner and dancing on board, there is a **Jolly Roger** (tel 68 15 74). And there are semi-submersible boats for a dry view of the corals; **Aquascope Seadom Explorer** at Pointe du Bout marina (tel 68 36 09) and **Aquascope Zemis** in St Anne (tel 74 87 41).

For longer hire, there are many companies on the island, in the marinas in Fort de France, Pointe du Bout and Le Marin. Contact **Korn Croisières**, PO Box 1161, 97247

Fort de France (tel 63 21 61), **Caraïbe Evasion** in Pointe du Bout marina, 97229 Trois Ilets (tel 66 02 85) and in Le Marin **Stars Voyages**, address Port de Plaisance, 97290 Le Marin (tel 74 70 92, fax 74 70 93).

Diving (la plongée) is popular and well-organized (a medical certificate and insurance is necessary) and is available from Fort de France and the resorts. The best dive-sites for corals are around the southern edge of the island, off St Anne, around Diamond Rock and on the southwest coast around Les Anses d'Arlets (excellent for **snorkelling**), where you will find forests of seafans and sponges. There are many other reefs along on the Caribbean coast, as well as some wrecks off St Pierre, sent to the bottom in 1902.

Many of the big hotels have diving and teaching facilities. In Schoelcher you will find **Tropicasub** (tel 77 15 02) and in the Pointe du Bout marina is **Planète Bleue** (tel 66 08 79). **Sub Diamond Rock** is on the south coast at the Novotel Diamant (tel 76 42 42) and nearby in St Anne is **Histoire d'Eau** (tel 76 92 98). In St Pierre contact **Carib Scuba Club** (tel 55 59 84).

The Yoles Rondes

The *yoles rondes* is a colourful spectacle that has grown out of the sailing races at the traditional Martiniquan *fêtes patronales*. These yawls, with huge square sails on a bamboo mast, are sailed by a crew of 11 or 12 men who clamber about on poles a good six feet out above the water.

OTHER SPORTS

There is one golf course on Martinique, the **Golf de l'Impératrice Joséphine** (tel 68 33 49), just south of Trois-Ilets, an 18-hole Robert Trent Jones course.

If you would like to see the rolling *mornes* or the beaches of southern Martinique on **horseback**, then there are several stables on the island. Try **Ranch Jack** at Galochas, above Anse à l'Ane (tel 68 63 97), or **Ranch Val d'Or** in the St Anne area (tel 76 70 58).

For **walkers**, organized outings into the rainforest are arranged by **Parc Naturel Régional de la Martinique**, 9 Blvd Général de Gaulle (tel 73 19 30) in Fort de France. They publish *Le Guide des Loisirs de Plein air et du Tourisme Vert à la Martinique* (in French). You can also fix up a guided tour of the northern part of the island through **Les Ombrages** (tel 52 32 09), down the hill from Ajoupa Bouillon.

Cockfights

Cockfighting can be seen in many islands in the Caribbean. It is quite a spectacle and may well appear cruel to a visitor, but it is a sport followed avidly by the Martiniquans. The *pitt* is a circular ring banked steeply with seats, which on Sunday becomes a mêlée of gamesmen with fistfuls of notes, shouting to place their bets. All goes silent when the cocks are brought in by their owners, carefully prepared for months with alcohol to make their skin hard and groomed especially for the fight. The owners posture in the ring for a while, showing off their beasts to the crowd, testing the sharpness of the knives attached to their claws. Eventually the two cocks are released at one another in the ring and all hell breaks loose: in the fury of the pit where the cocks lunge and lash, and in the stands, where men are standing and yelling, brandishing their fists. There are cockpits in Morne Rouge (Thurs 2), Ducos (Sun 2.30), Lamentin (Wed, Thurs 2) and Rivière Pilote (Wed, Sun 2.30).

The Mongoose (Mangouste) Versus the Snake

The mongoose was originally introduced to Martinique to reduce the snake population. Ironically, the animals promptly struck up a mutually beneficial arrangement in which the mongoose would avoid the snake by sleeping during the night and have a free run at the chickens in the daytime. As if in revenge, the islanders now wheel the two out against one another for sport.

Fort de France

The capital of Martinique is set on a huge bay on the leeward side of the island, looking out on to the Caribbean Sea. Framed with hills of dark green rainforest, it was chosen, like all Caribbean capitals, for its harbour and strategic value. Now, transatlantic yachts lie in the bay, attracted more to the waterfront cafés than the protective walls of Fort St Louis.

Though it has been the administrative centre of Martinique since 1681, it was a dozy and unhealthy backwater until the beginning of this century, when the eruption of Mont Pelée destroyed the illustrious town of St Pierre farther north. From just 10,000 inhabitants living in the gridiron streets between the Rivière Madame and the Rivière Monsieur, it has exploded to a city of over 100,000, spilling into suburbs along the coast and creeping steadily farther and farther up into the surrounding hills. The people of Fort de France are known as the *Foyalais*, from a corruption of the town's 17th-century name, Fort Royal.

The original settlement grew up around the looming battlements of **Fort St Louis** on the promontory, first established in 1639. The fort is still in the hands of the army and though it is quiet now, it has been assaulted any number of times. In 1674, 160 men were faced by the Dutch Admiral de Ruyter, who arrived at the head of 48 ships and 3000 men. The French evacuated the fort pretty quickly and so the Dutchmen, lulled into a false sense of security, paused over some kegs of rum, only to find themselves harried by

Fort de France

188

sober and determined Frenchmen. The Admiral cut his losses when a thousand of his men were killed and let the town be. Access to the fort is restricted. If you wish to visit, you must write to the officer in charge, who will arrange a visit to the network of caverns, dungeons and ramparts.

The fort juts into the sea, enclosing on one side the old *Carenage*, where ships would be 'careened'. Weights were tied to their masts and they were tipped up so that their hulls could be cleaned. Adjacent is the Baie des Flamands (flamingos), where hundreds of yachts ride at anchor.

Bordering Fort St Louis, the **Savane** is the large central park of Fort de France, towered over by a line of vast royal palms. Their solid grey trunks are like marble columns, soaring to 100 feet before they burst into curved fronds. Beneath such a regal canopy stands the statue of Joséphine, the Martiniquan who became an Empress. Her face is turned towards her home in Trois Ilets, across Fort de France bay to the south. Two other memorials are dedicated to the war dead and to Belain d'Esnambuc, the founder of the colony, who stands scouring the horizon for land.

The Savane, where the Martiniquans come in the evenings to 'promenade', is bordered by cafés and by the Boulevard Alfassa waterfront, the site of all major events such as carnival and military parades.

Facing the Savane on the Rue de la Liberté is the **Musée Départemental** (tel 71 57 05), which deals with the history of the island. The life of the Arawaks and Caribs, from their first arrival at the time of Christ to 1500, when the Spaniards appeared, is portrayed in a rich display of pottery and pictures. Open weekdays 9–1 and 2–5, Sat until noon, adm.

At the northwestern corner of the Savane is the **Bibliothéque Schoelcher**, a baroque iron agglomeration of arches, domes, fretwork and rivets, touched with russet and turquoise. The building was constructed by Henri Picq for the Exhibition of 1889 in Paris, at which the Eiffel Tower was the centrepiece, and then was dismantled and shipped out here to accommodate the library of Victor Schoelcher (see The French Antilles, introduction, p. 178)

The classical building opposite the Bibliothèque is the **Préfecture**, the seat of the administrator, appointed by the Interior Minister in Paris. Other attractive buildings in the town include the Palais de Justice and the old Hotel de Ville, now a theatre.

The streets of Fort de France are narrower and the buildings taller than in most Caribbean towns. The pavements are cluttered with small Peugeots and the shop windows decked out with chic-looking mannequins. In true French form, the street names commemorate many of France's political and literary heroes.

On the Place du Père Labat is the **Cathédrale St-Louis**, the sixth to be built on the site. This one dates from 1878, its predecessors having been destroyed by fire, hurricane and earthquake. It has beautiful stained glass windows, an impressive organ and metalwork balustrades. Next to the **Parc Floral**, where some of Martinique's floral profusion is on view and where there is a gallery devoted to island geology (Tues–Fri 9–12.30, 2–5.30), is a series of markets dotted among the streets, with ranges of tables sheltering under huge gaudy parasols, selling anything from locks of straight black hair (to be plaited into tight African curls) to avocados. Worth a visit is the fish market on the western bank of the Rivière Madame, where women sell the fish caught and landed by the fishermen, from dawn until about 5.

The hills surrounding the capital are covered with high-rise blocks and the 'instituts' of a developed French *département*. As in the other islands, the *bons bourgeois* build their homes high on the hills for the fresher air and the commanding view. Across the Rivière Madame, the suburbs clamber up into the hills both inland and west along the coast, to Schoelcher.

On the road towards St Pierre you will find the **Aquarium** (tel 73 02 29), with about 20 tanks of fish from the Caribbean and the Pacific, including a pirhana river, moonfish that look at you with huge foreheads and doubtful expression, filefish with quivering topknots and moray eels that seem to shout at you from their rocky retreats, as they pass water through their gills. Daily 9–7, adm expensive, adults Fr38, chidren FR24.

If you would like Fort de France's secrets to be revealed in a guided tour, contact **Azimut** (tel 60 16 59), who offer historical, shopping and nightime tours.

South of Fort de France

The many coves and white-sand beaches make Martinique's southwest coastline the magnet for the tourists. They centre around two areas, **Pointe du Bout**, near **Trois-Ilets**, within sight of Fort de France across the bay, and at **St Anne** at the southern tip of the island.

If you do not cross Fort de France bay by ferry, the main road skirts the bay, past the airport, and the D7 turns right at Rivière Salée. **La Maison de la Canne** is devoted to the history of sugar and is set in a restored sugar estate. It has impressive models and sugar hardware on display. Open daily 9–5, except Mon, adm expensive (tel 68 32 04).

Just before the town of Trois-Ilets another central piece of Martiniquan history is on view in **La Musée de la Pagerie**, the childhood home of the Empress Joséphine. Some of the sugar estate buildings have been restored and filled with the Empress's belongings, including portraits and some letters written to her by Napoleon. The setting, in a small valley of typical Martiniquan profusion, is idyllic. Open daily 9–5, except Mon; adm (tel 68 34 55). Close by is the **Domaine de la Pagerie**, a working horticultural garden where you will see Caribbean flora in all its extreme fertility. Open Mon–Fri, 9–5.

Trois-Ilets is a small town set around a square above the sea which takes its name from the three small islands in the bay. It was in the 18th-century church that the future Empress was christened Marie-Rose Joséphine Tascher de la Pagerie in July 1763. Her mother, Rose-Claire du Verger de Sannois, is buried in the church.

Just north of here is the tourist resort of **Pointe du Bout**, a conglomeration of hotels, cafés and boutiques and a marina which has grown up on the point and on the white-sand beach of Anse Mitan.

The coastal road rises into cliffs as it turns south and the land becomes drier and more windswept, where the shoreline is pitted with tiny coves with a profusion of coconut palms and small strips of sand. Some are used by fishermen, whose orange and green boats are slung with blue nets set out to dry.

The road winds up over the cliffs and down into **Grand Anse d'Arlet**. It is a charming bay, less known than the beaches at Pointe du Bout, but popular with yachtsmen. Two miles farther on is another cove with the picturesque village of **Les Anses d'Arlet** between the headlands and then a third cove called the Petite Anse d'Arlet.

The best route to take from here follows the vagaries of the coastline and descends from the heights of Morne Larcher to the town of Le Diamant, which is set on the magnificent sweep of the Grande Anse du Diamant and its two miles of beach with brown sand and crashing breakers.

Diamond Rock
Off the Point, a mile from the shore, is the **Rocher du Diamant**, a pitted outcrop that rises sheer from the water to over 500 feet. This rock, sometimes referred to as *HMS Diamond Rock*, witnessed one of the most curious of all episodes in the eternal struggles for empire between the French and British at the turn of the 18th century. The two nations were facing each other across the St Lucia Channel. From his look-out at Pigeon Island on St Lucia, Commodore Hood was stuck. All he could do was watch as the French ships dodged behind the Rock within the cover of their own guns, and sailed away unharmed. Hood decided to fortify the Rock.

For 18 months it stood as a British enclave within cannon-range of Martinique, denying the channel to French shipping. It was garrisoned by 120 men, who hoisted five cannon up on a rope from a ship, the *HMS Centaur*, 'like mice, hauling a little sausage' and built fortifications and outhouses. It became quite a community, with goats and rabbits and the Captain's dog and cat. Rope ladders were fixed to get from the upper battery to the shore and the mail and food were delivered in a communication bucket from the supply ship.

In May 1805 the French descended on the Rock in force. The two sides slugged it out for three days and two nights, until the British capitulated. When he eventually got back to Barbados the commander, Captain Maurice, was court-martialled for surrender, but then congratulated by Nelson himself for putting up such a good show. Ruins remain dating from the time the French sacked the Rock, but they are rarely visited and the crossing is often rough.

Heading further east, you will come to the **Trois Rivières Rum Distillery**, a working sugar and rum factory, where between February and July you can see the cane fed into the machines, cut to length, moved along a conveyor through three-stage crushers and the juice run down into a collecting vat while the bagasse is returned to fire the hundred-year-old steam engine. Hot and noisy, but interesting, and then you test the vintages; 1982, 1979 and then mellowest of all 1969. Mon–Fri, 9–noon, 2.30–5. There is another distillery at Rivière Pilote, **La Mauny**, with guided tours five times a day (10 am, 11 am, 12.30, 2, 3).

On the dry **St Anne** peninsula, where the beaches are excellent, stand the towns of Le Marin, which has an attractive coral-rock church and St Anne. Five miles farther on you come to the **Pointe des Salines**, where the land is covered in cactus scrub. From the point St Lucia is clearly visible on a fine day, beyond the lighthouse on the Ilet Cabrits. Beyond the salt flats (or salt ponds depending on the season) is the **Savane des Pétrifications**, a moonscape of petrified wood where nothing grows. Sadly, many of the pieces have been removed over the years, but it still looks pretty ghostly.

From Le Marin the road leads across to the Atlantic coast, on a leisurely return to Fort de France. **Le Vauclin** is the first town, with an active fish-market. Inland is the **Montagne du Vauclin**, at 1640 ft the highest in the south of Martinique. From the top, the panorama is fantastic, stretching as far as the Caravelle Peninsula in the north and to the southern tip of the island.

North of Vauclin is **Le François**, where the attractive old wooden houses are steadily being swamped by the new concrete suburbs. There is a classic French West Indian cemetery, with mausolea covered in black and white tiles, but the church looks as though it might be about to undergo a space-age transfiguration.

The road back to Fort de France passes through the Lamentin plains, the agricultural heartland of the island, which blow in green waves of bananas and sugar-cane.

N2–The Caribbean Coast, Fort de France to St Pierre

The road (N2) from today's capital to its spiritual ancestor, the once august city of St Pierre, runs along the Caribbean coast, clinging to the headlands that cast out into the sea and sweeping down into the bays. The land is steep and rugged, with a covering of scrub that makes it look a bit like Corsica. Above Case-Pilote the dry cliffs at sea level give way to tropical rainforest in the foothills of the Pitons du Carbet, Martinique's second highest peak.

Schoelcher, 5 km from the centre of Fort de France, was a fishing village by the name of Case-Navire until 1899, when it was renamed in honour of the abolitionist shortly after his death. Now the *commune* of Schoelcher, creeping ever higher into the hills, takes the overspill from Fort de France. It has one of the colleges of the University of the French Antilles.

A number of small towns, each with a town hall and church facing one another across the square, lie in the mouths of the valleys. Fishermen work from the black-sand beaches and you will see their blue nets spread out to be repaired. Their boats are painted bright colours to make them visible at sea and given lyrical evocative names such as *Regret de mon père* and *On revient toujours*.

Case-Pilote is named after a Carib chief who lived in this area and who welcomed the French when they settled, allowing Père du Tertre and the other Dominican missionaries to work amongst his people. Towards the end of his life he moved to Rivière-Pilote in the south of Martinique. **Bellefontaine** also shows its attachment to the sea in the curious house above the village, built as the prow of a ship steaming out of the cliffs.

The town of **Le Carbet** takes its name from the rectangular thatched houses in which the Caribs lived. The town fronts on to a coconut-lined beach on which Columbus is supposed to have landed during his visit.

In the hills above Anse Turin, sign-posted from the main road, is the **Musée Gauguin**, commemorating the French artist, who lived on Martinique in 1887 before he moved on to Tahiti in the Pacific. There is a permanent exhibition of Gauguin's letters and sketches, and of some of his paintings (in reproduction). Other traditional Martiniquan topics are covered as well, including the description of the checked *madras* head-dress and its codified intricacies by Lafcadio Hearn. There is also a revolving exhibition of work by local artists. Open daily 10–5; adm (tel 77 22 66).

St Pierre—The Paris of the Lesser Antilles

Until 1902, St Pierre was the cultural and commercial heart of Martinique and one of the prettiest towns in the Caribbean. The red-roofed warehouses of yellow stone were stacked in lines on the hillside, overlooking the magnificent bay, where 30 ships might sit, delivering luxuries to the *Pierrotins* and loading the sugar loaves and rum puncheons that were the town's stock-in-trade.

The oldest town on the island, it grew up around the fine harbour, protected from the Atlantic tradewinds by Mont Pelé and although the administrative centre soon moved to Fort Royal because of its superior strategic setting, the town thrived immediately from its beginnings in the 17th century.

The cobbled streets and the seafront promenade of 'Little Paris' were walked by the smartest Antillean ladies of the day, creole beauties with brown skin dressed in voluminous and brightly-coloured skirts, parasols over their shoulder to keep off the sun. Cafés and cabarets did a grand trade on Saturdays as did the Cathedral on Sunday. In 1902, the illustrious town of 26,000 inhabitants was the most modern in the area, with electricity and telephones, and connected from one end to the other by tram.

But for all the human endeavour, St Pierre was living beneath the Caribbean's most violent volcano, the **Montagne Pelée** (the bald mountain). It had stayed silent for the first 200 years of the town's existence, until 1851 when it grumbled, blanketing the town with volcanic ash and creating a lake in its crater.

Towards the end of April 1902 the rumblings started again, this time accompanied by plumes of smoke that flashed with lightning. Four people from St Pierre climbed to the lip of the crater and found that the lake had disappeared and that it was now a cauldron of boiling mud, with an icing of ash racing over the surface in the wind. The rivers were poisoned by sulphur emissions and ran with dead fish.

On 5 May, the crater split open and an avalanche of mud and lava slid down the the mountain, engulfing a factory and killing 25 workers. Despite the ever-increasing plumes of smoke, still lit by lightning, the Governor came from Fort de France to urge the Pierrotins not to leave. News came that the Soufrière volcano on the island of St Vincent had blown and it was thought that this would relieve the pressure on Mont Pelée. Though about 1000 did choose to leave for Fort de France at dawn the next morning, the majority were calmed and stayed put.

At a couple of minutes before eight the next morning the mountainside itself split and gaped open as the eruption began. A vast cloud of flames, molten lava and poisonous gases spewed up through the crater, thrown to a height of 300 feet before sweeping down the mountainside at 250 miles an hour. With a temperature of 400°C, the cloud engulfed the town of St Pierre and poured on down to the sea, turning it into a seething cauldron and setting the ships ablaze or capsizing them with a tidal wave.

30,000 people were killed within two minutes. They were knocked to the ground by the force of the *nuée ardente* and carbonized where they lay. Glasses wilted and pots and pans drooped in the heat. The city passed into complete darkness, pierced only by the light of burning houses.

There was one survivor in the city itself. Auguste Cybaris had been thrown into a police cell the night before for being drunk. No doubt he woke with a start at eight the next morning, but the thick stone walls of his cell protected him from the heat and the grilled window kept out the fumes. He lived out his days until his death in 1955 with the Barnum Circus, performing in a replica of his cell.

One ship also survived, the *HMS Roddam*, which was cut from its mooring by the tidal wave. Several of the crew were burned alive on deck by showers of molten lava and others died jumping overboard. The ghostly shell, heaped with grey volcanic ash, crawled into the harbour at Castries, St Lucia, later that day, its captain severely burned but still at the wheel.

The volcano continued to spit fire and lava over the next few months, but gradually calmed down. At the same time, there arose one of the most curious phenomena in the whole history of the Caribbean. In November of 1902, a glowing needle of solidified lava began to protrude from the crater. The plug steadily pushed upwards, until it reached a height of 800 feet. After nine months it eventually collapsed.

After so many stories about the cataclysm at St Pierre and the talk of the ruins, it comes as a bit of a surprise to discover that people actually still live there. It is a busy country town. No doubt the inhabitants have faith in the team of boffins who live on the slopes of the mountain listening out for future rumbles.

The cobbles of the old town can be seen protruding through the tarmac and the blackened walls and stairways still run down to the palm-lined promenade on the waterfront. The skeleton of the old theatre and the stone shells of the 18th-century warehouses have a slightly foreboding air, but the market and shops bustle happily around them. However, they still stand in the shadow of Mont Pelée, a monstrous and brooding colossus.

The **Theatre**, with its double staircase, is a copy of the one in Bordeaux. Just nearby is the cell in which Cybaris spent the night after his drinking spree. Across the Roxelane River is the Quartier du Fort, the site of the first settlement on Martinique. The ruined fort near the seafront was erected by d'Esnambuc in 1635 when he arrived, planted a cross and claimed the island for France.

Le Musée Historique de St Pierre on the rue Victor Hugo, contains a welter of pictorial exhibits of life in St Pierre before the disaster in 1902. Open daily 9.30–5, Sun 9.30–12.30, adm (tel 79 74 32).

Best known is the **Musée Volcanique**, established in 1932 by the American vulcanologist Franck Perret. Clocks that stopped at 8 am precisely and nails fused together in the heat of the *nuée ardente* are among the exhibits, alongside an explanation of the motions of a volcanic eruption. Guided tours do a circuit and release you to admire the view of the bay from the balcony. Open daily 9–12.30, 3–5, except Sunday afternoon, adm.

A commanding view of St Pierre Bay can also be had from the road that climbs past the cemetery at the back of St Pierre. From here it continues into the rainforest in the foothills of the Morne des Cadets in Pitons du Carbet and to Fonds St Denis, an agricultural village perched on the mountainside over hairpin bends. This road was the original approach from Fort de France to St Pierre; called *La Trace*, it was cut out of the hills by the Jesuits in the 17th century.

North of St Pierre

As the road follows the coast north, skirting the slopes of Mont Pelée, the 'developed' side of Martinique evaporates and a more typical West Indian simplicity takes its place. **Le Prêcheur** is a simple fishing village where you will see the daily catch hauled in and the washing spread out on the rocks in the river. It was one of the first areas to be settled in the 17th century and at that time the slopes above it were carved out with prosperous plantations. Le Prêcheur was the childhood home of Françoise d'Aubigné, who would

194

later become the Marquise de Maintenon. There are hot volcanic springs on the route up Mt Pelée.

Beyond the village is the bay of Anse Ceron, a black-sand beach of unmanicured beauty. The coastal road does not run all around the island, but stops a couple of miles beyond Le Prêcheur. However, it is possible to walk from here through the forest to the village of Grand' Rivière.

St Pierre to the Atlantic coast

The route to the Atlantic coast leaves St Pierre from the Quartier du Fort and cuts uphill into the botanical turmoil of the rainforest, climbing to **Morne Rouge** in the col between the Pitons du Carbet and Mont Pelée. A hundred years ago this route was walked by the *porteuses*, with huge trays on their heads, laden with anything that needed to be carried to the Atlantic coast. It is a route steep enough to make a car strain, but these young women would carry up to 100 pounds in weight for 15 hours a day with nothing but a drop of rum and some cake to keep them going.

Just beyond Morne Rouge is the dropping off point for hikes headed to the summit of Mont Pelée. If you attempt this, it is advisable to take a guide. Also, as there are often clouds parked on the summit, take a waterproof jacket to keep off the wind and wet. There has been only one rumble from Mont Pelée since 1902, but if it starts to rain pumice stones, clear out quick. The ascent takes around three hours.

Alternatively, the route passes over to the Atlantic coast, descending through the forest, where the road is overhung by vast sprouts of bamboo and 10-foot tree ferns. **Ajoupa-Bouillon** is a pretty town laid out either side of the main road, which is lined with flowers.

From here, two natural sites are worth visiting: the **Saut Babin**, a 40-foot waterfall half an hour's walk southeast of the town, and the **Gorges de la Falaise**. For the second you cut in from the road just above the town, going north on a path into the forest and you will come to the river, which has carved a narrow bed for itself out of the volcanic rock. In the dry season (Nov–June), it is possible to walk up in a swimming costume and a pair of gymshoes. Eventually, you will come to the falls, fed by the water of Mont Pelée. Guided tours of these sights can be arranged at Les Ombrages (tel 53 31 90) below Ajoupa Bouillon. At Les Ombrages there is a botanic path through the rainforest, shaded by hundred foot bamboo trees The plants are marked—*calathea ornata* (called musical paper) and *culotte du diable* (devil's trousers). Open 8–4.

As the mountainside descends and turns into plains, so the rainforest gives way to cultivation: pineapples, bananas and fields of sugar-cane. In the 18th century, this area was completely covered with plantations, cane as far as the eye could see, broken periodically by a cluster of buildings: the estate house, outbuildings and a windmill.

Basse Pointe, on the coast, is the birth-place of the mayor of Fort de France, Aimé Césaire, and has had strong East Indian influence since the Indians came to Martinique in the last century as indentured labourers. There is a Hindu temple just outside the town. Inland is the **Plantation Leyritz**, an old plantation house which has been restored as a hotel (with rooms in the slave quarters) and gardens. Machinery is scattered around the grounds and the old outhouses are fitted out as a restaurant. It was here that Presidents Gerald Ford and Giscard d'Estaing met in 1976. There is also a funny

195

exhibition of dolls made from vegetables. Open 8–6, adm to the plantation gardens (tel 75 53 92).

The village of **Macouba**, named after the Carib word for fish, stands on cliffs at the northern tip of the island, looking out over the channel to Dominica. It was a prosperous settlement in the 17th century, when it derived its wealth from the cultivation of tobacco.

The final stretch of road continues through wild country to **Grand' Rivière**, an isolated fishing village. The road ends here, though it is possible to walk over the cliffs and through the rainforest, skirting Mont Pelée, to Le Prêcheur on the Caribbean coast. The 20-kilometre walk over the cliffs of St Martin takes about six hours, though you should allow longer in the rainy season when the going is harder.

N3—Fort de France and the Pitons du Carbet

In the 17th century, the Jesuits cut a road through the mountainous interior of Martinique, linking the new administrative centre of Fort de France with the social and commercial hub at St Pierre. *La Trace* was initially just a track cut into the rainforest, used by horses and pedestrians, but in the 19th century it was enlarged by the army and then in the 20th it was made into a major road. Today it makes a spectacular drive through some of the island's best scenery.

Across the Madame River, La Trace climbs through the prosperous suburb of Didier, favoured by the creole ascendancy for its commanding panorama, where spectacular villas perch above Fort de France in gardens of tropical flowers. As the town thins, the road winds into primeval rainforest, clinging to the hillside.

Suddenly a mirage arises before you, the **Sacré Coeur** from Montmartre, transported to Martinique . . . It is an almost exact replica, but here its dome and spires stand brilliant white against the sparkling green of the rainforest. It was erected in 1923 to give thanks for the lives of those who died in the First World War.

Soon La Trace becomes buried in the rainforest and the mountains loom either side. Five miles above the capital, at the **Jardin de Balata**, the botanical pandemonium is momentarily set into order. Hundreds of species have been brought from tropical regions all over the world and cultivated in the garden, numbered so that you can put names to them: bananas, bamboos, orchids, cacti and endless palms. As you walk the paths you will see ferns like velvet, shrubs with flowers like little plastic animals or shaped like a fisherman's hat, and all around a plethora of palm trees. After a tropical shower the whole garden glints in the sunlight and the view opens out again as far as St Lucia. The gardens, an enjoyable tour even for uncommitted gardeners, give an idea of the absurd abundance of the Caribbean islands. Open daily 9–5, adm quite expensive Fr30 (tel 64 48 73).

The N3 then moves into the peaks and valleys of the Pitons du Carbet, running a contorted route as far as Deux Chous, where the old road descends into St Pierre and on to Morne Rouge.

N1—Fort de France to the Atlantic Coast

The N1 road leaves Fort de France heading east, past the airport at Lamentin, and into the central fertile plains, where much of Martinique's agriculture and industry is located. It emerges on the Atlantic coast at Le Robert, a fishing town on a wide bay.

Trinité is the second largest town on the island and an administrative centre for the northern Atlantic coast. The town is set on a sheltered bay and has an esplanade that teems with activity when the day's catch is brought in. In the hills above, the town of Morne des Esses is known for its weaving, techniques supposedly developed from their Carib heritage. The **Basket Weaving Workshop** is devoted to the art. Open Mon–Sat, 8.30–5, adm free.

The town lies in the lee of the **Caravelle Peninsula**, a windswept outcrop that juts seven miles into the Atlantic Ocean. It is mountainous, with a shoreline of cliffs and small coves, and a network of paths for walkers who wish to see the varied flora. Near the point are the ruins of the **Chateau Dubuc**, the remaining walls of a 17th-century castle with a magnificent view. There is a small museum and an assortment of sugar-coppers, from which the estate derived some of its wealth—the rest was made in smuggling. Open 8.30–5.30, except Sun afternoons, adm.

The N4 leads from Trinité back to Fort de France, cutting through the hills via Gros Morne, the seat of government during the patriots' rebellion in 1790.

Continuing north along the coast, the N1 comes to **Sainte Marie**, with an attractive church built in Jesuit style. Just beyond the town is the working **Rhum St James** distillery and museum. The old creole plantation house and the modern factory stand near one another, looking on to a garden full of sugar relics of all ages—crushing gear and steam engines. Inside the creole estate house is more sugar paraphernalia: rum barrels and boiling coppers, alongside a history of the sugar industry in Martinique. The informative tour is free and it culminates in a tasting-room, stacked to the ceiling with bottles of rum, which are of course available for purchase. Open weekdays 9–5, weekends 9–noon (tel 75 30 02).

L'Habitation Fonds St Jacques was once a thriving Dominican community and sugar plantation. It was run by Père Labat, who resided here in the 1690s, taking over a run-down plantation and turning it into the most prosperous on the island within two years. Some buildings have been restored and there is a small museum on the subject of sugar in the 18th century. The coastal road continues to wind through the plantations and along the shoreline to the town of Lorrain.

FESTIVALS

Bastille Day, 14 July, is celebrated in the Antilles as in France, but the major festival in the year is **Carnival**, which takes place in the run-up to Mardi Gras at the beginning of Lent. There are two days of street parades, in which many characters appear dressed in the traditional black and white, that culminate in the burning of momo, the Carnival spirit, on Ash Wednesday evening.

Many towns also celebrate their saint's day, in the *fête patronale*, with a round of races, competitions, outdoor dances and barbecued chicken legs. They take place mostly in the summer, in July and August, and it is well worth checking the newspaper or Tourist Board to find out if one is going on.

In April, the **Martinique Food Show** brings together the island's best cooks and their dishes in competition with one another and in July Fort de France stages a series of concerts and theatrical events at their **Cultural Festival**. November sees the annual sailing race to bring over the first case of Beaujolais Nouveau from the métropole and in

December Martinique clubs and venues come alive with an International Jazz Festival or the World Crossroads of the Guitar, held in alternate years.

WHERE TO STAY

Martinique offers a complete range of accommodation, from the modern Caribbean dream on the beach to tiny *auberges* set in old gingerbread houses, hidden in the rainforest. Many of the best hotels are quite isolated, particularly from Fort de France and so it is a good idea to have a car to get around. Rates quoted here are for a double room, though breakfast will usually be included. On top of the bill, expect to pay a 10% service charge and a 5% government tax.

Fort de France

The newest addition is the **Squash** Hotel on Blvd de la Marne, 97200 Fort de France (tel 63 00 01, fax 63 00 74), heading north out of the city. A shimmering twenty-first century building with views across the bay, Le Squash is convenient for town so it is good for businessmen, particularly the sport-minded exec, because of the sports club downstairs. The bar has a ringside view of the squash courts. US$130 a double in season. **Le Lafayette**, 5 rue de la Liberté, 97200 Fort de France (tel 73 80 50, fax 60 97 75) overlooks the craft vendors on the Savane if you would like to be in the middle of town. 42 rooms and action in the cafés downstairs. US$68 in season. There are some smaller hotels ideal for travellers who want to be in town rather than on a beach. At **Un Coin de Paris**, 54 rue Lazare Carnot (tel 70 08 52) a double room costs Fr250. 14 simple rooms.

Anse Mitan and Pointe du Bout

Across the bay in the Pointe du Bout area are some of the big beach resorts. The **Méridien** (tel 66 00 00) and the renovated **Bakoua** (tel 66 02 02) stand like factories on man-made beaches and dispense constant entertainment and high-pressure relaxation. They are the island's top resorts for international standard luxury and high-grade facilities, US$350 or rooms and suites. Close by is the **Hotel de la Pagerie**, Pointe du Bout, 97229 Trois Ilets (tel 60 05 30), fax 66 00 99), a friendly resort above the beach with 100 rooms around a courtyard and pool. Mock Louisiana architecture and chi-chi rooms, watersports arranged nearby. Double room US$110 in season. The **Auberge de L'Anse Mitan** (tel 66 03 19) is a retiring enclave of faded elegance hidden at the far end of the beach, overlooking the bay and the mornes one way and constantly under threat from the tropical jungle behind it. Built in the 1930s, it has 20 rooms furnished with dark wicker and hung with old prints. Rates for a double room only are US$70 in the winter and less in the summer season. Another option in the middle of Anse Mitan is the friendly **Bonne Auberge**, 97229 Trois Ilets (tel 66 01 55, fax 66 04 50) and its restaurant Chez André, both festooned in greenery. 32 comfortable rooms in blocks, from an earlier generation than today's high-pastel decor. No pool, but the sea is a minute's walk away, US$65 a double in season.

On **Anse à l'Ane**, a less crowded beach than Anse Mitan, is a comfortable hotel with the feel of a beach club, **Le Frantour**, 97229 Trois Ilets (tel 68 31 67, fax 68 37 65). The 77 rooms run in two-storey blocks around the gardens of heliconia and palm, furnished in primary colours and patterned in mosaic and rich turquoise. There are views of Fort de France, to which ferries leave regularly. Double room US$170 with breakfast in season. It is within a short drive or ferry-ride of the restaurants of Anse Mitan and Pointe du Bout. A little farther around the coast, on the grey sands of Grand Anse d'Arlet, a double room, simple but comfortable enough, is available in the **Hotel Tamarind** (tel 68 67 88) for around US$70 with breakfast.

In the **Diamant** area you will find cool and calm sumptuousness at the **Novotel Diamant**, Point de la Chéry, 97223 Le Diamant (tel 76 42 42, fax 76 22 87). Pretty in high pastel with a reasonable beach and good sporting facilities—diving, watersports, tennis and golf range. Double room US$230. In the town itself is the smaller **Hotel Diamant les Bains** (tel 76 40 14), with rooms in the hotel building and cabins scattered around the garden of palms and ginger-lily. The rooms are simple, but the hotel is friendly and serves good local food on the terrace above the garden. Miles of brown sand beach to walk along. The daily rate for a double in winter is US$92. Just above Sainte-Luce is a small and busy hotel, **La Petite Auberge**, 97228 St Luce (tel 62 59 70), which was built as a large, luxurious family home in the 70s and has now been converted to a hotel. There are twelve quite simple rooms overlooking a pool, and the downstairs floor is given over entirely to the restaurant and bar. Difficult to get a room sometimes, but worth the effort. Double room in season US$95. **The Last Resort**, 21 rue Osman Duquesnay (tel 74 83 88), is an amusing haunt buried in the back-streets of Le Marin (if that seems possible in so small a town). A young crowd filters through the simple rooms, walls covered with posters from all generations of rock music, of which the owner is a luminary. Some share baths, but a single goes at US$30 and a double at US$40.

The Sainte-Anne Peninsula
Club Med have a nice property sheltered by a forest of palms on the Pointe du Marin and so you will see pairs of chic bronzed body-vacationers promenading along the beach. If you wish to stay within walking distance of this beach, then a friendly hotel in town is **La Dunette** (tel 76 73 90, fax 76 76 05), with a view from the rooms and terrace restaurant across the southern coast as far as Diamond Rock. The 18 double rooms cost from US$85 in season. You can stay more cheaply in the town at the **Georges III** (tel 76 73 11), simple rooms at US$40 a double.

North of Fort de France
La Batelière (tel 61 49 49) in Schoelcher is one of the island's high-profile luxury hotels. It is not set on a beach, but has nightly entertainment and a casino. Around US$245.

There are not many places to stay around St Pierre, but you can get a cheap room at **Le Christophe Colomb**, 92771 Le Carbet (tel 78 05 38) with kitchenettes, double room US$46. Also **La Nouvelle Vague**, 97290 St Pierre (tel 74 83 88) with a waterfront restaurant on the terrace. Double room US$35, single $25. Perhaps the most congenial setting in this area is **Le Grain d'Or**, between St Pierre and Le Carbet, on Anse Turin. The attractive old wooden house has a pool and a terraced restaurant (myriade d'accras, lambi citron, Fr35). Eight rooms at US$35 a double.

The **Plantation de Leyritz** (tel 78 53 08) stands among the swathes of sugar-cane and bananas, on the hillside above Basse Pointe on the northern Atlantic coast. The 18th-century plantation house has been rebuilt as a hotel and the slave quarters turned into the hotel rooms (considerably improved since 200 years ago) and the old cane-crushing gear, a water-wheel and boiling coppers stand unused in the garden. The hotel tends to get a bit busy during the day, as a lot of visitors come by for lunch, but the early evening restores the plantation idyll. 24 rooms; US$115. In Grand' Rivière, the northernmost town, is a pension with seven rooms, **Les Abeilles** (tel 55 73 73), where a double room sets you back just US$35.

Travel down the east coast to Trinité and you will find one of the island's most attractive houses, the pink **St Aubin Hotel** (tel 69 34 77). The 18th-century house stands out on a hillside of tropical greens, with balconies running all the way around the outside. 15 rooms; US$90 for a double in season. There is a nice hotel on the northern side of the peninsula: **Le Madras**, 97220 Tartane (tel 58 33 95, fax 58 33 63); a dining room with a view and prints of the old houses of Martinique. 16 neat rooms, some looking out on to the fishing boats on the bay. Double rate US$85 in season.

Martinique is linked to the **Association des Gîtes Ruraux** and their office is at 9 Boulevard Général de Gaulle in Fort de France (tel 73 67 92). They have flats and houses for rent by the week and by the month.

For travellers who would like to stay with a Martiniquan family (often cheaper than the hotels) LVA (Logis Vacances Antilles) can place you in any area of the island, from US$20 per person per night.

Another cheap alternative is **camping**. **Courbaril Camping** (tel 68 32 30) has spaces in Anse à l'Ane, opposite Fort de France, for around US$5 per night. In St Anne, the **Camping Municipal** (tel 76 72 79) has spaces and facilities just off the beach.

EATING OUT

Martiniquan Fare

Martiniquan food has a traditional French flair and is considered by many to be the best in the Caribbean. Here, you can make your holiday almost entirely gastronomic, as there are cafés and open-air restaurants to linger in at every turn. You will find traditional *cuisine gastronomique*, but also its Caribbean or creole equivalent. Lovingly prepared, the dishes are often spiced and of course, it is all in the sauces.

Some creole dishes, many of them slightly more luxurious versions of usual Caribbean dishes, are: *crabe farci*, a very spicy stuffing of crabmeat in a crab-shell, traditionally served on Easter Monday; the avocado *féroce*, with a spicy fish filling; *blaff*, a way of cooking fish (the name is supposed to imitate the noise it makes when thrown into the water) with thyme, peppers, clove, parsley and onion; *accra*, seasoned cod or greens fried in batter; *écrevisses*, *soudons*, *oursins* and even *chatrous*, shrimps, clams, sea urchins and octopus; *colombo* is the delicate French Caribbean version of curry goat or chicken and *z'habitants* is a local preparation of crayfish. *Touffé* is a method of cooking in a casserole, as is *fricassé*, another popular dish. *Blanc manger* is a traditional pudding, a sort of coconut custard, ingredients: milk, coconut, cinnamon, vanilla and nutmeg.

Many of the hotels have fine kitchens, but it would be a pity to miss out on one of the island's best-loved pastimes by dining only there. Fort de France has its share of restaurants, some in the heart of town, others overlooking the mêlée from verandas on high. France's other colonial interests are also represented in Martinique in Vietnamese and African restaurants. *Bistros* can be found all over the island, so if you wish to join the Martiniquans in an afternoon's gastronomy, ask them when you come to a new town. Despite the local association with rum, which is drunk often as a liqueur, there is certainly something of the traditional French homage for wine, imported in large quantities.

The booklet *Ti Gourmet* lists many of Martinique's restaurants, with translations of the menu into English, recipes and useful facts about which are open on Sundays. Service is *compris*.

In and around Fort de France

EXPENSIVE

There are a number of excellent restaurants in and around Fort de France. **La Grand' Voile** (tel 70 29 29) on Pointe Simon, overlooks the yachts in harbour from an upstairs dining room decorated with beams and lanyards. *Nouvelle cuisine créole*, neatly presented local fare—*Farandole de petites specialités martiniquaises* (a combination dish) and *cassolette de soudons marinières* (local clams in onion and garlic). Follow up with a nougat glacé. Fr130 a main dish. **Le Privilège** on rue Perrinon (tel 60 27 32) is another top restaurant for lunch or a dinner out. The dining room is decorated in bright white wicker, peach and pink. Menus gastronomique and gersois, from southwest France, and creole *plats du jour*. A popular dish is the *magret de canard* in sauce Auscitane or for two people the *côte de boeuf de Charolars grillé aux deux sauces* (occitane and madeira). Fish Fr100 and meat dishes Fr130 plus. **La Mouïna** (tel 79 34 57), high up on the Route de la Redoute, has the lovely setting of a Martiniquan villa, where the dining room is set on the balcony above the garden. Smart and subdued, dinner is candle-lit and the menu is French and creole. A house speciality is the *filet de poisson en papillotte*—or try *canard à l'orange* with local vegetables. Fish Fr95, meat dishes Fr120. Lunch and dinner, reserve, particularly on a Saturday, closed Sun.

MODERATE AND CHEAP

Le Mareyeur (tel 61 74 70) is a seafood restaurant off the road north out of Fort de France. Quite a simple dining room with red and white chequered tablecloths, but the fish are exotic—*beignets de requin* (shark fritters), *palourdes farcies* (stuffed clams) and fish fricasséed, blaffed and paellaed. A welcoming place, Fr70 a main dish, music on Fridays, closed Sun. There is a vegetarian restaurant in the centre of town, near the Cathedral, **Le Second Souffle** (tel 63 44 11). Try *soufflé d'igname* and *parmentier de fruits à pain* (made with breadfruit), with fruit drinks. Main course Fr30, salads Fr20–40. For a very local bistro, try the **Perrinon** on the road of the same name. Also **Chez Gaston** on the Rue Félix Eboué, and **Le Lem** on Boulevard Général de Gaulle, where a *plat du jour* costs around Fr40. A fun and cheap way to eat is to go to the caravans parked between the Savane and Fort St Louis. Communal tables are set out under large awnings, where you will sit among Martiniquan families on an evening out, everyone shouting above the sound of *zouk* music and the roar of rebellious gas stoves. It stays open late, and the French Caribbean's equivalent of rice and peas, or a brochette, is yours for Fr15–20.

Anse Mitan and Pointe du Bout

MODERATE

The **Villa Créole** in Anse Mitan (tel 66 05 53) has a candle-lit veranda setting looking onto a garden. Creole and French cuisine accompanied by the serenading of the patron and then dancing. Try *poisson frit à l'Antillaise* or the *colombo aux trois viandes* (chicken, pork and lamb). Closed Sun, main dish Fr80 plus. There is another friendly restaurant close by, **Chez André**, under the awnings at the Bonne Auberge Hotel. Veranda setting draped in flowers for *velouté de lambi* (cream of conch soup) and *accras de crevettes* (shrimp fritters). Main course Fr60. Not far off, on the waterfront by the ferry jetty, **Le Langouste** gives a view of the yachts from the veranda. Fixed menu at Fr100, or *colombo de poulet* and *z'habitants à la carte*. Over the headland in **Anse à l'Ane**, try **Chez Jojo** (tel 68 37 43) which looks through the trees to the sea. Simple beach setting and regular creole fare—*boudin de lambi* (a sort of conch sausage) and *ananas flambé* (pineapple), Fr60 a main course. There are a string of waterfront watering holes, part bar, part restaurant, in the Anses d'Arlet. **L'Anse Noire** has a lovely setting in the profuse Martiniquan overgrowth, perched above Anse Noire and Anse Dufour. Local food— fish, chicken, lobster and salads, Fr45. You will find **Les Délices de la Mer** in the Grande Anse d'Arlet, good for fricassées and colombos (fixed menu, Fr90) or **L'Amandier**, all wickerwork on the waterfront, Fr35. Perhaps the nicest of all is **Le Flamboyant des Iles** at the southern end of the bay, another pretty veranda with a view over the yachts. *Touffé de requin* (shark casserole) or *steak tortue au beurre persillé* (turtle steak in parsley butter), followed by *beignets de grand-mère* (granny fritters), Fr55 plus. In Diamant town, the brightly painted **Le Diams** is a pleasant stop on the square, at lunch or dinner—huge *salades gourmandes*, or pizzas followed by *blanc manger* and coconut, Fr35–50.

Farther along the coast in St Luce you can get a nice meal on the main square at **Kaï Armande**. Seafood and local, but also some African specialities. Try a *yassa* or a *mafe* (with a nut base) or *écrevisses daube*, Fr55–80. For a barbecue fish or a brochette with rice, peas and ground provisions, try **Keep Cool** a little farther down the waterfront. A hip spot for a beer and a meal, Fr60. For such a large marina town, Le Marin is surprisingly short of restaurants. The **Beverly Hills** (tel 74 73 15) is probably the best bet for a meal—*gambas grillés* (grilled giant prawn) and duck in a mango sauce.

In **St Anne**, **Poï et Virginie** (tel 76 76 86) has a charming dining room on the waterfront, set with wicker furniture and walls lined with bamboo and hung with Haitian paintings. Brisk service and a sedate ambience. You might try the *plateau de fruits de mer* for two (*araignées, tourteaux, cigales, gambas, soudons, huîtres* and *palourdes*). Phone 24 hours in advance for this, Fr520. Otherwise lobstertail with mayonnaise. Humble fish costs Fr90, closed Mon. Another smaller restaurant, just along the seafront is **La Dunette** (tel 76 73 90), where you will find chicken pipiri (grilled and served with rice cooked in cinnamon and coconut), Fr65 a main dish. On the St Anne beach are a number of restaurants and bars to waylay you when the idea of tanning palls: **Le Touloulou**, with snacks and meals, or perhaps just an orangina and an *ananas flambé*; and **Les Filets Bleus** which looks through the palms to the beach. You can get a turtle steak with *christophene au gratin* for Fr100. There are smaller restaurants and snackette wagons in the area too where you can grab a sandwich. At the southern point of the island, at the end of Grand Anse des Salines, you will find **Aux Délices de la Mer** (tel 76 73 71), which has a fantastic view of the bay and the hills beyond from its terrace. *Oursins frits* and *colombo de crevettes*, Fr50. Also snackwagons on the bay here.

One of the most renowned kitchens on the island, for its local cuisine, is at **Le Colibri** (tel 61 91 95), in Morne des Esses. Clothilde Paladino has won prizes for her original variations on local recipes, including *tourte aux lambis* (conch pie), *écrevisses buisson* and *bisque, soufflé de christophene* and *flan au coco*. Family run and a West Indian welcome, Fr55–70 main course, so good value too. **Aux Fruits de Mer, Chez Fofor** (tel 65 10 33) has a pretty setting above the sea in Le Robert. French and seafood menu—for example *fricassé de z'habitants flambés au rhum*. Main dish Fr50, closed Mon. In St Pierre there is another waterfront view from the terrace at **La Vague de St Pierre** (tel 78 14 34). Here you can be served with an exotic version of conch (still in its shell) as well as more traditional stuffed crab-backs, Fr50. You get excellent value at the **Grain d'Or** in Anse Turin just south of the town. Also traditional Martiniquan fare, Fr35.

BARS AND NIGHTLIFE
The traditional Martiniquan apéritif is the *ti punch*, which is prepared with the same ceremony as the local food. The sugar (or cane juice) is heaped in the glass and the lime is squeezed quickly and dropped in before the white rum is poured and stirred vigorously. In times past only the cane juice would have to be paid for in bars because the rum was so plentiful. As everywhere in the Caribbean, bistros usually double as bars in Martinique. There is also an infinity of rum shops/supermarkets.

There are a number of bars in Fort de France, of which the most hip is probably **Le Terminal**, at the northern end of the Parking, with a video lounge and balcony upstairs and a mix of local execs and visitors. They loiter over absinthe cocktails or one of about 50 beers until 2 am. **L'Electra**, just off the Parking, has loud music, pool and pictures of motorbikes all over the walls, live music Thurs. Just out of town to the north, near the Rond Point in Didier is **Papagayo**, another chichi video cocktail bar, Latin music at weekends, closed Mon. You can also try **Chez Gaston** on the rue Félix Eboué and on the rue Lamartine **Le Carafe**, for Friday jazz.

Nightclubs and discotheques include the **New Hippo** on Blvd Allègre, Elysée Matignon, close by on the rue Ernest Deproge, for variétés, and **Club Bitaco**, with two bars and two dance-floors, high in the hills of Ravine Vilaine. (you have to follow the Route de Redoute off the bypass behind the downtown area), cover price Fr80 each.

Some of the hotels have discotheques and they also stage folklore shows. Classical cultural events are staged in the Hopital Civil on the road up towards Didier.

There are two casinos on the island, open from 9 pm until 3 am, one in the Méridien and the other in Schoelcher at La Batalière Hotel. Adm Fr50.

The Région of Guadeloupe
and La Désirade, Marie Galante and the Saints, St Martin, St Barthélemy

The *Région* of Guadeloupe is made up of a number of islands scattered over 150 miles of the Lesser Antilles. Altogether they have an area of 1705 square km and a population of around 400,000. Of the smaller islands, the Saints, La Désirade and Marie Galante lie close to Guadeloupe itself; St Martin (which shares an island with the Dutch colony of Sint Maarten) and St Barts (St Barthélemy), lie to the north, amongst the Leeward Islands. Guadeloupe is far the largest of the group and is shaped like a huge butterfly.

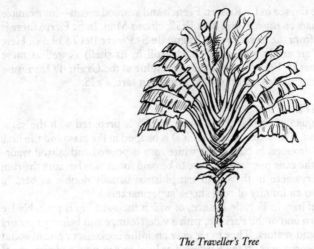

The Traveller's Tree

GUADELOUPE

Guadeloupe is in fact two islands, pushed together by geological movement, and each wing shows a different side of the Caribbean: Basse-Terre is mountainous and has the explosive luxuriance of the volcanic islands, its slopes covered with banana plantations and rainforest; the softer contours of Grande-Terre in the east have the coral reefs and white-sand beaches. The variety makes Guadeloupe one of the most rewarding islands to visit.

The small town of Basse-Terre on the west coast of the island is the capital of Guadeloupe, but Pointe-à-Pitre on Grande-Terre has long been the commercial centre. Grande-Terre is more populous and industrialized, and its gently sloping *mornes* are covered in 12-foot curtains of sugar-cane.

The island's economy has always been agricultural. Coffee gave way to sugar (and rum) and most recently to tropical fruits such as bananas. But as with so many Caribbean islands, tourism has grown here and become the primary industry most recently. Unemployment runs at around 30 per cent, but the standard of living is kept at a roughly similar level to that of France and so Guadeloupe appears far more prosperous than other islands nearby.

There is an old saying of the French Antilles which talks of *Les Grands Seigneurs de la Martinique et les Bons Gens de la Guadeloupe*. From the start Martinique was the senior, more prosperous island and its business interests in Guadaloupe continue today. But the Guadeloupeans have an independent cast of mind and they have always gone their own way. For the Guadeloupeans, the Martiniquans have too slavish an attachment to France. It is one thing to be 'Black Frenchmen', but if it has the effect of burying their own culture, then they will rebel against it.

Politically Guadeloupe has benefited from more autonomy in recent years, but they have also become more answerable for budget expenditure. France grants a huge amount of cash each year and the material benefits are clear to see, but there are some Guadeloupeans who would rather go it alone, without the protection of the Republic. The issue is an emotive one which erupts occasionally in violent campaigns, as it did in the late 1970s.

History

To the Caribs Guadeloupe was *Karukera*, thought to mean 'the island of beautiful waters'. Columbus was struck by the beauty of the waterfalls on the heights when he passed by on his second voyage in November 1493. He christened the island *Santa Maria de Guadalupe de Extremadura* but soon moved on. The 'Cannibal Isles' were dangerous country and apart from one attempt by the Spainiards in 1525 to settle Guadeloupe so that their ships could take on water and re-fit here after the Atlantic crossing, the island was left well alone.

It was another 100 years before the next Europeans arrived in force. Led by de l'Olive and Duplessis, 600 French settlers disembarked in June 1635. They attacked the Caribs, driving them off the island within a few years to the refuges in Dominica and St Vincent.

Guadeloupe was administered from Martinique. Not only did the Martiniquan Governor General have the ultimate say on affairs in Guadeloupe, but Martinique maintained its commercial hold. Trade to France had to be conducted through St Pierre, where the merchants would inevitably give a low price for Guadeloupean sugar, even after the extra costs of transportation. Revenge was sweet when four years under British rule (1759–63) turned out to be very prosperous ones for Guadeloupe because vast markets opened up to them in Britain and America.

During the Revolution the Guadeloupean *patriotes* gained the upper hand, ousting the planters. They welcomed the revolutionary Victor Hugues and the new régime was installed. A guillotine was erected and 300 were given the chop. From his base on Guadeloupe, Victor Hugues rallied the slaves and liberal Frenchmen on all the Windward Islands with the promise of freedom, but within two years the rebellions were crushed and Hugues' position in Guadeloupe was unsure.

A momentous event took place on 16 Pluviôse of Year 2 (4 February 1794). Following the declaration of the Revolutionary Convention in Paris, the slaves in Guadeloupe were set free. However, a reactionary régime was installed at the beginning of the 19th century and slavery was re-established in July 1802. There were bloody riots, and many Africans preferred to commit suicide rather than submit to slavery once again. Finally in 1848 the slaves were freed once more, largely due to the efforts of Victor Schoelcher (see p. 176), who then was elected deputy for Guadeloupe.

Guadeloupe was blockaded in the Second World War because it sided with the Vichy Government, but soon after the war Guadeloupe, like Martinique and French Guyana on the South American coast, became a French Overseas Département, with the same status as the mainland *départements*.

Flora and Fauna

Guadeloupe is a geographical oddity because the butterfly's two wings are islands of completely different geological origin, separated by a small stretch of sea, the Rivière

Salée. It is the meeting point of the two island chains that make up the Lesser Antilles; an inner chain of tall volcanic peaks that runs from Grenada up to Saba and the outer ring of coral islands from Marie Galante through Grande-Terre to St Martin and Anguilla.

Still odder are the names of the two islands: Basse-Terre and Grande-Terre. You might think that Grande-Terre would be the taller mountainous island, smothered in tropical rainforest, and that Basse-Terre would be lower. It is the other way around. There is a logical explanation, however, originating in now obscure sailing terminology. Basse-Terre is simply the 'lower ground' with regard to the prevailing wind. You can see the pattern repeated in the islands of the Saints, where Terre-de-Bas is downwind of Terre-de-Haut.

Guadeloupe can offer the best of the Caribbean in its two halves. Grande-Terre's coast is lined with mangrove bushes and the white coral beaches for which the Caribbean is famous. And in Basse-Terre there is the spectacular beauty of the rainforest as well as the fascinating, if smelly, attraction of the Soufrière volcano.

The **Parc National** covers some 30,000 hectares of the Basse-Terre mountains and they are as fertile as any in the Windwards. In the upper branches of the rainforest is another forest of hanging plants and explosive greenery—orchids and cycads, lianas grappling upwards to reach the sunlight and dropping aerial roots. Here you will see Guadeloupe's three hummingbirds and the woodpecker, a *tapeur* in French, and maybe the Hercules beetle, a six-inch monster that clanks. The elfin woodland in the wind-swept heights of the mountains has a whole new flora of dwarf palms and creepers.

Racing among the jumbled mountains are endless waterfalls that tumble into rock-pools; ideal spots for a dip. There are lakes, hot springs, and in the south, the curiosity of the volcanic peak itself, where the ground steams constantly. The mountains are also crossed by a series of tracks, many of which make a good day's walk. Some leave from and return to **La Maison de la Forêt** on road D23, others are more adventurous and cross from one side of the island to the other. (See the section on Basse-Terre.) Guided tours can be arranged through the **Organisation des Guides de Montagne de la Caraïbe** (tel 80 05 79) and the **Office National des Forêts**, Jardin Botanique, 97100 Basse-Terre (tel 81 17 20).

There is little wildlife on Guadeloupe, but what there is can be seen in the zoo on **La Route de la Traversée** (D23) that cuts across the middle of the park. In the hills you might be lucky enough to see the *raton laveur*, the racoon, that the Parc Naturel has adopted as its symbol, or an *agouti*, a little mammal introduced by man into many of the islands.

On the lower land of Grande-Terre the flora and fauna are completely different and you will see egrets and endless doves in the rolling mornes and sandpipers, snipe and yellowlegs (greater and lesser) around the mangrove swamps. On the coast there are pelicans and tropicbirds. You can find these, alongside a host of crabs and other crustaceans in the **Réserve Naturelle de Grand Cul de Sac Marin**, 1600 hectares of mangrove and swamp and 2100 hectares of marine park.

Guadeloupe was given a severe drubbing by Hurricane Hugo in 1989, which caused millions of dollars worth of damage and untold devastation to the natural life. It has grown back again quite quickly, but you will still see the broken stalks of coconut palms all over the island.

GETTING TO GUADELOUPE
Like Martinique, the main airline of Guadeloupe is Air France. Air Guadeloupe runs services to nearby islands from the airport at Le Raizet, a couple of miles from Pointe-à-Pitre.

From Europe: there are daily flights on Air France from Paris and a weekly service from Marseille and Lyon. There are also charter flights from other French cities.

From North America: Air France serves Guadeloupe from Miami and connections from the States can also be made via San Juan in Puerto Rico which is linked to Guadeloupe by American Eagle. From Canada there are flights from both Montreal and Toronto on Air Canada.

From other Caribbean Islands: Air France has flights at least once an hour between 7 am and 8 to Fort de France on Martinique. There are also services on LIAT, Air Guadeloupe, Air France and Winair to San Juan, Antigua, Sint Maarten (both airports), St Barts, Dominica.

By boat: Caribbean Express (tel 83 12 45) runs a hydrofoil service on the *Diamant Express* between Martinique and Guadeloupe, touching Dominica en route, about five times a week.

GETTING AROUND GUADELOUPE
The public **bus** system is a good way to get around Guadeloupe and it reaches all major towns, eventually. The buses can usually be heard before they are seen, as they are all equipped with extensive stereo systems. If you want to get on one, simply wave it down and if there is space the driver will stop. You will get to know the music of Guadeloupe, and your fellow passengers, well. There are bus-stops, but it is not necessary to use them unless you want to escape from the sun; to get off, you must either yell *Arrêt!*, or press the buzzer, which usually sounds like an air-raid siren. Buses leave when they have enough passengers and run from dawn until about 6 pm.

If you are catching a bus from Pointe-à-Pitre, your departure point will depend on the destination. The route along the south coast of Grande-Terre (Gosier—Fr8, St Anne—Fr10, St François—Fr15) is served from near the **Place de la Victoire**, on the eastern edge of La Darse, next to the ferries. To the northern part of Grande-Terre, buses depart from the **Mortenol Station**, across the dual carriageway from the Centre des Arts. Buses to the airport leave from the centre of town, on rue Peynier, cost Fr9.

If you are headed for Basse-Terre, all buses leave from the Bergeverin Station on **Boulevard Chanzy**. Ask around for the correct bus; some go just to Lamentin or around the northern coast to Deshaies, others turn south and run down the eastern coast and on to Basse-Terre, the island capital. The trip to Basse-Terre takes around two hours and costs Fr30 (Fr25 to Trois-Rivières). The last bus in both directions between the two major towns departs at around 6 pm. Miss it and you are stranded.

Guadeloupean **taxis** work on a fixed-rate basis and can be picked up in Pointe-à-Pitre (Place de la Victoire, Boulevard Chanzy and others), at the airport and at all the major hotels. Some taxi drivers speak some English and will give an impromptu tour. They are also happy to take a party out for the day at around US$60 for a half day and $85 for a full day (four people). Some numbers for taxis are: **CDL** (tel 20 74 74) and **SOS Taxis** (tel 83 63 94).

Sightseeing trips, usually with a lazy lunch-stop scheduled, can be arranged through

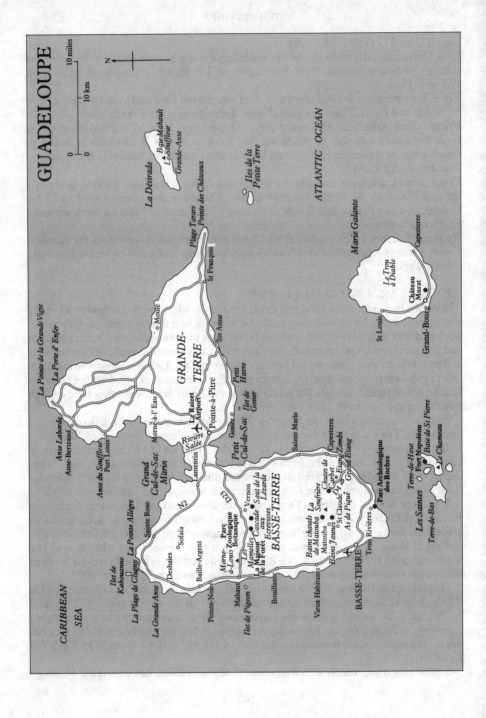

GUADELOUPE

CARIBBEAN SEA

ATLANTIC OCEAN

La Pointe de la Grande Vigie
La Porte d'Enfer
Anse Laborde
Anse-Bertrand
Anse du Souffleur
Port Louis
Grand Cul-de-Sac Marin
Sainte Rose
Ilet de Kahouanne
La Plage de Clugny
La Pointe Allègre
La Grande Anse
Deshaies
Sofaïa
Baille-Argent
Parc Zoologique Botanique
Morne-à-Louis
Les Mamelles
Cascade aux Écrevisses
La Maison de la Forêt
Mahaut
Ilet de Pigeon
Pointe-Noire
Bouillante
Vieux Habitants
Bains chauds de Matouba
Matouba
Bains Jaunes
La Soufrière
St Claude
As de Pique
BASSE-TERRE
BASSE-TERRE
Trois Rivières
Vernou
Saut de la Lézarde
Chutes du Carbet
Étang Zombi
Grand Étang
Capesterre
Parc Archéologique des Roches
Sainte Marie
N2
D23
Lamentin
Rivière Salée
Petit Cul-de-Sac Marin
Petit Gosier
Ilet de Gosier
Grand Cul-de-Sac Marin
Morne-à-l'Eau
GRANDE-TERRE
Le Raizet Airport
Pointe-à-Pitre
Sainte Anne
Petit Havre
Le Moule
St François
Plage Tarare
Pointe des Châteaux
La Désirade
Baie-Mahault
Le Souffleur
Grande-Anse
Iles de la Petite Terre

Les Saintes
Terre-de-Haut
Fort Napoléon
Baie de St Pierre
Le Chameau
Terre-de-Bas

Marie Galante
St Louis
Le Trou à Diable
Château Murat
Grand-Bourg
Capesterre

0 — 10 miles
0 — 10 km

N

the travel agents in town, or through any hotel lobby. Try **Petrelluzzi Travel**, 2 rue Jean Jaurès (tel 82 82 30). Charter excursions to other islands are available through **Safari Air Tourisme** (tel 84 30 73). If you would prefer to sightsee by helicopter, that is possible too through **Héli-Inter Caraïbes** (tel 91 45 00).

Car hire: with the benefits of the EEC, the roads in Guadeloupe are (usually) quite good, and Guadeloupean drivers push them to the limit. A foreign driving licence is valid for 20 days (a year's driving experience is necessary) and after that an international driving licence is needed. Deposit is around US$300, unless you pay by credit card. Rates start at about US$35 per day. Some firms are: **National-Europcar** (tel 82 50 51), **Carpentier** (tel 82 35 11) and **Avis** (tel 26 80 54), with offices at the airport. Local firms in Pointe-à-Pitre include **Karukera Car** (tel 83 78 79) and **Gordon's Car** (tel 84 18 61) in Gosier. You can even rent a camper van; **Antilles Locap Soleil** (tel 90 95 72) in Gosier and motorbike rental is possible through **Vespa Sun** (91 30 36). in Pointe-à-Pitre or **Dingo Location** (tel 88 76 08) in St François.

TOURIST INFORMATION
There are **Tourist Information Offices** in: **Pointe-à-Pitre**, Office Départementale, 5 Square de la Banque, 97110 Pointe-à-Pitre (tel 590 82 09 30, fax 83 89 22) just off the Place de la Victoire opposite la Darse; **Basse-Terre**, in the Maison du Port (tel 81 24 83); and **St François**, on the Avenue de l'Europe (tel 88 48 74). Office hours are 8–5 weekdays and 8–noon Sat. There is also a small information desk at **Le Raizet** airport, which is very helpful.

The Tourist Board produces a booklet called *Bonjour Guadeloupe*, full of useful facts like where to get your hair cut or which holiday villa company to invest in as well as advice on the beaches.

To **dial** directly to Guadeloupe, the international code is **590**, followed by six digits. On the island, the six digits suffice.

In a medical **emergency**, there is a casualty room at the main Pointe-à-Pitre **Hospital** at Abymes, emergency number 89 11 20. The **police** can be reached on 82 13 17 in Pointe-à-Pitre.

Guadeloupe is generally lower-key than Martinique, but you may find that the Guadeloupeans are quite private. This is not to be confused with unfriendliness, because if you ask for assistance, even in faltering French, they will usually go out of their way to help you. A refreshing fact, in comparison to other islands, is an almost complete absence of hustlers, who can be trying at times. Here, the state guarantees a certain standard of living and so there are very few of them.

MONEY
The **banks** open 8–noon and 2–4 on weekdays. Some banks open on Saturdays; try Crédit Agricole and Banque Nationale de Paris. Credit cards will be accepted anywhere that is accustomed to tourists. However, if you go off the beaten track be sure to take francs, the legal currency of Guadeloupe. Hotels will change money, at a slightly inferior rate to the banks. In restaurants service is *compris* and tipping elsewhere is the usual 10–15%. **Shops** keep similar hours to the banks in the morning and take a similar two-hour lunch, but usually stay open until 6 pm.

BEACHES

For soft white sand brushed by palm trees and susurrating waves, go to the southern side of Grande-Terre. This area is fairly built up with hotels, and some beaches become quite crowded. Go farther afield on Grande-Terre and you will find more secluded spots and have a better chance of being alone, but take a picnic with you because there are fewer cafés. Alternatively, there are the less typical beaches on the northwestern coast of Basse-Terre, where the sand is golden brown and comes in large granules. This area is much less populous, but has some excellent beaches which have a wilder charm about them.

Bathing topless is quite normal in Guadeloupe (though the West Indians themselves do not usually do it) and bathing nude is permitted in some places. All beaches are public and most hotels will allow you to use their facilities.

On the south coast of Grande-Terre, Gosier, with its strip of hotels, is best avoided unless you wish to hire windsurfing equipment or go waterskiing. Opposite the town, a few hundred yards out to sea is a small island, the **Ilet de Gosier** (where people generally bathe nude). Trips to the island can be arranged from the waterfront or in the hotels in the area.

Petit Havre and the other coves close to it are less populous and worth investigating. Heaped with blinding white sand, **Caravelle Beach** is crowded and popular. At one end is Guadeloupe's Club Med, a factory of entertainment, patrolled by peak-capped security monitors—just don't overstep the line of the high-tide mark.

St François also has a some stretches of sand, one called **Raisins-Clairs**, which are well served with watersports for those who want to be active while being grilled. There are a number of good, unpopulated beaches off the road to Pointe des Châteaux, on both the north and south sides of the peninsula. There is a nudist beach at **Plage Tarare**.

The eastern coast of Grande-Terre is not usually good for swimming because of the force of the Atlantic. However, there is a secluded spot in the north at **La Porte d'Enfer**. There are also two fine beaches on the northwestern coast, the **Anse du Souffleur** at Port-Louis and the **Anse Laborde** just out of Anse-Bertrand.

The spurs and shoulders thrown off the mountains of Basse-Terre produce small protected coves between steep headlands and in the northwest you will find a string of excellent beaches: **La Plage de Cluny**, near La Pointe Allègre, **Tillette**, **La Perle** and finally **La Grande Anse**, a huge bay backed with tall palms and stacked with golden sand, one of the most attractive beaches on the island.

The beach at **Malendure**, opposite Pigeon Island is a very busy beach even though the sand is dark. There is diving over on Pigeon Island and of course you can always bargain for an African carving.

BEACH BARS

In Grande-Terre you will find bars and bistros along the popular beachfronts, to which you can retreat when the sun is at its height. St Anne and St François have a string of cafés along the waterfront where you can cast a critical eye at the windsurfers' technique over a beer or two.

In easy-going Basse-Terre you will find beach bars spread out out in the isolated bays. On the **Plage de Malendure** there are snackwagons and pretty bars above the sand

210

and on the mile-long strip of Grand Anse near Deshaies there is a crêperie under the palms. But the best of all is **Chez Françine** on the Plage de Cluny at the northwestern tip of the island. Francine has a wooden house and a covered terrace swallowed in banana and bougainvillaea underneath the palms. Deck chairs on the sand and soursop or coconut milk to accompany *accras* (codfish batterballs). Well worth stopping for.

WATER SPORTS

Windsurfing (planche-à-voile) is very popular and equipment can be hired all along the southern coast of Grande-Terre, for around US$18 per hour. The winds are best in St François, where you will see the sailboards beating back and forth on the sideshore winds and in St Anne. **Waterskiing** can also be arranged on the major beaches. Hotel watersports shops also have smaller sailing dinghies like sunfish for hire to non-guests.

Bigger **yachts** can be chartered, bareboats or crewed, for a day, a week or more, from the companies in Bas-du-Fort, just outside Pointe-à-Pitre: **Soleil et Voile** (tel 90 81 81, fax 90 84 87) and **Star Voyages Antilles** (tel 90 86 26, fax 90 85 73). There are other marinas at St François, Deshaies and Basse-Terre.

If you are the sort for a more leisurely tour, rum punch in hand on a glass-bottomed boat, **Mélodie Marine** takes out day cruises and *Paoka* runs visits to the islands in the Cul de Sac Marin (tel 25 74 78). **Le Papyrus** leaves from the dock at Bas-du-Fort on daytime jaunts of tee-ree-ree and walking the plank and night-time sails where the mountains of Basse-Terre loom like Titans in the moonlight.

Deep-sea fishing can also be arranged, day and half-day tours in search of tuna and kingfish in the Caribbean Sea. This is particularly big on the west coast. The **Fishing Club des Antilles** (tel 90 70 10, fax 98 74 29) in Bouillante takes out trips, as does **Le Pigeonnier**, a hotel in Pigeon (tel/fax 98 83 45). In Grande-Terre you can contact **Caraïbe Pêche** (tel 90 97 51) in the Bas du Fort marina.

Diving (*plongée sous-marine*) is also at its best on the west coast of Basse-Terre off

Fishing Boats

211

Bouillante, where there is a marine reserve established by Jacques Cousteau around the Ilet de Pigeon. Contact **Chez Guy** (tel 98 91 72) or **Les Heures Saines** (tel 98 86 63), who dive under PADI and NAUI as well as CMAS, the French system. You can dive the reefs off **Grande-Terre** with **Aqua-Fari Plongée**(tel 84 26 26) in Gosier. Single-tank dives cost around US$35.

OTHER ACTIVITIES
On land, exploration of the National Park is best done on foot and there are two main drop-off points: **La Traversée**, the D23 road across the middle of the island and the foothills of **La Soufrière**. Guided walking trips can be arranged through the **Organisation des Guides de Montagne de la Caraïbe**, whose offices are at the Maison Forestière in Matouba (tel 80 05 79). Other adventurous tours—canoeing and river-hiking can be arranged through **Espace Loisirs**, 97118 St François (tel 88 71 93, fax 88 44 01) and **Guadeloupe Découverte**, 97190 Gosier (tel 84 2932, fax 26 80 10).

On Grande-Terre a number of other options are available, including **riding**, on the beaches or for a day's picnic, possible through **La Ferme de Campêche** (tel 82 11 54) and **Le Relais du Moulin** (tel 88 13 78), on the road between St Anne and St François.

Or you may prefer to travel by **bicycle**, which is quite popular. The companies will often suggest itineraries or provide a guide. Contact **Association Guadeloupéenne de VTT**, 97110 Pointe-à-Pitre (tel 82 82 67) or on Basse-Terre **VTT Evasion**, 97115 St Rose (tel 28 85 60). Also **Cyclo-Tours** (tel 84 11 34) in Gosier.

On the edge of St François there is an 18-hole Robert Trent Jones **golf** course (tel 88 41 87).

Grande-Terre

Pointe-à-Pitre

The town of Pointe-à-Pitre, the commercial capital of the island and major port, lies on the southern side of Grande-Terre, in the Petit Cul-de-Sac, the inlet formed as the two parts of the island have pushed together. It has a population of 28,000 concentrated in centre of the town, but 100,000 altogether including the suburbs along the coastline. The town first began to grow in the 1760s, during the British occupation of Guadeloupe, and supposedly takes its name from a Dutchman named Pieter, who had lived on the point near *La Darse* a century earlier.

Pointe-à-Pitre is hardly an attractive town, though some two-storey wooden buildings do give an inkling of its former mercantile pride. It has developed haphazardly, upset by earthquakes (1843), fires and hurricanes, the latest of which, Hurricane Hugo, cut through in 1989. In the centre, the old Pointe-à-Pitre has a similar charm to that of a French provincial town, buildings with louvred windows and balconies close on one another and the smells of coffee and patisseries exuding on to the street below. Beyond the Boulevard Chanzy, the newest *quartiers* have sprung up in a crop of ferro-concrete monstrosities from the 50s, proof against earthquake perhaps, but incredibly ugly. They have forced the traditional West Indian shacks farther out along the coast.

La Darse (meaning harbour) is still the heart of town-life. Markets appear on the wharves at dawn, as the ferries and the buses come and go, dropping people off for the day's work. Just above it is the main square, **La Place de la Victoire**, which commemorates victory over the British by Victor Hugues and the revolutionary army in 1794. This paved park, with its bandstand, royal palms and *flamboyant* trees (some sadly torn out by Hurricane Hugo), is lined with cafés and the *Pointus* (the inhabitants of Pointe-à-Pitre) take the evening air here. In his reign of terror, this is where Victor Hugues erected the guillotine.

On the Rue Alexandre Isaac is the **Cathedral of St Peter and St Paul**, built more to withstand the ravages of nature than to succour humankind. Its huge metal piles are riveted inside and out. It may be hurricane-proof, but it gives the effect of being an outsize boiler-house.

The main street, **Rue Frébault**, lined with shops and goods from mainland France, leads through the commercial heart of the town, down to **Le Marché St Antoine**, an iron market with a red corrugated-iron roof. If Guadeloupe is one of the most developed of Caribbean islands, this is a traditional institution. It pulses from early morning, with the smell of fruits and spices and offers anything from avocados to earrings for sale. Even for French speakers, the joking and haggling in creole is impossible to keep up with.

The **Musée Schoelcher** is set in an impressive townhouse with a double staircase on the Rue Peynier and contains some of the personal collections of the abolitionist, assembled in his 15-year struggle to outlaw slavery in the French colonies. General exhibits include a 'magnetic purifying filter' that provided clean drinkable water in the 19th century. Open weekdays 9–12.30 and 2–5.30, and Sat mornings until noon; adm.

Another leading light in Guadeloupe is celebrated in the **Musée St-John Perse**, set in an elaborate creole house on the rue Nozière. This poet and diplomat, Alexis Saint-Léger was born on the island of a long-standing family and was awarded the Nobel Prize for Literature in 1960. Open weekdays 8.30–12.30 and 2.30–5.30 and on Sat mornings, adm.

The Southern Coast of Grande-Terre

Protected from the Atlantic, the southern coast has the mildest climate on the island and has become the centre for the tourist industry. The action of the waves on the limestone coral shores has pushed up white-sand beaches, and on them the hotels have mushroomed. The main areas are just out of Pointe-à-Pitre to the south and the towns of Gosier, St Anne and St François.

Leaving Point-à-Pitre on the road to Gosier (N4), you pass the buildings of the University and come to Bas du Fort, where there are a number of tourist apartment blocks around a marina. Round the point is the Guadeloupe **Aquarium**, which exhibits tropical fish from all over the world in the twenty or so tanks. You will see lion fish with fancy dress tail and fins, fish that shine as though lit by ultra violet in a discotheque and a trapezoidal character called *lactophrys triqueter*, who will spit poison at you. It culminates in the walk-through shark tunnel. Open 9–7, adm.

Commanding la Grande Baie, a little farther round and covering the approaches to Pointe-à-Pitre, is the **Fort Fleur d'Epée**, a series of ramparts cut into the hillside. Constructed of coral rock, it is being rescued from the encroaching undergrowth and restored to its 18th-century glory, when it was fought over with empire-builders' fury, stormed and gallantly defended. The vaulted kitchens and dungeons are buried in the guts of the fort and the ramparts look out to the Saints and on to the island of Dominica. The Fort has attractive walks of *flamboyant* trees and a café, as well as a small museum. Open daily 9–6, adm free.

The town of **Gosier** spreads along the shore for several miles. It is the centre of the Guadeloupe tourist industry, and the hotels have encrusted around the old town, cluttering the hillside down to the beaches and bringing with them a plethora of restaurants, bars and discotheques. The name Gosier derives from the *grand gosier*, or pelican, that can be seen all over the Lesser Antilles and which occasionally fishes off the Ilet de Gosier, a couple of hundred yards off-shore.

St Anne and **St François** are two other towns whose incomes have switched from fishing to sport fishing, though among the motorboats with huge fishing-rods sticking into the air, you will still see *gommiers*, the brightly painted local fishing boats. Both towns still have a promenade, where fishermen's houses and restaurants mingle, looking across the sea towards Dominica.

In the early years of the 18th century, when the *Grands Fonds* inland were carpeted with ten feet of sugar-cane, St Anne was a commercial centre, but by the end of the century it was already in decline, its prosperity destroyed by Guadeloupe's internal turmoil. On the dock at St François, where the yachts are ranged in lines, you will also see local West Indian life as the ferry from La Désirade puts in. The inhabitants are poor farmers and they bring their sheep, stuffed into sacks with just their heads sticking out, to Guadeloupe to sell.

Beyond St François, Grande-Terre tapers to a spike pointing out into the Atlantic Ocean and culminates in the cliffs of **Pointe des Châteaux**. The wind blows strong off the ocean here and the waves have carved eerie shapes out of the rocks, including a blowhole that answers moments after a wave has disappeared under the lip of the rock. The landscape looks a little like Britanny, as though Guadeloupe had simply broken off the west coast of France and been transported 4000 miles west. From the cross on the point, high above the waves, it is possible to see La Désirade, a table-mountain emerging from the sea six miles away, and the uninhabited islands of Petite Terre. On the northern side of the peninsula is the **plage de Tarare**, a nudist beach.

The N5 leads north from St François through the canefields to **Le Moule**, on the Atlantic coast, where the waves come barrelling in relentlessly. Suffering continuously from the Atlantic winds, the houses were built with no doors facing east. The town knew some prosperity as the principal port on Guadeloupe's eastern coast in the sugar years, when ships would edge in on the waves to the anchor ports still visible, but now it is poor and broken down. Le Moule was wasted by Hurricane Hugo in 1989 and many of the buildings were destroyed.

A number of roads lead back to Pointe-à-Pitre through the rolling forested country-side **Grands Fonds**, where some white families have lived since they fled there in the turmoil of the Revolution.

Northern Grande-Terre

Alternatively, you can continue into the northern area of Grande-Terre, where the land lies lower and in places is covered with mangrove swamp. It is highly fertile land, and everywhere you will see the cone-shaped shells of abandoned windmills, some still with their crushing gear discarded inside. In **Morne-à-l'Eau** is one of the best examples of the French West Indian chequerboard cemetery, with acres of black and white tiles on the mausolea. On the Festival of All Saints there is a ceremony in which the whole graveyard is lit with candles.

At **Port Louis**, there is a view over the Grand Cul-de-Sac Marin enclosed between the two halves of the island. Basse-Terre rises spectacularly, grey-green in the distance, topped with vast clouds.

On the northwestern coast of the island is the town of **Anse Bertrand** another town that saw its most prosperous times in the sugar heyday of the 18th century. The most northerly point on the island is **La Pointe de la Grande Vigie**, where the cliffs stand 250 feet above sea level. On a clear day Antigua, 35 miles north, is visible from the point. Close by is **La Porte d'Enfer** (Hell's Gate), a massive fissure in the cliffs.

Basse-Terre

A coastal road circles Guadeloupe's mountainous volcanic wing and through the middle of the island *La Traversée* cuts a path up and over the rainforest to the Caribbean coast.

Leaving Pointe-à-Pitre, the N1 crosses to Basse-Terre over the **Rivière Salée**. Before the two parts of Guadeloupe were linked by bridge in 1906, the crossing was made by ferry. On one occasion, a party of Guadeloupeans were making for a ball in Pointe-à-Pitre, when they were swept out to sea. Garbed in evening dress, they drifted for five days before washing up on St Thomas in the Virgin Islands.

The main road (N1) to the town of **Basse-Terre**, takes a left turn and travels down the eastern coast, beneath the towering mountainsides, before crossing over to the Caribbean coast near the southern tip. **Sainte-Marie** is thought to be the place where Columbus landed on his second voyage in 1493, meeting his first Caribs.

Capesterre takes its name from its position (*Capesterre* means windward in French, and the village is upwind of *Basse-Terre*). In the town is one of the last *manioqueries*, where cassava flour is grated from manioc tubers. The Indians once used fan coral as a grater, before straining out the poisonous juices that the wet mix contains.

As you leave the town you pass along the **Allée du Manoir**, a tunnel of magnificent royal palms. They stand like living grey columns (the telegraph wires were once simply nailed into them), soaring to 100 feet, bursting with spiked fronds and tapering in a single ten-foot spine.

Inland and uphill from St Sauveur, at the end of the **D4** road that winds up through the banana plantations into the rainforest, are the three **Chutes de Carbet**. Two of the falls cascade into rockpools from over 300 feet. The middle one falls 350 feet and can be reached on a well-marked path, and the lowest tumbles 65 feet into a pool where you can take a dip after the short walk. From here the path leads on up into the rainforest, towards the summit of the Soufrière, a three hour walk. It is these falls that Columbus mentions in his diary when he talks of 'a waterfall of considerable breadth, which fell from so high that it seemed to come from the sky'. Back down the hill, there are several lakes just off the road: the **Etang Zombi** and the **Grand Etang**. The **As de Pique**, a lake in the shape of an ace of spades is beyond the serene Grand Etang.

The N1 coastal road continues to the village of **Trois-Rivières**. Down the hill, close to the harbour (where boats leave for the Islands of the Saints), is the **Parc**

215

Archéologique des Roches Gravées, where the main exhibit is a series of maniacal squiggles and outlandish faces on a rockface. They were carved by Arawak Indians before the Caribs bludgeoned their way on to the island in about AD 1000. The rock is set in a small botanical garden, in which the plants are marked. Open 9–5, adm. Another few miles brings you through a ravine to the Caribbean coast and down into Basse-Terre.

Basse-Terre (the town)

The town of Basse-Terre (15,000 inhabitants), the administrative capital of Guadeloupe, lies on the coast in the shadow of towering volcanic mountains. It is just 33 km from Pointe-à-Pitre as the crow flies, but the journey takes about two hours by road because it twists and turns so laboriously over its 70-km length. Some of the route is impossibly steep and windy, but take heart; lines painted on the road show that the Guadeloupeans actually compete in cycling races along here.

Founded by Houël in 1643, Basse-Terre is much more attractive than the commercial city of Pointe-à-Pitre and it retains an antique feel that the other town has lost. Just above the port, stone houses with upper storeys of shingle wood tiles and clapboard crowd over the narrow streets. The imposing official buildings, churches and town houses with wrought-iron balconies give it a gentrified air.

Behind the activity of the main streets, on the few areas of flat ground, there are two main squares, both pleasant to sit in: the Jardin Pichon and the Place du Champ d'Arbaud, surrounded by the old buildings of Basse-Terre.

Covering the harbour from the southern edge of town, Fort St Charles is another lumbering colossus of a fortress with huge embrasures that now stand unemployed. It expanded steadily from its beginnings in about 1650, when Houël erected the first battlements and has also seen plenty of action. There are acres of ramparts and it is easy to imagine the roar of the cannon and the smell of cordite. There is also a small museum in the fort, giving a good run-down of its history and of Basse-Terre. Open daily 9–5, adm free.

Like any prosperous Caribbean port, the town has spread up the hill as the wealthier inhabitants take a cooler and loftier view of the proceedings in the city centre. The district of St Claude, strung out over the bends of a sinuous mountain road, contains some the most attractive houses on the island.

A side road leads to the town of Matouba, which has a large East Indian population (who came here as indentured labourers in the last century). From the village, the Trace Victor Hugues leads up into the rainforest. Cut out of the hillside in 1795, it leads past the Bains chauds de Matouba (hot baths, where the water comes out of the earth at 59°C and is then channelled down to mineral baths) and on to the east coast of the island. It is a 10-hour, 30-km walk and very demanding.

High in the rainforest is the Maison du Volcan, a museum. It is set in a beautiful creole villa, in a garden festooned with greenery and tells of vulcanism in general and La Soufrière, which lurks just above it, in particular. Open 10–6, adm free. Also close by are the Bains Jaunes, hot water springs, and the Chutes du Galion, more waterfalls.

The road leads farther up on to the slopes of the volcano itself, an extremely steep path, wide enough for one car, that stops 1000 feet below the craters, at Savane à Mulets.

La Soufrière lives up to its name, as the summit is a morass of sulphurous fumaroles and solidified lava flows where plants are poisoned before they take root. It is still quite active, constantly letting off steam and occasionally rumbling and showering the neighbourhood with flakes of volcanic dust. It erupted in 1695 and in 1797. In 1837 the whole of Basse-Terre quaked but this was followed by 120 years of silence until 1956 and then considerable activity in the 70s. There were dust and gas explosions, geysers appeared from lakes, the rivers turned into mud and lava flows and at the height there were a thousand tremors a day. At one point 70,000 people were evacuated from the southern end of Basse-Terre.

From Savane à Mulets, you can make the summit in under two hours, on a path that passes between boulders tossed out by the eruptions. At 4813 ft (1467 m), La Soufrière is the highest point in the Eastern Caribbean. When the usual clouds are not in attendance (though this makes the whole climb that much more eerie), the view from the top is a cracker.

D23—La Traversée

La Traversée (D23) cuts across the middle of the island of Basse-Terre, climbing to the twin pyramids of the Mamelles (at 2500 ft) and emerging on the Caribbean coast at Mahaut. It gives an excellent view of the rainforest in all its luxuriance and occasional panoramic flashes between the trees.

At Vernou, a retreat where the wealthy have built their villas and set them in tropical gardens, is the **Saut de la Lézarde** (the lizard's leap), a small waterfall and rockpool. Higher in the rainforest, where it becomes dark because the canopy is so thick and grotesque mosses creep on the floor is the **Cascade des Ecrevisses**, a tame fall where the Guadeloupeans like to go for a day out at the weekend.

La Maison de la Forêt is a museum that describes Guadeloupe's natural life, from the *pâte calcaire* of Grande-Terre and early volcanic rumblings 15 million years ago to the flying cycads and bromeliads of today's tropical rainforest. It is well set out and explains the forest ecosystem. There are a number of marked walks through the forest that start and finish at the museum. Open daily, 9–5, adm free.

The Traversée reaches its summit at the Mamelles, from where there is a spectacular view, and then begins to descend in hairpins to the coast. From the heights a number of paths lead off into the forest, some of them the old *traces* that were walked by the *porteuses* with huge loads on their heads. The **Trace des crêtes** leads down to the Caribbean coast near Marigot and the **Route Forestière de Grosse Montagne** leads back towards Pointe-à-Pitre.

The **Morne-à-Louis**, unfortunately scarred by its television transmitter, offers more views over the cumulus of peaks in mountainous Basse-Terre. Just down the hill from here is the **Parc Zoologique et Botanique**, where a lack-lustre series of cages among the creeping vines exhibit Guadeloupe's limited fauna and unlimited flora. La Traversée joins the N2 on the Côte-sous-le-Vent, the rain-shadow, or Caribbean coast at Mahaut.

N2—Around the Northern Tip of Basse-Terre

From the Rivière Salée the N2 runs to the northern tip of the island and then down the length of the western coast. To begin with the land is blanketed with sugar-cane, but this changes as the road passes into the shadow of the mountains. At the **Domaine de Séverin** you will see a working sugar-cane crusher, a conveyor about two feet wide driven by a water-wheel (it gives an idea how labour intensive the industry was). Small museum and shop next door, where you can buy the eventual product, rum.

The **Musée du Rhum**, close by in Bellevue above Sainte Rose continues the story. It gives a history of cane—sweet bamboo—from Persian times to its use in Europe in the sweet drinks of the seventeenth century and of course in rum. Plenty of rum paraphernalia—machetes, carts and copper boilers. Rum on sale of course. Open daily 9–5.

Inland from Sainte-Rose is the village of **Sofaïa**, lost in the fertile valleys of the rainforest. Four km farther on is a sulphur spring, where bathers take the curative waters. It is possible to follow the **Trace Baille-Argent Sofaïa** through the rainforest, a four-hour walk that emerges on the Caribbean coast at Baille-Argent, just north of Pointe-Noire.

Pointe-Allègre is the northernmost tip of Basse-Terre and it was the spot chosen by the first settlers of Guadeloupe in June 1635. It was a shaky start, as they were constantly battling with the Caribs, so eventually they decamped and headed for the southwestern coast at Basse-Terre.

Deshaies is an attractive fishing village that lies in a small bay, from which the road winds up and over to **Pointe-Noire**, a town dating from the 17th century. The **Maison du Bois** is a small museum just south of the town, with exhibits of traditional machinery, tools and furniture from the French Antilles, all in tropical woods. The secrets of boat-building, straining the poisonous juice from manioc to make cassava meal, and the styles of gingerbread woodwork on the eaves of Caribbean houses are displayed. It is worth a visit, open 9–5, adm.

The **Trace des Contrabandiers** (smugglers' route) leads across the mountain range in the centre of the island from the Maison du Bois. A three-hour walk through the forest passes beneath Morne Jeanneton and will bring you into the hills above Lamentin.

At **Mahaut** La Traversée (D23) cuts across the island on the quickest route back to Pointe-à-Pitre. Alternatively, the N2 continues down the coast to **Vieux Habitants**. According to Père Labat, this town, founded in 1636, takes its name from its early inhabitants, who moved here after serving out their indenture (a three-year contract in exchange for their passage to the island), so as not to be confused with those who still had time to serve.

About four miles inland, lost in the hills on the D27, is **La Maison du Café** at La Grivelière, a delightful coffee and cocoa plantation from the last century that has been restored as a museum. Its setting is that of a tropical Gormenghast, with archaic and crumbling machinery, powered by a network of water-channels that rush and echo among the rambling buildings. The plants are on view—ripe red coffee berries and purple cocoa pods, as well as other tropical plants such as mahogany and apricots, and you can round it off with a taste of the coffee produced by the plantation. Open daily from 9 am, adm. La Maison de Café was due to open soon after publication.

FESTIVALS

Carnival gets going at the beginning of the year with Epiphany and culminates in a two-day street party on Mardi Gras and Ash Wednesday as they go into Lent. If you get a chance, join in with the streams of dancers as they parade around the town, dressed as

218

imps and buccaneers, to the relentless beat of French *zouk* music until *vaval* is burned on Ash Wednesday.

Other festivals include Bastille Day (14 July) and musical Saint Cecilia's day (22 Nov) and each individual town's saint's day, the *fête patronale*. One of the Caribbean's most enjoyable spectacles is the **Cook's Festival**, which takes place in August in Pointe-à-Pitre, in which island delicacies are dedicated and gastronomic parades take place before the customary over-indulgence. Every three years in July they stage FESTAG, a compendium of music, dance, folklore, painting and sculpture.

WHERE TO STAY

Guadeloupe caters for most tastes, with a few top of the range havens of discerning grandeur through to the small independent *relais créoles*, or inns—address: 12 Rue François Arago, 97110 Pointe-à-Pitre (tel 590 82 17 42, fax 82 17 63). *Gîtes* also provide cheaper alternatives for travellers—address c/o the Tourist Office, Place de le Victoire, 97110 Pointe-à-Pitre (tel 91 64 33, fax 91 45 40).

Gosier on Grande-Terre is the island's principal resort and has an authentic mix of factory hotels muscling in on beach space and small *relais* tucked away up the hill. Elsewhere on the southern coast, St Anne has a few beach resorts and St François has lately put in a challenge with several new hotels. After a week on the beach you might like to move to easy-going Basse-Terre, which has some fun places dotted around the countryside, lost in gardens of tropical luxuriance.

In the larger hotels they will probably speak English, but you will need some French if you step beyond the main tourist areas. Breakfast is usually included in the room rate. A service charge of 10% or 15% will be added to your hotel bill.

Grande Terre

EXPENSIVE
At the top of the range, **Le Hamak**, 97118 St François (tel 590 88 59 99, fax 88 41 92) is an enclave of rarefied luxury tucked away on its own just out of the town. The 56 rooms are hidden in magnificent gardens of bougainvillaea behind the sand and palms of a man-made beach. It is stately and quiet and lives up to its name—the veranda of every room is slung with a hammock. Double room US$350–500. If you like a more active beach club in equivalent luxury you can try the new annex of the Méridien, **La Cocoteraie**, PO box 37, 97118 (tel 88 51 00, fax 88 40 71). The 52 suites are in blocks ranged tightly around a huge pool, with dining room and pool bar on islands in the middle. Rooms are brightly decorated in pink, blue and green, or a sort of symphony in pastel. Watersports available, double in season, US$450. The **Auberge de la Vieille Tour**, Montauban (tel/fax 84 23 23), sits on a headland above the sea in Gosier and has recently expanded to 158 rooms, which makes it large, but the setting is still good overlooking attractive grounds that slope towards the hotel's own beach. It retains something of the an old colonial atmosphere in the plantation house, the two restaurants and bar, spiked only by the windsurfers down below and the boutique in the old windmill. Double US$250–320. **La Toubana**, PO Box 63 outside St Anne (tel 88 25 78, fax 88 38 90) is one of the most sympathetic hotels on the island. It stands high above a dark sand cove and has an open dining room terrace, a pool on the hilltop and views of the islands to Dominica (or Club Med the other way). The 32 rooms are scattered in bungalows on the hillside, very comfortable with kitchenettes. Double in season US$150–230.

MODERATE

The **Relais du Moulin**, Chateaubrun, 97180 St Anne (tel 88 23 96, fax 88 03 92) is also set around an old windmill. The 40 rooms are in bungalows and apartments scattered around charming tropical gardens, and although they are 600 yards from the beach, there is a pool. The inn has a family atmosphere and there is a good creole restaurant. Some rooms also have kitchenettes. Riding and bicycle touring on offer. Double in season US$120–140. Another pleasantly unassuming relais créole is the **Cap Sud Caraïbes**, route de la Plage, 97190 Gosier (tel 88 96 02, fax 95 80 39), on the hill at Petit Havre, halfway between Gosier and St Anne. A simply designed block stands on the hillside a few minutes' walk from the Petit Havre beach. Its atmosphere is private and friendly. A double room in season costs around US$110. The **Auberge du Grand Large** (tel 88 20 06) is on the edge of St Anne, 10 bungalows set in the garden, just above the beach, which they share with the St Anne fishermen. The hotel is run like a family and rooms go for around US$100 in the season. A charming small hotel high on the hill outside Gosier is **Les Flamboyants** (tel 84 14 11, fax 84 53 56), with a pool and open gardens out front, which overlook the Ilet de Gosier and Basse-Terre beyond—a moment of calm in the holiday hustle of the tourist town. The main house is an old villa, with trophies, sharks and turtles on the wall. Twelve rooms, quite simple, with breakfast only, though some have kitchenettes, doubles US$50–70.

Also in Gosier, **Serge's Guest House** (tel 84 10 25) is an amusing option, where the very simple studios are in a block on the outskirts of Gosier, overlooking a garden of Guadeloupean profusion. Around US$50 in season.

In the Bas du Fort area of Pointe-à-Pitre you will find a friendly and comfortable hotel in the **Village Soleil** (tel 90 85 76, fax 90 93 65). The 82 rooms are arranged in blocks, some overlooking the marina around the central pool and open terraced restaurant. Beach shuttle and good bars and restaurants nearby. Double in season US$120–140. If you need to be in town, you might try the space-age **Hotel Saint John**, 97110 (tel 82 51 57, fax 82 52 61), in which the 41 rooms lurk in a profusion of arches and overhanging eaves. Double rooms US$85. **La Maison de Marie Galante** (tel 90 10 41, fax 90 22 75) stands right on the Place de la Victoire downtown; a restaurant downstairs and nine slightly cheaper rooms at US$60–75 in season. At the **Relais des Antilles**, 38 Rue Denfert, 97110 Pointe-à-Pitre (tel 83 43 62) there are 10 simple rooms where you can stay for US$40 a double.

Basse-Terre

Here the hotels are a little bit more spread out—this half of Guadeloupe does not have so many of the picture-postcard beaches, but some of the hotels and inns have excellent settings above the water or hidden in the rainforest.

MODERATE

Just off La Traversée (D23) you will find a charming hotel at **L'Auberge de la Distillerie**, 97170 Petit Bourg (tel 94 25 91, fax 94 11 91), which is set on a hillside looking back towards Grande-Terre. Next to the main house stands a large covered terrace with the dining room and pool. It is friendly and low-key—the sort of place where you can entertain the other guests on the piano. The rooms are comfortable and have an air of old-time Guadeloupe, each with a balcony and a hammock giving onto a profuse garden. Double room US$100–120. At the southern tip of the island, in **Trois-**

Rivières, you will find a couple of good places to stay. The **Grand' Anse Hotel** (tel 92 93 69) is set on the hillside a few hundred yards up above the sea. There are 20 air-conditioned bungalows around the central pool and restaurant, which serves creole food. Good views from the balconies, double US$75. Alternatively you might try **Hotel Le Joyeux**, Faubourg (tel 92 71 24), where there are just six rooms with private baths and fantastic views of the Saints. Cock-fighting pit nearby if you feel like that sort of thing, otherwise a pool and a creole restaurant to keep you occupied. Double room US$35–45. In St Claude, perched on the slopes of the volcano is the **Relais Bleu de la Soufrière** (tel 80 01 27), a restored colonial house in period style with a panoramic view over Basse-Terre and the Caribbean Sea. It is isolated and has its fair share of tropical showers, but if you like the rainforest, a double room costs US$90. If you would prefer to be in town there is a good small hotel in **Le Houëlment**, 34 Rue de la République (tel 81 44 72), which has eight rooms looking out onto the Caribbean sea or back on to the Soufrière. Restaurant with traditional creole cuisine, double room US$60 in season.

Farther north you will find some waterfront hotels with a theme of sportfishing and diving. **Le Rocher de Malendure**, 97125 Bouillante (tel 98 70 84) has nine bungalows of which three sit on the *rocher* itself, double US$60. Another excellent sporting haunt is **Le Pigeonnier**, 97132 Pigeon (tel/fax 98 83 45), with the main house and superb terraced restaurant on the seafront and bungalows set across the road on the hillsides. Hip joint, rooms US$45 plus.

There are two **camp-grounds** on Basse-Terre—**Les Sables d'Or** (tel 28 44 60) in Deshaies and slightly further south, **La Traversée** (tel 98 21 23) in Pointe Noire.

EATING OUT

With French roots, Guadeloupean cooking is excellent and the island will not disappoint those who wish to partake in a gastronomic steeplechase or just take some time out from the rigours of sitting on a beach. And the settings are heavenly too, small cafés on the waterfront and verandas on a hillside grappled by bougainvillaea and slender fingers of hibiscus, with the tremulous thunder of the rain on an iron roof.

The Guadeloupeans cook a full range of French food, but the island is famed for its creole food, fish or island meats like goat, spiced sauces, tropical vegetables and fruits. There are Guadeloupean versions of many dishes you will find in Martinique (their point of origin is usually contested) and they will be stamped with the island flavour. Snapper, lambi (conch) and *langouste* (lobster) are favourites, in a *blaff* (a way of boiling fish) or goat in a *colombo* (a French West Indian curry), served with plantain or christophene and spiked with creole sauces. French wine is often drunk with a meal but, like their confrères in Martinique, the Guadeloupeans are slaves to the *petit punch*, rum-based and small only in name.

There are literally hundreds of restaurants and bistros in Guadeloupe; most are fairly relaxed, but in the smarter ones men are sometimes required to wear a jacket. Eating out is not exactly cheap, but service is *compris*.

Grande-Terre

EXPENSIVE

La Canne à Sucre (tel 82 10 19) has an ocean-liner-like setting right on the dockside in Pointe-à-Pitre, and you can sometimes look out on to cruise-ship hulls on both sides. The impression is really made in the dining room itself, where you dine on reproduction

221

antiques beneath gathered pink curtains, a menu of *nouvelle cuisine antillaise*—red snapper in passion fruit or tournedos in rhum vieux and green pepper, main course Fr100, closed Sun. Downstairs is an open-air bistro, plat du jour Fr50, an afternoon stop, which gets very full when the cruise ships are in port. Another restaurant in an elegant setting of mock-antiquity is **La Plantation** (tel 90 84 83), which overlooks the Bas du Fort marina just out of town. Only the clink of cutlery breaks the gentle murmur of conversation here, as you dine on classical French and créole cuisine—*friandise de langouste au sifflet de poireau et de saffron*, dishes served under *cloches*, which when removed reveal immaculate presentation on huge plates. Finish off with the colourful *eventail de feuilletage aux fruits*, a fan of tropical fruits. Main course Fr125, closed Sun. **Chez Deux Gros** (tel 84 16 20)—'Restaurant et Brocante' (restaurant and antique dealer)— is well worth finding for a meal. It is right on the main road heading east, about a kilometre beyond the second turning to Gosier. You approach it through an overgrown tropical garden and go into a house filled with weird and wonderful bric-à-brac—art deco lamps, clocks and bronze statuettes—and music from the 40s, 50s and 60s. Innovative local cuisine; papaya lambi followed by snapper in passion fruit and to finish with, *le collier de la reine*, a ring of exotic desserts on the plate. Main course Fr100, the antiques you can bargain for. Remember to reserve a table. **La Dampierre** (tel 84 34 76) is not far off, a seafood and fish restaurant set in a private villa with a simple setting for the dining room. *Lambis à la Santoise* (reddened conch to an old recipe from the Saints) or *snapper en papillotte*. Popular with the Guadeloupeans themselves, fish Fr90, meat Fr110, closed Mon.

On the outskirts of **St François** is **Le Vieux Carré** (tel 88 58 64), set in an old colonial house, where you take your cocktail to 50s jazz music or play a game of billiards before dinner, and then move out on to the veranda with a view of the well-tended garden. Menu à la blackboard and food intentionally simple but well-prepared—*filet de canard* or *tranche de gigot d'agneau*. Followed by local ice-cream, Fr80–150.

MODERATE
In **Gosier**, **La Fourchette** is a less expensive restaurant, small and friendly and set right on the road. Creole specialities—*oursins farcis* and *colombo de poulet*, Fr80 in a good West Indian setting of embroidered napkins and frilly curtains. You might also try the **Mérou d'Or**, down at the waterfront opposite the Ilet de Gosier. Fish restaurant—*blaffs* and *poissons en papillotte*. There are plenty of waterfront bistros in the Bas du Fort marina, where you can wander between video bars while you decide where to eat. **La Sirène** does a good crêpe for Fr50.

Close to **Le Vieux Carré** (see under expensive) in the outskirts of St François is **La Louisianne** (tel 88 44 34), also in a house surrounded by gardens. 'La Gourmandise n'est plus un vilain défaut'—*ragoût de requin au saffron* followed by *charlotte aux fruits exotiques*. Friendly and family run, main course Fr80. There is a string of bistros on the waterfront in both St Anne and St François and in the second you can get a nice meal in **Le Zagaya**, a *brochette de poissons à l'ananas et pruneaux* (fish kebab with pineapple and prunes), followed by a *clafoutis aux fruits*, Fr80 a main dish. You can eat more cheaply, with a view of the windsurfers at **Les Pieds dans l'Eau**. **Le Filibustier** (tel 82 23 36) has a certain style—set on a hill like a pirate's look-out and decorated inside with the beams of a galleon. Quite rumbustious, wine by the pitcher, chef with his hair tied back, who barbecues your meal and then presents it to you on a huge wooden platter. Naval battles and portraits of pirates on the walls. Closed Mon, Sun evening, main course Fr60–140.

An altogether more sedate spot for lingering over a long lunchtime visit is at **Le Château de Feuilles** (tel 22 30 30), which is set in a charming creole villa and garden miles from anywhere in the north of Grande-Terre, near Campêche. French and local fare—*choucroute de poisson de papaye verte*, charlotte soursop (mousse and cream) and an intercourse swim if you feel like it, just beside the tables. Also follow up with one of 20 different varieties of fruit-flavoured rums. Closed Mon, otherwise open daily for lunch, dinner Fri, Sat, ring to reserve. Main course Fr100 plus.

CHEAP

If you are feeling peckish late at night in **Pointe-à-Pitre** there are snackwagons on the Place de la Victoire. Afterwards you might like to grab an ice cream from the vendors with plastic buckets (they will explain how it works too).

Basse-Terre

Basse-Terre also has a number of good places to eat, dotted around the whole island, but particularly on the free and easy west coast around Malendure.

The **Domaine de Séverin** is on the northern slopes of the island on a sugar plantation. The restaurant is set in an old island villa with tiled floor, wooden walls and large veranda (sadly the outside is reinforced in concrete). *Ecrevisses* (crayfish, from the pond on the estate) *en civet au vin rouge* or *feuilletté de lambi*, Fr130.

MODERATE

If you are on Grand Anse, you can catch a good lunch on the tropical terrace at **Le Karacoli** (though you may find yourself dodging the tour buses). Creole food—*court bouillons*, *crabes* and *colombos* for Fr70. In nearby Deshaies there are a number of bars and restaurants strung along the waterfront. **Le Madras** (tel 28 40 87) offers creole fare inside a small, dark dining room set with madras tablecloths. *Boudin lambi* and stuffed crab backs. Lunch and dinner, closed Wed, Fr40 main course. **La Note Bleue** is at the other end of the waterfront, an open veranda with a creole fish restaurant—*court bouillon*, couscous or *fricassé*, followed by *noix de coco givré*, Fr70 a main course. Further south you come to **Le Rocher de Malendure**, overlooking Pigeon Island. Split-level dining room with a view, which you can retreat to after a morning's diving. Fish restaurant—kingfish or grouper—and seafood—local lobster in spiced butter. Fr50–90. **La Touna** also serves fish on the waterfront in the town of Bouillante just farther south. Here you eat the fish as it is landed on a rustic veranda with a view of the islands offshore—*darne de daurade* (dorado), *raie au beurre noire* followed by home-made ice-cream, Fr70 plus. But the best setting of all is at **Le Pigeonnier**, in the town of Pigeon, which is set on a rushwork and bamboo terrace lit with fairy lights. A hip crowd. The style is *nouvelle cuisine créole*, variations on the fish brought in that day—sailfish, swordfish and yellowfin tuna. Also seafood, blanquette of conch with freshly made pasta, followed by soursop flan. Main course Fr65 plus. In Matouba, high above the town of Basse-Terre, you can find excellent creole fare at **Chez Paul** (tel 80 29 20). Accras followed by *féroce* with hot pepper or a *fricassé* with a spicy sauce and of course a volley of local vegetables, Fr60 plus. In the town itself you might try **Massoukou** on Rue Victor Hugues for crayfish flambéed in Armagnac at Fr70, or **Le Houëlment**, which offers local food.

223

BARS AND NIGHTLIFE

Zouk is the current musical beat of the French Antilles, another bustling Caribbean rhythm with a double beat, often with echoes of West Africa. It can be heard on the buses and in the clubs, both about as crowded as each other, along with just about all the other Caribbean beats. You get to know the songs as they are played over and over again: hear them again when you get home and you will start to twitch. Most clubs have a door charge of around US$10, which includes the price of a drink.

Outside the hundreds of bistros and bars you will find a few spots where the hip chicks and lover-boys gather for an early evening drink. They are centred around the tourist areas.

At the Bas du Fort marina you will find a video bar and a list of cocktails as long as your arm at **Le Brésilien**. Perhaps try a *Soufrière* or a *Bounty*. Live music occasionally in season. In Bas du Fort itself you can catch a cocktail at **Le Grand Large** piano bar, before moving on, just next door, to the **Elysée Matignon** discotheque or the **Victoria**.

In Gosier you might start at **L'Endroit** in Montauban before going on for a dance at **La Cascade** or **New Land**. And in St François there are plenty of bars around the marina and there is a good local disco at **L'Acapulce** (open at the weekends).

LA DÉSIRADE

'Quand bleuira sur l'horizon la Désirade'

Apollinaire

La Désirade takes its romantic name from the Spanish *Deseata* (the desired one). In the 16th century the standard Atlantic crossing would arrive at Guadeloupe and after four or five weeks at sea the sailors would be longing for land. La Désirade was often the island they saw first.

La Désirade lies about six miles off the Pointe des Châteaux, the easternmost tip of Grande-Terre. It is a table mountain, eight miles by one, rising 200 m above sea-level, windswept and covered in cactus scrub. The northern coast is a line of rugged cliff-faces, cut into strange shapes. The south of the island is protected from the wind and it is here that the 1700 inhabitants have chosen to live, spread along the coast from the main settlement of Grande-Anse.

La Désirade is dry and was settled only by a few poor white settlers. Without the plantations there were no slaves and so the population of La Désirade remains predominantly white (also true on Terre de Haut in the Saints, but not so in Marie Galante). Today life is extremely simple and the economy of the island is mainly agricultural or connected with the sea (fishing and boatbuilding). It is one of the least developed islands of the Caribbean and so if you would like an utterly secluded escape, you can find it in La Désirade.

PRACTICAL INFORMATION

You can reach La Désirade by air from Le Raizet on scheduled flights (twice daily on Mon, Wed, Thurs and Fri) or by ferry, leaving daily from the marina at St François, price

Fr100. Yachts also cruise over there for the day from the marina and you might get a ride. When on the island, you can reach a taxi on tel 20 02 62 and hire a car or a bicycle through **Loca 2000** (tel 20 02 78), who will also take you on an island tour. Alternatively you can walk the length of the island in a day.

There are a couple of hotels on the island, **L'Oasis du Désert** (tel 20 02 12), with ten rooms, and **Le Touareg**, also in the Quartier du Désert, both quite simple and cheap. Restaurants include **Chez Marianne** in Quartier du Bourg and **O koubari** in Baie Mahault. Also, camping is possible at Baie Mahault. Beaches are at Grande-Anse, Le Souffleur, beneath the mountain and at Baie-Mahault, where you can arrange to **scuba dive**, with **Dinane Tony** (tel 20 02 93).

MARIE GALANTE

In contrast to La Désirade, Marie Galante has a more typical history for the Caribbean. The land was fertile enough to bear sugar and so in the 18th century it was covered with it down to the last square inch. Sweeps of cane blew in the breezes and every few hundred yards there were the cone and sails of a sugar-mill. The cane still grows, but Marie Galante's hundred mills, which once stood proudly at nearly two for every square mile, are run down and are steadily being devoured by tropical undergrowth.

Shaped like a football, Marie Galante is a flat 59 square miles and looks similar to Grande-Terre, just 20 miles to the north.

The 16,000 inhabitants live on the protected areas of the coast, around the main settlement of Grand-Bourg. Sugar is still important to the economy (there are three remaining distilleries and Marie Galante rum is renowned) and there is some agriculture. The rum is of course also the principal ingredient in the celebrations on Marie Galante, which are so popular with the people from Dominica that on public holidays they come streaming over in small boats to join the *fête*.

The island takes its name from Columbus's flagship, the caravelle *Santa Maria de Galante*, in which he led his second expedition to the New World in 1493. After coasting Dominica and failing to find a harbour, he saw Marie Galante and cruised north.

For a while the island became a refuge for the Caribs fleeing the larger islands but in the age of empire it quickly became a strategic base, the first stop on an invasion attempt on Guadeloupe. The Dutch stripped the island systematically in 1676 and the British occupied it a number of times before it finally settled to France in 1815.

There are some very attractive beaches on the western coast of the island, to which the Guadeloupeans come for the weekend. The best are the palm-backed strand at **Vieux Fort** in the northwest and **Plage de le Feuillère** in the southeast near Capesterre, where you will find the beach restaurant **Le Békéké** and the **Fun Evasion** Mistral windsurfing school.

Inland there are canefields and sugar-mills (*moulins*) on view of course; there is the **Moulin de Basse** and one at the **Château Murat**. In the Château, which has been restored to its 18th-century splendour, there is a **museum** dedicated to island traditions and, of course, the history of sugar. Open 9–1 and 3–6, adm free. At Capesterre, it is possible to see the **Distillerie le Salut**. Inland is a cave that goes by the name of **Le Trou à Diable** (the Devil's Hole), which goes quite deep underground. You should take a torch and the right footwear if you venture down it.

PRACTICAL INFORMATION

Ferries link Marie Galante to Pointe-à-Pitre several times a day, an hour's sail from La Darse off Place de la Victoire, and the journey brings you to Grand-Bourg, price Fr155. There are also regular flights (usually three a day) from Le Raizet to Basses airport in the south of the island. A tour to the island can be arranged from Pointe-à-Pitre that guides you around and yachts occasionally make the crossing from St François. Taxis can be contacted on tel 97 81 97 and there are cars for hire (best booked in advance) through Socagam (tel 97 80 38) or Dingo Location (tel 97 76 91). There is a marina at St Louis.

There are only a few places to stay on Marie Galante and all of them are family run and fairly simple. The **Auberge de Soledad** (tel 97 75 45) is in Grand-Bourg, with 18 rooms up to US$40 for a double and **Le Salut** is in the northwestern town of St-Louis (tel 97 07 67), double rooms at US$35. **Chez Hajo** (tel 97 32 76) has just six rooms. There are some *gîtes* on the island. (See Guadeloupe, Tourist Information, p. 209.)

Each of the hotels has a dining room, but you can find good classic French and creole food at **Le Touloulou** (tel 97 32 63), which is set on a veranda on the sand of Petite Anse de Capesterre—conch in puff pastry, or *oursins* (sea urchins), with a generous helping of local vegetables—christophene, breadfruit and sweet potato. You might also try **Le Neptune** (tel 97 96 90) on the waterfront in Grand Bourg where you can find creole food and seafood—*palourdes* (clams) and grilled crayfish—or **L'Arc en Ciel** in St Louis (tel 87 21 66). Worth phoning in advance to see if they're cooking.

THE SAINTS

The Saints are a collection of small islands that lie seven miles south of Basse-Terre. They are volcanic, and rise sharply out of the water to nearly a thousand feet, but they look tiny between the colossi of Basse-Terre and Dominica, the next Windward Island down the line. Stand on Le Chameau, the highest point on Terre-de-Haut, and you will feel as though you are on the lip of a swamped volcano crater; the islands make an almost perfectly round bowl.

Two of the islands are inhabited (3000 people in all) and their populations are curiously different. Terre-de-Bas was the usual plantation island and the people are mostly descended from the Africans taken there as slaves. Terre-de-Haut, on the other hand, was never planted and so there were never many slaves. Instead the original islanders were descended mostly from white Frenchmen, originating in Brittany and Normandy, and you can still see their blond hair and blue eyes. Their skin does not tan in the sun and it is clear that many of them are in-bred.

They are renowned fishermen, though, and before the age of baseball caps they would wear strange looking *salako* hats to protect themselves from the sun—white material stretched over a bamboo frame that sits close on the head like a small parasol. These 'coolie hats' are thought to have been brought by a Chinaman in the last century.

The Saints were supposedly named by Columbus in honour of All Saints' Day. They were settled in 1648 to defend the island of Guadeloupe. The ramparts can still be seen on the heights.

The Battle of the Saints

To British historians, the Saints' most famous moment came in 1782, when the islands had a ringside view of the most decisive naval battle of the period, one which established British dominance in the Caribbean for the next 30 years.

The Battle of the Saints (La Bataille de la Dominique to the French) was fought on 12 April 1782. The British were beleaguered at the time, having recently lost the American War of Independence. De Grasse had successfully cut the British supply lines, and now he was turning to the British Caribbean colonies. His target was Jamaica, the richest British colony, and he was on his way to join the Spanish navy at Santo Domingo to attack it.

Leaving Martinique, de Grasse headed north and the chase was on. For three days Rodney shadowed de Grasse without being able to commit him to a fight. Eventually they met off the Saints and the two lines, each of 30 ships, bore down on each other in slow motion in parallel and opposite directions, the French coming from the north. At eight in the morning the first broadside was fired. The fleets filed past one another, cannonading, until eleven o'clock when Sir Charles Douglas, with Rodney on the bridge of the *Formidable*, saw a gap in the French line, just a few ships behind de Grasse's flagship, the *Ville de Paris*. He steered for it and broke through the French line. The ships to his rear followed him through and in the manoeuvre they separated the French flagship from the bulk of the fleet. The French ships, so crowded and disordered that they made 'one object to fire at', were decimated. De Grasse stayed on his flagship, with 110 guns and 1300 sailors, throughout the conflict and when finally she was taken, he was one of only three men left uninjured.

The whole scene had been clearly visible from Dominica and the Saints, and as darkness fell ships were seen burning into the night. Five of the French ships were taken and one sunk and the rest of the tattered fleet headed for Cap Français under Admiral Bougainville and for Curaçao off the coast of South America.

When the two Admirals met, de Grasse is supposed to have said: 'You have fought me handsomely', and Rodney to have replied: 'I was glad of the opportunity'.

In the Second World War the islands saw no action, except that Fort Napoléon was used as a prison for those Guadeloupeans who disagreed with the decision to side with the Vichy Regime in France.

The Islands

There is one main settlement on Terre-de-Haut, called Bourg, which is set on a superb harbour. There are four or five streets of creole houses, almost all of them with red tin roofs. Between the cafés on the waterfront you will see the fishermen who sit and chat over a game of dominoes all afternoon.

The best **beach** is in Baie St Pierre, but there is also good sand at Marigot Bay. On the south coast you will find seclusion at Anse du Figuier and Anse Crawen, which sees quite a few nudists. Windsurfing can be fixed up through Guy Maisonneuve (tel 99 53 13) or Centre UCPA (tel 99 54 94), which also arranges sailing. For scuba, contact Diving Nautique des Saintes (tel 99 54 25).

The lumbering fortress on the hilltop, **Fort Napoléon**, is the island's principal sight. Open 9–noon, adm. It commands the bay and has a magnificent view to Guadeloupe and down to Dominica. The fort has exhibitions of modern art and a museum of local history (including pictures of the Battle of the Saints) set in the vast, cool stone ramparts. Outside, among the cannon runners in the grass on the once formidable battlements, there is a cactus garden. Another peak worth climbing is Le Chameau (camel's hump) at the other end of the island, where the *tour modèle* gives a fine view over the whole area and dwarfs Fort Napoléon.

PRACTICAL INFORMATION

The Saints are linked by ferry to Trois-Rivières (twenty minutes and Fr70) on the southern coast of Basse-Terre and daily to Pointe-à-Pitre (one hour, Fr150). Terre-de-Haut has a magnificent harbour and it is a pleasure to see the peaks glide by as you arrive. It is also possible to fly from Le Raizet airport at Pointe-à-Pitre, but if you do not like flying beware because the landing can be a bit hair-raising. There is an occasional scheduled boat crossing to Terre-de-Bas, but if you wish to cross for the day you will have to arrange it with somebody at the dock. Terre-de-Bas has an airstrip suspended on a spit of land a hundred feet above the sea. There are no cars for rent, but on Terre de Haut, you can hire a scooter through Logno (tel 99 54 08).

WHERE TO STAY

Only Terre-de-Haut has places in which to stay and the most charming of these is the **Auberge des Les Petits Saints** (tel 99 50 99) on the hills above town, one of the red-roofed houses with a terraced dining room and pool looking out over cracking views over the bay and on to the clouded Soufrière on Basse-Terre. One of the ten double rooms costs US$115. The **Bois Joli Hotel** (tel 99 50 38, fax 80 07 75) is tucked away in its own garden at the other end of the island at Anse à Cointre. Five rooms in the central house and 15 pink bungalows, double in season US$100. Back in Terre-de-Haut's beautiful main bay, beneath Fort Napoléon and beyond the house built like a boat that juts out into the water from a cliff, are two other small hotels, the **Kanaoa** (tel 99 51 94, fax 99 55 04), which is set in attractive creole style buildings with a waterfront dining terrace, and **Le Village Créole**, with 22 duplexes in a garden of croton and bougainvillaea. A double room at the Village Créole costs around US$120 and at the Kanaoa slightly less. There are also a number of small guest houses and rooms for rent at good prices (tel 91 64 33). The hotels have some good dining rooms, but there is also a clutch of bistros and salad bars set on the waterfront in Bourg.

St Jacques

The least known of all the Saints is the island of Saint Jacques. Christened *Santiago de los Vientos Alicios*, it was jokingly known as *Jack of all Trades* to the English filibusters who plied their trade of 'cruize and plunder' from its shores. The only historian to mention it is a certain Father Jerome Zancarol, who wrote that the food was good, girls were beautiful and that the islanders' morals were the worst he had come across anywhere in the world, a veritable Gehenna.

Apparently, sailors have heard the sound of violins on the 61st meridian, but the only record of the island's illustrious story I can find is in *The Violins of St Jacques*, by Patrick Leigh Fermor.

SAINT MARTIN

French Saint Martin shares an island with Sint Maarten, a member of the Netherlands Antilles (see p. 314), and it is the smallest island in the world to be shared by two nations.

228

The French half in the north is divided from the Dutch side by an imaginary line, marked only by an obelisk and a Bienvenue/Welkom sign.

Saint Martin looks across to British Anguilla in the north of the Lesser Antilles and is about 20 square miles in area (the Dutch half is around 17). Its beaches are supreme and inland the yellow-green scrubland rises to hills of 1200 ft. About 13 miles southeast is the other French island 'commune' of St Barthélemy.

Saint Martin is building fast and it is getting fairly crowded, but it retains a Gallic ambience in the pretty marinas and waterfront bistros. You will find real French West Indian villages there, with local markets and games of *pétanque*. You always know when you are leaving a town because the name is carefully crossed out with a red line. And of course the food is served with customary French flair.

If anything, over the past few years, Saint Martin has become more French than it was, as large numbers of investors and immigrants from France have come to the island. There is a certain French exclusivity, but it is possible to get by in English. The population has rocketed with the tourist industry, now by far the largest income generator.

The other major contributor is the French Government. Saint Martin is a *commune* in the *Région* of Guadeloupe and it is administered by a *sous-préfet* appointed from Paris. The islanders vote members on to the *Conseil Général* that sits in Basse-terre, Guadeloupe, and directly in the French elections.

History

Although the two communities on either side of Saint Martin tended to avoid each other where possible (a road between the two was not built until earlier this century), their pasts are quite similar. Saint Martin's history is included under Sint Maarten (see p. 315).

GETTING TO SAINT MARTIN

Most flights arrive at Juliana airport on the Dutch side of the island (code SXM), although some local services use Esperance airport (code SFG) near Grand Case: Air Guadeloupe from Pointe-à-Pitre and Air St Barts. There is a **ferry boat** from Marigot to Anguilla (20 min; US$20 return). (See Getting to Sint Maarten, p. 317, for details of flights into Juliana airport—from Paris, Frankfurt, Miami, New York—and connections to other Caribbean islands, and p. 316 for a map.) There is a departure tax of US$10.

GETTING AROUND

If you arrive at the airport on the Dutch side, the easiest way up to the French half is by taxi as no **buses** run past the airport. Buses do run from Marigot down to Philipsburg and up to Grand Case with the occasional link on to Orléans. They leave from the Rue de Hollande behind Marigot (fare to Philipsburg about US$1.50) from early in the morning for the workers and they run until about 10 pm. **Hitch-hiking** is the normal lottery; there are hundreds of cars, but few seem to stop, so you may need a fair amount of patience.

Taxis, however, come two a penny (except in price) and are easily available at both airports and at the hotels. A taxi rank also works from the Marigot waterfront (tel 87 56

54). Sample prices are: **Marigot** to Grand Case—US$10, east coast US$15–20, Baie Longue—US$10, Juliana airport—US$12, Philipsburg—US$18.

A morning's tour of the island is easily arranged, though there is not much to see except views across Saint Martin to the surrounding islands. Shopping stops and moments to pause in the bistros are built in to the tour. Hotel desks will fix it for you (safari buses will pick you up) or you can go through **Rising Sun Tours** (tel 87 85 31) or **Sint Maarten Sightseeing Tours** (tel 3–22753).

If you would like to take a tour by **helicopter**, Sint Maarten offers that too: **Héli-inter caraïbes** (tel 87 37 37).

For maximum mobility, to score a few duty-free bargains in Philipsburg or go out to dinner in the evenings, hire a car. There are plenty available at around US$40 per day. Any foreign licence is valid and driving is on the right. Hotels will arrange for cars to be delivered. The island's three towns do get congested, though, so leave plenty of time to get to the airport.

Some local firms as well as big international rental companies work from the Dutch side (see Sint Maarten section, p. 318) and **Avis** has an outlet in Marigot (tel 87 54 36). Local French hire-companies include **Saint Martin Auto** (tel 87 54 72) in Marigot and **Express Rent A Car** (tel 87 55 55). And if you want a scooter or a bicycle, contact **Location 2 Roues** at Galerie Commerciale in Baie Nettlé.

If you are fond of scams and are prepared to spend a couple of hours being given the hard sell about 'investment in vacationing' in a condominium complex, then you can sometimes score a '$50 off your rental bill' voucher.

TOURIST INFORMATION

There is a small Tourist Information Office (tel 87 57 23, fax 87 56 43) on the waterfront in Marigot. Open on weekdays 9–12.30 and 2–5, Sat 8 to noon. (For tourist information abroad see French Antilles, p. 178.) If you think you might be on the beach then, remember to make a selection from the superabundance of tourist literature that litters the airport when you arrive. Of all the magazines, the best one to get hold of is the joint publication *Discover*, which has some well-informed features alongside the normal tourist advice. In a medical **emergency**, there is a hospital in Marigot (tel 87 50 07).

To **telephone** Saint Martin from abroad, the code is 590 followed by the six-digit local number. Within Saint Martin, dial just the six digits. Phoning French to Dutch side, dial 3 and then the five-digit number, and Dutch to French side dial 06 followed by the six digits. There are no coin-boxes on the French side and so you will need to buy a *télécarte* from the post office or the few newsagents that stock them.

MONEY

The official currency of Saint Martin is of course the French franc, but with so many visitors from America, the greenback is accepted everywhere. In local shops and eateries you may receive your change in francs and centimes. Netherlands Antilles guilders or florins (the currency of the Dutch side) will not be accepted. Credit cards are widely accepted all over the island.

There are three **banks** in Marigot and they keep different hours, so you can usually find somwhere to change money during the day. Hotels are always willing to change money of course, but the rate will not be so good. **Shopping hours** are as they are in

France: 9–1 and 3–7. In Marigot you might try **Oro de Sol** for watches and **Cartier** for jewellery.

BEACHES

There are excellent beaches on both sides of the island (see also Sint Maarten in Netherlands Antilles Section), but the French side is less developed and so the beaches there tend to be a little less crowded. Topless bathing is perfectly acceptable here and there are a few nude beaches (Baie de l'Orient is the only official one, but it has been known to happen at Baie Rouge and Baie Longue). Unlike the Dutch side, where hotels often have a shower room which you can use, the beaches on the French side tend to be without changing facilities. On the larger beaches there are often concessionaires who will hire out snorkelling and windsurfing equipment. You may see the word *anse* on the French side; it means cove and there are one or two delightful ones to visit. There has been some theft on beaches all over the island and so you are advised not leave belongings unattended.

Probably the best beach on the island is **Baie Longue** (Long Beach), a cracking mile of soft golden sand on the west of the French side. The best swimming is at the bottom end (near the Samanna Hotel). Take food and drinks.

Just around the corner is the **Baie des Prunes** (Plum Bay), an afternoon suntrap with good snorkelling (but watch out for the rocks when swimming).

Baie Rouge is a lively beach, a fantastic stretch of golden sand with crystalline water that looks north toward Anguilla. Huts have snorkelling gear for hire and drinks for sale. From the eastern end you can swim round to an idyllic smaller cove, **Crique Lune de Miel** (Honeymoon Cove).

Nettle Bay or Marigot Bay is the built-up strip to the north of Simpson Lagoon that runs into Marigot. The sand is all right and most watersports can be arranged here.

There are two small isolated coves between Marigot and Grand Case—**Anse des Pères** (Friars Bay), where you will find a rasta beach bar and **Happy Bay**.

The town of Grand Case has some small hotels and guest houses along its strip of sand and so there is sports equipment available and plenty of bistros to retreat to at the height of the sun.

Anse Marcel has recently been built up and so the valley is dominated by an infestation of mock-classical gingerbread, but the beach has brilliant white sand enclosed by enormous headlands. A short walk round the western point takes you to the tiny and secluded **Duck Beach**.

Some of the island's best beaches are on the eastern Atlantic coast, even though the sea is rougher there. **Baie de l'Orient** is a stunning mile of fine white sand and clear blue water. It is a nudist beach.

To the south there are two other strips of sand before you come to the Dutch side, **Baie de l'Embouchure** or Galion Bay, a sweeping curve where windsurfing is popular and **Baie Lucas**, also known as Coralita Beach, which has excellent snorkelling and gets the full brunt of the morning sun. Both beaches have a hotel where you can get lunch and a drink to cool you down.

There are a few off-shore islands in the northeast of Saint Martin, favoured by some for the diving, where you go for a day's seclusion on your own strip of sand (remember to take a picnic and plenty to drink and arrange to be picked up again). A round-trip to **Ilet**

Pinel costs about US$25 and to **Ile Tintamarre**, with its beautiful Baie Blanche beach, around US$30.

BEACH BARS

There are a number of free and easy haunts above the waves in St Martin where you can linger over a beer after a dip. On Orient Bay you will find the **Kontiki Beach Bar** a little removed from the huddle of T-shirt shops and rum shacks, with a covered terrace and tables scattered around a sandy garden. There's no dress code here, so the odd stray nude might wander by from the club next door; otherwise it's salads, grills and creole dishes at US$6–10, noon–4. Also sailboards if you want to check out the winds. **Kali's** is another hip spot on the secluded Friar's Bay, where you might spend hours admiring the colours of the sea and the sunset to the tune of reggae and dub or just the susurration of the waves. Run by a rastaman, some food is ital, but you also get standard West Indian chicken and fish, served on the wooden deck above the sand. Full moon party.

The town of Grand Case is one long beach bar—plenty of restaurants to retreat to here, but you might try **Lucelia's Hideout**, off on its own at the top end of the town, or **Surf Club South**, a rock and roll bar in a neat shack under the trees, in the middle of the town.

WATERSPORTS

Windsurfing is very popular on the French side of the island and it is marginally cheaper there (about US$20 per hour). You can get a board in Nettle Bay or Grand Case, but the winds are best on the east coast, where the place to head for is Orient Bay if you like speed sailing. Try **Orient Watersports** (tel 87 33 85). The Baie de l'Embouchure is good for beginners because the onshore winds are gentler and the water is calmer. Contact **Patrick's**. Most hotels have sailing dinghies for hire and they will usually lend to somebody from outside.

There are a couple of marinas where larger yachts can be hired for a day, a week or a month out on the water, perhaps on a trip to a neighbouring island. At the **Port Royale Marina** on the lagoon in Marigot contact **Caraïbes Sport Boats** (tel 87 89 38, fax 87 89 89) and **Port Lonvilliers** in Anse Marcel (tel 87 31 94, fax 87 30 45). If you want a day's picnic cruise, **Dynasty** (tel 87 85 21), among others, works out of Marigot and you can also try **Seahawk Cruises** (tel 87 59 49) for a sunset cruise.

Deep-sea fishing trips can be arranged (about US$600 for a full day) at the marinas. There are good fishing grounds off the Anguillan islands, where you can cast for bonito and spiked-back wahoo.

Snorkellers will find excellent corals (do not pick any or use a spear-gun against the fish, though, as they are protected) in places off Saint Martin, where deep-blue angelfish and elongated needlefish lurk. The best beaches are Baie Rouge near the western point of the island and Green Cay opposite Orient Beach on the Atlantic side (also Ilet Pinel and Tintamarre). There is a glass-bottom boat *Karib 1* (tel 87 26 36).

There are also many colourful reefs, with fan corals waving in the currents patrolled by sergeant-major fish and trumpetfish, that make for good **scuba-diving**. In the reserve off the northeast coast you will find the best reefs —the bay of Grandes Cayes on the shoreline and the islands offshore, including Caye Verte, Ilet Pinel and a little farther afield the Ile Tintamarre.

Dives and instruction (PADI and NAUI) are available on the island. A single-tank dive costs around US$45. On the French side try **Blue Ocean Dive Centre** in Marigot (tel 87 89 73) at the Pirate Beach Hotel and **Lou Scuba Club** (tel 87 22 58, fax 87 20 14) on Baie Nettlé.

OTHER ACTIVITIES
A number of walking trails have been cut into the Saint Martin scrub, taking in heights such as the Mont des Accords and the Pic Paradis, both of which give cracking views of the surrounding islands and lowlands like the salt ponds. You will see Saint Martin's limited **flora** and **fauna**, from soldier crabs in their conical shells to the mournful white cattle egret on land and the yellowlegs who scurry around the mangrove swamps. Perhaps try the path leading over First Stick Hill from behind the airport, an hour's walk ending up in Anse Marcel, or the flatland on the east coast near Oyster Pond. More details can be found at the tourist office in town and they will arrange a guide if you should want one.

There is a **golf** course on the Dutch side, at the Mullet Bay Resort (tel 42081). The green fees are very high at around US$110 for the 18 holes, and residents of the hotel have preference in teeing off.

There are about 50 **tennis** courts on the island, many of them lit for night-play. Contact any of the larger hotels.

It is even possible to go for an early-morning dip on horseback through **Horse Back Riding** (tel 87 33 33) in Anse Marcel or through **OK Corral** in Oyster Pond on (tel 87 31 81).

Marigot
Like its Dutch counterpart Philipsburg, Marigot has four streets, clustered between the sea and a salt-pond, but where the Dutch town looks inwards to its shops, Marigot looks out across the water.

Marigot Balcony, Saint Martin

233

The esplanade, Boulevard de France, is lined with bistros and parasols, and it is possible to linger there all day, with just a few distractions between meals—a stroll around the marina on the lagoon or a visit to the waterfront market, watching the fishing boats land their catch and the sloops off-load their cargoes. Behind, the few streets have recently been restored and you will see the old wrought-iron balustrades of the few town-houses and municipal buildings among the pastel-fronted shopping arcades.

The town first grew up in the 1680s, when the danger of raids that had forced the islanders inland to Orléans was passed. In the 1760s the fear revived; this time it was navies on the rampage rather than marauding boatloads of pirates, and so **Fort St Louis** was constructed on the heights above the town. It is overgrown and littered with just a few cannon, but it has a fine view of Anguilla, from where the old adversaries would nip over at the first sniff of war. The path to the fort leads past the church, with its fresco of a black Virgin in a Caribbean scene, the hospital and the Sous-préfecture, the residence of the island administrator.

The **Saint Martin Museum** on the waterfront in Marigot gives an illustration of island history with Arawak ceramics and shells and other tools like the wicker squeezer used to extract the poisonous juice from cassava. Also old-time pictures of the island. Adm expensive $5.

Around the Island

The road leading north out of Marigot leads beneath the **Pic du Paradis**, the island's highest point, from which there are fantastic views of islands as far away as Nevis (about 60 miles).

Grand Case is a line of pretty, older houses and some new ones festooned in tropical greenery, strung out along the beachfront in a wide bay. There is something of a local West Indian life here beside the guest houses and hotels and you might even see a cock-fight in a pit at the western end of the village. Other spectator sports include watching the planes come in over the rooftops to land at the airstrip just behind the town. On Sundays there is often a *jump-up* on the beach, with a disco set up on the pier and braziers cooking chicken legs and soldier crabs in their shells.

Orléans, or French Quarter as it is sometimes called, a collection of villas and one or two shops, was the capital of the French half of the island in the early days.

FESTIVALS
Carnaval is celebrated at the beginning of Lent with street parades in Marigot and Grand Case (on the Dutch side, Carnival is at Easter) and in May there is the **Saint Martin Food Festival** in which island recipes, drinks and crafts are displayed (and offered for tasting) to steel band and 'old-time' band music. **St Martin's Day** is celebrated on 11 November, which brings joint ceremonies with the Dutch side.

WHERE TO STAY
Until recently it was the Dutch side that had the block resort hotels, thrown up by speculators as an investment, but lately they have been springing up in Saint Martin too. However there are still the local French West Indian inns dotted over the island, particularly around Grand Case. Except in guest houses, the rates quoted usually include breakfast. A small government tax (US$3) charge is added to your bill.

LUXURY

La Samanna, PO Box 159, 97150 St Martin (tel 87 51 22, fax 87 87 86), is a super-luxurious hotel set at the western tip of the island on Long Beach. It is a conglomeration of architectural styles—Mediterranean and Moorish shapes among the palms and a fantastic view of the sunset. It is quite large, with 85 rooms, but it is chic and very exclusive. Rooms are palatial, in sumptuousness, and some in size. Also in price, at US$980 a double in season.

EXPENSIVE

At the top of Orient Beach is the new **Esmeralda Resort**, PO Box 541, 97150 St Martin (tel 87 36 36, fax 87 35 18), with 56 units set in pretty terraced villas around a tiled and rock-walled garden. The rooms, which look onto their own pool, have all you need in the way of twentieth-century comfort with wicker furnishings, king-sized beds and TVs. There are sports on offer, a gourmet restaurant and a beachside club for simpler meals. Double rooms from US$200 and suites from $450. **La Belle Créole**, PO Box 118 (tel 87 58 66, fax 87 56 66), is set on the north coast of the island on its own beach. The style echoes the Mediterranean in its stucco and the tables arranged on the stepped courtyard. It is quite large, with a certain atmospheric grandeur and modern rooms in blocks. Plenty of watersports and tennis, a double room in season costs $385 plus. **Captain Oliver's**, PO Box 645 (tel 87 40 26, fax 87 40 84) has a nautical feel surrounded by the marina on Oyster Pond. All the rooms, which are decorated with white tiles and pastel colours, have balconies overlooking the marina or the offshore islands towards St Barts. Not on the beach, but there is a boat taxi across to Dawn Beach. Watersports and of course sailing, double room in season US$230.

MODERATE

The **Anse Margot Hotel** on Baie Nettlé (tel 87 92 01, fax 87 92 13) has 95 very comfortable air-conditioned and fan-ventilated rooms and suites in neat blocks. They overlook the lagoon and many have private balconies and terraces wrapped in gingerbread. Sports available and a large pool with jacuzzi on the deck next door to the restaurant and bar. Quite large but friendly; double room US$150 plus. **Grand Case** has a number of small mid-range hotels and guest houses. Most do not have pools, but they are right above the waves and most have no restaurant either; many have kitchenettes, but there is plenty of choice if you want to eat out. **La Belle Grand Case Beach Hotel** (tel 87 73 94, fax 87 98 60) has just eight rooms set in a modern building on the sand, with magnificent views of the bay and Anguilla from the balconies. Bright, breezy and comfortable apartments and studios with kitchenettes, US$175 in season. The Hotel **Pavillon Beach**, PO Box 313 (tel 87 96 46, fax 87 71 04) also stands above the sand, a little farther along the bay. It has 17 studios and suites with kitchenettes and a pretty terrace with balustrade from which to admire the sea. Double room US$110. The **Hévéa Hotel**, 163 Blvd de Grand Case (tel 87 56 85, fax 87 83 88) is set in an old colonial house across the road from the beach. Just eight rooms and suites redone in old West Indian style—muslin bed-netting and dark wooden furniture and beams. US$110 for a double room in season, including breakfast on the terrace.

On the beachfront not far off you can stay in high West Indian comfort—deep-pile carpets and large beds at the **Grand Case Beach Hotel** (tel 87 50 90), or write to PO Box 175 Philipsburg, Sint Maarten. Simple double rooms, US$70 in season. The

Morning Star guest house (tel 87 93 85) has similarly priced rooms in a block; clean and comfortable enough. Otherwise try **Rosely's** (tel 87 70 17, fax 87 70 20) in Concordia, where there are 48 comfortable rooms. At **Fleming's** (tel 87 70 25) the rate is US$25 per person.

EATING OUT

Eating out is something of a pastime in Saint Martin and there are some excellent restaurants on the island—offering both classic French cuisine and its creole counterpart, so if you are one for a gastronomic steeplechase, there is plenty to occupy you here. Grand Case calls itself the 'gourmet capital of Saint Martin' and there is a string of pretty restaurants along the waterfront (as there are in Marigot too). There is not really a need to dress up, but most restaurants would prefer you not to go in shorts. Prices are not cheap, but service is *compris*. There are also some good restaurants on the Dutch side.

EXPENSIVE

La Vie en Rose (tel 87 54 42) has a commanding view over the waterfront square from the first floor balcony and smart pink dining room, which is decorated with greenery and tended by lightning waiters. French cuisine—try pumpkin cream soup followed by *feuilletée de crabe homardine* or lobster in saffron. A rose for the lady at the end of dinner and a fairly big bill, main course US$15–35. Diagonally opposite, also dressed in pink, is another French restaurant, **La Maison sur le Port** (tel 87 56 38). You dine on an open terrace around an old creole house, backed with waterfalls and more greenery. Light sauces to go with the climate—duck and mango, swordfish and coconut, or sautéed shrimp and sea scallop in a curry sauce. Main course US$18–20. **Le Poisson d'Or** (tel 87 72 45) is slightly farther down the waterfront, in an old stone warehouse, restored with its arches and beams. You eat on the terrace, classic French cuisine—*matelotte de langoustine Bordeaux* or a snapper in red wine and puff pastry. Paintings for sale, main course US$20–23. **La Rhumerie** (tel 87 56 98) in the valley of Colombier, serves French and creole food on a small veranda in the countryside where you are surrounded by the encroaching jungle and the ringing of the tree frogs. The tables are set with creole madras material, and you might try *boudin créole* (a spicy blood sausage), followed by *blanquette pêcheur*, fish US$15–28. Then comes a volley of flavoured rums (in keeping with the name of the restaurant)—*maracudja* (passion fruit), *cajou* (cashew) and *quenette* (guinep). Dinner only, closed Mon. The water is lit at **Le Tastevin** (tel 87 55 45), where you dine under awnings or a wooden-roofed terrace. French cuisine—*croustillant de mérou* (crunchy grouper in white wine) or *mitonne de gambas* (prawns sauteed in red wine and butter). Main course US$22, closed Wed. Not far off is the **Fish Pot** (tel 87 50 88) which is set on a terrace with hanging plants high above the water. Fish and seafood in French style—Fish Pot *bouillabaisse* followed by *rouelle de queue de langouste* (lobster tail in a creamy fennel sauce in puff pastry), or a concoction of snails and hazelnut in garlic and basil. Main course US$20.

MODERATE

A restaurant with a difference in Grand Case is **Madrague** (tel 87 91 30), across the road from the beach and named after Brigitte Bardot's house. The bar inside the old town house is decorated with nets and fishing scenes, and from there you pass into the sandy garden of palms and an almond tree to eat. 50s music and a sail for shelter to go with barbecued meals—seafood kebab and grilled mahi-mahi at US$15. A classic spot in Marigot, well worth finding (it is hidden away in an alley), is the **Bistrot Nu** (no phone). The alley is on the left as you leave Marigot to the north, opposite the school. The restaurant is set in a small traditional clapboard house with overhead fans and there are about ten tables, with a fun, faintly chaotic feel. Set French and creole menu à la blackboard, with a variety from frogs' legs to *colombo*. Good value at US$14 fixed price. Haitian paintings for sale. Because it is small, you might have to be quite flexible about when you eat (open daily except Sun, 7.30–midnight). **Le Pêcheur** (tel 87 82 70) offers creole fare and seafood on a breezy bamboo terrace on the seafront just before the Sandy Ground bridge. *Court bouillon* of fish with spices or conch kebab and grilled catch of the day. Follow up with *banane flambée*. Good prices at US$10 for fish. Entrance in a building site, closed Tues. Close by is the **Case Créole**, which also serves local food.

CHEAP

In town you can eat relatively cheaply at **La Brasserie de la Gare**, upstairs on the waterfront; pizzas or salad at Fr50. People also speak highly of **Le Petit Bouffe** for everyday French food—in an alley off the main street in Marigot. Another good spot for a local meal with an atmosphere is at **Chez Bruno** (tel 87 80 05), up the hill out of Marigot on the road to Grand Case. It is set in a pink and white clapboard house, and you dine off plastic table-cloths on *brochette gambasse* (shrimp kebab), *ragout de cabrit* (stew goat) and other Haitian dishes. Main course US$7.

Finally **Les Lolos** in Grand Case are a great place for a standing lunchtime stop—for a chicken leg or some ribs with a johnny cake, pick them off the brazier. Three or four lean-tos in a row—Cynthia's, Starzie and Jimbo.

BARS AND NIGHTLIFE

In downtown Marigot you will find a couple of cocktail bars patronised by hip chicks and cool dudes—the **Bar de la Mer** occupies the side of a building on the waterfront and there is often live music. Along the waterfront is **La Fiesta**, an open lounge dressed up in pink, around a central bar. Music every night in season and a cocktail list as long as your arm. On the marina waterfront there are endless cafés where you can linger over an ice cream or a glass of wine, but at the end you will find a favourite haunt of sailors at **Le Lafayette**. **Le Circus** in Nettle Bay is a video bar with a stray car in the dining room—pizzas and beer, rock music.

There are some fun bars in Grand Case. Start with **Cocktail**, a terrace overlooking the water at the bottom end of the beach. Pool table, happy-two-hours and a dance floor. You can also try **Cha Cha Cha**, a tapas garden with flaming torches which attracts a hip crowd.

There are some more regular discotheques, including **Caribe Club** and **Heaven's** in Sandy Ground, where you will hear Caribbean music, and **Night Fever,** just by the turning to Colombier where you will be flexing your legs with the locals (weekends). If you want a late-night whisky after the dance-halls have closed, try the unaccountably smooth **Edouard's Bar** in Nettle Bay.

There are plenty more bars and of course casinos on the Dutch side.

ST BARTHELEMY

St Barthélemy is one of the most chic, civilized and least known parts of France. Here bronzed beauties cruise by on the beaches in just a nuance of a bathing costume and out in the bay the water whistles with windsurfers in red, white and blue; Dior, Chanel, Lacroix, jazz, restaurants to linger in, *haute cuisine* and Veuve Cliquot champagne. It is a chi-chi twentieth-century playground, as only the French could conceive. Even the tourist brochures are stylish and sexy in St Barts.

Fifteen miles southeast of Saint Martin in the Leewards, St Barts is a crooked six miles long—folds of volcanic lava and rubble that have been pushed up from beneath the ocean and sprouted a mantle of scrub. The fragmented coastline has some lovely coves, many of them culminating in perfect strands. St Barthélemy (pronounced San Bartailer-mee in French), is the island's formal name, but it is hardly ever used. It is usually known as Saint Barth in French and St Barts in English. There are 5050 islanders.

Strangely, for much of the 19th century, St Barts belonged to Sweden, but they wave baguettes happily in the streets nowadays. Despite their interlude as Swedes, the St Barthéléminois (sic) are mostly descended from French settlers and you might see a traditional bonnet or hear a snatch of a strange French dialect in one of the original villages. The population has always been quite white because there were never many slaves.

As the tourist industry has steadily grown in the last 30 years, St Barts has turned from one of the quietest islands in the area to a trusted home-from-home for expatriate French. It is a little *snob* at times, but is generally friendly. It has taken on an overlay of the République—there is practically no recognizable West Indian culture outside the cultivated prettiness of the tropical gardens—and it has gained a reputation as an exclusive tropical resort. It is the favoured haunt of a crowd of transient millionaires on their crusade against winter.

History

St Barts was not seen by Columbus, but later travellers called the island after his brother, Bartolomeo, who went with him to the New World. Like the rest of the Leewards it was given a wide berth by the Spanish colonists for their first 100 years because *Ouanalao*, as the Caribs knew St Barts, was dangerous cannibal country.

Settlers came in 1659, eking a living out of the ground with such crops as tobacco and indigo, but the main source of income for the next 100 years really lay in the island's position and in its well-protected coves. Smugglers and pirates, en route from South America to the Bahamas, would use the bays to repair their ships, and the islanders made a tidy profit by selling them the provisions they needed to refit.

The original St Barthians were Frenchmen from Normandy and Britanny. They had a few slaves, domestic ones only because there were no plantations. Even late in the 18th century there were still less than 1000 inhabitants on St Barts.

Then on 1 July 1784, the St Barthians woke to find that their island was no longer owned by France, but that they were on lease to Sweden. The King of France had simply swapped it for a warehouse in Gothenburg and for trading rights in the Baltic, without even consulting them. St Barts was Sweden's only colony in the Caribbean and little remains of their influence except the old stone warehouses on the waterfront and the street names in Gustavia, the capital. For the romantic story of how it all came about, see the history of Tobago (p. 83), King Gustav's original choice for his Caribbean base.

But the Swedish reign benefited the St Barthians. King Gustav promptly declared the island a free port and before long St Barts was prospering as a market on the trade routes from Europe to the burgeoning United States. While the other islands were held to ransom in the wars at the turn of the 18th century, St Barts continued to rake in money.

As soon as peace came to the Caribbean in the early 19th century and the seaborne trade waned, the island fell into a decline and the Swedish venture failed. The population, which had reached as high as 5000, began to tail off, particularly after the Swedish king emancipated the island's slaves in 1847. There was no land for the freed slaves to settle so they emigrated, mostly to the American Virgin Islands. In the end, King Oscar II put sovereignty to a referendum, and the islanders voted 351 to one to return to French rule. On 16 March 1878 St Barts was handed back to France.

The island was simply appended to Guadeloupe again and the decline continued. When Guadeloupe was made an overseas Département of France in 1946, St Barts became one of its *communes*, under its financial control.

Today it is administered, along with nearby Saint Martin, by a *sous-préfet* appointed from Paris. The islanders vote members on to the Conseil Général and the Conseil Régional, which sit in Basse-Terre, Guadeloupe, and directly in the French elections. Like Saint Martin, St Barts receives some assistance from the French Government via Guadeloupe for roads and large municipal projects. Tourism is the big earner at the moment and the island maintains an exclusive and luxurious style.

GETTING TO ST BARTS

St Barts cannot take international flights but it is well served from islands nearby, of which the best is Sint Maarten (most flights and good connections). Air St Barth has eight flights a day to Juliana airport in Sint Maarten, four a week from Puerto Rico and three from Guadeloupe. Winair (tel 35 42 30 Sint Maarten, 27 61 01 St Barts) has ten a day to Juliana. Air Guadeloupe flies from Saint Martin (Grand Case), Guadeloupe, Puerto Rico and St Thomas in the USVI. Virgin Air also fly from Puerto Rico and St Thomas.

The airstrip on St Barts, situated on the Plaine de la Tourmente(!), is one of the most exciting in the Caribbean. The main problem is that at whichever end you make your approach, there is a hill just where you should be lining up. And so from one end passengers get a close inspection of some hillside forest and the roof of a hotel and from the other they drop close enough to the road to read car-drivers' T-shirts. If you look over the pilot's shoulder, it may seem that he is going to miss the runway, but the small planes are so manoeuvrable that they can turn on a 20p piece. The runway closes at dusk, but you can usually make connections the same day from Europe and the USA.

If this all sounds a bit much, there are a couple of boat links from Saint Martin (both Marigot and Philipsburg) on the powerboat **St Barth Express**. Departs daily from Gustavia (8.15 am) for Saint Martin, and returns from Marigot (4.30 pm). There are only 12 seats, so book in advance (tel 27 62 38). A one-way fare is about US$30 and the return trip US$50.

If you just want a day trip to the island from Saint Martin, then there are plenty of yachts and launches that make an early start from Philipsburg. Try *White Octopus*, which

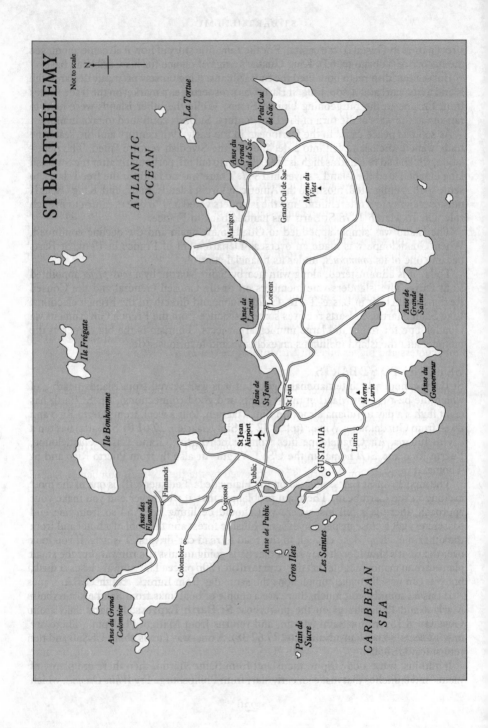

ST BARTHÉLEMY

Not to scale

ATLANTIC OCEAN

CARIBBEAN SEA

La Tortue

Petit Cul de Sac

Anse du Grand Cul de Sac

Grand Cul de Sac

Morne du Vitet

Marigot

Anse de Grande Saline

Anse de Lorient

Lorient

Anse du Gouverneur

Ile Frégate

Ile Bonhomme

Baie de St Jean

St Jean

St Jean Airport

Morne Lurin

Lurin

Flamands

Public

Corossol

GUSTAVIA

Anse des Flamands

Anse de Public

Gros Ilets

Les Saintes

Colombier

Pain de Sucre

Anse du Grand Colombier

leaves from **Bobby's Marina** (tel 599 5 23170). For a trip to one of the other islands, contact **St Barth Voyages** on rue Duquesne in Gustavia (tel 27 79 79).

If an hour's bouncing the waves against the Tradewinds still sounds like too much, then there are helicopters available from Sint Maarten airport.

GETTING AROUND

There is no bus service on St Barts, but hitching is a reasonably dependable way to get around the island. **Taxis** are readily available at the airport and in Gustavia. You can also order them through a hotel or through the central number (tel 27 66 31). Gustavia to the airport will set you back US$5.

Car hire is expensive across the board, though it gives you much more mobility. The island favourite is the mini-moke and its Volkswagen equivalent, the Gurgel and most recently the Suzuki jeep—they can just about cope with St Barts' many hills. Some of the big international names operate out of the airport and many hotels keep cars for their guests. If you will want one during the high season, you should order it in advance. A foreign driving licence is valid, credit cards are usually accepted, driving is on the right and many companies will deliver to your hotel. The minimum price in season is about US$35 a day plus taxes.

Some rental companies are: **Budget** (tel 27 66 30) and **Hertz** (tel 27 71 14) in St Jean, **Turbe Car Rental** (tel 27 71 42) and **Maurice** (tel 27 05 64) at the airport.

Scooters are also easily available for hire, though they are less likely to get you up the steep hills. Try **Chez Béranger** (tel 27 61 63) or **St Barth Moped Rental** (tel 27 70 95) for scooters and bigger bikes or **St Motobique** (tel 27 67 89).

TOURIST INFORMATION

The **Office du Tourisme** (tel 27 87 27, fax 27 74 47) is on the Quai Général de Gaulle in Gustavia. Open 8.30–noon and 2–6. An information bureau at the airport keeps the same hours. There is an annual glossy magazine **Tropical St Barth** with features about the island and some advice on sports, shopping and restaurants.

In a medical **emergency**, the Gustavia Hospital is on the seaward arm of the town, on the Rue Jean Bart (tel 27 60 00).

The **IDD code** for St Barts is 590 followed by the the the six-digit number. If you are calling within the island, dial just the six digits. There are no coin boxes on the island and to use a public phone you need a *télécarte*, bought in advance at the post office. If you do need to make a call, any hotel front desk will help out for a price.

MONEY

Generally speaking, St Barts is very expensive. Though the official currency is the French franc, the US dollar is accepted all over the island. If you are one to watch exchange rates, then you might find that you can get a marginally better deal in francs than in dollars. Credit cards are accepted by all shops, restaurants and hotels. Service is *compris* in restaurants (remember this when signing cheques) and hotels add 10–15% to your bill.

Banks are open on weekdays until mid-afternoon. BFC opposite the airport is open on Saturday mornings and Crédit Agricole in town has a hole-in-the-wall machine. **Shops** keep hours of 8.30–noon and 2–5. St Barts has been allowed to keep its tax-free status from Swedish days and so you may find some (relative) bargains.

BEACHES
St Barts has magnificent beaches, mounds of golden sand tucked away in coves, cut into the coastline and protected on both sides by mountainous headlands. Topless bathing is accepted and happens everywhere, but surprisingly on a French island, nudity is against the rules. All beaches are public, but you may have to get permission to cross somebody's land (ask if they stop you). *Anse* means cove.

The island's two best beaches are on the south coast—**Anse du Gouverneur** and the **Anse de Grande Saline**. Both have vast mounds of golden sand that shelve gently into the sea in their own deep bays, with views of the volcanic peaks of Saba, St Eustatius and St Kitts. Both are popular, as you will see by the hundred-yard line of mini-mokes and jeeplets, but as there are no beach bars, you will need to take all you need in the way of water and food. Anse du Gouverneur is approached via Lurin (south out of Gustavia) and Anse de Grande Saline from St Jean.

St Jean itself is the island's busiest beach; a conglomeration of bistros and bungalows where the tanned scooter-brigade congregate, exercising their windsurfers and wetbikes or taking an occasional dip.

In the northwest of the island are two cracking suntraps lined with talcum-powder sand: **Anse des Flamands** is 600 yards of gentle waves, with a stunning view of the deserted Ile Bonhomme and a couple of hotels with bars to retreat to; and **Anse du Grand Colombier**, a walk off the beaten track, palm-shaded and usually very secluded (take water and a picnic). **Lorient** is less known by tourists than by fishermen, but has a magnificent curve of white sand.

The **Anse du Grand Cul-de-Sac** receives winds straight off the Atlantic, but the bay is protected by a reef and so it is good for swimming and windsurfing. There are a couple of hotels here, where you can get a drink and a meal or borrow watersports equipment. The **Petit Cul de Sac** is a smaller secluded cove bordered by mangrove.

Ten minutes' walk out of Gustavia is the **Petit Anse de Galet** where shells are washed up in piles of pink and orange on the soft light brown sand—good for a walk. Beyond the town travelling north is another suntrap beneath the hills, in the fishing village of **Corossol**. Just down from the nets and the boats there is a strip of beige sand so soft that you sink up to your shins.

SPORTS
Windsurfers and small **sailing** boats are available for hire at two main beaches: on the **Baie de St Jean**, try the **St Barts Wind School** (tel 27 70 96) for BIC boards, or the **Mistral** school at Hotel Filao (tel 27 64 84) and on the **Anse du Grand Cul-de-Sac** at the eastern end of the island, where you will find **Wind Wave Power** (tel 27 62 73). Most hotels will have them to hire though if you ask, at about US$20 per hour. Lessons are also available.

Yachts are available for charter, on day sails around St Barts or a longer trip to other islands. **Yacht Charter Agency** (tel 27 62 38) make regular picnic trips and sunset cruises on *Zavijava*, as do **Marine Service** (tel 27 70 34) on *Ne me Quitte pas*. The latter also have a large number of boats if you would like to spend a day **deep-sea fishing** (pêche à gros), casting for marlin and kingfish, six people for a half-day for about US$350. Also try **La Maison de la Mer** (tel 27 81 00) for fishing or waterskiing.

Snorkellers will find the water around St Barts rewarding. You can try the reefs at

Petit Anse beyond Anse des Flamands, Anse Maréchal and the Grand or Petit Cul-de-Sac. Alternatively some hotels and the companies above offer snorkelling trips.

La Plongée (scuba diving) on the off-shore reefs and islands is also easily arranged. Expect to see striped sergeant-major fish gliding by followed by grunts, and long-spined urchins lurking in among the sea-fans and staghorn coral. Reefs include the off-shore rocks of Les Saintes, Gros Ilets and Pain de Sucre. A one-tank dive costs from US$45. In Gustavia contact the **St Barth Diving Centre** at Marine Service (tel 27 70 34) which is PADI certified. **Dan** (tel 27 64 78) works from the Emerald Beach Hotel in St Jean. Both companies offer resort and certification courses. If you would like to look at the corals in the dry, then contact **Aquarius** at La Maison de la Mer.

On land there is little in the way of sports other than **tennis** though there is a hilltop driving range and putting green if you feel like swinging a golf club, in Gouverneur (tel 27 62 49). There are courts at many of the hotels—Guanahani and the St Barth Beach Hotel—as well as the Sports Club of Colombier (tel 27 61 07). If you would like to explore the island on horseback, contact **Ranch des Flammands** (tel 27 80 72).

Gustavia

Only hints of a Swedish heritage remain in St Barts' capital after a hundred years and the recent tourist redevelopment. Almost all of the original Swedish town was destroyed by hurricane and a fire in 1850, and only a couple of houses remain in use (on the Rue Sadi Carnot and the Rue Jeanne d'Arc). But the streetnames: Drottninggatan, Hwarfsgatan, and Ostra- and Westra-Strandgatan on the harbour waterfront give an unusual impression for the Caribbean. The name Gustavia is taken from the enlightened despot King Gustav III who leased St Barts from France and gave the island the free-port status that enabled it to prosper.

Today the population of neat Gustavia is just a few hundred, a fraction of what it was 200 years ago when the harbour was filled with merchantmen and the warehouses were

The Swedish Belfry

243

overflowing. Sailing craft are filling the harbour once again as they cruise south from the Virgin Islands to Antigua. And the port still maintains its mercantile tradition with chic-looking mannequins displaying Christian Lacroix and Gucci clothes at duty free prices. But it is no longer Swedish in atmosphere: nowadays, with endless bistros and police wearing *képis*, the ambience is distinctly French.

At the four points around the harbour stand the tired old fortresses that once guarded Gustavia. It is possible to visit Fort Gustave on the road out of town, from where there is a magnificent view of the harbour.

Another remaining Swedish feature of Gustavia is the distinctive triangular-roofed clock-tower known as the Swedish belfry. It stands high above the town next to the **sous-préfecture** (formerly the island prison) and was originally built as a church-tower.

The **English anchor** at the head of the harbour is about 200 years old, but it has only been in St Barts since 1981 when it was dragged here by mistake from St Thomas in the Virgin Islands. It has just become part of the furniture.

The Municipal Museum can be found near the point of the bay (and will be installed in the Wall House when that is restored). On display you will see prints and pictures of old-time St Barts, alongside mock-ups of the traditional cottages and some rushwork articles made of the *latanier* palm. Open daily, 8–noon and weekday afternoons, adm.

Around the Island

For an island with no peak over 1000 feet, St Barts is extremely hilly and rough. There is little rain, not much cultivation, and the hills are infested with scrub, tall torch cactus and the distinctive St Barts palm tree, the *latanier*. For centuries the villagers were completely isolated from one another and would meet only in church after walking for hours along tortuous paths hacked out of the scrub. Nowadays the island is cut and crossed with impossibly steep and windy roads and the furthest reaches are occupied by holiday villas. In the narrow valleys you will see mournful white cattle egrets waiting for food while their companions graze.

You might catch snatches of a strange language in the country, the old speech of the islanders' Norman ancestors (the communities were so isolated that people living just five miles from one another spoke with a different accent). And you may just still see the womenfolk wearing their traditional frilled bonnets (calèches)—starched and prim white hats that keep the islanders' Norman skin protected from the sun. They are nicknamed *quichenottes*, supposedly a corruption of 'kiss-me-not', because it is rather difficult to get another face underneath them.

North of Gustavia the sea road cuts inland to St Barts' small industrial estate at **Public** and then emerges on the coast again at **Corossol**, a charming fishing village, where the houses clutter the slopes of a valley that opens on to the beach. In Corossol they wear the *calèche à platine*, with multiple hems, a frilly border and little chance of scoring a kiss. Farther up the coast in Colombier and in Flamands traditionally they wear the *calèche à batons*, strengthened with wooden slats. There is a private sea-shell collection on view in the town at the Inter Oceans Museum (tel 27 62 97), where you can see giant clams with wavy lips and some miniature creations of incredible intricacy. Open daily 9.30–5, adm.

All over this area you will see the *latanier* with its smooth trunk, a tangled confusion of stubs and then a series of fronds that grow like scratchy fans. When dried these leaves are very skilfully woven by the local women into hats, bags and table mats. Corossol is probably the best place to buy.

East of Gustavia St Jean, the site of the earliest settlement on the island, has become the centre of the tourist industry in St Barts—the old town has been almost swallowed by recent development and so when you arrive at the airport you are greeted by a neat collection of bistros and chi-chi boutiques.

As you go east the villas thin out on the hills and old St Barts begins to appear—dry-stone walls and distinctive houses with red roofs and sloping plastered walls. A few fishermen still work out of Lorient Bay. Boobies nest on the clifftops and in the mangroves you may see a pelican digesting a meal in the sun. The road rings the eastern end of the island, emerging on the southern coast where there are magnificent views as far as Statia and St Kitts.

FESTIVALS
St Barts stages a number of traditional French and Caribbean events as well as get-togethers for interested sportsmen and wine-drinkers. **Carnaval** takes place at Mardi Gras, with black and white parades on Ash Wednesday; on their **Saint's Days**, Gustavia (14 August) and St Barthélemy (24 August) come alive in trusted Caribbean style—*jump-ups* in the street.

Mid-January sees the **St Barts Music Festival**, with performers of chamber music, dance music and jazz, and May the **Golden Hammocks** Festival (a festival of tenderness and laziness.....). The **St Barts Regatta** runs parallel to Carnaval and windsurfers might want to join the **24 hours of the Lagoon** competition. In December, the St Barts Yacht Club organizes the **Route de la Rosé**, a race for 65-ft yachts and above to bring a case of rosé wine from St Tropez, followed by the usual partying.

WHERE TO STAY
St Barts has some extremely expensive and sumptuous hotels (none larger than about 60 rooms) to go with its exclusive image. And they are particular in the Caribbean for being set in delightful tropical gardens. Service is usually charged at 10%. There are also many villas to rent on the island; contact **Sibarth**, PO Box 55 Gustavia, 97133 St Barthélemy (tel 590 27 62 38, fax 27 60 52); 6 Rue Jacob, 75006 Paris (tel/fax 331 43 25 95 11); US PO Box 1461 Newport, Rhode Island 02840 (tel 401 849 8012, fax 847 6290).

EXPENSIVE
On the north coast, the **Hotel Manapany**, PO Box 114 (tel 27 66 55, fax 27 75 28) offers the best in Caribbean beach-front luxury. The 52 rooms and suites are located in 32 exquisite cottages, some fronting on to the sand, each with its own large veranda. All have VCR and room service at mealtimes. There are tennis courts and watersports and two restaurants above the pool. Double room US$400–435 in season. And the newest in beachborne sumptuousness can be found at the Hotel **Ile de France** (tel 27 61 81, fax 27 86 83) on the Baie des Flamands on the north coast. The mock-classical main house stands majestically above the sand, with twelve huge rooms, marble floors, English antiques and private jacuzzis in outsize bathrooms. 17 slightly smaller rooms, suites and bungalows across the road in the *latanier* garden, where you will also find the other facilities including the restaurant and sports room. Double rate in season US$365–670. At the end of the beach next door is the well-hip and idiosyncratic **Taïwana** (tel 27 65

01, fax 27 63 82). Difficult to recommend personally because guide-book writers (along

01, fax 27 63 82). Difficult to recommend personally because guide-book writers (along with anyone else they do not like the look of) are unceremoniously booted out, but the place seems to have an easy exclusivity about it. For the (outrageous) price of US$800–1200 a night, you get pretty well anything you want; from helicopter transfer from Sint Maarten to your own private wetbike, relative comfort in one of the nine bungalows, breakfast, a car, probably a couple of famous acquaintances, and of course privacy (from riff-raff). Another new hotel is **Le Toiny** (tel 27 88 88, fax 27 89 30) in the south-east of the island. Just twelve villas make up the resort, overlooking the Anse de Toiny, with views of St Kitts (there is no beach there, but there are pools). The villas are luxuriously decorated in old colonial style—wooden floors, mahogany furniture and four posters—but have all the twentieth century luxuries too, down to the video recorder and satellite TV. Kitchenettes, but also room service and there is a restaurant. Double room US$400, suite US$750. The **François Plantation** (tel 590 27 78 82, fax 27 61 26) stands high on the hillside above Colombier, from where some of the twelve rooms have a magnificent view of the north coast. The estate house has the old-time ambience of the plantation; an antique drawing room and dining room on a breezy terrace, where you will find classic French cuisine—*boeuf au Porto, saumon en papillotte*, with a julienne of vegetables, main course Fr130. The hillside rooms are furnished in dark-stained tropical wood, each with its own terrace. Double room US$350 or $380. Another hip spot, beautifully set in a garden of tropical profusion is **Club la Banane**, in Quartier Lorient (tel 27 68 25, fax 27 68 44). Just nine rooms in suitably eclectic style; antique furniture, colourful tiles and louvres on the windows, all in vaguely complementary colours. The bathrooms are excellent, part outdoor and overgrown with tropical flora. Share a shower with a banana plant. Also well worth going for the show—champagne bottle decorked with a cutlass and thoroughly OTT. Double rate US$300–400.

MODERATE

El Sereno Hotel (tel 27 64 80, fax 27 75 47) is a marginally less expensive resort (relatively speaking anyway), on the beach in Grand Cul de Sac. Comfortable rooms also lost in an explosion of greenery, painted garden walls and each room with a hammock. The gourmet restaurant **La Tocque Lyonnaise** serves French and exotic creole cuisine—*frivolités de saumon fumé* or filet of grouper in a seaweed duxeline, main dish Fr140. Also nine one-bedroom villas. Double room in season US$250–300. Close by is a mid-range beach hotel, the **St Barth Beach Hotel** (tel 27 62 73, fax 27 75 57), 36 rooms in a block above the beach. There is a French and creole restaurant (Le Rivage), but the hotel is best known for windsurfing. Double room US$150 in season. In Gustavia is **L'Hibiscus** (tel 27 64 82, fax 27 73 04) which has a fantastic view of the harbour from its balcony. Inside the open terrace of the main house is the piano bar, with early entertainment in season and the restaurant Le Vieux Clocher. The eleven rooms are set in bungalows on the hillside. Double rate US$200. There are one or two slightly cheaper spots on the island: **La Petite Anse**, PO Box 117 (tel 27 64 60, fax 27 72 30), stands on the clifftop at the end of the Anse des Flamands, where a double room in one of the 16 bungalows will set you back US$100–150, and close by is the Hotel **Baie des Anges**, PO Box 162 (tel 27 63 61, fax 27 83 44), with just nine rooms and kitchenettes overlooking a well-tended garden. Double room US$175–220. **Les Ilets Fleuris** up the hill in Lorient (tel 27 64 22, fax 27 69 72) is away from the sea but has a pool. Set in a tropical garden there are seven studios with kitchenettes for US$100–290. Finally **Le Petit Morne**, PO Box 14 (tel 27 62 64, fax 27 84 63) sits above the sea in Colombier; 14 apartments and a pool overlooking the offshore islands. Double room US$120–135. The only **guest house** on the island is the **Hotel Normandie** (tel 27 62 36) in Lorient, where a double room costs around US$50 in season.

EATING OUT
There are some excellent restaurants in St Barts, from the pretty hotel dining rooms (some recommended above) to the waterfront bistros and converted hilltop homes. The cuisine is sometimes heavyweight classical French, but you will also find concessions to the climate—lighter sauces and exotic ingredients—in *nouvelle cuisine créole*. It is, of course, expensive, but it is all part of the experience. The best hotel dining rooms are mentioned above. There are often set menus and service is *compris*.

EXPENSIVE
The **Wall House** (tel 27 71 83) sits in a glass-fronted modern house on the seaward arm of Gustavia, looking across the harbour from a bright white dining room. *Red snapper filet menuire* in curry and garlic or scallops in a grapefruit sauce, main dish Fr130. Not far off is the **Café Caraïbe** (tel 27 80 34). As well as a fine view of the marina from upstairs, there is a large selection of seafood—*parmentier de crabes aux gambas* (crab and shrimp) with *gratin* potatoes, or local catch in pepper and ginger, Fr150–180 a main dish. Out of town, **La Maison Blanche** has a very pretty setting in a private house on the hillside in Corossol. Tables are in an open, startlingly white dining room, with a view over the pool to the lights of the valley beyond. French cuisine but light—*panaché d'agrumes* (orange and grapefruit) with shrimps, or *magret de canard*. *Nouvelle* presentation, prix fixe, Fr180 or Fr230. **Chez Francine** (tel 27 60 49) is a good beachfront spot in St Jean Bay— seafood and fish. Try *carpaccio de requin* (shark) or *beignets de langouste*, Fr90. Back in town there are a couple of restaurants which are particularly worth visiting for their setting. At **Le Sapotillier** (tel 27 60 28) you eat at tables informally arranged in a walled garden, beneath the branches of a huge sasparilla tree. The menu is mainly French— *poulet fermier à la provençale*, but you might try couscous of scallop and prawn, followed by a fondu of three chocolates (white, milk and dark). Main course Fr100. Closed Sun out of season. And at **L'Ananas** you eat at tables on the breezy verandas or in the rooms of a beautiful, spruced up wooden town house, painted white inside and out. The walls are covered with huge paintings, for sale. Red snapper in passion fruit and ginger and *colombo de gambas*, Fr120 main course.

MODERATE
Cheaper options in town include **Marius and Fanny** (tel 27 66 19), a bistro just across from the waterfront, whose name comes from one of Marcel Pagnol's books (as do the pictures in the simple dining room). Provençal cuisine, or barbecue steak and fish. Prix fixe Fr130 or 160 with wine and pudding. At the **Côte Jardin**, just off rue Gambetta, you eat Italian food on a veranda, settled in canvas deck chairs, pizzas Fr70. If *cuisine créole classique* and *nouvelle* sounds a bit too much, you can always grab some Italian food at **Roland's Bar** on the Rue du Centenaire—juices and vegetable stews (Fr50) and reggae. **Chez Joe** will offer you something a bit more West Indian too; chicken or fish in a local bar for Fr20–50.

247

NIGHTLIFE

St Barts has a low-key attitude to entertainment (one tourism publication even warns that people looking for 'heavy action, glitter and gambling should be sent elsewhere'), but it is there in a few bars and piano lounges around Gustavia and the St Jean area. St Barts' famous names occasionally put in an appearance, but they are more likely to be on the drinks party and dinner circuit.

Hip chicks and tanned windsurfers collect in the garden at **Le Select** in the centre of town, an old warehouse redone in mock-brick. Lively. If you prefer to watch than be watched, then you might retreat across the road to the balcony of the the **Bar de l'Oubli**. You cannot miss the bright green sign of the **Pelican**, a bar and jazz haunt in St Jean—a beachfront terrace outside set with palms at tipsy angles and indoors a lounge with vast wicker armchairs where you recline to listen to the musician of the evening. In town **L'Hibiscus** will also give you a jazz accompaniment to your champagne.

248

The Leeward Islands

Antigua and Barbuda, Montserrat, St Kitts and Nevis, Anguilla

The Leeward Islands lie in the north of the Lesser Antilles, the link in the arc between the Virgin Islands and the mountainous Windwards in the south. They stretch over 150 miles, scattered around the Dutch Windward Islands and the French islands of Saint Barthélemy and Saint Martin.

In the west, Montserrat and the twin islands of St Kitts and Nevis soar from the water in a line, invariably capped in cloud. They are the peaks of extinct volcanoes, the northern extension of the chain of the Windward Islands (see p. 92). They have many of the features of the Windwards—the rainfall and stunning, luxuriant vegetation and the same massive majestic beauty.

Antigua, Barbuda and Anguilla, on the other hand, are coral based, and lie on the eastern lip of the Caribbean crust, pushed up as the Atlantic plate forces its way underneath. Their climates are milder (which is an advantage in the rainy season, when the other islands are often in cloud) and between them these three islands have the Caribbean's finest beaches.

The six islands were British colonies and a hundred years ago they were lumped together for administrative convenience as the Presidency of the Leeward Islands. Today, Anguilla and Montserrat remain British Crown Colonies, but since the early 1980s Antigua and Barbuda and then St Kitts and Nevis have gone their own way.

ANTIGUA and BARBUDA

The graceful and welcoming contours of Antigua inspired Columbus to name the island in honour of a statue of the Virgin in Seville Cathedral, *Santa Maria de la Antigua*. Its rolling yellow-green hills and the sweeping curves of its bays are soft on the eye after the

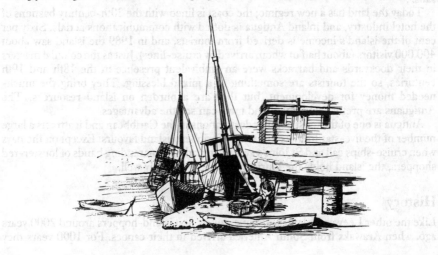

towering volcanic violence of the Windwards. Barbuda, Antigua's smaller sister island 30 miles to the north, is even gentler and more laid-back, not making it above 130 feet.

Antigua (pronounced more as in 'beleaguer' rather than in 'ambiguou(s)'), has a population of 65,000 and is the largest of the Leeward Islands (108 square miles). For years it was the linchpin of British influence in the area—St John's was the seat of government and the principal military and naval fortifications were here. Perhaps this past has given Antigua its feel of stability. The island has an air of confidence as it faces the future, having become fully independent from Britain only in 1981. Professionals who once might have stayed in the United States after their training are now beginning to return.

Antigua's shape has something of a confused amoeba about it, with pseudopodia headed off in every direction. These headlands enclose the bays used so successfully by navies and by smugglers over the centuries. Except for one corner of ancient volcanic outflow in the southwest, the island is entirely made of limestone coral. The Atlantic coast, beaten by the waves over the millennia, looks pitted and scarred like a Neolithic cake-mix, but on the protected shores of the Caribbean side, the gentler wave action on the reefs has pushed up miles of blinding white sand.

Antigua lies lower in the water than its southerly volcanic neighbours and its climate is gentler and drier. The same northeast trade winds blow in from the Atlantic, but Antigua does not collect the rain-clouds that linger above the Windwards. The early settlements were plagued by a lack of water and in 1731 a bucketful of it was even sold for three shillings. This is not to say that Antigua does not experience tropical rainstorms, however, as they can definitely catch you unawares and the proverbial bucketful will soak you in seconds.

For much of its history, Antigua's coastline bristled with forts and the land was covered to the last inch with canefields, dotted occasionally with a windmill and estate house. But now the 160 plantations have gone and their fields have turned into rolling scrubland, where the dilapidated conical shells of the windmills stand silent without their sails.

Today the land has a new regime; the coast is lined with the 20th-century bastions of the hotel industry, and inland Antigua is dotted with communications aerials. Sixty per cent of the island's income is derived from tourists, and in 1989 the island saw about 400,000 visitors (about half of whom arrived by cruise-liner). Just as the colonial masters in their dockyards and barracks were an ambivalent presence in the 18th and 19th centuries, so the tourists are something of a mixed blessing. They bring the much-needed money for development, but they are a burden on island resources. The Antiguans are pretty cool though and most can see the advantages.

Antigua is one of the most popular destinations in the Caribbean and it attracts a large number of the five-star tourists that every Caribbean island favours. Except on the days when cruise-ships call and St John's gets swamped with marauding bands of lobster-red shoppers, the island holds the tourist invasion remarkably well.

History

Like the other Leeward Islands, Antigua saw its first island-hoppers around 2000 years ago, when Arawaks from South America arrived in their canoes. For 1000 years they fished and tended small plots of cassava until their peace was interrupted by the intrusion of the Caribs.

Antigua's first permanent European settlement arrived from nearby St Kitts in the charge of Philip Warner in 1632. Like earlier settlers whose attempts had failed, they were plagued by a lack of water and by the Caribs, occasionally accompanied by the French, who nipped over on raids from the nearby Windwards.

A war of attrition followed, with the colonists determined to exterminate the native Indians. Law No 88 in the old Antiguan Statute Book for 1693 reads *'An Act to encourage the destroying of the Indians and Taking their Periagoes (canoes)'*. It took its course. By 1805, the law was simply marked down as *'Obsolete'*.

Antigua became the archetypal West Indian sugar factory. The technology was introduced by Christopher Codrington from Barbados in 1674, and within a few years every available inch of land was covered with sugar-cane. The cultivation of sugar involved large workforces of slaves and this gave Antigua its population of mainly African descent.

As the Caribbean empires flourished in the 18th century and the wars for territory hotted up, the British chose Antigua as their main military and naval base in the Leeward Islands, creating a link between their other defences in Barbados to the south and in Jamaica in the Greater Antilles. The fortifications at Shirley Heights above English Harbour on the south coast proved so formidable that the French and Spanish navies simply avoided them.

In the 19th century the wars came to an end and the empires crystallized. The abolition movement brought slavery to an end in 1834, but the freed slaves had no choice but to continue working the plantations. There was no other source of employment and although they were free, their situation hardly improved.

As sugar declined in the late 19th century (the price of West Indian cane sugar could not compete with subsidized European beet sugar), Antigua waned and the island became another poor and quiet outcrop in the Caribbean backwater. It was not until this century that things began to pick up again. The latest empire to make itself felt is of course tourism, which Antigua has developed cleverly for 40 years.

A wartime agreement granting the United States bases on the island brought a large influx of Americans during the Second World War, and this put the island on the map. The agreements are still retained and the US Air Force and Navy still have bases in Antigua.

Antiguan politics have a similar heritage to those of other British islands. Trade unions sprang up all over the Caribbean in the 30s and the islanders rallied to them, first as a way to organize political power in the face of colonial rule and later to develop into the movement for self-determination and eventually Independence.

Vere Bird, a President of the Antigua Trades and Labour Union in the 1940s, became the leading light in Antiguan politics, becoming Chief Minister, and later Prime Minister under 'Associated Statehood' in 1967. He became the first leader of independent Antigua and Barbuda on 1st November 1981. He dominates Antiguan politics and his Antigua Labour Party has only spent one term on the opposition benches, between 1971 and 1976.

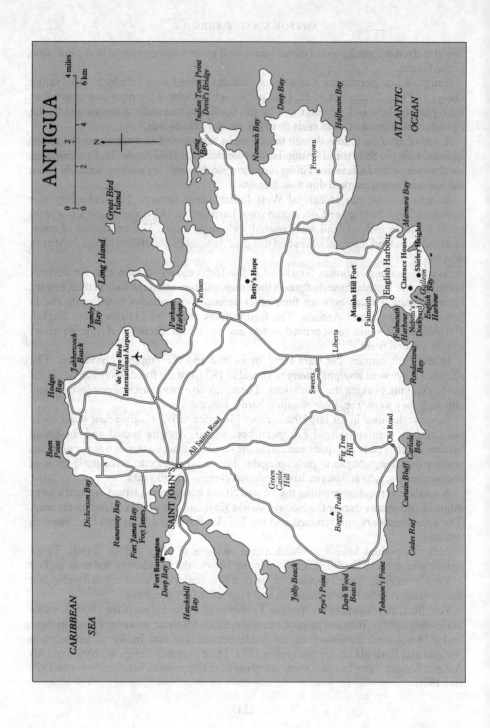

Flora and Fauna

Antiguan gardens are splendid with the bright pinks and purples of hibiscus and bougainvillaea. The closest the island has to rainforest is Fig Tree Hill, where you will see lusher slopes covered in elephant ears and of course fig trees (the local name for the banana). Flitting in its foliage you can find Antigua's two hummingbirds and several doves. On the plains you are bound to see the ever-present mournful cattle egret.

In the coastal ponds (there are many, behind the hotels on Dickenson Bay, in the creeks on the east coast and by Jolly Beach) you will see boobies, terns and sandpipers as well as the ubiquitous pelican. You can also visit the offshore islands, including Great Bird Island, which is particularly known as home to the red-billed tropicbird.

GETTING TO ANTIGUA
The highly developed tourism trade in Antigua means that there are frequent services to the island's Vere Cornwall Bird international airport, four miles northeast of St John's. Whether you are jetting in from Europe for a fortnight, or on a long island-hopping trip around the Caribbean, Antigua is easy to reach. All arrivals must have an onward or return air-ticket.

Departure tax of EC$25 (US$10) is payable except by those who have spent less that 24 hours in the country.

By Air
From Europe: British Airways has four flights each week between London and Antigua. Most of these are non-stop, taking just over eight hours. On other days, there are easy connections at Miami. BWIA also has two weekly flights from London. Lufthansa has two flights each week from Frankfurt.
From the USA: BWIA fly in non-stop from Miami every day and regularly from New York. **American Airlines** have direct and connecting flights from Chicago and Atlanta via San Juan. BWIA also fly from Toronto in Canada, as does **Air Canada**.
From other Caribbean Islands: Antigua is the headquarters of LIAT (tel 462 3142), so there are more flights to and from here on the airline's services than anywhere else. On LIAT and other carriers there are daily direct flights to Barbados, Dominica, Montserrat, Nevis, Guadeloupe, St Kitts, Sint Maarten, San Juan, St Thomas and St Lucia with easy connections to other Caribbean airports. There are three or four daily flights to **Barbuda**. If you need to charter a plane, contact **Carib Aviation** (tel 809 462 3147, fax 462 3125).

By Boat
The Geest Line runs a passenger-carrying cargo service from Barry in South Wales to Antigua approximately weekly. Services from other Caribbean islands are sporadic, though you might persuade a freighter captain to let you aboard for the ride.

GETTING AROUND
The **bus service** in Antigua is scant. It tends to run early in the morning, bringing workers into town from the outlying areas, and it finishes around 6 pm. You will have difficulty finding public transport after dark or on Sundays. There is a fairly regular service (leaving either when the bus is full or when the urge takes the driver) between St John's and **English Harbour** in the southeast of the island. Getting back at night is a

problem, though the All Saint's-St John's run continues until late. Other roads are run less frequently. No buses at all run to the northern tourist area, leaving you dependent on taxis, but a number of the hotels run buses for their workers, so you might be lucky enough to catch a ride with them.

The **East Bus Station**, on Independence Avenue on the outskirts of St John's serves the north and east of the island. Opposite the St John's market is the **West Bus Station**, from which buses leave for villages in the southern part of the island. Travelling on the buses is cheap, and the longest fare across the island costs around EC$3.

There are no buses from the airport to town and the taxi fare is EC$18. Hitch-hiking around the island works adequately. To attract the attention of both car and bus drivers the traditional Caribbean sign is to point rapidly at the ground.

Good tourists, of course, do go by **taxi**, and there is a superabundance of them in St John's and at the airport. They can also be ordered through all the hotels. The government fixes taxi rates and it is worth establishing the price (and currency) before setting off. Many of the taxi-drivers are knowledgeable about Antiguan lore and so you will often get an impromptu tour if you wish. A ride from the airport into St John's costs US$8 and from St John's to Nelson's Dockyard US$35.

Any taxi-driver would be happy to take you on a more formal tour of the island, which can cover many of the island sights. A half-day tour costs around US$45. Companies offering tours include: **Antours** (tel 462 4788) and **Bryson's Travel** (tel 462 0223). **Tropikelly Tours** (tel 461 0383) offers off-road tours in 4-wheel drive vehicles.

Hiring a car is probably the best way to get around the island, and there are plenty of rental firms. Drivers must obtain a Temporary Permit, available on presentation of a valid driving licence and payment of US$12. This can be dealt with by the rental company.

If you are driving out into the country take a reasonable map because there are few roadsigns. The roads are not brilliant (the 40-mile-an-hour speed limit is quite appropriate), and driving is on the left. If you wish to go off the main roads it is advisable to get hold of a four-wheel drive car, of which there are plenty for hire. The price of a day's hire starts at US$45.

Car rental companies, which work out of St John's and often from the airport include: **Carib Car Rentals**, PO Box 1258 (tel 462 2062), **National**, PO Box 405, All Saints Road, St John's (tel 462 2113), **Dollar Rent-a-Car** (tel 462 0362), and **Matthew's Car Rental**, PO Box 926, Sutherlands, St John's (tel 461 1776). You can rent a bicycle through **Sun Cycles** (tel 461 0324).

TOURIST INFORMATION
The **Antigua and Barbuda Tourist Board** has offices in:
UK: 15 Thayer St, London W1M 5LD (tel (071) 486 7073, fax 486 9970).
USA: 610 Fifth Ave, Suite 311, New York, NY 10020 (tel (212) 541 4117). Also 121 SE 1st St, Suites 508–9, Miami, Florida (tel 3–5 381 6762) and 3400 International Drive NW, Suite 4M, Washington DC 20008 (tel 202 362 5122).
Canada: 60 St Clair Ave East, Suite 205, Toronto, Ontario MT4 1N5 (tel (416) 961 3085).
Germany: Postfach 1147, Minnholzweg 2, 6242 Kronberg 1 (tel 06173 7091).

On Antigua itself, the main office is at the corner of Thames St and the High Street in the centre of St John's, PO Box 363 (tel 462 0480/462 0029, fax 462 2483). Downstairs there is an information office with helpful staff. There is also an office at the airport. The Tourist Board puts out the publication *Antigua and Barbuda Adventure*, a twice-yearly glossy magazine with articles and lists of restaurants and boutiques to help you deal with a shopping crisis.

In a medical **emergency**, there is a 24-hour casualty room at the St John's hospital, on Hospital Road (tel 462 0251). The **IDD code** for Antigua is 809 followed by a seven figure local number. On-island, dial the seven digits.

MONEY

Antigua and Barbuda share their currency, the Eastern Caribbean dollar, with the other countries in the OECS (Organisation of Eastern Caribbean States), from Anguilla in the north down to Grenada in the south. The EC$ is linked to the US$, at a rate of US$1 = EC$2.69. US dollars are accepted everywhere on the island, though change will sometimes be given in EC$. Credit cards are also widely accepted by hotels, restaurants and shops and as security for car hire. Though confusion rarely arises, it is a good rule to establish which currency you are dealing in.

Life in Antigua can be quite expensive. Not only do most necessities have to be imported, but the government imposes no income tax, preferring instead to raise taxes through sales of food and goods. Even in the markets, where fruit and vegetables might be relatively cheap, prices can be quite high.

Banking hours are 8 am–2 pm on weekdays with an extra two hours on Fridays, 3–5 pm. Exchange can always be made at the larger hotels, but the rate will not be as good. **Shops** tend to be open daily except Sundays between 8.30 am and 4 or 5 pm, with an hour off between noon and 1 pm. They will often stay open later when a cruise ship is in dock.

Antigua has a number of **galleries** in which you will see the works of Caribbean painters as well as arts and crafts. **Seahorse Studios** are located in Redcliffe Quay and you will find originals and reproduction prints and jewellery. **Harmony Hall** is difficult to find on the east coast at Brown's Bay, but there too you will find arts and craft from all over the Caribbean (Harmony Hall has a sister property in Jamaica). Haitian buses and colourful work with calabashes and baskets. It is good for a daytime visit; there is a restaurant and a bar in the old windmill.

FURTHER READING

Antigua was lucky in the English wife of a planter, a Mrs Lanaghan, who wrote her *Antigua and the Antiguans* in 1844, describing the island and the customs of its people.

A 20th-century Antiguan writer who now lives in the States is Jamaica Kincaid, author of *Annie John*, a disturbing book about a childhood on the island.

There are also one or two informative booklets that describe the historic sights of the island. *The Romance of English Harbour* deals with Nelson's Dockyard and *Shirley Heights* by Charles Jane tells the story of Shirley Heights and its defence of the island.

BEACHES

Between them, Antigua and Barbuda have some of the loveliest beaches in the Caribbean. Time was, not so long ago, that Antiguan families would simply move on if anyone

255

was already on their favourite beach when they arrived for the Sunday picnic. Now they are a little more crowded, but in fact, if you go off the beaten track, you are very likely to be alone.

There is something for every taste, and for once the tourist brochures claim is correct: you can walk alone on a mile-wide scalloped bay of silken sand, where coconut palms bend and brush the beach and the waves fizz around your toes; or you can cut a windsurfing dash on crowded strands where the body-beautiful roam. In some places, though, the sandflies do bite and mosquitoes dive-bomb you as you doze and so you might have to evacuate in late afternoon. Take some repellent if you go off the beaten track.

If you like an active beach, then your best bet is Dickenson Bay on the west coast north of St John's, where a clutch of hotels is situated. Superb sand and all the watersports and posing you will ever want; also plenty of watering holes to retire to. It extends into **Runaway Bay** to the south, which is also active and has lovely sand. **Fort James Bay** beach just to the south (closer to St John's) is popular with the Antiguans at the weekend, but tends to be uncrowded in the week.

There are a number of other beaches on the west coast and they become steadily more deserted as you go south. The **Hawksbill Bay** area has some small strips of sand. The farthest from the hotel is a nudist beach. Past the ever popular **Jolly Beach** (also called Lignum vitae after the wood) you come to some of the deserted, mile-long strips with fantastic sand: **Ffrye's Bay**, the palm-backed **Dark Wood Beach** and **Johnson's Point**.

On the south coast in **Carlisle Bay**, where the Curtain Bluff hotel stands, the waves splay in fans on the steep sand and there are reefs to explore. The rest of the south coast is indented with bays and you will find half-moon coves of soft and mounded sand, for instance, at **Mamora Bay** where the St James's Club is situated. On English Harbour, a water-taxi-ride from Nelson's Dockyard, is **Galleon Bay**, and nearby on Falmouth Harbour are one or two good strips of sand.

On the east coast, where the weather is a bit rougher, there are one or two protected spots such as **Half Moon Bay** and **Long Bay**. For those who would prefer to tame the Atlantic weather, the east coast is the best place for **windsurfing** and a couple of recommended places are **Jabberwock Beach** on the northeastern shore (you can hire equipment at the Beach Hotel) and **Hodges Bay** around the corner to the north.

In between these main beaches are any number of small coves where you can be alone. Ask an Antiguan.

BEACH BARS

There are a string of bars to retreat to on Dickenson Bay. Among them **Spinnakers** is popular, where there is usually a band playing in the afternoon. For something a little more secluded, head down to Fort James Bay, where there are a couple of bars right on the sand, including **Russell's Beach Bar**. The beach is only busy at the weekends, when the Antiguans themselves come here. On the endless strands of the southwest you will find the **Darkwood Beach Bar**, good for a beer and a view of the sunset. Finally there are all the nautical bars in Nelson's Dockyard, which collect an amusing crowd of yachtsmen, looking for a brawl, as they have for a couple of centuries.

WATERSPORTS

Antigua caters well for sport-minded people. It is particularly good for sailing, but like the other coral islands it has some extremely fine reefs, so snorkelling and diving are a great pleasure.

Antigua's sailing is centred around the traditional naval harbour sites on the south coast, and yachts of all sizes can be hired there; crewed or bareboats, for days, a week, or longer. Contact **Nicholson Yacht Charters** at English Harbour (tel 662 6066) and the **Catamaran Hotel Marina**, PO Box 958 (tel 460 1036, fax 460 1506) on Falmouth Harbour (tel 463 1036). There is a marina at Parham, east of St John's, where **Wadadli Watersports** (tel 462 2890) operate. The **Antigua School of Sailing** (tel 462 2026), also based in Parham, offers sailing instruction.

Antigua stages one of the major regattas in the Caribbean sailing year. **Race Week**, or Antigua Sailing Week, is held at the end of the winter season, before all the yachts take off across the Atlantic to spend the summer in the Mediterranean. It attracts sailors from everywhere, and so for two weeks around the actual event the Antiguan waters are busy with craft of all sorts. There are five major races, each with a number of different classes, all followed by another fleet of sails along for the ride. Many of the races skirt the island and so Antigua's hills offer a fantastic view of the proceedings if you would prefer a land-based vantage-point. But the races seem to be just an excuse for what the Caribbean does best, which is to mix a rum punch and get everyone to *jump-up* afterwards. There are plenty of silly races and wet T-shirt competitions for non-sailors and the week winds up with the Lord Nelson's Ball, a formal affair (for the Caribbean anyway) and prize-giving.

In the following week is the **Classic Yacht Regatta** which brings together yachts passed by the committee as of 'classic design', many of them fantastically beautiful yachts with long-forgotten configurations of sails (3 races). Contact the Classic Yacht Regatta (tel 809 460 1093, fax 460 1542).

Small craft such as sunfish and hobie cats are easily available, and can be hired out on Dickenson Bay or elsewhere through the larger hotels, for a small charge and a refundable deposit. In high season, hotel guests might have priority, but a chat with the concessionaire on the beach should fix it.

Windsurfing can also be fixed up there, or on the east coast of the island. You might try **Windsurfing Lord Nelson** (tel 463 3094), F2 boards, intermediate to advanced. **Waterskiing** is best arranged on Dickenson Bay beach, as is **parasailing** if you want a bird's-eye view of the tanning bodies.

Trips out into the ocean can be arranged for those who would like to go **deep-sea fishing** to cast for marlin and tuna. It can be fixed up through most of the large hotels, or on 463 2113. Also the catamaran marina in Falmouth (tel 460 1506). Full day on *La Giaconda* US$800.

If you want a rum-soaked voyage of walking the plank to the all-Caribbean tourist classic *Yellowbird*, then Antigua has a whole fleet of pleasure vessels. The red sails of the *Jolly Roger* (tel 462 2064) are the most familiar, but you might also try the catamaran *Sagitoo* (tel 460 1244) or *Bucanero* (tel 464 8587) a schooner from the last century. There are many tours to the offshore islands—Prickly Pear, Green Island and Bird Island—for a day's snorkelling and a picnic. You can even get a historical cruise in Antigua. **Shorty's** glass bottom boat (tel 462 2393) works out of Dickenson Bay.

Snorkelling is good in many places around the island and equipment can be borrowed from most hotels. There are reefs on all sides of Antigua, which offer excellent marine life for diving, down to 70 feet. Some good reefs are: Cades Reef, a two-mile protected reef off the south coast, and nearby Farley Bay and Rendezvous Bay, and at Boon Point, the northernmost tip of Antigua. The reefs have also claimed quite a few ships over the years and so there are plenty of wrecks to dive. You will see sergeant majors and parrot fish and larger fish-like rays and the occasional dolphin.

Dives can be arranged through Dive Antigua (tel 462 3483) on Dickenson Bay and Dive Runaway (tel 462 2626) on Runaway Bay. Dockyard Divers (tel 460 1058) operate from the Copper and Lumber Store in Nelson's Dockyard and cover the reefs and wrecks on the southern coast. Instruction is available at the above places and a one-tank dive costs around US$45.

On land, sports include golf at the 18-hole Cedar Valley Golf Club (tel 462 0161), which is found to the northeast of St John's. There is a nine-hole course just near the Half Moon Bay Hotel in the east of Antigua (tel 460 4300).

Riding through Antigua's rolling dry hills or along the beaches can be arranged with the Wadadli Stables (tel 461 2721).

Fortress Foraging

In the 18th century, Antigua's coastline bristled with forts and fortlets, many of which still exist, though they are mostly buried in 15 feet of scrub. Aficionados and fort boffins will enjoy rootling around the remains, and of course they still have the fantastic views for which they were built in the first place.

Fort James (early 18th century) and Fort Barrington guard the entrance to St John's harbour. Fort Barrington, on the south side, has a plaque commemorating William Burt, the Governor in whose tenure it was built. On it he signs himself *Imperator and Gubernator insularum Carib* (Emperor and Governor of the Leeward Islands). This Governor had some difficulties with the islanders, especially after drawing his sword at dinner and attacking some imaginary intruders supposedly lurking behind his chair.

Johnson Point Fort is at the southwestern corner of the island. Farther east, as you pass through Falmouth, Monks Hill Fort (as it is known to most Antiguans, though its name was officially Great George Fort) looms up on the hill. Built in the 17th century, it was a refuge for the women, children, slaves and cattle in case of attack by the French and their Carib allies. The track to the fort turns off the main road at the village of Liberta, and is only passable by four-wheel drive vehicles.

Fort Berkeley, a short walk beyond Nelson's Dockyard, was built in 1744 to guard the entrance to English Harbour. Its soldiers would haul up a chain boom if an invasion was threatened. Above Fort Berkeley the ground is crawling with earthworks and gun emplacements.

One of the oldest plantations on the island, Betty's Hope, is off the main road to Indian Town Point on the east coast. The estate house has gone, but the twin cones of the sugar works and several outhouses, including the boiling house, have survived.

258

St John's

Antigua's capital, St John's, stands on gently sloping ground above a large bay. The central streets are laid out on a grid-iron plan and although some are now being taken over by strips of concrete modernity, many of the older wood and stone buildings with overhanging balconies are still there, much as they were a century ago.

Over a third of Antiguans live in or around St John's, and the town is showing the fruits of the island's prosperity with shops full of computers and clothes from all over the world. But a more traditional West Indian life can be seen just a few minutes' walk out of the centre of the town, where fishermen make lobster pots or mend their nets in the boatyard.

Many visitors arrive in Antigua by the harbour, passing beneath the two defensive outposts at Fort Barrington and Fort James at the mouth of the bay. First steps ashore will lead into the airco environment of a duty-free shopping arcade, **Heritage Quay**, but the life of St John's is not far beyond.

Just close by, a stroll along the boardwalk is **Redcliffe Quay**, an area of old St John's, townhouses and warehouses with stone foundations and clapboard uppers, that has been restored. It is also a shopping complex, but worth a detour for its cafés and restaurants even if you're not on the hunt for a bargain.

Towering above the town's activity from its stately position at the top of the rising ground are the twin grey towers of the **Cathedral of St John the Divine**. The octagonal structure was erected in 1845 after one of Antigua's relatively frequent earthquakes, and to prevent similar damage the interior has been completely lined with pine. The two life-size statues that stand at the gates of the Cathedral, St John the Baptist and St John the Evangelist, were destined for French Dominica in the 18th century, but they were captured by a British warship and brought to Antigua.

The **Old Court House**, on the corner of Long St and Market St, dates from 1747, though it has been rebuilt a number of times, most recently after the earthquake in 1974. Now it is home to the National Archives and the **Museum of Antigua and Barbuda**, and houses an exhibition of Amerindian Antigua (known to them as *Wadadli*), with *zemies* from the 100 archaeological sites on the island, as well as Antiguan colonial memorabilia. The Museum opens weekdays, 8.30–4 and Sat 10–2, adm free (tel 462 1469).

A walk through downtown St John's will take you to the Market, an enclave of traditional West Indian mayhem, where the banter seems as much a part of the game as buying the local fruit and vegetables on display.

Since Antigua began to host West Indian Cricket Test Matches in 1981 the venue has been the stadium up above the Cathedral. In 1736 this area was used as an execution ground following a slave rebellion. The ringleader Prince Klaas and four others were broken on the wheel (a punishment where the victim was strapped to a cartwheel and his bones broken one by one), six were 'put out to dry' (hung in chains and starved) and 58 were burned at the stake. The Antiguans now enjoy watching the similar roastings meted out to visiting cricket teams. If there is a game on while you are in town, go to it.

259

The Northern Coastline

The area north of St John's is the most developed in the island, both by the tourist industry, which has built hotels on the beaches at Runaway Bay and Dickenson Bay, and by prosperous Antiguans who have moved out of town to live in large villas set in hibiscus and bougainvillaea gardens.

At the eastern side of the northern coast is **Long Island**, a low island lying a few hundred yards offshore, once used for grazing cattle and sugar cultivation. Now home to the Jumby Bay Hotel, it was traditionally famed for exporting far more sugar than it could possibly produce, all illegally shipped in from Guadeloupe. Having sworn in seven hogsheads for export before the magistrate, the owner would promptly add the letters 'ty' and ship out that amount to eager British markets.

The main road passes the Vere Bird International Airport and beneath hills littered with windmill shells and modern communications aerials before returning to St John's.

East of St John's

Travelling due east from the capital on the Old Parham Road you pass through lowlands that once were covered with canefields. A turn left leads to the old town of Parham, one of the first settlements and oldest harbours on the island. The few remaining old buildings are now surrounded by small clapboard houses set among the palm trees.

The main road proceeds to the east coast which has been buffeted and carved into limestone brittle over the millennia by the Atlantic's wave action. The coastline gives some cracking views. The much vaunted **Devil's Bridge** is a natural span cut out of the rock at Indian Town Point. On a rough day the area is spectacular as the full force of the ocean thrashes against the coral coastline and bursts up through blowholes.

But Antigua's coastline has many indentations here, creating deep and well protected bays, and just around the corner from all the spray are beaches tucked in the coves, as at Long Bay. At **Nonsuch Bay** there is no beach, but the cove is popular with yachtsmen as a sheltered harbour.

Just farther south, the village of **Freetown** was settled soon after Emancipation in 1834. The liberated slaves formed their own villages away from the plantations, often in remote areas such as this where they could settle on unused land.

St John's to English Harbour

If St John's was the administrative centre of the Leeward Islands, the British Navy maintained its rule of the Caribbean waves (often successfully) from the southeast of the island, at what is now English Harbour. The All Saints road leads south out of St John's past the market through the centre of the island, rolling scrubland dotted occasionally with the cone of a windmill.

The secluded cove of English Harbour is now considered one of the prettiest and most picturesque spots in the Caribbean, but 200 years ago the West Indies was a hardship posting, and one visitor considered Antigua 'one of the most infernal places on the face of the globe'. On his first visit, the future Admiral Nelson thought of Antigua as a 'barbarous island' and the dockyard now bearing his name as a 'vile spot'.

260

Nelson's Dockyard

Set on a point deep in the tortuous recesses of English Harbour, Nelson's Dockyard is a conglomeration of restored stone warehouses, workshops and quarters that once made up an 18th-century naval station. Were it not for the flowery tropical shirts on the tourists you might hear the whistles and drum-rolls of an active barracks. The waters are still plied by sailing craft, and it is a sight to watch the yachts manoeuvring between the headlands and making for open water much as they did 200 years ago.

You approach the dockyard on the road that skirts the eastern edge of Falmouth Harbour. At the entrance, once guarded to deter intruders, you will be waylaid by the inevitable T-shirt sentry. Once inside, the charm of the place takes over. The quarters, with gently sloping roofs that reach out and shade balconies, have all been repaired, as have the old sail-loft and workshops. Cannon and the odd anchor stand proud in mock activity and the boathouse pillars and sprays of tropical flowers give an air of groomed antiquity.

The dockyard was abandoned by the Navy in 1889 and fell into disrepair, but was restored by the Society of the Friends of English Harbour and re-opened in 1961 as Nelson's Dockyard.

Even if it has his name, Nelson himself certainly had no love for the place. He was based here for three years, as the young captain of *HMS Boreas*, between 1784 and 1787. He cruised the Leewards for much of the time, but during the hurricane season, when the French fleet was not in the area, he spent time in the dockyard, jokingly threatening to hang himself.

He fell out with the islanders by enforcing the Navigation Act, which made their profitable trade with American ships illegal (he had to stay on board his ship for eight weeks to avoid arrest when they took him to court). It was a pretty miserable time, though he found some solace in his marriage to Fanny Nesbit, a young widow from the nearby island of Nevis. He was happy to leave the Caribbean and did not return except briefly in 1805, hot on the tail of Villeneuve and the French fleet, in a chase of thousands of miles that culminated in the Battle of Trafalgar.

The dockyard is a bit of tourist trap, with hotels, bars and restaurants, and so you can expect to see a few blistering red package-holiday conscripts press-ganged on to tour-bus lunches. However, with all the yachts, the place also retains a nautical air and there are always a few latterday sailors loitering on shore for a few days, looking for grog and a brawl like their predecessors. There is a small **museum** in the Admiral's House, where you will see maquettes of naval ships, uniforms and buttons from the era of empire.

On the opposite shore from the dockyard, **Clarence House** stands on the hill. This Georgian-style house was built in 1787 for Prince William Henry, later to be King William IV, who was in command of *HMS Pegasus* stationed at Antigua. He was a friend of Nelson and gave away Fanny Nesbit at their marriage. Today Clarence House is the official residence of the Antiguan Governor General, though it is not often occupied. It is open to the public when he is not in residence (tel 463 1026).

Scattered all over the heights above English Harbour is the garrison of **Shirley Heights**. This is another extended family of barracks with arched walkways, batteries, cisterns and magazines. It was fortified in the 1780s by General Shirley, the Governor of the Leeward Islands from 1781 to 1791, in order to defend the harbour below, but since

261

THE CARIBBEAN

its abandonment in 1856 it has fallen into ruin. One or two buildings have been repaired, creating a visitors' centre as you enter the area and a restaurant at **Fort Shirley** itself. The fortifications were situated here because of their uninterrupted view across to Guadeloupe, giving advanced warning of any impending French invasion, which means that the view is exhilarating. Once the fortress was constructed, the French never considered invading again, of course.

The Southwest

Many of Antigua's fine beaches are on the west coast south of St John's and these include Deep Bay, Hawksbill Beach and Darkwood Bay. Inland is **Green Castle Hill**, where there are some odd rock formations that have come to be known in tourist lore as the megaliths, supposedly used by the Caribs as a sort of shrine. The view is particularly good from the top of the hill.

The road emerges on the sea and skirts the coastline for several miles, in the lee of the Shekerley mountains, Antigua's biggest hills. The tallest among them is the 1319 ft **Boggy Peak**, from which the view extends to Guadeloupe in the south and as far as St Kitts to the north on a clear day. It is also possible to see Barbuda, Antigua's sister island. To reach it you must take the steep road inland from Cades Bay on the south coast. The coastal road is a pleasant drive, through an undeveloped part of the island, where you can see the cultivation of the black pineapple, a small and succulent variety that Antigua exports.

At Carlisle Bay and the town of Old Road (from the old word 'roadstead' meaning harbour), the coastal road cuts inland into the island's lushest and most attractive area. At the village of **Swetes**, the road leads on towards English Harbour or makes a turn north back towards St John's.

CARNIVAL

For ten days or so in late July the carnival competitions wind up to the finals: Calypso King and Carnival Queen (Antigua also stages the Caribbean Queen competition which brings contestants from all over the area), steel bands (if you hear them practising, then just wander in) and junior competitions. The traditional *j'ouvert* (pronounced jouvé) takes place on the morning of the first Monday in August, and then the streets will pulse to the carnival parades.

WHERE TO STAY

Antigua has a host of fine resort hotels, tucked away in their own coves along the tortuous coastline. Many of them are extremely expensive retreats, ideal for the luxurious seclusion that the Caribbean does so well, and one or two sit in splendour in the historical setting of English Harbour. Some of the smartest hotels have shunned 'mod cons' like the television and air-conditioning, but most offer watersports, including snorkelling and diving. With echoes of a British heritage in Antigua, you might be expected to wear a jacket and even a tie at dinner, but where else could you be served afternoon tea in a hammock? The Antiguan government imposes a 7% tax and all bills will be supplemented with a 10% service charge.

EXPENSIVE
Perhaps Antigua's finest hotel is **Curtain Bluff**, PO Box 288 (tel 462 8400, fax 462

262

8409) on the south coast, where a glance at the beach from the cliff shows the scallop patterns on the sand created by the waves. This hotel is stately, and with just 60 suites and rooms scattered on the small promontory overlooking the two beaches, it has the air of a club. Fans whip round the sea air in preference to air-conditioning here and you can expect no intrusions from satellite TV, unless you particularly want it. The restaurant has an extremely fine wine list, and a jacket and tie are required for dinner. The hotel closes during the summer months and at US$500–800 for a double room in the high season (including meals), the rates are very expensive. Another stately resort with the air of a civilized country club is **Jumby Bay**, PO Box 243 (tel 462 6000, fax ext 144) on its own island a couple of miles off the northern coast. Once it was Long Island and did a good trade in smuggling sugar and as an extended cattle ranch, but now it is called Jumby Bay after the island's beach, itself called after a Caribbean word for 'ghost'. Roofed with Spanish terracotta tiles, sumptuous villas and rooms are dotted around the island, most within a half minute's walk of the vast strip of sand as well as the restaurants and bars. Any farther and you may wish to use bikes, which are provided in plenty. The ferry crosses from the dock near the Beachcomber Hotel, north of the airport on Antigua, about once an hour. For now, Jumby Bay has just 38 rooms and eight villas, but big development plans are in the air, and these will inevitably affect the atmosphere of seclusion. US$895 and above for a couple, with all meals included. A hotel with a difference is the **Galley Bay**, PO Box 305, St John's (tel 462 0302, fax 462 1187, US 800 223 6510), lying between a magnificent cove and a lagoon on the west coast. It is entirely unlike the factory hotels of the 1980s, and consists of individual cabins dotted around a park beneath a screen of palms, cottages overlooking the beach and palm-thatch cabins 'à la Gauguin' on the lagoon. *Berbice* planters' chairs (with extendable arms to support outstretched legs) for admiring the sunset, no phone or TV; fans chop the still evening air. A double room in the winter season costs US$300–400. The **Hawksbill Beach Resort** (tel 462 1515) takes its name from the oddly-shaped rock off one of its four beaches, looking like the bill of a Hawksbill turtle rising from the water (alternatively a frog with a crown). From an old plantation house and windmill on a promontory the 88 rooms and 40 cottages are strung out along the waterfront, where the palm trees burst in an explosion of scratchy fronds. Most watersports are available and winter rates are US$300 for a double room and $360 for a cottage on the beachfront. The **Long Bay Hotel**, PO Box 442 (tel 463 2005, fax 463 2439), is tucked into a typically secluded Antiguan cove on the eastern shore of the island, overlooking a lagoon one side and a pretty beach on the other. Family-run, it has just 20 rooms in a block and five cottages without phones or TV. Little known, it is ideal as a quiet retreat for tired execs, as you can tell by the magazines and books. Watersports—windsurfing, snorkelling and scuba—if you're feeling active. Winter rates vary between US$320 and 350. For a relaxed hotel on the sands of Dickenson Bay, you might try the **Siboney Beach Club** (tel 462 0806), where the garden threatens to take over. It has just 12 suites and a lively bar looking over the beach. Winter rates for a couple are US$200–300 per night.

If you would like to stay within the old English Harbour area, there are some good hotels, two of them in restored barrack buildings, the sail-lofts now converted into rooms. The **Copper and Lumber Store**, PO Box 184 (tel 460 1058, fax 460 1529), has been historically re-appointed with a Georgian dining-room, rum puncheons in the courtyard, and rooms and suites named *Hardy*, *Dreadnought* and even *Victory* . . . It is well

THE CARIBBEAN

restored and attractive, and does have an air of the 18th century in the brick arches, ship beams and stained wood staircases. Suites and rooms vary in price between US$160 and $300 per night. An aloof view of all this activity can be had from **The Inn at English Harbour**, PO Box 187 (tel 463 1014, fax 460 1603, US 800 223 6510), of which the main house commands the heights and has a fine view of the yachts manoeuvring into harbour as they have for centuries. The six cottages are dotted over the forested hillside and 22 rooms stand in a block on the beach, just a short trip by boat from the Dockyard. A double room in winter costs US$325–400, with good prices in summer.

MODERATE
It is possible to stay in Antigua without making a visit to the IMF beforehand, though very cheap beachside accommodation is hard to find. The **Admiral's Inn**, PO Box 713 (tel 463 1534, fax 460 1534), stands next to the odd pillars that once supported the boat-house near the entrance to English Harbour. The Inn has the same worn bricks that were shipped out as ballast and the dark wooden beams, but this is perhaps less the officers' accommodation and more the able seamen's—you could find yourself in the sail-loft. Still, you will not have to share a bathroom with 50 others and atmosphere is friendly, with a tar's tale or two told in the bar. Double room US$95–115 in season. One reasonable spot is the windsurfing hotel on the northeast coast, the **Lord Nelson Beach Hotel**, PO Box 155 (tel 462 3094, fax 462 0751), where the atmosphere is youthful and the 20 rooms simple, but they cost around US$100 per night. You could also try the **Catamaran Hotel**, PO Box 958 (tel 460 1036, fax 460 1506, US 800 223 6510), with just eight rooms right on Falmouth Harbour. It is set in a modern block with mock-classical pillars; comfortable rooms, some kitchenettes, beach passable, watersports on offer. Double room US$65–120 a night. Alternatively, look to the businessmen's hotels in town, where the **Barrymore Hotel** (tel 462 4062) offers rooms and a pool for US$85–100 per night. It is a short ride to Dickenson Bay, the island's main sporting beach. A town hotel with real Caribbean style is the **Spanish Main Inn** (tel 462 0660), set in an old wooden Antiguan house with creaking floorboards. There are just a few rooms with ceiling fans and private baths. Double rate US$45–60 in season.

CHEAP
Really cheap rooms can only be found in town and the area to head for is south of Heritage Quay, beyond the market. The **Montgomery Hotel** on Tindale Road (tel 462 2793) and **Miami Hotel**, Market Street (tel 462 0975), will offer a different side of Antiguan life for under US$25 for a double. There are some guest houses that can be contacted through the Tourist Board.

EATING OUT
Local Antiguan food is quite similar to that of other British West Indian islands, hardly auspicious, but a good mix of fresh fish and traditional Caribbean ground provisions. However it is fun to get out to the local (and tourist) haunts. And if you want an intimate evening out there are some good restaurants and hotel dining rooms, some with high quality (and expensive) continental fare. Restaurants add a service charge of 10% and there is a 7% sales tax on top too. They get quite busy in the winter, so it is worth making a reservation.

264

EXPENSIVE
Chez Pascal (tel 462 3232) is on Cross St in St John's and you dine in the breezy interior of a classic Caribbean town-house. Pascal serves French cuisine while using Caribbean ingredients, including the many ground provisions to their best advantage. Start with a pumpkin soup and home made-bread and follow with roast rack of lamb or grilled local catch à la creole, main course US$15–25. The **Ginger House Brasserie** (tel 462 2317) has a similar sophisticated ambience, set in one of the restored buildings of Redcliffe Quay. Salad lunches outside are popular and in the evening you retreat to the plush air-conditioned comfort of the main dining room where you will be served French creole fare—lobster bisque soup followed by a spicy *court-bouillon* of local catch, main course US$12–20. On Long St you will find the **Lemon Tree** (tel 462 1969), with a large and lively dining room upstairs, where there is often a piano player. A long menu, served both at lunch and dinner—from burgers and pastas to delicate shrimp in lemon butter sauce. Main course about US$8–20.

MODERATE AND CHEAP
There are a number of smaller, more local restaurants in St John's, good places to stop for lunch and to gather for a drink at the end of the day. **Calypso** (tel 462 1965) is on Upper Redcliffe St and has tables scattered around a courtyard garden. Mostly local fare, or a burger if you want it, closed Sun, main course US$7–12. **Brother B's** (tel 462 0616) is similar in style and stays open for dinner as well. You will find it in a courtyard on Long St and Soul Alley. **Hemingways** on St Mary's St has a charming veranda setting in an old gingerbread town house. Cool drinks and burgers, US$5–10. **Darcy's,** also on St Mary's St, is more local and you can grab a fungi with curry mutton or goat. Just out of town on the All Saints Road you will find **The Dolphin** (tel 462 1183), set in a small gingerbread house. Popular with the Antiguans, it offers classic Antiguan fare—fritters and pumpkin soup followed by local fish or perhaps a pepperpot. Closed for lunch at the weekends.

There is a also a clutch of restaurants around **English Harbour** in the southeastern corner of the island. At **La Perruche** (tel 460 3040) you dine on a cool terrace grappled with greenery. The fare is French and West Indian—local fish in a creole sauce with a volley of ground provisions, followed by tropical fruit ice creams. **Expensive** at US$15–30 for a main cours. **Le Cap Horn** (tel 460 1194) is also set on a pretty, open veranda, where you dine by candlelight—French and Argentinian cuisine, including huge churrasco steaks. Main course US$10–25. **Nations** is a much lower-key spot, a small shack with its own garden, where some of the food is grown. Chicken or fish (the menu depends on what has been landed that afternoon) in a coconut sauce and a number of exotic fruit juices. **Pizza Mac** is also a popular spot with the locals. In the Dockyard itself you will find a good crowd at **Abracadabra**, where there is often live music. The fare is Italian and so you get home-made pastas and pizzas. Farther east you will find another good restaurant that livens up in the evenings. **Albertos** (tel 460 3007) is in Willoughby Bay and also serves Italian cuisine along with some local fare—you will get an excellent grilled snapper with lemon and a tonnage of rice 'n peas. Sometimes dancing. Main course US$10.

BARS AND NIGHTLIFE
There are a string of excellent bars in English Harbour. In Nelson's Dockyard itself you will find the **Galley** on the waterfront, which has a happy hour in the early evening. You might try *twofers* (two for one) at the Copper and Lumber Store on a Tuesday and a popular place to move on to is **G & T's** at the Antigua Yacht Club in Falmouth. The **Shirley Heights Lookout** is something of an island institution on a Sunday afternoon when a band plays in the sunset high above English Harbour. A riotous crowd by the early evening.

There is a circuit of shows that perform in the hotels: steel bands and the usual limbo dancers. Discotheques include **Tropix**, an airco hang-out downtown at Redcliffe Quay, St John's.

There are three **casinos** on the island, where there are slot machines and betting tables open until four in the morning: **King's Casino** at Heritage Quay in St John's, the **Royal Antiguan** and the **St James' Club**.

BARBUDA

Barbuda's great attractions are its marine life and its beaches, which are measured in miles and where it is difficult not to be alone. The reefs are forested with corals that move gently with the water and teem with fluorescent fish. The sand on Barbuda is supreme. There is so much sand that they even export it.

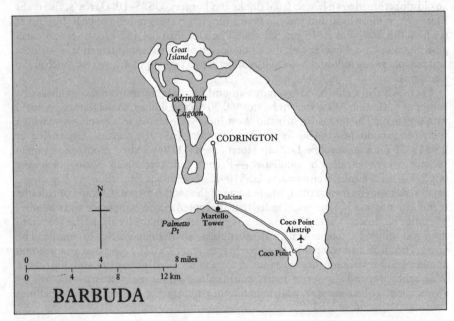

The island is 60 square miles of scrubland that barely clears the water, lying about 30 miles north of Antigua. It is made entirely of limestone coral deposits that have encrusted an outcrop on the same geological bank as Antigua. The contours of *Dulcina*, as the island was known to the Spaniards, are even gentler than Antigua's and the pace of life considerably slower. The Highlands, in the north of the island, struggle to top 130 feet.

Caribs prevented early settlement of the island, but when they were wiped out, Christopher Codrington leased the whole island as a private estate, paying rent to the Crown of 'one fat sheep, if demanded'. It stayed within his family from 1674 until about 1870 and, because the soil was not fertile enough to support sugar-cane, it was used as a ranch for stock and work animals, a farm for provisions, a deer-park and eventually a cotton plantation. Many of the animals are still seen wandering about much as they always have, and the ubiquitous Caribbean goat gets everywhere. There are even rumours of it having been used as a slave-farm, where the tallest and strongest slaves were encouraged to breed. Amateur anthropologists maintain that this is the reason for Barbuda's abnormally tall population.

In 1976 the 11-person Barbuda council was set up and the island was granted elected government (with just two appointed members). But, as in so many island partnerships, the Barbudans do still complain that they are neglected by the government in St John's. There are occasional words about the advantages of being independent of Antigua, but they are not very loud.

With just 1200 inhabitants, nearly all of whom live in the only village, Codrington, Barbuda is extremely quiet, and it is still surprisingly undeveloped as Caribbean islands go (petrol is hand-pumped here). The main activities are fishing and traditional West Indian subsistence agriculture. 'Wrecking' was another source of income as the reefs around Barbuda have claimed many ships in their time. Tourism amounts to a couple of extremely expensive hotels.

The few hundred Barbudans left on island (many have emigrated but revisit their families often) have a tight-knit community, and the island has a welcoming interest in visitors. One person claimed that on arrival at the airport not so long ago, he was greeted with the words: 'But nobody said you were coming . . .'.

GETTING TO BARBUDA

Barbuda (airport code BBQ) is 20 minutes north of Antigua by plane and **Codrington** is served by a return flight morning and afternoon by LIAT. If you have booked with the Coco Point Lodge then you will arrive at their airstrip in the south. It might also be possible to catch a ride on one of the ships that make the run with tinned food and essentials; ask around at the main dock in St John's.

There are just one or two cars available for hire. Bargain for them. Alternatively try to hitch a ride. Any cars that pass will pick you up, but with just 50 or so on the island it might be a long wait. Because most of the food and other essentials of life are imported it all tends to be quite expensive. Bring things that you cannot live without. You are advised to change any EC$s that you will want in Antigua (it is good to have a few here, though US$s are widely accepted). If you would like a tour of the island, contact the knowledgeable Ivan Pereira a couple of days in advance (tel 460 0258).

Island Sights

The **Codrington** family influence is everywhere on the island: in the only settlement, just a few streets of clapboard houses and an airstrip, in the lagoon on which it sits, and in **Highland House**, their estate house that was built in 1750 but never really occupied. Its ruins, just walls, outhouses and a cistern steadily being reclaimed by the scrub, are visible a few miles north of the village.

The island's other main sight is in better condition. **River Fort** is a martello (round) tower that stands on the south coast, its gun turrets without cannon now, but still guarding the approach to the original docking area and harbour.

For many years the island was a deer-park for the Codringtons and it is still possible to hunt them and to shoot duck. For those with a more peaceable interest in wildlife, a visit to the **Codrington lagoon** to see the thousands of frigate birds can be rewarding, when the birds are strutting around with their gullets puffed up. The best time to go is between October and February. To begin with there is the mating season and then in December the chicks begin to hatch. There are also **caves** in the northern part of the island, including **Dark Cave**, where a passage leads 100 yards underground.

Coral reefs grow off nearly all Barbuda's coasts, waving forests of staghorn and elkhorn where angelfish, trumpetfish and wrasses flit, and they make extremely good diving. Take your own snorkelling gear. Divers have to look after themselves.

WHERE TO STAY

The island's limited accommodation includes two incredibly expensive and luxurious enclaves, both located on the south coast. The smarter of the two is the **K Club** (tel 460 0300, fax 460 0305, US 800 648 4097), which is set on its own half mile of spectacular beach. The twenty villas and cottages are stretched along the waterfront, dressed in bright Caribbean pastel and white tiles, verandas open to the breeze. It is a luxury beach club—watersports, tennis and golf—and after all the activity, gourmet meals in the main house with the few other guests. Double room in season US$1000. **Coco Point Lodge** (tel 462 3186), where the emphasis is on seclusion from the outside world for its 50 or so guests. You will fly to the private airstrip near to the hotel and lodge in one of the cabins that look over the superb beach, where many watersports are available. There is a rather high, all-inclusive charge of about US$1000 per day for a couple in the winter season (the resort is closed over the summer). Another resort is the **Village Soleil**, PO Box 1104, St John's, where there are just eight rooms in thatched cottages dotted around the central area above the beach (along from Coco Point). Meals and watersports are included in the daily rate of US$250 to $300 for a double per day.

For those without spare millions there are a couple of guest houses in Codrington. The **Sunset View** has rooms for US$75 a double, or you can try **John Thomas's** Guest House (tel 460 0004), with double rooms for EC$65, or **Walter Thomas's** Guest House.

REDONDA

The chain of Caribbean volcanoes passes by about 30 miles west of Antigua and among its peaks rises the tiny pimple of Redonda, so named because of its nearly round shape. It stands between Montserrat and Nevis, a circle of cliffs sparse on top, and uninhabited except by birds.

For nearly 400 years after its discovery by Columbus it was ignored, but eventually in the 1860s somebody realized that centuries' worth of birdshit could be put to good use. Guano mining began, and at the height of production 30 years later the island produced 3–4000 tons of phosphate annually.

That the island should be worth something to somebody was enough to bring claims of sovereignty from all the powers in the area, and so before long the island was annexed by the British and attached to Antigua, capital of the Leeward Islands.

A rival claim, though, was staked by an Irishman who happened to sail past in 1865. One Matthew Shiell, born in Montserrat in 1865, decided to claim it as a 'fiefdom' for his son, later King Phillipe I. The courtiers to the sovereign were literary folk and the line passed to the poet John Gawsworth, self-styled King Juan I, whose peers included J. B. Priestley and Rebecca West.

This most illustrious of Caribbean lineages was thought to have gone into decline, but it was traced to the county of Surrey or Sussex in Britain, where it resides with the monarch, Jon Wynne-Tyson. The King made a visit in 1979 with his court historian and reaffirmed his suzerainty over the domain by planting his flag, blue, brown and green in colour and 'made from pairs of old royal pyjamas by Her Royal Highness, Jennifer Wynne-Tyson'.

Though Redonda is uninhabited now, there was once a post office there and it is possible to find Redonda stamps.

MONTSERRAT

Montserrat, the first of the Leewards, has a jumbled interior of rain-forested mountains worthy of one of the Windward Isles to the south, but its serried peaks are smaller, its slopes are gentler and island life is even slower.

Clapboard Shack

Even so, the island's 39 square miles (7 miles long and 11 miles at its widest point) are pretty inaccessible, and only a few houses are cut into the central hills of the island. Most of the 12,000 Montserratians live on the sheltered Caribbean coast. The flatlands all around the shoreline, where the villas and estates of modern Montserrat are springing up, are littered with estate ruins that speak of rich plantation days.

The island does not attract a large beach-bound crowd (it has few beaches anyway) and seems generally undeveloped, though tourism is in fact the main foreign exchange earner. It tends to attract a more stately visitor. Without the airborne invasion suffered by so many islands, Montserrat maintains some of the tranquillity now lost to the rest of West Indies. It can be relied upon. Many people retire here.

Montserrat has a considerable, if distant, Irish heritage which, along with its luxuriant appearance, has led to it being called the *Emerald Isle* of the Caribbean. Many of the place-names are clearly Irish, and although the islanders are clearly of African descent, at times it seems that you can hear an Irish lilt in their speech, momentary strains of brogue in the stream of West Indian. Whether this is imagined or not, Montserratian speech is one of the softest and most attractive of all variations in the English-speaking Caribbean.

For all the Irish heritage (and there is a shamrock on one of the eaves of Government House), the island has been a British colony for most of its history. It is one of just five British Crown Colonies remaining in the Caribbean, administered by a Governor appointed from London in partnership with the island legislature.

Life is easy-going in Montserrat and to judge by how often the locals have to say *Hello*, or *yeah man!* walking along the street, they must all know each other.

History

Alliouagana (thought to mean 'land of the prickly bush'), was deserted when Columbus passed on his second voyage. The Caribs were off raiding elsewhere. He paused long enough to name the island *Santa Maria de Montserrate* after the abbey near Barcelona in Spain. Only pirates braved the Caribs' attention over the next 140 years. The Spaniards gave the island a wide berth.

Montserrat was settled in about 1632 as a separate colony for the Catholics from mainly Protestant St Kitts, the English island about 40 miles to the northwest. Many of the settlers were Irishmen, as was the first Governor, and the island soon gained a reputation as a place where Catholics and the Irish were welcome. They came from Protestant Virginia, and the population was also swelled after the Battle of Drogheda in 1649, when Cromwell sent many of the Irish prisoners of war. Irish indentured labourers from the other islands would make their way here once their term was served on another island.

As with so many islands, the first half century of colonization was a litany of hurricanes, earthquakes and seaborne attacks. The raiders were French, Dutch and Spanish and, of course, the Caribs, who arrived in their thousands, burning and looting, killing the men and carrying off women and slaves. The Irish colonists had something of an understanding with their French co-religionists and often when the raids took place their property would be left alone.

But relations between the Montserratian settlers themselves were hardly any more peaceful. Laws had to be passed to prevent them from hurling insults at each other in the street, 'English Dog, Scots Dog, Cavalier, Roundhead and many other opprobrious, scandalous and disgraceful terms'.

By the late 17th century the land was covered with sugar-cane well up into the hills. Because of the steep terrain, the cured sugar was loaded on to mules and casked only on the shore before shipping. Sugar meant slaves and a large number of Africans were brought in to work the canefields, giving Montserrat its mainly black population today. The occasional rebellions were put down ruthlessly. One was arranged for St Patrick's day in 1768 and the slaves intended to take over Government House, but the plans were overheard by a slave-woman who told the planters and the rebels were captured and executed.

As sugar failed and Emancipation came, other crops were grown and Montserrat became famous for limes. It was the second Caribbean exporter of the fruit after the Windward Island Dominica and much of the crop, 180,000 gallons one year, went to Crosse and Blackwell in Britain. Cotton became an export crop at the end of the 19th century and formed the basis of the Montserratian economy well into this century. Like other Caribbean islanders, the Montserratians had moved on to small plots of land and were leading a simple agricultural existence. At the time of Emancipation they worked for sixpence a day, the lowest wage in the Caribbean, and 100 years later their situation was still the worst in the Leewards.

This pitiful state led to considerable emigration from the island when a better life seemed possible elsewhere, and so most Montserratians have a relative who left for the canefields in the Dominican Republic or to work in oil in Curaçao. The exodus culminated in the 1950s, when 5000 left for Britain. A recent influx of 'resident tourists', as they are known, many of them retired Americans, has brought the population back to about 12,000. Most recently there has been a wave of Dominicans and Guayanese, who have come to work in the construction industry in the aftermath of Hurricane Hugo.

On the political scene, Montserrat had a late start. Robert Griffith and William Bramble led the Montserratians in their efforts to obtain a fair wage and in their political aspirations. The Montserrat Labour Party took all five seats in the first elections in 1951 and again in 1955.

Today the island government, the Legislative Council, which has control over internal affairs, is led by Prime Minister Reuben Timide of the National Progressive Party. In elections in October 1991, they won four of the seven Parliamentary seats. Elections to the Council are held every five years. As a Crown Colony, ultimate executive power rests with the Governor, Queen Elizabeth II's appointed representative, but he would be very unlikely to use his overriding prerogative on internal matters. Independence is mentioned less now in island politics, but anyway it would not be considered before Montserrat is economically independent.

Hurricane Hugo, which struck in 1989, caused terrible destruction to both human and wild life and in places the damage is still visible. There were ten deaths. Not a single electricity pole was left standing and an estimated 95% of houses were damaged.

Apart from this upset, the standard of living in Montserrat has risen steadily over the last 20 years and though there is a visible disparity between foreigners and the simple Montserratian farmers, the island is very stable.

271

Blarney

Of all the echoes you hear in West Indian English, the strongest in the speech of Montserrat is the Irish. Some visitors have claimed that the Montserratians have the gift of the gab and a truly Irish wit. The West Indians have a pretty mean sense of humour anyway (just nip down to the market and catch the banter), but particularly after a few rum punches, you might think that you are in Galway.

In the 17th century, there were about 1000 Irish families on the island, but since then, most of the original white settlers have left. However, their names certainly live on in black Montserratian families, Farrel, Daly and Ryan, as a quick look at the Montserrat telephone directory will show. The Irish harp is a national symbol and appears on the Montserratian stamps.

There is a nice story from the 19th century about an Irishman who arrived from Connaught to find himself addressed by a black man in Connaught brogue. He asked how long the man had been in Montserrat. 'Shure, yer honour, and three years it is that I've been here.' Flabbergasted, the Irishman replied, 'Glory be to God. And do ye turrn black in thot toime?' and got on the first ship back home (*The Pocket Guide to the West Indies*, Sir Algernon Aspinall, 1938).

Flora and Fauna

'The confusion of soufrières or secondary craters and the mingling of mountains and hills make it like an enlarged picture of the moon.'

Montserrat has the same botanic exuberance as the Windward Isles to the south—the thick dark earth cultivates a luxuriant flora: explosions of bamboo, mosses on the march, creepers grappling down below, and above orchids and airborne ferns. The national flower is the yellow *Heliconia Caribaea*, known locally as lobster claw because of its odd shape.

The national bird, the *Montserrat Oriole*, is specific to the island. Its plumage is black and yellow and it can be found up in the mountains along with the purple-throated carib, one of Montserrat's three hummingbirds. Thrashers and bananaquits abound in the hibiscus and bougainvillaea of the lower slopes and you might be lucky and see a chicken hawk hovering, spying out a meal.

On the shoreline, particularly in the 15-acre mangrove swamp coastal reserve at Fox's Bay Bird Sanctuary you can see waders such as the common gallinule and some species of heron, alongside cattle egrets, kingfishers and the odd booby or a tropicbird with its long tail feathers. The bird population was badly affected by Hurricane Hugo.

Montserrat's landborne wildlife is limited to frogs, the odd lizard and the prehistoric-looking iguana, as well as agouti, 'mountain chickens' (frogs) and of course the tree frogs, which make their shrill nightime call all over the Caribbean.

The island is volcanic and though it does not erupt any more, one or two sulphurous patches have appeared in the hills quite recently.

GETTING TO MONTSERRAT

Blackburne airport, nine miles across the island from Plymouth cannot take long haul traffic, so you will have to make a connecting link. The best route is via Antigua, which has good connections from Europe and North America. LIAT has half-a-dozen flights

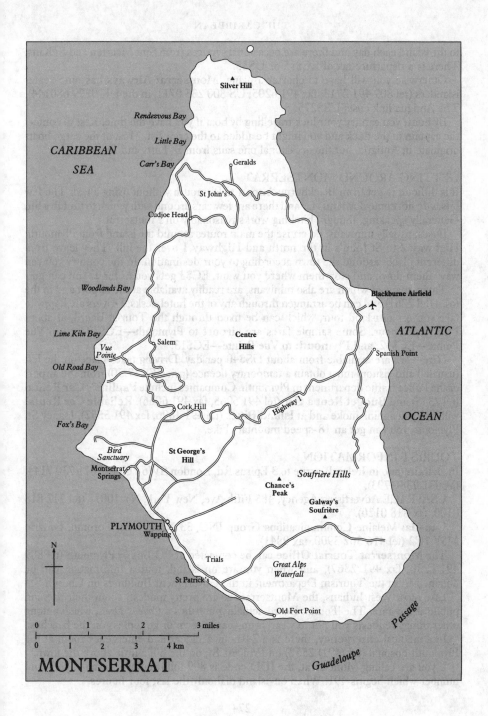

Silver Hill

Rendezvous Bay

Little Bay

CARIBBEAN
SEA

Carr's Bay

Geralds

St John's

Cudjoe Head

Woodlands Bay

Blackburne Airfield

Lime Kiln Bay

Salem

Centre
Hills

ATLANTIC

Vue
Pointe

Spanish Point

Old Road Bay

Cork Hill

Highway 1

OCEAN

Fox's Bay

Bird
Sanctuary

St George's
Hill

Montserrat
Springs

Soufrière Hills

Chance's
Peak

Galway's
Soufrière

PLYMOUTH

Wapping

N

Trials

Great Alps
Waterfall

St Patrick's

Old Fort Point

0   1   2   3 miles

0   1   2   3   4 km

MONTSERRAT

Guadeloupe   Passage

to the island each day and there are occasional services from Sint Maarten and St Kitts. There is a departure tax of EC$15 or US$5.

Otherwise you will have to charter a plane. **Montserrat Airways** has nine-seater islanders (tel 809 491 2713, fax 491 6205, US 800 235 0711, in the UK 0279 680144). The Antigua link costs US$275.

By boat: you can try your luck travelling by boat if you have the time. Best to contact the captain in the dock and you might be added to the crew list. Most of the cargo boats originate in Antigua, but the occasional one sails from St Kitts and Dominica.

GETTING AROUND MONTSERRAT
It is difficult to get from Blackburne Airport to Plymouth without using a taxi. The few buses do not come down this far and there are few cars around with which to thumb a lift. Generally speaking, though, hitching works reasonably on Montserrat.

Buses, usually minivans, do cruise the main routes around the island from Plymouth: **Highway 2** to St John's in the north and **Highway 1** over the hill. They leave from different places around the town according to your destination. In the country you can wave them down and stop them where you want. EC$3 gets you as far as you can go.

Taxis, many of which are also minivans, are readily available at the airport and in the town (tel 2261) and can be arranged through any of the hotel desks. Drivers are happy to take you on an island tour, which can be fixed through the Tourist Board, at about EC$30 per hour. Some sample fares are **airport** to Plymouth—EC$30 and to Vue Pointe—EC$42, and **Plymouth** to Vue Pointe—EC$13.

Hire-cars are available from about US$40 per day. Driving takes place on the left (usually) and visitors must obtain a temporary licence (price EC$7.50) from the airport or the Police traffic department in Plymouth. Companies include **Pauline's Car Rental** (tel 2345) and **Budget Rent a Car** (tel 491 6065, fax 491 6066). **Reliable Car Rental** will hire you a mini-moke and at **Island Bikes** (tel 491 4696, fax 491 5552), Haney St, Plymouth you can get an 18-speed mountain bike.

TOURIST INFORMATION
In **Britain** (and in Ireland), write to 3 Epirus Rd, London SW6 7UJ (tel 071 730 7144, fax 071 938 4793).

USA: PACE Advertising Agency, 485 Fifth Ave, New York, NY 10017 (tel 212 818 0100, fax 818 0120).

Canada: Melaine Communications Group INC, 33 Niagara St, Toronto, Ontario M5V 1C2 (tel 416 362 3900, fax 9841).

The **Montserrat Tourist Office** can be contacted at PO Box 7, Plymouth (tel 809 491 2230, fax 491 2367), and when you are on island, tourist information can be obtained from the Tourism Department in the Government Buildings on Church St.

Like most West Indians, the Montserratians are pretty modest, about their dress in public at any rate. The Tourist Board actually publishes a *Code of Dress*, which among other things requests you not to wear swimwear in town or go topless on the beaches.

In a medical **emergency**, there is a 24-hour accident and emergency room at the Plymouth hospital (tel (491) 2552) on Princess St, on the hill a little above the town.

If you are calling Montserrat, the **IDD code** is 809 followed by a seven-digit island number which begins 491. When on-island dial only the last four figures.

MONEY

The currency of Montserrat is the Eastern Caribbean dollar (fixed to the US dollar at EC$2.69 = US$1) which is used on islands fom Anguilla to Grenada. The US greenback is also widely accepted, but expect change in EC dollars. **Banking hours** are 8–1, Mon–Thur, and Fri 8–1 and 3–5. The Bank of Montserrat is open on Saturday mornings.

BEACHES

Most of Montserrat's beaches are strips of dark volcanic sand, some in coves lined with palms, but on the northwestern coast coral reefs have thrown up some light brown sand. There is not much in the way of beach facilities, so if you go far afield, take a picnic, but some beaches are close to the hotels and you can get a drink or lunch there.

Getting to the only white-sand beach, **Rendezvous Bay**, involves a difficult walk over the hills from Little Bay, or a boat trip. This can be arranged with a fisherman (reckon on about EC$50), or through the Vue Pointe Hotel which runs snorkelling trips there.

Carr's Bay and very secluded **Little Bay** are two other attractive bays in the north where fishermen keep their boats, but the best beaches are at (working south) **Woodlands Bay, Lime Kiln Bay, Old Road Bay** and **Fox's Bay**.

BEACH BARS

There is a nice beach bar, the **Nest**, on Old Road Bay, where you can get a snack or a drink, and on Barton Bay beneath the Montserrat springs you can linger at **Las' Call** until 8 pm at the weekends.

WATERSPORTS

Sailing is available on Montserrat through **Captain Martin** (tel 491 5738) who arranges a day's cruise to Rendezvous Bay in the north of the island aboard the *John Willie*, US$45.

Danny's Watersports at Old Road Bay will fix windsurfing, waterskiing and snorkelling (tel 5645). Scuba diving can be arranged with **Dive Montserrat**, who also offer resort courses for novices, or a deep-sea fishing outing to trail a line for tuna, barracuda and wahoo. Both on 491 8812.

Land-based sports include **golf**; there is an 11-green course at Belham Valley (tel 491 5220), where different tees make up 18 holes; green fees about US$35. The Montserrat Open is held each year on easter Weekend. There are **tennis courts** at the Vue Pointe Hotel (tel 491 5210) and the Montserrat springs Hotel (tel 491 2481).

Plymouth

The small capital of Montserrat, **Plymouth**, lies on an open bay on the southwest coast of the island and has a population of around 3500. It was supposedly named after the Pilgrim Fathers' Plymouth in Virginia, and became the capital town in 1640 when Kinsale to the south was abandoned. Set on the waterfront on the slopes of the gentle Montserratian mountains, it is a classical British West Indian town where the arched stonework of the old Georgian warehouses is topped with shaded balconies and red tin roofs.

The streets hardly bustle, but customary West Indian 'limers' hang around chatting at key points, and the odd policeman in a starched shirt and trousers will wander by. A short walk from the centre, the back streets soon become lined with simple wooden shingle houses shaded by breadfruit trees in small yards of beaten earth. Clambering up into the hills above the town and along the coast, the new Montserrat of concrete villas is establishing itself behind hedges and gardens.

On Fridays and Saturdays, the **Plymouth Public Market**, guarded by its cannon, becomes traditional West Indian mayhem. Country ladies sit, their skirts rolled above the knee, presiding over their stacks of ground produce, yam, tannia and eddoe and exotic Montserratian fruits, soursop, christophene and banana.

Parliament Street leads through the business centre of the town and past the government buildings to the Anglican **St Anthony's Church**, where there are two silver chalices presented to the church by the freed slaves: 'as a thank-offering to God for the blessing of freedom vouchsafed them on 1st August, 1838'. The church has been rebuilt a number of times, following military raids and hurricanes, since the first was erected on this site in 1636 by Anthony Briskett, Montserrat's first Governor. **St Patrick's Roman Catholic Church** stands on George St.

Across Fort Ghaut, heading south, the road descends into the area of Wapping, where the old stone warehouses have been restored. On the hill above is **Government House**, the official residence of the Montserrat Governor, an attractive wooden creole house built in the 19th century and decorated on one gable with a shamrock. The landscaped gardens are worth a visit (open on weekdays except Wed, 10.30–noon) and the house itself has paintings and period furniture.

North on Highway 2

Highway 2 leaves town in the shadow of the principal fort in the extensive ring of defences that guarded Plymouth in the 18th century. **Fort St George** stands 1200 feet above the town. Its battlements are overgrown now and the cannon lie around useless, but it was an impressive fortress in its time. Apart from a certain historic atmosphere, the best reason to go there is the incredible view, which covers the town and its approaches from north and south.

Down below, the road leaves the town via St Anthony's Church and **Sturge Park** where inter-island sports matches and carnival competitions take place. The **Montserrat Museum** (tel 491 5443) is situated in a restored 18th-century sugarmill and its exhibits cover Montserratian life from the time of the the Arawaks, through the sugar years to the island's success as a producer of limes in the 19th century. The museum is run on donations and contributions from the Montserrat National Trust, which you can join for EC$5. Open Sun 3–5 year-round, and Wed 1–5 in Dec–Apr winter season, adm free.

On the coast beneath the museum is the **Fox's Bay Bird Sanctuary** (see p. 222). Marked walks lead through the swamp. There is no admission fee. The remains of a fort can be seen on Bransby Point itself. You can see herons, mangrove cuckoo and kingfisher stalking and flitting in the mangrove and manchioneel.

Back inland, a side road (Highway 4) cuts up into the mountainside to St George's Hill, but the main road continues through a series of small villages, Salem and Weekes

among them, and the open slopes of the Centre Hills. At Waterworks stand the old
Montserrat Air Studios, the world-renowned recording studios that were opened in
1979 by George Martin, one-time producer of the Beatles. They are defunct now, but a
whole string of famous artists has worked there, including the Rolling Stones, the Police,
Stevie Wonder, Paul McCartney and Duran Duran.

North of Woodlands the expensive villas evaporate and the land becomes drier as the
Centre Hills tail off and the Highway wiggles through the West Indian villages of Cudjoe
Head, St John's and Geralds, where you will see farmers walking barefoot or riding a
donkey to their small plot of land in the hills. Carr's Bay and Little Bay, an idyllic fishing
cove, are on the Caribbean coast at the foot of Silver Hill.

From here the road crosses over to the uninhabited Atlantic coast, where the views are
spectacular and the mountains more rugged, eventually coming to the airport at Blackburne. This area is completely undeveloped.

On the flatlands around the airport the restored remains of the sugar estates with their
mills and chimneys stand out against the mountains. From here, it is a six-mile ride back
up into the fertile Montserratian hills on Highway 1, where there are a couple of simple
villages on the heights before the road descends into Plymouth.

South of Plymouth

Past Government House, a turn leads leads inland to the dropping-off point for the
climb to **Chance's Peak** (3002 ft), the highest on the island. The walk takes a couple of
hours and is quite steep, but the views from the summit (on a clear day) are stunning and
make it worthwhile. Do not let yourself feel too intrepid as you climb, because you will
find that civilization, in the form of a radio transmission tower, has beaten you to the top.

There is a legend, also heard elsewhere in the Caribbean that you might meet a
mermaid combing her hair on a rock at the summit, with a diamond snake as her
companion. If you can seize the comb, get it down to the sea and wet it before the snake
catches you, then her treasure will become yours. Island lore does not relate what
happens to you if you fail. A guide for this walk can be arranged at the Tourist Board.

The road comes to Galways Estate, where a sugar plantation was first established in
the 1600s and was worked for 200 years. It was excavated recently and you can see the
remains of a chapel, boiling house, estate house and windmill. Adm free.

To get to **Galway's Soufrière**, you can cut inland just beyond St Patrick's and walk
for 20 minutes from the end of the road. This large fertile area is Montserrat's vent to the
volcanic underworld, which periodically belches and continually lets off stinking gases
through discoloured sulphur pools and fumaroles (in 1902, when volcanic activity was
seen all along the island chain, the ashes were so bad that Plymouth had to switch on the
lights at midday). Water runs milky white, smelly and at near boiling point, discolouring
the rocks all around. The clay ground can be too hot to stand on, but as long as you are
careful then it is a good walk. The tourist board publishes a page of advice about how to
avoid scalding yourself on the visit. 'Persons who wear spectacles should make provision
to clean them regularly on the trail . . .' If you walk a little farther, there are spectacular
views over the other islands from the far side of the mountain.

The **Great Alps Waterfall** is 45 minutes' walk upriver into the hills from just outside
St Patrick's. The water, only really impressive in the wet season, cascades from 70 feet

THE CARIBBEAN

into a dank ravine strung with lianas and elephant ears and crawling with mosses. You can cool off with a 70ft shower when you get there, so take your swimming costume. The path is well marked. **White River Falls** are higher up the valley.

FESTIVALS
St Patrick's Day (17 March) has recently been resurrected in the Montserratian calendar and it is now celebrated with fêtes and beach parties, particularly in the southern village of St Patrick's. The Queen's Birthday on the second Saturday in June is a more formal affair, but August Monday (from Emancipation Day on 1 August 1834) is remembered with *jump-ups* and blow-outs, Caribbean style. On Labour day, May 6th, the festivities centre around a fishing competition. The major annual festival is **Carnival** at Christmas. The activities start at the beginning of December, with the early rounds of the calypso competition, and culminate in a week-long series of masquerade parades, calypsos, feasting and revelry. The main celebrations start on Christmas Eve and finish with Festival Day on 31st, when the island jumps up from dawn and then masquerades all day and night. On New Year's day they drag themselves out again, parading through the streets until late at night.

Fans of Caribbean *soca* music will immediately recognize the name of **(the Mighty) Arrow**, who comes from Montserrat and whose calypso *Hot Hot Hot!* made it to the top all over the world a few years ago.

WHERE TO STAY
There are few hotels in Montserrat, though they cover the range quite well. And Montserrat also offers a range of villas with two, three or four bedrooms for those who are happy to be independent. Many are on the hillside overlooking the west coast, with their own swimming pool, and all will have maid-service if you want it. Most are second homes that are rented out when the owners are not there.

There is a 7% government tax on hotel rooms and villas and usually a 10% service charge will be added to your hotel bill.

If you wish to hire a villa, there are plenty of companies to contact. **Isles Bay Plantation** (tel 809 491 4842, fax 491 4843) has a small number of sumptuous spots above the golf course in Belham—modern Caribbean luxury in pastel shades and cordon bleu cooking, villas sleep 8 people; **Villas of Montserrat**, PO Box 421, Plymouth (tel 491 5513, US tel 415 964 3498) has three units also in Belham Valley, also with pools, 6 people, US$200 for the week; **Neville Bradshaw Agencies Ltd**, PO Box 270, Plymouth (tel 491 5270, fax 491 5069).

The **Montserrat Springs Hotel**, PO Box 259 (tel 491 2481, fax 491 4070), gives bright and breezy Caribbean comfort in large rooms on the hillside above Plymouth. There are 46 air-conditioned suites and rooms set in blocks and a dining room and bar above a large pool. A double room in winter costs US$140 and a suite US$210. The **Vue Pointe Hotel**, PO Box 65 (tel 491 5210, fax 491 4813), has a more individual tropical island charm with octagonal rondavels ranged over the hillside among the tropical explosion of the gardens above Old Road Bay. A crowd of regulars at the bar and restaurant, beach bar down below and watersports on the bay. Double rooms US$126–166. There are two hotels in town; the **Flora Fountain**, PO Box 373 (tel 809 491 6092, fax 491 2568) on Parliament St, with 18 comfortable rooms set in an odd circular building, double room US$85–141; and the **Oriole Plaza Hotel**, PO Box 250 (tel 491 6982, fax 491 6690), with simple stopover rooms for US$65 a double in winter. There are one or two **guest houses** in the areas around Plymouth. **Marie's Guest House**, PO Box 28 (tel 491 2745), has just three simple rooms with a kitchen in a modern house, where you can stay for US$20 for a single and US$30 for a double year-round, rates negotiable for a longer stay. In Kinsale you will find the **Moose'e Guest House** (tel 491 3146), where a double comes at US$25–35 and in Belham Valley you will find **Rogie's Guest House** (tel 491 5591), 8 rooms at US$25 a single, $35 a double with a meal.

EATING OUT

Montserratian Food
Montserrat's culinary tradition is mainly West Indian, based on the tropical vegetables and fruits that you will find on sale at the market, and the fish and animals that can be caught here. Recently the supermarkets have catered for the large influx of Americans and Europeans by bringing in food from outside, which is quite expensive by comparison.

The island's Irish heritage is reckoned to reach as far as the food in *Goat water*, a stew of goat meat with herbs, often served at ceremonies. Another local delicacy, only served on Dominica and Montserrat, is *Mountain chicken*, which hops wild in the hills before it reaches your plate. In fact, it is not a chicken at all, but an outsize frog.

Restaurants
The hotels have popular dining rooms—the Vue Pointe has a barbecue on Wednesdays and a Sunday brunch and the Montserrat springs a barbecue with music on Fridays and a buffet lunch on Sunday afternoons—but it is worth looking elsewhere, particularly if you want local fare. Some of the old stone warehouses in Wapping have been restored to contain restaurants. You should reserve in season and you might request a dish while on the phone. A service charge of 10% is usually added to the bill.

At the **Belham Valley** restaurant (tel 491 5553) you look out from a veranda onto the golf course or the lights winking on the slopes opposite. The menu is varied and includes Montserrat fritters served with a dill mayonnaise or with West Indian hot sauce, followed by caroleen chicken, sautéed with shallots and cream brandy sauce. Finish off with a mango mousse. EC$50 average for a dish. With a more local West Indian feel about it is the **Blue Dolphin** (491 3263), which is set in a modern concrete Montserratian house in Parsons. Ask around if you're having trouble finding it. It has dolphins painted on a blue wall. Plastic tablecloths, local music or the television, fish, steaks and seafood with a volley of local vegetables, EC$25–50 (lobster). In **Wapping**, the **Emerald Café** (tel 3821) is a popular stopping point for visitors—seafood crêpe, sautéed lobster or mountain chicken diable—surrounded by an explosion of plant-life along the walls of the gallery, EC$30–50 a main dish. You might also try the nearby **Iguana** (491 3637) with a stone interior and a covered terace outside. Locals drop in here for a beer and a takeaway. Pizzas galore, but also veal marsala and shrimp scampi, EC$40. At **Oasis**, you can catch a calypso chicken or a burger for EC$15–20. There are plenty of very local Montserratian haunts and rum shops, which double as bars and simple restaurants. In Weekes, **Nep Co Den** (see bars) serves the best rotis (boneless) on the island. Just

279

farther north in Cork Hill is the **Golden Apple**, for rice and peas and in the far north, in the village of St John's is **Mrs Morgan's**, where you will get the best goat water on the island, or local fish if you want it. Concrete hut, plastic tablecloths and a crowd of limers. Goat water EC$8.

NIGHTLIFE
Montserrat is very quiet after dark, but being the West Indies you can always find a crowd and some rum somewhere. The hotels occasionally have a band and their bars are favoured haunts too. Everyone goes to the **Palm Tree** on George St on Friday nights. Just out of town in Weekes, **Nep Co Den** is a popular spot—fluorescent posters, cotton wool on the ceiling, crab-backs that flash and very loud music. You might stop for a game of pool in the **Village Place** in Salem, but there are rum shops all over the island.

ST KITTS and NEVIS

St Kitts and Nevis stand side by side in the arc of diminishing volcanic peaks in the Leeward Islands. The two islands are separated by the Narrows, a channel just two miles wide, across which each has a stunning view of the other.

The distance may be short, but it belies the gulf that exists between the two islands. Each island is proud of its distinct character and maintains its own identity. Internal rivalry is of course very strong—every Kittitian has a relative on Nevis and vice versa—the annual inter-island cricket match is a fiercely contested event.

Unless you hide out in the tourist ghetto or lock yourself away in plantation splendour (St Kitts and Nevis have a stunning collection of Plantation house hotels), you cannot help but notice life around you in St Kitts and Nevis. There is a strong and vibrant West Indian culture, unlike some of the other islands nearby, where life has been swamped by the international tourist industry. Expect to be accosted in the street. You may be asked for money or given a slug of rum. Either way, the Kittitians (pronounced as in 'petition') and Nevisians (as in 'revision') will let you know their thoughts on life. The country has a population of 46,000, of which about 9000 live on Nevis (many more Nevisians live in St Kitts of course).

Since their Independence in 1983 St Kitts and Nevis have faced a difficult economic future, so much must be bought in from outside. The remnants of the former sugar prosperity are visible everywhere—in the magnificent stonework of the estate houses, some of which have been restored to make superb plantation house hotels—but for now, the islands themselves are poor. Still, they are classic, laid back Caribbean islands and it is well worth making a visit there.

History

St Kitts was once known as the 'Mother Colony of the West Indies', because it was the first island in the Lesser Antilles to be settled permanently. *Liamuiga*, the Carib name for St Kitts, supposedly means 'fertile land' and it was the verdant growth that attracted European rovers in the early 17th century. Despite the hostility of the Carib Indians and risks from a local infestation of pirates, they came to plant tobacco.

The first settler was the Englishman Thomas Warner, who arrived in 1623 and started to plant. Next year he was joined by a French privateer, Pierre Belain d'Esnambuc, who called in to repair his ship after a fight with the Spaniards near the Cayman Islands. Welcomed by Warner, the Frenchman stayed for a while and then went to France to persuade settlers to return with him to St Kitts. The two men arranged to share the island and in 1627 divided it into three with the French in the north and around Basseterre, and the English in the middle.

One of the main reasons that the French and English were happy to team up was that they needed to protect themselves against the Caribs, who were none too pleased about this intrusion into their islands. The battles began even in 1626, with the Caribs rallying in their canoes from other islands including Dominica and Guadeloupe, but the Europeans held their own. Steadily the Caribs were forced out and *Liamuiga* became St Kitts.

The Spaniards were no more pleased at this intrusion into their backyard in the New World and in 1629 their fleet attacked the colony. During the skirmish the colony was destroyed, but the settlers soon filtered back and got on with planting their tobacco.

The islanders also started to look farther afield. Competition for empire was hotting up and English expeditions were sent to settle nearby islands. Nevis was one of the many 'Charibby Islands' made over arbitrarily to the Earl of Carlisle by Charles I in 1627 and the next year *Oualie* was promptly taken from the Caribs by the British. Montserrat and Antigua were settled in 1632. The French boldly took on the larger and more hostile Windwards to the south, heading for Martinique and Guadeloupe.

On St Kitts itself, the scene was set for the next 200 years—the French and British would be constantly at each others' throats. At one stage they managed to fall out on the basis that a tree had grown. A *banyan* marking the border in the north of the island had enlarged by putting out a few years' worth of aerial roots and the land enclosed by it just happened to include 250 French houses.

War was just averted on that occasion, but St Kitts passed from one power to the other like a shuttlecock. Brimstone Hill was built and sieged. And as the navies whittled through the islands Nevis took a fair beating too. In 1706 the French swooped in, destroyed what they could (about £1 million's worth), and left with around 3000 slaves.

At the beginning of the 19th century, the British finally gained the upper hand in the endless series of wars and both islands ended up in the hands of the British, with whom they remained until Independence. Only a few hints of French influence remain in St Kitts today: a *fleur de lys* on the national coat of arms and, most notably, the name of the capital, Basseterre.

When the islanders were not being besieged, they were planting sugar-cane furiously. Nevis stuttered on its route to prosperity, but prosperous it became. At one stage a fleet of 20 ocean-going ships was devoted entirely to serving that island, sailing out with luxuries and manufactured goods such as tools and returning loaded with sugar-loaves. She was dubbed the 'Queen of the Caribbees'. The sugar industry also needed slaves and in the late 17th century Nevis had a slave market. Vast numbers of Africans were brought over and when the ships arrived in port these frightened men and women would be oiled up before being made to parade through the streets singing, prior to being taken to auction.

With the 19th century, the West Indian sugar industry went into decline and the mansions into decay, though the planters kept up their balls and finery as long as they could.

281

After Emancipation in 1834, the apprenticeship system broke down in 1838 and the slaves were finally freed. On such small islands, many were forced to remain on the plantations, but eventually villages like Challengers on the leeward coast of St Kitts grew up.

The late 19th century was a lean period for all the Caribbean islands and St Kitts and Nevis slipped into obscurity. The sugar industry had more and more difficulty competing in the world market as Cuba and Santo Domingo gained the ascendancy.

Today, apart from a small income from sugar, the St Kitts-Nevis economy is dependent on a slowly expanding tourist industry.

Politics

St Kitts and Nevis are united in a constitutional Federation, in place since Independence from Britain in 1983. The two islands were originally shunted together in 1882, as the colonial authorities in London made one of their many political rationalizations, and formed a part of the *Presidency* of the Leeward Islands. The island of Anguilla was appended to the Basseterre administration in 1871.

The three islands followed much the same course as the other British colonies in the 20th century, led by the clamour for political change in Jamaica, Trinidad and Barbados in the 1930s. In 1951, the islanders were given the vote and the St Kitts and Nevis Labour Party, rallying the voices of people who had had no political say before, swept the board. 'Associated Statehood' in 1967 brought more self-determination, but at this point Anguilla, which had felt neglected by the government in St Kitts staged one of the world's lesser known revolutions and made its claims for secession heard. After a 15-year row, Anguilla eventually left the State of St Kitts-Nevis in 1982.

At Independence in September 1983, the Nevisians wanted to make sure that they would not end up in the same position as Anguilla and so they renegotiated the settlement, inserting an 'escape clause' that allowed them to secede from Federation with St Kitts if two thirds of the Nevisians choose to do so. Nevis has its own five-member elected assembly to govern its own affairs. For the moment, political unity between the islands is reasonably secure.

In the 11-member House of Assembly of St Kitts-Nevis, three of the seats are allotted to constituencies on Nevis and these can easily hold the balance of power. St Kitts-Nevis remains within the British Commonwealth. At the moment it is headed by Prime Minister Kennedy Simmonds, whose party, the People's Action Movement, is in coalition with the Nevis Reformation Party.

Flora and Fauna

Where the slopes of St Kitts are bright green with sugar-cane, cotton plants cut darker shades of green into the Nevisian forest. Above the lower plains of luxuriant grass and swathes of elephant ear, both islands have rainforest in the heights, where orchids and cycads explode in the upper branches of the gommier trees and vines tangle the trunks. Close to the summits of the mountains the rainforest gives way to stunted elfin woodland. The wildlife in St Kitts and Nevis is quite unspoilt.

Around the bright red flamboyant tree, poinciana (named after the island's first

French Captain General, de Poincy), and bougainvillaea you will see typical island birds such as the purple-throated carib and other hummingbirds, daring bananaquits and bullfinches. In the southern area of St Kitts (sometimes even offshore in Basseterre itself), you can see pelicans and the occasional frigate bird, as well as warblers and perhaps a pearly-eyed thrasher.

Both islands are home to the *green vervet* monkey, a shy character who was introduced by the French in the 17th century. It stands about a foot high and travels in packs of about 40. If you go up into the hills you have a good chance of seeing one. You can tell when they are angry by the white line above their eyebrow which they wiggle at you furiously.

GETTING TO ST KITTS AND NEVIS
Golden Rock airport, two miles from Basseterre on St Kitts, has a wide range of international services from the USA. Newcastle airport on Nevis is less well served, so most travellers whose final destination is Nevis end up travelling first to St Kitts; see below for connections between the two. There is a departure tax of US$8.

By Air
From the UK: there are no direct flights from Europe and the easiest connections to both islands are via Antigua, where LIAT flights link up with British Airways and BWIA services from London. It is possible to make same-day connections to the islands from Paris (Air France) or from Amsterdam (KLM) via Sint Maarten.
From the USA: BWIA operates a twice-weekly service from JFK airport in New York to St Kitts, and also flights from Miami via Antigua. The three daily flights between St Kitts and San Juan, Puerto Rico give good connections with numerous American cities.
From other Caribbean Islands: St Kitts is accessible by non-stop flights from Anguilla, Antigua, Sint Maarten and San Juan. Nevis is a little less easy to reach, having direct flights only from Antigua, Sint Maarten and San Juan. If you need to charter an airplane, you can contact Carib Aviation (tel 465 3055, fax 465 3168) which has 9-seater and 5-seater planes or Air St Kitts-Nevis (tel 469 9064, fax 469 9018).

By Boat
There are no scheduled services to St Kitts or Nevis, though plenty of cruise ships call in at Basseterre.

Travel between the Islands
LIAT flights operate half-a-dozen times a day, but are often fully booked. The local bus is really the ferry (usually twice-daily both ways; no services Thurs and Sun; about 45 minutes; EC$20 return). The views are magnificent as the mountains shift slowly above you. Kenneth's Dive Centre run a water taxi service for a minimum of 4 passengers (tel 465 2670).

TOURIST INFORMATION
The St Kitts and Nevis Tourism Offices are:
UK: c/o The High Commission for Eastern Caribbean States, 10 Kensington Court, London W8 5DL (tel (071) 376 0881).
USA: 414 East 75th St, New York, NY 10021 (tel (212) 535 1234).
Canada: 11 Yorkville Ave, Suite 508, Toronto M4W 1L3 (tel (416) 921 7717).

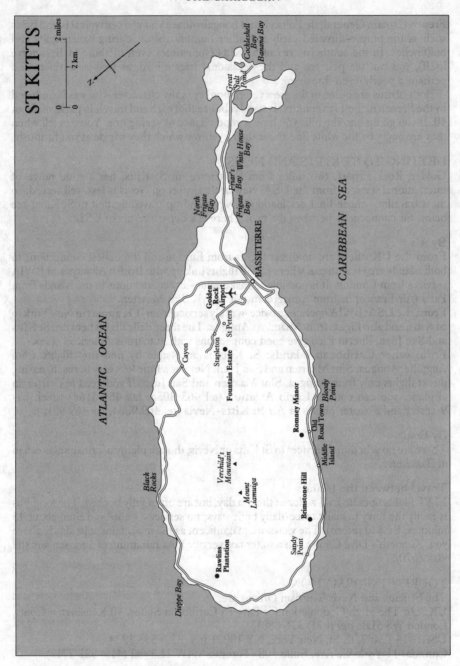

ST KITTS

2 miles
2 km

N

Cockleshell Bay
Banana Bay
Great Salt Pond
White House Bay
Friar's Bay
Frigate Bay
North Frigate Bay

BASSETERRE

CARIBBEAN SEA

ATLANTIC OCEAN

Golden Rock Airport
St Peters
Stapleton
Fountain Estate
Cayon

Romney Manor
Old Road Town
Bloody Point
Middle Island

Verchild's Mountain
Mount Liamuiga
Brimstone Hill

Black Rocks

Rawlins Plantation

Sandy Point

Dieppe Bay

The international direct dialling code for St Kitts and Nevis is 809 followed by a seven-digit local number, beginning with 465 in St Kitts and with 469 in Nevis.

MONEY
The currency of St Kitts and Nevis is the Eastern Caribbean dollar, shared with the other former British colonies in the area. It is fixed to the US$ at a rate of US$1 = EC$2.69. US dollars are accepted all over the island, though, as are the major credit cards. Make sure which dollar currency you are dealing in.

Banks are open daily 8–1 and many open for an extra two hours, Fri 3–5. The St Kitts and Nevis National Bank also opens on Saturday mornings, 8–11. Shopping hours are 8–midday and 1–4.

ST KITTS

The familiar name St Kitts (from St Christopher) has been used by the Kittitians since the 18th century. It is not known how the island took the name of the travellers' saint (Christopher Columbus did not call it this), but perhaps later explorers named it in his honour.

St Kitts is the larger of the two islands (68 square miles) and is shaped a bit like a paddle, set in the water so that the handle points southeast. The blade is covered in a ridge of volcanic mountains, tumbling steeply from the summits and then flattening out towards the sea. The slopes are traced with *ghauts*, or ravines, which look a bit like huge volcanic stretch-marks and give an idea of the upheaval that the mountains once underwent.

Like many islands in the Caribbean, St Kitts became immensely wealthy as a sugar factory in the 17th and 18th centuries (it was worth building the massive Brimstone Hill to defend it), but unlike most other islands, the slopes of St Kitts are still covered with canefields. The industry hardly pays its way—it was bought out by the government in 1975 and kept going because it employs a large number of islanders. Recently, however, cane-cutters have been brought in from Guyana and St Vincent.

GETTING AROUND ST KITTS
The ride to town is little more than a mile, but if you do not want to go by cab (EC$13), then it is a short walk over the sugar railway to the main road where a minibus will pick you up in a matter of minutes and take you to Basseterre for EC$1.

Buses, now Japanese minivans, run the roads of St Kitts intermittently from 6.30 am until about 8 pm. They leave from the waterfront in Basseterre when they are full or when the urge takes the driver. They do not generally circle the island, but run along either one coast or the other, which means that you can be stranded in the northern canefields if you are on a round-island tour. If this happens, hitch, which is a good alternative anyway.

Getting on to a bus is as easy as flagging it down on the roadside; to get off you must shout *Driver, Stop!*. The buses are inexpensive and EC$4 will get you to the north of the island.

Taxis are, of course, readily available; in Basseterre you will find them at the Circus and they can also be arranged through any of the hotels. Fares are fixed by the government. Some prices are **Golden Rock Airport** to: Basseterre—EC$13, Frigate Bay area—EC$25, Rawlins Plantation or Golden Lemon at the northern end of the island—EC$55; and from **Basseterre** to: Frigate Bay—EC$18, Brimstone Hill—EC$30, Rawlins Plantation or Golden Lemon—EC$50. Most taxi-drivers will also be willing to take you on an island tour, which costs around EC$130 for three hours. Taxis can be ordered through the St Kitts Taxi Association (tel 465 4253).

Organized island tours, to sights including Brimstone Hill and hikes up into the crater of Mount Liamiuga, can be arranged through **Kriss Tours** (tel 465 4042) and through **Greg's** (tel 465 4121).

Car hire gives the most mobility, particularly if you are staying in the north of the island, and a car can be hired for around US$40 per day or a mini-moke for slightly less. Before driving on St Kitts, you must purchase a local driving licence, obtained on production of your own licence and EC$30 at the police station in Cayon St, Basseterre. Driving is mostly on the left, though there are recognized chicanes to avoid the numerous potholes in the road. Some hire firms are: **Caines** on Prince's St, Basseterre (tel 465 2366), **Delisle Walwyn and Co.** on Liverpool Row, just off the Circus in Basseterre (tel 465 2631), **TDC Rentals** (tel 465 2991) and **Sunshine Car Rentals** (tel 465 2193).

TOURIST INFORMATION
On **St Kitts**, the main Tourism Office can be found in Pelican Mall on Bay Road, PO Box 132, Basseterre (tel 465 4040). There is also a helpful office at Golden Rock Airport. Shops are open 8–noon and 1–4. There are a couple of **art galleries** worth visiting in St Kitts. The **Spencer Cameron Gallery** (tel/fax 465 1617) is set in a pretty colonial Building on Independence Square. It exhibits some African, but mostly Caribbean paintings, some painted by Kittitians and residents on the island, but also artists from elsewhere in the Caribbean, Mon–Sat, 9 am–4 pm. In the north of the island you will find **Plantation Picture House** at Rawlins Plantation, with works painted over a ten-year period in St Kitts by Kate Spencer.

BEACHES
In the mountainous northern areas of St Kitts the beaches are mostly of black sand, but in the south, which has recently been opened up by the peninsular road the beaches have golden sand. **Frigate Bay** is still the island's most popular beach, and you will find all the facilities for watersports, a couple of hotels nearby and bars to get a drink. Its opposite number on the Atlantic side, **North Frigate Bay** is pounded by ocean waves. **Friar's Bay** is the best beach on the island and it is now easily accessible. Palm-backed, it has magnificent views and superb mounded golden sand. It can get quite busy, because cruise ships do put in here. Looking out to Nevis from the southern tip of the island there are other strips of sand—Banana Bay and Cockleshell Bay—due to be developed in a couple of years. Beyond them you will find seclusion at the thin strip of sand at **Major's Bay** There is windsurfing, kayaking and good snorkelling at **Turtle Beach**.

286

BEACH BARS

The **Monkey Bar**, an octagonal wooden hut at the bottom of **Frigate Bay** is a popular haunt with daytime bathers and at sunset when it collects a crowd. And beneath the palms on **Friar's Bay** there are a couple of lean-tos from paradise where you can get a grilled chicken or fish and a cool beer to stave off the heat. Definitely recommended, though opening times are a bit haphazard. One of the best spots for a drink and a view of Nevis (perhaps after windsurfing across) is the **Turtle Beach Bar**, which collects a lively crowd on its terraces and in the garden, particularly on Sundays. Follow the south peninsular road past Great Salt Pond and then take a left.

WATERSPORTS

The best place is **Frigate Bay**, in the hotel area south of Basseterre where many of the hotels are situated. Waterskiing and small boat sailing can be fixed up on the beach, as well as a **windsurfer** (hire about US$15 per hour). There is an annual windsurfing race in early July between Frigate Bay in St Kitts and Oualie Beach on Nevis. **Caribbean Watersports** at the Jack Tar Hotel can arrange most sports. Also try **Fisherman's Wharf** below the Ocean Terrace Inn in Basseterre (tel 465 2754).

Scheduled **catamaran cruises** (sunset or daytime picnic and snorkelling extrava-ganza) and charters can be fixed through **Tropical Tours**, PO Box 393, on Cayon St (tel 465 4167), and at the **Fisherman's Wharf**. Smaller yachts are available through the hotels and the watersports companies. **Deep-sea fishing** trips for steely-eyed shark-fishermen or women can also be arranged through the main companies above.

Scuba diving can be arranged and equipment hired through **Kenneth's Dive Centre** at the Fort Thomas Hotel (tel 465 2670), just west of Basseterre, At **Pro Divers** at the Fisherman's Wharf (tel 465 2754) and Turtle Beach (tel 465 9086). A single-tank dive costs around US$35 and operators have underwater photographic equipment. Snorkelling is good off Old Road Town on the leeward side of the island and Dieppe Bay on the northern coast.

OTHER SPORTS

On land there are well-organized **walking tours** around St Kitts, that make a close and informative inspection of plantation ruins (the conical windmills and square steam chimneys that you see from the road), and follow rivers up through the ever-encroaching undergrowth to hidden rockpools to seek out crayfish. The most rewarding walk takes you up 3792 ft to the top of St Kitts's highest peak, Mount Liamuiga (from Belmont Estate in the north), and down into its crater (400 ft down), a trip that lasts all day (US$25). Another trip takes you past Verchild's Mountain and across the island on the route of the old English military road from the 17th century, which linked the two coasts. It also passes close to the **Dos d'Ane** pond. You are advised to take a guide if you go high into the hills. If you wish to join a guided tour contact **Greg's Tours** (tel 465 4121) or **Kriss Tours** (tel 465 4042).

A more leisurely look at St Kitts's plantation history may be had on horseback, **riding** around the island or simply cantering along the beach. This can be arranged through **The Stable** (tel 465 3226). Off-season, you can sometimes ride on the sugar-cane train (tel 465 8157).

For **golfers** there are two courses on the island: the 18-hole championship course in the Frigate Bay area (green fees around US$25) and there is a nine-hole course at Golden Rock.

Basseterre

Basseterre, the small capital of St Kitts, has plenty of charm. It is home to about 15,000 Kittitians (just under half the island's population) and it is set on the mile-wide sweep of a southern-facing bay; a few streets of wooden West Indian houses ranged behind the waterfront, sheltered by the green slopes of Monkey Hill and the South Range.

The name Basseterre and its protected site have come down from the days when the French were settled here. It was adopted by the British in 1727, in preference to their capital at Old Road, but apart from this and the grid-iron layout of the town, nothing else French survives. Today, the church towers, stone Georgian buildings and even the pointed iron railings speak of the island's 350-year assocation with Britain. Life itself is changing as the colonial memory recedes, but echoes remain in the police's pith helmets, Bedford trucks and the clock-chimes.

Visitors in the 19th century entered Basseterre through the arch of the **Treasury Building**, the domed colonial structure on the waterfront that housed the customs. From here they emerged in the heart of the town at the **Circus**, where an elaborate brown Victorian clock-tower stands beneath a ring of royal palms. Fading 19th-century Basseterre, warehouses with dark stone foundations and bright white upper storeys, spreads out along Bay Road, parallel to the sea. St Kitts's notorious *ghauts* (pronounced gut), river-ravines, are channelled down the middle of the streets (when in flood they are fearsome and have been known to wash parked cars out to sea).

To the west of the Circus, the Government Buildings can be found on Church Street and **St George's Anglican Church** on Cayon St, built and rebuilt on the site of a French church of 1670. Travelling further west you come to the large villas in the gentrified district of Fortlands, known to the Kittitians as the 'old aristocratic area' of

Brush Salesman on the Circus, Basseterre

town. The Governor General's residence can be seen from the road, but it is not open to the public.

Walking east from the Circus you reach **Independence Square**, known until 1983 as Pall Mall Square, where the goats mowing the lawn spike the imposing grandeur of the imperious Georgian homes. The **Roman Catholic Cathedral** also overlooks the square, where *flamboyant* trees flame in summer. Further east on the waterfront, you quickly come to the boats and drying nets in the fishermen's district. In the yards of beaten earth, small clapboard houses are shaded beneath a breadfruit tree or a palm.

Visitors do not arrive by sea any more and so Treasury Pier has fallen into disrepair, used only by kids casting a line for fish or as a perch for pelicans between dive-bombing sorties. Instead, the new **customs pier** 50 yards away to the east is a hive of activity twice a day with the arrival of the ferry from Nevis. Traditional sloops also dock here to collect anything from crates of drink to building materials before sailing off to Nevis. With a boom as wide as their mast is tall they offer a graceful sight plying between the islands.

Clockwise around the Island

A coastal road runs around St Kitts, circling the island beneath the central mountain ranges, winding in and out of the ghauts, everywhere surrounded by canefields. Today the cane is crushed in one central factory, fed by a railway line, but the ruins of the old windmills and steam chimneys still stand proud behind curtains of bright green cane. Now that most of them are dilapidated, it is hard to imagine the atmosphere of a functioning plantation, but the rusting copper vats and the crushing gear still give a hint of the ceaseless human activity.

A couple of miles west of Basseterre, **Bloody Point** was the scene of an early massacre of the Caribs in 1626 when, in spite of their differences, the English and French teamed up. They were tipped off by a Carib woman that the Indians were preparing to attack and so the Europeans ambushed them, supposedly killing 2000. Strangely, the infant son of the Indian chief, Tegreman, was allowed to live and was brought up in the family of Ralph Merrifield in England.

At **Old Road Town**, capital of the English part of the island in the 17th century, you can see one of the Caribs' artistic memorials, their rock carvings: lozenge-bodied and antennaed cartoon characters waving at you from the face of black volcanic rock.

Just above the town is **Romney Manor**, a plantation that is the home of **Caribelle Batik**. The Indonesian process has been borrowed and has been turned to creating scenes with West Indian colour—anything from the fluorescent fish-life to the pastel nightlife, Mon–Fri, 8 am–4 pm.

A mile farther on is the town of **Middle Island**, where you will find the tomb of Sir Thomas Warner, the pioneer British settler, who was knighted at Hampton Court by Charles I for his efforts. He first arrived in 1623 and died here in 1648, a 'noble and much lamented gent'. From St Kitts, he had settled the islands of Nevis, Antigua and Montserrat.

Brimstone Hill

Beyond Middle Island, an 800-foot peak rises next to the coast, on the flank of Mount Liamuiga itself. Its contours appear square because a massive fortress sits on the summit—a 38-acre stronghold with a citadel presiding over miles of rampart, bastions, barracks, powder magazines and an amphitheatrical cistern. Brimstone Hill, named because of the sulphur which you can still smell nearby, is a fitting name for this monster—the whole edifice is built of burnt black stone.

The hill was first fortified in the 1690s, and with walls seven feet thick added almost 100 years later, it was considered impregnable, but it was stormed successfully by the French in 1782. They shelled it for weeks until there were breaches in the ramparts 40 feet wide and not a building was left standing. Once the fighting was over, the fortifications were rebuilt and this lumbering giant became known as the *Gibraltar of the West Indies*. It was never attacked again.

Today much of Brimstone Hill has been restored and it bristles with cannon once more. But despite the odd whiff of sulphur, the hellish aspect of Brimstone Hill has gone: the ramparts are overgrown with bougainvillaea, and cannon lie around useless. The view from the summit is magnificent and ranges from Montserrat and Nevis in the south to Statia, Saba, St Martin and St Barthélemy in the north. The citadel now contains a museum, displaying uniforms and weapons alongside the history of St Kitts. Open daily 9.30–5.30, Thurs and Sun 2.30–5.30; adm.

Sandy Point, a typical West Indian town, with clapboard rum shops and the odd old stone building jostling new concrete, is the second largest town on the island. **Charles Fort** was the island's leper asylum. From here, the road runs through the canefields around the northern point of St Kitts, in the shadow of Mount Liamuiga. In the 17th century, the Dutch were the great traders and they kept warehouses at Sandy Point. A fire in 1663 cost them 65 warehouses full of tobacco. The island five miles off the coast is Dutch St Eustatius.

Mount Liamuiga (pronounced 'Liar-mweagre') is the highest point on the island at 3792 ft, and there is a crater lake just below the lip. The volcano, which was known for most of its history as Mt Misery, is (almost) inactive; it has been known to rumble very slightly once in a while.

Dieppe Bay takes its name from its French heritage, which lasted until the early 18th century. The dilapidated stone and wooden buildings give an idea of the town's former prosperity as a sugar port.

Returning down the Atlantic coast to Basseterre, the road passes the **Black Rocks**, volcanic extrusions that have blackened into weird black shapes since their eruption millions of years ago.

At Cayon a road cuts inland to Basseterre, running through the villages of Stapleton and St Peter's. Just beyond Stapleton is the Fountain Estate House, built on the site of **La Fontaine**, the residence of illustrious French Governor de Poincy in the 1640s. Not only was he Captain General, but he was also Knight of Malta. He arrived with due pomp and circumstance and promptly erected himself a four-storey château in keeping with his station. The magnificent building was destroyed by an earthquake in 1689 and only the chapel and the steps remain.

The inland road rejoins the coast road as it approaches Basseterre, just by the central **Sugar Factory**. This monster is a proper factory, with conveyor belts feeding vast metal maws, banks of crushers that squeeze the very last drop of juice from the cane, and disgorge just a white pulp known as *bagasse*. All St Kitts' cane is brought in on the narrow-gauge railway track that runs around the northern part of the island. Among the modern equipment, vast brightly-coloured baskets full of cane, you can see the old coal-fired engines of seasons past. It does not take much persuasion to get an old hand on to stories of when cane was cut by gangs wielding bill-hooks.

There are no regular tours of the factory, but it is possible to visit it during the cane-crushing season, between February and June, by asking at the gate.

South of Basseterre
Passing through the last of the canefields, the road south from Basseterre descends into the Frigate Bay area, the tourist enclave, cut off from the heart of St Kitts. In 1989 a road was constructed that opened up the south of the island, and large international hotel companies have muscled in on the beaches. Once, Frigate Bay was the scene of early morning duels between slighted members of the St Kitts nobility, but now it tends to be clubs at dawn on the golf-course and a bit of jousting on jet-skis. The deer that used to live in this area have moved into the northern mountains.

From Frigate Bay, the new road leads past the old salt ponds, common property in the days when the island was shared by the French and English, and comes to Cockleshell Bay and Banana Bay, where there are magnificent views of Nevis.

FESTIVALS
The main event in the Kittitian calendar is **Carnival**, which takes place just after Christmas and lasts into New Year. It is a week of *jump-up*, singing and Beauty Queen shows. Not many tourists attend, though plenty of Kittitians return to the island for the festivities and it is fun to watch the events in the stadium at Warner Park and around the streets of Basseterre. Grab a chicken leg and a *Carib* lager from one of the ladies fanning braziers at the edge of the park and join the crowd. There are other smaller events in the year, more dancing in the streets of Basseterre: *Ghautarama* on the first Saturday in June, *Blockarama* and in November, *Village-arama* in St Johnston's, which sees fashion parades and the calypsonians sparring with one another in song.

Independence Day is celebrated on 19 September with traditional Caribbean feasting.

WHERE TO STAY
St Kitts (and Nevis) has far and away the finest collection of plantation house hotels in the Caribbean. Many are still surrounded by sugar cane as they were two hundred years ago and they still retain the grace and hopitality of the era—they are small and are run in the style of a private house. As former estate houses, most are not on the beach, and so you might like to hire a car for mobility, but the hotels also run beach shuttles a couple of times a day. Children are sometimes not encouraged at these hotels.

There are also purpose-built resorts in the Frigate Bay area, with more being constructed at the tip of the southeast peninsula. St Kitts also has a number of villas for hire all over the island. Details can be obtained from the Tourist Board.

Plantation Houses
Rawlins Plantation, PO Box 340, St Kitts (tel 465 6221, fax 465 4954) has one of the Caribbean's supreme settings in an old estate house on the slopes of Mt Liamuiga, looking north to Statia and Sint Maarten. There are just ten rooms, scattered in stone outbuildings and cottages among the tropical trees and hedges of the estate gardens. But

the house itself, with library and dining room, is the nerve centre, where you take cocktails and then dinner overlooking the grounds. A bewildering variety of tropical fruits for breakfast, followed by a buffet lunch (worth attending if you are not staying there, for the saltfish and funchi and the candied sweet potato) and then dinner of chicken and mango or lamb in guava sauce. If this sounds over-indulgent then you can walk in the forests above the estate or knock a ball about on the grass tennis court. Expensive, but there are few places like it anywhere in the Caribbean. Double in season US$375. Close by is the **Golden Lemon** (tel 465 7260, fax 465 4019), which is set in a 17th-century trading warehouse on the waterfront in Dieppe Bay. It is now beautifully restored and the old stone walls are more likely to echo with piano and singing accompaniment after dinner than the rumbling of rum barrels. There are 16 rooms, with wooden floorboards and louvred windows, gracefully furnished with antiques and with huge beds. But most charming are the ten suites in the Lemon Grove, which have been exquisitely decorated, each in a different style; tropical, oriental, Egyptian. Double room US$325, villas from $475 a night. **Ottley's Plantation Inn** PO Box 345 (tel 465 7234, fax 465 4760, US 800 772 3039) is set in magnificent grounds. From the colonial grandeur of the enormous rooms and balconies you look over restored stone outhouses and a superb lawn backed with royal palms to the Atlantic Ocean beyond. Again the private house atmosphere, centred on the stonework terrace of the old boiling house, where you will find the dining room and the pool. Prices for the 15 rooms are very good, at US$160–275 a double in season. The **White House**, PO Box 436 (tel 465 8162, fax 465 8275) used to be the military mess and the officers made sure to choose a superb site high above Basseterre for their retreat. The drawing room and dining rooms are furnished to suit the period (perhaps a little more luxuriously than the original), with rugs, chaises longues and rosewood chairs. The bedrooms are also far more comfortable than you might find in an old coach house. Just ten doubles, painted white with four posters. Tennis, croquet, golf nearby and other officer-like pursuits. Expensive at US$350 a double in season.

The **Ocean Terrace Inn**, PO Box 65 (tel 465 2754, fax 465 1057, US 800 223 5695) is close to town, but isolated from the relative hurly-burly in a walled garden that rambles cross the hillside. The 54 rooms make it sound large, but they are scattered around the main house, where you can swim and drink at the pool bar before dining before a view of Nevis. Watersports are arranged from the **Fisherman's Wharf** on the waterfront just below; US$105–205 a double. The **Fairview Inn**, PO Box 212 (tel 465 2472, fax 465 1056), is set in a classical Kittitian great house overlooking the Caribbean coast, with wooden floors and ceilings. It hasn't quite the style of the other inns of St Kitts, but prices itself accordingly. There are 23 rooms in stone cottages behind the great house, which has a busy and friendly bar. Double room in season US$120–140.

If you want to be on the beach, then you can get comfortable rooms and suites at the **Timothy Beach Resort**, PO Box 81 (tel 465 8597, fax 465 7723, US 800 621 1270) at the southern end of Frigate Bay. There are 60 rooms in blocks and a walkway of crotons and bougainvillaea down to the pool and **Coconut Café** just above the beach. There are kitchenettes in some rooms: double rate US$110–180 in season. Less expensive self-catering accommodation in Frigate Bay is available at the **Gateway Inn**, PO Box 446 (tel 465 7155, fax 465 1106). Walking distance from the beach, double room US$70. Also try **Conaree Beach Cottages**, PO Box 259 (tel 465 8110) on the Atlantic coast. US$65.

Guest Houses
There are two typically West Indian guest houses in Basseterre where local businessmen stay. Try the **Windsor Guest House** (tel 465 2894) on Cayon St (US$25–35) and the **Park View Guest House** (tel 465 2100), next to the bakery on Victoria Road (US$20–40).

EATING OUT
The food in St Kitts is fairly typical of the British Caribbean, chicken, fish or goat, often in a stew, served with a tonnage of Caribbean vegetables, but the more adventurous dining rooms will serve not only these, but also more exotic ingredients in tropical fruit sauces and some traditional European recipes. There is of course the rather less traditional burger to be found in the resort hotels, but it is well worth getting out to find a more Caribbean meal, either in the plantation houses, which serve excellent buffet lunches and set dinners, or in the side streets of Basseterre. Not many places accept credit cards and there is usually a 10% service charge added to the bill.

MODERATE
At the **Patio** (tel 465 8666) in Frigate Bay you dine on the veranda of a private house with tables lit by candle-lamps and served by waitresses in French creole *madras* costume. The menu is continental, with Caribbean adaptations—seafood pasta and lobster with crab, followed by tropical fruit parfait or chocolate mousse pie with a brownie crust. Main course EC$25–35, by reservation only. The **Georgian House** (tel 465 4049) is set in an 18th-century Caribbean town-house on Independence Square with antique dining rooms inside and a tropical garden at the rear. The menu is Mediterranean, with specials of local fish and seafood. Main course from EC$30. Closed Mon. The **Lighthouse** (tel 465 8914) sits on the cliff just above the deep water harbour, on the site of the old Fort Smith (from which it has taken its mock crenellations). It is air-conditioned and plush, with grill foods and gourmet dishes such as Dover Sole St Christopher, followed by fruit sorbets. There is a bar on the point itself and a couple of nights a week it hosts the Lighthouse discotheque. Main dish EC$40 plus, open Tues–Sat. Another popular spot in Basseterre, for a daytime drink or a cocktail at dusk, is the **Ballahoo**, upstairs above the Circus in the centre of town. Quite a few tourists, but some locals too—chilli shrimps or seafood platter and always a vegetarian dish, from EC$30.

CHEAP
Chef's Place on Church St serves West Indian food to a local crowd. Delicious local vegetable soups including pumpkin, carrot and dasheen, followed by turtle, saltfish and local fish. Open lunch and dinner, Mon–Sat, main course EC$12–40. There are plenty of local hide-outs in Basseterre where you can get traditional chicken or fish. Try **Victor's** in the New Town, where you dine on mock-leather benches and plastic table-cloths in a modern pink town-house. Local juices to accompany Kittitian fare— plates of curry goat heaped with green fig and sweet potato. **Victoria's Place** is on Victoria Rd and here you can taste more West Indian specialities—lobster or fresh fish with rice and peas or even a Montserratian *goat-water* (a goat stew with pepper, sweet pepper, onions, clove and thyme). EC$12–20. You can get an excellent take-away pizza

293

or a roti at the **Pizza Place** on Central St in town. And if you would like a classic fry chicken to go, try **Gilly's** on Sandown Rd or **Wendy's** on Cayon St. On Fridays and Saturdays the Kittitians cook up chicken and fish on braziers at the streetside.

BARS AND NIGHTLIFE

Much of the entertainment in St Kitts is centred around the hotels, whether it be singing along to Broadway tunes at the Golden Lemon or joining in the Jack Tar toga party. However, if you fancy a drink with some Kittitians after work, there are plenty of rum shops around the island. Try **Five-Ways**, on the junction of five roads at the western end of Central St, which collects a crowd of ministers and limers, and **Tiffin**, off Pond Rd. Turn at Uncle Jerry's corner.

There are a few clubs you can move on to. You can hear live music at the **Fisherman's Wharf** at the weekend. **Mingles** on Frigate Bay Rd, upstairs at the Flex Fitness Centre opens Thurs–Sat with a varied crowd and the **Lighthouse**, just out of town, has a clifftop bar with a view and a discotheque at the weekends.

NEVIS

At times it is the only cloud in the sky, but there is always a cloud on the summit of Nevis. Like all the tall volcanic Caribbean islands, Nevis blocks the path of the racing Atlantic winds which, as they rise and condense, stack in huge immobile cumulus clouds. This permanent white wreath supposedly reminded the Spanish travellers of the snow-capped peaks of home and so the island came to be called *Nuestra Señora de las Nieves*, Our Lady of the Snows. Gradually, the name has been shortened to Nevis (pronounced Nee-viss).

Nevis is almost circular (six miles by eight) and from the sea can look like a regular cone; deep green slopes rise in sweeping curves to the central Nevis Peak at 3232 ft. About 9000 Nevisians live in villages dotted all over the island.

Nevis is the smaller and quieter partner in the Federation with St Kitts and the vanishing stateliness of the old Caribbean is just visible here. Once, the island was known as the *Queen of the Caribbees* because the society was so august and the estate houses were so grand that ladies could walk down the stairs three abreast, panniered skirts and all. 'Old-time' Nevis is mostly gone now and the finely-crafted bridges and dark stone walls are being swallowed up in the ever-encroaching jungle, but the plantation house hotels retain the old grace and finery of centuries past and they are some of the most exquisite hotels in the Caribbean.

The Nevisians go more placidly than their fellow-countrymen. In school, the children learn that there were no slave rebellions in the island's history, in which fact Nevis would probably be alone in the whole Caribbean. Certainly the Nevisians are extremely polite and they all have time to stop and talk to a stranger.

A hundred years of association across the *Narrows* may have forged close relations, but it has not diminished Nevis's own traditions. When the Deputy Governor-General of St Kitts and Nevis is in residence you will always see two flags flying: one is for the Federation of St Kitts with Nevis and the other Nevis's own flag.

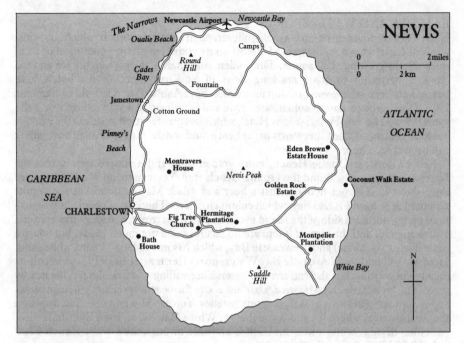

GETTING AROUND

There is a scant **bus** service that sets off from Charlestown in both clockwise and anti-clockwise directions. Buses leave from the town centre and run until 6.30 pm (8 pm on Saturdays), maximum fare possible is about EC$3. Hitching works well in Nevis, but there are just not many cars around.

Taxis are available near the pier in Charlestown, at Newcastle airport and through the hotels. Some sample prices are **Charlestown** to: Pinney's Beach—EC$10, Oualie Beach—EC$23, Newcastle airport—EC$30, Fig Tree Church—EC$18 and Golden Rock Hotel—EC$30. Taxis can also be hired for a three-hour island tour for around EC$120.

You need a local licence if you wish to drive in Nevis, and it can be obtained on presentation of your own licence and EC$30 to the Police in Charlestown. Mini-mokes are very popular and easily available. There is basically one road, about 20 miles long, that runs around the island, with one or two branches leading off it. Watch out for the goats who seem to find the tastiest grass at the roadside.

Car rental costs around US$45 per day and a mini-moke slightly less. Hire firms are: **Nisbet's** Car Rental on Main Street in Charlestown (tel 469 1913), **Gajor's** Car Rental, in Bath (tel 469 5367) and **Skeete's Car Rental** at Newcastle airport (tel 469 9458).

TOURIST INFORMATION

The helpful **Tourism Office** is on Main St in Charlestown (tel 469 5521).

BEACHES AND WATERSPORTS

Nevis has a stunning three-and-a-half-mile strand in **Pinney's Beach**, which starts just north of Charlestown and is backed almost on its entire length by a confusion of palm trees, trunks growing at all angles. The golden sand shelves steeply into the sea and the scene is perfected by some cracking views of St Kitts. Some of the hotels have beach-huts here, where you can stop for a drink. **Fort Ashby Bar**, a few old battlements just off the beach, is almost comatose in style and is well worth a stop to linger over the sunset view. The new Four Seasons Hotel, which has planted itself smack in the middle, has brought large-scale watersports to the beach, and windsurfing and small boat sailing can be arranged here.

Farther north is **Oualie Beach**, more golden sand and a superb view across the Narrows, where you will find the **Oualie Beach Bar**. You can fix up windsurfing here (hire about US$15 per hour) or just a beer and salad. May or June sees the annual sailboard race from Frigate Bay, which culminates here. There are a couple of indentations on the northern side of the island overlooking the Narrows; one long strip between Hurricane Hill and the airport (there are no facilities and not much shade, but you are quite likely to be alone) and **Newcastle Bay**, which has more steep-sloping white sand. Here you will find the **Newcastle Bay Watersports Centre** (tel 469 9395) which offers mainly windsurfing, but also can arrange waterskiing, sailing or snorkelling on the nearby reefs. The Newcastle Bay **Mariner**, a bar just above the beach, specializes in huge pizzas and is popular with locals as well as sports fanatics. You can also find a secluded spot on the Atlantic side, where the sea is rougher, at **White Bay** (down from Sheriffs).

Scuba-diving, rental and instruction is available through the **Oualie Beach Club** (tel 460 9735) in the north of the island.

OTHER SPORTS

For **walkers**, there are some worthwhile hikes into the Nevisian jungle, taking a look at the island's more exotic flora. From the slopes of Mount Nevis there are some spectacular views to the surrounding islands, when it is not shrouded in the cloud, of course. A good route to the peak leaves from above Zetlands Plantation, for which you are advised to take a guide. Another summit, usually unclouded, with supreme views is **Round Hill**, in the north of Nevis. The drop-off point is the village of Fountain, inland from Cades Bay.

The old sugar estates provide excellent foraging ground for the walker/historian. There are endless ruins on Nevis, where the skeletons of mansions gape in their decay and the long overgrown gardens are littered with cane-crushing rollers and boiling coppers. The Nevis Historical and Conservation Society is based at Alexander Hamilton House.

There was once an Upper Round Road which ringed Nevis above the plantation estates, linking Zion, Rowlands and Hamilton. Much of it is still walkable, if a little overgrown. **Montravers House**, inland from Pinneys Beach, was the finest on the island when Nevis was the Queen of the Caribbees (it even had a moat). **Bath House** is just south of Charlestown, and on the windward coast there are fine ruins at **Coconut Walk Estate** close to New River. Not far north on the Atlantic coast is the **Eden Brown Estate House**, famous for its ghost, the tortured bride who lost her husband in a duel with his best man on the very night of her wedding.

Riding: a ride in the foothills of Nevis Peak or a canter through the surf can be arranged through **Cane Gardens** (tel 469 5464) or the Hermitage Inn. Attached to the Four Seasons Hotel, on the Caribbean coast behind Pinney's Beach, is an 18-hole, Robert Trent Jones II **golf** course.

Charlestown

The island's capital and only town is Charlestown, a few streets of charming old stone buildings with balconies and gingerbread woodwork ranged along the Caribbean coast. It is home to 1500 Nevisians, whom you will see hanging out in the Court House square at the town centre—hucksters selling sweets and drinks, and a small crowd of *limers* passing the time of day. The odd countryman still rides into town on his donkey.

The town also has a strong spirit of 'when the boat comes in'—the atmosphere of sedation switches to one of hectic activity twice a day with the arrival of the ferry from Basseterre. Everything has to be brought in by boat and as the inter-island sloops or the ferry chug into harbour, loaded to the gunwhales with crates of bottles and boxes of tins, so the Nevisians race to the pier. Business complete, the activity is eclipsed and Charlestown snaps back into its customary slumber.

Just along the waterfront from the pier is the **Market**, at its busiest on a Saturday morning, when the fruits and spices are heaped on the tables and lightning banter fills the air from soon after dawn.

Alexander Hamilton

At the northern end of town, on a lane called Low Street, is **Alexander Hamilton House**, the birthplace and home for five years of the architect of the American Constitution, whose face you will see on the US$10 bill. The house was built in the late 1600s and Hamilton was born there in 1757 of a Nevisian mother and a Scots father. When he was five, they moved to St Croix, from where Alexander eventually left to complete his education in the States. A patriot during the American Revolution, he was George Washington's aide-de-camp. He was known as the 'Little Lion' because he was five foot seven inches tall and his blue eyes were said to turn black when he was angry. Trained as a lawyer, it was he who first suggested the Federation of the American States in the form that was eventually adopted, and with its founding he became First Secretary to the American Treasury. He died in a duel with a political opponent, Aaron Burr, in 1804. The attractive building houses the **Museum of Nevis History**, with pictures of 'old-time' Nevis as well as documents from the life of Alexander Hamilton himself. The Nevis House of Assembly holds its assemblies upstairs in the building. Open weekdays and weekends in season, 8–4, adm free.

It is a short walk back along Main Street, where the few shops and offices are situated, to the small square and War Memorial and the **Court House**. On the outskirts of the town is **Government House**, built in 1909, the official Residence of the Deputy Governor-General of St Kitts and Nevis.

Close by is the **Bath Hotel**, a huge block of a building constructed in 1778 in true Nevisian style, complete with ballroom, balconies and accommodation for 50 guests. In Nevis's heyday people would come and stay here in order to take the waters, which come out of the ground at as much as 108°F and supposedly resemble those of Baden-Württemburg.

The waters were first mentioned by some visitors before Nevis was even settled. Captain John Smith, leader of the Jamestown settlers of Virginia, called here first in 1607. Some of his fellow travellers had supposedly been scalded by manchineel sap when they sheltered under the tree in the rain, but here they found 'a great poole, wherein bathing themselves they found much ease ... they were well cured in two or three days.'

The hotel is a ruin now, although it has survived the earthquakes and hurricanes well. The bath-house is still there and it is still possible to 'take the waters', so if you are scalded by a manchineel tree, then you could rush around here. It has been taken over by the government, but it would be a surprise to find any officials around; it is open 9–4, bathing costs EC50c.

Anticlockwise on the Island Road

Once past Government House, the town quickly thins into countryside with scattered plots along the road. Here you will come across age-old stand-pipes, delivering water as they have for the last 100 years, and impromptu roadside markets which switch to the other side of the road at midday to take advantage of the shade.

In Belle View on the way out of town you will find the **Nelson Museum**, the collection of American writer Robert Abrahams. There are some of Nelson's documents and letters and porcelain from the marriage feast in 1787. Open weekdays 9–4 and Sat 10–noon, adm free.

Fig Tree Church, a small stone sanctuary in a tropical garden, is famous for the register of Horatio Nelson's marriage to the Nevisian girl Fanny Nisbet in 1787. He was based at English Harbour in Antigua on the *HMS Boreas* in the 1780s, but was unpopular with the West Indians because his job was to enforce the Navigation Laws which banned their very profitable trade with other countries (they even sued him once and he had to stay on board his ship for eight weeks to avoid being locked up). However, he found solace with the young widow Fanny, whom he first met at Montpelier House.

Fig-Tree Church

298

Prince William Henry, the friend of Nelson who later became King William IV, gave the bride away and his signature can also be seen in the register. The couple soon returned to England, but the marriage did not last as Nelson became involved with Lady Hamilton.

Saddle Hill is the site of a huge hilltop fort, started in 1740, which now lies in ruins. During his stays on Nevis Nelson would reputedly be seen each day on the hill with his spyglass pointed out to sea. Now it is a good place to rootle around and of course, as a lookout, the views are still magnificent.

At Camps near the northern side of the island, you can take a road that leads into the forest and through the hills, emerging on the Caribbean coast at Cades Bay at the **Soufrière**. This is an active volcanic vent that first appeared with a hiss and a sulphurous stench when an earthquake struck in 1950. It is a bit lukewarm now, with just the odd trace of stink-bomb and some heated and barren patches of earth, but is a reminder that the underworld is not so far away in the Caribbean.

The road returns to Charlestown along the Caribbean coast, behind Pinneys Beach. **Jamestown,** first capital of Nevis, which slid into the sea in 1680 when another earthquake struck the island, is visible to scuba divers just off the coast. It is said that one man escaped the quake when the jail collapsed around him. 'Redlegs Greaves', a Scots gentleman pirate who retired to an estate on Nevis after a lifetime of freebooting, had been recognized by a former comrade in revelry and had been thrown in jail. Having been spared by the earthquake, he was eventually pardoned.

FESTIVALS
In Nevis, the island festival goes by the rather unwieldy name of *Culturama*. There are displays of arts and crafts alongside many of the more regular Caribbean Carnival activities, so you can expect the streets of Charlestown to pulse to calypso, while beauty queens and dancing parades *jump up*. Culturama takes place in late July, coming to its climax on the first Monday in August.

WHERE TO STAY
Like St Kitts, Nevis has some extremely fine plantation hotels, where you can bask in 18th-century splendour; they are low key, but they are smoothly run. There has recently been a rather more frantic addition to this sedate bunch in the Four Seasons Hotel on Pinney's Beach, providing intensive beach-bound entertainment for those who need it, but generally Nevis is still gentle. It is still possible to have a cup of West Indian cocoa on the veranda as the day begins, just as the planters did 200 years ago. There is a 7% room charge and hotels add 10% to your bill for service.

There are also a number of villas and cottages dotted around the island, for those who would prefer to be independent and perhaps do the round of the restaurants in the evening. Contact the Tourist Board or Prendergast Services at Red Roof, Jones Estate, Nevis (tel 469 9600).

The **Hermitage Inn**, St John's Parish (tel 469 3477, fax 469 2481, US 800 223 9815) has a supreme setting on the southern facing slopes of Nevis. Around the great house, a classic West Indian timber-frame building from the 1740s, the rooms are set in neat cottages with traditional shingle walls and tin roofs, wrapped in gingerbread woodwork and bougainvillaea. There is the easy-going atmosphere of a private house. Guests meet

299

for a rum punch and tannia fritters before dinner on the veranda: Caribbean pumpkin soup, followed by batter-fried dolphin in caper and tarragon sauce or delicate local curry. Fixed price US$35. The rooms, beautifully presented with four-posters, wooden interiors and a balconies to savour the view, cost US$285–385 a double in winter (includes breakfast and dinner). **Montpelier Plantation Inn**, PO Box 474 (tel 469 3462, fax 469 2932, US 800 243 9240) is another tropical island idyll of centuries past, with the same gracious ambience, if a little more English in style. There are 16 rooms in cottages scattered around the grounds of a magnificent estate house, linked with brick paths through forests of flamboyant and frangipani. The plantation is lost in the southern hills of Nevis, but there are shuttles to the beach. The kitchen produces impeccable West Indian fare—pepper shrimp followed by local lobster and soursop ice-cream—which you eat on a huge veranda above the garden, before retiring inside for coffee and liqueurs. This place is quiet, luxurious and sedate and it will not let you down. About US$350 with breakfast and dinner. **Nisbet Plantation Beach Club**, St James Parish (tel 469 9325, fax 469 9864, US 800 344 2049) has the advantage among the plantation hotels of being on the beach, though as a larger hotel it lacks the intimacy of the others. The view from the great house to the seafront is superb—down an alley of tall palms beneath which the 38 rooms are situated. They are luxurious, with white wicker furniture and sea-facing balconies behind tropical screens. The great house is a fine setting for dinner—soursop soup followed by fresh salmon in saffron and puff pastry. Retire for piano accompaniment to your coffee in the drawing room and bar. Rates good at US$298–378 (includes breakfast, dinner and afternoon tea). The **Golden Rock Estate**, PO Box 493 (tel 469 5346, fax 469 2113, US 800 223 9815), is a smaller and simpler plantation hotel set 1000 ft up the mountain side and threatened with being swallowed up by its 25 acres of garden. Old estate buildings have been converted into drawing-room and bar, the cistern into the swimming pool and the shell of the windmill into the honeymooners' suite; the other rooms are a little disappointing in modern concrete villas. The hotel runs a number of special interest holidays, including nature and photography or ecology and painting as well as island exploration. Double room rate US$175, $235 with breakfast and dinner.

The **Four Seasons Resort**, PO Box 565, Charlestown (tel 469 1111, fax 469 1040, US 800 332 3442, Canada 800 268 6282, UK 071 834 4422) is a departure for Nevis. It is large, sumptuous, manicured and without much character, but good for a body-holiday—massage parlour, health centre, watersports and day cruises, tennis and golf, low cal meals and king-sized beds. Room service and five categories of rooms. Expensive at US$400–1000 daily.

The **Oualie Beach Club** (tel 469 9735, fax 469 9176) is situated on the golden sand of Oualie beach and has the feel of an original Caribbean beach club, small and laid-back. Just twelve bright and breezy rooms with screened balconies and superb views of St Kitts, which you can admire from the old planters' chairs (with arms that extend forward so you can rest your legs). There is an active bar and restaurant for West Indians meals and watersports are available. Double room US$115 in season. At the southern end of Pinney's Beach and on the edge of Charlestown is the fading **Pinney's Beach Hotel**, PO Box 61 (tel 469 5207), with its view along the strand and its three-mile jumble of palm trees from the rooms and cottages. The bar attracts a local crowd as well as visitors. Moderate, from US$140.

The **Seaspawn Guest House**, PO Box 489 (tel 469 5648), is also on the edge of Charlestown and offers no-nonsense rooms each with a private bath. It is a good place from which to explore Nevis if your hotel is not the main point of the holiday. Rooms charged as doubles, and singles have reductions; US$45. You can also try **Meade's Guest House** on Craddock Road in Charlestown, US$30.

EATING OUT
The finest food and the best settings are found on the verandas of the plantation house hotels (see above), but there are a few other restaurants where you can get a local meal with the Nevisians. Most restaurants add a 10% service charge to your bill.

At **Prinderella's** (tel 469 9291) in the northwest of the island, you dine on a tropical terrace just above the waves. Salads by day and grilled local catch in the evening, or sole with dill butter, followed by guava ice cream. Main dish EC$20. If you would like an original Trinidadian roti, then you could try **Miss June** (tel 469 9330), who serves in her home not far from here. For a pizza with a view, try the **Newcastle Bay Mariner** in the north of the island, which attracts a crowd of expats and locals. They also serve a volley of cocktails and Mexican and local foods, EC$12–40. **Unella's** (tel 469 5574) overlooks the Charlestown waterfront from an upstairs veranda. Local meals include callaloo and curry goat with rica and peas. Dinner daily, EC$10–25.

For an early evening drink you can try any of the beach bars or the restaurants, but you might check out the **Octagon Bar** in town or brightly painted **Dick's Bar** near Alexander Hamilton House. At Nisbet Plantation and the Jonathon Villa Hotel a pianist plays in season.

ANGUILLA

Anguilla is a flat, barren island, sixteen miles by three and mostly 15 feet deep in scrub. Inland, the 'eel' is hardly attractive, but along its writhing coastline Anguilla has the Caribbean's most spectacular beaches—mounds of sumptuously soft and blinding white sand, set in an electric blue sea. On a coast 45 miles long, there are about 30 of them.

Anguilla is the most northerly of the British Leewards and it lies about five miles from the French part of St Martin, looking north and east into the Atlantic. Sombrero Rock, its dependency, is the northernmost point in the chain of the Lesser Antilles.

The 7500 Anguillians are pretty cool—for a small island there is a remarkable air of independence and self-assurance. The island is quiet to the point of sedation and it seems that nothing could ruffle Anguilla's calm. But it is worth remembering that 20 years ago, when they wanted to secede from St Kitts and Nevis, they took to the scrub and staged a revolution.

As with so many Caribbean islands, the Anguillians you meet here are only half the story, as there are probably more abroad than there are on the island itself. The island has never been able to offer its people a living and so traditionally they have travelled. The money they send home and money from tourism has made Anguilla quite rich.

As you travel around the island you will see the grey skeletons of partially built houses protruding from the scrub. You might think they were the failed dreams of ex-patriots, paradise homes that have foundered on classic West Indian business inertia. But this is not the case at all, as most of them are owned by Anguillians abroad. When the traveller has earned enough, he returns to build the first storey of his house on the plot, then leaves again to earn more in order to decorate it. Steel reinforcements are left sticking into the sky ready for the time that the family outgrows the house and they need a second storey.

Apart from the impeccable beaches, it is the Anguillan people that make this barren islet a special place. As they greet you with the slightest wave and a soothing 'all right, all right', it is hard to imagine that there was ever a raised temper here, let alone a revolution.

History

In Amerindian times, Anguilla went by the name of *Malliouhana* and although it was probably christened Anguilla by a Spaniard, Spain ignored it because it offered no quick returns. Their only fleeting interest in the island was in 1633 when the Dutch moved into the area. They promptly attacked it.

In 1650 some Englishmen, an assorted bunch of rovers and misfits, made a go at settling Anguilla. They arrived to find an island 'filled with alligators and other noxious animals, but the soil was good for raising tobacco and corn, and the cattle imported multiplied very fast'. Salt could also be harvested on the island and this continues today.

Anguilla did not really turn out that well as a plantation island and soon it was a 'nest of pirates and smugglers and outlaws, dangerous to every neighbouring island and a disgrace to the British name'. But the islanders were still vulnerable to the usual raids and ransackings of the Caribs and other Europeans. The French occupied the island and the Irish attacked a number of times, leaving settlers behind in their turn (you can just hear echoes of Irish in Anguillan English).

But the defenders had more success in the 18th century. In 1744 they repelled a large French force that landed at Rendezvous Bay. The story goes that when the Anguillians ran out of ammunition, they loaded up the weights from their fishing nets in order to keep up their fire.

The early settlers had made what they could of the barren land, renting it from the Crown for the price of 'a fat capon, a kid, or one ear of Indian corn on every feast day of St Michael the Angel'. Slaves were brought to the island and yet the sugar estates could not support them, so they were left to grow their own food or fish for four days a week. They were also encouraged to go abroad, using their skills as coopers (barrel-makers) or carpenters to earn a living.

They ventured as far afield as Trinidad and Puerto Rico, dealing in merchandise and practising a bit of smuggling. A tradition of boat-building grew up on the island, rivalled only in the Grenadines. Even the Governor was known as an 'honest old sloop man' at one stage. As they sailed, they would send home contributions from the money they earned abroad, 'remittances' that were the back-bone of the economy until very recently.

Initially Anguilla had no Governor, but was administered by a notable on the island such as the doctor, who also acted as magistrate, but in 1825 the island was attached to St Kitts for administrative convenience. The Anguillians had very little in common with the people of this successful sugar colony founded on slave-labour, which in any case was about 60 miles away to the south. Occasionally they protested to the British Government, but without success. With little representation in the St Kitts House of Assembly, the Anguillians were treated as poor relations and they had to fight hard even to get their name added to the title of the country St Kitts and Nevis in 1951.

The Revolution
In 1967, when all the British Caribbean colonies were given internal self-rule as 'Associated States' with Great Britain, with the option of Independence not far off, Anguilla found itself faced with the possibility of Independence in Union with St Kitts and Nevis. The islanders promptly staged a revolution. On 30 May 1967, they rounded up the Kittitian policemen and shipped them out, refusing to recognize the authority of the Basseterre Government.

From the beginning the whole situation bemused outsiders and was written up as 'the mouse that roared' or 'the eel that squealed', but they did not reckon with the determination of the Anguillians, who even went as far as staging a tiny invasion (unsuccessful) of St Kitts to pre-empt attempts to take Anguilla by force. They held referenda and wrote a constitution for themselves.

Disbelieving colonial officials were dispatched to persuade the Anguillians to rejoin St Kitts-Nevis, but the islanders were adamant. With political tension mounting in 1969, British troops were sent to occupy the island in an operation which was later dubbed Britain's *Bay of Piglets* after the invasion of Cuba a few years before. Not a shot was fired, and the soldiers arrived to find themselves welcomed by people singing 'God Save the Queen'. When the troops were withdrawn, the London Metropolitan Police took over. All around them Caribbean countries were shaking off the colonial yoke, but Anguilla decided that it did not want Independence at all. It preferred to remain a Crown Colony of Britain.

The political solution was long in coming, but eventually in 1982 Anguilla was granted its own constitution, with Ministerial Government headed by a Governor and ministers chosen from an 11-member House of Assembly. The Government is led by Chief Minister Emile Gumbs, who was re-elected to office in 1989.

Today many Anguillians depend on fishing for their livelihood, sailing to catch lobsters, which sell for a very good price and are flown out to hotels as far off as Puerto Rico each evening. Others work in the hotels or in the construction industry. For now, fewer Anguillians work abroad as it is more difficult to get visas. Tourism has also taken off since the early 80s and the island specializes in a brand of low-key high luxury. On an island where life has been precarious for so long, Anguilla is probably more prosperous now than it ever has been.

GETTING TO ANGUILLA
The modest airport in the centre of the island has services only to other nearby islands, but most flights from Europe and the States can make the connection the same day. Transit points are Antigua, Sint Maarten and San Juan. The journey by sea from St Martin is perhaps a more charming way to arrive, and it is also cheaper; travellers departing Anguilla by air pay a departure tax of EC$16; those leaving by boat pay EC$5.

By Air
From the UK: the easiest connections are made in Antigua, where LIAT (tel 2238) links up with the regular British Airways flights to ensure a relatively trouble-free onward

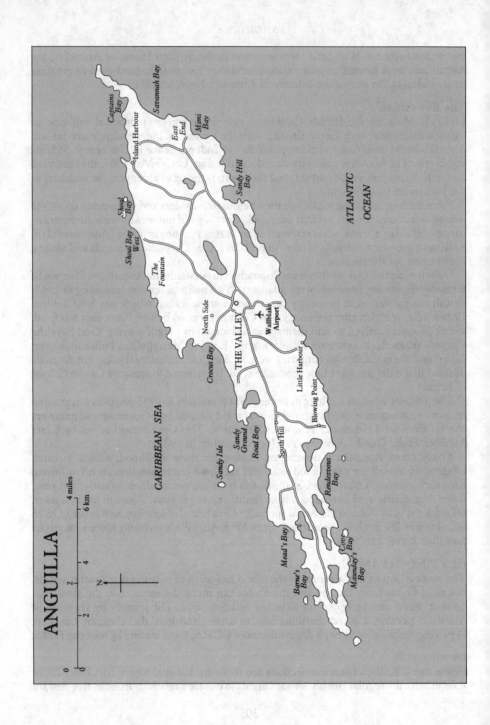

link. An alternative is to take the BA flight to San Juan on Puerto Rico, and connect there on American Eagle. Finally, travellers could take advantage of the competitive fares to St Martin/St Maarten, and continue from there by air or sea. From elsewhere in **Europe**, Air France, KLM and Lufthansa fly to Sint Maarten.
From the USA: the main gateway for Anguilla is San Juan. American Eagle (tel 3500) has two flights daily from San Juan, where there are easy connections on American Airlines and other carriers to all the large US cities.
From other Caribbean Islands: Winair (Windward Island Airways, tel 2748) provides an air link from St Thomas and Sint Maarten. LIAT serves Anguilla from Antigua and St Kitts. Finally, the island's carrier Air Anguilla has daily services from St Thomas and they will charter from San Juan or Antigua (tel 809 497 2643, fax 497 2982).

By Boat
Ferries link the port of Marigot in the French territory of St Martin with Blowing Point on the south of Anguilla. Services leave every 30 minutes during the day. The fare for the 20-minute journey is US$9 one-way, $11 in the evening. If you can, take the gull-wing powerboat built by Rebel Marine on Anguilla, with an engine that makes a sonorous rumble. You will have to pay a departure tax from St Martin of US$2.

GETTING AROUND
There is an almost mystical **bus** service in Anguilla, a couple of minivans that run from Blowing Point to the Valley, and occasionally on other roads, to an entirely unpredictable schedule. Track it down if you can. Hitching works all right; there are just not that many cars around.
   If you would like to travel the island by **bicycle**, contact **Sandy Island Enterprises** (tel 6395) in Road Bay or **Boo's Cycle** (tel 2323), just above Sandy Ground.
   Taxis can be arranged at the airport or at Blowing Point and at any of the hotels. Drivers are happy to deliver you to and collect you from a day spent on a remote beach. Most will give impromptu tours of the island, but organized tours cost US$40 for about three hours. Prices for journeys are fixed (quite expensively) by the Government. Some examples are: the **airport** to Shoal Bay—US$10 (and from **Blowing Point**—US$15), the Valley—US$5 (US$10), Sandy Ground—US$8 (US$10), Cove Castles and the southwestern end of the island—US$20 (US$17).
   Car hire gives the most mobility and cars are readily available. A local licence must be obtained, but this is easily done on presentation of a valid licence to the company at the time of hire, or with the police in The Valley, price US$6. The speed limit is 30 mph (!) and driving is on the left. Traffic usually does proceed at a stately pace, but watch out for the couple of roundabouts and the odd hanging traffic light. From around US$25 plus taxes. Some of the many companies are: **Island Car Rentals** on Airport Road (tel 2723), **Apex Car Rental** (tel 2462) and **Tripple K** (tel 2934), both in the Quarter.

TOURIST INFORMATION
UK and Europe: The Anguilla Tourist Office, 3 Epirus Rd, London SW6 7UJ (tel 071 937 7725, fax 071 938 4739).
USA and Canada: Medhurst and Associates Inc, 271 Main St, Northport, NY 11768 (tel 516 261 1234, fax 261 9606, toll free 800 553 4939).

On-island, information and assistance can be obtained from the helpful **Anguilla Tourist Office** in the social security building in the Valley, Anguilla, British West Indies (tel 809 497 2759, fax 497 2751), which is open 8–midday and 1–5.

If **telephoning** from outside the Caribbean, the code for Anguilla is 809 497, followed by a four-figure island number. From within the Caribbean just dial 497 and the four figures. If calling within the island, dial only the last four digits.

In an **emergency**, there is a 24-hour surgery at the **Cottage Hospital** in The Valley (tel 497 2551).

MONEY
The currency of Anguilla is the Eastern Caribbean dollar (fixed to the US dollar at a rate of about US$1 = EC$2.69). The US dollar, best carried in the smaller denominations, is perfectly acceptable, though you will occasionally receive your change in EC$. If you are on a tight budget, it is better to use EC$. Credit cards are accepted at the large and expensive hotels and in some shops, but do not expect to use them in small restaurants. **Banking hours**: Mon–Fri 8–3, with an extra couple of hours on Fri afternoons 3–5. **Shops** keep variable hours, usually with a respectable lunch-break.

BEACHES
Anguilla's beaches are probably the best in the Caribbean. There are miles and miles of them, with sand so thick and soft that you stumble through it. Breakers clap and hiss as they race in a flurry of surf towards the palms and sea-grape. Take sun-glasses; the sand is glaringly bright.

You will not find any crowded beaches on the island, though you can find watersports equipment at the hotels if you want action. There are miles of strand to walk in the cool of the early morning, and you can sizzle to your heart's content in the heat of the day. So much of the coastline is sand that even the harbours are usually on a good beach. Get a little off the beaten track and you will find a whole cove to yourself, glorious, calm and scorching. Two words of warning: *manchineel* trees, which bear a poisonous apple and will blister you if you sit under them in the rain, and skinny-dipping. Like many West Indians, the Anguillians are modest about nudity and so it is officially not allowed. If beaches are your thing, Anguilla is close to paradise.

Rendezvous Bay is a magnificent curving strand nearly two miles long on the southwestern coast. It has seen some development lately, but it is good for walking morning or evening and it is easy to find an isolated spot with the hills of St Martin in view. The next beach round, **Cove Bay**, is similar but more isolated.

To the west is the protected cove of **Maunday's Bay**, where it is possible to hire windsurfers. And farther round on the southwest coast you come to **Shoal Bay West**, where space-age villas cut the skyline and the swimming is impeccable.

On the northern side of the island, the coastline is cut by deeper, more protected, coves with steep-sloping shelves of sand and spectacular views of the sunset. At the western end, **Barnes Bay** and **Mead's Bay** have bars to retreat to in the hotels, and watersports equipment for hire.

Sandy Ground is a busy half-moon of ankle-deep sand with a line of bars and restaurants between the sea and the salt-flats in Road Bay. It is a working bay, with ships unloading at the jetty and yachts at anchor. It is possible to hire watersports equipment

306

here. Next along is **Little Bay**, a secluded cove to which you must go by boat, unless you are prepared to clamber down the rockface (where there are ropes to assist you). Again, lovely sand and some caves.

Shoal Bay is also one of the island's finest, with mounds of sand that the waves have carved into scallops, and there are one or two hotels and beach bars to retire to if the heat of the sun gets too much. All essential beach requisites are for hire at Skyline Beach Rentals—'beautiful lounge chairs, elegant floating rafts, long fluffy towels and reliable snorkelling gear'.

There are several isolated bays near the northeastern tip of the island, of which the best is **Captain's Bay**. You can also expect to be alone if you make it to **Mimi Bay** and the wilder **Savannah Bay**, but take drinks and a picnic if you will want them.

Even **Blowing Point**, the departure point for St Martin, has a good strip of sand where you can sunbathe while waiting for the ferry.

Anguilla's uninhabited off-shore islands—Deadman's Cay, Sombrero, Dog Island, Gorgeous Scilly Cay and the Prickly Pear Cays—may sound a bit like an absurdist's shopping-list, but if it is isolated beaches you want, with the usual superabundance of sea, sand and sun, then they are as good as anything on the island itself. It is easy to arrange a day's trip to one or other on a yacht. Try **Sandy Island Enterprises** (tel 6395).

Visible from Road Bay is **Sandy Island**, the archetypal paradise island, just a bar of sand and ten or so palm trees and excellent snorkelling. Perhaps this is where the Lamb's Navy Rum girl lives.

BEACH BARS

There are some cool and easy beach bars around the island where you can find a fruit punch or a beer and a salad to fill a gap during the day's beach activity. Between the (relatively) more formal restaurants of Sandy Ground you will find a couple of bars— **Palm Palm** and **Johnno's**—two lively spots that continue into the night. There is often evening entertainment here in season. At Shoal Bay on the north coast there are two more to retreat to: **Trader Vic's** and nearby **Uncle Ernie's**, which is festooned with photos of satisfied customers and where you can grab a burger or a grilled meal. Occasionally a barbecue.

Yet further east you come to Island Harbour, where **Smitty** has a shack under the palm trees covered with nautical buoys and nets, with chairs scattered in the sandy ground and TV relayed to the garden. Offshore you can have a fun day liming and snorkelling on **Gorgeous Scilly Cay**, which Eudoxie Wallace, Gorgeous to his friends, has landscaped with palms, conchshell walls and thatch shelters. Wave from the pier and they will come and pick you up. Both these two have music a couple of times a week in season.

WATERSPORTS

In Anguilla's electric blue water are some excellent coral reefs with good **diving** and **snorkelling**. The top spots for snorkelling are Little Bay (see beaches above) and Shoal (another name for reef) Bay. Dive sites are all around the island, particularly towards the western end, where reefs flash with butterflyfish and angelfish or a shimmering cloud of silverfish, and also on the offshore cays. There are wrecks (some deliberately sunk) and you might see a nurse shark or two. Go to **Tamariain Water Sports** (tel 2020) in

Sandy Ground, **Dive Tidbits** (tel 2759), or **Anguillan Divers** (tel 4750) in Island Harbour.

If you wish to go **windsurfing** or **sailing** in small sunfish and hobie cats, try one of the hotels. A day's sail farther afield (perhaps a picnic on Sandy Island) can be arranged through **Tropical Watersports** (tel 6666), **Suntastic Yacht Cruises (tel 3400)**, **Enchanted Island Cruises** (tel 3111) or through Tamariain Water Sports. You might also take a day's sailing trip to St Barts on the *Lady Maria*, which departs from Blowing Point.

Deep-sea fishing, for wahoo and tuna and sailfish, can be arranged through the Mariner's Hotel in Sandy Ground, which has a Boston Whaler for hire (tel 2671). A half-day's sail with full tackle costs around US$300.

There are **tennis courts** at a number of the big hotels.

Inland Sights

The Valley (population 500) is Anguilla's capital, though you should not think that this makes it a town; the density of houses is just slightly greater than elsewhere. Some official buildings and a few shops are bunched around a hanging traffic light. Blink and you will miss it.

Headed west from The Valley, the road passes into more open country very quickly, passing the airport and making towards the developed southwestern tip of the island. Anguilla's plantations were never very successful, but one estate house is on view at **Wallblake House**. Built in the late 18th century, this gingerbread house in a garden behind a white picket fence has been restored. You pass through a louvred veranda into a wooden interior, with carved rope motifs. The cistern in the garden is similar to those on the islands of Saba and Statia (Sint Eustatius) farther south. Telephone to arrange a tour of the house (tel 2405). Driving west, you will pass side-roads to **Sandy Ground**, a village on the last of the working salt pans, and to **Blowing Point**, the departure point for boats to St Martin.

Heading north and east from The Valley, you pass into open country once again, which is dotted periodically with Anguilla's attractive old wooden houses and the half-built newer ones. There are a couple of local settlements in this less developed area; one at **Island Harbour** on the north coast, from which many of Anguilla's fishermen set off. On the beach you will see the fishing boats, brightly painted so they are more visible at sea, built to a unique Anguillan design.

Anguilla's only historical sites can be found in this area. Just off the road close to Lower Shoal Bay, the **Fountain** is contained within a National Park and has a number of Amerindian rock carvings around the island's only reliable source of water, cartoon faces which are each struck by the sun's rays in the course of the year. At **Sandy Hill Bay** are the remains of a 17th-century fort.

FESTIVALS
The main event in the Anguillan calendar is **Carnival**, which takes place in early August. It borrows a lot from other Caribbean carnivals, with floats and dancers *jumping-up* as they cruise around town in masqueraders' costumes, and calypso competitions, where the Anguillians sing of island life and love.

Unique to Anguilla, the nation of seafarers and boat-builders, is **Race-week**, held each year at the beginning of August, in the which the traditional fishing boats are pitted with one another in races from bay to bay.

WHERE TO STAY
Tourism in Anguilla has always been geared to high-spending visitors who expect top-notch accommodation, and you will find some pretty luxurious resorts on this island. There is not much mid-range hotel accommodation in Anguilla, but you can find a room through the Inns of Anguilla at around US$100 a night for a double in season. There are a number of guest houses at the lower end of the scale. All of the hotels are set on one or other of Anguilla's pristine beaches. Hotel rooms can be booked in the UK through the **Anguilla Reservation Service** (tel 071 937 7725, fax 938 4793). An alternative is to stay in a villa. Some villas are set in hotel-like complexes, listed below, with pools and other facilities. Individual houses can be rented up through **Sunshine Villas**, PO Box 142 (tel 497 6149) or through **PREMS** (Property Real Estate Management Services) PO Box 256, The Valley (tel 809 497 2596, fax 497 3309). Perhaps check them out while you are there in preparation for a return visit. The Government levies a room tax of 8% and most hotels charge service at 10%.

EXPENSIVE
Cove Castles, PO Box 248 (tel 809 497 6801, fax 497 6051, US 800 348 4716), sells itself as a villa resort, but it has the facilities of the best hotel. The buildings look odd—the twenty-first century has come early to Anguilla—windswept geometrical faces staring over a superb vista to St Martin. Inside they are spacious super-luxury in rattan, terracotta and each one with a hammock with a view. Villas come with maids and villa (room) service and watersports on the supreme beach. Expensive but unforgettable, US$590–990. **Cap Juluca** (tel 497 6779, fax 497 6617, US 800 323 0139) has its own inimitable style—a Moorish mirage that rises out of Anguilla's southwestern sands. Its white domes are festooned with pink and purple flowers, giving a surreal impression after a day in the Anguillan sun. The 98 rooms are palatial, the tile floors covered by carpets from the east, and the bathrooms are no less than luxurious, jacuzzi in the sunlight. Room service comes course by course if you cannot make it to the restaurant, **Pimms**, where you sit beneath arches and awnings overlooking the bay. Expensive at US$390–600 plus for a double in peak season, half-price in the off-season. The **Malliouhana Hotel**, PO Box 173 (tel 497 6111, fax 497 6011), stands on the cliffs above the mile stretch of Mead's Beach on Anguilla's northwestern coastline. Arches and terracotta tiles (both floor and roof) give a Mediterranean impression here too, with fountains and a sumptuous divan in the main lobby. But the name *Malliouhana* is definitely Caribbean, taken from the Indian word for Anguilla. Many of the 67 rooms and suites have the same magnificent view of the sunset that the Arawaks would have seen 1000 years ago. In high season, the restaurant is reserved for hotel guests (it has perhaps the best food on the island), but in summer there is an extensive French menu complemented by a wine cellar of around 30,000 bottles. More reliable super-luxury, but expensive, as the cheapest double is over US$335–750. **Coccoloba**, PO Box 332 (tel 497 6871, fax 497 6332), also stands on the cliff at the other end of Mead's Bay, with its gingerbread cottages ranged above the golden sand of Barnes Bay. There is a slightly

more active buzz here than in many Anguillan hotels, with tennis courts and watersports for the physically fit. A room in the peak season costs over US$360–460. The cheapest room in the off-season is US$200. **The Mariner's**, PO Box 139 (tel 497 2671, fax 497 2901, US 800 223 0079), is at the southern end of the Sandy Ground beach, is a series of pretty West Indian cottages set in a sandy garden around a restaurant on the waterfront. It has a sporting feel, with tennis and watersports as well as a good bar with some entertainment. The package is all-inclusive (all meals and sports included in the price) and rooms are studios or suites. US$215–585 a double. The **Cinnamon Reef Beach Club**, PO Box 141 (tel 497 2727, fax 497 3727), is set in the horseshoe cove of Little Harbour on Anguilla's southern coast, with a view of the hills of St Martin five miles away. Villas and suites are set in squat modernist cottages splashed with bougainvillaea and hibiscus with hammocks on the terraces. With just 22 rooms, it has a friendly atmosphere and a 200-yard beach with plenty of watersports. The dining room, the Palm Court, is filled with palms and the food is a satisfying combination of French methods and local ingredients—chicken soup laced with coconut, orange and ginger catch of the day. Suites run at US$225.

Self-Catering Villas
There are two groups of villas on Shoal Bay where you can cater for yourself or eat in the restaurant downstairs. **Fountain Beach** (tel/fax 809 497 3491, US 800 633 7411) is set on its own half a mile from the main action of Shoal Bay, and the resort is small and private. The rooms are very comfortable, decorated in white and bright colours and furnished with antiques. The restaurant is Italian, an open veranda where you can eat duck breast in blueberry and wine or sautéed parrotfish. Double room US$225. The **Shoal Bay Villas**, PO Box 61 (tel 497 2051, fax 497 3631, US 800 722 7045) are set in a cluster around a pool. Just thirteen units ventilated by fan, with all the watersports of Shoal Bay nearby. The Reefside Restaurant stands beneath the palms on the sand. Speiality seafood and local catch including lobster and crayfish. US$150–360 a night.

MODERATE
At the upper end of the range of the **Inns of Anguilla** are **Harbour Villas** (tel 497 4433, fax 497 3723), seven self-catering apartments overlooking the translucent bay from their own verandas. Comfortable and good price in season for Anguilla at US$125 a double. You can also try the **Inter Island Hotel** on Lower South Hill close to Road Bay (tel 497 6259, fax 497 3091). In a modern West Indian house. Fourteen rooms for $60 a double in winter. There are less expensive **Guest Houses**, of which you might try Lloyds (tel 2351) above Crocus Bay, where a double room costs US$70 or **Florencia's** (tel 2319) in the Valley, price about the same. You will find simple accommodation at **Norman B's** (tel 2242) in North Side, just out of the capital, where a bed costs $20 per person.

EATING OUT
There are quite a few restaurants dotted around Anguilla, as well as the hotel dining rooms, the best of which are mentioned above. Many have good waterfront settings. Obviously there is plenty of fish and seafood and it is definitely worth tasting spiny lobster, caught in Anguillan waters (what remains after the rest has been shipped off to St Martin and San Juan). You will of course find local West Indian haunts where you can

pick up a pattie or a chicken leg for lunch and trusted local fare for dinner. Credit cards are accepted in the major restaurants.

EXPENSIVE

Mango's Seaside Grill (tel 6479) has a charming setting on Barnes Bay, with the waves crashing and fizzing just behind the sea-grape and the mounded sand. The arched veranda is open to the sea winds and the 'new American' cuisine gives exotic variations on Caribbean food and some southwestern American dishes—Caribbean red chicken soup, with pineapple, cheese and tomato, or calypso chicken, glazed and grilled with orange, apricot and Dijon mustard. Reservations necessary, main course, US$15–25. Sunday Brunch. **Riviera** (tel 2833) is one of the longest-standing restaurants on the island and has a great setting on a beach terrace on Sandy Ground. The menu is French, with Provençal specialities and you will start with a *ti punch* and the oyster bar, and then follow with a crayfish bisque and *darne d'espadon*, roasted swordfish in red butter. Light sauces and 'nouvelle' presentation. Main course about US$20 at dinner. Salads at lunchtime for a good break from the beach. Past the airport, **Smuggler's Restaurant** (tel 3278) is on the south coast at Forest Bay. You eat above the water, on a wooden deck with views of the lights of St Martin. French and seafood—shrimp creole or a brochette of lobster. About $20 a main dish. Closed Sun. The **Koalkeel** is on the road to Crocus Bay and is set on a large terrace with the antique feel of Anguilla's oldest houses. Menu French and English. Start with *christophene farci* and follow up with shrimp sautéed in olive oil with ratatouille and couscous. About US$20.

MODERATE

If you are feeling homesick for an English draught beer, then you might try **Roy's Place** just above the beach in Crocus Bay, a pub-style bar inside with a Caribbean terrace outside. Platters from across the Atlantic—ham steak and pineapple or fish and chips—to go with the darts. Popular with expatriates, meal US$12. Closed Mon. For something a little more local you can try **Lucy's Harbour View** (tel 6253), where you eat on a large veranda in a modern Anguillan house high above Sandy Ground. Classic West Indian dishes like conch fritters and curry goat with a tonnage of ground provisions. US$16 and up. Down below you can get a simple meal at **Ship's Galley** (tel 2040) on the beach. Whelks, sweet potatoes and fillet of local catch for US$15. Closed Wed.

NIGHTLIFE

Anguillan nightlife is quiet (the locals often take the ferry over to St Martin for the nightclubs there), though there is sometimes a barbecue or a band at one of the hotels, with the Anguillians often in attendance. It is definitely worth joining in the *jump-ups* at the bars in Sandy Ground. **Johnno's** and **Palm Palm** are both very popular and get wild at the weekends.

The Netherlands Antilles
Sint Maarten, Sint Eustatius, Saba, Aruba, Bonaire and Curaçao

The Netherlands Antilles are made up of two groups of three islands, separated by about 500 miles of Caribbean Sea. The **Dutch Windwards**, Sint Maarten, Sint Eustatius and Saba (the 3 S's in tourist jargon) are in the northern area of the Lesser Antilles, between the Virgin Islands and Antigua. Five hundred miles to their lee, off the coast of South America, are the trio of the **Dutch Leeward Islands**, Aruba (now autonomous), Bonaire and Curaçao (the **ABC** islands).

The Netherlands Antilles may be within the Dutch Kingdom, but they are by no means a tropical version of Holland. The Dutch were never great colonizers and what influence they had has been creolized. In Curaçao curly gables will take you momentarily back to Amsterdam; everywhere roadsigns are in Dutch and post-boxes are painted Royal Dutch red; money is Guilders and Florins; the tastes and sounds of Holland percolate through.

But the reminders are fleeting: the gables may be there, but the *Landhuisen* (Dutch country homes) look odd painted orange and surrounded by miles of cactus; drivers here are much more akin to their fellow West Indians than the good burghers of the Netherlands and the guttural sounds of Dutch have a curious ring when mixed in with Spanish in *Papiamento* (see p. 340). Neither group of islands actually uses Dutch as a mother-tongue.

The Dutch Windwards have been strongly influenced by the English-speaking islands around them and the Leewards are an enigmatic and exuberant mix of strains from all over the area—but they are both distinctly West Indian.

History

The Dutch first came to the Caribbean as traders in the early 17th century. Only they had the fleets and so they acted as middlemen for the new colonies that were springing up in the area. In an early piece of industrial espionage they introduced the cultivation of sugar to the islands of the Lesser Antilles; they provided the technology, the funding, the machinery and then shipped the produce back to eager markets in Europe.

They did not really colonize so much as occupy strategic ports in the New World, which they needed to carry on their trading and to attack the Spaniards. In the 1620s the Dutch West India Company settled some islands as entrepôts. They took Sint Maarten as it was en route from Europe to their possessions in Brazil and later moved in on the nearby islands of Saba and Sint Eustatius as well. And they chose the ABC islands because they needed salt for their herring industry.

At the beginning of the 18th century, the Dutch ports of Curaçao and Sint Eustatius were two of the three richest in the Caribbean (with Port Royal in Jamaica). Their warehouses were filled to bursting with goods; hundreds of ocean-going vessels would put in each year and off-load silks, slaves and gunpowder. Strictly speaking trade with other colonies was illegal because they were under monopoly trading laws, but their goods were in demand and so they made a tidy profit smuggling too.

Prizes so rich inevitably became targets and in the endless run of 18th-century wars the islands were at the mercy of the navies that chased each other around the Caribbean Sea. St Eustatius changed hands 22 times in all, its fortunes pilfered handsomely each time. But the wharves would fill up again almost as quickly, as trade with Venezuela and the North American colonies picked up.

The six islands eventually landed in Dutch hands for good in 1816 and like the rest of the Caribbean they were forgotten. Trading failed and the islanders turned to planting; crops like cotton and cochineal, sisal (for rope) and aloe. Even these died with emancipation, which was declared by the Dutch in 1863.

It was not until the early 20th century that prosperity returned to some of the islands when oil was discovered in South America. Royal Dutch Shell and Exxon built refineries in Curaçao and Aruba in the 1920s and these two islands boomed, receiving a wave of prosperity that only waned in the late 1980s.

Since the 60s the Netherlands Antilles have joined the tourism race, particularly in Sint Maarten and Aruba, where hotels have sprung up on any available beach space. The islands have also resurrected the Dutch tradition of entrepôts (like the freeports of Curaçao and St Eustatius two hundred years ago) to encourage 20th-century traders. These seaborne shoppers arrive in port just as they always did, with a fistful of dollars to spend, only nowadays they are off-loaded by the thousand from cruise ships.

Politics

For years the name Curaçao was used to refer to all the Dutch possessions in the Caribbean and it is only since the war that the different islands have become known in their own right. In 1936 the *Staten* (Parliament) was created and the colonies were made an integral part of the Kingdom of the Netherlands.

After the Second World War (when Holland was occupied by Germany and the islands had to look after themselves), self-determination became inevitable. *Autonomy*, internal self-government, was granted in 1954, but with the exception of Surinam, which took its independence in 1975, the islands have preferred to remain a part of the Kingdom of the Netherlands.

The administration was centred in Willemstad and as the Curaçaoans had a majority in the Staten they tended to neglect the welfare and progress of the other islands. The Arubians particularly, with political aspirations born of their oil wealth, resented the fact that decisions concerning their internal affairs had to be passed in Curaçao and so they struck out for their own self-government. (See Aruba, *Status Aparte*, p. 366.)

More recently Sint Maarten, also on a wave of prosperity because of its tourist industry, has voiced similar requests, but these have been turned down by the Dutch Government. Now that Aruba has left the Netherlands Antilles, Curaçao returns 14 senators to the 22-member Parliament, Bonaire—three, Sint Maarten—three and Saba and Sint Eustatius one each. The Governor of each island is appointed by the Queen of the Netherlands on the advice of Parliament. Since 1986, each island has been responsible for its own decisions and its budget, once it has been allocated by the central Government in Curaçao. Maria Liberia Peters, leader of the People's National Party, became Prime Minister of the five islands of the Netherland Antilles in a coalition government in 1988.

The Dutch Windwards

Sint Maarten, Sint Eustatius and Saba

SINT MAARTEN

Sint Maarten/Saint Martin is the smallest island in the world to be shared by two nations. The southern half is one of the Netherlands Antilles, a part of the Kingdom of Holland, and the northern area is a *commune* of France. (See introduction to Saint Martin p. 228.) The distinct personalities of the two sides of the island are still just recognizable, though with the building mania of the last 20 years it has taken on a universal wash of concrete, and the feel of the island has changed irreparably.

Of Sint Maarten's 17 square miles, between four and five are under water. Above the waterline, Sint Maarten is covered in yellow-green scrub and hills that rise to around 1200 ft.

It is rather like a modern-day Babel—overdeveloped and confused. It has excellent beaches and endless Caribbean sunshine, and together those are enough to have brought development corporations swooping in. They have built with abandon, throwing up resorts on any strip of sand they can find. Sint Maarten bulges with glittering casinos, shopping malls and fast-food joints. Hotels come in complexes here, and tourists by the jumbo-load.

And the languages of Babel are there too. You will hear the drawl of a Texan vacationer alongside the clipped vowels of an Englishman on holiday; Dutch, French and Spanish fill the air. English-speaking West Indians have flooded in from down-island, Dominican girls sit and chat in upbeat Spanish, you will hear Haitian *kreyol* and even the babble of *Papiamento* (see p. 340), the extraordinary language from the Dutch Windward Islands.

Sint Maarten has also adopted Sint Eustatius's traditional role as the Dutch entrepôt in the Windwards. The streets of the capital, Philipsburg, are lined with airco boutiques, brim-filled with duty-free bargains. And cruise-liners disgorge still more tourists on one-day shopping extravaganzas. It is mercantile mayhem.

The confusion is complete. But after centuries in the doldrums, the island is more prosperous now than it has ever been. The material benefits are obvious, and although tourism is a notoriously difficult industry, it could all be gone tomorrow, so who can blame them for taking advantage of it while the going is good?

But a million tourists arriving each year cannot but have an effect on island life—just imagine a national consciousness that is made up of waiters and maids. Dutch Sint Maarten officially has a population of around 34,000, and there are also a large number of illegals, perhaps as many as 10,000, who have poured in in search of work. If you go off the beaten track, some of the locals will ignore you, but being the West Indies there will be classic moments.

If you style yourself a traveller, then Sint Maarten is really a place to avoid, although the people who live there swear by it. You might take a look in passing to another more peaceful island nearby. But if you like a well-oiled vacation (often an impeccable package deal), with beaches, watersports, entertainment and a truly amazing variety of restaurants just a buggy-ride away, then Sint Maarten might be your place.

History

Though the PR moguls may swear otherwise, it is unclear whether Columbus ever saw Sint Maarten. He might have seen it on his second voyage, on 12 November 1493, as he sailed past Statia (Sint Eustatius) and Saba. He did name an island after the Saint (St Martin's Day is 11 November), but this was probably Nevis. As other sailors came by, the name was fixed as Sint Maarten.

The Caribs and Arawaks continued to live here on and off for 140 years after his arrival. Settlement was difficult as there was no permanent water-supply. But the Spaniards were not initially interested in the island anyway, and only made occasional raids to take people to work in their gold-mines. To the Indians, Sint Maarten was *Sualouiga*, supposed to mean land of salt.

It was the salt pans that attracted the first Europeans to Sint Maarten, as they ventured out from the original settlement in St Kitts. Some Frenchmen arrived in 1629 and in 1631 they were followed by the Dutch West India Company.

The Spaniards were spurred into action by the interest other countries showed in Sint Maarten, and in 1633 they arrived with a fleet of 50 ships and expelled the settlers. But whatever they did, the settlers kept creeping back into the area and so the Spaniards decided to put a garrison in the Eastern Caribbean. They chose Sint Maarten and fortified the point at the entrance to what is now Great Bay. By all accounts it was a miserable outpost, in which the soldiers had rats for company and for their food.

The Dutch soon occupied Curaçao off the coast of Venezuela, but they were still looking for a port in the northern Caribbean, en route from their colonies in Brazil back to Europe. In 1644, Peter Stuyvesant, a director of the Dutch West India Company, led an attack on Sint Maarten to take the island back. It was in this engagement that Stuyvesant (later Governor of New York, then Nieuw Amsterdam) was hit by a cannonball and lost his leg. In 1648 the Spaniards abandoned the garrison in Sint Maarten and the Dutch and French soon made their way back on to the island.

The agreement on sharing the island dates from 1648, and the traditional story tells of a Dutchman and a Frenchman setting off in opposite directions, with a bottle of liquour apiece to keep them going, walking around the coast until they met, whereupon a line was to be drawn between the two points. How the French got the bigger share is explained variously: the Dutchman's gin made him sluggish/he took time-out under a tree/the wily, wine-drinking Frenchman sent a girl to waylay him (delete as applicable).

The sad drab truth of the matter is that the two sides decided that they would do well to stop skirmishing and so they signed a treaty on a hill that came to be called Mount Concordia. The salt pans remained common property and the two sides arranged that they would not fight each other even if their mother-countries went to war. This happened many times and the treaty was broken with the same regularity. The island changed hands 16 times, often with British involvement. The communities had little to do with each other except to march over and skirmish on the other side, and so it was not until the 20th century that a road was built to link the two halves of the island.

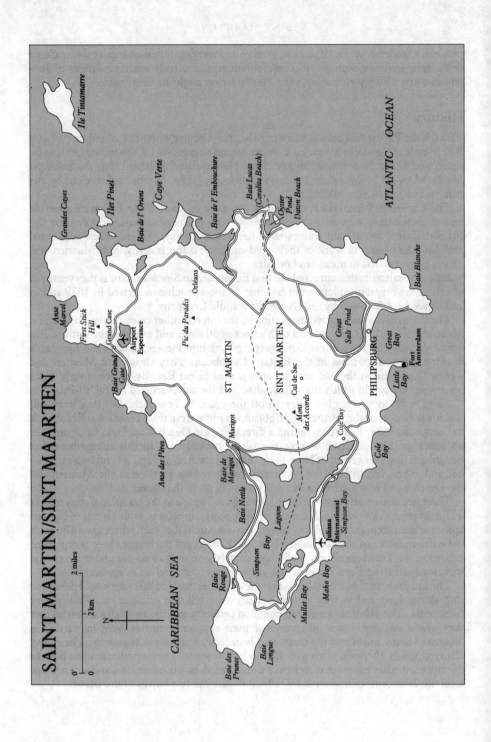

SAINT MARTIN/SINT MAARTEN

ATLANTIC OCEAN

CARIBBEAN SEA

Ile Tintamarre

Grandes Cayes

Ilet Pinel

Caye Verte

Baie de l' Orient

Baie de l' Embouchure

Baie Lucas
(Coralita Beach)

Oyster
Pond
Dawn Beach

Baie Blanche

Anse
Marcel

First Stick
Hill

Grand Case

Orleans

Airport
Esperance

Pic du Paradis

ST MARTIN

Baie Grand
Case

Cul de Sac

Great
Salt Pond

SINT MAARTEN

PHILIPSBURG

Great
Bay

Fort
Amsterdam

Little
Bay

Anse des Pères

Marigot

Mont
des Accords

Cole Bay

Baie de
Marigot

Cole
Bay

Baie Nettle

Simpson
Bay

Lagoon

Juliana
International
Airport

Simpson Bay

Baie
Rouge

Mullet Bay

Maho Bay

Baie
Longue

Baie des
Prunes

N

0'   2 miles
0   2 km

SINT MAARTEN

Sint Maarten saw some small prosperity as a plantation island, cultivating tobacco and growing provisions for nearby Sint Eustatius in the boom years of the 18th century. Sugar and cotton were also grown, and another industry that continued into the 20th century was the harvesting of salt from the inland ponds. At its height, Sint Maarten produced 4 million kg.

In 1848 the French emancipated their slaves in Saint Martin and so many of the Dutch slaves fled across the border, staying there until the Dutch declared emancipation in 1863. Gradually Sint Maarten's fortunes waned and it became poor and forgotten. Many of the islanders left in search of work elsewhere.

And so it remained until about 30 years ago, when the tourist industry started to grow. In the 1950s, the population of the Dutch side dropped as low as 1500. Now instead of emigration Sint Maarten is seeing floods of immigration, as people come to work in the hotels. (See also introduction to The Netherlands Antilles, p. 312.)

GETTING TO SINT MAARTEN

Most flights arrive at Juliana airport which is something of an air crossroads of the Caribbean. It is particularly busy on Sunday afternoons, when many organized tours change over. A departure tax of US$10 is payable except for destinations within the Netherlands Antilles.

From Europe: the French connections are the best. Air France operates three times a week from Paris and there are charter airlines to other French cities (including Mulhouse, giving access to Switzerland through the airport shared with Basel). There is also a weekly flight from Amsterdam on KLM, and one from Frankfurt on Lufthansa.

From the USA: American Airlines flies in direct from Miami and New York, with plenty of other connections to other American cities through their hub San Juan, Puerto Rico. Continental and ALM (the Netherlands Antilles carrier) also fly from New York.

From other Caribbean Islands: Sint Maarten is well served from around the Caribbean. Winair is based in Sint Maarten and flies to all the nearby islands. LIAT flies to many islands in the Eastern Caribbean, including Anguilla, Tortola (in the BVI), San Juan, St Kitts and Antigua (with connections further south). ALM flies daily to Curaçao, Aruba and Caracas, with occasional flights to San Juan, Santo Domingo and Port of Spain. Air Aruba flies to Aruba and to Santo Domingo. There is a **ferry boat** from Marigot on the French side to Anguilla (20 min; US$20 return).

GETTING AROUND SINT MAARTEN

Taxis wait in superabundance at Juliana airport to take you to your hotel. Competitive travellers who prefer not to use them will find that it is a long walk in the sun.

A rudimentary **bus** service links Philipsburg to Marigot and Grand Case, with a very occasional one going down the road past Juliana airport. The fares are US$1–2 depending on your destination and buses are quite frequent until 10 or 11 pm between Marigot and Philipsburg. Buses leave from Back Street in Philipsburg and in the country it is best to wait at the recognized bus stops. Hitch-hikers will find that a large proportion of the thousands of cars on Sint Maarten will pass without stopping. If you are patient, it works OK.

Taxis are, of course, the government-approved, quite expensive, tourist-recommended method of travel. They are not metered, but rates are fixed by the Tourist

317

THE CARIBBEAN

Board. Some sample prices are: Juliana **airport** to Philipsburg—US$8, Marigot—US$10, Grand Case—US$18–20. From **Philipsburg** to Marigot—US$8, Grand Case—US$18–20. In the unlikely case that you cannot hail one down, there is a taxi-stand just behind the court house in Philipsburg, and you can also arrange them through any hotel.

Tours of Sint Maarten are available, though there is not much more than views of the island and other islands to see. You will ride from shop to hilltop to restaurant in a little safari buggy. Tours can be arranged through any hotel desk (they will pick you up) or through **Sint Maarten Sightseeing Tours** (tel 52753) or **Calypso Tours** (tel 42858), US$15 for about 3½ hours.

If you would like to tour by **helicopter**, Sint Maarten offers that too: **St Martin Helicopters**, which flies out of Juliana airport (tel 44287).

If you want to test out the different beaches in the day and French restaurants at night, it is worth hiring a **rental car**, of which plenty are available from around US$30 per day or $35 for a jeep, plus insurance. Foreign driving licences are valid in Sint Maarten and driving is on the right-hand side of the road. You cannot drive away from the airport itself, but one or two of the rental companies have offices within walking distance of the airport terminal. Hotels will often book cars in advance for you and the companies will then deliver to the hotel. There are far too many cars on both sides of the island, so expect traffic jams in the three small towns.

Some local as well as big international rental companies are: **Opel Car Rental** (tel 54324), whose offices are just east of Juliana airport, **Caribbean Auto Rentals** (tel 45211) on Union Road in Cole Bay and **Speedy Car Rental** (tel 23893) just across from the airport, **Avis** (tel 42316), PO Box 315, in Cole Bay, **Budget** (tel 54274) within walking distance of the airport building and **Hertz** (tel 54314).

If you are fond of scams and are prepared to spend a couple of hours being given the hard sell about 'investment in vacationing' in a condominium complex, then you can sometimes score a '$50 off your rental bill' voucher in one of the many promotional rags.

Sint Maarten is an ideal dropping-off point for four other islands, all of which are served by air and also by boat. **Anguilla**, the enigmatic British Crown Colony, is just 20 minutes' ride out of Marigot (in a gullwing speed-boat) and **St Barts**, perhaps the chic-est piece of France anywhere, is 12 miles east of St Martin, reached daily from Bobby's Marina, Great Bay (tel 23170), in the *St Barth Express*. **Wish Tours and Services** (tel 53663) arranges tours by plane to nearby islands with Winair.

The two other Dutch Windward Islands are easily reached: **Saba**, where pretty gingerbread villages are clustered on sheer volcanic slopes, is an hour's sail away in the motorboat *Style* at the Pelican marina (tel 42640) and **Statia**, once the region's richest trading port (then known as the Golden Rock), is best reached by plane. **Winair** (tel 42230) flies to these islands a couple of times a day from Juliana airport, return about $60.

TOURIST INFORMATION
There is no Tourist Office dealing specifically with the Netherlands Antilles in **Britain**. You are best to write to New York or to the islands themselves. In **Holland**, contact the Cabinet of the Minister Plenipotentiary of the Netherlands Antilles at Badhuisweg 175, NL 2597 JP, 'S Gravenhage, The Hague (tel (070) 512811).

SINT MAARTEN

In the **USA**, you can get information from the Sint Maarten Tourist Office, 275 7th Avenue, New York, NY 10001 (tel (212) 989 0000, fax 627 1152) and in **Canada** from 243, Ellerslie Avenue, Willowdale, Ontario, M2N 1Y5 (tel (416) 223 3501, fax 223 6887).

On **Sint Maarten** itself the main Tourist Information Office is on the waterfront in Philipsburg, just where the launches drop the cruise-ship passengers—Sint Maarten Toeristenbureau, De Ruyterplein, Philipsburg (tel 22337) and a booth at Juliana airport. Open weekdays 8–noon and 1–5. On the French side, there is a small Tourist Information office on the harbour in Marigot, open 9–12.30 and 2–5.

The Sint Maarten tourist industry is well organized, and you will be bombarded with brochures and magazines telling you what to do and where to score your duty-free bargains from the moment of your arrival. If you can find a copy, the magazine most worth reading goes by the unlikely name of *Discover*, which is produced in tandem by the Tourist Offices from both sides of the island.

To **telephone** Sint Maarten from abroad, dial the code 599–5 followed by the 5-digit local number. Within Sint Maarten dial just the five digits, and from Saba or in Sint Eustatius, dial a 5 before it. Phoning Dutch to French side, dial 06 and then the six-digit number, and French to Dutch side dial 3 followed by the five digits. There are no coin-boxes on the French side and so you will need to buy a *télécarte* from the post office or the few newsagents that stock them.

In the case of a medical **emergency**, the Sint Maarten Medical Centre is on Front St in Philipsburg (tel 31111).

MONEY
All transactions in tourist hotels and restaurants can be carried out in US dollars on both sides of the island. The official currency on the Dutch side is the Netherlands Antilles florin/guilder, which is fixed to the US dollar (rate US$1 = NAFL1.77), but you will only see this money if you are in a local supermarket or on a bus. Where there might be confusion, make sure of which currency you are dealing in. NA florins are not accepted on the French side.

Credit cards are widely accepted in the Dutch side, as are traveller's cheques. Personal cheques are not widely taken. You can change money at any of the hotel front-desks, but the rate will not be as good as a bank. **Banks,** of which there are five or six in Philipsburg, keep hours of 8.30–1 on weekdays with an extra hour on Friday afternoons from 4–5.

General **shopping** hours are 8–noon and 2–6, Mon–Sat, with hours extended to Sunday morning if there is a cruise ship in town.

BEACHES
The beaches all over the island are excellent (see Saint Martin in the French Antilles section for the beaches on the French side). In the irregular, indented coastline, wave action has ground down the coral and pushed up the grains in blinding-white mounds of sand on the shore.

With so many resorts and complexes, every conceivable activity is available on Sint Maarten. Modern-day knights joust on their jet-skis, dipping and darting on the waves, inspected from above by para-sailors and by scuba divers from below. Screaming children can be frightened into rapt silence by being dragged around the bay on a high speed sausage. Senior citizens ply the water sedately in pedalos.

THE CARIBBEAN

If you go over to the French side, topless bathing is perfectly acceptable and there are also one or two nude beaches. This is becoming more common on the Dutch side. You will find facilities of some sort on all the beaches in Dutch Sint Maarten—some hotels have a shower room, for which they charge around US$3. A word of warning: there has been a certain amount of theft on the beaches and so you are advised not leave belongings unattended.

Cupecoy Beach is a series of suntraps close to the border with the French side at the western end of the island, all with a cracking view of the sunset. Coves with golden sand slope gently into the sea beneath 50-foot cliffs. At the northern end of the beach nude bathing is permitted. For Sint Maarten Cupecoy is relatively secluded, though you are hardly likely to be alone.

Mullet Beach is a classic stretch of Caribbean sand in the mile-long sweep of a gently curving bay. It is also Sint Maarten's busiest, with the thousands of guests of the nearby hotels, transported here by the buggy-load. All watersports are available and there are plenty of shaded retreats, palm-thatch umbrellas, where you can replace the fluids lost steaming in the sun.

There is a sign warning you that low-flying jumbos can ruin your bathing at the end of **Maho Bay**. Hotels hover above most of its length, making it another busy beach, buzzing with windsurfers and wetbikers. If the going gets too hot, you can always retreat to the terrace and watch the approach path of the in-coming aeroplanes.

Simpson Bay is a mile-long half-moon sweep just south of the airport, quite active and popular with windsurfers. One or two of Sint Maarten's smaller hotels and guest houses are located here, so you can get a drink or lunch in the unpressurized environment of a beach club.

Philipsburg itself has a reasonable strip of sand with a magnificent view of **Great Bay** and on to Saba just below Front Street. Perhaps a moment to recover before getting back into the shopping fray and exercising your credit card in another bout of impulse-buying.

There is a fine strip of sand on the Atlantic coast of the island at **Dawn Beach**. There are a couple of hotels here, but the crowds do not usually penetrate this far and so it is relatively quiet. The beach has a view of the dawn sun and of St Barts, but on a windy day the sea will be too rough for comfort.

WATERSPORTS
Sint Maarten's well-oiled tourist machine offers the full range of watersports if you are looking for an active vacation. Most large hotels have snorkelling and scuba gear, windsurfers and small sailing craft, jet-skis and motorboats on offer to their guests. If you are travelling independently and wish to hire sports equipment, you can use the hotels' rental companies. The main centres on the Dutch side are **Maho Watersports** (tel 44387), which works out of the Mullet Bay Resort and its opposite number on Simpson Bay Lagoon, **Lagoon Cruises and Watersports** (tel 52898). In Philipsburg you can hire equipment at **Watersports Unlimited** (tel 23434) in the Sint Maarten Beach Club. At Oyster Pond on the east coast go to **Red Ensign Watersports** (tel 25310). The French side also has rental facilities.

Windsurfers can get gear at the places above as well as in Simpson Bay and at **Little Bay Watersports** (tel 22333) in the Divi Hotel just outside Philipsburg. Rental in Sint Maarten costs around US$20 per hour.

320

Waterskiing can be fixed up in the main bays and lagoons. A half-hour outing costs around US$40. You will get a somewhat gentler ride behind a motorboat and the added attraction of a nice view of the hotels if you opt for **parasailing** at around US$30 for a 15-minute flight. And if you would like to take out a **jet-ski**, try **Yamaha Wave Runners** (tel 53663) on Simpson Bay Lagoon or **Westport Watersports** (tel 42557) on Simpson Bay itself.

Small **sailboats** (sunfish and hobie cats) are available at most hotels or from the rental companies. There is also a whole range of **charter yachts**, which make anything from a snorkelling and picnic trip to the off-shore islands to sunset booze-cruises. Outside the hotels, the *White Octopus* (tel 24096) departs on Fridays for a sunset cruise, or you can take a day's sail to Anguilla on the 60ft schooner *Gandalf* (tel 45427), from the Pelican Marina 9 am or a day on the catamaran *Quicksilver* (tel 22647), from Great Bay Marina.

Deep-sea fishing trips can be arranged at Bobby's Marina, as well as through **Blue Water Charters** at the Maho Beach Hotel (tel 42020). A half-day casting for tuna, tarpon and sailfsh costs around US$350.

Sint Maarten has some good off-shore reefs, some close enough in for **snorkelling**, where you will see shoals of pink and yellow fish dip and dart. Try the rocks at the end of Little Bay and Simpson Bay. On the rockier east coast the reefs at Dawn Beach are good, but best of all are the small islands off the French side, Ilet Pinel and Ile Tintamarre (also called Flat Island).

Scuba divers can arrange dives and instruction with the main concessionaires as well as through **Little Bay Watersports** (tel 22333) at the Little Bay Hotel, the **Tradewinds Dive Centre** (tel 54387) and **Sint Maarten Divers**, who work out of the Great Bay Hotel (tel 22446) in Philipsburg. Forests of coral, plied by angelfish and squirrelfish, can be found on the east coast of the island and off the south coast is the wreck of the *HMS Proselyte*, cannons and anchor encrusted, which sank in 1801. A single tank dive costs around US$40. There is also a glass-bottom boat tour; **Karib One** (tel 22366) in Bobby's Marina.

OTHER SPORTS
For landlubbers there is a variety of activities, including **golf** at the Mullet Bay Resort (tel 52801), where there is an 18-hole course backing on to the lagoon. All equipment can be rented and there are pros to improve your game. Green fees are very expensive at around US$105 for the 18 holes, includes cart. Residents of the hotel pay about half price and have preference in teeing off.

There are about 50 **tennis** courts on the island, many of them lit for night-play. Contact any of the larger hotels. It is even possible to go for an early-morning dip on **horseback** through the **Crazy Acres Riding Centre** (tel 42793).

Philipsburg

Philipsburg has just four streets, stretched out along the full length of a sand-bar that separates the Great Salt Pond from Great Bay. The Head of Town lies in the east and the Foot of Town in the west. Philipsburg is being rebuilt in concrete, but among the air-conditioned malls you will see a few old traditional gingerbread homes.

Front Street (Voor Straat) sells itself as the 'Shopping Centre of the Leewards' and

THE CARIBBEAN

the arcades and alleys (*steegjes*) manage successfully to delay most of the cruise-ship arrivals that come in safari-boats (the marine equivalent of the tourist bus), to Wathey Square, the little central square known locally as de Ruyterplein. Back Street (Achter Straat), where the harvested salt was once stored in vast white stacks, has the administrative buildings and churches.

There is a museum on Front St, set upstairs in an old town house, where island archaeology and history are revealed in pottery shards, Spanish buttons and pipes, colonial maps, china plates and recent marine recoveries. Open weekdays, 10–1, adm. There are also a number of galleries in the island, of which the best is probably Greenwith Gallery, set in an arcade off Front St (opposite Barclay's Bank), where you will see artists exhibited from Sint Maarten and the rest of the Caribbean.

Behind Philipsburg is the Great Salt Pond, which was common to both nations in the 17th century, when salt was important for preserving meats that could not be frozen. Since the industry folded in 1949, land has been reclaimed to expand Philipsburg.

Much of the local life has been squeezed out of Philipsburg, but it can still be lively to hear the medley of languages—the unaccustomed stream of not-quite Spanish is Papiamento.

Around the Island

The Sint Maarten countryside has little to offer. Much of it is as overgrown as the beaches, with houses rather than hotels. But the coast has superb views looking south to the other islands, grey stains on the horizon on a hazy day, but magnified and green if tropical rains have washed the sky. You can often see St Kitts about 45 miles away and Nevis is very occasionally visible from Cole Bay Hill.

An 'international' lifestyle has taken over in most areas of the island, but in the traditional villages (like Cul de Sac and Dutch Quarter) swollen with hotel-workers now, you get an idea of Caribbean life in the raffle-ticket booths (tickets for the Puerto Rican and Dominican raffles as well as the Dutch Antilles raffles) and the limers hanging around the *superettes*.

At the point on the western arm of Great Bay are the ruins of a fort built by the Spaniards in the 1630s. They demolished it when they abandoned the island and the remains were rebuilt by the Dutch and named Fort Amsterdam. There is a small zoo on the Madame Estate, where you will see Caribbean and South American animals including the racoon and the ocelot wildcat, with a special hands-on area for kids, adm.

The route to the French side of the island leads from Cole Bay. The border is marked by a small obelisk, but there are no formalities and unless you are looking out for it you will probably enter France without knowing.

SHOPPING

All visitors are encouraged to go shopping as part of their vacation, and maps are even provided to ease your passage through the jungle of Philipsburg's four streets. Sint Maarten is a free port and so there is no duty—clearly there are plenty of good bargains for professional and casual shoppers, though the island hardly has the status that Sint Eustatius had 200 years ago. For fashion you might try Ralph Lauren and Benetton, and for jewellery Gucci and Carat. Little Switzerland has good crystal and porcelain and you can find souvenirs at the Shipwreck Shop.

322

WHERE TO STAY

Many of the hotels in Sint Maarten have recently been built and seem to be not much more than speculative investments. There is an infestation of condominiums rather like fungus encrusting on the Dutch side, but buried among the rubble there are one or two with character and charm, particularly in the Simpson Bay area. Many offer 'efficiencies' (self-catering apartments). Hotels on the Dutch side usually add a 15% charge, 10% for service and the statutory government tax of 5%.

EXPENSIVE

The two most charming (and most expensive) hotels are on the island's secluded east coast: the **Dawn Beach**, PO Box 389 (tel 22929, fax 24421, US 800 351 5656) has attractive cabins lost in 16 acres of tropical grounds. They are well-decorated in pastel shades of pink and blue and with bamboo furniture. Quite large with 155 rooms, but the setting is a superb beach and there is a nice central area with a pool and a restaurant. Double room in season US$190–320. At the smaller **Oyster Pond Yacht Club**, PO Box 239 (tel 22206, fax 25695, US 800 365 8454) the rooms are arranged round a shady courtyard, looking outwards across Oyster Pond or out towards St Barts. Just 20 very comfortable rooms and a slightly rarefied atmosphere (no children under ten). This too is on the beach and there are watersports if you want them, also tennis courts. Double room US$170–310. On the south coast is the long-established **Caravanserai**, PO Box 113 (tel 52510, fax 53483, US 800 223 9815), with rooms in the gardens along the waterfront and its octagonal bar on the point; pool, tennis, double room in winter from US$135–450. The **Divi Little Bay Beach Resort**, PO Box 61 (tel 22333, fax 23911, US 800 367 3484) is just outside Philipsburg on the western arm of Great Bay, overlooking Little Bay on the other side. The 220 rooms stand in lines above the pool and in mock-Spanish blocks on the point, where you will find suites of high luxury with balconies and jacuzzis. Facilities include watersports and diving, tennis and entertainment around the pool or in the discotheque. Double room US$225–815 in season. **La Vista**, PO Box 40 (tel 43005, fax 43010, US 800 365 8484), is a purpose-built resort but it has very comfortable cottages with arches and pointed roofs. It is not on the beach and it is quite a way from town, but has a pool and terraces which look over the Caribbean Sea. 24 junior and penthouse suites decorated in high Caribbean pastel, with all mod cons, prices good at US$125–215. If you would like to stay in Philipsburg itself, the **Holland House Beach Hotel**, PO Box 393 (tel 22572, fax 24673, US 800 223 9815) has 54 good rooms above the sand of Great Bay with satellite TV and kitchenettes. Watersports available and restaurants and casinos nearby. Double in season US$140–250. Just along Front Street you will find the **Passanggrahan Royal Guest House**, PO Box 151 (tel 23588, fax 22885, US 800 365 8484), formerly the Government rest house. The reception area and restaurant are set in a charming green and white town house with gingerbread woodwork and louvred shutters, overlooking an overgrown palm garden. There is an old-fashioned air in the high-backed wicker chairs and the mellow portraits and it is right on the sand. Some of the 32 rooms are in the main house, but a new modern block has been built to take the rest. Double in season US$115–165. There are a few small and friendly beach club style hotels in Sint Maarten, many of them located together on Simpson Bay, a fantastic south-facing beach. **Mary's Boon**, PO Box 2078 (tel 54235, fax 53316) is right on the sand, rooms either side of the main house and linked by wooden walkways through the garden of palm and flamboyant. Classic beach club—a waterfront sitting area on the veranda, with a bar and a library. Twelve big rooms with white walls and rattan wicker furniture. Double room in season US$150.

MODERATE
The pink of the **Residence la Chatelaine**, PO Box 2056 (tel 54269, fax 53195) contrasts strongly with the turquoise of the sea and the swimming pool above which it sits. There are 17 suites surrounded by palm and sea-grape. Very neat and prettily decorated, with kitchenettes and some with four-posters. Double room US$95–215. The mellow **Trade Winds Inn** (tel 54206, fax 22269) has ten rooms on the beach for US$90–105 and if you go a couple of streets back from the beach you can stay at the **Calypso Guest House** (tel 44233) for US$69–115 in season.

CHEAP
The cheapest accommodation is in Philipsburg. All simple rooms at **Bico's Guesthouse** (tel 22294) on Zootsteeg off Back St. Not far off is **Lucy's Guesthouse** (tel 22995), both of which have rooms at US$30–60 a double. **José's Guesthouse** is also on Back St and the rooms cost US$22–40.

EATING OUT
Sint Maarten is as cosmopolitan in cuisine as it is in language and so you will find a bewildering selection of restaurants—anything from Mexican to Vietnamese, supported by a range of burger and pizza joints. Dutch food is not widely available, although Dutch East Indian (Javanese) is. The more upmarket restaurants are usually French or Italian, and it is not necessary to cross to the French side of the island for really good French cooking, though there are restaurants well worth visiting there too. Prices range from about US$20 per head to upwards of US$60 and all but the smallest restaurants accept credit cards. Reservations are advisable in season; a service charge of 10–15% is added to the bill.

Le Perroquet (tel 54339) has an attractive dining room hung with wooden parrots and tropical greenery and with a view through louvred windows to the garden. The menu is just as exotic, even if the style is French, because you can dine on curried lion, ostrich or even llama. If that sounds a bit much, you can always have an *escalope de veau* in calvados. Main course US$18–25, closed Mon.

Not far away in Cole Bay is **Spartaco** (tel 45379), an Italian restaurant, where lions stand guard at the entrance as you approach and you dine in the rarefied atmosphere of a stone house. *Gamberi giganti* (jumbo shrimps) or veal in mozzarella, tomato and oregano. From US$20.

There are some excellent restaurants just above the waves on the Philipsburg waterfront; you will find another very popular Italian restaurant there, **Da Livio** (tel 22690), set on a wooden terrace. *Aragosta fra diavolo* (lobster in spicy red sauce) or the *manicotti della casa* (with ricotta cheese, spinach and tomato). Wines from the Venice area. Closed Sun, main course US$18–30.

There are two attractive French restaurants on Front Street; **Red Snapper**, which lives up to its name by offering vivaneau in lime or in garlic butter and plenty of salads for US$20 a main course; and a little way down the street, **Antoine's** (tel 22946). You approach it through a courtyard and dine on a bright white terrace overlooking the water.

324

Canard montmorency or grouper in almonds, followed by *profiteroles* or a chocolate mousse. US$15–25 a main course. And if you would like the flavour of the Dutch East Indies in the Dutch West Indies, try the **Wajang Doll** (tel 22687) at the foot of town on Front Street. This is also in a pretty wooden creole house, but the fare is Indonesian— *nasi goreng* and dragon-mouthed *sambals* at $18–20.

Sint Maarten also has plenty of easy-going restaurants with a nautical setting, on a deck in the marinas or above the lagoon. The **Seafood Galley** is in Bobby's Marina, with a pub-style interior and a seafood restaurant at the side. Start with the **Raw Bar**— oysters, clams and rock crab claws—followed by creole shrimp or soft-shelled crabs in creole butter, US$15. And just before the bridge on the airport road you will find **the Boathouse**, which sits right on the lagoon. You approach through the side of a beached boat, on to which is built the restaurant, an upper deck with the dining room and a lower bar where you can dance or play darts. Netting and nautical flags on the walls and live music a couple of times a week. Shrimp scampi and conch fritters, US$10–15.

Cheaper meals can be found, particularly away from the tourist areas. Near the Boathouse is **San Yen**, where you can find simple Chinese fare for US$7 and in town you can get a pizza or some 'rice 'n peas' at **Ric's Place**, a sports and video bar on Back St.

BARS AND NIGHTLIFE
An excellent bar on the lagoon near the airport is the **Turtle Pier**, where you sit on wooden decks among the yachties or gather around the bar, which is always active, particularly at Happy Hour between 5 and 7. Music a couple of times a week. In Maho Bay just up the road you will find the ever lively **Chéri's Café**, which is good for a daytime ice-cream, an evening cocktail or an attack of the munchies any time. Live music. And just inside the Mullet Bay complex, looking over the golf course, you will find the **19th Hole**, usually crammed with tourists, all trying to be heard above the calypso music. Cheap drinks.

In town many of the restaurants have bars, but for a fun local spot go to **Reuben's Place** at the head of town, an open-air bar on a terrace with Latin music. You can also try the **Museum Café** on Front St.

You will find discotheques in a few of the big hotels—**Chrysalis** in the Great Bay Beach Hotel and **Studio 7** in the Mullet Bay Resort. Otherwise the **Greenhouse** in Great Bay Marina is a lively bar and disco. There are also some excellent bars on the French side (see St Martin).

There are eight casinos on the Dutch side, in the big hotels and along Front St in town.

SINT EUSTATIUS

Sint Eustatius is a tiny island with a glorious and glittering past. In the 18th century it was so rich that it was known as the *Golden Rock*; its warehouses were brim-full of silks, silver and guns from all over the world, but its fortune has waned. It was also the first country in the world to recognize the United States, when Governor De Graaff saluted the merchantman *Andrea Doria* in 1776.

Statia to her friends, the island has an area of just eight square miles and is situated close to St Kitts, about 30 miles south of Sint Maarten. Statia is of volcanic origin, and hills in the north descend to a central plain, where the capital and only town, Oranjestad, lies, rising again in the south to the Quill (1890 ft), a perfectly shaped volcano, now extinct.

The population of Statia (pronounced stay-sher) is now about 2000, a fraction of the numbers who lived and traded here in the 18th century. It is extremely quiet. If you go, remember that the glittering tradition remains in only a few dilapidated red- and yellow-brick walls. For now Statia is probably the poorest island in the area, and she can only wait until the waves of Caribbean fortune favour her again.

History

Settled by the Dutch West India Company in 1636 after a failed attempt on St Croix in the Virgin Islands, Statia's beginnings were modest—small cultivations of tobacco and sugar. But the company had its eyes on trade. Only they had fleets large enough to supply the burgeoning West Indian colonies in the 17th century and over the next 100 years Oranjestad in Sint Eustatius and Willemstad in Dutch Curaçao became two of the most important markets in the New World.

It started with slaves, for whom there was ceaseless demand in the sugar-islands nearby. The Statian merchants were often paid in kind (hogsheads of sugar and puncheons of rum were accepted currency), so the warehouses filled up and Sint Eustatius became a massive entrepôt, presided over by merchants from Europe and the Americas.

By 1750 the warehouses stretched all along the waterfront in Lower Town and as space ran out the merchants constructed dykes to reclaim land from the sea, so that they could build a second line of warehouses. Over the next 40 years, these became so full that the doorways were blocked up and the goods were hauled in and out through holes in the roof.

Strictly speaking, almost all of the trade was illegal because of monopoly trading laws imposed by the other European nations (which demanded that the colonies should trade only with the mother country). But the sugar-manufacturers in the West Indies knew that they would get a better price and immediate payment if they sold their goods to the merchants in Sint Eustatius, and so they were prepared to smuggle them there. In 1779 Statia grew around 500,000 pounds of sugar, but according to official records it managed to ship about 25 million pounds.

The Dutch in Sint Eustatius recognized no trading laws. Oranjestad was a free port and any ship that cared to come into harbour to trade was welcome. The port became famous as an arms depot, with rifles and ammunition passing through in vast amounts. Gunpowder turned in a profit of over 100 per cent. American blockade-runners would dodge the British Navy and smuggle arms to the colonists in sugar-barrels.

The First Salute

It was with this trade in mind that Governor de Graaff saluted an unknown flag on a ship that arrived in harbour on 16 November 1776. It was the American colonist merchant ship, the *Andrea Doria*. Even if the gesture was not deliberate, it was certainly a momentous event, as it was the first time that a foreign power had recognized the sovereignty of the United States. The British were furious and the Dutch apologized, recalling de Graaff.

So prosperous an island was a valuable prize and altogether Statia changed hands a ridiculous 22 times, as the different navies vied for supremacy in the Caribbean. Despite a ring of about 15 forts, Statia was never properly defended. It was too dangerous to fire the cannons in Fort Oranje anyway because the whole edifice was in danger of slipping down into the Lower Town.

Maverick Statia was attacked again soon after de Graaff's action when Admiral Rodney sailed into harbour with 14 warships on 3 February 1781. For the next few months he systematically plundered the island, confiscating all the goods in the warehouses and the personal fortunes of the Statian merchants. He even kept the Dutch flag flying above the port and lured in another 150 unsuspecting ships. When he auctioned off all the goods, the profits exceeded £3 million, of which he kept a sizeable proportion for himself.

Understandably, the merchants did what they could to save their riches and stories tell of an unusually high number of deaths and funerals. The coffins were loaded with gold and as soon as he discovered the trickery, Rodney promptly had them all dug up again. When he had had enough, the British abandoned the island.

Statia never really recovered, and since then the island has suffered an ever-declining spiral. As trading foundered, the plantations were started up again, but they failed quickly when slavery was abolished by the Dutch in 1863. Bricks that had been used to build the warehouses on the waterfront in the glorious days were sold on to other islands. The population dropped as the prosperity waned. Those that were left became subsistence farmers, or depended on remittances sent by relatives working abroad.

Today Statia is very quiet and has only a very small tourist industry (around 100 rooms). The government is the largest employer and the only other industry is an oil storage facility.

GETTING TO SINT EUSTATIUS
Sint Eustatius is served several times a day, by Windward Islands Airways from Sint Maarten (tel 844230); WIA also operate a daily flight from Saba. There are also a number of scheduled flights every week to the island from St Kitts. On approach, the plane often circles the volcano, the Quill, so remember to look out of the window. There is a departure tax of US$3 for travel within the Netherlands Antilles and US$4 elsewhere.

GETTING AROUND ST EUSTATIUS
Getting around Sint Eustatius is easy enough on foot, but there are also **taxis** if you do not want to walk up the hill. The ride into town from the airport costs US$3.50. A guided tour of the island can be made, and if you spin it out to a half day, it will cost around US$35. Taxis can be ordered at any hotel desk.

There are one or two **cars** for hire, at around US$40 per day. Present your driving licence to the **Avis** desk (tel 82421) at the airport, or a number of other outlets in town. Driving is on the right.

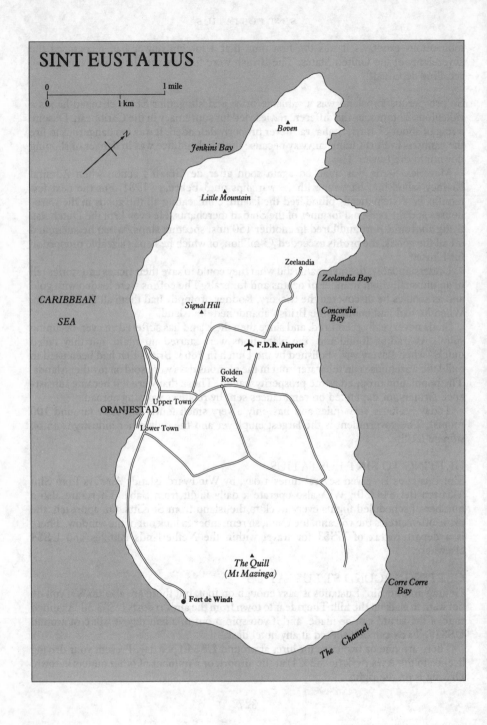

SINT EUSTATIUS

0   1 mile

0   1 km

Boven

Jenkins Bay

Little Mountain

Zeelandia

Zeelandia Bay

CARIBBEAN

SEA

Signal Hill

Concordia Bay

✈ **F.D.R. Airport**

Golden
Rock

Upper Town

ORANJESTAD

Lower Town

*The Quill
(Mt Mazinga)*

*Corre Corre
Bay*

● **Fort de Windt**

The Channel

TOURIST INFORMATION

In the **USA** contact Medhurst and Associates, 271 Main St, Northport, NY 11768 (tel 516 261 7474, fax 261 9608, US 800 344 4606). In the **Netherlands** you can contact the Antillenhuis at Badhuisweg 173–5, 2597 JP 'S Gravenhage (tel 070 3512811, fax 3512722).

The main **Sint Eustatius Tourist Office** (tel 82433) is in Upper Town, close to the entrance of Fort Oranje. Hours are 8–noon and 1–5 on weekdays. There is also a desk at the airport, open for the scheduled flights, and a small office in Lower Town.

One or two books deal with Statia's famous past, including a good, if a little academic, history, *Sint Eustatius, A short history of the island and its monuments* by Ypie Attema.

In a medical **emergency**, contact the Princess Beatrix Hospital (tel 82211) in Oranjestad.

To **telephone** the island from abroad, dial (599–3), except from Saba and Sint Maarten where you dial just (3), and then follow it with the 5-digit Statian number. On-island, use the five digits only.

MONEY

US dollars are accepted everywhere alongside the Netherlands florin, but credit cards are not that widely used. **Barclays Bank** (tel 82392) is open on weekdays from 8.30–1, with an extra hour on Friday afternoons, 4–5.

BEACHES AND WATERSPORTS

There are only a couple of beaches in Statia and they do not have the white sand for which the Caribbean is known. Off the road down to Lower Town is **Smoke Alley Beach** or **Oranje Beach**, which has an excellent view of the sunset and is popular among the Statians after work. Another sunning and snorkelling spot is **Crooks Castle**, beyond Lower Town.

On the Atlantic side of the island is a secluded cove, **Corre Corre Bay**. Skirt round the Quill to the southeast on Mountain road and the path down to the bay is marked. Generally, the Atlantic side is unsafe for swimming because of the undertow. The two miles of **Concordia and Zeelandia Bay** are good for walking and combing the sand for flotsam cast ashore by the Atlantic.

Watersports are limited in Statia (you might be able to borrow a windsurfer, but there are no small sailing boats for hire and there is no waterskiing). You can snorkel at Jenkins Bay in the north and **scuba divers** have plenty of opportunity among the remains of the warehouses in the water offshore at Lower Town. After a storm, the sea still turns up 18th-century bottles, blue trading beads and the occasional ducat. About 200 vessels are thought to have sunk off Statia. **Surfside Statia** and **Dive Statia** (tel 82435) operate in the town and send out two boats a day to the 20-odd dive sites.

On land, the Tourist Board has marked about 12 **walking** trails around the island, of which the most popular is up in the crater of the extinct volcano, the Quill. The Statians have a tradition of land-crab-hunting by torchlight in the crater at night, which is a fun way to spend an evening. A guide can be provided by the Tourist Board for an outing to the crater; if you go at night, you are advised to take one.

North of Oranjestad you might see coastal tropicbirds, distinctive with their long twin tail-feathers.

There is a floodlit **tennis court** at the Community Centre, in the southern area of town.

Oranjestad

Statia's only settlement, tiny **Oranjestad**, has two parts, Upper and Lower Town, which are separated by a 100-foot cliff. During Statia's supremacy as a trading port, goods were kept in the warehouses between the cobbled street and the waterfront and many of the traders would live up above in Upper Town. Today the Statians still live up above, in new 'gingerbread' houses that have forced aside the dark-stone 18th-century foundations and barrel-vaulted graves. Linked by an old stepped walkway, Lower Town has now fallen into almost complete dilapidation. There are just a few restored buildings among the ruins of red and yellow brick. On a calm day it is possible to see the base of the walls below the surface of the water.

The town takes its name from **Fort Oranje**, built by the Dutch in 1636 on the site of an earlier French fort. Even though the island was attacked so often, the fort saw little action. Still in danger of slipping down the hill, Fort Oranje is pretty and it has an attractive view across Lower Town. Among its monuments, the most significant commemorates the firing of the salute to the *Andrew Doria* on 16 November 1776. The fort also contains most of the island's administrative buildings and a Post Office.

The **Sint Eustatius Historical Foundation Museum** is located in Simon Doncker House (also known as de Graaff House after the Governor) just off the Wilheminaweg and central square. Admiral Rodney made it his headquarters when he ransacked the island in 1781. An exhibition covers Statian history from its beginnings as a haven for island-hopping Arawaks through settlement and siege, prosperity as the *Golden Rock* and the inevitable decline. On view are some small china pieces from the Nanking cargo, which was on order to the Dutch West India Company in Sint Eustatius when the Dutch East India Company ship that was carrying it sank in the South China Sea. They arrived 200 years late, but they made it. Open weekdays 9–5; adm.

Statia's sizeable Jewish community, who suffered most of all during Rodney's ravages in 1781 (not only was all their money taken, but they were deported), is remembered in the ruins of the **Honen Dalim Synagogue**, on the little alley, Synagoogpad. On the Kerkweg, the **Dutch Reformed Church** tower, with a cemetery full of barrel-vaulted graves, has been restored and gives a fine view of the harbour.

South of Oranjestad is Statia's volcano, known as **the Quill**, though its official name is Mt Mazinga. It is perfectly shaped, with sides sloping up to nearly 2000 feet and a circular crater, from which it takes its name (*kuil* in Dutch means pit). Inside the crater, which is 900 feet across and 550 ft deep, is a moist and tangled rainforest, where the trees grow tall in their efforts to reach the sun and mosses infest their trunks. Among the lianas and the moss-furred rocks, hummingbirds flit and the land-crabs scrabble.

There are thought to have been about 15 forts dotted around Statia's barren coastline; a couple are lost without trace. At **Fort de Windt** on the southern tip of the island, a couple of cannon look south over the superb view of St Kitts.

FESTIVALS

National holidays include **Statia Day** on 16 November, which remembers the event in 1776 when Statia saluted the young United States of America.

Carnival is the main event in the year and takes place for ten days from late July to early August. It is similar to other Caribbean carnivals, with a pyjama *jump-up* in the early morning at *jouvert*, with a Carnival Queen and a calypso competition, culminating in the burning of *Momo*, the spirit of the Carnival.

WHERE TO STAY

There are just three hotels on the island, two in Lower Town and one beyond the airport. There are one or two guest houses and it is possible to rent cottages through the Tourist Board. There is a 7% government tax on rooms and an energy tax of 5%. Service is generally charged at 15%, so the bills can mount fairly quickly.

The Old Gin House, PO Box 172 (tel 82319, fax 82555), has been rebuilt in the small red bricks of the old Statian warehouses and two centuries after the mercantilist mayhem they have taken on a rust of stateliness, festooned on the outside with tropical growth and a traveller's palm. There are 20 rooms, all neatly dressed up with antique furniture, some overlooking the sea, others tucked under the cliff, looking into the garden and pool. The restaurant, the Moonshay Publick House, takes advantage of the rarefied 18th-century atmosphere for candlelit dinners. More relaxed is the Terrace Restaurant across the road, overlooking the sea. A room costs US$150 in winter for a single or double. **La Maison sur la Plage**, PO Box 157 (tel 82256), is a collection of cottages set beneath a hill above the isolated Zeelandia Bay, a two-mile strip of brown sand dashed by Atlantic waves (swimming is not recommended because of the undertow). The main house has a bar and a fine French dining room looking out through trellis-work to the bay and the Quill volcano in the distance. On a small island this is a secluded retreat, with good trails all around. US$80 in winter. The **Golden Era Hotel**, PO Box 109 (tel 82345), on the waterfront in Lower Town, is a pre-fab construction that has none of the atmosphere of old-time Statia. However, it is in town, just a minute's walk from the Old Gin House or a stumble down the hill from the bars of Upper Town. The dining room serves West Indian and international fare. Under US$88 in peak season.

You can get a cheap and comfortable room at the **Country Inn** (tel 82484), just four secluded apartments, set far away from the hustle of Oranjestad in Concordia. Double room US$50, includes breakfast. The **Airport View Apartments** (tel 82299) are just next to the airport for about US$35 for a double, single $20. **Guest houses** include **Daniel's** (tel 82358) on Rose Mary Laan Rd, double US$35, single $25 and **Richardson Guest House** (tel 82378) at No. 3 Union Estate, double room US$35, single $20.

EATING OUT

Outside the hotels, each of which has a dining-room (standard roughly equivalent to the price of the rooms), there is **L'Etoile** (tel 82299), up the hill on Heiligerweg, where you will find local cuisine. Start with a callaloo soup and follow with creole catch of the day. Main dish US$8–15. **Talk of the Town** (tel 82236) in Golden Rock, on the way to the airport, offers more local creole meals like rice and peas and spicy chicken, as does the **Stone Oven** (tel 82247) on Faeschweg. A main course costs US$10–12 in both. If you feel like a Chinese meal, then you catch a chicken noodle soup and chow mein at the **Chinese Restaurant** on Prinseweg, US$8.

NIGHTLIFE
Nightlife in Statia is limited to the hotels and the local bars, of which the best is **Kool Corner**, where the Statians can be found 'limin' at all hours. At **Franky's** on the Ruyterweg you can get simple meals—burgers and a fry fish or chicken—or simply have a beer when the band is playing. Make sure to finish off with on of Franky's ice creams.

SABA

Saba is impossibly steep, a huge central cone surrounded by little lieutenants, a volcanic pimple 30 miles south of Sint Maarten. Just five square miles in area, Saba is the last peak in the chain of volcanic islands that run in an arc from Grenada in the far south.

Mount Scenery (2885 ft), the island peak smothered in rainforest, is the highest point in the Kingdom of the Netherlands. Near the summit, Saba can seem like a tropical Gormenghast—clouds swirl through the dripping greenery and the gnarled branches of ancient trees are clad in creeping diabolic green mosses.

Besides the capital, The Bottom, there are three main villages on the island's slopes (Windwardside, St John's and Hell's Gate). They appear almost alpine with their stepped alleys, switchbacks and steep retaining walls, the base of one house perched on the roof of the one below, and of course, spectacular views. There is a certain pastoral calm about the place as well.

Saba (pronounced as in sabre, the sword) is incredibly neat. Tidy gardens tamed from the tropical jungle nestle behind white wooden picket fences; fluorescent blooms stand out against the whitewashed clapboard walls of the houses with their horseshoe-shaped chimney-pots. Curiously, every single roof in Saba is painted red.

The population is just 1200 (mostly of British descent) and it is untypical in the Caribbean for being roughly half white and half black. With few plantations, most slaves on Saba were domestic servants and their numbers never exceeded those of the white

Windwardside roofs

population. Though the islanders all know each other, there are unspoken rules concerning skin colour (as there are in many Caribbean islands) and even today, there is little intermarriage between the races. And as with many small islands, much of the youth has left in search of work and adventure. The population appears to be mainly grandparents and infant grandchildren.

You have a good chance of getting a person's name right in Saba if you call them Mr or Mrs Hassell (about a quarter of the population are called Hassell). However, beware, because you might just come across a member of the two rival Saban dynasties, a Johnson or a Simmons.

History

A stream of famous visitors passed the island in the 16th century, among them Sir Walter Raleigh and Piet Heyn, the Dutch privateer—but most thought better of trying to land. Somebody must have done so, however, because in 1632 a ship-wrecked crew of Englishmen found a plentiful supply of fruit on the trees but no inhabitants. (It was a tradition that sailors would plant food-bearing trees for just this sort of occasion.)

The first permanent settlement of Saba was made by Dutchmen from nearby Sint Eustatius in about 1640, and they were joined by a succession of misfits, many of them English speakers. In 1665 Henry Morgan paused to capture the island, from which he promptly deported everyone who wasn't English.

Saba was almost impregnable. The terrain is so precipitous that storming the island presented quite a problem. For their part, the Sabans constructed platforms at the top of the ravines and loaded them with boulders. On the approach of an enemy, they simply knocked out the supports. In 1689 the French had a go after successfully capturing Sint Eustatius, but decided in the end to leave the island alone. From then on, most changes of allegiance were by political arrangement. In 1816 the island was handed back to the Dutch for the last time.

The great Caribbean rover, Père Labat, dropped by in about 1700 and found that the islanders' principal trade was in boots and shoes. Even the parson was a cobbler. Labat bought six pairs. Since then Sabans have been in many trades. They had some success growing sugar in the fertile parts of the island. For this they brought in some Africans, whose descendants are still on the island. Slavery was relatively benign here compared with other islands.

In the 19th century the Saban men took to the sea and became renowned sailors. They were much in demand by the shipping lines and they captained ships sailing all over the Americas. (Give them a bit of encouragement and old Sabans will gladly tell you of the days when 'the boats were made of wood and the men were made of iron'.) The economy of the island was supported by the contributions that they sent back to their families. At home, with no men around, the Saban women adopted lacemaking, or drawn-thread work, an industry that continues today. It was supposedly introduced to the island by a Saban woman who was educated in a convent in Venezuela.

As shipping waned in the 30s, the oil industry boomed in Curaçao and Aruba, the Dutch Leeward Islands off the coast of Venezuela, and the menfolk rushed away to get work there. All these departures have reduced the population of Saba from around 2500 to its present level.

Today the 'remittance money' sent home by Sabans abroad has dwindled but returns from tourism have increased. Saba also receives grants from the Central Government of the Netherlands Antilles in Curaçao, to which they send one elected senator.

GETTING TO SABA

The only scheduled flights that go to Saba are with **Windward Island Airways** (tel 599 5 44230) originating in Sint Maarten. Two of the five flights per day also touch down at Sint Eustatius.

You can also get to Saba by the powerboat *Style* (tel 599 5 22167), which departs three times a week from Great Bay Marina in Sint Maarten, returning at 5 pm. The round trip costs around US$50, and gives you most of a day's sightseeing on the island. Alternatively, you might be able to persuade a cargo-ship captain to give you a lift from Sint Maarten.

There is a departure tax of US$2 if you are travelling to Sint Eustatius or to Sint Maarten and US$5 for elsewhere.

Flying into Saba is a novel experience. Juancho E. Yrausquin airport is on Flat Point—named so because it is one of the only flat places on the island, even if there is a 130-ft cliff at either end. At 1312 ft, this strip is one of the shortest in the world, including most aircraft carriers, and as you look at it from the air, it seems impossible that anything could land on it. But be reassured, the STOL Twin Otters can land on a twenty pence piece and they usually take only half the runway.

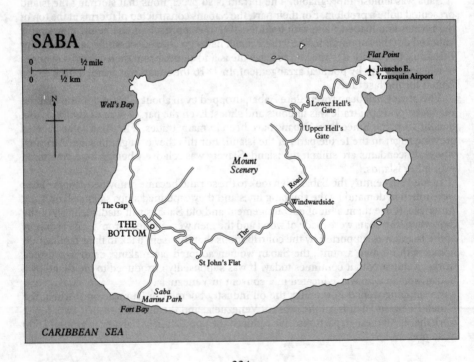

334

GETTING AROUND
With no buses, getting around Saba is really limited to **taxis**, and hitching, which works very well and will introduce you to the Sabans. There is only one road, so you cannot go wrong. It is usually enough to sit on the wall at the edge of town for someone to pick you up. The taxi-fare from one end of the island to the other comes to around US$12.

Taxi-drivers are willing to give a tour of the island, taking in the historical sights and views and a stop for lunch. They know about catching the last plane out, though it would probably not go without you anyway. A day's tour for two will cost around US$40, with a small charge for extra people.

There are 20 or so **hire cars** on the island and they can be rented for about US$35 per day. Remember to drive on the right, and that Saba's only petrol station is in Fort Bay (tel 63272), on the coast below The Bottom. Cars can be hired from **Doc's Car Rental** (tel 62271), **Hardiana** (tel 62205) and Johnson's Car Rental (tel 62469).

TOURIST INFORMATION
The **Saba Tourist Office** (tel 62231, fax 62350) is in Windwardside, in the same building as the Post Office. The staff are helpful and are in the office on weekdays 8–noon and 1–5.

The Tourist Office stocks a number of books about the island, including *Saba, the first guidebook* by Natalie and Paul Pfanstiel, a friendly tour of the island filled with historical nuggets and *Saban Lore, Tales from my Grandmother's pipe*, by Will Johnson, the island's Senator and editor of the monthly broadsheet, *Saba Herald*.

Not so many years ago, isolated Saba had only a weekly mail service, but now communications are rather easier. To **telephone** the island from abroad, dial 599–4 and then the 5-digit Saban number. If phoning within the island, dial the last four digits only.

In case of a medical **emergency**, contact the M A Edwards Medical Centre (tel 63288) in The Bottom.

MONEY
Barclays Bank (tel 62216) operates in Windwardside, hours 8.30 am to 1.30 pm on weekdays. Places accustomed to tourists, for instance hotels and dive-shops, will accept credit cards. Others will not.

SPORTS
Saba has no 'beaches' as beaches are generally thought of in the Caribbean. However, a patch of migratory grey volcanic sand returns annually to the north coast of the island in the spring, staying over the summer until about November. This is at **Well's Bay**, at the end of the road from The Bottom. On a calm day, it makes a good picnic spot. The other place occasionally referred to as the 'beach' is the concrete ramp down into the water at Fort Bay.

Saba has a name as a **scuba diving** destination. The island's slopes descend as steeply beneath the water as above and among the caves, pinnacles and lava flows are excellent gardens of coral. Visibility is good, often around 100 feet, and there is abundant fish life, with the occasional chance to see a turtle and even a migrating humpback whale. Expect patrols of sergeantfish (striped) and soldierfish to dart around the coral-forests and sponges.

The Saba Marine Park was established in 1987 to protect the marine life, and has placed mooring sites in the seabed (the coastline is so rough that all dives are made from boats). Spearfishing is illegal, as is the removal of any coral.

There are three dive operators on the island: **Saba Deep**, which works from Fort Bay (tel 63347) and offers instruction (NAUI and PADI), **Sea Saba** (tel 62246), located in Windwardside (offering PADI certification) and Wilson's Dive Shop (tel 63410). Saba has a four-person decompression chamber. A one-tank dive costs around around US$35.

For those content with a look at the marine life without getting wet, a slide show is staged at Juliana's Recreation Room every Tuesday, by the manager of the Saba Marine Park. Alternatively, you might like to take a sunset cruise around the island, which you can fix through either of the two dive shops.

WALKING

All over the island you will see the stone walls of old-time Saba, when the villages of the island were linked in a nexus of stepped pathways (before the arrival of cars in 1947). People would walk or ride a donkey to get around. Any older Saban will tell you about the morning rush-hour (a crowded ¾ hour's walk) over the hills from Windwardside to The Bottom, and how the islanders used to arrive at parties in their walking boots. A few of the ingenious old paths remain and they make good walking trails.

A favourite walk is up to Saba's summit, **Mount Scenery**, best when the peak is not engulfed in cloud. A sign on the road at the bottom forewarns you that there are 1064 steps. It is hot work and a good half hour's hike, though you can miss out the first bit out by taking the upper road. Cable and Wireless (who operate the radio mast on the summit and have to climb the hill quite often) have the right idea, and they have erected a shelter on the way up. The flora is fairly typical of the steep volcanic islands, with whole hillsides of *elephant ears* on the lower slopes and an ever-thickening rainforest with its profuse growth that eventually gives over to elfin woodland. Gnarled trees are covered with mosses that creep, tangles of lianas hang suspended and cycads and bromeliads explode from their perches in the trees. Perhaps you will see a *trembler* or a *garnet-throated hummingbird* in the elfin woodland.

There are a number of trails in the northern part of the island, between Well's Bay and Hell's Gate, where there are a couple of abandoned villages. In these remoter areas you may come across sea-birds like terns and brown noddies as well as shearwaters and tropicbirds. Further details of walks on the island, and a guide if you would like one, though it is hardly necessary, are available from the Tourist Office in Windwardside.

'The Road that could not be built'

Before the construction of The Road, anything from a bean to a grand piano had to be carried around on the pathways and so the Sabans decided that they needed a road. On seeking expert advice in the 30s, they were simply told: don't bother. But the Hassels and the Johnsons were made of sterner stuff than that, and so Lambertus Hassell, the architect of The Road, decided to take a correspondence course in civil engineering. In 1938 work began at Fort Bay, slowly winding its way uphill for the next five years to The Bottom. In 1947, the first car arrived and by 1951 it was able to drive to Windwardside.

The 19 miles of The Road clings to the mountainside, climbing to 1800 ft as it winds from village to village, so you get some unexpected and stunning views as you drive around. To the builders' credit, The Road was repaired for the first time in the late 1980s.

The Bottom

The Bottom is the capital of Saba and despite its name it is at 850 ft. It is a jumble of white walls, red roofs and green shutters set in neat little gardens, sitting in the bottom of a bowl (hence the name) thought to be the crater of Saba's extinct volcano. The evening shade comes early to The Bottom as it is towered over by vast forested escarpments.

The Dutch and the Saban flags fly alongside one another in front of the Lieutenant Governor's residence at the southern end of the town, a gingerbread house defended by a couple of fearsome cannon (at least four-ouncers). The present Lt Governor is Mr Sydney Sorton.

Close by is the road that leads down through the 'chicane' to **Fort Bay**. This is the island's main port, and all goods have been brought in here since the pier was constructed in 1972. Before that, landing was a skilled technique which involved beaching the row-boat on one wave and scrambling out before the next one broke over you.

At the other end of town, 520 steps lead down to **Ladder Bay**, the other main port, off the new road to Wells Bay. These steps have seen everything from shoes to the kitchen sink transported up them in their time. You might also see a charcoal-burner's pit on the way down.

The Road passes by way of St John's to **Windwardside**, Saba's second settlement, scattered over the mountainside at about 1960 ft. More white picket fences, barrel graves/cisterns and steep alleys. In one of the many neat houses, you will find the **Saba Museum**, dressed up as it was in its prime 150 years ago. It exhibits Saban memorabilia from Indian axe-heads to a Victorian mahogany four-poster with pineapple motifs. Open on weekdays 10–3, adm: a suggested donation of US$1. Outside the museum is a bust of *El Libertador*, Simon Bolivar, who recruited men here in 1816 for his struggle against the Spanish authorities in South America. There is a fantastic view across to Statia from the Lookout, just up the hill from Windwardside.

From Windwardside, The Road switchbacks its way through terraced cultivation to the alpine village of Hell's Gate (a curious adaptation of the original name of Zion's Hill), where each house is held in place and prevented from tumbling down the hill by the one above. The church was constructed only in 1962. From here The Road makes its 19 curves to get down to Flat Point, where the airstrip is situated.

WHERE TO STAY

There are few places to stay on Saba, but each has the cosy and friendly atmosphere for which the island is known (and of course, a red roof). Apart from the four hotels and guest houses there are about 20 villas for hire—more details of these can be obtained from the Tourist Board or through Saba Real Estate NV (tel 62299, fax 62415). There is a government hotel tax of 5%; hotels also add a service charge of 10% or 15%.

The **Queen's Garden Resort** (tel 62236, fax 62450) stands high above the Bottom, on a hillside smothered in rainforest, with views to the sea. The rooms are very comfortable, each with a pluge pool and mod cons like cable TV. Sports include tennis courts and a fitness centre and there is a restaurant in the main house. Double room US$150–200 per night in season. The **Captain's Quarters** (tel 62201, fax 62377), at the foot of the hill in Windwardside has ten very comfortable rooms in three gingerbread blocks; some have wooden floors and four-posters; from the balconies you look over banana trees to the Caribbean Sea 1500 feet below. The dining room is on a terrace beneath the main house, which is decorated as the sea captain's home that it once was. The bar is a popular gathering point after dark. A double room costs around US$125. Just up the hill is **Scout's Place** (tel 62205, fax 62388), with 15 simple rooms, overlooking the attractive roofs and jungle-like greenery. The hotel is in the centre of town and here also there is a lively open-air bar, where the Sabans stop off on their way home from work. The dining room is presided over by Dianna Medero, something of a local celebrity. Double room US$65–85, includes breakfast. **Juliana's** (tel 62269, fax 62389) is also in Windwardside, ten rooms with their own balconies facing the Caribbean Sea. There is a dining room, Tropics Café, and a pool with the hotel. Double room US$95 in season. **Cranston's Antique Inn** (tel 3203) is the former Lieutenant Governor's residence in The Bottom. As the name implies, the Inn basks in fading Saban glory, a pretty wooden creole house painted white with green shutters behind a picket fence. Some of the six rooms have four-poster beds (one of them slept in by Queen Juliana of the Netherlands). Some also share a bathroom. A double room in winter costs US$60, including breakfast. 10% service charge. In The Bottom you will find a friendly place to stay at the **Caribe Guest House** (tel/fax 62359). There are just five rooms with private baths and although there is no restaurant, the kitchen is for the use of the guests, double US$50 year round.

EATING OUT

You are likely to eat in the hotel dining rooms. Most serve a combination of local dishes—curry goat and callaloo—alongside standard American fare—burgers and steaks. The most sophisticated is the **Captain's Quarters**, set on the veranda—a good grilled catch of the day or a shrimp dish. The dining room at **Scout's Place**, set on the veranda, has another magnificent view of the Caribbean Sea, good for a cocktail with a view. Chicken or fish. **Tropics** at Juliana's is quite new and has a cracking view of the Caribbean Sea. **Cranston's Antique Inn** in The Bottom serves more local fare—kingfish and snapper or a fried chicken accompanied by a volley of local vegetables. It is worth making a reservation at the hotel dining rooms.

Outside the hotels you will find good seafood and creole fare at **Brigadoon** (tel 62380) in Windwardside. Try a lobster in butter or chicken in a creole sauce. If you feel like a Chinese meal, try the **Saba Chinese Restaurant** (tel 62268) where there is a huge selection of traditional Chinese dishes including sweet and sour and chow mein, US$10 a main course. And there is also an Italian restaurant, **Guido's** (tel 62230), with burgers as well as pizzas and pastas. Down in The Bottom you will get classic local cuisine at **Queenie's Serving Spoon** (tel 63225)—pumpkin soup or callaloo, followed by a curry goat and a topical fruit ice cream to finish. And **Lollipops** is another local bar and restaurant for classic West Indian fare; try fish or chicken with local vegetables—breadfruit, sweet potato and yam.

NIGHTLIFE
When Père Labat visited in 1701, he wrote: 'The settlers live as it were in a large club and frequently entertain each other.' It is pretty much the same today, except that they congregate in the bars dotted around the island, mainly in the hotels. If there is a party, you may find yourself invited. Many of the restaurants have bars where you can catch a crowd liming in the evenings. If you want to go dancing, the **Mountain High Club** is open at the weekend at Guido's Pizzeria in Windwardside.

The Dutch Leeward Islands

Aruba, Bonaire and Curaçao

The ABC Islands are long and thin, poised irregularly a few miles off the coast of South America. You can see the mountains of Venezuela from them on a clear day and yet the islands not are geologically connected to the continent. They are made up of packed lava and ashes pushed up from the sea floor over the millennia. As the sea has risen and receded around them, generations of coral have left reefs on their slopes, giving their coastlines a stone like a sort of limestone brittle, locally called *klips*.

Low-lying, the Caribbean winds race over them, hardly pausing to form clouds and rain as they do elsewhere, and so these islands have none of the lushness and exuberant fertility of other West Indian islands (rainfall here is just 20 inches annually as opposed to 300-odd in the Windwards). Instead they are semi-arid and look something like Arizona—parched flatlands covered with about 10 foot of thorny scrub and the occasional candelabra cactus standing around in an exclamatory pose. The rolling scrubland of all three islands is known in Papiamento as *cunucu*.

The average temperature is 82°F, but the Passatwinden (Dutch for the Tradewinds) take the edge off the heat. Sucked inevitably towards the equator, they are sometimes almost strong enough to lean against, particularly in the early months of the year when they are at their height. Like the Sirocco and the Föhn they actually send people a bit dotty, so you will know what's up when drivers seem psychotic in February. Another curious effect they have is on a native tree called the divi-divi; its branches become a gnarled and knotted brush pointing southwest, resembling a woman bent at the waist in a gale, her shawl and thigh-length hair swept away on the wind.

One of the most striking things about the ABC islands is the colours. The buildings here do not have the pastel wash of most Caribbean islands, nor the primary glare of Haiti, but a strong and distinctive colour scheme all of their own—ochre, orange and russet brown, with the occasional dark green and even vermilion. It was in 1817 that the Governor, Vice-Admiral Kikkert, whose eyes were suffering from the combination of the white-washed walls and the Caribbean sun, decreed that no building should be painted white. Highlighted by the white stucco of the Dutch colonial façades and the orange *dakpannen* (Dutch roof-tiles), the walls soak up the sunshine. You will see portakabins and mausolea imitating the colour scheme and even the Curaçao national bird, the *trupial*, is conveniently a shade of gold and orange.

With South America so close, Latin life runs strong through the islands. You will hear *salsa* and *merengue* on the buses; some Latin features are visible in the Dutch faces.

339

Spanish is clearly audible in the language and the islanders dress and often hold themselves with Latin poise.

And there is quite some competition between the islands. When Aruba took its Independence in 1986, the Curaçaoans threatened to take a shotgun to the Aruban bird on the Autonomy Monument in Willemstad. In return the Arubians will tell you that Curaçaoan waters are shark infested. They both dismiss the Bonaireans, who apparently sing their Papiamento.

Papiamento

Of all the creole languages that have developed in the Caribbean, the most enigmatic is *Papiamento*, spoken in the Dutch Leewards. Its heritage is thought of as almost mystical: a blend of strains from Spain, Portugal, Holland, England and France, from Africa and even from local Indian languages.

The language developed as a pidgin in the 17th century as the port of Curaçao grew. Into the mix of Dutch traders and African slaves came Portuguese-speaking Jews and other South Americans who spoke Spanish. In the 18th century, Papiamento (the word means 'babble' and is supposedly closely related to the word for Parliament) crystallized as the language of the three islands. It took on a life of its own, with expressions to reflect local existence: *Pampuna no sa pari calbas*, 'the pumpkin plant does not bear calabashes' (a Caribbean way of saying 'like father like son'), and *Un macacu ta subi palu di sumpinja un biahe so*, 'a monkey climbs a cactus only once'.

Unlike other Caribbean islands, where the creoles are usually treated with a certain ambivalence, Papiamento is spoken by islanders across the social spectrum. It is used in the home, in church and newspapers are published in it. Dutch may be the official language, used in schools, but Papiamento will receive official status in the Dutch Leewards soon.

Listening to Papiamento can give an impression that you are hearing a stream of Spanish; words will seem to offer meaning, but then the impression will dissolve as the unlikely guttural sounds of Portuguese and pursed Dutch noises jump out at you. Papiamento is a good language to get worked up in and no doubt you will hear the islanders do just that.

History

A succession of Indian tribes lived on the three islands before Columbus discovered the New World. For the last 300 years it was the Caiquetios, who came under a *cacique*, or chieftain, from the mainland. They had a peaceful enough life, fishing and trading in their *piraguas*, hollowed out canoes, and chewing chicle leaves (from the tree that provides the substance for chewing-gum), which they kept in bowls slung around their necks.

But things were to change with the arrival of the Europeans. The first came in 1498 as they explored the coast of South America—Alonso de Ojeda, one of Columbus's lieutenants, and Amerigo Vespucci, the Florentine explorer whose name was later mistakenly given to the whole continent of America. Vespucci called Curaçao the 'Land of the Giants' because the Indians were so large. Old prints show diminutive conquistadors clad in helmets and clutching pikes meeting vast Indians with clubs and bows and arrows.

The islands offered nothing to the Spaniards in their search for Eldorado and the Fountain of Youth, so all three were marked down as *islas inutilas* (useless) and passed over. *Indieros*, red slave traders who dealt in Indians from the South American continent, used the islands as a base and they shipped off those who lived there to work in the gold-mines in Hispaniola. Those they left behind were encouraged to chase off any other Europeans showing an interest in the island.

In 1527 the Spaniards did make a settlement of Curaçao and bred cattle there. Jack Hawkins, the English pirate, visited the island in 1565 and described it as 'one great cattle ranch'. He saw 100 oxen butchered in one day. The hides were stripped for curing and their tongues cut out to be eaten. The rest of the carcass was simply thrown into the sea.

'Isla inutila' or not, Curaçao proved a perfect base from which the Dutch could harry the Spaniards in the Indies in the early 17th century. The Dutch West India Company descended on it in 1634 and in a fairly typical invasion for the time, they chased the 20 Spanish settlers around the island for three weeks until, exhausted, they surrendered. To protect the rear approaches of Curaçao they put garrisons on Bonaire and Aruba in 1636.

The Spaniards, intent on keeping other Europeans out of their Empire in the New World, decided to sack Bonaire in 1642, but they arrived to find that, as usual, the Dutch had fled. They pillaged and burned the settlement for a week and then left, so before long the Dutch came back at their leisure.

In 1638 the governor of Curaçao was Peter Stuyvesant, perhaps best known nowadays for being on the front of a cigarette packet. Later he would become the Director General of all the Dutch possessions in the New World, which he administered from Nieuw Amsterdam, now New York. He set the island on course for its great prosperity and by the 1650s it was flourishing. Merchants flooded in and the Dutch fleets fed the trade.

The driving force behind the success of Curaçao was traffic in humans to work the burgeoning Caribbean sugar-plantations. Red Indians were replaced by black Africans, and the infamous slave trade was underway. On arrival after four to six weeks on the horrific 'Middle Passage', the slaves would be rubbed down with oil and paraded through the streets singing before being auctioned. Buyers came to Curaçao from all over the Caribbean, and at its height in the 18th century about two fifths of all slaves brought to the Americas came via Curaçao.

Meanwhile Aruba and Bonaire were kept as farms to supply the senior colony of Curaçao. They were left unsettled, except by ranchers and a few government farmers who scratched the infertile soil together to grow maize. Aruba was particularly known for its horses, which were sold on plantations in the Caribbean and in South America. Paardenbaai (Horses Bay), the original harbour off Willemstad, is where they were traditionally loaded and landed. Bonaire was more of a cattle ranch. Boca Slagbaai in the northwest is where the animals were slaughtered just before being shipped to Curaçao. Its main commodity, though, was salt (in the days before refrigeration it was essential for Dutch trading ventures between Europe and the New World). The harvesting took place in the shallow ponds in the south of the island and the industry has continued on and off to this day.

Curaçao became a valuable prize and its fortunes waxed and waned on the winds blowing from Europe—wars put the island under blockade, but brought untold riches in the supply of arms and gunpowder. The British invaded twice during the Napoleonic Wars, once capturing Curaçao while everybody was out celebrating the New Year, but by 1816 the islands were back in Dutch hands.

Connections with South America were strong and the islands, particularly Aruba, just 15 miles from the mainland, were often a political refuge. *El Libertador*, Simon Bolivar, came here after the collapse of the First Republic in 1812. As late as 1927 the Curaçaoans found themselves invaded by the Venezuelan rebel leader, Rafael Simon Urbina, who stormed Fort Amsterdam and stole all the weapons before departing with the Governor as a hostage. Two Curaçaoans buried in the Panteon Nacional in Caracas for their part in the Venezuelan War of Independence are Luis Brion and Manuel Carlos Piar.

Then decline began and even the trade failed. Successive governors tried different schemes to keep the islands afloat financially, including the cultivation of aloe, now used for cosmetics, cochineal dye and sisal for rope. The salt industry was continued in Bonaire and in 1825 gold was discovered in Aruba. Bonaire was so poor after the slaves were emancipated in 1863 that in their despair, the government put it up for sale.

The islands reached their lowest point at the end of the 19th century and many went abroad to look for work, sending money back to keep their families at home. They went off to the (then) Dutch colony of Surinam or joined the streams of West Indians who dug the Panama Canal.

The Ditch, as the canal was known, immediately reaffirmed Curaçao's status as a port, but it was the discovery of oil in Venezuela that would change Curaçao and Aruba so dramatically and secure the two islands' prosperity for the 20th century. Their Dutch heritage meant a stable political climate and their steep shores allowed the approach of ocean-going tankers which could not get to the South American coast. Crude oil was shipped in shallow-bottomed ships from Venezuela, refined and then shipped on in ocean-going tankers. Royal Dutch Shell moved into Curaçao in 1915 and built a refinery, and in 1924 the Lago Oil and Transport Company, a subsidiary of Standard Oil of New Jersey (EXXON) came to Aruba.

Workers flooded into the islands now to join the boom, from the Dutch Windwards and Surinam and from the English colonies. The populations rocketed, each multiplying by five times. The refineries directly employed as much as 15 per cent of the population of both islands.

The islanders talk in apocalyptic terms about *Automation*, which slashed the workforce in the 50s and 60s. The ageing plants were dealt another blow in the early 1980s when OPEC agreements forced up the price of crude oil and the industry foundered. The two giant oil companies have sold up and moved out, and now the refineries work at massively reduced capacity. The islands depend now mainly on tourism.

Flora and Fauna

The three islands have similar flora among their outsize boulders and sand dunes, and the blanket of scrub is broken by prickly pear and organ pipe cactus, locally known as *kadushi* (they are used as fences and also end up in soup here), and by several species of plant that were cultivated here on a commercial basis, for instance the spiky and fleshy-leafed aloe and the agave, also called the century plant, with its flowering, 30-foot stem.

There are very few land animals, just a few lizards and the iguana, who is shy because he also ends up in a traditional dish, though you might be lucky enough to see a deer on Curaçao.

However there is a large variety of birds here, partly because they stray over from South America, but also because the islands are a stop-over for the winter migration from North America. Among the usual bananaquits (which you will no doubt see because they will have a go at your sugar-bowl), there are yellow orioles, hawks and doves, the odd hummingbird and even burrowing owls. In the coastal ponds you will see herons and other wading birds trawling for food (among them the two magnificent colonies of flamingos on Bonaire).

CURAÇAO

Traditionally Curaçao has always been the heart of Dutch influence in the Caribbean; the powerhouse of their trading ventures and the administrative centre of the Netherlands Antilles. Even its name is fancifully thought to come from the Portuguese word for heart, *corazon*.

Curaçao is oddly shaped, a bit like a rebellious bow-tie, and at 38 miles by nine, it is the largest of the Netherlands Antilles. Like its neighbours it is low and scrubby, covered in *cunucu*, with cacti that strike theatrical poses. Its shores are cut with inlets that make perfect harbours.

With 150,000 islanders, Curaçao is heavily populated. Centuries of business as a trading port have brought racial strains from all over the world. Like Aruba, it experienced boom years earlier this century when Shell built a vast refinery and bunkering station on the island. The money poured in and population rocketed, from 33,000 in 1915 to 150,000 in 1975. Jokers claimed that the Curaçaoans liked to change their clothes twice a day and their car every three months in those days, but it all changed when *Automation* cut the workforce from 18,500 to 4000.

In the early 80s things got even worse with the oil-crash and the world economic recession. The price of oil plummeted and sales decreased, and eventually Shell sold the refinery and left in 1985. The volume of trade passing through the port (still one of the largest in the world, though) has rallied after the problems in Panama, as did off-shore finance, another important sector. The government of Curaçao is trying to increase tourism and this is now the island's second industry.

Its economy may be depressed, but that does not mean that the island itself is, for that would be to underestimate the Curaçaoans. A few may have left the island to find a better life elsewhere, but most have an irrepressible Caribbean spirit and a conviction that the future will see them right.

For details on Curaçao's history, see p. 340; for Flora and Fauna, see p. 342.

Curaçao Liqueur

On a still day, the Curaçao air used to hang with the tangy smell of orange peel drying in the sun. It was the skins of the *laraha* orange, which were being made into Senior Curaçao of Curaçao liqueur, original namesake of the more famous Bols. These green *Valencia* oranges, which grow normally elsewhere, grow small and bitter in the barren earth of Curaçao (the tree features on the national coat of arms) and you can see the distilling process at the **Curaçao Liqueur Distillery** (tel 613526) in the hall of the Landhuis Chobolobo on the outskirts of Willemstad. It is a small operation, just four or five vats. Distinctive round bottles with slim tall necks are corked by hand and labels are individually stuck on. The original orange is best, but there are three other flavours on offer. Open Mon–Fri, 8–noon and 1–5, adm free, samples on offer, plenty of opportunity to buy, of course. If you catch a whiff of something pungently sweet, then it is Curaçao's current smell, the refining crude, that hangs on the air around the oil refinery.

GETTING TO CURAÇAO

Curaçao has extremely good air connections; to Europe, the USA, South America as well as around the Caribbean. The airport at Hato, 7 miles (12km) north of Willemstad, is the busiest in the Netherlands Antilles. Other possibilities include a boat from Venezuela, though this is recommended only for the intrepid with plenty of time to spare. A departure tax of US$5.75 is payable upon leaving Curaçao.

By Air

From Europe: the most convenient service is on the Dutch airline KLM, which has several services each week non-stop from Schipol airport near Amsterdam. There are connections from most UK airports. The Portuguese airline TAP has one flight each week from Lisbon. A third alternative is to travel via Miami (see below).

From North America: there are no fewer than 20 flights each week from Miami to Curaçao on the national airline ALM, BWIA and Air Aruba. This is the best stopover point from the USA and Canada, although there are also direct and connecting flights from New York City on ALM and American Airlines. ALM also fly to Atlanta.

From Latin America: Curaçao is the best served island from which to begin a tour of the Caribbean. There are regular services from Valencia, Caracas and Maracaibo in Venezuela; Barranquilla and Bogotá in Colombia; Guayaquil in Ecuador; and Guatemala City.

From other Caribbean islands: there are numerous flights linking Curaçao with Aruba and Bonaire; there are more services at weekends, but these tend to be the most heavily booked. The other part of the Netherlands Antilles is served by a daily flight to Sint Maarten. For the rest of the Caribbean, the options are Kingston, Port of Spain in Trinidad and Port au Prince in Haiti and Santo Domingo in the Dominican Republic.

By Boat

There is an occasional ferry service from Coro in Venezuela, for which the fare is US$25. Check with Ferrys de Caribe in Caracas (tel 561 6520) to find out when it is running.

GETTING AROUND CURAÇAO

There is a public **bus system** in Curaçao and the important routes are run roughly every half hour. A florin will get you around town and two florins will take you up to Westpunt, as far as you can go. It is important to stand at the bus-stops (marked by lollipops) to ensure that you will be picked up. There are two terminals in Willemstad: the main one in Punda, behind the round market, which serves the east end of the island and the harbour area, and one at Riffort, just over the pontoon bridge, which serves the hotel area, the airport and beyond.

You will also see **share-taxis**, like South American *colectivos*, running the town routes. Again, it is best to wait at a bus-stop, but sometimes they will stop if you flag them down. One florin for a ride (US70c). Private minibuses will drop you off where you want to go, in an order that seems best to the driver; the further you go, the more you pay, up to about two florins.

Taxis are not metered so it is worth fixing the price before setting out. They can be found at any of the hotels and through the main despatch office (tel 616711). Some sample prices are: **Punda** to: the airport—US$11, Curaçao Caribbean Hotel area—US$10, Underwater Park area—US$10. **Airport** to Otrobanda—US$11, Curaçao Caribbean—US$10, Princess Beach—US$13. If you wish to take an island tour by taxi, the going rate is about US$20 per hour. You can arrange a bus-tour of the island through **Taber Tours** (tel 76713) or **Daltino Tours** (tel 614888), at about US$45 for a three-hour trip.

If you want the mobility to reach the Westpunt under your own steam, plenty of **rental cars** are available. Foreign and International licences are valid, and prices start at around US$35 per day. Driving is on the right, and where there are no road signs, traffic from the right has priority. If you do intend to hire a car, then look out for discount vouchers in the tourist magazines. Rental companies include some of the international names, **Budget** (tel 83466) and **National** (tel 803737). Local firms, which offer better basic rates, include **Caribe Rentals** (tel 613089) and **Simoons** rental at the airport (tel 82288). If you want to rent a bicycle, try **Cycle Rental** (tel 87447).

TOURIST INFORMATION

There is no Netherlands Antilles Tourist Office in the **UK**, so you are best to write to the USA or Curaçao itself.

Holland: Eendrachtsweg 69-C, 3012 LG Rotterdam (tel 4144 2639).
USA: 400 Madison Avenue, Suite 311, New York, NY 10017 (tel (212) 751 8266, fax 486 3024), and 330 Biscayne Blvd, Suite 330, Miami, FL 33132 (tel 305 374 5811, fax 374 6741).
Germany: Arnulfstr 44, 8000 München 2 (tel 0895 98490, fax 0895 232212).

In Willemstad, there is a helpful office in the arches at the **Waterfort Plaza** (tel 613397) on the Punda side. Other offices are at the airport (tel 86789) and in Schouwburgweg (tel 77121). Hours are 7.30–5, with an hour and a half off between noon and 1.30. The main office is at 19 Petermaai (tel 616000, fax 615999). The Tourist Board issues a yellow pamphlet called *Curaçao Holiday* with listings of current events.

Consulates include: Britain, 17 Chuchubiweg (tel 371698); Canada, Plaza Jojo Correa (tel 613515); France, 4 Andromedaweg (tel 370649); Germany, 42 Architectenweg (tel 613433); USA, 1 JB Gorsiraweg (tel 613066).

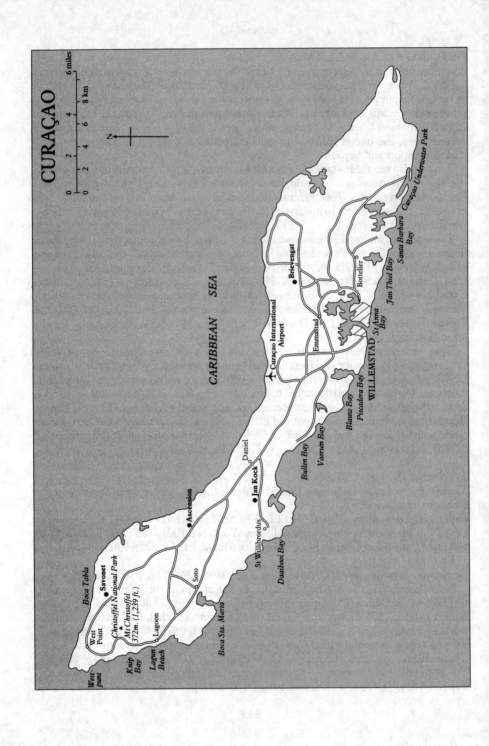

In a medical **emergency**, there is a 24-hour room at St Elizabeth's Hospital (tel 624900). The **police** can be reached on tel 44444. The **IDD code** to call Curaçao is 599 9 followed by the six- or five-figure island number. On-island use just the six or five digits.

MONEY
The currency of Curaçao is the Netherlands Antilles florin or guilder (NAFl), which is fixed to the US dollar at a rate of US$1 = NAFl1.77. However, the US greenback is very widely accepted all over the island and you might not even see florins except in change. US$ traveller's cheques and major international credit cards are accepted in all the hotels and any but the most off-beat restaurants and guest houses.

Banking hours are 8.30–noon and 1.30–4.30, Mon–Fri. You can change dollars and cash cheques with the hotel cashiers, but bear in mind that their rate will be marginally worse than the banks'.

Shopping hours are 8–12 noon and 2–6. Just as they did 200 years ago, traders will stay open longer if a large ship has come into town (though it tends to be cruise-ships now rather than merchantmen filled to the gunwales with porcelain and silks). Most will close for a couple of hours at lunch.

If you are looking to score a few duty-free purchases, then Curaçao is a good bet because it has some of the Caribbean's best shops—in fact your visit may even be billed as a 'shopping experience' anyway. A large proportion of the wares are mass-produced tourist rubbish (twee clogs and windmills made in Dutch *Delft Blue* china), but because Curaçao is such a massive trading-port, it is surprising what can turn up. A couple of shops worth considering are **Penha** (the distinctive building on the waterfront) for perfumes and chic clothes. You can find European fashion at **NafNaf** and Italian shoes at **Manhattan**. US residents returning home can take in up to $400 of duty-free goods.

BEACHES
Curaçao's coastline is not great for beaches and so the hotels have been known to build them. They are often small strips of hard sand on a substructure of coral rock, but in the west of the island you will find idyllic and secluded sun-traps cut into the *klips* where the water is warm and shallow. The north coast, battered by the onward swell of the Caribbean Sea, is too rough for swimming, but it does have some good spots for sunbathing if there is no wind. Some beaches have changing rooms and a small shop to buy a drink, but if you go farther afield remember to take a picnic. You might also take a parasol because the beaches are usually shadeless and the sun is extremely hot.

Beaches at the west end include **Westpunt** beach itself, where the water is fresh and translucent. In the heat, you can retire to the clifftops and the Playa Forti bar. At **Playa Abao** the water is jade in colour, as it is at **Knip Bay**, a beach popular with the Curaçaoans at the weekend, with changing facilities. **Lagun Beach**, with a few fishermen's huts, is a tiny secluded cove just below the Bahia Inn. **Daai Booi Bay**, down from St Willibrordus, is a small cove enclosed in cliffs, and **Vaersen Bay** close to the Bullen Bay oil terminal, is also secluded.

To the east of Willemstad the best beach is **Santa Barbara Bay**, also very popular with the Curaçaoans at weekends. There is a bar and changing rooms. There is a fee of US$4 to park a car. **Caracasbaai** is also popular with the locals.

There are also some good beaches on uninhabited Klein Curaçao, an outcrop off the east end of the island. Trips can be arranged through the big watersports shops.

WATERSPORTS

Watersports centre around the seafront hotels, but if you are staying inland you can usually hire equipment from them (ring and check before arriving). Try **Piscadera Watersports** (tel 625000) at the Curaçao Caribbean Hotel or **Dive Curaçao and Watersports** (tel 614944) at the Princess Beach Hotel. The Spanish Water lagoon to the east of Willemstad is another popular place for watersports.

The Curaçaoan winds are good for all sorts of sailing, including **windsurfing** and sunfish or hobie cats. Apart from the big operators, you can also arrange sailing trips out on a larger yacht through the **Curaçao Yacht Club** (tel 673038). If you want a day's cruise, you can join the yacht *Insulinde*, which stops for a picnic on Port Marie beach (tel 636310). The *Mermaid* makes a trip to Klein Curaçao for the day. **Taber Tours** (tel 76637) runs day-trips and picnics or a sunset tour. **Waterskiiers** can rent a boat for about US$20 for a quarter hour with the hotels.

The Curaçao Yacht Club arranges the 'Blue Water', a yearly fishing tournament in April, and they will also fix up **deep-sea fishing** trips on the high seas casting for marlin and bonito, cost around US$300 for a half day and tackle. Alternatively Piscadera Watersports (see above) will also take you out.

Curaçao's underwater world is excellent and the government have set aside 12 miles of reef and coastline on the southeastern shore of the island as the protected **Curaçao Underwater Park** (tel 624242). The office stages slide presentations of the park. Visibility is often up to 100 feet and the coral reefs, stacked with staghorn and gorgonians, teem with wrasses and snappers, while lobsters and the odd languid turtle cruise around. Wreck dives include the *SS Oranje Nassau* and the car wreck—a barge of cars that went down in a storm. Most hotels can lay on watersports and some run dive-boats down to the Underwater Park. Outside the big hotels mentioned above, operators include **Sammy's Scuba Centre** at Boca St Michel (tel 684444) and the **Lion's Dive Hotel** (tel 611644) which collects a friendly crowd.

Snorkellers will find excellent corals within a breath of the surface in many of the bays along the south coast, Knip Bay, Vaersen Bay and Blauw Bay for example. In the Underwater Park a snorkelling trail has been created, between the Seaquarium and Jan Thiel beach, but you must go by boat to reach it.

OTHER SPORTS

Most of the big hotels have **tennis courts** and you can usually book them as an outsider. **Golfers** can play at the Curaçao Golf and Squash Club (tel 73590) in Emmastad behind the harbour, where the 18 holes share ten oiled sand greens. If you wish to take a day out in the *cunucu*, **riding** on horseback, contact the **Rancho Alegre** (tel 79160), on the south coast beyond Piscadera Bay.

Willemstad

Willemstad has been a trading port for centuries. **Punda** at the harbour mouth, a Dutch port transported to the tropics, dates from the 18th century and in the recesses of Willemstad harbour is the Schottegat, Punda's 20th-century equivalent, all factories and

Willemstad

container wharves. Willemstad is still one of the busiest harbours in the world—so many ships use the channel that the hotel at the harbour entrance has had to take out marine insurance just in case.

The **Handelskade**, overlooking the St Anna Baai, is one of the Caribbean's most impressive and unlikely sights—an apparition of Amsterdam in the Caribbean sun, a line of tall coloured buildings with curly gables and orange roof-tiles. Two hundred years ago the waterfront at Punda (which takes its name from the point on which it sits) buzzed with ocean-going ships, offloading their cargoes for storage in these warehouses. Walled against a land-attack and built unusually tall because of the confined space, Punda's narrow alleys gathered around **Fort Amsterdam** at the beginning of the 18th century as the big Dutch trading houses sent their agents to Curaçao.

Willemstad's mercantile tradition is continued today and picturesquely precious Punda is bulging with goods on sale, now displayed in air-conditioned comfort for the benefit of the less hardy seagoers who arrive by cruise-ship rather than by clipper.

Another amusing and surprising feature of Punda is the **Koningin Emmabrug** (the Queen Emma Bridge), which links it to **Otrobanda**. It stands on 15 or so pontoons, which buck and sway, making it impossible to walk in a straight line (people jerk in unison as they cross, like a crowd of choreographed drunkards).

The first pontoon bridge was erected in 1888 by Leonard B. Smith, and was free to people without shoes. It is free to everybody today and so there is no need to take off your shoes as the toll-dodgers used to. But you may arrive at the shore to find that it has disappeared (there is an engine attached to the end pontoon). This is because the bridge has to open to let in the ships arriving in Willemstad harbour. While the Queen Emma Bridge is closed, a ferry (free to people with or without shoes) makes the crossing from about half-way down the Handelskade. It announces its departure with a siren.

On Sha Caprileskade, around the corner from the ferry terminal, is the **floating market**, where a line of Venezuelan sloops berth diagonally against the quay, shaded by vast awnings attached to their masts. Snapper and flying fish, stacks of melon and finger rolls of miniature bananas are piled on monumental slab tables on the wharf. The produce is mostly grown in Venezuela and is shipped to Curaçao overnight in time for the early morning market. The supply seems never-ending and if you ask for something not on display, the trader will rootle around on board ship and find it. Prices are very good here, but if you like to bargain, a couple of extra tangerines might be thrown into your bundle.

The original centre of the town is **Fort Amsterdam**, built by the Dutch immediately they arrived in 1634. It is now the seat of the Government of the Netherlands Antilles and also houses the Governor's Residence. **Fort Church** still has a British cannonball buried in its walls since they attacked in 1804.

On Columbusstraat is the **Mikve Israel Synagogue**, the oldest in the Americas. Modelled on the Synagogue in Amsterdam, it was built in 1732 by the large community of Jews that had taken refuge in Curaçao a century earlier. The floor around the mahogany altar is sprinkled with white sand in memory of the journey through the desert and the two of the four chandeliers date from 1707 and 1709. In the courtyard is the **Jewish Historical Museum**, where a 250 year-old *mikvah* (a ceremonial bath) and circumcision instruments are on display. Open weekdays 9–11.45 and 2.30–5, adm to the museum. The **Beth Haim Cemetery** (House of the Living), also the oldest in the Americas, dates from 1659 and is on the inner harbour, just outside Willemstad to the northwest.

As Punda expanded (the town walls were demolished in 1861), the wealthy Curaçaoan traders built their Dutch colonial town-houses away from the trading centre, in areas like Scharloo and Petermaai along the coast. The **Bolivar Museum**, on Penstraat, is tatty and run down, not really worth a detour except for the odd octagonal building in which it is housed, where his family took refuge in one of his two stays in exile on the island. Open 9–noon, 3–6 officially, adm.

They also crossed over St Anna Baai to **Otrobanda** (literally 'the other side'). The area is run-down and ramshackle now, but its 18th-century Dutch rococo architecture and elaborate gables give an idea of Curaçao's former grandeur. Today it is very much residential and also sees the seamier side of Curaçao life.

A classic Curaçaoan building with raised balconies and twin pointed roofs, the old sailors' hospital on Van Leeuwenhoekstraat, has been converted into the **Curaçao Museum**. Inside there are artefacts from the chicle-chewing Caiquetios, early Delft Blue china, a merchant's tablet advertising a tobacco shop, a revolving exhibition of island painters and a typical Curaçaoan kitchen, painted with red and white spots (supposedly it makes flies dizzy, but more likely it is superstition). Open daily except Mon, 9–noon and 2–5, adm.

On the sea as you leave Otrobanda is the Curaçao **Desalination plant**, which produces around 1.6 bn gallons of water from seawater annually. Time was when the oil tankers used to bring water as ballast and the Curaçaoans complained that it tasted of oil, but now the desalinated water is pure enough to brew Curaçao's Amstel beer. On the waterfront here, leading past the fishing huts, the Curaçaoans take the air in the early evening.

Fort Nassau, on the hill behind Punda, is no longer a fort, but still has the commanding view over the harbour and its approaches for which it was originally built.

Behind, it looks over Emmastad, the most modern extension of the capital, where you will find the container wharves and dry docks. Around the edge are the suburbs, with supermarkets, cinemas and fast-food joints, and where the majority of Curaçao's 170,000 population live, in neat fenced gardens with a satellite dish and two cars.

It also has one of the best views of the **Refinery** and on a still day you will recognize the pungent smell that hangs on the water (a cross between pitch and petrol). This monolithic assembly of silver chimneys and silos was once the largest refinery in the world, but has been run down since Shell sold the plant to the Curaçaoan Government in 1985. Recently it has been reactivated by Isla NV, owned by Petroleos de Venezuela.

On Fokker Weg you will see the futuristic **Autonomy Monument**, a sculpture of six birds commemorating the self-determination of the Netherlands Antilles in 1954. Aruba's bird remains despite its political separation in *status aparte* in 1986.

On Rijkseenheid Boulevard is the **Amstel Brewery**, the only one in the world that uses distilled seawater. Amstel, whose familiar red and white bottle tops you will see all over the Caribbean, started to brew under licence here in 1960 and today they produce three million gallons of lager annually. In a walk among the copper vats you will see the malt, germinated barley sent out from Holland, mixed with Curaçao water, fermented to make 'wort', and then matured, followed by a visit to the bar.

Curaçao Cunucu

Curaçao's 15 feet of cactus and *cunucu* is dotted occasionally with the orange roofs and white gables of the **landhuisen**, Dutch colonial country houses. Driving through the scrub, you will also see the original slave houses, with angled walls and shaggy maize-thatch roofs surrounded by cactus fences. Unlike other islands, where many slaves moved to the towns after emancipation, many more remained on the land in Curaçao, scratching a living from the earth. Hummingbirds and mockingbirds live in the scrub and along the northern coast you might be lucky enough to see an osprey.

A number of the *landhuisen* can be visited. Perhaps the best is the **Landhuis Brievengat**, once an aloe and cochineal plantation that has been restored to show life in the early 18th century when the house was built. Brievengat is just north of Willemstad, close to the sports stadium (tel 78344). Open Mon–Fri, 9–noon and 3–5, adm. Every Friday evening there is a public dance (entry NAFl 10) and one Sunday each month there is a day jamboree with music and folk dancing.

Other *Landhuisen* worth visiting include **Jan Kock** (tel 648087; irregular opening times, phone beforehand), and **Ascension**, restored and still used by the Dutch Navy (open first Sunday of each month from 10 am onwards). The 17th-century **Chobolobo Landhuis** on the outskirts of Willemstad is the home of the Curaçao Liqueur Distillery, well worth a visit (see p. 344).

Driving west from Otrobanda the coast road passes the main hotel strip and Bullen Bay oil terminal, where the storage tanks rise and fall as they are filled or emptied into the ocean-going tankers.

At the northwestern tip of the island you will find the **Christoffel National Park**, 4500 acres of nature reserve on the slopes of Curaçao's highest hill, Mt Christoffel (1239 ft). The park is laced with trails, for walkers and for vehicles, clearly marked and with displays of the semi-arid flora of the Dutch Leeward Islands, including the divi-divi and

351

THE CARIBBEAN

agave. Iguanas, like neolithic lizards, scuttle about and you might even see a Curaçao deer, a flitting orange *trupial* or an inquisitive-looking barn owl with a heart-shaped face peering at you. Some paths lead to the summit of Mt Christoffel, from where it is possible to see the mountains of Venezuela on a clear day. The entrance to the park is at the Savonet Landhuis (itself not open to the public), where there is a museum of Curaçaoan natural history, with exhibits of Caiquetio Indian life. Open 8–5, adm.

Passing **Boca Tabla**, a cave that can be entered from the landward side and which reverberates and echoes each time a wave crashes into the cave-mouth, the road leads to the sedate village of West Point and the kadushi cliffs at the western tip of the island.

East of Willemstad is the **Curaçao Seaquarium** where you can see the underwater world in a normal state of gravity— anything from an anemone or a panting shark with a beady eye to corals like 100 pink molar teeth. You can take a glass-bottom boat out to the reef from the Seaquarium and in the shop you might pick up an *Dutch onion skin* or a *continental squat* (bottles). Open all days 10–10, until midnight Fri and Sat, adm.

FESTIVALS
They do not really need an excuse for a party in Curaçao—Friday night is enough sometimes, and so you will see impromptu discotheques set up in the street, blaring out merengue, salsa and soca. The whole island gets down at **Carnival**, the big event of the Curaçaoan calendar—a week's worth of parades in the run-up to Lent, including costume masquerades and all-night *jump-ups*.

WHERE TO STAY
Curaçao is quite new to the tourism game and has few hotels. In contrast to Aruba and Bonaire, it is possible to stay cheaply in Curaçao—higglers and traffickers (travelling salesmen and women) come in their droves to buy wares and take them off home to sell them. There is a whole series of hotels where you can stay for as little as US$15 (per person), though their rooms are often hired by the hour as well as by the night. Curaçao gets pretty hot in summer and so it is worth paying extra for a fan or air-conditioning. There is a 5% government tax on all rooms and most hotels charge 10% for service.

EXPENSIVE
The **Avila Beach Hotel**, PO Box 791 (tel 614377, fax 611493) on Penstraat is still the most charming hotel in Curaçao. It has expanded dramatically to 145 rooms, adding a plush new block to the original antique building (that was the invading British Governor's residence in 1812), but it retains its rarefied and sophisticated air. A mix congregates on the two beaches and at the schooner bar. Rooms in winter US$150, suites $200. Perhaps the most sympathetic of Curaçao's large humming hotels is the **Princess Beach Resort and Casino** (tel 614944, fax 614131), east of Willemstad. The 336 rooms and suites are strung out along the waterfront in blocks above a beach that is not that exciting. Nightly entertainment, boutiques, beauty salon, pool bar, US$150 plus for a double room in season.

The **Lion's Dive Hotel and Marina** (tel 618100, fax 618200), just above the Seaquarium, is a statement in pastel pink and lime green, bananas, bougainvillaea and balconies. Rooms quite small, but comfortable. The hotel is home to **Rumours**, one of Curaçao's best bars and it attracts a young and lively crowd, who dive by day and booze by night. Double room US$100. The **Hotel Holland**, FD Rooseveltweg 524 (tel 688044, fax 688114) near the airport, has recently expanded to 40 luxury rooms and has introduced a dive shop. A bit isolated from town, but a friendly hotel with a casino, double room US$70.

CHEAP
Beyond here, on the road to West Point you will find a small hotel set in an old country house, the **Landhuis Daniel** (tel/fax 448400). Just ten rooms, small and friendly, double room US$35 in season. At the western end of the island at Westpunt you will find the small and cheap **Jaanchie's Hotel** (tel 640126), within easy reach of the island's best beaches. It is very simple and has a popular open-air restaurant which will serve you island delicacies like cactus soup and iguana stew. The six or so rooms are simple, but the asking price is good and you can bargain from there. There are plenty of hotels at the bottom end of the range in Willemstad, of which the best is probably the **Pension La Creole**, in the Saliña area of the town, double room US$15. **Hotel Stelaris** on de Rouilleweg (tel 625740), overlooking the St Anna Baai from the Otrobanda side, is a reasonably secure alternative, US$20. If you want full exposure to the intrigues of Curaçao life, try the **Park Hotel** on Frederickstraat in Otrobanda (tel 623112), where prices start at US$15. These hotels serve meals.

There are many apartments for hire in Curaçao, starting at about US$200 for a week's hire. You can contact the Tourist Board, or get in touch with **Sun Reef Village**, Redaweg 38 (tel 684959, fax 683594), or **Bulado Inn**, Kanasterweg Kaya B 27 (tel/fax 685960).

EATING OUT
With its tangled heritage, you will find food from all over the world in Curaçao. It is well worth venturing out of the hotels because you will find some fun places as well as local food.

A lively local spot for lunch Curaçao-style is the **Plaza Biejo** (the Old Market), in Punda just next to the monstrous circular new market. You eat at communal slab-top tables alongside bus drivers and local businesspeople and drink out of frosted glasses, while the food is cooked over charcoal stoves around the edge of the building. It is some of the island's best food because it is cooked in this way, though if you are obsessive about hygiene this place might not be for you.

Exotic *sopi* (soups) of local fish and traditional *juwana* (iguana) are available and to follow you can try a good Caribbean 'rice and peas' dish or another Curaçaoan favourite like *stoba*, meat stew made with papaya, or komkomber (cucumber) or even snijboonchi (if you dare). Other dishes include *giambo with funchi* (cactus fruit and maize meal) and *toetoe* (pronounced tutu), more maize meal with beans, bacon, sugar and all topped with melted cheese. The meal is served from steaming silver vats and is washed down with a sticky red drink like strawberry Ribena. Lunch is served Mon–Fri and is inexpensive at around US$4 for a main dish.

EXPENSIVE
Curaçao's two best restaurant, are both located in forts and the top one, both for its location and its reputation, is **Fort Nassau** (tel 613450). You take your cocktails on the

battery, where there is a cannon's eye view of Willemstad and then move through for new world cuisine—seared shrimp in pepper vodka or the day's catch in tropical fruit chutney on a bed of beans and pancake—surrounded by the old battlements. NAFl 30–45 a main course. **Bistro le Clochard** (tel 625666) is in the Riffort at the mouth of the St Anna Baai, where cocktails are accompanied by the hull of an occasional passing freighter. French and Swiss cuisine by candle light in the fort's cavernous jail and the old barrel-vaulted cistern—shrimp provençal and rösti in white wine and mushrooms. NAFl 35 a main course, take a constitutional on the battlements, closed Sun. **De Taveerne** (tel 370669) in the Saliña area is another excellent setting for lunch and dinner. The restaurant is in an old octagonal Curaçaoan landhuis, Groot Davelaar; candle-lit and furnished with antique furniture. Catch of the day creole and outsize steaks, main dish NAFl 25–35, closed Sun. **Alouette** (tel 618222), at 12 Orionweg in Saliña is decorated in art-deco style to smooth pastel colours and serves *cuisine vivante*— low calorie and colour co-ordinated dishes in life-sustaining portions. Try the goat cheese crêpe followed by red snapper Grand Marnier. Weekday lunches and dinner, NAFl 30 plus for a main dish. At the eastern end of the island, the **Queen's View** (tel 675105) indeed has a royal vista—overlooking the craft school and distant refinery from an airy wooden veranda. Piano accompaniment to French cuisine—tournedos and lobster thermidor followed by *crêpe suzette* for two. NAFl 30–40 for a main course.

If you want to eat Dutch in the Kingdom of the Netherlands, try **'T Kokkeltje** (tel 688044) in the Hotel Holland, with its windy view of the airport runway. There may not be the cockles from which it takes its name, but mussels are imported weekly in the months with a letter 'r' and served with white wine and lemon. One or two clogs and a Delft Blauw beer dispenser, but not Dutch stodge. Try *sliptong in loombooter gebakken* or *haring* in season, NAFl 25. And for a taste of the Dutch East Indies in the Dutch West Indies you can try **Surabaya** (tel 617388) under the arches of the Waterfort. *Rijstafel* and *pangsit* panckaes, NAFl 30 for a main course, closed Sun. And for something of Curaçao's Latin heritage try **Caribana** (tel 623088) on the St Anna Baai waterfront next to Rhum Runners. *Huachinango veracruzano* (Mexican snapper fillet) or *Anticacho* (Peruvian kebabs) for NAFl 30 a main course, closed Sun.

MODERATE

Fort Waakzamhied has a cracking position, around the battlements of another fort, where you sit on a breezy terrace and watch the lights of Otrobanda. All meals are grilled on the barbecue and accompanied by salads and chips. There is an nice informal atmosphere and often a crowd of Curaçaoans. NAFl 20. Two local restaurants definitely worth visiting are: **Chez Susenne** (tel 688545), where Susenne herself cooks Curaçaoan dishes, while her hip sons preside over the dining room; *balchi piska* (fishballs), *masbangoe* (sardines) and *snijboonchi* (stringbean soup) for NAFl12–15; and the **Golden Star** (tel 612746) on Dr Maalweg, a classic West Indian restaurant, airconditioned with plastic tablecloths, fake roses and excellent local food. Try *carni stoba* (meat stew) or *stoba de carco* (conch and vegetable in a strong creole sauce). Main course NAFl 13–15, open until 1 am, closed Sun. Particularly popular with the Curaçaoans is the **Cactus Club** (tel 371600), difficult to find at 6 van Staverenweg. International standard burgers and shakes, but always crowded, NAFl 10. At the western end of the island at the Christoffel Park you will find good local food at the **Oasis**

Restaurant—goat stew with funchi or seafood, NAFl 10–15. You might also try **Playa Forti** on the clifftops, with a cracking sunset view.

If you are still feeling peckish when the night's activity has wound up, you can grab a snack at a *pantruck* (literally a bread-truck), which can be found all over the island. You choose between a pan *galina* (chicken), pan *steak* or *porchop*, hacked in half, doused in hot pepper sauce and served up in a bread roll.

BARS AND NIGHTLIFE
Rum Runners is a popular bar dressed up in high fluorescence and cocktail paraphernalia on the waterfront above the St Annabaai channel, so you can watch the cruise ships and freighters as you sip a bahama mama or a piña colada. Out of town to the east is another very popular bar, **Rumours**, set on a terrace above the sea at the Lion's Dive hotel. In Spanish Water you might try the **Terrace à la Mer**.

For a cocktail and a view you can try the terrace at **Fort Waakzamheid** in Otrobanda and if you would like a drink in plantation estate surroundings, try the **Tinashi bar** at the Landhuis Brievengat. On the last Sunday of the month they hold open house with a folkloric show. Another good weekend venue, popular with the locals, is at Playa Canoa, a fishing bay on the north coast, where they dance on Sunday afternoons.

The **Brievengat** also has an excellent discotheque a couple of times a week, where the Curaçaoans like to shuffle and sway to loud bands playing merengue, soca and salsa. Wed, Fri, from 10 until the early hours.

Most of the regular **nightclubs** are in Saliña on what is known as *Hanchi macacu* ('monkey's parade' in Papiamento). The most lively place in the area is **Club LA** (L'Aristocrat) on Lindbergweg. Raised platform for a big band, but all styles of music, live Fri, Sat, when it is packed. Adm men NAFl 15, women NAFl 10. Close by on van Lindbergweg is **Façade**, which is a little more sophisticated. **L'Escape** on Caracasbaaiweg is a loud and active discotheque, full of Curaçaoans who shuffle all night long, and **The Pub** is an American-style bar with loud rock music; Blondie to Doble R. The **Campo Alegre** out near the airport is a government brothel.

There are a number of **casinos** in Curaçao, all of them in the big hotels.

BONAIRE

The underwater life of Bonaire is supreme. Miles of spectacular corals line its shores and the warm water teems with tropical fish, flashes of pastel and fluorescent colours—a *Diver's Paradise*. So says every car numberplate on the island, anyway. Shameless PR perhaps, but the island has managed its reefs well and it has a justified reputation as one of the world's top diving destinations.

Bonaire is the second largest of the Netherlands Antilles (a crooked 24 miles long by five) and it lies 30 miles east of Curaçao, 40 from the South American coast. It is mostly low and parched scrubland, with salt-ponds in the south and rolling land that rises to the 784-ft peak of Mt Brandaris in the northwest. The name Bonaire is supposedly derived from the local Indian *bo-nah*, meaning low country; the Netherlanders would have felt at home when they arrived in 1626.

French Angelfish

Bonaire has a population of just 10,500 and it is fairly quiet and secluded, unlike its brash neighbours in the Dutch Leewards. There are just two small settlements, Kralendijk the capital on the leeward coast and Rincon in the north. And the Bonaireans are quiet too. They think of the Curaçaoans as wild and spendthrift, whereas they consider themselves more measured and careful. Before the days of bank loans, the Bonaireans had a system called the *samm* in which they would club together, pooling a sum of money every month, which they would each receive in rotation, enabling them to buy an animal or building materials for a house.

Bonaire has never seen the extreme wealth of Curaçao and Aruba, but for the moment it is probably more prosperous than it has ever been. The traditional salt industry has been revived, automated to bring it into the 20th century, and the island earns some money from radio transmitting stations, Radio Nederland Wereldomroep (the Dutch World Service), and the religious broadcasting station, Trans World Radio. The biggest income earner is, of course, tourism, which sees a trusty crowd of tourists (about 30,000 each year), most of whom come for the diving.

Bonaire is changing fast. Outsiders are flooding in and the investment, once so difficult to come by, is now clearly visible. Hotels are springing up and the islanders are building houses for themselves too. The old feeling that time forgot the island is evaporating, but it is still possible to escape here for a rest-cure. And it is still pretty quiet after dark. Most visitors are in bed by about ten o'clock, building up their strength for another day underwater.

For details on Bonaire's history, see p. 340.

Flora and Fauna

Among Bonaire's 150 species of birds (boobies and pelicans, bananaquits, sand-pipers and oystercatchers), the king is certainly the pink flamingo. There are thought to be about 10,000 on the island, one of only a few colonies in the western hemisphere.

Flamingos are shy birds and quite easily disturbed (by humans at least, though they seem to have got used to aeroplanes), so the Bonaireans are understandably reticent about revealing the exact location of the two nesting sites on the island. However, you can fix up a guided visit through Bonaire Sightseeing Tours (tel 8300), usually to the southern colony near the salt pans in the morning and the northern colony by Goto Meer in the afternoon. If you have binoculars or a telephoto lens, take them because you will not be allowed too near, particularly while they are breeding in the early part of the year.

Flamingos nest on little round mounds of mud about a foot high, on which is poised a single large egg. When either parent is not occupied with incubation, you will see them standing around in groups, legs bent forward at the knee, passing the time of day.

To feed they have to visit the salt-water lakes dotted around the island, where they advance in ranks, heads moving left and right underwater as they trawl for food. It is a little water shrimp that they find there that gives them their striking pink colour.

Bonaire has little in the way of landborne animals, apart from goats, who nibble at everything in sight, but you will see plenty of lizards and the occasional example of its prehistoric antecedent, the iguana.

GETTING TO BONAIRE
Bonaire is traditionally the poor relation of the Dutch Leeward islands and it lacks the excellent international air links of Aruba and Curaçao. It is best approached from either of these islands. Note that passengers travelling to Aruba or Curaçao on the regional airline ALM are normally entitled to the Bonaire sector for no extra charge, so long as this sector is booked in advance.

GETTING AROUND BONAIRE
There is a sort of bus service in Bonaire. Minibuses run sporadically from the centre of Kralendijk up to Rincon. No buses run past the airport. Hitch-hiking around the island is relatively easy. **Taxis** meet the flights and can be ordered through hotels or from the central depot (tel 8100). They are unmetered, with fixed prices for each run. Some sample prices are: **airport** to Kralendijk—US$8, and to Habitat Hotel—US$10. If you wish to take a tour of the island, any taxi driver will oblige; the rate is around US$35 for half a day (which is about all you need).

You will be most mobile, of course, in your own vehicle and there are plenty available for **hire** on the island. A licence from an EC country, the States or Canada is valid and prices range from around US$35 a day for a small car, plus insurance. Driving is on the right. Some rental firms are: **ABC** (tel 8980), **Budget** (Boncar) (tel 8300 or 8315 at the airport) and **Erkar** (tel 8536). A number of hotels also have cars for hire, so check at the front desk.

Scooters and larger motorbikes are also available through **Happy Chappy Rentals** (tel 8407) for about US$15 per day, and you can even hire bicycles from **Divi Flamingo Beach Hotel** (tel 8285), at around US$5 per day.

TOURIST INFORMATION
There is no Tourist Office specific to Bonaire in **Britain**, or elsewhere in **Europe**. In the **USA**, the Bonaire Government Tourist Office is at 275 7th Ave, New York, NY 10001 (tel (212) 242 7707) and in **Canada** they can be contacted at 815A Queen St East, Toronto M4M 1H8 (tel (416) 465 2958).

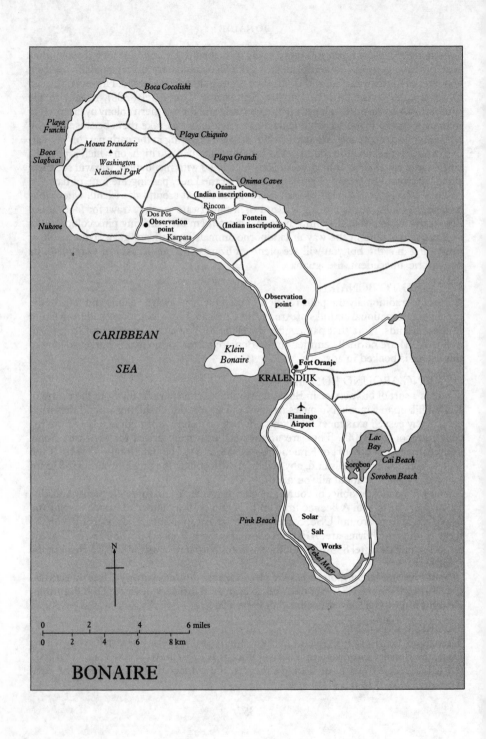

Boca Cocolishi

Playa
Funchi

Boca
Slagbaai

Mount Brandaris ▲

Washington
National Park

Playa Chiquito

Playa Grandi

Onima Caves

Onima
(Indian inscriptions)

Rincon

Nukove

Dos Pos
● Observation
point

Karpata

Fontein
(Indian inscriptions)

Observation
point ●

CARIBBEAN

SEA

Klein
Bonaire

● Fort Oranje

KRALENDIJK

✈
Flamingo
Airport

Lac
Bay

Sorobon

Cai Beach

Sorobon Beach

Pink Beach

Solar

Salt

Works

Pekel Meer

N

| 0 | | 2 | | 4 | | 6 miles |
| 0 | 2 | 4 | 6 | 8 km |

BONAIRE

On Bonaire itself, the **Tourist Bureau** (tel 8322 or 8649) is on Kaya Simon Bolivar, a little inland in Kralendijk.

In a medical **emergency**, there is a hospital in Kralendijk (tel 8900). To telephone Bonaire from abroad, the **IDD code** is 599–7 followed by the 4-digit island number. If phoning within the island, dial the last four digits only.

MONEY

Officially Bonaire's currency is the Netherlands Antilles Florin or Guilder (NAFl), which is fixed to the US dollar at a rate of US$1 = NAFl1.77. However, you may not even see this currency because the greenback is perfectly acceptable for all transactions. In local shops you may receive change in florins.

Restaurants and hire shops in Bonaire are prepared to accept most credit cards and the hotels take traveller's cheques. **Banking hours** are 9.30–noon and 2–4. **Shops** keep hours of about 8–noon and 2–6.

DIVING

Bonaire, ranked among the top three dive-sites in the world, is famous particularly for its range of incomparably colourful coral and its sloping drop-offs (not vertical walls, but slopes of between 45° and 60°) that start anything from 20 to 100 yards offshore. Visibility is dependably 100 ft, often more.

Brain corals with jigsawed hemispheres, sheet coral and star coral jostle for space on the reef with gorgonians and the forests of elkhorn and staghorn. Close to the surface, the corals tend to grow bunched together, reaching up for the sunlight, but as you descend and the reds, oranges and yellows fade, you find flat and bulky corals of blue, purple and brown.

Fish life glides by beneath the surface, dipping and darting in little shoals; peacock flounders change colour at you, a little school of needlefish will come and poke at you. Angelfish coloured a deep rich blue or bright yellow and black purse their lips and the four-eyed butterflyfish wink. Look out for seahorses and Christmas Tree worms, and you might even see a green turtle or a shovel-nosed lobster. While some fish grunt and swim away, crabs witness you with a fixed look of shock, eyes out on stalks and upturned in quizzical amazement.

At night the whole seascape changes: some corals close down for bed but orange tube corals wake up and transform into orange tubes. Nocturnal brittlestars light up if touched, and tarpons attracted by your flashlight will swim up and nose at you.

The reefs on Bonaire are managed by the **Bonaire Marine Park**, which has jurisdiction over nearly the whole of the coastline to a depth of 200 feet and imposes strict laws against the removal or killing of any marine life within the area. It has placed mooring sites in the reefs to protect them. The Bonaire Marine park charges an admission fee (US$10, valid for one year), payable by all divers.

Most of the 50-odd dive-sites are on the protected leeward coast of the island and around the islet of Klein Bonaire, none more than a few minutes' boat-ride away from Kralendijk. There is one wreck dive, the hulk of the *Hilma Hooker*, a ganja-runner that went down after its load of 25,000 lbs of resin was confiscated.

Bonaire is extremely well organized to cater for divers and many of the hotels have special dive-packages. Nearly all of them offer resort courses for those who want to learn.

359

A number of dive-centres also cater for underwater photography and you can hire the cameras and vast lighting equipment from **Captain Don's Habitat Dive Shop** (tel 8290), the **Bonaire Scuba Centre** (tel 8448) in the Bonaire Beach Hotel, and the **Flamingo Beach Hotel** (tel 8285). The **Dive Inn** (tel 8761, fax 8513) is an independent operator with good rates for equipment hire and instruction. Once you have arranged your equipment, it is quite possible to take off in a car and chose your own shoreline to dive off.

If you are not a diver, it is still possible to see the reefs with a mask and snorkel. And if you are not prepared to get wet, it is still possible to enjoy the marine life of the island in a glass-bottom boat; contact **Bonaire Dream** (tel 7080). Most of the hotels also stage **dive shows** (Capt Don's—Mon, Tues, Sand Dollar—Tues and Divi Flamingo Beach—Sun).

SNORKELLING
Many of Bonaire's reefs are close enough to the shoreline to be reached with a mask and snorkel and you will see crowds of tropical fish loitering close in too. As with diving, watch for fire corals—many colours, but always white fringes—which will give you a nasty sting. Equipment can be hired for the day from the dive shops.

If you take a tour to the north of the island, try **Playa Funchi**, for leaf corals and fire corals, and also in the Washington Park, **Boca Slaagbaai** where you will see tiger grouper and white-spotted filefish among mountainous star corals and cannon (from a film set). At **Nukove** nearby you can see redlip blenny and yellow pencil corals among the elkhorns.

South of Kralendijk you can also cast off the waterfront and be right among the reefs. Try **Punt Vierkant** just beyond the airport for the gorgonians and giant brain corals and the **Witte Pan** area by Pink Beach, where you will see staghorns patrolled by barracuda and octopuses.

BEACHES
The beaches in Bonaire are all right. One or two places have mounds of soft pink and white sand, but most are a hard strip of sand in a cove cut out of the limestone cliffs of former coral reefs. Unless you go to a hotel beach, usually small strips on the inner leeward coast, do not expect 'facilities', and remember to take food and drink. You are quite likely to be alone on the beaches in Bonaire; however, nudity is officially frowned on outside the area of **Sorobon** on the east coast.

The best beach on the island is **Pink Beach**, south of Kralendijk, along the side of the salt flats. Its name comes from the colour given by the corals that grow in the area (it is pink when wet and it dries to white). On the road back to town is **Bachelor's Beach**, a short drop off the klips into the warm water and sandy floor.

On Lac Bay on the opposite windward coast, where the mangroves grow in flying tangles, **Cai Beach** is protected from the Atlantic waves and is popular with the locals at weekends. On the other side of the bay, **Sorobon Beach**, which calls itself 'clothes-optional', has mounds of soft sand on a small half-moon cove. It is private and charges US$10 for admission.

In the north of the island are **Playa Funchi**, **Boca Slaagbaai** and **Playa Frans**, worth the detour for the snorkelling and some sand, though there is little shelter from the sun.

360

Take anything you will need in the way of a picnic as there are no shops in the area. On the route back to town, stop off at the the 1000 Steps.

There are also some unfrequented sandy beaches on Klein Bonaire. Any hotel will run you out and collect you later on (going rate US$13; if they forget, it is just a 20-minute swim back to Kralendijk).

WATERSPORTS

Apart from the diving, many of the hotels on Bonaire offer a few sports including **windsurfing, waterskiing** and small sailing boats. Even if you are not staying there, it is easy to arrange at the hotel front desk.

A superb spot for **windsurfing**—waist-deep water and constant onshore winds—is on Lac Bay, home of '**Jibe City**', **Windsurfing Bonaire**, PO Box 301 (tel/fax 5363, US 800 748 8733). Strip down and take a lunch break at Sorobon next door.

Deep-sea fishing trips are easily arranged at the Harbour Village Marina or through your hotel. **Piscatur** (tel 8774) will take out four fishermen for US$275, which includes tackle and bait, catch cooked on board. Also **Slam Dunk** (tel 5111). A deep-sea fishing tournament is held each spring.

For a **sailing** charter, contact the *Oscarina* (tel 8290) and for a day's picnic or a sunset cruise. A sailing regatta is held annually in October, five days of racing around the island. On land there is a nightly *jump-up* on the main square in Kralendijk.

OTHER SPORTS

There are not many land-based sports in Bonaire. There are a few **tennis** courts, in town (free) and at the Bonaire Beach Hotel (a fee for non-residents). A day's **riding** can be arranged with **Tinis Stables** through the Bonaire Beach Hotel. Bicycles can be rented at many of the hotels.

Kralendijk

Bonaire's small capital, Kralendijk (pronounced as in marlinspike), lies on the protected inner coastline of the island, looking across to the uninhabited coral football, Klein Bonaire. It has a few neat streets of russet and ochre Dutch Antillean buildings, gardens filled with banana and palm trees, and is patrolled by lazy dogs and lizards.

To the 1500 inhabitants, the town is known familiarly as 'Playa' (Papiamento for beach), really a bit of an exaggeration because there is only a measly strip of hard sand here. Kralendijk (meaning coral dike) is a rather more appropriate name because the shore-line is mostly a coral-limestone wall.

The town has always been a backwater and there was not even a pier until this century. Before that, ships would tie up to a cannon sticking out of the ground. Today the waterfront comes alive when the boats from Curaçao dock, but the main centre is on Breedestraat, which has recently come out in a profusion of duty-free stores and a shopping mall.

Back on the waterfront, **Fort Oranje** surveys the scene as it has since the middle of the last century, its cannon covering the bay. Inside you will find the **Instituto Folklore Bonaire**, the local museum, with exhibits of chicle-chewing Caiquetio Indian life before the Spaniards came and musical traditions of the later Bonaireans. Open weekdays 8–noon, adm free.

361

Close by is the **fish-market**, a mock-classical temple dressed in pink, which looks slightly out of place for the Caribbean, until it comes alive in the afternoon, selling the morning's catch of fish and imported vegetables.

Around the Island

Headed south out of Kralendijk the road skirts a lagoon and rejoins the coast at the airport, passing the antennae of Trans World Radio. The countryside is flat, desolate and wet. The southern toe of the island is really just a rim of land separating Bonaire's salt-pans from the sea.

Salt

Each salt-pond in Bonaire, dammed off with low mud walls, has a different colour—the faintest pink or lavender and then grey—before it turns to the bright white of the mature salt. You will see the harvested crop in huge blinding-white mountains, stacked by a conveyor belt and a vast double-armed crane.

Seawater, the sun and the constant winds are the essential ingredients for the salt industry. In Bonaire the process takes about 18 months from the moment that the seawater is introduced into the Pekelmeer (pickle lake). By opening and closing locks it passes through condensers where it becomes brine and then to crystallizers where the salt forms over the course of a year in depths of about 20 centimetres. It is washed and then stacked before export.

Slaves were brought in to work the salt pans. It was gruelling work and their existence was miserable. Their families lived 15 miles away in the north of the island and they were allowed home for one day a week.

The industry collapsed soon after emancipation in 1863 because it was unviable without forced labour. It was precarious at the best of times (too much rain would ruin the crop) and it lay dormant for 100 years before being revived in the 60s by the Antilles International Salt Company NV. The salt produced on Bonaire's 9000 acre 'farm' is used for industrial purposes.

Continuing around the coastline, you will see two small communities of **slave huts**, built in about 1850 in traditional Leeward Islands style, with square-topped gables and palm thatch. These two-man shelters were constructed on the slaves' wishes in preference to one single dormitory. There are also a number of obelisks, originally painted different colours (blue, orange, white and red), which were used to guide ships to the correct part of the coast. The road leads round the southern tip of the island and up the east coast, past Sorobon and back to Kralendijk.

Two roads lead north out of Kralendijk, one following the leeward coast past the hotels and the second cutting inland through the *cunucu* to the opposite coast. As the settlers crept in to the island in the early 1800s, they settled the area north of Kralendijk, and you will see human order imposed on the scrub—tall cacti trained to make hedges around the simple old Dutch Antillean houses of baked mud and maize thatch.

Before reaching the village of Rincon, a road leads out towards the coast and to the caves of **Onima** and **Fontein**, where there are Caiquetio inscriptions on the roofs of the caverns. Using the red dye for which the island was known early on by the Europeans, the Indians scrawled their diabolic squiggles and cartoon faces on the dark orange rock.

Rincon was settled early, its inland site giving the inhabitants a chance to escape marauding raiders, and it is now a sleepy Bonairean village dressed in Dutch Antillean orange.

The **Washington Slagbaai National Park** preserves 22 square miles of northwestern Bonaire, home to some of the island's 150 species of bird and the odd iguana, though these are shy because they fear the cooking pot. Traditional Bonairean crop plants are also there: aloe, divi-divi, sisal and agave, a small explosion of cactus leaves at ground-level with a stalk up to 30 feet in height. A number of trails are marked around the park, for drivers and for walkers, including a path to the summit of Mount Brandaris. Slagbaai, a cove on the western tip of the island, means 'slaughter bay', and it is where animals were killed before being shipped out to Curaçao. (Bonaire was used by the Curaçaoans as a ranch for a couple of centuries.) Open 8–5, adm, children free.

As one heads back down the leeward coast, the view is upset by the BOPEC oil terminal, the Radio Nederland antennae and the desalination plant. The road soon reaches the hotel strip and comes into Kralendijk.

FESTIVALS

The Bonaireans get out into the streets in costume at **Carnival** time (Mardi Gras) and at Easter, when they have parades and dancing. Late June (26th and 29th) sees local festivities and 6 September is Bonaire's **National Day**, when the celebrations are particularly strong in Rincon.

WHERE TO STAY

Bonaire's hotels are mostly ranged along the protected leeward coast of the island, many of them in a cluster north of Kralendijk. They are all new and few have much charm, but divers (who make up 60 per cent of tourists) do not care, generally, as they are there for the marine life. When diving is at issue, the atmosphere tends to be brisk and business-like, but with regard to anything else it is typically Caribbean and very low-key. There is a 5% government room tax and most hotels charge 10% for service.

Bonaire also has a number of villas for rent and the best company to contact on the island is **Bonaire Sunset Villas**, PO Box 115 (tel 599 7 8291, fax 8118) which has villas all over Bonaire, many near the diving centres in town. Their best villa is on the waterfront in Kralendijk, the Sunset Inn, which can be taken by a party of 14.

EXPENSIVE

Bonaire's top hotel is the **Harbour Village Beach Resort**, PO Box 312 (tel 7500, fax 7507, US 800 424 0004), luxury in a theme of Antillean orange and green. The 150 rooms and suites are ranged in villas around the central pool and bars, and each has a view of the marina or the hotel's fine beach. Watersports on offer. Rooms from US$220, suites $350. Also with a complete resort feel about it is the **Divi Flamingo Beach Resort** (tel 8285, fax 8238), which stands astride the promenade at the southern limits of Kralendijk. It is a hive of activity, relatively speaking, with two dive shops, a casino, a couple of pools, 110 rooms and the Chibi Chibi restaurant, which has a charming setting on stilts above the floodlit sea (reserve early if you want a waterfront table). It is Bonaire's first hotel and the regime has softened a bit since it was used as the island prisoner of war camp. US$150–185 plus. The **Sand Dollar Condominiums**, PO Box 175 (tel 8738), a mile or so north of Kralendijk, has a feel of cool modernity, where self-catering apartments are clustered overlooking the garden to the sea. The dive operation is on the seafront, the pool and tennis courts behind. The Green Parrot restaurant is lively, with burgers and some better dishes on the rocks above the sea. A studio apartment in winter costs US130; a 3-bedroom apartment around US$145–245. **Captain Don's Habitat**, PO Box 88 (tel 8290, fax 8240, US 800 327 6709) has added luxury suites and a pool to its villas and cottages. There are now 60 rooms in the sandy garden of cactus, palm and aloe, but the Habitat has kept the friendly feel of a diving inn. There is a small beach, but the gravitational pull is of course towards the diving pier. Some other watersports and entertainment a couple of nights in the week. Rooms US$150 (rates for singles), suites $240, but most stays are sold as diving packages.

MODERATE

The **Carib Inn**, PO Box 68 (tel 8819, fax 5295) is still an original dive inn, with just a few rooms on the waterfront in the south of Kralendijk. Very low key, no restaurant or bar, but most rooms and suites have kitchenettes. Also excellent prices, starting at US$50 for two in season. If you want to get away from the main strip you can try the **Bonaire Caribbean Club**, PO Box 323 (tel 7901, fax 7900), lost in the Bonaire cunucu. Just 20 rooms, some with kitchenettes, scattered around a garden. From US$60 a double in season.

CHEAP

There is a profusion of rooms on offer in guest houses. The **Leeward Inn** in town offers reliable and clean rooms for US$40–60 and in Rincon you can get a room for US$15 at the **Goede Hoop** (tel 6327).

EATING OUT

There is a clutch of surprising restaurants on tiny Bonaire. Generally the menus are international, particularly in the hotels, but you will find some good local restaurants. None are particularly cheap. Service is charged at 10%.

EXPENSIVE

In the middle of town, there is an easy atmosphere at **Rendez-vous** (tel 8454) where you eat on a streetfront veranda or just inside in an air-conditioned dining room. Some local dishes—*keshi yena* (chicken, vegetables and raisins, covered in gouda cheese) and international—chicken apricot and mango melba. Have your lighter framed as a memento of your visit. Main dish NAFl 25–30, closed Tues. At **Richard's** (tel 5263) you dine on a breezy Bonaire terrace overlooking the waterfront in the south of town. Tasty home-made soups and specialties in seafood and local fish. The bar attracts a crowd of locals. Closed Mon, NAFl 20–30. The **Beefeater** (tel 8081) is set in the rooms of an old Bonaire town house. You can expect the steaks of the title, but also more exotic fare such as shrimp au Pernod flambé (at the table) and an array of fruit ice creams. Main course NAFl 25–30. **Raffles** (tel 8617), just beyond the market on the waterfront (you will spot it by the London phone booth) has a lively atmosphere. The menu is mainly local fish and seafood, but people come just for the banana cheesecake, NAFl 20–30, closed Mon. Or go for a cocktail at the boat bar washed up on a coral dyke.

MODERATE AND CHEAP
Kilumba, a short walk north from the centre of town, is named after an African God of the sea. At lunch they serve local dishes to the Bonaireans, so it is worth stopping by if you fancy a big stew goat. Evenings you are more likely to find seafood and local catch NAFl 20. **'T Ankertje**, at the southern end of the waterfront promenade, serves simple Caribbean dishes alongside sandwiches and burgers, for a good price, NAFl 15.

NIGHTLIFE
The hip-est and really the only bar on the island is **Karel's**, which is perched over the sea in the centre of town—seats tightly packed around the cocktail counter with the waves washing back and forth beneath you. The owner runs the restaurants **Zee Zicht** and **Pirate House** (tel 8434) opposite, so you can always stumble over for a meal. The Bonaireans have their own favourite bars within the restaurants, so you will meet them as you take a drink before your meal.

E **Wowo** is an unaccountably chic nightclub for so small an island. International style, but musically dominated by *merengue* (fast and Latin, originating in Santo Domingo). Video baseball to occupy you between dances. Cover charge US$10.

ARUBA

Aruba lies within sight of South America, just 15 miles north of the Paraguana peninsula in Venezuela. It is 20 miles long by six wide; with a rainfall of about 17 inches a year (less even than Bonaire and Curaçao), its low-lying land and few hillocks are parched and scrubby with cactus, dotted only occasionally by diabolic boulders and divi-divi trees. The island's name is supposed to derive from the native Indian words for shell, 'ora' and island, 'oubao'.

Divi-divi tree

365

Like Curaçao, Aruba saw an explosion of prosperity earlier this century with the arrival of the oil industry. Exxon built the then largest refinery in the world on the island in 1929, and the population exploded from 8700 to 60,000 by 1972. For centuries a poor backwater, Aruba changed completely, and from nothing became very prosperous. Today the population is 71,000.

But in recent years the oil industry has foundered and so the islanders have thrown themselves with gusto into the latest Caribbean industry, tourism. The island has a façade of overwhelming modernity, and has geared itself up to the arrival of a quarter of a million tourists a year. It has opted for tourism on a grand scale—pristine and well packaged, in huge air-conditioned blocks, with glitzy floor-shows and in-house doctors. They do it pretty well. The new hotels in the high-rise strip are impressive and very comfortable. It is crowded and a little sanitized, but it is well organized and so you get a good body-holiday in Aruba. And the Arubians themselves are probably more gracious about the invasion of tourists than any other Caribbean islanders.

It is possible to spend a week on the island without actually meeting an Arubian, but not to would be a pity because they are a spirited bunch. In 1986, after 50 years of political wrangling, they achieved something which most Caribbean islands only ever dream of: they defied the colonial administration and won the consent to go it alone as an independent country, with *Status Aparte*. Aruba is the youngest country in the Caribbean.

So close to Venezuela, Aruba has a strong South American heritage. Aruban *Papiamento* is more Spanish than that of the other islands, and it is also clear in the faces. Aruba's tangled racial heritage has more South American Indian than African because there were never really any slaves on the island.

Every car that cruises by in Aruba proclaims 'One Happy Island' from its number-plate. So it may seem, now that the island has its freedom to guide its own affairs, but the country is not without its difficulties: unemployment is quite high, and the island is overwhelmingly dependent on tourism. However, beyond the tourism superstructure you will find a lively mix of West Indians of Dutch, Spanish and British heritage, steadily crystallizing into a nation and struggling to carve out a path for themselves.

Status Aparte

Aruba is an autonomous country within the Kingdom of the Netherlands and since 1986 it has no longer been a member of the Netherlands Antilles. Traditionally Curaçao maintained a dominance over its partners and this was particularly resented by the Arubians. They had earned their own wealth from oil, but still their money passed through the coffers in Curaçao before it was allocated back to Aruba. Parliamentary decisions affecting only Aruba had to be passed in the *Staten* (Netherlands Antilles Parliament) in Willemstad, where the Curaçaoans commanded a majority. The Arubians found that they depended on the Curaçaoans for everything down to the last typewriter, and so they pushed for autonomy. The movement began in the 40s as *Separacion*, steered by the charismatic politician Gilberto François Croes, known as Betico, and after endless lobbying, the Dutch Government agreed to their wishes and granted Aruba *Status Aparte*.

On 1 January 1986, Aruba raised its own flag and became a separate country, though still within the Kingdom of the Netherlands, with its own currency and elected Parliament, finally separate from Curaçao. They were due to take full Independence in 1996, but they have seen the difficulties that the other islands in the Caribbean have had and so these plans have been shelved indefinitely. Aruba is led by Nelson Aduber of the Social Democratic Party. Elections are due in late 1992.

GETTING TO ARUBA

By Air
The airport, Queen Beatrix, is a couple of miles from the main town of Oranjestad. Tax of US$10 is payable upon departure.
From Europe: there are several non-stop flights each week from Amsterdam. The national carrier **Air Aruba** has regular links to Cologne and Amsterdam (also flown by KLM), from where there are easy connections all over Europe.
From the USA: Aruba has good links from the USA: Air Aruba flies daily to Miami and to Newark and American carriers fly direct from JFK and Atlanta.
From other Caribbean Islands: there are countless links to nearby Curaçao (Air Aruba and ALM), some direct flights to Bonaire, and there are links to Maracaibo and Caracas in Venezuela. Further afield, BWIA fly from Port of Spain, Trinidad, Air Aruba twice weekly to Sint Maarten and American Airlines from San Juan, Puerto Rico. There are also good connections in Curaçao.

GETTING AROUND ARUBA

There is quite an efficient **bus service** in Aruba, linking Oranjestad to the southeast of the island and also running west and then north along the hotel strip (fare US90c). Buses also run from the airport into town (if you are booked in to one of the larger hotels, then you may find that there is a hotel bus waiting for you anyway). Buses run to an official schedule and the drivers almost stick to it. Roughly speaking, there is one an hour, or two on a major route, up until early evening. Minibuses also run local routes, price NAFl 2.

Taxis are available at the airport, in town and at all the hotels, or they can be fixed through the central depot at the Alhambra Bazaar (tel 22116). They can be quite expensive and they are unmetered, so fix the price before you set off. US$12 will get you from the airport to the high-rise strip, and US$8 as far as town. Prices increase in the evening. Taxi-drivers, who all speak English, are quite well versed about island history/lore and will happily give an island tour. The charge is around US$25 for an hour and a half on the road. Island tours by bus can also be fixed up through **De Palm Tours** (tel 24400) on LG Smith Boulevard in town, or **Aruba Friendly Tours** (tel 23230), also in Oranjestad.

If you wish to be more flexible about seeing the island and dining out, there are plenty of **rental cars** in Aruba and you can pick one up at the airport. Valid foreign driving licences are accepted and driving is on the right; roads are good. Daily rates start at around US$35 for the smallest car, with insurance on top. The usual large companies have operations on the island, with an office in town and one at the airport: **Avis** (tel 28787), **Budget** (tel 28600) and **National** (tel 21967). Local firms include **Marco's** (tel 25295). You can hire a bicycle through **Ron's Bicycle** (tel 32090).

367

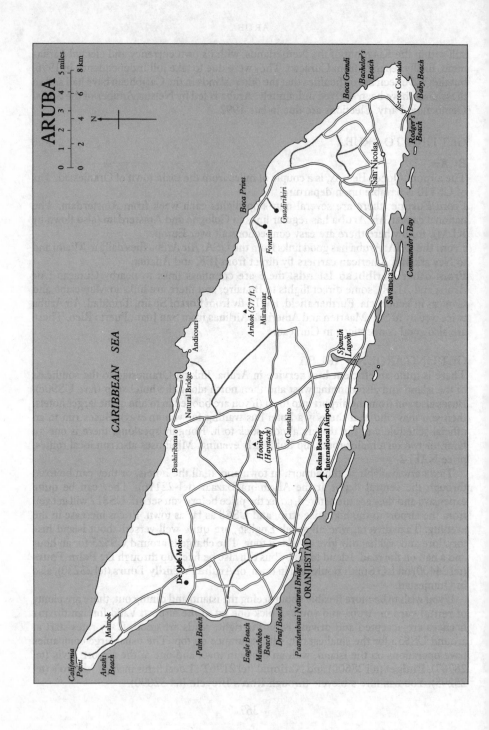

ARUBA

CARIBBEAN SEA

California Point
Arashi Beach
Maimok
Palm Beach
Eagle Beach
Manchebo Beach
Druif Beach
Paardenbaai Natural Bridge
ORANJESTAD
De Olde Molen
Reina Beatrix International Airport
Bushiribana
Natural Bridge
Andicouri
Hooiberg (Haystack)
Canashito
Spanish Lagoon
Savaneta
Commander's Bay
San Nicolas
Miralamar
Arikok (577 ft.)
Fontein
Guadirkiri
Boca Prins
Boca Grandi
Bachelor's Beach
Seroe Colorado
Baby Beach
Rodger's Beach

N

0   1   2   3   4   5 miles
0   2   4   6   8 km

TOURIST INFORMATION

There is no Tourist Office devoted to Aruba in the UK, but the Aruba Tourism Authority has offices in:

Holland: Amaliastraat 16, Den Haag 2514 JC (tel 703 566220, fax 604887).

USA: 521 Fifth Avenue, New York, NY 10175 (tel 212 246 3030, fax 557 1614, 800 TO ARUBA) and 85 Canal Drive, Suite 200, Miami, Florida 33144 (tel 305 267 0404, fax 267 0503).

Canada: 86 Bloor St West, Suite 204, Toronto, Ontario M5S 1M5 (tel 416 975 1950, fax 975 1947, 1 800 263 3042).

Germany: Victoriastrasse 28, D-6100 Darmstadt (tel 6151 23068, fax 6151 22854).

On Aruba itself, contact the **Aruba Tourism Authority** at PO Box 1019, 172 LG Smith Blvd, Oranjestad (tel 23777), who provide information and will arrange guides. There is a small but helpful office in the airport and one in the cruise-ship docking area.

In a medical **emergency**, there is a casualty room at the **Dr Horacio Oduber Hospital** on LG Smith Blvd (tel 24300). However, before phoning for an ambulance, check with the hotel front desk because there could be a house-doctor on call.

The **international code** for Aruba is 297 8, followed by a five-digit Aruban number. If you are phoning within the island then just dial the last five digits.

MONEY

With *Status Aparte* in 1986, Aruba adopted a currency of its own, the Aruban florin (AFl), which, like many Caribbean countries, they fixed to the US dollar (at a rate of US$1 = AFl 1.77). However, with their economy so closely geared to American visitors, they also accept US dollars in nearly all transactions (though you will need Aruban coins for pay telephones, etc.). Credit cards are widely accepted in any but the smallest restaurants, and traveller's cheques are accepted in the hotels. Service charges in Aruba are usually 15%. The Netherlands Antilles guilder (the currency of nearby Curaçao and Bonaire) is not accepted in Aruba.

Banks are open from 8 am to 5 pm on weekdays. You will get a slightly better exchange rate at the bank than at a hotel cash-desk. **Shops** are open 8 am–6 pm, longer if there are cruise ships in town. In case you are held up on the beach during the day, you can always go out and exercise your credit card with a bit of night-time shopping at the Alhambra Bazaar, where shops stay open until midnight.

BEACHES

Palm Beach and **Eagle Beach** are two of Caribbean's finest. 30 yards deep, they run for miles along the protected western coast of the island, heaps and heaps of sand like talcum powder, pushed up by the bluest of water. At the hotel strips they do become crowded, but it is here that you find the windsurfers and wetbikes for more active moments, or shade and a drink to cool you off. With the winds you may not feel the (very) strong Aruban sun, so be careful when you are out in the middle of the day. Eagle Beach is not officially topless, but it has been known to happen.

Elsewhere on the leeward coast there are other coves, not unknown to tourists, but not usually crowded with them. Towards the northern tip is **Arasji Beach**, where you can see the wreck of a German tanker sunk in the last war. There is good underwater life here and it is also popular for windsurfing.

At the easternmost tip of the island is a charming cove called **Baby Beach**, which is palm-lined and quiet. The water is just four feet deep right across the bay and there are shaded areas to retreat to. Close by is **Rodger's Beach**.

On the windward coast north of here there are one or two coves cut out of the limestone brittle of the northern coastline. The water can be rough as the waves barrel in off the Caribbean Sea, but particularly for windsurfers, **Batchelor's Beach** and **Boca Grandi** are worth a detour. **Boca Prins**, also on the Caribbean coast, is a tiny strip of sand between two cliffs, but it is usually rough, so you are advised not to swim.

There are one or two islands off the south coast of the island also mounded with sand. The most popular is **Palm Reef Island** (you can get a ferry from Balashi—$3 crossing), though it is worth checking with the skipper for other beaches that might be less crowded that day.

WATERSPORTS
Aruba has the whole range of opportunities for watersports, from waterskiing to fleets of wetbikes. The principal centre is Palm Beach, but hotels usually have equipment available for their guests. There are three large sporting outfits that operate from town and can be contacted through desks in the hotels: **Pelican Watersports** (tel 312288) and **De Palm Watersports** (tel 24400) and **Red Sails** at Palm Beach (tel 31603).

Windsurfing: the classic place to windsurf is off the upper end of the west coast, just beyond the high-rise strip, where the winds get a clean run across the island. Close in it is a good spot for beginners because the water is flat and shallow and farther out the winds build up. Instruction is easily available.

Intermediate and advanced sailboarders can sail waves at Boca Grandi (easiest because it has a sandy bottom), beyond the northwest point, and along the southern coast where there are sideshore winds. Some hire companies will allow you to take their boards to these places. Try **Vela Aruba**, the Mistral operators, at the top end of Palm Beach, or **Roger's Windsurf Place** (tel 21918), PO Box 461, Malmok. A windsurfing tournament, the Hi-Winds Pro Am, is held each year in May or June.

Waterskiing (about US$20 for 20 minutes), motorboat hire and **parasailing** are easily arranged on the high-rise hotel strip at Palm Beach. If you want to tame a jet-ski, you will find a little daytime colony of them at the top of Eagle Beach.

Most hotels have small sailing boats on hand, but if you would prefer to take a day's cruise on a larger yacht, this is also possible through the companies above or through individual operators: *Maria Monica* (tel 23334), *Wave Power* (tel 25520) or *Andante* (tel 47718). Trips will vary from a sunset cruise on a trimaran with full boozatorium and on-board steel band (try *Topaz*) to a full-blooded day's sail on the Trades. You can even arrange to go sailcarting if you don't fancy getting wet: contact **Aruba Sailcart**, Bushiri 23 (tel 36005).

Deep-sea fishermen can go out in search of sailfish, bonito and kingfish in the waters around Aruba. Six fishermen can hire a boat for a half day for around US$300. Aruba holds fishing competitions each year on Oct 25–27 and Nov 1–3. Yachts include *Driftwood* (tel 32515) and *G-String* (tel 26101).

A reef runs all along the protected leeward coast of Aruba, giving miles of diving, often with 100 ft visibility, for **scuba** enthusiasts. The best marine life is on the south coast between Spanish Lagoon and Commandeur's Bay, where there are a number of off-shore islands. Coral has also begun to encrust Aruba's two wrecks: the *Antilia*, a German freighter that was scuttled off Malmok, and the *Pedernales*, an oil transporter also sunk in the Second World War by a submarine.

Instruction is available through many of the hotels, starting in the swimming pool and venturing out on to the reefs. Dives cost around US$45 each and can be arranged through the hotel or through the major sports shops. Contact **Aruba Pro-Divers** (tel 25520), **Native Divers** on (tel 34763) or **Charlie's Buddies** (tel 43790).

If you wish to go **snorkelling**, there are reefs along the south coast at Arasji and Palm Beach and if you go farther afield, at Baby Beach in the southeastern area of the island. Trips can be arranged through the big operators, or if you would prefer not to get wet, you can try a glass-bottom boat: **ECO Destination Management** (tel 26034). There is also an **Atlantis Submarine** at the Seaport Village Marina in town (tel 36090).

Sports on land include **golf** at the **Aruba Golf Club** (tel 93485), which has up to 18 holes with oiled sand 'greens' and **tennis** which can be fixed up through any number of hotels. If you want to ride the cactus plains of the *cunucu*, then **riding** is available through **Rancho El Paso** (tel 23310), at Washington 44, US$15 per hour. You might also like to take one of a series of very worthwhile guided tours of the birds, architecture or archaeology of the island: **Corvalon Tours** (tel 21149) or **Private Safaris** (tel 34869).

Oranjestad (pronounced *Oran-yeh-stat*)

Named in 1824 after the Dutch Royal family, Oranjestad (population around 17,000) sits on Aruba's principal harbour Paardenbaai (Horse's Bay) in the southwestern corner of the island. Today, cruise ships arrive to deliver tourists in their thousands, but 200 years ago, when the island was really just a ranch, it was horses, which were simply driven off the side of the deck and left to swim for land. (As a tourist you can expect a gentler arrival.)

The oldest building on the island, **Fort Zoutman**, stands sentinel above the bay, where fleets of yachts glint at the quay's edge. Built in 1796, Fort Zoutman saw action only once, when the British invaded in 1799, and now it houses the **Museo Arubano**, where island history is illustrated with Indian artefacts and scenes from Dutch colonial days. Open 9–12 ans 1–4 Mon–Fri, adm (tel 26099). Close by at No. 1 Zoutmanstraat is the **Museo Archeologico**, which delves deeper into Aruban Indian life with displays of Caiquetio tools and a couple of 2000-year-old skeletons, found buried in vast clay pots and under turtle shells. Open 8–noon and 1.30–4.30 on weekdays, adm free (tel 28979).

Today, Oranjestad's front-line defences are glitzy duty-free shopping arcades in mock Dutch colonial buildings. Behind this pastel façade, plied by droves of tourists, is a more natural Oranjestad, much of it built in the boom period of the 30s, where Aruban homes and bars open on to the street. The old town-houses have angled tile roofs with dormer windows and tall louvred doors that encourage a breeze through the rooms.

The town has an impressive collection of coins from all over the world in the **Museo Numismatico** (tel 28831), behind St Francis Catholic Church on Irausquin Plein—30,000 pieces of money of all shapes and sizes from 400 countries across the world, from ancient Byzantium, through sunken treasure to the appearance of Aruba's own currency in 1986. Open 7.30–noon and 1–4.30 on weekdays. It is also possible to see a private collection of shells (700 species down to 1mm in length owned by the De

371

Man family, 18 Morgenster St (tel 24246), by appointment only, in the outskirts of the town.

Around the Island

As you fly in to land on Aruba, the island looks impossibly small, with just a few folds in the scrubland, but it can still take a while to get around it. If you venture further than the beach you will see farmsteads decorated with magical symbols—circus decorations like stars, kiss-curls and lozenges— surrounded by cactus fences. Just one or two of these simple old Aruban dwellings remain, clay houses with roofs of cactus wood and dried grass, built after Emancipation in 1863.

Travelling west along the coast from Oranjestad town centre you come to Aruba's commercial wharf and the industrial estates, and then you immediately emerge into hotel territory at Eagle Beach. As the road swings north you will see an unexpected sight: a genuine scarlet Dutch windmill from Friesland. Built in 1804, **De Olde Molen** was transported and reassembled here as a tourist attraction in 1961. Unfortunately the Aruban winds turned out to be so strong that they were forced to take off the sails. It is now a restaurant.

Close by is the **Bubali Pond**, once a salt-pan, but now an unofficial refuge for the island's birds, many of whom fly in at sunset to roost there for the night. Apart from the usual pelicans and frigatebirds who sit poised on rocks or in the bushes, you can see turnstones and sandpipers strutting around searching for food in the water.

East of the capital, headed towards the northern coastline, you pass through Ayo, where the *cunucu* is interrupted by an assembly of oddly-shaped boulders, granite rocks the size of buildings. At **Kristalberg** and **Bushiribana** you can see the ruins of the gold mines and the smelting works. Gold was discovered in Aruba in 1825 and the island experienced something of a gold rush, which lasted until 1913 (another explanation for Aruba's name is 'Ora uba', meaning 'gold was found here'). Many birds feed on the fruit of the organ cactus (they look like pipes) and hanging in the trees you may see the little bag nest of the oriole. Grassquits and orange troupials flit around the scrubby vegetation. At **Andicouri** the coastline has been carved into a **natural bridge**, a 30-yard span of coral wall, by the Caribbean waves.

Southeast of Oranjestad, the road passes the airport and beneath the **Hooiberg** (meaning haystack), a local landmark (with steps in it which make its 541 ft even easier to climb), on to Frenchman's Pass, an impressive gulley on an island so flat and on to Spanish Lagoon, and then to the island's industrial area and the site of the distillation plant, which produces 9.5 million gallons of water a day.

San Nicolas, Aruba's second town, has a population of 15,000. It grew up around the gates of the Lago oil refinery that opened here in 1929, and quickly it became bigger than Oranjestad itself. So many of the workers came from the British Caribbean islands that the streets of wooden shanties looked like a town in Trinidad. You will still hear English spoken in the streets.

North of San Nicolas you will come across caves with Amerindian hieroglyphs on the roof at **Guadirikiri** and **Fontein**. Some of these exploding squiggles and schematic faces are thought to be genuine, but others were more likely drawn by a European film-crew that was here about ten years ago. Inscriptions (genuine) can also be found on rocks at **Arikok** on the route back to Oranjestad.

FESTIVALS

The major event in the Aruban calendar is **Carnival** held in the run-up to Lent. Starting with the Lighting Parade, there is a kiddies' romp, and then musicians' competitions, and it all culminates eventually in the Old Mask Parade on the Sunday before Lent along the waterfront in Oranjestad, to music so loud that the streets seem to vibrate.

At New Year the Arubians have a tradition of open house, in which choirs and troupes of singers go from home to home singing a more melodic version of medieval Gregorian chants.

WHERE TO STAY

Aruba's hotels have gravitated around two main areas. The strip at Palm Beach is affectionately known as the 'high-rise hotels' and it is easy to see why. It looks a bit like Miami Beach, with a mile's worth of skyscrapers humming above ant-like vacationers. Activity is intense—casinos, Vegas-style shows and serried ranks of jet-skis. The newest additions are very large and impressive. Slightly lower-key, but on an equally good beach (Eagle Beach), are the 'lower-rise hotels', where some less imposing structures lurk among the ferro-concrete monsters. If conferences are your thing, then they do those too. For villas and apartments you can contact the Tourist Board. All hotels charge a 5% government room tax and usually 10% for service on top of their bills.

EXPENSIVE

In the high-rise strip, the **Hyatt Regency** (tel 297 8 31234, fax 21682, US 800 233 1234) stands tall with 360 luxurious rooms and suites. You glide up to an atrium set with pillars, dark-stained beams and wrought-iron chandeliers, passing into a palm garden with split-level pools, waterfalls, waterslide, a restaurant in mock ruins and finally to the beach. All the requisites for a body-holiday—tennis, watersports, massage and aerobics. Double rate US$270. The **Americana Aruba Beach Resort** (tel 24500, fax 23191, US 800 223 1588), just along Palm Beach, is also dressed in the strong pastel shades of today's Caribbean. Again a good feel, with international service. 420 rooms, three restaurants, watersports, swim-up bar, casino, nightly show. Double rate in winter, US$245–350. Just around the southwestern point of the island, on Druif Beach is the **Divi-divi Beach Resort** (tel 23300, fax 34002, US 800 367 3484), which has 200 rooms in blocks strung along the seafront and partially hidden in a tropical garden. All the sports and a couple of restaurants, and bar by the pool. You can also exchange with the facilities at the nearby Divi Tamarijn Beach resort. Double winter rate, US$245–430.

MODERATE

A less expensive option on Palm Beach is the **Palm Beach Resort** (tel 23900, fax 21941, US 800 345 2782), another high-rise from which you could abseil from the upper floors to the pool and bar and then make a quick dash to the beach. 173 rooms, two restaurants, tennis, watersports, casino and evening entertainment. US$175–195 a double. To the south are the low-rise hotels, which have a rather more relaxed feel than their high-rise counterparts. On the point of the vast Eagle Beach is the twin hotel combination of **Manchebo Beach** and **Bucuti Beach Hotels** (both tel 23444, fax 32446, US 800 223 1108). The 'Bucuti Wing' is pastel and plush, a counterpoint to the Manchebo Beach Hotel, which has 70 rooms and retains something of a beach-club feel. You dine in a

373

concrete galleon half submerged in the sand of Eagle Beach. About US$150 for a double. **Talk of the Town**, PO Box 564 Oranjestad (tel 23380, US 800 223 1108) is in the outskirts of town on the road to the airport, a sympathetic businessman's stopover. The 63 rooms are set around the pool and palm courtyard. It is low-key and away from the main beach area (it has its own small strip across the road). The hotel takes its name from its restaurant, considered to be one of the best on the island. Double room in season US$105–130.

CHEAP

A small hotel off the traditional Aruban tourist track is a the **Vistalmar**, Bucutiweg 28, Oranjestad (tel 28579, fax 47739). Rooms set in a villa on the seafront, with kitchens, maid-service and watersports. Double room US$65. Other reasonably priced rooms, usually with kitchens, include **Inocencia Apartments** at Patriastraat 4, in Dakota, just east of town (tel 22274), **Aulga's Place**, Sero Blanco 31 (tel 22717) and near the high-rise strip **Coconut Apartments**, Noord 31 (tel 21298), all about US$45. In town you will find the **Hotel Central** (tel 22260) is at 23 Elleboogstraat, double room US$40–45 and in San Nicolas there is the **Astoria Hotel** (tel 45132) at 6 Crijñssen-straat, price similar.

EATING OUT

As befits the mix of population, there are restaurants of almost any nationality in Aruba—Argentinian, Chinese, German, Japanese—as well as almost any style—grills, seafood, bistros, pizza huts. And of course do not forget Aruban food itself, for dishes such as *sopito* (fish chowder with coconut), *calco stoba* (conch stew) and *keshi yena* (spiced chicken covered with Dutch cheese). Many restaurants are set in old Aruban town and country houses. Portions are usually large and most restaurants add a 10% service charge to your bill.

EXPENSIVE

The place to linger over the best meal on the island is outside on the terrace at **Papiamento** (tel 24544) at Washington 61, in Noord. The plantation house is one of the oldest in Aruba and you can eat French and Caribbean specialities here, presented in clay pots (which you break with a hammer), or on a marble slab, which sizzles at your table. The seafood combination is superb (lobster shrimp, crab, scallop and others on a bed of home-made noodles), or local catch, home-smoked by the owner, Eduardo Ellis, a man with a compelling chuckle. Main dish US$20–30. **Chez Mathilde**, at Haven-straat 23 in town (tel 34869), is set in an Aruban townhouse. The menu is French, tournedos and thermidor served in candlelit intimacy, complemented by an extensive wine-list. Dinner only, main course US$20–30.

MODERATE

La Paloma, at Noord 39, behind the high-rise strip (tel 24611) is a bright and breezy Italian restaurant serving northern Italian fare and seafood. *Linguine scampi marinara* or Caribbean shrimps, local crowd at the bar. Main dish $15. There are a number of restaurants serving Aruban food, of which the nicest is **Gasparito**, at Gasparito 3 (tel 37044), also close to the high-rise strip. It is set in a pretty Aruban house—tiled floors, white-washed walls and dakpannen and all over the walls inside you will see Aruban paintings as the dining room doubles as a gallery. Aruban and seafood dishes; you might try the *combo* (fish cake, *kari kari* and chicken stew) or shrimp *en coco* (in coconut milk and brandy), followed by *banana na forno* (banana baked in cinnamon syrup). Open for lunch and dinner, main course $12–15. Not far off is **The Old Cunucu House**, 150 Palm Beach (tel 31666), where you can eat outside on the terrace or in another Aruban homestead. The menu is a bit more international, but you can have the house veal escalope in white wine cream sauce or pan-fried, brandy-flamed conch. Entrées $15–20. More local restaurants can be found heading east from Oranjestad. In a neat Aruban house in of all places the Dakota shopping centre is **The Mamas and the Papas** (tel 26537). You eat outside, by the cactus, or in the air-conditioned interior—*keshi yena, galina horna* (roast chicken) and *funchi* (cornmeal). Closed Sun, main dish US$10–15. Another excellent spot in the eastern suburbs is **Mi Cushina** at Noord Cura Cabai 24 (tel 48335), just short of San Nicolas. *Kreeft stoba* or *lasa* (lobster stewed or fried) or *bestia chiquito stoba* (stewed lamb). Open for lunch and dinner except Thurs, main dish US$10–15. A seafood restaurant with a difference is the **Nueva Marina Pirata** (tel 27372), a barge in the mangroves of Spanish Lagoon. Grilled catch of the day in spicy creole sauce and some Aruban dishes—*casuela de mariscos*, main course US$15–20. Or you might try **Brisas del Mar** (tel 47718) at Savaneta 222A, a small seafood restaurant also on the waterfront, with views of the departing freighters, US$10–15.

At the *refrisquerias*, a cross between a bar and a bakery, where you can sit out on the pavement with a beer, you can get *pan bati*, a sort of flat johnny cake and *rotis*, pastry envelopes stuffed with meat that originate from Trinidad. If you are peckish and see a vision of a white truck coming at you out of the night then stop it because it is a snack unit, the mobile equivalent of a *refrisqueria*.

BARS AND NIGHTLIFE

Aruba's well-oiled tourism machine has a whole smorgasbord of entertainment laid on with Carnival shows and cabaret extravaganzas, or join-in limbo shows and congas to steel bands. There are even Country and Western evenings for the homesick. Details are available through the hotels.

There are eight casinos on the island, but the best has to be the Alhambra Bazaar, where if your luck is out, at least you can be sure of getting something for your money in the all-night shopping arcade.

Outside the hotels are some fun bars: in Oranjestad you will find locals at the **The Celler** on Klipstraat—not in fact a cellar, but a classic cocktail bar, walls decorated with atmospheric shots of other capital cities. Live music on Saturdays. You might also try **Café Jimmy's**. On Main St in San Nicolas, **Charlie's** is something of an institution— for fifty years a drinking man's bar, now the second generation of Charlies has allowed women in. The ceiling is festooned with anything from car numberplates to their favourite videos. You can also try **Joey's Drive-in Bar** or any one of the hundreds of rum shops.

If you want to join the Arubians and a younger crowd of tourists for a dance, try **Club Visage**, beyond the Bushiri Beach Hotel. And if you want to flex the legs to merengue, you can try the **Blue Wave** near the marina, where the walls and ceiling are hung with fluorescent green seaweed. Other discotheques include **Reflections**, for old-time (60s) music. **Chesterfield** nightclub in San Nicolas opens on Fridays.

The Virgin Islands

The Virgin Islands must have been a nightmare for an early cartographer—more than 100 islands scattered over 1000 square miles; forested volcanic colossi that soar from the water and tiny cays that barely make it above the surf. To sail among them is a glorious sight, as beautiful as it was 500 years ago when Columbus himself passed through. He was so awestruck that he thought of St Ursula and her 11,000 virgins—a name which has remained ever since.

The Virgin Islands lie at the eastern extremity of the Greater Antilles, 50 miles east of Puerto Rico. Across the Anegada Passage, 80 miles to their east, are the Leeward Islands. The Virgin Islands are nearly all of volcanic origin (now completely inactive) and so they rise steeply out of the water to as much as 1200 feet within a few hundred yards of the coastline. From their summits the views over the islands are stunning. The island peaks run in two main lines, facing each other across Sir Francis Drake Passage.

Politically the islands fall into two groups, both of them possessions—in the west the

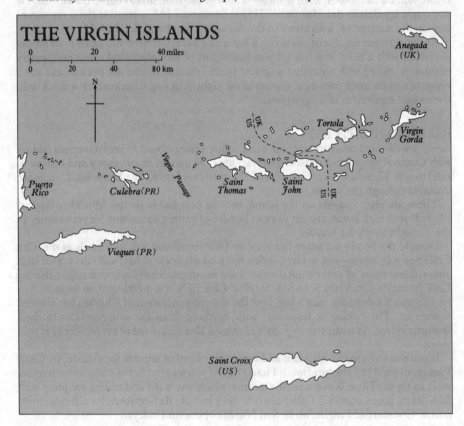

THE VIRGIN ISLANDS

0   20   40 miles

0   20   40   80 km

N

Anegada (UK)

Tortola

Virgin Gorda

UK US

Puerto Rico

Culebra (PR)

Virgin Passage

Saint Thomas

Saint John

UK US

Vieques (PR)

Saint Croix (US)

United States Virgin Islands are an unincorporated Territory of the USA and to their east lie the smaller BVI, one of Britain's five Crown Colonies in the Caribbean. The USVI has a much larger population (about 120,000 compared with the BVI's 12,000). However, many more BVIers have moved to the USVI to live and work. The population of both groups is mainly of African origin, descended from former slaves, but besides the Virgin Islanders themselves, there are large communities of Puerto Ricans, mainland Americans and West Indians from down-island.

The United States Virgin Islands are far more developed than their British counterparts. In St Thomas, life is upbeat and clearly American—you will see the big cruising cars and drive-thru fast-food joints, and hear 10-year-olds chatting about HBO satellite TV. Even in St Croix and St John, which are less developed than St Thomas, the traditional West Indian life has all but disappeared.

Life in the BVI is far gentler and less pressured, and you will still see the old West Indian farming life continue behind the modern encrustation of marinas and duty-free shops. The USVIers of course consider them a bit backward, but it is a bit more relaxed in the BVI and they prefer it that way. The British, who have all but withdrawn from this tropical colony, remain only in the scarlet pillar boxes and the peaked caps of the customs officials.

In the past there has been talk of the two groups of islands forging closer political links, with the BVI attaching themselves in some way to the USVI to gain from the investment that tourism has brought to the economy. However, having seen how recent development has changed things next door, the majority would prefer to remain autonomous. Many of them already work in the USVI and take their money back home to the BVI to build a home for their retirement. The tourism and sailing industries are making themselves felt in a smaller way in the BVI anyway.

Most people who come to the Virgin Islands will spend some time on the water; on a ferry, belly-flopping over the water in a seaplane, or cruising the secluded coves in a yacht. The cartographer's nightmare is now a sailor's paradise.

SAILING AND CHARTERS
Cruising Sir Francis Drake Channel is one of the best experiences the Caribbean can offer—nearby small islands move with you as you sail and the volcanic colossi on the horizon do not budge. You can moor in coves where headlands enclose a horseshoe of white sand and a few palms and where the water is so clear that the boat seems to be suspended in the air. When it gets too hot on board, swim to the beach and collapse there. At sunset there is nothing better to do than to watch for the Green Flash as the sun vanishes.

The Virgin Islands offer some of the best sailing in the world—it is safe and sheltered by the large islands, but there are constant breezes. Anchorages are good and the distances between them is short. Sailing is also relatively easy (with the exception of Anegada, there are few reefs) and so the area is ideal for bareboat chartering.

You can hire for a half day, a week or as long as you please. Yachts of all sizes are available, complete with cordon bleu cooks, on-board video and windsurfers and snorkelling equipment. Prices start at around $100 per day per person and for extreme luxury expect to shell out around $400. Hire is, of course, considerably cheaper in the summer months (as much as 40% off) and you will find the channel and coves a little less crowded. For more details on charter companies and marinas see USVI p. 381 and BVI p. 410.

The United States Virgin Islands

St Thomas, St Croix and St John

The US Virgin Islands consist of three main islands and around 70 cays, most of which are too small to be inhabited. The largest is St Croix (84 square miles), which lies on its own, 40 miles south of the main group. St Thomas (33 square miles) is the next largest, and the islands' capital, Charlotte Amalie, is situated on its southern shore. Five miles east of here is the third in the group, St John (just 16 square miles).

The islands were purchased by the USA in 1917. For 250 years before that they were Denmark's only colony in the Caribbean. Echoes of the Danes remain in the pretty waterfront towns with their warehouses and narrow stepped alleys (still with names like Raadet's Gade and Gamle Gade) and the plantation windmills out in the country. Danish was never really spoken here so the language has gone, but it seems strange that in a part of America they should still drive on the left.

Each car that cruises by in the USVI announces *American Paradise* on its numberplate. And as somebody thrusts a rum punch into your hand as soon as you arrive at the airport, in the tropical heat, while strains of calypso fill the air, you might imagine that you are there after all. You can have a good holiday here, but the paradise façade hides many of the same problems as the other Caribbean islands.

The tourist invasion is relentless. It is big business, the islands are almost completely dependent on it and it appears that development often proceeds with more regard to the tourist playground than the needs of the islanders themselves. However, wages are far higher here than elsewhere in the Caribbean and the islanders can reap the benefits. After a boom period in the mid-80s, the last couple of years have been harder on the islands. Visitor numbers and cruise ship arrivals are down.

The US Virgins (with the exception of St John) are among the most developed islands in the Caribbean and they receive well over a million and a half visitors each year. Hotels and condominiums cover the hillsides and there can be as many as 10 cruise ships in Charlotte Amalie harbour at one time. This is tourism at its most advanced—with stateside entertainment shipped in, carefully packaged 'vacationer's investment opportunities' and even the plastic cards of corals and tropical fish to take underwater with you so that you can identify them.

The American Virgins are obviously too developed for some (St John is the exception), yet they remain very popular. The towns are as pretty as any in the West Indies and, of course, the sea, sand and sailing are impeccable.

History

At the time that Columbus arrived in the Caribbean in 1492, the Virgin Islands were seeing the first waves of Carib attacks on the Greater Antilles. The belligerent island-hoppers, who decorated themselves with red warpaint and feathers, had come up all the

378

way from South America and had squeezed out the Arawaks as far as the Leewards. They would would pass through the Virgin Islands in their vast war canoes on raids from down-island, make a lightning attack and steal a few women, and then paddle back again.

The Spaniards battled with the Caribs over the next century, trying to keep them away from Puerto Rico, but as the first scourge receded another arrived. Pirates began to infest the islands, taking refuge there after their raids on Spanish shipping and settlements.

In the 1620s adventurers started to arrive and to plant crops—the Dutch and English and French settled in St Croix—and buccaneers took over the smaller islands, curing the meat they killed and selling it to passing sailors. These islands became stopping-off points for ships travelling up and down the island chain and for those that had just crossed the Atlantic. They became known as markets, where pirates would off-load their loot and spend time ashore waiting for another expedition.

The Danes moved in to St Thomas in 1665 and allowed the trading to continue. They were so successful that by the end of the 17th century the British Admiral Benbow described St Thomas as 'a receptacle for thieves'. In 1724 they declared it a freeport and it was soon on its way to being the richest port of its day. They claimed St John in 1684 (though they did not settle it until 1717) and they bought St Croix from the French in 1733 for 750,000 francs. Both islands were soon covered with sugar-cane.

The Danish islands' neutral status sheltered them from the worst effects of the wars between Spain, France and Britain. In wartime they were entrepôts and a haven against the marauding freebooters (hired by the warring nations to harry enemy and neutral shipping) and in peace they were the headquarters of the smuggling trade in the area. Slave auctions also brought in huge revenue. In the War of American Independence they shipped arms to the colonists. British objections to the trade led to two occupations in the Napoleonic Wars (1801 and 1807), but the islands were handed back to Denmark in 1815.

The Danes were the first to abolish the slave trade, in 1792, but slavery itself was not abolished until much later. In 1848 the Danish King Frederik VIII issued an edict that all slaves would be emancipated in 1859, but hearing this the slaves revolted. When the Governor-General Peter von Scholten, a man with a mulatto mistress, faced the crowd on St Croix, he realised that he was unwilling to impose the law and simply announced that he was freeing them then and there. The slaves remained free, but the Governor was tried for dereliction of duty. He was eventually acquitted.

In the middle of the 19th century the islands went into decline: sugar failed in St Croix and St John as it did all over the West Indies, and trading in St Thomas fell off too. Eventually the islands became a burden to the Danish government and so they began to look for a way of getting rid of them.

The United States first showed interest in the Islands in 1866, but at that stage the Virgin Islanders themselves vetoed the transfer. The subject came up again when the Americans were concerned about German naval movements in the Caribbean in the First World War. This time the islanders voted for cession to the United States and the Americans bought the islands for $25 million. Early on the islands were administered purely as a naval base because of their strategic position, but by 1932 the islands were under civil jurisdiction and the people had been granted citizenship of the USA.

Initially the Governor was appointed by the President in consultation with the elected

Senate of the USVI, but this has changed and since 1970 the Governor has been elected by the Virgin Islanders themselves every four years. Since 1972 they have sent a delegate to the House of Representatives, though he has no vote and so has more of a lobbying role. Though the islanders are US citizens and taxpayers, they do not vote in national elections. Unlike Puerto Rico, which is part of the Federal banking system, taxes paid in the USVI stay within the islands. The current Governor is Mr Alexander Farrelly.

In 1931 the American President, Herbert Hoover, described the US Virgin Islands as 'an orphanage, a poor house' and so soon after, the Virgin Islands Company was established to improve the infrastructure of the islands. The production of sugar was centralized and industry was stimulated through tax incentives. In 1966 a huge oil refinery was established on St Croix by the Hess Oil Company, capable of producing over 700,000 barrels a day. Other industries in operation today include the production of rum, some light manufacture and the assembly of parts from outside the islands.

The USVI have one of the highest per capita incomes in the Caribbean. By far the largest income-generator today is the tourist industry, which reached its height in 1988 (before Hurricane Hugo struck), when between them the islands saw 1.8 million visitors, of whom about 60 per cent arrived by cruise ship.

GETTING TO THE US VIRGIN ISLANDS

By Air
The USVI have international airports on the two largest islands, St Thomas and St Croix.

From the UK: there are no direct services, but British Airways' twice-weekly flights from London Gatwick to San Juan, Puerto Rico, offer the best connections. You might also consider flying via Miami. Lufthansa fly to San Juan from Frankfurt and Iberia from Madrid.

From the USA: St Thomas and St Croix are served by numerous airlines, notably American Airlines and Continental. Between them, they fly in direct from Atlanta, Boston, Miami, Newark and New York City. Note that most services stop first at St Thomas then continue to St Croix. From other points in the USA, passengers can either make a connection at one of those cities or fly to San Juan and take a commuter flight from there.

From other Caribbean Islands: San Juan on Puerto Rico has numerous shuttle services to and from the USVI, both St Thomas and St Croix. Going east and south, there are also direct links to Anguilla, Antigua, St Kitts and Sint Maarten.

GETTING AROUND THE US VIRGIN ISLANDS

A different way to get between St Croix and St Thomas is by seaplane. These beasts (known as the 'Goose' or the 'Mallard' on island) bounce over the waves as they struggle to get airborne and thrum like an outsize tuning fork in the air; they are fun to ride. The terminal in St Croix is in the north of Christiansted and in St Thomas it is right on the waterfront in Charlotte Amalie. In St John it is in Cruz Bay. Contact: the VI Seaplane Shuttle (tel 773 1776).

If you would prefer not declare your body weight, then you might try Sunaire Express (tel 778 9300), which flies to the Virgin and Puerto Rican islands, or GAS (Gorda Air Services).

USVI Ferries

With so many islands, a good way to get around is by boat. Many of the islands are served. Be careful of timings. It may seem unlikely for the West Indies, but many ferries do leave on time. Ferries leave St Thomas for **St John** (Cruz Bay) from Red Hook, at the eastern end of the island, every hour on the hour, 8–midnight daily, with sailings as early as 6.30 am, Mon–Fri. Crossings the other way start earlier, running 6 am–11 pm. The crossing takes 20 minutes, price $3. There is no reason to book as the ferries rarely reach their capacity.

There is also a 30-minute ferry from Charlotte Amalie to Cruz Bay, departing six times a day—9 am, 11 am, 1 pm, 3 pm, 5.30 pm and 7 pm—with return sailings at 7.15 am, 9.15 am, 11.15 am, 1.15 pm, 3.45 pm and 5.15 pm. Daily except Sundays, fare $7.

There are no ferries from St Thomas or St John to St Croix.

USVI to BVI

There are plenty of ferries from St Thomas to **Tortola** in the BVI. Most depart from the Charlotte Amalie waterfront, touching West End on Tortola and then continuing to Road Town. The crossing takes about an hour with customs. Companies include Native Son Inc (tel 495 4617) and Smith's Ferry Services (tel 494 4430). Speedy's (tel 495 5240) runs a service three times a week from St Thomas to Virgin Gorda, a two-hour ride through Sir Francis Drake Channel, return fare about $40. St John also has links to West End on Tortola (usually three a day) and an occasional sailing to Jost van Dyke and Virgin Gorda.

Charter Companies and Marinas

In the USVI, of the many charter companies, the **Virgin Islands Charteryacht League,** Homeport, USVI 00802 (tel 774 3944), works out of the bay off Charlotte Amalie, close to the cruise-ship dock. It oversees a large number of charter yachts. Another hire company offering week-long cruises is **Fairwind Charters** (tel 776 3650), PO Box 7332, St Thomas, USVI 00801. There are marinas at Homeport, the Sub Base and at Red Hook. The annual Charterboat exhibition takes place in November each year in Charlotte Amalie harbour in St Thomas.

If you want to go on a day cruise, you can turn up at the marina offices and tailor make one. Among the many regular yachts there is even the odd traditional West Indian schooner or sloop from down-island in the USVI. Most yachts carry snorkelling equipment with them. They will take you to an isolated cove on a nearby island for a picnic, or if you would prefer to be surrounded by a crowd, you could fix up an evening cocktail sail or a 'booze cruise'. Expect to pay from around $50 for a day's sail.

TOURIST INFORMATION

The United States Virgin Islands Division of Tourism has offices at:
UK: 2 Cinnamon Row, Plantation Wharf, York Place, London SW11 3TW (tel/fax (071) 924 3171).
Germany: Postfach 10–02–44, D-6050 Offenbach, (069 892008, fax 898892).
USA: 1270 Avenue of the Americas, New York, NY 10020 (tel (212) 582 4520, fax 581 3405); 3460 Wilshire Blvd, Suite 412, Los Angeles, CA 90010 (tel (213) 739 0138, fax 739 2005); 2655 LeJeune Rd, Suite 907, Coral Gables, FL 33134 (tel 305 442 7200, fax

445 9044; 900 17th St NW, Suite 500, Washington, DC 20006 tel (202) 293 3707, fax 785 2542).

The Head Office of the **USVI Division of Tourism** is at PO Box 6400, Charlotte Amalie, St Thomas 00804 (tel (809) 774 8784, fax 774 4390).

You are advised to be careful with regard to personal security after dark in Charlotte Amalie and to keep an eye on belongings left on the beach while you go for a swim.

The **IDD** code for the USVI and the BVI is 809, followed by a seven-figure number on the island. If you call in the islands, dial just the seven figures.

MONEY
The currency of the Virgin Islands (USVI and BVI) is the US dollar. Credit cards are accepted in hotels and all but the smallest shops and restaurants. Tipping is the same as in mainland USA, about 10–15%.

Banking hours are 9–2.30, Mon–Fri, with an extra hour and a half on Friday afternoons 3.30–5. **Shops** are open from 9–5 every day except Sunday, though they will often open up for the cruise ship trade.

FURTHER READING
One of the best books to come out of the Caribbean is Herman Wouk's *Don't Stop the Carnival*, which tells the story of a statesider who comes down to the islands and sets up as a hotelier. Every conceivable disaster befalls him in a book that is excruciatingly funny and ruthlessly tense (very unlike later books by Wouk). Budding hotel managers would be advised to read this book; the hoteliers themselves swear by it. It is rather difficult to look them in the eye after reading it.

Another amusing read about West Indian life and love is *Star Spangled Virgin*, by Du Bose Hayward, a story set in St Croix, in which a missionary tries to persuade West Indian women to persuade West Indian men to marry them rather than live in 'sin'. The Dockside Bookshop in Havensight Mall has an excellent selection of Caribbean books.

ST THOMAS

The life of St Thomas has always centred around the island's magnificent harbour—a steep-sloped bowl partly closed by islands—which attracted shipping from the earliest days. The lines of 18th-century trading warehouses in Charlotte Amalie are just as busy today and the harbour teems with yachts, motorboats and cruise ships.

St Thomas is one of the most developed islands in the whole Caribbean. About 50,000 people live on its 33 square miles, most of them in the extended suburb of Charlotte Amalie, the capital town in the USVI. Buildings have sprung up everywhere—villas, hotels and vacation condominiums—and there is even a rush hour. Only in the west end of the island, beyond the airport, is it less built up. In such a crowded place there is some tension (some of it racial) and it occasionally spills over into violence.

But overdeveloped as it is, the island is attractive to many for its upbeat tempo. Top entertainment acts come down to perform in the island hotels, maintaining St Thomas's tradition as the 'nightclub of the Virgin Islands' and, of course, if you want to join the fray, St Thomas has some of the best shopping in the Caribbean.

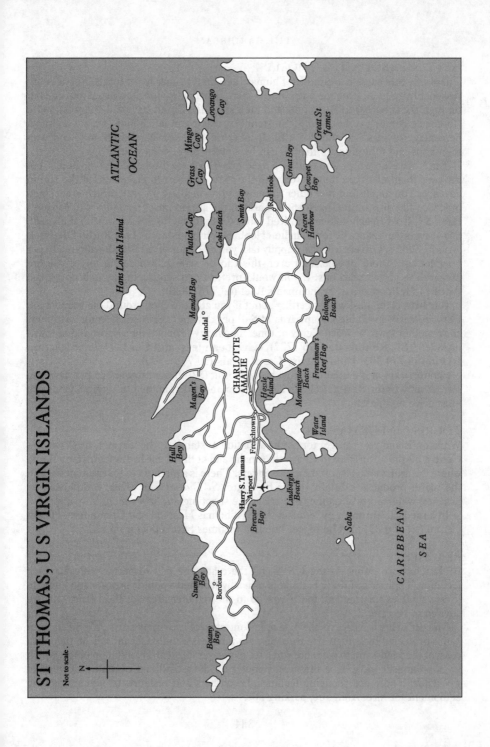

ST THOMAS, U S VIRGIN ISLANDS

Not to scale.

N

ATLANTIC
OCEAN

Hans Lollick Island

Loeango
Cay

Mingo
Cay

Grass
Cay

Great St
James

Thatch Cay

Coki Beach

Smith Bay

Red Hook

Great Bay

Cowpet
Bay

Secret
Harbour

Mandal Bay

Mandal

CHARLOTTE
AMALIE

Frenchman's
Reef Bay

Bolongo
Beach

Magen's
Bay

Hassle
Island

Morningstar
Beach

Hull
Bay

Frenchtown

Harry S. Truman
Airport

Brewer's
Bay

Water
Island

Lindbergh
Beach

Saba

CARIBBEAN

SEA

Stumpy
Bay

Bordeaux

Botany
Bay

GETTING AROUND ST THOMAS

There is a **bus** service around St Thomas, designed primarily for locals. Services are reasonably frequent from the outskirts of Charlotte Amalie (along the waterfront and out through the suburbs) to Red Hook and then along the Smith Bay road and west out to Bordeaux, running until about 8. No standees, maximum fare about 75c. A very small percentage of cars will stop for a hitch-hiker on St Thomas, and on an island with thousands and thousands of them it can be a pretty depressing wait.

Taxis are everywhere and work to a fixed rate (these are displayed in some hotels, but the taxis themselves are unmetered). All the same it is best to make sure of the fare in advance. You might find that other passengers hop in along the way, which is accepted practice. The trip from **Charlotte Amalie** to the airport costs around $5, to Magen's Bay—$7, Coki Beach—$8 and to Red Hook—$8. If you do not see one on the street, taxi-drivers can always be found in hotel lobbies. **Virgin Islands Taxi Radio Dispatch** is on 774 7457. Drivers will also happily take you on a tour of the island—about $30 per hour for up to four people. However, this can be arranged more cheaply if you are prepared to go by safari bus. If you would prefer to go sightseeing by helicopter, call **Antilles Helicopters** at Frenchman's Reef (tel 776 7880).

Car hire is the best way of getting about if you are travelling around the island a lot. Cars are easily available for upwards of $40 per day, but the roads become extremely congested in town, so leave plenty of time. The many firms (at the airport and in town) include: **ABC Rentals** (tel 776 1222), **Caribbean Jeep and Car** (tel 776 6811), **Sun Island** (tel 774 3333) and **Thrifty Car Rentals** (tel 776 2500).

Scooters are also available, with a hefty deposit ($200), for around $25 per day from **Paradise Scooter Rental** (tel 775 2724). Remember that in the US Virgin Islands you must drive on the left.

TOURIST INFORMATION

While on island you can get tourist information at stands at the **airport**, the **Visitor's Centre** on the waterfront in Charlotte Amalie and at the **West India Company dock**, where the cruise ships let off their passengers. There is a plethora of tourist material and the island produces a bright yellow brochure, *St Thomas This Week*, with advice on beaches, watersports and other essentials like shopping and investment in real estate.

In a medical **emergency**, contact the St Thomas Hospital and Community Health Centre (tel 776 8311). The bigger hotels sometimes have a doctor on call.

BEACHES

All beaches are public in the USVI and there are one or two places with changing facilities. Topless and nude bathing is officially frowned upon. It is not a good idea to leave valuables unattended and if you go to the remoter areas of the island, you are advised to be careful.

Magen's Bay is a superb beach, a mile-long strip of extremely fine sand and coconut palms protected by a huge arm thrusting out into the Atlantic Ocean. It is on the north coast of the island and to get there you have to go over the central mountain range, which gives a fantastic view. It is the most popular on the island and becomes crowded at weekends. There are changing facilities, beach bars and restaurants, and snorkelling equipment for hire. Adm 50c, parking 50c.

There are one or two tiny strips of sand along the arms of Magen's Bay where you can sometimes be alone. **Paradise Beach** is on the south side (the road leads down from the E&M grocery on the Hull Bay road). **Community Bay** is on the opposite side near the point. To the east of Magen's Bay is **Mandal Bay**, which is quite secluded and though the surf can get up, there is excellent snorkelling.

On the south side of the island, **Brewer's Bay** and **Lindbergh Beach** are just beyond the airport from Charlotte Amalie and are relatively free of crowds. The latter has hotels nearby where you can get a drink and a windsurfer.

Out of Charlotte Amalie to the east is **Morningstar Beach** at the Frenchman's Reef Hotel, where you can hire snorkelling and windsurfing gear. Beyond it you eventually come to **Bolongo Beach** and at the eastern end, **Cowpet Bay**. Both beaches have a hotel where you can hire watersports equipment.

On the Atlantic-facing east coast, try **Sapphire Beach** for the snorkelling and Sunday afternoon entertainment. **Coki Beach**, next to Coral World, gets very busy. Some snorkelling and diving, but mainly a people beach—sunbathing, hair-braiding, jetskis and loitering by the snackwagons.

There are some isolated beaches in the northwest of the island, some of which need a four-wheel drive to get to and then a walk. Try palm-backed **Hull Bay**, a cove just west of Magen's Bay where there are often 6–10 ft breakers for surfing and there is a beach bar, or **Stumpy Bay**, close to Bordeaux.

If you want real seclusion, it is worth considering a trip to some of the off-shore islands. Recommended are **Hans Lollick** island to the north of St Thomas and **Great St James** to the east and **Saba** and **Buck Island** off the south coast.

WATERSPORTS

The hotels also have smaller sailing craft for their guests if you wish to sail around the bay in a hobie cat or a sunfish. If you want to get hold of a wetbike, again try the big hotels, or go to Coki Beach off the east end. **Parasailing**, in the comfort of a flying deck-chair and complete with stereo, can be arranged at Morningstar Beach among others.

Windsurfing can be fixed up at the hotel beaches on the south and eastern sides—try Morningstar, Sapphire Beach, Cowpet Bay at the southeastern tip of the island.

Deep-sea fishing is good off St Thomas and is easily arranged. Wahoo, skipjack, sailfish, tuna and white and blue marlin cruise the depths in abundance and there is something to catch at all times of the year. At the **American Yacht Harbour** (tel 775 6454), Red Hook, you will find the sleek chrome machines waiting for another day's preying on the high seas. Others include the **St Thomas Sport Fishing Center** (tel 775 7990) and **Nauti Nymph Watersports** (tel 775 6858) is located at Cowpet Beach.

The Virgin Islands are surrounded by reefs and St Thomas has some excellent **snorkelling** grounds where you can hang around in a school of triggerfish and butter-flyfish or linger among the sea fans. **Coki Beach** is often busy and other spots include **Sapphire Beach**, **Secret Harbour**, **Great Bay** and **Botany Bay**. Off-shore islands with good reefs include **Hans Lollick** and **Lovango Cay**, **Mingo Cay** and **Grass Cay** off the east coast.

A whole new world opens out for **scuba divers** in St Thomas. The crystalline water often has visibility up to 100 feet, and the Virgin Island outcrops, forested above the surface, are covered in coral below. Simple dive-sites off the south coast include Cow and Calf and the shelves of St James Island, and more advanced sites are the tunnels at Thatch Cay and the spine of Sail Rock off the west coast.

Once again, the hotels usually lay on equipment and often they can give instruction, but there are outside dive operators if you are travelling independently. A veteran St Thomas navy diver is **Joe Vogel**, PO Box 7322, St Thomas (tel 775 7610), who works out of the West Indies Inn in Frenchtown, or there is **Chris Sawyer Diving Centre** (tel 775 7320) and **Caribbean Divers** (tel 775 6384) at Red Hook. Dives cost from $40 per tank. There is a decompression chamber on the island (tel 776 2686).

If you would prefer not to get wet, you can still get a tame view of the fish and corals from **Coral World**, off Coki Bay (see p. 387). Alternatively, the **Atlantis Submarine** runs excursions under the waves for a close inspection of the submarine underworld. It leaves from the Havensight Mall, near the cruise-ship dock (tel 776 5650 for reservations, price around $50).

OTHER SPORTS
On land there are other sports to keep the body active. The **Mahogany Run Golf Course** is on the northern side of the island, east of Magen's Bay. Green fees $45.

There are endless **tennis** courts on the island and a game is best fixed through a hotel. Guests usually play for free but visitors will be charged a fee.

Charlotte Amalie

Charlotte Amalie is a classically pretty Caribbean town—red roofs and bursts of palm fronds that scatter the hillsides around a bay and steep alleys that lead down to the harbour. The warehouses on the waterfront are doing a roaring trade as they have on and off for over 300 years.

In 1700 Père Labat, the roving Dominican monk and gastronome from Martinique, found silks from India and gold-embroidered Arabian muslin cloth. It was all off-loaded by pirates who stopped in port to spend their loot before heading seawards again for more 'cruize and plunder'. The infamous Blackbeard, Edward Teach from Bristol, was known to have hidden out here when he was not on the high seas.

Encouraged by the Danes, the trade became a little more regularized and at its height the harbour would see as many as 1300 vessels in a year. In the late 18th century, the future architect of the American Constitution, Alexander Hamilton (on the reverse of the $10 bill), decided the town was so rich that 'gold moved through the streets in wheel-barrows'.

The seaborne arrivals continue—marauding characters pour off the ships, with fists full of dollars to spend—but nowadays they race past the rum shops and load up into little safari buses instead, ready to go shopping. The wares still come from all over the world; they are just shipped in legally, that is all. It is fascinating mercantile mayhem and it gets quite frantic, so you are advised to avoid Charlotte Amalie on a busy day (when as many as ten cruise ships have been known to call in). Originally the town was known as Tap Hus (roughly translated as the rum shop), but in 1730 the Danes renamed it after the wife of their King Christian V, Charlotte Amalie. As well as the name, many Danish buildings also remain in Charlotte Amalie.

The heartland of Charlotte Amalie is, of course, the alleys of trading warehouses from the 18th century, which are still buzzing with trade. Like in all West Indian islands, the main **market** in the middle of the town sells fruit and vegetables to the St Thomians who dare venture that far into town.

Dark red **Fort Christian**, built in 1672 when the Danes first arrived, stands on the waterfront guarding the bay. In its time it has housed the Governor's house, the garrison and recently the prison, police station and courts. Now home to the **Virgin Islands Museum**, the underground cells have displays of the simple island existence of the Arawaks and the planters' and traders' sumptuous life when St Thomas was in its prime. Open Mon–Fri, 9–noon and 1–5, adm free.

Over the road is the island **Legislature**, formerly the Danish barracks, a grand structure from the 1870s that is dressed up in lime-green, where the 15 US Virgin Island Senators sit. Open 8–5.

On the hillside behind, aloof from all the trading activity on the waterfront, is **Government House**, a three-storey building with wrought iron balconies that was built in 1867 for the Danish colonial council and is now the official residence of the Islands' Governor. Inside the floors are wooden and you will see the names of the early Danish Governors and their American counterparts. Some paintings by the impressionist painter Camille Pissarro are on display (he was born on the island). Open during working hours, 8–noon and 1–5, adm free.

Climbing the **99 Steps** to the top of Government Hill you come to what is called **Blackbeard's Tower**, an extremely fine look-out, where the pirate was supposed to have lived around 1700. He was an extremely violent man, who would occasionally shoot one of his sidekicks to keep the others on their guard and liked to adopt an especially demonic appearance when going into battle by burning fuses in his hair. He was eventually killed in a shoot-out with the British navy in 1718.

On the western outskirts of the town you come to **Frenchtown**, still a distinct community that is descended from settlers from the island of St Barthélemy in the Leewards, who first came over in 1852. Many are fishermen and the restaurants in the area are renowned.

At the opposite end of town is **Homeport**, St Thomas's main yachting marina, and close by is the West India Company Dock, where you will find the **Havensight Mall** another community of tourists shops in warehouses.

Around the Island

The island of St Thomas is highly developed all around. The hills above Charlotte Amalie are covered with homes to their summits and wherever you go on the island you are not far from a residential area. On top of the central range is **Drake's Seat**, the vantage point supposedly used by Sir Francis Drake in his privateering days in the 1580s. The view is magnificent and looks across to the BVI.

The southeast of the island is built up with condominiums and vacation homes that take advantage of the beaches in that area. **Coral World** is a small underwater world complex at Coki Beach in the east of the island, with good displays—walk-in observatory 20 ft underwater, a predator tank where sharks and tarpons patrol and Reef Encounter, in which you will see over a hundred sorts of fish including filefish and barred hamlets (which need no mate to reproduce), lionfish like fans and fluorescent corals. Adm expensive, adults $12, children $7. The west end is the least developed area of St Thomas, and you will find some more typical West Indian villages in that area.

SHOPPING

St Thomas (particularly) and the other Virgin Islands offer some of the Caribbean's finest hunting grounds for shoppers. As you step off the cruise ship, the dockside warehouses are ranged in front of you and there is literally no manufactured accessory you cannot find. In St Thomas prices will occasionally be marked at about 60 per cent of their stateside price. American citizens are encouraged to spend with special tax concessions when they return home—their duty-free limit is doubled from $400 worth of goods to $800, with yet more concessions on drink (USVI rum).

There are two main areas on St Thomas, the **Havensight Mall**, by the West India cruise ship Dock, where three lines of air-conditioned glass-fronted boutiques jostle for business, and central Charlotte Amalie, which has been involved with trade for over 300 years and is really an outsize emporium. It is a network of alleyways and streets with everything on sale from Swiss watches and jewellery from the world over to Chanel perfumes and the chic-est French modes. There is even a small mall at Mountain Top, so you can shop with a view if you want.

You can try La Romana for Italian clothes and AH Riise or Little Switzerland for jewellery purchases. Gucci have just one shop for leather clothes and you might pick up a bargain at the Ralph Lauren Polo Shop.

WHERE TO STAY IN ST THOMAS

St Thomas has its share of large and expensive luxury beach resorts, but it also has a surprising collection of excellent small hotels in Charlotte Amalie, many of them set in charming antique townhouses on the hillside with a view of the town below. The government adds a 7.5% room tax to all bills and most places charge 10% for service.

EXPENSIVE

The **Frenchman's Reef Beach Resort**, PO Box 7100 (tel 809 776 8500, fax 774 6194, US 800 524 2000), is a flagship among the resorts, like a luxurious cruise ship on the point at the harbour mouth that outshines the other liners that pass beneath it at night. It is large, with 500 rooms in the main blocks and the more private Morningstar Beach Club on the sand down below. All watersports, tennis, six restaurants, extravaganza entertainment, double room in season $250–425. The **Grand Palazzo** (tel 775 3333, fax 775 4444, US 800 283 8666) is set on Great Bay in the east of St Thomas, 150 one- and two-roomed suites, each with a balcony overlooking the islands towards St John. The suites are set in Italian-style blocks above the mangrove lagoon and the beach, where there is a beach bar and restaurant (one of two) and watersports including excellent windsurfing. Otherwise there are tennis courts, a fitness centre and evening entertainment. Double room $210–865. A little further away from Charlotte Amalie is the **Limetree Beach Hotel**, Box 7337 (tel 775 1800). Each of its 84 rooms faces the narrow beach. Rates are about $300 for a double room in peak season, but include free watersports and numerous other benefits. Its sister hotel is the **Bolongo Bay Beach Club** (tel 775 180), with similar rates and an emphasis on watersports and tennis; it has more of a clubby atmosphere, with numerous organized activities. At the quiet East End of St Thomas, a mile from the ferry to St John and close to Sapphire Bay is **Pavilions & Pools** where each of the 25 rooms has its own private pool. The smaller of the room sizes, known as Caribbean, costs around $250 for two people in peak season, while the larger size—the International—is about $300.

MODERATE
Overlooking the waterfront in the centre of town is the **Windward Passage Hotel**, PO Box 640 (tel 774 5200, fax 762 3577, US 800 542 7389), central and convenient for the airport. All mod cons and assistance with business and with transport to the tourist areas of the island, entertainment, $135–190 in season. On the other side of town, quite close to the airport, the **Island Beachcomber Hotel**, PO Box 2579 (tel 774 5250, fax 762 3577, US 800 982 9898), is lower-key and less expensive than the rest of St Thomas's beach hotels. The 50 rooms are in blocks, but they are hidden in a forested tropical garden. Friendly and comfortable, some watersports, double room $140 in winter. Another informal spot, overlooking Hassel island from just beyond Frenchtown is the **West Indies Inn**, PO Box 4976 (tel 774 1376, US 800 448 6224). It is set around the red roofed Villa Olga, an old holiday home which is now the restaurant. Rooms air-conditioned and inexpensive at $90–150 (inc breakfast). Dive packages available through Joe Vogel. A cheaper option just above the beach is the **Sea Horse Cottages**, PO Box 2312 (tel 775 9231), which overlooks St John from the eastern end of the island. 25 cottages with kitchens, pool and snorkelling a breath off the coast. About $50 in season.

Plantation House Hotels
If you would like to experience some of St Thomas's antique charm, Charlotte Amalie itself has some sophisticated and tranquil retreats. The colonial echoes of the **Mark St Thomas** (tel 774 5511, fax 774 8509, US 800343 4085) make for one of the most congenial places on the islands. The façade of the yellow-brick house is decorated with filigree wrought-iron balustrades around its balconies and inside the rooms are fitted with original and reproduction antiques. All twentieth-century comforts available too. Eight double rooms at $145–215 in season. Nearby the **Hotel 1829**, PO Box 1576, Government Hill (tel 776 1829, fax 776 4313, US 800 524 2002) is another spot with old-time island ambience. The original town house, with dark backgammon bar and balcony restaurant, has been extended behind with some rooms overlooking the court-yard garden. 15 rooms, some a bit small, $80–280 in season. The **Galleon House** is also close by, PO Box 6577 (tel/fax 774 6952, US 800 524 2052), with cracking views of the red roofs of Charlotte Amalie. 14 comfortable rooms, pool and best of all, central dining tables on the terrace where you can listen to the wind-up piano—anything from the Blue Danube through ragtime to James Bond theme tunes. Double room $69–115, good value, includes breakfast. The **Danish Chalet Inn**, PO Box 4319 (tel 774 5764, fax 777 4886, US 800 635 1531) has the friendly feel of a family guest house. 13 comfortable rooms, some with share bath, $75–95.

CHEAP
The **Miller Manor**, PO Box 1570 (tel 774 1535), with the faded elegance of a town house and a fantastic view of the bay, is the cheapest deal on the island at $40–45.

At a pinch, if you are down to your last few dollars, go to the marina and ask a yacht owner if you can sleep in a berth on board while the yacht is not on charter; some owners are prepared to allow this in exchange for a few hours' work.

EATING OUT IN ST THOMAS
Quite highly developed, St Thomas has a grand variety of restaurants and so you can eat anything from 'contemporary exotic' cuisine through to good local rice 'n peas. Menus are mostly reliable American—burgers and steaks—but everything can be imported, so you will find fine French fare as well as Caribbean seafood and fish. A 15% service charge will be added to your bill, for your convenience... 'Tipping is not a city in China...'

EXPENSIVE
Some of the best local food can be found in Frenchtown, just outside Charlotte Amalie. It is also a popular area for an early evening drink. **Café Normandie** (tel 774 1622) is set in an upstairs drawing room decorated with the works of local artists and presided over by hip waiters in white coats. Classical French cuisine with some light sauces—catch of the day caribe in white wine and seasoning or cognac-flamed veal Normandie. Open daily in season, worth reserving a table, main course $20.

In town you will receive minutely attentive service and presentation on the veranda at the **Fiddle Leaf** (tel 775 2810). Echoes of nouvelle in the contemporary exotic dishes—scallops with mango and papaya relish and spicy coconut sauce, or jumbo shrimp sautéed in saffron, polenta and hazelnut dressing. Closed Mon out of season, main course $20 plus. Nearby on Back St you will find **Virgilio's** (tel 776 4920), which serves classic Italian dishes in a drawing room, quite sophisticated even with the stained-plastic windows. *Scampi della casa* with linguini oil and garlic. There is an extensive wine-list and it is worth going just for the cappucino, to which is added a blend of galliano, Bailey's and Kahlua. Main course $20–25.

MODERATE
In Frenchtown, **Chez Jaques** (tel 776 5797) has a brasserie and a gourmet dining room, also offering a traditional French menu—escargots in puff pastry with roquefort and some of the most calorific chocolate pudding you will find anywhere. 30 different wines by the glass, main dish $12–18, closed Sun. **Alexander's** (tel 776 4211) serves Italian and Austrian food in plush air-conditioned comfort—pastas, wursts and a variation on the Wiener Schnitzel (made with conch). Lunch and dinner, main course $12–20, closed Sun.

Little Bo Peep (tel 776 9292) on Back St is an airco lounge with brick walls and is a favourite gathering point of St Thomians and visitors alike for local food—curried and stewed meats (chicken, conch, goat) accompanied by bewildering local vegetables. Main course $15. Yet more local, and set in a traditional Caribbean clapboard house is **Tasha's** on Gamle Gade just above Market Square. Start with Tasha's rum punch (ingredients undeclared) and then callaloo, curry goat, fried plantain and paes and rice. Just seven tables, main course $7–10.

CHEAP
Finally, a great setting for a local meal is the snackwagon on the waterfront in downtown Charlotte Amalie. If you do not mind dining out of a polystyrene box on your knees, then try **Bill's Texas Pit BBQ**—batter chicken or ribs swimming in barbecue sauce and coleslaw, $5–7.

Beyond Charlotte Amalie you will find excellent local seafood at **Eunice's** (tel 775 3975) in Smith Bay on the east coast, wicker tables on an upstairs veranda. Stewed conch in lime ginger and garlic or filet of yellowtail for about $17, closed Sun. Near Red Hook is **East Coast** (tel 775 1919), a breezy wooden terrace and American style TV bar. Cajun shrimp for a starter followed by burgers or ribs, $15.

BARS AND NIGHTLIFE
An excellent bar to start the evening with in Frenchtown (whether you'll eat nearby or not) is the **Epernay Champagne Bar**, where hip chicks and execs gather after work for sushi and duck tacos. Otherwise you might try one of the small town hotels—**Blackbeard's, the Mark St George** or **1829**, where the bars often have piano players. The **Agave Terrace** at the Point Pleasant Hotel has a regular full moon jazz evening and **Mona's** at Magen's Point Resort has evening music.

Downtown there are lively pub-style bars at **Coconuts** on Paradise Alley and straight opposite, **Rosie O'Grady's**. If you want a game of pool or air-hockey with a few locals you can try **Wet Willie's** at the eastern end of town or the **Surf Club** opposite the Ramada Hotel down by the marina. You can also catch a beer in a London bus just across from the waterfront near the ferry terminal.

There are also bars in the Sub Base area, another yachties' hangout, so it gets quite lively. Try **Barnacle Bill's**, which you will spot by the lobster on the roof, or by the noise of a band playing. And if you want to go dancing, **Club Z** is worth the climb up the hill. Out of Charlotte Amalie, try **For the Birds** at Compass Point, **Horsefeathers** and **East Coast** in the Red Hook area and **Sib's Mountain Bar**.

ST CROIX

St Croix (pronounced St Croy) is the largest of the Virgin Islands. Unlike the hillier islands of St Thomas and St John, St Croix has stretches of flat and fertile land between its hills and so it has traditionally been agricultural. Once, its 84 square miles were divided up into about 100 sugar plantations. In the last 50 years agriculture has declined and recently the tourist industry has taken over as the main source of revenue.

But tourism is not as intensive in St Croix and you can still find deserted beaches on the island. The streets of Christiansted simply do not have the pressure-cooker effect of Charlotte Amalie. Things are more low key here, but you will find some surprisingly good places to stay and eat. Like so much of the Caribbean, it feels a little haphazard.

The island's name is French (a straight translation of Columbus's original name for it, Santa Cruz), but this is one of the few legacies of French ownership in the 17th century. The island was bought by the Danes in 1733 after they had established themselves in St Thomas.

Mural, St Croix

From time to time, St Croix has been the senior island of the three US Virgin Islands, because of its successful plantation economy and because it had the largest population (now about 55,000). The Governor resided here in the 19th century and it was in Frederiksted on St Croix that he declared that the slaves should be freed in 1848. There is little love lost between the St Thomians and the Cruzians, who consider St Thomas over-developed and stressful.

Earlier this century the island's importance declined as agriculture failed, while St Thomas boomed with the tourist industry. Only recently have the Cruzians started to catch up with their neighbours. There is a large Puerto Rican community in St Croix who have made their way on to the island over the last 100 years, escaping the poverty of the larger island. There are many 'down-islanders' and there is even a small community of Danes, the strongest remnant of the colonial legacy. It is not very strong, but one commentator claimed that a week among the Cruzians was like a tropical version of a tortured Ibsen play! Generally the Cruzians are slow and polite.

Christiansted, the capital, and Frederiksted (traditionally the more important because of its better harbour) are traditional West Indian waterfront towns, where the arched walkways can transport you back to the days of clippers and ocean-going trading ships and wharves heaving with barrels and tea-chests. They have been well restored.

St Croix received a severe drubbing from Hurricane Hugo in 1989. Over 90% of the islanders were left homeless and there were outbreaks of looting, but it has basically recovered. About 20 per cent of the population moved off the island after the hurricane, some of whom have now returned.

GETTING AROUND ST CROIX
There are no public **buses** on St Croix, but share-taxis run the principal routes (Christiansted to Frederiksted costs $2, other journeys less), leaving when they are full or the driver has the urge. You can pick them up at the supermarkets. If you want to get to

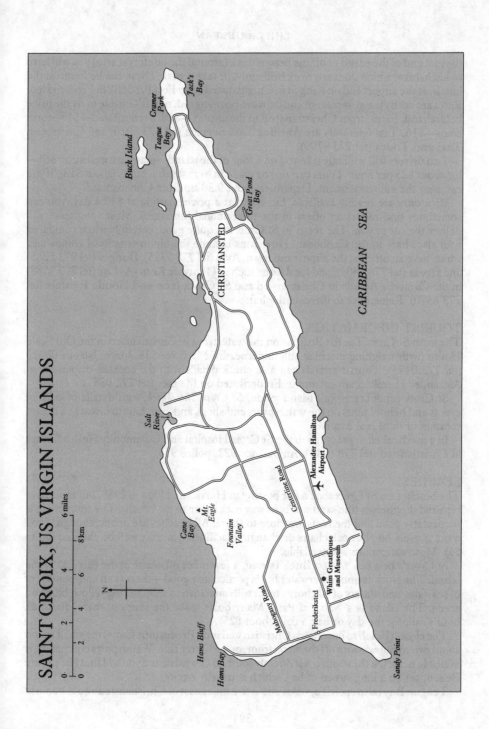

SAINT CROIX, US VIRGIN ISLANDS

Buck Island

Cramer Park

Jack's Bay

Teague Bay

Great Pond Bay

CHRISTIANSTED

CARIBBEAN SEA

Salt River

Mt. Eagle

Cane Bay

Fountain Valley

Centerline Road

Alexander Hamilton Airport

Hams Bluff

Hams Bay

Mahogany Road

Frederiksted

Whim Greathouse and Museum

Sandy Point

N

0   2   4   6 miles
0   4   6   8 km

the east end of the island or off the beaten track (around the rainforest area) you will have to hitch-hike, which does not work brilliantly, or take a **taxi**. These can be found at the hotels, at the airport and on King St in Christiansted or by Fort Frederik in Frederiksted. Rates are set by the government and cabs are not metered, so it is sensible to fix the price beforehand. Fares: from **Christiansted** to the airport—$10, Frederiksted—$15, north coast—$16. Taxi operators are **Antilles Taxi Service** (tel 773 5020) and **Caribbean Taxi and Tours** (tel 773 9799).

Taxi drivers will willingly take you on a tour of the island—many are well informed—for about $25 per hour. Tours can also be made in tourist safari buses (about $18), if you can bear the embarrassment. Departure about 9.30 am from Christiansted.

Hire cars are readily available, but come at a price, starting at $40 a day (you can sometimes find reduction offers in the promotional literature). Most companies will deliver the car to you. The roads in St Croix are quite good, certainly when compared with elsewhere in the Caribbean. Hire firms include the big international companies, which have an office at the airport and town: **Avis** (tel 778 9355), **Budget** (tel 773 2285) and **Hertz** (tel 778 1402), and local firms such as **Olympic Rent-A-Car** (tel 773 9588) in the Caravelle Arcade in Christiansted and **St Croix Jeep and Honda Rentals** (tel 773 8370). Remember to drive on the left.

TOURIST INFORMATION
The main St Croix Tourist Board is on the waterfront in Christiansted in the Old Scale House (with weighing machine still underneath), PO Box 4538, Virgin Islands 00822 (tel 773 0495). Tourist arrivals can also check details with the cocktail-dispensers at Alexander Hamilton airport and in Frederiksted on the pier (tel 772 0357).

St Croix produces a pink island guide, *St Croix This Week*, with details of current events and helpful hints on the watersports and shops and even how to invest in a dream vacation or local real estate.

In a **medical** emergency, go to the St Croix Hospital and Community Health Centre in Christiansted (tel 778 6311), Ambulance 922, police 915.

BEACHES
The beaches on St Croix took a fair beating in Hurricane Hugo in 1989, but most have repaired themselves (the sand works its way back up on to the beach). The snorkelling is particularly good and the reefs are close to shore. All beaches are public, though if you want to use a hotel's deck chairs or changing facilities, you may well be charged (up to $5). Most watersports are available.

St Croix's best beach is on **Buck Island**, a few miles off-shore at the east end of the island. The Buck Island underwater life is particularly good—there is an enormous reef of sea-fans, and antlers of staghorns teem with angelfish in shimmering yellow, blue and green. The island is a National Park. Many boats make the tour out there, about an hour's sail, for the day or half a day (about $25).

The closest beach to downtown Christiansted is on **Protestant Cay**—the small island about two minutes' swim off the waterfront, or a $1 ferry ride. Watersports equipment is available here. On the south coast directly south of Christiansted you will find **Ha'penny Beach**, set on a long sweep of bay, which is usually empty.

Teague Bay (also spelt Tague) is about five miles east of Christiansted and is home to a couple of hotels and the St Croix Yacht Club. It is a broad strip of sand curving around a large bay, where you can get windsurfers and small sailing boats or fix up some time on waterskis. There are a couple of snack bars to retire to if the action gets too hot.

Cramer Park (at the eastern tip of the island on the north side) is popular with the Cruzians and so it fills up at weekends. There is a changing room, but take drinks and a picnic and also snorkelling gear because of the underwater life. On the other side of the point and even more isolated is **Isaac's Bay**, where the snorkelling is even better. The best way to get to this beach is from the eastern end of Jack's Bay.

The sand comes ashore in mounds at the southwestern tip of St Croix at **Sandy Point**. It is quite isolated here, and you are advised to be careful about locking your car and leaving belongings unattended. Take food and drinks. In season (May to July), leatherback turtles come ashore here at night to lay their eggs.

Cut into the cliffs of the north coast are a number of coves, of which the best is **Cane Bay**, where the palm-backed sand comes and goes, but the reef remains, giving superb snorkelling. Jewel fish glint among the coral heads and striped sergeant majors cruise around on patrol. There are hotels nearby.

BEACH BARS

There is a string of beach bars with a cracking view of the sunset on the west coast of the island, north of Frederiksted. The **Sundowner** is rustic but gets quite lively with live music three days a week and the **La Grange Beach Club** is a little more formal—parasols on the terrace where you can order sandwiches and salads (up to $10), adm $3 for the day. The **West End Beach Club**, set on the best stretch of sand is probably the liveliest; volleyball and crowds at the weekend. Salads and burgers $6–7 and cocktails for a view of the Green Flash.

WATERSPORTS

Most sports can be arranged in the shops that line the waterfront in Christiansted—wetbikes are for hire if you want to scoot around among the yachts and waterskiing ($25 per person) can also be arranged. Most resort hotels have watersports equipment too. If you wish to go **parasailing**, you can get airborne in Christiansted practically without wetting your feet. Contact **Paradise Parasail** (tel 773 7060) on the Christiansted boardwalk.

Windsurfing is well-served on the island. The winds are good at the eastern end of the island and **Mistral** has a school at the Chenay Beach Resort. Also **Tradewind-surfing** (tel 773 7060).

Small sailing boats like sunfish are available through the hotels and if you want to go out on a larger yacht you can charter for a day or join the organized cruises. To hire a yacht (crewed or a bareboat) try **Mile-Mark Charters** (tel 773 2628), in Christiansted or **Llewelyn's Charters** (773 9027) for a trimaran trip. Daytime snorkelling trips and sunset and rum-punch cruises are available through the same operators, and if you would like to sail away on a 118 ft transatlantic schooner, you can contact the *Elinor* (tel 773 7171).

Deep-sea fishing is well organized in St Croix, with fleets of sleek cruisers in which to ply the deep for six-foot marlin, sailfish and wahoo. A full day can cost from around

$600 and a half day from $400. Try the big firms, or opt for **Ruffian** (tel 773 6011), which leaves from the King's Alley Wharf.

The best **snorkelling** grounds are listed in the beaches section, but the reefs also offer extremely good **scuba diving**. The island is almost completely ringed by barrier reefs and there are endless dive-sites, some of which drop off just a few hundred yards off shore. It is particularly good for its soft-coral life. There is a wall off the north coast between Christiansted and Hams Bay in the west: the Salt River drop-off starts in 20 feet of water, dropping to thousands, as with the Cane Bay drop-off (from 35 ft). Frederiksted has good corals and off-shore at Buck Island is another popular spot.

Many of the hotels offer dive-packages and it is also easy to fix up lessons if you wish to learn. A single-tank dive costs from $40. Outside operators include **Dive Experience** (tel 773 3307) at Club Comanche in Christiansted, **Cruzian Divers** (tel 772 3701) in Frederiksted and the **Cane Bay Dive Shop** (tel 773 9913).

OTHER SPORTS
There are two 18-hole **golf** courses on the island, the Carambola (tel 778 0747) on the northern shore and at the Buccaneer Hotel, east of Christiansted (tel 773 2100). Green fees are around $25. The Reef is a nine-hole course in the eastern Teague Bay area (tel 773 8844), fee $15 for nine holes.

Horse riding can be fixed up through **Paul and Jill's Equestrian Stable** at Sprat Hall Estate in Frederiksted (tel 772 2880), for a ride through the diminutive rainforest, or in Christiansted at **Buccaneer Stables** (tel 778 8670), from where you can visit old-time St Croix, the land of the windmills.

Tennis courts are available in practically every hotel on the island, and some have a tennis pro who can give lessons.

Christiansted

With its waterfront walkways and arched Danish storage houses, Christiansted is an alluring harbour town that rings with echoes of another age. The inevitable invasion of airco boutiques and fast-food halls that makes it a 20th-century trading town has been kept out of sight—neon signs must not protrude beyond the original façades—and so you have the impression that a colonial official in serge with gold epaulettes might round the corner at any minute. But instead of a clipper at anchor, the harbour is ranged with yachts and from time to time the seaplane belly-flops into the bay.

The town was laid out by the Danes when they arrived in 1733 and is named in honour of King Christian VI. It is protected by a large barrier reef, on which the waves break a few hundred yards out from the shore. Any potential invading force would have had to negotiate the reef and then face unformidable **Fort Christiansvaern**. Nobody did and so the yellow fort never saw action, but it is pleasant to visit (it seems that the walls were used mainly to lock the soldiers in at night rather than keep invaders out). It was started in 1733, with stones brought from Denmark as ballast, and since 1878, when it was abandoned by the military, it has functioned variously as a police station and courthouse. Open weekdays 8–5 and weekends 9–5, adm (which also admits you to the Steeple Building across the way).

The fort's guns have a a good view over **Protestant Cay**, an island-hotel just a few

396

minutes' swim out to sea. It takes its name from the French era when only Catholics could be buried on the mainland, and so Protestants were buried here. It is mostly referred to as the Hotel on the Cay, supposed to be the setting for Herman Wouk's classic novel about the nightmarish life of a Caribbean hotelier, *Don't Stop the Carnival*.

Back on the mainland, newly-arrived captains would first check in to the **Old Danish Customs House** before unloading. It was built in the 1750s, and the staircase, a suitably imposing entrance for the captains, was added later. Next stop was the **Old Scale House** (weighing scales still in place) which would measure their cargo. The building also contains the Tourist Information office.

Beyond the **Old Danish West India and Guinea Company Warehouse**, which the company used as its headquarters from 1749 (now the post office) is the **Steeple Building**, a Lutheran Church constructed in 1753 (the steeple itself was added in 1794). Today it houses the **National Park Museum**, where you can see exhibits of Indian calabashes, maps of Danish St Croix and diagrams of rum production. Open Mon–Fri, 9–4, adm (with fort).

On King St (Kongens Tvaergade), you will find **Government House**, with its arched veranda and red pillar boxes. It is two private homes set around a garden, joined together when Governor van Scholten bought them in 1830s. The staircase at the entrance leads to the main hall, now redecorated with chandeliers and mirrors like those under which the islanders danced a hundred years ago (the Danes took the originals with them when they left in 1917, but gave some others back to the islands in 1966). Today the buildings house the court and government offices.

Those looking to score a few duty-free bargains will find the main shopping streets just behind the waterfront around King Street and King's Alley, in the old trading houses. Another echo of the old West Indies (from before the age of the supermarket) can still be seen in the covered **market** (weekdays and Saturdays), which has been there in one form or other since 1735. A few Cruzians have stalls selling ground provisions to other islanders.

Around the Island

St Croix's 84 square miles were once divided into about 100 sugar plantations and the windmills once used to crush the cane (without sails and steadily more dilapidated) seem to be on every hilltop. From them there are splendid views across the island and often as far north as the other Virgin Islands, grey stains on the horizon 40 miles to the north.

Travelling west from Christiansted on the north shore road you pass **Salt River**, a mangrove bay where Columbus put in for water in 1493, and then you come to Cane Bay, where the road twists and drops into small coves forested with palm trees that are cut into the northern cliffs. The views are spectacular. Eventually the road turns inland past Fountain Valley to the Centerline road.

The **Centerline Road** runs west from Christiansted to Frederiksted on the west coast, mostly in a direct straight line. As it leaves the town it passes close to St Croix's small industrial area, where you will find the Hess Oil Refinery on the south coast, now running at a reduced capacity and the aluminium plant. The road eventually passes the Alexander Hamilton airport. (Alexander Hamilton came to St Croix from Nevis as a boy and grew up in Christiansted until he left for North America in the 1760s.)

397

Across the road you come to the **St George Village Botanical Gardens,** laid out over a 16-acre site that was a plantation estate and before that an Arawak village. Some buildings around the great house have been restored and on the various trails you will find many Caribbean favourites including the bulbous *sandbox tree* (the pods of this spikey-barked tree were used to hold sand that was then sprinkled on ink to stop it smudging), the *autograph tree* (you can write on its leaves) and the dildo cactus, named for its shape! The garden is making a collection of all the plants in St Croix that are endangered. Concerts are sometimes given in the grounds on Sundays (tel 772 3874). Open daily, guided tours, early—3.30 pm, adm.

Sugar-cane was the source of St Croix's wealth and it blanketed the land as late as 1966, but the distillation of rum has continued, with imported molasses at the **Cruzian Rum Distillery** (tel 772 0799), just off Centerline road to the south. A half-hour guided tour will lead you among the vats of distilling molasses, where the smell will have you teetering on the walkways. Some rum is bottled here for sale in the USVI, but most is exported. Tours finish with a snifter in the bar, 8.30–11 and 1–4.15, adm free.

A couple of miles farther along the road is the **Whim Greathouse and Museum,** which will cast you back to the days of plantation glory, when planter Mr McEvoy lived in this house with the air of a church, surrounded by a moat. It has been restored by volunteers and refitted with period furniture. In the dungeon-like outhouses you can see the tools of all the island artisans—cooper (barrel-maker), logger, wheelwright, joiner and blacksmith. Open Mon–Sat, 10–5, adm.

Frederiksted

St Croix's second town is Frederiksted, set on the west coast, 17 miles west of Christiansted. Founded in 1751, Frederiksted has always been important because it has a better harbour than Christiansted, and large ships were able to dock there. Until the pier was destroyed by Hurricane Hugo in 1989, the cruise ships would unload their passengers here.

Even 100 years ago liners were passing by; in 1887 Lafcadio Hearn stopped off in the town, describing it in his *Two Years in the West Indies.* To him the town had 'the appearance of a beautiful Spanish town, with its Romanesque piazzas, churches, many arched buildings peeping through breaks in a line of mahogany, bread-fruit, mango, tamarind and palm trees'. The town, much of which was rebuilt after it was burned in a riot in 1878, was well-known for its elaborate West Indian gingerbread architecture. The pretty arches are still along the waterfront, but the feel of the Spanish town has gone.

As usual, the harbour is watched over by a fortress, **Fort Frederik,** now run down. Constructed in 1752, it was here that Governor van Scholten made his announcement that he was abolishing slavery in the Danish islands in 1848, against the orders of his king. Close by is the **Old Customs House,** where the duty would be paid on the incoming and outgoing cargo.

Well worth a visit is the **St Croix Aquarium and Marine Education Centre** on Strand St, which has a series of small aquaria. They are brought alive by Lonnie Kaczmarsky, who will tell you stories of the dentist shrimp (which cleans the teeth of other fish without them eating him), sponge crabs who disguise themselves with sponges and then eat them if they cannot find a meal, and the triangular arrow crab who looks like a cartoon character. He takes guided snorkelling tours.

The **market**, on Queen St, can be as lively as Hearn described it, with all the tropical fruits and vegetables, presided over by the brightly-dressed market ladies.

The Rainforest

A mile out of Frederiksted, towards the north coast of the island, is St Croix's miniature 'rainforest'. It does not receive enough rain to be a real rainforest, but the vegetation is different from the rest of the island and as you drive along **Mahogany Road**, the creepers and lianas will reach down to grapple with you. Orchids perch and ferns explode in the upper branches, just beneath the 100-foot canopy, and you may see a hummingbird flit by. There are a number of roads leading from the top of West End Road into the forest (many unpaved and so you are best to go by jeep), and there are endless footpaths if you wish to walk. In the forest you will find **St Croix LEAP** (from Life Experience Achievement Programme), which has a wood mill and craft shop selling products from local timber.

The East

The eastern end of St Croix is drier and less lush than the west. The beaches are worth a visit (some active, others reclusive), but all you will see among the windmill cones and the modern villas are a few goats and the dildo cactus.

WHERE TO STAY IN ST CROIX
Like St Thomas, St Croix has a good variety of hotels with a string of beach-front resorts and some smaller hotels with antique (and mock-antique) charm, set in the older Danish buildings. **Villa Rental** can be arranged through **Island Villas**, 14A Caravelle Arcade, Christiansted (tel 773 8821) or **Tropic Retreats in Paradise**, PO Box 5219, Christiansted (tel 778 7550, US 800 233 7944). USVI government tax of 7.5% is levied on all hotel bills.

EXPENSIVE
The **Buccaneer Hotel**, PO Box 25200 (tel 773 2100, US 800 223 1108) is set in 300 acres of rolling grounds that descends to a string of private beaches just east of Christiansted. It is large, with 150 rooms around the central estate house of coral rock, but very comfortable. Four restaurants, watersports and a golf course. Double room $200–330 in season. A smaller beach hotel with real Caribbean island charm is the **Cormorant Beach Club**, 4126 La Grande Princesse (tel 778 8920, fax 778 9218, US 800 548 4460). It has everything for the luxurious escape—sumptuous high-pastel rooms with their own balconies and a view of the ocean, afternoon tea and no telephones. And when you feel like emerging from your seclusion there is an excellent restaurant looking out through the palms. Just 37 double rooms, which go for $285 in season. Close by, the **St Croix by the Sea**, PO Box 248 (tel 778 8600, fax 773 8002, US 800 524 5006) also has a low-key, beach club feel, with hammocks slung between the palm trees. The 65 brightly decorated rooms stand in two blocks overlooking the sea and swimming pool and there is nightly entertainment in the restaurant. Double room $170. High on a hill at

the eastern end of the island you will find a luxurious enclave at the **Villa Madeleine**, PO Box 24190 (tel 773 8141, fax 773 7518, US 800 548 4461). Built in the formal style of a plantation house, the villa itself is new, but it has a comfortable ambience with billiard room and piano bar. The 43 rooms, all villas with their own pool and a view, are sumptuous—bamboo four-posters and wicker furniture—and have all the necessities for 20th century comfort including cable TV and VCR. Villa $350–450 in season.

MODERATE

In town, the **Pink Fancy**, at 27 Prince St a little way from the centre of town (tel 773 8460, US 800 524 2045) has good old West Indian charm. The ten rooms are set in a old town house with arched brick foundations and a clapboard upper, with louvred windows and shutters. It is of course pink, but the rooms are decorated with Brazil wood in keeping with the antique style. An echo from St Croix's illustrious past. A charming spot, double rooms at $150 a night (includes breakfast), no restaurant. There is a clutch of other small hotels in Christiansted, set in the trading streets and converted warehouses along the waterfront. A comfortable place is the **Hotel Caravelle** at 44A Queen Cross St (tel 773 0687, fax 778 7004, US 800 524 0410), with 43 rooms overlooking the pool and Christiansted harbour beyond. Neat and friendly, double deluxe $125 in winter. **Club Comanche**, 1 Strand St (tel 773 0210, US 800 524 2066) is in the thick of it in the centre of town. The 40 rooms are reached in a network stairs, walkways and balconies from the old wooden main house. Rooms are air-conditioned with cable TV and some have kitchens; a double costs $80–110. For marginally less you can stay at the **Danish Manor Hotel**, 2 Company St (tel 773 1377, fax 773 1913, US 800 524 2069), where the fourteen rooms give on to the brick courtyard with pool and explosive greenery. Double room $60–90.

At the other end of the island you will find an extremely fine setting at the **Sprat Hall Plantation**, PO Box 695 (tel 772 0305, US 800 843 3584), a couple of miles north of Frederiksted. The estate house, in which three rooms are decorated with period furniture, including four-posters, dates from the late 1600s. It stands in open grounds just in from the coast, where there is a private beach. Small with just 18 rooms, but friendly. Double $125–150 in season, some with kitchens. You can stay at the **Frederiksted Hotel**, 20 Strand St (tel 773 9150, fax 778 4009, US 800 524 2025), a comfortable hotel in the middle of town for $115–130.

EATING OUT IN ST CROIX

Like the hotels, many of Christiansted's restaurants and bars are set in the pretty town houses and along the harbour waterfront. Restaurants accept credit cards and most charge service at 10%.

EXPENSIVE

At **Kendrick's** (tel 773 9199) on King St you climb stone stairs to reach an antique drawing room where bow-tied waiters ply back and forth to multiple dining rooms in smaller annexes. Start with the rum punch and follow with shrimp in puff pastry with chutneys of Caribbean fruit and finish with any one of a number of exotic coffees. Nouvelle presentation, at $17–25 a main dish, worth reserving in season. The **Top Hat** restaurant (tel 773 2346) on Company St is run by Danes and retains some Danish elements in its menu. There is a lively bar where you can linger before moving in to the wooden walled dining room with its tray roof and network of supporting beams. Home-made sausages followed by *Flikadeller* (meatballs) with red cabbage and mashed potato, or duck à la Danish (crisp with apples). Main dish $18–25, closed Sun.

MODERATE

At the **Tivoli Gardens** (tel 773 6782) you eat on a breezy veranda surrounded by white trellis work and hung with greenery. Filet mignon in mustard and gorgonzola or chicken tivolese in tomato sour-cream sauce, $12–20. On the road east out of town, beyond Fort Christiansvaern, you will find **Dino's** (tel 775 8005), a small and friendly Italian restaurant. Seafood canelloni and home-made pastas, tables air-conditioned inside or al fresco. Dinner only, closed Sun, Thurs, main course $15. At the eastern end of the island, **Duggan's Reef** (tel 773 9800) looks over the waterfront to Buck Island, a good spot for lunch. Crêpes and salads at $10 and an international menu for dinner.

CHEAP

Back in town you will get an excellent local meal at **Harvey's** on Company St. It has a classic West setting, plastic tablecloths and foldaway chairs. No written menu—chat with Sarah through the stable door into the kitchen. Try callaloo followed by conch in butter sauce, or chicken or goat (curried or stewed). It comes with a tonnage of ground provisions—sweet potato, plantain and yam. Main dish $5–10. You might also try **Kim's** restaurant (tel 773 3377), a cosy streetfront café on King St, where you can gat a shrimp and fries for $6–10.

Frederiksted also has some good restaurants and you will be well entertained at the **Blue Moon** (tel 772 2222), which is set in the vaulted interior of an old trading house on the front street. Cajun BBQ shrimp, or Florida-raised, pan-seared catfish, followed by hot fudge rum cake, about $15 a main dish. Friday nights is liveliest, when the jazz is live; Sunday brunch is also popular. The menu at **Le Crocodile** (772 5700) is French and you dine in a tropical garden and courtyard. Frogs legs and veal in mushroom and cream, $18. **Le St Tropez** (tel 772 3000) on King St also serves French food on the veranda. French onion soup followed by a quiche or a salad, lunch and dinner.

BARS

There are some fun bars on the waterfront in Christiansted, where the yachties crawl ashore for a beer. You can start an evening at **Stixx Hurricane Bar**. The bar at the Comanche Hotel is mellow, good for an early evening drink listening to the paino player. The **Company St Pub** is a loud and lively video bar. In **Frederiksted** you can catch a beer and a game of darts at the **Brandy Snifter** on King St.

ST JOHN

First appearances are enough to tell that St John is altogether different from St Thomas. Unlike its larger neighbour, where houses dot the hillsides to their very summits, St John is almost entirely green and forested. As you make the short crossing over the Pillsbury Sound, the pressurized tempo of St Thomas will evaporate and low-key St John will welcome you with a nonchalant calm.

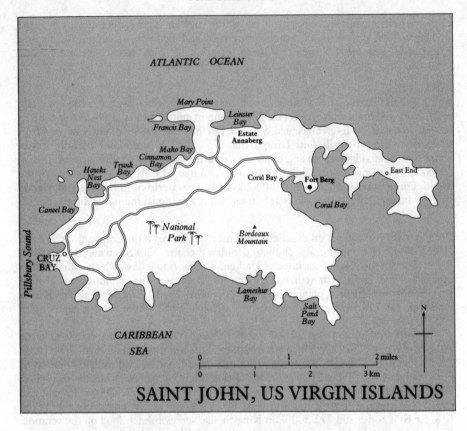

ATLANTIC OCEAN

Mary Point

Leinster
Bay

Francis Bay

Estate
Annaberg

Maho Bay

Cinnamon
Bay

Hawks
Nest
Bay

Trunk
Bay

Coral Bay

Fort Berg

East End

Caneel Bay

Coral Bay

Pillsbury Sound

National
Park

Bordeaux
Mountain

CRUZ
BAY

Lameshur
Bay

Salt
Pond
Bay

N

CARIBBEAN

SEA

0   1   2 miles
0   1   2   3 km

SAINT JOHN, US VIRGIN ISLANDS

Since 1956 St John has taken a different path from the other Virgin islands. Laurence Rockefeller and his Jackson Hole Preserve Corporation granted two-thirds of the island to the National Parks. It has remained undeveloped since then and much of the land has now returned to second generation forest. The National Park has opened up the forests with walking trails and holds seminars on the wildlife.

St John feels almost pastoral and of the three USVI it is the most similar to the BVI. Its capital, Cruz Bay, has just a few streets and the only other settlement consists of a few houses on Coral Bay at the east end. It is not hard to imagine how life was 50 years ago when the islanders travelled everywhere by donkey on small trails cut out of the forest. The island now boasts a bank, a post office and a petrol station.

All may be quiet today, but once St John was as much a hive of plantation activity as the rest of the Caribbean islands. 200 years ago the slopes were cut with terraces for the sugar-cane. In 1733 St John saw one of the Caribbean's most successful slave rebellions, in which the Africans revolted and held out for over nine months, successfully beating off attempts by Danish and British troops to put them down. When they were eventually defeated by French soldiers brought in from Martinique, many preferred to commit suicide by jumping off the cliffs at Mary's Point rather than allow themselves to be returned to slavery. Just a few plantation ruins remain, throttled by the jungle.

Like all the islands, the vast majority of St John's income derives from tourism and that has been developing too. It has a feeling of the modern Caribbean playground—neat and tidy with little complexes of shops and restaurants and day-trippers shifted around in little safari buses, but it has a pleasant holiday spirit about it. The island also goes out of its way to provide a nature-based holiday for those who want it (the campsites are often booked up well in advance).

The 4500 people who live here now are fewer than were here in the island's plantation heyday. Nowadays the island is tranquil, favoured by campers and a few writers and recluses. The desperation suffered by the rebellious slaves seems as far away as the mercantile mayhem of St Thomas.

GETTING AROUND ST JOHN

There is no **bus service** in St John and so if you do not want to pay for a taxi, then you will have to hitch a ride, which is not that easy, or walk.

Taxi rates: **Cruz Bay** to Trunk Bay—$6, Cinnamon Bay—$7, Annaberg—$12. People will often team up because that brings the price down. You may find that somebody hops in anyway. A two-hour tour of the island by taxi will cost $30.

Cars are available for hire, though the roads are pretty hairy—watch out for safari buses and water delivery trucks. Jeeps are popular here and daily rates start at around $35. Companies include **Delbert Hill Jeep and Auto** (tel 776 6374), **Varlack Rental** (tel 776 6695) and **Spencer's Jeep** rental (tel 776 6628), all of them in Cruz Bay. Remember to drive on the left.

TOURIST INFORMATION

The Tourism Office is in Cruz Bay (tel 776 6450), PO Box 200, USVI 00830, near the post office, and the **National Park Service** has a visitors' centre in Cruz Bay, just near the ferry terminal (tel 776 6201). For more information you can write to VI National Park, PO Box 7789, St Thomas VI00801. Open 8–4.30.

If you are making a visit to St John for just the day, check in the tourist magazines to see which day there are fewest cruise ships in dock.

In a **medical** emergency, contact the DeCastro Clinic in Cruz Bay (tel 776 6252).

St John National Park

The 12,900 acres of the St John National Park are cut and crossed with about 20 **walking trails**, and you can get information on them (along with films) and maps from the office in Cruz Bay, opposite Mongoose Junction. Many species of plants in the forest are marked. Some 5,600 acres of the National Park are offshore, covering reefs and marine life. The guides (with an encyclopaedic knowledge of island flora, fauna and history) take out walks a number of times a week, which include picnics and snorkelling breaks. A popular hike leads from Centerline Road in the middle of the island over to Reef Bay, from where they arrange a trip back by boat to save you the walk. There are also evening slide shows in the camp grounds.

The walks cover all the terrain of St John, from the mangroves on the shoreline at Leinster Bay, where you may see gallinules and a mangrove cuckoo among the leafy

403

THE CARIBBEAN

sprouts, and into the lusher vegetation on the upper mountainsides. On the offshore islands you may can see frigatebirds and the usual boobies and pelicans.

If you would prefer to hike on **horseback, Pony Express** (tel 776 6494) will take you on guided tours through the island's blanket of forest and to hidden coves where you can ride along the sand.

BEACHES

St John's beaches are mostly along the northern coast and they are more secluded than the beaches on St Thomas, although this does not prevent crowds building up on the more popular ones. Between the forested fingers of the coastline, the water in the coves is crystalline and will glow in the richest shades of blue on a sunny day.

Trunk Bay is St John's answer to Magen's Bay, mounds of blinding white sand backed by palm trees. There is a snorkelling trail through the corals, where you should be surrounded by tropical fish like parrotfish and tangs. There are changing rooms and a snack bar which hires out equipment.

Cinnamon Bay and in the next cove **Maho Bay** and **Francis Bay**, where there is excellent snorkelling, are two broad curves rimmed with the softest sands and with a view out over the other Virgins. There is a snack bar in the campsite and changing rooms at Cinnamon Bay.

Off the road to Cruz Bay there is a thin strip of sand at **Hawksnest Bay** and the many small beaches at **Caneel Bay** (you may have to swim in because you are sometimes not allowed over the hotel's private land).

If you want to get off the beaten track, try **Salt Pond Bay** and **Lameshur Bay** on the south coast, where there are few people, the water is calm and the snorkelling good. Take a picnic and drinks if you plan to stay for the day.

There are also one or two off-shore cays which are worth the visit for their sands, including Henley Cay (out from Caneel Bay) and Lovango Cay (farther out), and off Leinster Bay in the north, Waterlemon Cay, where the snorkelling is good.

WATERSPORTS

Watersports are handled by the hotels and by a few outside companies, including **St John Watersports** (tel 776 6256), **Low Key Watersports** (tel 776 7048) and **Cinnamon Bay Watersports** in Cinnamon Bay (tel 776 6458). They will fix up windsurfing, kayaking and snorkelling gear (see beaches for the best sites). They will also arrange day trips on a yacht to the nearby cays, as will **Cruz Bay Watersports** (tel 776 6234), who also do **deep-sea fishing** trips.

Scuba divers can go to any of these companies or to **Coral Bay Watersports** (tel 776 6857) at the east end of the island. Favourite dive-sites include the reefs and cays to the north of the island, Eagle Shoal to the south, Ten Fathom Pinnacle and also the steamship *Rhone* off Salt Cay in the British Virgin Islands. You can parasail **Windseekers** (tel 776 7048) or take a glass-bottom boat, the *Calypso Queen* (tel 776 6922). A day's sail can be fixed up through *Serenity* and sportfishing through **World Class Anglers** (both tel 776 6922).

On the island there are a few **tennis** courts in the hotels as well as four public courts in Cruz Bay.

404

Cruz Bay

Cruz Bay, the miniature capital of St John, is a typically sleepy West Indian town set on a west coast bay just a few miles across the Pillsbury Sound from St Thomas. The houses scattered on the hillside tumble down to the waterfront, where a pint-size pastel-painted arcade has sprung up to catch the day-trippers.

The small island **museum** is downstairs in the public library as you go up the hill. Alongside the St Johnian schoolchildren, you can discover old-time St John through prints and the descriptions of their slave revolt in 1733. Open Mon–Fri, 9–5.

Around the Island

In its plantation days the slopes of St John were completely covered in sugar-cane, but since the early 19th century the land has been left, and so the island is now carpeted with 50 feet of jungle. Just a few mill-ruins poke out from beneath the overgrowth.

To drive along the north coast, follow the bay and turn left at Mongoose Junction from where the road starts to switchback, clambering up the slopes and sweeping down into the successive bays. On each headland there is a view of the other Virgins. At Mary Point is a ravine called Minna Neger Ghut, where the last survivors of the slave rebellion in 1733 are thought to have jumped to their deaths rather than submit themselves to slavery once more. Eventually you come to the best preserved and most accessible of the estate ruins at **Estate Annaberg**, a former sugar plantation with displays showing the process and describing the buildings. Open in daylight hours, no guides, adm free.

Centreline Road carves a path into the forested hills, wiggling over the impossibly steep slopes and passing beneath Bordeaux Mountain, St John's highest peak. From **Coral Bay Overlook** there is a superb view of the islands to the northeast, looking along Sir Francis Drake Passage towards Virgin Gorda about 20 miles away. From here the road descends towards St John's only other settlement at Coral Bay, a light smattering of houses around the harbour. Coral Bay was the first area settled by the Danes and Fort Berg, the dilapidated fort on the point-dates from 1717, the year they arrived.

WHERE TO STAY

There is a small selection of hotels on St John, concentrated around Cruz Bay. Another option is to consider taking a villa, of which there are plenty on the island (see below). There are also a couple of camp-sites, if you want to see the National Park from close up. Government tax of 7.5% is levied on all hotel bills.

EXPENSIVE

Caneel Bay, PO Box 720 (tel 776 6111, fax 776 2030) is set on a magnificent sweep of bay overlooking Pillsbury Sound and St Thomas. The hotel has been offering low-key, high luxury to generations of returning visitors. Echoes of the old Caribbean in the restored buildings and the colonial atmosphere. Double rooms $325–535. The **Hyatt Regency**, PO Box 8310 (tel 775 3858) has a more modern beach front resort feel about it. It is large, with rooms in blocks lurking around landscaped gardens and has water-sports and entertainment and three restaurants—as the name suggests, Chow Bella serves Chinese and Italian cuisine. Double room $300–870. The **Gallows Point** Suite Hotel, PO Box 58 (tel 776 6434, fax 776 6520, US 800 323 7229) is a very comfortable and attractive hotel set in wooden buildings on the clifftop just out of Cruz Bay. Suites with balconies and a restaurant with a view of the other islands, double room $225–275.

MODERATE
The **Raintree Inn**, PO Box 506 (tel/fax 776 7449) is a busy spot on one of Cruz Bay's few tiny streets. Nice wooden verandas and the Fish Trap restaurant, double room $70–95. The **Cruz Inn**, PO Box 556 (tel 776 7688, fax 776 7449) stands on the hillside over a bay behind town. Friendly with quite simple rooms at $50–90. Cheaper rooms can be found at the **Inn at Tamarind Court**, PO Box 350 (tel 776 6378) just beyond the library, double room $55–75. There are two **campgrounds** on the island, both 'luxury camping' in which permanent 'tents' (raised floors with walls and netting at either end) are ranged on the forest and connected to the central area, washrooms and beach by a lacework of paths. Hikes, watersports, environmental lectures and supermarket. Try **Maho Bay Camps Inc**, PO Box 310 Tel 776 6240, US 800 392 9004) in Maho Bay, or **Cinnamon Bay**, PO Box 720 (tel 776 6330, fax 776 6458). Both sites are comfortable and get booked up in the winter season. Double tent $75.

There are plenty of **villas** on the island and the companies will usually send brochures and photographs on request. **St John Properties**, PO Box 700, St John USVI 00831 (tel 776 7223, fax 776 6192) has some very attractive villas for hire, or you can try **Vacation Vistas**, PO Box 476 (tel 776 6462). Prices range from $100–400 per day for a single bedroom villa.

EATING OUT
The most stylish dining in St John is to be found in the big hotels, but the new shopping centres have brought some chi-chi new eateries around town. The larger restaurants will accept credit cards.

Paradiso Restaurant, bistro and cocktail bar (tel 776 8806) is in the new shopping centre at Mongoose Junction II. Hardwood and imitation marble and pastel colours and a lively crowd. The menu is Italian—try the seafood *puttanesca* with shrimp scallops and olives. Main dish $15. The **Café Roma** (tel 776 6524) also serves Italian food in a pretty tropical dining room upstairs on Main St in Cruz Bay. Venetian shrimp in lemon and garlic and a multiplicity of pizzas. Main dish $12. The **Lime Inn** (tel 776 6425) is a lively restaurant with tables around a breezy gallery set back from the street. Fresh seafood— shrimp Dijon—or a New York strip if you feel too far from home. The **Old Gallery** (tel 776 7544) is set in a classic West Indian town house with wooden dining room upstairs and on the veranda. Rice 'n' peas as well as steaks and pizzas, $12. Or you can try nearby **Fred's** (tel 776 6363) for a chicken or fish, or a goat stew. $8 for a main course. Finally, to round off an evening drop in to the **Garden of Luscious Licks** on Main Street, where you will find health foods and ice creams. Fresh salads, good veggieburgers, juices, brownie bars and peace pops. 'The heart knows the soul better than the mind does...' Cheap.

At the other end of the island you will also find good places to eat in **Coral Bay**, where the waterfront settings pick up the daytime and evening breeze. **Shipwreck Landing** (tel 776 8640) is right on the sea and will serve you local catch in batter or a fried chicken for about $10. Not far off, **Sea Breeze** serves barbecued and grilled food (a different menu by the day) for around $10.

BARS
St John can get surprisingly lively and at the weekend you will find Cruz Bay buzzing until at least midnight. Some of the bars employ bands. Wharfside Village is the busiest area, where **Beni Iguana** seems to attract a fun crowd. The **Pusser's Pub** is done up in the brass and polished wood of mock nauticalia—there is an oyster bar in the **Crow's Nest** with a good view of the harbour. **Larry's Landing** is a beer and pool bar. Two local bars are **Back Yard** and **Cap's Place**, the haunt of the Puerto Rican community, audible by the blaring salsa music.

The British Virgin Islands

Tortola, Jost van Dyke, Virgin Gorda, Anegada and others

The British Virgin Islands—50-odd reefs, rocks and raging volcanic towers—are sprinkled across the sea to the northeast of the USVI. They run in two lines about three miles apart, enclosing the Sir Francis Drake Channel. The bays make magnificent anchorages, as good now as when Columbus passed by and later when the pirates skulked here. The British Virgin Islands are great islands on which to be marooned (particularly in five-star luxury).

The British Virgins are undeveloped in comparison with their American counterparts. There is none of the hustle and bustle of St Thomas; life is run at a far more stately pace. Construction is only beginning to break the green continuity of the hillside scrub and there are no high-rise buildings anyway. They say the BVI are twenty years behind the USVI, but in recent years at least, the islanders are happy with it that way.

There are about 17,000 inhabitants in the BVI, most of whom live on Tortola. However, for generations they have been travelling to the USVI and so there is probably

Yachts in the BVI

a larger number than this living in the American Virgins. These *belongers* go there to work, returning regularly to see their families and to build a house for their retirement. The old traditional West Indian life of fishermen or farmers, working a small plot of land in the hills with a few domestic animals has all but gone now. The BVIers are building frantically at the moment, cashing in as investors come to look for holiday homes.

The islanders have occasionally considered some sort of union with the USVI. The opportunity was there in the 1950s, but the general mood today is that they are right not to have made the link. They are happy to have the US dollar as their currency and with their special status of belongers in the USVI, but they also talk fearfully of how the USVI has been overdeveloped and of the crime-levels. In the BVI the policemen carry truncheons rather than guns. Some islanders claim that the very word British adds a stability of sorts.

Most BVIers admit that American influence will inevitably increase and the old British ways recede. There is continual American investment and most consumer goods originate in the USA anyway. Most sides of life seems to be headed in that direction. Nowadays the BVIers are just as likely to play softball as cricket.

About 200,000 tourists visit the BVI each year, of which the majority come for the sailing and the BVI angles its tourism at the upper end of the market. Recent developments have brought to the BVI a feel of a Caribbean playground, so you can get a very good tropical break here and for a price you can get the seclusion of a tropical island.

History

History and legend are closely intertwined in the Virgin Islands—the coves and bays that make such perfect anchorages were for centuries a pirate hangout and so the two have become confused. As late as 1792, when the British had officially been in control for over 100 years, Tortola was still described as a 'pirates' den'. The islands' most important industry, smuggling, was never recorded anyway.

When Columbus first arrived here in the late 15th century, the Virgin Islands were seeing waves of the belligerent Carib Indians from down-island passing through, stopping by before they raided Arawak Borinquen (now Puerto Rico) in the quest for enemies to barbecue. The fact that the Spaniards settled Puerto Rico made no difference, they were still a good target and were just as tasty. But the Spaniards turned out to be more of a match than the Arawaks and in 1555 they bore down on the Caribs in the Virgin Islands and wiped them out.

Soon after the Caribs were eliminated another threat began appearing in the Virgin Islands—pirates. They used the bays to anchor and climbed the heights to watch for a sail to appear on the horizon. Jack Hawkins and Sir Francis Drake also passed through, the latter giving his name to the channel through which he escaped in 1585 after raiding the Spanish *flota* with the riches of Mexico aboard. There are of course endless legends of buried treasure in the BVI.

The first permanent settlers on the islands were Dutch buccaneers and cattle ranchers, who arrived on Tortola in 1648. They barbecued beef rather than human limbs and sold the smoked meat to passing ships. In 1672 they were ousted by English buccaneers and the eastern Virgin Islands were taken over by England. Despite the official status, the smuggling continued as the buccaneers became settled.

Although the islands are not particularly fertile, they were able to grow cotton and experienced some prosperity in the sugar era of the 18th century. Slaves were brought here and the steep hillsides were terraced and planted with cotton and cane. Quakers who came to the islands had a hand in freeing some of the slaves (they thought slavery immoral and rallied against it) and the plantations folded quickly, even before emancipation in 1838. As they failed, so the white population left. In 1805 the population was about 10,500 (9000 slaves) and a century later there were 5000, of whom two were white. The islanders became subsistence farmers on the land abandoned by the white settlers. This has only changed in the last few years with the advent of the tourist industry.

Early on the British Virgin Islands were governed by an elected council, but in 1867 this was abolished and the islands were simply appended to the Leeward Island Federation as a 'Presidency'. The British Virgin Islands are still a Crown Colony of Britain and are nominally administered by a Governor appointed in London, but since the war the Virgin Islands have steadily taken on internal self-government. There is a 12-member elected council with a ministerial system. The Chief Minister is the Hon H Lavity Stoutt of the Virgin Islands Party.

Lying so close to their American counterparts, the British Virgin Islands have often considered political union with the USVI. In the 50s, as the other British Caribbean countries moved together in Federation, the British Virgins turned away and seemed to be on the point of making the link. There were even rumours in the 1960s that the British Government had offered to sell the islands to the United States. But no union was formed and most of the islanders feel that it was the right decision.

The biggest foreign exchange earner is tourism: of the 200,000 visitors each year, there are 60,000 cruise ship arrivals and of the rest 60 per cent come for the sailing. Other industries include some light manufacturing and an expanding off-shore finance sector.

FESTIVALS

The highlight of the BVI calendar is the three-day **Carnival** held in early August, when the floats and dancers parade along the waterfront in Road Town, Tortola. Go if you get the chance. The main **regatta** arranged by the BVI Yacht Club is held each year in April, but smaller events are held all year round.

GETTING TO THE BVI

The islands are still relatively remote—the biggest aircraft that can land on the BVI is a 49-seater. Airstrips on the islands include Beef Island (for Tortola), Virgin Gorda and Anegada. The main hub in the area is San Juan in Puerto Rico and plenty of airlines make this connection—LIAT (tel 494 3888), Sunaire Express (tel 495 2840), American Eagle (tel 495 2559) and GAS (Gorda Air Services) (tel 495 2271).

From the UK: British Airways has connecting flights, some on the same day, via Puerto Rico and Antigua. BWIA also makes a twice weekly link between London and Antigua, in time to make connections.

From the USA: connecting flights can be arranged via San Juan, Puerto Rico (e.g. American Airlines and Delta from Atlanta) and through the USVI.

From other Caribbean islands: There are flights to Tortola from St Thomas, Puerto Rico, Antigua, Anguilla and Sint Maarten. Services to Virgin Gorda are more limited.

There are also many charter companies. For details on air and sea services between the BVI and USVI, see USVI p. 381. There is a departure tax of $5 if you are leaving by air and US$3 if departing on a boat or ferry.

GETTING AROUND THE BVI
GAS (Gorda Air Services) flies from Tortola to Virgin Gorda and to Anegada.

BVI Ferries
The islands are well served with ferries (the main terminals are at West End and Road Town on Tortola; the Valley and North Sound in Virgin Gorda). For sailings between the USVI and the BVI, see details on p. 381.

There are four or five sailings each day between Road Town and the Valley, Fare $10. Two companies run the route: **Speedy's** (tel 55240) and **Smith's Ferry Services** (tel 44430). Up to the minute schedules can be found in the BVI *Welcome* Tourist Magazine. The North Sound Express (tel 809 494 2746) meets flights in Beef Island if you want to go to the northern end of Virgin Gorda (Leverick Bay and Bitter End). Four trips a day, Price $15. The boats are sleek and fun to ride as they skim across the water with a sonorous rumble. There is also a link from the Valley on Virgin Gorda to Beef Island for the airport.

There are five or six daily sailings from West End to Jost van Dyke—Reel World (tel 59277) and Jost van Dyke Ferry Services (tel 52775). Peter Island is served by the Peter Island Boat, which departs from the CSY Marina in Road Town. About six crossings a day, $10.

An alternative in all the Virgin Islands is to go to the marinas and talk somebody into taking you to the island that they area sailing to.

Charter Companies and Marinas
The **Moorings** have the largest selection of bare-boats for charter in the BVI and they are based in Wickham's Cay II in Road Town. Address PO Box 139, Road Town (tel 809 494 2331, fax 494 2226). Rates run at $85–110 per person per day in the winter season. For a skippered yacht you can contact **BVI Sailing**, PO Box 146 (tel 494 2774, fax 494 6774). You could also try **Sun Sail Yachts** at Frenchman's Cay, PO Box 609, West End (tel 495 4740), or **North Sound Yacht Vacations** at Nanny Cay, PO Box 281 (tel 494 0096), both of which hire yachts at between $1700 and $3500 per week.

In Virgin Gorda you can contact the **Bitter End Yacht Club** in the North Sound, PO Box 46 (tel 809 494 2746) or **Misty Isle Yacht Charters**, PO Box 1118 (tel 809 495 5643, fax 495 5300).

There are many marinas in the BVI where you can dock and service a yacht, including Wickham's Cay II, Village Cay, PO Box 1456 (tel 494 2771) and Soper's Hole at West End, PO Box 601 (tel 809 495 4553). In Virgin Gorda you can go to the Virgin Gorda Yacht Harbour, PO Box 1005 (tel 809 495 5555) and the Bitter End Yacht Club.

TOURIST INFORMATION
The BVI Tourist Board has offices in:
UK: 110 St Martin's Lane, London WC2N 4DY (tel 071 240 4259, fax 240 4270).

410

THE BRITISH VIRGIN ISLANDS

USA: 370 Lexington Ave, Suite 511, New York, NY 10017 (tel (212) 696 0400, toll free 800 835 8530), or 1686 Union St, San Francisco, CA 94123, (tel (415) 775 0344, toll free 800 232 7770).
Germany: AM Kappelgarten 42, D 6000, Frankfurt am Main (tel 069 477223, fax 069 477235).

In the BVI itself, the main Tourist Board is in the Social Security building in Road Town on Tortola, PO Box 134, Road Town (tel 494 3134, fax 494 3866). The Tourist Board put out the quarterly *Welcome Tourist Guide*, in which you will find plenty of useful information about current events and the latest investment opportunities.

In a medical **emergency**, dial 998 or contact the Peebles Hospital in Road Town (tel 43497), Tortola. On Virgin Gorda there are two clinics: in Spanish Town (tel 55337) and at North Sound (tel 57310).

The **IDD code** for the BVI is 809 49 followed by five digits. On island, you dial just the last five figures of the number.

MONEY

The currency of the BVI is the US dollar (adopted in 1967). You will find that major credit cards are very widely accepted in the hotels, restaurants and shops. Traveller's cheques carry a 10c stamp duty. **Banking** hours are weekdays 9–2.30 with an extra slot on Friday afternoons, 4.30–6. Shops generally keep hours of 9–5, Mon–Sat.

TORTOLA and BEEF ISLAND

Tortola (the Turtle Dove) is the largest of the British Virgins (21 square miles) and set in a huge bay on its south coast is the BVI capital, Road Town. The island is irregularly shaped, long and thin, and ten miles by three, but it is so mountainous that you cannot cross over from one side to the other without ascending to about 1200 feet. **Mount Sage**, whose upper slopes are covered with lush and explosive greenery that is almost rain-forest, is the highest point in all the Virgins (1780 ft). About 10,000 of the 17,000 population live on the island, but this makes it almost sound busy, which is not the case.

GETTING AROUND TORTOLA

There is a rudimentary **bus service** that runs along the south coast of Tortola, (fares $1–3, timings unpredictable). Catch it if you can find it. Hitch-hiking is possible and about as haphazard as anywhere else. The most reliable method of travel is via **taxi** and these are easily found in town and the airport/ferry terminals. Fix the price beforehand. Rates are pretty high, about US$14 from **Road Town** to West End, Cane Garden Bay or Beef Island. You can order one through the **BVI Taxi Association** (tel 42322). There are also one or two safari bus tours around the island arranged for the cruise-ship arrivals. Price around US$12 for an island tour if there are enough people. Contact the Taxi Association or **Style's Taxi Service** (tel 42260).

Of course maximum flexibility comes with your own **hire car**, but at a price (from $35 per day). If you wish to drive in the BVI, you must obtain a BVI temporary driving licence (from the car rental agency or traffic department on production of $10 and a valid licence from elsewhere). There is often a hefty deposit (credit cards OK). Driving is on the left

411

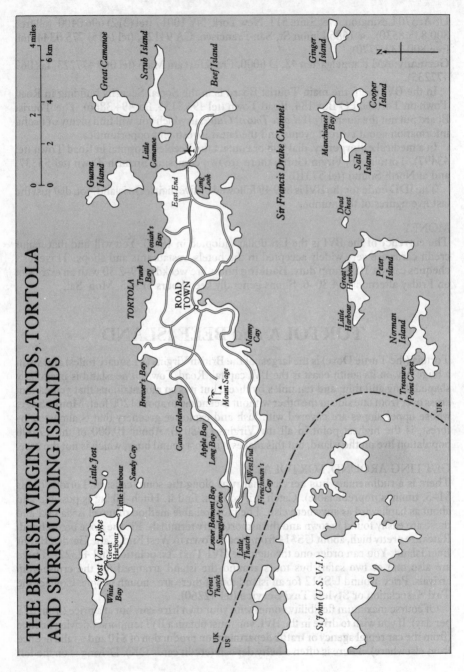

THE BRITISH VIRGIN ISLANDS, TORTOLA
AND SURROUNDING ISLANDS

and the speed limit is a princely 30 mph in the country and 10 or 15 in town. Some rental firms are, **Anytime Car Rental** at Wayside Inn (tel 43107), **Island Suzuki** near Nanny Cay (tel 43666) and **Budget Rent-a-Car** (tel 42639) at Wickhams Cay II in Road Town.

BEACHES

The best beaches on the island are along the north coast, protected by the massive volcanic shoulders that lumber out of the water. If there is a busy beach then it will be there. On the south coast the sand is not so good, but you will have good winds for windsurfing and sailing in the channel.

The most popular beach is **Cane Garden Bay**, up over the hill from Road Town, where there is a little collection of houses and a couple of hotels and a cracking view of Jost van Dyke. You can get hold of windsurfers and small yachts here when frying in coconut oil loses its appeal.

Travelling west of Cane Garden Bay you come to **Apple Bay** and **Carrot Bay**, and then over the hill to **Long Bay** and **Belmont Bay**. **Smuggler's Cove** (or Lower Belmont Bay) is the most secluded of them all, down towards the west end of the island and there is good snorkelling there.

Off the incredibly steep road over to town there is a jeep-trail down to **Brewer's Bay**, which is secluded and has a campsite, with a bar on the sand. Both these two bays are good for snorkelling. **Trunk Bay** and **Josiah's Bay**, which has excellent sand, when it is not being carted off for construction, are further east and very isolated. They are a good stop in a yacht, though Josiah's Bay can be reached by land. Take a picnic.

There is another **Long Bay** on Tortola, or at least on Beef Island just close to the aiport. Looking across to Great and Little Camanoe, this Long Bay arches in a stunning half-mile strip of soft white sand and shelves gently into calm translucent water. The snorkelling on the Camanoes and Scrub Island is excellent.

BEACH BARS

The BVI has some classic beach bars, of which Tortola's best is **Bomba's Surf Shack** on Apple Bay. True to its name it is a shack, made of driftwood (Bomba's was one of the few places to benefit from Hurricane Hugo; the flotsam became an extension). Great spot for chilling out, particularly at the monthly full moon party, famous for its jars of unusual drinks additives. Who knows, perhaps you too will feel like decorating the walls with your knickers after a heavy evening's liming. Surfing when the waves are up.

Cane Garden Bay has a number of bars right on the sand where you can retreat for a beer and a chicken or fish platter, for about $10 and watch the yachts run over to Jost van Dyke. You can chill out at **Stanley's Welcome Bar** or play darts as you drink at the **Paradise Club** next to Rhymers. At the end of the beach is the orange and blue bar **the Wedding**, where you can get a bride's delight cocktail if it's appropriate.

If you are in Trellis Bay on Beef Island you can stop for a snack at **De Loose Mongoose**, a friendly bar on the beach.

WATERSPORTS

Windsurfers will find equipment and lessons at **Boardsailing BVI** at Nanny Cay (tel 42512) and in the northeast on Trellis Bay (tel 52447), a good place to learn because the

413

winds are funnelled between the islands into the bay where the water remains calm. Hire costs around $15 per hour, $45 per day. If you would like to test out the Virgin Islands winds and waters, but would rather not take out a 50ft yacht, many of the hotels have sunfish or hobie cats. You can get instruction at the Treasure Isle Offshore Sailing School (tel 45119).

The BVI have some superb reefs for **scuba diving**, where staghorn and elkhorn stand tall by sponges and sea-fans and patrols of sergeant majors and triggerfish follow wrasses, grunts and groupers. Spiked urchins and spiny lobster lurk in the depths. The most renowned dive is the *RMS Rhone*, a Royal Mail ship that sank off Salt Island in a hurricane in 1867. Some of it lies in 40 feet of water; other bits of this 310 ft vessel are at 90 ft.

For all the islands that soar to 1000 feet from the sandy bed there are also plenty of coral-clad pinnacles that do not quite make the surface, and these make good diving grounds. Other dive-sites include the *Chikuzen*, a ship in 70 feet of water, six miles north of Beef Island; **Blonde Rock** and **Painted Walls** between Dead Chest and Salt Island; the **Indians** near Norman Island and the **Dogs** off Virgin Gorda. Anegada in the north, the only coral-based island in the group, has extremely rich marine life too.

Dive companies include **Island Diver** from Road Town (tel 43878), which offer resort courses and photographic equipment, **Underwater Safaris** (tel 43235) at the Moorings in town, **Baskin in the Sun** (run by Alan Baskin), who also offer lessons (tel 42858), or **Blue Water Divers** at Nanny Cay Marine Centre (tel 42847). Single tank dives cost from $40.

You can find deep water for **sport-fishing** close to the BVI, so if you wish to cruise after wahoo, marlin and kingfish, go to **Charter Fishing Virgin Islands** (tel 43311) at the Prospect Reef Hotel, where a day's outing will cost around $650. The BVI Yacht Club arranges about five tournaments in the year.

OTHER SPORTS
There are **tennis courts** in many of the hotels on the island and at the **Tortola Tennis Club** in Road Town (tel 43733). If you would like to explore the island on **horseback**, contact **Shadows** (tel 42262), who will take you through the hills and down to Cane Garden Bay.

WHAT TO SEE
Strung along the water's edge, **Road Town** takes its name from the bay on which it sits, Road Harbour (a 'road' was an open anchorage in the 17th century) and it is the centre of government and most business activity. It is a pretty ugly town. The ferries dock on the southwestern side of the bay and you can walk just across the way to the shops, set in the old-time BVI buildings. A little deeper into the bay are newer office buildings, which have been thrown up with abandon, without any thought to the appearance of the town. At the foot of the hillside behind them is a clutch of local BVI homes, clapboard wood with shingle tiles.

A quick look will suffice at the **BVI Folk Museum** on Main Street, where there are displays of Arawak pottery, plantation tools and chinaware from the *RMS Rhone*, the mail-packet that sank off Salt Island in 1867. Open Mon, Tues, Thur, Fri, 10–4 and Sun, 10–1. There are some small **Botanical Gardens**, where the familiar flamboyant and bougainvillaea throw out their magnificent blooms around the lily pond and the fern house, just off Main Street farther inland. Open Mon–Sat, 9.30–5.30 and Sun, noon–5. Roads follow the wiggly coastline to Tortola's other small settlements, West End and Long Look, where many 'Belongers' have returned to build their homes, but to get to Cane Garden Bay (a popular north-coast bay), you must head inland and up. The ridge road runs the backbone of Tortola and gives some superb views of the other islands.

In the **Sage Mountain National Park** trails are cut through the small patch of (almost) rainforest, where hanging vines grapple you as you pass and the ferns and philodendrons quiver on the breeze. Since the 1960s, the park has been allowed to grow naturally and the vegetation, which looks more like that on the bigger Windward Islands, is thought to be similar to the island's original growth, before the land was cleared for planting. From here, as from many parts of the island, the views are superb.

Frenchman's Cay is at the western end of the island. Once it was a favoured pirate hideout—it was easily defended and had good look-outs. It is still a working shipyard with a collection of pretty pastel boutiques and bars. Opposite, West End is the ferry terminal for the USVI and Jost van Dyke.

Across the toll bridge at the eastern end of Tortola is **Beef Island**, the site of the airport. It takes its name from its former use as a cattle ranch by buccaneers, but now all there is to see are a few goats and guest houses, private villas and the occasional 48-seater plane pitching and reeling as it comes in to land.

Great Camanoe and **Scrub Island** also lie off the northeast tip of the island and they have a few private homes. To visit them, take a boat from Beef Island. **Guana Island** is private and is devoted to a hotel, a classic island retreat (see below).

WHERE TO STAY
The BVI's smartest hotels are on Virgin Gorda or on their own island, but there are some comfortable spots on Tortola as well as some cheaper places to stay. You can also arrange a villa through **Rockview Holiday Homes** (tel 494 2550, US 800 782 4304), or **Virgin Holidays** (tel 494 0014). A government tax of 7% will be added to all bills.

EXPENSIVE
The **Guana Island Club** (tel 494 2354, fax 495 2900, US 800 544 8262) offers some of the best in Virgin Islands' luxury and seclusion, on a private island of 850 acres just north of Beef Island. Tennis and watersports are there—windsurfing, sailing, fishing trips and seven beaches—but the club is most special for its gracious atmosphere amid superb hillside settings. From solitude in one of the very comfortable rooms you can venture to the company of the main house (relative company anyway because there are a maximum of 30 guests), with dining room and of course library. Afternoon tea, honour bar and you dress for dinner (a shirt and trousers at least). Seclusion in luxury for $385–530 a double or $7400 the whole island if you feel like it. The **Long Bay Beach Resort**, PO Box 433 (tel 809 495 4252, US 800 729 9599), has some excellent new rooms among the cabanas that stand high above the seagrape on Long Bay beach. There are 65 rooms in all (some new and plush, others a bit more rarefied rustic), and there are villas on the hillside behind, but the grounds are large and there are sports for the active in body. Position relative to the superb beach determines price, which ranges from $240–340 for a double in season. The **Sugar Mill**, PO Box 425 (tel 495 4355, fax 495 4696, US 800 462 8834)

retains something of the planters' West Indies, set in the restored estate buildings. The 20 rooms are modern, white and bright with a view of Jost van Dyke from the balcony, over the pool and seaside restaurant. The dining room, considered one of the best on the island, is set in the antique stone walls of the old boiling house and you eat to the tune of water falling into copper kettles. A set menu revolves every fortnight—roast turkey breast with mango and plantain or spicy chicken with pineapple salsa, price $35. Rooms cost $150–215 in season. The **Frenchman's Cay Resort Hotel**, PO Box 1054, West End (tel 495 4844, fax 495 4056, US 800 235 4077) is another haven of high Tortolan luxury. The one-bed and two-bedroom villas overlook the tennis court, pool and restaurant away to the sails of the yachts on Sir Francis Drake Channel. Full kitchens; 1 bed villa $170 in season, 2 bed $270.

MODERATE

If you want a comfortable spot in town, you might try **Treasure Isle**, PO Box 68 (tel 494 2501, fax 494 2507, US 800 334 2435), which stands above the marinas on the hillside. Pretty in yellow and pink, with pool and restaurant. Double room $155 in season and $215 for a suite. There is a friendly guest house in Trellis Bay, the **Beef Island Guest House**, PO Box 494 (tel 495 2303). Just four rooms a little past their prime, but a fun spot with De Loose Mongoose nearby. Double room $100 in season.

CHEAP

The **Cane Garden Bay Beach Hotel**, best known as Rhymer's, PO Box 570 (tel 495 4639) has quite simple rooms, superb views and a good beach. Double $70 in season. The **Tamarind Country Club**, PO Box 509 (tel 495 2477) has rooms at about the same price. It is also worth asking around in Cane Garden Bay. Mrs Hodges has rooms for $40. There is a camp-ground in Brewer's Bay on the north coast, with showers, loos and a concessionary shop; bare site costs $7 and a fixed-base tent $20.

EATING OUT

EXPENSIVE

The two top dining rooms on Tortola are probably the **Sugar Mill** (tel 54355), set price $35 exclusive of wine (see where to stay) and **Brandywine** (tel 52301), east of Road Town, towards Beef Island. The menu is international with a twist of Florence in the lobster ravioli and *pollastrella alla Daviola*. Striking views of Sir Francis Drake Channel from the terrace. Main course $18 plus, closed Sun. There are a number of good spots in town—perhaps try the **Fort Burt** (tel 42587), which sits on a stone terrace with a nice view over the harbour. Local soups followed by lobster in butter sauce or shrimp sautéed in garlic for $18 dollars a main course. At lunch you might ask for the *trenchman's menu*, same dishes, $10. **Pusser's Outpost** (tel 42467) is a leading light in town, upstairs from the bar where the tourists and the yachties mix—stained wood and wicker chairs and maquettes of sailing ships and figure-heads. International menu; beef Wellington or tenderloin in flaky pastry. $20 a main course. On the harbour itself is the **Captain's Table** (tel 43885), which overlooks Wickham's Cay marina from a terrace festooned with greenery. French menu—duck in sweet cherry sauce—with some Cajun—blackened fresh catch—followed by crêpe suzette—$17 a main course.

Close by, the **Wharf** (tel 43626) has a nightly barbecue—chicken, fish or ribs on the veranda. The best in West Indian food can be found at **C&F Bar and Restaurant** (tel 44941) just out of Road Town. Classic setting on a porch with plastic tablecloths and waiters watching the telly. Delicious shrimp in lemon butter and a tonnage of ground provision, $12. Go east from town, turn left at the roundabout, left again and it's at the next turning right. Alternatively you might try **Mrs Scatliffe's** Restaurant (tel 54556), set on the balcony of her home in Carrot Bay, where you will be fed callaloo with home-made bread, coconut chicken, and superb ice creams. Finally you might also try the **Roti Palace** on Abbott Rd in town, for a spicy envelope of bread with chicken or beef.

The **Last Resort** (tel 52520) is a final exotic spot for dinner in Trellis Bay—open veranda with barrel chairs and a donkey that wanders among the tables occasionally. Pumpkin soup followed by chicken in curry and honey (or roast beef and Yorkshire pudding) and particularly noted for a show in which the owner takes the mickey out of life, the universe and yachtsmen. Set dinner $23.

BARS

There is always a lively drinking crowd out in Tortola—yachties and newcomers alike. There are plenty of tourist bars, with the pretty mock-nautical setting of the Pusser's Pubs, but there are also classic West Indian rum-shacks too. The national drink of the BVI (for the tourists anyway) is the *Painkiller*, usually mixed with local Pusser's Rum—cream of coconut, orange juice, pineapple juice and rum, topped with nutmeg, but you might pick up an exotic cocktail like a *Gulf Crisis*. Most bars have a happy hour to catch you early.

In town an ever-popular haunt is the **Pusser's Store and Pub**, just across from the ferry terminal in Road Town, where the dark-stained wood and brass is a bit reminiscent of an English pub, as is next door, the **Tavern on the Town**. A more traditionally Caribbean waterfront bar is the **Paradise Club**, set around a courtyard beneath Fort Burt. The **West End** has some good bars—**Pusser's** on Frenchman's Cay is pink and ever-popular, and across the bay, garish in even more outrageous lavender and fuschia is the **Jolly Roger**, which has seen some riotous excesses in its time, as the name would suggest. And the **beach bars** in Apple Bay and Cane Garden Bay are of course lively. Finally, if you want a cocktail and a fantastic view you can go to **Skyworld**, where you can get yourself a *Gulf Crisis* or a *SCUD*.

Many of the bars and beach bars have live music in season—ask around. More regular discotheques include **Pegleg Landing** at Nanny Cay and the disco at Fort Burt marina.

JOST VAN DYKE

The little island of Jost van Dyke lies about four miles off Tortola's West End. It is a perfect place to be marooned. There is hardly anything there—just a couple of square miles of scrub, about 120 inhabitants and idyllic beaches and bars to retreat to. A dirt track leads from Great Harbour, the port of entry, to Little Harbour at the east end of the island, but there are hardly any vehicles and the island has only just received electricity. There is nothing to see above the waterline.

THE CARIBBEAN

And yet Jost van Dyke, which supposedly takes its name from a Dutch pirate, used to be cultivated from the shoreline to the tops of the hills (highest 1070 ft), terraced to grow cotton and sugar-cane. In those days this barren outcrop was quite prosperous. It is also the birthplace of two famous men.

Dr John Lettsom was born to a Quaker planter family in 1744 and eventually became the founder of the London (later British) Medical Society and the Royal Humane Society. He is remembered for his efforts in the rhyme:

> *I, John Lettsom,*
> *blisters, bleeds and sweats 'em*
> *If, after that, they please to die*
> *I, John Lettsom.*

His fellow Quaker, born on the island in 1759, was William Thornton, another medical doctor, who campaigned against slavery in the islands. He became a US citizen and won the competition to design the Capitol in Washington, later serving as the first superintendent of the US Patent Office.

BEACHES
There are two fantastic bays on the south coast: **Great Harbour** and **White Bay**, where the snorkelling is particularly good. And off the east end of the island there are other superb strips of sand. **Sandy Cay** is a blip with a fine beach and good snorkelling and **Sandy Spit**, off Green Cay, is the archetypal sandy spit with nothing but a few palm trees and luscious, foot-deep sand.

WHERE TO STAY
There are few places to stay on Jost van Dyke. The **Sandcastle** is a Caribbean dream. Just four breezy cottages lost in the sea grape and the palms on White Bay, a stunning white-sand cove with absurdly blue water. Very secluded and low-key—hammocks, watersports if you want them, an honour bar and passing yachtsmen who drop by. Few places like it, $295 a double in season. Address: Suite 237, Red Hook Plaza, St Thomas, USVI 00802 (tel 809 496 0496, USVI 809 775 5262, fax 775 3590). **Rudy's Mariner Inn**, Great Harbour (tel 495 9282 or 775 3558) is friendly and has just three rooms with kitchenettes. Prices vary, $75–220. Over in Little Harbour you can get a room for $60 at **Harris's Place** or a tent for two for $35 at **Tula's N&N Campground**, $15 a bare site (both tel 495 9302, fax 495 9296).

EATING OUT AND BARS
All the restaurants in Jost van Dyke double as bars and some of them have entertainment and a barbecue in the week. You can have a candlelit dinner above the surf at the Sandcastle—fresh local fish and vegetables done to a turn or continental dishes like duck à l'orange. Reserve on channel 16 by 4 pm, about $30 for a set meal. If you are stopping by just for a drink, try **Gertrude's**.

Great Harbour is really one long string of beach bars where you can also get a meal. **Club Paradise** will fix you a soup or a salad for $5 or a fish for $15. **Ali Baba's**, is a covered terrace on the sand and then an attractive wooden bar. At the eastern end of the bay is **Foxy's** (reserve Channel 16 or call 59258), a riotous place under the palms on the

418

waterfront. Foxy himself will occasionally sing to you over the barbecue and in season he has live music a couple of times a week, but the highlight of the year is the New Year's Eve party, which attracts as many as 2500 people from 300 yachts. All the bars along the waterfront have bands and so there is drinking and *jumping up* until near dawn. Also very popular is Foxy's wooden boat regatta.

VIRGIN GORDA

Virgin Gorda lies within sight of Tortola across Sir Francis Drake Channel, and when you get there Road Town seems almost like an uncaring metropolis. Life proceeds at an even more sedate pace and you will find that the people all greet each other here. Come to that, they may all know each other anyway, because there are only 1500 of them.

Virgin *Gorda* was the 'fat Virgin' according to the Spaniards, because they thought its shape from the south was like a pregnant woman reclining. The island is eight square miles in area and, like Tortola, it is long and irregularly shaped, rising from plains in the south to 1370 ft at Gorda Peak in the north. Generally speaking, the island is furred with scrub and cactus, inhabited by lizards and geckos. Supposedly there is also a very rare five-foot iguana who lives in the hills. Birds include warblers and the usual cattle egrets on the plains and you may find that the odd cheeky pearly-eyed thrasher takes a fancy to your lunch.

For a while Virgin Gorda was the capital island among the British Virgins, but in 1741 Tortola took over. The island splits quite neatly into two, with settlements at each end, barely connected through the hilly scrubland between. To the south is Spanish Town, or the Valley as it is known, the closest thing to a town; its few houses are scattered over the plain. In the north is the North Sound, a huge bay almost enclosed by islands and reefs.

The south of the island is best known for the curious assembly of vast rocks called **the Baths**, a giant's playground of granite boulders at the southwest tip of the island. These smooth rocks, which hardly seem to belong in the Caribbean, are buried to their necks in sand and jumbled on one another, creating caverns where the waves crash and the water races. The remains of a very early copper mine can be found close by on the southeastern tip of the island. More granite boulders like those at the Baths make up **Fallen Jerusalem** off the south coast of the island. It has this name because it looks like a ruined town crumbling into the water. The island is a National Park and so fishing is prohibited, as is collecting the corals. You are asked to be careful when anchoring a yacht or swimming near the reef.

Overlooking the North Sound you will find Leverick Bay, a tourist development of hotels and villas, and **Gun Creek**, a local town scattered over the hillside. Opposite them are the Bitter End Yacht Club and Biras Creek and enclosing the North Sound are Mosquito and Prickly Pear Islands and tiny Saba Rock. Slightly further out are Eustatia Island and **Necker Island**, a small green lump rimmed with sand set in the translucent blue. It is owned by Richard Branson, founder of Virgin Records, who has built a house there in Balinese style, complete with outsize furniture and a split-level jacuzzi/pool. It is private (above the high-water mark), but you can hire it for the meagre sum of $7500 per day (up to 10 people), or $9000 for 11–20 people), contact in UK, 5 The Lanchesters,

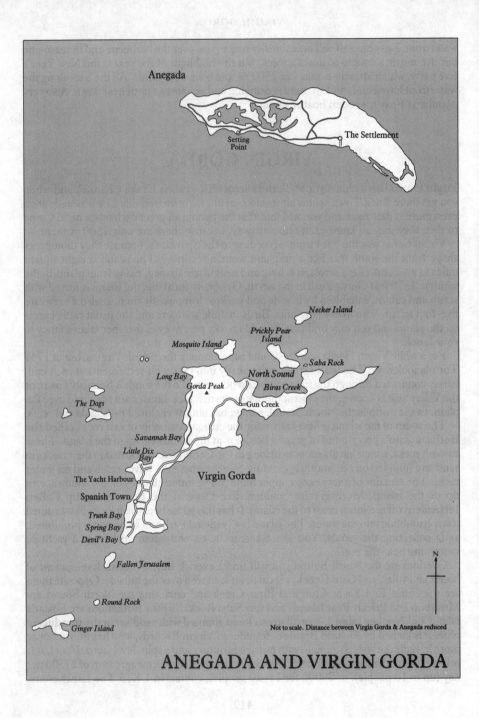

Anegada

Setting
Point

The Settlement

Necker Island

Prickly Pear
Island

Mosquito Island

Saba Rock

Long Bay

North Sound

Gorda Peak ▲

Biras Creek

The Dogs

Gun Creek

Savannah Bay

Little Dix
Bay

Virgin Gorda

The Yacht Harbour

Spanish Town

Trunk Bay

Spring Bay

Devil's Bay

Fallen Jerusalem

N

Round Rock

Ginger Island

Not to scale. Distance between Virgin Gorda & Anegada reduced

ANEGADA AND VIRGIN GORDA

162–164 Fulham Palace Rd, London W6 9ER (tel 081 741 9980, fax 741 9968, in the US toll free 800 926 0636).

GETTING AROUND
There is nothing like a bus service on Virgin Gorda, but hitching is no problem. Taxis will let you hop in on someone else's a fare and will ask for a few dollars for the ride. There are **hire-cars** and jeeps available (for regulations and prices see under Tortola). Contact **Mahogany Car Rentals** (tel 55542) or **Andy's** (tel 55252), both in the Valley. Taxis can be found through both these operators as well. Hotels often have cars available for their guests too.

BEACHES
In the whiplashes and switchbacks of Virgin Gorda's coastline are some classic Caribbean coves crowned with coral sand, Virgin Gorda also has a fine collection of beach bars. In season the more popular ones can be crowded, but it is usually possible to find a solitary spot. Watersports have to be arranged through the hotels. Some beaches are a little isolated and difficult to get to from the landward side but of course many people will approach from the sea.

The most popular beaches are in the southwest, near the Baths. Here you will sink into the sand up to your ankles and you can swim among the boulders as the waves break over you. You can reach **Devil's Bay** and **The Baths** on marked paths through the scrub, which lead off from **Mad Dog Bar**, a wooden house with a veranda, where you can get a hot dog or a BLT. Shaded by the vast rocks of the Baths is the **Poor Man's Bar**, a shack with some benches where you can get a beer and a snack. Going north are **Spring Bay** and **Trunk Bay**, also known as the Crawl, two other superb spots, often with yachts in the bay.

Other beaches on the west coast include **Savannah Bay**, a broad sweeping arc between towering volcanic hills. Two miles north of here, at the end of a dirt track, is the isolated **Long Bay**, a suntrap backed by mangrove and palms and a view of Tortola.

Leverick Bay is a lively spot with a bar—you can windsurf over to the beaches on Mosquito Island, where there are some good strips of sand to collapse on to. You will find a classic beach bar on Prickly Pear Island—the **Sandbox** is a long wooden shack with seats outside, where you can take time out from the snorkelling and sizzling.

SPORTS
Windsurfing and **sailing** (hire and lessons) can be fixed up through the **Nick Trotter Sailing School** at the Bitter End Yacht Club on North Sound. In the Valley, contact **Misty Isle** (tel 55643), who arrange day sails. Hotels also have equipment. **Scuba diving**, among the snappers and squirrelfish, can be arranged with **Dive BVI** in their shops at the Yacht Harbour near Spanish Town (tel 55513) and in Leverick Bay (tel 57421), or through **Kilbride's Underwater Tours**, which works off Saba Rock in North Sound, PO Box 40, Virgin Gorda (tel 59638, fax 59369). Leverick Bay also has plenty of watersports on offer.

Deep-sea fishing can be fixed up with **Classic** at Biras Creek (tel 43555) and **Kingfisher** (tel 55230) at the Yacht Harbour.

On Virgin Gorda, the Little Dix Bay Resort keeps **horses**, if you would like to explore by riding or to gallop through the surf. **Tennis** courts are also available there (tel 55555), though the guests have priority. If you are in the north of the island, go to Biras Creek (tel 43555) or Leverick Bay (tel 57421).

WHERE TO STAY

EXPENSIVE

In the northern peninsula, **Biras Creek**, PO Box 54 (tel 809 494 3555, fax 494 3557), has been proffering high-grade, low-key luxury to returning guests for years. The thirty rooms are strung out on the breezy Atlantic side (the sweltering beach is tucked in a Caribbean cove. The restaurant is renowned—a superb view from the terrace and the finest local ingredients. Double room $425–475 in season. If you would prefer a busier, more active hotel, you could try the **Bitter End Yacht Club**, also on the North Sound, PO Box 46 (tel 494 2746, fax 494 4756). It is run as a yacht club , with the feel of the nautical life in the dark stained wood and brass and pewter tableware, as well as the constant waterborne activity. And a feeling of desert-island seclusion within a shout of civilization can be found in their luxurious, mock-rustic cabins on the hillside. A couple of restaurants and entertainment in season. Hammocks everywhere. winter rates $350–475, some liveaboard yachts. **Drake's Anchorage**, PO Box 2510 (tel 494 2254, US 800 624 6651) is another idyllic island retreat overlooking the North Sound. Beach club and very low-key, comfortable cottages with louvred windows and fans, strung along the beachfront in a sandy palm garden just out of earshot of one another. Rooms $330–475. People speak highly of the restaurant, where you dine in wicker chairs on a waterfront terrace—dolphin (*mahi-mahi*) in curry and banana, or striploin à la Drake's, $25 for dinner; lunch prickly-pear soup and sandwiches or Anegada conch, $10, call in advance to reserve. The **Leverick Bay Resort**, PO Box 63 (tel 495 7421, fax 495 7367, US 800 848 7081) offers the last expensive deal in this area, a double room on the hillside for $119 (**Moderate**). You can also hire a villa in the north of the island through **Virgin Gorda Villa Rentals Ltd**, who work through the same office.

In the southern half of the island, **Little Dix Bay**, PO Box 70 (tel 495 5555, fax 495 5661, US 800 223 7637) is a grand and luxurious resort where guests have been returning for decades. It is quite large (102 rooms), but it is well spread out in tropical gardens around the central sugar mill. Watersports, tennis and all meals accompany Caribbean island tranquillity for a cool $480–495 a double in season.

MODERATE

A more affordable but just as charming place to stay is the **Olde Yard Inn**, PO Box 26 (tel 495 5544, fax 5968, US 800 633 7411), just off the road to the north of the island. The 14 rooms, fan ventilated (some a/c if you want) overlook a charming garden, and over the main house and the library, two important gathering places. A writer's retreat with a touch of traditional West Indian charm. Double in winter $165–230 in winter. **Guavaberry Spring Bay**, PO Box 20 (tel 495 5227), in the southern part of the island, is a surprising resort; hexagonal chalets on stilts, swallowed in explosions of tropical plants and the rocks of the Baths. You can cater for yourselves in a single bedroom villa for $130–185 in winter. You will find marginally cheaper accommodation at the **The Wheelhouse**, PO Box 66 (tel 495 5230) in the Valley. Double room $70–80.

EATING OUT

In the north of the island, the **Biras Creek Hotel** (see above) has a magnificent setting high on the hill; *haute cuisine* and a superb wine list, five course dinner for a fixed price of $35 plus service. **Drake's Anchorage** is also renowned (see above). If you are in Leverick Bay you might try the **Pusser's Restaurant**, mock gingerbread and a nautical ambience, plush armchairs and painkillers; Cajun fish or swordfish for $15 and John Courage Beer on tap. For something a little less manicured try the **Pirate's Pub** on Saba Rock, a blip opposite the Bitter End Yacht Club. It flies the skull and crossbones and the bar is tended by washed up yachtsmen and women. Barbecue, booze and a riotous assembly on a good night.

In the southern half of the island try **Chez Michelle** if you would like to eat outside the hotels. The setting is simple and candle-lit, but you might enjoy the lobster Rémy, flambéd in cognac and served with cream and mushrooms or roast rack of lamb in Dijon mustard, garlic and honey, $17 plus for a main course. Be sure not to miss **Teacher Alma's** in the Valley for a local meal—callaloo followed by a curry chicken and local vegetables. Finally the **Sea Turtle** (beached over a hundred yards inland) is an amusing spot frequented by the locals—a bar in a boat with awnings now attached.

ISLANDS IN THE CHAIN

Headed south-west along the line of amoeba-shaped islets and cays on the southern side of Sir Francis Drake Channel, you pass Round Rock and Ginger Island, an uninhabited island, before coming to **Cooper Island**, with its popular anchorage and beautiful curved beach at Manchineel Bay. There are just a few holiday homes built on the scrubby dry hills. There is a single bar and restaurant on the island: the **Cooper Island Beach Club** (VHF Channel 16), which offers daytime meals—conch fritters and chicken roti for $7— and dinner—sautéd shrimp in butter, white wine and garlic for $17, barbecue on Thursdays. It depends on the crowd, but it can get very lively. Watch out for Henry. **Underwater Safaris** runs a dive operation from here, for guided dives and tank refills.

Next in the line is **Salt Island**, 200 hundred acres of scrubland that enclose a salt pond. Once the population of this island was as high as 100 people, mostly involved in the collection of salt, which they would sell to passing ships (the rent of the island is still set at one sack of salt a year payable to the Queen of England, but it is apparently not often demanded any more). Today the population is not usually more than about four or five people.

Nowadays, most people come to Salt Island to visit one of the Caribbean's finest wrecks, the shell of the 310-ft *RMS Rhone*, which lies on her side in two bits in depths from 30–80 ft. Swimming around the hull, now fuzzed with coral growth and home to clouds of grunts that nose at the exhaled bubbles, is an eerie experience. The area around the wreck is a Marine National Park and so the usual rules apply.

Peter Island, which lies about five miles across the Channel from Road Town harbour, is almost entirely devoted to an extremely luxurious hotel. The only other inhabitant lives in a small wooden house across the bay. The **Peter Island Resort**, PO

Box 211 (tel 494 2561, fax 494 2313, US 800 346 4451) has 50 rooms in all, of which the best are on the beach on Deadman's Bay (also one villa). There are two restaurants, newspapers on hand-held sticks in the drawing room and low-key entertainment each night in season. And there are good uncluttered beaches (Deadman's Bay, where the waves break in scallop shells, is charming, and White Bay is reclusive and isolated), watersports and bicycles to get around. Rooms $475–595 a night. If you would like to go over for dinner, or for a day out on the beach (you can use the resort's facilities), the ferry sails about six times a day from the CSY marina on the eastern side of Road Town harbour. Return fare $10.

Just off the island is a cay called **Dead Chest**, a reminder of the pirates who used these anchorages before the sailors arrived. Blackbeard is supposed to have dropped 15 of his more rebellious sidekicks here with just a cutlass and a cask of rum. The pirates did not survive long, but the island was immortalized in the sea-shanty:

> *Fifteen men on a dead man's chest*
> *Yo ho ho and a bottle of rum.*
> *Drink and the Devil have done the rest*
> *Yo ho ho and a bottle of rum.*

The last BVI island in the chain, next to the US Virgin Island of St John, is **Norman Island**, which also features in pirate lore. Treasure has supposedly been found here. Ruins remain from past settlement, but Norman Island is home only to a few goats and seabirds today and the island's only industry is apparently smuggling. The snorkelling at the Treasure Point caves, which are partly submerged in water, is supreme.

ANEGADA

Anegada lies out on its own about 15 miles north of the main group of the British Virgins, visible only from the mountaintops of Tortola and Virgin Gorda. It is unlike the other islands because it is not of volcanic origin. Rather it is a coral cap that just makes it above sea level (there is nothing over 28 ft), rimmed with reefs and about 14 miles of beach. *Anegada* means 'the drowned one' in Spanish, a fitting name because it is full of lagoons and marshes and is occasionally further soaked by passing tidal waves.

At 15 square miles, Anegada is the second largest of the British islands. It is arid and scrubby and supports little life other than goats and donkeys. However, there is a ancient colony of about 400 20-lb, five-ft iguanas. Once these animals lived all over the Virgin Islands, but they featured heavily in a local stew and so they are now endangered. Moves have been made to protect them by taking some to Guana Island off Tortola.

Only about 250 people live on Anegada, centred around **The Settlement**, and traditionally the islanders have depended on the sea for a living. When they were not away pirating or smuggling they fished, or looted the ships that were wrecked on the reefs.

Anegada's underwater life is superb. The coral reefs are endless, forests of sea-fans, barrel-sponges and gorgonians, and they abound with fish—parrotfish, squirrelfish and thin trumpetfish hanging upright in the water. There are an estimated 300 wrecks on Horseshoe Reef which make for good exploring. Dives dropping on to the miles and miles of Horseshoe Reef can be arranged through the Anegada Reef Hotel at Setting Point (tel 58002).

Sport-fishing is also popular because the deep water of the Atlantic is so close by; if you would like to cast for 1000-lb blue marlin or a kingfish, you can contact the same hotel.

There are one or two cars for **hire** on Anegada if you want them. Contact the hotel.

WHERE TO STAY

There is one hotel on the island, the **Anegada Reef Hotel** (tel 809 485 8002, fax 495 9362). With just 12 rooms, the place is small and friendly. The restaurant prepares an excellent lobster as well as other seafood and fish on the beach barbecue. Double rooms $155–215 in winter. There is a campsite on the island, where a tent will set you back about $30.

In town you can eat at **Del's** Restaurant and bar—shrimp or cracked conch for $8 and on the north shore you can get a drink and a snack at the **Big Bamboo** on Loblolly Bay.

Part IV
THE GREATER ANTILLES

Balcony, Old San Juan, Puerto Rico

PUERTO RICO

By American law the Puerto Rican flag must always fly side by side with the Stars and Stripes. For the last hundred years Puerto Rico has been owned by the United States and it has brought a fascinating overlay of America to this Latin Caribbean island nearly a thousand miles southeast of Miami.

The duality runs throughout Puerto Rican life. Side by side you will see air-conditioned high-rise buildings and tiny wooden West Indian shacks, pristine neon-lit shops and chaotic Caribbean markets, dog-stands and *kioskos*, chocolate-chip cookies and *chicharrón* with spicy sauce. The currency is the US dollar, but it is often referred to as the *peso*.

Even the languages exist in tandem. Traditional Spanish is the tongue of the Puerto Rican Parliament and of the poor country man, but much of daily life takes place in English. Business-like American order has been imposed on the Latin Caribbean chaos.

Puerto Rico is the smallest and most easterly of the four Greater Antilles and it lies between the larger island of Hispaniola and the archipelago of the Virgin Islands. It is oblong in shape, about 100 miles from end to end by about 35 from north to south. It seems much larger though; like many of the mountainous Caribbean islands, the interior is very rough. Just a thin band of coastal plain runs around the Cordillera Central, a cumulus of peaks that rise to over 4000 feet, mostly clad in thick rainforest. In the northwest of the island there is an odd geological phenomenon in the *karst* country, a

426

conglomeration of hill-sized pimples and sinkholes shaped by aeons of water dripping through the limestone rock. The climate varies across the island—on the Atlantic coast in the north it is wetter and cooler than across the mountains. In the southwest the country is hotter and almost desert-like in places. Different crops and fruits grow there such as aloe and pineapple.

There are over three million Puerto Ricans on the island (3352 square miles), of whom about a third live in and around San Juan, the capital, towards the eastern end of the north coast. The islanders have a mixed ancestry, a blend of the early Spaniards and the original Arawak Indians (some towns in the centre of the island have distinctly Amerindian names) and then Africans. Over the centuries, migrants from all over Europe and the Caribbean have added to the mix, followed in this century by the Americans. Puerto Rico has a population noticeably whiter than the other Latin Caribbean islands.

Traditionally Puerto Rico has had a rural economy, but that has changed over the last 50 years as the island has been encouraged to develop an industrial base. American firms have invested in Puerto Rico, and, whilst this has brought huge opportunities for employment, unemployment is still running at 20 per cent. Notwithstanding, Puerto Rico has one of the highest standards of living in the Caribbean. The material benefits are clear.

Even with all the pharmaceutical and manufacturing concerns, tourism is still one of the most important industries on Puerto Rico. It is very well organized. If you like a high-pressure vacation—a mugged-by-sunshine holiday with day-long beach activity and Vegas-style entertainment—there are plenty of places on offer. But Puerto Rico is big enough for tourism not to swamp local life and off the beaten track you will also find some superb Caribbean retreats. The hilltop towns of the Cordillera and off-shore islands of Vieques and Culebra are charming and show the Spanish Caribbean at its most rural and laid-back.

Latin Heritage and the American Legacy

In places Puerto Rico can seem exactly like America itself. Kids wear jeans, sneakers and T-shirts and cruise around in large gas-guzzlers, spending their evenings in drive-in cinemas and fast-food joints. Buses cost a quarter, exact fare only please. The billboards scream at you: *Buy Buick!* and *Drink Bud!* Its just that the models have Puerto Rican faces.

For all the superficial change, once you are beyond the coconut suntan oil on Condado beach and the glass-fronted skyscrapers of Santurce and the coastal factories, once you are out into the country, Puerto Rico becomes far more like the other Caribbean islands, and stateside USA seems to belong to another age. In the hilltop towns the islanders pass the time of day chatting on the *plaza*, surveyed calmly by the local church, or wait patiently to sell their fruits at a roadside stall. And in the evenings they promenade and take the night air.

And for all the changes that America has brought, the Latin heritage also rings clear in modern Puerto Rican life. Besuited executives wilt as soon as they emerge from their air-conditioned offices, but the islanders prefer to wear the *guayabera*, a square-tailed,

427

pleated long shirt. Cotton *guayaberas* are worn by the islanders instead of a suit; pineapple-fibre is for more formal evening occasions. You will certainly hear the bustling and compulsive rhythms of *salsa* blaring in the street and the *macho* poise and swagger is all too evident. The country is strongly Catholic—there are convents and monasteries and even one or two shrines where the Virgin Mary has appeared to the faithful. The Caribbean-wide desire for a *jump-up* expresses itself in the week-long *fiestas patronales*, in which each town celebrates its saint's day.

There have been changes, of course, in traditional island life. The role of the family, traditionally an extended collection of uncles, aunts and grandparents, has taken a turn for the nuclear and romantic old gents lament the demise of the serenade, impossible now that she lives on the 13th floor.

Another issue that has changed with the American presence is the feeling of being Puerto Rican. Perhaps more than any other American nationality, the Puerto Ricans are Puerto Rican first and American second. Hopes for independence at the end of the last century never came to pass, killed by the arrival of the American army, uninvited. Since then the island has been a Commonwealth of the United States. The issues still remain—they still name streets and plazas after the *Independentistas* of the 19th century, but with the easing of the relationship with the USA and the material benefits that the association has brought, the desire for independence has faded and it is hardly a practical solution now.

As citizens of the USA, the Puerto Ricans can move to the mainland if they want to. There are large communities of Puerto Ricans all over the States (Puerto Rico is a crowded island and this emigration acts a pressure valve), particularly in New York, where there are supposed to be more Puerto Ricans than in San Juan. Many of these *Neorriqueñans* as they are known maintain close links with their island.

For their part, the Americans have pumped huge amounts of money into the island, in health care, food stamps, unemployment benefit and tax concessions. The island is strategically important and they maintain huge military bases there. Puerto Rico has some of the best schools in the Caribbean.

Suggested Itinerary
In two weeks, you can tour the coast of Puerto Rico (about a week) and spend time in San Juan as well as on the offshore islands. You may even be able to fit in a quick visit to the Virgin Islands. You are likely to arrive in San Juan, where there are some fun bars and restaurants and many museums. From here head east, to the eastern beaches and natural parks such as the El Yunque rainforest and Las Cabezas. Do not miss a trip to one of the large offshore islands, either Culebra or Vieques, both of which have small-island charm. If you choose Vieques, make sure to visit the phosphorescent bay. Back on the mainland, Ponce is a pretty town and is worth a quick look; from here head for the southwest coast—maybe with a stop in the lazy town of San German—visit Boqueron or perhaps Cabo Rojo, both seaside towns where the Puerto Ricans themselves take their holidays. From here it is a short ride up into the mountains, along the *ruta panoramica*, where there are two superb *paradors* hidden away in the rainforest—the Casa Grande in Utuado and best of all the Hacienda Gripiñas. It is worth tailoring your trip around any festivals in the countryside. Ask at the Tourist Board.

History

The native Tainos called Puerto Rico *Borinquen*, which was supposed to mean 'Land of the Noble Lord'. These Arawak Indians, who had come up from South America along the island chain, were the most advanced of the Indian tribes who had lived on the island (the Archaics and the Igneris were hunter-gatherers who had come to the island as fishermen). Their skin was copper-coloured and they had long dark hair. They lived in thatched huts in villages, around a ceremonial area called a *bateye*, a few of which can still be seen on the island, where they would dance and play games with balls and shuttlecocks.

Columbus was the first European to come to Puerto Rico, as he worked his way along the islands back to Hispaniola on his second voyage to the New World, on 19 November 1493. He named it San Juan Bautista (St John the Baptist). Travelling with him was a man called Juan Ponce de Léon, who was to return as the first Governor of the island in 1508. In 1511 the island was given the romantic name of Puerto Rico (Rich Port).

The 30,000 Taino Indians were immediately divided among the settlers who set them to work searching for gold in the rivers. Inevitably there was war, though not before the Indians had confirmed their suspicion that the Spaniards were not immortal (by drowning one). The Indians were soon defeated and retreated to the hills or fled the island. Ponce de León himself died in Havana of wounds received while hunting for the Fountain of Youth in Florida and his body was returned to Puerto Rico, where eventually it was placed in San Juan Cathedral.

By the late 1500s the mines were exhausted and the few remaining Spaniards made a hard living out of cultivating sugar, cotton, ginger and indigo. They suffered the usual natural scourges of the Caribbean, including disease and hurricanes. They also were visited periodically by the canoe-borne Caribs from down-island, who would make lightning raids (5000 attacked them in 1525).

Another human scourge was the arrival of pirates in the Caribbean from the middle of the 16th century. These men arrived with gold in mind too—Spanish gold—or, if they could not find that, then any loot they could lay their hands on.

Puerto Rico was a strategic port and the pirates infested its waters trying to capture Spain's riches as they were shipped back to Europe. Funded from Mexico, San Juan was fortified in defence against them. Perhaps the most famous pirate to attack the island was Sir Francis Drake. He made it into the harbour past the guns of El Morro and set the Spanish ships alight, but was bombarded in his turn—legend says he was forced to retire when a cannon-ball tore through his cabin, mortally wounding Jack Hawkins. The Dutch had a crack in 1625 and burned the town as they were forced out.

Meanwhile the island was neglected by Spain, and the smuggling industry grew. Officially the Puerto Ricans could trade with no ships except those from Spain—but at one stage not a single Spanish ship called for seven years, so they carried on brisk illegal trade in tobacco, ginger and cattle with other Caribbean islands. Puerto Rico was nearly given to Britain in exchange for Gibraltar.

It was not until 1765 that the Spanish King sent an envoy to develop the island. Alejandro O'Reilly advised that sugar should become the main agricultural crop as in the other Caribbean islands and the trading laws be amended, and Spaniards should be encouraged to settle here. Within a few years the ships of the New American Republic were doing a brisk legal trade.

As the 19th century began Puerto Rico was not much better off than it had been 100 years before, but as the century progressed, the political scene became more important. The Puerto Ricans became citizens of Spain in 1809 during the Napoleonic Wars and rights were granted with a more liberal Spanish constitution in 1812. Steadily an island identity crystallized and the struggle for autonomy began, encouraged by the wars of independence in South America.

Spain started to clamp down in 1825, and sent over a series of ruthless military Governors, later called the 'Little Caesars'. One Governor even banned goatees because they were emotive of revolution. In 1856, the reformer Betances was exiled for his anti-colonial views. Encouraged by the revolution in the Dominican Republic in 1862, he and other exiles plotted revolution in Puerto Rico and Cuba.

On 23 September 1868 their first uprising came in the town of Lares in the northwest of the island and the Republic of Puerto Rico was declared. But the colonial authorities responded quickly, crushing the revolt at San Sebastian. It is remembered as the *Grito de Lares* (the cry of Lares) and became symbolic of the struggle for Independence. On 22 March 1873, slavery was abolished in Puerto Rico.

The Puerto Ricans divided into two camps, the autonomists, who wanted independence and the conservatives who wished to remain connected with Spain, with self-government. They hoped that a new Republican government in Spain would grant them autonomy without a war.

This came on 28 November 1897, and at last the Puerto Ricans were able to govern themselves. They elected their own Lower House and half the Senate. The Governor was appointed from Spain, but his powers were restricted. But it was not to last for long. Within nine months the Americans had invaded as part of the Spanish-American War. The campaign lasted 17 days. In December of that year, after 400 years as colonial masters, the Spaniards handed Puerto Rico to the Americans at the Treaty of Paris.

Initially the Puerto Ricans were hopeful that American intervention and severance from Spain would improve their political status, but it steadily became clear that the USA would impose its political will. The Jones Act of 1917 granted the Puerto Ricans American citizenship and an elected bicameral legislature, but still the key administrative posts were appointed from the US government. Political struggle was by no means dormant for long. In 1937, 19 people were killed at an *Independentista* rally when police fired on the crowd and there were attacks on the government.

On 5 August 1947 Harry Truman signed the Bill that created the Commonwealth of Puerto Rico, ratified by the islanders themselves in 1952. Like the USA, the government is divided into executive, judicial and legislative branches. There are two Houses of Parliament, a 51-member House of Representatives and a 27-member Senate. The Governor is elected for four-year terms in line with the elections on the mainland.

The island does not pay taxes to the Federal Bank as a State of the Union would and consequently they have no representation in Congress. The elected Resident Commissioner, Jaime Fuster, has observer status—more of a lobbying role. The island also receives financial support in grants for public works, the universities and food stamps ('pan' cheques).

Today the politics of Puerto Rico are dominated by the status of the island with regard

430

to the USA and there are two main possibilities (the desire for Independence seems to have faded and the *Independentistas* only ever poll a small percentage of the vote nowadays). The majority of the voters swing between maintaining the Commonwealth status and becoming the fifty-first State of the Union.

The governing party is the Popular Democratic Party (PPD), led by Rafael Hernandez Colon , which advocates continued Commonwealth status with more autonomy (there are elections in November 1992).

Flora and Fauna

Puerto Rico has the full variety of Caribbean wildlife, from the coral reefs that skirt the island and the coastal mangrove swamps to rainforest at 4000 feet. In El Yunque and the rough mountains of the Cordillera you will see trees that soar and explode into canopy at 100 ft, tangled with lianas and creeping vines, montane forests of extraordinarily lush ferns and palms and on the upper slopes at 4000 feet, stunted elfin forest where mosses fur the prehistoric looking tree bark.

In the heights you might see the Puerto Rican parrot, recently so close to extinction, but now flourishing, lizard cuckoos, warblers and screech owls—and, of course, hummingbirds, tiny delicate creatures with a metabolic rate so high that they must fly all day to keep up their intake of nectar. In the lower mountains, among Puerto Rico's man-made inland lakes, you will see kestrels and hawks on the hunt, hovering and casting a drilling eye over the undergrowth and the dumbstruck cattle egret.

There are mangrove swamps all around the coastline, where you will see crabs with their eyes out on stalks, surprised to see you perhaps. These monstrously tangled waterways are refuge to hundreds of different birds, including the exotic green-backed heron and the purple gallinule. You might also see a mockingbird or a whistling duck. On the off-shore islands you will come across boobies and the mournful pelican and maybe even a red-billed tropicbird with an eighteen-inch tail.

There are 14 Forest Reserves (see pp. 438, 442, 446, 450) and there is usually a ranger's hut in each, where you might get information to help you get the best out of the natural life. They publish information (usually) in both Spanish and in English. For more information, contact the Natural Resources Department, PO Box 5887, San Juan 00906 (tel 723 0028).

GETTING TO PUERTO RICO

By Air
From Europe: British Airways run two flights a week from Gatwick; Lufthansa fly from Frankfurt and Iberia from Madrid. There are many transfer flights from Europe, mostly via John F. Kennedy Airport, New York or via Miami.
From the USA: Puerto Rico is a domestic destination for US airlines and an American Airlines hub: American Airlines, American Eagle, US Air, Eastern and Delta all run frequent flights from Miami and many others US cities (including Atlanta, Baltimore, Boston, Dallas and Orlando) to Luis Muñoz Marin airport in San Juan. Eastern and American Airlines also do cheap night flights to and from New York.
From other Caribbean islands: San Juan is very well served from the Caribbean and South America by: BWIA (from Trinidad, Antigua, Jamaica and Barbados); ALM (from

THE CARIBBEAN

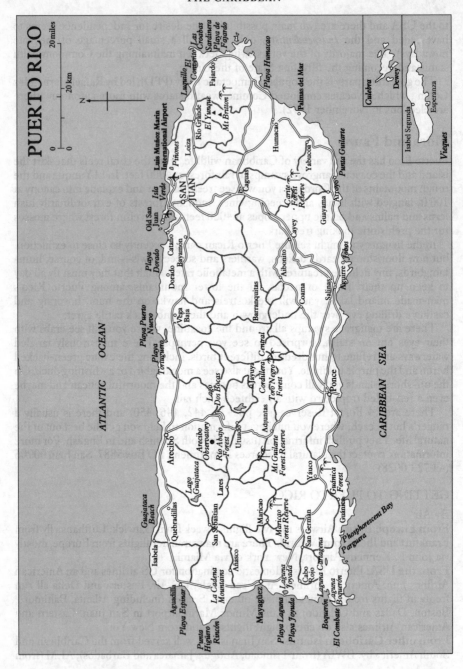

PUERTO RICO

432

Sint Maarten and Curaçao); Air France (from Guadeloupe and Martinique); and LIAT (from St Kitts, Antigua and many other smaller islands like the Virgin Islands and Anguilla).
Puerto Rico has the same entry requirements as the US.

GETTING AROUND PUERTO RICO
Travel between towns is mainly by **público** (Ford vans, marked with P or PD), that run between the central plazas. Travelling like this works, though it can take a while, because you may have to take successive públicos from one town to the next (their beat is not usually longer than two or three towns). The system is typically Caribbean and works to a vague schedule, with *públicos* leaving when they are full or when the urge takes the driver. You can flag them down on the roadside to let you on or shout to get off. Service is more limited at the weekend, but travelling in them is fun because there is the latest salsa music to sing along to and you will get to know your fellow passengers fairly well. Destinations are marked on the windscreen. The *público* terminals in San Juan for journeys around the island are at the **Luis Muñoz Marin International airport** and the plaza in **Rio Piedras** (Plaza del Mercado at end of metropolitan bus routes 1 and 2). Some sample prices are **San Juan** to Fajardo—$3.50, Humacao—$4, Ponce—$6, Arecibo—$5 and Aguadilla—$6, Mayagüez—$7. From **Ponce** (main square or the market place) to Utuado—$3, Guayama—$3, Yauco—$2, San German—$3. From **Mayagüez** to San German—$1.50, Cabo Rojo—$1.50, Aguadilla—$2 and Arecibo—$3.

The metropolitan area of **San Juan** is served by air-conditioned buses from the US locally known as **guaguas** (pronounced wahwah). From Old San Juan (Plaza Colon and the harbour area) you can get to Bayamón, Cataño, Country Club and Rio Piedras (close to the Plaza del Mercado *público* terminal). The fare is 25c, exact change only. Wait at the yellow posts (*paradas*). *Guaguas* do not run very often (about every 20–30 minutes), but they go on until around 10 pm. There are some recently privatised routes around the city, with smaller and faster buses, price 35c.

A word of warning about getting to and from the airport by bus is that the *guagua* drivers will sometimes not let you aboard with luggage, so basically you are forced to go by taxi.

If your feet get tired within Old San Juan itself, you might consider using the little safari buses (free) that run a circular route around the area.

Taxis are, of course, readily available at the airport, at all the hotels and in areas like the dock in Old San Juan. Cabs are metered according to a fixed scale set by the government and the arm is supposed to be up when you set off. A cab from the airport to Old San Juan costs around $12, Condado—$10 and Isla Verde—$4. Taxi drivers will happily take you on a longer tour at around $25 per hour.

Island **tours** can be arranged to the principal sights—a day's excursion to El Yunque and Luquillo or over to Ponce, for instance—through **VIP Coach and Tours** (tel 782 0435) and the **Tour Co-op of Puerto Rico** (tel 723 8060). Most companies will pick you up and deliver you to your hotel.

Car-hire is really the best way to see the island for the independent traveller and there is a limitless supply of them in Condado and Isla Verde. Most companies will deliver and pick up rental cars for you. Driving is on the right and, although speed limits are indicated in miles, distances are in kilometres. US licences are valid for three months.

433

UK licences are valid, as are international licences. If you wish to travel around the island, in the Cordillera or around the less populous south coast it is essential to have a good map. Make sure to get one from the hire company. Road signs are not brilliant, but the roads themselves are good. Small cars start at around $40 per day inclusive of insurance, mileage unlimited.

Hire companies include the big international names: **Avis** (tel 721 4499), **Budget** (tel 791 2418), **Charlie** (tel 728 3685) in Isla Verde and **National** (tel 791 1805). Other island companies are: **Afro** on Ponce de León (tel 724 3720), **L & M** on Ashford Avenue (tel 725 8307) and **Target** on Baldorioty Avenue in Santurce (tel 783 6592).

Ferries operate within San Juan harbour (linking Old San Juan and Cataño every half hour 6 am–10 pm, fare 50 cents). *Aqua Expresso* also links San Juan to Hato Rey and Cataño (75c). From **Fajardo** on the east coast you can reach the off-shore islands of **Vieques** (weekdays twice daily, 9.30 am and 4.30 pm, weekends three times daily, fare $3, crossing 1 hour, ferry originates in Vieques) and **Culebra** (weekdays once a day at 4 pm, returning next morning at 7 am, with additional sailings at the weekend, fare $2.50, crossing 1¼ hours). Ferries are rarely full, but you can reserve on 863 0705. There are no ferries to the island of **Mona**, so you must go by fishing boat or charter a private plane.

There are small airstrips dotted around Puerto Rico which can be reached by short hop from **Isla Grande airport** in Condado or from San Juan International airport: Ponce—about $35 from San Juan, Mayagüez—$40, the Dorado area—$30 and Palmas del Mar—$35. You can also fly to the off-shore islands: Vieques and Culebra—both $30 (the Fajardo—Vieques link is considerably cheaper ($15) and so it may well be worth considering), and Mona.

TOURIST INFORMATION
UK: the **Commonwealth of Puerto Rico Tourism Company** can be contacted at 67–9 Whitfield St, London W1P 5RL (tel 071 636 6558, fax 071 255 2131).
Spain: Calle Capitan Haya 23, 1–7–4, 28020 Madrid (tel 341 555 6811, fax 341 556 7286).
France: 10 Rue de l'Isly, 75008 Paris (tel 331 429 30012, fax 429 34729).
Germany: Bahnhofstrasse 55–7, 6200 Wiesbaden (tel 49 611 302064, fax 611 303801).
Italy: Bodo Associates, Via le Maino 35, 20122 Milan (tel 392 27022966, fax 392 780937).
Scandinavia: Sergat Scandinavia, Kammarkargatan 41, S111 24 Stockholm (tel 468 115495, fax 468 206317).
USA: the Puerto Rican Tourism Co. at 575 Fifth Ave, New York, NY 10017 (tel (212) 599 6262 or 800 223 6530), at 3575 W Cahuenga Blvd, Suite 248, Los Angeles, CA 90068 (tel (213) 874 5991) and Peninsula Building, Suite 903, 200 SE First St, Miami, FL 33131.
Canada: 11 Yorkville Ave, Suite 1003, Toronto, Ontario M4W 1L3 (tel (416) 925 5587).

On **Puerto Rico** itself, you can write to the Head Office at Calle San Just 301, Box 4435, Old San Juan, PR 00905 (tel 721 2400). However, the island is dotted with Tourist Information offices, including at the International Airport (tel 791 1014), at El Centre Convention Centre in Condado (tel 723 3135), and the very helpful office near Pier 1 on the cruise-ship dock in Old San Juan (tel 722 1709). Outside the capital, each major town will have an Information Bureau in the Alcaldía, the Town Hall, on the main plaza. In Ponce go to the Casa Armstrong-Poventud off the central square (tel 840 5695). Open 8–noon and 1–4.30.

The Tourist Board publishes a monthly guide *Qué Pasa*, with listings of current events as well as the hotels and restaurants. English is widely spoken in the tourist areas of Puerto Rico, but if you venture off the beaten track into the country you will find it very useful to speak Spanish. It is also worth requesting an English-speaking guide in some places if you need one.

In a medical **emergency** you can contact the 24-hour emergency rooms at Ashford Memorial Community Hospital at 1451 Ashford Ave (tel 721 2160) or the San Juan Health Centre, 200 De Diego Ave (tel 725 0202). Ambulances can be reached on tel 343 2550. You are advised to have extensive medical cover, because charges for treatment in Puerto Rico are high. If you wish to contact the **police**, the central number is tel 343 2020. In the Condado area they are on Vieques St (tel 722 0738). The **IDD code** for Puerto Rico is 809, which is followed by a seven-digit island number. There is an international telephone exchange on Baldorioty de Castro in Miramar. Alternatively, some hotel will put calls through for you.

MONEY

The currency of Puerto Rico is, of course, the US dollar, but it is often known as the *peso*. Quarters are called *pesetas* and cents *centavos*. Traveller's cheques and credit cards are widely accepted in the tourist areas, but out in the country you will need to pay in cash. Small notes are useful for this and for tipping (the usual dollar or 10–15%). **Banks** keep hours of 8.30–2.30 on weekdays and 9.45–noon on Saturday mornings.

Shoppers will find endless hunting grounds in Puerto Rico and with no sales tax it is quite good sport. Individual shops and even malls are often found in the big hotels, but they are thickest on the ground in Old San Juan. **Shops** open from 9–6 and will accept credit cards quite happily.

BEACHES

Puerto Rico's hundreds of miles of coastline have a great variety of beaches—from protected coves on the southwestern shore where the snorkelling is excellent to the crowded action-packed strands in San Juan and the surfing beaches at the northwestern tip of the island. Going to the beach is a popular day out at the weekend among the Puerto Ricans and the government has developed some of the more popular spots with *balnearios*. These 13 public beaches have changing rooms with lockers, lifeguards, a car park and usually a small restaurant. Open Tues–Sat, 9–5, adm usually a dollar parking and 50c entrance. Some also have sites where you can pitch or hire a tent for a minimal fee. There are also good beaches on the off-shore islands, with particularly good reefs for diving (see pp. 438, 461).

The Eastern End of the Island

In the bays of northeastern Puerto Rico are some superb curving strands. The two most famous are **Condado** and **Isla Verde**, two crowded and highly-developed strips in San Juan, backed by high-rise hotels that make them look a bit like Miami beach. Here you will find every conceivable watersport on offer (parasailing to sailing-boat trips) and endless restaurants. The beach is always busy at the western end beneath the high-rise complexes; the eastern end (Ocean Park) has become popular with the gay crowd. Condado Lagoon also teems with windsurfers and jetskiers. Bus T1 passes Isla Verde. There are good snorkelling reefs at the eastern end, at Boca de Cangrejos (crab mouth). There is also surfing close by.

As soon as you round the point heading east the action evaporates and the skyscrapers turn to palm trees in the remoter area of **Piñones**. Here the Atlantic waves barrel in on to red-golden sand and on the roadside there are plenty of *kioskos* where you can get a crabstick or a fried codfish batter in a seagrape leaf with a chilled coconut to drink. Thirty miles out of San Juan is one of the island's most popular beaches, **Luquillo**, another stunning mile-long half-moon bay backed with forests of palm trees. This *balneario* becomes very crowded at the weekend as the San Juañeros pour out of town in search of sun and sand. There are some watersports available, including windsurfers.

Close by are several other beaches, approached from Fajardo, **Las Croabas** on the eastern coast where the old and new, villas and fishing shacks, are side by side on the shore. To the north are two remote but just as enticing strands, **El Convento** and **Soroco** beaches at the eastern tip of Puerto Rico. The coastline and the offshore cays (Icacos, Palominos), reached by boat from the marinas around Fajardo for just a few dollars, are good for snorkelling. Icacos also has an excellent strip of sand if you want a beach to yourselves midweek. Take what you want in the way of a picnic.

Punta Santiago about 15 miles south of Fajardo, and the *balneario* at **Playa Humacao** are two more deserted strips of sand that suddenly explode with activity at the weekend. At the huge development in Palmas del Mar, five miles further south, you can find watersports for all the family. There is a *balneario* at **Punta Guilarte** near Arroyo. Generally speaking, the south coast towards Ponce does not have the sand and the reefs of the northeast, but in the mangroves and the seafront towns you will find small coves where you can be alone.

The Southwest, Ponce up to Mayagüez

There is just one rather disappointing cove at Parguera before you reach the western coast, where you will find many of the island's most glorious beaches and of course the best view of the sunset and the Green Flash. The magnificent curve of **Boquerón** beach is one of the best known on the island—ever popular at the weekend and less crowded during the week. Backed by a forest of palms the three miles of sand gently slopes away into the warm limpid water where the laziest of waves play.

Towards the southwestern tip of the island is another beach idyll called **El Combate**, lined with fishermen's shacks on the shore and their boats in the jade-coloured water. A perfect view of the sunset. You can also find deserted suntraps around the *salinas*, the salt flats, in this area.

Headed north again, there is a small beach at **Playa Buye** to the west of Cabo Rojo, overlooking the bay of Puerto Real where more fishing boats lie at anchor. North of here the seafront is developed between Playa Joyuda and Playa Laguna, so you can hire a windsurfer or bask on the thin beach before retreating inside for another piña colada.

North of Mayagüez the coastline becomes rougher where the cliffs of the Cordillera and the Atlantic waves meet. There are a few passable stretches of sand in the area (there is a *balneario* at Añasco), but Punta Higüero and Rincón are most popular among surfers and windsurfers. There are a number of surf shops in the area. **Playa Espinar**, close to Aguadilla, is half a mile of white sand and water good for lively bathing.

The North Coast back to San Juan
The north coast of Puerto Rico is pounded by the Atlantic waves and so it can get pretty dramatic, but the miles of sand are protected by reefs in places which creates good swimming beaches. Protruding through the sand you will see the limestone base of old coral reefs, like a sort of stone peanut brittle.

Close to Isabela is **Jobos beach**, a stretch of sand between the cliffs, where you can escape the crowds. Take water and a picnic. There is a *balneario* among the palms at Guajacata just outside Quebradillas.

There are a number of beaches around Vega Baja, including Playa Tortuguero and a beach among the cliffs at Playa Puerto Nuevo. A few miles east of here the beaches of **Dorado** have become encrusted with hotels and are good places to get hold of water-sports equipment if you want to pause for an afternoon on the beach in an island tour. **Playa Sardinera** is a popular strip with a *balneario* and *kioskos*, where you can stop for a chat and buy a drink to stave off a thirst in the height of the sun.

WATERSPORTS
Most watersports can be arranged in the resort areas, through the hotels and beach concessionaires in Condado, Isla Verde, Dorado (20 miles west of San Juan), the Fajardo area, Palmas del Mar and to a lesser extent the west coast resort towns of Parguera and Cabo Rojo. **Jet-skiing** ($30 for half an hour), **waterskiing** and **parasailing** and outings in small **sailing craft** can all be fixed up here.

Windsurfing is popular all over the island (particularly in Condado lagoon) and rental equipment is easily found. There are also small concessionaries on the beaches around the coast, particularly in the northwest, Aguadilla and Añasco and Rincón, where the wind and waves are often high (**surfing** is also a popular sport here). Hire is around $20 per hour for a board and instruction is available through all the main beaches.

A more adventurous **sailing** trip can be arranged through the marinas, of which there are plenty on Puerto Rico: **San Juan Bay Marina** in Miramar and one at **Boca de Cangrejos**, Fernández Juncos Ave (tel 721 8062) and four in the area of Fajardo, among them **Puerto Chico** (tel 863 0834) and **Villa Marina** (tel 728 2450). The eastern coast around Fajardo has excellent sailing among the cays and reefs, driven by Atlantic winds. Bareboats or crewed, a day or a month, simple or luxurious, all are possible through the marinas. **Castillo Watersports** (tel 791 6195) works out of Isla Verde, and for an organized trip to Icacos Island off Fajardo, try **Caribe Aquatic Adventures** (tel 724 1882), which works out of San Juan or **East Wind Catamaran** in Puerto del Rey (tel 863 2821) or **Captain Jayne Sailing Charters** (tel 791 5174), half day about $35.

The northern shore of Puerto Rico drops away to 6000 ft within a couple of miles, and there are some extremely fine waters for **deep-sea fishing**. Cast for white and blue marlin, wahoo and sailfish and perhaps you could improve on one of Puerto Rico's many world records. You can set off from the Club Náutico in San Juan, with **Benitez Deep Sea Fishing**, Fernández Juncos Ave (tel 723 2292) or **San Juan Fishing Charter** nearby (tel 723 0415). If you are on the west coast you can contact **Western Tourist**

Services (tel 833 4328) in Mayagüez. A boat for six people costs around $650 for a full day's sail.

Fajardo and its islands also have the best of the **snorkelling** and **diving** on the reefs and sandbars. The reefs teem with schools of grunts and solitary graceful angelfish and butterflyfish. Most hotels will fix it up for you, but in Fajardo contact **Caribbean Divers** at the Ferry Terminal (tel 723 0145) and **Borinquen Sub-aqua** (tel 863 3483). In San Juan, try **Ocean Sports** (tel 268 2329) and **Mundo Submarino** (tel 791 5764), both in Isla Verde. Parguera is another good diving area; contact **Parguera Divers Training Centre** in Lajas (tel 899 4171).

OTHER SPORTS

There are about ten **golf** courses in Puerto Rico, some of them attached to the big hotels. On the outskirts of San Juan is the **Luis Ortiz** course (tel 786 3859). There are two 18-hole courses in Río Grande just east of the capital, the **Berwind Country Club** (tel 876 3056) and **Club Riomar** (tel 887 3964). These courses are open to the public at varying times, so it is best to ring before arriving. At the Dorado resort area there are a number of courses. Try the **Hyatt Dorado Beach Hotel** (tel 796 1234). Near Humacao the **Palmas del Mar** development has an 18-hole course (tel 852 6000).

Tennis courts proliferate around the tourist hotels, though you may find it difficult to get a court in the winter season. If the hotel you are staying in does not have one, they can arrange it elsewhere. Outside the hotels you can play at **San Juan Central Park**, off Route 2 (tel 722 1646).

Hiking has endless possibilities in the mountainous interior of the island. Most National Parks have trails, and so you can struggle up switchback paths in the mountains, taking a quick dip in the waterfalls, or stalk pelicans and tropicbirds in the mangrove swamps. The parks are co-ordinated by the Natural Resources Department, PO Box 5887, San Juan 00906 (tel 723 0028). The best known Forest Reserve is **El Yunque**.

Other mountain parks a little more off the beaten track are: the **Carite Forest Reserve**, in the Cayey mountains south of Caguas or the **Toro Negro Forest**, just east of Adjuntas in the centre of the island (this park contains the mountain Cerro de Punta, Puerto Rico's highest peak) and **Río Abajo Forest**, in the karst country south of Arecibo. If you would prefer somewhere less hilly, you could try the coastal mangrove swamps, for instance at **Guánica Forest**, on the south coast to the west of Ponce, which has extensive bird-life, or **Piñones Forest**, just a stone's throw out of San Juan to the east.

You might prefer to go **riding** through the mountains or to gallop through the breakers. Around Luquillo you can go to Hacienda Caribali (tel 793 8585). In El Yunque rainforest itself, contact Rancho Criollo, and in the southeast of the island you can go to the large centre at Palmas del Mar (tel 852 4785) or Ranchos Guayama.

Puerto Rico's underground rivers have carved out some extremely impressive cave systems in the limestone rock. There are tame, trolley-borne tours on offer, but if you are a **pot-holer** (spelunker), then you might want to check out the lesser known caverns in an independent party: contact the Puerto Rico Speleological Society, PO Box 31074, 65th Infantry Station, Rio Piedras, Puerto Rico 00929.

A favourite spectator sport in Puerto Rico, as in the other Latin Caribbean islands of Cuba and the Dominican Republic, is **baseball**. The season runs over the winter months here, from October to April, and some Puerto Rican sportsmen in the major leagues return here to play. There are stadia in San Juan, Santurce, Caguas, Ponce, Mayagüez and Arecibo.

Another very popular sport in the Latin Caribbean islands is **cockfighting**. There is an organized and rather plush *gallera* in Isla Verde, at the Club Gallístico, open Sat 1–7, adm $5–10 (tel 791 6005), but if you go to a *gallera* in a country town, you will see all the frenzied passion of a local tournament, where pride as well as money ride on the result. It is cruel and often ends with one of the birds being killed. Usually Sun afternoons.

San Juan

The capital of Puerto Rico captures best the duality of this American-Caribbean island. Side by side here you will see charming Spanish colonial town houses and modern glass-fronted offices, West Indian shanties and massive airco tourist hotels.

Since it was founded in 1520, San Juan has expanded from a little collection of shacks huddled together for protection near the point at *El Morro*; it crept along the peninsula and over to the mainland and then splurged over the lagoons and beaches into suburbs, eventually becoming a city of over a million. It has its own University, a huge international airport, and is the top financial centre of the whole Caribbean area.

The original seven blocks of **Old San Juan**, which have recently been restored to their state as an 18th-century Spanish colonial city, are one of the most charming spots in the Caribbean. Among the steep and narrow alleys, you will see the old gas lanterns and wrought-iron balconies. The houses are painted in pastel blue and yellow, cut with white door-frames and window sills.

The whole of Old San Juan is surrounded by massive defensive walls 30 ft thick and studded with lumbering fortresses. *Garitas*, little stone sentry-boxes perched above the sea, run around the town. The whole town is laid with *adequines*, cobblestones of a rich blue-grey colour that were brought out as ballast in the ocean-going ships. They speak of the days when the island was the 'Rich Port' of its name and San Juan a very wealthy harbour town. At its less crowded moments the colonial city has such an aura of history that you might expect to see a bearded merchant or a cleric in flowing vestments swish past.

Despite being slightly tourist-precious, Old San Juan is fun because it is also a living city, with banks and bookshops, business-people and domino players and when there are not too many cruise-trippers around, it has real charm. After dark the islanders promenade, and the bars and restaurants come alive as crowds of young Puerto Ricans loiter around the nightclubs.

On the western point of the peninsula is **San Felipe del Morro** (*morro* means headland), a fortress and a half. Its walls, 20 ft thick, rise from the sea to a height of 140 ft, and inside it contains an network of tunnels, dungeons and bastions on six levels. On the uppermost level, the cannon were placed on runners so that they could get a better angle of fire. Construction began in 1540 and it was not completed until 1783. Sir Francis Drake was one of the first to attack it in 1595, and it was last shelled by the Americans in 1898. Open daily 9.15–6, a small historical museum and slide shows for the studious visitor (tel 729 6960); adm, children free.

Two of the few buildings older than El Morro are: the crenellated **Casa Blanca**, built in 1521 as the Ponce de León family home, which it remained for the next 250 years, eventually to be restored as a museum of island life in the early colonial days (open Tues–Sun, 9–noon, 1–4.30, tel 724 4102), and **La Fortaleza**, which overlooks San Juan bay from the top of the city walls. This mansion (the 'fortress' that was originally built here in 1532 as a defence against Carib Indians has long been swallowed up by plaster walls), is the official residence of the Governor of Puerto Rico. It sells itself as the 'oldest executive mansion still used as such in the Western Hemisphere', but for all the tourist twaddle it is a pleasant visit to see the corridors of power, ceremonial rooms and gardens. Hourly tours in English and Spanish, 9–4, adm free (tel 721 7000).

Another pillar of the Spanish establishment was **San Juan Cathedral**, overlooking the steep alleys down on Calle Christo, a magnificent Spanish colonial church dressed in beige with white stucco and topped with three red and white cupolas. It was begun in 1521, but the first thatch-roofed building had to be rebuilt after a hurricane. There is a marble tomb containing the remains of Ponce de León himself, brought here in 1913. Open daily 8.30–4.

When León's remains were originally returned to Puerto Rico he was buried in his family chapel, the **San José Church** on the Plaza San José, a little north of the Cathedral. Like the Cathedral, it is of medieval design, its domes supported by coral rock walls and Romanesque arches, and laid with ochre tiles. Open Mon–Sat, 8.30–3.30.

Dominating the Plaza de San José, where a statue of Ponce presides over the markets during the day and the young San Juañeros loitering at night, is the old **Dominican Convent**, where two cool floors of arched cloisters surround an inner courtyard. Built in 1523 by Dominican Friars, it has offered sanctuary to besieged citizens, pious besiegers (the Earl of Cumberland in 1598) and until 1966 it was the headquarters of the US Army Antilles Command. Now once again it has a more peaceful mission as the home of the **Institute of Puerto Rican Culture** (tel 724 0700). Inside is the **Chapel Museum** (open Wed–Sun, 9.15–noon, 1–4).

Next to the Convent on Calle San Sebastian is the **Pablo Casals Museum**, dedicated to the cellist who came live in Puerto Rico in 1957—as well as hearing recordings of his concerts, you will see his favourite cellos. Open Tues–Sat, 9.30–5.30, Sun 1–5, adm free (tel 723 9185).

A short walk away, at the corner of Norzagay and MacArthur is the **San Juan Museum of Art and History**, where there are exhibitions of Puerto Rican art and an audiovisual presentation (11 am) of the history of San Juan. Concerts are also staged here in the courtyard. Open Mon–Fri, 9–noon and 1–4, recommended donation $1 (tel 724 1875).

Back in the heart of town is the **Plaza de Armas**, once the parade ground and now an open piazza with fountains and bandstands, department stores and a tourist information booth. Originally it was larger, to accommodate military manoeuvres, but it became San Juan's central square. On the northern side is the **Alcaldía** (City Hall), with two layers of rounded arches and a beautiful inner courtyard, a copy of the City Hall in Madrid. Started in 1609 and completed in 1789, it was the nucleus of the San Juan social life.

Just south of here on Calle Cristo are two more museums set in San Juan's charming 18th-century town-houses. The **Museo de Arte de Puerto Rico** (Fine Arts Museum), open 9–noon and 1–4.30, adm free (tel 723 2320), is home to the collection of the

Institute of Puerto Rican Culture and the **Casa del Libro** has exhibits of the art of printing and bookbinding, with a library of books, including some from the 15th century. Open Tues–Sat, 11–4.30.

Across the way you will find the tiny, ornate **Capilla del Christo**, where behind a grille a silver altar commemorates the apparently miraculous survival of a rider who plunged off the cliff on a round-the-city horse-race. You get a good view over the harbour and the city beyond from **Parque de las Palomas** (pigeon park, with special nesting holes), but do not go too close to the edge or you could end up in **La Princesa** prison, 50 ft below. It is no longer a jail, but is used by the Tourism Company.

If you walk down the hill beneath the city walls you come to the dock in San Juan Bay, where the vast and gleaming cruise ships tie up before they each off-load their thousand-odd passengers. Behind the Customs building and Coast Guard Station on the headland is **El Arsenal**, the old Spanish naval base, where more art exhibitions are staged in the three galleries. Open Wed–Sun, 9–4.30, adm free (tel 724 5949).

Back up top, Calle Fortaleza is full of shops and bars (one claims that the *piña colada* was invented there) and runs the full length of Old San Juan from La Fortaleza itself to **Plaza Colon** (Columbus Square), where a statue commemorates the explorer, at the entrance to the colonial city.

Just above the Plaza Colon, the eastern extent of Old San Juan is guarded by another fortress, **El Castillo de San Christobal**, a vast and lumbering affair worthy of its counterpart on the western point of the peninsula. Completed in 1678, it is a classic piece of 17th-century military architecture, with five bastions, each of which had to be captured before the main keep could be taken. Its 27 acres are a maze of ramparts, tunnels and arches, bristling with cannon, overlooking the Atlantic approaches to the island. Open daily, 8–6, tours in Spanish and English, adm (tel 729 6960).

Just outside the northern city walls beneath San Christobal, you will see another side of Puerto Rico. The rundown area of **La Perla**, with its wooden shacks and forests of TV aerials, an alter-ego to neat and tidy Old San Juan. You are advised to be careful if you go there.

As you travel farther east you come to a more modern Puerto Rico in the white, pillared and domed **Capitol**, the seat of the island Legislature (Senate and House of Representatives). Started in 1925, the Capitol contains the Puerto Rican Constitution in an urn and inside the elaborate dome friezes depict Puerto Rican history. Open Mon–Fri, 8.30–5, guided tours by appointment (tel 721 6040, ext 253).

San Juan Suburbs

Soon after you pass the Capitol the hotels and the expressways begin to appear and you cross from the peninsula on to the mainland. On the Atlantic waterfront is the high-rise **Condado** strip, where a range of humming factory hotels jostle for beach space, and fast-food joints and designer shops muscle in on Ashford Avenue beneath them. A few miles farther along the coast is **Isla Verde**, another extremely fine beach lined with luxury hotels and high-rise condominiums. These two strips are developed to bursting point, and you can expect canned music, cable TV and Vegas-style entertainment. (see Beaches p. 435)

Across the Condado Lagoon, where the windsurfers fly back and forth, you come to the business/residential districts of **Miramar**, and **Santurce**, with the grand, walled homes of San Juan's wealthy. Among the industrial estates on the shores of the San José lagoon. There are shanty towns where the poorest San Juaneros live.

Following Highway 1 south out of Santurce you come to **Hato Rey**, the business capital of Puerto Rico. On the **Golden Mile** you will see the glass-fronted head-offices of the corporations and banks that operate on the island. Nearby is the other suburb of **Rio Piedras**, home of the **University of Puerto Rico**, its faculty buildings scattered around the distinctive clock-tower. In the **University Museum** there are exhibitions of contemporary sculptures and paintings from Puerto Rico and Latin America. Open Mon–Fri, 9–9 and weekends 9–3, adm free; entrance on Avenue Ponce de León.

South of here at the bus terminal is the **Plaza del Mercado**, San Juan's biggest market, where the island produce, tropical fruit and vegetables, are shipped in from the country and stacked in colourful piles on the tables and the Puerto Ricans haggle.

Further on to the south are the **Botanical Gardens**, 200 acres that are peaceful and green after the mayhem of the city. Among the walks and waterways are endless variety of palm (from the tall spiked Royal palm to the scratchy sable), 60-ft bamboos, an orchid garden and everywhere Puerto Rican lovers. Open Tues–Sun, 9–5, adm free (tel 766 0740). Entrance off the intersection of Route 1 and Route 847.

West of Hato Rey, a 50c ride on the ferry across the bay from Old San Juan is the suburb of **Cataño** and the vast **Bacardi Rum Plant**, on Route 888, where you can whizz around the outsize stills in trolley buses, zip through the museum and then claim a free daiquiri. Open Mon–Sat, 9.30–3.30, adm free (tel 795 1560).

On Route 2 travelling towards Bayamón are the ruins of **Caparra**, the island's oldest settlement, founded in 1508 by Ponce de León, but only used for ten years before the pioneers decamped for Old San Juan. A small museum, the **Museum of the Conquest and Colonization of Puerto Rico**, has about as many excavated artefacts on view as there are words in its title. Open daily 9–4, adm free (tel 781 4795).

Route 3—East of San Juan

Driving east on the north coastal route 187 beyond Isla Verde you pass palm-backed sand beaches and mangrove for six miles and then turn south before eventually coming to Loíza on the main road east from San Juan. The area has a strong African influence and is best known for its church, **Iglesia San Patricio**, built in 1645, and its saint's day festival, dedicated to Santiago Apostol (from 25 July). (see Festivals, p. 450–1)

You can visit the **Piñones Forest Reserve**, a vast mangrove swamp behind the *kioskos* and the coconut trees of Playa Piñones, where as well as the crabs that support their huge claws across their body like broken arms, you will see herons (green-backed and tricoloured), pelicans and the ubiquitous and mournful snowy egret. Boats can be fixed up at the Cangrejos Marina on the Laguna Torrecilla.

El Yunque Rainforest

Luquillo, 35 miles outside the capital is best known for its beach, a mile-long strip backed with more palm trees, which is very popular with the San Juañeros at the weekends. Visible from the beach is the **Sierra de Luquillo**, a 3000-ft mountain range with a mantle of rainforest, where the Atlantic winds stack in vast rainclouds and then go at it hammer and tongs, dropping as much as 200 inches of rain a year (something around a hundred billion gallons of water). **El Yunque** (the Anvil) is a spectacular rainforest, where the air fizzes with mist and rain among 100-ft trees and exotic birdlife (60 species), flits among the perfectly formed ferns and scratchy sierra palms and the *tabanuco* trees, which seeps a sap smelling like *Vicks*. (see Flora and Fauna, p. 431). The rainforest is home to the Puerto Rican parrot, and if the squawking was not enough, the forest also rings with the dual tone of millions of tiny tree frogs (*coquís*).

El Yunque is a popular place to visit and you can get information at the **Sierra Palm Visitor Center** on route 191. There are two waterfalls worth the detour, **La Coca Falls**, not far into the park and **La Mina Falls**, which are more remote (approach from the Palo Colorado Recreation Site). A number of concrete trails have been laid in the forest to give you a close-up of the intricate beauty of the individual plants—tiny orchids the size of a cent coin—and panoramic views as far as the coasts.

The trails, which are well maintained, start from Route 191 or 186, and include **El Yunque, Mt Britton** and the relatively easy eight miles of **El Toro**, also known as the Tradewinds. Take a pair of training shoes (or better) for the slippery rocks, and waterproofs if you do not want to get too wet. Although the locals drink the water, you are better to take your own to be absolutely safe.

Route 3 continues from Luquillo Beach to **Fajardo** on the eastern tip of the island, a sleepy town around a typical paved plaza. On the coast a few miles away (Playa de Fajardo) you will still see the town's traditional side—fishermen from the fleet of small boats selling their catch on the beach—but the bay between here and Las Croabas has also become a major tourist centre, with three marinas and ranges of villas perched on the hills above. You can hire boats to reach the tiny off-shore cays where the snorkelling and diving are excellent. La Playa is also the ferry terminal for the islands of **Vieques** and **Culebra**.

At the northeastern tip of the island is **Las Cabezas de San Juan Nature Park**, with the central visitors' centre set in an old lighthouse, El Faro (the park also goes by this name). Quite tame, you are guided along forest paths and boardwalks that give you a close-up view of the mangroves. There is also a phosphorescent lake in the park which is well worth a visit (see Vieques, p. 459). Open at weekends, unless you can claim to be a group, call to reserve (tel 722 5882, at weekends 860 2560), adm.

Turning south, the road passes Roosevelt Roads, a vast US Naval Base, **Playa de Humacao** and Humacao itself (turn off on Route 30 for a trip back through the mountains to **Caguas** and eventually San Juan) before it disappears south into the cane-covered hills to **Yabucoa** and the south coast. Arroyo, Guayama and Aguirre are sleepy and charming rural and waterfront towns where the old wooden buildings around the plaza have been encrusted with concrete suburbs. At Salinas, Route 3 meets Route 1, which continues to the city of Ponce.

From San Juan to Ponce
Two freeways (tollway Route 52 and untolled Route 1) carve a way up into the mountains south of San Juan en route for the Caribbean coast and fifteen miles out of the capital

they meet at **Caguas**. Named after an old Amerindian chief, the city is set in the massive foothills of the Cordillera Central. From here Route 172 switchbacks up into the mountains to be swallowed by tunnels of bamboos and ferns. Both the main roads cross the Panoramic Route near **Cayey**, where the land is dotted with small private tobacco plantations and drying sheds, and then descends to the south coast, from where they head west towards Ponce.

Back up in the hills on Route 153 is the town of **Coamo**, established in 1579, the third oldest on the island. The old church and the town houses of its former splendour can still be seen set around the classic mountain plaza. There is a small **museum** in the inner courtyard of one of the houses on the plaza, with a display of family life 100 years ago, but Coama is best known for its **thermal springs** just south of the town. They were used by the Arawaks and are thought to have been visited by Ponce de León in his search for the Fountain of Youth. They became popular as a resort in the 19th century but fell into disrepair, and have recently been rebuilt as a *parador*, with the spring water brought to the pool at 110°C.

Ponce

Ponce (pronounced *Pon-tsé*, with pursed Spanish vowels) is Puerto Rico's second city and it is situated across the Cordillera on the southern coast of the island. Founded in the late 17th century, Ponce takes its name not from the first governor of the island, Ponce de León, but from his great-grandson. It may only be an hour and a bit to drive from the capital nowadays, but 50 years ago the journey of 70 miles was daunting and Ponce was cut off from the capital. The 200,000 Ponceños have a proud tradition (and an idiom of speech) all of their own and they refer to their city as *la perla del Sur* (the Pearl of the South). It is very attractive at the moment as it has recently been restored.

As you come to the outskirts on the freeway you pass the old clapboard shanties alongside the new residential villas and a plethora of sports stadia and drive-in fast food joints, eventually coming to the centre of the town, where the old plastered and wooden buildings are embellished with intricate latticeworks of wood and iron.

Plaza Central

The heart of the city is the old **plaza central**, where the Ponceños gather by day in the shade of the neatly trimmed figtrees and promenade at night. It is guarded on one side by the **Cathedral** of Our Lady of Guadeloupe, a 17th-century Spanish creole church (designed by Puerto Rican architects who had studied in Spain) with classical pillars and devotional statues, topped with rounded silver towers.

Ponce's most famous sight is its fire station, the **Parque de Bombas**, a striking red and black wooden structure with towers and arched windows, built in 1883 for an agricultural fair held on the plaza.

The **Casa Armstrong Poventud**, a restored neo-classical town-house from the turn of the century, is home to the Ponce Tourism Information Centre, open Mon–Fri, 8–noon and 1–4 (tel 844 8240) as well as a small display of antique furniture.

The renowned **Ponce Museum of Art** on Avenue Las Americas has over 1000 paintings and 400 sculptures and is probably the best collection of European art in the

Caribbean. The Puerto Rican artists Jose Campeche (1751–1809) and Francisco Oller (1833–1917) are exhibited there, along with Latin-Americans Murillo and Rivera, and Reubens, Velasquez and Gainsborough. Open Mon–Fri, 10–noon and 1–4 and Sat, Sun 10–4 with no break for lunch, adm (tel 840 1510).

Around the Plaza

Like many Puerto Rican coastal towns, the plaza is a few miles from the sea. **Playa de Ponce** is on the shore, and from here you can get a ferry (Sat, Sun 9 am, tel 848 4575) at the weekend to mile-long **Caja de Muertos**, a rough and rocky protrusion a few miles off-shore, so named for its coffin-like shape. It is a popular day out with the locals, both for the beaches and the reefs that are alive with fish and corals. There are also guided nature walks through the dry terrain of the island. Take what you will need in the way of a picnic.

Like many West Indians, the wealthy Ponceño traders built their mansions on the hill above the town. The hillside community is called **El Vigia** because they would look out from here for merchant ships approaching the harbour. The outsize cross that dominates the town has replaced a wooden one that guided the ships to the right part of the coast.

The **Castillo Serailles** is probably the most sumptuous of these mansions and it is now open to the public. It was built in 1933 as a family home (on the proceeds of the local rum *Don Q*), in Spanish revival style (which has Moorish influences) in a grand hillside garden. A lovely indoor courtyard leads to a wood-panelled living room and library and an extraordinary medieval dining-room with metalwork grilles. Downstairs in the kitchen are the original fridges, stoves and the massive sinks. Open 10–7, adm.

Behind the town is the **Tibes Indian Ceremonial Center**, an Amerindian site discovered in 1974. An Arawak village of thatched *bohíos* has been reconstructed, and also some *bateyes*, stone-lined ceremonial grounds used for sports (using a shuttlecock or a ball), dancing and inhaling their hallucinogens (cajoba seeds). Among the skeletons unearthed by the archaeologists were decorated ceramic pots, axe-heads and *zemies* (ceremonial idols). The park and Museum are open Tues–Sun, 9–4.30, adm (tel 840 2255).

The **Hacienda Buena Vista** (about seven miles north out of Ponce on Route 10) is a restored coffee and corn plantation from the late 19th century, a time when Puerto Rico produced some of the most famous coffee in the world, drunk in coffee-houses as far afield as Paris and Vienna. You can see original machinery restored and working: pulping, fermenting, rinsing, drying and husking the coffee berries. The whole complex is driven by a network of waterways—collected from a waterfall at the top and channelled for 200 yards to the estate, where it is sluiced off to run the different machines (waterwheels, crushers and turbines). Not a pint of the water is wasted as it is all channelled back to a waterslide where it is frothed up and dropped into a communal bath, the 19th century's answer to the jacuzzi. Among the exhibits at the estate house museum are a dripstone (to provide cool and clean drinking water) and stencils that were used to mark up the bags of coffee beans. Open Fri–Sun, they do not accept casual callers, so reserve (tel 722 5882), adm.

Ponce to Mayagüez on Route 2

The southwest coast of Puerto Rico is the driest part of the island, but inland the slightly wetter mountains manage to support coffee (now almost gone) and the traditional crop, sugar-cane. Route 2 follows the southern coastline, in the shadow of the vast Cordillera, past small fishing villages where vendors sell oysters at the streetside, and then cuts inland into the hills and the Spanish colonial hill towns.

Yáuco, where the stepped alleys lead up to classic wooden houses with shaded verandas, was the coffee capital of Puerto Rico 100 years ago. They hold a coffee festival each year in February and celebrate the day of their patron saint Nuestra Señora del Rosario on 7 October.

Guánica sits on the waterfront among the cactus and mangrove forest. The beaches are placid nowadays, but they saw action in July 1898 when a force of 16,000 American troops landed there and began a 17-day campaign (called a picnic by one journalist) that culminated in the surrender of Puerto Rico to America.

Just south of here is the **Guánica Forest Reserve**, where ornithologists will have a field day, so to speak. The 1600 acres have been designated a 'World Biosphere Reserve' by UNESCO and are part of the US National Forest network. The reserve is home to about half of the species to be found on Puerto Rico and among the knotted *guayacan* trees (lignum vitae, a wood so hard it was used to replace metal propeller shafts and ball-bearings) you will see bullfinches, hummingbirds and possibly even the *guabairo* or whippoorwill, a bird that was thought to be extinct for 80 years, but which was found in the reserve in the 50s. If you are a fisherman, you can arrange a trip to the island of Guilligan.

Farther along Route 116 is the resort town of **Parguera**, which has sprung up around an old fishing village where the cabins sit on stilts above the water. It is lively holiday spot, popular among the Puerto Ricans themselves. Just west of Parguera, among the coastal mangrove swamps, is a well known phosphorescent bay, though reports say that Parguera has lost much of its luminescence (there is an excellent bay on Vieques).

San German

San German is the oldest settlement on Puerto Rico after San Juan and it is one of the island's most charming Spanish colonial towns. It had to be moved a number of times to be safe from the Caribs and pirates in the 16th century but eventually it settled here in the foothills of the Cordillera in 1573. Today the town has 30,000 inhabitants and a university.

The central streets of old San German remain intact, running parallel to enclose a series of paved plazas lined with trees above which the old white colonial buildings stand proudly in the sun and the town houses from the coffee era display their elaborate gabling.

The **Porta Coeli Church** (meaning 'Heaven's Gate') was built in 1606 by Dominican friars, and is one of the few examples of baroque Spanish architecture in the Caribbean. Recently restored, it stands above the Parque de Santo Domingo, an old market-place, and is approached by brick steps. Inside the wooden beams and ceiling are thought to be original, though the balcony is not. Statues and paintings from the 19th century are on view. It is really more of a museum of religious art than a working church, as Mass is celebrated only three times a year. Open Tues–Sun, 9–noon and 1–4.30.

The Southwest

The remote Cabo Rojo district in the southwestern corner of the island is the driest area of Puerto Rico and it has long been known as a vacationers' spot because of the beaches. Puerto Real on the coast was once the principal harbour for merchandise off-loaded for this part of the island and it is still an important fishing area.

Boquerón is well known for its balneario (many say it is the best beach on the island) but less known for the Boqueron Nature Reserve, which includes two swamp areas, the Laguna Boqueron and the Laguna Cartagena. Paths are cut through the mangrove, where you can expect to see plenty of birds sporting spiked haircuts and glaring plumage—including ducks, herons, pelicans and the purple gallinule. Laguna Joyada to the north of Cabo Rojo is also designated as a wildlife reserve.

At the southwestern tip of the island, where there are sandy salt pans once used by Ponce de León, is the Cabo Rojo lighthouse, built on the 100-ft clifftops by the Spaniards a century ago. This area was a favourite pirate haunt in the 17th century, used by the Spaniard Roberto Cofresi. North of Boquerón you pass the other resort town of Joyuda, a string of restaurants along the waterfront with a good beach just out of the town. Continuing north you come to Puerto Rico's third town of Mayagüez.

San Juan to Mayagüez

The north coast, running west from San Juan, is the most developed area of the island. Routes 2 and 22 eventually emerge from the sprawl of suburban San Juan and cruise the 80 miles to the northwestern corner of the island at Rincón, by-passing tourist resorts, towns and factories. They follow the coastal plain, five miles broad, in the shadow of the mountains—minor roads labour tortuously up into these forested peaks of 1500 feet, known as karst country, where the rainwater has carved a landscape of sharp pinnacles and caverns out of the limestone rock over the millennia.

Bayamón has been all but swallowed up by the ever-encroaching San Juan, but it seems that modernity has already arrived anyway in the form of shopping malls and the Alcaldía, a massive space-age construction of glass and yellow beams that seemingly hovers above the road. One of the island's finest artists, Francisco Oller (1883–1917), came from here. His work is on show at the Museo Francisco Oller in the old Alcaldía, along with Arawak figurines; open Tues–Sat, 9–4.

The beaches around Dorado have been developed as a tourist resort—the quarter-mile waterslide at Cerromar being the next most appealing feature after the sand—though the town itself retains something of the sedated feel it had before the tourists arrived. Fifteen miles farther down the coast, Vega Baja is set among fertile grounds that once riffled with sugar-cane.

Arecibo, set on a bay 50 miles west of San Juan, was founded in the late 16th century and is now home to about 80,000 people. It was named after an Arawak Indian chief, Aracibo, whose tribe used a cave, the Cueva del Indio, a few miles west of the town, for their ceremonies. There are petroglyphs visible on the cave walls. Arecibo is one of the industrial centres of Puerto Rico—pharmaceutical companies established themselves here during 'Operation Bootstrap', the American investment programme, in the 1940s.

In the mountains, 15 miles south of the town, you will find the **Arecibo Observatory**, the largest radio telescope in the world. It is simply vast; a 20-acre dish that fits neatly into a *karst* sinkhole 1300 feet across, the sort of place where James Bond might hang out. Radar and radio waves bounce off the dish and are collected by the huge triangular measuring gear, slung 600 feet above the bowl and then analysed by the batteries of computers in the buildings nearby. The Observatory is run by Cornell University and was responsible for discovering the first pulsars and quasars. Open weekdays, 2 pm for a tour, open day Sun 11–4, no tour, adm free (tel 878 2612).

Route 10 leads across the island to Ponce via Utuado and Adjuntas, the heartland of the *jibaro*, the self-reliant Puerto Rican farmer who cuts a living out of the mountains and cultivates the fertile ground of the rainforest. About 8 miles west of Utuado is the **Caguana Indian Ceremonial Park** and museum, towered over by mountain peaks. The stone-lined playing fields (called *bateyes*) were built about 800 years ago by the Arawaks for their ballgames and religious ceremonies. It is a bit sad and empty because the activity is long gone, but the gardens are pleasant enough to walk in. Open daily except Tues, 9–5, museum open Sat and Sun 10–4, adm free.

For a close up of the **karst country**, a sea of forested cones, take the minor roads south and west of Arecibo to the forest reserves of **Río Abajo** on Route 621, where you will see the forest at its richest and may come across a Puerto Rican parrot (you can also get a boat trip on **Lago Dos Bocas** from nearby) and **Lago Guajataca**, on Route 446 to the west.

The karst cones are mirrored below ground by a series of sinkholes and caverns. The limestone base of this area has been eroded over the millennia by acidic water, and all the dripping has created stalactites, stalagmites and caves. Rivers emerge momentarily in the base of a sinkhole and then disappear again underground. It is one of the largest cave-systems in the Americas.

The **River Camuy Cave Park**, on Route 129, puts all of this on view in a regimented way, with bilingual lectures followed by a trip in a little trolley bus and then a walk, strictly monitored to keep you on the concrete path (you are asked not to touch anything because human oils quickly destroy aeons of work on the limestone by dripping water). You wind down the overgrown walls of a sinkhole into the depths of the karst to a cavern 170 ft high where mighty and bulbous stalactites continue to drip and stalagfruitcakes of goo below rise to meet them at a speed of about an inch per million years. You will see the 'witch', complete with a drip on the end of her nose, and you will even discover the secret of curving stalactites. The underground Rio Camuy can be seen crashing through the base of the Tres Pueblos sinkhole. Open Wed–Sun, 8–4, adm (tel 765 5555). The Cueva de Camuy is a different venture on Route 486, where there are go-carts and horses to keep you amused as well as the cave. Open daily 9–5, adm (tel 898 2723).

The town of **Lares**, perched on the hillside at the southern edge of the karst country, has a special place in the Puerto Rican soul. The *Grito de Lares* (the cry of Lares), a revolt which many feel was the first expression of Puerto Rican national consciousness, took place here in 1868. When liberals such as Betances were expelled from the island in 1867 by the Spaniards, from their exile they tried to raise the Puerto Ricans. Their plans were rumbled, but they went ahead anyway, capturing Lares and declaring a Republic of Puerto Rico. But their first crack at independence was short-lived because they were defeated the next day when they advanced on the nearby town of San Sebastian. The 'cry' is celebrated every year by *Independentistas* on 24 September. An obelisk in the town square commemorates the heroes of the revolt.

Back on the coast, Route 2 hits the west coast at Aguadilla, spread along the seafront. Christopher Columbus is supposed to have landed between here and Añasco on his second voyage in 1493. The controversy over exactly where still continues, each town claiming the honour. The waves can get up in this area and **Rincón**, backed by the massive foothills of La Cadena mountains, is a very popular surfing spot. The world championships were held here in 1968 and 1988.

Fifteen miles south, **Mayagüez** (pronounced Majjawezz) is Puerto Rico's third town, an industrial centre and important port. Rebuilt after it was completely destroyed by an earthquake in 1917, Mayagüez now has a population of around 100,000 and is dotted with modern blocks, but it still pulses around the traditional square, the Plaza Colón, where Columbus and the classical Alcaldía (Town Hall) face one another through the trees. In the outskirts you will see the factories that process over 50 per cent of the tuna fish eaten in the USA.

The gardens of the **Tropical Agricultural Research Station** are attached to the University of Puerto Rico and are sited on a former plantation in the north of the town, on Route 65. Tropical plants from all over the world are neatly set out. Check out the smells of the leaves—cinnamon, citrus and clove—and oddities such as the cannonball tree (with fruit like wooden cannon balls and yet the most ephemeral flowers that die at dusk), the Panama canoe tree and pink torch ginger. Open Mon–Fri, 7.30–4, adm free (tel 834 2435).

At the **Mayagüez Zoo**, a little farther north out of the town on Route 108, the compounds of the several hundred animals from all over the world are laid out in another garden of Caribbean tropical exuberance. As well as Bengal tigers and the Andean condor, you can see the outsize rat called a capybara. Open Tues–Sun, 9–4.30, adm (tel 832 8110).

La Ruta Panoramica—West to East

The Panoramic Route follows a tortuous path along the chain of mountains in the Cordillera Central, running for a hundred miles (as the crow flies, though he might have some difficulty over these mountains). Starting at Mayagüez the road climbs quickly into the hills, often touching heights of 3000 ft and passing close to the island's highest peak, the Cerro de Punta. It crosses the main San Juan—Ponce road near Cayey and then descends to Yabucoa on the southeastern coast. The vistas are quite spectacular; with just a small turn in the road whole new valleys and views of the coast can open up. There are also some strategically placed look-out towers. Some days you will find yourself in the rainclouds at this height, but whatever the weather the flora is as exuberant and stunning as the views. The road seems to be swallowed up in a tunnel of foliage: strangled mahogany, bamboos, sierra palms and 10-ft tree ferns of luminescent green, as powerful a colour as the night-time glow of the fireflies. The Ruta Panoramica is marked (though the Route numbers vary along the way) and it takes a couple of days at least to cover the ground at leisure. You could take far longer over it, perhaps stopping at the mountain paradors.

From Mayagüez the road climbs into the traditional coffee country around the town of Maricao. The **Maricao** and (a little further east) the **Mt Guilarte Forest Reserves** are two of the lesser known and less developed reserves on the island, but there are trails that will lead you among the mahogany, tabanuco and trumpet trees of the forest (ask around because many are unmarked and you might decide to take a guide). Woodpeckers, cuckoos and hawks as well as the more delicate hummingbirds live in the luxuriant trees. In the ponds of the **Maricao Fish Hatchery**, set in tropical gardens off Route 120, they raise around 25,000 fish each year for the freshwater lakes around Puerto Rico. Open daily 8–noon and 1–4, adm free.

At Adjuntas the Ruta Panoramica joins the main Ponce to Arecibo road for five miles before turning east to the **Toro Negro Forest Reserve**, where a path leads from the road up Cerro de Punta, at 4390 ft the highest peak on the island. On a clear day you can see 50 or 60 miles, beyond the coasts of the island. Unfortunately you will find that you are not alone up there, because there are some communications antennae on the peak. Many rivers rise in this area and so there are plenty of waterfalls and rock pools beneath them in which to swim. Try the Inabón river, which thrashes out a ravine for itself heading south from the reserve. The Dona Juana Falls in the **Dona Juana Recreation Centre** are 60 m high. Most of the trails in the forest are unmarked and so you should ask directions.

Thirty-five miles farther on you come to the towns of **Aibonito**, the highest town on the island, and **Barranquitas**, birthplace of the 19th-century Puerto Rican leader Luís Muñoz Rivera.

The **San Cristóbal canyon** is a spectacular river ravine that runs between the two towns. Its sides are almost sheer and in places they plummet for 500 feet, but they are still infested with tropical growth. There are two easy descents (though you will have to ask because they are not marked). From Aibonito go north on Route 725 and after three miles descend on a path to a 100-ft waterfall on a rocky face. Outside Barranquitas on Route 156 you can climb down into the other end of the ravine among the riotous mosses and greenery.

Not far after crossing the main San Juan—Ponce Expressway (Route 52) you come to the **Carite Forest Reserve**, a 6000 acre reserve in the Sierra de Cayey, where 50 species of bird live, including the Puerto Rican tanager and hummingbirds. There are waterfalls and a small pool called Charco Azul about ten yards across where the water is a strong blue colour. From the Reserve, the road descends to the southwestern coast at Yabucoa and to the tourist world of Palmas del Mar.

FESTIVALS
Every town in Puerto Rico celebrates its saint's day in a week-long blow-out of masses, feasts, candle processions with statues, dances and masked street parades. These are fun to attend, and you will certainly be included in the activities if you are around. The daytime parades are a riotous procession of masked figures and diabolos dancing in ghoulish, brightly coloured masks and everywhere the streets are alive with impromptu *kioskos* and games. A favourite is the horse-races on a crank-up merry-go-round where you bet on tin horses.

PUERTO RICO

Some of the main towns and their *fiestas patronales:*

2 Feb—Mayagüez, a very spectacular celebration in honour of *La Virgen de la Candelaria.*
19 March—Lares, *San Jose*
1 May—Arecibo, *San Felipe Apostol*
13 June—Barranquitas, *San Antonio de Padua*
17 July—Culebra, *La Virgen del Carmen*
25 July—Loíza, *Santiago* one of the best known on the island.
25 July—Fajardo, *Santiago*
21 Aug—Adjuntas, *San Joaquin and Santa Ana*
3 Sept—Jayuya, *Nuestra Señora de la Montserrate*
29 Sept—Utuado, *San Miguel Arcangel*
29 Sept—Cabo Rojo
7 Oct—Yauco, *Nuestra Señora del Rosario*
4 Nov—Aguadilla
8 Dec—Humacao
16 Dec—Ponce, *Nuestra Señora de Guadelupe.*

At **Christmas** Puerto Rican towns are strung end to end with fairy lights and coloured tinsel, often with a life-size nativity scene, but the most spectacular and riotous event over the Christmas period is the **Festival of the Innocents**, which takes place in the small town of Hatillo, near Arecibo, on 28 December. Groups of men (mainly) dress in suits of brightly coloured ruff-like material, wearing ghostly masks and spend the day driving around the country on decorated floats. In the afternoon they converge on the town square, where they bounce their vehicles from side to side until they nearly tip over. Well worth a visit for a riot of colourful excess.

WHERE TO STAY
Puerto Rico has something to suit every taste. It is well known for the large glitzy casino hotels along the coast in San Juan, but behind these you will find smaller, more personable inns. And away from the city there are some unexpected gems (particularly the luxurious Horned Dorset Primavera on the west coast), both in the resort towns on the seafront and also in the mountains where there are some charming paradors. If you are travelling around the island it is useful to have a comprehensive list of hotels in *Qué Pasa*, the tourist brochure. A government tax of 7% is applied to all hotel bills (9% in hotels with a casino). Most hotels accept credit cards.

San Juan
If you would like to be in the historic surroundings of Old San Juan you can stay at the **Gran Hotel El Convento**, PO Box 1048 (tel 809 723 9020, fax 721 2877, US 800 468 2779) on Calle Cristo just near the cathedral. The former 17th-century Carmelite convent has been completely refitted but it retains an atmospheric air with its old beams and chequerboard tile floors and the arched balconies above the courtyard and swimming pool. The dining room is in the old chapel and the rooms are certainly more comfortable than the former occupants' cells. Double in season: *Abbot* $150, *Monsignor* $175, *Cardinal* $200. Not far off is the **Casa San José**, 159 Calle San Jose (tel 723 1212, fax 723 7620), a beautifully restored town house just off the Plaza de Armas, with

wrought-iron balconies, a tiled interior with colonial furniture and four-poster beds. No children, just nine rooms, at $160–400 for a double in season. A good and **cheap** place to rest your head right in the centre of town (a travelling businessman's rather than a tourist hotel) is the **Central Hotel** (tel 722 2751), just off the Plaza de Armas. Simple fan-ventilated rooms with share or private bathrooms, restaurant downstairs, $30 a double.

Condado and Isla Verde

EXPENSIVE

If you like a large hotel with all the glitz then in the **Condado strip** you might try the **Hotel Condado Beach**, PO Box 41226 (tel 721 6888, fax 722 5062, US 800 468 2775), a pink colossus on the waterfront. In the swish foyer with arches, palms and vaulted ceilings you will see pictures of the Vanderbilt family, whose holiday home it was (before expansion). It has something of the manicured sophistication of those years and international standard comfort in the rooms. No casino, but plenty nearby. The Vanderbilt Club within the hotel caters for businesspeople. Double room in season $130–420. In Isla Verde the **El San Juan Hotel and Casino**, PO Box 2872 (tel 791 1000, fax 791 6985, US 800 468 2818) has a similar humming quality as it towers above the beach. Pith-helmeted guards greet you and you pass into the massive elaborate foyer of dark-stained wood, imitation gas-lamps and chandeliers. Huge lounging area and pool outside with swim-up bar and then the superb sand. The rooms are high-luxury, down to the third telephone in the bathroom. Ten restaurants, bars, clubs and casino on the premises. Double room $285–385.

MODERATE

Behind these monumental blocks on the seafront you will find smaller, friendlier (and better priced) hotels in both Condado and Isla Verde. The **Canario Inn**, 1317 Ashford Ave (tel 722 fax 722 0391) has a hint of old-time Puerto Rico in the façade and the foyer, though inside the inn is modern. Just 15 rooms, no pool, but a pleasant stop in town, double room $75, includes breakfast on a communal veranda, no restaurant. Close by is the **Canario by the Sea**, 4 Condado Ave (tel 722 8640, fax 725 4921), which also has a friendly feel, with just 24 rooms. Small bar and courtyard, rooms air-conditioned with television. Double room $80–95, includes breakfast. **El Prado Inn**, 1350 Calle Luchetti (tel 728 5925, fax 725 6978, US 800 468 4521) is set in an old suburban villa in Condado. It has just ten rooms and a pool (though, like the others, the beach is just a couple of minutes away) in a courtyard dripping with bougainvillaea. Some rooms have a certain style of times past, others just a bit past their prime but comfortable nonetheless. Another nice stop in town, double room $60–80. In Santurce you can find a simple double room at the **Hotel Castle Sutherland** (tel 724 1577, fax 724 7169) for $60 or at the **Hotel Toro** (tel 725 5150). In Isla Verde **La Casa Mathieson**, Calle Uno 14 (tel 762 8662, fax 268 2415, US 800 223 1588) is a stone's throw from the beach (if you can clear the condominiums). Twenty rooms with air-conditioning, ceiling fans and private baths for $65–70. Also kitchenettes, though there is a bar and a restaurant in the hotel. Next door you will find the **Green Isle Inn** with 17 rooms at similar prices. At the **Borinquen Royal Guest House** (tel 728 8400, fax 268 2411), right on the main Isla Verde Ave you can get a double room for $65.

In **Fajardo**, east of San Juan, you will find a friendly parador, **La Familia**, PO

Box 21399 (tel 863 1193), 22 air-conditioned rooms in a modern villa, beaches and watersports not far off. Good stopover for a trip to the islands, double room $62. You might also try the parador **Martorell**, PO Box 384 (tel 889 2710) in Luquillo, also set in a modern house, double room $55.

Ponce
The **Hotel Meliá**, PO Box 1431 (tel 842 0260, fax 841 3602) is the most charming place to stay, situated in the historic area in the centre of Ponce. It keeps some of the old-time feel of the town in the period foyer and courtyard, though the rooms are modern. Comfortable double rooms for $65–75 year round. The **Hotel Belgica** (tel 844 3255) is across the main square at 122 Villa, in a large town-house with wrought iron balconies. Double at $40. The cheapest place to stay in town is the **Hotel Colville** on Avenida Muñez Riviera at the corner of Las Américas (tel 843 1835), simple rooms at $25. Call before 10 pm or you'll end up at the **Hotel Eden**, a drive-in knocking shop way out of town, $21 for a garage and large double bed and mirrors all over the walls.

There is a parador off the San Juan–Ponce road; **Baños de Coama** (tel 825 2186, fax 825 4739), just off Route 153. The 'baños' are the hot springs that attracted so elegant a crowd in the last century. They have lost most of their refinement now, the rooms are sparse and functional, but there are still one or two fine buildings around the courtyard and the dining room has been restored nearly to its former elegance. Not a bad stop if you are travelling through. Double room $65. Beyond Ponce you will find one of the nicest paradors, in the centre of San Germán, the **Oasis**, PO Box 144 (tel 892 1175, fax 892 1175 ext 200). It is set in an old town house and so you pass through the colonial foyer furnished with ornate woodwork and wicker-backed rocking chairs. The dining room overlooks the pool, as do some of the 55 rooms. Another agreeable stopover for the setting and the friendly crowd, double room $60.

Around the Island
In the southeastern corner of the island you will find three seaside resort towns with small and friendly hotels. They are popular with the Puerto Ricans at the weekends and in the holidays and their prices tend to rise for the summer months rather than in the winter season.

In **Parguera** the nicest place to stay is one of the paradors, the **Villa Parguera**, PO Box 273 (tel 899 3975, fax 899 6040), which overlooks the lagoon and the mangrove islands where the holiday houses stand on stilts. The 61 rooms stand in two-storey blocks with balconies giving on to a palm garden and the pool. There is no beach, but you can find sand just a boat-ride away. There is a good restaurant, double room $74. Not far along the waterfront is the **Posada Porlamar** PO Box 405 (tel 899 4015), also a parador, which is slightly simpler, but has comfortable, air-conditioned rooms in a cabin. There is no restaurant, but the rooms have kitchenettes, double room $65. There are a number of **guest houses** in the streets behind the waterfront, of which the most comfortable is probably the **Parguera** guest house (tel 899 3993) opposite the Porlamar where double rooms with private bath and air-conditioning come at $50. **Hilda's** guest house, Calle 2 (tel 899 4055) is set in a modern villa—two apartments built with all mod cons for $65 and $75 a night. On Calle Principal there are rooms at the **Flamboyan** (tel 899 3524), kitchen facilities, private bath, air-conditioning, rooms from $30. Not far off the **Villa Andujar** also has cheap rooms (tel 899 3475).

The small town of **Boquerón** has a similar seaside feel about it, and excellent sunset views from the superb beach, which is just a short walk from the town. The best place to stay is the **Parador Boquemar**, PO Box 133 (tel 851 7600), in a modern block in the centre of the town. The 63 air-conditioned rooms are fitted out with TV and fridges and balconies that overlook the pool. Double room $65 in season.

There is a (much) simpler alternative across the road at the **Villa del Mar** on the waterfront, where you can get a double rooms for $25. There are plenty of villas for rent in the town. On the other side of Cabo Rojo, between Playa Joyuda and Playa Laguna you wil find a string of hotels and restaurants. The most comfortable is **Perichi's**, a parador, PO Box 16310 (tel 851 3131, fax 851 0620). The inn is in a modern block, but the service is personal and friendly and there is a popular restaurant downstairs. 22 rooms with balconies and a pool, double room $71 year round. There are rooms at **Tony's** (tel 851 2500); pool, simple accommodation and a seafood restaurant.

North of **Mayagüez** there is a good beach hotel in the **Parador Villa Antonio**, PO Box 63 (tel 823 2445, fax 823 8380), just south of Rincón. The hotel itself is modern and air-conditioned and the rooms are comfortable if a little uninspiring, but the sand and palms just outside are superb. And of course there are fine sunset views, double room $50–85.

Not far up the coast is a surprising find all on its own; the most elegant hotel in Puerto Rico, the **Horned Dorset Primavera**, PO Box 1132 **Rincón** (tel 809 823 4030, fax 823 5580). The 24 suites look through a beautiful tropical garden towards the sea and the sunset and beneath them the main house has the grace and finery of the old Spanish colonial days. Above, approached by the 'embracing' staircase, is the restaurant, with chequerboard floor, wrought-iron lamps and candles, and downstairs are the classical balustrades of the terrace just above the waves, together with the rarefied atmosphere of a country house in the drawing room and library—John Stuart Mill's autobiography and Harry Truman's memoirs, as well as copies of the New Yorker magazine. Double room $275–300.

There are not many hotels in the **northwest** of the island, and those that exist are a bit disappointing. The best is probably the parador **Vistamar** (tel 895 2065, fax 895 2294) a modern block on a hilltop off Route 113, where the comfortable double room costs $55–80.

However, **inland** you will find two of the island's finest paradors, lost in the mountains and the rainforest. The **Hacienda Gripiñas**, PO Box 387 (tel 828 9750, fax 828 1717) is one of the loveliest spots on the island. The inn is set in a charming wooden West Indian house, formerly the estate house of a coffee plantation, built in 1853. There is a superb veranda overlooking the explosive tropical flora where you can take an early evening cocktail in time-honoured Caribbean style. The 19 rooms are in the main house and an extension—many have the gracious atmosphere of the planters' days. It is high in the mountains and so it can get quite cold at night (the pool's freezing in the winter). Good value at $60 a double. A few valleys away in **Utuado** is another parador, the **Casa Grande**, PO Box 616 Utuado (tel 894 3939), which is also set on a former coffee plantation. The main house stands on the hillside with the wooden cabins containing the 20 rooms strung out beneath it. Lost in the rainforest, the inn is private and quiet, another good weekend retreat from the city or the high-pressure tourism race, double room $55.

EATING OUT

Puerto Rico, and particularly its capital San Juan (which is both a large city and the centre of the tourist industry) has a grand variety of places in which to eat out, with endless styles—Spanish, Chinese, seafood and *nouvelle*—and as many settings—sophisticated dining rooms, waterfront fish restaurants, milk bars and local *fondas*. The hotels tend to have international and continental menus and of course, as Puerto Rico is a part of America, there are endless burger bars. You will find the service slightly snappier than in much of the Caribbean. Restaurants accept credit cards and service runs at 10–15%.

This is not to forget Puerto Rican food itself. Food can often be quite heavy, the main course a thick soup or a stew, such as *asopao*, which is made with pork, chicken or seafood. You also get a mound of rice in *arroz con pollo* (chicken or another meat with rice cooked in coconut). To accompany it you will have *mofongo*, battered spiced plantain, or *arroz con habichuelos*, rice and beans (*cristianos y morros* are white and black beans). *Lechón asao*, roast suckling pig, is a popular dish, and otherwise seafood and goat meat are often used.

Snacks are also very popular in Puerto Rico and you will see *kioskos* at the roadside all over the island (there is a string of them at the roadside in Luquillo). They sell a bewildering variety of snacks—seafood appears in crab sticks, or deep fried crab with yucca which is then presented to you in a sea-grape leaf, and you will find lobster and chicken tacos. *Alcapurrias* are meat or crab fritters and traditional Caribbean codfish also comes frittered as *bacalao*. *Chicharrón* are pieces of fried pork rind like outsize pork scratchings. Sweet potato and banana are often fried too. Cheese is often used to best advantage. Try a *sorullo*, a sugared cheese roly-poly. *Picadillos* are meat patties and *empanadas* and *pasteles* are made with fried cassava dough inlaid with meat or raisins and beans.

San Juan

The capital has the greatest concentration of restaurants and bars, many of them in the old buildings of the colonial area, which are pleasant surroundings.

EXPENSIVE

La Zaragozana (tel 725 3262) on Calle San Francisco has an old-time ambience—dark-stained panels and wooden furniture, overseen by brisk bow-tied waiters. Caribbean food, but also international fare on a huge and varied menu—sautéd chicken in almonds, raisins and white wine or *zarzuela de mariscos* (a medley of seafoods). Open seven days, main course $20. A chic restaurant in town is **Pikayo** (tel 721 6194), which is dressed up pastel-coloured, geometric panels and huge mirrors and peopled by hip San Juañeros. The menu is creole and cajun, presented immaculately on big plates which are colour-coded with the decor. Shrimp popcorn, followed by blackened fish or 'canoe' eggplant with shrimp and *sofrito* sauce. Main course $17–20, with a set spa menu (700 calories) for $23. At 315 Recinto Sur, just above the port, dinner only, closed Sun.

455

MODERATE
Just close by is another cool spot, the lively Italian restaurant **Al Dente** (tel 723 7303), with a dining-room slung with greenery. Pumpkin *linguini* in basil and olive oil or scallops sautéed in garlic and white wine. $14 a main course, closed Sun. Among the bars of Calle San Sebastian (see below), you will find a chi-chi retreat at **Amadeus**, which also serves Italian food—*funghi porcini tortellini* with mushrooms, ham and cream sauce, or grilled chicken in its mayonnaise, main course $7–20. Nearby **El Patio de Sam** (tel 723 1149) is another haunt popular with the locals, set in an attractive town house. Fun crowd, particularly at the weekends, and good food, lobster tail broiled or scampied, or kingfish in an almond sauce, $7–20. Another good daytime spot, particularly if you need a rest after touring the cavernous recesses of the San Cristobal fortress, is **Amanda's**, which overlooks the ocean from Calle Norzagaray. You can sit outside at a special bar or inside in the bright and breezy dining room. Mexican food—*fajitos* and *guacamole* and plenty of vegetarian dishes for $7–10. **La Mallorquina**, on Calle San Justo (tel 722 3261) has been something of an institution in the city since it was built in 1848. It has seen generations of San Juañeros out for political discussion over a meal (the broken vase in the corner is witness to a flared temper apparently). Nowadays the visitors tend to be tourists, but you get a good local meal in historic surroundings—house speciality *asopao* or you might try sherry seafood, main course about $15.

CHEAP
Less pretentious, but just as central a city institution is **La Bombonera** on Calle San Francisco, a popular gathering point, particularly after mass on Sundays. Past the pastries section at the entrance you can sit at the long bar on round stools or at the bench tables along the walls. Busy and full of waiters in red coats storming past, tending to singles reading the paper, doting pairs of lovers and noisy families. Local dishes or an omelette for $5–9. Best of all is the lemonade served in crushed ice.

Condado and Isla Verde

EXPENSIVE
Outside the colonial area there are also a host of restaurants and of course there are endless dining rooms inside the hotels. **Torreblanca** (tel 725 8496) is situated in a mock-Spanish villa at 1110 Magdalena in Condado. The dining room is calm and plush, laid with deep red velvet and presided over by brisk waiters. The menu is mainly Spanish—vegetable *menestra a la Bilbaina* and *camarrones al ajillo* (shrimp in garlic). Main course $20 plus. Not far off is **Don Pepe** (tel 723 4593) at 72 Condado, which is similar in price and its setting in a modern villa. International menus with paella specialities—*marinera or valencia*—followed by tropical fruit ice creams.

MODERATE
Ajili Mojili, downstairs in the Condado Lagoon Hotel is very popular with the Puerto Ricans themselves—an airco dining room serving local food and seafoods including *asopaos* and rice dishes, price from $12. Across the lagoon you will find local and Spanish fare at **Fornos** restaurant (tel 722 3120), which is set in a dark and sumptuous airco dining room. Huge menu of chicken, seafood and trout, $12 plus. One of the best

restaurants in the island is **La Casita Blanca,** a classic Puerto Rican *fonda*, set in the *barrio* (the ghetto). You feel that you have come into someone's home when you arrive—you sit either outside in the courtyard, under the guinep trees, or indoors on foldaway chairs at tables with bright yellow plastic table cloths. The waiters wear neckerchiefs and are generally pretty hip. Appetizers arrive in a banana leaf; codfish or sugary corn fritters and you eat them with *mariada*, a local mix of wine, rum, mavi and fruit juices. Follow up with goat stew or fish dishes and finish with coffee and their own additive (with rum and cinnamon). Well worth a visit, some of the best local food, main course about $10.

Around the Island

You will find good local *fondas* everywhere in the country, though they will not usually be gourmet dining. However, the Tourist Board sponsors a list of restaurants called the *Mesones Gastronomicos* which are located throughout the island. There are about 40 of them and they are listed in *Qué Pasa*.

In **Fajardo** you will find two restaurants: **Rosa's** seafood restaurant and steakhouse in an ugly concrete house, good local food though—shrimp, crayfish or BBQ chicken Rosa style; and the **Anchor's Inn**, on the road to Las Croabas, with excellent seafood and *mofongo* to a musical accompaniment.

Ponce has a few good dining rooms—in the Playa area south of the town you will find **El Ancla** (tel 840 2450), where you can eat seafood, including the house speciality *asopao de mariscos* or a lobster and shrimp combination. Open daily, main dish $15.

Along the coast heading west are two waterfront restaurants which collect a lively crowd at the weekends. Try **Pito's** (tel 841 4977), with seafood and Spanish fare. You can eat under parasols on a deck above the Caribbean Sea. Try shrimp in white wine sauce with linguini, $17. Not far off is **Las Marguaritas** Café (tel 841 6617) where you can have a fresh fillet of local fish in Cajun spices or butter sauce for $15. Both have live music occasionally.

In **Boqueron** you will find a nice veranda setting at **RUICOF** Restaurant (from Ruiz Cofresi), where you can get a *tortilla camarrones* or a *carrucho* (conch) mayonnaise, from $7. North of here in **Playa Joyuda** there is a good restaurant at **Perichi's**, a *meson gastronomico*, but you might also try the **Vista Bahia** restaurant, which as the name suggests looks out on to the bay from a deck. Octopus salad or seafood for $15. **El Bohío** also stands on the waterfront and serves local food and seafood for $10 a main course.

BARS AND NIGHTLIFE

Old San Juan's bars may be frequented by cruise-ship tourists by day, but they are more local at night when the San Juañeros venture outside to take the evening air in a promenade (or its car-borne equivalent, in which they cruise by, stereo blaring). One of the most charming spots is the cocktail bar **La Violeta**, at the top end of Calle Fortaleza. Here you are cast back in time in an old colonial drawing room with rocking chairs, wicker armchairs and family photographs above the piano. Nice crowd at the bar, or hidden away in the private rooms off the courtyard. Extremely tasty strawberry and banana daiquiris. If you would prefer a beer and a game of pool, then you can go just round the corner to the **Small World Bar**. Posters of cars if you're homesick for the Caddy and bicycles hanging from the ceiling.

The liveliest street in Old San Juan (one long traffic jam in the late evening) is Calle San Sebastian, where there are chichi cocktail bars alongside more raucous drinking and dancing bars. **El Quinqué** sees an arty crowd, and on the Plaza San Jose at the top end wasted execs gather around **El Pub en los Balcones**, with latterday pirates serving at the bar, and at **Naco's**, where you are watched closely by a bull's head while you drink. Round the corner is another fun drinking dungeon, **El Batey**, where the walls are smothered in graffiti. Opposite the Mallorquina you will find a hip video bar, **El Fausto**.

One of the best bars in the city is on Calle Loíza, in the Santurce area, **Shannan's Pub**, an Irish bar with a very lively crowd at the weekend—videos, sleek chicks in black and cool guys. Close by is the **Apple Jazz Club**. **Peggy Sue** on Roberto H. Todd is more of a dancing club and back in old San Juan you will find **Lazer Disco**. Some of the larger hotels in Condado and Isla Verde also have discotheques.

The **Black Angus** is one of the best-known brothels in the world.

Culebra, Vieques and Mona

There are a number of islands and plenty of tiny cays off the coasts of Puerto Rico. To the east lie **Vieques** and **Culebra**, midway between Puerto Rico and the Virgin Islands, to which they are geographically related. You can fly or take the ferry from Fajardo. **Mona** stands out on its own, 50 miles off the west coast, half-way between Puerto Rico and the Dominican Republic. These islands are quite remote and it is helpful to speak Spanish in order to get the best out of them.

VIEQUES

Vieques (pronounced 'Byekess') lies seven miles from the eastern shore of Puerto Rico and is twenty-five miles by five, larger than Culebra. With 9000 inhabitants and about as many horses, it is a good example of a small Spanish Caribbean island, easy-going and well worth a visit. It connection with the military has meant that it has remained relatively undeveloped—there is an easy tranquillity when the island is not being invaded. As for beaches, Vieques has some of Puerto Rico's best. On a coastline of 60 miles, there are about 40 of them.

Vieques played a part in the merry-go-round of colonial possession, being occupied by the French and the British in turn before finally winding up in Puerto Rican hands in 1854. For a while the island was covered in sugar-cane and it was a successful plantation island. Today there are none of the cane-cutting gangs and so life has become considerably quieter.

Unlike Culebra, Vieques is still two-thirds owned by the US Navy—they own the western fifth, the NAF, and the eastern half of the island, Camp Garcia—and there are annual naval exercises (the dummy runs for the invasion of Grenada in 1983 were carried out here and there was a lot of activity during the Gulf War). When there are no exercises, some of the Navy land is open to the public and you can visit the excellent beaches on the south coast. Many of the islanders object to the Navy presence, and sometimes squat on the land, but for visitors it brings an unexpected benefit. Were it not for this, so stunning an island might look a bit like Condado or Miami Beach. As it is Vieques is rustic and not really that well known.

The town (and ferry arrival point) is **Isabel Segunda**, on the north coast, where you will see the locals pursuing life's necessities like playing dominoes and chatting. On the plaza is a bust of Simon Bolivar, El Libertador, who came to the island in 1816. Overlooking the town is a fort, built in 1843 and restored to its original state, though it was never finished, with wooden staircases and the statutory rusting cannon. It is now a **museum**, open irregularly, ask at the Tourism Office.

The only other settlement is **Esperanza** on the south coast, a string of villas, guest houses and restaurants along the Malecón, where the Viequenses lime and take the evening air. This is the island's principal tourist area. The pier was connected to a railway and was the loading point for the island's sugar crop, but the bay is used mainly by fishermen and sunbathers now. The quay at Mosquito on the northwest coast was built in the Second World War as a port for the British Navy, in case Britain was captured by the Germans. From the Punta Mula Lighthouse the views are spectacular.

GETTING TO AND AROUND VIEQUES
There are many daily flights from San Juan (both the international airport and Isla Grande), St Thomas and Fajardo, from where the flight is good value at $14. The **Vieques Air Link** (tel 722 3736 in San Juan and 741 8211 in the island). The ferry ride from Fajardo costs $3. *Públicos* will take you around the island. If none seem to be around, sit under a tree at the edge of town and somebody will probably stop to pick you up. To hire a car, contact **Island Car Rentals** (tel 741 1666) or **Sammy's Car Rental** in Esperanza (tel 740 0106). There is a helpful **Tourist Office** on the northern side of the plaza in Isabel Segunda (tel 741 5000), though you will find the hotel managers well informed.

BEACHES
Sun Bay, often written Sombe, just east of Esperanza is the best known of the island's beaches and there are public facilities. You can hire watersports equipment there and in Esperanza. Other beaches, many of which have taken on the colours of military speak, are in Camp Garcia. Enter by the gate on Route 997 and you will come to a sign to **Red Beach**—roads lead off this to **Barracuda** and **Garcia** beaches—and then half a mile beyond here you will come to a turning to the best beach on the island, **Secret** or **Hidden beach**. Farther on is a cracking bay called **Blue Beach**. Finally, in the far northwest of the island is another good beach **Green Bay**, which is approached by the airport road. **Snorkelling** is best off Esperanza and there are reefs in Hidden Bay and Blue Bay. **Scuba** diving can be fixed up through **Vieques Divers** (tel 741 8600).

The Phosphorescent Bay
A trip to Mosquito Bay, one of Vieques' three phosphorescent bays is one of the most extraordinary sights in the Caribbean. The bio-luminescence arises from a chemical reaction in microscopic protozoa living in the water, which glow when they are agitated. They shine in weird bright green whorls and clouds as you move through the water, or as you kick and splash. You will see fish dart away ahead of you (huge mantas are known to

glide by too) and if you flick the water with your canoe paddle you can set off a bright green arc of spray. Launch trips can be arranged (the motor makes an impressive trail), but you are best to go by canoe, which can be arranged through the Esperanza Hotel, $15.

Trips around the island on **horses** can be fixed up through Casa del Frances, a parador with an inimitable style and manager in Esperanza, about $10 per hour, minimum two hours.

WHERE TO STAY AND EATING OUT

There are no large hotels on Vieques, which is part of the charm of visiting the island, and so you will find personal service and an easy-going atmosphere, along with well-stocked libraries to which you can help yourself during your stay. If you wish to hire a villa, of which there are plenty, contact **Vieques Villa Rentals** at Calle Gladiolas 494, Esperanza, Puerto Rico 00705 (tel 741 8888). Government tax on hotel rooms is levied at 7% and service is usually 10%.

MODERATE

La Casa del Francés, PO Box 458 (tel 809 741 3751, fax 741 0717), just outside Esperanza, is a charming island retreat in the best West Indian tradition. It is set in a classic Caribbean great house with an inner courtyard and terraces smothered in tropical greenery. There are just twelve rooms and a fine dining room, run by a latterday Hemingway. This is the sort of place that writers retreat to. Double room $79, plus $20 for breakfast and dinner. A more conventional Caribbean beachfront hotel and one of Puerto Rico's paradors is the **Villa Esperanza**, PO Box 1569 (tel 741 8675). The parador has a beach club atmosphere, with 50 breezy and comfortable rooms looking through the garden to the bar and the waterfront (watersports available). The restaurant is a *meson gastronomico*, where you can get seafood or an excellent grouper in garlic and lime, $15. Double room in the winter season $76–96. Just above **Isabel Segunda** is a friendly guest house, the **Crow's Nest**, PO Box 1521 (tel 741 0033), eight self-catering rooms around a modern villa. There is a pool and a bar with a view. Also an excellent seafood restaurant—Cajun spiced chicken grilled and served with mango salsa or shrimp *de la casa*, main course $14. Double room $60 in season with better rates by the week. Also in a modern house above town, overlooking the fort and on to Culebra is the **Sea Gate Hotel**, PO Box 747 (tel 741 4661), patrolled by dogs, of which the owner has about twenty. Double rooms $50 with breakfast.

There are a number of **guest houses** in Esperanza, including **Tradewinds** (tel 741 8666), where rooms go for about $50, and you will find **Christina's Restaurant**— seafood or steamed fish *en papillotte* for $10—and the **Posada Vistamar** (tel 741 8716) in a similar range. **Tito's**, a couple of streets behind the main drag, is a cheaper option: no phone, $25 for a double room.

There is a string of bars and restaurants to retreat to in Esperanza when the sun gets too hot or from where you can watch the sunset of an evening. Try **Bananas**, a busy joint set on a terrace on the street front, steaks or shrimp for $12, or **El Quenepo**, a simple spot where you can get an octopus, conch or snail salad for $8. Finally, **El Gringo Loco** is a fun bar—benches around the walls of a wooden deck bar in the mangroves.

460

CULEBRA

Seven miles by four, Culebra rises lazily from the water in a range of low scrubby hills, surrounded by its satellites, a host of rocks and cays. Around them stretch a series of spectacular coral reefs.

Life is extremely peaceful for the 2000 Culebrans, many of whom live around the only settlement of **Dewey** (locally known as Puebla), just a few ramshackle houses and the odd grocery shop. Not much seems to happen here, just a few fishermen working from the bays and once-domestic animals wandering around the scrub, much as there was two or three centuries ago when the pirates would drop by. There is a sleepy atmosphere, a tropical island idyll Spanish-style.

Life wasn't always that peaceful, though. For 40 years, Culebra was used as a gunnery range by the US Navy and for whole days and nights the island would reverberate to the sound of exploding shells. The islanders became so sick of it that they mobilized in protest against it—with strategically placed picnics in the target area and the odd petrol bomb. Eventually in 1975 bombing was halted and peace returned.

Information and assistance can be obtained from the Tourist Office in the Alcaldía (Town Hall) in Dewey. The town does come alive once a year, during the *fiesta patronales* on 17 July.

BEACHES AND WATERSPORTS
There are some spectacular beaches on Culebra, the best known of which is **Flamenco Beach**, a cracking strip of bright white sand. Other beaches worth visiting are **Resaca** and **Zoni** on the east coast. You might also consider a trip over to one of Culebra's 23 satellites—Pirate's Cay in Ensenada Honda, Culebrita, Luis Peña—fix it up through a fisherman and remember to arm yourself with a picnic and snorkelling gear.

A few watersports (windsurfing, sailing and snorkelling) can be arranged through the hotels and through the small shops in the town. **Diving** among the excellent coral reefs, where deep blue angelfish glide and groupers pout, can be fixed up through the **Culebra Underwater Diving Association** (tel 742 3839).

WILDLIFE
Seeking out the wildlife can be rewarding. Four species of sea turtle come to the beaches to nest—they crawl up the sand at night, dig a hole with their back flippers in which they lay their eggs, and then bury them before disappearing back into the sea. You might have to stay up most of the night, but if you get a chance to see the giant Leatherback laying its eggs between April and July, it is well worth it. You might wish to go through a guide, but if not, the best beaches are Resaca and Brava.

In the flatlands around the coast and the mangrove swamps you might come across such characters as the sandwich tern or the black and white sooty tern, the red-billed tropicbird or red-footed booby. Culebra has an extensive Wildlife Refuge, which includes all its offshore rocks. Inland you may see a large iguana, a sort of four-foot armoured lizard.

WHERE TO STAY
La Hamace (tel 742 3516), one of the *paradors*, or **Villa Fulladoza** (tel 742 3576), an apartment complex backing on to the marina with double rooms from $55.

461

MONA

Mona Island is the remotest of them all—fifty miles from Puerto Rico and further from civilization. An oval 25 square miles, Mona lies half-way to Santo Domingo and it soars out of the water to 200-ft cliffs. It is surrounded by coral reefs which make the best diving in Puerto Rico.

Mona is administered by the Department of Natural Resources (tel 722 1726 on Puerto Rico) as a reserve and it is deserted now except for passing fishermen and the lighthouse keeper. There are a few animals, descended from the stock once farmed here, but now running wild. The only way to get there is by plane or by persuading a launch owner in Mayagüez to take you there. Take everything you need (including water), because there is not so much as a grocery store on Mona.

Apart from the reefs, Mona's attraction lies in its caves inland, where there are stalactites and stalagmites, where the pirates used to brawl after their 'cruize and plunder' and guano miners came to collect bat droppings as fertilizer. If you run out of water, there are pools in here. On the rocky land you may come across a four-foot iguana or two, but beware the wild boars. The only place to stay is at the camping ground at Playa Sardiniera on the west coast.

Hispaniola

Hispaniola is the second largest island in the Caribbean (after Cuba) and it is shared by two countries, each with a distinct heritage. In the east is the Latin bustle of the Spanish-speaking Dominican Republic. In the western third of the island is the press of Haiti, where the echoes of Africa are the strongest of any Caribbean country.

THE DOMINICAN REPUBLIC

The Dominican Republic is one of the poorest countries in the Caribbean, but a quick walk down to the Avenida del Puerto beneath the Colonial City in Santo Domingo, where the Dominicans take the evening air, will show you that it is also one of the liveliest. The country is large, and so beyond the coastal encrustation of beach resorts tourism is barely visible. Here you will find a charming Latin people and, particularly if you speak Spanish, the country can be very rewarding to travel.

The Dominican Republic is the second largest country in the Caribbean, 48,600 square kilometres in area or about the same size as Scotland. It is cut by three main mountain ranges running west to east. In the middle is the massive Cordillera Central, where you will find the Caribbean's highest mountain, Pico Duarte (10,417 ft). In the north the rainfall is high and there are extremely fertile plains. Just 100 miles away, the southwest of the country is so arid that it is desert.

The capital, Santo Domingo, is situated on the south coast and is the oldest city in the Americas. Around two million of the total population of seven million live in the shanties of greater Santo Domingo. Despite this increasing urban population, the majority of

Refrisceria, Santo Domingo

Dominicans still lead a rural life in small towns or in *bohío* shacks out in the country, where they make a living through sugar, tobacco, cocoa and coffee or small agricultural concerns. The country also has large reserves of ferronickel (25% of export earnings) and bauxite, as well as some gold and silver.

The biggest sector of the Dominican economy nowadays is tourism, but despite its million annual visitors, the Dominican Republic has not been swamped by the industry. It is possible to combine a tourist's beach-based holiday with travel to the towns of the interior to discover the buoyant style of Dominican life.

The Dominican heritage is both Latin and Caribbean. The men are *macho* here; they will strike up a matador's pose as a woman walks by, or maybe just grab her and dance in the road. After dark the tree-lined streets come alive as people take the evening air and the portable stereos strike up with the latest sounds of *merengue*, the national rhythm.

A look at the faces will show what a vibrant and thorough mix the Dominicans are. In colour they range from white (about 15%) to pure African (about 15%), but the majority of the Dominicans are a melting pot, with some Arawak Indian features thrown in and still visible. There is not much overt prejudice, but it is clearly a social advantage to have a lighter colour. There is, however, a certain racism against the Haitians. There is not much love lost between the two countries.

The country is extremely poor (one recent estimate puts two thirds of the country on the poverty line and unemployment at around 25%) and this is immediately visible if you venture beyond the enclave of the tourist hotels into the country or into the outskirts of Santo Domingo. The islanders put up with a chronically inefficient infrastructure, plagued by powercuts and without a reliable water supply. The dissatisfaction has occasionally erupted in riots. Some express it by trying to escape to the USA.

But for all the difficulties the Dominicans have a natural exuberance and a country of considerable natural beauty. Package tourists get a good deal in the Dominican Republic at the moment, but as an independent traveller you will find some surprisingly cool and pleasing hang-outs in the beach towns—Las Terrénas and Cabarete (renowned for windsurfing)— and some mountain retreats, as well as the small but attractive colonial glory of the oldest city of the New World.

Suggested Itinerary
In two weeks you can make a good tour of the Dominican Republic. If you arrive in Santo Domingo it is worth spending a few days looking around the colonial city, with an outing to the Columbus Lighthouse or a day on the beach at Boca Chica. After this head for the north coast: on your way make a detour in the Cordillera Central, to Constanza and Jarabacoa. Santiago has not much to recommend it, but there are places to stay overnight. Puerto Plata and particularly Sosua are lively tourist resorts; if you want something slightly more relaxed, then move straight on to Cabarete (which still has a fun crowd because of the windsurfing). Do not miss the resort of Las Terrenas on the Samana Peninsula, an excellent place to settle for a few days. From here take the ferry over to Sabana de la Mar (an experience in itself) and look around the agricultural southeast of the country. There are also tourist hotels to retreat to in this area if you feel like a night of luxury along the way. Alternatively you could head the other way from Santo Domingo, to the desert-like southwest, well away from the crowds. If you are feeling adventurous, take a few days in Haiti, which is thoroughly recommended.

History
Columbus discovered 'Quisqueya' on his first voyage, reaching the north coast of the island on 5 December 1492, as he sailed down from the Bahamas. He named it Hispaniola, 'Little Spain', and he chose it as the headquarters of the Spanish Empire in the Americas, establishing the first settlement in the New World with a thousand colonists who accompanied him on his second voyage in 1493. Initially they settled the north coast, but the site proved to be unhealthy and so they moved to the south coast, nearer to the gold mines.

Columbus was not a great administrator and in 1502 he was recalled to Spain in disgrace, but his son Don Diego oversaw the expansion of the Spanish Empire from the glorious city of Santo Domingo. The conquistadors and colonizers set out from here: Hernándo Cortéz departed for his invasion of Mexico, Ponce de León went to settle Puerto Rico, and Diego Velázquez to Cuba. As the gold in Hispaniola dried up and the mines of Colombia and Peru were discovered, Santo Domingo lost its lustre. It remained the official capital, but the colonists simply moved on and eventually the island was eclipsed, ignored by Spain.

Buccaneers moved into the remote northwestern part of Hispaniola in the late 1500s (see Haiti, History p. 497). Finally, at the Treaty of Ryswick in 1697, the Spaniards acknowledged their presence and ceded the western third of the island to France. Over the next hundred years Saint Domingue, as the French part of the island was known, became the archetypal West Indian sugar factory, the richest colony in the world. In the east, Santo Domingo languished.

But it was the fall of the French colony that was to stir the torpor of Santo Domingo. In 1793 Saint Domingue was involved in a civil war as the slaves rose up in rebellion. The Spaniards stepped in on the side of Toussaint and the slaves, but then soon found themselves without an ally as Toussaint switched sides to the French. In 1801 he invaded Santo Domingo and the whole of Hispaniola was in his hands.

In 1809, with the help of the British, the Spaniards forced the Haitians out of the eastern part of the island and the colony was restored to Spanish colonial rule. But, following the lead of other colonies on the South American mainland, the creole Dominicans started an independence movement to drive out the colonists. In 1821 they succeeded and the eastern part of the island became independent.

It was not to last. In 1822 the Haitians, under General Boyer, occupied the new country, unifying the whole island under the name of Haiti. Some of the Dominicans welcomed him (slavery was abolished), but the occupation fostered a spirit of Dominican nationality and an underground independence organization, *La Trinitaria*, was formed, led by Duarte, Sánchez and Mella. In 1843 Boyer was ousted from power in Haiti in a coup, and then on 27 February 1844 the Dominican rebels took their chance, storming the Ozama fortress and freeing the Dominican Republic once again.

Since independence, Dominican politics have swung between a state of ineffective liberal democracy and the extreme of, repressive dictatorship. Dictatorial rule was maintained by terror tactics—many died in office at the hands of assassins. In the chaos, the United States has decided to step in to maintain order more than once.

The Trinitaria found themselves ousted from power almost immediately in 1844 and for the next 45 years the power swung between two self-appointed generals, Buenaventura Báez and Pedro Santana. Santana even invited the Spaniards back in to administer the country in 1861, but the colonizers were forced out in a violent campaign, culminating in the *Restoration* of 16 August 1865.

The Americans also were beginning to show an interest. In the 1870s, the US Senate failed to pass a Bill for the annexation of the country by just one vote. By 1907, having reneged on its foreign debts, the bankrupt Dominican Republic was placed in the receivership of the US. In 1916, after an invasion of Haiti the previous year, the Americans occupied the country, staying for the next eight years. A few Dominicans resisted the occupation, but others welcomed the stability it would bring after years of turbulent internal politics. The Americans brought many improvements in island infrastructure—roads, schools, sanitation and public health, but there was a brooding political resentment at the military rule and eventually in 1924 the Marines left.

Within a few years another despot was in control. Rafael Leonidas Trujillo, the Army chief of staff, had himself elected in a rigged ballot in 1930. His 30 repressive years in power are still remembered with horror and bitterness. It is true that he turned the economy round to begin with, but the price was ruthless dictatorship. The country became his personal fiefdom, a police state. Trujillo himself was responsible for the disappearance of thousands of people. He renamed Santo Domingo Ciudad Trujillo in his own honour, and helped himself to a personal fortune estimated at a billion dollars. Finally, in 1961, he was assassinated and the country was plunged into chaos. Fearful of another Cuba, the Americans took it upon themselves to invade again in 1965.

Next year Joaquín Balaguer, once a moderate associate of Trujillo, was overwhelmingly elected President in what seemed like a vote for peace. He was re-elected twice, but was ousted in the elections of 1978 (only after he returned ballot boxes that had been stolen, under pressure from the USA). He was elected once again in 1986, taking his fifth Presidency at the age of 78.

As in many Caribbean islands, politics is a source of considerable dispute and sometimes erupts into violence in the streets, so it is best to avoid the cities in the run-up to election time.

Merengue

Dancing is something of a way of life in the Dominican Republic—they take music with them everywhere on noisy portable stereos and you will see even two-year-olds moving to a beat, developing their sense of rhythm. The buses are like mobile discotheques and it is not unusual to find that the passengers sing along. The national sound is *merengue*, a typically Latin beat, relentless, bustling and compulsive.

Most popular *merengue* is produced on modern instruments now, but you will certainly still see the traditional three-piece band of the *perico ripiao*, made up of a drum, an accordion and a *güira* (a cheese grater scratched with a metal stick or a soul comb).

An annual **Merengue Festival** is held in Santo Domingo in the third week of July. It is one of the year's liveliest, a week's blowout of dancing, drinking and local food in the capital. If you cannot make that, there are endless discotheques, even in the smallest Dominican towns. After an evening's promenading around the town square the locals end up there. Friday, Saturday and particularly Sunday nights are most popular.

Amber

The Dominican Republic possesses one of the world's largest reserves of amber, a semi-precious gem. It is not a stone, but petrified sap from trees that grew on the island 50 million years ago. It has been known as a 'touchstone' in the past because of its static qualities. The word electricity derives from the Greek for amber, *elektron*.

The featherweight gem varies from an almost transparent variety that has undergone the least chemical reaction, through the familiar yellow and amber to a deep red (the price increases with the depth of colour). Value is increased further by wisps of blue smoke within it, gases that were caught as the sap formed in the old rainforests millions of years ago. Most exquisite (and most expensive of all), are pieces in which leaves and insects have been caught.

There are three main mining areas in the Republic, the largest being in the mountains just south of Puerto Plata on the north coast. The other two are in El Valle and close to Santo Domingo.

Several museums exhibit amber, including **Joyas Criollas** at the Plaza Criolla in Santo Domingo and the **Amber Museum** in Puerto Plata (see p. 482). There are pieces for sale in these places as well as any tourist shop you might go into. It is possible to visit the amber mines, though you will have to do much of the organizing yourself. Start off at the museums. It is illegal to export unpolished amber from the Dominican Republic.

Larimar

Larimar, or Dominican Turquoise is unique to the Dominican Republic. It is a very hard, semi-precious stone, slightly lighter in colour than other turquoise and it is mined in the southwestern corner of the country. You will find examples of jewellery made from Larimar in all the tourist shops and markets.

Flora and Fauna

The Dominican Republic has rainforests, lowlands, deserts and coastal swamplands (and land more than a hundred feet below sea level at Lago Enriquillo). There are the barren or 'bald' plains near the summits of the Caribbean's highest peaks, where the vegetation is stunted, 'dwarf forest' of ferns and grasses, but this soon descends into pines and into the dripping, tangled rainforest. Among the buttressed mahogany trees, infested with lianas and creeping vines, you will see rufous-throated solitaires, the greater Antillean elaenia and the Hispaniola parrot, the green *cotorra*. Lower down you will also come across the Hispaniolan woodpecker, a noisy character and plenty of hummingbirds, including the Hispaniolan emerald and the tiny *zumbadorcito*, one of the most minute birds in the world.

In the coastal areas you will find many of the Caribbean's most elegant birds, including ibises, herons and flamingos and the magnificent frigatebird, as well as terns, todies— red and green plumage and a long, straight bill—and turnstones.

Trees include lignum vitae, or tree of life, and satinwood, with a grain so fine that it is used in veneers. The coconut palms are endless and, of course, the towns are decorated with ceiba, or kapok, and many species of flowering tree like the flaming poinciana, the flamboyant. There has been considerable deforestation in the Dominican Republic as people have gone higher into the hills to chop wood for burning and for cultivation. Efforts have been made to improve the situation, with limited success.

Island fauna is more limited, though there is a variety of reptiles, from tiny lizards that crawl around upside down on the ceiling, through iguanas to crocodiles. You might come across the odd vast spider, the size of a man's outstretched hand—a tarantula.

There are five main **National Parks** in the Dominican Republic (two in the Cordillera Central, Isla Cabritos on Lago Enriquillo, Los Haitises on Samaná Bay and Parque Nacional del Este) and you will need permission to visit them. This can sometimes be obtained from the Park Office at the gates, but it is best to make sure by visiting the main office in Santo Domingo, Calle las Damas 6, in the colonial city (tel 685 1316). If you do go off on your own, stock up on food and water because it is often difficult to find provisions in the remoter areas.

For more details on the National Parks, see under separate entries in text.

GETTING TO THE DOMINICAN REPUBLIC

The main airport is at Santo Domingo, about 25 km east of city itself (internal flights leave from Herrera airport in the west of the city), but most flights to the tourist resorts of the north coast will fly into Puerto Plata. The national carrier is *Dominicana*.

By Air

From Europe: There are almost daily flights to Santo Domingo from Madrid (Iberia or Dominicana), where most connections are made from the major cities in Europe. Air France has two flights a week from Paris.

From the USA: There are daily direct links to both Santo Domingo amd Puerto Plata from Miami and New York (Dominicana, American Airlines and some Continental), with connecting flights from other cities in the US. Other cities with direct links are Boston and Chicago.

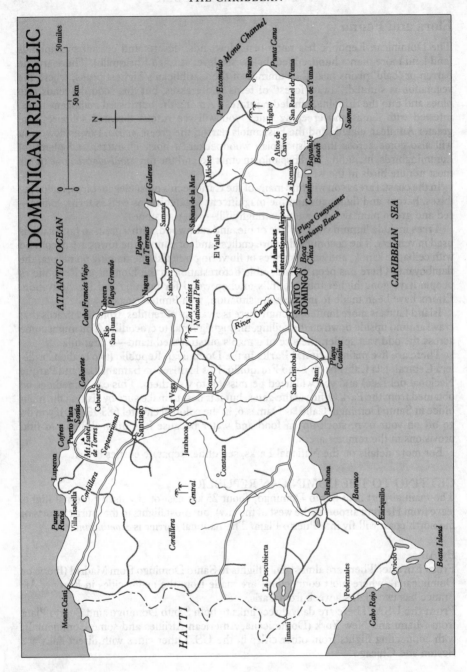

DOMINICAN REPUBLIC

ATLANTIC OCEAN

CARIBBEAN SEA

HAITI

50 miles
50 km

Punta Rucia
Monte Cristi
Villa Isabella
Luperon
Cofresi
Puerto Plata
Sosúa
Cabarete
Mt Isabel
de Torres
Cabarete
Septentrional
Cordillera
Santiago
La Vega
Jarabacoa
Constanza
Cordillera
Central
Bonao
San Juan
Rio San Juan
Cabrera
Playa Grande
Nagua
Sanchez
Playa
las Terrenas
Samaná
Las Galeras
Sabana de la Mar
El Valle
Los Haitises
National Park
River Ozama
San Cristobal
Bani
Playa Catalina
Baní
Barahona
Baoruco
Enriquillo
Oviedo
Pedernales
Jimani
La Descubierta
Cabo Rojo
Beata Island

Cabo Francés Viejo
Miches
Altos de Chavón
La Romana
Catalina
Bayahibe Beach
Playa Guayacanes
Embassy Beach
Boca Chica
Playa
Las Américas
International Airport
SANTO DOMINGO
Higüey
San Rafael de Yuma
Boca de Yuma
Soana
Bavaro
Punta Cana
Puerto Escondido
Mona Channel

From other Caribbean Islands: There are many daily flights to Santo Domingo from San Juan (American Airlines and Dominicana) and from Curaçao on most days (ALM). Occasional services link the city to Sint Maarten, Martinique and Guadeloupe and Aruba. There are also plenty of links to **South America**, including Caracas, Lima and Bogota.

There are direct flights to **Puerto Plata** from Miami and New York, and also from San Juan (daily service by American Airlines). There is also a link to Grand Turk and Providenciales in the Turks and Caicos. La Romana is served daily from San Juan too, mainly for guests at La Romana.

Entry Regulations
Visitors from Britain, Germany, Spain and most other European countries can enter the Dominican Republic on a valid passport and can stay for 90 days without a visa. Citizens of Belgium, Canada, France, Holland, Jamaica, Portugal and the USA must purchase a **Tourist card** on arrival. It costs US$10 and is valid for 60 days (it can be renewed twice at no further cost). You must surrender it when you leave. There is a departure tax in the Dominican Republic of US$10. They insist that foreigners pay this in US dollars.

GETTING AROUND THE DOMINICAN REPUBLIC
The Dominican Republic has an extensive transport system, on which you can reach almost anywhere from Santo Domingo within the day. At the top end of the range you will get the pleasure of your own seat in an air-conditioned bus with Bruce Lee videos to keep you amused. Lower down the scale, buses are a bit ramshackle and you will get to know your fellow passengers pretty well: they tend to be fairly crowded. The back row of the bus, the source of all gossip, is known as *la cocina* (the kitchen).

Within **Santo Domingo** (and other towns), the quickest method of transport are the crowded *públicos*, or share taxis. These are private cars, which run along the main drags, picking up and setting down passengers as required. Fare 2 pesos, 4 pesos, depending on the distance. You can also take the big yellow public buses that run fixed routes for 2 pesos, but it can be a long wait as there are no schedules.

The cities of the Dominican Republic are linked by **coach service**, with as many as five daily runs to the north coast by each company. Most routes originate in Santo Domingo, so be prepared to change or to stay overnight there. Coaches leave according to a schedule from a terminus, or the main *plaza* in a smaller town. There is a system of reservations, but this is not all that reliable. To be sure of a seat, you must be in the queue about an hour before departure.

Terrabus (sic) has the smartest and most comfortable buses, with on-board snacks and videos. They work from the Plaza Criolla in Santo Domingo (tel 541 2080). Other companies include **Caribe Tours**, which depart from Avenida 27 de Febrero (corner Leopoldo Navarro), not far northwest of the colonial city (tel 687 3171/76), or from Avenida Estrella Sadhala in Santiago and from Calle 12 de Julio in Puerto Plata. **Metro Buses** (tel 566 6587) leave from the corner of Ave Winston Churchill and Hatuey in Santo Domingo (Puerto Plata tel 586 3736). **Mota Saad** at Avenida Independencia 7 (tel 688 7775) and **Apolo** can be contacted on tel 541 9595. Approximate fares to the north coast is about RD$70, Santiago RD$35, Samaná RD$45, Barahona RD$32 and La Romana RD$20.

Guaguas are privately operated minibuses which operate between the towns, picking up passengers in the villages on the way. These are the loudest, most crowded and best fun of all, particularly if you join in when they sing along to the latest *merengue* and *salsa* on the stereo. You will see the best side of Dominican life here, cooped up with the shopping and the chickens. One of the few problems with *guaguas* can be the drivers, many of whom drive as fast as their engines will take them and some of whom have been known to drink. Take your chance.

Guaguas are slightly more local buses and they leave when all the seats and any room in the aisles have been filled, starting about 6 am and running until dusk and beyond. Out in the country just hail them down; in town go to the plaza. In Santo Domingo a large collection of them leave from the **Parque Enriquillo** at the intersection of Avenida Duarte and Calle Caracas, north of the colonial city. Listen out as they drive around the square shouting for passengers. You can catch a bus from here to the **airport**. Fares are low. **Santo Domingo** to Boca Chica costs RD$7 and La Romana around RD$20.

Between the smaller towns the local *guagua* will often be a pick-up truck, brim-filled with Dominicans and their produce and animals. **Hitching** works adequately, though you might be expected to sub the driver. Women passengers will often be offered the front seat. This is merely politeness rather than a way to get to know you better.

Taxis are available in the tourist areas and at the airports. They are expensive in comparison with local transport. They are unmetered, so be sure to arrange the price beforehand (rates are fixed in hotels, but you can bargain if you want). The going rate for a trip from Las Américas International airport to downtown Santo Domingo (about 25 miles) is about US$20 (RD$250). Taxi firms include **Taxi la Paloma** (tel 562 3460) and **Taxi Radio** (tel 562 1313). In the towns you can catch a motorbike for a peso and recently rickshaws (*motoconchos*) have made an appearance in Santo Domingo.

Organized **tours** will take you to all the recognized sights and beaches as well as night-time excursions around Santo Domingo. Hotel front desks can arrange them for you (and you will be picked up there), or you can go to the tour companies direct. In Santo Domingo contact **Metro Tours** in Avenida Winston Churchill (tel 567 3138), **Prieto Tours**, Avenida Francia 125, Santo Domingo (tel 688 5715) or **Turinter**, Leopoldo Navarro 4 (tel 685 4020). Prieto Tours also work out of Puerto Plata (tel 586 3988), as do **Puerto Plata Tours** at Beller 70 (tel 586 3858) and **Apolo Tours** (tel 586 2751), who will take you up the mountain, by cable car. **Tropical Tours** work from La Romana (tel 566 2512) and Casa de Campo nearby (tel 556 3636).

In such a large country it is convenient to have the freedom of travelling by **hire car**, but these come only at an outrageously high price. Your licence is valid for 90 days. Driving in the Dominican Republic is mainly on the right and is quite an experience. In town it is chaotic, with cars and buses nosing for position and generally ignoring the unspoken rules that govern driving elsewhere. On the country roads it is downright dangerous as all the same manoeuvres are performed at high speed. The main routes are quite good, but in remoter areas the surfaces will often be quite rough. Leave plenty of time if you are going off the beaten track. There are not that many petrol stations in the remoter areas of the country. All in all you might prefer to go by bus.

Insurance is not usually comprehensive and some companies will expect you to pay the first US$500 of a claim against you. Rates start at US$100 per day for the smallest car, or

$60 for an old banger (you might consider ordering a car from abroad through one of the large international hire companies). You will have to leave a hefty deposit.

Hire firms in Santo Domingo include **Avis** on Ave Abraham Lincoln (tel 533 3530), **Budget** on J F Kennedy (tel 562 6812), **Hertz**, Ave Independencia (688 2277), **National**, Ave Abraham Lincoln 1056 (tel 562 1444), and local firms **Auto Rental** at O y Gasset (tel 565 7873) and **Nelly** at José Contreras 139 (tel 535 8800). In Puerto Plata, try **Abby** on John F Kennedy (tel 586 2516) and **Budget** on Avenida L Ginebra (tel 586 4433). Budget and National also have offices at the airport. In La Romana contact **Honda** (tel 556 3835) and **Nelly** (tel 556 2156), both on Avenida Santa Rosa.

There is something of a **motorbike** culture in the Dominican Republic and you can easily hire a motorcycle or a moped in the tourist areas. If you get one be extremely careful to lock it up, and put it behind closed doors at night. In the remoter areas, away from the most dangerous traffic, motorbike is probably the best method of travel. However, do not take any risks with larger vehicles. Be ready to get off the road if the situation requires. Hire costs from at least US$20 a day.

Finally, it is possible to travel in the Republic by **air** as there are a number of airstrips around the country capable of taking small aircraft; in Santo Domingo's western suburbs is Herrera airport (tel 567 1195) and there are strips in Santiago, Puerto Plata, Cabo Rojo, La Romana (for Casa de Campo) and Samaná at Las Terrenas and Portillo. There are no scheduled internal flights, but you can charter small aircraft through **Servicios Aeros Turisticos** (tel 562 2351) and **Unicharter** (tel 567 0481).

TOURIST INFORMATION
There is no Dominican Republic Tourist Office in the UK. Your best bet is to go through a tour operator or contact the office in the USA.
USA: 485 Madison Ave, New York, NY 10022 (tel (212) 826 0750, toll free (800) 752 1151).
Canada: 24 Bellair St, Toronto, Ontario, Canada M5R 2C8 (tel (416) 928 9188).
Spain: Nuñez de Bilbao 37, 4to Izquierda, Madrid (tel 01 431 5354).

The main Tourist Information centre in the **Republic** is on Avenida Mexico (at the corner with Avenida 30 de Marzo) in Santo Domingo (tel 682 8181), where you will find helpful staff. There is a Tourist Office at Long Beach, Puerto Plata (tel 586 3676). In Santiago go to the Ayuntamiento (the Town Hall), second floor. Hours are 7.30 am–2.30 pm.

Most **museums** are captioned in both Spanish and English and generally admission is about RD$10. In certain places men are not allowed to enter in shorts as a mark of respect (at the Cathedral, however, there is usually somebody on hand to lend you a pair of track-suit bottoms for a few pesos).

The Dominican Republic's leading **newspaper** is the Spanish daily *Listín Diario*. English language papers include *Hispaniola Business*, the *Santo Domingo News* and *Touring*, which include plenty of tourist information and listings of current events. American newspapers and magazines make their way down after a few days and are available in the Santo Domingo bookshops.

In an **emergency** you can contact the Santo Domingo **police** on tel 682 3000 or Puerto Plata on tel 586 2331. Few police speak English and so if the problem is not urgent it might be best to contact the tourist authorities/hotel.

In a **medical** emergency, there are 24-hour casualty rooms available in **Santo Domingo**, Clínica Abreu, Calle Beller (tel 688 4411) or Clínica Gomez Patiño, Avenida Independencia 701 (tel 685 9131), and in **Puerto Plata**, Grupo Medico Dr Brugal (tel 586 2342).

International and local calls can usually be arranged by hotel receptionists, but you may find it easier to go via the *Codetel* offices, open daily 8 am–10 pm or midnight, depending on the size of the town. The **IDD code** for the Dominican Republic is 809. Dialling into the country is far easier than dialling out.

Britain has no Embassy in the Dominican Republic. Affairs are handled by a consul at Ave Independencia 506 in Santo Domingo (tel 682 3128). The US **Embassy** is at César Nicolás Penson in central Santo Domingo (tel 682 2171).

MONEY

The currency of the Dominican Republic is the *peso* (RD$), divided into a hundred *centavos*. At present it stands at US$1 = RD$12.50 (about RD$20 = £1) and this rate makes travel quite cheap in the Republic. Most banks have exchange facilities for dollars into pesos. The authorities are strict about changing pesos back into dollars and it is not that easy (it is theoretically possible, up to a small amount, at the airports or at the Banco de Reservas in Santo Domingo, on presentation of a recent exchange receipt, and your air-ticket and passport).

You are quite likely to be accosted in the street by someone whispering furtively, 'dollars, dollars, I give fifteen for one', and flicking through a wad of notes. The best advice is to say no, their rate is not that much better than the official one and you always run the risk of their sleight of hand and quick turn of speed.

Credit cards are widely accepted by hotels, tourist restaurants, travel agents and the car hire firms. Outside these areas you will be given a blank look if you flash your plastic at somebody. Take pesos in small denominations.

Banking hours are weekdays, 8.30–4.30, with an extra stint on Saturday morning for foreign exchange 8–midday. **Shops** are open morning and afternoon, with a long siesta over lunchtime, Mon–Sat, 9–noon and 2.30–7. Government offices are open 7.30–2.30. Dominicans will expect you to bargain, not only in the markets. You can also buy duty-free goods in US$ inside the *free zones*, some of which are at Las Atarazanas in the colonial district of Santo Domingo, Centro de Los Héroes and the airport. Goods must be bought a couple of days in advance and then they will be given to you once you are past the ticket barrier at the airport.

TRAVELLERS' ADVICE

To get the best out of the Dominican Republic, it is essential to speak at least some Spanish. English is enough in the tourist areas, but if you go off the beaten track, you will find few people who understand it.

It is a good idea to lock your bags when you send them into the aeroplane hold. Once you are beyond the airport, you are unlikely to encounter any trouble. However, you will definitely come across hustlers, particularly in downtown Santo Domingo. They are persistent and quite persuasive, and have a whole inventory of drugs and services on offer. Most of them are also tricksters. If you want to be sure of a guide's reliability, find him through the Tourist Office. You will not be hustled that much beyond the tourist towns, though you may find yourself surrounded by a crowd of inquisitive kids. A stock of pencils or small presents to give away would help.

Unfortunately travellers who venture out and about are at the mercy of unscrupulous traders and so you will find yourself outrageously overcharged for snacks, drinks and sometimes bus-fares. It is of course haphazard, but this practice has become quite widespread over the last few years as tourism on the island has increased.

There are often power cuts in the Dominican Republic (if you are staying outside the big tourist hotels, which usually have their own generating system). Take a torch or candles. Spare batteries are easily available here. Remember, the water supply will probably be cut off too. Mosquito coils are also available and make life a bit more comfortable. You may consider using a mosquito net (available in Santo Domingo). It is a good idea to have a room with a fan in the summer months because the nights can be hot.

Do not drink unpurified tap water. It is quite easy to get hold of purified water in the main towns (most cheap hotels have it), but off the beaten track you will have to stock up. Drinks bought on the street are dodgy because they will not be made from purified water. Key words are *filtrada* and *purificada*.

Women travellers may find themselves the centre of some macho attention, usually verbal but occasionally tactile. You are advised not to make long journeys alone or to go to the downtown areas alone at night. All white foreigners are, of course, *gringos* to some of the Dominicans, and so you may find that you get some odd reactions. If someone moves away on the bus, or shouts *SIDA* at you, they probably think you have AIDS.

The authorities take a very hard line with drugs and you are liable to find yourself in an unpleasant Dominican jail for a few weeks before they think about bringing you to trial. There are less drugs here than in most other Caribbean countries.

In the remoter tourist areas you may find yourself stopped by the road police for no apparent reason and they will check around your car or bike until they find something wrong with it. The going rate for an easy time is a few pesos (it increases around Christmas time). If you wish to make a moral stand, prepare for an argument.

Prostitution is pretty big in the Dominican Republic (there is a considerable trade in sex tourism) and so single men particularly will find themselves approached by *aviones*, as they are known (often with some pretty surprising tactile introductory lines). The country is very poor and so it is inexpensive. Apart from all the weird and wonderful strains of clap you may catch, the island is fizzing with HIV.

FURTHER READING

The Dominican Republic's most famous book is *Enriquillo*, by Manuel de J. Galvan, which tells the story of the Taino nobleman who took to the hills and waged a guerrilla war against the Spaniards in the 1520s. He is something of a national hero. Sumner Welles's *Naboth's Vineyard* gives an excellent view of the country in the 1920s. It was republished by Arno Press in 1972. Samuel Hazard wrote a enlightening account of the island in *Santo Domingo Past and Present with a Glance at Hayti*, published in 1873. There are some factual errors, but it is interesting reading because it was written at a time when the Dominicans were considering joining the United States.

BEACHES

There are miles and miles of beach in the Dominican Republic, many of them developed with hotels or condominiums and with every conceivable watersport on offer, but in remoter areas you will find seemingly endless stretches of sand that are completely deserted. Beaches with hotels tend to be well kept and sprayed to get rid of sandflies, but off the beaten track, remember to take insect repellent. You are advised to watch your possessions closely on the beaches.

North Coast
In the remote area between the Haitian border and Puerto Plata you will find a small, secluded bay at **Punta Rucia**, close to Columbus's La Isabella. There are hotels in the area. Better known is the beach at **Luperón**, set on a wide bay with excellent golden sand and palm trees with a hotel to retreat to in the heat of the midday sun. **Cofresi** has a mile-long strand and a single hotel and is relatively untainted despite being so close to Puerto Plata.

Heading east from Puerto Plata the beaches and hotels really start. The beach in the town itself is disappointing, but at **Playa Dorada**, three miles east, you will find a superb strand; active and busy with all the watersports. Officially the hotels each have their strip of beachfront on the two miles of sand and palms. You can negotiate with the concessionaires for a windsurfer or a waterskiing trip.

The next resort beach, with a more relaxed feel than Playa Dorada, is at **Sosúa**, a crescent curve of mounded white sand brushed by more palms. It is a very busy beach and inevitably you will be accosted to buy a wood carving, a T-shirt or any number of other exotic services. There are bars around the whole length of the beach. Watersports available. There are other smaller coves with fantastic sand and less of a crowd close by.

Cabarete is nine miles farther down the coast and is best known for its winter-season winds, which blow off the Atlantic with such force that they held the 1987 world windsurfing championships here. It is a very laid-back and friendly town strung along miles of excellent, light-coloured sand, where you can, of course, hire a sailboard.

And there are beaches scattered along the coast right down to the eastern tip of the island, many of them picture-postcard Caribbean—white sand and palms and ridiculously blue sea. Many are face on to the Atlantic and so the waves are big and the undertow is strong. Try **Playa Grande** close to Cabrera, and **Playa la Preciosa** and the secluded beach at the headland of Cabo Francés Viejo.

There are some good beaches on the Samaná Peninsula, though not many near to the town itself. The best are on the northern shore, where they run, seemingly endlessly east and west from from Playa **Las Terrenas** (do not swim off the town itself because of the sewage). Watersports are available at the hotels. It is well worth exploring because you will find superb, deserted strands. You can find transport in Sánchez.

On Samaná Bay itself you can go to **Puerto Escondido** in the town (over the hill to the southwest and behind the Bahia Beach Resort). Otherwise head for **Cayo Levantado**, off the southern shore, six miles east of Samaná—take a boat from the quay (RD$50 return), or from the beach opposite the island. Buses run to **Las Galeras** on Bahia del Rincón at the northeastern tip of the peninsula for 15 pesos. The beach here is OK, and there are places to get a drink or a meal.

East of Santo Domingo
Boca Chica, about 20 miles east of Santo Domingo, is the busiest of all the beaches, particularly at the weekends when the Dominicans stream out of the capital. It is noisy,

with hundreds of portable stereos blaring out the latest *merengue*. In the area of Juan Dolio you will find palms and snackbars and a smaller crowd at **Embassy Beach**, where the waves roar in between two arms of coral-rock and the gentler **Playa Guayacanes**. Or you can find your way down to **Playa Real**, a quieter spot where there is a hotel and restaurant to retreat to.

There is a beach in Casa de Campo, **Playa Minitas**, but it is surrounded by private land and so entrance is restricted (it is man-made anyway and gets quite crowded). All watersports are available. Preferable is the wilder and remoter **Bayahibe Beach**, yet another strip of stunning white sand lapped with gentle waves and fringed with palms and with a small fish restaurant for a drink when the going gets too hot. There is a fantastic beach on **Playa Catalina**, an uninhabited island offshore opposite La Romana, trips (expensive) arranged from the front desk at Casa de Campo, otherwise hire a boat to run you across, but take a picnic.

The beaches run in an almost continuous stretch from south of **Punta Cana**, the island's most easterly point, up to **Miches**. An occasional hotel breaks the isolation, but they often do not allow you in. The waves can be quite big as they come straight in off the Atlantic so be careful when you swim, but if you want untouched sands to walk, you will find 20 miles of them here.

West of Santo Domingo there are few beaches, the coastline is mostly rocky until the Barahona peninsula, where the white sands resume. If you are exploring the area, you will find a small beach at **Baoruco**, with a hotel that has facilities.

WATERSPORTS
Watersports gravitate around the tourist centres. The larger hotels usually have them on offer, but as an outsider you may not be allowed into the hotel compound, so if you are travelling independently the best bet is to go to more off-beat areas like Sosúa, Cabarete and Las Terrenas. Boca Chica, the favourite with the Dominicans themselves, has most sports on offer too.

Windsurfing is extremely good in the Dominican Republic, and you can pick up a board in most places on the north and east coasts, but the best area for advanced sailboarders is Cabarete, a few miles east of Sosúa, where the hotels are devoted to windsurfing. The winds run across the bay, slightly onshore and several hundred yards out there is a reef where you can sail waves. Winds are at their highest in the early part of the year. World champion Mickey Bouwmeester runs a windsurfing centre here in the winter months and Mistral and Vela High Winds also have their shops. **Surfers** will find big waves at this time off Playa Grande near Rio San Juan and at Macao.

For small **sailing craft**, two-person hobie cats and sunfish, you will depend on the hotels, but if you wish to charter a larger **yacht**, you can go to the marinas at Boca Chica, the **Sailing Club of Santo Domingo (Club Nautico de Santo Domingo)** (tel 566 4522), at La Romana and at Boca de Yuma in the far south east.

Deep-sea fishing trips, on the hunt for magnificent 10-ft marlin in the Mona Channel can also be arranged from Boca de Yuma, which holds a fishing tournament each year in June. Alternatively try **Club Andres** in Boca Chica (tel 685 4940) or the quay in Samaná. The fishing is also good off the north coast in the region of Monte Cristi, where they hold a couple of yearly competitions.

Diving is not that developed in the Dominican Republic and your best bet is the hotels, some of which run instruction courses for beginners. There are reefs off all sides of the coast, some of which can be reached by swimmers (try Punta Cana area). Diving reefs are at Catalina Island and Bayahibe near La Romana, and there are wrecks on the reefs off Monte Cristi and near Miches. There is a marine park near the airport at La Caleta (make arrangements in Boca Chica) and other good areas include Las Terrenas. Try **Buceo Dominicano** in the capital, Abraham Lincoln Ave 960 (tel 567 0346). Another useful contact in Santo Domingo is **Mundo Submarino** (tel 566 0430), who arrange trips for trained divers and sailing and snorkelling excursions.

OTHER SPORTS

On land there are plenty of sports for the active vacationer—it must be one of the only places in the world where you can hire **polo ponies** (at Casa de Campo). **Tennis** courts are everywhere. Once again, go to a nearby hotel.

Golfers will find three courses at Casa de Campo in the east, and two near Puerto Plata (nine holes at Castambar). Around Santo Domingo you can go to the Country Club (through the hotels).

Walkers will not find anything organized, except occasionally by the National Parks Service (see Flora and Fauna p. 467). However, if you are prepared to rough it a bit, the parks can provide excellent hiking.

Baseball is the Republic's national sport and some of the Dominicans play in the National leagues in the States, returning home to winter in the warmth, where they keep their eye in with the local teams. There are stadia in Santo Domingo, Santiago, Puerto Plata, La Romana and San Francisco de Macoris.

Cockfighting is popular in the country areas and, last but not least, if you get a chance to see a Dominican **wrestling** match, go to it because it is a great spectacle. The fervour is extraordinary, and is matched only by the suspension of disbelief.

Santo Domingo

The capital of the Dominican Republic, Santo Domingo (called La Capital), is the oldest city in the New World. In the early 1500s it was the seat of the Viceroys of the Americas, replete with fittingly glorious coral-stone palaces, among them the earliest Cathedral, University and Hospital in the New World (the oldest surviving building dates from 1503). From here the *Conquistadors* departed on their expeditions to conquer the mainland and to settle the other islands.

But the glory was eclipsed within a couple of generations as the riches of the Spanish Main were revealed and the administrators moved there. In 1562 much of the town was destroyed in an earthquake and by 1586, when Sir Francis Drake had had his twopenny-worth (25,000 ducats to be precise), it was in ruins and it never really recovered.

Today, though the colonial city has largely been restored and the streets retain some of their former splendour, there is little glorious about Santo Domingo outside this immediate area. It is a working city of about 2 million inhabitants—the streets teem with lottery ticket vendors, fruit sellers and of course the endless traffic. Away from the city centre are prosperous-looking villas set in tree-lined boulevards running down to the seafront, the lively Malecón. Behind this screen of prosperity, in the ever-expanding shanties are some of the Caribbean's poorest slums.

The Colonial City

The centrepiece of the colonial city is the **Alcazar de Colón**, a two-storey, coral-stone palace with enclosed arches, for 60 years the seat of the Spanish Crown in the Caribbean. It was constructed in 1510 by Don Diego Columbus, son of the discoverer, during his tenure as Viceroy, reputedly without the use of a single nail (doors and windows turned on pivots sunk into the walls). It was restored in 1957 with stone from the original quarry and period 16th- and 17th-century pieces, including outsize earthenware water-carriers and pint-size chairs. It is a nice place in which to pass the time of day, beneath the gargoyles and 17th-century tapestries and among such viceregal paraphernalia as the leather- and velvet-covered travelling trunks. Open daily except Tues, 9–6, adm.

La Atarazana is opposite the Alcazar and runs down to the river beneath the square. The eight 16th-century buildings housed the royal armoury, the customs house and the official warehouses of old Santo Domingo; they have a similar role once again in that they are stuffed with duty-free goods shipped in for sale—you will find idyllic courtyards in which to rest when you are gorged with buying and strolling the art galleries. There are also a couple of fun bars among the buildings of La Atarazana.

In the last building you will find the **Museum of Marine Archeology**, with relics from wrecks that have foundered on the island's coasts—the *Guadeloupe, Tolosa* and *Concepción*. Also discover about life on board ship in the seventeenth century, including why the poop deck is so called. Open 9–5, adm.

The oldest surviving building in the Americas, the **Casa del Cordon**, is just up the hill from the Alcazar, on the corner of Calle Emiliano Tejera and Calle Isabel la Catolica. Built in 1503, it is named after the cord of the Franciscan order that is carved in stone above the lintel. Today it is the Banco Popular, but they permit tours during working hours, adm free.

South of the Alcazar, by the **Calle de Las Damas** (where the court ladies would take the evening air in colonial times), you come to the **Capilla de Nuestra Señora de los Remedios**, a recently restored 16th-century chapel. Opposite is the **Museo de las Casas Reales**, formerly the palace of the Governors and Captains General, with some of the finest exhibits of the Spanish colonial heritage in the Americas, including handblown glass, armour and weapons. Also there are reconstructions of Columbus's voyages and his ships the *Niña*, the *Pinta* and the *Santa Maria*. Open daily except Mon, 9–6, adm (tel 682 4202).

Across Calle las Mercedes is the monumental **Panteon Nacional**, with an eternal flame to the heroes of the Republic, including the assassins of Trujillo. The building dates from 1714 and was a Jesuit monastery. The Calle de las Damas continues south, lined with attractive old palaces, until it reaches the old fortress of the colonial city, the **Fortaleza Ozama** on the banks of the river. Its heart is the Torre del Homenaje (the Tower of Homage), a minor colossus with walls four feet thick, where for centuries prisoners were held. Fortress open daily except Mon, 9–6, adm free.

Nearby there is a good art gallery and café in which to sit in an alley, the **Plaza Toledo**, which is named after the wife of Bartholomew Columbus. You can see the works of Dominican painters—Alberto Ulloa, Freddy Javier and Martos Garcia. Off the Calle de las Damas is the **Casa de Bastidas**, which has a pleasant courtyard in which to recover from the fray of Santo Domingo.

Not far off is **Parque Colón** (Columbus Square), where a statue of the explorer stands pointing to the horizon surrounded by arched walkways and coral-stone town buildings. On the south side is the **Catedral de Santa Maria la Menor**, the first cathedral in the New World, which was built between 1523 and 1540. It is an attractive conglomeration of styles, with friezes and statues and gracefully curved roofs of rusty dark rock, though it is not particularly magnificent. Its grandeur lies in its status as the Catedral Primada de America (the senior Cathedral in the Americas). Sir Francis Drake had no fitting respect for it in 1586, and used it as a place to hole up during his raid, chipping off the nose and hand of Bishop Bastidas's statue in a fit of anger.

It is also one of the many resting places of Columbus (other claims are from Seville and Cuba). A huge marble tomb contains his remains, supposedly brought here by his daughter-in-law in 1544, many years after he died. His next journey was in 1796, when the whole of Hispaniola was ceded to France—he was moved to the Cathedral in Havana so that he would remain in Spanish soil—and then in 1898 he was supposedly taken back to Seville. However, in 1877 a Padre Francisco Billini discovered a small crypt containing some ashes. He declared them the ashes of Columbus. There are many other things to see, including a huge mahogany throne and gold and silver ware from across the centuries. Open Mon–Sat, 9–6, adm free (tel 689 1920).

The main street of old Santo Domingo is **El Conde**, which leads west from the Parque Colón towards the **Parque Independencia** and the Puerto del Conde, one of the old city gates. In a mausoleum constructed in 1976 you will find a monument to the 1844 Independence leaders, Duarte, Mella and Sánchez. El Conde is now only for pedestrians and you will find crowds of Dominicans out promenading and browsing there, among the city's best shops.

Within the crumbled city wall of the Santo Domingo colonial city you will find endless other ruins and monuments, some of them modern, but many which will cast your mind back to the glorious days of 16th century. On Parque Colón stands the **Palacio de Borgella** built in the Haitian occupation of 1822–44 and seat of the Dominican Congress until 1947 until it moved to the Palacio Nacional. You can also visit the ruins of the **Hospital Iglesia di San Nicolás de Barí**, the first hospital in the New World and, also dating from 1510, the Convento de los Dominicos, which once housed the first university founded here in 1538. On Calle Padre Billini you will find the **Convento de Santa Clara**, a refuge for the Clarissa Sisters dating from 1522 and the **Museum of the Dominican Family**, with exhibits of the good life in the 19th century. Open daily 9–6, adm (tel 689 5057). In the Puerta de la Misericordia you will find the old refuge of the city dwellers during hurricanes, and the spot where Mella initiated the revolt against Haitian occupation in 1844.

The Modern City

The modern city of Santo Domingo lies north and west of the **Parque Independencia**, leading off in broad streets lined with trees where the villas stand back from the endless motorbikes and the red and blue share-taxis. **The Malecón** (the promenade, officially Avenida George Washington), under an avenue of *palm cana* on the seafront, is one of the liveliest spots in town. The road has recently been extended to the east, running beneath the walls of the colonial city and along the Ozama River. The whole strip comes alive at dusk when the Dominicans take the evening air, walking up and down past the hundreds of portable stereos blaring out *merengue*. Unfortunately many people seem to take the air in Toyota convertibles and so it becomes one big traffic jam, but it is fun to be a part of. The Malecón is particularly lively during carnival and the *merengue* festival (see above), when the parades go by.

Another scene of Dominican mayhem is the **Mercado Modelo**, to the north of the colonial city on Avenida Mella (another major shopping street). It is one of the main Santo Domingo markets and so you will find anything on sale from plantains and root vegetables to T-shirts and arts and crafts.

The **Plaza de Cultura**, on the Avenida César Nicolás Penson, is the site of a number of museums. The **Museum of the Dominican Man** (tel 687 3622) has excellent exhibits from Taino life and more recent Dominican lives like those of the cane-cutters and modern carnival players. The **Museo Nacional de Historia y Geographica** has more Arawak Indian exhibits and also Trujillo memorabilia. Open daily except Mon, 10–5, adm. You will also find the **Galeria de Arte Moderno** and the **Teatro Nacional** (the National Theatre and home of the Symphony Orchestra) and the **Bibliothéca Nacional** (National Library).

The **Palacio Nacional**, on Calle Dr Delgado just to the northwest of Parque Independencia, is an imposing mock-classical edifice of rose-coloured marble that might come from 17th-century Europe. In fact it was built in the 1940s and for a while it was the home of the Congress of the Dominican Republic. It is quite closely guarded, but is open to visitors by guided tour, adm free, by appointment only (tel 686 4771).

In the northwest of town you will find a quiet retreat from the mayhem of Santo Domingo, the kempt botanic violence of **Jardin Botanico Nacional**, just off the Avenida John F Kennedy. More than 200 species of palm are on display and there is a Japanese garden and an orchid pavilion. Train and boat rides are available with screaming Dominicans. Open 9–midday and 2–6, adm. To the northeast of here, is the **Parque Zoologico**, where in the 10 acres of landscaped gardens above the river you will find dromedaries roaming, more miniature train rides and a vast aviary. Open daily 10–6, adm.

Across the River Ozama is the immense **Faro a Colón** (the Columbus lighthouse), a monumental construction in the Discoverer's honour, due to open during the 500th anniversary celebrations in 1992. It will contain six museums and libraries, most of them dedicated to Columbus and his journeys as well as a lighthouse with an 80-mile radius and a laser that can throw a cross up into the Santo Domingo sky. Columbus is destined to make yet another journey as his ashes are to be brought to a chapel in the lighthouse.

The idea of a lighthouse was first mooted in the last century, but this design was submitted for a 1929 competition by a student of architecture from Manchester, J Gleave. Construction was undertaken by Trujillo but was abandoned until it was taken up again by Balaguer in 1987. It is vast, and will have a fine view over Santo Domingo. It will also have its own generator, essential because the Santo Domingo lights seem to cut out often enough as it is.

A little farther out along the coast is the **Parque de los Tres Ojos** (the three 'eyes', four in fact), limestone sinkholes with pools. In the caves there are some impressive stalactite and stalagmite formations. From here the Avenida de las Américas, lined with the flags of all the American nations, leads along the south coast to Boca Chica and the airport.

Around the Island

The road from Santo Domingo to Santiago and the north coast climbs into the Cordillera Central, the Republic's largest mountain range and then descends into the fertile Cibao valley before rising again into the hills of the Cordillera Septentrional on the north coast. You will see the plots of the subsistence farmers cut into the deep brown earth and their small thatched *bohíos* right by the side of the road.

The town of **Bonao**, halfway to Santiago, has recently been transformed by the discovery of mineral deposits (nickel and bauxite) and the arrival of the mining industry, an overlay of modernity on the traditional town centre.

A side route runs into the Cordillera to the towns of **Constanza** and **Jarabacoa**, set among the pineforests and mountains as high as 10,000 feet. The temperature here is cooler than on the coast and so these valleys have become the favoured retreat of the Dominican wealthy. There is a community of Japanese in Constanza, brought here by Trujillo. The **Aguas Blancas** are a run of two waterfalls visible from the road a few miles south of the town. It is an invigorating walk to get to them, followed by an even more invigorating swim in the cold water. There is occasionally frost up here.

From Jarabacoa you can see the **Jimenoa Waterfall**, a 100-ft cascade that crashes into a rockpool large enough to swim in. Go south to El Salto, about six miles, and ask for directions down to the falls, an easy descent, but harder on the way back.

Jarabacoa is also the dropping-off point for the climb of **Pico Duarte**, at 10,416 ft the island's highest peak, lost in the Bermúdez and Ramírez National Parks. The mountain has only recently been called after Duarte the Independence hero. Before that it had a spell as Pico Trujillo after the dictator, but for most of its history it was known as Pico la Pelona (the bald mountain) because of the barren plains near the top. A bust of Duarte has been placed at the summit. The usual route passes Monabao and La Ciénaga, via Casa Tabalone, through the changing vegetation of palms and tangled rainforest to pines and ferns and diabolic dwarf growth.

It is possible to hike, without the use of mountaineering gear, but you need to be reasonably fit. Take food for four days and warm clothing for the evenings. Arrange a guide and make sure to inform the National Park staff at La Ciénaga that you are going.

A number of wealthy towns draw their prosperity from the fertile Cibao Valley, the breadbasket of the Republic that sits between the two Cordilleras. The people are renowned for their pride and the area is referred to jokingly by Dominicans from elsewhere as the 'Republic of Cibao'. As you descend into the Cibao valley you come to **La Vega**. For a spectacular view, climb to the top of the Santo Cerro (just north of the town). Nearby are the ruins of Columbus's original settlement of Vega Real (Royal Valley), which were abandoned for the present site after an earthquake.

Santiago de los Trienta Caballeros

Santiago (population 400,000) is the Dominican Republic's second city and quite a change from the mayhem of the capital. The romantic sounding, 'St James of the thirty noblemen' is set on the banks of a river gorge, inland where it was less vulnerable to attack, and it has a stately and confident air. There are some grand town-houses from the last century, when Cibao agriculture was the engine of the Dominican economy. The city is generally by-passed by tourists, but a traveller may enjoy the pace of life here after the capital, before rejoining the fray on the north coast. You will not be pestered by hustlers in Santiago.

A striking and rather ugly 200 ft obelisk stands above the town, commemorating the heroes of the Restoration of 1844, when the Dominican Republic forced out the Haitian occupation (it was originally built by Trujillo in honour of himself). There is a fantastic view from the top. The **Museo del Tabaco**, on Calle 30 de Marzo, shows the processing of tobacco from cultivation to cigars (available for sale). In the town centre **Museo de Arte Folklorico**, set in an elegant old town-house, exhibits local arts and crafts as well as the 'lechones', the mischievous imps of the Santiago Carnival. Ruins fans will enjoy the old colonial ruins at Jacagua in the north of the city.

As you head northwest along the Cibao from Santiago towards the Haitian border the land becomes steadily drier. The town of Monte Cristi is known as 'Estamos muriendo de sed' (we die of thirst), because it is so windswept and desert-like.

The North Shore—the Amber Coast

The 150 miles of coastline from Monte Cristi to the Samaná peninsula contain the bulk of the island's tourist industry. You will come across vast factory hotels in complexes, but in other places you will find palms and beaches as far as the eye can see, offset with the glorious blue of the reef-protected sea.

Northeast of Monte Cristi (the northwesterly point of the island), beyond the cacti and the salt pans, is the **Parque Nacional El Morro**, on a point (*el morro*) that sticks into the sea like a pimple, where you will find an undeveloped reserve that has extensive birdlife, including oyster-catchers, ruddy turnstones, plovers and seabirds like noddies and terns. Cayo Cabrito just offshore takes its name from the goats that were left there to graze.

The coastline is remote from the road for several miles as you head east (you can get to the stunning beach at Punta Rucia), but you can turn north to **Luperon**, a fishing village, where the country starts to get a bit greener. Close by are the remains (archaeological only now) of Columbus's first settlement, La Isabella. Just before Puerto Plata is **Cofresi**, named after a buccaneer (he got about a bit, there is another town named after him on the west coast of Puerto Rico). (See Beaches, p. 474.)

Puerto Plata

The 'Silver Port', founded at the beginning of the 16th century, lies on the Atlantic coast in the shadow of the Cordillera Septentrional. At the western end of the Malecón (so long that it never becomes busy, though people do collect at the eastern end), you will find the **Fortaleza de San Felipe**, a lumbering brute that was built in 1577 to defend the town from pirates. They managed to take the place over eventually and so Spain sacked it in 1605. (Fort open daily except Thurs, 9–noon and 3–5, adm) Puerto Plata now has a faded charm in its many elaborate wooden gingerbread houses and Spanish plazas. Tourists are well known here, but they have not swamped the local life. Playa Dorada, a few miles through the canefields to the east of Puerto Plata, is the main tourist area. It is a gaggle of modern hotels all collected together in a little complex.

The **Amber Museum**, 61 Calle Duarte, has a series of exhibits about the origins and mining of amber, with pieces containing prehistoric creepy-crawlies on show, in an elegant old town-house. There is a sales room with amber jewllery on sale. Open Mon–Sat, 9–5, adm (tel 586 2848).

At the **Brugal Rum Distillery**, on the Avenida Colón, a tour will take you through the Republic's second industry (for years the backbone of the economy), from cane-cuttings to rum punch, with samples to taste if you have not already had enough from the fumes. Open Mon–Fri, 9–midday and 2–5.

One of the stranger sights in the Caribbean is a cable-car (*teleférico*) that runs from behind the town to the summit of **Mt Isabel de Torres** (2600 ft), from where the view is magnificent, when it is not in cloud. There are botanical gardens and a restaurant at the top. Working daily except Wed (summer season restricted), 8–5, fare RD$5.

East to Samaná

The town of Sosúa splits into two halves, **El Batey**, the tourist area in the east with restaurants shoulder to shoulder and buzzing nightlife, where you might notice a residual European influence from an influx of German Jews who settled here to escape persecution in the 1930s. On the other side of the glorious half-mile bay is **Los Charamícos**, the more traditionally Dominican part.

Soon after Sosúa you come to **Cabarete**, a resort town strung along the coastal road just by a huge bay. It is renowned for windsurfing, and so it attracts a fun, active crowd who spend the day on the waves and the evenings in the beach bars and restaurants. Hotels are springing up here as the crowds discover it.

At Cabarete the endless beaches begin, all of them undeveloped. The coastal road leads through Rio San Juan and Cabrera down to the town of Nagua, towards the Samaná peninsula.

The Samaná Peninsula

North and slightly east of Santo Domingo, the Samaná Peninsula is one of the most beautiful parts of the island. Its mountainsides are cut by swathes of light green coco palm and deep green pine trees, with the small clapboard *bohíos* of the Dominicans painted in pastel washes of pink or purple. In Samaná Bay you will see the fishermen standing in their flat-bottomed boats casting their nets for snapper. There are spectacular beaches on both sides of the peninsula, some of which can only be reached by boat. There is a ferry link to Samaná from Sabana de la Mar on the other side of the bay, but it tends to get overfilled.

Columbus appeared in the bay in 1493, but was met by such a volley of arrows from the local inhabitants (probably Caribs from down-island on a raid against the Tainos) that he named it 'Golfo de las Flechas'. The original town of Samaná was populated by escaped American slaves who came to the free island of Haiti in the early 19th century. It is just possible still to hear the locals speaking old American English. Samaná is also the home of President Balaguer.

Today Samaná is an ugly concrete infestation along a four-lane seafront boulevard (the old wooden houses were destroyed in the name of tourism development) that was destined to be big but never took off. The odd-looking aqueduct in the bay was supposed to lead to a hotel on the offshore island, but that too was never built. However, the town can be quite lively all the same.

Las Terrenas on the north coast of the peninsula is a very low-key resort town with an easy manner and some small and hip places to stay, on what are some of the country's best beaches. No package tourists make it here, so it is the best resort on the island for the independent traveller.

The **Báhia de Samaná** is the winter home of about 3000 humpback whales, who come here to give birth. There are occasional excursions to see them at the Silver Bank in January and February. The actual sanctuary is 50 miles from the shore and so the trip takes about eight hours, but you may see the odd one blowing in the bay. In the hills above Samaná (on the road to Las Terrenas), you can visit the **Río Limón Waterfall**, which falls 160 feet in a number of chutes.

To the south and west of Sanchez is **Los Haitises National Park**, an area of karst limestone and coastal mangrove swamps. There are also a number of small offshore cays where you will see hawks, pelicans, noddies and roseate terns. Deeper in the swamps you will see the ungainly jacana, with overlong toes that help it walk over water-lilies, and herons and ibises. You can arrange a trip from Samaná.

East of Santo Domingo

Headed east from Santo Domingo on the Avenida de las Américas, you first come to **Boca Chica**, just past the airport, a good beach that becomes very crowded and noisy at the weekends as the Dominicans escape in droves from the capital. At **La Caleta** you can see an Arawak burial site. Passing by San Pedro de Macoris you come to **La Romana**, still a sugar town and cattle grazing area, but now famed for the vast (and very expensive) resort a few miles to its east, Casa de Campo, where there are a whole host of hotels, villas, golf courses and polo pitches. In this area you will still meet English-speaking West Indians from down-island whose parents came to work in the sugar industry earlier this century.

Altos de Chavón is a medieval clifftop town built of rusty coral rock, everywhere festooned with bougainvillaea and sprays of hibiscus and inhabited by a colony of artists. Its heart is the **Iglesia St Stanislaus**, and all around are aged cobbled alleys and streets. There is even an amphitheatre, where Frank Sinatra and Julio Iglesias have sung in recent years. And yet, there is something slightly wrong about Altos de Chavón. Somehow there is an unruly Gothic air to the medieval idyll—it is slightly overdone, very neat and really rather twee. It comes as no surprise to find out that it was all designed in 1978 and that Frank Sinatra actually inaugurated the amphitheatre. Free bus service from Casa de Campo, and worth a look if only for the novelty, some good restaurants and the fantastic view over the Chavón river valley.

About 20 miles northeast of La Romana, lost in the cattle and sugar-cane flats of the southeast, is the genuine 16th-century town of **Higüey**. A charming church lies at its centre, the **Basilica de Nuestra Señora de la Merced**, supposedly erected on the site of a battle in which the early Spaniards fended off the Caribs. It had long been a place of pilgrimage and then in the 1950s the massive new church was built. The monumental **Basílica de Nuestra Señora de Altagracia** (the patron saint of the Dominican Republic) is built of concrete and shaped like a 200-ft pair of hands held in prayer. The town has certainly seen tourists—they tend to pass through in busloads—but it has an easy, parochial air. Pilgrims arrive on 21 January and 16 August.

Beyond Higüey the countryside becomes wilder and you will see the *campesinos* riding around on their horses and their palm-thatch bohíos. Many of the roads turn to dirt tracks. Heading south, on a metalled road, you will come to the small town of **San Rafael de Yuma**, where you will find the restored house of Ponce de León, who lived here for three years before he went to settle Puerto Rico in 1508 and then travelled on to Florida. The road reaches the coast at **Boca de Yuma**, a quiet fishing village.

On the western road, past several caves, is the **National Park of the East**, which contains much of the V-shaped point of land and the island of Saona off the southern shore. The western entrance to the park is at Bayahibe, not far from La Romana. Paths do cross the park, but you will need to find a guide. On the south coast is Catalinta Bay, a phosphorescent bay where the water glows in orange and green luminescent whorls as you drag your fingers through the water. In the park you may see lizard cuckoos and orioles and on the coast oyster-catchers and other seabirds like pelicans and magnificent frigatebirds.

If you head northeast of Higüey you reach the coast at **Bavaro**, where the beaches begin. They run almost uninterrupted for the 30 miles from here to Laguna Nisibón, and they are spectacular and developed only with the occasional huge hotel complex. They are bordered along their whole length by palms and sea grape and they are excellent for walking, though you should be careful of swimming because of the Atlantic currents. Beyond Miches you enter wild farming country and eventually you come to the sleepy town of Sabana de la Mar, from where you can get a ferry across to the Samaná peninsula (twice a day).

West of Santo Domingo

The southwestern corner of the Dominican Republic is the remotest area and in places it is barren and desert-like, though this means that the sun is more reliable than on the north coast, of course. Not much organized tourism happens in the region (though there are recent developments in Barahona) and so you get a good view of local Dominican life. As you get closer to the frontier with Haiti you can expect army activity to increase and you will be stopped and may be subjected to searches.

Taking the Carreta Sanchez out of Santo Domingo you come to **San Cristóbal**, most infamous for being the birthplace of Trujillo. During his life he built it up in a grandeur that befitted his status as dictator—see the plaza and the ornate church and his mausoleum (he is not buried there, though; his remains were taken to France). **Casa las Coabas**, his family home, overlooks the town from a hill. It is now in disrepair, but it is due for restoration. Open 9–5, adm. Also being restored is the **Castillo del Cerro**, another of Trujillo's palaces, a monstrous over-elaborate affair on another summit. It too is being restored and you can visit for a small fee. Also worth a visit are caves at El Pomier.

Passing through endless canefields you come to the prosperous town of Baní, birthplace of Máximo Gómez, a hero of the Cuban Independence movement, and eventually to Barahona, an industrial but nonetheless sleepy town. The countryside in this area turns to barren hills covered with organ-pipe cactus trained into fences and prickly pear. From here, one road runs south into the V-shaped Barahona peninsula, passing through poor fishing villages like Enriquillo and Oviedo, with excellent beaches, before heading north to the town of Pedernales on the Haitian border. It was from the Baoruco mountains that Enriquillo led his guerrilla campaign against the Spaniards in the 1520s.

The **Jaragua National Park** lies in the southwestern tip of the island, 500 square miles of cactus plains, sea and discoloured limestone shoreline. You will see pelicans and terns on the coastline. The park is remote. Go by jeep and take plenty to eat and particularly to drink if you are going off the beaten track. **Beata Island** off the southern tip of the island has excellent bird life too.

From Barahona a road inland leads towards Jimaní on the Haitian border. The town is close to the **Lago Enriquillo**, a saltwater lake that lies 140 ft below sea level. **Isla Cabritos** (Goat Island, after the livestock left to forage there) is a national park in the centre of the lake. The five-mile long island is dry and scrubby but supports a wide variety of wildlife, including alligators and iguanas. Among the birds that live on the island are flamingos, clapper rails and roseate spoonbills. You can usually get permission to go to the lake at the park office in the village of **La Descubierta**, a hot and desolate town (you should also request permission in the National Parks Office in Santo Domingo before you set off). If you make the trip, make sure to stock up on food and drink, which is not that easily found in the remote areas beyond Barahona. About half a mile before La Descubierta there are Arawak petroglyphs carved on a cliffside. In the town is a *balneario*, a freshwater swimming pool.

The grandly named **Carretera Internacional** is in fact not much more than a dirt track in many places, running basically along the inland border of the Dominican Republic and Haiti. It is very rough in the south, but offers a great way to see some of the Dominican outback.

FESTIVALS
As a Catholic country many of the Dominican festivals will be based on church celebrations. However, as well as religious processions, the Dominicans make sure to get a week or so's dancing out of a festival. Apart from the major dates in the Christian festival calendar—New Year's Day, 21 Jan (Our Lady of Altagracia, the patron saint of the Dominican people), **Carnival** in the days before Lent, Good Friday and Christmas Day—Dominicans also remember Independence Day (27 Feb) with carnival parades and Restoration Day (16 Aug), when the Dominicans finally became free from Spain in 1865.

Each town also celebrates the day of its patron saint (with an associated blow-out) in its *fiesta patronal*. These start with a mass in the early morning and continue with dancing and street games, culminating with the parade of the carnival queen.

In remoter areas the celebrations can have a strong trace of Dominican *santería*, similar to Haitian voodoo, in which drums produce such a relentless rhythm that the dancers go into trance.

Some of the major *fiestas patronales* are:

13 June—*San Antonio* in Sosúa
29 June—*San Pedro Apostol*, San Pedro de Macoris
5 June—*San Felipe*, Puerto Plata
22 July—*Santiago Apostol*, Santiago
25 July—*San Cristóbal*, San Cristobal
15 Aug—*Nuestra Señora de Antigua*, La Vega
24 Sep—*Nuestra Señora de las Mercedes*, Constanza
4 Oct—*Nuestra Señora del Rosario*, Barahona
24 Oct—*San Rafael*, Boca Chica
4 Dec—*Santa Barbara*, Samaná

A list of the upcoming *fiestas patronales* can usually be winkled out of the tourist offices. It is worth attending if you hear of one happening.

WHERE TO STAY

The Dominican Republic has a full range of hotels—large, self-contained resorts of international standard luxury set on glorious sand, through to the smaller, more personal beach clubs; and in the mountains, small, hillside retreats. If you are travelling the island you will probably spend some time in the capital, Santo Domingo, where you will find restored colonial palaces as well as good guest houses. The Dominican Republic offers well-priced package tours at the moment and with a bit of shopping around, independent travellers will find some very good prices in the off-beat tourist resorts. In the larger tourist hotels you can pay with credit cards and traveller's cheques, but in more local hotels you will have to pay in pesos, so prices are indicated in RD$. Government tax of 6% is added to all bills and service is usually charged at 10% or 15%.

Santo Domingo

EXPENSIVE

The hotels in Santo Domingo are not near to the beaches, but if you want high Caribbean comfort in glitzy pink right in the city, try the **Jaragua Hotel** on the Malecón, 367 Ave George Washington (tel 809 686 2222, fax 686 0528, US 800 223 9815). Four restaurants (one low-cal), casino, club, tennis courts and 300 rooms in high pastel decor with TVs. Double room in season US$170–210. A slightly more Dominican version of this international standard fare can be found at the **Santo Domingo Hotel**, farther along the Malecón (tel 532 1511, US 800 223 6620). The hotel was decorated by the Dominican designer Oscar de la Renta and there are echoes of another era in the arches, dark-stained louvres and palms in the courtyard. It is very much a modern hotel though, with the 216 rooms all in one block and with a special floor devoted to business travellers. It is low-key; they serve afternoon tea and there is no discotheque or casino. Two restaurants and a swimming pool. Double room US$135, or $155 on the executive floor. Across the road you will find its sister hotel, the **Hispaniola**, PO Box 2112 (tel 5357111), which is slightly more up-beat. The Hispaniola is also a modern town hotel with 165 rooms in a block, but it has a nice feel. Bar, casino and CNN to keep you in touch. Double rooms US$100.

MODERATE

If you would prefer the surroundings of the **Colonial City**, where you can stay in a restored *palacio*, there are a couple of comfortable options. The best known is the **Hostal Nicolas de Ovando** (tel 687 3101, fax 688 5170) on the Calle de las Damas in the oldest part of town. It is set in the house of a sixteenth century governor—from the days when Santo Domingo was a gracious viceregal capital. The rooms are set around three charming tiled courtyards, each surrounded by colonnades. Within, the hallways are inlaid with dark mahogany beams and hung with tapestries and paintings on exhibit. Sixty rooms, some dressed up in colonial grandeur (rooms at the rear above the new Avenida del Puerto are quite noisy). There is a good restaurant in the *Extremadura*. Double rate in season US$70. A smaller and quieter, but equally gracious palace is the **Hostal Nicolas Nader** (not to be confused) on the Calle Luperón (tel 687 6674). This is a charming retreat from the bustle of the town, set around a lovely stone courtyard, with arches and mahogany beams that speak of the sixteenth century when generals and conquistadors would pass through. With just ten rooms, furnished in dark colonial style but with air-conditioning, this is a charming and friendly retreat. No restaurant, but a lively bar, and a parrot. Double room in season, US$45 (includes breakfast). Not far off you will find the less appealing **Hotel Palacio** on Calle Hostos, where there are nine comfortable rooms around a courtyard. Air-conditioning and TVs, no restaurant, double room US$50.

There are plenty of **guest houses** around the town, many of which offer a single rate. At 62 Calle Danae you will find **Hotel La Residence** (tel 682 4178) with clean and comfortable rooms for RD$350–450 a double, no restaurant. Close by, at 26 Calle Danae is **La Mansion Guest House** (tel 682 2033), rooms with private baths, cafeteria, double RD$250–300. There are yet cheaper places to overnight around the Parque Independencia. Try the hotel training school, the **Hotel Bolívar** at 62 Avenida Bolívar (tel 685 2200). All mod cons—cable TV, air-conditioning, a restaurant and of course excellent service. Double room RS$300. The **Hotel Aida** on Calle Espaillat (tel 685 7692) has simple double rooms from RD$200 and at the **Independencia** on Estrella you can stay for RD$160 plus.

The Central Mountains

There are not many places to stay in the central mountains, but in Constanza you will find the **Hotel Nueva Suizza** (tel 539 2233). Sixty simple rooms with superb views. In Jarabacoa you can stay at the friendly **River Resort** (tel 574 2918), where the rooms are set in cabins on the hillside. The **Pinar Dorado** (tel 689 5105) offers double rooms at US$30 year round.

The North Coast

West of Puerto Plata there are few hotels. However, at **Punta Rucia** you will find the small and friendly **Orquideria del Sol** (tel 583 2825), which overlooks the beach through a garden of orchids, as the name suggests. 28 rooms.

In the town of **Puerto Plata** the most sympathetic place to stay is the small **Hostal Jimessón**, at 41 John F Kennedy (tel 586 2177), where there are 22 rooms set behind the tiny 19th-century foyer—wood-panelled and tiled, with rocking chairs, antique mirrors and a collection of clocks and gramophones. Beyond the foyer the courtyard and rooms are modern, but well kept and comfortable. A double room in season costs RD$250. There are standard rooms at the **Hotel Caracol** on the Malecón (tel 586

2588), which sees quite a few Dominicans and if you want to stay cheaply you can find rooms at Long Beach at the end of the Malecón for RD$120.

Playa Dorada itself is set on a fantastic beach. If you are happy in a large complex, the resort has excellent facilities—all the watersports, sports on land, restaurants, clubs and casinos. The **Princess Golf, Tennis and Beach Resort** is very comfortable. It has 336 rooms in suites; air-conditioned with cable TV, huge double beds and large balconies. The resort also has tennis courts and golf right next door, as the name implies. The beach is a short walk away. Gourmet restaurant or buffet meals, and evening entertainment. Double room US$150–200. The **Victoria Resort**, PO Box 22 (tel 586 1200, fax 586 4862) also has a certain style. The main house stands above the lake and swimming pool, finished with Spanish colonial trimmings and classical motifs. In spirit the hotel is more twentieth century, with high pastel decoration in the rooms and wicker furniture. All the sports; dining on the breezy terrace to the sound of a band. Double rooms US$110–160. If you would like to stay on the beach (or at least just a dash over the lagoon by boardwalk), the best hotel is probably **Villas Doradas**, PO Box 1370 (tel 586 3000, US 800 332 4872). The villas themselves face on to explosive tropical gardens of bougainvillaea and golden palm. The hotel is large with 207 rooms, but it is comfortable and friendly. Double room in season US$90–120.

A few miles along the coast you come to **Sosúa**, which has one or two resort hotels, but also plenty of small and friendly retreats, in keeping with the spirit of the town. The best place to stay is the **Tropix Hotel** (tel 571 2291), which you will find a couple of minutes' walk across the main road. There are just ten rooms, in blocks overlooking the pool behind the main house, set in a cool garden. There is a communal kitchen, a daily vegetarian menu on offer if you do not want to cook and outside in the shed is an honour bar. Laid back and well away from the hustle of the town, a charming place to stay. And well priced at US$40 a double for the night (includes taxes).

If you would like more customary Caribbean comfort (international standard design, but at good prices) try the **Sand Castle Resort** (tel 571 2420, fax 571 2000, US 800 446 5963). The hotel stands on a cliff above the sea, a space-age conglomeration of Spanish colonial arches overlooking tropical gardens and a pool with a dip and sip bar. It is set on its own beach, double room in season US$70–150.

In El Batey you can find a double room at the **Casa Marina** (tel 571 3690, fax 571 3110), a resort-style hotel set on its own, often crowded, beach. All the watersports and evening entertainment, with good prices; double room US$60 in season.

Behind the Casa Marina there are a number of hotels in the town. The **Yaroa Hotel** on Calle Dr Rosén (tel 571 2651, fax 571 3814) is pleasantly low-key and offers double rooms for around US$40. You can find a cheap room, with terrace and kitchen at the **Sosúa Ocean-front Guest house** for US$25.

Cabarete has a number of laid-back hotels in the easy-going spirit of the town. At the top end of the range the nicest is **Casa Laguna** (tel 571 0725, fax 571 0704), just across the road from the beach. The airy rooms stand in blocks around the tropical garden and pool and they are spacious and breezy, with louvred windows and their own balconies. A good restaurant to loiter in and all the sports for when you want to shed a bit of the weight you have gained. Double room from US$100. You will find very comfortable villas at the **Nanny Estate** (tel 571 0744, fax 571 0655), a couple of miles outside the town. The apartments are ranged shoulder to shoulder, looking diagonally through the palm garden to the sea. Each one has two huge bedrooms and a roof terrace where you can trap the sun for bronzing. Pool, watersports and a good restaurant. Double apartment US$1000 a week. Right on the beach in town is the friendly and sporty **Auberge du Roi Tropicale** (tel 571 0770), where the Micky Bouwmeester windsurfing centre is based. The hotel is set in a modern villa engulfed in palm trees, with a pool and restaurant, massage and sports—including mountain bikes and of course, endless windsurfing. Double room US$70. You can stay more cheaply across the road, for instance at **Don Pedro**, where rooms go for US$28 a double.

The Samaná Peninsula

The best beaches of the peninsula are on the Atlantic coast and so the place to head for is **Las Terrénas** (best approached from Sanchéz), where there are some cool and low-key haunts in which to pass your time. The best fun is the **Hotel Tropic Banana**, PO Box 25 Sanchéz (tel 566 5941, fax 552 7399), which has held hip sway over the town for seventeen years. There are about 30 rooms scattered in small blocks around a palm garden and pool, but the heart of the hotel is the main house, where the hip chicks and pig-tailed windsurfers loiter listening to a local band afternoon and evening. Comfortable rooms furnished in rattan, with a veranda to take it easy after action on the beach or in the bar. Double room US$50 plus. Not far off is another excellent small hotel, the **Hacienda**, just five rooms in a private house in the lovely setting of a superb tropical garden. Very friendly, double room US$50. You can stay cheaply in the town at the **Hotel Restaurant Dinny** (tel 589 9530). Simple, functional rooms US$20. And just a little way out of town there is another charming place to stay at **Isla Bonita** (tel, in Santo Domingo, 562 6209, fax 562 4648), two villas side by side in a sandy garden that overlooks a superb beach. Very low key, fan ventilated with muslin nets on the veranda, hot and cold water, watersports nearby and an Italian restaurant. Just nine room, double rate US$50–90.You will find a more typical Caribbean beach resort at **El Portillo Beach Club** (tel 589 9546, fax 548 4747), a few minutes east out of the town. 75 cabañas are scattered around their own palm garden, with a view on to the cracking, reef-protected beach, and there are other rooms in a block too. Plenty of watersports on the endless beaches, tennis and entertainment. Double rate, inclusive of meals, US$170.

At the northeastern tip of the **Samaná Peninsula** you will find the small and comfortable **Moorea Beach** Hotel (tel 689 4105, fax 538 2545), which overlooks the sand at Las Galeras. Just 12 rooms, with hot and cold water and a restaurant, US$90.

There are not many hotels in the town of Samaná itself, but you can find a comfortable room at the **Tropical Lodge Hotel** (tel 538 2480) just outside the town, US$50 a double. There are simpler rooms at a good price at **Cotubanama** (tel 538 2557), just up from the Malecón. Clean and comfortable, if simple, private baths and a good French restaurant. Double room US$30.

East of Santo Domingo

The beaches begin to appear, and the hotels with them, beyond the airport. **Boca Chica** is active by day and by night, and it is very popular with the Dominicans themselves. A lively hotel, the best of the tourist haunts, can be found at the **Don Juan Beach Hotel** (tel 687 9157, fax 688 5271). As the name suggests, life centres around the beach and nighttime activity. The 124 rooms stand in a block above the pool, which is in spitting distance from the sand, where there is every watersport imaginable, and entertainment. Quite a few package tourists but a lively hotel, double rate US$70–100. There are plenty of **guest houses**, many of them a bit sultry, along the strip (sic), but you will find clean and comfortable rooms at the **Don Paco Guest House** (tel 523 4816) at 6 Calle Duarte. Just ten rooms, friendly, double rate US$35. You can also find rooms at **El Cheverón** (tel 523 4333), simple, US$30 a double. Or if you would prefer to rent an apartment, contact **Caribe Sol** on Calle Rafael (tel 523 4010, fax 523 4140).

Heading east, just beyond La Romana you will find **Casa de Campo** (tel 523 3333, fax 523 8548), the Dominican Republic's leading resort. It is set on a huge estate with 900 rooms and villas, in landscaped grounds, golf courses (there are three), tennis courts (14), and set on cliffs overlooking the sea. The rooms are luxurious, designed by Dominican designer Oscar de la Renta. Buses shuttle the length and breadth of the complex continually, racing you from villa suburb to the beach and from the massage clinic to the hilltop restaurants at Altos de Chavón. High luxury and very expensive, US$250–1000 a double per night. There are also rooms at the **Posada Inn** in Altos de Chavon (same contacts as Casa de Campo), a small hotel (just ten rooms) where there is a pool and rooms with a superb view of the river valley below. High luxury and a faintly Gothic twist on medieval Spain. Double room US$90–120.

A few miles along the southern coastline you will find the **Dominicus Beach Village** (tel 533 4897), which is isolated from the rest of the island in both space—on its own beach away from the crowds—and time—it has an air of the pre-Columbian Caribbean in the mock-rustic bohío thatch cabañas, each with a hammock. Well away from it all, a comfortable retreat for those weary of the twentieth century, double room US$60.

The far northeastern coastline is dotted with an occasional, but usually huge hotel complex. The best is probably the **Bavaro Beach Hotel**, PO Box 1 Higüey (tel 682 2161, fax 682 2169), really four hotels rolled into one, set on a magnificent mile-long sweep of impeccable sand backed along its entire length by palm trees. All the watersports; pools, golf and plenty of evening entertainment. You will have a good, active beach holiday here even if you do not see much of Dominican life. Double room US $130–180. The **Punta Cana Beach Resort**, Higüey (tel 541 2724), is scattered over 100 acres, beach and pool, with swim-up bar. Rooms cost from US$100 per day. At Playa Macao you will find the **Hacienda Barbara** (tel 565 7176), a small and exclusive guest house set in a family villa on a cliff above the beach and surrounded by coconut palms.

West of Santo Domingo
There are few hotels to the west of Santo Domingo, but a few miles beyond the town of Barahona try the **Barahona Beach Club** (tel 685 5184), where there is a complex of suites and apartments with watersports, riding and tennis. The **Hotel Guayocura** (tel 685 6161) is in the town itself, a small and simple hotel. There are guest houses in all towns.

EATING OUT AND NIGHTLIFE
Food and Drink
Like dancing, eating is a favourite pastime in the Dominican Republic and the islanders savour it as they dine out with their families in the evenings. The food is heavy by most standards and many of the meals are centred around a meat stew with a side-salad. Starters are *sopa* (soup), or *chicharrones*, crispy pork rind or chicken pieces that are served

with a spicy dip. *Sancocho* is a thick stew made with seven or more different meats and vegetables, redolent with herbs, and other favourites include *mondongo*, a stew made with tripe and *mofongo*, plantain mashed with spices and garlic. Seafood is good in the Dominican Republic and so you can get a delicious paella and a crab or a lobster dish for US$10. Finally, for a filling local meal, try *arroz con pollo* (chicken and rice) with fried plantains at the side. The Republic grows its own coffee in the northern mountains, which is really quite good.

The Dominicans make the best of their fruits, which grow in profusion in the island and end up in ice-creams and in drinks served in the small bars open on to the street. *Jugos* are drinks made from fresh fruit, water, sugar and crushed ice—extremely refreshing—*bastidas* are a milk shake version of the drink, the best of their kind in the Caribbean. China (orange) is exceptionally good. The Dominicans brew a number of beers; *Presidente* is an excellent light-coloured beer and *Quisqueya* is a slightly darker brew. Rums are *white*, the traditional tipple and mixing drink, *dorado* (gold) and *añejo*, aged in the barrel, which is drunk as a liqueur.

Restaurants

There are literally thousands of restaurants, cafés, local bars and ice-cream halls in the Dominican Republic. Part of the pleasure is simply to wander until you find one you like the look of. As you walk, you get the idea that entertainment is the country's biggest industry. Santo Domingo has an extraordinary variety of restaurants in both style—gourmet, seafood, Italian, Argentinian—and setting—in the old colonial palaces of the Alcazar and along the Malecón. In restaurants outside the hotels, if you do not pay by credit card, you must pay in Dominican pesos.

Santo Domingo

EXPENSIVE

In the capital, the top gourmet restaurant is **Vesuvio** (tel 221 3333), right on the Malecón. Glass-fronted and modern, Vesuvio is always full, at both lunch and dinner. You start with a cocktail about the size of a swimming pool, on the veranda or indoors where the walls are decorated with murals. The owner is Italian, but there are also Spanish and Dominican menus. Try the creole shrimp on *tortellini* in pink vodka sauce or *spaghetti posillipo*, topped with seafood. Main course RD$120. **El Mesón de Castila** (tel 688 4319) also serves Spanish and international dishes at lunch and dinner. The dining room is set in a villa in the suburb street west of the Parque Independencia, at 8 Calle Dr Baez. Brisk service in a vaulted dining room with tiles and beams and you will see all the food neatly displayed as you enter. Try the *paella gran mesón* in cream or brandy. Dishes about RD$80. Not far off is the renowned **Don Pepe** (tel 689 7612), also set in a converted suburban villa, on Calle Santiago at the corner with Calle Pasteur. It is a bit stuffy and formal, presided over by major-domos in tuxedos, but it serves good Spanish fare—suckling pig and variations on the vast crabs that are on view as you come in through the door. There is also a good wine cellar. Main course RD$120.

MODERATE

At the opposite end of the scale, full of the joys of life and with a riotously informal air, is **El Conuco** (tel 686 0129) at Calle Casimro de Moya 152. 'Conuco' means 'country' and the theme is current throughout the restaurant, as is obvious immediately you walk under

491

the rustic thatch roof and palm supports. Huge pestles and mortars, pitchforks and fishtraps adorn the walls, between the *cibaeño campesino* (farmer's sayings) on wooden plaques. And the menu is farmers' food, dressed up a little for the capital—all the tripe dishes you can imagine and some a little less of an adventure, for example *chicharrones de pollo* (deep fried chicken). A fun place. When the waiters have had enough, they turn the music up, grab their instruments and dance for you. Main course RD$50. **Paco's Bananas** (tel 682 3535) at 64 Calle Danae, is also quite hip. The restaurant is set in an open house with covered courtyards and the walls decorated with brightly painted calabashes and atmospheric pictures of rock stars. Menu Spanish and creole—sea bass in a coconut sauce—and there is a lively bar. RD$70. There are limitless restaurants along the Malecón. If you would like a simple meal with a spectator sport thrown in, then try the **Capri Club**, where you can watch the waiters taking food to the tables on the other side of the road, dodging the traffic. A few dishes have gone end-up, but they haven't lost a waiter in 27 years. **El Llave del Mar**, in an air-conditioned dining room on the Malecón, has a distinct sea theme about it. The walls and ceiling are hung with nauticalia—stuffed birds and fish, outsize lobsters, fishermen's floats and even seaweed. Snapper stuffed with shrimp at RD$100 (expensive).

In the **Colonial City** there are plenty of stopping points for when you tire of the sightseeing. The **Fonda de la Atarazana** is in the Alcazar down by the Columbus palace and you can eat upstairs in air-conditioned comfort or in the courtyard set with parasols and greenery. Kingfish or tuna *criollo*, RD$60. Just off the Cathedral Square, at the very foot of El Conde you come to a paved alleyway set with tables and chairs that have spilled out of restaurants. **Che Bandoneon** is one half of the array of tables, and you will be served French and Argentinian food, fillet steaks, *pasta pesto* and *crêpes de la passion*, RD$65 a main dish, with a *bandoneon* (accordion) and guitar accompaniment. A pleasant place to sit and eat for an evening. Not far off is the **Mesón Bari**, a lively joint at the corner of Calle Salome Ureña. It is the favourite gathering point of Santo Domingo's writers and artists on a Friday night, so the diet is as much philosophy, gossip and beer as it is creole food; RD$50. A seafood restaurant in a garden setting, very popular with the Dominicans, is **Captain Crusty** on Avenida Tiradentes, quite far to the northwest of the city. A good lunchtime stop, in the shade of a flamboyant tree. Fish and seafood menu—shrimp *ceviche* or crêpe or a St Peter fillet of fish (breaded). Also, *para los alergicos*—chicken; RD$75. And back in the very centre of the town, just south of the Parque Independencia is another favourite local restaurant, where you linger over your meal and the staff stand around chatting to one another most of the time. The **Independencia** has some of the best in local food, main course about RD$50.

There are three good **vegetarian** restaurants in Santo Domingo. On Calle Luperón you will find the **Bethel**, the most health-conscious of the three. **Ananda's** on Calle Casimiro de Moya and **Ojas** on Calle Gazcue both serve a huge variety of tropical vegetables and fruits in Dominican sauces.

VERY CHEAP

One of the best Dominican meals, a take-away, can be found at **De Nosotros Empanadas**, just down Avenida Independencia at the corner with Dr Delgado. Superb patties—chicken, shrimp and even lobster in creamy sauces—and a soft drink to accompany them. RD$20–30. You can also find very local meals at one of hundreds of **pensions** around the city. They are family kitchens that open up to all-comers. *Un servício*, a plate of rice n' beans (also known as the *bandero nacional* because it is an unofficial national dish) will cost RD$25. Finally, you might consider a snack on Vicini B (leading down to the obelisk on the Malecón), where you sit in a rocking chair as they cook your *chimichurri* (a spicy sausage burger).

Santo Domingo Bars

Just as there are hundreds of restaurants in Santo Domingo, the bars seem to go on forever. Once again, set off until you find one you like the look of. Popular with the locals for a daytime stop are **Kilometro Zero** (all official distances in the country are measured from the square) on the Parque Independencia. Following El Conde down to the colonial city you will find lots of bars and *heladerias* (ice cream bars). Look out for the **Café Colonial** and the **Polo Ground**, where the walls are covered in baseball memorabilia. There are a clutch of bars in the Atarazana, overlooking the Columbus palace: **Drake's Pub** is always a lively option and next door is the marginally quieter **Café Montesinos**. Both are set in the fantastic restored surroundings of the oldest part of town. You might also stop by at **Don Roberto** at the Hostal Nader on Calle Luperón. Popular with the Dominican youth are the **Café Atlantico** at the corner of Avenida Mexico and Abraham Lincoln and **Exquesito**, on Avenida Tiradentes, a cheese and wine/Seven Up/beer bar that collects a lively crowd early on in the evening. If you feel like watching the Dominicans at it, dancing the merengue (and maybe dare have a go yourself), the popular **discotheques** include **Neon 2002** at the Hispaniola Hotel and **Bella Blue**, next to Vesuvio on the Malecón, with lots of glass, pillars and palms, which attracts a slightly older crowd. Discotheques usually have a cover charge of RD$10–20. If you simply want to hang out with the Dominicans to loud music, then it is simple enough to wander down to the Avenida del Puerto, which warms up at about 10 and buzzes till 2 am.

The North Coast

The top restaurant in **Puerto Plata** is **De Armando** (tel 586 3418), on Calle Separación in the centre of town. It is set in an old wooden house which has been refurbished and enclosed with glass to make it air-conditioned. You can still take cocktails on the veranda, though, because they have set up a gazebo inside. The decor is pink and luxurious and the food is top knotch. Try the *Mero Larimar*, sea bass in white wine, or the *filete de Armando* in a celery cream sauce. Main course RD$150. **Valther's** (tel 586 2329) has a superb tropical setting in a lovely open-sided creole house lost in explosive Caribbean overgrowth, on Calle Hermanas Mirabal. You sit out under the banyan tree with the frogs singing all around you and then move on to the veranda for grouper in lemon or orange (RD$85) or a pasta ($60). Just down the road is another **Paco's Bananas**, set on an open veranda with thatch covering and banana plants as decoration. Brisk and often busy, the restaurant serves Spanish and Dominican food—paella or creole-flavoured fish, RD$80. The **Jardin Suizo** is on the Malecón, a simple terrace looking onto the sea where you can get a salad for RD$30 and a full platter like a Wiener schnitzel for RD$100. **Uncle Dick's** is a fun bar and restaurant set in a clapboard house in the centre of town. A hip crowd crawls out of the woodwork and gathers here, not all of them for the exchange library in the corner of the bar by the look of it. Quite lively. You can have a very Dominican meal at the stalls in the alleyway opposite the stadium at the eastern edge of town. **Deportivo** is particularly popular on Sundays.

In **Sosúa** the **Café Atlantico** is famous for its seafood. It has an excellent position on the Charramícos side of the town, with a lovely view of the palms and activity of Sosúa Beach. It is set on its own veranda, with rafters and wooden seats and tables. The menu will vary according to the catch of the day, but there is always a casserole and the house speciality, the paella. Main course RD$100. On the other side of town, **El Batey**, the Pavillon also has a nice setting, a mock Arawak cabana with bohío thatch and pillars and walls of coral rock inlaid with pebbles. Simple menu, steaks and seafood and a lively crowd, main course, RD$90. There is usually a **vegetarian** menu at **Tropix Hotel** (ring and ask on 571 2291), just over the main road. Good poolside setting and friendly crowd. Varied fixed menu—Indonesian, Tex-Mex, crêpes, about RD$50 per person. Another good hotel dining room is **Sonya's** at the Yaroa Hotel. The setting is modern and hardly special, but the French menu is good. Steak in raspberry vinegar or *écrevisses à la provençale*, RD$80–120. On the main street, Calle Pedro Clisante, you will find the restaurant **Don Juan**, where tables spill out on to a terrace from a bar. The speciality is paella, but you might try the shrimp in creole sauce with spaghetti. On the other side of the road is the **Cactus Club**, where there is a Mexican menu—*burritos, enchiladas* and sautéd shrimp, RD$75.

Most of these restaurants have **bars**, but you will find a popular haunt upstairs at **Barock**. Alternatively you get a great view of the beach from the cliffs at the **Marco Polo** bar and restaurant.

Cabarete has a surprising clutch of beach bars and restaurants where you might easily find yourself lingering, escaping the sun during the day and over a meal in the evenings. There are good dining rooms in a couple of the hotels; at the **Casa Laguna** and **Chez Cabarete** at the Nanny Estate, where you can even get a fondu for RD$160. Outside the hotels, a very popular restaurant for local food is **Leandro's**, an open dining room with a thatch roof just off the road. Good for a rice 'n peas, *chicharrones de pollo* or *chivo grisado* (goat stew). Main dish about RD$60. **Lucimar** is more expensive and has a good setting on a veranda giving on to the beach itself. The roof is supported by palm pillars and there seems to be an active, sporting crowd around, while the waves sound in the background. Excellent spiny lobster and king crab are on the menu at RD$160 and fish for RD$100. Another hip spot is **Las Brisas**, which also overlooks the beach from a breezy seaside terrace with palm thatch and a stereo playing the latest rock and merengue. A salad and a beer by day, RD$50–60 and Bar BQ or kebabs in the evening, RD$100, and a wind-surfing crowd (as the name would suggest), so it is quite fun. The **Tex-Mex** Restaurant on the main road also pulls a lively crowd.

But the coolest of them all is a bar across the road from the beach, the **Kao-Ba**. The chairs and benches are scattered around a garden of spotlit tropical greenery, beneath the most enormous coconut palms. Beer if you want it, but also rum cocktails in an easy tropical atmosphere.

In **Las Terrénas** on the Samaná Peninsula there are some surprising and excellent restaurants too. You arrive at **Jikaco** along a pathway flanked by huge gladioli and lit with flaming torches. The dining room is open to the still air and is a pleasant enough place to spend the time drinking anyway. But it is well worth eating; the menu is French—*poulet basquaise* or *mérou grillé* about RD$100. Another superb Caribbean beach setting can be found at **El Rincón**, right on the seafront. The menu is also French here, and you dine on a cosy wooden deck with soft lighting, soft jazz and the gentle wash of the waves. Shrimp and avocado salad, lots of varieties of kebab and then *banane flambée* in rum. RD$100 a main dish. The most formal restaurant in the town (and that is not saying much) is **Chez François**, farther down the waterfront. After a drink in one of the rocking chairs at the beachfront bar, you retreat to the subdued, candlelit dining room. Cangrejo (crab) guisado or camarrones al ajillo (garlic shrimp) for RD$100. The hotels also have some good dining rooms too. You can try the **Tropic Banana**, which has a particularly lively bar, well worth a visit; and the very low-key **Isla Bonita**, where there is an Italian kitchen serving five or six pastas a night as well as the day's catch. If you want a cheap local meal, go to the **Hotel Dinny**.

You will pass through the town of **Samaná** itself, where there are some good cafés overlooking the Malecón. **El Nautico** is decorated with fishing nets and palms and you can sit out on the airy veranda. The menu is fish and seafood, with the special selected according to what was landed by the fishermen that day. **Camilo's** is straight across from the pier if you need to recover after the trip from Sabana de la Mar. Quite simple, breaded kingfish or shrimp and rice, about RD$50. A good stop if you are waiting for, or have just got off the bus to the capital is the **Café de Paris**, a bistro where you can get a salad for RD$40 or a pizza *au feu de bois* for RD$75. Follow up with a crêpe or an ice cream.

East of Santo Domingo
At Boca Chica you will find one long string of snack bars and beach restaurants specializing in fish and seafood. The veranda at the **Casa del Mar** is slightly removed from the hurly-burly of the beach activity and you can get a plate of seafood or a steak for RD$80.

There are a number of restaurants in the Altos de Chavón village above Casa de Campo. The smartest is probably the **Casa del Rio**, from which in the evening you get a superb view of the river, floodlit below. All very atmospheric and mock-medieval, and then rather nouvelle dishes to go with it. Caribbean lobster roasted and baked in vanilla and vinegar or lamb loin in orange marmalade and pastry, main course RD$180 plus. Then take a constitutional on the battlements. If you are on for something simpler and rather less expensive, you can try the **Café del Sol** where you can get a pizza for RD$100. **Papa Jack's** is a fun bar, with a drinking crowd downstairs and a gallery upstairs.

HAITI

The rhythms and reverberations of Africa echo more strongly in Haiti than in any other Caribbean country—in the speech and the faces, in the sheer effervescence of its people and of course in the spiritual world and the relentless beat of African drums. Haiti, which staged the Caribbean's only successful slave rebellion, fighting for its Independence in 1804, is the oldest black republic in the world.

Haiti was originally an Arawak name for the island and supposedly meant 'mountain-ous land' (a good guess at translation if nothing else because the island has three vast

The Citadelle

mountainous ranges). Haiti has the western third of the island of Hispaniola. Like its neighbour it has the same rainforested mountains and fertile valleys, as well as areas that are practically desert. It is about 10,700 square miles.

If Santo Domingo has a pastel wash, Haiti is a land of primary colours, where scarlet, yellow and overpowering blue dominate life, on windowframes and doors, on the buses and in the 'naive' art. There are around six million Haitians and they are almost entirely of African origin, brought here as slaves to the French colony of Saint Domingue. They speak *kreyol*, a language in which French and African strains are clearly audible. Officially the Haitians do not distinguish between white and black, but skin colour has long been a point of controversy in Haiti, enough to cause massacres and political violence.

There is grinding poverty—Haiti is the poorest country in the western hemisphere. As in many Caribbean countries, the people are poorly dressed, but here they are also poorly fed. You will see 50 children clamouring at the only standpipe for miles around, collecting water which they take home balanced on their heads in vast plastic buckets. Out in the country they go to church if they can afford shoes. In Haiti, shoe-shine boys are grown men, not children.

Politics has also been hard on the Haitians and in this they have an ingrained pessimism. Over the last two centuries they have seen endless internal strife as a succession of corrupt dictators jockeyed for position and then administered with a brutal disregard for their population's pitiable situation. Despite a desire for stability among the people themselves, it seems a forlorn hope that the situation should improve radically in the near future. On the international scene, Haiti has been embattled from the beginning, shunned as a stronghold of black magic and most recently as the home of AIDS.

However, most Haitians are not resigned in their poverty. The country has an irrepressible spirit, and they escape their drab physical existence in many ways. The most notorious is of course the religious cult of *voodoo* (see below), but the islanders also

496

express themselves in vibrant traditions of naive art and a lively street culture. Get out into the streets of Port au Prince and you will soon see. Haiti seems to have taken all the strains essential to Caribbean life and amplified them to a blare. And unlike so many Caribbean countries, who have hang-ups about a colonial past, Haiti has no problem about its national identity.

Haiti is hardly a tourist destination, though it has the beaches and the reliable winter sun, but the joy of Haiti lies well behind the screen of palms and coconut oil. It is a thoroughly rewarding place to travel, though it can be very tiring and at times of political difficulties it can be dangerous.

History

Columbus discovered Haiti on 5 December 1492 on his first voyage to the New World, as he sailed east from Cuba. His ship, the *Santa Maria*, was wrecked there and so with the wood he constructed a fort, La Navidad (Christmas), leaving 40 men to discover the reserves of gold that they had already seen and which Marco Polo had reported as 'inexhaustible' (Columbus thought he had discovered Japan). When he returned a year later the men were all dead.

A hundred years later, as the colony of Hispaniola was languishing, pirates and sea-rovers began to creep into the inaccessible northwestern corner of the island. They holed up on the island of Tortuga, fortifying themselves so that they were almost impossible to winkle out. Often they would disappear on jaunts around the Caribbean as mercenaries, but when there was peace they crept on to the mainland to kill cattle, which they smoked over a frame called a *boucan*. They came to be known as the buccaneers.

The buccaneers were mostly French (English pirates had a similar hide-out in Port Royal, Jamaica) and eventually, at the Treaty of Ryswick in 1697, the Spaniards ceded the western third of the island to the French crown. Over the next century, Saint Domingue became the richest colony in the world, supplying sugar, coffee and indigo to France in a fleet of 700 ocean-going ships. With annual exports worth $40 million, it was far more prosperous than any of the American colonies and its capital, Cap Français, was known as the Paris of the New World. The regime was as brutal as it was successful. The half million slaves were treated with abominable cruelty—the planters would flog them close to death for the most minor offence and slaves were starved and buried alive.

With so many slaves, and internal rivalries between the whites, mulattos and free blacks, the colony was a powder keg which was sparked off by the French Revolution. The National Assembly in Paris granted political rights to the mulattos, but the whites would not permit it in the colony itself and so the rebellions started. The mulattos Ogé and Chavannes made a call to arms and were publicly broken on the wheel.

Rebellion and Revolution

These events were overtaken in August 1791, when the first major black rebellion took place. It was initiated by Boukman, a voodoo *houngan*, who gave instructions to torch the northern plains with the call of a conch and with the voodoo drums. The slaves pillaged and burned, subjecting the white slave-owners to the tortures they had undergone themselves, killing any they could find. The few who escaped fled to Cap Français and left the country, many settling in eastern Cuba. Over the three years of the rebellion the northern part of the colony was devastated and the lines were drawn for civil war between the blacks in the north and the mulattos in the south. The French colonial authorities were powerless to intervene.

The rebel leader in the north was the remarkable Toussaint L'Ouverture (called so either because of an opening he created in a battle or for the gap between his teeth) who sided with the French Republicans after they abolished slavery in 1793. Toussaint had educated himself with the sanction of his white master (whom Toussaint helped to escape during the 1791 rebellion) and he entered the rebel army as a herb doctor. His skill as a military man, supposedly learned from a book about Alexander's campaigns, soon became clear, and by 1796 he was the undisputed leader of the former slaves in the north. He then showed his brilliant colours as a politician and he administered his country humanely, ending the massacres and managing to restore some of Saint Domingue's former prosperity. He was the unofficial governor of a colony that was independent from France in all but name.

But when he tried to introduce a constitution that allowed the country autonomy and appointed him Governor for life, it was too much for Napoleon, who wished to re-establish his power in the Americas. In 1801 Bonaparte despatched an army of 34,000 men, led by his own brother-in-law Leclerc, with instructions to subdue the slave armies and to retake the colony for France. Leclerc treated with Toussaint and during a dinner to discuss the affairs of the colony in Cap Français, he had him seized and deported to France. Toussaint was held in a castle in the Jura mountains, ill-fed and without warmth. His letters to Napoleon were left unanswered and within a year he was dead. His final words on departure from Saint Domingue were, 'In overthrowing me, they have cut down in Saint Domingue the trunk of the tree of black liberty. It will shoot up again through the roots, for they are numerous and deep.'

The blacks did not revolt immediately, but they buried their arms rather than turn them in. In May 1802, the Convention in Paris reintroduced slavery and the blacks rose up against the French once more. More whites were massacred and the French army, decimated by disease and guerrilla war, evacuated. On 1 January 1804 Jean Jacques Dessalines tore the white strip out of the *tricolore*, and proclaimed the independent black Republic of *Haiti*.

Dessalines was a tyrant, but he started to rebuild the economy, forcing the former slaves back to their plantations. Ever-fearful of an attack by the French to retake the colony, he maintained a large army, introducing into Haitian society a traditional power which has continued even to today. But soon he became unpopular, particularly with the mulattos, and he was assassinated in 1806.

His death led to civil war again between the mulatto south, under the General Pétion, and the north, which adopted the negro Henry Christophe as its leader. As leader of Haiti, Christophe, a megalomaniac and an immense man in size and energy, wished to show that the first black Republic was as capable as any European power. He had himself crowned King (Dessalines had made himself an Emperor in imitation of Napoleon) and he built a magnificent palace worthy of any European kingdom at Sans Souci near Cap Haitian in the north (his court still sounds faintly comical to European ears as it included the Counts of Limonade and Marmelade). Nearby, his Citadel is one of the most extraordinary feats of engineering in the world. But his reign was also tyrannical and in 1820, as armies closed in on him, he committed suicide by shooting himself with a silver bullet. He was buried in the Citadel. After his death, the two sides of the country were united again, under the southern General Boyer.

Boyer treated with France, who finally admitted Haitian Independence at the price of 150 million French francs as compensation (later reduced to 60 million). He also invaded Santo Domingo which had just won Independence from Spain.

In the 72 years between Boyer's flight in 1843 and 1915, Haiti saw 22 Heads of State, most of whom left office by violent means. Some tried to improve the infrastructure of the country, but the aspirations of the early leaders foundered with a succession of corrupt and self-seeking dictators. Rivalry continued between the whites and the mulatto elite and the blacks, who dominated the army, flaring up from time to time in politically motivated massacres. In the fields, the Haitian peasants suffered a steady decline in their standard of living, scraping barely enough food from the soil to survive.

In 1915, after the dismemberment of President Guillaume Sam, the Americans invaded the country, concerned with the influence of the German community in the country at the time of the First World War. There followed 19 years of heavy-handed administration. It brought considerable development in roads, sanitation and in schools, but the Haitians opposed it with a nationalist movement which erupted increasingly in violence. Eventually Haiti was flourishing in 1930 and they wanted independence again. In 1934 the Marines left.

The mulatto elite had come to prominence again during the American occupation and it was not long before internal political troubles started along the traditional lines. Coloureds found their way into the positions of power. They also led campaigns against voodoo. Until the accession of François Duvalier in 1957, and since the deposition of his son in 1986, Haiti has suffered the political turmoil it has always faced.

The Duvaliers

The Duvalier regime was another brutal chapter in Haitian history, in which the country was hijacked by a ruthless despot who then arranged to hand over power to his son. It was characterized by repression, particularly through his private militia, the notorious *tontons macoutes* (the name means 'uncle knapsack' and comes from a character in Haitian folklore who carries off children in the middle of the night). Father and son amassed vast personal fortunes from the Haitian national coffers.

François Duvalier, a doctor and union leader and a member of Haiti's emerging black middle class, was elected President at the age of 50 in 1957. For the first few years in his 14 year rule 'Papa Doc' terrorized the country, consolidating power and rooting out potential rivals in the army, the church and the mulatto elite. 'Papa Doc' was a shrewd manipulator and ensured that there was no organized resistance to his regime. He was also a practising vodunist—his loa was *Baron Samedi*, the guardian of cemeteries and a harbinger of death. Thousands of Haitians died in his regime. In 1964 he had the constitution changed so that he could be elected President for life, which he remained until his death in 1971. He appointed his son, Jean Claude, then 19 years old, President for life.

There was initially some political liberalization and there was foreign investment as the regime became less isolationist. But the status quo was maintained by the usual terror tactics and once again, the poorest Haitians benefited little. Haiti was the poorest country in the western hemisphere. Many Haitians took their chance and tried to get illegally into the USA. Corruption ran rife. In the face of the poverty, 'Baby Doc' lavished an estimated US$7 million dollars of national money on his wedding in 1980.

In the early 80s he cracked down on any liberalization and the new political parties were banned. Riots broke out as the regime began to founder in 1984 and by late 1985 the country was in open revolt. Eventually, in what was known as *Operation Deschoukay*, the regime collapsed on 6 February 1986 and 'Baby Doc' fled the country for France.

Haiti continues to suffer political turmoil. There seems to be a general will among the people for internal stability, but for the moment, with endless suspicions of corruption and involvement in drug-trafficking at the highest levels and the unpredictable activities of the rival security forces and traditional political power-blocs, it is impossible to say what will be the outcome. The future is by no means bright. Many Haitians are still trying to escape to the USA.

The economy is in a mess and three quarters of the population of Haiti is on the breadline. The majority are subsistence farmers, but many work in the coffee industry. The low wages make a certain amount of industry possible, including the manufacture of some electronic goods, shoes and baseballs. The usual Caribbean mainstay, tourism, has fallen off because of the political problems. For the same reason, mineral resources remain untouched. There is only 20% literacy in Haiti.

Voodoo

Voodoo is an essential part of Haitian life, but one that is little understood outside the country—with all the sensationalized stories of frenzied drumming and dancing and of sacrificial black magic ceremonies, it is one of the sources of the country's mystery and bad PR. The saying has it that 90% of Haitians are Catholic, but 99% of them believe in voodoo.

Voodoo (vodun in Haitian kreyol) is a religion (a system of beliefs at least), in which the spiritual world is inhabited by *loas* (pronounced 'lwa'), spirits who have a direct effect on human life. There is no overall voodoo theology, complete creed of beliefs or order of service and the spirits will be different in different parts of the country. Voodoo started on the slave plantations as a form of celebration, in which some of the spirits from Africa were invoked, but over the years many have taken on noticeably Catholic characteristics; other new spirits were discovered in Haiti. Good and evil are not so clear cut as in the monotheistic religions. Spirits can be angry or content and will bring happiness and good luck if treated well, but they can also be vengeful. Over the years it has been used as a political weapon and denied as quackery and superstitious nonsense. However, voodoo runs very deep in Haitian society. It is one of the strongest expressions of the Haitian spirit, in defiance of their poverty.

The principal loas are *Papa Legba*, the guardian of doors, gates, roads and crossroads, who acts as a sort of go-between for the believers and their other loas. *Erzulie* is a female loa and resembles the Virgin Mary, though she does not perform any specific function. *Damballa*, on the other hand, is the spirit of water and so he can send rain enough to provide for the crops, but when angry he will cause destruction in floods. Others include *Papa Zaca*, the father of agriculture, *Ogun*, the spirit of war and the well-known top-hatted *Baron Samedi*, who watches over cemeteries, and spirits who control the livelihoods of fishermen, hunters or tradesmen. Christian deities are acknowledged, but they are far more remote than these spirits, except of course Erzulie. Each spirit has its favourite colour, often white or grey, but sometimes red, and animals that are sacrificed to them must be of that colour.

The voodoo ceremony itself takes place in a *hounfort*, a building with an altar and an area of beaten earth where the dancing takes place. It begins with a ritual very similar to Catholic liturgy, but then the drumming strikes up (on drums of different sizes, carved out of mahogany, with a skin stretched over the top and held taut with vast pegs) and the dancing begins. A loa will reveal him or herself to the *houngan* (the nearest thing to a priest) and the particular rhythms of that loa will be played. A *véver*, a patterned symbol, is drawn on the ground with cornmeal or with ash to appease the specific loa.

Eventually, if the conditions are right, the loa may come and 'mount' a dancer, who will then go into trance, sometimes screaming and flailing around, often intoning predictions. The first loa to mount a person becomes their guardian angel for life. This possession does not necessarily happen at every ceremony, but is expected at most important events.

There is another side to Haitian spiritual life, occasionally connected to voodoo, in which magic can be used in curing an illness or warding off evil spirits or to change the course of events. An illness might be the act of a loa, and so the sick person would seek the advice of the houngan or perhaps a *bocor* (a sorcerer), to find out why it is. Some cures will resemble old wives' brews, other have more sinister ritual. The sorcerer has a powerful hold over his devotees, but the final arbiter is, of course, his success.

One of the most sensational aspects of Haitian life is, of course, that of *zombies*, of which little evidence exists, but which still make fascinating and ghoulish stories. Supposedly a person is fed a potion which makes their metabolic rate drop so low that they appear to be dead. After they are buried, the administrator of the poison will then dig them up, restoring them to full physical capacity, but keeping their mind in limbo. The zombie is then transported to the other end of the country and used as a slave.

Voodoo ceremonies take place according to a calendar and to celebrate special events. You will hear the drumming blow on the still night air, and if you are driving around at these times you may well see streams of people heading for the local *hounfort*. It is very difficult for a white stranger to attend a local voodoo ceremony. Unless your contacts are very good, the best you can really hope for are the various shows that admit foreigners. These are impressive sights nonetheless and it is difficult to tell how authentic they are. You can try the Le Péristyle de Mariani, of which the houngan is Max Beauvoir, who will explain the ceremony as it is performed. The going rate is around US$15–20. You can even contact some houngans in the telephone book. Try 'V' for voodoo.

Taptaps

Taptaps are the brightly decorated buses that you see barging their way through the traffic in Port au Prince or chasing from one town to the next, loaded to the gunwales. They take their name from the old lorries, whose engines would labour over the hills with a *tap-tap-tap*, but now they can be anything from a Mitsubishi van with a cage on the back to a vast seven-ton MACK lorry with multiple horns and flashing lights.

The decorations on the cage are all important and look a bit like an old circus or gypsy caravan. The basic wooden frame on the back is often red, but it is carved in graceful

Taptaps on Dessalines

sweeps, with curves and cresting waves. It is embellished with stars and diamonds in red, gold and green, kisscurls and unwinding squiggles. Along each side you will see a kreyol maxim, often religious, lit by a stream of coloured flashing bulbs, 'Pran courage fre la Tribilation', 'A Koua Bon' (Béni Soit L'Eternel NISSAN looks a bit odd). There is often a biblical scene painted on the bonnet.

There are, of course, more normal looking buses around, but these coloured ones are very popular and are a sort of Haitian street art. You can get a large lorry on longer journeys (as a foreigner you might be offered the front seat, take it because it gets pretty crowded in the back), but within the towns there are smaller versions on the back of pick-ups, cages with whirligig fans on the front, coloured plastic windows and loud *compas* music on the stereo, making the whole thing like a mobile discotheque. Be careful walking through the traffic in Port au Prince, otherwise you might look up and receive a final sacrament as you are run over by a bus screaming 'Dieu Te Bénisse!'

Haitian Art

Another of Haiti's most vibrant traditions is that of 'naïve' art. It is unique, and uses a simple, almost childlike style, usually without the use of perspective, and invariably using very bright primary colours. As well as on canvas, it appears all over the island—in churches, on the taptaps and in a profusion of murals in the wake of *Operation Deschou-kay*, the ousting of the Duvaliers. Catholicism, the loas of the voodoo world and rural Haitian life are typical themes in Haitian painting.

Haitian naïve painting became known outside the country when the American teacher De Witt Peters came to Haiti in the early 40s. The form was frowned on initially by the Haitian elite, who tended to look to French culture for their inspiration, but Peters recognized the extraordinary flavour of the primitivists and helped the artists to develop their skills by setting up the Centre d'Art, which provided materials for the painters and sponsored them. The school produced the likes of Philomé Obin, Hector Hyppolite, a

HAITI

voodoo houngan, Bazile, Dufont, Benoit and later Lafortune Félix. Sculptors were also encouraged and Liautaud, Brierre and Jasmin Joseph became famous.
There are many places to view and to buy Haitian art. It can literally be bought by the yard and you will even be approached in the street by people clutching their latest masterpiece, but the galleries, both downtown and in Pétionville, contain the best (and most expensive) works. You can buy at the renowned **Centre d'Art** (tel 222018) in the Musée d'Art Haitien on the Champ de Mars. In Pétionville there is a selection of galleries, including the **Mapou Galerie** at 8 Rue Panaméricaine (tel 576430), and the **Galerie Nader** at 48 Rue Grégoire (tel 575602), both of which have a good selection.
Selden Rodman has written a number of histories of Haitian art. He described the growth of the primitive school in *Haiti: The Black Republic* (published 1954) and later wrote *The Miracle of Haitian Art* (published 1974). His most recent book, published in 1988, is *Where Art is Joy. Haitian Art: the first forty years*.
There is also a strong tradition of arts and crafts on the island, and if you go to the Marché de Fer, you will be inundated with offers of gaudy religious paintings, mahogany work and ghostly faces in shawls made of leather. The best place to go for ironwork and metal sculptures is an alleyway that leads off Avenue John Brown as you leave Port au Prince for Pétionville.

Flora and Fauna

The 'mountainous land' of Haiti is extremely fertile, particularly in the well-watered heights of the northern and southern massifs, each of which has developed unique flora. The nearest park to Port au Prince is in the hills above Kenscoff; **Morne la Visite** lies between Furcy and Seguin and in the lush montane forests you will find parrots and parakeets and the Hispaniolan hummingbird. Similar vegetation and birdlife can be found at the western end of the peninsula, at the remote **Macaya Peak National Park**. Take all you will need if you go exploring here.
At **Saumâtre Lake** near the Dominican border you will see crocodiles and extensive birdlife including flamingos and jacanas with rebellious toes and an embarrassing splurge on their faces. Across the cactus plains in the centre of the island where the hawks and hummingbirds hover, the Massif du Nord has more rich red earth and precipitous slopes which can be treacherous after rain.
There is considerable deforestation in Haiti as the islanders chop down trees for burning. If you go out into the country you will see the charcoal pits in which the Haitians prepare their fuel.
There is little organized about the National Parks in Haiti, though there is sometimes a ranger's hut available. Take all you need in the way of food and water and a four-wheel drive car. You should get permission in Port au Prince before you visit the Parks, through ISPAN (Institut pour la Sauvegarde du Patrimoine National), PO Box 2484, 86 Ave John Brown in Port au Prince (tel 225286).

GETTING TO HAITI
The main airport is at the capital Port au Prince, but some flights and charters fly into **Cap Haitien** on the north coast. There is a departure tax of US$20, usually payable in dollars.

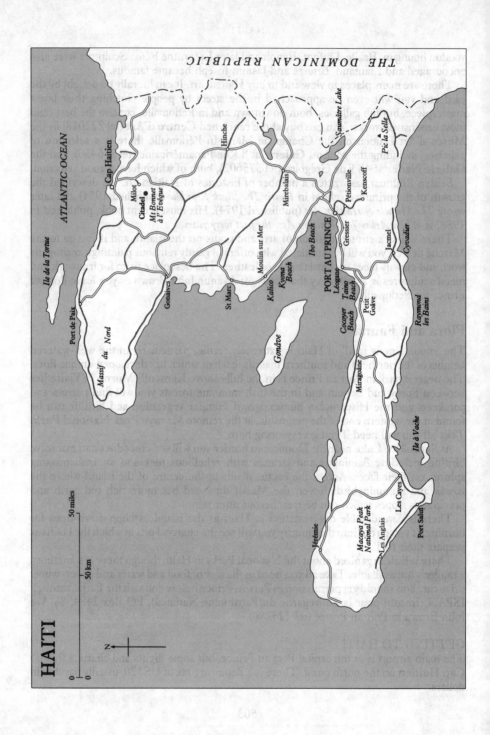

HAITI

THE DOMINICAN REPUBLIC

ATLANTIC OCEAN

Île de la Torture

Cap Haïtien

Milot
Citadel
Mt Bonnet
à l'Evêque

Port de Paix

Gonaïves

Massif du Nord

St Marc

Moulin sur Mer

Kaliko
Kyona
Beach

Gonâve

Hinche

Mirebalais

Saumâtre Lake

Pic la Selle

Pétionville
Kenscoff

Gressier

Ibo Beach

PORT AU PRINCE
Léogâne

Tano
Beach

Cocoyer
Beach

Petit
Goâve

Jacmel

Cyvadier

Raymond
les Bains

Miragoâne

Île à Vache

Jérémie

Les Cayes

Macaya Peak
National Park

Les Anglais

Port Salut

N

50 miles

50 km

HAITI

By Air
From Europe: There is a weekly Air France flight from Paris. From other cities in Europe you will need to change planes, usually in Miami.
From the USA and Canada: Direct links to Haiti can be caught from **Miami**, mainly with American Airways and Haiti Trans Air, with a couple of flights a week with Air France and ALM. American Airways offer daily services from New York. Air Canada flies once a week from Montreal.
From other Caribbean Islands: Many links have been cut since the recent troubles, but ALM flies from Curaçao.
Cap Haitien on the north coast, is linked four days a week to the Turks and Caicos Islands and directly to Miami.
There are two points of entry on the Haitian border with the Dominican Republic, at Jimani in the south and at Ouanaminthe in the north. Crossing into Haiti is quite easy, but getting out again is problematic (see Travellers' Advice below).

GETTING AROUND HAITI
Around Port au Prince you can take *camionettes*, like small taptaps, which run specific routes through the town, picking up and setting down where you please. They do not have a schedule, but they are frequent, starting at dawn and running until dusk (only infrequently on the important routes after dusk). A ride costs two gourdes. Otherwise take a *publique*, recognizable by the red cloth tied to the rear-view mirror. These pick up any passenger and the driver decides who to let off first. If you want to get up to Pétionville, flag down a *publique* on Avenue **John Brown**, which leads out of the Place du Marron Inconnu or catch it earlier down by the Marché de Fer.
Taptaps run the length and breadth of the country, but if you are on a long journey, you may find it more comfortable to ride in one of the more regular buses, though these can be crowded enough as it is. Once again, they leave when they are full (ask around for the next one to leave). Jacmel and Cap Haitien are quite well served, other towns have only a couple of services a day. Get to the bus stop early. If you are going to a beach, ask the driver to drop you off.
Buses going **south** and **west** leave from behind the customs building, towards the waterfront from the Marché de Fer. If you are going **north**, you leave from the top of Boulevard Jean Jacques Dessalines. A few sample fares from Port au Prince are: Jacmel—US$3 (2½ hrs), Les Cayes—US$6 (4 hrs), Jérémie—US$10 (8 hrs), Go-naïves—US$4, Cap Haitien—US$10 (4–5 hrs). To Kenscoff from Pétionville costs US40c or 2 gourdes. Hitch-hiking in Haiti is not really recommended.
Taxis are available at the airport and at major hotels and restaurants. They are not always in the best condition, but usually get you home. They are unmetered and rates are officially set by the government, so you should establish the price (don't forget to bargain) and make sure of the currency before you set off on the journey. Port au Prince to Pétionville costs US$16 and the journey out to the airport from downtown costs about US$15.
Taxi-drivers would be happy to take you on a **tour** for about US$15 per hour, though not all speak English. You will probably get the runaround, and be taken only to the galleries where the driver gets a commission on your purchase, but be firm if there is a place you particularly want to visit. You can arrange a 'gingerbread' tour of Port au

505

Prince and Pétionville, visiting the best of the old-style mansions. Usually Thurs, check the day before at the Musée d'Art (tel 222510), US$15.

Car hire is another option, but not one to be taken lightly because it comes with its hazards. Driving in town is chaotic, and on the country roads it can be pretty dangerous as larger vehicles have little sympathy for cars. Officially driving is on the right. Drivers can use a licence from home for the first three months. You are best to use the large international firms, and you might consider arranging it before you leave home. Most of them have offices at the airport and in town. Weekly rentals will bring the price down. Cars are available at around US$40–45 per day, plus insurance. Companies usually accept a credit-card deposit. Try **Zénith** (tel 456179), or **Budget** at the airport (tel 462324) and in town (tel 461366). **Dynamic** can be reached on 460700 or at the airport (tel 460236).

You might be able to hitch a ride on the graceful old boats that ply between the ports taking produce.

TOURIST INFORMATION
There is not much tourism in Haiti at the moment and there are no tourist boards around the world. You might get some information by contacting the embassies. In **France**, the Ambassade d'Haiti is at 10 Rue Théodule Ribot, 75017 Paris (tel 47 63 47 78).

There is no Tourist Board in Haiti itself at the moment. However, if you are travelling there you will find that travel agents and hotel managers are quite well informed. There are many missionaries in Haiti and in remote areas they can be helpful.

In a **medical** emergency, contact the Hôpital L'Asile Français, Rue du Centre, Port au Prince (tel 222323). If you are having problems, most hotels have an English-speaking doctor on call.

The **IDD code** for Haiti is 509, followed by a six-figure national number. Just the six digits should be dialled within Haiti.

The **US Embassy** is near the waterfront in Port au Prince on Harry Truman Boulevard (tel 220354) and the **British Consulate** is at the Hotel Montana, PO Box 1302, Port au Prince (tel 221227).

Strangely, the official **language** in Haiti is French. You will find that in the towns French is enough to get by, but in the country it is not that widely understood. English is understood in the tourist hotels.

Around 90% of the Haitians communicate in *kreyol*, an extraordinary mix of French and African that has grown into a new language. Of all the French creoles in the Caribbean (there are others in the French Antilles), this is the hardest baked and it is certainly not mutually comprehensible with French. You will see expressions written in kreyol on the taptaps and daubed on the walls. There is a different spelling system from the official French, but if you read it out loud you can sometimes hear the French meaning.

MONEY
The official currency of Haiti is the *gourde*, which is fixed, officially at any rate, to the US dollar (US$ = 5 *gourdes*). The currency was introduced by King Christophe at the beginning of the last century, when he supposedly made the gourde or calabash (a large fruit with a hard exterior that can be used as a bowl) into the currency, slowly introducing

notes to replace them. The name remains. Five gourdes is referred to for ease as a *'dollar haïtien'*. If you go off the beaten track, you should get hold of some gourdes.

The US dollar is not really legal currency beyond the tourist hotels and restaurants, which can accept traveller's cheques and credit card bills in dollars. The banks give a flat rate of five gourdes to the US dollar with no commission as there are on other currencies. However, the US dollar (*'dollar US'*) does trade at about eight gourdes on the very open black markets. You will be approached in the streets by characters flicking a wad of notes. Dealing on the street is obviously illegal and so you are advised not to be too flagrant. However, businesses that deal in foreign goods do need hard currency to buy in their products, so they have been known to buy dollars at a preferential rate. Carry around plenty of small change. **Banking** hours are weekdays 9–1. **Government offices** keep hours of 8–noon and 1–4.

TRAVELLERS' ADVICE
Because of the political unrest, there is practically no tourism in Haiti at the moment. There are hardly even any hustlers any more. However, it is a fascinating country in which to travel, even for the fact that it is quite hard work.

A white traveller in Haiti will soon become familiar with the word *blanc* (white), which the islanders will say at every turn. It is not a racist insult, it merely registers that you are white and that you are in Haiti, a cross between an exclamation and a greeting to a stranger (if a Haitian wants to insult you he will do it with a babble of incomprehensible expletives in Haitian kreyol). There is no reason to feel threatened by the word *blanc*, but it may not be a request for you to stop and talk. You are quite likely to be shouted at in the street, but this is not always with malicious intent, it is often a humorous quip in the Haitian street-theatre (though it can still be a little disconcerting to find that the whole road collapses in raucous laughter).

Dollar on the other hand, is definitely a request for money, and you sometimes get the idea that this is the first word that a Haitian baby learns. White travellers, who must have money to have got to Haiti in the first place and are therefore all assumed to be rich, will find themselves surrounded by crowds of kids requesting a dollar, or five. The best advice is not to give even though they are quite persistent.

When they are out and about, Haitian **hustlers** are far and away the best in the Caribbean: they will pester you relentlessly if you are alone (to be fair they are also the poorest). And they are pretty sophisticated, suddenly they will be there and they will stick to you like a limpet. Some of them are good guides, others are just small-time dealers. It can be extremely tiring being alone in Haiti, as you spend all day explaining that you wish to be alone, and so it may be easiest to come to an arrangement with one guide just to keep the others away. Offer a daily rate (perhaps US$15) and pay for meals that you eat together. It is important to distinguish between the hustlers who nobble you at the gates of your hotel and in downtown Port au Prince (making a reasonable living out of it), and the genuinely poor countryman to whose life the donation of a dollar would make an appreciable difference.

There is not much **crime** against white travellers in Haiti. However, as in any city you are advised to be aware when in Port au Prince (watch your pockets in public places). Violence in Haiti tends to be political, and will surface at election time and the fairly regular coups d'état. Consider getting out of town then, though there is not usually any trouble directed at foreigners. Women do not usually suffer sexual harassment in Haiti. There is a problem with venereal diseases in Haiti, most notably with AIDS. When visiting Haiti you should take a preventive medicine against **malaria**.

You are advised not to drink the **water** in Haiti, or to buy the iced drinks off the streets, sold from the tricycles with a box of concentrates on the front. Stick to soft drinks and coconuts. Purified water (Culligan is an accepted term for purified water) is easily available in the shops. The electrical supply in Haiti is hopeless. Expect it to be off for most of the day and to come on at any time between 6 and 8.

The Haitian **bureaucracy** is all-encompassing and the best advice is to avoid it if at all possible. If not, you will need a French/kreyol speaker and a lot of patience. Whatever government office it is that you must visit, get there early. For instance, in order to go overland to the Dominican Republic, you must go through the following steps (leaving at least a couple of days for it all to be complete):

1. Get a form from Immigration on 173 John Brown.
2. Take it to the Impôts (price about US$20), and then get a *Laisser-passer* letter with the stenographers outside, price 3 gourdes.
3. Return to Immigration with form and passport for stamping.
4. Visit Grand Quartier-Général des Forces Armées d'Haiti (Army HQ) for a final stamp.

Bureaucratic trouble over? Not a bit of it. When you get to the border, you must:

1. Visit Immigration and pay the departure tax of US$20.
2. Visit the Army.
3. Visit the Border Police.

If you are lucky you can circumvent any one of these steps; however, remember that if the relevant authority is in a bad mood you may get further delays and that the first few steps can only be arranged in Port au Prince. Sometimes the officials will go as far as asking for a backhander if you forget to produce one. It is probably easier to fly—you can complete all the formalities at the airport.

Lastly **photography** is something of a problem in Haiti and it can be quite entertaining as all the Haitians dive for cover at the sight of a camera. If you look too determined, they will remonstrate at you and tell of their soul being stolen. The odd Haitian has been known to sell his soul for a few dollars—take your choice. If you go ahead without paying, expect to be screamed at and cursed in kreyol and for the whole street to collapse in giggles again.

Literary Tradition and Further Reading

Haiti has quite a literary tradition of its own and has inspired plenty of books by writers from other countries. One of the country's earliest literary sons was Alexandre Dumas, author of *The Three Musketeers* and *The Count of Monte Cristo*. The Cuban Alejo Carpentier wrote a magical representation of life under Christophe, including the building of the Citadel, in *A Kingdom of this World*.

In the 1930s the Haitians re-evaluated their culture and their African heritage much as other Caribbean writers did. Perhaps the best novel from this period was about

Haitian peasant life, called *Les Gouverneurs de la Rosée*, by Jacques Roumain. It was published posthumously in 1944 (Heinemann put out a translation under the name *Masters of the Dew*). Other works by Roumain include *La Montagne Ensorcelée*. Another excellent author of the period was Jacques Stephen Alexis, who wrote a number of novels including *Compère Général Soleil, Romancero aux Etoiles* and *L'Espace d'un Cillement*. More modern, *The Beast of the Haitian Hills*, by the brothers Philippe and Pierre Marcalin, tells a fatal tale of peasant and voodoo life.

The Trinidadian historian CLR James treated the subject of the Haitian revolution in *The Black Jacobins*, an angry and extremely powerful book that was first published in 1938.

Many books look at the sensational side of Haitian life and mystery, of which the most famous is probably *The Magic Island* by WB Seabrook, published in 1929. An authoritative and scholarly view can be found in Alfred Métraux's *Le Vaudou Haïtien*.

Graham Greene's novel, *The Comedians*, describes the oppressive life under 'Papa Doc' Duvalier in the 60s. The inspiration for the hotel is the Oloffsen in the South East of town. This book was once banned in the country.

From Dessalines to Duvalier by David Nicholls is an excellent history of Haiti for those who would enjoy a detailed and well-researched account of the country since the rebellion and Independence. Two recent travel books are *Best Nightmare on Earth*, by Herbert Gold (Grafton 1991) and *Bonjour Blanc*, Ian Thomson (Hutchinson 1992).

Audubon, the great bird artist who was the inspiration for all the Audubon birding societies, was from Haiti.

BEACHES

Haiti has a full range of beaches, from strips of idyllic white sand to secluded coves which you can only reach by row-boat, and with the political trouble they have become generally deserted. The more popular beaches, if they are owned by a hotel or have been developed by a cruise ship company, will charge an entrance fee. You will find most watersports available here. You can also go further afield and discover fishing villages on idyllic half-moon coves. Remember to take all you need: picnic, mosquito repellant, water and snorkelling gear.

The nearest beaches to Port au Prince are to the south, off the route to Miragoane. You will come to **Guilou**, near Gressier, and then **Taino**, both well served with watersports huts and snack shops. Nearby is **Sun Beach** and the very attractive and slightly more isolated **Cocoyer Beach**, close to Petit Goâve.

Jacmel Beach on the south coast is not very attractive (it has dark sand), but not far east are **Raymond les Bains** and **Cyradier**, where the sand is whiter. There are no facilities here.

In the area of Les Cayes the best beaches are on **Ile à Vache** (again, take provisions, though the island is inhabited), and around **Port Salut** to the west, where there are some cracking strips of white sand brushed by palms. The **Jérémie** area also has some superb coves that can only be reached by hiring a boat.

To the **north** of Port au Prince the most popular beaches run up the coast from Cabaret (it was Duvalierville) towards St Marc. **Ibo Beach** on Cacique Island (30 mins ride, five minutes by boat, adm), **Kyona Beach** (50 mins from Port au Prince, adm) are both developed with watersports and get crowded at the weekends. Close by is **Kalico** (adm $1) and **Ouanga**, a little lower key. At **Moulin sur Mer** you will find restored plantation ruins and an aqueduct. The most attractive beach in this area is palm-backed **Amani-y Beach** just south of St Marc, where there is a splendid view of the sunset.

On the north coast there are beaches not far from the Cap. **Rival**, with its colonial ruins, is a few minutes' walk out of town. The most popular in the area is at **Cormier** (adm), a fishing village five miles to the west. **Coco Beach** has been developed by a cruise-line company and charges admission ($20 if a ship is in port and the facilities are available, $3 if not).

SPORTS
Haiti is not very well organized for sports, but it is possible to find most watersports, windsurfing and sailing, through the beach hotels. Try the beach hotels north of the capital particularly at Ibo and Kyona beach. There is a marina at Ibo beach where you can fix up a deep-sea fishing trip.

Divers will find a superb coral reef at Sand Cay out in Port au Prince harbour (it is also good for snorkelling). The other main reefs are on the island of Gonâve in the bay, a half-hour boat trip from the hotels. Labadie on the north coast has good snorkelling.

On land there are few sports on offer. **Tennis** courts can be fixed up through the hotels. If you have the stomach for a cockfight after Sunday lunch then you can go to a *Guaguère* and watch the frenzy of the audience and the two poor battling cocks. In the Haitian streets you will also see a fascinating version of **miniature football**, played with five a side and a goal two-foot high. It is very skilful and fun to watch.

Port au Prince

The capital of Haiti is tucked deep into the southeastern corner of Haiti's huge bay and is backed by the mountains of the southern peninsula. It was founded in 1749, and became capital of the new Republic in 1806. Today it has a population of over half a million.

The small commercial area downtown is set out in a grid-iron of unattractive streets, scattered at intervals with old-time churches, gingerbread mansions, a few glass-fronted structures and with large classical official buildings. The human activity is immeasurable—vendors stand three deep on the pavement in places and there is a constant rush of traffic—and the street theatre is ever-present. Clustered around the town centre are the *cités*, the poorest shanties you will see in the Caribbean, where the stoves light up long before dawn as families prepare their cassava bread. On the hill, aloof from the bustle of Port au Prince, is the capital's prosperous alter-ego, Pétionville. Here, villas sit in stately calm behind 10-ft walls and wrought iron gates.

The heart of the town is around the imposing **Palais National** downtown, a vast white pile with classical columns and cupolas, the former home of the President Duvalier and the seat of the Government. Built in 1918, it is heavily guarded (with anti-aircraft guns as well as soldiers) and is not accessible to the public. It looks across the square to the statue of the **Marron Inconnu** (the unknown maroon soldier), a runaway slave with a machete who is blowing into a conch horn, raising the slaves to rebellion.

Just east of the Palais National is the **Place des Héros de l'Indépendence**, or Champ de Mars, an open park where other national heroes are commemorated— Toussaint L'Ouverture, Jean Jacques Dessalines, Christophe and Pétion. The bunker-like **Musée National** is also on the square and contains national treasures like the pistol with which Christophe shot himself and the cloche de la liberté, rung by Toussaint himself at Ennery. The crown of Emperor Faustin I is on display and there is even an ancient 13-ft anchor, supposedly from Columbus's *Santa Maria*, which was wrecked off the island in 1492. Open Mon–Fri, 10–2 or 3.30 (tel 228337), adm 5 gourdes.

Close by is the **Musée Defly**, in a restored timber mansion with towers and verandas embellished by intricate gingerbread decoration. Inside, the setting is a turn of the century town-house, where you will see old irons and openers for glove-fingers like massive tweezers. Open daily except Sun, 10–noon, adm. There is a shop selling Haitian antiques, of which the proceeds go to the handicapped children of Haiti. Also close by is the **Musée d'Art Haitien du College St Pierre** in which many of the country's finest works of art are displayed. De Witt Peters' Centre d'Art was moved here. The exhibitions change, but there are often paintings by Hector Hippolyte, Sénèque and Philome Obin. Open weekdays 9.30–1.30, Sat till 12.30, adm free (tel 222510).

You will find other permanent exhibits of Haitian art in the Episcopalian **Cathédrale de la Sainte-Trinité**, where the apse was painted by Obin, Benoit, Bazile and Leveque. Scenes from the birth of Christ to the Crucifixion are represented in the bright colours of the naïve school.

The main thoroughfare in Port au Prince is the **Boulevard Jean-Jacques Dessalines**, a little closer to the waterfront, where the vendors line the street. Each person has their beat and in the covered walkways in front of the buildings you will find music vendors with elaborately arranged stacks of cassettes, tables of sweets and cigarettes, watchmenders and moneychangers fanning a wad of notes. Trade becomes more hectic as you approach the **Marché de Fer**, where the vendors stand three deep, women standing in line, their arms slung with towels and a huge basket of soap and flannels on their heads, or seated in front of rebellious piles of tropical fruits.

The Marché de Fer (the ironmarket) itself is magnificent and seems to cover whole acres with its iron columns and huge riveted arches. Its corrugated tin roofs are painted red as all Caribbean markets are. Erected by President Hyppolite in 1889, it looks slightly odd with minarets—originally the Marché de Fer was intended for India. But around it, the human endeavour is uniquely Haitian. Expect to be accosted to buy at every turn—most of what you are offered will not be much good, but who knows, you could pick up a bargain in there.

The **Oloffson Hotel** at the head of the rue Capois is something of an institution around the city, and a good place to retreat to for an afternoon drink or a rum punch in the evening. The hotel and the rum punch were made famous by Graham Greene, who used the setting for his novel, *The Comedians*, about life in Haiti under Papa Doc. You may still meet the man on whom he modelled the journalist Petit Pierre (Aubelin Jolicoeur). The hotel also attracts a transient crowd of journalists and researchers, so there is often good company there. Plenty of pictures to buy on the walls and the occasional show of Haitian dancing. Worth a visit for the building itself, which is a gingerbread masterpiece.

Around Port au Prince

Removed from all of the activity of downtown Port au Prince, on the cooler heights of the mountainside, **Pétionville** is stately. The large hotels and fine restaurants have a magnificent view of the town and the bay beyond from 1500 ft. By the look of the number of grand houses going up, fortunes are still being made in Haiti. The buildings are grand, but there is not much to see here. There is a beautiful forested valley, where the lianas creep and the trees block out the sun—leave the town on the rue Borno.

The **Barbancourt Rum Distillery** is on the road to Kenscoff, set in a mock Teutonic castle. The family has been distilling rum on the island since 1765. You are invited to sit on the veranda, surrounded by vast rum puncheons and cane-crushing gear, tasting their various 19 varieties of flavoured rums—hibiscus, apricot, coffee, mango, coconut. Free tasting, bottles US$5 (tel 557303).

Ten miles beyond Pétionville and 3000 feet higher up into the cultivated slopes you come to **Kenscoff**, another retreat with an excellent climate (take a jersey if you stay there) and more superb views. The fruit and vegetable market held every Friday seems to go on for ever. There is a handicraft centre and a café at the nearby Baptist Mission, the Mountain Maid, which sells excellent woodwork at good prices, 8–5. Fort boffins will enjoy the ruins of Fort Jacques and Fort Alexander, with their thousands of cannonballs. Beyond Furcy is the Morne La Visite National Park and east of there is Haiti's highest mountain, Pic la Selle (see p. 503).

Gonâve Island lies in the bay off the capital, with mountains that rise to 2500 feet and superb coral reefs. 30 miles long, it is skirted with mangrove swamps, where you can come across herons, clapper rails, roseate spoonbills and the occasional flamingo.

Around the Island

Two and a half hours in a taptap will get you over to **Jacmel** on the south coast of the island. A few magnificent old gingerbread town-houses remain from its glorious days as a coffee port at the turn of the century, but its trade was cut off by Duvalier in the 50s and it has decayed. Founded in 1698, it is more accessible now since a good road has been built, and it is the usual Haitian press, particularly around the ironmarket. In the hills west of the town is the **Bassin Bleu**, a triple waterfall where each cascade drops into a rockpool. You will be told the legend of a goddess who combs her hair with a golden comb, but vanishes with the approach of humans. You are advised to take a guide (you would be lucky to get away without one) and they will encourage you to go by horse ($5).

On the northern side of the peninsula, where the rugged landscape has a rare physical beauty, you pass through **Léogane**, supposedly the city of the Arawak Queen Anacoana who ruled at the time of the Spaniards' arrival, and then climb into hills of banana and coffee plantations before descending into **Miragoâne**. Off the road to Les Cayes is a lake where birdwatchers can spot many of the great Caribbean shorebirds—magnificent frigatebirds, blue herons, white ibises and ungainly purple gallinules with overlong toes.

The tarmac road crosses over the mountains, passing the *cailles*, the wattle and daub shacks of the small Haitian farmers, and then skirts the south coast and comes to **Les Cayes**, situated on a large fertile agricultural plain. Vache Island sits in the bay about thirty minutes from the town. You can hire a motorboat to get there for the day.

From Les Cayes the increasingly rough road crosses back over to the north coast towards the town of **Jérémie**, where the old colonial-style buildings stand in faded grandeur, its coffee wealth now diminished. The town was the home of the father of Alexandre Dumas, the author.

North of Port au Prince

The main road to the north and to 'the Cap', as Cap Haitien is called, runs along the coast as far as the town of St Marc, from where it descends into the Artibonite Valley, flooded in places to create ricefields, but dry enough in others for cacti to line the hills. At **Gonaïves**, just under a hundred miles from the capital, Dessalines proclaimed Independence in 1804. From here, the main road climbs to over 2000 feet into the extraordinarily lush hills of the Massif du Nord.

There are two spectacular waterfalls inland north of Port au Prince. Closest to the city is the **Ville Bonheur** waterfall, south west of Mireblais (also the scene of a very popular pilgrimage for the Haitian Catholics and vodunistes each year on 16 July, in memory of an appearance of the Virgin Mary). The 'saut d'eau' is made up of several streams that cascade 100 feet on to rocks in a maelstrom of spray. More remote from the capital is the **Bassin Zim**, close to the town of Hinche, where two cascades tumble 100 feet out of the thickest rainforest.

The **Cap**, as Haiti's second city is known, lies on the north coast about 150 miles from Port au Prince. In French colonial days, Cap Haitien was the island's capital (called Cap Français), a city so illustrious that it was known as the 'Paris of the Antilles' (as St Pierre in Martinique also was later on). Some of the grand buildings remain, but most were destroyed in the slave rebellions in the 1790s. Isolated from Port au Prince, it always had an independent attitude, but this was too much for Papa Doc Duvalier who cut it off and let it fall into decay. Today it has a population of around 70,000.

Close by is the town of **Milot**, from where Christophe ruled his northern kingdom. His magnificent palace, the **Sans Souci**, was built in 1813 above the town, and was supposed to rival Versailles. It was partly destroyed in an earthquake in 1842 and the marble floors of the galleries are gone, but the design of the palace can be seen in the surviving walls and the last of the yellow plaster remains in places.

But Christophe's most lasting monument stands at the top of a mountain, 3000 feet above the town. The **Citadelle** broods like a vast colossus on the peak of Mt Bonnet à l'Evêque, a tropical Gormenghast. It is a two-hour walk in the heat of the Caribbean sun to get there, and yet every stone that was used to build it was carried up between 1804 and 1817. The whole population of the north was involved, about 200,000 people, of whom an estimated 20,000 died. Their megalomaniac leader Christophe just mixed their blood into the mortar. When it was completed, he was supposed to have impressed visiting dignitaries with the loyalty of his troops by marching them into the abyss. The walls are more than 100 ft high and 30 ft thick in places, arrowslits (for cannon) were four feet wide, there were 365 5-ton cannon and 250,000 cannonballs. 10,000 soldiers could hold out here for a year. The Citadelle is so vast that it makes the mountain on which it squats look square from 20 miles. From Milot you can walk the 4 to 5 miles and 3000 feet, or you can take a horse (about $4). If you have a car, you can drive to within half a mile.

Open until 5, adm (includes Sans Souci). **Bois Cayman**, also near the town, is reputedly where the slaves would meet at the time of their rebellions two hundred years ago.

If you explore the northwestern peninsula, one of the least touched parts of Haiti, you will find no restaurants or guest houses. Stock up with food and drink in Gonaïves or Port de Paix and take extra fuel as there are no petrol stations between the two towns. Roads (tracks) are rough, particularly after rains, and many of the villages are linked to the road by footpath. It is possible to visit **Ile de la Tortue**, the old stronghold of the buccaneers. Life is very basic there too.

FESTIVALS
Carnival is the principal festival in the Haitian calendar and celebrations take place each Sunday starting on Epiphany (6 January) and culminating on Mardi Gras just before Lent. Costumed dancers fill the streets, all strutting in time to *ra-ra bands* and following the bandwagons (articulated lorries stacked with speakers).

The Haitian Independence Day is 1 January, also known as *Jou d'lan*, on which wreaths are laid at the statue of the Marron Inconnu in Port au Prince. Each town and village has its *fête patronale*, in honour of their patron saint. For forthcoming celebrations, ask around.

WHERE TO STAY
There are a few hotels and guest houses in the centre of Port au Prince. Most of the best hotels are off the road leading to Pétionville or in Pétionville itself. There are not many traditional Caribbean beach hotels in Haiti, but you will find some wonderful creole town houses. Few visitors mean that prices are fairly low at the moment. An energy tax is often levied and service is usually charged at 10%.

Port au Prince and Pétionville
El Rancho, PO Box 71 (tel 572080, fax 574926) is five km from the city centre, perched on the hillside above the plain, with a terrace for tea and dinner overlooking the swimming pools and dip and sip bar. The hotel has a touch of colonial Spain in the arches and orange roof-tiles and some rooms are sumptuously decorated, with massive mahogany furniture and local works of art. Also tennis courts and a masseur. A double room costs US$60–145. Close by is the **Montana Hotel**, PO Box 523 (tel 571920), with just 24 rooms set around a modern town-house with spectacular views over the city and the bay beyond. Glorious swimming pool and a tennis court and gardens. Double room US$55–85 (all taxes included). A particularly nice hotel in Pétionville is the **Villa Creole**, PO Box 126 (tel 571570, fax 574935, US 800 223 9815), another elegant retreat. You are luxuriously cocooned from Haitian life on the balcony—large poolside veranda and restaurant, tennis courts and comfortable rooms, US$77–110, meal plan for US$24. Not far off is the **Hotel Caraïbe**, PO Box 15423 (tel 572524) a modern town house in a quiet Pétionville street. Attractive dining rooms and bar. Rooms US$40–70, includes breakfast. On the Place St Pierre in the centre of town you will find the **Hotel Kinam**, (tel 570462, fax 74410), which has excellent prices. It is set in an old town house that has been restored, and the rooms, neat with white tiles and wicker furniture, have been added behind in mock-gingerbread blocks on two sides of the swimming pool.

There is also a good restaurant. The menu is French and creole (or a *menu léger* if you want it)—*poulet djon-djon* or *cabrit boucane* (grilled goat) in *sauce 'ti malice*. Rooms US$44–60 for a double, $75–105 for a suite.

The **Hotel Oloffson**, PO Box 260 (tel 234000, fax 230919) is on the Rue Capois not far from the Port au Prince city centre. It is one of the Caribbean's classic hotels, a magnificent gingerbread town-house, tin-roofed and turreted and dripping in the most luxurious fretwork. It was made famous by Graham Greene as the setting for *The Comedians*. The bar and balconies, which overlook the gardens above the town, collect an interesting crowd and serve excellent rum punch. Rooms in the main house are decorated with antiques and there are more modern rooms in a block behind. The owner has a band, who make a fair amount of noise when they are practising. Double room US$50. In the town centre, on the eastern side of the Place des Héros is the **Holiday Inn Le Plaza**, blocks set around a pool in a garden festooned with tropical plants. It is mainly used by businessmen. Rooms from around US$60. Close by is the **Hotel Park**, with clean and simple rooms for about US$30.

Guest Houses

On the road up to Pétionville you might try **La Griffone** on the rue Jean Baptiste (tel 454095) in the foothills an in Pétionville itself is the **Marabou** (tel 571934), with just 15 rooms at around US$25. The **Villa Kalawes** (tel 570817) is just out of the town on the road to Kenscoff, rooms US$35 a double and in Kenscoff itself is the **Florville** (tel 452092 in town), double room $25. The cheapest rooms, around US$10, can be found in the downtown area of the city, though many are not that salubrious.

South of Port au Prince

In **Jacmel** you will find more of Haiti's spectacular creole town houses now acting as hotels and guest houses, including the **Manoir Alexandre** on the hill, surrounded by palms, about US$25. **La Jacmelienne sur Plage**, PO Box 916 (tel 224899) is a beach hotel set on the black sand bay of Jacmel, soulless because of the lack of visitors during the week, pool, double room US$35. Also try **Guy's Guest House** (tel 883241). Farther afield in Les Cayes is the **Concorde** (US$25) and in Jérémie there are two small hotels, the **Trois Dumas**, where the author Dumas was born, set in a hillside garden with a view of the town (room US$15), and the **Pension Fraenkel**, simple rooms at US$18.

North of Port au Prince

Thirty minutes along the coast is the **Jolly Beach Hotel** (tel 229653), just 20 rooms near Kaliko, pool, tennis and some watersports, about US$80 with meals. Another good beach hotel close by is the **Moulin sur Mer** at Montrouis (tel 221844), built in the walls of an old sugar mill. The 30 rooms in newer blocks are comfortable, but the main lure is the beach, where there are watersports and snorkelling, about US$70 for a day's stay. If you stop over in Gonaïves on the trip north to the Cap, there are a couple of guest houses, including **Pension Elias**, about US$10, and just outside the town, **Chez Frantz**.

In **Cap Haitien** the best hotel is the **Mont Joli**, PO Box 12 (tel 620300), on the hilltop above the town, where the bar and the swimming pool below it have a fine view of the bay. Rooms around US$80 with meals. Just below is the **Roi Christophe**, PO Box 34 (tel

620414), an old colonial mansion (used by General Leclerc as his headquarters in Napoleon's invasion of the island in 1801), with antique furniture inside and shaded gardens around the hotel. Rooms US$40–50 in season. The **Hotel Beck** offers clean rooms and wholesome meals on the hill above town for about US$35 per person. There are a number of guest houses in the town, cheap, simple and mostly clean. Try **A à Z**, an old colonial town-house on the main square across from the Cathedral and the **Pension Colon** on the waterfront.

About five miles west of the Cap is the **Cormier Plage Hotel**, PO Box 70 (tel 621000), where the 30 rooms are scattered along the seafront, shaded by a screen of trees. Good restaurant, especially for the locally caught fish and seafood. Rooms about US$80 with meals.

EATING OUT

Though the colonial connection was severed almost two centuries ago, the Haitians maintain a sympathetic link with the French in their treatment of food, and Haitian creole cooking is excellent. They use the fish and the seafood of the Caribbean and cover them with strong creole sauces—lobster and lambi swim in thick and spicy oil and the traditional Caribbean chicken comes crisp and flavoured with lime or coconut. The French expatriate community make sure that there is plenty of traditional French cuisine too, and you will even be offered snails and frogs' legs. Haiti's fertile hills produce all the Caribbean vegetables, including plantain and breadfruit, which are served at all creole tables, and fruits, from pineapple to papaya, which make their way into the delicious ice creams and sorbets. Even in the few small places in downtown Port au Prince the food is good—you will find traditional Caribbean cook-ups with rice and peas or *tassot* (dried and grilled chicken or pork)—as are the barbecued roadside snacks, though these are best left alone for the first few days unless you think that your stomach is up to it. The local beer, *Prestige*, is quite drinkable. Prices are mostly listed in Haitian Dollars (H$).

The smartest restaurants around the capital are in Pétionville. **Chez Gérard** (tel 571949) is set in its own profuse tropical garden. You start at the bar, in large leather armchairs and then move on to tables set out on terraces beneath columns and arches, for French and creole fare—poached red snapper or duck in green pepper sauce followed by chocolate marquise, main course H$17, closed Sun. At **Les Cascades** you take cocktails upstairs before descending to the level of the waterfalls and the tropical greenery to dine. The menu is French with a lot of seafood, and so you can try scallops topped with shrimp or veal in a creamy ginger sauce, main course H$15, closed Sun. **La Belle Epoque** (tel 570984) on the rue Grégoire, has a lovely setting in an old town-house with tall open shutters. The bar and dining room are on the terrace and the menu is both French and kreyol. Try a *griot* (Haitian fried pork) or crevettes in a creole curry sauce. Closed Sun, main course H$10–20. You might also try the **Souvenence**. If you happen to be homesick for a game of darts and a burger, you can wander along to **Richard's Place**, which is set in an open house with a corrugated iron terrace. Collects a rum crowd and gets quite riotous late on. On the Rue Grégoire.

There are very few restaurants in downtown Port au Prince now. However, you will find a nice vegetarian restaurant for lunch 8–4; **Ananda's** on the Place d'Italie near the waterfront. Fixed menu, H$4, which includes soup and a salad, or accras and juices. Just off the Rue de Delmas heading down to Port au Prince, **Le Recif** (tel 462605) is a seafood restaurant set in a garden of bougainvillaea, where you can have crab, turtle, lobster or red snapper in creole sauce, spiced or even *boucanned*, as they would have been cooked up by the buccaneers a couple of centuries ago. Prices about H$30 for a meal. In the centre of the town the best restaurant is **Aux Cosaques** (tel 452339) at around H$25. There are some smaller haunts, including **Au Bec Fin** (tel 462929) on the Rue de Delmas in town. You will also find a string of very local stall restaurants on the Champs de Mars, where you can get a simple fish meal or chicken to a merengue or compas accompaniment.

There are two **casinos** on the island, at the Christophe Hotel and at El Rancho.

CUBA

Cuba is the only communist country in the western hemisphere. The Revolution is everywhere in Cuba—in the revolutionary art, in the rhetoric of the leader, Fidel, in the wearing bureaucracy and the queueing that is a way of life, in the hideous concrete buildings. And yet, beneath the communist overlay, the typical themes of the Caribbean ring through, in the beaches and palms, in the relentless *salsa* music and the easy-going West Indians.

At 750 miles from east to west and averaging around 60 miles in width, Cuba is by far the largest island in the Caribbean (its 44,000 square miles make it about the same size as England). It lies at the mouth of the Gulf of Mexico in the northwest of the Caribbean, just south of the Tropic of Capricorn, and is shaped something like an alligator—with a switch of its tail, Cuba might propel itself east, out into the Atlantic Ocean.

There are three main mountain ranges in this stunningly beautiful island—in the west, the Sierra de los Organos; the Sierra Escambray in the centre and the Sierra Maestra in the southeast. In between, the glass-flat and undulating plains are immensely

Colonial Havana

517

fertile. Seeds seem to explode in the rich red-brown earth, growing into the swathes of sugar-cane and the tobacco for which Cuba is so well known.

There are around eleven million Cubans, of whom a fifth live in and around Havana, the capital, in the northwest of the island. As in the other former Spanish Caribbean colonies, the population has a range of complexions from blackest African to European blond. The mix is thorough and the majority of the Cubans are coloured somewhere in between. Although there is still a certain draining of colour as you move to more privileged areas of society, there is little overt racial discrimination (black Cubans are considerably better off now than they were 50 years ago). Cuba has a remarkably equal and homogenous society.

The Revolution, which came to power in 1959, touches almost every aspect of Cuban life. The changes are widespread and the achievements considerable (certainly in comparison with other Latin American countries). Nobody goes to bed hungry, education is free to all those who want it up to university level, and health care is the best in Latin America (Cubans no longer suffer from the diseases of the developing world but those normally associated with the developed world).

The art and the rhetoric of Revolution is everywhere too—on the billboards the thoughts of Lenin and of Fidel stand side by side and you will hear the Cubans refer to one another as *compañero* and *compañera* (comrade). At national celebrations, the red and black of the Revolutionary flag of Cuba flies all over the country, marked with M–26–7 (for Moncada, 26 July, the date of Castro's first attack on the Batista regime). Che Guevara, a hero of the Cuban Revolution, has lost none of his lustre here. Dot-matrixed now, this *'Knight without flaw and without fear'* stares benevolently out on the Cubans, exhorting them to fulfil their social duties.

But the rhetoric is beginning to look overwrought now that Cuba stands alone in its beliefs. The excitement of the 60s is long gone. The leadership seems to have no intention of changing its path and the situation can only get more serious, because the United States will not relax their stance.

The Cubans are solidly nationalistic and many of them have a genuine affection for their leader and a pride in the achievements of the last 30 years. The former Soviet Union subsidized them to the tune of billions of dollars, but Cuba has struggled under a total embargo from the USA, its natural trading partner, since 1961. There is an ambivalence towards the United States—with plenty of state-sponsored anti-American propaganda and a strong Latin feeling against the overbearing attitude of the 'colossus in the north', but, of course, many Cubans, particularly the youth, who take the benefits of the last 30 years for granted, like the American goods that are smuggled in via Central America.

Cuba has something of a siege mentality: partly sloganeering, but not without some good reason (since the Bay of Pigs, there have been attacks on its leader and some on its industry too). Around 13% of Cuba's national budget is spent on defence and the Cuban leaders can call on literally millions of militarily trained personnel. Inside the country the Revolution defends itself ruthlessly—anti-revolutionary sentiment is not tolerated.

All this seems a little unlikely for a Latin and Caribbean country and it need not have much effect on the visitor. Negotiating the bureaucracy can be wearing at times, especially for travel and in the restaurants, but the Cubans have an explosive vitality that filters into everyday life. They love children, and as a foreigner you can expect to be treated with kindness and genuine interest.

Music is a national pursuit, and you will hear the compulsive rhythms of *rumba, son* and the distinctly Latin *salsa*, played loudly on stereos, by impromptu bands at the street corner and in the bandstands in town squares. Dancing is another national pastime.

Four centuries of Spanish heritage also ring clear in Cuban life. In the old colonial town centres you will find *plazas* overlooked by beautiful churches and old houses with wrought-iron balconies. Old Havana is absolutely stunning—a square mile of colonial palaces. The position of women in Cuban society may have been improved considerably by the Revolution, but the Latin tradition of *machismo* remains with the Cuban men (they joke that the best thing that the Spaniards did for them is the *mulatta*, a Cuban girl with the looks of a Spaniard, who can move like an African).

All of this makes Cuba a compelling place to visit. It is possible to have a typical Caribbean sun, sea and sand holiday here—Cuba has the resorts and beaches, 10-mile strips in places with idyllic off-shore cays—but for the traveller who wants to explore beyond the coconut oil and jetskis, there is a stimulating and vibrant island.

The present economic difficulties are making Cuba more difficult for the independent traveller, however. The logistical problems are even worse than usual and cut-backs mean that much of the fun of life has been removed for the Cubans themselves. Tourists are able to have what the Cubans cannot, so you will feel conspicuous. Cuba is also not exactly cheap at the moment either, because foreign currency is in high demand.

Suggested Itinerary

If you have just a couple of weeks in Cuba, the best way to divide your time would be to spend the first part in Havana, checking out Cuban ballet or cinema and at the same time planning a couple of days on the following recommended trips. A journey into the tobacco plantations and cigar factories west of the capital in Pinar del Rio, making sure to take the coastal road one way. Take the train to Matanzas and on to the superb if touristy beach at Varadero, Cuba's best place for watersports. A visit to Trinidad and the Sierra Escambray (mountains) nearby. A flight for a few days down to Santiago, making sure to visit the *casa de la trova*, and then travelling off the beaten track in the remote eastern area of the island. Finally, a trip to the Isle of Youth (Isla de Juventud) off the south coast for a laid-back couple of days' beaching and clubbing with the Cubans.

History

Columbus landed in Cuba on his first voyage to the New World, touching the eastern end of the island on 27 October 1492 as he sailed south from the Bahamas. Confidently he sent off emissaries to find the Imperial court of Japan (he presumed he had discovered the East Indies), but all they found were 50 Arawak huts. He explored the south coast on his second voyage in 1494, but he never accepted that Cuba was an island. It was not circumnavigated until 1508 by Sebastian de Ocampo.

Spanish settlers were sent from Santo Domingo by his son Diego in 1511 and the *conquistador* Diego de Velásquez arrived with 300 men, to be met by the Arawak chief Hatuey, originally from Hispaniola, who roused the Indians into resistance. Hatuey besieged the Spaniards in their fort for three months, but was betrayed and captured. He was offered salvation if he became a Christian, but preferred not to go to heaven, fearing that it was full of Spaniards. Hatuey's name lives on in Cuba as the country's first revolutionary and on the country's leading beer. His people were wiped out within 50 years—just a few Amerindian features can be seen in the faces in the Baracoa region in the east.

Velásquez founded seven *villas*, or fortified towns. Cuba was eventually to become one of the jewels in the Spanish Crown, but initially development was slow as the settlers grew tobacco and cured hides. The settlers were also constantly at the mercy of pirate raids. Sir Francis Drake besieged Havana in 1586 and failed, but the likes of Henry Morgan and Montbars the Exterminator held whole towns to ransom. Their main target, though, was the yearly *flota*, the fleet that transported the combined riches of Central and South America back to Spain. It would assemble in Havana harbour and steadily the town grew in importance, becoming capital in 1589. In 1628, Piet Heyn, at the head of the Dutch West India fleet, captured the entire *flota* and its treasure worth millions within 100 miles of Havana.

Along with Mexico City and Lima, Havana became the richest and finest Spanish colonial city. Spain officially maintained a monopoly of the trade and the merchants became incredibly wealthy—their magnificent houses are still to be seen. Away from the city, the country languished, involved mainly in small agriculture, and making a bit on the side through smuggling. It was not until a British invasion in 1762 opened up the island to traders of all nations that the economy boomed.

The British introduced sugar, a crop that was to change the face of the island to this day (Cuba is still the world's largest exporter of sugar). At the end of the 18th century, when France's richest colony, Saint Domingue (now Haiti), collapsed, Cuba became the main sugar island in the West Indies. Slaves had to be brought in their thousands to cultivate the cane and over the next 100 years, Cuba developed into one of the most brutal slave regimes. The unfortunate Africans were worked for as much as 19 hours in the day, seven days a week. About 10% died each year and as many as a quarter would be ill at any time. Despite the abolition of slavery in most other Caribbean islands by 1848, slavery continued in the Spanish colonies until 1886. The industry was run on mutual fear, with the call 'Remember Haiti!', as a reminder of what would happen in a slave rebellion. The Torre de Iznaga, a slave watchtower near Trinidad, was the tallest building on the island when it was built in 1820.

After the Independence of the South American republics and Mexico at the beginning of the 19th century, Cuba was the last remaining 'Jewel in the Spanish Crown'. There was anti-colonial unrest and an Independence movement began to crystallize, calling for the abolition of slavery. The Cubans rebelled in 1868, led by Carlos Manuel de Céspedes, who freed his slaves as a gesture and then armed them, and there followed 10 years of war against the Spanish authorities. Céspedes died in 1874, but his movement was carried on by men such as Antonio Maceo and Máximo Gómez, whose vast statue stands on the Malecón in Havana. A truce was drawn up in 1878, but within two years the Cubans had rebelled again under Calixto García, and this time were brutally crushed.

The Spaniards sent 250,000 troops to control the population of 1 million, but fighting broke out again in 1895. This insurrection was inspired by José Martí, an author and journalist. José Martí was killed in an ambush before he had fired a shot, but he is still considered the hero of Cuban Independence and you will see his bust in every town on the island. The whole country rose up against the colonial authorities and by 1897 the rebels had forced the Spaniards to concede autonomy, but they were set to fight for complete Independence. In 1898, however, the Americans intervened, officially because their warship, the *USS Maine*, was blown up in Havana harbour (by whom, it was never discovered). With Roosevelt at their head, the Americans defeated the last of the Spanish troops. They would not even allow the Cuban rebels the pleasure of accepting the Spanish surrender. In 1899, in the Treaty of Paris, the Americans took possession of Cuba and Puerto Rico in the Caribbean, and the other Spanish territories of Guam and the Philippines. Cuban Independence had been denied at the last minute. The Americans installed the government, piled in money in investments and reserved the right to intervene again in Cuban affairs 'to preserve its Independence'. As José Martí himself had warned when he spoke of 'historical fatalism', the Americans were in control of the island and it would now be impossible to be independent of American influence. Cuba became a colony in all but name.

For the next 30 years the Cuban Republic was headed by corrupt and ineffectual leaders before it degenerated into dictatorship and gangsterism in the 30s. General Gerardo Machado, elected in a landslide vote in 1924, was ousted in 1933. Eventually the infamous Batista, who had been in the background for 20 years, seized power in a military coup in 1952 and tightened his ruthless and brutal grip on the country. Though the economy had grown considerably over the previous few years and some Cubans lived in style in Havana, the lot of the average Cuban was pitiful. Unemployment was around 50% and nearly a quarter suffered from malnutrition.

The Revolution
The Revolution, as it is officially documented, began on 26 July 1953, when 130 young men and women, led by the lawyer Fidel Castro, made an attack on the highly fortified Moncada garrison in Santiago. Militarily it was a failure and most of the rebels were rounded up and tortured or killed. But at his subsequent trial, Castro was to make his mark with a five-hour indictment of the Cuban system that has become known as the 'History will Absolve Me' speech. He was sentenced to 15 years in jail, but his revolt had caught the imagination of the Cuban people. After 20 months he was released and went into exile in Mexico, from where he launched the revolutionary 26 July Movement (M–26–7), devoted to the overthrow of the Batista. It was here that they were joined by Ernesto Che Guevara, an Argentine doctor.

In October 1956, 82 rebels sailed to Cuba in the tiny boat *Granma* (on display in Havana), only just making land, and with most of their equipment lost. Within a month they had been found and ambushed by Batista's troops and only 12 of them were left to make their way to the Sierra Maestra, the mountains in the southeast of the island. But the guerrillas survived and began to pick off military outposts. Steadily their numbers swelled. Supported by underground movements in the cities, who in turn were rallied to general strikes by the guerrilla radio station, *Radio Rebelde*, the insurrection gained ground all over Cuba. In May 1958, Batista put in 10,000 men into the Sierra Maestra to defeat the rebels, still numbering only 300, but they were defeated and the soldiers went over to the guerrillas. The morale of the Batista regime was broken, and the troops refused to fight as the Revolution spread westwards. It was only a matter of time before the regime collapsed. In the early hours of 1 January 1959, Batista fled the country. Castro accepted the surrender of the Moncada garrison that he had stormed so unsuccessfully five years earlier, and on 8 January the 31-year-old lawyer entered the capital in triumph.

The M–26–7 movement assumed control of the country and they started to institute educational and agricultural reforms. A huge literacy campaign was introduced, in which students left their schools to live and work in the country for a year, cutting illiteracy to 4%, the lowest in Latin America. The casinos and brothels for which Havana was so famous were closed down. There were immediate agricultural reforms and the maximum private landholding became 1000 acres. This was followed by further nationalization of foreign banks and other businesses. These moves understandably alienated the USA, whose interests in Cuba amounted to about $800 million.

The US reacted by sponsoring the Bay of Pigs invasion attempt by Cuban exiles. Castro oversaw the defence personally and defeated it with ease. The Cubans rallied behind him. And so began the US trade embargo, which has held out for 30 years, in which the US does not permit trade either way with Cuba. The island was forced to look elsewhere for oil and for much of its basic supplies.

There was little evidence of initial communist inclination on the part of Fidel, his actions were nationalist and anti-imperialist, but in mid-1961, just at the time of the Bay of Pigs, he proclaimed the Revolution a socialist one. Later in the year, as the press was muzzled and promised elections were shelved, he said that he was a Marxist-Leninist and would be until the day he died. Opposition and the other groups who had worked independently of him for change in Cuba were shunted aside.

In October 1962 the situation flared up again with the Cuban missile crisis, in which the Soviet Union began to move nuclear missiles to the island, which was a valuable strategic outpost in the western hemisphere. Kennedy sent out the US Navy and threatened war unless they were removed. Without consulting Castro, the two superpowers eventually agreed that the missiles would be withdrawn by the Soviet Union if the USA did not invade the island.

The optimistic early dreams of the Revolution, the intention to industrialize, had to be revised. Sugar remained the island's economic base and it became clear that the 'moral incentives' of working for the state alone were not enough to encourage the Cubans into high productivity. But sufficient food was made available at minimal prices and education was made available to all. The improvement in health care was something of a miracle. Cuba has eradicated the diseases of poverty and the major health concerns are now those of the developed world, such as heart disease and cancer. Microbrigades were sent out to provide housing for the rapidly expanding population (it has doubled in the last 30 years). There are people in Cuba who still live in thatched *bohío* huts, but only by choice.

Thirty years on from the Revolution, Cuba is run by the authoritarian control of the Communist Party, headed by the Central Committee and ultimately the Politbureau. Fidel is President of both. At grassroots level, the primacy of the party is maintained by the CDRs (Committees for the Defence of the Revolution), which monitor every aspect of Cuban life, from cleaning up the streets to providing marital advice and informing on black marketeers. Apart from respected 300,000 armed forces, the Revolution also has a militia of half a million men and women. Theoretically there is elective power through the National Assembly of People's Power, but the ideological leader of the country is the Communist Party. There have been many accusations of human rights abuses against Cuba, though the number that the government admits to are low by Latin American standards. However, there are definitely restrictions on personal freedoms such as travel and political activity, which is closely monitored.

The economy is still not efficiently run. With the exception of the tobacco farms, it is mostly state controlled. After Brazil, Cuba is the world's largest sugar producer, with an annual production of around $8\frac{1}{2}$ million tonnes. Using this as a basis, the intention is to expand the light manufacturing sector and tourism. There is a considerable hard-currency debt, around $6 billion, and at least as much is owed to the Soviet Union.

The lack of consumer goods and the austerity programmes have caused some unrest among the population, which is now educated and has economic and political aspirations. The youth particularly, who do not remember the country before 1959 and who take for granted what the government provides, tend to envy the States for their material advantages. A few try to leave. In 1980, as the tense situation with America was relaxed under Carter, 125,000 took the decision to leave the country for an uncertain future in the States.

Politically Cuba has shown no inclination to move with the changes in eastern Europe. There has been no talk of *perestroika* or of the Communist Party relinquishing ultimate control. The Commonwealth of Independent States ended all subsidies to Cuba on 1 January 1992 and the economic situation has become steadily worse since then. The queues are becoming longer and the fuel shortages are dire. There are hardly any cars on the roads and Cuba has imported a huge number of bicycles.

Fidel

Fidel Castro Ruz has been leader of Cuba since his M-26-7 Movement swept the Batista regime out of the country in 1959 and even after 30 years, this charismatic leader still commands the admiration and respect of many of his people. He has improved their material situation dramatically and he has carved out a path of Cuban self-respect and independence, in defiance of José Martí's 'historical fatalism' (the inescapable dominance of the USA). To them he is affectionately known as *Fidel*.

Of course, he is correspondingly unpopular with the Cubans in exile, many of whom live just a couple of hundred miles from Havana in Miami. Many Americans, too, regard him as a harbinger of the communist scourge and would therefore like to see him toppled. The CIA are known to have made attempts on his life (stories abound of exploding cigars and poisonous wetsuits that would make his beard fall out, so that his *macho* image would disappear). He uses each attempt to vilify the over-bearing attitude of the 'colossus in the north'.

Fidel still appears in his battle fatigues and cap when he addresses his people, but they have the lustrous sheen of good quality material nowadays. The nine-hour speeches and rapturous applause from half a million people are gone now, but he is still an impressive speaker, who will hold forth eloquently and persuasively without notes.

He appears less in public nowadays and he is officially reluctant about his position as the personification of the Revolution. Even so, you will see him on some of the revolutionary posters around the country and his thoughts appear at the foot of the pages of the Havana telephone directory. For the moment, his successor is supposed to be his brother, chief of the military, Raul Castro.

Cigars

It is an ironic twist that Cuba, the arch enemy of the capitalist world, makes the world's finest cigars, beloved of fat-cat businessmen. In Cuba you will find bricklayers and taxi-drivers puffing on Size 4 Monte Cristos. Your average eight-inch cigar is available for the equivalent of about US$1.

The tobacco plant cannot be mass-cultivated like sugar, it is best tended by an individual farmer and so many of the Cuban tobacco plantations are still in private hands. West of Havana, you will see the tobacco fields and the distinctive *vegas* (drying sheds)—clapboard buildings with shaggy thatch or more modern aluminium roofs—where the leaves are hung over bamboo spars to dry. Then they are baled up according to age and the position on the plant in which they grew and sent off to the factories.

In the factory itself, the roller stretches out the leaves and cuts the youngest one to size and holds it in his (or her since the Revolution) open hand, placing two slightly older leaves with stronger flavour on top. Offcuts and tobacco shavings are then packed in the centre and the cigar is hand-rolled. It gets its shape between boards in a vice, pressed for 20 minutes, turned and pressed again. On removal it is cut at one end for length and the outer cover, the tenderest leaf of all, is rolled around the exterior (this leaf is slit down the middle and the cigars are rolled alternately left and right). The mouthpiece is sealed with a touch of glue, the labels slipped on and the cigar is sent off to be packed, between thin layers of cedar wood to keep them dry, or in a palm leaf if they are for local consumption.

Monte Cristo, H. Upmann, Romeo y Julietta and Davidoff are of course the most famous cigars in the world and you can see them being packed in the factories around the island (especially in Pinar del Río). In Cuba these brands can be bought for around US$25–45 for a box of 25 (outside they are worth around US$500, though, of course, it is illegal to sell them in the States, but this can offset the cost of the airticket). Visits are arranged most easily through Cubatur, for a few dollars. You will have difficulty talking your way into a factory, but you can try. Cigars are on sale in all the tourist shops.

Music

Music is a particularly vibrant part of Cuban life and where most Caribbean islands have a rhythm of their own, Cuba has several, most notably *salsa*. Cuban *salsa* is distinctly Latin, but it is different from the *salsa* of Puerto Rico, which has been influenced by the Neoriqueñans (Puerto Ricans living in New York). *Salsa* grew out of *son*, with a guitar and a *guiro* (washboard) and heavy drum backing. The best known *salsa* artists are Los Van Van, Ritmo Oriental and Orquestra Revé.

Other Cuban rhythms include *rumba*, *danzón* and *cha-cha-cha*. *Guantanamera* (the girl from Guantanamo) is an example of yet another style, the *guajira*. In every major Cuban town you will find a *casa de la trova*, where musicians (many of them old gents) play the *trova*, a sort of ballad with a guitar accompaniment. Another lively Cuban tradition is the bands that come out to play on Sunday evenings in the town square, blasting out all the Cuban rhythms on brass instruments. At carnival time, look out for the wind-up organs that play old *son* rhythms. Cuban **jazz** is also excellent, and you might just catch groups such as *Irakere* while you are in town.

Cabaret

There are cabarets all over the island, many of them in the tourist hotels, but the most spectacular of them all is definitely the **Tropicana**, still as it was when Havana was at its sleaziest in the 50s. It is set in the outskirts of Havana, a show of hundreds of dancing girls (and a few men), who appear on catwalks, on trapezes, descending out of trees…

Voluptuous matriarchs act as commères, singing and spurring on their cohorts of thrusting beauties to feats of dancing and athletic daring. In unison 30 of them strut around the stage high-kicking, skirts flailing, head-dresses quivering and cascading, thighs up to their ribs, scrunching up their noses at moments of high exertion. A familiar *salsa* pulse drives them on, backed by relentless African drums. It is a celebration of bodies as only the Latin Americans know how.

$60 will get two people to and from your hotel, a ringside view of the action and a couple of drinks, probably cheaper than it was in the 1950s. Book through Cubatur or ring direct (tel 6 6224).

Flora and Fauna

Cuba, like many of the Caribbean islands, is extremely beautiful and it has a grand variety of flora, varying from thick mountain forest through the extraordinarily fertile plains where the rich brown earth sprouts in sugar-cane (*guarapo*) and tobacco, to the dry cactus flats and the coastal mangrove swamps that are home to endless birds and reptiles.

Of the 60 species of palm, the *royal palm* is the most magnificent—100 ft tall, with an explosive bush and a topmost spike—and it is the national tree. Other palms include the barrigona, rather rudely called the palma puta because it looks pregnant (Cuban *macho* men will also point out tiny grasses like legs that close up at the touch and make jokes about their women), the traveller's tree that opens like a fan and the stunted fossil palm, recently almost extinct. Cuban forests were once an excellent source of hardwoods, including mahogany, teak and ebony, of which some still grow. There are many flowering trees, such as the African tulip tree and the flamboyant which explodes into a scarlet bloom in the summer months. There is one that grows lots of wooden pineapples on its branches.

Real pineapples grow on spiky plants at ground level and are one of the many Cuban fruit crops, some of which are exported. You will also see huge citrus orchards of orange, lemon, lime and grapefruit and more exotic fruits such as soursop, mango and guava. The white *mariposa*, the butterfly flower, is Cuba's national flower.

Cuba has a greater variety of animals than the other Caribbean islands, including a range of reptiles from 12-ft crocodiles (you can see them in the Zapata peninsula, where they are farmed for their meat), tank-like iguanas, endless lizards and geckos, down to the tiny almiqui, a shrew-like reptile found only in Cuba. There are 14 species of snake, but none of them is poisonous. Rodents include the agouti and the jutia. There is the odd wild boar, introduced by the Spaniards as meat in buccaneer days. In the coastal waters there are five species of turtle and the occasional endangered manatee or sea cow.

525

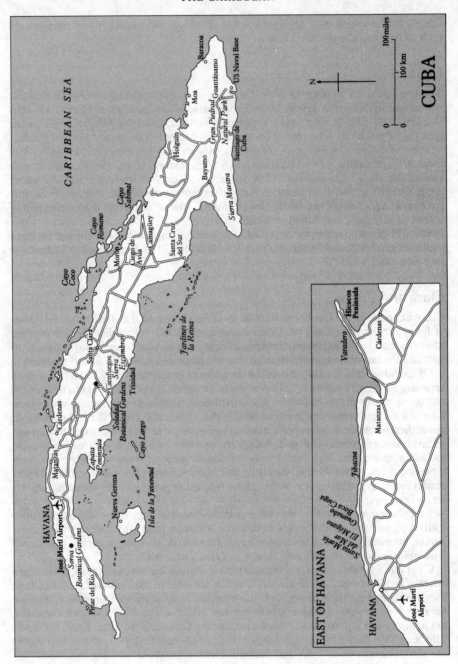

CUBA

CARIBBEAN SEA

Baracoa
Moa
Gran Piedra
Guantánamo
Natural Park
US Naval Base
Holguín
Santiago de
Cuba
Bayamo
Sierra Maestra
Cayo
Sabinal
Cayo
Romano
Morón
Camagüey
Ciego de
Ávila
Santa Cruz
del Sur
Cayo
Coco
Jardines de
la Reina
Santa Clara
Cienfuegos
Sierra
Escambray
Soledad
Botanical Gardens
Trinidad
Cárdenas
Matanzas
Cayo Largo
Zapata
Peninsula
HAVANA
José Martí Airport
Soroa
Botanical Gardens
Pinar del Río
Nueva Gerona
Isla de la Juventud

N

100 miles
100 km
0
0

EAST OF HAVANA

Hicacos
Peninsula
Varadero
Cárdenas
Matanzas
Jibacoa
Santa María
del Mar
Guanabo
El Mégano
Boca Ciega
HAVANA
José Martí
Airport

526

Insects include nearly 200 species of butterfly and hand-sized tarantulas which will give you a bit of a fright. The zunzuncito hummingbird is one of the world's smallest birds and one of Cuba's 380 local and migratory species. In the forests you will find solitaires, owls and parrots, and on the plains there are hawks and the mournful cattle egrets that keep a daytime vigil with the grazing cattle. Vultures gather in small and ominous groups by the roadside. The Cuban trogon, with its green, red, white and blue colouring, is the national bird.

Around the shoreline you will see single pelicans diving and magnificent frigatebirds soaring looking for other birds to prey on, and in the swamps there are herons that stand around on one leg waiting to strike for food, and flocks of flamingos that strut in unison.

GETTING TO CUBA

All the normal rules are suspended for travel to Cuba. US citizens are denied free access through a series of regulations imposed by the Treasury Department in Washington, which effectively prohibit Americans from spending money in Cuba except under certain circumstances. Some US citizens have by-passed these rules by entering Cuba through a third country, but it is easier and safer to join a tour operated by the USA's specialists in travel to Cuba. Marazul Tours (tel (212) 586 3847) knows the regulations inside out, and organizes trips which conform to them. Western visitors need to obtain a Tourist Card in advance, which most agencies specializing in travel to Cuba can obtain easily.

From the UK: Cubana has a weekly flight from Stansted to Havana. If you know you want to go to the eastern end Cuba, you can fly via Amsterdam with Martinair (weekly). There are also Aeroflot flights which can be joined in Shannon in Ireland. There is a daily link with Madrid on Iberia.

Two UK tour operators work specifically to Cuba and they will book packages for you or suggest itineraries: **Regent Holidays** of Bristol (tel (0272) 211711) and **The Travel Alternative** (0865 791636).

From Canada: There is a weekly sceduled flight from Montreal on Air Canada, and there are many charter flights from both Montreal and Toronto to Havana and Varadero.

From the USA: there are regular charter services between Miami and Havana, though these are never shown on departure boards at Miami airport. Flights cost around US$250 for the round trip, and can be booked only through agencies such as **ABC Travel and Tours** in Miami (tel (305) 871 6522).

From other Caribbean Islands: there are several flights each week from the Dominican Republic and a twice-weekly service from Kingston, Jamaica, as well as charters from Montego Bay. There are also flights to Nassau and to Latin American countries including Mexico, Panama and Venezuela.

GETTING AROUND CUBA

Travelling around the island is one of the main problems with a visit to Cuba, particularly at the moment, with all the shortages. The buses, trains and planes are usually heavily booked and often slow and chaotic. If you try to book a seat, you will often have to wait for a few days before a space is available. Arrange everything as far ahead as possible, expect delays and changes of plan, and be very patient—unlike elsewhere in the Caribbean,

527

playing the irate foreigner with officials will not work here. If nothing else, though, it is cheap.

Buses, known locally as *guaguas* (pronounced wawa), are the best form of transport around the island. They are quicker than the train and marginally more expensive. They run long-distance (Interprovincial), and between the towns within a province (Intermunicipal). The two terminals are often in different places.

Interprovincial services (usually large coaches) link the major cities of Cuba. From **Havana** there are direct services to towns as far afield as Santiago and Baracoa in the east. Book as far ahead as possible (if you are on an island tour, perhaps try to book your onward leg as soon as you arrive in a new town). If this is not possible, turn up and try to get a seat at short notice; it may just work. Some services run overnight, which cuts out the next problem of accommodation for one night at least. The Interprovincial terminal in Havana is near the Plaza de la Revolución, on the Avenida Rancho Boyeros (tel 709401). Some sample prices are: Havana to Matanzas—2 pesos (about 10 services daily), Varadero—3 pesos (5 services), Cienfuegos—6 pesos (6 services), Trinidad—8 pesos (2 services), Camagüey—12 pesos (3 per day), Holguín—20 pesos (twice daily), Santiago de Cuba—25 pesos (twice daily) and Guantanamo—28 pesos (once a day).

Intermunicipal guaguas link the towns within a province, for a fare of a couple of pesos. These buses tend to be a bit less comfortable and more crowded, but they are one of the best exposures to Cuban life. It is theoretically possible to use the municipal services to link you from one province to the next to cover a longer distance, but progress will be slow. At the provincial border you will simply be left to wait for the corresponding bus from the next town, or to hitch.

A similar service is performed by *colectivos* (long distance, share-taxis), which have taken up some of the overspill of the national bus network. These cars, some of them old Caddies and Pontiacs of pre-revolutionary Cuba, usually leave from the intermunicipal bus station and they depart when they are full, or when the urge takes the driver. Ask around for your destination; they travel as far afield as 100 miles and prices are roughly twice the fare by bus. The *colectivos* offer some of the best possibilities for getting around the island. You can also persuade the drivers to take your further afield at a price, but they may turn up late if they get a better offer or if they feel like the day off.

Hitching is difficult at the moment because there are hardly enough vehicles for the Cubans to get around, but it brings the usual lottery. Women will often get the front seat.

Good tourists are, of course, encouraged to travel on organized **bus tours** and it is possible to see many of the main sights within a day's drive of Havana or Varadero if you are prepared to go on a 'day trip', e.g. Trinidad or Pinar del Río. Regular tours are booked through the Cubatur offices in the hotel foyers. Independent travellers can always try to catch a ride in an empty seat as the bus leaves from the hotel or returns at the end of the day.

It is possible to make the same tours independently by taking a taxi, if you can get a good rate, and then split it between four people. Negotiate with a *colectivo* driver.

Cuba has an extensive **train** network which can give another good introduction to Cuban society as well as offering a cheap method of travel. The Central railway station in Havana is on the southern edge of the colonial city, overlooking Havana harbour, ticket office across the road (open 6 am–midnight) and it serves most areas of the country. Trains travelling west and south to Cienfuegos leave from the station on Calle Tulipán, southwest of the Plaza de la Revolución. Matanzas is served six times daily from the station at Casablanca, across the water from the colonial city. Some sample fares are **Havana** to Pinar del Río—3.50 pesos, Matanzas—3.30 pesos, Ciego de Avila—6 pesos, Santiago—11 pesos. In the present difficulties it is very hard to book a seat.

A number of cities are also linked by air, and though this is generally a more reliable service than any other, it also gets booked up. To assure your reservation, book it in person. Payment is US dollars with Cubatur or better still a Cubana Airways office. Cubana in Havana is at the bottom end of La Rampa (Calle 23) in Vedado. Some approximate one-way fares are: **Havana** to Camagüey—$40, Holguín—$50, Santiago de Cuba—$60 and the the Isle of Youth—$20.

Within the cities there are local *guaguas* on fixed routes (fare 10 centavos, exact change only), which run on an infrequent schedule and tend to be very crowded. **Taxis**, or *los incapturables* as the peso taxis are known, are marked with a black and white chequerboard strip on their front doors. If you see one hail it, even if there are already people inside, there may just be room for you—the driver will split the fare and drop you off in the order that seems best to him. Some prefer not to take foreigners on the grounds that they are not supposed to, others will stop because you might give them a dollar fare. Negotiate as you get in. Private cars will often act as an impromptu cab service, price 1 peso. In outlying towns, you will occasionally see a pony and trap used as a taxi. Look for the taxi-despatcher somewhere around the main square.

Easier to get hold of around the main resort areas (Havana, Varadero, Santiago) are the **turistaxis**, payment due in dollars. Go to the front desk of any dollar hotel.

Car hire in Cuba gives independence of travel, but it is expensive. Cuban driving is fairly typical of the Caribbean and so you are advised to keep your eye on the road, rather than the landscape. Once again, if you decide to hire a car, do so as far in advance as possible. It is possible to book one before you fly and it will usually be waiting for you on arrival. Your home driving licence is valid and the roads in Cuba are good.

Fuel must be paid for in advance with coupons, which are then exchanged for petrol. Buy enough to cover the journey and a little more, the surplus is (theoretically) reclaimable when you return the car. Foreigners are only allowed to buy the higher grade *especial* petrol, and off the beaten track not every station sells it. Cars range from US$40 per day for the smallest (air-conditioning $5 more on average) to over $100, with reductions for hire by the week.

The main hire firm in Cuba is **Havanautos**, which has offices in all the major tourist areas; head office Calle 36, No 505 in Miramar (tel 225891). In Havana there are other offices at José Martí airport and the main tourist hotels.

TOURIST INFORMATION
Cubatur is the government agency that brings most foreign tourists to the island. They have no office in **Britain**. Contact the Cuban Consulate in the same building as the Cuban Embassy on High Holborn, entrance in the side-alley at 15 Grape St, London WC2H 8DR (tel (071) 240 2488). There are two Cubatur Offices in **Canada**: 55 Queen St East, Suite 705, Toronto, Ontario, M5C 1R5 (tel (416) 362 0700), and 440 Boulevard Dorchester West, Suite 1402, Montreal (tel (514) 857 8004) and one in **Germany**, Steinweg 2, D 6000 Frankfurt am Main 1 (tel (069) 288 322). **Havanatur** has an office in **France** at 24 rue du Quatre-Septembre, 75002 Paris (tel 47 42 58 58).

On the island itself, **Cubatur** keeps an information desk in every tourist hotel (they will try to sell you tickets on organized excursions, but they also have a wealth of information, which you can try to tap). The Cubatur head office is at No 156, Calle 23 (known as La Rampa) in Vedado, open weekdays 8–5 and Sat 8–noon, for some information and complaints (tel 32 4521–7).

Intur is primarily concerned with internal Cuban tourism, but if you speak Spanish and you find the right person, then they can also be quite helpful, perhaps in booking a hotel or advice about local travel. They have offices in all the main towns. Otherwise, the independent traveller might try to winkle some information and advice on the intricacies of Cuban bureaucracy and travel at the **Oficina de Turismo Individual** on La Rampa (No. 156) (there is also an office at Havana airport). Foreign tour guides, employed by **Havanatur**, also know the ropes and can provide invaluable advice. They are often to be found in the tourist hotels.

Cuban **newspapers** are not that interesting or enlightening. *Granma*, the official government paper (named after the boat in which Fidel arrived in Cuba from Mexico), is published daily, with a weekly edition in English. There is not much hard international news. Others include *Trabajadores* (Workers), the trade union paper, and *Juventud Rebelde* (Rebel Youth). You will find some foreign magazines on the racks.

Cuba's **medical** services are excellent, though they are no longer free to foreigners. Small complaints can be dealt with in local clinics (where you will pay for drugs), but if you need extensive medical attention in Havana, the main clinic for foreign patients is the **Cira García Clinic**, on Avenida 20 in Vedado (tel 26811). Treatment here is quite expensive and payment is due in dollars.

The **IDD code** for Cuba is 53, but only numbers in Havana can be dialled direct. Outside the city, you must go through an operator. The telephone system is chaotic—try, try again. There are coin-boxes (5 centavos) and hotel front desks are usually helpful. International calls must be settled in dollars and collect calls out of Cuba are not permitted.

The **British** Embassy in Cuba is on the eighth floor of the Edificio Bolívar, Calle Cárcel, just north of Old Havana (tel 79 1086–89). The **Canadian** Embassy is at Calle 30, No 518, in Miramar (tel 2 6421) and the **German** Embassy is at Calle 28, No 313, also in Miramar (tel 22 2560). US interests are under Swiss auspices, but their consulate is at the eastern end of the Calzada in Vedado, overlooking the Malecón (tel 32 0551). You are most likely to notice it when you are told to walk on the other side of the road.

MONEY

As with most communist countries, there are two parallel currencies in Cuba, local money and hard currency, and the divide between the tourist and the local is most visible here. Dollars can buy luxury goods in the tourist shops, to which the Cubans themselves have no access. There is, of course, a flourishing black market.

The local Cuban money is the **peso** (symbol $), officially set at the (unrealistically inflated) rate of US$1 = 1 Cuban peso. The peso is divided into 100 centavos. You will need at least some pesos and centavos for bus fares (10 centavos), stamps and an ice-cream at the *Coppelia* or a cup of coffee. The basics of Cuban life are cheap. Do not change much money at a time and make sure to get small denominations of pesos and coins if you can, because change is in short supply.

530

You can change money in the bank, the Banco Nacional de Cuba (open weekdays, 8–midday and 1–3), but they tend to be slow. Preferable are the front desks in the tourist hotels, where you get the same rate and quicker service. There is a *bureau de change* at José Martí airport outside Havana. Keep your exchange receipts. You will need them to change pesos back into hard currency (to a maximum value of 10 pesos) and sometimes restaurants will not accept pesos unless you can show that they were exchanged legally. Again, take small denomination notes and traveller's cheques to Cuba, or you will be left with a fistful of pesos that you cannot spend. They will be useful only in local shops, in cafés, taxis, the occasional restaurant, and in local 'peso hotels'.

Most credit cards and traveller's cheques are accepted in payment for hotel bills, restaurants and other tourist activities, but because of the US trade embargo, no credit cards or cheques may draw directly on accounts in the USA. AMEX credit cards are not accepted at all. On dollar traveller's cheques, you are asked not to indicate where the cheque was cashed.

There is nonetheless an increasing need for convertible currency, in particular the US dollar, and so this has produced a pressure for foreign visitors to pay in dollars. In restaurants, often the first question you are asked is whether you are paying in dollars. If so, you will go to the front of the queue, past those who are paying in pesos.

You may receive change in a third, tourist currency, valid only in the hard currency shops. These notes are theoretically convertible, but you are encouraged to think of them as souvenirs. Officially, tipping is discouraged, but it is becoming more common. A gratuity is not likely to be refused.

Visitors to Cuba are encouraged to spend, spend, spend and so special **dollar shops** are provided for tourists, offering some good duty-free deals when compared with prices at home (e.g. whisky, Caribbean rums and musical hardware). The best buy, of course, is cigars (see above). As the name suggests, payment is made in dollars. Dollar shops are restricted to foreigners and so you might be asked to buy something on behalf of a Cuban. Strictly speaking it is illegal, but the Cuban stands to lose more than you. Occasionally food is available, mainly snacks, if you are frustrated with queueing in the restaurants, but you cannot count on it. Dollar shops keep hours of 8–8, roughly speaking.

There is little of interest in the local shops—Cuban clothes are hardly in the vanguard of fashion (except in *guayaberas*), or the records up to the minute. Bookshops (*librerías*) occasionally turn up Cuban classics. Many things are in short supply. Staple items like meat, eggs and rice, which are sold very cheaply to the Cubans, can only be bought with ration tickets and are not on sale to foreigners. There is an occasional run on milk or yoghurt which you can snaffle up, if the locals haven't got there first, but do not count on it. Local shops are open erratically 9–5 or 6, usually with a break of an hour or so for lunch.

The Black Market

The demand for dollars is pressing among the individual Cubans as well as with the government—with hard currency they are able to get hold of the luxury items which are officially reserved for tourists. This has spawned a considerable black market for exchange.

The going rate is anything between around 5 pesos to the dollar and occasionally you will be quoted as much as 20 or even 30 (the higher the rate, the more suspicious you should be, because there are a number of rip-off artists around). Living in Cuba suddenly becomes far cheaper at this rate, but it does not come without its risks, presuming that you can use the money at all. To change money illegally is a crime against the economy and therefore counter-revolutionary. You will not be popular if you are caught (theoretically you risk a two-year jail term, but in practice you will be detained and fined). The most persistent exchange hustlers will appear outside the big hotels and on the Malecón in Havana. If you decide to do it, the risks are minimized (and the rate lowered a bit), in a taxi (if you can find one)—simply ask the driver if he knows where you might change money and he will probably offer three or four pesos to the dollar.

TRAVELLERS' ADVICE

Outside the established tourist network, life in Cuba can be pretty wearing. A fearsome bureaucracy hampers an overloaded system. It can be infuriating, particularly when it comes to travel (see above) and to mealtimes (always allow at least an hour for the simplest plate of food). You will need a fair amount of patience and it is a good idea to take plenty of books to Cuba, to while away time spent in queues. They will be gratefully received when you have finished reading them (English is the Cuban's second language in school). Altogether it may be easier to be a package tourist.

As far as food is concerned, the best advice is to use the dollar shops and the restaurants and hotel dining rooms when you come across them, and pick up anything that you can as you go along the way. When travelling around, buy fresh fruit where you can (you sometimes see farmers with avocados or pineapples on offer by the side of the road). Not much is available to foreigners in the local shops. If you will be going off the beaten track, it is a good idea to stock up on your favourite tins before you leave home.

The Cuban system does not bend easily to the needs of the traveller at the best of times. From the end of July into August and over the Christmas period, when the Cubans themselves like to go on holiday, things are yet more hectic. You will find that you are in competition with them for the scarce resources.

Queueing is something of a way of life in Cuba. Sometimes you have to queue to buy a ticket and then queue to collect your purchase. The Cubans themselves are inured to it and simply wait patiently (it can be three or four hours in a restaurant sometimes). Dollars are the answer to avoiding this. If you have to queue, check that you are at the back by asking *ultimo?* or *ultima?* if it is a woman (it means 'last') and then take your place.

With regard to **personal safety**, Cuba is generally safe, both during the day and after dark, though there are a few places where you need to keep a beady eye on your possessions—on the Malecón and in some run-down districts of Havana and on Varadero beach. As everywhere, watch your pockets in a crowd, but most Cubans would never dream of thieving from you. **Women** should have no problem in Cuba other than the occasional attentions of Latin men—verbal, but rarely physical, and not usually directed against foreigners in any case. A 'wedding ring' can be a convenient defence against a persistent man.

Hustlers will accost you from time to time, particularly around the hotels in town, usually to change dollars (see under Money, p. 531), but sometimes simply asking for money. They can be very persistent, but clearly it is better not to give in. There are no beggars on the island as elsewhere in the Caribbean. A gift of money may seem a friendly gesture to a person who is genuinely poor, but it could get you both in trouble. Perhaps take cigarettes or other small presents.

Lastly, the Cubans place restrictions on **photography**. No photography is permitted in museums and the Cubans are particularly sensitive about uniformed personnel and industrial or military installations (this includes happy snaps of Cuban sugar factories and any old forts with aerials sticking out of them). Also, don't be seen wielding a camera when some Cubans are having an argument in a public place. You will probably be detained. Cuba is quite closely monitored by an effective intelligence service, so if you do not want to end up in a pickle like Wormold in *Our Man in Havana*, then do not get caught making detailed plans of the inside of a Cuban hoover.

FURTHER READING
There are many histories of the Cuban Revolution. One of the most readable is Peter Marshall's *Cuba Libre—Breaking the Chains?* and *Fidel—a critical portrait* by Tad Szulc gives a very detailed and well-researched account of the Cuban leader, and is an informative and easy read.

Alejo Carpentier was a Cuban journalist and writer, author of *El Reino de este Mundo* (A Kingdom of this World), about the Haitian revolution, and other works that have influenced Latin American authors. Ernest Hemingway lived for 20 years on the island and is remembered for his Nobel Prize-winning *The Old Man and the Sea*, which gives the most poignant picture of a poor fisherman's life in 50s Cuba.

Our Man in Havana is another classic by Graham Greene, in which the vacuum-cleaner salesman Wormold gets in a pickle as his ring of fictional agents starts to take on a disturbing life of its own. Carlo Gébler's *Driving through Cuba* is an enjoyable and well-informed personal view about a trip through the island in 1987.

BEACHES (Clockwise from Havana)
On its thousands of miles of coastline, Cuba has some of the best beaches in the Caribbean. The island is relatively flat, at least when compared to other Caribbean islands, and the 1200-odd offshore cays have given coastlines that slope gently into the sea, the softest sand and superb coral reefs. Around 50 of the beaches (*playas*) have facilities and hotels for the thousands of Cubans who pour out of the cities in lorries at the weekend, others have been developed with tourist hotels in response to the stepped-up tourist race and most watersports are available there. If you get off the beaten track you can find idyllic strands, tucked between the 'dark teeth' of the coral coastline or behind the mangrove forests. All beaches in Cuba are public, and topless bathing is not really allowed.

Closest to Havana are the **Playas del Este**, which are strung out over several miles of the northern coastline of Havana province. **El Mégano** and the busier **Santa María del Mar** have good strips of crystalline sand and as you travel farther east on the Vía Blanca, the northern coastal road, you will come to the most developed beaches of **Boca Ciega** and **Guanabo**. There are other smaller beaches between here and the idyllic bays of **Jibacoa**, where the snorkelling is particularly good. The mountainous area to the west of Havana has fewer beaches, though there are some attractive bays that are enclosed by lumbering headlands. Try Puerto Esperanza.

At 12 miles, **Varadero** beach is one of the longest beaches in the Caribbean—a supreme strand, as much as 40 yards wide and mounded for most of its length with satin smooth granules of sand that trickle through your toes. It is understandably very popular, mostly with foreigners—it offers all watersports, evening fun in the bars and discotheques. It is Cuba's best resort. All in all it is rather built up. Varadero is about 80 miles from Havana and 20 from Matanzas, from where it can be reached by share taxi.

The northern coastline of Villa Clara province is not developed and it is off the beaten track anyway, but among the mangrove swamps you will find small beaches with fishing villages and offshore there are more idyllic sands on the cays. Try **La Panchita** and **Playa Juan Francisco**. North of the remote town of Morón in Ciego de Avila province you can go to **La Tinaja** and the oddly name **XI Festival** beach on the Punta de San Juan.

In contrast, the islands of the Archipiélago de Camagüey have been chosen for development and so it is easier to get out on to the superb sands and coral reefs of **Cayo Coco** (with an airstrip), **Cayo Guillermo** and **Cayo Paredón Grande**. Farther east is **Cayo Guajaba** and then **Cayo Sabinal**, which can be reached by the day from Santa Lucía. **Santa Lucía** is another 10 miles of idyllic, palm-backed sand with 20 miles of brilliant off-shore coral reefs, good for snorkellers as well as divers. It is built up with a marina and hotels with watersports.

As you head east from here the beaches are undeveloped and do not have facilities, so remember to take food and water. They tend to be populated by the Cubans and only the odd adventurous traveller. Northeast of the city of Holguín, however, is another resort area set on a magnificent beach at **Guardalavaca**. And at **Don Lino** you will find a small cove with a hotel where you can get refreshments and a windsurfer or snorkelling gear. The reefs continue to the eastern tip of the island. For swimming, try **Playa Corinthia**, a few miles west of Moa.

Rounding the eastern tip of the island, you come to **Yateritas**, also popular with the locals, and as you approach Santiago de Cuba from the east, there are beaches with facilities at **Punta Berracos, Daquiri** beach and at **Siboney** beach.

There are fewer beaches on the protected southern shore of the island. Much of the shoreline is mangrove swamp, impenetrable forest of the sort that the cruiser *Granma* landed in in 1956 (near Las Coloradas). If you are dying for a beach in Camagüey, instead of going north, you might try going south through the hill and cattle country to **Santa Cruz del Sur**, where there is an attractive beach and offshore cays and reefs.

Close to Trinidad you will find the beaches of **La Boca** and **Ancón**, each with hotels nearby for a drink, and near the mouth of Cienfuegos Bay there is the hotel and beach of **Rancho Luna**.

West of here you will find more mangrove swamp in the Zapata peninsula, into which the Bay of Pigs takes a large bite, famous as the site of the failed invasion by the Cuban exiles in 1961. There are beaches and hotels at **Playa Girón** and at **La Larga**, which are backed with sea-grape and palms and shelve very gently into the water. Offshore is the **Cayo Ernst Thálmann**, where you will find more sun-bleached sand and water the colour of aquamarine.

Island Beaches off the South Coast

There are two main archipelagos off the south coast of Cuba, with hundreds of islands, cays and sandbars. In the Batanabó Gulf south of Havana you will find a string of islands stretched between the Isla de la Juventud and Cayo Largo. On the former there are beaches on the south coast, at **Playa Larga** and **Punta del Este**. A series of subsurface reefs and sandbars that just break the waves run east, past the undeveloped Cayo Avalos and Cayo Rosario to **Cayo Largo**, another island that has been developed as a tourist resort. This island is nearly all beach and the water is stunningly blue, and so you can go to any bit of 15 miles of sand between **Playa Sirena** in the southwest and **Playa Tortuga** in the northeast.

The Archipiélago de los Jardines de la Reina (the Gardens of the Queen) is another another 100-mile string of islands and barrier reefs teeming with tropical fish, off the province of Ciego de Avila. Another tropical island idyll. The problem is getting there. There is one boat hotel that moors out there along with the fishermen, who offer the only other form of transport.

WATERSPORTS
Windsurfers and small **sailing** craft can be hired through the hotels at all the main areas, for good prices (around US$12 per hour) and you can even get a bird's eye view of all the roasting bodies on a **parasailing** jaunt at the major resorts. Go to the Playas del Este, Varadero, Playa Santa Lucía and the offshore islands. **Waterskiing** is also popular in Cuba and easy to arrange.

Yacht tours are limited, but are available through the Hemingway Marina, west of Havana and at Varadero. Out on Cayo Largo, you can take a boat trip to Cayo Avalos or Cayo Rosario, for snorkelling and a picnic. Much more popular in Cuba is **deep-sea fishing**, and you can take a launch out into the Gulf Stream and cast for blue, white or black marlin, yellowfin tuna, sailfish or wahoo. Again, try the Hemingway Marina at Calle 248, Santa Fe, La Habana, Cuba (tel 22 5590–3). The other principal resorts also have boats equipped for off-shore fishing and for deep-sea trips, including the Playas del Este, Varadero, Playa Santa Lucía, Guardalavaca, Santiago de Cuba and on the Isla de la Juventud. It is very cheap compared with most Caribbean islands and you can reckon on US$150 to charter a boat for the whole day.

Scuba divers will find some superb reefs off Cuba. Whole forests of black coral, sponges and gorgonians fur the submarine walls and the sloping drop-offs, and in the shallow sandy bottoms between the islands whole schools of tropical fish dip and dart in unison, while single angelfish float and lobsters and crabs scuttle. On the north coast, dives can be arranged at the tourist resorts and instruction is available. On the protected south coast there are stunning underwater landscapes in the cays of the two archipelagos—between the Isla de la Juventud (go to the Colony Hotel) and Cayo Largo there are some supreme reefs with crystalline water, good also for snorkelling, and the cays of the Jardines de la Reina are yet more beautiful and remote. Underwater photographic equipment is also on hand at the bigger dive shops.

OTHER SPORTS
Tennis courts are available in most of the larger hotels and in the resort areas (courts around US$2 per hour). Inland fishing and hunting (for anything from quail and snipe to wild boar and even an alligator if you so desire) is possible in season. Book through Cubatur; the resorts will provide guides, boats and shotguns.

If you wish to go **hiking**, you will have to look after yourself, but it is possible to set up horseback outings along the beach or into the hills in many of the resorts; it is popular with the Cubans and so there are plenty of stables.

Spectator sports in Cuba are free and the country has some excellent sportsmen and women, rating highly in sports like boxing (extremely popular in Cuba). There is no bull-fighting in Cuba. It is well worth taking time out to watch a Cuban game of **baseball**—there are stadia all over the island. In the back streets you will see a scaled down version of baseball played by children in which they are not allowed to run, which is quite fun to join in. You will also see games of dominoes played in the town squares (dominoes is a popular game all over the Caribbean), played quickly and demonstratively.

Havana

Cuba's capital, La Habana, lies on the northern shore of the island, towards the western end, about 90 miles across the Gulf Stream from Key West in the USA. Its population of just over two million makes it the largest city in the Caribbean islands. The city was founded in 1514 as San Cristobal de la Havana, on a magnificent natural harbour, and its importance grew as ships put in here, their last stop before the Atlantic crossing back to Europe. By 1558, the small collection of coral-stone buildings and palm thatch *bohíos* was made the capital of Cuba.

Heading west from the harbour along the Malecón (the Embankment, or sea wall) you will see the history of the city mapped out before you, from the stunning colonnaded courtyards of 16th-century *palacios* in Old Havana, past the stately 19th-century colonial edifices of Habana Central and then the vast and luxurious art deco palaces thrown up in the 30s and 40s in Vedado, to the imposing ferro-concrete monstrosities of the Revolution. The city has an air of decay in places—the Revolution has put a higher priority on developing the country instead, and it has discouraged farmers from moving into shanty towns as they have on the outskirts of most other Caribbean capitals.

Old Havana

Habana Vieja is by far the most beautiful town in the Caribbean. It is a square mile of glorious colonial palaces ranged in lines along narrow alleys and around the plazas. Behind the grey façades of coral rock, embellished with wrought-iron balustrades and stained-glass windows, you will disover idyllic courtyards, forested in greenery and overlooked by cloistered walkways. On the cobbled streets and in the colonnades you can almost imagine the merchants of the 17th century clattering past in their carriages. You can wander for hours.

Much of it is in disrepair. The stucco and plasterwork has crumbled and in places whole façades are shored up with timber spars and scaffolding. It has been designated a city of world heritage by UNESCO and restoration continues.

A few bits remain of the old city wall. This was started in 1633 to keep out the plague of pirates and freebooters who were roving the islands at that time, but it was not completed until over a century later in 1767. You may hear a cannon fired at 9 pm each day, which once warned the citizens to get within the city walls. To protect themselves from the sea attack, they slung a chain across the entrance of the harbour.

The oldest part of Havana is the **Plaza de Armas**, where the city's first mass was said in November 1519, in the shade of an old ceiba (silk cotton) tree and where the neoclassical **Templete** has stood since 1754. Murals by the French artist Vermay commemorate the event. From here you can see the tiny **Giraldilla**, Havana's symbol, a statue of a woman holding a cross, who stands atop the tower of the **Castillo de la Fuerza** Museum. Constructed between 1538 and 1542, la Fuerza is Cuba's oldest surviving fortress.

At the centre of the square, surrounded by the royal palms of Cuba, stands a statue of Manuel Céspedes, the father of Cuban Independence and hero of the 1868 War of Independence. But his old adversaries still dominate the square around him in the massive **Palacio de los Capitanes Generales**, the seat of the Spanish colonial government. Today this huge palace, which was built between 1772 and 1776, is home to the **Museo de la Ciudad** (the museum of Havana City), dedicated to the history of Cuba. On view are the splendour of colonial days and mementoes of 20th-century Cuban triumphs. A statue of Columbus stands in the cloistered courtyard. Open Tues–Sat, 2.30–9.30, Sun 9–1 (tel 60 0722), closed Mon. The colonnaded **Palacio del Segundo Cabo**, which stands next to the museum and was built in the same period, is occupied by the Ministry of Culture, but you are permitted to go into the inner courtyard. There are one or two cafés on the square.

A number of other gracious old *palacios* look on to the square and on to the nearby Calle Obispo, including the **Méson de la Flota**, the 'Fleet's Tavern' (which it still is to a limited extent, serving beer and snacks), the **Palacio Intendencia**, now the Letras Cubanas Publishing House and **La Casa del Agua**, where you can get stone-filtered water in metal beakers for 5 centavos. There is also the old University bell, an old pharmacy and herb shop, dressed up as it would have been in the last century, and the **Casa de Las Infusiones**, where you can stop for a vanilla or lemon tea. The **Casa de la Obrapia** is set in a 17th-century town house with a delightful courtyard and has an exhibition of 18th-century and 19th-century furniture. Downstairs there is a room devoted to the Cuban journalist Alejo Carpentier.

On the Calle Oficios, which runs south from the Plaza de Armas, you will find the old **Monte Piedad** (the pawn shop), now the **Museo Numismático**, with Cuban notes and coins on display, Tues–Sat, 1.30–8, the **Casa del Árabe**, with Arabic memorabilia and the **Automobile Museum**, with some of Cuba's stately old motor cars on view.

The **Plaza de la Catedral**, just northwest of the Plaza de Armas, is another cobbled square enclosed by stunning colonial balconies and colonnades. At its head stands the baroque Cathedral itself, originally built by the Jesuits in 1704, with towers of different size. Though it is dedicated to the Virgin Mary, it is usually known as the Columbus Cathedral—the bones of Christopher Columbus were reputed to have spent some years here between 1796 and 1898, brought from Santo Domingo and then taken to Seville. Open Mon–Fri, 9–11.30 am. The rest of the square was built in the first half of the eighteenth century. Directly opposite the Cathedral is the **Museo de Arte Colonial**, where there are exhibits of 19th-century furniture and carving. Check out the washstand. Open Tues–Sat, 1.30–8.30 and Sun, 9–12.30 (tel 61 1367). In the square you will see a shocked-looking face built into one of the walls. It is in fact a postbox, Cuba's oldest.

The colonial city is studded with colonial masterpieces: churches, seminaries and convents and old family *palacios*. A third stunning square in Old Havana is the **Plaza Vieja**, to the south of the Plaza de Armas. Look out for the Palacio de la Artesanía on Avenida Tacón, the Palacio del Arzobispo de la Habana, on Calle Chacón, the old Convento de Santa Clara on Calle Sol, now restored, and the nearby Iglesia de Nuestra Señora de la Merced. The **Museo de la Música**, with Cuban musical instruments and drums on display, is near the Máximo Gómez monument, open Tues–Sat, 10–6, closed Tues and the **Museo Casa Natal de José Martí**, which traces the Independence hero's life, is on Calle Leonor Pérez, close to the railway station.

Beyond the western edge of Old Havana you come into **Central Havana**, which dates from the last century and is where you will find most of the capital's shopping streets. Parallel to the **Prado** (a boulevard with raised gardens and wrought-iron street lamps where Cuban gents congregate to read the paper and foreigners inevitably get nobbled by the exchange hustlers) are a number of Revolutionary monuments and museums, on the open street between Calles Zulueta and Montserrate. As you walk south from the Máximo Gómez statue at the harbour mouth, you come first to a tank that was involved in the Bay of Pigs battle, and then the former **Palacio Presidencial**, where Batista only just escaped an attack by 40 students in March 1957 by hiding in a lift. The palace has been turned into the **Muséo de la Revolución**, and on its three floors it gives a detailed history of Cuba from the arrival of the Spaniards to the Revolution and beyond, covering moments such as the conquistadors, Eduardo Chíbas's suicide as he addressed the nation on the radio, and conflicts to the Bay of Pigs. It is worth a look. Open Tues–Sat, 1–8, Sun 10–1 and 2–8. Outside, the *Granma* sits behind a glass screen.

The modern building next in line is the **Museo Nacional de Bellas Artes**, the National Art Museum, with Cuban rooms and foreign artists including Goya, Velazquez, Rubens and Turner. Open Tues–Sat, 1.30–8.30, Sun 4–8. And at the top of the hill is the old **Capitolio**, the centre of the modern town, an imposing edifice in the style of the US Capitol (built by the Henderson Corporation in the 30s), the old Cuban House of Assembly. It contains an uninspiring museum of science, the **Museo de Ciencias Naturales**.

Vedado

As you travel west from Central Havana, you pass through run-down residential streets, but the streets soon open out into **Vedado** district. Built in the 30s and 40s, the huge art deco palaces and villas are a reminder of just how luxurious and rich Havana was at its height as the sleaze capital of the Americas. The best view of all is from the top of the **Havana Libre Hotel**.

The central street is Calle 23, better known as **La Rampa**, which runs from the Malecón up towards the Columbus Cemetery. On La Rampa you will find the Havana **Coppelia**, the ice cream parlour, the Havana Libre Hotel, and close by the Palacio de los Matrimoniales, where the Cubans formalize their marriages in the absence of a church service. Close to the University, on Calle San Miguel, is the **Museo Napoleónico**, which exhibits furniture and arms from the Napoleonic period. Open Tues–Sat, 1.30–8, Sun 9–1. North of La Rampa, at No 502 17th St, you will find the **Museo de Artes Decorativas**, with 18th- and 19th-century porcelain and furniture including Meissen, Wedgwood and Chippendale, and an art deco bathroom. Open Tues–Sat, 10–6.

In the southern area of Vedado, between the Avenidas Rancho Boyeres and Céspedes, you will find the the vast open space of the **Plaza de la Revolución**, dominated by a massive mural of Che Guevara and Fidel. The square only really comes into its own when hundreds of thousands collect there to hear Fidel speak, usually at the New Year celebrations. Its heart is a statue of José Martí and behind it a 116-metre obelisk, a masterpiece of supremely ugly concrete architecture. Beyond here are the Headquarters of the Cuban Communist Party, not open to the general public.

The **Cemetario Cristóbal Colón** is a vast acreage of imposing mausolea and marble statuary set around an octagonal chapel. Among the graves of the martyred revolutionaries there are areas dedicated to the particular professions. It was in a speech outside the Columbus Cemetery that Castro declared the Revolution a socialist one in 1961.

Across the harbour mouth (a 10 centavo ferry ride) you come to Casablanca, where you will see a 17-metre statue of Christ and the distinctive Morro lighthouse. In the Morro itself, a massive lumbering fortress that guarded the harbour approaches, there is the **Museo de Armas**, with weaponry from across the ages and an art exhibition downstairs. Open Tues–Sat, 1–7, Sun 9–noon (tel 66 0216). Beyond here you come to the suburb of **Cojimar**, the setting of Hemingway's *Old Man and the Sea*. It was a fishing village, but now most of the fishermen have moved to more comfortable houses—it is only just possible to imagine a marlin's huge tail and backbone discarded on the beach. A bust commemorates him. More interesting is his house, **La Vigía**, where the writer ('Ernesto' to the Cubans) lived in the 40s and 50s, in the suburb of San Francisco de Paula, southeast of Havana. It is maintained exactly as he left it in 1960. The walls are lined with hunting trophies and you can see his typewriter at chest height (he wrote barefoot standing up) and the sad record of his decreasing weight in the bathroom (he was dying from cirrhosis and eventually he shot himself in 1961 in the USA). You are only really supposed to look in through the windows and doors. The small estate stands on a cliff and has an excellent view looking north from the garden—La Vigía means lookout. Open Tues–Sat, 9–12 and 1–5; Sun, 9–1. Ring beforehand (tel 91 0809), or you may prefer to make a US$10 organized tour. The Hemingway Marina, five miles west of the capital, is Hemingway's only in name and in his love of sport fishing. It is a modern tourist complex and marina.

South of Havana itself is the **Parque Lenin**, just outside the Havana ringroad, a huge area of parkland with lakes, an amusement park, art galleries, a spiral aquarium, and a massive, blinding-white bust of Lenin himself. There are also stables to hire horses, a diminutive train to ride, and in the evening you may like to visit the drive-in cinema (Autokine), if you can get hold of a car. There is a railway terminal in the park, reached from Central Station. It gets very busy at the weekends, when the Habañeros pour out of the city. Close by to the south are some **Botanical Gardens**, with an effusion of Caribbean flora and **Expocuba**, a series of pavilions that illustrate the country's successes in industry and social progress.

Around the Island—West of Havana

The province of **Pinar del Río** occupies the western tip of Cuba, and with the Sierra de los Organos (which seems to collect rainclouds) along its northern shore, it is fantastically beautiful and incredibly fertile. It is here that Cuba's finest tobacco is grown. Among the royal palms and the *karst* limestone outcrops, the hills are smothered in bright green plantations and dotted with aluminium and shaggy-roofed *vegas*, the tobacco drying houses. If you take a trip out to the west of the island, make sure to travel on the northern coastal route between Cabañas and La Esperanza on one of the journeys.

In the hills north of San Cristóbal are the botanical gardens of **Soroa**, with a walkway through Cuba's explosive vegetation. The garden, which covers a hillside, was built by a Spaniard in memory of his daughter who had died in childbirth. Besides *mother-in-law's tongue* and the *elephant's foot* tree from Mexico there is an **orquidearía**, where most of the island's 250 varieties of orchid (including the extraordinary *Queen's shoe*) are on view. Orchidarium open 8.30–noon and 1.30–4 for a guided tour, best in November and December.

The city of **Pinar del Río**, 110 miles from Havana, grew on the back of the tobacco industry—until a few years ago it was nicknamed Cinderella because it was so poor. You can visit any number of cigar factories, or the **Museo del Tabaco**, in the west of the town, on Calle Ajete, where there is an illustration of the industry from seed to cigar. Some of the many other museums include the **Museo de Historia**, with Cuban life from the local Indians onwards (on Calle José Martí, open Tues–Sat, 2–10) and the **Museo de Ciencias Naturales** (also Calle Martí, open 2–10), set in one of the city's grand old buildings.

North of Pinar del Río, the valley of **Viñales**, has an extraordinary geographical phenomenon in its *karst* mountain outcrops, once the supports of a vast plain which collapsed through water erosion millions of years ago. (Called *mogotes* in Cuba, they look similar to the haystack mountains of South China.) From the Hotel las Jasmines is one of Cuba's most attractive views, where these vast neolithic fruit cakes soar from the lush tobacco fields. The mogotes are laced with cave-systems where the *Guanahatabeyes*, cave-dwelling Indians who were Cuba's earliest inhabitants, lived and where you can take boat trips. Try the **Indian Cave**. West of Pinar del Río the mountains subside and the province becomes more Cinderella like.

East of Havana

Beyond the beaches of Playas del Este to the east of Havana and past the drilling heads of Cuba's oil industry, you come to the city of Matanzas, set on a deep bay about 60 miles from the capital. You can also make the journey by the 'Hershey Railway' (called so because because it was constructed with money from the American chocolate company), which departs Havana from Casablanca.

Matanzas, which takes its name from a massacre (perhaps of Spaniards, but more likely of bloodstock), was founded in 1690, but it did not really develop until the 19th century, when it became immensely wealthy through the sugar industry. It became a Cuban leader in matters cultural and it is full of grand old buildings from the period, including the **Cathedral** and others ranged around the Parque Central and the **Teatro Sauto**, built in 1863. It is a gentler town after the bustle of the capital.

The **Museo Farmacia** (Pharmaceutical museum) is near the Parque Central and has an original display of old wives' remedies and medicinal plants (open Tues–Sun, 2–9), and nearer the waterfront, you will find the provincial museum in the **Palacio de Junco**, a beautiful mansion built by a sugar planter in the last century, which recounts Matanzas' history and its connection with sugar. Open Tues–Sun, 2–9. There are two Casas de la Trova, on Calle 83 and Calle 85.

Matanzas is a dropping off point for **Varadero**, Cuba's premier resort, set on a fantastic beach 12 miles long on the Hicacos Peninsula. It specializes in sun, sea and sand vacations, with exotic cabaret and subterranean discotheques (names like Pirate's Cave) to keep you satisfied in the evenings. The town, which consists mainly of high-rise and beachfront blocks interspersed with villas, is strung out along the half-mile-wide peninsula (gaps are rapidly being filled with new development in a drive to increase beds from 3000 to about 25,000 by the turn of the century).

There is a historical **museum** on Calle 57, with an exhibition of the town's past, since it was established as a resort 100 years ago, but more interesting is the **Indian Museum**, which deals with the life of the Taínos on the island before the Spaniards arrived. At the end of the peninsula is the vacation home of the Du Pont family, an impressive villa with a view that now doubles as the Restaurant Las Américas.

The town of **Cárdenas**, is not far south of Varadero, lost in the sugar flats and totally untouched by the tourist race. It is a sleepy place, and gives a good idea of rural Cuba. It is known as the 'City of Flags' because the Cuban flag was first raised here in 1850, in a failed insurrection. It was also the birthplace of José Echevarría, a militant student leader who was killed by the Batista regime in March 1957. A **museum** of Cárdenas's sugar tradition has been created in his home on the street now named after him. Open Tues–Sun, 9.30–noon and 1–6 (closed Sun afternoons).

On the southern seaboard of Matanzas province is the swamp of the Zapata Peninsula—as you travel south from the provincial capital you pass through the endless canefields, the source of Matanzas' wealth—most renowned among the Cubans for being the site of the 'First major defeat of Imperialism in Latin America', the **Bay of Pigs**. Fidel himself returned to the battlefield in April 1961 in order to repel the landing by Cuban exiles, supported by the USA. It is a proud piece of Cuban history, with memorial stones along the route to those who died and a **Museum** in Playa Girón with tanks and aeroplanes on view. Open Tues–Sat, 9–6. At Playa Larga you will find **Guamá** Indian village, a hotel built of palm-thatch *bohíos* and decorated with sculptures by Rita Longa, and a **crocodile farm**, best visited at feeding time in the early evening.

The city of **Cienfuegos** is about 40 miles east of Playa Girón, and it is set on an almost landlocked bight on the south coast of the island. It is an industrial and port town, with a population of 100,000 and a large naval base. The city centre has some elaborate old Spanish colonial buildings, including the **Cathedral** with its octagonal cupola and the **Thomas Terry theatre** on the attractive and open square of the Parque Martí. The waterfront Prado is uninspiring, but it leads south to the extraordinary folly of **Valle Palace**, a conglomeration of the styles of the three religions of Christianity, Judaism and Islam.

A further 50 miles east of Cienfuegos, along a spectacular coastal road that winds over the headlands thrown off by the peaks of the Sierra Escambray, you come to the extraordinary and charming town of Trinidad.

Trinidad has been restored entirely to its early 19th-century glory—cobbled streets, Spanish colonial town-houses, wrought-iron street lamps, cannon at the street corners

541

with muzzles buried in the ground to stop the carriage wheels clipping the walls. Two hundred years ago Trinidad was one of Cuba's richest trading ports and its fleets would sail as far afield as Brazil and the Baltic. Today the streets may be festooned with telephone wires, but the narrow streets still have a pleasant and antique feeling, overlooked by wrought-iron balconies and pastel plaster façades. The cannon still do a useful job too, defending the stonework from wayward lorry wheels. Along with Old Havana, Trinidad has been placed on the world heritage list.

The town is one of Cuba's oldest and was founded by Diego Velásquez in 1514. In 1518 Hernán Cortéz embarked on his conquest of Mexico from a house on the beautiful central square, the Plaza Martí. The site is now occupied by the **Museo de Archeológico**, which has a lacklustre display of pre-Columbian Indian life, including burial pots. Open Mon–Sat, 10–5. Diagonally opposite is the **Museo de Arquitectura Colonial**, which illustrates the development of Trinidad's buildings and their embellishments in pictures, including the pineapples that appear all over the town. Look out for the ingenious 18th-century steambath and the loos with a communicating door—men and women; and see which side you can lock it from. Open Mon–Sat, 9–6, Sun 9–1. The **Museo Romántico** is also on the square, a classically beautiful colonial palace set around a courtyard, stuffed with elaborate furniture and with marvellous views from the upstairs windows. Open daily 9.30–5.30. The **Museo de la Lucha Contra Bandidos** tells the story of the struggle against counter-revolutionaries. Open daily, 10–5.30. The Casa de Cultura and the Casa de la Trova are both just south of the Plaza Martí.

The **Torre de Iznaga** is a reminder of Trinidad's other career as a centre of sugar. This folly, a few miles out of the town on the Sancti Spíritus road, was actually an observation tower for plantation overseers to watch the slaves.

Above Trinidad, straddling the three provinces of Villa Clara, Cienfuegos and Sancti Spíritus are the mountains of **Sierra Escambray**, Cuba's central mountain range, where immensely fertile peaks and valleys reach 3000 feet in places. The northern slopes are covered in tobacco plantations and their shaggy drying houses. The highest summit is Pico San Juan (3800 ft) just northwest of Trinidad on the south coast. A trip to **Topes de Collantes** is a good day out from Trinidad—the views are magnificent. The **Soledad** botanical gardens are east of Cienfuegos and you will see 60 sorts of palm among the 2000 species of plant in the pleasant parkland. Look out for the 'pineapple tree'.

In the centre of the island, directly north of Trinidad is the city of **Santa Clara**, capital of Villa Clara Province, a city of 175,000 and the home of one of Cuba's four universities. It is quite industrialized, but still supports a tradition of agriculture, surrounded by fields of maize, beans and yuca (cassava) as well as ranches of cattle—no doubt you will come across the *vaqueros* sitting on their huge saddles, driving the herds along the local roads.

Villa Clara has one of Cuba's oddest museums in the **Tren Blindado** (the armoured troop train), still at the site where it was stormed by Che Guevara in the closing moments of the war against the Batista regime. The exhibits are set inside the old wagons, which still sport their old military colours. Open Tues–Sun, 8–noon and 3–7. There is a Museum of Decorative Arts in the Parque Vidal.

The province of Ciego de Avila is also agricultural, with more sugar-cane flats and pineapple plantations. Its capital (the city of Ciego de Avila) is quiet and lacklustre, and is only really visited because it happens to lie on the main east-west road. A pleasanter town to visit goes by the unlikely name of Morón, with the atmosphere of a 19th-century country town and horse-drawn carriages. If you wish to fix up a shooting trip, you can do so on the Laguna de Leche and in the swamps north of the town.

Camagüey, city and province, are altogether a better prospect. The city of Camagüey, originally called Puerto Prinicipe, was one of Cuba's earliest settlements, established on the coast in 1514, but moved inland to save it from pirate raids. Today it is Cuba's third largest city and it sits on the plain among the canefields and cattle ranches. The city has many old Spanish colonial buildings, among them the **Teatro Principal, La Soledad** church and the 18th-century **Palace of Justice**. The large earthenware pots that you can see all around the city were used for storing and keeping water cool and have become the symbol of the province.

There are two museums bearing the name of Ignacio Agramonte, a hero of the Cuban War of Independence born in the town. The **Museo Ignacio Agramonte**, which is the provincial museum, is set in a magnificent building on the Avenida de los Mártires and depicts local history and the many moves the town has made. Open Tues–Sat, 3–11. The **Museo Casa Natal de Ignacio Agramonte** gives a more personal view of the rebel leader's life and achievements in the house where he was born. There are two Casas de la Trova, one in the Parque Agramonte.

Holguín and **Granma** provinces straddle the island as it widens towards the south-eastern tip and they consist mainly of agricultural plains, rising into the foothills of the Sierra Maestra on the south coast. **Holguín**, a small colonial town with three main squares surrounded by an infestation of concrete, is scattered in the lee of a large hill, the Loma de la Cruz, from where the views are magnificent. The **Museo de Ciencias Naturales** is set in a stunning colonial house on Calle Maceo and has displays of Cuban animals from mammals to crustaceans (open Tues–Sat, 9 am–11 pm), and the **Museo de Historia** which follows Cuba from Taíno Indian to revolutionary times. Open Tues–Sat, 12.15–7.15, on Calle Frexes.

Beyond the town are the beaches and resorts around Guardalavaca on the north coast. **Gibara** is supposed to be Columbus's landfall on the island in 1492, when he thought he had discovered Japan. In **Banes**, an hour away into the hills by bus, there is the excellent **Museo Indocubano**, with an extensive collection of Siboney and Taíno artefacts, including their illustrated pottery and descriptions of their cere-monies.

The capital of Granma province is **Bayamo**, one of Cuba's oldest towns, founded by Diego Velásquez in 1513. The **Church of San Salvador** is one of the oldest buildings in Cuba. The town was also the home of Céspedes, who initiated the Cuban War of Independence here in 1868 by freeing his slaves and arming them against the Spaniards. He is remembered in the Parque Céspedes and the **Museo Casa Natal de Carlos Manuel de Céspedes**, a colonial house on Calle Maceo, which tells of his life and struggle. Open daily, 8–noon and 2pm–8. The **Museo Nico Lopez** tells the story of the Bayamo people who staged a rebellion in 1953 to coincide with the Moncada garrison attack. Open Tues–Sun, 8–8. The province is named after the boat in which the revolutionaries sailed from Mexico. Las Coloradas has a concrete memorial to the landing.

Santiago de Cuba

In Oriente province, 60 miles east of Bayamo, is Cuba's second city, **Santiago de Cuba**. The town sits on the edge of a massive harbour, where the Sierra Maestra mountains tumble down to the south coast. It has a special place in the panoply of modern Cuba as the spiritual home of the Independence movement and of the Revolution. Independence heroes such as Céspedes and José Martí are buried in the city and it was here that Castro made his first attack in 1953. He returns to speak here often, usually in the summer celebrations in July each year.

Santiago de Cuba is the third oldest city on the island, founded in 1513 by Diego Velásquez, and for 40 years it was the colony's capital. Some buildings survive from the earliest period (among them is the oldest building on the island, Velásquez's palace), but the town's charming atmosphere comes from all the 19th-century town-houses, with their wrought-iron balconies and shuttered windows, that line the steep streets and stepped alleyways. It is a good town to wander in. Santiago also has a complex heritage as refugees have come here in floods with every conflict in the islands nearby. A strong French heritage dates from the influx of 30,000 planters who fled Saint Domingue at the time of the Haitian Revolution in 1791.

The centre of the town is **Céspedes Square**, set on the hill a few hundred yards above the harbour and here you will find the house of Diego Velásquez, built in around 1514, on the west side of the square. Recently restored, it is a charming house with balconies set around inner courtyards. It is now home to the **Colonial Museum**. Open Tues–Sat 8–10. On the south side is the **Cathedral**, first built on this site in 1524, but the imposing edifice has been enlarged since then.

To the east of the square, past the famous Santiago Casa de la Trova (one of the best loved in Cuba) is the **Bacardi Museum**, with exhibits of Cuban archaeology and history up to the Revolution and 19th-century painting. Open Tues–Sat, 8 am–10 pm, Sun afternoon, Mon morning, on Pío Rosado. Over the road is the **Museo del Carnaval**, with an illustrated history of *Carnaval* in Santiago, which has a strong French influence, and costumes from the latest carnival parade. Open Tues–Sat, 8 am–10 pm, Sun afternoon. **José Martí** is buried in a vast concrete mausoleum in the Santa Efigenia cemetery to the west of the town.

As the spiritual home of the Revolution there are plenty of museums dedicated to the armed struggle in the 1950s. The most famous is of course the **Moncada garrison**, restored (with all its bullet-holes) as it was after the attack on 26 July 1953. It is now a school (many of Batista's barracks were turned into educational establishments), but there is a small museum showing the attack. Open Tues–Fri, 8–8, Sat till noon and 2–6, Sun until noon, off the Avenida de los Libertadores. Other museums include the **Museo Casa Frank País** on Calle General Banderas, set in the home of one of the revolutionary leaders, and the **Museo de la Lucha Clandestina**, set above the town on the Padre Pico. There is a superb view from here.

Farther out of town to the south is the lumbering **Morro** fortress several hundred feet above the sea, built on the point at the harbour mouth in 1643. Inside is the **Museo de la Piratería**, with exhibits of Caribbean piracy, including an assault on the Morro itself by Henry Morgan in 1662. There are supreme views along the south coast and into the mountains above the town. Open daily 8–noon and 2–6. It is worth ringing to check before you set out (tel 9 1569).

On the road east out of the town, towards the south coast beaches, is **Siboney farm** (another museum), from where the Revolutionaries set out, some of them in taxis, to storm the Moncada. The road is dotted with memorial stones to the dead. Soon after, you come to one of Cuba's most curious parks as outsize pterodactyls and brontosauri in concrete appear around you in the 'Dinosaur Park'. North of here is the nature park of **Gran Piedra**, set around the 4000-ft mountain of the same name, where you can walk among the explosive vegetation of the Sierra Maestra. It is best avoided at the weekends as the Santiagueros pour out of the city to get here. On a clear day you can see the Blue Mountains of Jamaica 80 miles to the south, and Haiti 70 miles east.

The remote and unpopulous province of Guantánamo runs from Santiago to the eastern tip of the island. The capital, also called Guantánamo, is not an attractive town and is probably best known for the song *Guantanamera*. It is also the site of a political oddity in the US naval base, 45 square miles of America in the socialist state of Cuba. It was leased by the USA in 1902 and the Americans pay a handsome $2000 each year for the pleasure. You are not allowed near it, but can get a view from the hills above. Take the road south out of the city to the visitor centre.

The road continues along the south coast and then cuts into the mountains to the north coast to the city of **Baracoa**, Cuba's oldest town, established in 1510. It is a sleepy port town of 60,000 inhabitants. In the central square, where the locals gather to play dominoes, is a statue of Cuba's first rebel, the Indian Hatuey. The town is guarded by a series of forts, of which one, **Matachíne**, has been turned into a museum.

ISLA DE JUVENTUD

Sixty miles south of the mainland, in the bay made by the alligator's tail, in the west of Cuba, is the flat **Isle of Youth**. Discovered in 1494 by Columbus, it was a pirate haunt for several hundred years and until 1978 it was known as the Isle of Pines. The main town is the lively Nueva Gerona, in the north of the island. Good roads run to the southwest and southeast coast where there are good beaches, but much of the country in the south is swampland. There are regular flights to the island, but if you prefer, you can catch the ferry from Surgideno de Batananó, south of Havana.

Today the Isla de Juventud has a population of 60,000 and it has a youthful atmosphere to go with its name—students come to take courses here, many of them from African countries. It has a slightly remote and a distinctly relaxed feel after the mainland, and it is fun to travel there. Surrounded by reefs, it has excellent diving and the fishing, one of the island's main occupations, is good too.

There are several museums, of which the most impressive is in the **Presidio Modelo**, the former high-security prison with its five round cell-blocks, where Castro did a stint after the Moncada garrison attack. It has been turned into a school. Open Tues–Sat, 9–5, Sun till 1.

Cayo Largo, at the other end of the archipelago, has been developed solely as a tourist resort, and no Cubans go there except to work. Consequently it is far more expensive, but if you want to spend a few days uninterrupted in the relentless pursuit of beach lounging and of watersports this place is as good as any in Cuba. You can go even further afield and be more remote, to the nearby cays of **Cayo Rico** and **Cayo Pájaros**.

FESTIVALS
Carnaval is the brightest and liveliest event in the Cuban calendar and it is held each year at the time of the *zafra*, the end of the sugar harvest. Like other Caribbean carnivals, it consists of a series of weekend events that culminate in a three-day street party in the last weekend of July. Then the streets of the major towns fill up with floats, bandwagons (articulated lorries) and hundreds of choreographed dancers in fancy dress. Dancing is one of the principal Cuban occupations anyway, and so you will find whole streets closed off and turned into impromptu discotheques. In the larger towns, congas (not holding each other by the waist, but an exuberant rabble of hundreds) snake their way through the sea of bystanders, shuffle-stepping after the relentless beat of a three-man band of drums, trumpet and a cowbell. Stalls and bars on the street give it a feel not unlike a race-meeting. As a foreigner, you can usually get near the judging of the *Carnaval* parade, but make sure to get out into the crowd as well.

Havana has a lively carnival, in which the different city districts compete for the best pageant, but **Santiago** is different because of its strong French influence that came with the refugees from Haiti at the turn of the last century. Other major towns hold carnivals at different times (ask Cubatur if any are forthcoming). In **Varadero**, there is a winter carnival staged for the tourists, during the second week in February each year. Go to it if you are around, the Cubans will be out for a dance, anyway.

Fidel's first strike against the Moncada garrison was carried out under cover of ·*Carnaval* in 1953 and so the annual revolutionary celebrations, the **Remembrance of the National Rebellion**, happens each year at the same time. It is possible to hear him speak during this time (usually in Santiago). The New Year also coincides with the Anniversary of the **Victory of the Revolution** and at that time Fidel often appears to a crowd of hundreds of thousands in the Plaza de la Revolucion. Other public holidays tend to commemorate revolutionary and historical moments, including the birthday of José Martí (28 January), the Bay of Pigs Victory (19 April), the death of Che Guevara (8 October) and the landing of the *Granma* (2 December).

WHERE TO STAY
The sheer magnificence of a building like the Hotel Nacional at the foot of La Rampa in Havana gives an idea of the opulence and splendour (their decadence aside) of the hotels of Cuba in the 40s and 50s. The exterior remains, in decay, but the hotel has a very different atmosphere now. Like much of Cuban life, negotiating Cuban hotels can be a wearing process. Beyond the normal tourist areas it may be difficult to find a room, and then when you are finally in it, the plumbing and the service can be a bit of a let down. Package travel may suddenly seem delightfully simple. Tourist hotel rooms are usually air-conditioned with private bath and in Havana, most will have a television showing American films. A number of hotels have recently been built in joint ventures with foreign companies, bringing styles and fittings to which westerners are more accustomed.

Foreigners are encouraged to use the 'dollar hotels' in which payment has to be in hard currency. These vary in price and in standard, with many in Havana (the most expensive), and in the main beach centres, and usually a couple in each major provincial town. There are also 'peso hotels', and although they are theoretically set aside for the Cubans themselves, it is possible to stay in many of them. However, it can be difficult to get a room as they often claim to be full. This is not always true and so it sometimes helps to enquire a little further and more insistently. They will also demand payment in dollars sometimes. Check-in time is also usually late in the day, often not before 4.

On arriving in Cuba, if you do not have accommodation arranged in advance, you must book at least one night with the Individual Tourism desk at the airport in order to be allowed through immigration. (It is not a bad idea anyway as a couple of days in Havana will help you get your bearings and give you a bit of time to look at the city, while at the same time arranging onward travel.)

Reservations while in Cuba can be made through Cubatur, who will give details and make reservations only in the 'dollar hotels', and also the Intur offices. You will often pay in advance. If you are moving around, you can try to get reception at your current hotel to book the next night. Finding a room is most difficult in the Cuban summer holiday season (July and August) and over the winter (December, January and February). Unlike the rest of the Caribbean, single travellers can expect a reduction of about a third on the double-room rate. It is also possible to **camp** while travelling around the island and many towns have well-equipped campsites where you can stay for a couple of dollars, tent and facilities included.

In **Havana** there are not many hotels in Old Havana or in Havana Central. You may well have to head for Vedado, where most of the dollar hotels are situated. However, you should avoid the Miramar area (Tritón, the Commodoro and the Sierra Maestra), because its distance from the centre of Havana will mean wasted time or money on taxi fares.

On the edge of the Colonial City you will find one of Havana's smartest hotels, the newly restored **Plaza Hotel**. There is a breezy tiled foyer with echoes of grander colonial days, decorated with palm trees and hints of art deco in the stained glass. The rooms are large and comfortable and there are two restaurants (one à la carte) and two bars. Double room in season US$90. Not far off is the **Hotel Inglaterra** (tel 61 8351) standing next to the Teatro Nacional on the Paseo de Martí, the Prado in the heart of town, set in an ornate and grand old building that has recently been restored. Some of the large rooms have balconies overlooking the street, the restaurant is good and the bar downstairs is a popular gathering point for travellers. US$60 for a double. Also on the Prado, down towards the Malecón, is the **Caribbean Hotel** (tel 6 9896), which is a good bet for the independent traveller, with clean and safe accommodation, US$35 for a double room.

In Havana Central, quite well positioned between Old Havana and the Vedado district, is the **Lincoln** (tel 61 7965), a large and faded building on the Calle Virtudes, with a double room going for about US$45. At the bottom of the Avenida Italia, just off the Malecón, is the **Hotel Deauville** (tel 61 6901), with less good rooms for US$45 for a double.

Close by you will find the large, imposing hotel blocks that were erected in the decades before the Revolution in the district of Vedado. The former Havana Hilton, taken over by the revolutionaries, is now the **Havana Libre** (tel 30 5011), which stands tall at the top of La Rampa. There is a fantastic view of the city, over Old Havana and the harbour, from the Turquino bar on the top floor and there is entertainment. Double rooms at

US$80–100, suites $130–260. Similar in style, a huge and imposing block, is the **Capri Hotel** (tel 32 0511), across La Rampa, pool and cabaret, rooms US$82 or the **Vedado Hotel** (tel 32 6501), on Calle O just down from Havana Libre, with a cabaret, where a double room costs US$55. Cheaper alternatives, but without any charm, include the **Colina** (tel 32 3535), on Calle L and the **St John's**, on Calle O, both around US$40.

The most comfortable place to stay in the **Vedado** district is the **Hotel Victoria** (tel 32 6531) on Calle 19 and M. Close to the commercial centre of the town, the Victoria is probably the best hotel for business travellers—business facilities available, also a pool. US$100 for a double room, $130 for a suite. Farther into the Vedado district, a taxi ride or a long walk from the centre of the town, the **Hotel Presidente** (tel 32 7521), on Calle Calzada has a certain style, with awnings on the outside and a foyer with marble floors, chandeliers and huge vases. Even the rooms have a grander feel than elsewhere, though they are not that large. There is a good bar on the top floor and a swimming pool, double room about US$68–75. On the coast is the **Havana Riviera** (tel 30 5051), a tall, ugly block on the Malecón with a similar feel to the Havana Libre, with pool and cabaret, US$90.

West of Havana

In the city of Pinar del Río to the west of Havana you will find the **Hotel Pinar del Río** (tel 5071) on the eastern outskirts, a 136-room hotel with a swimming pool and nightclub, costing US$35 for a double room. On the western edge of town is the **Hotel Vuelta Abajo** (tel 2303) on Calle Martí, US$20, and in the town centre itself is the **Hotel Globo**, set in an old Cuban town house, about US$15 for a double. In the area of **Viñales** to the north the **Motel Los Jazmines** (tel 9 3205) has a superb view of the valley from up above. There are 14 rooms and a pool and a good restaurant upstairs, double room about US$35. On the other side of the town is the 18-room **Motel La Ermita** (tel 9 3204), also with a pool and a good view from the hillside, US$30 double room. On the way back to Havana, in the hills of Soroa, you can stay at the **Villa Turística Soroa** (tel 2122), sometimes difficult to get a room, but you can use the pool, US$35.

East of Havana

In the **Playas del Este** you can find beach hotels, though they tend to be full of package tourists and they become very booked up at the weekends anyway as the Habañeros escape from the capital. In Santa María del Mar the best is probably the 20-room **Atlántico** (tel 2551) on the Avenida de las Terrazas, where the local Intur office is situated (they can help find you a room) or the cheaper **Villa las Brisas** (tel 2469).

There are four small peso hotels in the city of **Matanzas**, set in the graceful old town-houses of the city's sugar prosperity and all of them 'full' almost all the time. You will be encouraged to move on to Varadero where you will spend dollars like dutiful tourists, but it is worth a try. The **Hotel Loubre** (tel 2745) and the **Yara** (tel 4418) look out on to the Parque Central and the **Velazco** (tel 4443) and **Los Amigos** (tel 3609) are down towards the harbour.

There are not many places along the **Varadero** strip with faded grandeur or style; like many Caribbean resorts, the whole place has been thrown up in a fair hurry and quite recently, to service the tourists. The building continues.

At the top of the range you will find the **Paradiso** and the **Punta Arena** hotels, assemblies of villas around a pool and central area, right above the superb beach. The rooms are very comfortable by Cuban standards. All the watersports and evening entertainment, double room in both US$150 a night in season. The newest addition in the town is the **Melia Varadero**, with luxurious rooms in blocks around tropical gardens overlooking the beach. Double room US$150 per night. You might also try the **Hotel Y Villas Internacional Oasis** (tel 6 3011) on the Carretera las Américas, with 160 rooms in blocks giving on to the beach, swimming pool, sauna, bars and cabaret, where a double room costs around US$100 in the season, or the **Hotel Kawama** (tel 6 3113), at the western end of the resort, comfortable, costing US$65. The **Complejo Centro Copey Oasis** (tel 6 3013) on Avenida 3 at Calle 61, is also large, price US$85. The **Villas del Mar Oasis** (tel 6 2217) is on the Carretera Las Américas, with 50 cabins and pool and tennis court, US$50.

There is some cheaper accommodation available, of which the best is the **Hotel Los Delfines** (tel 63815), set in a small block on the beachfront, 38 rooms around a small coral-rock courtyard. It has been discovered by the tour operators, but it is small and friendly. Double room in season US$40. You might also try the **Hotel Pullman** (tel 62575), on Avenida 1 at Calle 49, just 14 rooms at US$34 a double. Otherwise try the **Herradura** (tel 6 3703), with rooms and some self-catering apartments as well as a cafeteria, rooms US$40. Finally, try the **Varazul**, Ave 1 at Calle 14, about US$35 and the **Barlovento** and **Sotovento** Apartments, both of which are on the beach, double US$37. The Varadero Hotel reservation office is on Calle 20 and Ave 3. Many of the hotels hire bicycles which are convenient for getting around the flat peninsula.

There are three hotels on the **Zapata Peninsula**, of which the most distinctive is undoubtedly the **Villa Turística Guamá** (tel 2979), on the Laguna de Tesoro, a reproduction of an Arawak village, complete with thatch-roof bohíos on stilts and wooden walkways over the lagoon. It is a little isolated, but has a pool and of course a nearby crocodile farm for your amusement, US$40. Less comfortable is the **Villa Turística Playa Larga** (tel 7119). On the southern coast is the **Villa Turística Playa Girón** (tel 7610), with 130 rooms in concrete cabañas, one of which has been left, collapsed, since it was shelled in the abortive 1962 Bay of Pigs invasion. Good swimming pool, US$40.

Along the coast at **Cienfuegos**, where the most comfortable hotel is the **Jagua** (tel 6362), in the south of the town: 140 rooms with a good pool, double rooms US$50 in season. The **Pascabello** sits on the heights above the harbour mouth, pool and a good view, but 15 miles out of the town and the **Rancho Luna**, 10 miles out of Cienfuegos on the same road, has cabins on a good beach for US$40 in season. There are a couple of peso hotels in downtown Cienfuegos, of which the best is the **Hotel San Carlos**, on Avenida 56, where there are rooms with unreliable regularity.

In **Trinidad**, the **Las Cuevas Motel** sits on the hill above the town, double rooms US$40, and on the nearby beaches are the large **Hotel Ancón** (tel 2552), US$45 and the **Costa Sur**, about six miles out of the town, US$50 at an all-inclusive rate. It is difficult to get into the peso hotels in Trinidad as a foreigner, though you can try the Hotel Canada in the central square.

In **Ciego de Avila** there are a couple of dollar hotels, including the large **Hotel Ciego de Avila** (tel 2 8013) in the north of the town, with pool, a bar and a night club, double room about US$30, and the **Hotel Santiago Habana** (tel 2 5703) on the Calle Honorato del Castillo in the centre of the town, room US$30.

At **Camagüey** there are a couple of dollar hotels, of which the larger is the **Hotel Camagüey**, (tel 6218), two miles outside the town on the Carretera Central, with 140 rooms, pool and a cabaret, US$35, but far preferable is the peso **Hotel Colón** (tel 2553), set in a grand old building on Calle República. It is usually full, so you might head for the **Isla de Cuba** on Oscar Primelles. Beach resorts at **Santa Lucía** on the north coast include the 220-room **Hotel Mayanabo** (tel 8184), with a pool, bars and watersports facilities and the apartments of the smaller **Villa Tararaco** (tel 8222).

In the area of **Holguín**, the **Pernik** (tel 4 4802), large (200 rooms), but with a good pool, restaurant and friendly atmosphere, where the locals gather, US$45 per double. Otherwise try the cheaper **Motel El Bosque** (tel 4 2188) on Ave XX Aniversario, with 70 lacklustre cabins and a pool, US$30. Peso Hotels in Holgín include the **Santiago** on Calle Maceo and the **Praga** on Calle López.

On the coast to the north of Holguín, the 220-room **Hotel Guardalavaca** (tel 4 2685) is set on the stunning Guardalavaca beach, with watersports and double rooms a snip at US$35 in season. The smaller **Don Lino Beach** Hotel has good cabanas and watersports for US$15. Five miles southeast of Holguín is the **Hotel Mirador de Mayabe** (tel 4 2160), with 20 rooms and a cracking view of the valley, pool and night club, US$25. In **Bayamo** in Granma Province you will be steered towards the **Hotel Sierra Maestra** (tel 4 5013), large and ugly and US$45 for a double room.

Santiago de Cuba

Rooms in Santiago must be booked through the central reservation system, from where you will be dispatched to a dollar hotel, usually with scant regard to your stated preference—go to the **Carpeta Central** on Calle Lancret, just off Céspedes Square. It is difficult for foreigners to circumvent the system, but it is worth a try, particularly as it will be much cheaper.

The big hotels include the **Las Américas Hotel** (tel 8040), with 64 rooms, to the east of the town centre, with pool and entertainment, US$40 and slightly further out the **Motel Leningrado** (tel 29049), on the Carretera de Siboney, with a pool and nightclub, US$32. High on the hill is the **Rancho Club** (tel 3 3202), to be avoided if you do not have a car, despite the good views, because of the difficulties of getting into town, US$35.

You may prefer to base yourself in the centre, in which case try for the **Hotel Casa Granda** right on the central square. The building is an attractive old *palacio* with a busy atmosphere of locals and travellers. Cheap, US$15 for a double, if a little poky. Other local hotels include the nearby **Venus**, just behind the Casa Granda, **Imperial** on José A Saco (tel 8917), 47 small rooms and the **Rex** on Ave Victoriano Garzón, all around US$15.

If you are catching a flight you might consider going to the **Hotel del Balcón del Caribe** (9 1011), near the Morro fortress on the point, pool, US$40, or the **Motel Versalles** (tel 91016), small with 44 rooms, also in another modern construction on the airport road, with a pool and tennis court. These two are inconveniently far out of town if you want to visit Santiago.

Twenty-five miles east of Santiago is the beach hotel **Sol**, with tennis courts and other tourist facilities. In **Baracoa** you will find the renovated **Hotel Castillo** (tel 2103), with a fantastic view over the town, about US$35. On the seafront, the **Rusa** is named after a Russian woman who lived there, price about 10 pesos, and also in the town is the **Plaza**, cost 10 pesos.

On the **Isla de Juventud** there is just one dollar hotel, the **Colony** (tel 9 8282), in the bight in the southwest of the island, about 25 miles from Nueva Gerona, with 77 rooms looking over the sea, pool bars night club and watersports, US$75 a double in the winter season. You might also try the **Rancho el Tesoro** (tel 24081), about two miles out of town on the road to La Fe, no pool, or if you wish to be in the town go to **La Cubana**, on Calle 39, or the **Hotel Bamboo**, both around 15 pesos.

Cayo Largo has a number of beach hotels with pools, bars and endless watersports, reserved entirely for tourists where the dollar is the ticket. **Club Aventuras Cayo Largo** now has an all-inclusive package with reates from US$150 per couple.

EATING OUT

Of Cuba's three logistical frustrations (travel, accommodation and food), eating out is the most trying and when you go into a restaurant, you should reckon on at least an hour from arrival to payment for even the simplest meal. The menu too is often frustrating, because you will find many of the dishes not available. You will often be asked as you arrive whether you will be paying in dollars. If you are, you will be taken immediately to the front of the queue. If you are staying in a dollar tourist hotel the problems are not so bad and meals, often in self-serve cafeterias, will be available more quickly. You may even find yourself retreating into them after a while. Most large towns have a *pizzeria*, marked by the queue, the very sight of which will probably make your stomach rumble. The *coppelia* is the local ice cream parlour, same queueing system and rewarding when you finally get one.

The Cubans like to start their meals with fresh fruit—it gets the gastric juices working, they say, though supply is somewhat erratic. In Cuban cooking, outside the finest *criollo* restaurants, main meals tend to be meat and two tropical veg, which gets quite heavy on the stomach (especially crocodile meat), but it is usually welcome. Only in the top Havana restaurants will you find menus employing seafood and fish with more adventurous sauces. Coffee, referred to jokingly as 'American' if you go for English-style dishwater, is usually drunk by Cubans as Expresso, and this is available in bars on the street.

A great way to start any evening in Havana is a cocktail in the **Turquino Bar** on the top floor of the Cuba Libre Hotel. It gives a fantastic view of the city as the sun goes down. In **Old Havana** one of the best restaurants is the **Floridita** on the corner on Montserrate and Obispo, a low-lit salon hung with velvet curtains and a slightly rarefied atmosphere, specializes in fish, seafood—try the Hemingway plate of lobster, shrimp and fish in garlic sauce—and of course, daquiris, as drunk by Hemingway himself. Main course US$20–30. Another famed spot on the Hemingway trail is the **Bodeguita del Medio**, on Calle Empredado, where there is always a lively crowd, who are encouraged to sign their names on the wall, as drunken writers have since the 1940s. Ask about the chair (the upside-down one on the ceiling). Hearty creole food, *pierna de puerco asado rollo* or cooked *en su jugo*, main course US$10–20. You might also try the **Zaragazona** near the Floridita, for fish dishes and ubiquitous international fare but reasonable service. You

551

eat in an air-conditioned dining room lined with stained wood and tiles—*pavo asado al jugo* or *camarrones enchiladas*, main course US$7–15. For the setting alone, go to the **El Patio** restaurant on the Plaza de la Catedral, with a view across the cobbled square from beneath the arches and stained glass windows; *langosta enchilado* and Cuban fried chicken, main course US$8–12. There is a café downstairs on the colonnaded patio itself. On the Plaza de Armas, next to the Casa de Agua, there is another café which is good for a pit-stop—juices and cakes. Often a queue. And you will find a pizzeria in a colonial town-house on Calle Tacon, the **Don Giovanni**; pizzas and simple platters US$6–9. On the waterfront in Central Havana, try **La Ostionera**, where you can get oysters by the bucketful, which you dip in sauces provided.

In **Vedado** there are a number of restaurants outside the hotels of which the best, certainly for the view anyway, is **El Torre** in the edificio Fosca on Calle 17, quite expensive but with reliable Cuban and international fare. For more of the same you can try **La Rica** at No 102 on Calle 21, but you can always dine on rabbit at the **Conejito** down from the edificio Fosca on Calle 17. You can, of course, get an ice cream at the *coppelia* on La Rampa for a few centavos.

In **Miramar**, the best restaurant is **La Cecilia** (tel 22 6700) on 5th Ave between 110 and 112, which specializes in Cuban cuisine, food and service good, but expensive at around US$35 a head. On the waterfront just over the bridge from Vedado on the Malecón is the restaurant **1830** (tel 3 4504), set in a small and attractive *palacio* with tables inside and out, Cuban and international fare, service average. Across the harbour in the Morro Castle (beneath the Havana lighthouse) you will find a couple of good restaurants: **La Divina Pastora**, which has a fantastic view over the Malecón and the buildings of Havana—specializes in seafood, *camarrones al ajillo* (shrimp in garlic), US$15 a main course, and **Los Doces Aposteles**, at about the same price.

At the Hemingway Marina in the west of Havana there are two dollar restaurants, including **Papa's** and **Fiesta**. There is a good club at the Marina if you wish to go out dancing. At **Cojimar** in the east is the **Las Terrazas** restaurant, which has seafood on offer. Supposedly Cuba's finest restaurant, and certainly one of the most expensive, **Las Ruinas** (tel 44 3336) is in the Parque Lenin, a few miles to the south of the city. International and Cuban food of a high standard and reliable service.

In the **Pinar del Río** area the best restaurant is the upstairs dining room in the **Los Jazmines** hotel (tel 9 3205), with its stained glass windows and fantastic view over the Viñales valley. You can also get lunch not far off in the **Cueva del Indio** (tel 9 3202). In the town itself you are really dependent on the hotels. The **Castillo de las Nubes** in **Soroa** is not really recommended, but you can find food at **El Centro**.

In Matanzas, you can get a meal for pesos at the **Pekin** on Calle 83, but in **Varadero** you will have to pay in dollars everywhere, and the prices are quite high. **Mi Casita** (tel 3787) is a surprising find, on the Avenida Playa between 11 and 12. It is a charming spot, set in an old seafront villa made of coral rock, with an odd elegance in the old furniture and tropical plants. Fixed menu, lobster, chicken or steak with local vegetables, US$20. Also **El Meson de Quijote** for good Spanish food (evening only, but crowded so reserve) and **El Bodegón**, on the Ave de la Playa near Calle 40, which serves good criollo food and has a bohemian atmosphere about it. Finally you might try the nearby **Las Americas** restaurant, set in a spectacular house on the cliff in the eastern area of the peninsula.

In **Cienfuegos**, go to the **1819**, set in an old town-house on the Prado for Cuban food or the nearby **Mandarín** for Chinese dishes. Both are payable in pesos, but queues are long. If the wait is too much, you can head off to one of the dollar hotels. **Trinidad** has restaurants with a delightful setting, but with the usual problems about the food. Go to the **Guamuhaya** or the **Trinidad Colonial**, both in colonial buildings. The pizzeria is on the main square. The hotel dining rooms are also OK in this area.

The **Hotel Pernik** in Holguín has an excellent dining room, which you can hope to get into as a passer by, and even pay in pesos, but if not there are a couple of other restaurants downtown, including the **Trópico** on the Calle Libertad.

In **Santiago**, head for the **1900** restaurant (tel 23507), on Calle San Basilio, which serves criollo food in a salon of faded grandeur at about US$15 a head, or the **Taberna de Dolores** (tel 23913) on Aguilera, local food and clientele mainly. The **Pizzeria Fontana** on Lacret just down from the Parque Céspedes, serves a good pizza when supplies are in. In Baracoa, **La Punta**, at the western end of the town, is the best restaurant.

On **Cayo Largo** you will be dependent on the hotel dining rooms, but on the **Isla de Juventud** the possibilities are slightly better. In Nueva Gerona go to **El Corderito**, on Calle 39, which after its name specializes in lamb, or the **Avión**, set in an old aeroplane on Calle 41. There are one or two smaller cafés where you can pick up a drink and a snack. However, if you feel like splashing out, go to the **Hotel Colony**, quite a way from town to the southwest.

JAMAICA

Everyone has an image of Jamaica: the island idyll of palms and beaches, a hedonist's paradise of rum, reefers and reggae rhythm, a fantastically beautiful tropical garden. It is often considered to be a little threatening. But Jamaica's allure is the strongest of all the Caribbean islands.

Jamaica lies south of Cuba and, at 4411 square miles, it is the third largest of the Greater Antilles and about half the size of Wales. It is so mountainous that parts are barely accessible. The coastline rises immediately into mountains, and within a few hundred yards of the sea you can be at 1000 ft (about two-fifths of the island is above this height). Starting in the east are the John Crow and Blue Mountains, and from there the peaks continue west along the spine of the island to the Cockpit Country, a moonscape of forested limestone hillocks, and to the west coast. The island is immensely fertile.

On a map Jamaica may look as though it languishes like a turtle, but nothing could be further from the truth as far as the Jamaicans themselves are concerned. About 2.4 million Jamaicans live on the island (more than this number live elsewhere in the world). The streets are something of a theatre, the liveliest and most compelling in the British Caribbean as the Jamaicans shout and quip with one another. Markets, from downtown Kingston to the three or four people selling fruit at the roadside, are mayhem. The Jamaicans do not suffer authority or formality gladly (queueing died soon after the British left) and they are very forward; some stop you to give advice or to say hello, others to hustle you.

Jamaica has always been exuberant and at times slightly rough, but the reports that call it unsafe are ill-founded, as long as you use as much care as you would in any poor country. Occasionally the fervour spills over into violence, but this is rarely directed against foreigners. Avoid Kingston at election time when political tensions are at their highest.

Jamaica became independent from Britain on 6 August 1962, but the echoes of three centuries of British colonial rule still ring through. Churches and Georgian great houses were constructed by the planters in the style of buildings at home, and clock chimes sound as they do in Britain. Jamaica has moved on since Independence, but many British institutions remain in creolized form, including the Westminster model of democracy and the belts, peaked caps and serge trousers of uniformed policemen.

And yet things are never quite as they seem. The Jamaican marching bands may wear scarlet tunics with trimmings of gold braid, but their movements are not the clipped and formal procession of the British, they have the rhythmic swagger of the Jamaican. Cricket is still played in whites, but it has developed its own, typically West Indian, expression and is now thrown back at the English with a vengeance.

Many visitors to Jamaica go for the sun, sea and the ganja, but beyond the beach Jamaica has a special appeal which over the centuries has attracted men as diverse as Henry Morgan and Noel Coward. Tropical paradise or tricky destination, Jamaica offers the most romantic liaison with the Caribbean.

Suggested Itinerary

You can make a good tour around Jamaica in a couple of weeks (the longer the better); this will give you some time in the well known tourist resorts as well as a look at something more Jamaican, the magnificent interior of the island and maybe Kingston. Whether you arrive in Kingston or in Montego Bay, you can follow the coastline. Stay a few days either in Montego Bay or Ocho Rios, until you get the urge to look beyond the beaches and bars. Go east to Port Antonio, a charming and laid-back town in the far northeast, the lushest and most strikingly fertile area of the island. From here, you might make a visit to the John Crow mountains. Alternatively, go to the Blue Mountains from Kingston, when you have made your way to the south coast. The capital will also show you the Jamaicans' Jamaica—check out the markets downtown and make a ferry trip over to Port Royal. From here you should head west to the sleepy towns of Treasure Beach and Black River, where the Jamaicans themselves take their holidays. Leave enough time for Negril, which is a tourist town with a difference; great for a few days' 'hanging out' waiting for the sunset and the flight home. An alternative way of crossing the island is to take the train from Montego Bay to Kingston, a six-hour ride through the fantastically beautiful centre.

History

There are thought to have been 100,000 Arawaks living on Jamaica when Columbus arrived on 5 May 1494, on his second voyage. He went to investigate reports of gold on *Xamayca* (the land of 'Wood and Water'), as the Indians knew the island. To him it was the 'fairest isle that eyes ever beheld; the land seems to touch the sky . . .'. There was no gold and so he left. It was another nine years before he returned, on his fourth voyage, washed up here after exploration of the Central American coast, his ships worm-eaten and unfit for the Atlantic crossing. They sank off St Ann's Bay and the Admiral was stranded for a year before he was rescued (two of his sailors braved the high seas and the Indians in a canoe and paddled to Hispaniola, from where they fetched him).

Spaniards came to Jamaica to settle the island in 1510 and initially the island was used to supply the senior colony on Hispaniola (now the Dominican Republic). Colonization was a failure, but it succeeded in wiping out the Arawaks within 100 years. They were worked as slaves, killed for sport and tortured to death, and they died like flies from European diseases.

The Spaniards' first town, Sevilla la Nueva, was on the north coast, near St Ann's Bay, but it proved to be an unhealthy spot, so the town was moved to the south coast. St Jago de la Vega (now Spanish Town) became their principal settlement. They planted some crops, but their main occupation was the farming of pigs for the fat and the hides. The colony was neglected in favour of Havana and the mainland coast and, facing regular attack by pirates in which hard-won wealth could disappear overnight, it languished for 150 years until the British arrived in 1655.

Little remains of Spain's influence on Jamaica apart from a few names now, but in the hills, the *cimarróns*, later known as the maroons (initially slaves armed and set free by the Spanish to attack the British), were to have an effect on Jamaican life until the 19th century.

With the arrival of the British, a base opened up in Port Royal for the *buccaneers*, where they would repair their ships and sell their loot. In time of peace these 'brethren of the coast' could not be officially approved because they ran too fine a line between freebooting and piracy, but when the islands were at war, they were an invaluable fighting force. Port Royal received its come-uppance in 1692 when it was destroyed in an earthquake (see p. 574).

The pirates continued to plague the coasts though, and the likes of Charles Vane, Blackbeard (a natty dresser who would go into battle with lit fuses in his hair), 'Calico' Jack Rackham (supposedly called so because of his penchant for calico underclothes) and his women pirates Anne Bonney and Mary Read, would use the bays along the coast to drink captured rum and to refit their ships before setting off again on the high sea.

But at the same time, Jamaica was growing into Britain's wealthiest colony in the West Indies. Every available piece of land was planted as the island became a massive sugar factory and for a while, Jamaica was the largest sugar producer in the world. The planters and merchants at any rate enjoyed immense wealth and they built their great houses on the estates and town houses in the capital. The whole venture depended on a massive workforce, made up of slaves from Africa, shipped in to the market in Kingston. The slaves were subjected to brutal treatment in what was a cruel age and the estates were run on the basis of mutual fear. The planters maintained their law with a rod of iron and with a liberal use of the whip, while always living in the fear that the slaves would rebel, which from time to time they did.

Some slaves ran away to the mountains and formed communities of *maroons*, hunting pigs and planting a few crops, and descending from the hills at night to attack the plantations, torching the fields and stealing cattle. They settled in townships in the Cockpit Country and in the mountains of the east and became expert at defending themselves from the raiding parties sent out against them. They fought a guerrilla war and would disguise themselves with jungle foliage, ambushing the routes through the hills and then filtering away into the forest. Led by men such as Cudjoe, Accompong and Cuffee (and the woman maroon Nanny, one of Jamaica's national heroes), they eventually forced the government to sue for peace, and in 1739 the maroons were granted an area of land to themselves, in which they would not be disturbed. In return they promised to cease hostilities against the plantations and to return runaway slaves. A treaty was also made with the maroon leader Quao in the Blue Mountains in the east.

The maroons were quiet for half a century, but the slaves themselves revolted. Tacky's Rebellion took place in 1760 as a band of Coromantee slaves broke into a fort and stole arms and ammunition, attacked a few plantations and then took to the hills. Tacky was killed by one of the maroons who had been called out against them, and his followers committed suicide rather than surrender, but revolts broke out all over the island and it was months before the old order was reimposed.

In 1795, when the French Revolution had an explosive effect on the French colony of Saint Domingue, and the slaves took over the country in open revolt, a second maroon war broke out in Jamaica. This time 300 of them held out against 4500 trained troops and militia, once again waging a guerrilla war against the government and torching estates. Tracker dogs were brought from Cuba to find them and the maroons knew their time was up. Under the terms of the treaty they should have been allowed to settle elsewhere on the island, but the majority were deported to Nova Scotia and then eventually shipped to Sierra Leone.

At the beginning of the 19th century the abolitionist movement was gaining ground in Britain, and despite the objections of the West Indian planters, the slave trade was banned in 1808. Slave laws were passed in Britain but the planters refused to institute them. Unrest continued on the island, and Jamaica erupted in another massive revolt in 1831. It was led by Sam 'Daddy' Sharpe, who has since become another of Jamaica's national heroes. He was hanged for his action, but it was enough for Parliament in London to force the Emancipation Act for all the West Indian islands in 1834. There was a period of 'apprenticeship' for four years, in which the slaves were tied to the plantations, but in 1838 the slaves were set free unconditionally.

They left the estates and took plots of land where they could find them and turned to subsistence agriculture. With the help of Baptists, Methodists and other missionaries, who had sided with the slaves against the planters, they formed free villages (one called Wilberforce after the leading abolitionist). For their part, the planters fared badly, despite waves of immigrant workers (East Indians mainly, but also some voluntary Africans), and steadily the sugar industry declined.

The pressure for political change came soon after the slaves were freed. Their cause was adopted by men like the mulatto lawyer George William Gordon and the preacher, Paul Bogle. Matters came to a head under Governor Eyre and in 1865 there was a rebellion in Morant Bay in the southeast of the island, led by Bogle. The riot was put down brutally. The blame for it was laid at Gordon's door and he was hanged. Bogle was hunted down and he was tried in Morant Bay, where he was sentenced and hanged in the arch of the Court House where his rebellion had taken place. Statues of him stand at the Court House today and in National Heroes Park. Eyre was recalled and dismissed from the colonial service, but his last act was to get the Jamaican Assembly to vote its own demise and give power to the Colonial Office in London. In 1872 the capital was removed to Kingston.

In the 20th century as the original plantocracy declined, more black and mulatto Jamaicans began to be elected to the local Assemblies and to enter the civil service. Changes were particularly influenced by another Jamaican national hero, Marcus Mosiah Garvey.

Garvey was born in St Ann's Bay in 1887 and as he travelled around the Americas he resolved to unite the African race and to better their situation in the white-ruled world. In 1914 he founded the Universal Negro Improvement Association, which by the 1920s had become an international movement, with offices all over the Americas, in African countries, and even as far off as Australia. They were all linked with the newspaper, the *Negro World*. The UNIA ran successful businesses and banks and a shipping line, the Black Star Line (after the White Star Line), in competition with the whites. There was even an aim to go 'back to Africa', to create a model state in which the blacks could be proud. Garvey's ideas helped to define the Jamaican faith of Rastafari.

Garvey became a champion of the blacks everywhere because he brought them pride and self-respect in a way that had never been possible under colonial rule, but he was generally disliked by the white establishment and in 1922 he served a jail-term in the States for supposed fraud. He returned to Jamaica in 1927 and set out aims for a political party in 1929. In 1935 he moved his offices to London. Garvey had had a profound effect on Jamaica and blacks all over the world and he set the pattern for Jamaican politics for the coming years. Though his movement was eclipsed after his death in London in 1940, his remains were flown back in triumph to Jamaica in 1964. He was proclaimed the country's first national hero soon afterwards.

Pressure for political change grew ever stronger in the 1930s, in the wake of the Depression. There were riots all over the Caribbean in 1938 and soon after this, the Jamaican trade unions and then political parties were born. The two leaders who emerged were the flamboyant Alexander Bustamante, later leader of the Jamaica Labour Party (JLP) and Norman Manley of the People's National Party (PNP). In 1944 adult suffrage for all Jamaicans was introduced, the first in the Caribbean, and in 1957 cabinet government and full internal autonomy were granted. In a referendum put to them by Bustamante in 1961, the Jamaicans decided not to remain in the West Indies Federation, and within the year they had taken Independence, the first British Caribbean island to do so, on 6 August 1962.

After Independence, politics continued to be dominated by these two men, who are also Jamaican national heroes. The PNP, now lead by P. J. Patterson, and the JLP (leader Edward Seaga) are the main parties to this day. The Jamaican Parliament is made up of a 60-member House of Representatives, elected every five years, and a smaller Senate, to which members are appointed on the advice of the Prime Minister and leader of the opposition. The country remains within the Commonwealth and the Queen is represented by the Governor General, at present Sir Howard Cooke. The Judiciary is based on British law and the highest court of appeal is the Privy Council in London.

Elections in Jamaica tend to be somewhat traumatic, despite efforts to calm them in recent years (the violence for which Jamaica has gained a reputation is mainly political) and they are always hard, if not entirely honourably, fought. The 1980 election was extremely bloody (500 people died) and it returned the JLP, led by Edward Seaga with a massive majority. He followed monetarist policies that reversed the decade of left-inclined government from the PNP under Michael Manley. But no Jamaican leader has stayed in office for three consecutive terms and in 1989, Michael Manley was re-elected on a less radical ticket than before. In early 1992 Michael Manley resigned his leadership and P.J. Patterson took over.

The Economy

The three most important sectors of the Jamaican economy are mining of bauxite (which provides alumina for aluminium), agriculture, and increasingly tourism. Agriculture is the largest employer at around 35% (about half of Jamaica's population lives in rural areas) and export crops include sugar, bananas, coffee and cocoa. Since the drop-off in the 1970s, tourism has increased over the last 10 years and it is now the largest foreign exchange earner.

The best known unofficial export earner in Jamaica is, of course, marijuana, and at one stage this was thought to top all others. Recently, however, with the assistance of the United States DEA, there has been a heavy clampdown. The Jamaican farmers say they can no longer grow whole fields of the stuff (the helicopter pilots can spot their plantations a mile off), but they still reckon to be able to grow it in hedgerows and in areas of thick vegetation.

Rastafari and Revivalism

Jamaica has a proliferation of religions, including the Baptist and Methodist Churches, as well as Islam and Judaism—many of them introduced by missionaries in colonial times, others adapted by the slaves from their African beliefs, but perhaps the most recognizable outside the country is the Rastafari belief. It is known for its dreadlocks and reggae music and also for its connection with ganja (there are many opportunist pseudo-rastas around the tourist areas in Jamaica), but it is less appreciated for the quiet and peaceful ideals that its true adherents follow, in fear of Jah (God).

Rastafari was born in the 30s at the time of Marcus Garvey and his ideas of black self-respect. His rejection of the white world clearly had its effect on the religion. The rastas were brought to 'Babylon' by the white man (they think of themselves as one of the lost tribes of Israel), and their aim was eventual return to Africa. Their spiritual leader was the Emperor of Ethiopia Haile Selassie, or *Ras* (prince) *Tafari* (to be feared), King of Kings, Lord of Lords, the Conquering Lion of Judah. He was the Black Messiah and his Kingdom was the Promised Land. He died in 1975, but is still revered by the rastas, who do not believe that he is dead.

There are different rasta sects, but as a rule genuine rastas are gentle people who follow their avowed beliefs of 'peace and love'. They are vegetarians, and many are herbalists living in the mountains; many are teetotal and do not smoke tobacco. They do regard ganja as sacred and the 'chalice' (pipe), as it is known, is supposed to bring inner wisdom.

There are a number of semi-religious sects in Jamaica, part Christian, part animist, with a view of the spirit world not dissimilar to the voodoo of Haiti. The best known are *pocomania*, *kumina* and *Revival Zion*. They are particularly strong in the countryside and

558

some involve ceremonies with drumming and dancing to drums, with the eventual possession of one of the participants by the spirits. *Obeah* is another system of beliefs in which individuals are able to affect the outcome of their lives. Quite a lot of Jamaicans believe in *duppies* and *deads* (the ghosts of people who have died, but who are not at peace), some of whom remain in conflict with the living over issues dating from their lifetime.

Jamaican Music—Ska, Reggae and Dancehall

Visitors joke that the Jamaicans switch the roll of their gait as they walk the street, passing each successive shop and its stereo system. This is not far from the truth, as music is played everywhere, constantly and almost always at high volume. Buses are like mobile discotheques, usually audible before they come into view, and out in the country you can see a stack of speakers higher than the bar that has the stereo.

Mento tended to be slow and rhythmic, and would traditionally be jokingly rude about life and love, but it was overtaken by *ska* in the early 1960s. Ska is a riotous and often compulsive beat in which the strains of danceable *rocksteady* are audible. Like the steel pans of Trinidad, these sounds came from the yards of downtown Kingston and were disapproved of initially by the authorities, but they are an elemental expression of Jamaica and unique in their inventiveness.

Reggae developed in the 1970s as singers like Jimmy Cliff and, of course, Bob Marley and the Wailers began to have their success on the island. It was not until around the time of his death in May 1981 that Robert Marley and more generally reggae gained international fame. Other leading groups and singers incude Toots and the Maytals, Burning Spear, Third World, Black Uhuru, Peter Tosh and Gregory Isaacs. And abroad, among the large expatriate Jamaican community in Britain, reggae groups, including Steel Pulse, flourished.

And like many other Caribbean rhythms, *dancehall*, the current popular reggae beat, addresses the issues of the day, from sex to corruption (a fair dose of the former, which are known as slack songs), although it is nigh incomprehensible unless you can understand *patois*. *Dancehall* is a compulsive and monotonous rap rhythm grafted on to the original reggae beat, and it has become the leading sound in Jamaica today. You will hear it everywhere—from tiny portable radios to the vast sound-systems in the nightclubs. Its rhythm makes it danceable, but it is the lyrics, often rude or controversial, that make it so popular. There are *singers* (who tend to be slower and more melodic) and *DJs*, who rap their lyrics to a number of established rhythms (cherry-o, scandal, taxi). Leading DJs include Shabba Ranks, Yellowman, Ninjaman and Admiral Tibbet.

The central date of the reggae calendar is the annual **Reggae Sunsplash Festival**, which takes place in July or August in Montego Bay. It is a six-day bonanza of reggae, featuring individual singers, dancehall and big bands. It is a fun event, more like a day at the races than a concert in the European style, with games being played at the rumshops and stalls that line the back of the concert area. Reggae artists from all over the world come to it and they play a set of around five or six songs, so you see about 20 performers in a night. It usually gets started at about 10 pm and goes on until dawn, and beyond.

You get a good idea of Jamaican music from just wandering around the streets of Kingston, but to see it Jamaican-style, you have to get out into the concerts and clubs.

You may find a world-famous band playing to a crowd of just a few hundred here. (The tourist hotels tend to play calypso, which comes from Trinidad and Barbados at the other end of the Caribbean anyway.) During the day you can listen to non-stop reggae on *Irie FM* (105.5 or 107.7). Any club or record shop will sell you a cassette of the latest tunes.

Jerk

Jerk is a special Jamaican way of barbecuing seasoned meats slowly over a wood fire set in the ground. The technique was supposedly developed by the maroons, runaways who lived in the mountains in the 18th century, who would cure meat for sale. Traditionally they would kill early in the week and cook it in an underground oven for a couple of days before taking it to market on Friday or Saturday. Meat is 'jerked' all over the island now, but the home of jerk is Boston Bay, beneath the John Crow Mountains in Portland parish in the east, where the maroons lived. There are a number of shacks at the roadside, where they start to cook early in the morning—don't arrive after about 4 pm or it will all be gone.

Jerk Centres are among the best local Jamaican restaurants. Despite their name, they are not for the socially ungainly (there are even Executive jerk centres), but a place where you order jerk (pork, chicken, 'spear ribs', sausage and even fish), which you eat with a special sauce and with a festival, a sweet and heavy cassava roll. As you order, the cook will suddenly pull out a machete before you and proceed to chop the food into bite-size pieces and throw it on to a piece of paper. You will then be asked if you want hot pepper sauce. Try one tiny dash on a corner of the meal on your first time out, because Jamaican hot pepper sauce has a vicious and searing scourge and a habit of affecting everything edible for miles around.

Flora and Fauna

From its wet and mountainous northeast corner where the jumble of the John Crow Mountains and Blue Mountains soar to thousands of feet, Jamaica's stunningly beautiful countryside descends through dwarf and montane forest, where mahogany and mahoe trees are grappled by creeping vines, lianas and ferns, and through hilltop coffee and spice plantations, where you will see miles of overgrown telephone wires, down into the immensely fertile banana plots in the rich red earth of the lower hills and on to the sugar flats. In the southwest of the island, the rainfall is low (by Jamaican standards), and you will find the Great Morasses of Black River and Negril, acreages of swampland covered with mangroves.

The national tree is the mahoe and the national flower, which also grows on a tree, is the lignum vitae (the wood of life). There are, of course, endless palms, from the magnificent royal palm, which grows to over 100 ft, to the typical seafront coco palms that lean out over the beach into the sunset. Jamaica has many botanical gardens, some of them left to decline into riotous growth, but most worth visiting even for botanical novitiates, excellent for escaping the hustle and bustle of the towns for a while. They were set up in order to encourage Jamaica's agricultural development for most of the food crops were brought in to Jamaica, from the breadfruit shipped by Bligh to the mango from the south seas. The Jamaicans all keep flowering gardens too, so you will constantly see bougainvillaea and hibiscus reaching out into the road. Even the traditional farmer's hedge, made with quick-stick (called so because it takes from just a cutting placed in the ground) comes out in a riot of lavender blooms.

With the extraordinary variety of terrain and vegetation comes an equal diversity of bird life, with over 250 species during the year; 25 of these are endemic and about half are migratory. In the heights you may hear the mournful solitaire, or see the Jamaican eleania or the Blue Mountain vireo and a handful of warblers. In the lower mountains are hosts of grackles and grassquits, the Jamaican euphonia and woodpecker and two rare parrots, yellow-billed and black-billed. The Jamaica nightingale sings at dawn and sunset. You will also see hummingbirds, including the Jamaican national bird, the doctorbird, or red-billed streamertail, whose forked tail is about twice as long as his emerald green body. The smallest bird on the island is the tiny vervain or bee humming-bird. The Jamaican tody, called robin redbreast, is odd because it lays its eggs at the end of a 2-ft tunnel underground. Among the lilies and aerial roots of the mangroves in the morasses are gallinules and green-backed herons, and whistling ducks. Offshore you may see sooty and noddy terns.

The animal life is not so varied, though there are many reptiles, ranging from the crocodiles of the Black River swamp and the Jamaican boa (rarely seen), which grows up to 15 ft in length, to the tiny geckos that find their way on to the ceiling. The snoring frog is the second largest tree frog in the world and there are many other varieties to be heard chirruping at different altitudes. The iguana was thought to be near extinction, but some have been sighted in the Hellshire Hills up to seven feet long. The few rodents include jutia, but this is rare. Manatees, lumbering great walrus-like creatures without tusks, are occasionally sighted off the south coast and turtles come to the island. Some terrapins live in the rivers.

GETTING TO JAMAICA

The main airport for tourist arrivals in Jamaica is the Donald Sangster Airport in **Montego Bay,** which serves the resort towns of Negril, Montego Bay, Runaway Bay and Ocho Rios. If you are travelling on to Port Antonio or to Kingston itself you should fly to the Norman Manley airport just outside Kingston. Long haul scheduled flights often make a stop at both airports. The National carrier is Air Jamaica. You need an onward or return ticket to get into the country and there is a departure tax of J$200.

By Air
From Europe: Direct flights to Jamaica from Europe include the Air Jamaica and British Airways Joint Service from London and Lufthansa from Düsseldorf. There are charter flights from Holland, Switzerland, Italy and also from Britain.
From the USA: Direct scheduled flights on either Air Jamaica or American Airways reach Jamaica from Atlanta (1 or 2 per week), Baltimore (twice weekly), Los Angeles (twice a week), Miami (plenty each day), New York (several flights daily, also on Continental), Orlando (twice weekly) and Washington (daily). Most connections from South America are made via Miami, from where there are at least six flights a day into Kingston and Montego Bay.
From Canada: There is a daily scheduled service on either Air Jamaica or Air Canada

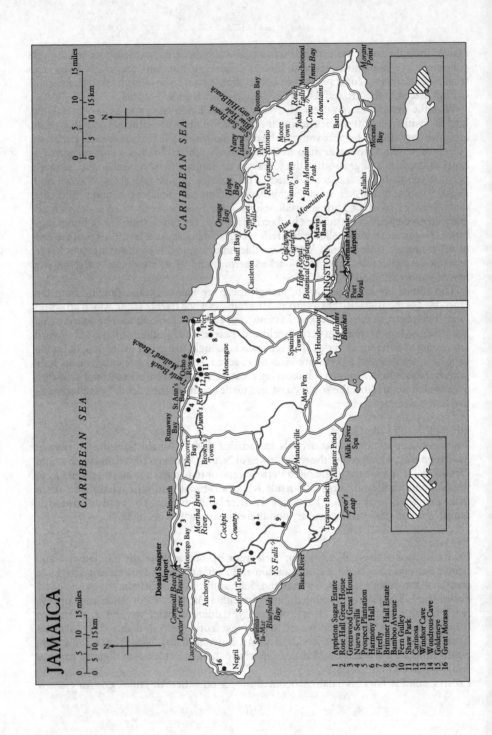

from Toronto to Kingston, sometimes stopping at Montego Bay, a weekly service from Montreal to Montego Bay and a multitude of charter flights.

From other Caribbean Islands: Flights from other Caribbean islands tend to fly into Kingston rather than Montego Bay. There are a couple of flights a day from Grand Cayman on either Air Jamaica or Cayman Airways (also stopping at Montego Bay), a weekly flight to Nassau in the Bahamas and a twice-weekly flight to Havana in Cuba on Cubana (there are also charter flights from Montego Bay to Cuba). There are links with San Juan, Puerto Rico (daily), Sint Maarten (once a week), Antigua (4 times a week), Port of Spain in Trinidad (daily on BWIA, which flies a lot of the links) and Curaçao (4 times a week, Air Jamaica or ALM).

GETTING AROUND JAMAICA
Within the large towns, particularly Kingston, there is a good **bus** system (minibuses and larger), which will give you an excellent exposure to Jamaican life. They are noisy (a relentless pulse on the stereo), and usually crowded. If you are sitting, you may well find that a 'standee' hands you their bag to hold. In Kingston, many buses run to and from the Parade in the downtown area. If in doubt about which bus to take, ask a fellow passenger, or one of the lads with dollar notes folded around their fingers (and then expect to be hustled aboard). In town the buses will stop only at official stops. Fare J$2–4; they run until 6.30 pm. There is a bus service (roughly every half hour) from the airport to the Parade, downtown. You can also flag down the cars, share taxis, which run the same routes for the same fare.

If you wish to travel **beyond Kingston**, out on the island, the limited number of government coaches are supplemented by endless private minivans (more mobile stereo systems). Buses seem to run every road on the island, eventually. It is best to travel in the morning, but they run until dusk. Check the fare as you get on, though you may not actually hand over the money until later in the journey. In the country, flag buses down from the side of the road with a frantic wave.

Buses to towns on the north coast leave from downtown **Kingston**, west along Beckford Street from the Parade. Fare to Port Antonio—J$45, Ocho Rios—J$45 and Montego Bay—J$60. For Spanish Town and Mandeville (J$25), go to the station at Half Way Tree.

In **Montego Bay**, north coast buses leave from below Sam Sharpe Square, towards the waterfront and by the craft market. To Ocho Rios—J$30. Buses for Negril—J$20, leave from Creek St.

In **Negril**, buses leave from near the roundabout at the southern end of the beach, over the bridge from the crafts market, in **Ocho Rios** from the clocktower off from the roundabout that leads up to Fern Gully and to Kingston; and in **Port Antonio** on the foreshore road behind the Bank of Nova Scotia. In **Mandeville** they leave from beneath the church on the main square.

Hitch-hiking in Jamaica is usually a bit slow, but is acceptable if you're on for an adventure. To signal to a driver point repeatedly and rapidly at the ground and shout.

Taxis are readily available in Jamaica, through any hotel lobby if you cannot find one yourself, which is pretty unlikely around the tourist areas. Steel yourself to run the gauntlet as you emerge from the airport. The Tourist Board sets a standard fare, posted in JUTA taxis. With the others, bargain. Taxis are not usually metered in Jamaica and so you are advised to settle the fare before you set off, making sure of the currency. All licensed taxis have the red PPV plates. Some sample fares are: New Kingston—downtown J$50, to Port Royal—J$130. **Norman Manley Kingston Airport** to New Kingston—J$200, downtown—J$150. From **Donald Sangster International Airport** (Montego Bay) to Doctor's Cave Beach area and downtown—J$70, Rose Hall area—J$150. Some restaurants will send a car to pick you up and return you to your hotel if you request. There are **taxistands** at the following numbers: Mo Bay (Montego Bay) (tel 952 0521), Ocho Rios (tel 974 2971) and Port Antonio (tel 993 3144).

Many of the taxi drivers make good **tour guides** if you wish to take a ride to the local sights or up into the hills. Any hotel lobby will find a driver for you; the going rate is J$500 per hour, which makes a reasonable price when divided between four.

Jamaica is very well served with organized **tours**—there is endless information in the hotel lobbies. Among the classic spots are Rose Hall Great House, Dunn's River Falls, Fern Gully and rafting on the Rio Grande or the Martha Brae (all of them crowded but OK nonetheless). There is also a large variety of tours that go into the mountainous interior and the lesser known towns and plantations. From Montego Bay you can try the Appleton Estate Rum Tour (tel 952 3692), the Hilton High Day Tour, most days (tel 952 3343) and a tour to the Maroon country and Accompong near Cockpit Country (tel 952 4546). Just out of Ocho Rios, you can visit Prospect Plantation (tel 974 2058). Tour companies operating out of the tourist towns include, in **Montego Bay**: Glamour Tours (tel 952 0640), Forsythe's (tel 952 0394) and Greenlight (tel 952 2650); and **Ocho Rios**: Blue Danube Tours (tel 974 2031) and JUTA (tel 974 2292), who are also in Port Antonio (tel 993 2684). Tours can be arranged very easily through the hotel lobbies.

Many of these tours are a little tame and so if you want to look at Jamaica in more depth there are organisations who are able to tailor-make tours for you. SENSE, PO Box 216, Kingston 7 (tel 927 2097, fax 926 0727) can arrange tours as varied as a river-canoeing trip, an architectural tour or even a jam session in a Trenchtown yard.

A **train** links Montego Bay and Kingston, stopping at Magotty, Mandeville (Williams-field) and Spanish Town. The journey takes about six hours, twice daily, and passes through the most fantastic Jamaican scenery. The Kingston station (tel 922 6620) is downtown, at the western end of Barry St, to the southwest of the Parade and in Montego Bay the station (tel 952 4842) is south of the town, off Barnett St.

You can **fly** to a number of towns on the island. There are regular scheduled flights between Kingston (Tinson Pen airport) and Montego Bay and the other tourist areas. Contact Trans Jamaican airlines: tel 952 5401 in Montego Bay, tel 923 8680 in Kingston, tel 974 3254 in Ocho Rios and tel 993 2405 in Port Antonio. Fares from **Kingston** to Mo Bay—US$40 ($60 return), to Negril—US$45 ($65), Ocho Rios or Port Antonio—US$38 ($45). You can take a sight-seeing flight over the Cockpit Country from Donald Sangster airport in Montego Bay for about US$40 and in Ocho Rios you can even go sight-seeing by helicopter. Helitours (tel 974 2265), call a couple of days in advance.

Car hire: the Jamaicans joke that you buy the car each time you hire one because it's so expensive. However, if you can afford it, it is well worth having one to explore the mountain roads and the successive headlands and bays. There are plenty of hire cars available, but it is still a good idea to arrange a few days ahead in season.

564

The Jamaicans are pretty awful drivers and the roads are notorious for being pot-holed. Avoid driving in downtown Kingston except for sport. It is chaotic and the Jamaicans perform some remarkable manoeuvres in their constant hurry. Driving on the high roads is correspondingly more dangerous, as all the same manoeuvres are performed at high speed. The country is not that well sign-posted, so take a good map (easily available from the hire companies and the Tourist Board). Driving happens, mainly, on the left. Finally, watch out for goats and cows.

A driving licence from home is acceptable, minimum age 25. Take a credit card for the hefty deposit. There are many hire companies, with a variety of different contracts—read yours. The Jamaica U-Drive Association represents a number of car-hire companies with a standard code of business and rates. You can get their list at the Tourist Board offices. Reckon on rental of around US$60 for the smallest car for a single day with reductions for a week's hire. There are other smaller, local enterprises which offer lower rates.

All the big hire companies have offices at the **Montego Bay** airport: Avis (tel 952 4543), Budget (tel 952 5061), Hertz (tel 952 4472) and Island (tel 952 5771). Caribbean Car Rentals can be reached on tel 952 0664, and Anna Car Rentals on tel 952 3274, and there are a number of local companies along Sunset Ave, the road into town from the airport, including Sun Island (tel 952 3322) and Central (tel 952 1982). In **Negril** there are a couple of firms at the airstrip or you could try the Rite Rate Rent a Car (957 4267).

In **Ocho Rios** contact Avis on (tel 974 2641) on Main Street, or Budget (tel 974 2178), Caribbean (tel 974 2513) and National (tel 974 2266), and in **Port Antonio** try Dollar (tel 993 2625) or Eastern Rent a Car (tel 993 3624). The big firms are represented in **Kingston**, at the Norman Manley airport and in town, Avis (tel 924 8013) or on Haining Rd (926 3690), Dollar (tel 924 8462) and on Knutsford Blvd in New Kingston (tel 926 1535), Island (tel 926 8861) and at the airport (tel 924 8075). Caribbean Car Rental are on 926 6339.

For the very brave and for PHDs (pot hole dodgers), there are **mopeds** and **motor-bikes** for hire in all the tourist areas. Drive defensively, and be prepared to get off the road in a hurry. Make sure to get hold of a helmet somehow. They are quite expensive, at around US$35 a day for a motorbike and $12 for a bicycle.

TOURIST INFORMATION
The Jamaica Tourist Board has offices in:
UK: 111 Gloucester Place, London W1H 3PH (tel (071) 224 0505, fax 224 0551).
Germany: Schmidstrasse 12, 6000 Frankfurt am Main 1 (tel 069 75 800317).
France: c/o Target International, 595 Ave Champs Elysées, 75008 Paris (tel 01 45 61 90 58, fax 42 25 66 40).
Italy: c/o Sergat Italia, Piazza dei Cenci 7A, 00186 Rome (tel 06 686 9112).
USA: 801 2nd Ave, 20th Floor, New York, NY 10017 (tel (212) 688 7650, fax 856 9730).
Canada: 1 Eglington Ave East, Suite 616 Toronto, Ontario M4P 3A1 (tel 416 482 7850, fax 482 1730).

In **Jamaica** itself there are offices in Kingston, the Tourism Centre in New Kingston, at 21 Dominica Drive, PO Box 360, Kingston 5 (tel 929 9200, fax 929 9375), and at the airport (tel 924 8024). In Montego Bay the office is north of the town, near Cornwall

Beach (tel 952 4425) and another in Donald Sangster airport. In Negril they are in Adrija Plaza (tel 957 4243), in Ocho Rios in the Ocean Village Shopping Centre close to Turtle Beach (tel 974 2570), Port Antonio at the City Centre Plaza (tel 993 3051) and in Mandeville, 21 Ward Ave (tel 962 1072). You will also find a posse of small octagonal tourist information booths around the main towns, with helpful staff.

The principal Jamaican newspaper is the *Daily Gleaner*, released in the morning. The same company, a formidable Jamaican institution, puts out *The Star* in the afternoon. The Jamaican tourist publications are quite good, with current events as well as advice on shopping opportunities. Try *The Visitor*.

In a medical **emergency**, you may find that there is a doctor on call to the larger hotels. If not, contact the University Hospital in **Kingston**, Mona campus in the east of the town (tel 927 6621), the Cornwall Regional Hospital in **Montego Bay**, in Mt Salem behind the main town (tel 952 5100) and in **Port Antonio** there is the General Hospital on Naylor's Hill (tel 993 2646).

The **IDD code** for Jamaica is (809), followed by a 7-digit number. On island, you should prefix a zero if you are dialling long-distance; for local calls just dial the seven digits.

The British High Commission is at 26 Trafalgar Road, Kingston 5, in New Kingston (tel 926 9050). The American Embassy is in the Jamaica Mutual Life Centre building, 2 Oxford Rd (tel 926 4220) and the Canadian High Commission is on Knutsford Boulevard, both in New Kingston.

MONEY
The currency of Jamaica is the Jamaican dollar (J$), which fluctuates on the international exchange. At present it exchanges at a rate of about US$1 = J$25 or Sterling £1 = J$40. US dollars are not legal tender in Jamaica. You will certainly need some Jamaican dollars for getting about on the buses and for a patty and a skyjuice at the roadside. Travel in Jamaica has become considerably cheaper (and life for the Jamaicans more expensive) since the Jamaican dollar was floated. There are foreign exchange desks in most of the hotels, at the airports and in many of the banks.

Occasionally you will be offered a black market rate on the streets, but as it is only marginally better than the bank rate, it is not worth the attendant risks. Jamaican officialdom is quite strict about exchange. Keep your receipts if you want to change Jamaican dollars back into another currency on departure.

Tourist activities tend to be linked with the US dollar, and you can pay for restaurant and hire bills with a credit card or traveller's cheques. These are accepted all over the tourist areas and in the shops in Kingston, though places have started to charge for exchange on traveller's cheques. The going rate for tipping is 10–15%.

Banks are open Mon–Thurs, 9–2 and Fri 9–noon and 2.30–5. **Shopping** hours are weekdays, 8–4 and Sat, 8–1, but if you are looking to score duty-free bargains then hours in the hotel boutiques and in-bond warehouses are extended for your leisure and pleasure.

TRAVELLERS' ADVICE
Particularly as a new arrival, you will be accosted by higglers (street vendors) and hustlers on the street in Kingston and on the beaches in the main tourist areas, and you will be

asked to buy goods and then offered a whole inventory of services. Until you get a tan or learn to 'give them the eye', they can be quite persistent.

While travelling in Jamaica, take the same precautions you would in the cities of any foreign country, and be wary. Do not flash a full wallet around or hang an arm with a bracelet out of a bus window. You are advised not to walk around downtown Kingston alone after dark. If you wish to go to an area you think might be dodgy, you can always get a Jamaican to go with you.

The Jamaican authorities have a strong disapproval of illegal **drugs** and they nobble offenders from time to time (there are quite a few foreigners serving time in Jamaica for drug possession). In practice, you will be offered almost anything by the beach hustlers, from a single spliff to a hunnerd-weight of cullyweed, along with other drugs, including cocaine, dropped in en route from South America. Buying and consuming proscribed drugs is against the law and the risks are clear.

FURTHER READING

Two early travelogues of Jamaica are Lady Nugent's *Journal of Residence in Jamaica 1801–3* and Matthew 'Monk' Lewis's *Journal of a West Indian Proprietor*, written in 1834 and published after his death at sea on his return from the West Indies.

Andrew Salkey's *A Quality of Violence* looks into the life of a Jamaican village during a drought at the turn of the century. John Hearne's *Voices under the Window* gives an idea of the mercurial nature of the Jamaicans in the frenzy of the crowd. Herbert G. de Lisser has put some of Jamaica's traditional tales into novels in *Morgan's Daughter*, *The White Witch of Rose Hall* and *Psyche*.

There is some good contemporary literature coming out of Jamaica, including *Bake Face*, short stories by Opel Adisa Palmer, and collections by Olive Senior, *Summer Lightning* and *The Arrival of the Snake Woman*.

If you can track down a copy of *How to Speak Jamaican* by Ken Maxwell, read it. *Jamaica Labrish* will give you a chance to read some of Louise Bennett's hysterical machine-gun poetry at a gentler pace, and the *How to be JAMAICAN Handbook* takes a chuckling look at all aspects of Jamaican life and love, from the north coast hustler to the ICI (a higgler for the 90s).

The best driving guide to Jamaica is put out by the Gleaner Co, *Tour Jamaica* by Margaret Morris, with well documented pieces about the country and its personalities. The *Insight* guide gives a colourful look at Jamaican life and history.

BEACHES

There are innumerable, excellent beaches on Jamaica, from the seemingly endless strand at Negril with its fantastic view of the sunset, to the tight bays in the east where the mountains tumble into the sea.

Many Jamaican beaches are private and so there is limited access if you wish to explore beaches at the other hotels, but you will have some privacy on your hotel beach. Some hotels allow people from outside to use their facilities for a small fee. There are, of course, public beaches in Jamaica which are usually lively. The Jamaicans are far too modest (in public, about their bodies at any rate) to go nude on the beaches. However several of the resorts do have designated nude beaches.

567

THE CARIBBEAN

In **Montego Bay**, the popular public beaches are Cornwall Beach (well known for its beach parties) and Doctor's Cave beach, both popular with the locals, lively and usually crowded (entry J$10 for the day). There are bars where you can get a drink to cool you off. Beyond the airport is the charming curve of sand at Burwood Beach, a quieter spot.

Negril has an almost uninterrupted five miles of golden sand running north from the roundabout at the centre of the town (south of here it is nearly all 'ironshore' cliffs). It is good to walk, or if that seems too energetic, there are hip places to loiter and wait for the Green Flash at sunset. There are beach concessionaires who will arrange most watersports. There is a wide curve of sand in **Bloody Bay**, steadily being developed and beyond here you will find other tiny inlets with lovely sand. On the coast road back to Montego Bay, try Gull Bay, just before Lucea, and strikingly beautiful Miskito Cove.

Around **Ocho Rios** the busiest beaches, with all the watersports and the hustlers, are Turtle Beach and Mallard's Beach, at the centre of the town. Less known is Mammee Bay a few miles to the west.

35 miles east of Ocho Rios, Port Maria is a sweep of beaches backed by palm trees, enclosed by vast headlands. Cabarita Island in the bay has some sand and palms—persuade a fisherman to take you out. Port Maria is less touched by the tourist trade, but there are local bars to get a drink or a patty once you have found a spot of sand. On the road east there is a beach at Orange Bay.

In **Port Antonio** itself you can go to Navy Island off the bay, Errol Flynn's old haunt. Call up and catch the ferry over from the market in town. East of Port Antonio, try San San beach, a hotel beach with facilities, a restaurant and watersports equipment, and the famous Blue Hole nearby. Fairy Hill beach has some facilities and is free. At **Boston Bay** big waves whipped by the trade winds roll in from the east and surfers get out and do their stuff occasionally. There is a good strip of sand at the head of the bay and of course you can grab a jerk chicken or pork for lunch. Further along the dramatic northeastern coastline you come to Long Bay, where there is a fishing village and a lovely deserted stretch of sand; and then Innis Bay and other coves sheltered between mountain spurs that rarely see a tourist. There are no watersports here, of course, just coconut palms and sand.

There are beaches along the southeastern coastline. En route to Kingston, you can stop off at Morant Bay and Yallahs, where there are small strips of sand. For a snack and a skyjuice wander into the town.

Around **Kingston** itself the local favourite beaches are Fort Clarence and Hellshire to the southwest of the town, where there are facilities. They are crowded at the weekends, but they are quite hard to reach (buses from the parade). The thing to eat there is fried fish and *bammy*. There are dark-sand beaches on the Palisadoes peninsula, or alternatively, you can catch a ferry over to Port Royal and then hire a boat to take you over to Lime Cay, where the snorkelling is excellent.

The few beaches west of Kingston along the south coast are all remote (completely untouched by the lobster-pink scourge of the north coast) and you should take snorkelling gear, towels and drinks, and pick up a picnic in town if you are stopping over at Alligator Pond, the fishing village in Manchester Parish, Treasure Beach or Bluefields Bay.

568

INLAND BATHING AND RIVER-RAFTING

Some of the best bathing in Jamaica is in the rockpools beneath the waterfalls. Some rivers disappear in the limestone caverns and flow underground, emerging in a pool. If you go off the beaten track, ask around, because the locals will know where the best spots are. It is better not to swim after rain because the mud will have been stirred up.

Somerset Falls, off the road a mile east of Hope Bay (near Port Antonio) are a little tame, though tour buses do come here, adm. Preferable are **Reach Falls**, inland from Manchioneal, 20 miles beyond Port Antonio, a series of pools, a stunning waterfall and a cave, adm free. If you go into the John Crow Mountains to Ginger House south of Port Antonio, there is a cascade and rockpool called **Jupiter**. At Upton near Port Maria (ask around), you will find good swimming and rapids at **Spanish Bridge**. The **YS Falls** in St Elizabeth Parish, have unfortunately been developed with trolley buses, though the falls themselves (seven in sequence that flow into rockpools) are still as beautiful as ever, if there are not too many people around. There are also falls off the beaten track at **Maggotty** and at the **Black River Gorge** near Apple Valley.

Another classic tourist activity (but nonetheless good· fun) is **river-rafting**, which takes place on several rivers: the Martha Brae near Falmouth and the Great River at Lethe near Montego Bay, the White River just out of Ocho Rios and best of all, the Rio Grande near Port Antonio, winding up at Rafter's Rest (tel 993 2778), adm exp. Wear a bathing suit because when you have finished your rum punch you'll be expected to dive in.

WATERSPORTS

Watersports are laid on by all the beach hotels in Jamaica and so you can just go down to the concessionaires. Independent travellers can sometimes hire here, or they can go to the watersports shops on the larger public beaches. The full range of watersports is on offer in Jamaica, from a ride in a stately pedalo or on a trusty wetbike to a high-speed ride on an inflated sausage or an evening cruise to catch the sunset.

The going rate for **windsurfers**, which are available all over the island, is around J$300 per hour. The best beach on the island for windsurfing is Burwood Beach, a public beach beyond Trelawny Beach just outside Falmouth. Small sailing boats, a hobie cat perhaps, cost around the same, as does **waterskiing**, for a ten-minute ride. On the major beaches in Montego Bay, Negril and Ocho Rios you can also get a jetski or a ride strung beneath a **parasailer** (about J$180 for 10 minutes). Glass-bottom boats are available on most beaches too for a trip to a nearby reef.

Day and half-day **yachting** trips are available through the hotels in the major resort areas. In Mo Bay try *Calico*, which departs daily from Pier 1 (tel 952 5860) or Jamaica Yacht Charters (tel 952 2578), and in Ocho Rios you can even sail on the yacht *Red Stripe* (tel 974 2446). There are lots of silly excursions also on offer, so if you are in the mood for an afternoon of rum-soaked fun and tee-ree-ree, you can fix these through any hotel. In Ocho Rios try the Pirate Ship Cruise (tel 974 2323) or Heave Ho (tel 954 5367). A more stately alternative in Mo Bay is the dinner-cruise on the *Reggae Queen* (expensive at US$55 all inc, tel 952 2988). In Port Antonio, the *Lady Jamaica* makes day and evening cruises around the area (tel 993 3318).

The Montego Bay Yacht Club holds an annual regatta at Easter and the Miami to Mo Bay Yacht Race in February, and the Royal Jamaican Yacht Club (tel 924 8685) on the

Palisadoes peninsula just near the airport and Port Royal holds a regatta in August. Keen sailors will find themselves taken on as crew during the friendly weekend regattas.

Deep-sea fishing is possible in all the resorts, but reckoned to be at its best off Port Antonio in the east. There is an annual fishing tournament for all fish held there in March and there are marlin fishing tournaments held in Montego Bay and Ocho Rios in September and early October, before all the fishermen return to Port Antonio for the year's major event in mid-October (tel 923 8724). Other fish inhabiting the waters off the Jamaican north shore are kingfish and sailfish with a fin like a sail, as well as wahoo and tuna. In Ocho Rios contact *Ninja* on (tel 974 2442).

Scuba diving: Jamaica is surrounded by offshore reefs, furred with sponges and corals, where tropical fish play and barracuda stalk their lunch. The reefs are supposed not to be in the best condition because they have been depleted for their corals, but many are now protected and there are still enough around the north coast resorts to keep divers occupied. The major operators of the Jamaica Association of Diver Operators work under PADI specifications—you must show your certification—and most can provide instruction. Some smaller operators do not. Underwater photographic equipment is for hire at the bigger rental companies. A single tank dive costs around US$35.

Dive operators around **Montego Bay** include Poseidon Nemrod Divers on Gloucester Ave (tel 952 3624) and Seaworld Resorts (tel 953 2180). In **Negril** operators are Dolphin Divers (tel 957 4481) with three locations, Blue Whale Divers (tel 957 4438) and the Negril Scuba Centre at the Negril Beach Club (tel 957 4425). In **Runaway Bay** go to Sundivers (tel 973 3509). **Ocho Rios** has many outfits including Fantasea Divers at the Sans Souci, PO Box 103 (tel 974 5344) and Sea and Dive Jamaica at Shaw Park Hotel (tel 974 5762). And in **Port Antonio** try Aqua Action (tel 993 3481) at San San Beach. In Kingston contact Morgan's Harbour Hotel in Port Royal (tel 924 8140).

OTHER SPORTS
There are **tennis** courts at most of the hotels and if not it can easily be arranged through a front desk.

There are many **golf** courses in Jamaica. The best around **Montego Bay** are Half Moon (tel 953 2280), at the hotel north of the town, and Tryall, set out beneath the Tryall resort about 15 miles west. Also Ironshore (tel 953 2800) and the Wyndham Rose Hall course (tel 953 2650) to the east. In **Runaway Bay** there is a course at the Super Clubs Golf and Country Club (tel 973 2561), and in **Ocho Rios** there is the Upton Golf Club, fee J$90 (tel 974 2528). There are two clubs near Kingston: the Caymanas Golf and Country Club, fee J$100 (tel 923 7538) and Constant spring Golf Club, fee J$75 (tel 924 1610).

If you wish to go **horse-riding**, for anything from a beach canter at dawn to a day-long trek into the Jamaican highlands, there are stables in all the main towns. Riding out costs roughly J$200 per hour. You are advised to call a couple of hours before arriving to book the horses.

In **Montego Bay**, try the Half Moon Hotel Stables and Trelawny Beach Hotel (tel 954 2289). At **Mandeville** contact Marshall's Pen Great House (tel 962 2260). Polo is quite big in Jamaica, and you can even hire polo ponies at Chukka Cove Farm (tel 972 2506) near **Ocho Rios**, or get a refresher course if you haven't hit a nearside forehand for a while. There is good riding out from Chukka Cove. In **Port Antonio** rides into the mountain foothills are available through the Bonnie View Hotel (tel 993 2752). If a nag seems a bit much, you can take a cycling tour of the Blue Mountains from Port Antonio instead. Sounds like quite hard work, but this is a specifically downhill tour. Blue Mountain Tours (tel 993 2242).

Walkers will find good hiking in the Hellshire Hills, around the Cockpit Country southeast of Montego Bay and in the trails of the Blue Mountains in the east. The Blue Mountain Peak is usually climbed very early in the morning, so that you are at the 7402 ft summit at dawn, with the best chance of seeing Haiti and the Sierra Maestra in Cuba. However there are many other trails in the Blue Mountains. You can contact SENSE Adventures at PO Box 216, Kingston 7 (tel 927 2097) and the Forestry Dept, 173 Constant Spring Road (tel 924 2667) for information and a few ideas. Both organizations can call on some accommodation in the remoter areas and they will help you out with a guide. If you do go, take a waterproof and a woolly jersey because it gets cold in the mountains.

If you have a screw loose then you might enjoy Jamaica's recent addition in Ocho Rios, bungee-jumping; **Jamaica Bungee**, James Ave (tel 974 5660).

Spectator sports include **cricket**, which is something of a national preoccupation. You will see it played in the streets (join in), yards, country roads, on the beaches and in Kingston at Sabina Park (go to a match if there is one on). The only time when the radios stop playing dancehall music is when the cricket is on. And even the hustlers are magnanimous if the West Indies are winning. **Horse racing** is popular in Jamaica and you will find details of coming meetings in the local press. The main stadium, to the west of Kingston, is Caymanas Park.

Kingston

Jamaica's capital, a sprawling city of a million people on the south coast, is the hub of the Jamaicans' Jamaica and it is certainly well worth visiting. It is the political, cultural and

Skyjuice, Kingston

571

the business centre of the island and it buzzes with the most vibrant and vigorous of Jamaican life. Downtown on the Parade the press is incessant as the busmen shout and the higglers tout their wares; goats wander oblivious and the traffic bobs and weaves, everywhere the deafening rap of dancehall; the occasional policeman in dark serge trousers and a peaked cap tries to keep order. All the extremes of Jamaican life are there: the poor urban shanties in the 'ghettos of the west', the markets in the downtown area, the grand old institutions in the few remaining Victorian buildings close by, the gleaming airco offices of New Kingston and the fortified villas that take a cool view of it all from the Kingston mountainsides.

The city owes its birth to the death of Port Royal in the earthquake of 1692 (see p. 574). The new city was originally laid out on a grid-iron pattern and within a few years it was the commercial and social centre of the island. Hundreds of ships would put into Kingston's magnificent harbour and the city grew as the planters built town-houses to match the splendour of their estate houses in the country. Kingston became the capital of the island in 1872. Another earthquake struck in 1907, killing 800, and much of the old town was destroyed. Modern Kingston is not an attractive city as far as its buildings are concerned.

The waterfront, the heart of the town until earlier this century, is quiet now that the big passenger liners and the fruit ships no longer call. The docks are in decay and a few characters 'lime' on the Boulevard and around the **Victoria Crafts Market**, where the Kingstonians sell their tourist souvenirs, straw hats and wooden carvings, and among them one or two finer pieces. The **National Gallery** is at the foot of Orange St and has exhibitions of Jamaican art, including the works of sculptresses Edna Manley and Mallica Reynolds. Open Mon–Fri, 10–5 (tel 922 1561).

King Street, one of Kingston's main shopping streets, leads from the waterfront up to the Parade, from where the **Coronation Market** spills out into the road. This is the heartland of the downtown area and it is mercantile mayhem. Outside the shops of King St, watchmenders, clothes vendors and sweet and cigarette salesmen tout their wares from countless stalls and from blankets laid out on the pavement. This is *ben dung* plaza at its best—many higglers prefer to lay their wares out on the ground than use tables. Periodically the higglers are cleared off the street and told to go back into the market buildings (built after the original one at the bottom of King St on the waterfront was destroyed), but they always come back because they prefer it here.

The **Parade**, called so because the colonial soldiers would parade here, is officially called William Grant Park. It is the terminal for Kingston's bus system—yet more chaos. The hawkers tout iced drinks from their handcarts with a shout of *Juice! Skyjuice!* and the busmen practically kidnap you to put you on their bus (your intended destination seems only a secondary consideration). The small square, a park shaded by trees where more limers hang out, is overlooked by the **Ward Theatre** on the north side, built after the 1907 earthquake.

To the west of the downtown area, which itself has become run down since many of the businesses moved to New Kingston in the 1960s, are Kingston's poorest shanty towns, including Trench Town, immortalized by Bob Marley. These are some of the most vibrant areas of Kingston, but it would be unwise to go there as a white, at least not without a guide.

East of the Parade, on Duke St, is the modern **Gordon House**, the seat of the

Jamaican Parliament, where the Representatives and Senators sit. Next door you will find **Headquarters House**, which also was the seat of Parliament earlier this century. It was built in the 18th century by a merchant, Thomas Hibbert, and its present name comes from its one-time use as the headquarters of the military. Its 'crow's nest', the lookout on the roof, was used by Hibbert to see what ships had recently come into harbour and what goods they might be carrying. To the east, on South Camp Road, is the Sabina Park Cricket stadium, where the international tests are played.

At the top of Duke St, past the Gleaner Building on North St, is **National Heroes Park**, which followed Independence in 1962. There are monuments to Paul Bogle and George William Gordon, champions of the poor in the last century, and to Nanny the Maroon and Sam Sharpe. The graves of Marcus Mosiah Garvey, founder of the UNIA, and the fathers of modern Jamaican politics, Norman Manley and Alexander Bustamante, are also there. Simon Bolívar, *El Libertador*, the hero of South American Independence, who stayed in exile in Jamaica, is remembered here as well. On East St is the **Institute of Jamaica**, which has a natural history museum. Open Mon–Sat, 8.30–4, adm free (tel 922 0620).

The buses run up Slipe Road from the Parade towards **New Kingston**, the commercial centre of modern Kingston. Knutsford Boulevard is the principal street, with the shops and banks. On Hope Road is the classical **Devon House**, set in gardens of palms and flowering trees. It was built in 1881 for a Jamaican merchant and it has been restored as a museum, furnished with period antiques. Quite touristy, but worth a look, particularly for the ice creams on sale in the stables. Gardens open daytime and evenings, Devon House open daily 9–4.30, tour adm.

In a large area of parkland just up from here are **Jamaica House**, built in the 1960s as the residence of the Prime Minister, now just his office, and **Kings House**, the official residence of the Jamaican Governor General. You can visit the grounds. The red, green and black house at 56 Hope Road is the old **Tuff Gong** recording studio, where Bob Marley lived and recorded. It is now the **Bob Marley Museum**; you can see his golden disks and album covers, and a tour culminates with your favourite track on the video. Open Mon–Sat, 9.30–4.30, Wed, Sat afternoons only, adm. At the top of Old Hope Road are the **Hope Botanical Gardens** which were established in 1881. The vast lawns are lined with royal palms, and bougainvillaea explodes in colourful blooms. The 150 acres are a good retreat from the humdrum of downtown Kingston, as well as a favoured spot for Jamaican limers and lovers. There is a collection of orchids on view. Open daily 8.30–6.30, adm free. Close by is the Mona Campus of the **University of the West Indies** on an old sugar estate between the hills, the old aqueducts and some buildings still visible.

There is a lively art scene in Jamaica and in Kingston there are a number of good galleries. Try the Contemporary Art Centre at 1 Liguanea Ave, Kingston 6; Babylon Jamaica, 10A West Kings House Rd; Makonde at the Wyndham Hotel; and the Bolivar Bookshop and Gallery, 1A Grove Rd.

Port Royal
At the end of the Palisadoes Peninsula, past the Royal Jamaica Yacht Club and the Norman Manley airport, is the settlement of Port Royal. The peninsula almost encloses the bay, making the harbour one of the best in the Caribbean. The British fortified it

573

immediately they arrived in 1655 and very soon it became a haunt for the buccaneers, who had been driven out of the island of Tortuga off Hispaniola. These men were possessed in their hatred of the Spaniards and were useful as an unofficial army for the governor.

They also brought back vast piles of loot from their raids on Cuba, Hispaniola and the Spanish Main. Port Royal was the sorting station for it all and it quickly became the richest town in the area. Silks from the east, grog by the cask, chests of jewels and gold and silver were auctioned off by the returning buccaneers, who then gambled and drank and generally made whoopee until the money ran out and they had to go off again to find more. Full of pimps and prostitutes, there was one ale-house to every ten inhabitants at Port Royal's height in the 1680s and in the opinion of one man, 'this place has been one of the lewdest in the Christian world, a sink of all filthiness and a mere sodom'.

When it came, a few minutes before noon on 7 June 1692, the earthquake seemed like divine retribution, as 2000 people died in three minutes. Whole streets of the 'Gilded Hades' slid into the sea, fissures opened in the ground and a tidal wave threw a ship into the middle of the town. Some continued drinking and others started to loot the shops. One Lewis Galdy had a story to tell, after being swallowed up by the earth and then thrown out again into the sea as another shock came. His tomb, with his story on the stone, is in the graveyard of St Peter's Church.

The merchants rebuilt their town, but in 1703 a fire destroyed it again and the last of the inhabitants went to Kingston. The area remained a naval base, where Horatio Nelson served at the time of the American War of Independence. **Fort Charles** was his base and you can still visit it today, castellated ramparts and cannon and a fantastic view of the Kingston mountains. There is a small **Maritime Museum** in the fort with model ships and Arawak canoes, open daily 10–1 and 2–5. Beyond the fort is the **Giddy House**, which lurched to its present position in the earthquake of 1907. The **Museum of Historical Archaeology** is located in the old naval hospital, where there are displays of Arawak, maroon and Spanish artefacts and remnants from the earthquake.

A visit to Port Royal is a good day out from Kingston. After the few sights and a meal of fried fish and johnny cakes, you can take a trip to one of the offshore cays or across to Port Henderson. The ferry leaves Pier 2 on the Kingston waterfront about 6 times a day, fare J$2.

Into the Blue Mountains

As soon as you leave Kingston you will be winding up into the mountains. The A3 road goes via Half Way Tree and Constant spring and then up to Castleton and over to the north coast at Annotto Bay. In **Castleton** are some Botanic Gardens that date from 1869, set in 39 acres in the incredibly fertile (and pretty wet) Wag River valley. The plants are marked and there are guides who will explain the 35 palms among the 60 ft explosions of bamboo and point out the lair of the trap-door spider (sealed watertight and lined with silk). You can visit the **Cinchona Gardens**, close to Clydesdale, spectacular for their ridgetop setting 5000 thousand feet above Kingston (pick a clear day). They were established in 1868 and their name comes from the Cinchona tree that was farmed to produce quinine.

At World's End above Guava Ridge is the Sangster's 'Old Jamaica' liqueur factory which you may visit, and where there is an excellent view of Newcastle. At **Mavis Bank** is one of the area's many coffee plantations (Blue Mountain Coffee is reckoned to be the best in the world), which you can visit during picking time between September and February. You will see the berries pulped, sweated and husked and then the beans dried and sized.

The **Blue Mountain Peak** is Jamaica's highest (7402 ft) and the ascent can be made in seven hours from Mavis Bank. The mountains are often lost in cloud and mist in the day and so to get the best chance of a clear view you should aim to reach the peak soon after dawn, when you might be able to see as far as Cuba. On the way down you will pass through elfin growth, stunted grasses, knee-high trees and lichens, and then into montane woodland, still swirling in cloud, where the ferns and orchids sit in the upper branches and trees reach tall to catch the sunlight. For a tour, see the addresses under Other Sports, p. 471.

Clockwise from Kingston

Twelve miles west of Kingston, across the sugar flats, is **Spanish Town**, the capital of Jamaica until 1872, except for a brief interlude (1755–8), when the Kingston merchants managed to force through a bill moving the capital there. The town is set around a few streets of old-time stone buildings of colonial elegance, and has mushroomed with modern villas and poor shanties.

Santiago de la Vega was laid out by the Spaniards when they moved here from the north coast in 1523, but there is nothing left of the original *plaza* in the central square of Spanish Town. The Georgian architecture and the iron railings around the park give the square a distinctly British feel and it was the social hub of Jamaica for three centuries. The **Rodney Memorial**, sculpted by John Bacon, commemorates Admiral George Rodney following his victory at the Battle of the Saints off Guadeloupe in 1782. Opposite is the **Court House**, a lively centre still as parish business is done here. The colonnaded building with wooden upper storeys and a balcony, on the east side of the square, is the former **House of Assembly** and opposite that stands **King's House**, built in 1762, which was burned down to its façade in 1925. Look out for the Cathedral Church of St James, head of the Jamaica Diocese, on Barrett St. It was built in 1714 on the site of an original Spanish church, but there are commemorative tablets from the earliest English settlers to Jamaica.

Beyond this rarefied square with its colonial echoes, Spanish Town is a busy Jamaican town, partly industrialized, partly fading timber businesses and homes. The **White Marl Arawak Museum**, set in a reconstruction of an Arawak house, is between Kingston and Spanish Town and has exhibits of Arawak life and some artefacts, open Mon–Fri, 10–5, adm.

Past the massive ruins of 17th-century Colbeck Castle near Old Harbour you come to **May Pen**. There are many *Pens* in Jamaica; the name refers to a farmstead where animals were kept. At Toll Gate you take the turning to the south coast, along the Milk River valley and canefields, past a village called Rest, down to the **Milk River Spa**, where the highest levels of natural radioactivity in the world occur in the water—about 50 times the radioactive levels of Baden-Baden. The water comes out of the ground at

120°F and they are popular for their supposed healing powers (tel 925 9544). There are occasional day trips from Kingston (tel 929 8990).

Set on a 2000-ft plateau, **Mandeville** is the capital of Manchester Parish. The area calls itself the *feeding tree* (the Jamaican equivalent of the breadbasket) because of all the cultivation—there are endless stalls at the roadside selling cashews and strings or bags of whatever fruits are in season. In British days Mandeville was a hill station, to which the colonial authorities and the planters would retreat in the heat of the summer (in those days nobody lay on the beach because the heat was thought to be degenerative). It was even laid out like a village green, with the Georgian court house and the Parish Church standing opposite one another across the open square, though they stand rather oddly aloof among all the Jamaican chaos. There is also an impressive iron market in the town, in which the ground provisions and fruits were traditionally sold. The town retained a stately and faded air until the 1950s when the area suddenly became the centre of the Jamaican bauxite industry. Not far off at Shooter's Hill, in the shadow of the huge bauxite plant, you will find the **Pickapeppa** sauce factory, the source of the pungent concoction that the Jamaicans dash liberally on their food (tel 962 2928).

Following the main road west out of Mandeville you descend to the plains of St Elizabeth at Spur Tree. The views are fantastic, as they are on the south coast at **Lover's Leap**, a 1600-ft drop sheer into the sea from the Santa Cruz mountains. The story goes that two slave lovers were chased here by an ardent planter who fancied the girl, and they jumped to their death rather than be split up.

On the road to Black River is **Bamboo Avenue**, one of Jamaica's best known sights; a little touristy really but impressive nonetheless as it is a tunnel of bamboo, still mostly complete along its three-mile length, constantly creaking in the breeze. Throughout this area you will find vendors at the roadside selling bags of 'swims' (shrimps cooked in pepper sauce).

Black River itself is a faded and rundown Jamaican town on the south coast, but one which was clearly prosperous at the turn of the century as there are magnificent gingerbread houses decaying on the waterfront. It made its wealth through exporting dyes—indigo and logwood, which were used in jeans. You can take boat-trips into one of Jamaica's two swamps called the *Great Morass* (the other being in Negril). Tendrils hang like curtains from the extended families of mangrove trees and Great Blue herons and jacanas or purple gallinules creep and strut around. You may also see a crocodile flop into the water and cruise lazily away in the swamp or, if you're lucky, a very rare and ponderous manatee at the river mouth. **Treasure Beach** is a lovely, laid-back seaside town, untouched by tourists, except by the Jamaicans themselves, who come here for their holidays.

The coastal road continues through Bluefields, from where Henry Morgan set off to sack Panama in 1670, to **Savanna-la-Mar**. The town is run down and is still used as the port for sugar brought from Frome inland, but its position on the coast is not always a blessing as it is scourged by storms—in 1912, a schooner ended up in the main street of the town.

Twenty miles further on is the resort town of **Negril**, which stretches along seven miles of spectacular beach and four of ironshore cliffs on the western tip of Jamaica. Its remote position and its well-known 'hippy' history have made Negril the most easy-going of Jamaican tourist towns.

It was a pirate haunt, and the crews of corsairs would lie in wait for ships en route from the Spanish Main to Havana. Calico Jack Rackham and his disguised women companions Anne Bonney and Mary Read were captured here in 1720, while on a rum blow-out. They were taken off to Spanish Town and found guilty of piracy, robbery and felony. Rackham was executed and then 'hung out to dry' (in an iron frame) on Rackham Cay off Port Royal, but the two women, who were renowned as being just as fierce as their male counterparts, pleaded pregnancy and were jailed.

The town remained a backwater until a road was built in 1959 and hippies began to wash up here. They rented space on the floor in the local houses and enjoyed the magic mushroom omelettes, the weed, the palm-backed beach and the sunsets. Things have become a little more formal since then as the big hotels have muscled in on the beachfront, but it is still fairly easy and relaxed. However, it has had the worst of the hustlers and pseudo-rastas in Jamaica, since they descended on the town after their eviction from Mo Bay a few years ago.

There are no sights in Negril unless you wish to go to the top of the lighthouse at the southern tip of the West End Road (south from the roundabout), but then hanging out is much more the style here. Running parallel with the main beach, behind the Norman Manley Boulevard, is Jamaica's other *Great Morass*, a vast swamp where you can see herons and other waders among the mangroves. Bloody Bay, off the road to Montego Bay, takes its name from the whales that were beached and cut up here, or possibly from pirate battles of centuries past.

The road northeast to Montego Bay follows the magnificent coastline, skirting the bays and clambering over lumbering headlands to **Lucea**, the capital of Hanover Parish, which is set on a wide harbour overlooked by cliffs.

The North Coast

The north coast of Jamaica is legendary as a tourist destination, the favoured haunt of Britons such as Winston Churchill and Noel Coward and Royal families from all over. The villas of the rich and famous have dotted the hillsides since the 30s and although Port Antonio is quiet now, it was so popular at the turn of the century that there was a 400-bedroom hotel there. People would come on packages on the banana boats for the winter season. Today's tourists fly into Montego Bay by the jumbo-load; it is the main airport for the north of the island.

Montego Bay

Situated in the northwest of the island, Montego Bay, or **Mo Bay**, as it is usually known, is Jamaica's second city. It is the tourist heartland of the island; its coastline has become infested with humming factory-like hotels for miles and the beaches are awash with lobster-red trippers sizzling in coconut oil. Rude-boys joust on their jetskis and higglers apply their high-pressure selling techniques from the roadside downtown. It is mayhem as the goats and boys pushing handcarts compete for road space and relentless horns and shouts of *Skyjuice!* interrupt the pulse of dancehall music. Old-time Montego Bay looks on from its Georgian stone buildings and timber houses as it has done for two centuries.

The Bay was first named by Columbus for its favourable winds, the 'Golfo de Buen

Tiempo', but when the Spaniards settled the area it was called 'manteca' after the butter or pig fat that was its trade. Development was slow because of the maroons in the mountains, but in the 18th century there was big business in sugarloaves ('Monk' Lewis thought it the prettiest town in Jamaica), and then in bananas in the 19th century, but it was in 1906 when the latest boom, tourism, began with the opening of Doctor's Cave Beach.

The centre of the town itself is **Sam Sharpe Square**, still occasionally called Charles Square as it was originally known. Sam Sharpe, now a Jamaican national hero, was hanged here, near where his statue stands. His 1831 rebellion went far further than his intended sit-down strike—plantations were torched and riots continued for months—but it speeded the eventual end of slavery. In one corner of the square is the **Cage**, once used as a lock-up for slaves out after curfew at 3 pm and drunks or sailors in the town after their curfew at 6 pm. It is now a visitor's information centre.

The St James Parish Church is behind the Square, an imposing structure straight out of England with arched windows and a mahogany interior, that was first erected in 1778. On East St is the amphitheatrical **slave ring**, thought to be a slave auction area, but also perhaps a cock-fighting pit. The **Creek Head** monument is the hexagonal building on Creek St, built where two girls discovered Montego Bay's permanent water supply while catching crabs. Montego Bay's town **market** (as opposed to the craft market) is on Fustic St, down at the end of Railway Lane, and it is well worth a visit to see the traditional way of buying ground provisions West Indian style.

Modern Mo Bay has spread north into hotel and beach territory and south of the old town, where villas have sprung up in the vast background of forested hills. The surrounding countryside is dotted with the remnants of 18th-century Jamaica in the plantations and their great houses, many of them restored or turned into hotels. Hiking trails lead into the mountains from **Sign Great House**, about 6 miles east of the town. Many of the places mentioned below can be visited on the endless tours arranged from Montego Bay.

South of Montego Bay

The **Rockland Bird Sanctuary**, in Anchovy, three miles south of Reading, is open to the public in the afternoon, when a stream of Jamaica's colourful birdlife heads in for feeding—hummingbirds including the vervain, the Jamaican mango and the doctor bird—you might even get one to sit on your finger while it feeds (see Flora and Fauna, p. 560). You can also see warblers, tanagers and the yellow and black Jamaican oriole. Open daily, 3–5.15, adm.

Belvedere Plantation is off the road to Savanna-la-Mar and you approach the old estate buildings through citrus, pineapple and banana plantations. You will see a riverside garden with plants such as puss-tail, anato, which provides red food dye (and lipstick of a sort) and, no connection, shame a lady. The great house is in ruins, but a post-emancipation village has been created with traditonal village skills on view—weaving, blacksmithing, a herbalist's garden and a small crusher where you can get a drink of cane-juice, adm.

The road follows the railway and the valley of the Great River to Cambridge, high in the absurdly fertile Jamaican mountains. **Seaford Town** is the home of the descendants of German families who arrived in 1835. The community has become inbred and many have emigrated, but the blond features and blue eyes of the 200 or so that remain are clearly visible, even if they hold themselves more like Jamaicans when they dance. Passing the village of Magotty the road and railway come to **Appleton Sugar Estate**, set in swathes of cane that make Jamaica's most famous rum. During working hours there is a tour of the distillery, which produces 10 million litres of rum each year in the column stills and the oak barrels of the cool storage house. You might be lucky and get a tour of the sugar factory itself, where the canes are crushed on conveyors and the liquid is boiled and then granulated in a centrifuge. Adm.

North of this area is the **Cockpit Country**, a remote and weird landscape of shaggy limestone hillocks like 300-ft haystacks. This was the maroon heartland, and in the south is the infamous area known by soldiers as the 'land of the look-behind'—they had to ride back to back on their horses because it was so treacherous. The maroons held out here (see History, p. 555), in settlements where the charming villages of Accompong, Maroon Town and Quick Step are today, descending to attack the plantations at night. The Cockpit Country is laced with caves, including Peace Cave near Accompong and Wondrous Caves near Elderslie.

East from Montego Bay

Rose Hall Great House is Jamaica's most famous great house, an imposing Georgian mansion that stands on the hillside 10 miles east of Montego Bay. Built in 1770, Rose Hall has been restored to its former splendour as the most illustrious manor on the island, with period antiques. But it is most famous for the legend of its mistress Annie Palmer, who came to Rose Hall in 1820. A renowned beauty, feared as a black magician, she is supposed to have got through three husbands (by poison, stabbing and strangling) and innumerable lovers, including slaves, whom she simply killed when she was bored of them. She was murdered in her bed. There is apparently no evidence for the legend, but an amusing version was written up by H.G. de Lisser in his *White Witch of Rose Hall*. Open daily 9.30–6, adm exp (tel 953 2323).

Greenwood Great House, on the hillside four miles farther on, was a home of the Barrett family from which the poet Elizabeth Barrett Browning was descended. Built in the early 1800s, it is still lived in. On view are musical instruments, the old carriages and portraits and the Barrett family library. There is a stunning veranda. Open daily, 9–6, adm.

Six miles east is the town of **Falmouth**, capital of Trelawney parish. The town was founded in 1790 and for a time was the busiest port on the north coast, but the sugar trade declined and the town faded with it. Many of the Georgian buildings are still standing, with verandas supported on stilts, reaching out over the pavement, and timber frame upper storeys on stonework bases. Look out for the court house on Water Square, and Market Street, with the post office and the Methodist manse. The parish church is another elegant building that might have been lifted straight out of England.

Just east of Falmouth is a phosphorescent lagoon at **Rock**. If you take a boat out you can run your hand through the millions of bioluminescent protozoa that are returning after being threatened a few years ago.

Twenty miles farther along the coastal road you come to Discovery Bay, the supposed

579

site of Columbus's arrival in 1494, though many disagree (he is commemorated with a lacklustre museum/park all the same, adm free) and then Runaway Bay, where the last Spaniards gathered in 1655 before making a break for Cuba 90 miles to the north. Slaves are also known to have holed up in the caves around here. The **Runaway Caves** and the **Green Grotto** are over-touristed (yet more carvings for sale), but are worth a visit for the trip across the underground lake, open 9–5. Inland, beyond the stunningly fertile areas of the Orange Valley, **Brown's Town** has a classic Caribbean iron market, to which the local farmers bring their produce from the hills around. At Nine Mile beyond Alexandria is the **Bob Marley Mausoleum**, on a hillside in the town of his birth. You'll be hustled like mad and told all sorts of tall stories about Bob, adm, no video cameras if you please. Further east, on the road south to Kellits in Clarendon parish, you come to the remains of **Edinburgh Castle**, seat of the 'Mad Doctor' Lewis Hutchinson, who would watch the road and kill lone travellers who happened by in the 1760s, disposing of their bodies in a nearby sinkhole. Eventually he went too far when he shot a neighbour, and he was arrested and hanged.

Back on the coast, past the site of Nueva Sevilla, the first Spanish settlement of 1510 (where a few remains are still visible), is the town of St **Ann's Bay**, capital of the parish of St Ann. The town is the birthplace of Marcus Garvey, the Jamaican national hero and founder of the UNIA (see History, p. 557) and he is remembered with a statue in front of the town library. Seven miles farther on you come to the resort town of Ocho Rios, announced by a small fortress (don't bother to investigate, it contains the local sewage plant) and the enormous bauxite shipping station just before the town.

Ocho Rios

Ocho Rios, or 'Ochee' as it is often known, is Jamaica's second tourist town, about 70 miles over the hill from Kingston and the same from Montego Bay. It is another businesslike tourist town that was created in the 60s from a tiny fishing village on a magnificent beach. It is a little soulless, but it is business as usual as two or three cruise ships call in some days and the tourists come in droves. Ocho Rios contains some of the island's best beaches and a couple of Jamaica's smartest hotels as well as a string of high-pressure fun factories.

The name, which looks as though it might come from 'eight rivers' in the vicinity, is in fact a corruption of Las Chorreras, meaning waterfalls, of which there were many coming off the hills that rise immediately behind the town. Ocho Rios has no traditional centre, apart from the clocktower—it is scattered along the coastline for several miles.

Dunn's River Falls is probably Jamaica's most famous sight, a series of waterfalls that tumble 600 ft from top to bottom, and although you have to join a conga of other tourists holding hands and dice with death as you edge gingerly up among the relentless cascades, it is quite beautiful and a surprising feature. Open daily, 8–5, start at the bottom and buy another carving at the top, adm.

The road to Kingston leads south out of town from the roundabout up into the mountains towards Moneague. **Shaw Park Gardens** are set out on the hillside off the road, ranges of bougainvillaea and hibiscus with streams linking lily ponds. It is a pleasant retreat from the hustle and bustle of Ochee. Open daily, 9–5, adm. As it climbs, the road passes through **Fern Gully**, an absurdly fertile chasm three miles long where the vegetation makes a tunnel over the road. Creepers and lianas tangle and many of Jamaica's 500 varieties of fern explode in the upper branches of the trees. Until a few years ago the gulley was alive with fireflies at night, but now the petrol fumes have killed them off.

Headed east from Ocho Rios, over the White River (good swimming if you follow it up on the backroads), you come to the **Prospect Plantation**. There are three daily tours of its grounds, where many of Jamaica's plantation crops are set out on view, including cassava, banana, coffee and of course sugar-cane. Horseback rides are available into the mountains. Open daily 10.30–3.30, adm. Close by is **Harmony Hall**, a turreted estate house with gingerbread fretwork which has been restored and now houses a collection of Jamaican arts and crafts, including paintings by the Jamaican 'intuitives'.

Following the coastal road farther east you come towards **Port Maria**, the capital of St Mary parish, set on a stunning bay. The poor and remote east of the island begins here. The parish church is attractive and the only other sight in this ragged town is the monument to the Tacky Rebellion in 1760 that stands in front of the court house.

On the hill above the town is Noel Coward's house **Firefly**, chosen with customary discernment because from its 1000-ft vantage-point it has perhaps the finest view in the whole of the Caribbean. The view takes in the Blue Mountains in the south and the northern coastline where the successive headlands outreach one another into the Caribbean Sea. Coward lived here for the last 23 years of his life until he died in 1973 (the same site was chosen by Henry Morgan 300 years before him, and Morgan's old kitchen is still standing). Noel Coward is buried in the garden under an elaborate white grille, surrounded by hibiscus. The house was severely damaged by Hurricane Gilbert in 1988 and has been restored as he left it, with his musical scores and some paintings still on view, adm.

Author Ian Fleming, creator of the character James Bond, lived on the coast nearby from 1946 until his death in 1964, in a house called **Goldeneye**. The name James Bond itself was borrowed from the cover of one of Jamaica's other renowned birdwatchers, the author of *The Birds of the West Indies*. Goldeneye is privately owned, but it can be taken as a villa. **Brimmer Hall Estate** is inland, southwest of Port Maria, and offers tractor tours through the banana and coconut plantations and traditional Jamaican fare of ackee and salt fish and a dip in the pool (the house itself is closed to visitors). Open daily 9–5, adm.

From Port Maria the main road heads inland into the hills, re-emerging at Annotto Bay from where it heads into Portland parish and Port Antonio, following the magnificent coastline beneath the massive and beautiful foothills of the Blue Mountains. Buff Bay (in name only) is now a faded parish town, with its old buildings in decay, and Hope Bay is a small fishing village best known for the Somerset Falls just above the town, falls, pools and a swimmable channel, open 10–5, adm. Soon afterwards the road crosses the **Rio Grande**, Jamaica's largest river, and best known for river-rafting since Errol Flynn joined the banana growers who shipped their fruit downriver on bamboo rafts.

Port Antonio

Port Antonio is the capital of Portland parish and both the town and its parish are simply spectacular, among the most beautiful places on the island. The town's heyday is clearly passed, for the moment at least, as the grand old buildings show in their distressed decay, but the setting of the town, on the point between two bays and with vast and fertile mountains behind it, makes Port Antonio incomparable.

Port Antonio was a Spanish settlement, and although it was laid out in 1723, it remained a sedate coastal town until the late 1880s, when it became the centre of the banana trade and exploded into prosperity. By the turn of the century it was the most important town on the north coast. Tourists poured in from the US and the place was so popular that there was a 400-room hotel, three storeys high with verandas on all sides, an Italian orchestra to play at mealtimes and a massive ball-room. In the winter season it was patronized by the likes of Rudyard Kipling. As the banana trade failed in the 30s, so did the hotel and with it the tourist trade in Port Antonio. The town received a fillip in the 50s with the arrival of the film star Errol Flynn. He bought Navy Island in the West Harbour and the glamour returned with his parties, to which guests like Bette Davis and Ginger Rogers came.

Once described as the 'most exquisite port on earth', Port Antonio still has a romantic feel about it, and you are inclined to believe the locals when they make their predictions that after your first fleeting visit you will return one day.

The most attractive area of the town, where you will find the classic Caribbean gingerbread houses built in timber and wrought iron, are on the point between the two bays, or 'The Hill'. The remains of Fort St George, a few embrasures and some mean-looking cannon on rollers, have been turned into Titchfield School. The centre of the town itself is the clocktower at the head of West St, where you will find the market, always worth a visit, but particularly active on Thursdays and Saturdays. The view from the Bonnie View Hotel is superb.

Above Port Antonio, between the Blue Mountains and the John Crow Mountains, is the maroon settlement of Moore Town. In the 18th century, the Windward maroons occupied this area and they are supposed to have lived in Nanny Town, beneath the Blue Mountain Peak. They were forced out of the town by the British in 1730, but in 1739 they signed a treaty allowing them to live in peace. Legends grew up around the place and around their leader Nanny, who was supposed to have supernatural powers. Locals say that the spirits of the maroons still inhabit the area. Nanny became a national heroine of Jamaica in 1975. If you wish to visit, get the Port Antonio Tourist Board to contact the Maroon Colonel in advance, who might give you a tour of the town. **Bump Grave**, opposite the school in Moore Town, is supposed to contain the remains of Nanny. Close by is Ginger House, where there is a stunning waterfall called **Jupiter**, lost in the densest greenery, and a rockpool where you can swim. Ask around for directions.

Back on the coast the main road leads east out of Port Antonio, passing some of Jamaica's expensive villas, including Folly 1, a vast classical pile that was never finished, on the headland across the East Harbour. Folly 2 is a Bavarian castle farther down the road. More villas cling to the coastline at the **Blue Hole**, another of Jamaica's most popular sights. This beautiful pool is a limestone sinkhole with a royal blue colour, which is fed by freshwater rivers underground, a cracker of a place to swim.* **Nonsuch Caves** are made up of nine chambers in Athenry Gardens up in the hills behind Port Antonio—

---

* As the café/restaurant here was still closed due to hurrican damage at the time of writing, there was no official access route and one recent report indicated that visitors were accosted by menacing hustlers, although the author himself did not experience this and still rated the spot highly on his last visit. More reports please.

JAMAICA

walkways and lighting to see the stalactites and stalagmites (shapes include a woman with a basket on her head, a man riding a camel and the Hush Puppy dog), set in gardens with a magnificent view of the town from above. Open daily except Sun, 9–5, adm.

Beyond Boston Bay, home of jerk (see p. 560), the road follows the rugged southeast coast past Reach Falls into the parish of St Thomas and to the tip of the island, where the views from Morant Point lighthouse are spectacular. Morant Bay is the capital of the parish and the site of the famous 1865 rebellion, after which over 400 people were executed, including Paul Bogle and George William Gordon, who were hanged outside the town hall.

Inland is the town of **Bath**, Jamaica's favourite resort two centuries ago because of the hot and cold springs, and home to the second oldest botanical gardens in the western hemisphere (now dilapidated). At the Bath Fountain Hotel you can have a dip in the waters, which are supposed to have curative properties (tel 982 2132). The road follows the coast from Morant Bay through Yallahs and on to the capital.

FESTIVALS
The annual Jamaican Independence celebrations take place on the first Monday in August with parades, parachutists and marching bands in the National Stadium in Kingston. All a bit staid but quite fun. About a week earlier is the Reggae Sunsplash Festival in the Bob Marley Performing Centre in Montego Bay, a gathering for rastas and reggae fans from all over the world. There is a carnival week with celebrations all over the island and particularly in Kingston in April and you might wish to visit the Maroon Festival held at Accompong in January. The National Dance Theatre Company stages performances twice a year that are well worth attending. The Jamaica Tourist Board publishes a twice-yearly list of forthcoming festivals and events giving exact dates.

WHERE TO STAY
Jamaica has a superb selection of hotels—among them some of the smartest in the world, set in their own beautifully manicured grounds on a stunning beach—and recently a new generation of all-inclusive hotels that offer the champagne treatment and *à la carte* dining (the older fun-factory style of hotel; wet T-shirt competitions, drink and dance until you drop is still going strong). But there is something for everyone in Jamaica and so you will also find small guest houses tucked away in the hills and along the south coast, as well as the odd fantastic old plantation house which takes in guests; great stops if you are travelling around the island. You can book direct, or through the **Jamaica Reservation Service**, 1320 South Dixie Highway, Suite 1180, Coral Gables, FL 33146 (tel US toll free 1 800 JAMAICA and in Canada 800 432 7559). For some alternative retreats, contact **JATCHA**, the Jamaica Alternative Tourism Camping and Hiking Association, at PO Box 216, Kingston 7 (tel 809 927 2097, fax 926 0727).

Villa Rental
Individual villa rental, with anything from a studio to seven bedrooms on offer, can be arranged through **JAVA**, the Jamaica Association of Villas and Apartments, based in Ocho Rios, PO Box 298, Pineapple Place (tel 974 2508). The London address is TC Ltd, 21 Blandford St, London W1H 3AD (tel (071) 486 3560) and they can be contacted in Miami on 1320 South Dixie Highway, Suite 845, Coral Gables, Miami, Florida 33146 (tel (305) 667 0179, toll free (800) 221 8830).

All hotel rates are quoted in US Dollars—you can pay with credit cards and traveller's

583

cheques in all hotels. There is a General Consumption Tax of 10% levied on all purchases and hotel bills. Some hotels also charge 10% for service.

Kingston

MODERATE

Most of the hotels in New Kingston, are a couple of miles from the waterfront and downtown area. The most charming and comfortable is the **Terra Nova Hotel** at 17 Waterloo Rd, Kingston 10 (tel 809 926 9334, fax 929 4933). It is set in an expanse of gardens, a town-house with classical balustrades and a rarefied atmosphere away from the hustle of town. It is still very much an uptown meeting place. There are just 33 rooms in the main house and a newer block, a pool and a good dining room. Double room US$90–150. There is a clutch of other small hotels in the area. Try the **Hotel Four Seasons**, 18 Ruthven Rd (tel 929 7655, fax 929 5964), in an Edwardian town house, with veranda at the front for the bar and restaurant. The interior is a little unlikely for the Caribbean—panelled walls and sumptuously thick carpets, but it has a pleasant atmosphere for a stopover in town. The 39 rooms are not luxurious but perfectly comfortable, double US$50–58. No pool, but the front desk will arrange for you to go to one. The **Courtleigh Hotel**, 31 Trafalgar Rd (tel 926 8174, fax 926 7801) is also quite friendly and attracts an amusing crowd on the veranda bar. There are two pools, one with a bar and tropical flowers all around and rooms are in a block, while the suites are in their own annexe. Double room US$60–70.

CHEAP

You can find cheaper rooms at the **Indies Hotel** on Holborn Rd nearby (tel 926 2952). Just 14 rooms around a small courtyard. Private baths and phones and a restaurant over the road. Double room US$40–45. There are also **guest houses** in this area of town. You can try the **Sandhurst** at 70 Sandhurst Crescent, Kingston 6 (tel 927 7239). Simple, with private baths for US$40. Next to the Indies Hotel is **Mrs Johnson's** Guest House (tel 926 0296), rooms also with private baths. Both have a single rate of US$20.

BUSINESS

If you are on business in this area of Kingston you might try the **Wyndham Hotel**, 77 Knutsford Blvd (tel 926 5430, fax 929 7439), which has complete business services. Double room US$115–190. And if you would prefer to be downtown, then you can stay at the **Oceana Hotel** on the waterfront, 2 King St (tel 922 0920, fax 922 3928). The hotel is set in a block with views of the harbour and has business and conference facilities, and international standards of comfort and services. Double room US$125–145.

Rooms with a View and into the Blue Mountains

Within a shout of town (a short ferry ride across the harbour) is **Morgan's Harbour Hotel** at Port Royal (tel 924 8468, fax 924 8562). There are 60 air-conditioned and fan-ventilated rooms set in their own grounds. Pretty rooms decorated with Jamaican wood furniture and of course superb views over Kingston and the hills beyond. Some watersports, double room US$105.

A corresponding view over the town from the other side (just as spectacular) can be had from the ridge at Jack's Hill, at **Ivor Guest House** (tel 977 0033, fax 926 7061). At 2000 feet above the town, the old colonial house has a superb setting—one of the best on the island. And there is even a telescope on the veranda for a closer look at the hustle of the town below. Inside there are still the wooden floors, door-frames and the antiques of times past, to go with the gracious hospitality. Just three rooms, with four-posters, and home Jamaican home cooking. Afternoon tea and cocktails on the veranda (worth going up there for that). Double rate excellent at US$80. Another good Jamaican retreat is close by at **Maya Lodge**, PO Box 216 (tel 927 2097, fax 926 0727). There is a main house, with endless information on Jamaican wildlife and walking, and terraces outside from where you can admire the scenery. But it is an activity place, with birding and walking tracks all around, as well as a good stopover for longer expeditions. It gets quite cold on winter evenings, so take a jersey. Cool and quiet, local Jamaican food, 4 cabins $20, hostel space and tent-sites, US$7.50. Facilities are quite basic. Higher up into the Blue Mountains you will find the **Pine Grove Hotel**, c/o 62 Duke St (tel 922 8705, fax 922 5895), with 14 rooms scattered on the hillside beneath the central house, where there is a restaurant and bar. Double room US$45. Yet higher in the mountains, on an old coffee plantation at 4000 ft is **Whitfield Hall Hostel**, contact 8 Armon Crescent, Kingston 6 (tel 927 0986), another retreat lost in the grandeur of the Jamaican peaks. Very remote (you need a four-wheel drive to get there, which can be arranged with the number above) and you must take your own food. No electricity, gas lamps, single rate US$10. It is a favourite drop off point for those climbing the Blue Mountain Peak.

Clockwise from Kingston
There is nowhere good to stay in Spanish Town, so you are advised to stay in Kingston, but there is a small hotel in May Pen; the **Versailles** on Longbridge Ave (tel 986 2775), with a double room at US$34. There are also rooms on the south coast at the **Milk River Mineral Baths** (tel 924 9544). Simple accommodation, massage clinic, restaurant and of course the mineral baths themselves. Bicycles can be hired. Not many tourists. Double room, US$25–30.

In **Mandeville**, the old hill station in the centre of the island, you will find the **Astra Hotel**, PO Box 60 (tel 962 3265, fax 962 1461), a family-run hotel up the hill on Ward Avenue. It is in a modern house, with 40 rooms, which are comfortable, but the charm is in the people. Double room US$50–100 in season. You might also try the **Mandeville Hotel**, 4 Hotel St (tel 962 2138, fax 962 0700), also in a modern block, with rooms overlooking the pool and gardens. Double room US$90–130. Cheaper rooms can be found at the **Roden Guest House** down the hill on Wesley Road (tel 962 2552), US$30. In the town of Christiana, in the hills to the north of Mandeville you will find a nice retreat in the **Hotel Villa Bella**, PO Box 473 (tel/fax 964 2243). The hotel harks back to the 50s; the building is quite modern, but there is a gracious air of times past, in the drawing room and on the veranda (an old sign says ring twice for ice water, three times for the maid). Very well kept, comfortable rooms upstairs at US$50.

The area to the west of Mandeville has some charming small, typically Jamaican guest houses and some inns off the beaten track. The **Treasure Beach** Hotel, PO Box 5 (tel 965 2305, fax 965 2544), has simple and comfortable rooms above a good stretch of beach. It is a quiet resort with just 16 rooms in cottages, with pool and watersports, US$80 a double. A cheaper alternative at Treasure Beach is the **Four M's Cottage** on the beach, restaurant and kitchens, just US$35 for a double. There are also villas for hire in this area. You will find a guest house not far off, the **Ital Rest**—two rooms for just US$25 and camping space available. There are cheap rooms available in Black River at the **Hotel Pontio** (tel 965 2255).

In the hills above Black River you will find another guest house, set in the grand and fertile splendour of **Apple Valley** at Maggotty (no phone). The guest house is by the river itself and there is swimming and walking around the area, though accommodation is simple. Just five rooms at US$20 a single, US$30 a double, camping available. And to the west of Black River you will find the **South Sea View Guest House**, Whitehouse Post Office (tel 965 2550), set on its own beach, with eight comfortable rooms, single US$37, double US$75. **Natanias's Guest House**, is just up from Whitehouse and has 16 rooms in a modern house set right on a small secluded beach, with some watersports, very quiet, no phone, US$50 for a double. Close to Bluefields, the **Wilton on the Sea Guest House**, PO Box 20 (tel 955 2852) is set above the sea, a classic writer's retreat in a family home. There are just four bedrooms in the main house and a cottage in the garden, US$75.

Negril
Long renowned for its pleasure-seeking and sensual way of life, Negril has excellent and easy-going places to stay, on both sides of town (the beach and the cliffs). The resort is peopled by latterday hippies and the odd original one. The laid-back style has also been updated and repackaged for 90s man and woman, in some excellent all-inclusive hotels.

EXPENSIVE
Hedonism II, PO Box 25 (tel 957 4201, fax 957 4289, US 800 858 8009) is the naughtiest club in town. Set at the northern end of the Negril Beach, the resort allows couples, but encourages singles in a seemingly endless volley of hedonistic activities; bar open 19 hours a day, nudes and prudes beaches, watersports, diving, trapeze and juggling instruction, wet T-shirt competitions, body-painting lessons (your's or some-body else's), singalong piano bar, drink and dance till you drop (or find a partner), mirrors on the bedroom ceiling, breakfast served until late (and then it all begins again). US$200 per person per night in high season; you may be put in a room with a stranger if you arrive as a single. 'Be Wicked for a Week'! Next door, the **Grand Lido**, PO Box 88 (tel 957 4010, fax 957 4317, US 800 858 8009), on a lovely strip of sand in Bloody Bay is a much more stately affair. It has taken the all-inclusive concept up-market—you are received with champagne and there are three dining rooms, two of them *à la carte*. The formal French restaurant—abstract of grilled pork followed by snowball chiffon, jackets required (but they can lend you one if you forgot yours)—and an Italian dining room. The hotel is large with 200 sumptuous rooms with stunning sea views, good beaches (one nude) and endless watersports. The daily rate for a couple is expensive at US$490 for a couple and $345 for a single.

MODERATE
There are a number of smaller hotels in the middle price-range. The calm and quiet **Charela Inn**, PO Box 33 (tel 957 4277, fax 957 4414) sits on a prime piece of Negril sand, with a fantastic sunset view through the palm trees of course. It is a small and friendly hotel, 36 bedrooms with balconies overlooking a lush courtyard or the beach itself; some family units. Windsurfers and sunfish. Double rate US$130–155. Good restaurant with French cuisine.

On the cliffs at the other end of town are some hip spots where you can stay, many of them available at quite good prices. There is of course no beach there (jumping off the cliffs and swimming the coral reefs are the favoured activities), but it is a good place to hang out (the other main pastime). The best hotel is probably **Xtabi on the Cliffs**, PO

Box 19 (tel 957 4336). There are just 14 fan-ventilated rooms in cabins on the clifftops and a central house with a hip bar and restaurant, though the rooms have cooking facilities. Pool and watersports can be arranged. Double room US$45–105. Another excellent spot, with rooms overlooking the sea or buried in the tropical profusion of the garden is **Banana Shout**, PO Box 4 (tel 957 4007). Comfortable wooden cottages with a hammock on the terrace, just ten rooms. There is no restaurant (breakfast can be delivered), but there are good bars around. Rates in winter US$50–100. The **Rock House**, PO Box 24 (tel 957 4373) also has a spectacular setting on the clifftops. The cabins are quite simple, wooden and rustic palm thatch, but they have private baths and fan ventilation and of course, a superb view. Double rate in winter, US$80–120. For a truly Jamaican experience, perhaps a weekend away from you hotel, you might try **Dream Scape Villa** (tel 957 4495). The villa is modern, aggressively air-conditioned, with thick-pile carpets, boxing gym (if you like that sort of thing), jacuzzi, king-sized waterbeds and a line of Mercedes with tinted windows in the car-park. Double room US$150.

CHEAP
There are cheaper rooms throughout the town. On the beach you will find the 'finest in rooms and campings' at **Roots Bamboo** (tel 957 4479). Double rooms with private baths and porch looking out onto a sandy garden, US$40–45, tent sites $20. Restaurant. You can find comfortable rooms at a small spot with the unlikely name of **Perseverance Resort** (tel 957 4333) Simple but clean, US$30 a double. And just south of Negril Lighthouse there are cabins, cottages and tent-sites at **Lighthouse Park** (tel 957 4490), US$30–60, tent-sites $15.

The North Coast—Montego Bay
Montego Bay is the leading resort area in Jamaica and you will find the town itself studded with huge towerblocks of hotel rooms. Farther afield, tucked away in their own coves, are some of the Caribbean's most luxurious resorts.

EXPENSIVE
The **Half Moon Golf, Tennis and Beach Club**, PO Box 80 (tel 953 2211, fax 953 1731, US 800 237 3237) lies eight miles out of the town to the east, an enclave of colonial splendour set on a lovely half-moon curve of beach. A neo-classical great house stands in sumptuous tropical gardens, where you will find hidden 17 swimming pools, 13 tennis courts and 4 squash courts. There are plenty of watersports (jetskis excluded) and the golf course is just across the road. The 209 rooms are in a single block and in assorted suites and villas around the grounds—the Royal suites on the beachfront are superbly comfortable, high sumptuousness in the Half Moon colour-scheme of black and white. The **Sugar Mill** Restaurant serves creole and international fare in a colonial-style house with chequerboard tiles or on the veranda overlooking the golf course—sautéed pork mignon with mango sauce or snapper in almonds and cashews. Double room US$250–660. **Round Hill Hotel and Villas**, PO Box 64 (tel 952 5150, fax 952 2505) lies eight miles to the west of the town. It has maintained a reliable air of stately exclusivity since 1954 and sees generations of returning guests. The 27 villas stand in their own gardens on the slopes of the Round Hill and other rooms are in a block above the private beach.

THE CARIBBEAN

Watersports are available if the library palls, rooms US$250–440 in winter. A third enclave of low-key, high luxury lies a few miles further on at the **Tryall Golf, Tennis and Beach Club**, PO Box 1206 (tel 952 5110, fax 952 0401). The great house, an elegant conglomeration of buildings in colonial style, stands amid the palm trees on the crest of a hill, with the 52 luxurious rooms lined out on the hillside overlooking the golf course. Scuba and other watersports are available if you are feeling active, otherwise croquet and afternoon tea on the veranda. Double room US$250–410. If you like an action-packed, all-inclusive holiday in a crowded beach hotel, then you will find two **Sandal's** Resorts in Montego Bay, of which the better is probably Sandal's Royal Caribbean.

MODERATE
The town has a number of smaller hotels with style, a lower-key atmosphere and easy access to the restaurants and bars of Montego Bay. The **Reading Reef Club**, PO Box 225, Reading Post Office (tel 952 5909, fax 952 7217) is across the bay from the town, on a small beach with some watersports There are just 21 rooms in small blocks and a friendly bar. Quiet and well off the beaten tourist trail. Double room in season US$100–185. If you do not need to step straight from your bedroom on to the beach, you can try the **Richmond Hill Hotel**, PO Box 362 (tel 952 3859, fax 952 6106), which has a commanding view of the bay from a hillside above the town. The columns and balustrades around the old estate house and pool give a feel of classical colonial grandeur and inside you will find the antique ambience of a planter's retreat. US$107 for a double room in season. The **Coral Cliff Hotel**, PO Box 253 (tel 952 2147, fax 952 6532), on Gloucester Ave also has a certain style. Unlike most of the hotels in the area, it was built as a private home rather than as a hotel, and it retains some homely comforts and charms—the wooden floors, breezy corridors, garden setting of the old house and its antique telephone exchange. There are 21 rooms in the older style and a pool above near the newer block. The hotel sees a crowd of friendly repeat visitors. Double rooms US$54–60.

CHEAP
There are also plenty of **guest houses** in Montego Bay. You will find that people will offer to take you to them if you are looking a bit lost at the airport. Registered guest houses include **Caribic House** (tel 952 5013, fax 952 0981), which is near all the bars on Gloucester Avenue, rooms US$40–60 and the **Comfort Guest House** (tel 952 1238) on Jarrett Terrace, where a double is US$40. And on Sunset Boulevard, above the airport, the **Ocean View Guest House** has rooms for US$20 per person. Finally there is an excellent guest house and camp-ground outside the town at **Orange River Lodge**, PO Box 822 (tel 952 1145, fax 952 6241). It is set in a thousand acres of wild Jamaican land on the edge of the Cockpit Country. Excellent walking and swimming. Rooms US$35 a double, hostel $10 per person, tent site $5.

In **Runaway Bay** (most of the way to Ocho Rios) you will find good all-inclusive fare at **Jamaica Jamaica**, PO Box 58 (tel 973 2436, fax 973 2352). All the watersports are on offer (including diving on the barrier reef) from the lovely stretch of beach (there is a nudist beach and jacuzzi) and there is a golf course with school attached and an exercise gym. Evening entertainment includes a piano bar, mixology (the theory and practice of

588

cocktail mixing) live accompaniment to dinner and then band and discotheque. US$175–230 per person per day. Next door, **FDR** (Franklyn D Resort), PO Box 201 (tel 973 3067, fax 973 3071) sells itself as a 'giant step for kid kind'. The package is all-inclusive here too, but the activity is centred mainly around taking the children off your hands for a week. A 'girl Friday' will put them through their paces at finger painting, early computer programming, kiddies disco technique or simply run them around until they tire out so that you can busy yourself with more important things like windsurfing and sitting at the pool bar. She also cooks and babysits for you. 67 modern, high-pastel suites, US$213–235 per person per day. The **Runaway HEART Club**, PO Box 98 (tel 973 2671, fax 973 2693), has just 20 rooms with balconies looking on to well-kept gardens above the coast. The service is superb as many of the staff are drawn from the hotel training school next door, but it is also a quiet and fun place to stay. Double rooms at US$50 in season. The **Caribbean Isle**, PO Box 119 (tel 973 2364), a small hotel with good Jamaican informality, has clean and simple rooms, meals available, for US$60 plus per double; and the oddly named **Accommodationer** in Discovery Bay (tel 973 2559, fax 973 3020) has just seven rooms with kitchens at US$44. Some watersports and other sports nearby.

Ocho Rios

Ocho Rios has put in a late bid as Jamaica's leading tourist centre (it used to be a sleepy fishing village, but it has a string of good beaches) and there are some excellent hotels in the town, and a string of restaurants, bars and clubs to keep everyone occupied in the evening.

EXPENSIVE

The **Jamaica Inn**, PO Box 1 (tel 974 2514), two miles from the centre of the town, is set in its own bay, a cove with a fantastic stretch of sand protected by small headlands on either side. There is a refined and graceful air in the old estate house and each of the impeccably decorated rooms has its own colonnaded balcony looking down on to the sea. Pool and watersports if you are feeling active, library and scrabble if the desire should pass. Just 45 rooms ranging from US$350–400 per night in season. Another hillside enclave, all but hidden in an explosively fertile Jamaican garden, is the **Sans Souci Hotel**, PO Box 103 (tel 974 2353, fax 974 2544), a more modern version of Jamaican luxury. It lies four miles beyond the town centre and the 70 rooms with balconies stand on the hillside above the hotel spa, with its pool and work-out area, around the point from the beach, where most watersports are available. Sumptuous and expensive at US$330 a double room in season. The **Plantation Inn**, PO Box 2 (tel 974 5601, fax 974 5912), is another luxury hotel, with 80-odd rooms in blocks overlooking a 200-yard strip of golden beach, enclosed either end by headlands. You cruise up to a classical atrium and inside, the halls and the rooms and suites are bright, airy and very comfortable, US$250–320 a day.

ALL INCLUSIVES

A new addition in Ocho Rios is **Ciboney**, PO Box 728 (tel 974 1027, fax 974 5838), a deluxe all-inclusive resort with 250 rooms in suites, set on the hillside above a huge mock-colonial plantation house. There are tennis courts and squash courts, a spa for manicures, pedicures and water-jet treatment etc etc and if you are feeling hot you can always take a dip in one of the resort's 90 swimming pools. A regular shuttle takes you to the beach, where there are watersports. There are five restaurants, including one with light menus (five courses for just 1,000 calories—breast of chicken with papaya or shrimp sausage with pasta. It is large and busy, but not too crowded and the honeymoon suites are an excellent retreat. US$200–380 per person in the winter season. In a rather different style is **Couples**, PO Box 330 (tel 974 4271, fax 974 4439), another all-inclusive resort to the east of the town, where you will find an action-packed régime of daytime watersports (or intensive lazing around on the offshore island, where there is a nudist beach) and other essential activities like massage and pool volleyball. Everything happens in pairs here, from the beach chairs to the cocktails (the bar is open all day of course). And love is in the air, certainly if you follow the example of the lions on the hotel logo. Breakfast and lunch are buffets, but dinner is *à deux, à la carte*. $2400–3400 per couple per week in season. You must arrive in a man-woman couple. Not far off, the **Boscobel Beach**, PO Box 63 (tel 974 3331, fax 975 3270) is also all-inclusive in plan, but it caters specifically for families with children. They will be taken off your hands at all moments and put through their paces in arts and crafts and given lessons in Jamaican *patois* while you follow the more urgent pursuits of tanning and windsurfing. There are 200 rooms in the complex, which is set on a cracking beach. The charge starts at around US$180–335 per person per day.

MODERATE

The **Shaw Park Beach Hotel**, PO Box 17 (tel 974 2552, fax 974 5042) has a certain style, a mock-colonial house that stands above a protected cove and beach. It is not too large at 128 rooms and suites, comfortable and modern and all with a view across the sea. Plenty of watersports down below and a dining terrace that makes the best of the waterfront setting too. Double room in season US$150–238. You will find a good price at the **Silver Seas Hotel**, PO Box 81 (tel 974 2755, fax 974 5739, US 800 544 5499), which stands on the clifftops in the centre of town, rooms overlooking the balustraded terraces and the restaurant to the ocean. There are 80 rooms above the small beach, where there are windsurfers and sailing boats on offer. Double rate in season US$70. The **Hibiscus Lodge Hotel**, PO Box 52 (tel 974 2813, fax 974 1874) also stands in nice gardens on the clifftops, and on stepped terraces beneath you will find the restaurants, bars and swimming pool, shaded by tropical greenery and a huge almond tree (from which the restaurant takes its name). Watersports down below for the daytime and some entertainment in the evenings, particularly at the bar with its chairs slung from the ceiling. Rooms comfortable if not luxurious, double rate US$62–68 in season.

CHEAP

Cheaper rooms can be found at **Pier View Apartments**, PO Box 134 (tel 974 2607) in the centre of town, a short walk from Turtle Beach. The 14 rooms have private baths and ceiling fans. No pool or dining room, but all the restaurants are close by. Double rate just US$40 in season. At 25 St James Ave, near all the bars you will find **Seeker's Guest House and Lounge** (tel 974 5763), where there is a hip bar with heavy reggae and rooms at US$20 a single or $30 a double, private baths, no pool. Just up from the White River on the main road is the **Hummingbird Haven**, PO Box 95 (tel 974 5188, fax 974

2559), a garden retreat set in six acres of forested hillside, just up from the beach. Simple cabins (only six of them) at US$20, endless tent-sites for $5. There is a restaurant that serves breakfast and snacks, but not kitchen facilities. A friendly stopover for travellers and walkers and you can pick up good advice about where to walk in the area. Up the hill you get a fantastic view from the very simple **Murphy Hill** guest house, about US$25. Finally there is a charming spot at Buff Bay between Ocho Rios and Port Antonio, at **Crystal Springs Guest House** (contact Stuart's Travel, King's Plaza, Kingston, tel 929 4222, fax 926 0727). It is well off the beaten trail, set slightly inland, in a tropical park with hiking and bird-watching all around. There are cottages, US$50 a couple, a camping area, $10 and a swimming pool and restaurant.

Port Antonio

The **Trident Villas and Hotel** are one of the most low key and luxurious spots in the Caribbean, PO Box 119 (tel 993 2602, fax 993 2590), just east of the town. 12 rooms and 14 cottages are set neatly in luxurious gardens, of palms and pine hedges with roaming peacocks and doves, on a dramatic ledge of Jamaican ironshore. The rooms are exquisitely decorated—tiled, with stained wood panelling and solid furniture in the black and white colour scheme that runs throughout the resort. Ventilation is still by fan and sea breeze here rather than air-conditioning and each room has its own veranda. In the winter season double rooms cost US$250–320 and up to US$800 for the magnificent Imperial Suite. A little closer to town is the surprising and sumptuous **Jamaica Palace Hotel**, PO Box 277 (tel 993 2020, fax 993 3459), set in a recently converted private house (more of a palace really). It stands stark white in the luxurious greenery of the forest. Everywhere there are marble floors, candelabra, Persian rugs and antique furniture. 60 luxurious rooms, a pool in the shape of Jamaica, beaches and watersports nearby and low-key evening entertainment, including a dining room with a sculpted waterfall. Double room US$100–165 and suites US$280. The **Goblin Hill Villas** at San San further east of the town, PO Box 26 (tel 925 8108, fax 925 6248), are 28 villas set in 12 acres of peaceful, luxuriant Jamaican garden on a hillside. Pool up top, beach down below with watersports, maid service included, US$1280 per night for a two-bedroomed villa. In Port Antonio harbour is **Navy Island**, with the **Admiralty Club Hotel**, PO Box 188 (tel 993 2667, fax 993 2041), the former haunt of Errol Flynn and in the 50s the most hip resort on the island. The glitz has faded, but the island still has an inimitable allure—staff predict lazily that you will return here, and they may just be right. There are about 30 rooms hidden in villas in the mantle of palms on the 60-acre island, with three beaches (one 'clothes optional'), and watersports. The restaurant and bar stand out over the water on an enclosed terrace. Double rooms US$100–150 in season. The **Bonnie View Hotel**, PO Box 82 (tel 993 2752, fax 993 2862, US 800 448 5398) is set on the summit of the hill in the town and has a fantastic view of the red roofs and the two harbours of Port Antonio. It is past its best, and is simply decorated, but it is a good stopover if you are travelling the island. Double room US$72–82.

Down on the point itself you will find several smaller hotels and guest houses, some of them set in the classic old Jamaican town-houses from the turn of the century, set with shingle tiles and wrought-iron balconies. **De Montevin Lodge**, PO Box 85 (tel 993 2604), has 15 rooms in the three storeys, some with their own balconies. Quite simple and expensive at the moment, from $66 a double. Not far off is **Ivan Owen's Guest**

House on Queen St, with rooms at about US$20 and you will find very cheap, if simple rooms, or a villa at the **Holiday Home** (tel 993 2882), on Ffrench Avenue and King St.

EATING OUT

Once the staple diet of the plantation slaves, ackee and saltfish is now a Jamaican national dish. Ackee is the yellow fruit of the *ackee* tree from Africa, which cooks and tastes like scrambled egg, and salt fish is salted cod, originally imported as food for the slaves. Other classic Jamaican dishes include curry goat, callaloo and rice and peas, cooked in coconut milk. Good use is made of the Caribbean vegetables—*pepperpot* is a thick soup based on okra; popular traditional vegetables are breadfruit and plantain. Fruits—soursop, sweetsop, coconut, mango, pawpaw and pineapple—are served at breakfast, as midday thirst-quenchers and in the ice creams. Many restaurants will offer you Jamaica's own Blue Mountain coffee, widely thought to be the best in the world. It rounds off a dinner well.

In hotel dining rooms you are most likely to come across international type food (with the occasional Jamaican buffet), but some are becoming more adventurous, and there is a greater variety on offer within the hotels now. You have to go outside the hotels or go local to get good Jamaican food. *Jerk* centres (see p. 560) are well worth the visit, and an excellent lunchtime snack is a patty and a soft drink, rounded off with a rock cake with sultanas or coconut. Some restaurants and particularly hotel dining rooms require a jacket and occasionally a tie for dinner. Credit cards can be used in the larger restaurants. There is a General Consumption Tax of 10% and many restaurants also charge service.

Kingston and Surrounding Area

EXPENSIVE

The top dining in the capital at the moment is at **The Restaurant** (tel 942 4430) at the Temple Hall Estate, a few minutes beyond Stony Hill, on the heights above the town. (If you are driving, it is off the Constant Spring Road.) The Restaurant is set in the bright white decor of a 17th century great house and retains an atmosphere of antique colonial splendour. The menu is Jamaican, with an exotic Caribbean variation on *nouvelle cuisine*—home made *fettuccine* with grilled Black River shrimp in Chardonnay cream, lamb Londonderry and garlic papchoy in escovitch sauce. A set meal of five courses costs J$450, wine from the extensive cellar costs extra. In a vast cleft in the mountains, on the road to Gordon Town is the **Blue Mountain Inn** (tel 927 7400), with a lavish interior to match the prices of the mixed menu, where steaks are served as well as local creole dishes of chicken and fish, followed by Jamaican ice creams. Sometimes music, but always a brilliant view of the river from the terrace, J$350 plus for a main course.

In town, **Norma's** (tel 929 4966) is an excellent spot for lunch, and dinner on Thurs and Fri, at 8 Belmont Rd off Oxford Rd. You eat on a pretty, open veranda or in the paved garden, at tables with blue and white striped cloths, sitting on metal garden chairs. The menu varies daily according to what's fresh, but you can expect such exotic delights as chicken stuffed with cream cheese and garlic, glazed with orange sauce, or roast Cornish game hen in a *flambé* of raisins. Main course J$200–350. There is also a good dining room at the **Terra Nova Hotel** (tel 926 9334) on Waterloo Rd, where you dine in the colonial setting of a neo-classical villa built at the turn of the century. Dinners include thermidors and chowders of local Jamaican seafood, and average at J$350. At **Ivor Guest House** you can dine in the gracious antique setting of a small plantation house high above the town, in Jack's Hill. The food is West Indian, with local seafood and vegetables, cooked and served much as it has been for the last 100 years, from J$200.

MODERATE
Something of the Port Royal of the 1680s exists in the old warehouse building of the **Grog Shoppe** at Devon House in New Kingston—the guests behave rather better now though. You will see locals as well as visitors here; after you have tucked into a list of exotic and colourful cocktails, you will be served local Jamaican callaloo and hot pot, as well as burgers and steaks. An easy spot under the mango tree, main course about J$180. In a similar style with tables set on a terrace beneath a mango tree is **Heather's** in Haining Rd. Heather's is popular with expats, who cluster here for a drink after work, J$150. A popular seafood restaurant in downtown Kingston is the **Pirates Cave** near the Port Royal ferry terminal. Chowders or a crab-back followed by grilled catch of the day with rice'n peas, J$80–120. In Port Royal itself you will find a cool joint on the water front, **The Cabins**. Local Jamaican food—chicken and fry fish or maybe lobster, with a tonnage of ground provisions. Not far off is **Gloria's**, the Jamaican's favourite for a snack. The thing to order is fish and bammy and *Red Stripe* to wash it down. Back in **New Kingston** the **Indies Pub** collects a croud after work, and at lunchtime when it is popular with the New Kingston business people. Simple chicken and fish with chips, or a pizza, J$100 a main course. And for local Jamaican fare try the **Hot Pot** on Altamont Crescent behind the Wyndham Hotel. Wooden tables set with plastic tablecloths around a sparse courtyard and rice 'n' peas or a fricassée chicken, served with dumpling and plantain, J$50 a main course.

CHEAP
Minnie's Ethiopian Herbal Healthfood Restaurant (tel 927 9207) has a style all of its own. At the top of Old Hope Road it is built entirely of wood, a conical cabin with thatch roofing. The menu is only partly Ethiopian, and you can expect Jamaican *ital* (rasta vegetarian) food and juices, perhaps a stew fish in coconut milk or gungo (pigeon) pea stew. Breakfast, lunch and dinner, dishes J$55–100 and juices J$16, closed Sun. You can get a **vegetarian** meal at the **Eden** Restaurant, 7th Ave Plaza, 29 Constant Spring Road—home-made breads with ground provisions in a *run down*. Closed Sat. You might also try **Lyn's** Restaurant at 7 Tangerine Place (tel 929 3842) Kingston 10, which also has a good selection of vegetarian fare.

There are several **Jerk Centres** in town. Perhaps the most popular is the **Chelsea Jerk Centre** on Chelsea Avenue in New Kingston, where you can get chicken or pork doused in hot pepper sauce, closed Sun. Also try **Peppers** on Waterloo Road. You can always get a barbecued half-chicken from one of the ladies on the roadside cooking on upturned braziers.

Mandeville
In Mandeville, apart from the hotels, the best place to eat is **Bill Laurie's Steak House**, which stands in the hillside high above the town in an old gingerbread house, with licence plates and visiting cards from the world over stuck on the walls, and a number of old classic cars in the garden. Good steak accompanied by Jamaican

593

vegetables—entertainment is made by the guests (there's a piano there if you want to play); J$250–350 a main course.

Negril

Negril has a full range of restaurants, many in keeping with the laid-back air of the town. You can grab a simple meal with an excellent view of sea and sunset. If you want something formal you will have to choose one of the hotels.

MODERATE

You will find a classic Caribbean setting and fare at **Tanya's** (tel 959 4041), where the tables are set aroung the pool, just a hop from the beach. A superb lemon shrimp or *chicken sunset* with white wine, mushroom and cheese. Some French dishes, about J$200. The **Hungry Lion**, on the cliffs, has a style all of its own, with benches and tables in the open air around a forested tropical courtyard. Exotic nature foods and juices—lobster in lemon butter or kingfish in coconut milk, attended by hip waiters. It is quite small and popular, so it fills up quickly—get there early, main course J$180–250. One of the mellowest dining rooms in town is the **Paradise Café**, about half a mile inland from the roundabout, on the road to Savanna-la-Mar. The tables are set on open terraces in a wooden cabin with a tin roof and sheltered beneath flamboyant and palm tree. The best in local cuisine—chicken fricassée, curry goat or a rasta pasta, J$100–200. Another excellent spot, set on its own strip of Negril beach is **Cosmo's**—simple bamboo decor open to the sea breeze. Similar fare—grilled catch of the day or curry conch with *bammy*, J$150–200. The **Bar-B-Barn**, also stands among the palms on the beach front, and you eat on the terrace or in a glass-fronted dining room. Shrimp in lemon butter J$350, or barbecued ribs, chicken and fish.

CHEAP

At **Erica's** (on the cliffs), a local dining room with bright red tablecloths and curtains and roses on the tables, you can get a chicken or a fish for J$70. And for a take-away chicken in a box try **Chicken Lavish**, not far from the roundabout leading south, about the same price.

Montego Bay

EXPENSIVE

Norma's of Kingston fame has recently opened up just outside the town, in Reading (tel 979 2745). You dine at the water's edge beneath coloured awnings on the jetty of an old sugar warehouse. The fish dish will vary with the catch of the day—otherwise grilled devilled crab-back followed by fresh local shrimp in Jamaican spicy sauce J$200–350. There are two stalwart restaurants around town, set in the manicured antique surrounds of Montegonian town houses. The **Town House** is in an elegant Georgian mansion. Start with a cocktail and baked coconut chips (while you decide which painting to buy from the walls around you). The dining room is in the brick-walled cellar—chicken in orange and ginger or Jamaican stuffed lobster, US$15. Not far off is the **Georgian House** (tel 952 0632) on Orange Street, which has a classic English West Indian setting. Once again, you dine in gracious colonial splendour. The fare is international with variations on the theme of shrimp—in garlic butter or barbecued—and steak—fillet maurier, with exotic fruit salads and ice creams to follow, main course US$21–29. There is a nice bar downstairs in the cellars, where you can take a rum punch or a Red Stripe.

JAMAICA

The Diplomat (tel 952 3353) is set on the hillside on Queen's Drive; a modern town house, but there is a refined air about the restaurant because of its open-terraced dining room overlooking the pool and fountains. The menu offers continental and Jamaican dishes—a catch of the day in creole sauce or lobster in butter, main course around US$20. Among the hotels, the Half Moon has an excellent restaurant at the Sugar Mill (see Where To Stay) and the Coral Cliff has a good dining room specializing in local fish and seafood, and if you would like a Thai meal, try the Sandals Royal Caribbean.

MODERATE
Downtown, among the bars of Gloucester Avenue you will find a couple of lively places, first for a drink, and then a light meal. Marguerite's is set on a terrace just above the sea and you can catch a soup and a salad or a cocktail while you are watching satellite TV, US$8. And at Willoughby's you can play a game of pool between courses—deep fried shrimps or grilled chicken kebab US$15. If you feel that you would like a fondu, you might try the Houseboat (tel 952 5817), where you dine on the bay while cooking your own food on the table.

There are a couple of good local Jamaican restaurants in Montego Bay—plush plastic bench seats and aggressively air-conditioned, but classics of their kind because of the food. Try Smokey Joe's, in a little alley off St James's Avenue. Delicious pumpkin soup, followed by curry goat and rice 'n' peas, J$80 a main dish. And not far off is Greg's, a little more expensive, set upstairs in a house on Church Lane. Lobster or other seafoods and juice for J$200. A classic among Jerk Centres is the Pork Pit, at the corner of Kent Avenue and Sunset Boulevard. Benches outside where you can savour pork, chicken, spear rib and a festival with a chopped coconut to drink. At Patsy's you can get good local chicken or fish, and there are plenty of stalls around for a lunchtime patty and an ice cream.

On the north coast between Mo Bay and Ocho Rios there are plenty of small and local restaurants, good stopovers for a beer and a chicken or fish. At the village of Rock on the coast you can get a tasty conch and a beer at Glistening Waters, on a terrace at the waterfront. After dinner it is well worth taking the tour of the lake to see the phosphorescence. Between Discovery Bay and Runaway Bay are some breezy shacks where you can pick up a fish and bammy. And at Runaway Bay you will find the Seafood Giant, an octagonal cabin with open sides and pointed thatch roof—fry fish or steam fish in peppers in okra butter, all barbecued on pimento wood and eaten to a loud reggae and rock accompaniment. Daytime and evening popular with the Jamaicans J$100. Also very popular with the locals is The Mug, which you will find on the waterfront at St Anns. It is mainly a bar in the evening, but during the day you can get a good fry fish and bammy or shrimps swimming in garlic butter.

Ocho Rios
Ocho Rios has a string of good dining rooms in its smarter hotels and there are several excellent independent restaurants as well as a whole array of local haunts where you can get a wholesome Jamaican meal. At the Carib Inn (tel 974 2445) you dine on an open terrace looking out onto a lovely floodlit tropical garden, where the tree frogs peep their night song. It is presided over by brisk, tuxedoed waiters. A seafood menu, lobster flamed at the table or pan-boiled shrimp with delectable vegetables, US$15–30, simpler lunchtime salads at US$10. The Almond Tree restaurant, at the Hibiscus Lodge

Hotel, on the main street, is reckoned to be one of the best dining rooms in town. It is set on a terrace high above the sea, with gingerbread fretwork surrounded by greenery and of course a huge almond tree. Superb pumpkin soup followed by snapper or kingfish in coconut and then a volley of tropical fruit ice creams, US$10–30. Perhaps the best known restaurant in town is **The Ruins** (tel 974 2442) on da Costa Drive. It gets very crowded, so it's hardly one for a romantic meal à deux, but it still has a nice setting. Limestone waterfalls like those at Dunn's River are floodlit and you eat on platforms as the water flows past, serenaded from time to time. Beef in oyster sauce or fish creole, Chinese dishes too, US$15–20. **Evita's** (tel 974 2333) on Eden Bower Road, has a cracking view from the hillside above the town near the Old Carinosa Gardens. Pastas, pizzas and southern Italian fare, main course US$20–25.

If you wish to go a bit more local try the **Parkway** Restaurant on Main Street. A true West Indian dining room, air-conditioned and with the TV playing and tables set with plastic table-mats—Jamaican chicken or a fried rice and shrimp followed by banana cake, US$9. In a similar style and setting is **Jeff's** Restaurant, as you walk west from downtown. Formica tops with wicker chairs and Jamaican music on the stereo. Curried chicken US$10 or conch creole, US$10. **Mom's** Restaurant, on Evelyn Street opposite the police station, will also serve you a good Jamaican meal with a Red Stripe. Yet more local, there are two **Jerk Centres** in Ocho Rios, one on Main Street close to Jeff's and the other on the road out of town to the east, **The Double V**, a wooden cabin open to the winds and the tropical garden.

There are few places in which to eat in **Port Antonio**. If you want to dine out you will have to go to the hotels. **Trident Villas** has a delightful veranda setting in classic old West Indian style, and you will get good Jamaican fare at the **Bonnie View** (tel 993 2752). The **Admiralty Club** on Navy Island (tel 993 2667), has a cracking setting for dinner, on a terrace.

The **Port Antonio Marniers** is across the bay on the mainland and collects a crowd of passing yachties. Good for a drink or a meal throughout the day—a rustic wooden cabin and an easy going feel, on West St, burgers and grilled or fried fish about US$10. Down the street you will find a fine Jamaican restaurant in **Daddy D's**—plastic tablecloths and flowers, curry goat and conch, US$7 a main course. You will also get a good local meal at **Tri-me** for about the same price. And if you suddenly feel like a jerk (pork or chicken) you can try **Stop Brap Jerk** on the road east out of town.

A few miles east of Port Antonio is **Boston Bay**, home of jerk, if you want the original thing. There are three or four centres on either side of the road—**Sufferer's Jerk** and **The Front Line**. You sit on open-air terraces while the barbecueing process happens around you. About J$60 for a portion, *festivals* and beer extra.

BARS AND NIGHTLIFE

Entertainment in the hotels is varied—in some places it owes nothing to Jamaica, and is as packaged as the holiday that gets you there (wet T-shirt competitions, pot-belly contests, fire-eating, and limbo competitions that nobody wins because they all fall over backwards). However, there are good discotheques in some of the larger and more sophisticated hotels, and there is often a lively crowd at the all-inclusives if you can get in for the evening.

The clubs are fun and worth a visit to see the Jamaicans themselves at play, though you should be slightly wary in some areas of Montego Bay and Kingston about going in alone.

Perhaps go with a Jamaican guide. There are plenty of venues for concerts around the island—keep an eye on the papers because sometimes world famous reggae bands will play a gig in a small club. And of course there are limitless bars around the island, from the hillside setting of plantation house restaurants or a local rumshop to the cliffs and beachside bars of Negril, where the crowds gather to watch the sunset with almost religious adoration.

The national brew of Jamaica ia *Red Stripe* beer, though you will also find many imported beers. *Appleton* is the best known rum—the smoothest is Appleton *Gold*, but the most popular among the Jamaicans is Appletons *Overproof*, a white rum which is also known as John Crow Batty because of its fearsome strength.

A great place to start any evening in Kingston is at **Ivor Lodge** in Jack's Hill. It has a fantastic view across the city from the veranda, as far as Port Royal in the distance. Good for a rum punch in old Jamaican surroundings. Back down in the thick of the town there are plenty of haunts, part bar, part restaurant, frequented by Kingstonians. The **Indies Pub** on Holborn Road is always popular, as is **Heather's** on Haining road. Both have a garden where you can sit out beneath a huge floodlit tree and they attract a lively crowd at the weekend. You might also pass by **Peppers** on Waterloo Road or **Chancers Bar**. If you want to gou out dancing in Kingston you can try **Illusions** in the Lane Plaza on South Avenue or **Epiphany**. Live bands play occasionally in **The Club** on Knutsford Boulevard.

Negril has a multitude of bars and clubs along its ten miles or so of seafront. Watching the sunset is one of the highlights of the day and traditionally this is popular at **Rick's** (so popular now that they bus them in.) If you want something a little less crowded, try the **LTU Pub** a couple of hundred yards further on—still lively, but fewer lobster-red tourists. Two other fun spots are the **Awee Maway** bar and **Kayser's**, where you sometimes get music and a sunset drink on little sitting areas on the limestone rock. On the other side of town there are some cracking bars right on the beach. The **Hurricane Bar** is an octagon of bamboo on a superb strip of sand—plenty of music and plenty to drink. And at **De Buss**, last resting place of a pink and green double decker that washed up here, perhaps in the 60s, you will find another beach bar with live music. For more regular concerts, check the reggae parks—**Central Park** and **MX3** and for dancing try **Compulsion**, at Plaza de Negril at the roundabout, or **Close Encounter**, at the Kings Plaza.

In **Montego Bay** things are a bit more up-beat—the major gathering joint is along Gloucester Avenue. Perhaps start at **Marguerite's** where there is a waterfront setting and a cocktail list as long as your arm. **Hemingway's Pub** is popular, an air-conditioned lounge-bar with leather benches, stained wood and brass, and close by is **Walter's**, a garden bar with TV (you can keep up with the NFL at most bars in the area), popular with locals and with tourists. If you're one for a game of pool and a beer, go to **Willoughby's Bar** just close by. There is a cracking view of the sunset from up the hill at **Mickey's Bar** on Queen's Drive. **Pier 1** is a very lively meeting and pairing off bar, particularly on Fridays. Monday night in Montego Bay sees a *jump-up* on Gloucester Avenue, which is quite fun and there is usually a live show on Fridays at Walter Fletcher Beach. The two most popular discotheques in town are **The Cave** at the Seawinds Hotel and, a much more Jamaican affair, **Sir Winston's**, a dungeon-like dance-floor with mirrors, car-numberplates and loud dancehall music.

Ocho Rios is similarly upbeat and so outside the hotels, where there are plenty of shows, you will find a string of bars and clubs. To the west of the town, in St Anns, you will find **The Mug**, a waterfront bar which attracts a fun crowd—the hotel workers like it. Going out of town the other way you will find **Sid's on the Bay**, an easy-going haunt down by the White River with a view of the Caribbean sea and waves washing up to your feet. But Ocho Rios centres around Main Street and St James's Avenue, where you will find **Bill's Place** upstairs, a laid back bar that attracts a loud crowd, and **Ocean Sands**, on a terrace above the water. The **Little Pub** plays loud rock in an air-conditioned lounge and often has a band in the evening. Finally if you need a beer after a spot of bungee jumping, or just to watch someone else at it, try **Ease the Tension**, down on St James's Avenue.

At the **Grotto** you can grab a cocktail to piano accompaniment before moving on to the clubs: the **Acropolis** on Main Street, the **Limelight** at Burger King plaza, and best of all the **Roof Club** on St James's Avenue, an open air lounge and roof top where you will hear the latest in dancehall as well as some more traditional reggae.

Port Antonio is of course much more mellow, but there are some good bars—you could catch a drink at the **Rafter's Rest**, at the bottom of the Rio Grande. Two good restaurant bars in town are the **Admiralty Club** on Navy Island, where you can get a cocktail above the water and **Shadows** Restaurant and lounge. If you want to go dancing, try **Blue Jay's Club** or best of all, the **Roof Club** on West Street, a wild and hip spot which is well worth checking out.

THE CAYMAN ISLANDS

The tiny Cayman Islands are well known internationally as an offshore banking centre, the official home to massive corporations, but they are equally celebrated among diving fiends as having some of the finest coral grounds in the Caribbean. The two industries have combined to make the Caymans highly developed and for their size the most prosperous islands in the Caribbean.

The three Cayman Islands lie in the western Caribbean, northwest of Jamaica and south of Miami and Cuba. They are the coral-encrusted summits of a submarine mountain range (around them the slopes descend to the Bartlett Deep and the Cayman Trough, at 3500 fathoms, the deepest water in the Caribbean). The islands are in two groups, separated by 89 miles of sea. In the south is Grand Cayman, where the capital George Town is situated. Its two partners are to the northeast: Cayman Brac and Little Cayman are just two miles apart.

No point on the Caymans rises to more than 140 ft, and so they do not have the rainfall and the luxurious greenery of other Caribbean islands. They are mainly covered in a tangle of scrub forest with mangrove swamps, with superb beaches along the coasts. There is not much wildlife on land, just the ubiquitous Caribbean goat and a few indigenous iguanas (though there is an endemic parrot on Cayman Brac). Turtles still visit the islands, but the marine crocodile, from which the name *cayman* comes, is no longer seen. Beneath the waterline though, the Caymans have a stunning variety of corals, sponges and tropical fish.

598

There are about 28,000 Caymanians and they are extremely easy-going. Most live on Grand Cayman; Cayman Brac has a population of about 1500 and Little Cayman just 40. About half the islanders have a mix of African and European blood—you will recognize the familiar red of the Caymanian hair. There is no black-white animosity in the Cayman Islands. Caymanian English is easy to understand—if you hear a different *patois*, it is probably Jamaican. The islands are strongly influenced by the USA—home-delivery pizzas, satellite TV, and in places Grand Cayman looks as though it is in danger of becoming an outsized shopping precinct.

The Cayman Islands package is very slick. It caters well for high pressure 90s execs who are looking for a by-the-hour, percentage return on their watersports time (if you begin to feel out of touch you can always hire a cellular phone and call the broker). You can even take an extra-curricular course in the advantages of offshore banking in the Caymans. However, the Caymans are still slow and gentle and the people are some of the most approachable in the Caribbean, so it is a good place for a break.

History

As Columbus passed Cayman Brac on his fourth voyage in 1503, he saw 'two very small and low islands, full of tortoises, as was the sea all about'. He named the islands the *Tortugas* after them. A while later they were known as *los lagartos*, after the alligators, but eventually the name *Caymanas* stuck, taken from the crocodiles and iguanas seen on the island.

Initially, Little Cayman became a stopover for the water supply and the easily available food—iguanas and turtles (the latter will stay alive for weeks if laid on their backs). It was not until the invasion of nearby Jamaica in 1655 that the islands were settled. Supposedly two soldiers by the name of Walter and Bowden came to Grand Cayman (their names are still evident in the Caymanian names Watler and Bodden). In 1670 the Spaniards gave up Jamaica and the Caymans to Britain at the Treaty of Madrid. This did not make the islanders any safer, though, as they were still harassed by the Spaniards and roving bands of pirates who put in occasionally. The settlers farmed cotton and turtles (as many as 40 turtling ships would set out from Kingston in the season) and they became wreckers—taking what they could find from the ships that foundered on the reefs. The wrecks are still happening, though laws are stricter about salvage now; off the east end of Grand Cayman, there is a magnificent hulk a few hundred yards out to sea.

In 1802 the population on Grand Cayman had climbed to 933, of whom just over half were slaves until Emancipation in 1834. Cayman Brac and Little Cayman were only settled permanently in 1833. By the turn of the century, there were 5000 Caymanians, and without employment on the islands, the men went to sea to make a living. They were renowned for their seamanship and were in particular demand by National Bulk Carriers of New York.

For three centuries the Cayman Islands were administered as a part of Jamaica, but on 4 June 1960, as the Jamaicans prepared for Independence, the Caymanians seceded, preferring instead to become a Crown Colony directly dependent on the UK. Today the Cayman Islands are administered by the representative of Queen Elizabeth, Governor Michael Gore, who presides over the Executive Council. The Governor is in charge of defence, foreign affairs, police and internal security. Elections to the 12-man Legislative Assembly take place every four years.

Alongside tourism, the central pillar of the Cayman economy is offshore finance, and among the reams of tourist bumf (the Cayman seems to produce more than anywhere else in all the Caribbean) you will find brochures on how to invest in the Caymans. The islands are basically tax free (though visitors will find themselves paying a 6% government tax on their hotel room) and the handling of money is made as easy as possible (no direct taxation, laws of confidentiality, absence of exchange controls, teams of lawyers and accountants to handle it all, good communications). The islands are famous for it and they have attracted over 500 banks and 20,000 companies to register on the island. Hardly any even have an office; they are simply a plaque on the wall.

GETTING TO THE CAYMAN ISLANDS

By Air
You will fly into Grand Cayman (from where local connecting flights can usually be taken on the same day to Cayman Brac or Little Cayman). The National Carrier is Cayman Airways, Grand Cayman (tel 92311), in Cayman Brac (tel 83235) and in Kingston, Jamaica (tel 926 1762). There is a departure tax of CI$6 (US$7.50).
From Europe: there are no direct flights from Europe. Connections are best made in Miami or New York.
From the USA: the main centre for flights to the Cayman Islands is Miami, from where five or six flights originate each day (Cayman Airways, American Airlines and Northwest Airlines). Other direct links in the States, some of them stopping at Miami, include those from Atlanta (twice a week on Cayman Airways), Baltimore (5 times weekly on Cayman Airways), Chicago (daily on American Airlines), Houston (2 or 3 a week on Cayman Airways), Memphis (daily on Northwest), New York (3 times a week on Cayman Airways) and Tampa (once or twice a week on Cayman Airways).
From other Caribbean Islands: there are five flights a week to Kingston, Jamaica, on Air Jamaica or on Cayman Airways, with a stop in Montego Bay on Thursdays and Cayman Airways have a service to the Turks and Caicos Islands.

GETTING BETWEEN THE ISLANDS
Cayman Airways usually make a daily flight between Grand Cayman and Cayman Brac in a light plane or a 737. It is possible to arrange a day's return flight to Little Cayman, returning to Grand Cayman around 6 pm (price about US$70).

GETTING AROUND THE CAYMANS
There is a **bus** service running along the seven-mile strip on Grand Cayman, but it is quite difficult to spot. It departs from the main square hourly and runs to West Bay in the north, where most of the Caymanians live. Fare $1. Except on the seven-mile strip, **hitching** is quite a reliable way to get around. Elsewhere on the island, and on Cayman Brac, you will find that the Caymanians stop without you even flagging them down.

There is an abundance of **taxis**, many of them Dodge vans, in Grand Cayman, and if there is not one to hand, just wander into the foyer of the nearest hotel. Fares are fixed by the government: **airport** to George Town—US$8, mid-way up Seven Mile beach—US$11.50, West Bay (top of Seven Mile beach)—US$18.50, Spanish Cove—US$21.50, Bodden Town—US$21–50, East End and North Side—US$40, Water Cay—US$50.

Taxi-drivers would be happy to take you on an island **tour**, with up to five people in the cab. Reckon on an hourly rate of US$30. Tours are also available by bus. Contact **Evco Tours** (tel 92118), **Majestic Tours** (tel 97773) or **Tropicana Tours** (tel 90944).

Cars are readily available. Everything in the Caymans proceeds at a stately pace, the driving included, which is something of a relief after other Caribbean Islands. There are so many cars on Grand Cayman that there is even a traffic jam going into town sometimes. You need a local driving licence (issued by the hire firm, price US$5) and a credit card or cheque deposit. Better rates for a week's hire, but all the firms have roughly similar prices. Driving is on the left. Rates start at US$35 for the smallest car, with charges on top (cheaper rates in summer). Contact **Ace Hertz** (tel 92280), **Andy's Rent a Car** (tel 93391), **Coconut**, with good rates (tel 94037) or **National** (tel 94790).

Scooters and motorbikes are widely available and are a very good way of getting around, though hoteliers sometimes try to bully their guests into not using them because they send so many honeymooners home in plaster. Rates around US$25–30 per day, driving licence required. Contact **Cayman Cycle Rentals** (tel 74020) or **Soto Scooters** (tel 74652) in Coconut Place. **Bicycles** are available through the same companies for about US$10 per day (the only hill on the Cayman Islands is at the eastern end of Cayman Brac).

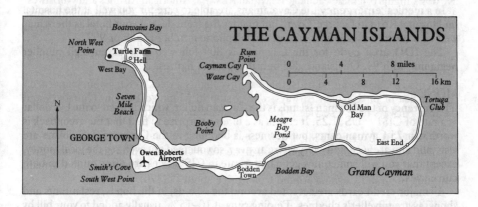

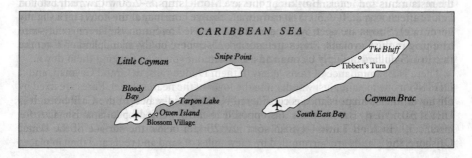

601

TOURIST INFORMATION

In **UK**, the Cayman Islands Department of Tourism, 100 Brompton Rd, Knightsbridge, London SW3 1EX (tel (071) 581 9960, fax 071 584 4463).

Germany: contact Hans Regh Associates, Postfach 930247, Elbinger Str 1, D–6000 Frankfurt/Main 90, (tel (69) 704013).

Italy G & A Martinengo, Via Fratelli, Ruffini 9, 20123 Milano (tel 39 3 48 01 20 68).

USA: there are many offices. In New York, write to 420 Lexington Ave, Suite 2733, New York, NY 10170 (tel (212) 682 5582, fax 212 986 5123), in Los Angeles; 3440 Wilshire Blvd, Suite 1202, Los Angeles, CA 90010 (tel (213) 738 1968).

Canada: contact Earl B Smith Travel Marketing Consultants, 234 Eglington Ave East, Suite 306, Toronto, Ontario, Canada M4P 1K5 (tel (416) 485 1550).

On island, you can write to the Cayman Islands Department of Tourism at PO Box 67, George Town, Grand Cayman, British West Indies (tel 949 0623, fax 949 7607). There is an information desk in the Tower Building in North Church St, George Town, one at the airport and one at the Craft Market, which opens up when the cruise ships are in town.

Tourist magazines, with advice about extra-curricular banking courses and where to buy a pin-striped bathing costume, include **Key to Cayman,** published yearly and the Cayman Airways in-flight magazine, *Horizons.* The local newspaper is the *Caymanian Compass,* which is published on weekdays.

In a medical **emergency** the Caymanians are able to care for you well at the hospital on Hospital Road in George Town, but first try the front desk at your hotel as there may well be a doctor on call. The emergency telephone number is 555 or 999.

The **IDD area code** for the Caymans is 809 followed by a seven-digit number beginning with 94. On-island, dial only the last five figures.

MONEY

The currency of the Cayman Islands is the Cayman dollar, which is fixed to the US dollar at a rate of CI\$1 = US\$1.25. It comes as a bit of a surprise to find that the greenback is worth just 75 Cayman cents, but business is booming in the Caymans. US dollars are also valid and are accepted everywhere anyway, so you need not even see the local money, except that you will sometimes get a better rate in CI\$. Prices are often quoted in both currencies.

All major credit cards are accepted around the islands, in the hotels, restaurants and shops, as are traveller's cheques. Tipping runs at 10–15%, usually added to your bill by the restaurants and hotels. **Banking** hours are Mon–Thurs, 9–2.30 with an extra slot on Friday afternoons 2.30–4.30. You can always change currency at the hotels (at a slightly lower rate). **Shops** are open 9–5 and are usually closed on Sundays. There is duty-free shopping in the Caymans. Prices are usually only quoted in Cayman dollars. To get the rate in US dollars multiply by one and a quarter.

DIVING

Diving in the Cayman Islands is considered by many as the best in the Caribbean. It is known particularly for its 'walls' (as opposed to the sloping drop-offs of Bonaire, for instance), which off Little Cayman start just 20 feet below the surface of the water. Offshore, the islands are surrounded by a few miles of sand and reefs and then in places the submarine mountain walls drop sheer to 20,000 ft. Visibility is superb in the Caymans, often as much as 150 ft.

Elsewhere there are caverns, pinnacles and underwater ravines, all of them encrusted with a vast array of corals, sponges and gorgonians: corals like tufts of shaggy white wool, thin tube sponges and vast barrel sponges, the jigsaw pattern of a purple seafan standing against the tide, and deep down the fingers of black coral.

Single damselfish pout and shimmering schools of wrasses and tangs dip and dart in unison in the exhaled bubbles. Camouflaged crabs eye you with suspicion from their hide, and little red and white banded coral shrimps tangle with their spindly feet and antennae. Shy and tiny seahorses, suspended, lunge to find the cover of the coral, starfish flip as they move. At 'sting-ray city' in the North Sound, you can spend the afternoon cavorting with tame rays five feet across.

There are reefs on all sides of Grand Cayman—off George Town and Seven Mile beach, but most popular is the **North Wall** off the north shore. Cayman Brac is less known than Grand Cayman, but according to many the diving is even better. The main sites are around the West End. On Little Cayman, the Jackson Wall and Bloody Bay are off the north shore. There are endless wrecks to choose from off the Caymans, the best known being the *Balboa* off George Town.

The Cayman Islands have strict laws for the protection of their reefs and fish, with different zones. Spearfishing and setting traps are prohibited and there are strict rules about anchoring. You are not allowed to take any corals or sponges. However, many of the diving outfits have underwater photography equipment, so you can take photographs of them, at least. If you happen to stumble across any buried treasure, then you have to work out an agreement with the Cayman government, because all wrecks and hordes officially belong to the Crown.

There are about 30 dive outfits on the islands. Most are attached to a hotel, but there are some self-contained live-aboard cruisers which will go where you want them to. With the land-based concessionaires, a single tank dive costs from US$35 with all equipment and two tanks US$50. Night dives cost around US$45. Divers should have a 'C' card or take a resort course (about US$75), available with most dive shops. There is a decompression chamber on the island (tel 94324). Good dive outfits on Grand Cayman include **Sunset Divers**, PO Box 479 (tel 97111), south of George Town, **Fisheye**, PO Box 2123 (tel 74209), **Quabbin Dives**, PO Box 157, just north of George Town (tel 95597), **Bob Soto's**, PO Box 1801 (tel 74631) and **Cayman Kai**, PO Box 1112 (tel 79056), a little out of the way on the north side, but good prices. In Cayman Brac, contact the **Divi Tiara Beach Resort** (tel 87553) and on Little Cayman contact **Sam McCoy's Diving Lodge** (tel 82249) or the **Southern Cross Club** (tel 83255).

For those who do not dive, but who would like to see the reefs' colourful growth, there is always the **Atlantis Submarine**. The dives are quite expensive at US$58, but the guides are informative and knowledgeable. The submarine leaves from South Church St, just down from the Museum. Find out how groupers cope with the boredom of middle age. You get a deeper and personalised tour in the three man submersibles of **Research Submersibles Ltd**, PO Box 1719 Grand Cayman (tel 98296, fax 97421). They dive the wall down to 800 ft with lamps to illuminate the corals as the sunlight fades and so you will find yourself suspended between huge barrel sponges and turtles and visiting the odd wreck. Price $200.

BEACHES

Grand Cayman's Seven Mile beach is one of the world's most famous, and its gently shelving sands run from just north of George Town to West Bay, up the west coast of the island. It is the centre of the island's tourism, and the majority of the hotels, watersports and diving operations are located along it. It is marginally less crowded at the northern end, though it is steadily becoming more and more built up. Facing west, it has one of the finest views of the sunset anywhere, with a good chance of seeing the Green Flash, of course. The Caymanians ask you not to wander around the town in your bathing costume, and nudity or even toplessness is not really on unless you get right off the beaten track. There are many beach bars attached to the hotels where you can stop for a drink and admire the sunset.

There are other less busy beaches, all of them public below the high-water mark, scattered along the coastline. It is easy to find a secluded spot if you are prepared to travel a bit. A favourite with the Caymanians is **Smith's Cove**, a mile or so south of town. Otherwise head for the south coast with beaches protected by fringing reefs and to the **East End**, where isolated suntraps are hidden behind bushes of sea grape at the end of sandy tracks. The same goes for the north coast, where among the 'ironshore', the pitted and pointed remains of old coral reef, there are particularly good spots at **Cayman Cay** and **Water Cay**.

In **Cayman Brac** there are beaches at the southwestern end of the island, where the hotels are situated. All along the southern edge of **Little Cayman** there is silken sand and idyllic shallows where the water glares with a power of blue. Try **Sandy Point** in the east and hidden strips of blinding white sand down the southern coast towards Owen Island and the hotels.

SPORTS

Windsurfers and small **sailing boats** can be hired at many of the hotels and watersports shops along Seven Mile Beach. The best winds are out towards the East End. The going rate for a board is US$20 per hour and for a hobie cat around US$30. Try **Sailboards Caribbean**, half way up the beach (tel 91068), **Aqua Delights** at the Holiday Inn (tel 74444), or **Surfside Watersports**, north of town (tel 97330) and at Rum Point (tel 79098). You can also take a bird's eye view over the island by **parasail** (about US$35 for 15 mins), or test out your biking skills on a jetski (US$35 per ½ hour). A more stately option is available in a **pedalo** at US$25 per ½ hour and a **glass-bottom boat** trip costs around US$22 for 2 hours. Some watersports shops will also take you **waterskiing** (US$50 per ½ hour). You can even take a high speed ride around the bay on an inflatable banana . . . (it'll shut the kids up anyway).

Yacht tours can also be arranged through the watersports shops, at about US$60–80 for a day's sail. Try **Sailboat Charters** (tel 79561), with day sails, dinner cruises and even trips to the Brac or Little Cayman, or **Charter Boat Headquarters** (tel 74340), opposite the Holiday Inn. An excellent tour is offered by the *Spirit of Ppalu*, which is based at the Hyatt Regency. Lunchtime visits to sting-ray city and sunset cruises. The going rate is US$50 for a half-day or a sunset cruise. There are two marinas on Grand Cayman, one either side of the North Sound; Morgan's Harbour (tel 93099) is at West Bay, and Kaibo (tel 79064) is on North Side. If you want a silly pirate cruise, with lots of rum and tee-ree-ree, you could try the Rock & Roll Booze Cruise at Aqua Delights (tel 947 4786).

Deep-sea fishing, casting for tuna and wahoo or six-ft marlin, is another popular day out on the high seas, and the Caymans have a host of sleek vessels. Rates are around US$500–600 for a full day for six people, US$300–400 for a half day. Try **Captain Eugene's** (tel 93099) at Morgan's Harbour in West Bay, **Standin' Tall** (tel 72348) in George Town, and **Crosby Ebanks** (tel 74049) near George Town. There are two operators on **Little Cayman**: Southern Cross Club (tel 83255, fax 69503) and Sam McCoy's Lodge (tel 84526). The rates are better in Little Cayman.

All the Cayman Islands have reefs close enough to the shore and shallow enough for excellent **snorkelling**. In Grand Cayman, there are reefs off the south coast and in the northeast, though you should be careful of the currents here. Some of the best snorkelling is at Eden Rock and Devil's Grotto south of George Town and at Soto's Reef (now known as Cheeseburger Reef because it is opposite Burger King). Also try the Cemetery at the top end of Seven Mile Beach. In **Cayman Brac** the best place is the western end of the north shore. All the watersports shops and most of the dive shops rent gear and have regular snorkelling trips. For **diving** see above.

On **land**, the most popular sport is **tennis**. There are plenty of courts available. If there is not a court at your hotel, arrange through the front desk to play elsewhere, fee about US$8–10 per hour, US$14 at night. There is a 9-hole **golf** course at the Hyatt Regency Hotel. Book well in advance, green fee US$40.

GRAND CAYMAN

George Town
The Cayman Islands' capital is situated on a broad bay in the southwest of Grand Cayman. Nothing remains of the *Hogstyes* after which it was originally called, before it was renamed after King George III at the beginning of the 19th century, but there are one or two timber buildings from old-time Cayman, including **Fort George**, at present being restored. The town is mostly modern concrete and among the few official buildings there is a superabundance of air-conditioned shops selling trinkets, clothes and coral jewellery to cruise ship passengers. To the east of the town centre is a small area which looks a bit more like the rest of the West Indies, where you will find local restaurants and the odd goat.

The **Cayman Maritime and Treasure Museum** is on the waterfront north of the town centre. There are some captivating exhibits about sailing and shipbuilding as well as the Blackbeard recordings. Test the weight of a gold bar at the exit. Open Mon–Sat, 9–4.30, adm exp. **McKee's Treasure Museum** has displays of loot discovered off the shores of Cayman in recent years from wrecks dating from the 17th century. Open 9–4.30, adm exp.

Out on the island, away from the tourist areas, you will see something of the Caymanian pride in the charming older houses. They are invariably neat, with verandas and white picket fences. Others of course have satellite dishes, but they are all set in pretty gardens festooned with blooms of tropical flowers.

Seven Mile Beach is not actually seven miles long (more like 5½), but it must have seemed like it to the inhabitants of West Bay who had to walk each morning to George Town to work. Many Caymanians, whose ancestors moved here when they were emancipated in 1835, live in this area, jokingly called the 'Republic of West Bay'. **Hell** is a small moonscape of inland ironshore, a petrified goo of limestone cake-mix. You can send a postcard from the special postbox which will be stamped Hell.

On the north shore is the **Turtle Farm**, a breeding farm and research station which breeds the green sea turtle, up to six or seven feet long and 200–600 lbs, in a series of tanks, where thousands of nippers scrabble over one another, and on a mock beach, where you will see the trails like tractor tracks where the females crawl up at night to lay 100 or so eggs. Five per cent of the turtles are released into the wild each year—others only make it into soup. Discover the secrets of what sex a turtle will be. Loggerheads, hawksbills and ridleys are also on view and there is a small menagerie of iguanas and alligators. Open daily 9–5, adm.

Headed east from George Town you come to Bodden Town, the island's only other town, which was the first capital. East of the town is Meagre Bay Pond, a bird sanctuary where you may well come across sandpipers and shovellers. Out in the country you will see the cattle and their companions, cattle egrets, that maintain daily silent vigil by their side. A road rings the east end of the island and inland the scrub is occasionally dotted with a Caymanian house or the rare Cayman iguana.

CAYMAN BRAC

Ask a 'Bracker' and they'll tell you that all the success has gone to their heads in Grand Cayman and that Cayman Brac still has the easy-going tranquillity that Grand Cayman had 20 years ago, before there were any hotels along Seven Mile Beach. The island takes the name from its cliff (Brac means cliff in Gaelic) that rises to a vertiginous 140 ft in the northeast. Scrub- and cactus-covered Cayman Brac is 12 miles long and about a mile wide and surrounded by reefs.

There is a small museum in Stake Bay on the north coast, with some old-time household utensils, but mostly more modern mementoes. You can take a trip around the island with a taxi driver, but you are best to set off on your own, perhaps from Spot Bay in the northeast, on the hunt for the Brac's parrot or a grebe.

LITTLE CAYMAN

Five miles to the southwest of the Brac is Little Cayman. It is just 10 miles long, about a mile wide and makes it to a massive 40 ft in height. Once Little Cayman had a population of 400 and was the most visited of the three islands because of the availability of fresh water, but it is inhabited by just 40 people today. The population of birds is far greater and around the ponds on the south coast you will find herons, ducks and stilts, and a flight of piratical magnificent frigatebirds with their huge red gullets.

A track runs along each coast from the airstrip in the southeast corner. The hotels are located in the southwest. Bloody Bay on the north coast was supposedly so called because of the blood on the beach after a conflict between the British and Spaniards.

FESTIVALS

The big event in the Caymanian calendar is **pirates week** in October, a swashbuckling affair of fake eye-patches and tee-ree-ree. It all gets a bit over the top, with choreographed invasions to amuse the tourists (the Caymanians themselves would surely never need an excuse like this for a booze-up), but the evenings are enjoyed by all in the bar. There is also a carnival, **Batanabo**, held in April each year, in which the islanders and visitors dress in theme costume and shuffle-step through the streets to steel bands and to loud soca music. It happens over a weekend in George Town. Cayman Brac also stages its own carnival, **Brachanal**, a week later, following a similar format. **Million Dollar Month** (June) is a month-long fishing competition, in which you might just catch US$250,000 prize-money if you hook and land a record-breaking blue marlin (584lbs). Other smaller prizes for other classes of fish. Winning catches mounted free of charge by the official Tournament Taxidermist.

WHERE TO STAY

Grand Cayman

The majority of the hotels are strung out along the 5 miles of Seven Mile Beach to the north of George Town and they range from simple and quite expensive guest houses (relative to the rest of the Caribbean, that is) to the height of luxury. Many of the hotels offer diving packages. All hotels add a government tax of 6% and usually a service charge of 10%. There are also a large number of condominiums and villas for rent if you wish to look after yourselves. Contact Reef House Ltd, PO Box 1540, Grand Cayman (tel 949 7093), Cayman Rent A Villa, PO Box 681 (tel 947 4144) or you can go through the Department of Tourism Reservations Office in London.

EXPENSIVE

At the top end of the scale, the **Hyatt Regency Hotel** on West Bay Rd, PO Box 1698 (tel 949 1234, fax 949 8528, US 800 223 1234), is the most luxurious place to stay, or to hold a conference. It is large (with 236 rooms), modern and decorated in plush Caribbean pastel, but harks back to a colonial era in the mock-classical columns and tall Georgian windows. The style is quite up-beat though, with a dip and sip bar, watersports across the road on the beach and *cuisine naturelle* in one of the four restaurants. Very comfortable, double room US$165–450. On the beach, the nicest of the large, factory-style hotels is the **Holiday Inn**, PO Box 904 (tel 74444, US 800 421 9999). The four storeys stand above a central pool area with palm thatch parasols and palms. And from there it is a short hop to the sea and the watersports. Good if you are happy to be in a large hotel, double room US$148–278. Unlike all the big pastel palaces, the **Beach Club**, PO Box 903 (tel 949 8100) has a gentler, more West Indian feel about it, with the venerable status of one of the island's oldest hotels. The 40 rooms look down from balconies or give straight on to the sand of Seven Mile Beach, with the restaurant and bar on a terrace, from where you get a superb view of the sunset. Watersports facilities. US$165–235 for a double.

MODERATE

The **Cayman Islander Hotel**, PO Box 509 (tel 949 0990) is north of George Town, across the West Bay Rd from the beach. With 64 rooms it has a friendly and more laid-back feel than the bigger hotels, but the rooms are comfortable and there is a pool. The beach is about 200 yards away, and restaurants not far down the road. Quite good value, from US$79 a double room, with good reductions in the summer. The **Sunset House Hotel**, PO Box 479 (tel 949 7111, fax 949 7101), is a lively inn, with a bar frequented by the Caymanians themselves. It is situated to the south of the George Town on a fringe of ironshore, but the reefs begin close by, and this is the primary advantage of the hotel which runs three dive boats. There are good packages for divers and 57 rooms from US$110–150 in winter. Similar prices are offered by the **Villa Caribe Inn**, PO Box 16 (tel 947 9636), on the north side (half an hour's drive from George Town and the airport). Very friendly, away from the relative hustle of the West Bay area, it has a dining room and charges US$105–125 for a double in season. A small hotel with the unlikely name of the **Ambassador's Inn**, PO Box 1789 (tel 949 7577), lies to the south of George Town, opposite the Grand Old House Restaurant. It is a low-key establishment set around a pleasant garden, with 18 reasonably priced rooms—US$80.

There is nowhere really cheap to stay on the Cayman Islands. The least expensive is **Irma Eldemire's Guest House**, PO Box 482 (tel 949 5387), south of George Town, where a simple double room will set you back US$70 in winter (perhaps worth bargaining).

Cayman Brac

There are two main hotels on the island, both specialists in diving, and with a classical beach-club feel, on the southwestern shore of the island. The **Tiara Beach Hotel** (tel 948 7553), run by the Divi chain, has 70 rooms on a strip of powder-soft sand sprouting with palms and tropical flowers. Tennis courts, a pool, some jacuzzis, watersports and snorkelling will set you back US$100–200. Not far off is the smaller (40-room) and even quieter **Brac Reef Beach Resort**, PO Box 56 (tel 948 7323, 947 5167), with comfortable rooms set around a pool area and sand shelving gently into clear turquoise water. A double room in winter is good value at US$140.

Little Cayman

There are just three small places to stay, including **Pirate's Point** (tel 948 4210, fax 948 4210) to the southwest of the island, with just 6 rooms. Luxurious accommodation and food, with daily diving and snorkelling and fishing, costs from US$140–150 per person per day (all in). The **Southern Cross Club** (tel 948 3255, US reservations 317 636 9503), set on a beach overlooking Owen Island on the south shore, has 10 rooms. Activity revolves around the central house, with expeditions down into the swamp to go bird-watching, as well as watersports on the beach. US$260 a double with meals. On the north shore of Little Cayman is **Sam McCoy's Guest House** (tel 948 2249), with just eight rooms, run by easy-going Sam McCoy. The rooms have ceiling fans as well as air-conditioning and private baths. Diving and fishing are the two main activities; the former is included in the good price of US$148 per person per day.

EATING OUT

As Grand Cayman has developed over the last twenty years, so too has a wide range of restaurants—from gourmet establishments with celebrity chefs from the USA, and successful local ventures serving West Indian food, to imported dial-a-pizza parlours, burger joints, and tiny local Caymanian restaurants in the back streets of George Town. There are also restaurants specializing in Italian, French, Mexican and Chinese food. A lot of what the hotels serve up is imported, but there is generally good seafood, so you can have spiny lobster, conch or turtle (farmed on Grand Cayman). You are advised to reserve tables in winter, when there will be a waiting list of up to three days in the popular expensive restaurants. Most restaurants except the smaller local ones add a 15% service charge to your bill.

EXPENSIVE
The **Grand Old House** (tel 99333) has the charming setting of an old gingerbread town-house on stilts, with tables scattered about the rooms and on the verandas. Chef Tell Erhardt of US television fame is the Master Chef here. The menu is international, with some variations on traditional Caribbean themes, including *wahoo* or turtle steak, garnished with local vegetables, followed by some heavyweight puddings. There is a long wine list of good quality, and a main dish costs US$25–35. Open seven days for dinner and on weekdays for lunch. The **Ristorante Pappagallo** (tel 91119) has a spectacular setting on a lake in West Bay north of Seven Mile Beach (though you might think it should really be in the South Pacific). As dusk falls, the mangroves around the lakeside are lit up—a good setting for a cocktail before you move into the tall thatched building to eat. The noisier parrots are kept at a safe distance from the dining room (which looks rustic, but is air-conditioned). They specialize in northern Italian cuisine, with good Caribbean seafood, including lobster and shrimp in a cream and brandy sauce. Main course about US$20. The **Almond Tree** (tel 92893) in the north of George Town has a fun, mock-rustic setting, where you sit in a tropical garden, under floodlit trees—guinep, breadfruit, almond. Start with callaloo, followed by mango chicken, or with a seafood combo of turtle and lobster. Also a nice bar and tables inside. Main course, US$15–25. The **Periwinkle** restaurant (tel 92927) on West Bay Rd, is set in a pink bungalow 3 miles north of George Town, with tables outside in a pretty Caymanian garden. It is always busy. The menu is European, but there is good local conch in creole sauce and swordfish or snapper in coconut, US$15–25. There are always vegetarian dishes on offer. The **Cook Rum** (tel 98670) offers excellent West Indian cuisine, in the comfortable surroundings of an air-conditioned Caymanian townhouse. Excellent seafood; lobstertail and shrimp in herbed butter sauce, or conch or turtle creole, a strong and tasty flavour, followed by delectable ice creams, costs about US$20 a main dish. The **Wharf** (tel 92231) is right on the waterfront on Seven Mile Beach and serves excellent local fare. You eat inside, or under parasols on the terrace above the waves. Good seafood—lobster and shrimp combination, steaks à la Madagascar or Bearnaise. Main dish US$20.

MODERATE
The **Cracked Conch** on Selkirk Plaza (tel 95717), is a relentlessly lively venue if you want an active night out. Some steaks and local fish, but mostly conch (pronounced 'conk'), marinaded, stewed, chowdered, curried, scalloped or even in a burger, around US$12 for a main course and entertainment.

CHEAP
The **Crows Nest** restaurant is on the beach just north of George Town, looking west to the sunset, and offers the best value in local fare; conch fritters followed by chicken curry

in coconut or garlic and rum shrimp, US$6–8. The **Jammin by the Sea** on on Harbour Drive in the centre of town has Jamaican jerk pork and chicken, roti, curry goat and other West Indian specialities like rice 'n' peas, open until 2 am if you feel like a drive and a midnight snack. About US$10. **Wellie's Cool Spot** is a local restaurant to which the Caymanians escape at lunchtime, about US$10.

BARS
Many of the restaurants have bars in which you can stop for a drink while you decide whether to eat there. And of course there are plenty of bars along the beach strip, from where you can admire the sunset. The **Lone Star** gets pretty rowdy in the evening. It is set in a wooden cabin, its walls covered in T-shirts (left by satisfied customers perhaps). TV playing continuously, so you can catch up on the NFL. The **Pirate's Den** is also quite a cool venue—dark-stained wood and drinking booths in of all places a shopping arcade. The restaurant is famous for its wings. There is a fine spot for liming at the **Rum Point Club**, rustic and on the shoreline. But **Apollo 11**, a bar in the North Sound is the coolest of them all. It is set in a large shed, with vast tree stumps carved out to resemble chairs and shutters held open on pegs. It is a bar from paradise at sunset.

In Cayman Brac you will find some easy-going local restaurants outside the hotels. Try **Angie's** in West End, or **Sonya's** in White Bay. In Little Cayman you will have to eat in the hotels or arrange to have a picnic on the beach.

THE TURKS and CAICOS ISLANDS

The Turks and Caicos stick out like a spur at the southeastern tip of the Bahamian archipelago. There are eight main islands and a host of tiny cays, sandbars and coral heads that just protrude from the sea. Like the Bahamas, the islands are set in shallows, with fringing reefs and superb corals, but here the sun glares so strongly and the sea is so intensely turquoise that it all appears almost surreal.

The islands, with an area of about 195 square miles in all, are situated 90 miles north of Haiti and about 575 miles southeast of Miami, in two separate groups. On the Caicos Bank in the west are the Caicos Islands (of which the best known is Providenciales), a string of scrub-covered coral-limestone shelves just a few feet above sea level. The highest point on the islands is 250 ft on Providenciales. The name Caicos is supposed to derive from the Spanish for 'islands' (*cayos*).

A further 22 miles east, across the 7000 foot depth of the Turks Island Passage, Grand Turk and Salt Cay are the cap of an outcrop that broke away from the main Bahamian archipelago millions of years ago. The 'Turks' in the name is supposed to come from the red flower of the Turk's Head cactus, which looks a bit like a fez. East of Grand Turk, the sea floor drops sheer into the the the Atlantic Ocean.

The 14,000 islanders are quiet and private and almost a little reserved, but friendly if you get to know them. Most of the original inhabitants are black or a mix of African and European, the descendants of slaves brought by white settlers, who left after their plantations failed. If you hear an incomprehensible gabble that sounds a bit like French, it is *kreyol*, spoken by the many Haitians who have fled here over the last few years.

Windsurfers, Providenciales

The Turks and Caicos are one of five remaining British Crown Colonies in the Caribbean. You still occasionally see the British imperial regalia paraded in the guise of military bands and peaked police caps, but as the islands, particularly Providenciales, develop, the American influence rings ever louder. The islands' economy rests on two principal industries—tourism and offshore finance.

The Turks and Caicos are not very well known and are visited by only a few people. For 100 years, they even had an igloo on the national flag because a colonial flagmaker, who presumed that they were near the Arctic, mistook their symbol, a pile of salt, for an igloo and kindly added a door. But those who do visit often return, for the islands' magnificent beaches and superb diving. For the moment, most of the Turks and Caicos Islands still retain the tranquil feel of the British West Indies as they were 40 years ago, but as the developers move in with their JCBs, this may not be so for long.

History

There are occasional claims that the Turks and Caicos were the original landfall of Columbus in the New World. The Bahamians claim that this is nothing more than an idle rumour put out by the Turks and Caicos Tourist Board, but it has credibility with some historians. If it was not Columbus himself, then the next contender was Ponce de Léon, who is supposed to have dropped by in 1512, while on his quest for the Fountain of Youth.

At any rate, there were Arawak Indians living on the islands at the time of Columbus's arrival (some remains have been uncovered recently) and their thousands of years of peace were destroyed within a few decades by the European newcomers. They were within easy reach of Hispaniola and so were rounded up and shipped out to work in the Spanish gold mines.

The population gone, the islands had nothing to offer the Spaniards and so they left them alone for the next couple of centuries. It was a convenient stopover for the

611

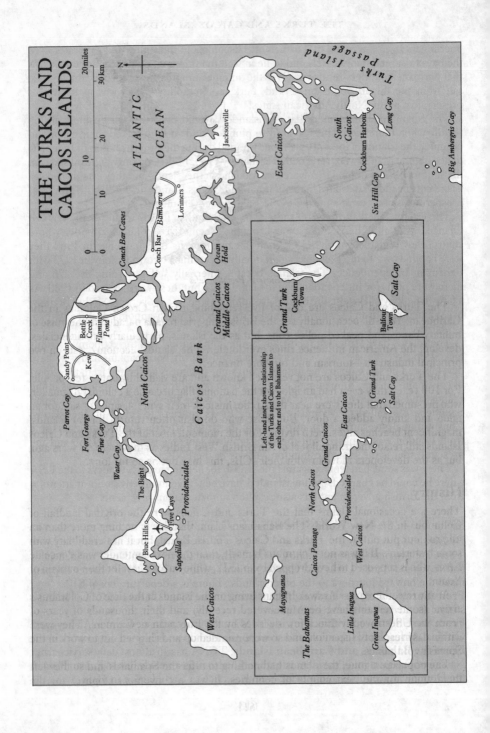

THE TURKS AND
CAICOS ISLANDS

ATLANTIC

OCEAN

20 miles

30 km

N

Turks Island Passage

Jacksonville

East Caicos

South Caicos

Cockburn Harbour

Long Cay

Six Hill Cay

Big Ambergris Cay

Conch Bar Caves

Bambarra

Lorimers

Conch Bar

Ocean Hold

Grand Caicos
Middle Caicos

Caicos Bank

Bottle Creek

Flamingo Pond

Kew

Sandy Point

North Caicos

Parrot Cay

Fort George

Pine Cay

Water Cay

The Bight

Providenciales

Blue Hills

Five Cays

Sapodilla

Grand Turk
Cockburn Town

Salt Cay

Balfour Town

Left-hand inset shows relationship
of the Turks and Caicos Islands to
each other and to the Bahamas.

Grand Turk

Salt Cay

East Caicos

Grand Caicos

North Caicos

Providenciales

West Caicos

Caicos Passage

Mayaguana

The Bahamas

Little Inagua

Great Inagua

West Caicos

buccaneers from the island of Tortuga off Hispaniola to the south, and so pirates used the bays to careen their vessels and to lie in wait for shipping, but it was not until 1678 that permanent settlers returned. Over the summer months Bermudians came to rake salt from the inland ponds on Grand Turk, a commodity which was in need as a preservative in the North American states.

The Spaniards complained that the islanders would drop the salt business all too readily when there were ships around to plunder, and so they staked their claim and occupied the islands in the 1710s. France invaded during the American War of Independence but the islands were returned to Britain by 1783. Following the war, loyalists from the southern states of the USA were granted land in the islands and they established sea island cotton and sisal estates in the uninhabited Caicos Islands. In 1799, both groups of prosperous islands were annexed to the Bahamas government.

The estates failed and most of the planters left, and so in 1873, after many years of financial difficulty, the islanders voted to annex themselves to Jamaica, under whose control they remained until 1959. When Jamaica took its Independence in 1962 they were handed over to the Bahamas again, finally becoming a Crown Colony in 1973 with Bahamian Independence. The islands became internally self-governing in 1976 and there were plans for Independence in the late 1970s, but these were shelved in 1980. As a Crown Colony of Britain, the islands are administered by a Governor, Michel Bradley, in conjunction with an Executive Council (partly elected, partly appointed) and a 13-man Legislative Council.

The islands have struggled financially in the 20th century and the economy has only picked up over the last few years as tourism and the offshore banking industry have developed. The salt industry has finished, but some income is generated from the export of conch and lobster. Smuggling has always been one of the principal industries in the islands and it came to the fore again in 1985 when the Chief Minister, Norman Saunders, was jailed in Miami for allowing drugs couriers to refuel on the islands. Constitutional government was suspended by the British after the scandal and direct rule from London was imposed, but the ministerial system was restored in 1988 and the present leader is the Hon Washington Missick of the PNP.

There was some bad feeling against the British for helping to get Saunders to the USA where he could be charged, but the islanders have benefited indirectly as closer attention from the British government has also resulted in material improvements.

GETTING TO THE TURKS AND CAICOS

By Air

There are two main airports of entry in the Turks and Caicos Island, on Providenciales and on Grand Turk. Turks and Caicos National Airlines (TCNA) or charter hoppers make the onward journeys to the other islands. There is a departure tax of $10.

From Europe: there are no direct flights from Europe to the Turks and Caicos Islands, so you are advised to change in Miami.

From the USA: the only direct link is with Miami. Between them, Cayman Airways and Carnival Airlines have six services a week to the islands.

From the Bahamas and Caribbean Islands: TCNA has an almost daily service from Nassau or Freeport into Providenciales. TCNA also runs a weekly link to Puerto Plata in the Dominican Republic and a twice-weekly service to Cap Haitien in Haiti.

By Sea
There are no scheduled passenger links to the Turks and Caicos, but you can always try hitching out of the islands by asking at the container ship wharf at South Dock on Providenciales.

GETTING BETWEEN THE ISLANDS
As with most buses in the West Indies, you will find that the islanders say good morning when they board the TCNA 'bus service'—the twice-daily, eight-seater shuttle that flies along the chain of islands, departing Grand Turk and touching South Caicos, Middle Caicos, North Caicos and Providenciales (occasional services also go to Salt Cay and Pine Cay). If you cannot get a seat, ask around; you may well find that someone is chartering a plane and wants other passengers to share the cost (TCNA; tel 946 2350). Charter companies include Charles Air Services (tel 946 4352), Blue Hills Aviation (tel 946 4388) and Flamingo Air (tel 946 2108).

The **Caicos Express** (tel 946 7111) ferry links Providenciales (known as Provo), Pine Cay and North Caicos four times daily, Mon–Sat. Occasional ferries link other islands (e.g. North and Middle Caicos). Otherwise try your luck at hitching a ride from Five Cays docks on the south side.

GETTING AROUND THE TURKS AND CAICOS
There is no **bus** service (except for the schoolkids on Providenciales) and so you must either walk, hitch (usual lottery, but quite reliable) or take a **taxi**, which works on fixed rates and is expensive. Taxi drivers will ferry you from one sight to the next for about $25 per hour.

Island tours are available on Provo through **Executive Tours** (tel 4524) or **Turtle Tours** (tel 4393), who will also fly you to one of the smaller islands for the day—Salt Cay, Pine Cay, Middle Caicos.

Cars and **scooters** are available for hire on the major islands. Rates are around $35 per day for a small car. Remember to drive on the left. On **Grand Turk** try the Island Reef Hotel (tel 2055) and on **Provo** contact Provo Rent-A-Car (tel 4404) or Pride (tel 4325) and for a motorbike 'Scooter' (tel 4684) in the central square (rates exorbitant at $25 per day). On South Caicos, ask at the hotels.

TOURIST INFORMATION
The Turks and Caicos Islands have Tourist Boards in:
UK: 3 Epirus Rd, Fulham, London SW6 7UJ (tel (071) 376 2981).
USA: R Keating and Associates, 425 Madison Ave, New York, NY 10017 (tel 212 888 4110, fax 212 888 5817). From the USA you can call the islands toll free on (800) 441 4419.

On island, contact the Department of Tourism on Front St, Grand Turk (tel 2321), where they keep hours of Mon–Thurs 8–4.30 and Fri till 4. There is also a Tourism Office in Providenciales at No 17, Turtle Cove Landing (tel 946 4970).

The magazine *Times of the Islands* is published quarterly and contains some features as well as advice for sun-worshippers and investors alike. In a medical **emergency**, contact the 24-hour casualty room at the hospital on Grand Turk (tel 2333) or the Medical Centre on Providenciales, on the airport road (tel 4201). The **IDD code** for the Turks and Caicos is 809 946, followed by a 4-figure island number. On island dial just the four digits.

The Turks and Caicos have some of the fattest mosquitoes in the area. Take plenty of repellent and coils to burn at night.

MONEY

The currency of the Turks and Caicos is the US$. Major credit cards and traveller's cheques are usually accepted in any tourist area. If you go off the beaten track or to one of the less inhabited islands, you should take sufficient cash. **Banking hours** are Mon–Thurs, 8.30–2.30, until 5 on Fri. **Shops** are open 9–5, with a long Caribbean lunch-break.

BEACHES

For the sand, the crystal-clear water and the extraordinarily powerful blue of the sea, the Turks and Caicos beaches are supreme—some of the best in the Caribbean and Bahamas. There are one or two strips where you can hire watersports equipment (through the hotels), but along the vast majority of the islands' estimated 200 miles of pristine strand, often only accessible by boat, there is complete isolation.

The most active beach on the islands is on the 12-mile curve of **Provo's** northern shore, fringed a couple of miles out by a reef. There are a few hotels dotted along it (still miles and miles for a dawn walk in between them), with bars to retreat to and watersports equipment for hire. Other beaches on Provo include **Sapodilla** in the southwest.

In the line of cays stretching northeast from Provo, **Pine Cay** has the best of all the beaches in the islands, a simply stunning 2 miles of silken sand that shelves gradually into the shallows. There is a private resort on the island where you can get lunch and watersports equipment if they are not too full and if you call in advance (tel 5128). **Parrot Cay** is another sandbar fringed with white coral sand and washed by the azure, a former favourite of pirates. Some tours go here for the day. **North Caicos** has miles and miles of sandy beach, much of it protected from the Atlantic swell by offshore islands and reefs, where you can find a suntrap for a day's picnic and snorkelling.

In the northern area of **South Caicos**, minutes from the airstrip, there are idyllic curves where the waves clap and hiss—miles and miles of them, utterly uninhabited (take a picnic and snorkelling gear if you wander off there for the day). From its town, Cockburn Harbour, the island throws off a string of cays to the south with more stretches of total isolation—arrange a boat from South Caicos to **Six Hill Cay**, **Long Cay** or to **Big Ambergris Cay**.

In the Turks Islands you will find more excellent beaches on the leeward coasts (away from the full force of the Atlantic). On **Grand Turk** the best known is Governor's Beach which runs south from Cockburn Town. There are hotels dotted along it where you can get drinks and watersports gear, but there are miles of sand to walk—also a good spot to see the Green Flash at sundown. If you go to **Salt Cay**, there are beaches enough for when you tire of inspecting the salt flats and windmills.

SPORTS

Watersports are most easily arranged through the hotels or the dive operators (see below). On Provo you can also go to **Provo Jetski hire** (tel 4644). A **windsurfer** costs around $20 per hour and a **sunfish** or other small sailing boat about $25 per hour. **Waterskiing** is available in some places for $35 for half an hour.

Yacht tours are arranged by Turtle Tours (tel 4393)—the trimaran *Tao* goes out for a sunset cruise—who sail out to the other cays. **Snorkelling** trips are available from most hotels at around $30 per person. Try Turtle Divers (tel 4232).

Fishing is also quite popular, close to the shore or over the deep-sea channels, where you might hook a yellow tuna or a marlin. Try the hotels again or contact the companies above. To go out into the deep expect to pay $400 for a half day for six people and $650 for a full day. **Bonefishing**, casting in the sandy shallow flats, is also extremely popular and can be arranged through the same companies. There is an annual bill-fishing tournament in July.

The **scuba diving** on the Turks and Caicos is excellent, and divers return year after year to the submarine walls (which drop sheer for thousands of feet) around Grand Turk and the caverns along the northern edge of the Caicos Bank. Elsewhere there are pinnacles of coral surrounded by an expanse of sand and ravines plied by flotillas of tiny fish and scoured by a barracuda, even the odd coral-encrusted anchor offshore. There are plenty of areas off the Turks and Caicos that have not been extensively explored.

Beds of soft corals are near the surface—like tussocks of wool that float on the currents—and lower down are forests of gorgonians and black coral. Lobsters scrabble on the sea-bed (they are one of the islands' major exports) and above them groupers and yellowtail snapper hang around with vibrant blue butterfly fish and the odd long, thin trumpetfish. Turtles cruise by and occasionally a whale is seen in the area.

The Grand Turk Wall starts in 35 ft of water in places and has ledges and overhangs to explore just below the lip. Off Providenciales there are pinnacles and ravines that attract fish of all kinds as well as caves and tunnels on the wall at the northwest point. The slopes of North Caicos have superb coral grounds, relatively unexplored, with ravines and caverns leading down to the northern wall of the Caicos Bank. Other dive sites include West and South Caicos.

Divers must present their certification cards. If you have not dived before, introductory courses are available for around $100. Many of the dive operations are run out of the hotels. On **Providenciales** try Third Turtle Divers at the Third Turtle Inn (tel 4230, USA contact, tel (800) 323 7600), Flamingo Divers (tel 4193, USA contact Neal Watson's Undersea Adventures, tel (800) 327 8150), or Provo Aquatic Centre in Sapodilla Bay (also called Wet Pleasures in the USA, on island tel 4455).

In **North Caicos** contact Dolphin Cay through the Prospect of Whitby Hotel (tel 4250) and on **Grand Turk** contact Blue Water Divers, PO Box 124 (tel 2432) or Omega Diving at the Kittina Hotel (tel 2232) and on **Salt Cay**, contact Porpoise Dovers (tel 6927).

There are also **liveaboard** dive-boats based in the Turks and Caicos waters, which include *Aquanaut* off Grand Turk (US contact (414) 434 3400), and off Provo, the *Sea Dancer* (tel (800) 367 3484).

Tennis courts are available in many of the hotels—check any front desk. You will occasionally see cricket matches played by the local teams.

The Islands

Grand Turk (about 7 miles by 2) is the senior island (population 5800) and site of the capital **Cockburn Town**, situated on the sheltered leeward coast. Overlooking the waterfront are some classic old West Indian buildings, timber-framed houses with grille-work windows and verandas (some of which have been turned into attractive inns). Among them are the official buildings, guarded by a couple of cannon. Behind the waterfront are the old *salinas* (salt flats), now rundown, and the poorer districts of the island, where, despite the satellite dishes, other aspects of life have changed little and you will still see islanders riding around on donkeys. The attractive island church and its graveyard are on the island in the middle of the Town Pond. Beyond Government House (called Waterloo) is a former US airbase to which the astronaut John Glenn was welcomed back to land after the first voyage into space. At the southern tip of the island is where some islanders believe that Columbus made his first landfall in 1492.

Seven miles southwest of Grand Turk is $2\frac{1}{2}$ square mile **Salt Cay** (as the name indicates, another of the original salt-raking settlements). The industry is defunct, but the sun still does its work and you will see the blinding-white expanses of sea salt on the island and the old windmills. There are just 300 islanders, centred around Balfour Town, living in attractive colonial stone and wooden houses.

The Caicos Islands were traditionally the poorer islands of the two groups. They had a few prosperous plantation years in the late 1700s, but it is only recently that anyone has actually wanted to go there. Originally only **South Caicos** (population 1600) was inhabited, again for the collection of salt. It retains its slow, old-time atmosphere, but recently it has become the centre of the islands' fishing industry, with conch and lobster available on the bank to its west, and excellent bonefishing.

East Caicos is uninhabited, but once was the site of the large sisal and cotton plantations set up by loyalists fleeing the American War of Independence. There is a supreme beach (17 miles long) on the north coast. **Middle** or **Grand Caicos** is the largest island and is inhabited, just, (population 530) in the towns of Conch Bar and Lorimers. There was a thriving guano industry in the lacklustre caves, but now the main occupation is working for the government. Bambarra is the islanders' beach. Separated by a channel in the west, **North Caicos** has a few more inhabitants (1600) in the villages of Bottle Creek, Sandy Point and Kew. There are a couple of plantation ruins, but the island is known for its fruit and its wildlife—there is a colony of flamingos at Flamingo Pond.

On the cays strung out between North Caicos and Provo are the ruins of a fort on **Fort George Cay**, its cannon in the sea close by encrusted by corals, and **Pine Cay**, a privately owned and luxurious resort, fringed by a fantastic beach. The sand continues through Water Cay and Little Water Cay to the tip of Providenciales.

Providenciales is the centrepiece of tourist development and has shot from a tiny and barely inhabited backwater to a resort island with a population of 5590, rapidly usurping the position of Grand Turk. The hotels are mostly strung along the northern shore and its fantastic beach. The **Caicos Conch Farm** is in the east of the island and you will see the development of a conch from a pinhead sized egg which grows a claw and then hides in the sand for a year while it starts to grow its shell. They carry on growing in their spiral shell throughout their life, moving around with their claw, but retracting it when you pick them up. One in 10,000 grows a pearl. (Elsewhere on the islands you will see conch hanging out to dry on the line like laundry after they have been extracted.)

West Caicos is also uninhabited now, except by passing flamingos. There is a stunning beach in the northwest and the diving is superb.

WHERE TO STAY

Grand Turk has some fine old creole coral stone houses, with shuttered windows and wooden balconies, which have now been turned into guest houses. These have a family atmosphere and none have more than about ten rooms, so you get to know the managers and the other guests quickly. **Providenciales** on the other hand, has been developed more recently, and has the large modern hotels of the sort that have sprung up all over the Caribbean, strong on watersports and entertainment. All hotels add a 7% government tax and often charge service at 15%.

Grand Turk and Salt Cay

The **Salt Raker Inn** (tel 2260, fax 2866) is across the road from the beach, in the southern part of Cockburn Town, and is something of a centre with the islanders, who gather here for a beer and a meal after work. The main house is an old island home, restored with 10 rooms and a couple of suites in the garden, $60–105. The **Guanahani Hotel** (tel 2135, fax 1152) has 16 air-conditioned rooms set in a two block above the beach just to the north of the town. All mod cons, a restaurant and watersports. Friendly, double room $75. A larger hotel, more typical of Caribbean resorts, is the **Kittina Hotel** (tel 2232, fax 2877), a bit pre-fab, but comfortable, some rooms set above the beach and others in the main house across the road, where the restaurant, pool and the bar are located, from $150–210; diving packages, some rooms have kitchenettes. The **Island Reef Hotel** (tel 2055, fax 2877) has 21 air-conditioned units with kitchens linked by a wooden walkway, south of Cockburn Town. Pool, tennis, and good beach not far off, $125.

Inns include **Captain Kirk's** (tel 2227), with just three rooms set on the beach, double room $65. Finally there is **Columbus House** (tel 2517), also set on the beach, with a dive shop right next door. Double room in winter $50.

Salt Cay has just three places to stay—small and quiet guest houses. **Windmills** (tel/fax 6962, US 800 822 7715) is set on 2½ miles of superb beach, a fantastic retreat on an already secluded island. There are just ten rooms and suites around the central bar and pool area, each decorated in bright Caribbean pastel colours with period antiques and reproduction furniture made with Costa Rican mahogany. Some watersports, double room $415–550 year-round (all inclusive rate). If money is a concern then you can contact the **American House** (tel 2485), $85 a double or **Mount Pleasant Guest House**, $85.

The Caicos Islands and Cays

The smartest place to stay in **South Caicos** is the **Club Caribe Beach Resort** (tel/fax 3386), with 24 rooms set on a superb strip of sand. Quiet and comfortable, double room in season, $120. And in **Middle Caicos** try the **Eagle Rest Villas** (US tel 215 255 4640), four villas on the beach, scuba and fishing available. Or there are very simple rooms at **Taylor's Guest House**, $40 for a double, no meals.

North Caicos has a few of hotels, of which the most comfortable and friendly is the **Prospect of Whitby Hotel** (tel 7119 fax 7114, US 800 346 4295), with 28 rooms set on seven miles of sand. Pool, tennis, watersports and scuba packages through Dolphin Cay Diving, double room $150. The **Pelican Beach Hotel** (tel 7112) stands on six miles of sand, quiet, with a restaurant and bar, just six double rooms from $110.

Pine Cay is home to the exclusive and expensive **Meridian Club** (US 800 331 9154), which has 12 sumptuous suites on a stunning two-mile strip of blinding white sand with palm-thatch sun-shades. Watersports, pool, tennis court, restaurant and bar, bird-watching trips to the inland lakes or just seclusion if you want it, double room $200–450.

Providenciales

The **Erebus Inn** (tel 4240, fax 4704), on the cliff, 30 comfortable rooms, with balconies looking down to Turtle Cove, a good French restaurant and pool and bar. Two tennis courts, dive packages, from $100. If you need an all-over-body-holiday, then Club Med's **Turkoise** (tel 4491, US 800 258 2633) can give you a 21st-century rest-cure; communal jacuzzis, pool volleyball, all-night dancing, classical music seminars and of course all the watersports you could mention from pedalos to deep-sea fishing. Large and busy, $250 a double. **The Deck** (tel 4343, fax 5770) is set just along the beach and has a similar modern beach club abandon about it. Pastel pink surroundings, pool and watersports, about $170. A lower-key beach resort can be found at the **Island Princess Hotel** (tel 4260, fax 4666) east of the Turtle Cove area, with 80 rooms in lines overlooking a sandy garden. Watersports on the miles and miles of sand, bar and a good island restaurant, children accepted, from $80 a double room. The **Mariner Hotel** (tel/fax 4488) at Sapodilla Point has a charm all of its own. It is in a secluded spot on the southern side of the island with 25 timber-built rooms overlooking a garden and pool. Not on the beach, but most people are concentrating on the diving anyway, $110 for a double room.

There is nowhere really cheap to stay on Provo.

EATING OUT

Seafood is the speciality in the islands, lobster is superb, as is conch, which you will see hanging out to dry like a string of handkerchiefs on the washing line. Fish is also good, trawled straight from the deep around the islands and some vegetables are grown here, but meat and most fruits have to be imported.

Grand Turk

Most of the small inns have good kitchens, turning out some international food like burgers, but also some local fare. Try the **Salt Raker Inn** (tel 2260), which is a gathering point anyway, for the lobster tail in spiced melted butter and banana puddings, $20 meal.

Papillon's Rendez-vous (tel 2088) sits right on the waterfront in the town, with just a few tables on the terrace. The menu is French, with many Caribbean ingredients, so besides a bourguignonne you can get snapper or conch creole, about $30. **Xavier's** is a lively restaurant and bar in town, frequented by island luminaries, who come here for a meal, and then stay for a beer or two at the bar; island and continental cuisine, $20, and the **Royal Beagel** has simpler island meals for around $15.

Providenciales
The popular pre-fab **Fast Eddie's** downtown serves an exceptional lobster, with other seafoods on offer for about $20 a meal. Some of the hotel dining rooms have good food, but can be quite expensive. Try the panoramic setting of the **Erebus Inn**, for its French menu, onion soup, escargots and turtle chasseur, $15–25 a main dish. The **Banana Boat** at the Turtle Cove marina, has a lively atmosphere, with simple burgers and plates of seafood at $20. **Dora's** on the Leeward Highway has good island seafood in a modern concrete West Indian villa, $20 for a meal. More rustic is **Henry's Road Runner** in the Blue Hills area, a classic West Indian bar, where you sit down next to anyone and strike up a conversation. Rice 'n' peas or lobster with butter and honey, $10.

On the smaller islands you will be dependent on the hotel dining rooms, or on the local snack bars.

Part V
THE BAHAMAS

Fishing for Marlin

The Bahamas are favourites with satellite photographers—700 emerald-green islands and cays scattered over 100,000 square miles of absurdly blue sea. The water is gin-clear and glistens over the banks of sand that stretch for miles and miles, where you must walk hundreds of yards into the sea to get as deep as your waist. The activity is there too—the reefs are superb and make bewildering diving, and the fishing and sailing are world-renowned. Since Columbus first made land in 1492, these cays have been plied by generations of pirates and gun-runners, and more recently rum- and drug-runners.

For the purposes of tourism the islands are divided into three separate groups. **Nassau, Cable Beach and Paradise Island** are on the senior island of New Providence at the heart of the Bahamas, where the capital Nassau is situated. To the north is **Freeport/Lucaya** on Grand Bahama, a complete resort area that has sprung up from a barren and virtually uninhabited island 30 years ago. The 697 others are known as the **Family Islands** and they are less developed and mostly far gentler in their lifestyle, much the same as they were 50 years ago. The only problem is choosing which to go to. They include islands such as Bimini, the Abacos, Eleuthera, the Exumas and Andros.

Named by the Spaniards after the *baja-mar* (the shallow sea) in which they lie, the Bahamas are not geographically in the Caribbean. These splinters and fragments of land stretch from the northern limit of the Greater Antilles (Haiti and Cuba), across the Tropic of Capricorn, and up alongside the coast of Florida, separated from the USA only by the 50 miles of the Gulf Stream. In all there are about 3000 of them if you include the rocks, fringing reefs and the ribbons of sand that just make it above the surf.

The Bahamas are low-lying, coral limestone outcrops that sit on top of the Great Bahama Bank (stretching from Bimini to Cat Island and Ragged Island) and the Little

621

Bahama Bank (in the north, with Grand Bahama and the Abacos). Most do not make it above 50 ft—the highest point among them is 206 ft, on Cat Island. They are lush in places, mostly covered with scrub and wispy *casuarina* pine trees and there are many inland lakes, usually salt water. Altogether the islands cover about 5380 square miles.

The 240,000 Bahamians do not consider themselves West Indians (despite their claim that Columbus discovered the Indies on San Salvador). They have a long-standing association with the USA, and this is clearly audible in their voices—there is an American drawl on the West Indian English. Most of the islanders are of African descent, but there are one or two communities that have remained determinedly white since they arrived here as loyalists in the late 1700s. There are also a large number of expatriates in the islands.

The Bahamas were a colony of Britain until they took their Independence in 1973 and the connection with Britain still rings clear in parts of Bahamian life. You will actually come across garden fêtes here. The Parliamentary system is based on the British model and the policemen are recognizable in their uniforms of black serge and red stripe, complete with white helmet. But in recent years the Bahamians have been strongly influenced by the States. The cars, many of them left-hand drive even though the Bahamians drive on the left, are big American cruisers, and though they have trouble in the tight streets of Nassau, a quick look at Freeport will show them more at ease on the boulevards of the recent development there.

Traditionally commerce has come from outside the islands, as the Bahamas are not fertile. The Bahamians have muddled along, scraping a living from the land, but with each war and each new wave of people has come a momentary flood of prosperity, often beyond the law. The monuments to the different eras are visible in Nassau, from the early stone and timber houses of the Bahamian gun-runners on the hill to the Nassau mansions that have been built on the prosperity of prohibition and most lately tourism.

The Bahamas have a highly developed tourist industry and the islands see about three million tourists a year, half of whom arrive by cruise ship (as many as 10 a day can call at Nassau). About two thirds of the the work force are employed in tourism one way or another and some 70% of GNP is derived from the industry. The Bahamas offer an extraordinary variety to the visitor. In the traditional centres you can take in glitz and gambling in the vast pink palaces of Cable Beach and Freeport. And yet just a few nautical miles away are the idyllic castaway cays of the Family Islands.

Suggested Itinerary

If you are travelling independently around the Bahamas it will probably be necessary to spend some time in Nassau (most flights arrive there). To see the real Bahamas you must get beyond here, but if you need to change planes (or mail-boats) in Nassau, there are good bars and restaurants to occupy you while you wait. Two weeks gives enough time to see a variety of the Bahamian islands. Start with a trip to a developed island, to Harbour Island and North Eleuthera or to the lovely cays of the Abacos. Great Exuma is also worth a visit—from here you can reach the lovely Exuma Cays. If you cannot persuade a yachtsman to take you on down to the other islands you may have to return to Nassau and set off again, but the further south you go from here, the more remote the islands become. For a taste of small-island life, try Andros, Cat Island, Long Island or San

Salvador. Another option, to help you see as much as possible, is to fly in or out of the Bahamas through Bimini, Eleuthera or the Abacos.

History

The recorded history of the New World begins on one of the Bahamian islands. On 12 October 1492, after more than a month at sea sailing into the unknown, Columbus made land on the island of *Guanahani*—and named it San Salvador or 'the saviour'. He landed with the banners of Ferdinand and Isabella and immediately claimed the island for Spain, greeted by no doubt dumbstruck native islanders, the *Lucayan* Indians. They were fascinated by the bells and mirrors that Columbus gave them in return for food, beads and the gold ornaments that they wore through their noses. It was the gold that attracted his attention, and the Indians explained that it came from the south. Soon afterwards Columbus sailed off to search for it, touching other islands before leaving Bahamian waters and heading for Cuba.

The Lucayans (an Arawak tribe) had lived in the Bahamas for around 500 years before the arrival of the Europeans, living off fish and turtles and growing a small amount of cassava. Columbus noticed scars on their bodies, received in raids by the Carib Indians from the islands farther south. There were about 40,000 Lucayans when the Spaniards first came to the Bahamas, but within 40 years there were none left—they had all been transported off the island to work in the gold mines in Hispaniola.

The Bahamas, rejected as 'islas inutilas', were simply left alone by the Spaniards for the next 100 years. They were avoided because the *bajamar* was a treacherous sea in which to sail. Many ships were to founder over the next four centuries and 'wrecking' became one of the principal Bahamian industries in an otherwise barren place. There are even stories of the islanders putting out false lighthouses to lure passing ships on to the reefs.

Others were more open about their profligacy. Pirates discovered the islands in the 16th century and they would lie in wait for the Spanish *flota*, the yearly fleet which collected in Havana harbour and set off into the Gulf Stream for Spain, loaded with the riches of the Spanish Main. Just as they are today, the coves and bays were the perfect hideaways for small sailing vessels.

The first British interest in the island came in one of the many royal grants, in which chunks of uninhabited land were handed out as favours in the courts of Europe. Charles I granted the Bahamas to Sir Robert Heath in 1629, in addition to the Carolinas on the mainland, just as the French King was to grant other islands a few years later. Settlement was another matter, and it was not until 20 years later that the first serious attempt was ventured from Bermuda.

Religious troubles, mirroring the disputes in England itself, led a group of Puritans under the governor William Sayle to leave Bermuda in 1648 for the Bahamas, settling an island that they called *Eleuthera* (from the Greek word for freedom). The colony had difficulties from the start and most of the settlers returned to Bermuda, but it was at this time that Sayle discovered by accident a fine harbour on another island, which he called New Providence.

Nassau soon became the important island and the pirates and privateers swarmed to it in the late 1600s. Pirates like Charles Vane and Blackbeard, Benjamin Hornigold and

Jack Rackham with his two women companions, Anne Bonney and Mary Read, made their way up here from Port Royal in Jamaica and from the Virgin Islands. Working for the British as 'privateers' or on their own account, they looted any Spanish ship or settlement they could find and returned with their loot to Nassau. In revenge, the Spaniards sacked the town four times in 25 years.

The town flew the British flag, but it was almost completely lawless, and so in 1718, the British sent out a governor to bring it under control. When he arrived Woodes Rogers was popular, with the merchants and pirates alike, but within months he had stopped piracy, persuading the freebooters to become privateers only in time of war, and hanging those who did not want to give up the trade.

And so the Bahamas took shape, muddling through in times of peace, but flourishing as an entrepôt when there was a war. In the American War of Independence the 3000 Bahamians did not side openly with the rebelling mainland colonists, but there was an undercover trade of arms and gunpowder through the islands. Some took to the seas as privateers on the hunt for American shipping. Nassau was captured in 1766 by the colonist fleet and all the island's military supplies shipped off to the colonies.

Following the war, the population of the islands trebled as 8000 loyalists fled the southern states for the Bahamas, setting up cotton estates on the out-islands (now called Family Islands), which prospered for a while. To work the plantations they brought slaves, whose descendants form the majority of today's Bahamian population. As their plantations failed the white settlers left the islands, simply leaving the slaves to fend for themselves. Emancipation was declared in 1833.

In the American Civil War Nassau saw another wave of prosperity as blockade runners made the dash over to the coast of the States with boatloads of arms. It lasted just four years and then the islands were eclipsed again, and so the Bahamians continued to scrape a living growing sisal and fruits, and collecting sponges from the sea-bed. *Prohibition* in the States, from 1920 to 1933, turned the wharves of Nassau into a forest of bootleg barrels and casks waiting for the run across to Florida in fast boats. It took a few years before the Coast Guard could hope to catch them. The tradition continues in a similar way today—in recent years the cargo has been marijuana and cocaine, to be shipped to the States in powerboats, but of course the DEA are considerably better equipped to deal with it. The planes parked along the runway at Nassau airport are mostly impounded drug-running planes.

The Bahamian tourist industry has mushroomed over the last 40 years, to the point today where there are 10 times as many visitors each year as the entire population of the islands. After the Second World War, Hog Island was sexily renamed Paradise Island and it exploded with hotels. Freeport was conceptualized and then appeared in the 'pine barren' of Grand Bahama, and the 'Out Islands' became the 'Family Islands'. The Bahamians flooded into the centres from the other islands to get a piece of the action. Tourism is the mainstay of the economy, worth over a billion dollars annually and employing over two thirds of the workforce. Other industries include offshore finance and agriculture, fishing and some light industry in Freeport on Grand Bahama. There is still visible poverty in certain parts of the Bahamas, but the situation is better than in most of the Caribbean islands, and far better than it was 40 years ago. Considerable money is invested in the country by expatriates who have built houses in estates like Lyford Cay on New Providence Island or taken over an island for private development.

Traditionally the colonial Bahamas were administered by a small group of mainly white Bahamians called the 'Bay Street Boys', but after the Second World War their predominance came to an end. Universal suffrage did not come until 1962 when their power began to be shared with the Bahamian blacks. Led by Lynden Pindling, the charismatic leader of the Progressive Labour Party, the Bahamas became Independent on 10 July 1973, and the same party has held power ever since. Despite scandals, most Bahamians associate their leader with the new Bahamas and they continue to support him. The main opposition party is the Free National Movement.

Bahamian government follows the British model, with a 16-member Senate and a 49-member House of Assembly elected for four-year terms. The country is a member of the British Commonwealth and is headed by a Governor General, Sir Clifford Darling.

FESTIVALS

Junkanoo is celebrated at the turn of the year, with masquerades in the streets on 26 December and 1 January to Bahamian *Goombay* and other Caribbean rhythms, mainly in Nassau and Freeport, but also with smaller events in the Family Islands. The festival **Goombay** itself runs over the summer months starting in June with a wider series of cultural events as well as more carnival parades through the streets. Independence Day is celebrated on 10 July and Discovery Day on 12 October.

Sailing regattas include the **Family Islands Regatta** out of George Town in the Exumas in April, **Regatta Time in Abaco** from April into June and immediately afterwards the **Green Turtle Cay Regatta** in early July (also in the Abacos). The Long Island Regatta is held in May.

GETTING TO THE BAHAMAS

By Air

The two main centres for air arrivals are the islands of Grand Bahama, for the Freeport/Lucaya area and New Providence, for Nassau and from where flights can be taken on to other destinations in the Bahamas. There are direct scheduled flights to some of the Family Islands and it is possible to charter a light plane from Florida to almost any of the islands. Bahamasair is the national carrier and they can be contacted on (US toll free, (800) 222 4242). There is a departure tax of $13.

From Europe: there are no direct scheduled flights from Europe to the Bahamas, so you are advised to change in Miami or perhaps in New York. Miami to Nassau is 35 minutes flying time.

From the USA: the major carriers into the Bahamas from the USA are Bahamasair, American, Delta, US Air, TWA and Chalk's International (which has scheduled flights into Paradise Island). Connections can be made in Miami, Fort Lauderdale and West Palm Beach in Florida and also New York, which have several flights a day into Nassau and Freeport. There are direct flights to Nassau from many other US cities, including Atlanta (2 daily), Baltimore (weekly), Cleveland (daily), Dallas (daily), Orlando (daily), Tampa (twice daily) and Washington (daily).

Some of these flights also touch Freeport. There are also some direct flights to Marsh Harbour and Treasure Cay in the Abacos, Governor's Harbour in Eleuthera and George Town in the Exumas.

Finally, if none of the above happens to be convenient, there are a number of air

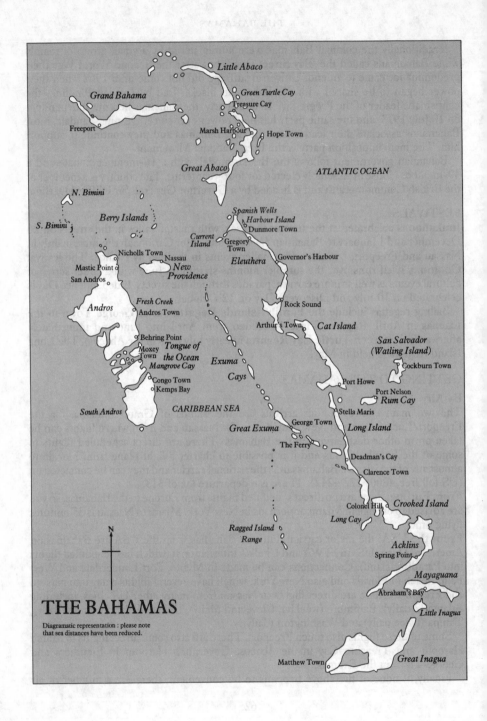

THE BAHAMAS

Diagramatic representation : please note
that sea distances have been reduced.

charter companies that fly light planes ideally suited for a short hop down to the islands. Contact **Trans-Island Airways** (tel 327 8329, fax 327 7413) or **MD Air Services Ltd** (tel 327 7335).

From Canada: there is a weekly flight on Air Canada to Nassau from Toronto and three from Montreal (also touching Freeport). Charter companies also fly to the Bahamas from these two cities.

From the Caribbean Islands: there is a daily link to Providenciales in the Turks and Caicos Islands on TCNA (Turks and Caicos National Airlines). There is a twice-weekly service to Kingston, Jamaica on Air Jamaica. And there is an occasional link to Cap Haitien in Haiti and to Santo Domingo in the Dominican Republic (on TCNA).

There is also a seaplane service, **Chalk's** (US tel (305) 371 8628, US (800) 327 2521), which links the coast of Florida (Watson Island off Miami and Fort Lauderdale), with several points in the Bahamas including Paradise Island (tel 363 2845) and Bimini (tel 347 2024). Charters are also available with Chalk's.

By Sea
A ferry, the *Discovery 1*, links Fort Lauderdale in Florida with Freeport in Grand Bahama, departing daily (US tel (305) 525 7800, fax 763 7074, 800 226 7800). Endless cruise-ship lines pass through the Bahamas, some on weekend cruises out of Miami (see cruise lines in introduction).

There are **ports of entry** for sailors in the following islands: **the Abacos**: Green Turtle Cay, Marsh Harbour, Sandy Point, Treasure Cay, Walker's Cay. **Berry Islands**: Chub Cay, Harbour Cay. **Bimini**: Alice Town, at any marina facility. **Andros**: Congo Town, Fresh Creek, San Andros. **Eleuthera**: Cape Eleuthera, Governor's Harbour, Harbour Island, Hatchet Bay, Rock Sound. **Exuma Cays**: George Town. **Cat Island**: Cat Cay Club at Government Dock. **Long Island**: Stella Maris. **San Salvador**: Cockburn Town. **Mayaguana**: Government Dock.

TRAVELLING BETWEEN THE BAHAMAS
Bahamasair flies from Nassau to about 20 different islands dotted around the archipelago. The more isolated islands are served only a couple of times a week, but to most there are a couple of flights each day. Hotels usually have a connecting motorboat if you need to make a hop to an offshore cay. All flights are routed via Nassau and so if you wish to travel from one out island to another, you will find that you have to return to the capital.

The same goes for the **mail boats**, which do a weekly run from Nassau to an island with the mail, the stores, and any locals heading home, accompanied by their goats and chickens. Spaces on mail boats are offered on a first-come, first-served basis and they leave from Potter's Cay docks in downtown Nassau, close to the bridge over to Paradise Island (tel 323 1064). The boats are fun to travel on, though they can take up anything to 24 hrs to reach their destination. Typical one-way fares are: from **Nassau** to the Abacos—about $35, Grand Bahama—$35, Andros—$20, South Andros—$30, Bimini—$30, the Exumas—$25–30, Cat Island—$35, Rum Cay—$30, San Salvador—$45, Mayaguana—$65. Finally, you might consider hitching a lift on a yacht by turning up at the marina and asking around.

THE CARIBBEAN

TOURIST INFORMATION
There are **Bahamas Tourist Offices** in:
UK: 10 Chesterfield St, London W1X 8AH (tel (071) 629 5238).
France: 9 Blvd de la Madeleine, 75001 Paris (tel 1 42 61 61 30).
Germany: 6000 Frankfurt am Main, Poststr 2–4 (tel 069 25 20 29).
USA: 150 East 52nd St, 28th Floor North, New York, NY 10022 (tel (212) 758 2777);
3450 Wilshire Blvd, Suite 208, Los Angeles, California 90010 (tel (213) 385 0033); and
255 Alhambra Circle, Suite 425, Coral Gables, Miami, Florida 33134 (tel (305) 442
9797).
Canada: 1255 Phillips Sq, Montreal, Quebec H3B 3G1 (tel (514) 861 6797) or 121
Bloor St East, Suite 1101, Toronto, Ontario M4W 3M5 (tel (416) 968 2999).

In the Bahamas themselves there are tourist information offices at Nassau International airport; a booth in arrivals (tel 327 6806) and departures (tel 327 6782)—they
can be very helpful, but if you are not having any luck, you can always take away an armful
of brochures for ideas. Downtown there is an office at the cruise-ship terminal, Prince
George Wharf (tel 325 9155), and one at Rawson Sq on Bay St (tel 326 9781). Hotels
will also help out usually. Most hotel rooms in the Bahamas can be booked through the
Bahamas Reservation Service (US and Canada toll free 800 327 0787, UK and
Europe in London (081) 876 1296).

Information about Freeport/Lucaya and the Family Islands is available from the main
office in Nassau.

There are two daily newspapers published in Nassau—the *Nassau Guardian*, which
appears in the morning, and the evening *Tribune*. A wide selection of US dailies are flown
in on the day of release. There is a proliferation of tourist literature, where some quite
useful information is hidden. *What to do* contains mainly adverts about jewellery, watches
and even advice on which perfume might be best suited to your sign of the zodiac, along
with a little practical advice. The Family Islands issue the *Getaway* magazine which
contains some features and some practical information on things other than shopping.

There is direct dialling to and from the major Bahamian islands. The area code is
(809), followed by a 7-digit number. Dial the seven digits when calling between islands.
Hotels sometimes add a hefty service charge to your bill for telephone calls. You may
wish to avoid this by going direct to the **Batelco** Bahamas Telecom office in the main
towns.

MONEY
The Bahamian dollar and the US dollar, set at par with one another, are both valid
currencies in the Bahamas. You may receive change in either currency or even both,
including Bahamian $3 and 50c notes. You are best to exchange money in the banks, but
hotels do change money at a slightly worse rate. Traveller's cheques and credit cards are
accepted almost everywhere in the hotels, restaurants and shops. If you go off the beaten
track then take cash with you. Personal cheques are not readily accepted. Tipping runs at
a high 15%.

In Nassau and Grand Bahama, **banks** keep hours of 9.30–3, Mon–Fri (until 5 pm on
Fri). In the smaller islands you may find that the bank only opens for a few hours a couple
of times a week.

628

Shops are generally open Mon–Sat, 9–5 (later in the hotels), but they often close one afternoon in the week.

SCUBA DIVING

The clear waters of the Bahamas have superb diving, with a variety not offered by other areas in the Caribbean. There are shallow reefs on the slopes close to shore off some of the islands; canyons and pinnacles that rise close to the water's surface; walls, where the Bahama banks drop sheer down to the deep ocean floor; 'blue holes', inland lakes that are connected to the ocean by tunnels below the ground and, of course, many wrecks, that were beyond the famed Bahamian 'wreckers'.

Visibility is excellent, often over 100 ft, and it reveals fantastic landscapes of corals: gorgonians like vast fans standing among the fingers and branches of fur-covered corals, stark white mounds of brain coral and pink and blue sponges. The fishlife is bewildering and you will come across single rays cruising and groupers loitering, while little shoals of blue tang race in time. Luxuriously coloured angelfish twitch as they glide past and trumpetfish hang vertically beneath the surface of the water.

Diving is available at all the main centres and there are some spectacular reefs right off Nassau itself (these have been used in a number of film sets), but if you go farther afield into the Family Islands, there is stunning variety. Off the eastern coast of Andros is the third largest barrier reef in the world, where the colours of the corals and sponges are supreme. In places you can actually join shark-feeding time, and off the Abacos and Eleuthera, wreck dives include the wrecks not only of ships, but of two trains that went down while they were being transported. You could also take a ride in the tidal race at Current Cut off Eleuthera. Lessons are available in all the resorts.

NEW PROVIDENCE

Nassau, Cable Beach and Paradise Island

The island of New Providence is small (just 21 by 7 miles), but it has always been the hub of Bahamian life. It lies in the northern area of the islands and is the site of the Bahamian capital, Nassau. 160,000 people, two thirds of the Bahamas population live on New Providence, most of them in Nassau, which has flourished periodically over the centuries as an entrepôt because of its magnificent harbour. It is on the crest of a wave at the moment, as up to 10 cruise ships dock each day.

Traditionally, since the 20s at least, the island has been the engine room of Bahamian tourism, and the three main resort areas now see as many as 1¼ million tourists a year. You can see the successive generations of hotels, each one falling into decay as a newer and more exciting one is built. The old colonial houses on the hill which are now old-time hotels of 'character', were overtaken in the 30s by art deco piles and in the 50s by high-rise hotels downtown. The newest and most exciting are the pastel palaces on Cable Beach, with the cabarets and gambling halls with their acres of slot machines.

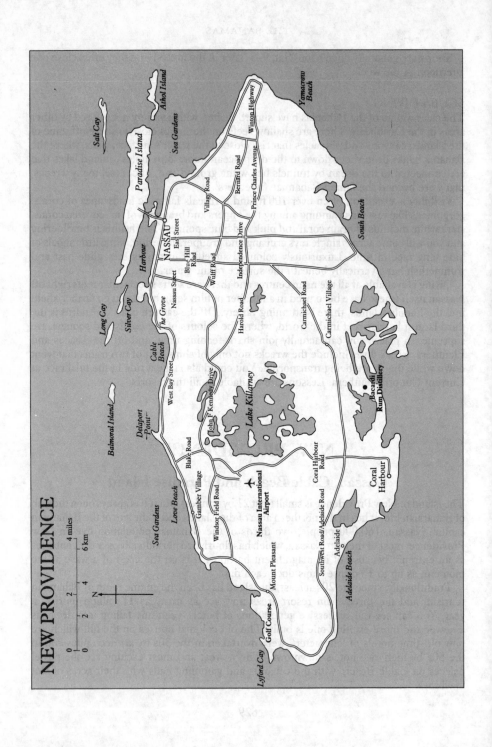

NEW PROVIDENCE

0 ____ 4 miles
0 __ 6 km

N

0 2 4

0 2 4

Lyford Cay

Golf Course

Mount Pleasant

Sea Gardens

Love Beach

Windsor Field Road

Gamber Village

Blake Road

Delaport Point

Balmoral Island

West Bay Street

Cable Beach

The Groove

Silver Cay

Long Cay

Harbour

NASSAU

Nassau Street

East Street

Blue Hill Road

Wulff Road

Independence Drive

Prince Charles Avenue

Bernard Road

Village Road

Winton Highway

Paradise Island

Sea Gardens

Salt Cay

Athol Island

Yamacraw Beach

South Beach

Harold Road

Carmichael Road

Carmichael Village

Bacardi Rum Distillery

Lake Killarney

John F Kennedy Drive

Coral Harbour Road

Coral Harbour

Nassau International Airport

Southwest Road/Adelaide Road

Adelaide

Adelaide Beach

With all the cruise ships and straw-hat vendors, Nassau has a pretty fearsome tourist race, but there is a more sophisticated side to it too. There are good restaurants and a lively expatriate crowd. And there are a few more noticeably 'West Indian' parts of the island—'over the hill' in Nassau and in outlying towns on the island.

GETTING AROUND

Endless minibuses link downtown Nassau and Cable Beach and around the town itself, but only occasionally does one run further to the residential areas out on the island (until about 6.30 pm). The Nassau terminal is at the western end of Bay St, beneath the British Colonial Beach Resort. Stand at the stops and flag them down, fare $1. Around the town itself, you might just prefer to travel by horse-drawn carriage, about $10 for half an hour.

Hotels often transfer guests from the **airport** on arrival and departure and many of them run a complimentary safari bus service into town. If you **hitch**, a daunting number of cars will drive straight past, but it works in the end. You may be expected to give a little towards the fare.

Ferries run across the harbour from the dock in downtown Nassau to Paradise Island for a couple of dollars. A minibus circles Paradise Island every 30 mins.

Taxis are always available at the airport, along Bay Street and in town. Fares are fixed by the government and theoretically metered. From the **airport** you can expect to pay $12 to Cable Beach, downtown Nassau—$17 and Paradise Island—$20 (includes $2 toll). If you hire a taxi by the hour for a trip around the island, negotiate a rate of around $25.

Car rental is convenient and the cars are easily available, but expensive at anything from $50 per day. You will be required to leave a hefty deposit by credit card imprint. Drive on the left and avoid downtown Nassau if humanly possible. Island companies include the big names with desks at the airport and in the major hotels: Avis (tel 327 7121, 326 6380) on West Bay St, Budget (tel 327 9000, 327 7956), Hertz (tel 327 8684) and National (tel 327 7301). **Scooters** can be rented at around $30 per day. Drivers and passengers must wear crash helmets by law. Try **Holiday Scooter Rental** (tel 325 3949) or **Bowe's Scooter Rental** (tel 326 8329) at Prince George Dock.

Island **tours**, visiting the few sights beyond Nassau, or sailing off for a day's snorkelling or a sunset cruise, can be booked through the front desks of most large hotels or direct with **Majestic Tours** (tel 322 2606), **Happy Tours** (tel 323 5818) or **Tropical Travel Tours** (tel 322 3802).

In a medical **emergency**, contact the Princess Margaret Hospital on Shirley St, Nassau (tel 322 2861).

BEACHES

Within a shout of downtown Nassau there are beaches at **Lighthouse Beach** on the western esplanade leading out of town, crowded but close; a bus-ride away at the resort area of **Cable Beach**, where there are all the sporting activities on offer; or a ferry-ride over on Paradise Island—go to **Paradise Beach**, another active beach on the west of the island (adm), or if you want to be a little less crowded, farther round on the northern shore.

Elsewhere on New Providence Island, many of the smaller beaches are privately owned by the hotels, but you might go to **Adelaide Beach** on the south shore, or

631

Delaport Point or **Love Beach** beyond the Cable Beach area. In the southeast is **Yamacraw** beach. They are not usually deserted, but you will not be one of a thousand.

SPORTS
Most hotels have **windsurfers** on offer to their guests. Otherwise, go to the concessionaires on Cable Beach or Paradise Island (more expensive). Rates around $20 per hour. The same goes for **parasailing**, which is expensive at $40 for 10 minutes. **Waterskiing** averages at around $20 per 15 mins and you can even fix a ride on a pedalo (about $15 for 30 minutes) or shut screaming children up on an aqua-sausage for a high-speed view of the harbour ($10). **Glass-bottom boat** tours can be made from the Bay Street Dock or from Cable Beach, price around $10 for an hour and a half.

Many hotels also have sailing **dinghies** for hire (about $25 per hour), but there are endless yacht tours on offer, from an outing of snorkelling, boozing and dancing (try the *Calypso*, tel 363 3577), or a picnic trip to Rose Island with the **Keewatin Sailing** (tel 325 1821) or **Topsail Yacht Charters** (tel 393 0820). For a full-blooded day's yachting check with the **Nassau Yacht Haven** (tel 322 8173) or the **East Bay Yacht Basin** (tel 322 3754).

Deep-sea fishing trips are easily arranged through the above marinas or through the **Nassau Harbour Club** (tel 323 1771) and **Hurricane Hole Marina** on Paradise Island (tel 326 3601). Rates run from $230 for a half day with tackle and bait provided (6 people) to $600 for the full day.

Scuba shops on the island include **Bahama Divers** on East Bay St (tel 326 5644), **Coral Harbour Divers** at the west end (tel 326 4171), **Dive Dive Dive** (tel 362 1401) at the Smuggler's Rest Resort and **Nassau Undersea Adventures** (tel 362 1964). If you are not a diver, you can still take an underwater walk with a sealed helmet through **Underwater Wonderland** (tel 322 8234) at Nassau Yacht Haven.

On **land** there are plenty of **tennis** courts in the hotels, often free to guests. If you are travelling independently you can try the hotels (fee usually around $8 per hour), or go to the **Nassau Squash and Raquet Club** on Independence Drive (tel 323 1854).

There are three **golf** courses open to visitors on the island (fees $25–30), at **Cable Beach Hotel** (tel 327 6000), the **South Ocean Golf Club** in the southwest of the island (tel 326 4391) and on the eastern end of **Paradise Island** (tel 326 3926).

Horses are available if you would like to explore the pine barren interior of the island or take a canter along the beach, through **Happy Trails** (tel 326 1820), $25 per hour, and on Paradise Island at **Harbourside Riding Stables** (tel 326 3733).

Nassau

The capital of the Bahamas has always centred around its harbour as the source of its prosperity—waves of gun-runners and rum-runners have traded in the port and brought huge prosperity for a few years. The old waterfront buildings now look on to Bay Street, where the commercial buzz still continues, now driven by shiploads of cruise-trippers—*hackers* tout their goods in the street (usually offering to braid your hair nowadays or sell you a conch shell) and the warehouses contain air-conditioned boutiques with cut-price bargains. You will even hear the cruise liners calling their passengers by blowing their foghorns. The inhabitants of Nassau are not always very forthcoming, but most will oblige if you need help. You should also be careful about your valuables.

Settled in 1666, the city was originally called Charles Town, but it was renamed Nassau after William III of Orange Nassau. The town divides into three areas: the commercial district down by the waterfront with its colonnaded warehouses, the colonial mansions and the large town-houses built by the merchants, set back from the activity on top of the cliff, and the area 'over the hill', where the poorer inhabitants of Nassau live in streets of clapboard houses—an extremely lively part of Nassau life.

The commercial hub of the city is still **Bay Street**, an outsize shopping precinct as it always has been, running parallel to the waterfront. Its heart is the **straw market** (constructed on the site of the traditional market building in 1974), with endless stalls selling anything from rush matting to a straw hat, carvings and beads to plait into your hair. Its activity is infectious and the saleswomen are persuasive—more mercantile mayhem.

Not far down Bay Street, close to the cruise ship wharf and Rawson Square, is the traditional heart of the Bahamas government in **Parliament Square**, where a statue of Queen Victoria sits surrounded on three sides by classical buildings dressed up in Nassau pink. Here you will find the Bahamas **House of Assembly**, the old Treasury and Supreme Court. Taking Parliament Street out of the square you come to an octagonal building, which once was the town prison, decommissioned in 1879 and now the Nassau public library. The alcoves with the books were the original cells. The *surreys* (horses and traps) that you see everywhere, are tourist taxis.

The **National Historical Museum** is in the Bahamas Historical Society building on Elizabeth Ave, and houses a collection of paintings, photographs and maps from Bahamian history, starting in Arawak times, through pirates and loyalists. The **Queen's staircase** leads to the top of the cliff to **Fort Fincastle**, built in 1793 with the shape of a ship's prow. It is restored and has a commanding view and a few hefty cannon that were never used. Open in office hours, adm free. The view is better still from the watertower nearby.

Farther along the clifftop, where many of Nassau's finest old stone town houses with louvred verandas were built in the 19th century (like the attractive restaurant, Graycliff), you will come to **Government House**, a neoclassical mansion built in 1801 and dressed in Nassau pink, now the residence of the Governor General. On the stairs leading down to the street is a statue of Columbus.

Near the toll bridge that leads over to Paradise Island is a lively piece of Bahamian life, the market, where fruit vendors sit and conch salesmen extract the animal from their shells. Fruits and ground provisions are shipped in from the out islands and sold here on the dock. The mail boats also dock here.

There is not much to see on **Paradise Island** itself unless you are a student of the tourist industry—the best reason to go over is for the beaches. However, the island, which was called Hog Island until 1961, is quite pretty and some of the hotels are set in attractive grounds. One sight to aim for is the **Cloisters** in Versailles Gardens (near the Ocean Club in the east of the island), where a walkway of stairs and statuary lead down to a 14th-century cloister that has ended up thousands of miles from its monastery in Lourdes. The toll to **Paradise Island** costs $2 for cars and 25c for walkers.

Bahamian theatre is on view at most times of the year at the **Dundas Centre for the Performing Arts** on Mackey St in eastern Nassau.

Around the Island

Leaving downtown Nassau to the west you pass the old British Colonial Hotel and rejoin the seafront on the Western Esplanade. To the left is the lumbering **Fort Charlotte** on the hill, built at the beginning of the 19th century; it once manned a fearsome 42 cannon, but they never fired a shot in anger. Open daily, adm free.

Behind the fortress are the **Nassau Botanical Gardens**, where trails lead through the 16 acres of flowering trees and shrubs, a cactus garden, and past ponds of tropical fish to a grotto. Open daily 9–4.30, adm (tel 323 5975). Nearby the **Adastra Gardens** shows off the Bahamian national birds, the pink flamingos to their best advantage when they perform a bit of precision marching at the orders of their drill sergeant. In the five acres of tropical luxuriance there is an aviary of birds and a few animals. Open daily 9–5, adm (tel 323 5806). Down on the waterfront, **Coral World** has a shark tank and turtle pools and an underwater view of a coral reef and its tropical fish in action. On Silver Cay, open daily, adm (tel 328 1036).

Cable Beach is called so because the Bahamas' first cable link to Florida was made from here, along the magnificent stretch of sand. It is the Bahamas' most built up resort area—the first hotels appeared here in the 1950s and the building continues. Travelling further west, the road eventually reaches **Lyford Cay** on the western tip of the island, an exclusive and extremely rich housing estate mainly peopled by expatriates. It is private.

The south of the island is less densely populated, though there are a few local Bahamian towns like Adelaide that the tourism race seems to have by-passed. Some were settled by emancipated slaves, others by Africans who were being transported on Spanish slave ships caught by the British Navy after the abolition of the slave trade in 1807.

Midway along the south coastal road you can visit the **Bacardi Rum Distillery**, where tours and the odd sample of rum or their cocoa liqueur are available until around 4.30 pm. In the east of the island is the **Retreat**, the headquarters of the Bahamas National Trust, where there are some 200 species of palms and other exotic plants in the five acres of garden. Tours Tues–Thurs, adm (tel 323 1317).

WHERE TO STAY
Nassau, Cable Beach and Paradise Island is the largest resort area in the Bahamas, and it has around 4000 rooms for rent in all, in hotels ranging from the most modern, massive, pastel pink palaces of Cable Beach, through the tower block hotels of the 70s and early 80s and the sumptuous splendour of post-war palladia, to small and comfortable guest houses, the family homes of the last century, built 'on the hill' in Nassau. If you feel like splashing out, you'll find the Caribbean's most expensive hotel room (a whole floor in fact, complete with robot servant) in the Crystal Palace on Cable Beach. A snip at $25,000 a night, but you'll be pleased to hear that they'll throw it in free if you are a high roller on the casino downstairs ($100,000 stake). There is a 6% government tax on hotel rooms and service charges usually run at 15%.

THE BAHAMAS

EXPENSIVE

The **Ocean Club Golf and Tennis Resort**, on the north side of Paradise Island (tel 326 2501, fax 363 2424, US 800 321 3000) has the finest setting in the area, with its 71 villas with their own jacuzzi and rooms on either side of the charming main courtyard laid with coral flagstones, sprouting with small palms, a fountain and pool and gingerbread trimmings or in villas with their own jacuzzis. In the luxuriant gardens are the tennis courts and swimming pool, leading down to the resurrected French cloister. All mod cons, cable TV, beach nearby, $200–850. Also on Paradise Island, the **Club Méditeranée** (tel 326 2620) has a good setting in a large garden, where the lawns are littered with follies and classical statues and where a string quartet might suddenly strike up. Lots of tennis, private beach, evening entertainment, canned classical music, musculation, 300 rooms, $150 per person per day. Unlike most Club Meds, it is possible to sign in for a day or a weekend, but otherwise it is not accessible.

The most attractive hotel on **Cable Beach** is the **Le Meridien Royal Bahamian** (tel 327 6400, fax 327 6961, US 800 543 4300), with a neoclassical façade dressed in Nassau pink on the outside, and inside very much the English country residence, right down to afternoon tea and bell boys in braid. But there is also twentieth-century comfort in the satellite TV, health spa, weights and cabaret. 170 rooms and villas linked by coral paving stones in the manicured garden, private beach, $160–300, $500 for a villa. Set in its own grand and luxurious landscaped gardens on the south coast of the island is the **Ramada South Ocean** Hotel, (tel 362 4391, fax 362 4728, US 800 408 4488). The 250 rooms are set in wings around the central great house and there are plenty of sports (there is a golf course) and watersports, including diving, on the beach just across the road. Country club luxury; the hustle of Nassau is miles away. Double room from $200. In downtown Nassau, the **Graycliff Hotel** is set in one of the magnificent old town houses on West Hill St (tel 322 2796, fax 326 6110). Downstairs is the restaurant, but on the creaking floors upstairs, behind the breezy screened balconies, and in the explosive walled garden are 14 sumptuous rooms—including Hibiscus, Jasmine and Mandarino, all dressed up in traditional colonial style. Double rate $145–363 per night.

MODERATE

Not far off is the **Buena Vista Hotel**, on Delancy St (tel 322 2811), also set in an old colonial town house. There are just a few rooms upstairs, comfortable and decorated in old style. Double rate in winter $105. **Casuarinas Hotel and Villas**, PO Box N-4016, Nassau, (tel 327 8153, US 800 327 0787) is in Cable Beach, just across the road from the beach itself. It is a bit pre-fab, but it is friendly. The rooms are set around the pool and gardens, with air-conditioning and satellite TV. Double Room 85–120

CHEAP

The **Pink House**, PO Box N-1968, Nassau (tel 363 3363, fax 393 1786) is a guest house on Paradise Island, set in a colonial great house—tiled verandas and wooden balconies with louvres, surrounded by bamboo and palms. Old time island charm, with watersports and beaches nearby. Double room $60–80. The **Parthenon Hotel** (tel 322 2643) on West St, just out of the downtown area of Nassau, has 18 neat and clean rooms at $60 for a double in season. The best place for cheap accommodation is in Nassau, where there are a number of reasonable guest houses: try the **Diplomat Inn**, 4 Delancy St (tel 325

2688), a nice old town-house on the hill in town, where a double room costs $40 in winter, kitchen available and bar. **Mignon Guest House** on Market St in central Nassau (tel 322 4771) has 6 air-conditioned rooms, about $34 a double.

EATING OUT
There are some good restaurants to be found in the islands, and you should look beyond the hotels, which tend to serve standard international fare. Like most other things in the Bahamas, there is a West Indian lilt, but the accent is also distinctly American. The top restaurants serve gourmet food, ingredients imported from the States as well as local fish and seafood, but traditional Caribbean dishes are readily found—rice 'n' peas is peas 'n' rice here—and, of course, the Bahamians do a mean seasoned chicken. Goat and tropical vegetables find their way in from the Family Islands and are then served up curried and stewed. Souse is a watery stew in which you will find vegetables and odd looking parts of animals, eg 'pig foot'. And the Bahamians make good use of seafood, of the lobsters and crabs (stoned crab and cracked conch), and of the fish that they trawl in the shallows and haul out of the deep, from grouper to kingfish. **Kalik** is the beer of the Bahamas and it is quite good—light and quite bitter for a lager, and of course always served chilled.

There is a strong influence from a hundred miles across the Gulf Stream, and apart from the universal 'continental menus of the hotels', you will find fast-food joints with the familiar names of McDonalds and Kentucky Fried.

Nassau has the largest selection of restaurants (many of the best local Bahamian eateries are 'behind the hill'). Most restaurants add 15% government tax and service, 'for your convenience...'

EXPENSIVE
The **Graycliff** Restaurant (tel 322 2796) has a magnificent setting in an old town house on West Hill St, and serves probably the finest food in Nassau. Before the meal you take cocktails in the drawing room, to a piano accompaniment, and then you move into one of the three dining rooms, candlelit with huge windows and polished wooden floors and tables. It is pleasantly formal for an evening out; the menu is French—*filet de mérou sauce dijonnaise* or grilled spring lobster *aux deux sauces*. The wine list is like a Bible and to follow you can have a brandy or try an aged Caribbean rum. Main course $30 plus. Not far off is the **Buena Vista** restaurant (tel 322 2811), also set in a West Indian town house with a large and airy dining room. The cuisine is French and the menu long—Bahamian fish, Dover Sole and Norwegian salmon, and a speciality of veal in chanterelles and mushrooms, main course $30. At the other end of town, in Lakeview Drive off East Bay St you will find **Sun and....** (tel 393 1205) in a modern Nassau villa. The tables stand around the courtyard garden, overlooking the fountain and ornamental pool. The menu is French and continental—tournedos rossini with Madeira truffle sauce or blackened shrimp cajun style. Closed Mon, main dish $25. On Paradise Island **Café Martinique** luxuriates in its sophisticated setting of red deep-pile carpets and patterned wall paper, overlooking the lagoon. *Grenadins de veau au calvados* or *fruits de mer au gratin*. 'Jacket required', main course $30–35. It is also known for its Sunday brunch.

MODERATE
At **Coconuts** you eat in a small waterfront dining-room—smoked game fish fritters in Andros and Asian sauce, followed by grouper in a coconut and almond crust. Slightly less expensive at $15–20 for a main course. There are plenty of touristy spots around, lively restaurant bars where you can grab a burger and a beer at lunch and hear a band over a more substantial meal in the evening. You might try **Pick A Dilly** (tel 322 2836) on Parliament Sq in the centre of town. Grills seafood and pastas at around $8 and of course daquiris, made with just about every tropical fruit imaginable. **Twin Gables** (tel 393 8566) on Mackey St has a pretty setting in an old creole house with wooden gables and a louvred terrace. Huge steaks or seafood dishes. Conch steak is the speciality or you might try a seafood platter of grouper, conch and shrimp, $10–15, closed Sun.

If you would like something a little more Bahamian, there are some great local restaurants. The **Shoal** (tel 322 4400) on Nassau St by the Texaco garage, has a classic West Indian setting—an air-conditioned dining room with thick carpets and formica on the walls. And the best in local food—Bahamian broiled crawfish, or stew-fish and johnny cake, all washed down with a *Kalik* beer, main course $8–13. The **Three Queens Restaurant and Lounge** (tel 393 3512) on Wulff Rd is also popular with the Bahamians and serves good local fare. You sit on bench seats and will be served superb scorched conch and other traditional West Indian meals such as curry chicken, $10. You can't miss **23 Delancy Street**, the former residence of the Anglican bishop in the Bahamas; it is pink. And the atmosphere is somewhat less austere than it would have been as a clerical seat. It is a fun bar and restaurant, with the sports channel playing on the TV and good local food on offer—chicken and fish, steamed conch or curry mutton, or souse, $6 or $7.

If you want to go even more local, you can find some superb and authentic Bahamian take-away food in small shacks in Nassau. You should be quite careful at night if you go 'over the hill'. Try the **Dirty's** on Boyd Rd or best of all **Roselle's**, where you are served through an iron grille. The thing to have is a conch snack—conch cracked (beaten and then covered in batter), which usually comes swimming in tomato sauce and with chips. At **Bertha's Go-go Ribs** on Mackey St you can take away ribs cooked in Bertha's secret mellow sauce.

BARS AND NIGHTLIFE
You will find that many of the bars around Nassau fill up with sunburnt tourists making whoopee, so if you want something a bit more sophisticated, perhaps a cocktail in colonial surroundings, then you might try one of the smarter restaurants. Otherwise, you can head for a boozy early evening scrum at the **Poop Deck**, above the marina on East Bay St. It collects a lively crowd of tourists and some locals, testing out their exotic cocktails—*nut-washer, bra-opener* and *pantie-dropper*.... Not far off or dissimilar in style is **Captain Nemo's**, another lively bar and snack style restaurant. More tourists on a blow-out and more exotic cocktails. A lower-key bar in the area is **Le Shack**, in the same building as Coconuts Restaurant. Light beer or a rum punch and light music. There is a mellow waterfront bar out of town to the west, the **Traveller's Rest**, West Bay St in Gambier—daquiris among the palm trees. Heading back into town, the **Rock 'n Roll Café** is in Cable Beach and collects a lively crowd. Hip chicks and dudes in sun-glasses (a permanent fixture even at night it seems) gravitate around the **Deep End**; MTV and

light beer. You might also try **Hammerheads** next to the IBM building in the east of town. If you feel like going dancing you can try **Roselawn** in Parliament Sq, **The Ritz** or the best club **Waterloo**, quite a long way out on East Bay St—*No hats, no plaits, no singlets, no portable phones (!).*

There are discotheques, cabaret shows and casinos in the large hotels on Paradise Island and Cable Beach.

GRAND BAHAMA

Freeport/Lucaya

The tourist area of Freeport/Lucaya is unlike anything else in the Caribbean or the Bahamas. It is visibly American in style, with wide tree-lined boulevards and spacious suburbs, satellite dishes and air-conditioned supermarkets. Freeport/Lucaya is run as a company, the Grand Bahama Port Authority.

The island of Grand Bahama itself is the third largest of the Bahamian islands and with 40,000 inhabitants, its city Freeport has become the second largest in the country. But 40 years ago none of the Freeport/Lucaya area existed. The resort was simply dreamt up and created in the 60s.

Until 1955 there were no more than 1000 islanders on Grand Bahama, a few lumbermen and fishermen, except during the Civil War and Prohibition, when the village of West End was one of the prime gun- and rum-running centres and had around 400 boats. Otherwise, the islanders scraped a living by catching sponges and cutting wood.

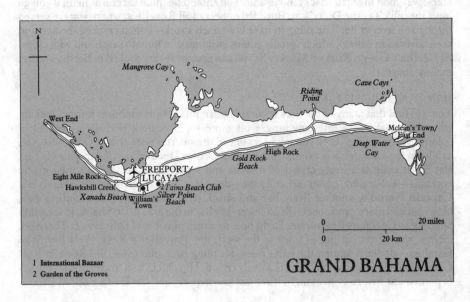

1 International Bazaar
2 Garden of the Groves

GRAND BAHAMA

Freeport was the brainchild of American financier Wallace Groves, to whom the Bahamian government signed over 50,000 acres of land for development as a duty-free port in 1955, with agreements over tax exemptions for 35 years. Industry came—oil refining and bunkering. As tourism boomed the company began to build hotels on the island's magnificent beaches and Freeport/Lucaya took off. The resort sells itself on the ticket of a truly 20th-century cure for your woes—endless watersports by day, and gambling, glitz and cabaret at night.

GETTING AROUND GRAND BAHAMA
Within the Freeport/Lucaya area there are **buses**, some of which run beyond the central area to the local villages: Eight Mile Rock, West End and East End. They do not run to the airport, but many hotels have a shuttle service for arriving guests, and buses down to the beach or to the shopping areas. **Taxis** are easily found in the tourist centres and through hotel lobbies. To hire a taxi by the hour costs $25–30.

Island **tours** to the island's few sights can be arranged (again through any hotel lobby, where they will pick you up) with **Executive Tours** (tel 352 8858), **Sun Island Tours** (tel 352 4811) or **Reef Tours** (tel 373 5880). If you would like to tour by plane, contact **Taino Air** (tel 352 8885).

Plenty of **rental cars** are available. There is a deposit and a steep rental charge ($55–70 per day). Remember to drive on the left. Hire firms, some of which have offices in the hotels, include **Avis** (tel 352 7675) in Freeport and (tel 352 7666) at the airport, and **National** (tel 352 9308) at the Xanadu Beach and (tel 352 9308) at the airport. Other firms are **Courtesy Car Rentals** (tel 352 5212) and **Star** (tel 352 5953), both at the airport.

Scooters, again steep at around $30 per day or $45 for a two-seater, can be hired at **Bowe's** in the Holiday Inn (tel 373 1333).

In a medical **emergency**, contact the Rand Memorial Hospital on East Atlantic Drive, Freeport (tel 352 6735).

TOURIST INFORMATION
In Grand Bahama there are tourist offices at the airport, at the cruise-ship dock, in the International Bazaar and at Port Lucaya. The main office is on East Mall Drive (tel 352 8044) and is very helpful.

BEACHES
The southern shore of Grand Bahama is ribboned with strips of idyllic white sand interspersed among the coral limestone coast, and the beaches in the Freeport/Lucaya area have become built up with hotels. **Silver Point Beach** in Lucaya and the **Radisson Xanadu Beach** are the most developed and the best place for watersports (see below for companies).

Beyond the tourist hotels there are some superb suntraps with casuarina trees down to the sand and with excellent snorkelling and swimming. There are no jetskis or windsurfers for hire there, but there will often be a small town where you can get a drink and a snack. South of Freeport is a cracking beach at **William's Town** and just to the east of Lucaya, try **Taino Beach**, a stunning stretch of beach that runs for miles. Off Midshipman Road is the **Club Caribe Beach** and further along the same stretch is **Fortune**

639

Beach, south of the Garden of the Groves. The other side of the Lucayan Waterway is **Barbary Beach**, more perfect white sand and isolation. There are other isolated strips farther along the southern coastline. Try **Gold Rock Beach** which you can reach from the Lucayan National Park (no facilities).

SPORTS
Watersports companies outside the hotels include **Reef Tours** (tel 373 5880), **Executive Tours** (tel 352 8858) or **Forbes Charter** (tel 352 7142).

Windsurfers are on hire from all the beach hotels, at a rate of around $15 per hour. Try the **Club Caribe** east of Lucaya or **Paradise Watersports** (tel 352 2887). *Mistral* have a school at the Atlantik Beach Hotel in Lucaya (tel 373 1444). Small sailing **dinghies** are also available through the major hotels ($25–30 per hour), as is **parasailing** ($20 for 10 mins) at the Atlantik and Radisson Resort on Lucaya Beach, and **waterskiing**, about $15 for 10 minutes. **Glass-bottom boat** tours can be fixed up through the tour companies and hotels (about $20 for two hours) and you can even also get hold of a jetski.

Yacht tours can also be arranged with them, anything from a day's roistering with rum-punch in hand to a hard day's yachting. Contact the tour companies for the booze cruises: on the *Jolly Roger*, *Triwind Cruise B* and *Island Time* (tel 373 8001). If you wish to sail try the marinas—the **Lucayan Harbour marina** (tel 373 1639), the **Xanadu Beach Hotel marina** (tel 352 6780) or the **Running Mon marina** (tel 352 6834).

These marinas also serve **deep-sea fishing** boats. There are good fishing grounds off the island and you can set off into the Gulf Stream to cast for marlin and sailfish. A boat with tackle and bait for half a day comes at $400 and a full day at $650.

Snorkelling is good in many places on the south coast, but it is superb at Peterson Cay east of the resort areas. **Dive** operators include **UNEXSO**, the Underwater Explorer's Society, based at Lucaya marina (tel 373 1244), **Sun Odyssey** (tel 373 8211) at the Atlantik Beach and **Club Caribe** (tel 373 6866). There is another UNEXSO outfit at the **West End Diving Centre**, and at the East End is the **Deep Water Cay Club** (US tel (305) 684 3958).

On land there are endless **tennis** courts in the hotels, usually available to non-guests (fee about $7 per hour). Check any hotel front desk.

There are a number of **golf** courses on the island, fees around $15–25, with club and cart rental. Try the **Lucayan Golf and Country Club** (tel 373 4500), set in the hills above Lucaya, or the **Bahama Reef Golf and Country Club** in Freeport (tel 373 1055). The Bahama Princess **Emerald** and the **Ruby** courses are close to the International Bazaar area (tel 352 6721).

Riding is available through **Pinetree Stables** on Beachway Drive in Freeport (tel 373 3600). Riding out costs $20 per hour and you can expect to canter along Grand Bahama's fantastic beaches.

Freeport/Lucaya

There are very few sights on the island, but in Freeport you will definitely come across the **International Bazaar**, an odd conglomeration of buildings in imitation of styles from all over the world, from a Japanese arch of welcome to a Turkish bazaar. You can eat and shop here. It feels a little odd and soulless, but most people do not worry because they are on the hunt for bargains (prices are around ⅓ lower than the mainland USA). Occasionally there is some entertainment. The real centre of the town of Freeport is **Churchill Square**, near the Port Authority Building, where you should buy groceries if you are catering for yourself.

There is a botanical garden in the area. The **Garden of the Groves** is set in 12 acres of Bahamian greenery laced with lagoons, streams and with a hanging garden at the entrance. The plant species are named. Open daily exc Wed, 10–5, adm free (tel 352 4045). The **Grand Bahama Museum** is in the grounds, with displays of Arawak artefacts and explanation of their rituals, as well as more modern Bahamian traditions such as Junkanoo costumes that derive from African traditions. Open weekdays 10–4, weekends until 2, adm.

UNEXSO in the Port Lucaya area is a diving school, or perhaps a diving college, where there are courses in diving for beginners and instructors and even in dive medicine. The dolphin experience, where you can cavort with several bottlenose dolphins who are kept in captivity while being studied, has been moved to Sanctuary Bay. They are eventually to be let back into the wild if they wish to go. **Port Lucaya** is a shopping complex and marina.

Beyond Freeport to the east you come into the pine barren, endless pine forest with just a few local towns which are a bit more typical of the rest of the Bahamas and where you can usually get a meal or a drink. At the Lucayan National Park and Caverns, trails lead through the scrub to a couple of limestone sinkholes, Ben's Cave and Burial Mound Cave. Beyond the park you come to the old Gold Rock missile tracking station, the first down-orbit of Cape Canaveral, and eventually the road comes to McLean's Town at the east end.

To the west of Freeport is Hawksbill Creek, the centre of Grand Bahama industry, where the liners and tankers put in. The town of Eight Mile Rock is strung along eight miles of coral shoreline and you will see some of the attractive old Bahamian homes that were here before the recent concrete development. At West End you can still see the remnants of the old warehouses and decaying piers from the days of Prohibition, where the boats tied up before making the dash over to the coast of Florida loaded up with liquor.

WHERE TO STAY

The most comfortable hotels in the Freeport/Lucaya area are set in the large high-rise blocks, often with an acreage of casino attached. If this sounds a bit too much, there are one or two smaller places where the atmosphere is a bit more personal and the prices lower.

Of the large hotels try the low rise **Princess Country Club** (tel 352 6721) in Freeport, across the road from the International Bazaar and the Moorish casino. It hums; with 565 rooms, five dining rooms, multiple jacuzzis, golf, nightclub; $140–160. Next to the Ruby Golf course you will find the comfortable suites of **Chillingsworth Court**, Bahama North, Freeport (tel 352 7632, US 800 621 1274). The rooms overlook the pool and courtyard and they have all modern conveniences—full kitchens and cable TV. Double room $150 in season. The **New Victoria Inn**, 'in town', (tel 373 3040), offers cheaper rooms at $50 a double. A small, more luxurious hotel is the **Silver Reef**

Health Spa, PO Box F773 Freeport (tel 373 7761, fax 373 3332), off Bahama Reef Boulevard. The hotel is small, with 22 guests at the most. As the name suggests, the hotel offers a healthy rest-cure—massage, facials, body wraps and a library if you should tire of the treatment. But the beach is nearby—there are watersports, activities for land and evening entertainment to accompany the light meals served in the restaurant. Double room $445 per person for a two-night (minimum) stay, all inclusive rate.

If you are looking for a beach resort go to the Lucaya area, to the **Genting Lucayan Beach Resort and Casino** (tel 373 7777): 248 rooms, endless watersports, tennis, fishing, restaurants, shopping arcades; $220 for a double. Smaller and less expensive properties include the **Caravel Beach Resort** (tel 352 4896), with self-catering suites with maid service. Central bar and restaurant, on beach not far from Xanadu Hotel, where watersports can be arranged, from $130 per night.

EATING OUT
Freeport and Lucaya have a limited selection of restaurants and although there are one or two good local snack bars in the outlying towns, you may find yourself eating in the hotels. You will find fine cuisine in the Polynesian setting of the **Captain's Charthouse** (tel 373 3900), on East Sunrise and Coral Rd, which serves high quality continental fare; try lobster tail with melted seasoned butter, followed by soursop or banana ice creams; $15–20 a main course, music and dancing.

The **Stoned Crab** (tel 373 1442) has a brilliant seaside setting on Taino Beach and offers a wholesome candlelit dinner for two, main course $12–20. Farther down the way at Smith's Point is **Outrigger's** (tel 373 4811), where you can get a cheaper beachside meal, main course $10. You might also try the **Buccaneer Club** (tel 349 3494) at Deadman's Reef, a beach bar with a fine view of the sunset. Lots of volleyball and crab races to go with grilled ribs and chicken, as well as some Bahamian platters like breaded shrimp. Main dish $10 approx. **Freddy's Place** (tel 352 2931) is a favourite with the Bahamians, serving conch, snappers and broiled lobster; main dish $10.

You will get extremely fine Bahamian fare at **Ruby Swiss**, next to the Princess Tower Hotel: conch fritters followed by a fry fish. Main course from $15. Other local restaurants include **Scorpio's** on Explorer's Way (tel 352 6969), where you can get a cracked conch for $7; **The Place** on the Grand Bahama Highway, which also has good seafood as well as traditional curry goat; and the **Native Hut** on Sergeant Major Drive. You might also try the **Three Kings** and **Sip Sip**. If you take a trip out to the outlying towns like Eight Mile Rock, you will find waterfront snack joints where you can pick up a good seafood platter for around $5.

The Family Islands

The Family Islands (or *Fambly* as they are sometimes pronounced) comprise the hundreds of Bahamian out islands and their cays and sandbars that just make it above the waves. They leave the casinos and cabarets of New Providence and Grand Bahama far behind. Instead you will find a more traditional Bahamas—pretty and well-kept timber houses with shingle roofs, set in gardens of tropical flowers and surrounded by white picket fences. There is some tourism development, and with it has come the odd shopping precinct, but generally it is very low-key, slow island life.

In the remoter islands you will see poorer clay houses with thatched roofs and little ovens built away from the house. In the most barren areas, where the topsoil is so thin that it cannot support much growth, the islanders have developed a system of planting in holes in the ground. They make a compost in there in which they plant. Traditionally self-sufficient and more remote from the capital than the few miles of sea would imply, many of the Family Islands have changed little in 50 years.

Scattered in splinters and shards over the *baja-mar*, most of the islands rise no more than 100 feet from the sea. Many are just a couple of miles wide, but they can stretch for a hundred miles. On their sheltered coastlines the beaches are superb—they descend gently into shallows of warm and crystal clear water, rising again as sandbars a few hundred yards offshore before descending into deep green or blue. Fly over them and the views are fantastic—back on land you can walk for miles and hardly see a soul.

But besides the superb natural surroundings and the gentle island lifestyle, certain islands have gained renown for their sports—Bimini is known for its deep-sea fishing and in the north the Abacos, among others, have superb sailing. Andros has recently gained a reputation as a dive-site. In the east is San Salvador, supposedly Columbus's first landfall in the New World. Alternatively, you may just want to get away to the tranquillity of a tropical island idyll.

GETTING AROUND
In the **Family Islands** there are rarely any buses, but you can often catch a pick-up. Activity tends to centre around the arrival of the boat or the plane and so there are usually people around. Alternatively, hitch. It is perhaps polite to offer something towards petrol, though it is unlikely to be accepted. People often walk or go by boat as much as they travel by car.

Taxis, either boats or cars, are usually available at all the main airstrips. If not, ask around and one will either be found or you will be offered a lift by someone going that way. The taxi drivers often also operate as tour guides around the islands and they will be happy to take you out for about $25 per hour for a full car.

Hire cars and **boats** are available in the larger resorts and tend to be expensive, as are scooters. Bicycles are also on hire in many places. If you are sailing by and want to stop in for a meal, many restaurants can be called up on VHF channel 16.

THE ABACOS

In the northeast of the Bahamian archipelago are the Abaco Islands and their offshore cays, stretched in a 140-mile curve around the east of Grand Bahama. They have a population of over 7300 and outside the two major resorts they are the most developed area of the Bahamas. There are two main areas, each served by an airport, to which a string of smaller islands are linked by water-taxi: Marsh Harbour in the south with nearby Hope Town on Elbow Cay; and farther north Treasure Cay and Green Turtle Cay. Walker's Cay, which has its own airstrip, is a self-contained resort 10 miles off Little Abaco Island in the far northwest of the island group.

Marsh Harbour, long the site of a lumbering industry as well as the Abacos' traditional lifeline of shipbuilding, is the third largest town in the Bahamas. As well as building ships, the islanders traditionally helped to destroy them with their other invisible industry, 'wrecking', in which they would clean up after passing ships had been washed on to the reefs. Eventually things were regularized when the lighthouse at Hope Town was built in the 1830s, despite the islanders' best efforts at sabotage. The east coast of Great Abaco (in the south) is fringed by a string of cays, many of which were settled, along with the mainland, by loyalists following the American War of Independence. These islands are still the focus of much of Abaco life. Abaconian 'loyalty' came to the fore once again as the Bahamas headed towards Independence in 1973, when there was a movement to remain part of Britain rather than go along with Nassau.

Marsh Harbour is set on a north-facing cove about midway down Great Abaco. Here you will find some concessions to the 20th century, with shops and tourist restaurants, but the old-time charm of the timber houses is still there. Above the town stand the turquoise turrets of the house of Dr Evans Cottman, author of *Out Island Doctor*. From here, a ferry service will take you out to the other islands.

Elbow Cay and its settlement of **Hope Town** are easily reached from Marsh Harbour and they are best known for the 120-ft pink and white lighthouse that stands above the town. The **Wynnie Malone Historical Museum**, restored as it was in the last century, gives a good idea of the old-time life of the Abaconians. There are bicycles for hire to explore the ribbon of land that leads north and south of the town.

Man-of-War Cay has a slightly unreal feel about it, untypical of the Bahamas. The small community is almost entirely white—until Independence, the islanders would demand that blacks left the island at sundown. They are proud and polite, and their island, one of the traditional boat-building areas of the Abacos, is clearly prosperous. No alcohol is sold on the island and they have not allowed hotels to be built, but visitors are welcome to visit. You will still see some of the traditional hulls taking shape in the dockyards.

Great Guana Cay, with a population of around 100, is visited principally for its fantastic seven miles of beach, excellent swimming and snorkelling.

Back on the island, about 30 miles northeast of Marsh Harbour, is the resort area of **Treasure Cay** and the surrounding villages. Despite the name, which implies an island, it is set on a peninsula of Great Abaco, overlooking a fantastic three-mile beach.

A couple of miles offshore is **Green Turtle Cay**, two miles by four, where the town of New Plymouth is situated—more clapboard houses with gingerbread fretwork set in flowering gardens, and on the ocean shore another superb beach. The **Albert Lowe Museum** is in a Victorian home in the town and it traces the history of the island back to the loyalists. Model boats built by Albert Lowe himself are on view alongside works by his artist son, Alton.

Walker's Cay, the most northerly point in the Bahamas, has been a game-fishing haunt since 1939.

SPORTS

Sailing is the main sport on the Abacos and you will find facilities on all the islands mentioned above. Marinas include **Abaco Bahamas Charters** in Hope Town. They hire out crewed and bareboats for a day or a week or more, as do **Bahamas Yachting Services** in Marsh Harbour. The islands hold their regattas in late June and July.

Windsurfers are cheaper than on the bigger islands and are hired out by the day for around $45. Try the Abaco Inn or the Elbow Cay Club in Hope Town, and the Treasure Cay Beach Hotel.

Waterskiing is possible at Treasure Cay ($15 for 15 mins) and **deep-sea fishing** is easy to arrange through the centres: Green Turtle Cay Club (tel 367 2572), the Elbow Cay Club (tel 367 2748) and Great Guana Cay (tel 367 2207). Rates good at around $350 for a full day.

Tennis is on offer in many of the hotels (check at the front desk of your hotel, who will arrange it if they have no court) and **golf** is available at the Treasure Cay Resort ($20 green fee, tel 367 2570).

WHERE TO STAY

In **Marsh Harbour** on Great Abaco there is a string of hotels, the smartest is the **Abaco Towns by the Sea**, PO Box 486 (tel/fax 367 2227, US 800 468 9876) a low-key resort with the 68 villas hidden in the hibiscus, casuarina pines and palms between the sea of Abaco and Marsh Harbour. The villas are dressed up in high Caribbean pastel and are well-equipped with full kitchens and terraces. All the watersports are on offer and there is a central swimming pool. Villas sleep up to six people $170–180 per day. Not far off is the **Great Abaco Beach Hotel**, PO Box 511 (tel 367 2158, fax 367 2819, US 800 468 4799) and Marina (tel 367 2736). The hotel is quite upbeat, 65 rooms in blocks overlooking the pool and swim-up bar, tennis and watersports, boat rental, evening entertainment. Double room $165. The **Conch Inn Resort** and marina, PO Box 434 (tel 367 2800, fax 367 2980) has just ten rooms in a sandy palm garden in Marsh Harbour. Quite simple but comfortable enough, air-conditioned, pool and all the sports are available nearby. Double room $75. If you want a **cheaper** place to stay, try the **Ambassador's Inn Hotel**, PO Box 484 (tel 367 2022). Classic West Indian pre-fab air-conditioned comfort, Double room $42.

On **Elbow Cay** a twenty-minute water taxi ride from Marsh Harbour you will find isolated beach-club comfort in the **Sea Spray Resort** and villas, White Sound (tel 366 0065, fax 366 0383) set between the sea of Abaco and the Atlantic. Just five clapboard villas in pretty pastel colours overlooking the beach. Double room $120. Another good spot on Elbow Cay is the **Abaco Inn** (tel/fax 366 0433, US 800 327 0787) a small retreat just out of Hope Town. There are twelve rooms, standing among the windswept greenery above the beach, each with a hammock on its private terrace. Pool, tennis, and watersports. Rooms have a full kitchen. Double in season $135. In **Hope Town** itself you will find **Hope Town Harbour Lodge** (tel 367 3590 fax 366 0286, US 800 626 5690). Quite simple, but comfortable and friendly just above the beach. Double room, $65–75. The **Guana Beach Club Resort and Marina**, PO Box 474 (tel 367 3590) is another retreat on an isolated cay off the main island. Just 15 rooms standing above the beach (all 7 miles of it), windsurfers and small sailboats on offer. Double room $125 in season.

The next inhabited cay in line is **Green Turtle Cay**, where you will find the **Green Turtle Club and Marina** (tel/fax 365 4271, US 800 327 0787) a low-key club style hotel on the waterfront. The hotel rings with colonial echoes in the decoration and hardwood floors and dark-stained antique-style beds and overhead fans. Rooms and villas look over the harbour, but there are beaches a few minutes' walk away. A trusty retreat with rooms at good price—in season double costs $120–140 and villas $250. The **Bluff House Club and Marina** (tel 365 4248 fax 365 4247) stands above the sea and beach on a cliff, 25 air-conditioned rooms in a block and in suites and villas. Tennis, pool and bar and of course fantastic water just beyond the palm trees. Double room in season $85. A charming place to stay is The **New Plymouth Club and Inn** (tel 365 4161, fax 365 4138), which is in one of New Plymouth's picture postcard town houses. The atmosphere of the inn fits the colonial elegance of the building itself. Very low-key and comfortable in an enchanting gingerbread setting. Just 9 rooms in old-time Bahamian style, some sports, beaches nearby, but generally a congenial atmosphere centred on relaxation on the pool terrace or at the Galleon Bar. Double room $110.

Finally at the north-western limit of the Abaco Cays you will find a very comfortable hotel on Walker's Cay. The **Walker's Cay Hotel and Marina** (tel in Miami 305 359 1400, fax 359 1414, US 800 432 2092) is set on its own 100-acre island, and is particularly popular for deep-sea fishing, for which it holds many records. There are 62 rooms and two restaurants and the island has its own airstrip for easy access. Also scuba diving, tennis and a friendly crowd passing through the marina. Double room $95.

There are many cottages and villas for rental in all the main towns in the Abacos. Try *Abaco Life* Magazine.

EATING OUT
In the remoter areas in the Abacos you will be dependent on the hotels, but there are plenty of places to eat in Marsh Harbour. **Wally's** (tel 367 2074) has the nicest setting, in a classic gingerbread house on Bay St. Bahamian food and some concessions to continental style—seafood fritters followed by catch of the day in a local sauce—lively, sometimes live music in the evenings, four course fixed-price dinner at $25. **Mangoes** (tel 367 2366, VHF channel 16) overlooks the harbour from the waterfront and you dine on the veranda or in the air-conditioned interior. Local and international fare such as crawfish and pizzas, main course about $15. You will find a good local meal at the **Golden Grouper** (tel 367 2301) in a modern Bahamian setting—Dove Plaza. But you can eat exotic variations on local fish, as the name suggests, or land-based Bahamian fare like a stew or a souse. You might also try **Cynthia's Kitchen** (tel 367 2268), which offers turtle steaks and seafood, eaten in or taken away. You can also grab a beer with a lively crowd of yachties at **Below Decks** or **Penny's Pub** (at the Harbour Lights restaurant) and there is dancing to all the Caribbean rhythms at the New Oasis Club in Dundas Town.

In **Elbow Cay** the finest dining can be found at the **Club Soleil** (tel 366 0003, VHF channel 16) which overlooks the harbour in Hope Town. Bahamian and continental cuisine—lobster in melted and seasoned butter, or a steak done to a turn. Main course about $20. Local Bahamian dishes are on offer at **Cap'n Jacks**, also on the waterfront and you can catch a beer and a game of pool at **Harbour's Edge**.

In **Green Turtle Cay** you will get a fine meal at the **Captain's Table** (tel 365 4161) in the old-time Bahamian setting of the New Plymouth Inn. You start off with cocktails at the bar and then retreat to the dining room for grilled local catch, crawfish or rack of lamb with local vegetables. Reserve by 5, main course about $20. **Roosters Rest** has good local food—souse or a stew goat as well as cracked conch; and you can get other Bahamian specialities, perhaps a plate of peas 'n' rice with shrimps at **Laurie's Kitchen**. At **Man O' War Cay** try the **Dock and Dine** Restaurant, a yachties stopover, for a burger or a grilled fish, or **Sally's Take-away**.

BERRY ISLANDS

The Berry islands are scattered over 40 miles of the Great Bahama Bank to the northwest of Nassau, en route from the capital to the American mainland and a regular stop-off for the cruise ships and yachts. A population of shorebirds (noddies and terns) and just 500 people is scattered across the islands, mainly living in Bullock's Harbour on Great Harbour Cay in the north. Many of the islands are private estates (Wallace Groves of Freeport fame owns Little Whale Cay). There are airstrips in Great Harbour Cay and Chub Cay. **Diving** in the nearby Tongue of the Ocean is superb, and is available through **Chub Cay Undersea Adventures** (US tel (305) 763 2188). Fishing is excellent, also from Chub Cay.

WHERE TO STAY AND EAT

The **Great Harbour Cay Club** (US tel 313 689 1580, fax 689 1594, US 800 343 7256) has just 16 rooms in beachfront villas. The hotel also services the passing yachts and so there is plenty of activity and an easy-going feel. Sports for those not sailing include tennis, a nine-hole golf course and bicycles. Double room $150. The **Tamboo Club** attached to the hotel is probably the best bet for a meal; you dine on the waterfront on ribs and chicken dishes. **Basil's** bar and restaurant catches a crowd of yachties who are making whoopee either at the very beginning or end of their trip. Burgers and snacks and plenty of beer. You can grab a more local meal at the oddly-named **Graveyard Inn**, or a fry chicken or fish at the **Watergate Chicken Shack**.

At the other end of the Berry Islands is the **Chub Cay Club** (tel 809 325 1490, fax 322 5199, US reservations 800 662 8555), which also sees a number of yachts passing through. There are 15 rooms overlooking the swimming pool. Also tennis and of course excellent fishing and diving; $85 for a double.

BIMINI

The string of the Bimini Islands, famed as the game-fishing capital of the world, are the westernmost of the Bahamian islands and they lie a bare 50 miles from downtown Miami. In between there and the mainland the Gulf Stream has carved out its path over the millennia, and it is here that the biggest marlin and giant tuna are to be found. In the past the island have been rich and raw—drug money poured through at one stage (Bimini is one of the traditional staging posts en route to the States), and it would become quite riotous as fishermen, fresh from the day's fight on the seas, would return and booze at night. Bimini is the setting of the novel *Islands in the Stream* by Ernest Hemingway, who visited often in the 30s. It is all a bit tamer now, and it is a pretty nice spot for a few days, though it is expensive. It can get quite lively at the weekends when the Florida vacationers drop in for a break.

South Bimini was one of Ponce de León's stop-offs on his hunt for the Fountain of Youth, and he supposedly came here in 1513 before discovering Florida. The northern island is the main fishing haunt and the inner coastline around Alice Town is furred with marinas, and all the bars are inland. Most of the islanders live in Bailey Town on the King's Highway leading north. A superb white-sand beach runs along the west coast of the island. You will find watersports at the Anchorage and if you want to be a little more isolated you can go to Paradise Beach and Radio Beach farther north. There is a **museum** devoted to Hemingway in the Compleat Angler Hotel; the walls are hung with pictures of the great man showing off his catches and there are illustrations and excerpts from the *Old Man and the Sea* as well as general fishing memorabilia, adm free. Cays to the south of Bimini include Gun Cay and Cat Cay, a private club, founded in the 1930s. There is a bank in Alice Town, open Mon–Fri, 9–1. **Chalk's** Airline serves the islands (twice daily from Miami and Paradise Island) and there is an airstrip on South Bimini which operates during daylight hours. There are also many marinas on the islands.

Deep sea fishing is obviously the biggest sport on the island and marinas include the **Bimini Big Game Fishing Club** (tel 347 2391), the **Blue Water Resort** (tel 347 2166) and **Weech's Bimini Dock** (tel 347 2028) in Alice Town. Fishing tournaments are held throughout the year, with the blue marlin tournament held in June. **Diving** is another growing sport on Bimini. Contact **Bimini Undersea Adventures** (US tel (305) 736 2188). Dive-sites include the reef to the west of the island and a wreck known as the concrete ship.

Bimini holds a host of **fishing tournaments** through the year, including the March Hemingway Billfish Tournament and the April Championship Billfish Tournament (both part of the Bahamas Billfish Championship). In June the Bimini Big Game Fishing Club holds the Blue Marlin Tournament and in July is the Jimmy Albury Blue Marlin Tournament. Two all-fish tournaments are held in August and there are competitions to catch wahoo in November.

WHERE TO STAY AND EAT

The most modern and comfortable hotel in the island is the **Bimini Big Game Fishing Club**, PO Box 669 (tel 809 347 3391, US 800 327 4149) on the sheltered shore of Alice Town, North Bimini. There are 49 rooms overlooking the central pool in the courtyard. A good restaurant, local fish at $15–25; diving, and of course endless fishing packages. Double room $140–170. The **Bimini Blue Water Resort**, PO Box 601 (tel 347 3166, fax 347 3292) also in Alice Town has a bit more traditional island charm with an attractive old timber-frame house and an ocean view towards Miami and the sunset. There are twelve air-conditioned rooms in suites and in a cottage. Close to all the activity of the town, double room in season, $90. The **Compleat Angler** (tel 347 3122, fax as above) also offers the best in Bimini charm, just a few rooms in one of the island's classic buildings. The interior is lined with wood and the walls are strung with nauticalia (and the exhibits of the Hemingway Museum). Rooms quite simple, a couple of good bars downstairs, which can get quite lively, and evening entertainment in season. Double room $75–85. You can find **cheaper** rooms at **Weech's Marina** (tel 347 2028), simple rooms at $60, located on the dock, but the cheapest deal is at **Brown's Hotel**, just up from the seaplane terminal, where a double room costs $55 in season.

You will find a string of **restaurants** and **bars** in Alice Town in North Bimini, none of them that cheap. Elsewhere you will be dependent on the hotels. At the **Red Lion Pub** you sit in a wooden-walled dining room, where a lively crowd collects, boozing and watching the TV while they tuck into baked turtle or a platterful of shrimps in fluffy batter, $13–17. The **Fisherman's Paradise** is a classic West Indian restaurant, air-conditioned and modern and a liming point for a few locals. Chicken or fish, quite expensive at $10–15.

Activity at the **Island Bar** centres around the pool table—loud, and quite fun, judging by all the satisfied customers who have left their calling cards attached to the beams. The **Sand Bar** is lower-key and good for a beer or two; set in a small shack with sand on the floor. The Compleat Angler bar is also excellent, particularly when they have live music—the whole town stops in for a beer and a dance.

ANDROS

At 100 miles by 40, Andros is the largest island in the Bahamas, and it has a population of 8400, the third largest. It lies just 20 miles from New Providence, across the Tongue of the Ocean, a 6000-ft trench that cuts into the Great Bahama Bank. The island is flat and crossed in places by 'bights' (channels), and inland there are many 'blue holes'. It is so low that parts of it are mangrove flats, forested swamp impenetrable except to terns, whistling tree ducks, the island's six-foot iguana and the island gremlin, the *chickcharnie*. This tiny character supposedly has three fingers, three toes, red eyes and hangs upside down in trees, and he has been attributed with a mischievous turn of mind if you do not believe in him. The island was first settled by loyalists who grew cotton, and later sponges and sisal (for rope) were the mainstays of the economy. In recent years the government has encouraged agriculture and farming of livestock on Andros.

The settlements are scattered along the east coast, where there are superb, pristine beaches. There are airports at San Andros and Andros Town on the northern island, at Moxey Town on Mangrove Cay and Congo Town on the southern island. There is a bank in San Andros, open 10.30–2.30 on weekdays.

A mile off the island's eastern shore the sea floor drops sheer for 6000 feet into the Tongue of the Ocean. On its submarine 'wall' is the third largest barrier reef in the world, 140 miles of corals and sponges plied by surgeonfish, soldierfish and angelfish. **Diving** is possible at a number of resorts on the island, including the **Small Hope Bay Lodge** just north of Andros Town (tel 368 2014) and **Andros Undersea Adventures** near San Andros in the north (US tel (305) 736 2188). **Windsurfers** and limited other watersports are available through the hotels. Bone-fishing, casting in the shallow sandy flats, is reputed to be some of the best in the world.

WHERE TO STAY AND EAT
In **Nicholl's Town** near San Andros the most comfortable place to stay is the **Conch Sound Resort Inn**, PO Box 23029 (tel 329 2060). It is a bit pre-fab, but friendly, just six rooms with satellite TV and ceiling fans or air-conditioning, double room $80. Another retreat is the **Andros Beach Hotel** (tel 329 2582), with 24 simple rooms on a superb

strip of sand. $75 a double in season. Sports include scuba and of course fishing. At **Donna Lee's Guest House** (tel 329 2194) there are twelve rooms which go for $60 a double in season. If you wish to eat out, you can try the **Palm Tree** or **Riley's Rest**, both of which serve local Bahamian food—conch fritters followed by grilled local catch, hauled in that afternoon, perhaps by you. Main course about $10. **Lilley's Bar** is a local favourite, as is **Rumours**, between Nicholl's Town and San Andros, where there is live music and dancing in the evenings.

At **Fresh Creek** is a charming small hotel, the **Small Hope Bay Lodge** (tel 368 2014, fax 368 2015, US 800 223 6961). This is a classic Caribbean retreat, with a speciality in diving. There are just 20 rooms, built of local coral rock and island pine wood, each overlooking the sand and the sea. The atmosphere is extremely low-key, particularly as most people have been out diving all day and are building up their strength for the following day's activity. There is an all-inclusive rate of $280 per person. The **Lighthouse Yacht Club** (tel 368 2305, fax 368 2300) is centred around sailing and there is a small marina there. Twenty rooms and villas on the beach and watersports including scuba and fishing, double rate about $120 a night. You can find a cheaper rate at the **Cickcharnie Hotel** (tel 368 2025) on the waterfront; eight rooms and a restaurant, double room $50. If you want a local meal in the area, you can try the **Land Mark Restaurant**, where you can pick up some peas 'n' rice or a curry goat for about $8.

Not far off, the **Cargill Creek Lodge** (tel 329 5129, fax 329 5046, US 800 942 6799) specializes in fishing and has a fleet of boats to take you off to the deep waters and the bone-fishing flats. Also diving and a pool and central sunning area. The air-conditioned rooms look out to sea and have TVs, double rate $250 a night in season. A good local restaurant in this area is the **Gateway Restaurant and Bar**, where you can get a grilled fish or a burger. In **Mangrove Cay** you can stay quite cheaply at the **Mangrove Cay Resort** (tel 369 0004), twenty rooms in a modern block on the beach. Double room $55. **Cool Breeze Cottages** (tel 329 4465) are just four cottages on the beach, double rate $50.

On **South Andros** you will find one of the Bahamas most luxurious hotels, the **Emerald Palms by the Sea** (tel 329 4461, fax 329 4467, US 800 835 1018 for reservations). High Caribbean comfort on the five-mile, palm-backed ocean-front—just twenty rooms with four-posters and muslin netting, also a fine restaurant. Sports include tennis, windsurfing, small sailing boats and scuba, or just sunning by the freshwater pool, armed with a book from the library. Double room $175 in season. For a cheaper room you can try the **Royal Palm Lodge** (tel 329 4608), where a double room costs $60.

ELEUTHERA

Eleuthera was the first of the Bahamas to be settled when the company of Eleutherian Adventurers arrived in 1648, escaping religious persecution in Bermuda and England. They called their island *Eleutheria* after the Greek word for freedom. The settlement was quickly overtaken by New Providence (about 50 miles to the east), but Eleuthera has flourished steadily, helped by an influx of loyalists in the 1780s, making a living from agriculture and the sea. Today Eleuthera is among the most developed of the Family Islands with regard to tourism.

The island is 100 miles long and barely more than 2 miles wide, and on its sheltered side the beaches and sandbars stretch for tens of miles into the jade green water. On the ocean side the waves barrel in, and are big enough to surf on. Eleuthera is quite fertile, traditionally a farming area, nowadays mainly producing pineapples and tomatoes, though you will still see grain silos along the road.

There are three airstrips: North Eleuthera which serves the north of the island and the offshore islands of Harbour Island and Spanish Wells; Governor's Harbour which serves the centre of the island and Rock Sound for the south. Make sure to get off at the correct one because it can be a 100-mile drive to the other end of the island. There is a tourist information office in Governor's Harbour (tel 332 2142).

Harbour Island with its inhabitants, the 'Brilanders', was once the second most prosperous place in the Bahamas after Nassau, but the docks are quiet now compared with when the shipbuilding industry was at its height. Dunmore Town is a pretty and slumberstruck village that lines the protected shore of the island—sugary pink gingerbread houses sit snug behind the white picket fences as they always have, only now they are accompanied by satellite dishes. Some of the hotels are set in these old antique houses and so they are quaint and comfortable. The islanders are laid back, and only too happy for you to join in their musings. The famous Pink Beach, miles of sand a delicate shade of pink, is on the ocean side of the island.

Another offshore island close by, **Spanish Wells**, is almost as picturesque, and has the beaches to match Harbour Island, but it has a different feel altogether. The islanders are among the richest in the Bahamas because of the fishing industry. They fish mainly for lobster or craw fish, sailing off for three weeks at a time in their refrigerated boats, scouring the Bahamian waters as far south as Cuba, reaping vast profits. They reappear and make whoopee back home before setting off again a couple of weeks later.

But the island, just 3 miles long and less than a mile across, has an untypical feel for the Bahamas because there are very few black faces. Until quite recently black Bahamians, even the doctor, would be asked to leave the island at sunset.

On the main island of **North Eleuthera** you can visit Preacher's Cave, where the early settlers are supposed to have worshipped. Current Cut is a popular dive at the change of the tide because the water races through it at around 7 knots. Heading south past Gregory Town, a fishing village, you come to the 'Glass Window' (named after a natural bridge that has collapsed), where the difference between the ocean and the protected leeward coast is most clearly visible). At Hatchet Bay there is a more extensive underground cave system, which culminates in a clifftop at 70 ft above the sea.

Governor's Harbour is another tired town of timber houses set on the curve of Cupid's Bay, now overlooked by the island's Club Med. Not far off, the Windermere Island Club is one of the Bahamas' most exclusive resorts, favoured by royalty from the world over. **Rock Sound** is the largest settlement on Eleuthera and a good place to stock up, but still little more than a village of fading gingerbread houses above the bay. Not far off is one of Eleuthera's famous 'Blue Holes', an inland lake connected to the ocean deep underwater.

Watersports (windsurfers, dinghies and waterskiing) and **tennis courts** are available through the hotels, which will often allow outsiders to use their equipment if it is available. **Bonefishing** is good off the northern resorts and if you wish to take a day's

651

deep-sea fishing, contact the resorts, including Spanish Wells Beach Resort (tel 332 2645), or at the Cotton Bay Club (tel 334 2156).

Divers can check out the tidal race at Current Cut and explore the wreck of the train that was on its way to Cuba on the Devil's Backbone reef off the north coast of the island. Contact the Romora Bay Club (tel 333 2324) and Valentine's Dive Centre (tel 333 2309), both on Harbour Island, and the Spanish Wells Dive Centre (tel 332 2645). Also the Cotton Bay Club near Rock Sound, where there is a golf course.

WHERE TO STAY AND EAT

Harbour Island, off the northeast coast of Eleuthera, is a charmed spot, with some extremely smart hotels and guest houses set in the old Bahamian island-homes or hidden in luxurious gardens. Named after the east coast beach, **Pink Sands**, PO Box 87 (tel/fax 333 2030), is approached through a rickety gate, but once into the garden, the informal luxury of the place is immediately upon you. 35 rooms are scattered across the grounds and on the beach itself. There is a good library and a delightful dining room and you can expect extra pampering at moments like afternoon tea. Watersports are available, but the atmosphere is very low-key; $275 for a double room in season. The **Romora Bay Club**, PO Box 146 (tel 333 2325, US 800 327 8286) is an active hotel which offers diving and other watersports just a short walk from Pink Sands beach. There are 37 rooms with air-conditioning and ceiling fans and a central area with a dining terrace slung with greenery. Double room $150–180. The **Runaway Hill Club**, PO Box 31 (tel 333 2150, US 800 327 0787) is a charming inn of just eight rooms set in a traditional Bahamian house, not far from the centre of Dunmore Town. Still, in its own garden, it is quiet and isolated from the buzz if that's what you want. Double room in season $160. Not far off, **Valentine's Yacht Club and Inn**, PO Box 1 (tel 333 2142, fax 333 2135, US 800 327 0787) is busy town hotel where passing yachtsmen gather. It is a neat inn, with cottages gathered around an old town house and its tropical garden courtyard. The marina is right over the road and there is evening entertainment in season. Double room $120. There are one or two cheaper places to stay on Harbour Island, including the **Rock House** (tel 333 2053), 6 rooms, dining room, sports arranged; $70 for a double room and **Tingum Village** (tel 333 2161), 12 simple rooms in cottages, with bar and dining room; $60.

The restaurants have some good dining rooms, but at the Tingum Village, Rubi Percentie cooks the best in local food at **Ma Rubi's**—excellent conch fritters and grilled lobster and shrimp, about $10. Otherwise you might try the **Harbour Lounge** on the waterfront or **Angela's Starfish Restaurant** for local seafood. **Willy's Tavern** is a fun bar for a beer or a cocktail and **The Reach** is a favourite with the passing yachtfolk, on the waterfront opposite Valentine's. **Gusty's** is the local night-spot, where you can get a beer and catch up on the latest sports news on the satellite TV, and you can often see a band at **Seagrapes**.

On the island of **Spanish Wells** there are two main hotels; on the eastern shore is the **Spanish Wells Beach Resort**, PO Box 31 (tel 333 4371, fax 333 4565), with 21 airy and simple rooms overlooking a massive expanse of fantastic sand and waist-deep water. There is a restaurant and a lively local bar, where the fishermen collect when they are home from the seas. Double room $110. The **Spanish Wells Harbour Club** (same phone and fax no) overlooks the harbour side of the island and has its own bar and dining room. Fishing and diving trips leave from the dock below, $75 a double room in season. Cheaper rooms can be found at the **St George's Hotel**, PO Box 48 (phone the island exchange and ask for ext 255), about $45. Eating out is limited to the other hotel, though you will be able to pick up a lunchtime snack from the local bakery.

At the western tip of Eleuthera itself you will find the **Current Club Beach Resort and Marina** (tel 359 1531, fax 392 5133, US 800 832 2772). There are just 18 suites in modern villas and a central club house with a restaurant that specializes in seafood dishes. Fishing and diving are on offer and of course the beach is right there if you just want to soak up a few rays. Double room $100. In **Gregory Town** you will find the **Cove Eleuthera**, PO Box 1548 (tel/fax 335 5142), where there are 24 rooms dressed up in Caribbean pastel colours and white rattan furniture. Pool and tennis court and a restaurant. Double rate $110. Not far off, at Hatchet Bay you will find the **Rainbow Inn** (tel 332 0294, US 800 327 0787), which is set on an expanse of white sand beach, lost among the palm trees. Surfing when the waves are up and tennis, or a pool bar if you are feeling lazy, double rooms $90.

At **Governor's Harbour** you can find one or two less expensive places to stay. The **Cigatoo Inn**, PO Box 86 (tel 332 2343, fax 332 2159, US 800 327 0787) has 26 rooms in a modern block and a restaurant. Some sports on the superb beach, double rooms go for $65–100. And at the **Laughing Bird Apartments** you can stay for $60–75 a night, scuba and tennis are on offer. You can eat out at the **Buccaneer Club**, which offers local Bahamian food for lunch and dinner, closed Sun.

You will find one of the Bahama's smartest hotels at the **Windermere Island Club** (tel 332 6009, fax 332 6002, US 800 237 1236), which is hidden away on its own island 18 miles north of Rock Sound. Here you will find sophisticated castaway seclusion on five miles of pristine private beach. There are just 21 rooms on the island and the usual sports are available to occupy you should you so wish. Otherwise you might like to concentrate on the dining room, which is reputedly excellent—jacket and tie required in keeping with the formality of the place. Double rate for a room $230. The **Cotton Bay Club**, PO Box 28 (tel 334 4055, fax 334 6082, US 800 334 3523) at Rock Sound is another sumptuous enclave of low-key luxury where you can expect high-grade pampering. The 77 rooms are dressed in bright pastel fittings and are very comfortable. Sports include an 18-hole golf course, tennis and all the watersports. Lovely beach, double rate $250. And the **Winding Bay Beach Resort**, PO Box 93 (tel 334 4055, fax 334 4057, US 800 835 1017) is another expensive and charming seafront resort where you can expect to be alone on miles of superb beach. The 36 rooms are set around the central great house which is lost in the palm trees. The hotel offers an all-inclusive package which includes tennis and watersports and evening entertainment in the winter season. The rate is $150 per person.

At the other end of the scale, you can get a cheap room at **Edwina's Place**, PO Box 30 (tel 334 2094), just a mile from the airport, dining room, pool, and beach nearby; $70 for a double. An even cheaper option is **Hilton's Haven Motel** (tel 334 4231), simple rooms in a modern block, with a restaurant and a lively bar; good prices at $50 for a double. At Rock Sound you will find the **Haven Restaurant**, good for a local meal of grilled fish or curry goat, and the **Hide Out** bar, where a local crowd of limers stops in for a beer.

653

EXUMA CAYS

The 350-odd Exuma cays are strung out over more than 100 miles of magnificent sea, in a line running southeast, starting 50 miles from Nassau and heading southeasterly towards Great Exuma in the south, where most of the population lives. Most are uninhabited and some, just sandbars, disappear with the one-foot tides. Others, like Allen's Cay is home to just a crowd of iguanas. In the string of islands Staniel Cay has a small marina. You will hear stories of Norman's Cay, which was used as a smuggling base by cocaine barons until it was raided by the DEA. All that remains are a few buildings and cars, with bullet holes and an airstrip. The Exumas are famed for their sailing and there are excellent grounds for snorkelling and of course washing up on superb beaches. The Exuma **Land and Sea Park** is based around Warderick Wells Cay. The islands have some small agriculture.

There are two main airstrips and settlements; on Great Exuma in the south, the largest island and home to most of the 3500 population (about half of whom have the name Rolle), and a few people live on Staniel Cay about midway up the chain.

George Town sits on a hillside above a stunning blue harbour, protected by the offshore cay of Stocking Island, which has beaches along its entire shoreline. There is a tall obelisk on Stocking Island, erected to guide ships in to load up with salt in the last century. Rolle Town in the south has some attractive old-time Bahamian buildings and from here you can get across (on a bridge) to Little Exuma Island and its town, The Ferry.

Sailing is the principal occupation in the Exumas. In April George Town comes alive with the Family Island Regatta, in which you will see local boats competing. For watersports on Staniel Cay, contact the Staniel Cay Yacht Club (tel 335 2011). On Great Exuma, go to Exuma Docking Services in the George Town Harbour (tel 336 2578). Diving trips can be fixed up through **Exuma Divers** in George Town (tel 336 2030) or **Exuma Aquatics** (tel 336 2600). Deep sea fishing can also be arranged through the above.

WHERE TO STAY AND EAT

Most of the hotels in the Exumas are on Great Exuma in the far south and there is a clutch of small resorts in George Town itself. The **Club Peace and Plenty**, PO Box 29055 (tel 336 2551, fax 336 2093, US 800 525 2210) has 35 rooms set around one of the original wooden George Town houses—it is named after a ship that brought colonists here in 1783. The faded gentrification of the colonial days remains, but all the twentieth century's sports are available within a short ride. Double room $105–130. The **Peace and Plenty Inn**, PO Box 29100 (tel 336 2552, fax and US 800 no as above) has continued the same theme in a purpose-built villa, so there is a slightly different air, but the 16 rooms are air-conditioned and comfortable and cost $115–125. You can use the facilities and the dining room of either resort. **Regatta Point**, PO Box 6 (tel 336 2206, fax 336 2046, US 800 327 0787) sits on its own peninsula just out of George Town, a secluded resort, but still within a shout of all the activity of the town, if you can call it that. Just a few apartments with fully equipped kitchens. There are boats to take a fishing trip and there are windsurfers and sunfish for shorter sails. Double rate $110. The **Two Turtles Inn** (tel 336 2545, fax 336 2528) is another pleasant out-island inn in George

Town. There are 14 air-conditioned rooms around the stone courtyard and all the sports can be arranged. Double rate good at $78. The **Three Sisters Inn**, PO Box 29196 (tel 358 4040, fax 358 4043, US 800 253 2771) is set on the magnificent Bahama Sound Beach away from the town. There are twelve large rooms in a single block looking out over a sandy garden. Quiet and cut off, double room $105 in season. Finally, the **Staniel Cay Yacht Club** (tel 335 2024, fax 335 2044) is situated on its own island, Staniel Cay, about half-way along the string of the Exuma Cays. The hotel, with just six rooms in cottages, sees plenty of passing yachts and so it has a lively crowd at times. Diving and fishing available and of course simple isolation if that's what you're there for. Double rate in winter, $180, includes all meals. Sailors who want to stop in for dinner should contact the kitchen well in advance.

There are a number of recommendable eateries in George Town outside the hotels. Try **Eddie's Edgewater Club** for all the variations on conch and local catch and **Gemelli's**, overlooking Elizabeth harbour where you can order a pizza and some local fare. There is occasionally a band at the **Silver Dollar**. In the day, you might wish to go over to the very popular **Stocking Island Beach Club**, which will keep you topped up with beer and rum punch while you spend the day lazing around in the sun.

CAT ISLAND

Cat Island is also a sliver of land, 45 miles by 1 on average, that lies northwest-southeast, across the prevailing ocean winds, ribboned on both coasts by pristine beaches. Named after the British sea captain Catt, the island has a line of cliffs (at 206 ft, Mt Alvernia is the highest in the Bahamas) and it is fertile, as the walls and the derelict houses of its former plantation prosperity show at a glance. But if it was developed for cotton and sisal 100 years ago, Cat Island is one of the least developed of the Bahamian islands today. Old-time Bahamian life continues here, small plantations cut out of the hillside, and traditions such as *obeah*, the West Indian magic, of which you will still see the signs hanging in the trees.

There are three airstrips on Cat Island; near Port Howe in the south, Fernandez Bay in the centre and the main airstrip in the north at Arthur's Town, to which Bahamasair flies.

Arthur's Town is the most populous on the island, and it is much the same as when Sidney Poitier grew up here. It is the commercial centre, but there is not much to see and so you are best to set off along the island where you will find the traditional Bahamian thatch-roofed cottages and their outdoor ovens set in the tropical gardens.

The Bight is a large cove with two seafront villages (New Bight and Old Bight) linked by a stunning beach. Pigeon Bay Cottage is the ruin of a 19th-century estate house nearby, and on top of Mt Alvernia above the town you will find the Hermitage, a monastery built in miniature by Father Jerome, who designed many of the Bahamian churches, including the Augustinian monastery on New Providence. He came to live as a hermit on Cat Island in his last years. South of the Bight the road passes the Deveaux Mansion, an impressive ruined plantation house, and heads towards Columbus Point and the small town of Port Howe, famed as a wrecking town in years past. Hawks Nest Creek in the southwest has a large number of herons. Hire cars and sports, including tennis, diving and deep-sea fishing, are available through the few hotels on the island.

THE CARIBBEAN

WHERE TO STAY AND EAT

Fernandez Bay Village is the smartest hotel on the island and it is a classic castaway resort, set on its own magnificent beach. There are just eleven rooms in villas overlooking the sea, with full kitchen facilities, though there is a restaurant if you want it. Some watersports are offered; cottages $180–210 per day. The hotel can arrange transportation from the USA. There is a slightly cheaper alternative in the **Bridge Inn** (tel 354 5013, fax 354 5041, US 305 634 1014) which has twelve airy rooms in a modern block just up from the beach, each with satellite TV. The bar and restaurant are a gathering point for all comers. Double rate $80 in season. The **Hotel Greenwood Inn** (reservations US 800 825 5099) also has rooms at the same price, as well as offering diving and boat rentals. If you want to eat out you can try **Pilot Harbour**, where you can get a grilled local fish in creole sauce overlooking the harbour.

LONG ISLAND

Long Island, which stretches southeast from the tip of the Exuma Cays and cuts the Tropic of Cancer, is 57 miles long and 4 wide at most. In the north are rugged headlands and at the southern tip of the island the hills subside into salt flats. There are over 40 small communities scattered along its almost entirely undeveloped western coastline of reefs and beaches, of which the largest are Deadman's Cay, midway down the island and Clarence Town, set on a beautiful harbour farther south. The main airstrips are at Stella Maris in the north and Deadman's Cay.

Though some of the 3500 islanders work in the tourist industry, most are involved with fishing and farming. The produce, much of which is grown in fertile 'pot holes' in the limestone ground, is sold to the government and shipped out on the weekly boat to Nassau.

The beaches around the Stella Maris Inn and up to the north of the island at Cape Santa Maria are spectacular and they have the best of the Bahamas' superbly clear water. Travelling south you will see the island littered with the walls and the skeletons of former plantation prosperity. Deadman's Cay is the largest town and the best place for provisions. Clarence Town, which is still the island capital, is dominated by two of Father Jerome's churches (see above on Cat Island). St Paul's Anglican Church was topped when he turned Catholic and constructed St Peter's Catholic Church.

WHERE TO STAY AND EAT

The **Stella Maris Resort Club**, PO Box 105 (tel 336 2106, US 800 426 0466), has 60 rooms and self-catering units in low pre-fab buildings scattered around a sandy garden of pines and palms. There are three pools, and a bar and dining room in the central area, which can get quite lively because there is a marina in the property too. Windsurfing, sailing, fishing and diving and you can hire cars from them to explore the island; from $110. **Carroll's Guest House** at Deadman's Cay (no telephone) has just six rooms and a dining room; $55 a double.

For a meal outside the hotels try **Conchy's** in the Stella Maris shopping centre or **Salty's Bar**, where you will get a dish of Bahamian peas 'n' rice. At **Sabrina's** in Burnt Ground Village you can also get local Bahamian fare.

656

SAN SALVADOR

San Salvador takes its name (the Saviour) from Columbus's first landfall in the New World on 12 October 1492. Just 12 miles by 5, San Salvador is out on its own, a little farther into the Atlantic than the other islands, and historians decided what the Indian inhabitants called *Guanahani* was the best site for Columbus's island (in the mean time it had become known as Watling's Island, the lair of a pirate). Just as there are other islands that dispute the claim, so there are four sites on the island that vie for the title of the first bay where he put in and you will see several monuments commemorating them. Long Bay with its simple white cross has the most favoured claim.

For all the controversy, the island is inhabited by only a few hundred people, undeveloped and much like the other out-islands. It is mainly flat, with a series of inland lakes, and offshore reefs that the Navigator had to avoid. There is one airstrip on the island, just north of the main village of Cockburn Town (pronounced Co'burn), which is served twice a week.

There is a spectacular view of the island from the 160-ft lighthouse (still wound up by hand) on Dixon Hill in the northeast. On the hill above the south coast is 'Watling's Castle', supposedly the pirate's lookout. In fact it is one of the plantation houses of the American loyalists who settled the island in the late 1700s.

A few **sports** are available through the Riding Rock Inn, including a tennis court, diving with three boats, and a dark-room for film shot on the dives. There are also marina facilities.

WHERE TO STAY AND EAT

The **Riding Rock Inn** (tel 332 2631, US 800 272 1492) is on the beach north of Cockburn Town, with 24 air-conditioned rooms and villas around the freshwater pool, dining room and bar; tennis, full diving operation and fishing on offer, double room $100. Cheaper options are the smaller **Ocean View Villas** in the town which have kitchenettes. A **Club Med** opened on San Salvador at the time of the Quincentennial anniversary.

You can eat out at the **Ocean View Club**, where the island limers gather for a beer, and the **Halem Square Club**, where you can get some conch fritters and a lobster platter and some live music at the weekends.

RUM CAY

About 35 miles from San Salvador, and supposedly Columbus's second island stop, which he named after the Virgin Mary, Rum Cay is another former pirate haunt surrounded by spectacular reefs. Just ten miles by four and with a population of under 100, it is perhaps the most slumberstruck and friendliest of them all. Port Nelson, the only village, is hidden among the palms on the southeast coast and the island is fringed with supreme sand. Apart from piracy, salt manufacture was the only major industry. The reefs are as spectacular as they are dangerous for shipping—a shipload of rum that foundered here gave the island its name, and there is a superb dive to the *HMS Conqueror*, wrecked in 1861, which lies in just 25 ft of water. There are marina facilities at the head of the harbour. Watch out for the wild boars.

The **Rum Cay Club** has its own airstrip. Otherwise you are dependent on the mail boat. **Watersports** can also be arranged through them.

WHERE TO STAY AND EAT
You can stay cheaply at **Dolores** and there is good local fare at **Kaye's Bar** next to the pier in Port Nelson and at the **Ocean View**.

CROOKED ISLAND—ACKLINS

About 300 miles southeast of Nassau, Long Cay, Crooked Island and Acklins enclose on three sides the stunning Bight of Acklins, where crystal clear water runs on to sandbars and palm-lined beaches. The population of the Crooked Island district (500 on Crooked Island and 600 on Acklins) is far lower now than it was a century ago when the islands were a major port of call. Life here is gentle and friendly. Long Cay has about 20 inhabitants, most of whom are fishermen by trade.

The twice-weekly flight from Nassau touches both major islands: Colonel Hill on Crooked Island and spring Point on Acklins. There is a twice-daily boat link from one island to the other across The Going Through, the strait that divides Lovely Bay and the Ferry (Crooked Island).

The reefs are excellent and diving can be arranged through the hotel Pittsdown Point Landings on Crooked Island. Bonefishing in the bay is also excellent.

WHERE TO STAY AND EAT
At Landrail Point is **Pittstown Point Landings** (tel 336 2507, US reservations 513 732 2593), which has 14 rooms set on a magnificent beach (one of a number on the island). It is very low key, with an honour bar and huts on the beaches where you cook up your own catch at lunchtime. Boating, snorkelling and scuba on offer; $95 a double in season. At Colonel Hill is the **Crooked Island Beach Inn** (tel 336 2096), eleven rooms with ceiling fans in beach cottages; kitchenettes, but also a dining room with local food and some sports on offer; rooms $60 a double. **T and S** guest house is three miles from the airstrip at Cabbage Hill and has five simple rooms and a communal kitchen; $50 for a double. At Landrail Point, try **Wilfred and Hanna Gibson's Restaurant**.

MAYAGUANA

Mayaguana is still rarely visited except as a stopover for yachts headed south to the Caribbean. And then only for shelter in Abraham's Bay on the south coast, the capital village because there are no organized facilities there. Life is extremely slow for the 600-odd islanders, many of whom have left because there is no work other than farming. There is a twice-weekly flight to Inagua. There is one guest house and bar, **Reggie Satellite Lounge**, which collects anybody who is out liming at the time.

THE INAGUAS

Most southerly of the Bahamas, Great Inagua is just within sight of Cuba to the south, about 60 miles across the Old Bahama Channel. The island is remote, over 350 miles away from the bustling centre of Nassau, and less than 1000 people live there. Its remoteness and size (at 35 miles by 25 it is the third largest of all the Bahamas) have meant that it has become the last resort of a large colony of birds, including spoonbills, ducks and most spectacular, pink flamingos; an estimated 40,000 of these birds, which now survive in just a few places in the Americas, are protected in the Inagua National Park, set around Inagua's inland lakes. Trips can be arranged through the Bahamas National Trust (Nassau tel 323 1317).

The traditional industry on this low, windswept island is salt manufacture, and miles of brilliant white salt flats of the Morton Salt Company make up the second largest in the world. The main town is Matthew Town in the southwest, where the airport is located for the twice-weekly flights to Nassau. You might also be able to arrange a ride on the ships of the Morton Salt Company, based in Port Canaveral, Fort Lauderdale.

WHERE TO STAY AND EAT
There are a couple of guest houses in Matthew Town, a mile from Great Inagua airstrip, both simple rooms, with a dining room and beach nearby. **Ford's Inagua Inn** (tel 277) has five rooms at $40 a double and the **Main House** (tel 267) has six at $45.

FURTHER READING

Any number of travellers have left memoirs of their island-hopping journies, and although it is difficult to get hold of originals James Pope Hennessy has collected many of the best known names in *West Indian Summer*, including Raleigh, Trollope, Froude, Waller and Henry Coleridge. He also published a book about the slave trade entitled *Sins of the Fathers* (Cassell). It is possible to find a copy of Père Labat's travels in the 1690s (see Martinique) and Trollope's *West Indies and the Spanish Main*, about a journey undertaken in the last century, re-issued in paperback by Alan Sutton.

More recent island-hoppers include: Patrick Leigh Fermor, whose *Traveller's Tree* (John Murray and Penguin) derives from a journey in the late 1940s; his *Violins of St Jacques* (Oxford's 20th Century Classics) is a charming novella about life in a mysterious French Caribbean island; also Alec Waugh, who wrote books of Caribbean travel including *The Sugar Islands*; Quentin Crewe, *Touch the Happy Isles* (Michael Joseph); Zenga Longmore, who visited a selection of islands, *Tap Taps to Trinidad* (Hodder and Stoughton)—it is interesting to see the West Indies viewed from a woman's perspective; Hugh O'Shaughnessy, who published revealing stories of journalistic visits to several Caribbean islands in *Around the Spanish Main* (Century) and most recently a musician, Henry Shukman, who has written a musical tour of the Caribbean in *Travels with my Trombone* (Harper Collins).

Daniel Defoe's *Robinson Crusoe* is of course a Caribbean classic, set in Tobago, so they say. Pirates are remembered in some old classics, by Exquemeling and by Captain Johnson, in his *History of the Pirates*.

Simple modern histories include Parry and Sherlock's *A Short History of the West Indies* (published by Macmillan). Eric Williams, the Prime Minister of Trinidad wrote two major historical perspectives of the Caribbean, *From Columbus to Castro* and *Capitalism and Slavery*. Warwick University and Macmillan publish a series of papers of West Indian history. If you want a softer, layman's view of Caribbean history, James Michener's *The Caribbean* (Mandarin) races through it at a lightening pace.

Macmillan also publishes good natural history books such as *Trees of the Caribbean* and *Flowers of the Caribbean*.

Two well-known writers who spent some time in the Caribbean are Ernest Hemingway, remembered particularly for his Nobel Prize winning classic *The Old Man and the Sea*, written about the fishermen of the town of Cojimar, just east of Havana in Cuba and other classics such as *Islands in the Stream*, and Graham Greene, the best of whose Caribbean novels are: *The Comedians*, set in Haiti, and *Our Man in Havana*, about Cuban life.

Heinemann has the best series of Caribbean literature including works by Trinidadians, Michael Anthony, Earl Lovelace and Sam Selvon; Derek Walcott from St Lucia; and Jamaicans, Roger Mais and V. S. Reid. One of the most interesting anthologies of Caribbean writing is *From the Green Antilles* (Granada and Panther).

American author John Shacochis has followed up his award-winning book of Caribbean short stories *Easy in the Islands* (Penguin America) with *The Next New World*.

For titles specific to particular places, see under the Further Reading sections in the islands.

INDEX

INDEX

jerk xvi, 560, 568, 582, 592, 593, 595–6
John Crow Mountains 553, 554, 560, 569
Kingston 2, 143, 345, 527, 554, 559, 561–3, 565, 566,
568, 571–4, 584–5, 592–3, 597, 627
Mandeville 563, 564, 570, 576, 585, 593–4
Montego Bay 2, 554, 561–3, 566, 568–70, 577–8,
587–9, 594–5, 597, 600
music 20, 559–60
Negril xx, 21–2, 554, 560, 561, 563, 565, 567–9,
576–7, 586–7, 594, 597
nightlife 596–8
Ocho Rios 554, 561, 563, 568, 569–71, 580–1,
589–91, 595–6, 598
Port Antonio 554, 561, 563, 565, 566, 568–70, 577,
581–2, 591–2, 596, 598
Port Royal 33, 554, 555, 568, 572, 573–4, 593
Rastafarianism 558–9
restaurants 592–6
revivalism 558–9
Rockland Bird Sanctuary 578
Rose Hall 579
St Ann's Bay 555, 580
Spanish Town 555, 564, 575
sports 18, 570–1
travel 561–5
watersports 16, 569–70, 587–8
jazz 20, 21, 23, 59, 63, 525
jetskis 16, 104, 186, 319, 321, 370, 420, 437, 519, 547,
580, 615
JOST VAN DYKE xvi, xx, 5, 381, 410, 417–19
junkanoo 21, 23, 567

kreyol 12, 314, 496, 500, 506, 507, 508, 610

La Désirade xvii, 203, 214, 224–5
languages 12
Leeward Islands, see Anguilla; Antigua; Barbuda;
Montserrat; Nevis; St Kitts
limes 159, 271
Lucayan Indians 29, 623

manchineel tree 8, 43, 70, 76, 298, 306
Marie Galante xvii, 170, 203, 224, 225–6
Grande-Bourg 225
MARTINIQUE xviii, 178–203, 182
accommodation 198–200
Balata Gardens xx, 181, 196
beaches 185–6, 190, 195, 198
Bellefontaine 192
Case-Pilote 192
Diamond Rock 191
festivals 20, 21, 23, 197–8
flora & fauna 14, 181
Fort de France 174, 179, 180, 183–4, 188, 189, 197–8,
201, 203
Grand' Rivière 193, 194, 196, 199–200
history 94, 175–6, 179–81, 188–9, 191
Le Carbet 180, 199
Le François 192
Le Prêcheur 194–5, 196
Le Vauclin 191
Les Anses d'Arlet 190, 198–9
Les Trois-Ilets 190
Macouba 196
Mont Pelée 87, 179, 180, 188, 193–4, 195
Morne Rouge 195
nightlife 203
Plantation Leyritz 195–6, 199
Pointe du Bout 198, 201–2

restaurants 200–3
St Anne 191, 199, 200, 202
St Pierre 128, 175, 178, 180, 183, 192–4, 199, 203
Sainte Marie 197
Schoelcher 192, 199, 203
sports 187–8
travel 8, 181–4
Trinité 197, 200
watersports 186–7
medical services 42, 69, 85
Bahamas 631, 639
French Antilles 184, 209, 230, 241
Greater Antilles 435, 472, 506, 530, 566, 602, 614
Leeward Islands 255, 274, 298, 306
Netherlands Antilles 319, 329, 335, 347, 359, 369
Virgin Islands 384, 394, 403, 411
Windward Islands 103, 121, 163
merengue 20, 22, 339, 352, 355, 365, 375, 463, 466, 470,
479
MONTSERRAT xviii, 269–80, 273
accommodation 278–9
beaches 275
Chance's Peak 258
festivals 21, 278
flora & fauna 272
Fox's Bay Bird Sanctuary 272, 276
Galway's Soufrière 277
history 270–1
Irish heritage 270, 272, 279
nightlife 280
Plymouth 275–6, 278–9
restaurants 279–80
travel 272–4
watersports 275
mosquitoes 8–9, 14, 256, 473, 615
music xi, 3, 19–20, 21–2
MUSTIQUE xviii, 133, 136–7
Lovell Village 136
nightlife 130

Nelson, Lord Horatio 46, 191, 260–1, 298–9, 574
Netherlands Antilles
history 312–13
politics 313
see also ARUBA; BONAIRE; CURAÇAO; SABA;
SINT EUSTATIUS; SINT MAARTEN
NEVIS xviii, 294–301, 295
accommodation 299–301
beaches & watersports 296
Charlestown 295, 297–8
festivals 22, 299
Fig Tree Church 298, 298
Jamestown 299
Mount Nevis 296
nightlife 281
restaurants 301
Soufrière 299
sports 296–7, 300
travel 283, 295
NEW PROVIDENCE 629–38, 630
accommodation 634–6
beaches 575, 631–2
Cable Beach 621, 622, 629, 631, 632, 634–5, 638
flora & fauna 5634
history 33, 623
Nassau 1–2, 23, 613, 621, 622, 623–4, 625, 629–31,
632–7
nightlife 637–8
Paradise Island 621, 624, 627, 632, 633, 634–8

666